Businesses and Organizations Cited in this Book

3M Dental Products Division

Accenture
ADAC Laboratories
Advanced Circuits
Airbus
Alcoa
Alliance for Work-Life Progress
Allied Signal
Amalgamated Clothing and Textile Workers
Amazon.com
American College of Surgeons
American Electric Power
American Express
American Honda Motor Co.
American Management Association
American National Standards Institute
American Productivity and Quality Center
American Quality Foundation
American Red Cross
American Society for Quality
Ames Rubber Corporation
AMR Research, Inc.
Corning, Incorporated
American National Standards Institute
Armstrong Building Products Operations
Artesyn Technologies
AT&T
Australian Business Review Weekly
Avis

Bama Companies
Bank of Montreal
Baptist Hospital Inc.
Baxter Healthcare International
Bell System
BellSouth
Best Buy
Bethesda Hospitals of Cincinnati
BI
Big Bear Stores
BMG Music Service
BMW
Boeing
Boeing Aerospace Support
Boeing Airlift and Tanker
Borders Books
Bose Corporation
Branch-Smith Printing Division
British Standards Institute
Bronson Methodist Hospital
Budapest Festival Orchestra

Cadillac Motor Car Company
Cardinal Glennon Children's Hospital, St. Louis
Caterpillar Financial Services Corporation
CBS
Center for Creative Leadership
Center for Quality of Management
Centers for Medicare and Medicaid Services
Chase Manhattan Bank
Chick-fil-A
Chrysler Corporation
Chugach School District (Alaska)
Cincinnati Fiberglass
Cincinnati Milacron
Citibank
Clarke American Checks
Clifton Metal Works
CNH Capital
Coca-Cola Company
Compaq
Computer Associates
Consolidated School District 15 (D15)
Consumer Product Safety Commission
Consumer's Checkbook
Continental Airlines
Convergys Corporation
Coors Brewing Company
Copeland Companies
Corning, Incorporated
Corning Telecommunications Products Division
Crawford Consumer Products
Cummins Engine Company
Custom Research Inc.

Daimler-Chrysler
Dana Corporation-Spicer Driveshaft Division
Datsun
Day Industries
Deere & Company
Delcor Homes
Dell Inc.
Domino's Pizza
Douglas Aircraft
Dover Corporation
Dow Chemical Company
Doyleston Hospital, Philadelphia
DuPont
DynMcDermott Petroleum Operations Company

Eastman Chemical Company
Economic Club of Chicago
ENBI Corporation
Enron
Enterprise Resource Planning
Environmental Protection Agency
European Foundation for Quality Management
European Organization for Quality Control

continued in back of book

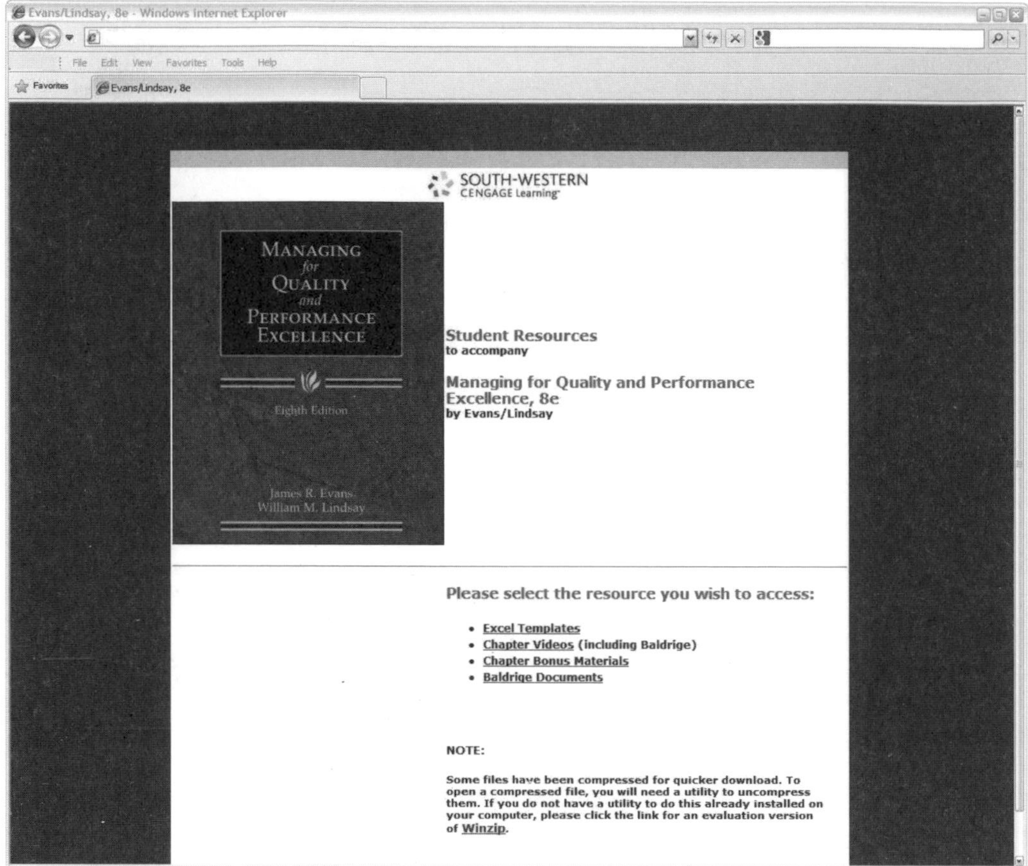

Attention Students:

The Student Premium Website is accessible via an access code. The code is bound in the front cover of your new textbook along with instructions on how to register.

Materials on the Premium Website include additional cases, videos showcasing quality in action, datasets, and much more!

For information, visit: www.cengage.com/decisionsciences/evans today!

Managing for Quality and Performance Excellence

1. 5 chap
2 " 222
3 11 544 400 chp8
4 5 239
5 13 706 712
6 12 604-607
7 11 568-569

5, 11, 12, 13

Managing for Quality and Performance Excellence

Eighth Edition

James R. Evans
University of Cincinnati

William M. Lindsay
Northern Kentucky University

Australia • Brazil • Japan • Korea • Mexico • Singapore • Spain • United Kingdom • United States

Managing for Quality and Performance Excellence, Eighth Edition
James R. Evans and William M. Lindsay

Vice President of Editorial, Business: Jack W. Calhoun

Publisher: Joe Sabatino

Senior Acquisitions Editor: Charles McCormick Jr.

Development Editor: Elizabeth Lowry

Marketing Manager: Bryant Chrzan

Content Project Manager: Lindsay Bethoney

Media Editor: Chris Valentine

Senior Art Director: Stacy Jenkins Shirley

Print Buyer: Miranda Klapper

Text Permissions Manager: Mardell Glinski Schultz

Image Permissions Manager: Deanna Ettinger

Production Service: Pre-Press PMG

Internal Designer: Pre-Press PMG

Copy Editor: Christine Hobberlin

Cover Designer: LouAnn Thesing

Compositor: Pre-Press PMG

Library of Congress Control Number: 2009937733

ISBN-13: 978-0-324-78320-9

ISBN-10: 0-324-78320-5

South-Western Cengage Learning
5191 Natorp Boulevard
Mason, OH 45040
USA

Cengage Learning is a leading provider of customized learning solutions with office locations around the globe, including Singapore, the United Kingdom, Australia, Mexico, Brazil, and Japan. Locate your local office at: **international.cengage.com/region**

Cengage Learning products are represented in Canada by Nelson Education, Ltd.

For your course and learning solutions, visit **academic.cengage.com**

Purchase any of our products at your local college store or at our preferred online store **www.ichapters.com**

Printed in the United States of America
1 2 3 4 5 6 7 13 12 11 10 9

Brief Contents

Preface xix

1 The Quality System 1

Chapter 1 Introduction 3
Chapter 2 Total Quality in Organizations 47
Chapter 3 Philosophies and Frameworks 89

2 The Management System 151

Chapter 4 Strategic Focus for Performance Excellence 153
Chapter 5 Focusing on Customers 189
Chapter 6 High Performance Workforce Management 245
Chapter 7 Process Management 305
Chapter 8 Performance Measurement and Information Management 363
Chapter 9 Leading, Building, and Sustaining Performance Excellence 421

3 Six Sigma and the Technical System 477

Chapter 10 Statistical Thinking and Applications 479
Chapter 11 Six Sigma and Process Improvement 527
Chapter 12 Design for Quality and Product Excellence 581
Chapter 13 Statistical Process Control 659

Appendixes A-1

CONTENTS

Preface xix

1 THE QUALITY SYSTEM 1

CHAPTER 1 INTRODUCTION 3

THE HISTORY AND IMPORTANCE OF QUALITY 4
- The Age of Craftsmanship 5

QUALITY PROFILES: CLARKE AMERICAN CHECKS, INC., AND MOTOROLA, INC. 6
- The Early Twentieth Century 7
- Post–World War II 8
- The U.S. "Quality Revolution" 8
- Early Successes 10
- From Product Quality to Total Quality Management 10
- Disappointments and Criticism 11
- Performance Excellence 12
- Emergence of Six Sigma 12
- Current and Future Challenges 12

DEFINING QUALITY 14
- Judgmental Perspective 15
- Product-Based Perspective 15
- User-Based Perspective 16
- Value-Based Perspective 16
- Manufacturing-Based Perspective 17
- Integrating Perspectives on Quality 17
- Customer-Driven Quality 19

TOTAL QUALITY: PRINCIPLES, PRACTICES, AND TECHNIQUES 20
- TQ Principles 20
- TQ Practices 25
- TQ Techniques 25

Quality and Competitive Advantage 25
Quality and Business Results 27
Three Levels of Quality 29
Quality and Personal Values 30
Summary of Key Points and Terminology 31
Quality in Practice: From Leadership Through Quality to Lean Six Sigma at Xerox 31
Quality in Practice: Quality Practices in Modern China 36
Review Questions 38
Discussion Questions 38
Projects, Etc. 40
Cases Skilled Care Pharmacy 41
Designing a Quality-Based Business 43
Deere & Co. 43
Notes 45

Chapter 2 Total Quality in Organizations 47
Quality Profiles: Jenks Public Schools and the City of Coral Springs 48
Quality and Systems Thinking 50
Quality in Manufacturing 50
Manufacturing Systems 51
Quality in Services 56
Contrasts with Manufacturing 57
Components of Service System Quality 58
Quality in Health Care 61
Quality in Education 64
Koalaty Kid 66
Quality in Higher Education 69
Quality in Small Businesses and Not-for-Profits 71
Quality in the Public Sector 73
Quality in the Federal Government 73
State and Local Quality Efforts 75
Summary of Key Points and Terminology 76
Quality in Practice: Service Quality at The Ritz-Carlton Hotel Company, L.L.C. 76
Quality in Practice: Kenneth W. Monfort College of Business 78
Review Questions 80
Discussion Questions 81
Projects, Etc. 82
Cases The Nightmare on Telecom Street 83
U.S. Water Resource Agency—Flagstaff District 84
Walker Auto Sales and Service 85
Notes 86

CHAPTER 3 PHILOSOPHIES AND FRAMEWORKS 89
QUALITY PROFILES: TEXAS NAMEPLATE COMPANY, INC., AND THE CEDAR FOUNDATION 90
THE DEMING PHILOSOPHY 91
Foundations of the Deming Philosophy 92
Deming's 14 Points 99
THE JURAN PHILOSOPHY 104
THE CROSBY PHILOSOPHY 106
COMPARISONS OF QUALITY PHILOSOPHIES 108
OTHER QUALITY PHILOSOPHERS 109
A. V. Feigenbaum 109
Kaoru Ishikawa 110
Genichi Taguchi 110
QUALITY MANAGEMENT AWARDS AND FRAMEWORKS 111
THE MALCOLM BALDRIGE NATIONAL QUALITY AWARD 111
History and Purpose 112
The Crite ria for Performance Excellence 114
Criteria Evolution 119
Using the Baldrige Criteria 119
Impacts of the Baldrige Program 121
Baldrige and Deming 121
INTERNATIONAL QUALITY AWARD PROGRAMS 122
The Deming Prize 122
European Quality Award 123
Canadian Awards for Business Excellence 125
Australian Business Excellence Award 125
Quality Awards in China 127
Baldrige and National Culture 128
ISO 9000:2000 128
Structure of the ISO 9000:2000 Standards 129
Factors Leading to ISO 9000:2000 130
Implementation and Registration 132
Benefits of ISO 9000 132
SIX SIGMA 133
Evolution of Six Sigma 133
Six Sigma as a Quality Framework 135
BALDRIGE, ISO 9000, AND SIX SIGMA 135
SUMMARY OF KEY POINTS AND TERMINOLOGY 138
QUALITY IN PRACTICE: ISO 9000 AND SEARS' QUALITY MANAGEMENT SYSTEM 138
QUALITY IN PRACTICE: INTEGRATING QUALITY FRAMEWORKS AT VERIDIAN HOMES 139
REVIEW QUESTIONS 141
DISCUSSION QUESTIONS 142
PROJECTS, ETC. 145

CASES SANTA CRUZ GUITAR COMPANY 145
CAN SIX SIGMA WORK IN HEALTH CARE? 147
NOVEL CONNECT: UNDERSTANDING THE ORGANIZATIONAL ENVIRONMENT 147
SHARE FOOD CASE STUDY: UNDERSTANDING THE ORGANIZATIONAL ENVIRONMENT 148
NOTES 148

2 THE MANAGEMENT SYSTEM 151

CHAPTER 4 STRATEGIC FOCUS FOR PERFORMANCE EXCELLENCE 153
QUALITY PROFILES: PAL'S SUDDEN SERVICE AND PREMIER, INC. 155
STRATEGIC LEADERSHIP 156
UNDERSTANDING THE ORGANIZATIONAL ENVIRONMENT 157
STRATEGY DEVELOPMENT 162
STRATEGY DEPLOYMENT 165
Hoshin Kanri (Policy Deployment) 167
Linking Human Resource Plans and Business Strategy 169
THE SEVEN MANAGEMENT AND PLANNING TOOLS 171
ORGANIZATIONAL DESIGN FOR PERFORMANCE EXCELLENCE 171
CORE COMPETENCIES AND STRATEGIC WORK SYSTEM DESIGN 175
STRATEGIC PLANNING IN THE BALDRIGE CRITERIA, ISO 9000, AND SIX SIGMA 177
SUMMARY OF KEY POINTS AND TERMINOLOGY 178
QUALITY IN PRACTICE: INTEGRATING SIX SIGMA WITH STRATEGIC PLANNING AT CIGNA 178
QUALITY IN PRACTICE: STRATEGIC PLANNING AT BRANCH-SMITH PRINTING DIVISION 180
REVIEW QUESTIONS 182
DISCUSSION QUESTIONS 183
PROJECTS, ETC. 184
CASES A STRATEGIC BOTTLENECK 185
CLIFTON METAL WORKS 185
NOVEL CONNECT—CORE COMPETENCIES AND WORK SYSTEMS DESIGN 186
NOVEL CONNECT—STRATEGIC PLANNING 187
NOTES 187

CHAPTER 5 FOCUSING ON CUSTOMERS 189
QUALITY PROFILES: PARK PLACE LEXUS AND MERCY HEALTH SYSTEM 191
THE IMPORTANCE OF CUSTOMER SATISFACTION AND ENGAGEMENT 192
The American Customer Satisfaction Index 194
IDENTIFYING CUSTOMERS 195
Customer Segmentation 196

UNDERSTANDING CUSTOMER NEEDS 198
Gathering and Analyzing the Voice of the Customer 201
LINKING CUSTOMER INFORMATION TO DESIGN, PRODUCTION, AND SERVICE DELIVERY 205
BUILDING A CUSTOMER-FOCUSED CULTURE 208
Commitments and Customer Support 209
Selecting and Developing Customer Contact Employees 210
Customer Contact Requirements 211
Complaint Management and Service Recovery 212
Strategic Partnerships and Alliances 215
Customer-Focused Technology 215
MEASURING CUSTOMER ENGAGEMENT 217
Designing Satisfaction Surveys 218
Analyzing and Using Customer Feedback 222
Why Many Customer Satisfaction Efforts Fail 224
Customer Perceived Value 225
CUSTOMER FOCUS IN THE BALDRIGE CRITERIA, ISO 9000, AND SIX SIGMA 226
SUMMARY OF KEY POINTS AND TERMINOLOGY 227
QUALITY IN PRACTICE: UNDERSTANDING THE VOICE OF THE CUSTOMER AT LAROSA'S PIZZERIAS 227
QUALITY IN PRACTICE: CUSTOMER FOCUS AT AMAZON.COM 228
REVIEW QUESTIONS 230
DISCUSSION QUESTIONS 231
PROJECTS, ETC. 235
CASES PAULI'S RESTAURANT AND MICROBREWERY 237
FIRST INTERNET RELIABLE BANK 238
GOLD STAR CHILI (A) 241
NOVEL CONNECT: CUSTOMER FOCUS 242
NOTES 242

CHAPTER 6 HIGH PERFORMANCE WORKFORCE MANAGEMENT 245
QUALITY PROFILES: SUNNY FRESH FOODS AND PRO-TEC COATING COMPANY 247
THE EVOLUTION OF WORKFORCE MANAGEMENT 248
PRINCIPLES OF ENGAGEMENT AND MOTIVATION 250
Workforce Engagement 250
Motivation 253
DESIGNING HIGH-PERFORMANCE WORK SYSTEMS 256
Work and Job Design 257
Empowerment 259
Teamwork 261
Developing and Empowering Teams 268
Workplace Environment 270
Engaging the Workforce in Process Excellence 271

Skills for Team Leaders 272
Skills for Team Members 272
MANAGING HIGH-PERFORMANCE WORK SYSTEMS 273
Compensation and Recognition 274
Performance Management 278
Assessing Workforce Engagement, Satisfaction, and Effectiveness 281
SUSTAINING HIGH-PERFORMANCE WORK SYSTEMS 282
Workforce Capability and Capacity 282
Workforce Learning and Development 286
WORKFORCE FOCUS IN THE BALDRIGE CRITERIA, ISO 9000, AND SIX SIGMA 288
SUMMARY OF KEY POINTS AND TERMINOLOGY 289
QUALITY IN PRACTICE: TRAINING FOR IMPROVING SERVICE QUALITY AT HONDA 289
QUALITY IN PRACTICE: IMPROVING EMPLOYEE RETENTION THROUGH SIX SIGMA 292
REVIEW QUESTIONS 294
DISCUSSION QUESTIONS 295
PROJECTS, ETC. 298
CASES GOLDEN PLAZA HOTEL 298
THE HOPEFUL TELECOMMUTER 299
NORDAM EUROPE, LTD. 300
NOVEL CONNECT: WORKFORCE FOCUS 302
NOTES 302

CHAPTER 7 PROCESS MANAGEMENT 305
QUALITY PROFILES: DYNMCDERMOTT PETROLEUM OPERATIONS COMPANY AND BOEING AEROSPACE SUPPORT 306
BUSINESS PROCESSES 307
Process Requirements 310
PROCESS MANAGEMENT FRAMEWORKS 311
DESIGNING WORK PROCESSES 312
Process Design Approaches 313
Mistake-Proofing Processes 317
PROCESS CONTROL 319
Quality Control in Manufacturing 322
Quality Control in Services 323
PROCESS IMPROVEMENT 326
Kaizen 327
Improvement Opportunities 329
PROCESS IMPROVEMENT METHODOLOGIES 330
The Deming Cycle 333
Creative Problem Solving 336
Custom Methodologies 336
BREAKTHROUGH IMPROVEMENT 338
Benchmarking 338
Reengineering 340

Process Management in the Baldrige Criteria, ISO 9000, and Six Sigma 341
Summary of Key Points and Terminology 342
Quality in Practice: Gold Star Chili: Process Management 342
Quality in Practice: Building Japanese Quality in North America 345
Review Questions 347
Discussion Questions 348
Projects, Etc. 356
Cases The State University Experience 357
The PIVOT Initiative at Midwest Bank, Part I 358
Novel Connect: Process Management 359
Notes 359

Chapter 8 Performance Measurement and Information Management 363
Quality Profiles: Wainwright Industries, Inc. and Baptist Hospital, Inc. 366
The scope of performance measurement 367
The Balanced Scorecard 368
Product Outcomes 370
Customer-Focused Outcomes 372
Financial and Market Outcomes 372
Workforce-Focused Outcomes 372
Process Effectiveness Outcomes 373
Leadership Outcomes 373
Designing Effective Performance Measurement Systems 374
Selecting Measures and Indicators 374
Linking Measures to Strategy 375
Process-Level Measurements 376
Identifying and Selecting Process Measures 379
Aligning Strategic and Process-Level Measurements 381
Analyzing and Using Performance Data 383
The Role of Comparative Data 386
Performance Review 387
The Cost of Quality 388
Quality Cost Classification 389
Capturing and Using Quality Costs 390
Quality Costs in Service Organizations 391
Measuring the Return on Quality 392
Managing Information Resources 393
Knowledge Management 395
Knowledge Transfer 397
Measurement and Information Management in the Baldrige Criteria, ISO 9000, and Six Sigma 400
Summary of Key Points and Terminology 402

QUALITY IN PRACTICE: USING THE BALANCED SCORECARD AT THE UNITED STATES POSTAL SERVICE 402
QUALITY IN PRACTICE: KNOWLEDGE MANAGEMENT FOR CONTINUOUS IMPROVEMENT AT CONVERGYS 404
REVIEW QUESTIONS 408
DISCUSSION QUESTIONS 409
PROBLEMS 410
PROJECTS, ETC. 413
CASES SKYHIGH AIRLINES 413
COYOTE COMMUNITY COLLEGE 414
NOVEL CONNECT: IDENTIFYING KEY PERFORMANCE MEASURES 417
NOVEL CONNECT: MEASUREMENT, ANALYSIS, AND KNOWLEDGE MANAGEMENT 417
NOTES 418

CHAPTER 9 LEADING, BUILDING, AND SUSTAINING PERFORMANCE EXCELLENCE 421
QUALITY PROFILES: SAINT LUKE'S HOSPITAL OF KANSAS CITY AND AMERICAN ELECTRIC POWER 422
LEADERSHIP FOR PERFORMANCE EXCELLENCE 423
Leadership Systems 426
Leadership, Governance, and Societal Responsibilities 429
LEADERSHIP THEORY AND PRACTICE 432
Contemporary and Emerging Leadership Theories 433
New Perspectives on the Practice of Leadership 437
BUILDING PERFORMANCE EXCELLENCE IN ORGANIZATIONS 438
Implementing ISO 9000, Baldrige, and Six Sigma 438
Organizational Culture and Performance Excellence 442
Changing Organizational Culture 443
Barriers to Change 447
Best Practices 448
THE JOURNEY TOWARD PERFORMANCE EXCELLENCE 449
The Life Cycle of Quality Initiatives 450
Organizational Learning 453
Self-Assessment 456
LEADERSHIP IN THE BALDRIGE CRITERIA, ISO 9000, AND SIX SIGMA 459
A VIEW TOWARD THE FUTURE 459
SUMMARY OF KEY POINTS AND TERMINOLOGY 461
QUALITY IN PRACTICE: LEADERSHIP CHANGES AT ALCOA 461
QUALITY IN PRACTICE: MERGING DIVERGENT QUALITY SYSTEMS AT HONEYWELL 463
REVIEW QUESTIONS 466
DISCUSSION QUESTIONS 467
PROJECTS, ETC. 468

CASES DISTINGUISHED AD AGENCY 469
NOVEL CONNECT—LEADERSHIP 470
THE PARABLE OF THE GREEN LAWN 470
THE YELLOW BRICK ROAD TO QUALITY 471
NOTES 472

3 SIX SIGMA AND THE TECHNICAL SYSTEM 477

CHAPTER 10 STATISTICAL THINKING AND APPLICATIONS 479
STATISTICAL THINKING 480
QUALITY PROFILES: GRANITEROCK COMPANY AND BRANCH-SMITH PRINTING DIVISION 481
Deming's Red Bead and Funnel Experiments 484
STATISTICAL FOUNDATIONS 490
Random Variables and Probability Distributions 490
Sampling 491
STATISTICAL METHODOLOGY 495
Descriptive Statistics 496
Statistical Analysis with Microsoft Excel 497
Statistical Inference 501
Enumerative and Analytic Studies 505
Design of Experiments 506
Analysis of Variance (ANOVA) 510
Regression and Correlation 512
SUMMARY OF KEY POINTS AND TERMINOLOGY 513
QUALITY IN PRACTICE: IMPROVING QUALITY OF A WAVE SOLDERING PROCESS THROUGH DESIGN OF EXPERIMENTS 514
QUALITY IN PRACTICE: APPLYING STATISTICAL ANALYSIS IN A SIX SIGMA PROJECT AT GE FANUC 516
REVIEW QUESTIONS 519
PROBLEMS 520
PROJECTS, ETC. 523
CASES THE DISCIPLINARY CITATION 523
THE QUARTERLY SALES REPORT 524
THE HMO PHARMACY CRISIS 524
NOTES 525

CHAPTER 11 SIX SIGMA AND PROCESS IMPROVEMENT 527
QUALITY PROFILES: KARLEE COMPANY AND CATERPILLAR FINANCIAL SERVICES CORPORATION 528
THE STATISTICAL BASIS OF SIX SIGMA 529
SIX SIGMA DMAIC METHODOLOGY 531
PROJECT MANAGEMENT FOR SIX SIGMA 536
Six Sigma Project Selection 537

Tools for Process Improvement 540
The "Seven QC Tools" 541
Lean Tools 556
Lean Six Sigma 560
Six Sigma in Services and Small Organizations 560
Summary of Key Points and Terminology 563
Quality in Practice: An Application of Six Sigma to Reduce Medical Errors 563
Quality in Practice: Applying Quality Improvement Tools to an Order Fulfillment Process 565
Review Questions 568
Discussion Questions 568
Problems 570
Projects, Etc. 573
Cases LT, Inc. 574
Janson Medical Clinic 577
Readilunch Restaurant 578
Notes 579

Chapter 12 Design for Quality and Product Excellence 581
Quality Profiles: Spicer Driveshaft and 3M Dental Products Division 582
Product Design Processes 583
Concurrent Engineering 585
Design for Six Sigma 586
Concept Development 587
Concept Engineering 587
Design Development 589
Quality Function Deployment 589
Design for Manufacturability 599
Design and Environmental Responsibility 600
Design for Excellence 601
Target and Tolerance Design 602
Design Optimization 603
The Taguchi Loss Function 604
Design Failure Mode and Effects Analysis 607
Reliability Prediction and Optimization 609
Design Verification 621
Design Reviews 622
Reliability Testing 622
Measurement System Evaluation 623
Calibration 629
Process Capability Evaluation 630
Summary of Key Points and Terminology 637

Quality in Practice: Testing Audio Components at Shure, Inc. 638
Quality in Practice: Applying QFD in a Managed Care Organization 639
Review Questions 642
Problems 643
Projects, Etc. 650
Cases Applying Quality Function Deployment to a University Support Service 651
Black Elk Medical Center 653
Notes 656

Chapter 13 Statistical Process Control 659
Quality Profiles: MESA Products, Inc., and Operations Management International, Inc. 661
Implementing Statistical Process Control 662
The Difference between Control and Capability 662
SPC Methodology 664
SPC Metrics 665
Control Charts for Variables Data 666
Constructing $\bar{x}$- and R-Charts and Establishing Statistical Control 666
Estimating Process Capability 667
Process Monitoring and Control 667
Case Study: La Ventana Window Company 668
Interpreting Patterns in Control Charts 674
Special Control Charts for Variable Data 681
$\bar{x}$- and s-Charts 682
Charts for Individuals 683
Control Charts for Attributes 687
Fraction Nonconforming (p) Chart 688
Variable Sample Size 691
np-Charts for Number Nonconforming 694
Charts for Nonconformances 696
Choosing Between c- and u-Charts 699
Summary of Control Chart Construction 701
Designing Control Charts 703
Basis for Sampling 703
Sample Size 703
Sampling Frequency 704
Location of Control Limits 705
SPC, ISO 9000:2000, and Six Sigma 706
Controlling Six Sigma Processes 707
Pre-Control 707
Summary of Key Points and Terminology 709
Quality in Practice: Applying SPC to Pharmaceutical Product Manufacturing 709
Quality in Practice: Using a u-Chart in a Receiving Process 713

Review Questions 716
Problems 717
Cases Morelia Mortgage Company 724
Murphy Trucking, Inc. 725
Day Industries 727
Notes 727

Appendices
A Areas for the Standard Normal Distribution A-2
B Factors for Control Charts A-3
C Random Digits A-4
Bibliography B-1
Index I-1

PREFACE

The American Society for Quality (ASQ) monitors news items reported in the press (you can add the *ASQ Quality News Today "app"* to an iGoogle website). What types of stories do we find? Food safety and toy recalls, health care, the automotive industry, and various product glitches dominate. Indeed, quality—or lack of quality—is a vital issue in everyone's life. That's why this book is relevant and important for today's students and future business leaders, as well as those already in the workforce. Today's business and not-for-profit organizations need to capitalize on the knowledge and "lessons learned" that excellent organizations have acquired.

With each new edition of *Managing for Quality and Performance Excellence,* we strive to present the most current information about quality management and performance excellence approaches used in the top organizations. As the Malcolm Baldrige National Quality Award framework has been described as "the leading edge of validated management practices" by a former chair of the Baldrige Panel of Judges, we feel that one of the best ways of obtaining such knowledge is from the national role models that have emerged from the Baldrige program in the United States and similar programs throughout the world. Thus, in this new edition, we continue to use Baldrige as the fundamental framework for organizing and presenting key issues of performance excellence. In addition, we continue to provide a comprehensive focus on the technical tools by which quality can be achieved and improved in organizations.

CHANGES IN THE EIGHTH EDITION

The eighth edition of *Managing for Quality and Performance Excellence* continues to embrace the fundamental principles, criteria, and historical foundations of total quality, while providing a foundation for understanding and applying technical tools. In an effort to provide the best coverage and continue to be a leader in the field, we have made several significant changes to the organization of some of the material in this edition. This was done to eliminate some redundancy and improve the logical flow and topical coverage of the material. Specifically, we have consolidated topics in process management, process improvement tools, and quality in product design into new chapters; have expanded the strategic focus on performance excellence into a separate chapter; and have integrated leadership with building and sustaining high-performance organizations. In doing so, we have trimmed the number of pages and eliminated one chapter.

All chapters have been updated to provide the most current coverage available. New topics in this edition include strategic leadership, core competencies and strategic work systems design, customer engagement, workforce engagement, workforce capability and capacity, the life cycle of quality initiatives, lean tools and lean Six Sigma, and design for excellence.

We have also developed new and interesting *Quality Profiles* and *Quality in Practice* cases and a wide variety of examples from organizations around the world. These profiles and QIP cases emphasize the importance of quality in the global economy. We also added new cases and revised many end-of-chapter problems from the previous edition.

Some highlights that continue from the previous edition include:

- Contrasts and comparisons of Baldrige, ISO 9000, and Six Sigma in the managerial chapters of the book
- Student-friendly layout highlighting important concepts
- "Bonus Materials" on the student Premium website that includes additional cases, summaries of key points and terminology, supplementary topics, and additional cases and *Quality in Practice* features
- Text coverage of most of the body of knowledge (BOK) required for ASQ certification as a Certified Quality Manager

As in the previous edition, Part 1 introduces fundamentals, Part 2 concentrates on the management system, and Part 3 focuses on Six Sigma and basic technical topics. This organization provides the instructor with considerable flexibility by focusing on both managerial and technical topics for audiences ranging from undergraduate students to MBA students or executives.

Part 1 provides an introduction to quality management principles.

- Chapter 1 introduces the notion of quality, its history and importance, definitions, basic principles, and its impact on competitive advantage and financial return.
- Chapter 2 explores the role of total quality in all key economic sectors: manufacturing, service, health care, education, and the not-for-profit sector.
- Chapter 3 presents the philosophical perspectives supporting total quality, chiefly those of Deming, Juran, and Crosby, as well as quality management frameworks defined by the Malcolm Baldrige National Quality Award and the Criteria for Performance Excellence, ISO 9000, and Six Sigma.

Part 2 focuses on the management system, which is concerned with planning the organizational systems for performance excellence, focusing on customers' needs, accomplishing goals through the actions of people and work processes, managing information to support good decisions, and leading and sustaining performance excellence efforts. Each of Chapters 4 through 8 summarizes the key relationships and importance of the topics to Baldrige, Six Sigma, and ISO 9000.

- Chapter 4 provides the strategic context for performance excellence, including strategic leadership, strategic planning, organizational design, core competencies, and strategic work systems design.
- In Chapter 5, the focus is on understanding customers and their needs, and practices to build a customer-focused culture and achieve high levels of customer engagement.

- Chapter 6 deals with workforce management practices specifically focused on achieving good business outcomes and engaging the workforce through designing, managing, and sustaining high-performance work systems.
- Chapter 7 focuses on frameworks and techniques of process management, including the design of work processes, process control, and process improvement. The topics are more tightly integrated than in previous editions.
- In Chapter 8, the focus is on the use of data and information to measure and manage organizational performance. This chapter includes discussion of balanced scorecards and modern approaches to knowledge management.
- The final chapter in this part, Chapter 9, deals with leading, building, and sustaining high-performance organizations. Concepts of leadership have been moved to this chapter to emphasize the importance of leadership in driving all the approaches in the previous chapters.

Part 3 includes basic technical issues, tools, and techniques that underpin Six Sigma and process improvement, product design, and process control.

- Chapter 10 focuses on statistical thinking and applications, which provide a foundation for subsequent chapters.
- Chapter 11 introduces Six Sigma and process improvement tools and methodology in a unified fashion.
- In Chapter 12, we focus on quality in product design and the variety of tools and techniques that support it.
- Finally, Chapter 13 provides a basic coverage of statistical process control (SPC). The material has been updated to leverage the capabilities of Microsoft Excel in applying SPC through a comprehensive case study.

Features and Pedagogy to Enhance Learning

Each chapter begins with a single-page *Quality Profile* of two role-model organizations. Significant points of learning are highlighted in distinctive boxes. Quality Spotlight icons in the margin identify examples of unique organizational practices, and computer mouse icons in the margin indicate that extensive supplementary materials may be found on the accompanying Premium website.

The *Quality Profile* presented at the beginning of each chapter provides background, important practices, and results for organizations that embrace total quality principles. Most of these organizations are Baldrige recipients. In each chapter, *Quality in Practice* case studies describe real applications of the chapter material. They reinforce the chapter concepts and provide opportunities for discussion and more practical understanding. Many of the case studies are drawn from real, published, or personal experiences of the authors.

End-of-chapter materials for each chapter include Review Questions, which are designed to help students check their understanding of the key concepts presented in the chapter. All of the chapters in Parts 1 and 2 also have Discussion Questions that are open-ended or experiential in nature, and designed to help students expand their thinking or tie practical experiences to abstract concepts. Chapter 8 and those in Part 3 include Problems designed to help students develop and practice quantitative skills. Most chapters have a section entitled Projects, Etc. that provides projects involving field investigation or other types of research. Finally, each chapter includes several cases, which encourage critical thinking through application of quality concepts to unstructured or comprehensive situations.

Student Premium Website

The URL for the website for the new edition of *Managing for Quality and Performance Excellence* is www.cengage.com/login. The Premium website is accessible with a code that is provided with new copies of the text. "Bonus Materials are available on the student premium website and include additional cases, videos showcasing quality in action, datasets, and more. For information, visit: www.cengage.com/decisionsciences/evans today! Bonus Materials, including the following:

Instructor Resources

Instructor's Resource CD (0-538-45220-X): Place all of the key teaching resources you need conveniently at your fingertips with this all-in-one source for planning, teaching, grading and assessing student understanding and progress. This CD now includes the full Instructor's Manual/Solutions Manual with teaching suggestions and answers to all cases and problems in the text, Test Bank in Word and ExamView® computerized format, and PowerPoint® presentation slides.

PowerPoint® Slides: Created by text coauthor, James Evans, these clear presentation slides help bring your lectures to life, clarify difficult concepts, and provide guides for student note-taking and study. Available on the IRCD and for download on the companion website.

Companion Website: In addition to the quality management strengths, insights into the Baldrige Award, Six Sigma, and ISO 9000 found within this edition, you can access a rich array of teaching and learning resources at the interactive companion website. You can easily download password-protected teaching resources, including brief videos highlighting winning practices of Baldrige award winners, the PowerPoints, Instructor's Manual/Solutions Manual, and Test Bank whenever you need them to support your course.

Instructor's Manual/Solutions Manual: Prepared by text coauthor, William Lindsay, this critical teaching tool contains insightful teaching suggestions and notes as well as answers to all end-of-chapter questions, exercises, problems, and cases for your convenience. Available on the IRCD and online.

Note on Company References and Citations

In today's ever-changing business environment, many companies and divisions are sold, merged, or divested, whereas others have declared bankruptcy, resulting in name changes. For example, Texas Instruments Defense Systems & Electronics Group was sold to Raytheon and is now part of Thales Raytheon Systems Company, and AT&T Universal Card Services was bought by CitiBank (which is now CitiGroup). Although we have made efforts to note these changes in the book, others will undoubtedly occur after publication. In citing applications of quality management in these companies, we have generally preserved their original names to clarify that the practices and results cited occurred under their original corporate identities.

ACKNOWLEDGMENTS

We are extremely grateful to all the quality professionals, professors, reviewers, and students who have provided valuable ideas and comments during the development of this and previous editions, especially Bertie Greer of Northern Kentucky University.

Many people deserve special thanks for their contributions to development and production of the book. Our regards go to our senior acquisitions editor Charles McCormick, Jr., who we regard as a close and valuable friend, developmental editor Elizabeth Lowry, production manager Lindsay Bethoney, technology project manager Chris Valentine, and Mardell Glinski Schultz and Paula Sutherland of the Permissions Coordination Group at Cengage Learning, and Richard Fenton, Mary Schiller, and Esther Craig, our previous editors at West Educational Publishing, and our long-time, now-retired developmental editor at Thomson Higher Education Division, Alice Denny.

Quality expert Joseph Juran was asked in an interview in 2002 what advice he would give to someone just starting out in quality today. He replied, "I would start out by saying 'Are you lucky!' Because I think the best is yet to be. In this current century, we are going to see a lot of growth in quality because the scope has expanded so much . . . away from manufacturing to all the other industries, including the giants: health care, education, and government." We will continue to do our best to improve this book in our quest for quality and to spread what we truly believe is a fundamentally important message to current and future generations of business leaders.

James R. Evans (james.evans@uc.edu)
William M. Lindsay (lindsay@nku.edu)

Managing for Quality and Performance Excellence

PART 1

THE QUALITY SYSTEM

H. James Harrington, one of the leading quality management consultants in the world, and a columnist for *Quality Digest* magazine, lamented the lack of a true quality focus in the United States and around the world, from both organizational and personal perspectives. He observed

> *From where I stand, CEOs around the world have lost much of their interest in quality . . . we are more interested in reducing cost, removing waste, and reducing cycle time . . . Maybe it's time we got back to basic quality measurements. We talk about getting to the root cause of problems. Well, I think we need to get to the root results of our actions by measuring the level of customer satisfaction improvement, the increase in mean time to failure, reducing percent defective during the first 90 days of usage, stopping product recalls, and lowering return rates—not dollars saved, inventory turns, or output per hour. We are trying to do everything for everybody, and as a result we are missing the real quality objective—better and better products and services.*
>
> *We need to take pride in what we do. When you go home at night and look in the mirror, will you able to smile and say, "I did my very best"? Too many of us stop short of being our best. We say, "That's good enough," never knowing how good we could be . . . To make up for these sloppy work habits, we are using information technology to offset the lack of interest in the job and the lack of commitment to the organization . . . What we need to do is get back to basics. The things that made us great in the first place are hard work, pride in accomplishment, technical education, and strong family values.*[1]

Does quality matter to you personally as a consumer and future employee or manager? We certainly hope so, because that is what this book is about. While poor quality can be a source of irritation and frustration to you as a consumer, it can be costly to businesses (and investors) in the form of product recalls or lost customers, and can be lethal—a poorly programmed altitude warning system was partly responsible for a 1997 Korean Air crash that killed 228 people. The economic welfare and survival of businesses and nations depends on the quality of the goods and services they produce, which depend fundamentally on the quality of the workforce and management practices that define their organization.

Quality has become a vital component of every modern organization and will remain an important part of a continual quest for improving performance across the globe.

Joseph Juran, one of the most respected leaders of quality in the twentieth century, suggested that the past century will be defined by historians as the century of productivity. He also stated that the current century has to be the century of quality. "We've made dependence on the quality of our technology a part of life."[2] As a member of the emerging generation of business leaders, you have an opportunity and a responsibility to improve the quality of your organization and society at large, not just for products and services, but in everything you say and do.

Part 1 introduces the basic concepts of quality. Chapter 1 discusses the history, definition, basic principles of quality, and the impact of quality on competitive advantage and business results. Chapter 2 describes the role of total quality in different types of organizations—manufacturing, service, health care, education, and not-for-profits—and stresses the importance of taking a systems perspective of quality throughout an organization. Chapter 3 introduces the management philosophies on which modern concepts of quality are based, and managerial frameworks—the Malcolm Baldrige Criteria for Performance Excellence, ISO 9000, and Six Sigma—that guide today's organizational approaches to quality improvement and performance excellence. These topics provide the foundation for the key quality principles and practices that are the subject of the remainder of the book.

NOTES

1. H. James Harrington, "Are We Going Astray?" *Quality Digest*, Feb 2008; "The Decline of U.S. Dominance—Part 1" *Quality Digest*, April 2008; "The Decline of U.S. Dominance—Part 2" *Quality Digest*, May 2008. www.qualitydigest.com . Reprinted with permission.

2. Thomas A. Stewart, "A Conversation with Joseph Juran," *Fortune*, January 11, 1999, 168–169.

Chapter 1

Introduction

Outline

The History and Importance of Quality
- The Age of Craftsmanship

Quality Profiles: Clarke American Checks, Inc., and Motorola, Inc.
- The Early Twentieth Century
- Post–World War II
- The U.S. "Quality Revolution"
- Early Successes
- From Product Quality to Total Quality Management
- Disappointments and Criticism
- Performance Excellence
- Emergence of Six Sigma
- Current and Future Challenges

Defining Quality
- Judgmental Perspective
- Product-Based Perspective
- User-Based Perspective
- Value-Based Perspective
- Manufacturing-Based Perspective
- Integrating Perspectives on Quality
- Customer-Driven Quality

Total Quality: Principles, Practices, and Techniques
- TQ Principles
- TQ Practices
- TQ Techniques

Quality and Competitive Advantage
- Quality and Business Results

Three Levels of Quality

Quality and Personal Values

Summary of Key Points and Terminology

Quality in Practice: From Leadership Through Quality to Lean Six Sigma at Xerox

Quality in Practice: Quality Practices in Modern China

Review Questions

Discussion Questions

Projects, Etc.

Cases Skilled Care Pharmacy
- Designing a Quality-Based Business
- Deere & Co.

Quality is by no means a new concept in modern business. In October 1887, William Cooper Procter, grandson of the founder of Procter & Gamble, told his employees, "The first job we have is to turn out quality merchandise that consumers will buy and keep on buying. If we produce it efficiently and economically, we will earn a profit, in which you will share." Procter's statement addresses three issues that are critical to managers of manufacturing and service organizations: *productivity*, *cost*, and *quality*. Productivity (the measure of efficiency defined as the amount of output achieved per unit of input), the cost of operations, and the quality of the goods and services that create customer satisfaction all contribute to profitability.

Of these three determinants of profitability, the most significant factor in determining the long-run success or failure of any organization is quality. High-quality goods and services can provide an organization with a competitive edge. A reputation for high quality generates satisfied customers, who reward the organization with continued patronage and favorable word-of-mouth advertising, often resulting in new customers.

Restoring a damaged quality reputation can be very difficult. Just consider Ford Motor Company. During the 1980s, Ford fought its way from the bottom of Detroit's Big Three automakers to the top of the pack through a concerted effort to improve quality and better meet customer needs and expectations. It quickly became a highly profitable business. However, on January 12, 2002, a newspaper headline read, "Ford to cut 35,000 jobs, close 5 plants." CEO William Ford is cited as stating "We strayed from what got us to the top of the mountain, and it cost us greatly . . . We may have underestimated the growing strength of our competitors. There were some strategies that were poorly conceived, and we just didn't execute on the basics of our business." The article goes on to observe that Ford "has been dogged by quality problems that forced the recall of several new models, including the Explorer, one of the top money-makers."[1] One of the key elements of Ford's 2002 Revitalization Plan was to "Continue Quality Improvements." Their top *two* "vital few priorities" set by Ford's president for North America are "Improve quality" and "Improve quality"! The new strategy seems to be paying off. In recent years, Ford has received numerous quality-based awards from Strategic Vision, J.D. Power, and other automotive industry organizations, and has appeared to weather the recent economic crisis better than other domestic automobile manufacturers.

If achieving quality were an easy task, there would be little need for this book. The mandate for focusing on quality is clear. In working with Chrysler Corporation to improve quality several decades ago, a vice president of the United Auto Workers (UAW) succinctly stated the importance of quality: "No quality, no sales. No sales, no profit. No profit, no jobs."

In this chapter, we examine the notion of quality. We discuss its history, its importance in business, and its role in building and sustaining competitive advantage. At the beginning of each chapter we profile two leading companies that have developed exemplary quality management practices (see the Quality Profiles on page 6). These examples will help you understand some of the key cultural issues that comprise the foundation of high-performing organizations.

Building—and maintaining—quality into an organization's goods and services, and more importantly, into the infrastructure of the organization itself, is not an easy task.

THE HISTORY AND IMPORTANCE OF QUALITY

In a broad sense, **quality assurance** refers to any planned and systematic activity directed toward providing consumers with products (goods and services) of appropriate quality, along with the confidence that products meet consumers' requirements. Quality assurance depends on excellence of two important focal points in business: the design of goods and services and the control of quality during execution of manufacturing and service delivery, which is often aided by some form of measurement and inspection activity.

Quality assurance has been an important aspect of production operations throughout history.[2] For instance, Egyptian wall paintings circa 1450 B.C. show evidence of measurement and inspection. Stones for the pyramids were cut so precisely that even today it is impossible to put a knife blade between the blocks.

The Egyptians' success was due to good design, the consistent use of well-developed building methods and procedures, and precise measuring devices.

The birth of modern quality asssurance methods actually began the twelfth century B.C. in China during the Zhou Dynasty. Specific governmental departments were created and given responsibility for:

- Production, inventory, and product distribution of raw material (what we now call supply chain management)
- Production and manufacturing
- Formulating and executing quality standards
- Supervision and inspection

These departments were well organized and helped establish China's central control over production processes. The system even included an independent quality organization responsible for end-to-end oversight that reported directly to the highest level of government.

The central government issued policies and procedures to control production across China—including production of utensils, carts, cotton, and silk—and prohibited the sale of nonconforming, inferior, and substandard products. An example of one of the decrees of the Zhou Dynasty is: "Utensils under standards are not allowed to be sold on the market; carts under standards are not allowed to be sold on the market; cottons and silks of which the quality and size are not up to the standards are not allowed to be sold on the market." In ancient China, inspection at various stages by the workers themselves was important in establishing responsibility for quality. When a product was found to be nonconforming, the responsible worker was identified and the root causes for the failure evaluated. A Quality in Practice feature at the end of this chapter examines the role of quality in modern China.

The Age of Craftsmanship

During the Middle Ages in Europe, the skilled craftsperson served both as manufacturer and inspector. "Manufacturers" who dealt directly with the customer took considerable pride in workmanship. Craft guilds, consisting of masters, journeymen, and apprentices, emerged to ensure that craftspeople were adequately trained. Quality assurance was informal; every effort was made to ensure that quality was built into the final product by the people who produced it. These themes, which were lost with the advent of the Industrial Revolution, are important foundations of modern quality assurance efforts.

In the middle of the eighteenth century, a French gunsmith, Honoré Le Blanc, developed a system for manufacturing muskets to a standard pattern using interchangeable parts. Thomas Jefferson brought the idea to America, and in 1798, the new U.S. government awarded Eli Whitney a two-year contract to supply 10,000 muskets to its armed forces. The use of interchangeable parts necessitated careful control of quality. Whereas a customized product built by a craftsperson can be tweaked and hammered to fit and work correctly, random matching of mating parts provides no such assurance. The parts must be produced according to a carefully designed standard. Whitney designed special machine tools and trained unskilled workers to make parts following a fixed design, which were then measured and compared to a model. He underestimated the effect of variation in production processes, however (an obstacle that continues to plague many companies to this day). Because of the resulting problems, Whitney needed more than 10 years to complete the project. Nonetheless, the value of the concept of interchangeable parts was recognized, making quality assurance a critical component of the production process during the Industrial Revolution.

Quality Profiles

Clarke American Checks, Inc., and Motorola, Inc.

Headquartered in San Antonio, Texas, Clarke American supplies personalized checks, checking account and bill-paying accessories, financial forms, and a growing portfolio of services to more than 4,000 financial institutions in the United States. In the early 1990s, when an excess manufacturing capacity in check printing triggered aggressive price competition, Clarke American elected to distinguish itself through service. Company leaders made an all-out commitment to ramp up the firm's First in Service® (FIS) approach to business excellence. Comprehensive in scope, systematic in execution, the FIS approach defines how Clarke American conducts business and how all company associates are expected to act to fulfill the company's commitment to superior service and quality performance.

From orientation and onward, associates are steeped in the company's culture and values: customer first, integrity and mutual respect, knowledge sharing, measurement, quality workplace, recognition, responsiveness, and teamwork. They are schooled regularly in the application of standardized quality tools, performance measurement, use of new technology, team disciplines, and specialized skills. Individual initiative and innovation are expected. Associates are encouraged to contribute improvement ideas under Clarke American's S.T.A.R.—suggestions, teams, actions, results—program. In 2001, more than 20,000 process improvement ideas saved the company an estimated $10 million.

Motorola, Inc., is among the largest U.S. industrial corporations. Its principal product lines include communication systems and semiconductors, and it distributes its products through direct sales and service operations. Motorola was a leader in the U.S. quality revolution during the 1980s and was one of the initial group of organizations to receive the Malcolm Baldrige National Quality Award in 1988. Two key beliefs guide the culture of the firm: respect for people and uncompromising integrity. Motorola's goals are to increase its global market share and to become the best in its class in all aspects—people, marketing, technology, product, manufacturing, and service. In terms of people, its objective is to be recognized worldwide as a company for which anyone would want to work.

Motorola was a pioneer in continual reduction of defects and cycle times in all the company's processes, from design, order entry, manufacturing, and marketing, to administrative functions. Employees in every function of the business note defects and use statistical techniques to analyze the results. Products that once took weeks to make are now completed in less than an hour. Even the time needed for closing the financial books has been reduced. What used to take a month now requires only four days.

Although the corporation has had its share of difficulties in tough competitive markets and the economic environment that technology companies have encountered, Motorola's focus on quality has not waned. In 2002, the Commercial, Government, and Industrial Solutions Sector (CGISS) was recognized as a Baldrige Award recipient. CGISS is the leading worldwide supplier of two-way radio communications and products and is recognized around the world for its environmental, health, and safety efforts. Customers report high levels of satisfaction, and the division demonstrates strong financial, product quality, cycle time, and productivity performance. These results stem from exceptional practices in managing human assets, sharing data and information with employees, customers, and suppliers, and aligning all its business processes with key organizational objectives.

Source: Adapted from Baldrige Award Recipient Profiles, National Institute of Standards and Technology, U.S. Department of Commerce.

The Early Twentieth Century

In the early 1900s, the work of Frederick W. Taylor, often called the "father of scientific management," led to a new philosophy of production. Taylor's philosophy was to separate the planning function from the execution function. Managers and engineers were given the task of planning; supervisors and workers took on the task of execution. This approach worked well at the turn of the century, when workers lacked the education needed for doing planning. By segmenting a job into specific work tasks and focusing on increasing efficiency, quality assurance fell into the hands of inspectors. Manufacturers were able to ship good-quality products, but at great costs. Defects were present, but were removed by inspection. Plants employed hundreds, even thousands, of inspectors. Inspection was thus the primary means of quality control during the first half of the twentieth century.

Eventually, production organizations created separate quality departments. This artificial separation of production workers from responsibility for quality assurance led to indifference to quality among both workers and their managers. Concluding that quality was the responsibility of the quality department, many upper managers turned their attention to output quantity and efficiency. Because they had delegated so much responsibility for quality to others, upper managers gained little knowledge about quality, and when the quality crisis hit, they were ill-prepared to deal with it.

Ironically, one of the leaders of the second Industrial Revolution, Henry Ford, Sr., developed many of the fundamentals of what we now call "total quality practices" in the early 1900s. This piece of history was not discovered until Ford executives visited Japan in 1982 to study Japanese management practices. As the story goes, one Japanese executive referred repeatedly to "the book," which the Ford people learned was a Japanese translation of *My Life and Work*, written by Henry Ford and Samuel Crowther in 1926 (New York: Garden City Publishing Co.). "The book" had become Japan's industrial bible and helped Ford Motor Company realize how it had strayed from its principles over the years. The Ford executives had to go to a used bookstore to find a copy when they returned to the United States.

The Bell System was the leader in the early modern history of industrial quality assurance.[3] It created an inspection department in its Western Electric Company in the early 1900s to support the Bell operating companies. Although the Bell System achieved its noteworthy quality through massive inspection efforts, the importance of quality in providing telephone service across the nation led it to research and develop new approaches. In the 1920s, employees of Western Electric's inspection department were transferred to Bell Telephone Laboratories. The duties of this group included the development of new theories and methods of inspection for improving and maintaining quality. The early pioneers of quality assurance—Walter Shewhart, Harold Dodge, George Edwards, and others such as Joseph Juran and W. Edwards Deming—were members of this group. These pioneers not only coined the term *quality assurance*, they also developed many useful techniques for improving quality and solving quality problems. Thus, quality became a technical discipline of its own.

The Western Electric group, led by Walter Shewhart, ushered in the era of statistical quality control (SQC), the application of statistical methods for controlling quality. SQC goes beyond inspection to focus on identifying and eliminating the problems that cause defects. Shewhart is credited with developing control charts, which became a popular means of identifying quality problems in production processes and ensuring consistency of output. Others in the group developed many other useful statistical techniques and approaches.

During World War II the United States military began using statistical sampling procedures and imposing stringent standards on suppliers. The War Production Board offered free training courses in the statistical methods developed within the Bell System. The impact on wartime production was minimal, but the effort developed quality specialists, who began to use and extend these tools within their organizations. Thus, statistical quality control became widely known and gradually adopted throughout manufacturing industries. Sampling tables labeled MIL-STD, for military standard, were developed and are still widely used today. The discipline's first professional journal, *Industrial Quality Control*, was published in 1944, and professional societies—notably the American Society for Quality Control (now called the American Society for Quality, www.asq.org)—were founded soon after to develop, promote, and apply quality concepts.

Post–World War II

After the war, during the late 1940s and early 1950s, the shortage of civilian goods in the United States made production a top priority. In most companies, quality remained the province of the specialist. Quality was not a priority of top managers, who delegated this responsibility to quality managers. Top management showed little interest in quality improvement or the prevention of defects and errors, relying instead on mass inspection.

During this time, two U.S. consultants, Dr. Joseph Juran and Dr. W. Edwards Deming, introduced statistical quality control techniques to the Japanese to aid them in their rebuilding efforts. A significant part of their educational activity was focused on upper management, rather than quality specialists alone. With the support of top managers, the Japanese integrated quality throughout their organizations and developed a culture of continuous improvement (sometimes referred to by the Japanese term *kaizen*, pronounced kī-zen). Back in 1951, the Union of Japanese Scientists and Engineers (JUSE) instituted the Deming Prize (see Chapter 3) to reward individuals and organizations who meet stringent criteria for quality management practice.

Improvements in Japanese quality were slow and steady; some 20 years passed before the quality of Japanese products exceeded that of Western manufacturers. By the 1970s, primarily due to the higher quality levels of their products, Japanese companies' penetration into Western markets was significant. Hewlett-Packard reported one of the more startling facts in 1980. In testing 300,000 16K RAM chips from three U.S. and three Japanese manufacturers, Hewlett-Packard found that the Japanese chips had an incoming failure rate of zero failures per 1,000 compared to rates of 11 and 19 for the U.S. chips. After 1,000 hours of use, the failure rate of the U.S. chips was up to 27 times higher. In a few short years, the Japanese made major inroads into a market previously dominated by American companies. The automobile industry provides another, more publicized, example. The June 8, 1987, *Business Week* special report on quality noted that the number of problems reported per 100 domestic models (1987) in the first 60 to 90 days of ownership averaged between 162 and 180. Comparable figures for Japanese and German automobiles were 129 and 152, respectively. In the 1980's the U.S. steel, consumer electronics, and even banking industries also were victims of global competition. U.S. business recognized the crisis.

The U.S. "Quality Revolution"

The decade of the 1980s was a period of remarkable change and growing awareness of quality by consumers, industry, and government. During the 1950s and 1960s, when "made in Japan" was associated with inferior products, U.S. consumers purchased domestic goods and accepted their quality without question. During the 1970s, however, increased global competition and the appearance of higher-quality foreign products on the market led U.S. consumers to consider their purchasing decisions more carefully. They began to notice differences in quality between Japanese- and U.S.-made products, and consequently began to expect and demand high quality and reliability in goods and services at a fair price. Consumers expected products to function properly and not to break or fail under reasonable use, and courts of law supported them. Extensive product recalls mandated by the Consumer Product Safety Commission in the early 1980s and the intensive media coverage of the Challenger space shuttle disaster in 1986, in which the Challenger exploded shortly after takeoff killing all seven astronauts, increased awareness of the importance of quality. Consequently, consumers are more apt than ever before to compare, evaluate, and choose products critically for total value—quality, price, and serviceability. Magazines such as *Consumer Reports* and Internet reviews make this task much easier.

Obviously, the more technologically complex a product, the more likely that something will go wrong with it. Government safety regulations, product recalls, and the rapid increase in product-liability judgments have changed society's attitude from "let the buyer beware" to "let the producer beware." Businesses now see increased attentiveness to quality as vital to their survival. Xerox, for instance, discovered that its Japanese competitors were selling small copiers for what it cost Xerox to make them at the time, and as a consequence, initiated a corporate-wide quality improvement focus to meet the challenge. Xerox, and its former CEO David Kearns, who led their "Leadership Through Quality" initiative, were a major influence in the promotion of quality among U.S. corporations. In the five years of continuous improvement culminating in the firm's winning the Malcolm Baldrige National Quality Award in 1989, defects per 100 machines were decreased by 78 percent, unscheduled maintenance was decreased by 40 percent, manufacturing costs dropped 20 percent, product development time decreased by 60 percent, overall product quality improved 93 percent, service response time was improved by 27 percent, and the company recaptured much of the market it had lost. The company experienced strong growth during the 1990s. However, like Ford Motor Company discussed earlier in this chapter, Xerox lost focus on quality as a key business driver, much of it due to short-sightedness on the part of former top management. Fortunately, new corporate leadership recognized the crisis and renewed its focus and commitment to quality (see the Quality in Practice case at the end of this chapter).

A Westinghouse (now CBS) vice president of corporate productivity and quality summed up the situation by quoting Dr. Samuel Johnson's remark: "Nothing concentrates a man's mind so wonderfully as the prospect of being hanged in the morning." Quality excellence became recognized as a key to worldwide competitiveness and was heavily promoted throughout industry.[4] Most major U.S. firms instituted extensive quality improvement campaigns, directed not only at improving internal operations, but also toward satisfying external customers.

One of the most influential individuals in the quality revolution was W. Edwards Deming. In 1980, NBC televised a special program entitled "If Japan Can...Why Can't We?" The widely viewed program revealed Deming's key role in the development of Japanese quality, and his name was soon a household word among corporate executives. Although Deming had helped to transform Japanese industry three decades earlier, it was only after the television program that U.S. manufacturers asked for his help. From 1980 until his death in 1993, his leadership and expertise helped many U.S. organizations to revolutionize their approach to quality.

Early Successes

As business and industry began to focus on quality, the government recognized how critical quality is to the nation's economic health. In 1984, the U.S. government designated October as National Quality Month. In 1985, NASA announced an Excellence Award for Quality and Productivity. In 1987, the Malcolm Baldrige National Quality Award (see Chapter 3), a statement of national intent to provide quality leadership, was established by an act of Congress. The Baldrige Award became the most influential instrument for creating quality awareness among U.S. businesses. In 1988, President Reagan established the Federal Quality Prototype Award and the President's Award for governmental agencies.

From the late 1980s and through the mid-1990s, interest in quality grew at an unprecedented rate, fueled in part by publicity from the Malcolm Baldrige National Quality Award. Manufacturers as well as service organizations made significant strides in improving quality. In the automobile industry, for example, improvement efforts by U.S. automakers reduced the number of problems reported per 100 domestic cars in the first 60 to 90 days of ownership from about 170 in 1987 to 136 in 1991. The gaps between Japanese and U.S. quality began to narrow, and U.S. firms regained much of the ground they had lost. (The rate has continued to improve, and many domestic models now rank among the top in recent J.D. Power and Associates' Initial Quality surveys.)

In 1989, Florida Power and Light was the first non-Japanese company to be awarded Japan's coveted Deming Prize for quality; AT&T Power Systems was the second in 1994. Quality practices expanded into the service sector and into such nonprofit organizations as schools and hospitals. By 1990, quality drove nearly every organization's quest for success. By the mid-1990s, thousands of professional books had been written, and quality-related consulting and training had blossomed into an industry. Organizations began to share their knowledge and experience through formal and informal networking. New quality awards were established by the federal government under the Clinton administration. The majority of states in the United States developed award programs for recognizing quality achievements in business, education, not-for-profits, and government. In 1999, Congress added nonprofit education and health care sectors to the Baldrige Award, and all other nonprofit organizations became eligible in 2007.

From Product Quality to Total Quality Management

In the 1970s, a General Electric task force studied consumer perceptions of the quality of various GE product lines.[5] Lines with relatively poor reputations for quality were found to deemphasize the customer's viewpoint, regard quality as synonymous with tight tolerance and conformance to specifications, tie quality objectives to manufacturing flow, express quality objectives as the number of defects per unit, and use formal quality control systems only in manufacturing. In contrast, product lines that received customer praise were found to emphasize satisfying customer expectations, determine customer needs through market research, use customer-based quality performance measures, and have formalized quality control systems in place for all business functions, not just for manufacturing. The task force concluded that quality must not be viewed solely as a technical discipline, but rather as a management discipline. That is, quality issues permeate all aspects of business enterprise: design, marketing, manufacturing, human resource management, supplier relations, and financial management, to name just a few.

Managers began to realize that the approaches they use to listen to customers and develop long-term relationships, develop strategy, measure performance and analyze data, reward and train employees, design and deliver products and services, and act as leaders in their organizations are the true enablers of quality, customer satisfaction, and business results. In other words, they recognized that the "quality of management" is as important as the "management of quality." In this fashion, quality assurance gave way to *quality management*. Many began to use the term **Big Q** to contrast the difference between managing for quality in all organizational processes as opposed to focusing solely on manufacturing quality (**Little q**).

As organizations came to recognize the broad scope of quality, the concept of **total quality management (TQM),** or simply **total quality (TQ),** emerged. A definition of total quality was endorsed in 1992 by the chairs and CEOs of nine major U.S. corporations in cooperation with deans of business and engineering departments of major universities, and recognized consultants:

> *Total Quality (TQ) is a people-focused management system that aims at continual increase in customer satisfaction at continually lower real cost. TQ is a total system approach (not a separate area or program) and an integral part of high-level strategy; it works horizontally across functions and departments, involves all employees, top to bottom, and extends backward and forward to include the supply chain and the customer chain. TQ stresses learning and adaptation to continual change as keys to organizational success.*
>
> *The foundation of total quality is philosophical: the scientific method. TQ includes systems, methods, and tools. The systems permit change; the philosophy stays the same. TQ is anchored in values that stress the dignity of the individual and the power of community action.*[6]

Procter & Gamble uses a concise definition: Total quality is the unyielding and continually improving effort by everyone in an organization to understand, meet, and exceed the expectations of customers.

Actually, the concept of TQ had been around for some time. A. V. Feigenbaum recognized the importance of a comprehensive organizational approach to quality in the 1950s and coined the term *total quality control*.[7] The Japanese adopted Feigenbaum's concept and renamed it *companywide quality control*. The term *total quality management* was developed by the U.S. Naval Air Systems Command to describe its Japanese-style approach to quality improvement that is based on participation of all members of an organization in improving goods, services, and the organizational culture.

Disappointments and Criticism

Unfortunately, with all the hype and rhetoric (and the unfortunate three-letter-acronym, TQM), organizations scrambled to institute quality programs in the early 1990s. In their haste, many failed, leading to very disappointing results. Consequently, TQM met some harsh criticism. In reference to Douglas Aircraft, a troubled subsidiary of McDonnell Douglas Corporation (since merged with the Boeing Corporation), *Newsweek* stated, "The aircraft maker three years ago embraced 'Total Quality Management,' a Japanese import that had become the American business cult of the 1980s . . . At Douglas, TQM appeared to be just one more hothouse Japanese flower never meant to grow on rocky ground."[8] Other articles in *The Wall Street Journal* ("Quality Programs Show Shoddy Results," May 14, 1992) and the *New York Times* ("The Lemmings Who Love Total Quality," May 3, 1992) suggested that total quality approaches were passing fads

Although quality initiatives can lead to business success, they cannot guarantee it, and one must not infer that business failures or stock price dives are the result of poor quality.

and inherently flawed. However, reasons for TQM failures usually were rooted in organizational approaches and management systems, such as poor quality strategies or good strategies that were poorly executed, and not in the foundation principles of quality management. As the editor of *Quality Digest* put it: "No, TQM isn't dead. TQM failures just prove that bad management is still alive and kicking." A poor strategic business decision such as an inappropriate merger or acquisition, over-emphasis on financial performance, or a change in top management can easily undo years of effort to build a quality-focused organization, as was apparent at Ford and Xerox.

Performance Excellence

As TQM changed the way that organizations thought about customers, human resources, and manufacturing and service processes, many top executives began to recognize that *all* fundamental business activities—such as the role of leadership in guiding an organization, how an organization creates strategic plans for the future, how data and information are used to make business decisions, and so on—needed to be aligned with quality principles, work together as a system, and be continuously improved as business conditions and directions change. From this perspective, the notion of quality has evolved into the concept of **performance excellence**, which can be defined as an integrated approach to organizational performance management that results in

1. Delivery of ever-improving value to customers and stakeholders, contributing to organizational sustainability,
2. Improvement of overall organizational effectiveness and capabilities, and
3. Organizational and personal learning.

As we shall see in Chapter 3, the Malcolm Baldrige National Quality Award provides a framework for organizations that wish to achieve high levels of performance excellence.

Emergence of Six Sigma

In the quest to remain competitive, and after learning from the failures of TQM, a new approach to quality improvement re-emerged in the late 1990s, called **Six Sigma**. Six Sigma is a customer-focused and results-oriented approach to business improvement that integrates many traditional quality improvement tools and techniques that have been tested and validated over the years, with a bottom-line and strategic orientation that appeals to senior managers, thus gaining their support. Many organizations have adopted Six Sigma as a way of revitalizing their quality efforts. Recently, Six Sigma tools have been integrated with lean tools from the Toyota production system to address not only quality problems, but other key business problems involving cost reduction and efficiency. We will discuss the concepts of Six Sigma as they relate to the topics in many chapters of this book and delve into it in more depth in Part III.

Current and Future Challenges

The real challenge today is to ensure that managers continue to apply the basic principles of quality management and performance excellence. Unfortunately, a recent survey sponsored by ASQ found significant gaps between executives' awareness of quality improvement processes and implementation, suggesting that many organizations either are not using these proven approaches or simply don't realize that approaches they do use are rooted in the quality discipline (and may miss key opportunities to improve them).[9] As former Xerox president David Kearns observed, quality is "a race without a finish line."

The global marketplace and domestic and international competition have made organizations around the world realize that their survival depends on high quality.[10] Many countries, such as Korea and India, are mounting national efforts to increase quality awareness, including conferences, seminars, radio shows, school essay contests, and pamphlet distribution. Spain and Brazil are encouraging the publication of quality books in their native language to make them more accessible (this book has been translated into Spanish and Chinese). Several quality-related professional groups united to form the Middle East Quality Association. In addition, the e-TQM College in the United Arab Emirates initiated a master's degree in quality management, and continuing education classes and conferences in the region are full.

These trends will only increase the level of competition in the future. Approaches, such as Six Sigma, require increased levels of training and education for managers and front-line employees alike, as well as the development of technical staff. Thus, a key challenge is to allocate the necessary resources to maintain a focus on quality, particularly in times of economic downturns. However, businesses will require an economic justification for quality initiatives: Quality must deliver bottom-line results. An executive at Texas Instruments observed that "Quality will have to be everywhere, integrated into all aspects of a winning organization." Companies such as Ford and Xerox recognized that the process is not easy; true quality requires persistence, discipline, and steadfast leadership committed to excellence.

In 2008, the American Society for Quality identified seven key forces that will influence the future of quality:[11]

1. *Globalization:* Globalization is driving global supplier networks and the need to manage global quality platforms. Organizations are no longer bound by location and space. Likewise, entirely new consumer markets are being created—often by the Internet, which creates opportunity and concern. Globalization will influence trade policy and trading partners in new, unimagined ways.
2. *Social responsibility (SR):* As organizations begin to realize that social responsibility is not only the moral thing to do, but that it's also good for business, the world will continue to embrace SR philosophies and practices at an increasing rate. Consumers are demanding more knowledge of organizational practices, and corporate reputation will play a greater role in consumer buying choices. Organizations that seek to improve their practices will need to know the concepts, techniques, and tools of quality to deliver on their goals. Issues such as ethics, transparency, social behavior, and environment coincide with the broader considerations of SR and formulate what some have called a "triple bottom line" impact that encompasses people, planet, and profits.
3. *New dimensions of quality:* A new collection of quality-related competencies will be required if quality is to maintain relevance in a quickly changing world. Organizations are looking for leadership in innovation—the ability to develop new ideas and manage change. This necessitates the commingling of quality and innovation. The emerging focus must work within the systems of

organizations—not just be focused on products and services. Organizations must master change and these emerging capabilities, or give way to smaller, newer, and more agile competitors.

4. *Aging population:* The world's population is getting older, and with that trend come problems and solutions. According to a 2008 report from the United Nations on global population changes, the median age is projected to increase from 29 to 38 years between 2009 and 2050. The fastest growing segment of the population will be people 60 years or older.[12] This aging population will push economies and organizations to respond to the resulting market needs. Aging workers will leave the workforce, and organizations will be charged with replacing those skills. This, in turn, may cause traditional retirement to be redefined as organizations seek to tap into the skills of those who have left the workforce.
5. *Health care:* A by-product of the other forces on this list, globalization and the aging population have heightened the need and expectation for quality health care. Quality can play an important role in health care by taking waste out of the system so that more people can benefit. Policymakers must also address equity of access—inefficiencies in the system only exacerbate these problems. On the positive side, advancements in biotechnology and nanotechnology will result in cures for diseases and prolonged lives. This will require increased focus on quality in the waste-free development of these technologies. Quality can also help ensure operational efficiencies in health care delivery.
6. *Environmental concerns:* The world has come to understand that much of the environmental damage that has been done cannot be reversed, and that increasing consumption will put even more strain on finite resources. Quality provides the concepts, tools, techniques, and standards to foster change.
7. *21st century technology:* Technology's impact is difficult to forecast and will most certainly surprise us in terms of how it affects current models we think we understand. Some believe technology will deliver solutions to address energy, food, and water shortages, and the need for clean air. Information technology and advances in genetics, biotechnology, and nanotechnology will change everyday life and drive our future state. A new, innovative definition of quality is required for this innovative age.

A number of implications arise out of these forces. As the business world becomes more complex, quality must be approached from a systems, rather than a process, perspective. Management systems are becoming more integrated; for example, quality, environmental, safety, and health must be viewed together. Quality has transitioned from control, to assurance, to management; the next era will focus heavily on quality of design. Quality will take on more of a strategic, rather than tactical, function. These will challenge both managers and quality professionals.

DEFINING QUALITY

Quality can be a confusing concept, partly because people view quality subjectively and in relation to differing criteria based on their individual roles in the production-marketing value chain. In addition, the meaning of quality continues to evolve as the quality profession grows and matures. Neither consultants nor business professionals agree on a universal definition. A study that asked managers of 86 firms in the eastern United States to define quality produced several dozen different responses, including the following:

1. Perfection
2. Consistency
3. Eliminating waste
4. Speed of delivery
5. Compliance with policies and procedures
6. Providing a good, usable product
7. Doing it right the first time
8. Delighting or pleasing customers
9. Total customer service and satisfaction[13]

Thus, it is important to understand the various perspectives from which quality is viewed in order to fully appreciate the role it plays in the many parts of a business organization.[14]

Judgmental Perspective

One common notion of quality, often used by consumers, is that it is synonymous with superiority or excellence. In 1931, Walter Shewhart first defined quality as the goodness of a product. This view is referred to as the *transcendent* (*transcend*, "to rise above or extend notably beyond ordinary limits") definition of quality. In this sense, quality is "both absolute and universally recognizable, a mark of uncompromising standards and high achievement."[15] As such, it cannot be defined precisely—you just know it when you see it. It is often loosely related to a comparison of features and characteristics of products and promulgated by marketing efforts aimed at developing quality as an image variable in the minds of consumers. Common examples of products attributed with this image are Ritz-Carlton hotels and Lexus automobiles.

Excellence is abstract and subjective, however, and standards of excellence may vary considerably among individuals. Hence, the transcendent definition is of little practical value to managers. It does not provide a means by which quality can be measured or assessed as a basis for decision making.

Product-Based Perspective

Another definition of quality is that it is a function of a specific, measurable variable and that differences in quality reflect differences in quantity of some product attribute, such as in the number of stitches per inch on a shirt or in the number of cylinders in an engine. This assessment implies that higher increasing amounts of product characteristics are equivalent to higher quality. As a result, quality is often mistakenly assumed to be related to price: The higher the price, the higher the quality. Just consider the case of a Florida man who purchased a $262,000 Lamborghini only to find a leaky roof, a battery that quit without notice, a sunroof that detached when the car hit a bump, and doors that jammed![16] A product—a term used in this book to refer to either a manufactured good or a service—need not be expensive to be considered a quality product by consumers. Also, as with the notion of excellence, the assessment of product attributes may vary considerably among individuals.

User-Based Perspective

A third definition of quality is based on the presumption that quality is determined by what a customer wants. Individuals have different wants and needs and, hence, different quality standards. This leads to a user-based definition: Quality is defined as fitness for intended use, or how well the product performs its intended function. Both a Cadillac CTS and a Smart car are fit for use, for example, but they serve different needs and different groups of customers. If you want a highway-touring vehicle with luxury amenities, then a Cadillac may better satisfy your needs. If you want a vehicle for commuting in a congested urban environment, a Smart car might be preferable.

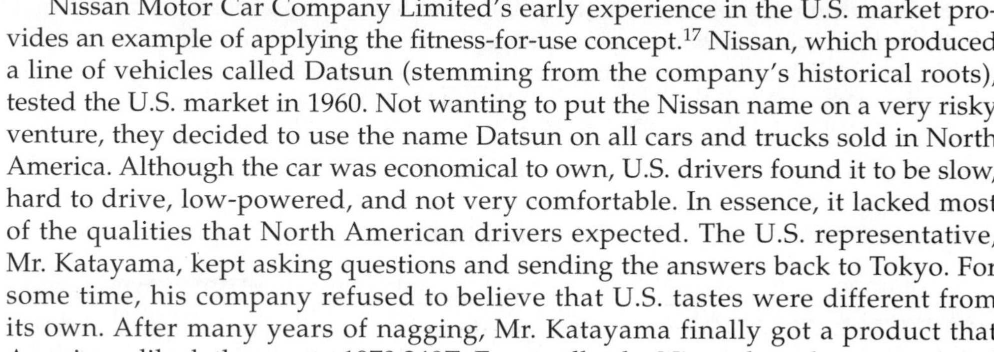

Nissan Motor Car Company Limited's early experience in the U.S. market provides an example of applying the fitness-for-use concept.[17] Nissan, which produced a line of vehicles called Datsun (stemming from the company's historical roots), tested the U.S. market in 1960. Not wanting to put the Nissan name on a very risky venture, they decided to use the name Datsun on all cars and trucks sold in North America. Although the car was economical to own, U.S. drivers found it to be slow, hard to drive, low-powered, and not very comfortable. In essence, it lacked most of the qualities that North American drivers expected. The U.S. representative, Mr. Katayama, kept asking questions and sending the answers back to Tokyo. For some time, his company refused to believe that U.S. tastes were different from its own. After many years of nagging, Mr. Katayama finally got a product that Americans liked, the sporty 1970 240Z. Eventually, the Nissan brand name replaced Datsun. Car enthusiasts will know that Nissan reintroduced a modern version of this classic vehicle in 2002.

A second example comes from a U.S. appliance company whose stoves and refrigerators were admired by Japanese buyers. Unfortunately, the smaller living quarters of the typical Japanese home lack enough space to accommodate the U.S. models. Some could not even pass through the narrow doors of Japanese kitchens. Although the products' performance characteristics were high, the products were simply not fit for use in Japan.

Value-Based Perspective

A fourth approach to defining quality is based on value; that is, the relationship of usefulness or satisfaction to price. From this perspective, a quality product is one that is as useful as competing products and is sold at a lower price, or one that offers greater usefulness or satisfaction at a comparable price. Thus, one might purchase a generic product, rather than a brand name one, if it performs as well as the brand-name product at a lower price. An example of this perspective in practice is evident in a comparison of the U.S. and Japanese automobile markets. A Chrysler marketing executive noted "One of the main reasons that the leading Japanese brands—Toyota and Honda—don't offer the huge incentives of the Big Three (General Motors, Ford, and Chrysler) is that they have a much better reputation for long-term durability." In essence, incentives and rebates are payments to customers to compensate for lower quality.[18]

Competing on the basis of value became a key business strategy in the early 1990s. Procter & Gamble, for example, instituted a concept it calls value pricing—offering products at "everyday" low prices in an attempt to counter the common consumer practice of buying whatever brand happens to be on special. In this way, P&G hoped to attain consumer brand loyalty and more consistent sales, which would provide significant advantages for its manufacturing system.

Competition demands that businesses seek to satisfy consumers' needs at lower prices. The value approach to quality incorporates a firm's goal of balancing product characteristics (the customer side of quality) with internal efficiencies (the operations side).

Manufacturing-Based Perspective

A fifth view of quality is manufacturing-based and defines quality as the desirable outcome of engineering and manufacturing practice, or *conformance to specifications*. **Specifications** are targets and tolerances determined by designers of products and services. Targets are the ideal values for which production is to strive; tolerances are specified because designers recognize that it is impossible to meet targets all of the time in manufacturing. For example, a part dimension might be specified as "0.236 ± 0.003 cm." These measurements would mean that the target, or ideal value, is 0.236 centimeters, and that the allowable variation is 0.003 centimeters from the target (a tolerance of 0.006 cm.). Thus, any dimension in the range 0.233 to 0.239 centimeters is deemed acceptable and is said to conform to specifications. Likewise, in services, "on-time arrival" for an airplane might be specified as within 15 minutes of the scheduled arrival time. The target is the scheduled time, and the tolerance is specified to be 15 minutes.

Conforming to specifications establishes consistency in goods and services. For the Coca-Cola Company, for example, quality is "about manufacturing a product that people can depend on every time they reach for it," according to Donald R. Keough, former president and chief operations officer. Through rigorous quality and packaging standards, the company strives to ensure that its products will taste the same anywhere in the world a consumer might buy them. Even service organizations strive for consistency in performance; The Ritz-Carlton Hotel Company, which we discuss further in Chapter 2, seeks to ensure that its customers will have the same quality experience at any of their properties around the world. Conformance to specifications is a key definition of quality, because it provides a means of measuring quality. Specifications are meaningless, however, if they do not reflect attributes that are deemed important to the consumer.

Integrating Perspectives on Quality

Although product quality should be important to all individuals throughout the value chain, how quality is viewed may depend on one's position in the value chain, that is, whether one is the designer, manufacturer or service provider, distributor, or customer. To understand this concept more clearly from a manufacturing perspective, examine Figure 1.1. The customer is the driving force for the production of goods and services, and customers generally view quality from either the transcendent or the product-based perspective. The goods and services produced should meet customers' needs; indeed, business organizations' existences depend upon meeting customer needs. It is the role of the marketing function to determine these needs. A product that meets customer needs can rightly be described as a quality product. Hence, the user-based definition of quality is meaningful to people who work in marketing.

The manufacturer must translate customer requirements into detailed product and process specifications. Making this translation is the role of research and development, product design, and engineering. Product specifications might address such attributes as size, form, finish, taste, dimensions, tolerances, materials, operational characteristics, and safety features. Process specifications indicate the types

Figure 1.1 Quality Perspectives in the Value Chain

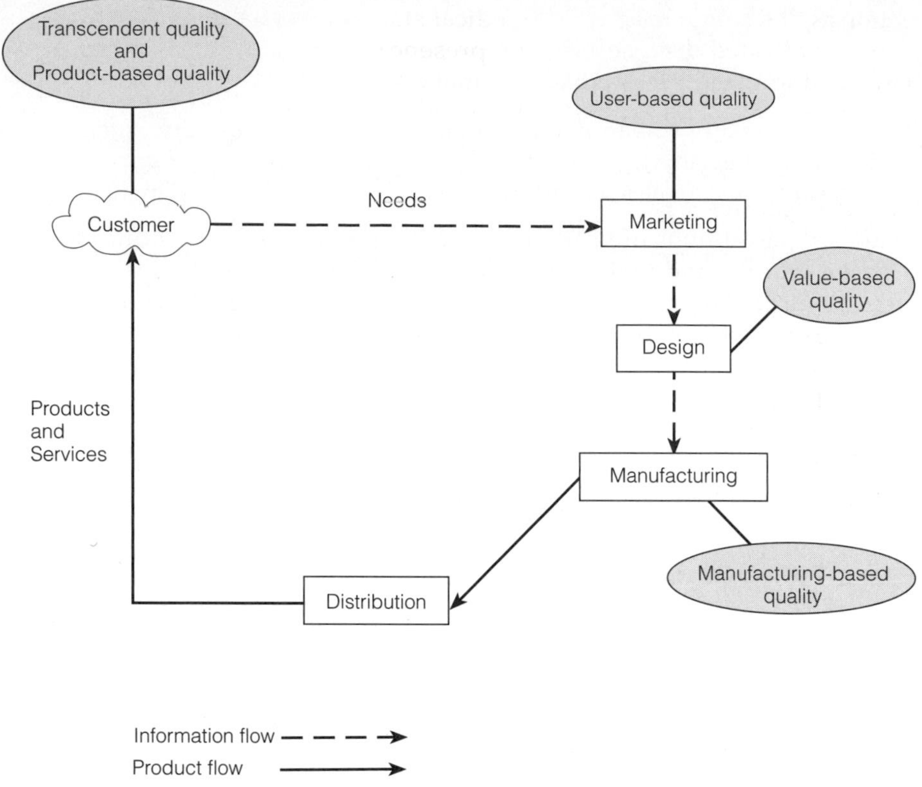

of equipment, tools, and facilities to be used in production. Product designers must balance performance and cost to meet marketing objectives; thus, the value-based definition of quality is most useful at this stage.

A great deal of variation can occur during manufacturing operations. Machine settings can fall out of adjustment; operators and assemblers can make mistakes; materials can be defective. Even in the most closely controlled process, specific variations in product output are inevitable and unpredictable. The manufacturing function is responsible for guaranteeing that design specifications are adhered to during production and that the final product performs as intended. Thus, for production personnel, quality is described by the manufacturing-based definition. Conformance to product specifications is their goal.

The production-distribution cycle is completed when the product has been moved from the manufacturing plant, perhaps through wholesale and retail outlets, to the customer. Distribution does not end the customer's relationship with the manufacturer, however. The customer may need various services such as installation, user information, and special training. Such services are part of the product and cannot be ignored in quality management.

Because individuals in different business functions speak different "languages," the need for different views of what constitutes quality at different points inside and outside an organization is necessary to create products of true quality that will satisfy customers' needs.

Hospital care offers a good illustration of how different views of quality can affect a single product in a service context. The transcendent definition of quality applies to the hospital's need to promote and maintain an image of excellence by ensuring the competency of its medical staff, the availability of treatments for rare or complicated disorders, or the presence of advanced medical technology. Patients and third-party organizations make subjective judgments about this kind of quality. Those who audit hospital efficiency and monitor treatment consistency and resource consumption define quality according to product-based dimensions. This view of quality is predominant among government and health care accrediting agencies.

Patients' perceptions of health care quality are focused on product-based and user-based criteria, and their expectations are high because of widely publicized improvements in medical care, advances in therapeutic drug treatments, and innovative surgery. These expectations increase the pressure on hospitals to provide a variety of services to meet these expectations. As demand for flawless service increases, the medical staff and ancillary services must turn their attention to a manufacturing-based definition of quality. This view of accrediting agencies and the medical profession mandates conformance to various practices and determines licensing requirements for practice.

Customer-Driven Quality

The American National Standards Institute (ANSI) and the American Society for Quality (ASQ) standardized official definitions of quality terminology in 1978.[19] These groups defined quality as "the totality of features and characteristics of a product or service that bears on its ability to satisfy given needs." This definition draws heavily on the product- and user-based approaches and is driven by the need to contribute value to customers and thus to influence satisfaction and preference. By the end of the 1980s, many organizations had begun using a simpler, yet powerful, customer-driven definition of quality that remains popular today:

Quality is meeting or exceeding customer expectations.

To understand this definition, one must first understand the meanings of "customer." Most people think of a customer as the ultimate purchaser of a product or service; for instance, the person who buys an automobile for personal use or the guest who registers at a hotel is considered an ultimate purchaser. These customers are more precisely referred to as **consumers**. Clearly, meeting the expectations of consumers is the ultimate goal of any business. Before a product reaches consumers, however, it may flow through a chain of many firms or departments, each of which adds some value to the product. For example, an automobile engine plant may purchase steel from a steel company, produce engines, and then transport the engines to an assembly plant. The steel company is a supplier to the engine plant; the engine plant is a supplier to the assembly plant. The engine plant is thus a customer of the steel company, and the assembly plant is a customer of the engine plant. These customers are called **external customers**.

Every employee in an organization also has **internal customers** who receive goods or services from suppliers within the organization. An assembly department, for example, is an internal customer of the machining department, and managers are internal customers of the secretarial pool. Most businesses consist of many such "chains of customers." Thus, the job of an employee is not simply to please his or her supervisor; it is to satisfy the needs of particular internal and external customers.

Failure to meet the needs and expectations of internal customers can result in a poor-quality product. For example, a poor design for a computerized hotel reservation system makes it difficult for reservation clerks to do their job, and consequently affects consumers' satisfaction. Identifying who one's customers are and understanding their expectations are fundamental to achieving customer satisfaction. This focus is a radical departure from traditional ways of thinking in a functionally oriented organization. It allows workers to understand their place in the larger system and their contribution to the final product. (Who are the customers of a university, its instructors, and its students?)

Customer-driven quality is fundamental to high-performing organizations. For instance, Hilton Hotels Corp. implemented its Ultimate Service program, which trains employees to anticipate guest needs, personalize service, and if necessary, deal with complaints quickly and seamlessly in an effort to ensure high levels of customer satisfaction. Hilton also uses rigorous inspections and satisfaction loyalty tracking surveys.[20]

TOTAL QUALITY: PRINCIPLES, PRACTICES, AND TECHNIQUES

In a classic research article, James W. Dean, Jr. and David E. Bowen characterize total quality by its *principles*, *practices*, and *techniques*.[21] Principles are the foundation of the philosophy, practices are activities by which the principles are implemented, and techniques are tools and approaches that help managers and employees make the practices effective. All must work together.

TQ Principles

Total quality is based on three fundamental principles:

1. A focus on customers and stakeholders
2. Employee engagement and teamwork by everyone in the organization
3. A process focus supported by continuous improvement and learning

Despite their obvious simplicity, these principles are quite different from traditional management practices. Historically, firms did little to understand external customer requirements, much less those of internal customers. Managers and specialists controlled and directed production systems; workers were told what to do and how to do it, and rarely were asked for their input. Employee engagement and teamwork were virtually nonexistent. A certain amount of waste and error was tolerable and was controlled by postproduction inspection. Improvements in quality generally resulted from technological breakthroughs instead of a relentless mindset of continuous improvement. With total quality, an organization actively seeks to identify customer needs and expectations, to build quality into work processes by tapping the knowledge and experience of its workforce, and to continually improve every facet of the organization.

Customer and Stakeholder Focus The customer is the principal judge of quality. Perceptions of value and satisfaction are influenced by many factors throughout the customer's overall purchase, ownership, and service experiences. To accomplish this task, an organization's efforts need to extend well beyond merely meeting specifications, reducing defects and errors, or resolving complaints. They must include both designing new products that truly delight the customer and

To meet or exceed customer expectations, organizations must fully understand all product and service attributes that contribute to customer value and lead to satisfaction and loyalty.

responding rapidly to changing consumer and market demands. An organization that is close to its customer knows what the customer wants, how the customer uses its products, and anticipates needs that the customer may not even be able to express. It also continually develops new ways of enhancing customer relationships.

A firm also must recognize that internal customers are as important in assuring quality as are external customers who purchase the product. Employees who view themselves as both customers of and suppliers to other employees understand how their work links to the final product. After all, the responsibility of any supplier is to understand and meet customer requirements in the most efficient and effective way possible.

Customer focus extends beyond the consumer and internal customer relationships, however. Employees and society represent important stakeholders. An organization's success depends on the knowledge, skills, creativity, and motivation of its employees and partners. Therefore, a TQ organization must demonstrate commitment to employees, provide opportunities for development and growth, provide recognition beyond normal compensation systems, share knowledge, and encourage risk taking. Viewing society as a stakeholder is an attribute of a world-class organization. Business ethics, public health and safety, the environment, and community and professional support are necessary activities that fall under social responsibility.

Employee Engagement and Teamwork Joseph Juran credited Japanese managers' full use of the knowledge and creativity of the entire workforce as one of the reasons for Japan's rapid quality achievements. When managers give employees the tools to make good decisions and the freedom and encouragement to make contributions, they virtually guarantee that better quality products and production processes will result. Employees who are allowed to participate—both individually and in teams—in decisions that affect their jobs and the customer can make substantial contributions to quality.

In any organization, the person who best understands his or her job and how to improve both the product and the process is the one performing it.

This attitude represents a profound shift in the typical philosophy of senior management; the traditional view was that the workforce should be "managed"—or to put it less formally, the workforce should leave their brains at the door. Good intentions alone are not enough to encourage employee involvement. Management's task includes formulating the systems and procedures and then putting them in place to ensure that participation becomes a part of the culture.

Empowering employees to make decisions that satisfy customers without constraining them with bureaucratic rules shows the highest level of trust. Marriott and Nordstrom are examples of two organizations that empower and reward their employees for service quality. Marriott calls its customer service representatives "associates." Associates are permitted wide discretion to call on any part of the company to help customers and can earn lush bonuses for extraordinary work. Nordstrom's customer service stories are legendary, and include employees who have ironed a new shirt for a customer who needed it that afternoon, one who warmed customers' cars in winter while they shopped, and even one who refunded money for a set of tire chains, even though Nordstrom does not sell them![22]

Another important element of total quality is teamwork, which focuses attention on customer–supplier relationships and encourages the involvement of the total workforce in attacking systemic problems, particularly those that cross functional boundaries. Ironically, although problem-solving teams were introduced in the United States in the 1940s to help solve problems on the factory floor, they failed, primarily because of management resistance to workers' suggestions. The Japanese, however, began widespread implementation of similar teams, called quality circles, in 1962 with dramatic results. Eventually, the concept returned to the United States. Today, the use of self-managed teams that combine teamwork and empowerment is a powerful method of employee involvement.

Traditionally, organizations were integrated vertically by linking all the levels of management in a hierarchical fashion (consider the traditional organization chart). TQ requires horizontal coordination between organizational units, such as between design and engineering, engineering and manufacturing, manufacturing and shipping, shipping and sales. Cross-functional teams provide this focus.

Partnerships with unions, customers, suppliers, and education organizations also promote teamwork and permit the blending of an organization's core competencies and capabilities with the complementary strengths of partners, creating mutual benefits. For example, many organizations seek suppliers that share their own values. They often educate them in methods of improvement. If suppliers improve, then so will they. For instance, Motorola requires suppliers to take courses in customer satisfaction and cycle time reduction at Motorola University. It also established a 15-member council of suppliers to rate Motorola's own practices and offer suggestions for improvement.[23]

Process Focus and Continuous Improvement The traditional way of viewing an organization is by surveying the vertical dimension—by keeping an eye on an organization chart. However, work gets done (or fails to get done) horizontally or cross-functionally, not hierarchically.

*A **process** is a sequence of activities that is intended to achieve some result.*

According to AT&T, a process is how work creates value for customers.[24] We typically think of processes in the context of production: the collection of activities and operations involved in transforming inputs (physical facilities, materials, capital, equipment, people, and energy) into outputs (products and services). Common types of production processes include machining, mixing, assembly, filling orders, or approving loans. However, nearly every major activity within an organization involves a process that crosses traditional organizational boundaries as illustrated in Figure 1.2. For example, an order fulfillment process might involve a salesperson placing the order; a marketing representative entering it on the company's computer system; a credit check by finance; picking, packaging, and shipping by distribution and logistics personnel; invoicing by finance; and installation by field service engineers. A process perspective links together all necessary activities and increases one's understanding of the entire system, rather than focusing on only a small part. Many of the greatest opportunities for improving organizational performance lie in the organizational interfaces—those spaces between the boxes on an organization chart.

Figure 1.2 Process Versus Function

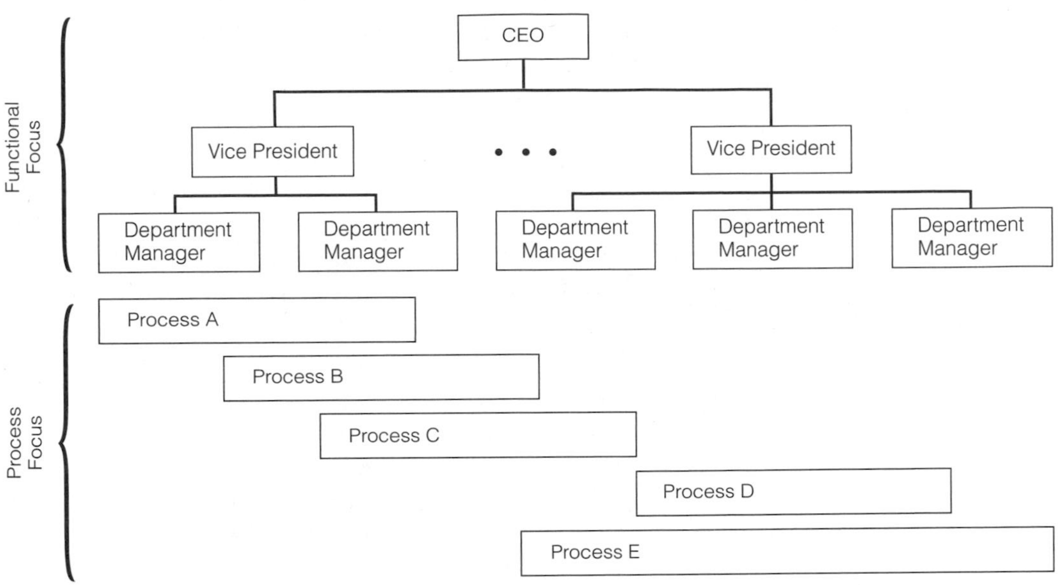

Continuous improvement refers to both incremental changes, which are small and gradual, and breakthrough, or large and rapid, improvements. These improvements may take any one of several forms:

1. Enhancing value to the customer through new and improved products and services
2. Reducing errors, defects, waste, and their related costs
3. Increasing productivity and effectiveness in the use of all resources
4. Improving responsiveness and cycle time performance for such processes as resolving customer complaints or new product introduction

Thus, response time, quality, and productivity objectives should be considered together. A process focus supports continuous improvement efforts by helping to understand these synergies and to recognize the true sources of problems.

Major improvements in response time may require significant simplification of work processes and often drive simultaneous improvements in quality and productivity.

In 1950, when W. Edwards Deming was helping Japan with its postwar rebuilding effort, he emphasized the importance of continuous improvement. While presenting to a group of Japanese industrialists (collectively representing about 80 percent of the nation's capital), he drew the diagram shown in Figure 1.3. This diagram depicts not only the relationships among inputs, processes, and outputs, but also the roles of consumers and suppliers, the interdependency of organizational processes, the usefulness of consumer research, and the importance of continuous improvement of all elements of the production system. Deming told the Japanese that understanding customers and suppliers was crucial to planning for quality. He advised them that continuous improvement of both products and production processes through better understanding of customer requirements is the key to capturing world markets.

Figure 1.3 Deming's View of a Production System

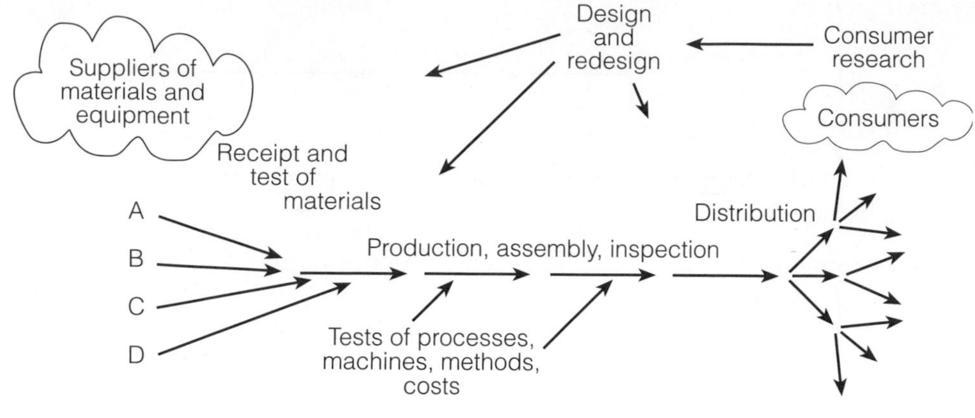

Source: W. Edwards Deming, *Out of Crisis*, p. 5. Copyright © 1986 MIT Press and the W. Edwards Deming Institute. Reprinted by permission.

Deming predicted that within five years Japanese manufacturers would be making products of the highest quality in the world and would have gained a large share of the world market. He was wrong. By applying these ideas, the Japanese penetrated several global markets in less than four years!

Real improvement depends on *learning*, which means understanding why changes are successful through feedback between practices and results, leading to new goals and approaches. A **learning cycle** consists of four stages:

1. Planning
2. Execution of plans
3. Assessment of progress
4. Revision of plans based upon assessment findings

The concept of organizational learning is not new. It has its roots in general systems theory[25] and systems dynamics[26] developed in the 1950s and 1960s, as well as theories of learning from organizational psychology. Peter Senge, a professor at the Massachusetts Institute of Technology (MIT), has become the major advocate of the learning organization movement. He defines the learning organization as

> *. . . an organization that is continually expanding its capacity to create its future. For such an organization, it is not enough merely to survive. "Survival learning" or what is more often termed "adaptive learning" is important—indeed it is necessary. But for a learning organization, "adaptive learning" must be joined by "generative learning," learning that enhances our capacity to create.*[27]

The conceptual framework behind this definition requires an understanding and integration of many of the concepts and principles that are part of the total quality philosophy. Senge repeatedly points out, "Over the long run, superior performance depends on superior learning." Continuous improvement and learning should be a regular part of daily work, practiced at personal, work unit, and organizational levels, driven by opportunities to affect significant change, and focused on sharing throughout the organization.

TQ Practices

TQ practices can be classified into six basic areas of management that are generic to any organization:

1. Strategic planning and design of organizational and work systems
2. Customer engagement and knowledge acquisition
3. Workforce management
4. Process management
5. Information and knowledge management
6. Leadership

These areas represent the focus of Chapters 4 through 9 in this book. Some examples of TQ practices are ensuring that complaints are resolved effectively and promptly (a customer engagement practice); setting organizational vision and values (a leadership practice); allocating resources to support action plans (a strategic planning practice); gathering employee satisfaction data (a workforce management practice); coordinating design and production/delivery processes to ensure trouble-free introduction and delivery of products and services (a process management practice); and reviewing and analyzing organizational performance (an information and knowledge management practice). As we shall see in Chapter 3, the Malcolm Baldrige Criteria for Performance Excellence provides a framework for such TQ practices.

TQ Techniques

TQ techniques include a wide variety of tools and statistical methods to plan work activities, collect data, analyze results, monitor progress, and solve problems. For instance, a chart showing trends in manufacturing defects as workers progress through a training program is a simple tool to monitor the effectiveness of the training; the statistical technique of experimental design is often used in product development activities. Throughout this book we will introduce many techniques that are useful in quality planning, control, and improvement activities.

QUALITY AND COMPETITIVE ADVANTAGE

Competitive advantage denotes a firm's ability to achieve market superiority. In the long run, a sustainable competitive advantage provides above-average performance. S. C. Wheelwright identified six characteristics of a strong competitive advantage:[28]

1. It is driven by customer wants and needs. A firm provides value to its customers that competitors do not.
2. It makes a significant contribution to the success of the business.
3. It matches the organization's unique resources with opportunities in the environment. No two organizations have the same resources; a good strategy uses the firm's particular resources effectively.
4. It is durable and lasting, and difficult for competitors to copy. A superior research and development department, for example, can consistently develop new products or processes that enable the firm to remain ahead of competitors.
5. It provides a basis for further improvement.
6. It provides direction and motivation to the entire organization.

Each of these characteristics relates to quality, suggesting that quality is an important source of competitive advantage.

The importance of quality in achieving competitive advantage was demonstrated by several research studies during the 1980s. PIMS Associates, Inc., a subsidiary of the Strategic Planning Institute, maintains a database of 1,200 companies and studies the impact of product quality on corporate performance.[29] PIMS researchers found the following:

- Product quality is an important determinant of business profitability.
- Businesses that offer premium-quality products and services usually have large market shares and were early entrants into their markets.
- Quality is positively and significantly related to a higher return on investment for almost all kinds of products and market situations. (PIMS studies showed that firms whose products were perceived as having superior quality earned more than three times the return on sales of firms whose products were perceived as having inferior quality.)
- Instituting a strategy of quality improvement usually leads to increased market share, but at the cost of reduced short-run profitability.
- High-quality producers can usually charge premium prices.

These findings are summarized in Figure 1.4. A product's value in the marketplace is influenced by the quality of its design. Improvements in design will differentiate the product from its competitors, improve a firm's quality reputation, and improve the perceived value of the product. These factors allow the firm to command higher prices as well as to achieve a greater market share, which in turn leads to increased revenues that offset the costs of improving the design.

Improved conformance in production or service delivery leads to lower costs through savings in rework, scrap, resolution of errors, and warranty expenses. Philip Crosby popularized this viewpoint in his book *Quality Is Free*.[30] Crosby states:

> *Quality is not only free, it is an honest-to-everything profit maker. Every penny you don't spend on doing things wrong, over, or instead of, becomes half a penny right on the bottom line. In these days of "who knows what is going to happen to our business tomorrow," there aren't many ways left to make a profit improvement. If you concentrate on making quality certain, you can probably increase your profit by an amount equal to 5 percent to 10 percent of your sales. That is a lot of money for free. The net effect of improved quality of design and conformance is increased profits.*

Figure 1.4 Quality and Profitability

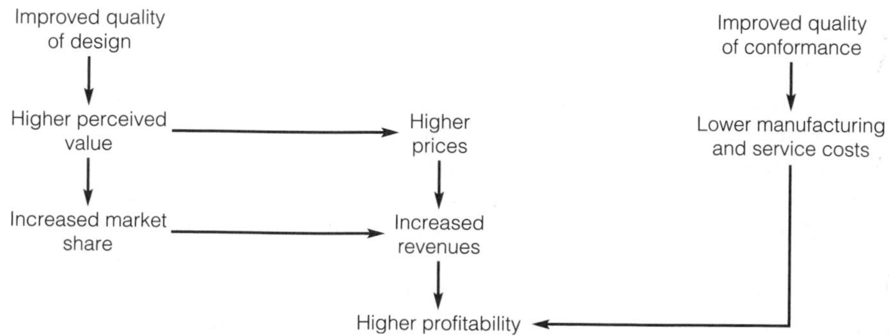

It is vital to focus quality improvement efforts on *both* design and conformance. Many organizations simply confine their quality efforts to one dimension; for example, they might focus on defect elimination but fail to design products that customers really want, or they design great products that are plagued with defects and service errors. A case in point is the auto industry. In 2003, *Business Week* noted that "The Big Three are catching up in quality, but they have miles to go on the wow factor"—that is, designs that excite consumers. Defect rates have fallen more than 80 percent since 1980. For example, the Buick Regal beat out the Toyota Camry and Honda Accord in *Consumer Reports'* reliability rankings, but did not make the recommended list because of ho-hum design compared to its competition. To remedy this, the Big Three have recruited European designers to improve interior amenities and create more exciting exterior styling.[31] On the flip side of the coin is Nissan, which designed and launched many new hot-selling vehicles in the United States, but fell dramatically in J.D. Power & Associates' Initial Quality Survey, resulting in part from using cheaper materials at the expense of manufacturing precision and lacking the engineering resources to check thoroughly for defects during manufacturing.[32]

In today's global marketplace, high conformance is considered "entry into the game," rather than a source of competitive advantage. Quality is simply the foundation for achieving competitive advantage. Competitive success in today's market depends on such attributes as the speed of new product development, flexibility in production and delivery, and extraordinary customer service. For example, *Business Week* reported in 1998 that several wireless communications providers had replaced products from Motorola—a long-time quality leader—with other companies' technologies. A BellSouth spokesman said the products did not pass its "shake and bake test." After Qualcomm, Inc., released digital phones the size of cigarette packs, Motorola was nearly a year behind, and as a result, was quickly losing market share.[33] However, within a year, Motorola's wireless communications returned to profitability, including making a $1 billion, 10-year pact with Sun Microsystems to build wireless telecom equipment for the Internet with a 99.999 percent reliability. Only the most agile companies could make such a quick turnaround.

Quality and Business Results

As an old saying goes, "The proof is in the pudding." Companies that invest in quality management efforts experience outstanding returns and improvements in performance. Various research studies show that quality-focused companies achieved better employee participation and relations, improved product and service quality, higher productivity, greater customer satisfaction, increased market share, and improved profitability.[34]

Considerable evidence exists that quality initiatives positively impact bottom-line results.

Kevin Hendricks and Vinod Singhal published one of the most celebrated studies in 1997.[35] Based on objective data and rigorous statistical analysis, the study showed that when implemented effectively, total quality management approaches improve financial performance dramatically. Using a sample of about 600 publicly traded companies that received quality awards either from their customers (such as automotive manufacturers) or through Baldrige and state and local quality award programs, Hendricks and Singhal examined performance results from six years before to four years after receiving their first quality award. The primary performance measure tracked was the percent change in operating income and a variety of measures that might affect operating income: percent change in sales, total assets, number of employees, return on sales, and return on assets. These results were compared to a set of control firms that were similar in size to the award recipients and in the same industry. The analysis revealed significant differences between the sample and the control group. Specifically, the growth in operating income averaged 91 percent versus 43 percent for the control group. Award recipients also experienced a 69 percent jump in sales (compared to 32 percent for the control group), a 79 percent increase in total assets (compared to 37 percent), a 23 percent increase in the number of employees (compared to 7 percent), an 8 percent improvement in return on sales (compared to 0 percent), and a 9 percent improvement in return on assets (compared to 6 percent). Small companies actually outperformed large companies, and over a five-year period, the portfolio of award recipients beat the S&P 500 index by 34 percent.

A sample of specific operational and financial results achieved by recent Baldrige recipients includes:

1. Among associates at Clarke American, overall satisfaction improved from 72 percent to 84 percent in five years. Rising associate satisfaction correlates with the 84 percent increase in revenue earned per associate. Annual growth in company revenues increased from a rate of 4.2 percent to 16 percent, compared to the industry's average annual growth rate of less than 1 percent over the five-year period.
2. Business satisfaction with the city of Coral Springs, Florida, has risen from 76 percent in 2004 to 97 percent in 2008; 90 percent of businesses would recommend the city to others, up from 82 percent in 2004. In 2006, *Money* magazine named Coral Springs as one of the Best Places to Live. In 2005, 2006, and 2007, the city was named as one of the 100 best communities for young people by America's Promise Alliance.
3. PRO-TEC Coating Company consistently achieves the quality expectations of its customers by delivering products with a defect rate of less than 0.12 percent and has scored better than its competition on product quality, on-time delivery, service, and product development. Its return on assets, a measure of long-term viability, has had a sustained upward trend since 2002.
4. Between 1999 and 2005, Sharp Healthcare gained more than four percentage points in market share, an unprecedented achievement in a mature health care marketplace. Sharp exceeds the national benchmark for first-year functional improvement following joint replacement, the result of a program that tracks parameters such as pain, function, deformity, and range of motion for 10 years following surgery.
5. In 2003, 2004, and 2005, North Mississippi Medical Center (NMMC) was recognized by *Solucient*, a leading source of information for the health care industry, as one of the top 100 performance improvement leaders. NMMC is one of only four hospitals nationwide to be recognized for this distinction three years in a row. In 2006, physician overall satisfaction, measured by Press Ganey Associates, surpassed NMMC's benchmark by 8 percent to 9 percent with overall satisfaction and ease of practice scores at 99 percent and leadership score at 98 percent.
6. Operating margin at Premier, Inc. grew from 35 percent in 2003 to 50 percent in 2006 and exceeded that of Premier's largest competitor in all years, while operating expenses have remained well below those of that competitor. Between 2003 and 2006, operating income per employee grew from $144,000 to $225,000.

7. Sales at MESA Products, Inc. have increased 93 percent since 2000, growing total revenues from $14 million to $27 million in 2006, and return on equity improved from −5 percent in 1999 to more than 25 percent in 2005 and presently exceeds that of industry competitors by 20 percent.
8. Drop-out rates, a measure of student satisfaction for students at Jenks Public Schools in Oklahoma, have decreased steadily from 6.3 percent in 1999 to 1.2 percent at the close of the 2004 school year.

THREE LEVELS OF QUALITY[36]

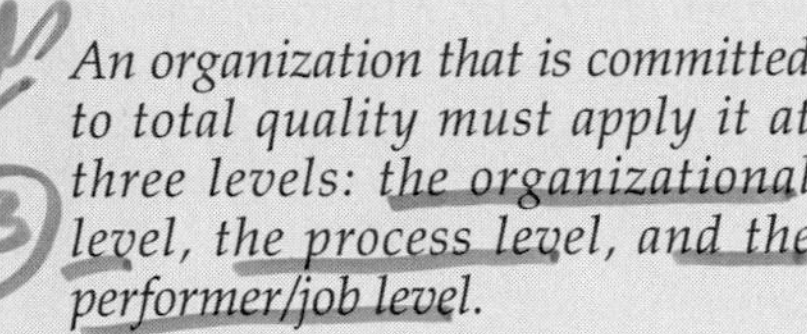

At the organizational level, quality concerns center on meeting external customer requirements. An organization must seek customer input on a regular basis. Questions such as the following help to define quality at the organizational level:

1. Which products and services meet your expectations?
2. Which do not?
3. What products or services do you need that you are not receiving?
4. Are you receiving products or services that you do not need?

Customer-driven performance standards should be used as bases for goal setting, problem solving, performance appraisal, incentive compensation, nonfinancial rewards, and resource allocation.

At the process level, organizational units are classified as functions or departments, such as marketing, design, product development, operations, finance, purchasing, billing, and so on. Because most processes are cross-functional, the danger exists that managers of particular organizational units will try to optimize the activities under their control, which can suboptimize activities for the organization as a whole. At this level, managers must ask questions such as the following:

1. What products or services are most important to the (external) customer?
2. What processes produce those products and services?
3. What are the key inputs to the process?
4. Which processes have the most significant effect on the organization's customer-driven performance standards?
5. Who are my internal customers and what are their needs?

At the performer level (sometimes called the job level or the task-design level), standards for output must be based on quality and customer-service requirements that originate at the organizational and process levels. These standards include requirements for such things as accuracy, completeness, innovation, timeliness, and cost. For each output of an individual's job, one must ask:

1. What is required by the customer, both internal and external?
2. How can the requirements be measured?
3. What is the specific standard for each measure?

Viewing an organization from this perspective clarifies the roles and responsibilities of all employees in pursuing quality. Top managers must focus attention at the organizational level; middle managers and supervisors at the process level; and all employees must understand quality at the performer level. Getting everyone involved is the foundation of TQ.

QUALITY AND PERSONAL VALUES

Today, organizations are asking employees to take more responsibility for acting as the point of contact between the organization and the customer, to be team players, and to provide more effective and efficient customer service. Rath & Strong, a Lexington, Massachusetts-based management consulting firm, polled almost 200 executives from Fortune 500 companies about activities that foster superior performance results for an organization.[37] The survey revealed that personal initiative, when combined with a customer orientation, resulted in a positive impact on business success and sales growth rate. However, although 79 percent of all respondents indicated that employees are increasingly expected to take initiative to bring about change in the company, 40 percent of the respondents replied that most people in their company do not believe that they can make a personal contribution to the company's success. Alan Frohman, a senior associate with Rath & Strong, stated, "These results are significant because they suggest that although people are being expected to take personal initiative, most organizations have not figured out how to translate those expectations into positive behaviors."

Unless quality is internalized at the personal level, it will never become rooted in the culture of an organization. Thus, quality must begin at a personal level (and that means you!)

Such behaviors reflect the personal values and attitudes of individuals. Employees who embrace quality as a personal value often go beyond what they're asked or normally expected to do in order to reach a difficult goal or provide extraordinary service to a customer. A good example involved a young girl who laid her dental retainer on a picnic table at Disney World while eating lunch.[38] She forgot about it until later in the day. The family returned to the spot, found the table cleaned up, and were at a loss to know what to do. They spotted a custodian, told him the problem, and the custodian sought permission from his supervisor to have the garbage bags searched by the night crew that evening! Two weeks later, the family received a letter from the supervisor explaining that, despite their best efforts, they had been unable to locate the retainer.

Robert Galvin, former CEO of Motorola, once told the Economic Club of Chicago, "Quality is a very personal obligation. If you can't talk about quality in the first person . . . then you have not moved to the level of involvement of quality that is absolutely essential." The concept of "personal quality" has been promoted by Harry V. Roberts, professor emeritus at the University of Chicago's Graduate School of Business, and Bernard F. Sergesketter, vice president of the Central Region of AT&T.[39] Personal quality may be thought of as personal empowerment; it is implemented by systematically keeping personal checklists for quality improvement. Roberts and Sergesketter developed the idea of a personal quality checklist to keep track of personal shortcomings, or defects, in personal work processes. The authors defended the use of a checklist to keep track of defects:

> *The word "defect" has a negative connotation for some people who would like to keep track of the times we do things right rather than times we do things wrong. Fortunately, most of us do things right much more than we do things wrong, so it is easier in practice to count the defects. Moreover, we can get positive satisfaction from avoiding defects—witness accident prevention programs that count days without accidents.*

A personal quality checklist can be developed by listing eight or ten items that reflect personal "defects" in separate lines in a column of a spreadsheet. Some examples might be not responding phone calls or emails within 24 hours or failing to exercise at least three times during a week. Adjacent columns for dates and checkmarks that denote defects when items were not accomplished can be added to the spreadsheet (see the project later in the chapter). Note that each item on the checklist should have a desired result, a way to measure each type of defect, and a time frame. Both work and personal defect categories may be listed on the sheet.

Sergesketter plotted defects that he observed during the first 18 months of his use of his own personal quality checklist on a run chart. Many of the results were surprising.[40] For instance, he was surprised at the extent to which he was not returning phone calls the same day. He discovered that he had no way to count defects related to correspondence. As a result, he started to date stamp correspondence when it arrived and date stamp the file copy of the response. None of the items he measured were in the "four-minute mile" category, and yet he started out at a rate of 100 defects per month, but dropped drastically simply because he was aware of them. He also observed that when a person shares a defect list with others, they can help in reducing defects. Sergesketter noted, "I encourage and challenge you to start counting defects. It is impossible to reduce defects if we don't count them, and we can't reasonably ask our associates to count defects if we don't! I really believe that if several thousand of us here in the Central Region start counting defects, we will reduce them and differentiate ourselves from our competitors in a significant way."

In the daily attempt to bring about change in the individual parts of the organizational universe, managers, employees, professors, and students can find that personal quality is the key to unlock the door to a wider understanding of what the concept really is all about.

Personal quality is an essential ingredient to make quality happen in the workplace, yet most organizations have neglected it for a long time. Perhaps management, in particular, operates under the idea that promoting quality is something that organizations do *to* employees, rather than something they do *with* employees.

SUMMARY OF KEY POINTS AND TERMINOLOGY

The Bonus Materials folder for this chapter on the Premium website, provides a summary of key concepts and terminology introduced in this chapter.

QUALITY IN PRACTICE

FROM LEADERSHIP THROUGH QUALITY TO LEAN SIX SIGMA AT XEROX[41]

The Xerox 914, the first plain-paper copier, was introduced in 1959. Regarded by many people as the most successful business product ever introduced, it created a new industry. During the 1960s Xerox grew rapidly, selling all it could produce, and reached $1 billion in revenue in record-setting time. By the mid-1970s its return on assets was in the low 20 percent range. Its competitive advantage was due to strong patents, a growing market, and little competition. In such an environment, management was not pressed to focus on customers.

Facing a Competitive Crisis

During the 1970s, however, IBM and Kodak entered the high-volume copier business—Xerox's principal market. Several Japanese companies introduced high-quality low-volume copiers, a market that Xerox had virtually ignored, and established a foundation for moving into the high-volume market. In addition, the Federal Trade Commission accused Xerox of illegally monopolizing the copier business. After negotiations,

Xerox agreed to open approximately 1,700 patents to competitors. Xerox was soon losing market share to Japanese competitors, and by the early 1980s it faced a serious competitive threat from copy machine manufacturers in Japan; Xerox's market share had fallen to less than 50 percent. Some people even predicted that the company would not survive. Rework, scrap, excessive inspection, lost business, and other problems were estimated to be costing Xerox more than 20 percent of revenue, which in 1983 amounted to nearly $2 billion. Both the company and its primary union, the Amalgamated Clothing and Textile Workers, were concerned. In comparing itself with its competition, Xerox discovered that it had nine times as many suppliers, twice as many employees, cycle times that were twice as long, 10 times as many rejects, and seven times as many manufacturing defects in finished products. It was clear that radical changes were required.

Leadership Through Quality

In 1983, company president David T. Kearns became convinced that Xerox needed a long-range, comprehensive quality strategy as well as a change in its traditional management culture (see Figure 1.5). Kearns was aware of Japanese subsidiary Fuji Xerox's success in implementing quality management practices and was approached by several Xerox employees about instituting total quality management. He commissioned a team to outline a quality strategy for Xerox. The team's report stated that instituting it would require changes in behaviors and attitudes throughout the company as well as operational changes in the company's business practices. Kearns determined that Xerox would initiate a total quality management approach, that they would take the time to "design it right the first time," and that the effort would involve all employees. Kearns and the company's top 25 managers wrote the Xerox Quality Policy, which states:

> *Xerox is a quality company. Quality is the basic business principle for Xerox. Quality means providing our external and internal customers with innovative products and services that fully satisfy their requirements. Quality improvement is the job of every Xerox employee.*

Figure 1.5 Origin of the 1983 Xerox Quality Imperative

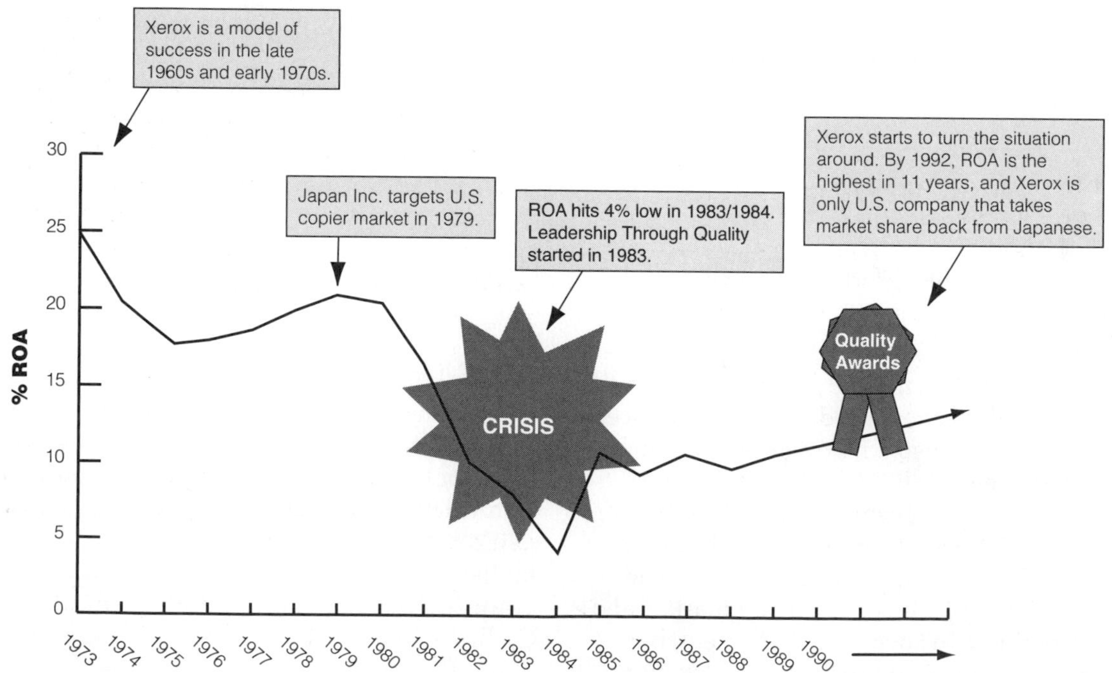

This policy led to a process called Leadership Through Quality, which had three objectives:

1. To instill quality as the basic business principle in Xerox, and to ensure that quality improvement becomes the job of every Xerox person.
2. To ensure that Xerox people, individually and collectively, provide our external and internal customers with innovative products and services that fully satisfies their existing and latent requirements.
3. To establish, as a way of life, management and work processes that enable all Xerox people to continuously pursue quality improvement in meeting customer requirements.

In addition, Leadership Through Quality was directed at achieving four goals in all Xerox activities:

- Customer Goal: To become an organization with whom customers are eager to do business.
- Employee Goal: To create an environment where everyone can take pride in the organization and feel responsible for its success.
- Business Goal: To increase profits and presence at a rate faster than the markets in which Xerox competes.
- Process Goal: To use Leadership Through Quality principles in all Xerox does.

Leadership Through Quality radically changed the way Xerox did business. All activities, such as product planning, distribution, and establishing unit objectives, began with a focus on customer requirements. Benchmarking—identifying and studying the companies and organizations that best perform critical business functions and then incorporating those organizations' ideas into the firm's operations—became an important component of Xerox's quality efforts. Xerox benchmarked more than 200 processes with those of noncompetitive companies. For instance, ideas for improving production scheduling came from Cummins Engine Company, ideas for improving the distribution system came from L.L. Bean, and ideas for improving billing processes came from American Express.

Measuring customer satisfaction and training were important components of the program. Every month, 40,000 surveys were mailed to customers, seeking feedback on equipment performance, sales, service, and administrative support. Any reported dissatisfaction was dealt with immediately and was usually resolved in a matter of days. When the program was instituted, every Xerox employee worldwide, and at all levels of the company, received the same training in quality principles. This training began with top management and filtered down through each level of the firm. Five years, 4 million labor-hours, and more than $125 million later, all employees had received quality-related training. In 1988, about 79 percent of Xerox employees were involved in quality improvement teams.

Several other steps were taken. Xerox worked with suppliers to improve their processes, implement statistical methods and a total quality process, and to support a just-in-time inventory concept. Suppliers that joined in these efforts were involved in the earliest phases of new product designs and rewarded with long-term contracts.

Employee involvement and participation was also an important effort. Xerox had always had good relationships with its unions. In 1980, the company signed a contract with its principal union, the Amalgamated Clothing and Textile Workers, encouraging union members' participation in quality improvement processes. It was the first program in the company that linked managers with employees in a mutual problem-solving approach and served as a model for other corporations. A subsequent contract included the provision that "every employee shall support the concept of continuous quality improvement while reducing quality costs through teamwork."

Most important, management became the role model for the new way of doing business. Managers were required to practice quality in their daily activities and to promote Leadership Through Quality among their peers and subordinates. Reward and recognition systems were modified to focus on teamwork and quality results. Managers became coaches, involving their employees in the act of running the business on a routine basis.

From the initiation of Leadership Through Quality until the point at which Xerox's Business Products and Systems organization won the Malcolm Baldrige National Quality Award in 1989, some of the most obvious impacts of the Leadership Through Quality program included the following:

1. Reject rates on the assembly line fell from 10,000 parts per million to 300 parts per million.

2. Ninety-five percent of supplied parts no longer needed inspection; in 1989, 30 U.S. suppliers went the entire year defect-free.
3. The number of suppliers was cut from 5,000 to fewer than 500.
4. The cost of purchased parts was reduced by 45 percent.
5. Despite inflation, manufacturing costs dropped 20 percent.
6. Product development time decreased by 60 percent.
7. Overall product quality improved 93 percent.

Xerox learned that customer satisfaction plus employee motivation and satisfaction resulted in increased market share and improved return on assets. In 1989, president David Kearns observed that quality is "a race without a finish line."

Crisis and Quality Renewal

Throughout the 1990s, Xerox grew at a steady rate. However, at the turn of the century, the technology downturn, coupled with a decreased focus on quality by top corporate management, resulted in a significant stock price drop and a new crisis (see Figure 1.6). A top management shake-up, resulting in new corporate leadership, renewed the company's focus on quality, beginning with "New Quality" in 2001 and leading to the current "Lean Six Sigma" initiative.

The New Quality philosophy built on the quality legacy established in the 1983 Leadership Through Quality process. Soon afterward, as Six Sigma became more popular across the United States, this approach was refined around a structured, Six Sigma-based improvement process with more emphasis on behaviors and leadership to achieve performance excellence. The new thrust, established in 2003 and called "Lean Six Sigma" (see Chapter 11 for a detailed discussion), includes a dedicated infrastructure and resource commitment to focus on key business issues: critical customer opportunities, significant training of employees and "Black Belt" improvement specialists, a value-driven project selection process, and an increased customer focus with a clear linkage to business strategy and objectives. The basic principles support the core value "We Deliver Quality and Excellence in All We Do" and are stated as:

- Customer-focused employees, accountable for business results, are fundamental to our success.
- Our work environment enables participation, speed, and teamwork based on trust, learning, and recognition.

Figure 1.6 Restrengthening Quality to Address a New Crisis

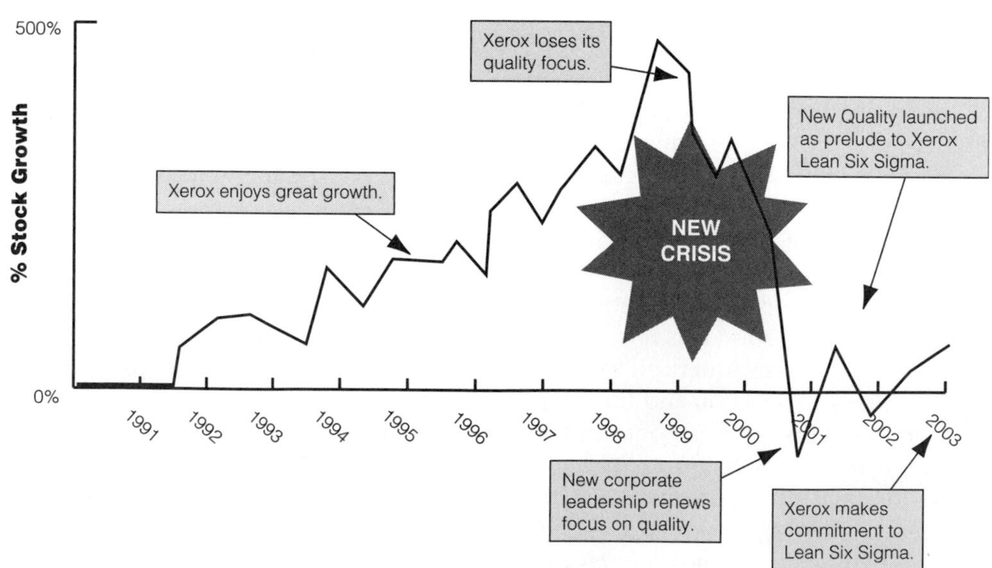

- Everyone at Xerox has business objectives aligned to the Xerox direction. A disciplined process is used to assess progress towards delivery of results.
- Customer-focused work processes, supported by disciplined use of quality tools, enable rapid changes and yield predictable business results.
- Everyone takes responsibility to communicate and act on benchmarks and knowledge that enable rapid change in the best interests of customers and shareholders.

The key components of Xerox's Lean Six Sigma are as follows:

1. Performance excellence process
   - Supports clearer, simpler alignment of corporate direction to individual objectives
   - Emphasizes ongoing inspection/assessment of business priorities
   - Clear links to market trends, benchmarking, and Lean Six Sigma
   - Supports a simplified "Baldrige-type" business assessment model
2. DMAIC (define, measure, analyze, improve, control) process
   - Based on industry-proven Six Sigma approach with speed and focus
   - Four steps support improvement projects, set goals
   - Used to proactively capture opportunities or solve problems
   - Full set of lean and Six Sigma tools
3. Market trends and benchmarking
   - Reinforces market focus and encourages external view
   - Disciplined approach to benchmarking
   - Establishes a common four-step approach to benchmarking
   - Encourages all employees to be aware of changing markets
   - Strong linkage to performance excellence process and DMAIC
4. Behaviors and leadership
   - Reinforces customer focus
   - Expands interactive skills to include more team effectiveness
   - Promotes faster decision making and introduces new meeting tool

The heart of Xerox's Lean Six Sigma is the performance excellence process, illustrated in Figure 1.7. It consists of three phases: setting direction, deploying direction, and delivering and inspecting results. It starts at the top of the organization—even the chair and CEO, Anne Mulcahy, has an individual performance excellence plan with objectives that are aligned with organization goals and measures and targets for assessment. This approach provides clear communication of direction and accountability for objectives. A structured approach is used

Figure 1.7 Xerox Performance Excellence Process

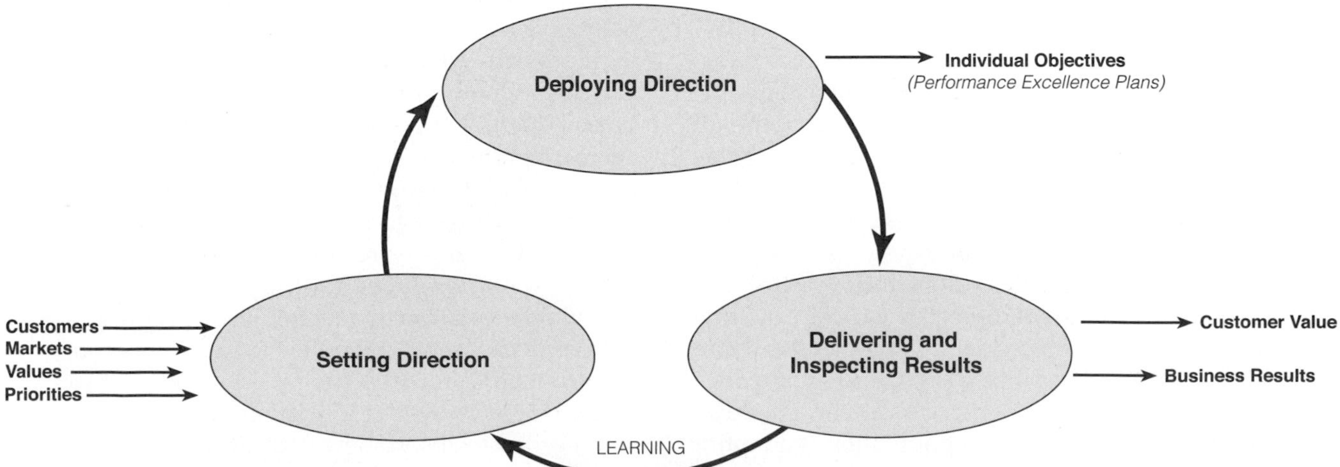

to prioritize and select projects that have high benefits relative to the effort involved in accomplishing them. Statistical methods, lean work flow methods, and other process management skills are used to drive improvement from a factual, objective basis, driven by the DMAIC methodology.

Market trends and benchmarking help provide an external perspective required to lead the market with innovative products, services, and solutions and add value to the customer experience. This component encourages all people to share information and knowledge that enables changes in the best interest of customers and shareholders. Finally, behaviors and leadership reinforce customer-focused behaviors, based on the principle that "Quality is the responsibility of every Xerox employee."

In 2003, Xerox trained more than 1,000 senior leaders across the company and communicated this business approach, the key differences from their quality legacy, and expectations to every employee, and is rapidly moving Lean Six Sigma concepts from manufacturing and supply chain into all business areas. They recognize that full leadership commitment is the key ingredient. As Anne Mulcahy noted, "What I worry most about is how to return Xerox to greatness . . . Lean Six Sigma is not the only answer, but it's a significant part of the equation."

Key Issues for Discussion

1. Contrast Leadership for Quality and Lean Six Sigma as quality initiatives for Xerox. How did their motivations differ? What differences or similarities are evident in the principles behind these initiatives and the way in which they were implemented?
2. What lessons might this experience—particularly in responding to the new crisis—have for other organizations?
3. Discuss the meaning of "Quality is a race without a finish line." What is its significance to Xerox, or to any organization?

Quality in Practice

Quality Practices in Modern China

In this chapter, we noted that many of today's quality approaches evolved in ancient China. Jack Pompeo, a telecommunications professional who relocated to lead quality initiatives at Huawei Technologies, provides a first-hand look at quality in modern China.[42]

Quality processes today continue to be influenced by remnants of ancient policies and practices established 3,000 years ago. China continues to exercise strong centralized oversight over end-to-end production processes, extending from the purchase of incoming materials and in-process testing through final acceptances and customer care. Today's Chinese quality systems strongly emphasize tools, methodology and measurement, and place great importance on key quality management processes, including self-inspection, traceability, and recruiting and training of workers. However, even in light of recent and highly-publicized recalls, China's population is adapting and learning rapidly and is hungry for best practices and new challenges.

Today, China is seeking to introduce new ideas like total quality management and team empowerment, which have taken Western society decades to adapt and integrate into business management, in a fraction of the time. China is striving to improve its education, health, living standards, and, most important, its manufactured consumer products, and is embracing modern quality management philosophies. In just the past few years, Chinese manufacturers have adopted a wide array of quality tools and techniques. This has created a clash in China's desire to maintain balance between a centuries-old culture and the demands placed on the nation by technological progress.

China has an official policy to grow the economy about 8% annually, the rate state officials calculate would create the 15 million new jobs each year needed to absorb new entrants into the labor market and discards from the shrinking state sector. Every policy is calibrated to ensure economic output continues to expand at this rapid pace. Like businesses in the rest of the world, Chinese organizations are driven by numbers. They identify gaps in their quality management systems and are closing them quickly. They understand that they have a narrow window of opportunity to transform themselves from low cost producers to competitive and high quality global leaders.

Huawei Technologies is one of China's largest telecommunications manufacturers, with annual sales of more than $10 billion. The company is located in Shenzhen, in the southern portion of the Guangdong Province on the eastern shore of the Pearl River Delta, neighboring Hong Kong to the south. Huawei's products provide reliable telecom services to more than 100 countries. But the company's goal is not to be just another telecom manufacturer; it is to be the quality leader in the telecommunications industry. Huawei's senior management recently declared the company's desire to be the "Toyota of the telecom industry." To achieve this, Huawei has studied Western telecom manufacturing in great detail and has invested heavily in the latest tools and technology. It is constantly looking for better tools and techniques that will make it a world leader, moving away from its current emphasis on low-cost production.

Huawei's rapid economic growth parallels the company's desire to be the world leader, and Huawei is now in the midst of understanding the critical role that quality processes play in its future expansion. The company places a strong focus on measurements, tools, and methods to enforce strict quality control of production processes. Its management systems are based on accepted worldwide processes and standards and are applied across all of Huawei's product lines in design, development, manufacturing, sales, installation, and service. Huawei also has a complete end-to-end integrated product development process that was implemented with the support of IBM in early 1998. In 2002, Huawei started Six Sigma quality initiatives in its manufacturing center and migrated them into R&D product lines. A Six Sigma steering committee oversees the deployment and reviews and approves projects to ensure they meet the launch criteria and resources are available to support the teams.

The QuEST Forum is a unique collaboration of telecommunications service providers and suppliers dedicated to telecom supply chain quality and performance. The Forum supports its member organizations to pursue performance excellence through implementing a common quality standard, emphasizing industry best practices and delivering a benchmarking measurement system. There are 11 benchmark measurements, including number of problem reports, problem report fix response time, on-time delivery, network element impact outage measurement, and field replacement unit returns. Huawei recently launched an initiative in partnership with the QuEST Forum's integrated global quality workgroup. The goal is to set up a benchmark study team to better understand causes of variability in the benchmark data and raise industry performance.

The benchmark data are a critical component of Huawei's quality management system and are integrated into top management's personal business commitments and the executive management team balanced scorecard. The balanced scorecard measures four key areas in corporation health: financial and profit, customer and quality, growth and learning, and internal business performance. The report cards and quality metrics are linked to both the executives' performance reviews and bonuses.

Huawei Technologies is just one example of the progress that Chinese companies have made in quality. Today, its automobile industry is beginning to distribute in the United States and in Europe. The government has embarked on a nation-wide program to improve product quality and safety throughout the supply chain that includes a safety tracking and accountability system and a national product quality-monitoring network.[43] However, the nation is not without its obstacles. The continued rapid growth of the Chinese economy is threatened by infrastructure limitations, pollution, logistical bottlenecks, a young banking system, and the imbalance between male and female births. Also, China cannot continue progressing by copying foreign technologies forever. China might need another decade to overcome a long list of quality manufacturing problems, such as weak design, before its companies can compete with those in Japan and America.

Key Issues for Discussion

1. Do you see any parallels between today's China and post-World War II Japan? What differences are evident?
2. What opportunities does China have in learning from the progress made in quality in Japan and the West over the past half-century?

Additional Quality in Practice features can be found in the Bonus Materials folder on the Premium website.

Review Questions

1. Briefly summarize the history of quality before and since the industrial revolution. What caused the most significant changes?
2. What factors have contributed to the increased awareness of quality in modern business?
3. Explain the various definitions of quality. Can a single definition suffice? Why?
4. Distinguish among consumers, external customers, and internal customers. Illustrate how these concepts apply to a McDonald's restaurant, a Pizza Hut, or a similar franchise.
5. What is the concept of total quality? What does it mean for the way an organization is managed?
6. Explain the differences among quality principles, practices, and techniques.
7. Describe the three fundamental principles of total quality.
8. What is a process? How does a process focus differ from a traditional organization?
9. List some examples of the types of improvements an organization can make.
10. What is the difference between improvement and learning?
11. How does quality support the achievement of competitive advantage?
12. What did Philip Crosby mean by "Quality is free"?
13. Explain the role of quality in improving a firm's profitability.
14. What evidence exists to counter the claim that "Quality does not pay"?
15. Explain the three levels of quality and the key issues that must be addressed at each level.
16. Why is it important to personalize quality principles?

Discussion Questions

1. Discuss how either good or poor quality affects you personally as a consumer. For instance, describe experiences in which your expectations were met, exceeded, or not met when you purchased goods or services. Did your experience change your regard for the organization and/or its product? How?
2. Discuss the importance of quality to the national interest of any country in the world. Given China's emergence as a global economic power, of what importance do you believe that quality will play in their future?

3. A reader wrote to *Business Week* (July 9 & 16, 2007, p. 16) and noted: "Americans have switched from Detroit Big Three vehicles to Honda and Toyota vehicles not for visual design features but for durability, reliability, good fuel consumption, and low full cost of operation. Detroit needs to offer five-passenger, 35-mile-per-gallon vehicles with 100,000 mile bumper-to-bumper warranties over 10 years of ownership to cause satisfied Honda and Toyota buyers to switch." What definitions of quality are implied in these comments?
4. How might the definitions of quality apply to your college or university? Provide examples of consumers, external customers, and internal customers, and ways in which their expectations can be met or exceeded. Do you feel that your college or university is applying the principles of total quality? Why or why not?
5. Think of a product or a service that you are considering purchasing. Develop a list of fitness-for-use criteria that are meaningful to you.
6. A top Ford executive stated "You can't have great value unless you have great quality." Comment on this statement. Do you agree? Why or why not?
7. Select a service activity with which you are familiar. If you were the manager of this activity, what "conformance to specifications" criteria would you use to monitor it?
8. Choose a product or service (such as the hospital example on page 19 in this chapter) to illustrate how several definitions of quality can apply simultaneously.
9. What definition of quality is implied by the following consumer advertisements?
   a. A McDonald's ad stating "Dollar Menunaires know you don't have to spend a lot to taste the rich life . . . . From Double Cheeseburgers to fries. Eight deluxurious items, each for only a dollar."
   b. A Tag Heuer watch ad featuring Tiger Woods with the caption "What are you made of?"
   c. Symantec, a software firm that makes anti-virus software and performs e-mail storage and security services advertises:
      - No viruses
      - No spam
      - No downtime
      - E-mail done right
   d. A Samsung ad that states "The Samsung BD-UP5000 gives you the best of both HD worlds by bridging Blu-ray and HD DVD capabilities together in one player . . . . at an incredible Full HD 1080p resolution, which delivers up to six times the picture quality of standard definition DVDs."
10. What are some processes that you personally perform (for example, as a student, in your job, or in your leisure time)? What opportunities can you think of for improving them?
11. Suggest some TQ practices that organizations might perform other than those described in this chapter within the six basic areas that we discussed that support the principles of TQ.
12. Choose an organization that you have read about or with which you have personal experience and describe their sources of competitive advantage. For each, state whether you believe that quality supports their strategy or does not support it.
13. Explain how the "three levels of quality" might apply to a college or university.
14. What do you think is more important to achieving quality, technology or culture? Why?

Projects, Etc.

1. Develop a portfolio of advertisements from newspapers and magazines and illustrate how quality is used in promoting these products. Do the ads suggest any of the different definitions of quality?
2. Visit the Malcolm Baldrige National Quality Award website at http://www.baldrige.nist.gov and summarize the key results of award recipients for the past two years.
3. Prepare a Quality in Practice case similar to those in this chapter using sources such as business periodicals, personal interviews, and so on. Focus your discussion on how their approach to total quality supports their competitive strategy.
4. Examine the annual reports of one company over a period of years. Summarize how quality is discussed or implied in the company's statements and philosophy. Are any changes in the perspectives of quality evident over time?
5. Many countries around the world have professional organizations similar to the American Society for Quality; however, each has its own unique history and offers exclusive activities to its corporate and individual members. They include Excellence Finland, Excellence Ireland, German Society for Quality, Hong Kong Society for Quality, Instituto Profesional Argentino para la Calidad y la Excelencia, Israel Society for Quality, Union of Japanese Scientists and Engineers (JUSE), National Quality Institute (Canada), Programa Gaucho da Qualidade e Produtividade (Brazil), Singapore Quality Institute, and the Spanish Association for Quality. Conduct some research on several of these societies and contrast their similarities and differences.
6. Develop your own personal quality checklist and analyze the results over an extended period of time. After you have gathered data for a week or two, review the data for the purposes of analysis and improvement. Use charts to plot and analyze weekly results. Use the following guidelines.
   - Each participant should initiate a personal quality improvement project and maintain and improve it during the rest of the study period.
   - Consistent effort, rather than elegant precision in pursuing the project will be rewarded; that is, individual benefit, rather than "a grade," or perfection, is to be the major objective.
   - Eight to ten items for personal tracking and improvement should be chosen. The listing of possible checklist standards can be seen below. However, participants are not required to use only items from this list. Whatever is meaningful to you may be tracked.
   - After a week's data are gathered, plot a simple graph to determine the level of "defects" encountered.
   - A suggested practice is that you share your personal checklist items and goals with your instructor, a colleague, spouse, or friend. Have that person ask you about your progress every week or so. If you are making regular progress, you should be happy to discuss it, and to show your charts and graphs. Even if your progress is uneven, you should be able to show that you've improved on one or two items, which is progress. Don't be too self-critical!
   - An intermediate progress report should be built into the process around the middle of the pilot study period. The final report on the pilot project should be made at the end of the study period. Consideration should be given to making personal quality a permanent part of your personal planning and improvement process.

After completing the project, answer these questions:

a. What did your analysis reveal?
b. Did you experience the same thing that Sergesketter did when he found that certain items disappeared as problems in a short period of time, simply because he began to measure them?
c. How did you feel about discussing your "defects" with others?
d. How does the personal quality process tie into processes in a work environment?

The listing of possible checklist standards might include:

- Review class notes after each class
- No text messaging during classes
- Limit phone calls to ten minutes
- No more than ½ hour per day spent on social networking websites
- No more than X hours of TV per week
- Update schedule daily on PDA or computer calendar
- Get up promptly—no snooze alarm
- Ensure that team members are informed on project progress, each day or each week
- Complete all reading assignments as due
- Inform professor of essential absences via e-mail, text, or phone message at least 24 hours in advance
- Work in library (or other quiet place) to avoid interruptions
- No more than one "junk food" snack per day
- Exercise in gym for at least one hour, twice per week
- Turn off cell phone during classes
- Prepare or buy, and eat, breakfast every day
- E-mail or call parents at least once per week
- Ensure that bank account is never overdrawn by checking balance online at least every other day

Adapted from Harry V. Roberts and Bernard F. Sergesketter. *Quality Is Personal: A Foundation for Total Quality Management*, Copyright © 1993 with the permission of The Free Press, a Division of Simon & Schuster Adult Publishing Group.

Cases

Additional cases are available in the Bonus Materials folder on the Premium website.

BONUS MATERIALS

Skilled Care Pharmacy[44]

Skilled Care Pharmacy, located in Mason, Ohio, is a $25 million dollar privately held regional provider of pharmaceutical products delivered within the long-term care, assisted living, hospice, and group home environments. The following products are included within this service:

- Medications and related billing services
- Medical records
- Information systems
- Continuing education
- Consulting services to include pharmacy, nursing, dietary, and social services

The key customer groups that Skilled Care provides services to include the senior population housed within the extended and long-term care environments. Customers within this sector depend on Skilled Care to provide their daily pharmaceutical needs at a competitive rate. Because of the high risk factor of its business, these needs require that the right drug be delivered to the right patient at the right time. Moreover, depending on the environment being served, different medication dispensing methods may be used such as vials, multidose packaging, or unit dose boxes. Also, depending on the customer type, specific delivery requirements may be implemented to better serve the end user.

Skilled Care's dedication and commitment to continuous quality improvement is evident throughout its internal and external operations. By reflecting on the principles needed to attain quality success across all levels of customers, Skilled Care adopted the quality policy statement shown in Figure 1.8.

Skilled Care's employee population includes 176 culturally diverse associates committed to a substance-free workplace. The team includes associates with all levels of educational training representing many of the following disciplines: pharmacists, pharmacy technicians, medical data entry, accountants, billing specialists, nurses, human resources, sales/marketing, purchasing, administrative and administrative assistance, delivery, customer service representatives, and IT certified personnel. At times, multifaceted work teams are formed through cross-functional approaches to complete the task(s) at hand.

Skilled Care's deliverables are generated from its sole 24,000-square foot location in Mason, Ohio. The pharmacy, which is open 24 hours a day, 365 days a year, is secured by a Honeywell alarm system. The company's primary technology rests within its pharmacy software, Rescot. This system enables Skilled Care to process, bill, and generate pertinent data critical to the overall operations of the company. Other partnerships have also been established within Skilled Care's multidosed packaging capabilities and wholesaler purchasing interface.

SCP utilizes the Internet for publishing pertinent information and news as well as hosts a Web-enabled customer service application called Track-It to report specific information about customer issues for companywide resolution. Advantages of e-commerce include quicker customer service response time for all areas of service including placing the order, pharmacist's review, delivery, and billing of the product.

Skilled Care Pharmacy faces key strategic challenges from the rapidly evolving financial structure of health care, a shortage of licensed pharmacist personnel, the constant evolution of medical practice, and employee retention at all levels. These, as well as future challenges, are always balanced with the responsibility to the stakeholders.

Discussion Questions

1. How might the various definitions of quality apply to Skilled Care?
2. How are the principles of total quality reflected in Skilled Care's policy and operations?
3. Given the nature of Skilled Care's operations and the challenges it faces, discuss how a total quality approach can help the company meet these challenges and improve its ability to provide the services its customers need.

Figure 1.8 Skilled Care Quality Policy

Source: Courtesy of Nancy Milnarik, VP of Quality, Skilled Care, Inc., Mason Ohio. Reprinted with permission.

DESIGNING A QUALITY-BASED BUSINESS

Chuck, a young entrepreneur who has worked in various restaurants throughout high school and college, has decided to develop a new type of restaurant that focuses primarily on takeout of home-cooked meals for busy professionals on their way home from work. The restaurant would also have a small dining area for customers who wish to eat the food there. Because this prospective business will have to compete with national franchises and other traditional local restaurants, Chuck wants to ensure that this business will compete on quality and develop a strong quality reputation. He has asked you to help him understand the issues that he must address in designing and managing this restaurant.

Using the principles of TQ and the six basic areas of management that defined TQ practices as discussed in this chapter, provide Chuck with specific advice on how he might "bring to life" the principles of TQ in this new venture, and what specific practices he should consider to help develop a quality-based business.

DEERE & CO.

Deere & Company (http://www.deere.com) (also known as John Deere, after it's founder) is a world-leading manufacturer, distributor, and financier of equipment for agriculture, construction and forestry, and commercial and consumer applications (lawn and grounds care). Deere's objective has consistently been to be the low-cost producer in the markets it serves. However, it seeks to do so while maintaining an image of quality and customer focus. Its company values are quality, innovation, integrity, and commitment. Because of the company's close ties to the agricultural industry, corporate performance in both sales and profits was highly variable over the last several decades due to cycles of low prices and oversupplies of many agricultural products. During that period, the company made various adjustments in its product mix and manufacturing processes to enable it to better compete and survive in the global environment.

The excerpts below come from various Deere annual reports.

> *1984*
>
> *In spite of the industry environment of low demand, the challenge is to do what we do better. Provide more value per dollar of purchase price. To accomplish this will require cost-effectiveness in all facets of our business, which includes being more flexible and more aggressive in adopting the most modern design and manufacturing technologies . . . Product design is being systematically reviewed to provide improved performance and quality at a lower cost . . . New manufacturing technologies such as robot welding have enabled Deere employees to become more efficient while producing parts of higher and more consistent quality.*
>
> *1987*
>
> *John Deere is determined to be the lowest-cost producer in our industries and to sustain a competitive advantage on a global basis. However, we all must perpetuate the company's reputation for providing the best quality and value to our customers. While we're making structural changes in our operations we must continue to adhere to these business principles . . . John Deere leadership in the agricultural equipment business is based on a line of products that has earned a reputation for excellent quality and reliability, on the skills and services we have to support the product line, and on our strong network of independent dealers . . . In our continuing effort to improve the quality and performance of John Deere agricultural equipment, we have traditionally invested a higher percent of sales in product R&D than any of our major competitors . . . The industrial equipment improvement reflects our strong product line and dedicated organization and our employees' determination to reduce costs, improve quality, and deliver the best value to the customer . . . The total value of John Deere equipment is quality, reliability, dealer support, finance plans, resale value, and the company that stands behind it all.*
>
> *1989*
>
> *We must continue to ensure that John Deere products offer the customer the*

best value in all respects—in quality, reliability, features, resale price, and especially in value added by an independent network of well-placed, full-servicing dealers people can rely on.

1995

Deere's focus on continuous improvement takes a wide variety of forms, but is based on the simple concept that any product or process can be improved. We have placed great emphasis on enhancing the team-based culture of the company, in which salaried and hourly employees work cooperatively toward the common goal of creating ongoing, meaningful gains in productivity . . . A key component of this operating philosophy is the company's growing utilization of team-based compensation systems that reward continuous improvements in productivity.

1996

As we move ahead in the pursuit of genuine value, we continue to follow twin strategies of continuous improvement—embodying innovation, efficiency, effective business processes and a passion for excellence—and profitable growth, which is being accomplished through the global pursuit of new markets and products . . . Nothing stands as a better illustration of Deere's commitment to continuous improvement than our long record of investment in capital programs and research and development . . . Continuous improvement initiatives are setting the stage for our other strategy—that of profitable growth . . . Our company's pursuit of genuine value as our primary strategic initiative provides a strong point of focus. In reaching to create value for our many constituencies, we have embarked on a series of exciting journeys that are fundamentally remaking our enterprise. For example, a strong company-wide total quality program continues to expand and intensify, yielding improved customer responsiveness, shortened cycle times, and reductions in costs and asset levels.

1999

Highlighting our pursuit of genuine value through continuous improvement is an aggressive series of process-based initiatives targeting six-sigma levels of performance and customer satisfaction. During the year, some 900 projects involving the efforts of several thousand employees, were completed or in progress. Their goal: Streamlining business processes, large and small, and pursuing operational excellence throughout the company . . . In support of the initiative stressing customer focus, our operating divisions are structuring their activities around the core processes of customer acquisition, order fulfillment, product development and customer support.

2003

A totally new compensation and rewards system, which began taking effect in 2003, is supporting the attainment of our goals and promoting true alignment among the interests of customers, employees and investors. Thousands of management employees at all levels are now eligible for a bonus payable when our service to customers earns a return above the cost of capital over a multi-year period.

2005

Deere employees are tightly aligned with our business objectives and are being evaluated and compensated accordingly. Virtually all 21,000 of our salaried employees worldwide follow detailed performance plans tailored to their own responsibilities and development potential. The plans spell out how each individual's efforts contribute to meeting unit and company goals . . . A prime example of how product innovation is driving higher sales, the John Deere 2500 E greens mower is the golf and turf industry's first mower that uses hybrid technology. Result: Lower noise and better fuel efficiency but plenty of power (18-hp) . . . Building on a tradition of stewardship, the company has continued to develop product solutions that are less disruptive to the surrounding environment. Deere's newly introduced Tier 3-compliant PowerTech Plus engines use the latest technology to deliver better fuel economy and more power while meeting stringent emissions regulations. In another case, the company in 2005 became the first equipment manufacturer to use biodiesel as a factory fill at its U.S. manufacturing locations.

Assignment

On the basis of this information, prepare a brief report discussing Deere & Company's evolution of quality. Relate your discussion to historical trends, future challenges, the various definitional perspectives of quality, and other issues discussed in this chapter such as the principles of TQ and infrastructure. For example, how has their perspective of quality and the practices used to implement it changed over the years? Update the case by reviewing Deere's latest annual report and include any new information in your analysis.

NOTES

1. *The Cincinnati Enquirer*, January 12, 2002, pp. A1, A9.

2. Early history is reported in Delmer C. Dague, "Quality—Historical Perspective," *Quality Control in Manufacturing* (Warrendale, PA: Society of Automotive Engineers, 1981); and L. P. Provost and C. L. Norman, "Variation through the Ages," *Quality Progress* 23, no. 12 (December 1990), 39–44. Modern events are discussed in Nancy Karabatsos, "Quality in Transition, Part One: Account of the '80s," *Quality Progress* 22, no. 12 (December 1989), 22–26; and Joseph M. Juran, "The Upcoming Century of Quality," address to the ASQC Annual Quality Congress, Las Vegas, May 24, 1994. A comprehensive historical account may be found in J. M. Juran, *A History of Managing for Quality* (Milwaukee, WI: ASQC Quality Press, 1995). Discussions of quality in China were adapted from the first chapter, "Ancient China's History of Managing for Quality," in Juran's book and from Jack Pompeo, "Living Inside China's Quality Revolution," *Quality Progress*, August 2007, 30–35.

3. M. D. Fagan (ed.), *A History of Engineering and Science in the Bell System*: The Early Years, 1875–1925 (New York: Bell Telephone Laboratories, 1974).

4. "Manufacturing Tops List of Concerns Among Executives," *Industrial Engineering* 22, no. 6 (June 1990), 8.

5. Lawrence Utzig, "Quality Reputation—Precious Asset," *ASQC Technical Conference Transactions*, Atlanta, 1980, 145–154.

6. Procter & Gamble, *Report to the Total Quality Leadership Steering Committee and Working Councils* (Cincinnati, OH: Procter & Gamble, 1992).

7. A. V. Feigenbaum, *Total Quality Control*, 3rd ed., rev. (New York: McGraw-Hill, 1991), 77, 78.

8. "The Cost of Quality," *Newsweek*, September 7, 1992, 48–49.

9. Kennedy Smith, "Managers Disagree on Quality's Definition" *Quality Digest*, May 2004, p. 6.

10. Lori L. Silverman with Annabeth L. Propst, "Quality Today: Recognizing the Critical SHIFT," *Quality Progress*, February 1999, 53–60.

11. Reprinted with permission from Seiche Sanders, "What's Up? ASQ's Futures Study Offers Insights into Where Quality is Headed," *Quality Progress*, October, 2008, pp. 42–49. Copyright © 2008 by American Society for Quality (ASQ). No further distribution allowed without permission.

12. Source: http://www.un.org/esa/population/publications/wpp2008/pressrelease.pdf

13. Nabil Tamimi and Rose Sebastianelli, "How Firms Define and Measure Quality," *Production and Inventory Management Journal* 37, no. 3 (Third Quarter, 1996), 34–39.

14. Four comprehensive reviews of the concept and definition of quality are David A. Garvin, "What Does Product Quality Really Mean?" *Sloan Management Review*, 26, no. 1 (1984), 25–43; Gerald F. Smith, "The Meaning of Quality," *Total Quality Management* 4, no. 3 (1993), 235–244; Carol A. Reeves and David A. Bednar, "Defining Quality: Alternatives and Implications," *Academy of Management Review* 19, no. 3 (1994), 419–445; and Kristie W. Seawright and Scott T. Young, "A Quality Definition Continuum," *Interfaces* 26, 3 (May–June 1996), 107–113.

15. Garvin (see note 13), 25.

16. "Lamborghini owner says he got $262,000 lemon," *Cincinnati Enquirer*, June 23, 1998, B5.

17. Gregory M. Seal, "1990s—Years of Promise, Years of Peril for U.S. Manufacturers," *Industrial Engineering* 22, no. 1 (January 1990), 18–21. We also thank Ben Valentin for providing some historical facts about Nissan and Datsun.

18. Alex Taylor III, "Detroit's Used-Car Blues," *Fortune*, September 16, 2002, 147–150.

19. ANSI/ASQC A3-1978, *Quality Systems Terminology* (Milwaukee, WI: American Society for Quality Control, 1978).

20. "Quality Pays at Hilton Hotels," *Quality Digest*, August 2005, p. 9.

21. James W. Dean, Jr. and David E. Bowen "Management Theory and Total Quality: Improving Research and Practice Through Theory Development," *Academy of Management Review*, 19, 3, 392–418, 1994.

22. Ron Zemke and Dick Schaaf, *The Service Edge* (New York: New American Library, 1989), 352–355;

William Davidow and Bro Utall, *Total Customer Service* (New York: Harper & Row, 1989), 86–87.

23. Myron Magnet, "The New Golden Rule of Business," *Fortune*, February 21, 1994, 60–64.

24. AT&T's Total Quality Approach, AT&T Corporate Quality Office (1992), 6.

25. L. von Bertalanffy, "The Theory of Open Systems in Physics and Biology," *Science*, 111 (1950), 23–29.

26. J. W. Forrester, *Industrial Dynamics* (New York: John Wiley & Sons, 1961).

27. Peter M. Senge, *The Fifth Discipline: The Art and Practice of the Learning Organization* (New York: Doubleday Currency, 1990), 14.

28. S. C. Wheelwright, "Competing through Manufacturing," in Ray Wild (ed.), *International Handbook of Production and Operations Management* (London: Cassell Educational, Ltd., 1989), 15–32.

29. *The PIMS Letter on Business Strategy*, no. 4 (Cambridge, MA: Strategic Planning Institute, 1986).

30. Philip Crosby, *Quality Is Free* (New York: McGraw-Hill, 1979).

31. Kathleen Kerwin, "When Flawless Isn't Enough," *Business Week*, December 8, 2003.

32. David Welch, "Nissan: The Squeaks Get Louder," *Business Week*, May 17, 2004, p. 44.

33. Roger O. Crockett, Peter Elstrom, and Gary McWilliams, "Wireless Goes Haywire at Motorola," *Business Week*, March 9, 1998, 32.

34. U.S. General Accounting Office, "Management Practices: U.S. Companies Improve Performance Through Quality Efforts," GA/NSIAD-91-190. (May 1991); "Progress on the Quality Road," *Incentive*, April 1995, 7.

35. Kevin B. Hendricks and Vinod R. Singhal, "Does Implementing an Effective TQM Program Actually Improve Operating Performance? Empirical Evidence from Firms That Have Won Quality Awards," *Management Science* 43, 9 (September 1997), 1258–1274. The results of this study appeared in extensive business and trade publications such as *Business Week*, *Fortune*, and others.

36. Adapted from Alan P. Brache and Geary A. Rummler, "The Three Levels of Quality," *Quality Progress* 21, no. 10 (October 1988), 46–51.

37. Rath & Strong Executive Panel, Winter 1994 Survey on Personal Initiative, Summary of Findings.

38. David Armstrong, *Management by Storying Around* (New York: Doubleday Currency, 1992), 117–119.

39. Harry V. Roberts and Bernard F. Sergesketter, *Quality Is Personal: A Foundation for Total Quality Management* (New York: The Free Press, 1993). Another good source that addresses the history and application of personal quality tools is Bernard F. Sergesketter, "Create a Better Life With Quality Tools," *Quality Progress*, August 2004, 25–30.

40. Roberts and Sergesketter (see note 39), 13–14.

41. Information for this case was obtained from "Xerox Quest for Quality and the Malcolm Baldrige National Quality Award" presentation script; Norman E. Rickard, Jr., "The Quest for Quality: A Race without a Finish Line," *Industrial Engineering*, January 1991, 25–27; Howard S. Gitlow and Elvira N. Loredo, "Total Quality Management at Xerox: A Case Study," *Quality Engineering* 5, no. 3 (1993), 403–432; *Xerox Quality Solutions, A World of Quality* (Milwaukee, WI: ASQC Quality Press, 1993); and "Restrengthening Xerox: Our Lean Six Sigma Journey," Presentation slides, May 2003. Courtesy of Xerox Corporation. Our thanks go to George Maszle of Xerox Corporation for providing the information on current Six Sigma initiatives.

42. Reprinted with permission from Jack Pompeo, "Living Inside China's Quality Revolution," *Quality Progress*, August 2007, pp. 30–35. Copyright © 2007 American Society for Quality. No further distribution allowed without permission.

43. Scott M. Paton, "Is China Another Japan?" *Quality Digest*, January 2008, p. 128.

44. Appreciation for materials in this case is expressed to Nancy Mlinarik, VP of Quality, Skilled Care, Inc.

Total Quality in Organizations

Outline

Quality and Systems Thinking
Quality Profiles: Jenks Public Schools and the City of Coral Springs
Quality in Manufacturing
Manufacturing Systems
Quality in Services
Contrasts with Manufacturing
Components of Service System Quality
Quality in Health Care
Quality in Education
Koalaty Kid
Quality in Higher Education
Quality in Small Businesses and Not-for-Profits
Quality in the Public Sector
Quality in the Federal Government
State and Local Quality Efforts
Summary of Key Points and Terminology
Quality in Practice: Service Quality at The Ritz-Carlton Hotel Company
Quality in Practice: Kenneth W. Monfort College of Business
Review Questions
Discussion Questions
Projects, Etc.
Cases The Nightmare on Telecom Street
U.S. Water Resource Agency—Flagstaff District
Walker Auto Sales and Service

The sparkly smiley-face stickers and pink crayons in first-grade teacher Carly Laurent's classroom at Washington Elementary School in Mt. Lebanon, PA, don't look as if they came from the world of Total Quality Management. They are being used that way, however, as part of the same "continuous improvement" management model that made Toyota the world's top-selling automobile company. At Washington Elementary, the "workers" are the pint-sized pupils, the end products are better spelling, reading, and math scores, and the day-to-day management techniques might sound a little different than those used in the corporate world. "All right, sweet pea, let's look at your spelling test," Ms. Laurent says to 6-year-old Tiausa Brown, who gets a high-five and an "awesome" for her perfect score of 10 out of 10. Tiausa then places a smiley sticker to mark her score on a class graph of the test performance and, after conferring with a classmate, uses a pink crayon to fill in a bar graph in her personal data binder. After all of her pupils receive their scores and chart their progress in their binders, Ms. Laurent calls the class together to compare this week's spelling performance (all 8s, 9s, and 10s) to the previous week's (some 5s and 6s). They also discuss what worked well (spelling in their heads, practicing in the car) and what could be done differently to improve next time (checking their work, decorating the bathroom with words on Post-it notes). "What we try to do in an educational setting is apply the theory from the boardroom, the central office, down to the individual student, where even kindergartners are saying, 'Can I be better tomorrow than I am today?'" said an associate superintendant in Cedar Rapids, IA. After the continuous improvement plan was implemented in Cedar Rapids in 2004, fifth-graders increased their math proficiency by 6.9 percent by the time they reached eighth grade. Reading groups increased 9.6 percent over the same period.[1]

As noted in Chapter 1, modern quality management in the United States began in the manufacturing sector. By the 1990s, many manufacturers discovered that service quality is as critical to retaining customers as the tangible products they buy, and turned attention to such support processes as order entry, delivery, and complaint response. Pure service companies began to think in terms of "zero defections" and to explore new ways of developing customer loyalty. A hospital in Detroit, for example, promises to attend to its emergency room patients in 20 minutes or less. If it is unable to keep this promise, the care will be free.[2] Slogans such as "Whatever It Takes" and service guarantees are the norm in today's competitive environment. Nevertheless, many service industries, such as airlines and wireless communications, still struggle with quality. Today, the concept of quality has moved far beyond its manufacturing roots, and has become an important focus in education, health care, government, and other nonprofit agencies. The *Quality Profiles* in this chapter provide two examples of quality management in education and city government.

As consumer expectations have risen, a focus on quality has permeated other key sectors of the economy, most notably health care, education, and not-for-profits.

For all types of organizations, quality is absolutely vital to keep customers, sustain profitability, and gain market share. This chapter explores the role of quality in manufacturing, service education, health care, and not-for-profit organizations. We begin with the importance of viewing all organizations as systems, and focus on the role that each component of an organization plays in achieving high quality. We then present a variety of examples of quality efforts in these organizations.

Quality Profiles
Jenks Public Schools and the City of Coral Springs

Jenks Public Schools (JPS) is the 11th largest public school district in Oklahoma. JPS has established four "pillars"—Strong Quality Leadership, Continuous Improvement, Customer Focus, and Systems/Process Focus—that serve as a foundation for the school district. Through the district's Strategic Planning Process, JPS senior leaders, create a focus on the future, set organizational vision, values, goals, and strategic objectives, and ensure that site and department goals and action plans support the district's goals, strategic objectives, core values, mission, and vision.

JPS sets an expectation for performance excellence that supports its Pillar of Continuous

Improvement. Continuous improvement is evaluated using four processes: the Performance Appraisal Review Process; the Comprehensive Local Education Plan (CLEP) in which sites include a Plan, Do, Study, Act (PDSA) component; the Performance Measurement System; and surveys and committee evaluations. JPS's key learning-centered system is determined by its mission of preparing all learners for productive, responsible citizenship in an ever-changing world and the Comprehensive Local Education Plan mandates of the state, which include continuous improvement cycles. JPS has adopted a team-based learning approach that has resulted in multiple awards and recognition of its students, faculty, and staff for a variety of achievements of its academic programs and services. JPS's system addresses students' education, well-being, and success by organizing curriculum and decision making around the entire period of a child's education, through the use of research-based instructional strategies and differentiation of instruction, by providing performance data to support instructional decision making and to keep parents informed, and by addressing safety, communication, teamwork, and educational experiences to develop character and citizenship. JPS is among the top 1 percent of schools in Oklahoma, and the dropout rates—a measure of satisfaction—have decreased steadily from 6.3 percent in 1999 to 1 percent by 2004, while faculty turnover has also decreased from 15 percent to 6 percent.

During the 1980s, Coral Springs, Florida, was one of the fastest growing cities in the nation and now is home to about 132,000 people. In 1993, the City of Coral Springs began its journey to be a high-performing "municipal corporation," a city government following a corporate management model. The city's organizational culture is reflected in its four core values: ***customer focus***—demonstrate a passion for customer service; ***leadership***—establish an inspiring vision that creates a government that works better and costs less; ***empowered employees***—empower the people closest to the customer to continuously improve the organization's quality and services; and ***continuous improvement***—commit every day, in every way to getting better and better.

The city's strategic plan, which is reviewed and updated annually, represents a shared vision for the future of the community and spells out its priorities: customer-involved government; financial health and economic development; excellence in education; neighborhood and environmental vitality; youth development and family values; strength in diversity; and traffic, mobility, and connectivity. The strategic planning process has been cited by a number of organizations, including the American Productivity and Quality Center, as a "best practice."

A number of mechanisms make it as convenient as possible for customers to get information on services, conduct business, and communicate with city officials and employees. They include the city's website, podcasts and streaming video, e-mail, the CityHelpDesk (automated comment and complaint system), and the City Hall in the Mall, which offers services such as paying cable and water bills and applying for a passport and permits.

The city's flat organizational structure, training, and recognition encourage employees to be innovative in addressing customer concerns and make on-the-spot improvements. Teams of employees from across the organization work together to solve problems and review processes, promoting cooperation and driving organizational innovation. For the past 10 years, more than 90 percent of employees have been satisfied with their jobs and are willing to recommend the city as a place to work, outperforming a comparison group of federal government employees. The City of Coral Springs is the first state or local government agency to receive the Malcolm Baldrige National Quality Award.

Source: Jenks profile: Courtesy of Jenks Public Schools. Text was written by a team of four authors for the Malcolm Baldrige Application; Coral Springs profile: Baldrige Award Recipient Profiles, National Institute of Standards and Technology, U.S. Department of Commerce.

QUALITY AND SYSTEMS THINKING

*A **system** is a set of functions or activities within an organization that work together for the aim of the organization.*

A production system is composed of many smaller, interacting subsystems. For example, a McDonald's restaurant is a system that includes the order-taker/cashier subsystem, grill and food preparation subsystem, drive-through subsystem, purchasing subsystem, and training subsystem. These subsystems are linked together as internal customers and suppliers. Likewise, every organization is composed of many individual functions, which are often seen as separate units on an organization chart. However, managers need to view the organization as a whole and concentrate on the important organizational linkages among these functions. For example, strategies need to be linked to human resource plans and key processes in order to effectively align resources; human resources activities such as training and work system design must be linked to the processes that manufacture products or deliver services; and data collected from processes must be fed back to strategic planning as a means for improvement.

Russell Ackoff, a noted authority in **systems thinking**, explained the importance of systems thinking in the following way:

> *. . . a combination of the best practices by each part of a system taken separately does not yield the best system. We may not even get a good one. A company that has 12 facilities, each producing the same variations of the same type of beverage, had broken the production process down into 15 steps. It produced a table showing each factory (a column) and each of the 15 steps (rows). The company then carried out a study to determine the cost of each step at each factory (a costly study), which identified for each step the factory with the lowest cost. At each factory, the company tried to replace each of its steps that was not the lowest cost with the one used in the factory that had the lowest cost. Had this succeeded, each factory would be producing with steps that had each attained the lowest cost in any factory. It did not work! The lowest-cost steps did not fit together. The result was only a few insignificant cosmetic changes that did not justify the cost of the exercise.*[3]

Ackoff concluded that management should focus on the interactions of parts and of the system with other systems, rather than the actions of parts taken separately. As we discuss quality in different types of organizations, think about how important a systems perspective is in achieving quality.

Successful management relies on a systems perspective, one of the most important elements of total quality.

QUALITY IN MANUFACTURING

Well-developed quality assurance systems have existed in manufacturing for some time. The transition to a customer-driven organization has caused fundamental changes in manufacturing practices, changes that are particularly evident in areas such as product design, workforce management, and supplier relations. Product design activities, for example, now closely integrate marketing, engineering, and manufacturing operations. Workforce management practices concentrate on empowering employees to collect and analyze data, make critical operations decisions, and take responsibility for continuous improvements, thereby moving the responsibility for quality from the quality control department onto the factory floor. Suppliers have become partners in product design and manufacturing efforts. Many of these efforts were stimulated by the automobile industry as Ford, GM, and Chrysler forced their network of suppliers to improve quality during the 1980s. As they did so, quality efforts were pushed down the supply chain to many smaller companies.

Traditional quality assurance systems in manufacturing focus primarily on technical issues such as inspection, defect prevention, equipment reliability, and process control.

Exemplary quality leaders in the manufacturing sector include large companies such as Boeing, Medrad, Eastman Chemical Company, Motorola, and Solar Turbines Incorporated; and small companies such as Stoner, Inc., Sunny Fresh Foods, KARLEE, Texas Nameplate Company, and PRO-TEC, Inc. Practices of these and other outstanding manufacturing companies are featured throughout this book.

Manufacturing Systems

Figure 2.1 illustrates a typical manufacturing system and the key relationships among its functions. The quality concerns of each component of the system are described next.

Marketing and Sales Milton Hershey, the founder of Hershey Foods Corporation, understood the relationship between quality and sales. He used to say, "Give them quality. That's the best advertising in the world." For the first 68 years it was in business, Hershey Foods did not see a need to advertise its products in the mass

Figure 2.1 Functional Relationships in a Typical Manufacturing System

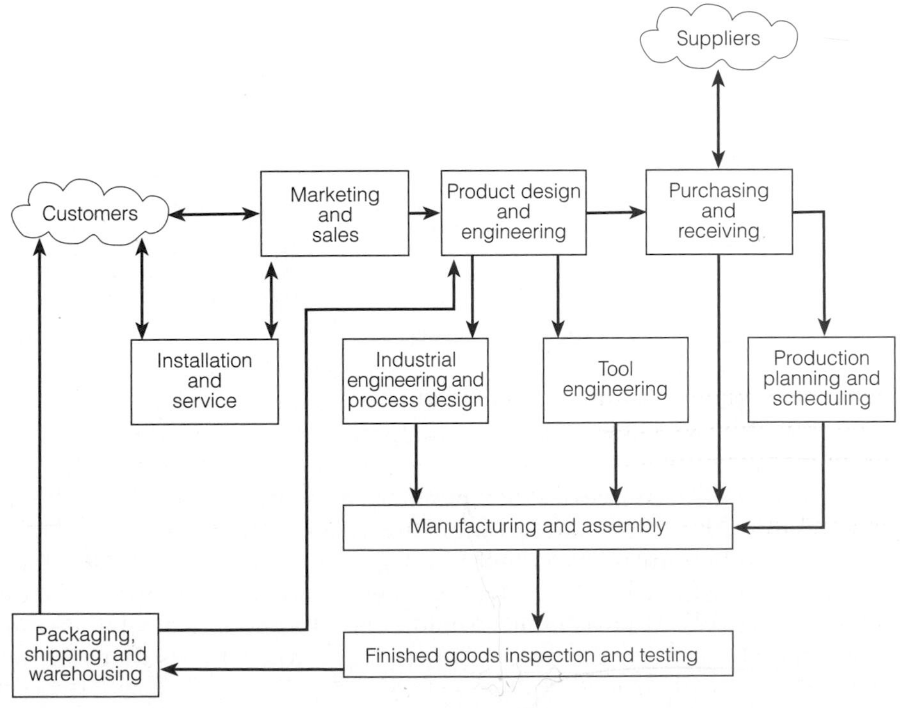

media.[4] Marketing and sales involve much more than advertising and selling. Today, marketing and sales employees have important responsibilities for quality. These responsibilities include learning the products and product features that consumers want, and knowing the prices that consumers are willing to pay for them. This information enables a firm to define products that are fit for use and capable of being produced within the technological and budgetary constraints of the organization. Effective market research and active solicitation of customer feedback are necessary for developing quality products. Salespeople can help to obtain feedback on product performance from customers and convey this information to product designers and engineers. They should also help to ensure that customers receive adequate assistance and are completely satisfied.

Marketing and sales personnel are responsible for determining the needs and expectations of consumers.

Ames Rubber Corporation

Ames Rubber Corporation, based in Hamburg, New Jersey, produces rubber rollers used to feed paper, transfer toner, and fuse toner to paper in office machines such as copiers, printers, and typewriters. All products are made to order to customer design and specification. Its warranties are among the best in the industry and include a refund of the customer's portion of development costs for prototype parts if Ames fails to achieve the specifications. Sales representatives take special note of such things as the volume of work a customer or prospective customer expects, the product features the customer seeks, and the customer's cost, service, and delivery requirements. Ames's sales department also conducts quarterly customer satisfaction surveys and monthly customer contact surveys. Customer satisfaction surveys collect data in the areas of products, service, information, and relationships. Customer contact surveys, which take the form of informal conversations, explore quality, cost, delivery, and service. The company uses all of this information to improve customer satisfaction.

Product Design and Engineering Underengineered products will fail in the marketplace because they will not meet customer needs. Products that are overengineered, those that exceed the customer requirements, may not find a profitable market. Japanese automakers, for instance, discovered in the early 1990s that many consumers were unwilling to pay for some luxury features they had designed into their cars as standard features. Overengineering can also create a complacency that leads to poor quality. Poorly designed manufacturing processes result in poor quality or higher costs. Good design can help to prevent manufacturing defects and service errors and to reduce the need for the non-value-adding inspection practices that have dominated much of U.S. industry.

Product design and engineering functions develop technical specifications for products and production processes to meet the requirements determined by the marketing function.

Motorola, one of the pioneers of corporate quality initiatives, places considerable emphasis on improving manufacturing quality through its product and process design activities. Motorola sets an ambitious goal of *six sigma quality*—a level of quality representing no more than 3.4 defects per million opportunities—for every process in the company. To reach this goal, Motorola knows that before it manufactures a product it must first determine the product characteristics that will satisfy customers (marketing's role); decide whether these characteristics can be achieved through the product's design, the manufacturing process, or the materials used; develop design tolerances that will assure successful product performance; conduct measurements to determine process variations from existing specifications; and then hone the product design, manufacturing process, or both, in order to achieve the desired results.

Purchasing and Receiving The quality of purchased parts and services and the timeliness of their delivery are critical. The purchasing department can help a firm achieve quality by:

- Selecting quality-conscious suppliers
- Ensuring that purchase orders clearly define the quality requirements specified by product design and engineering
- Bringing together technical staffs from both the buyer's and suppliers' companies to design products and solve technical problems
- Establishing long-term supplier relationships based on trust
- Providing quality-improvement training to suppliers
- Informing suppliers of any problems encountered with their goods
- Maintaining good communication with suppliers as quality requirements and design changes occur

An example of the quality consciousness of Japanese customers was presented to a college class by the manager of a U.S. plant that was supplying stock to a Japanese manufacturer of semiconductor devices for electronics applications. The U.S. manager was justifiably proud of having the best-quality material of this type available from any U.S. supplier, which was why his company had been chosen as a supplier. However, when the Japanese firm tested the first shipment of 9 million parts, it was quite upset with the lack of quality and informed the U.S. firm that it would have to do better or face being replaced by a Japanese supplier. The incoming inspection had detected five bad parts in the total shipment!

A purchasing agent should not simply be responsible for low-cost procurement, but should maintain a clear focus on the quality of purchased goods and materials.

The receiving department is the link between purchasing and production. It must ensure that the delivered items are of the quality specified by the purchase contract, which it does through various inspection and testing policies. If the incoming material is of high quality, extensive inspection and testing is not necessary. Many companies now require that their suppliers provide proof that their processes can consistently turn out products of specified quality and give preferential treatment to those that can.

The quality of incoming materials and parts becomes more critical as the use of flexible automation increases. Many U.S. firms have implemented just-in-time (JIT) scheduling. JIT requires that inventories be reduced to the barest minimum. To maintain production, the quality of materials must be high because no buffer inventories are available to take up the slack. Motorola, for example, provides extensive assistance and training to its suppliers to improve their capabilities and quality and expects results in return. Suppliers are evaluated on the quality of delivered product and the timeliness of deliveries. Only those suppliers that meet the company's expectations for superior quality are retained.

Production Planning and Scheduling A production plan specifies long-term and short-term production requirements for filling customer orders and meeting anticipated demand. The correct materials, tools, and equipment must be available at the proper time and in the proper places in order to maintain a smooth flow of production. Modern concepts of production planning and scheduling, such as small batch and single piece flow, have been shown to lead to quality improvements and cost savings.

Poor quality often results from time pressures caused by insufficient planning and scheduling.

Manufacturing and Assembly The role of manufacturing and assembly in producing quality is to ensure that the product is made correctly. The linkage to design and process engineering, as noted earlier, is obvious; manufacturing cannot do its job without a good product design and good process technology. Once in production, however, no defects should be acceptable. If and when they do occur, every effort must be made to identify their causes and eliminate them. Inspecting-out already defective items is costly and wasteful.

Ames Rubber Corporation, for example, produces more than 17,000 custom parts by means of a wide range of manufacturing operations such as casting, extrusion, spraying, and molding. Each operation requires appropriate measuring methods and devices that can closely monitor the manufacturing process. Sophisticated measuring and testing equipment, such as laser-measuring devices, ensure in-line process control. All Ames manufacturing staff must understand the importance and use of statistics in controlling processes. At each production step, operators, inspectors, and supervisors collect and evaluate performance data. This practice allows Ames to detect deviations from the processes immediately and to make the necessary adjustments.

Both technology and people are essential to high-quality manufacturing.

Tool Engineering The tool engineering function is responsible for designing and maintaining the tools used in manufacturing and inspection. Worn manufacturing tools result in defective parts, and improperly calibrated inspection gauges give misleading information. These and other tool problems lead to poor quality and inefficiency. Engineers at Ames Rubber use statistical techniques to evaluate tooling and equipment and conduct periodic studies to ensure that Ames continues to meet or exceed product requirements. If they cannot, the result is excessive scrap, waste, and higher costs.

Industrial Engineering and Process Design The job of industrial engineers and process designers is to work with product design engineers to develop realistic specifications. In addition, they must select appropriate technologies, equipment, and work methods for producing quality products. For example, Nissan Motor Manufacturing has a fully automated paint system in which robots are programmed to move along with cars. Because the robots always know where the body is, the robot will stop if the line stops but continue the paint cycle until finished as a means of keeping paint quality consistent.[5] Industrial engineers also work on designing facilities and arranging equipment to achieve a smooth production flow and to reduce the opportunities for product damage. Recently, industrial

Manufacturing processes must be capable of producing output that meets specifications consistently.

engineering as a profession has been incorporating the types of activities more often taught in business schools.

Finished Goods Inspection and Testing If quality is built into the product properly, inspection should be unnecessary except for auditing purposes and functional testing. Electronic components, for example, are subjected to extensive "burn-in" tests that ensure proper operation and eliminate short-life items. In any case, inspection should be used as a means of gathering information that can be used to improve quality, not simply to remove defective items.

The purposes of final product inspection are to judge the quality of manufacturing, to discover and help to resolve production problems that may arise, and to ensure that no defective items reach the customer.

Packaging, Shipping, and Warehousing Even good-quality items that leave the plant floor can be incorrectly labeled or damaged in transit. Packaging, shipping, and warehousing—often termed logistics activities—are the functions that protect quality after goods are produced. Accurate coding and expiration dating of products is important for traceability (often for legal requirements) and for customers.

Installation and Service Products must be used correctly in order to benefit the customer. Users must understand a product and have adequate instructions for proper installation and operation. Should any problem occur, customer satisfaction depends on good after-the-sale service. At one company, truck drivers saw the opportunity to do more than merely deliver materials to receiving docks. Where labor relations permit, they make deliveries to specific locations within plants and assist with unloading, stocking, and inventory counts. Many companies specify standards for customer service similar to the dimensions and tolerances prescribed for manufactured goods. For example, associates are expected to arrive for all appointments on time and to return customer phone calls within a prescribed time period. They are also responsible for knowing and observing their respective customers' rules and regulations, especially those that concern safety procedures.

Service after the sale is one of the most important factors in establishing customer perception of quality and customer loyalty.

In addition to the functions directly related to manufacturing the product, certain business support activities are necessary for achieving quality. Some of these activities are discussed here.

Finance and Accounting The finance function is responsible for obtaining funds, controlling their use, analyzing investment opportunities, and ensuring that the firm operates cost-effectively and—ideally—profitably. Financial decisions affect manufacturing equipment purchases, cost-control policies, price-volume decisions, and nearly all facets of the organization. Finance must authorize sufficient budgeting for equipment, training, and other means of assuring quality. Financial studies can help to expose the costs of poor quality and opportunities for reducing it. Accounting data are useful in identifying areas for quality improvement and

In many organizations, quality is seldom considered in financial analysis and decision making.

tracking the progress of quality improvement programs. Furthermore, inappropriate accounting approaches can hide poor quality.

Financial and accounting personnel who have contacts with customers can directly influence the service their company provides. At many companies, for example, employees chart invoice accuracy, the time needed to process invoices, and the time needed to pay bills. In addition, they can apply quality improvement techniques to improve their own operations. Financial personnel at Motorola, for example, were able to reduce the time needed to close the books from one month to four days.

Quality Assurance Because some managers lack the technical expertise required for performing needed statistical tests or data analyses, technical specialists—usually in the "quality assurance department"—assist the managers in these tasks. Quality assurance specialists perform special statistical studies and analyses and may be assigned to work with any of the manufacturing or business support functions. It must be remembered that a firm's quality assurance department cannot guarantee quality. Its proper role is to provide guidance and support for the firm's total effort toward this goal.

Every manager is responsible for studying and improving the quality of the process for which he or she is responsible; thus, every manager is a quality manager.

Legal Services A firm's legal department attempts to guarantee that the firm complies with laws and regulations regarding such things as product labeling, packaging, safety, and transportation; designs and words its warranties properly; satisfies its contractual requirements; and has proper procedures and documentation in place in the event of liability claims against it. The rapid increase in liability suits has made legal services an important aspect of quality assurance.

We see that manufacturing is a rather complex system that can be viewed as a "chain of customers." This approach suggests that a customer-driven quality focus must involve everyone in the organization. Quality is indeed everyone's responsibility.

QUALITY IN SERVICES

Service can be defined as "any primary or complementary activity that does not directly produce a physical product—that is, the non-goods part of the transaction between buyer (customer) and seller (provider)."[6]

A service might be as simple as handling a complaint or as complex as approving a home mortgage. The North American Industry Classification System (NAICS) describes service organizations as those

> *...primarily engaged in providing a wide variety of services for individuals, business and government establishments, and other organizations. Hotels and other lodging places, establishments providing personal, business, repair, and amusement services; health, legal, engineering, and other professional services; educational institutions, membership organizations, and other miscellaneous services are included.*

This classification of service organizations includes all nonmanufacturing organizations except such industries as agriculture, mining, and construction. Also usually included in this category are real estate, financial services, retailers, transportation, and public utilities.

Pure service businesses deliver intangible products. Examples would include a law firm, whose product is legal advice, and a health care facility, whose product is comfort and better health. However, service is a key element for many traditional manufacturing companies. For instance, manufacturers such as IBM and Xerox provide extensive maintenance and consulting services, which may be more important to the customer than its tangible products.

The service sector grew rapidly in the second half of the twentieth century. In 1945, 22.99 million people were employed by service-producing industries, and 18.5 million were employed by goods-producing industries. Today more than 80 percent of the non-farm employees in the United States are working in services, and more than half the jobs in manufacturing industries are service-related.

The service sector began to recognize the importance of quality several years after manufacturing had done so. This lag can be attributed to the fact that service industries had not confronted the same aggressive foreign competition that manufacturing faced. Another factor is the high turnover rate in service industry jobs, which typically pay less than manufacturing jobs. Constantly changing personnel makes establishing a culture for continuous improvement more difficult. Also, the very nature of quality changed from a focus on product defects to achieving customer satisfaction.

Companies nationally prominent in the service industry for their quality efforts include large organizations such as DynMcDermott, Caterpillar Financial Services, FedEx, and The Ritz-Carlton Hotel Company; and small companies such as Park Place Lexus and Pal's Sudden Service. These award-winning companies will be featured throughout this book.

The American Management Association estimates that the average company loses as many as 35 percent of its customers each year, and that about two-thirds of these are lost because of poor customer service.

The importance of quality in services cannot be overestimated. Studies show that companies can boost their profits by almost 100 percent by retaining just 5 percent more of their customers than their competitors retain.[7] This drastic difference is because the cost of acquiring new customers is much higher than the costs associated with retaining customers. Companies with loyal, long-time customers—even with higher unit costs and smaller market share—can financially outperform competitors with higher customer turnover.

The definitions of quality that apply to manufactured products apply equally to service products. The very nature of service implies that it must respond to the needs of the customer; that is, the service must "meet or exceed customer expectations." These expectations must be translated into performance standards and specifications similar to standards of conformance that direct manufacturing activities. For example, a quick-service restaurant might be expected to serve a complete dinner within 5 minutes. In a fine restaurant, however, one might expect to have 10 to 15 minutes between courses, and might regard the service as poor if the time between courses is too short.

Contrasts with Manufacturing

The production of services differs from manufacturing in many ways, and these differences carry important implications for quality management. The most critical differences are described here.

1. Customer needs and performance standards are often difficult to identify and measure, primarily because the customers define what they are, and each customer is different.

2. The production of services typically requires a higher degree of customization than does manufacturing. Doctors, lawyers, insurance salespeople, and food-service employees must tailor their services to individual customers. In manufacturing, the goal is uniformity.
3. The output of many service systems is intangible, whereas manufacturing produces tangible, visible products. Manufacturing quality can be assessed against firm design specifications (for example, the depth of cut should be 0.125 inch), but service quality can only be assessed against customers' subjective, nebulous expectations, and past experiences. (What is a "good" sales experience?) Also, the customer can "have and hold" a manufactured product, but can only remember a service. Manufactured goods can be recalled or replaced by the manufacturer, but poor service can only be followed up by apologies and reparations.
4. Services are produced and consumed simultaneously, whereas manufactured goods are produced prior to consumption. In addition, many services must be performed at the convenience of the customer. Therefore, services cannot be stored, inventoried, or inspected prior to delivery as manufactured goods are. Much more attention must therefore be paid to training and building quality into the service as a means of quality assurance.
5. Customers often are involved in the service process and are present while it is being performed, whereas manufacturing is performed away from the customer. For example, customers of a quick-service restaurant place their own orders, carry their food to the table, and are expected to clear the table when they have finished eating.
6. Services are generally labor intensive, whereas manufacturing is more capital intensive. The quality of human interaction is a vital factor for services that involve human contact. For example, the quality of hospital care depends heavily on interactions among the patients, nurses, doctors, and other medical staff. Banks have found that tellers' friendliness is a key factor in retaining depositors. Hence, the behavior and morale of service employees is critical in delivering a quality service experience.
7. Many service organizations must handle large numbers of customer transactions. For example, on a given business day, the Royal Bank of Canada might process more than 5.5 million transactions for 7.5 million customers through 1,600 branches and more than 3,500 banking machines, and FedEx might handle several million shipments across the globe each day. Such large volumes increase the opportunity for error.

These differences make it difficult for many service organizations to apply total quality principles, and foster misguided perceptions that quality management cannot be effectively accomplished in services.

Components of Service System Quality

Many service organizations such as airlines, banks, and hotels have well-developed quality systems. These systems begin with a commitment to the customers. For example, Amazon.com has pioneered a number of innovative approaches to improve customer satisfaction, ranging from easy-to-use website design to fast order fulfillment.

Service quality may be viewed from a manufacturing analogy, for instance, technical standards such as the components of a properly made-up guest room for a hotel, service transaction speed, or accuracy of information. However, managing

Two key components of service system quality are the workforce and information technology.

intangible quality characteristics is more difficult, because they usually depend on employee performance and behavior. This dependence does not imply that these factors are not important in manufacturing, of course, but they have special significance in services—just as engineering technology might have in manufacturing.

The two most important drivers of service quality are people and technology. In discussing *Fast Company* magazine's selection of the best customer-focused companies, editor John Byrne stated:

> *What do these companies and the people who run them teach us? First, leaders must be champions of the customer experience. By example and by emphasis, they must set high expectations for satisfying customers in their organizations. Second, employee empathy is what creates distinctive service. It's not enough to put on a happy face. Our champions of the customer understand that their employees must know what it feels like to be on the other side of the counter. And while technology is often central to providing a superior customer experience, it must be used to benefit customers, not just to replace the human element. . . . Boosting productivity and treating customers well are not mutually exclusive.*[8]

The Workforce Customers evaluate a service primarily by the quality of the human contact. A *Wall Street Journal* survey found that Americans' biggest complaints about service workers are of delivery people or salespeople who fail to show up when you have stayed home at a scheduled time for them; salespeople who are poorly informed; and salesclerks who talk on the phone while waiting on you, say "It's not my department," talk down to you, or cannot describe how a product works.

Researchers have repeatedly demonstrated that when service worker job satisfaction is high, customer satisfaction is high, and that when job satisfaction is low, customer satisfaction is low.[9]

Many service companies act on the motto "If we take care of our workforce, they will take care of our customers." At FedEx, for instance, the company credo is stated simply as People, Service, Profits. All potential decisions in the company are evaluated on their effects on the employees (people), on their customers (service), and the company's financial performance (profits), in that order. FedEx has a "no layoff" philosophy, and its "guaranteed fair treatment procedure" for handling grievances is used by firms in many industries as a model. Workers are encouraged to be innovative and to make decisions that advance quality and customer satisfaction goals. Front-line workers can qualify for promotion to management positions, and the company has a well-developed recognition program for team and individual contributions to company performance. FedEx management continually sets higher goals for quality performance and customer satisfaction, investing heavily in state-of-the-art technology, and building on its reputation as an excellent employer.

In many companies, unfortunately, the front-line workers—salesclerks, receptionists, delivery personnel, and so on, who have the most contact with customers—receive the lowest pay, minimal training, little decision-making authority, and little responsibility (when workers receive authority and responsibility, that is termed *empowerment*, which we discuss further in Chapter 6). Recruiting and selecting the right types of individuals and training them are particularly important, because service workers need to be skilled in handling every customer interaction, from greeting customers to asking the right questions. High-quality service workers also require effective reward systems that recognize customer satisfaction results and customer-focused behaviors, appropriate skills and abilities for performing the job, and supervisors who act more as coaches and mentors than as administrators.

The Ritz-Carlton Hotel Company, L.L.C.

The Ritz-Carlton Hotel Company, L.L.C. (see the Quality in Practice case at the end of this chapter) is one service company with an exemplary focus on its people.[10] The Ritz-Carlton motto is "We Are Ladies and Gentlemen Serving Ladies and Gentlemen," and all workers are treated as guests would be treated. The company's focus is to develop a "skilled and empowered workforce operating with pride and joy" by ensuring that everyone knows what they are supposed to do, how well they are doing, and have the authority to make changes as necessary. For example, the role of the housekeeper is not simply to make beds, but to create a memorable experience for the customer. Each hotel has a director of human resources and a training manager, who are assisted by the hotel's quality leader. Each work area has a departmental trainer who is responsible for training and certifying new employees in his or her unit. The Ritz-Carlton uses a highly predictive "character-trait recruiting" instrument for determining candidates' fitness for each of 120 job positions. New employees receive two days' orientation in which senior executives personally demonstrate Ritz-Carlton methods and instill Ritz-Carlton values. Three weeks later, managers monitor the effectiveness of the instruction and then conduct a follow-up training session. Later, they must pass written and skill-demonstration tests in order to become certified in their work areas. Every day, in each work area, each shift supervisor conducts a quality line-up meeting and briefing session. The workforce receives continuous teaching and coaching to refresh skills and improve performance, reinforce the purpose of the job, and to provide recognition for achievements. Through these and other mechanisms, workers receive more than 100 hours of quality education aimed at fostering a commitment to premium service, solving problems, setting goals, and generating new ideas. Workers are empowered to "move heaven and earth to satisfy a customer," to enlist the aid of others to resolve a problem swiftly, to spend up to $2,000 to satisfy a guest, to decide the business terms of a sale, to be involved in setting plans for their particular work area, and to speak with anyone in the company regarding any problem. The Ritz-Carlton has improved the turnover rate of the workforce steadily to well below industry averages.

Information technology is essential for quality in modern service organizations because of the high volumes of information they must process and because customers demand service at ever-increasing speeds.

Information Technology Information technology incorporates computing, communication, data processing, and various other means of converting data into useful information. Intelligent use of information technology not only leads to improved quality and productivity, but also to competitive advantage, particularly when technology is used to better serve the customer and to make it easier for customers to do business with the company.

Many service industries exploit information technology to improve customer service. Restaurants, for example, use handheld order-entry computer terminals to speed up the ordering process. An order is instantaneously transmitted to the kitchen or bar, where it is displayed and the guest check is printed. In addition to saving time, such systems improve accuracy by standardizing the order-taking, billing, and inventory procedures and reducing the need for handwriting.

Credit authorizations, which once took several minutes by telephone, are now accomplished in seconds through computerized authorization systems. FedEx's handheld "SuperTracker" scans packages' bar codes every time packages change hands between pickup and delivery.

The Ritz-Carlton Hotel Company exploits information technology to remember each of its 800,000+ customers. Knowledge of individual customer preferences, previous difficulties, family and personal interests, and preferred credit cards is stored in a database accessible to every hotel. This guest-profiling system allows each customer to be treated individually, by giving front-desk employees immediate access to such information as whether the guest smokes, whether he or she prefers scented or unscented soap, and what kind of pillow he or she prefers.

Another example is provided by Fidelity Investments.[11] Fidelity receives about 200,000 telephone calls each day, more than two-thirds of which are handled by a computer system without human intervention. A computer switching system monitors the call loads at Fidelity's four telephone centers and distributes calls among its more than 2,000 representatives. Fidelity developed a "workstation of the future" that allows its representatives to call up any customer's account on their terminal screen. Using this capability, Fidelity will be able to offer its customers up-to-the-second, personalized information and service while improving internal productivity.

Without a doubt, the largest impact of information technology for service has been in e-commerce. Customers can shop for almost any product; configure, price, and order computer systems; and take virtual test drives of automobiles and select from thousands of possible combinations of options on the Internet in the convenience of their homes. Information technology can be used to develop and enhance customer relationships. Amazon.com, from which many readers have probably ordered, has been extremely successful at this. They provide extensive information about products, such as reader reviews to help customers evaluate books, search used bookstores for out-of-print books, and even provide e-mail thank you letters a month or so after purchase. However, while information technology reduces labor intensity and increases the speed of service, it can have adverse effects on other dimensions of quality. Some people, including some customers, will argue that customer satisfaction is decreased when less personal interaction takes place. (Have you ever gotten irritated when wading through multiple menus on an automated telephone answering system?) Thus, service providers must balance conflicting quality concerns.

QUALITY IN HEALTH CARE

One service industry that faces continuing pressure to improve quality—and one with the fastest-growing interest in quality—is health care. Quality has been a focus for the industry for some time. In 1910, Ernest Codman, M.D., proposed the "end result system of hospital standardization." Under this system, a hospital would track every patient it treated long enough to determine whether the treatment was effective. If the treatment was not effective, the hospital would then attempt to determine why, so that similar cases could be treated successfully in the future. The American College of Surgeons (ACS) developed Minimum Standards for Hospitals in 1917 and began inspections the following year. The Joint Commission on Accreditation of Healthcare Organizations (JCAHO)—the principal accreditation agency for health care—was created in 1951 through a collaboration of ACS and several other agencies to provide voluntary accreditation. Its mission is "to continuously improve the safety and quality of care provided to the public through the provision of health care accreditation and related services that support performance improvement in health care organizations." By 1970, accreditation standards were recast to represent optimal achievable levels of quality, rather than minimum essential levels of quality. JCAHO issued new standards in 1992 requiring all hospital CEOs to educate themselves on CQI (continuous quality improvement—the term used in the health care profession to denote quality initiatives) methods.[12] The new standards emphasize performance improvement concepts and incorporate quality improvement principles more fully in areas such as surgical case review, blood usage evaluation, and drug usage evaluation.

Despite these accreditation efforts aimed at quality, the industry has faced many challenges. A 1998 study by the President's Advisory Commission on Consumer Protection and Quality in the Health Care Industry entitled Quality First: Better Health Care for All Americans, noted several types of quality problems in health care.[13] They include:

1. *Avoidable errors*. For example, a study of injuries to patients treated in hospitals in New York State found that 3.7 percent experienced adverse events, of which 13.6 percent led to death and 2.6 percent to permanent disability, and that about one-fourth of these adverse events were due to negligence.
2. *Underutilization of services*. An estimated 18,000 people die each year from heart attacks because they did not receive effective interventions.
3. *Overuse of services*. Millions of Americans receive health care services that are unnecessary, increase costs, and often endanger their health. For example, an analysis of hysterectomies performed by seven health plans estimated that one in six was inappropriate.
4. *Variation in services*. A pattern of wide variation continues in health care practice, including regional variations and small-area variations. This pattern clearly indicates that the practice of health care has not caught up with the science of health care to ensure evidence-based practice in the United States.

BONUS MATERIALS

The Commission's report included more than 50 recommendations to address these issues. These recommendations, which include the use of measurements, stakeholder participation, error prevention, and continuous improvement, support the underlying philosophy of total quality that we described in Chapter 1. Details of the Recommendations of the President's Advisory Commission on Health Care can be found in the Bonus Materials folder for this chapter on the Premium website.

In 2000, the Institute of Medicine (IOM) issued a report "To Err is Human," which quantified shocking stories of medical errors.[14] The report showed that the majority of medical errors do not result from recklessness, but are caused by faulty systems, processes, and conditions that lead people to make mistakes or fail to prevent them. The report provided a comprehensive strategy by which all stakeholders—government, health care providers, and consumers—can reduce medical errors. A follow-up report focused more broadly on how the health care system can be reinvented to foster innovation and improve the delivery of care.

Many organizations, both public and private, have developed models and guidelines aimed at improving health care quality. The National Committee for Quality Assurance (NCQA) is a private, not-for-profit organization dedicated to improving the quality of health care.[15] The organization's primary activities are assessing and reporting on the quality of the nation's managed care plans, work that has led to partnerships and collaborative efforts with many states, the federal government, employer and consumer groups, and many of the nation's leading corporations and business coalitions. NCQA's mission is to provide information that enables purchasers and consumers of managed health care to distinguish among plans based on quality, thereby allowing them to make more informed health care purchasing decisions. This greater information encourages plans to compete based on quality and value, rather than on price and provider network. Efforts are organized around two activities, accreditation and performance measurement, which are complementary strategies for producing information to guide choice. These activities are integrated under NCQA's Accreditation program, which includes selected performance measures in such key areas as member satisfaction, quality of care, access, and service.

NCQA began accrediting managed care organizations (MCOs) in 1991 in response to the need for standardized, objective information about the quality of these organizations. Although the MCO accreditation program is voluntary and rigorous, it has been well received by the managed care industry, and almost half the HMOs in the nation, covering three-quarters of all HMO enrollees, are currently involved in the NCQA Accreditation process. For an organization to become accredited by NCQA, it must undergo a survey and meet certain standards designed to evaluate the health plan's clinical and administrative systems. In particular, NCQA's Accreditation surveys look at a health plan's efforts to continuously improve the quality of care and service it delivers.

The Agency for Healthcare Research and Quality (AHRQ) is an integral part of the government's plan to improve health care quality and safety. Congress mandated that AHRQ produce an annual report on health care quality in the United States, resulting in the National Healthcare Quality Report, which has been published annually since 2003. The Centers for Medicare and Medicaid Services (CMS) launched quality initiatives in 2001 that are based on accountability by requiring public disclosure of quality measures for nursing homes, home health agencies, hospitals, and kidney dialysis facilities. The Association of American Medical Colleges (AAMC) formed a panel dedicated to incorporating quality of care issues into medical school and residency curricula.

Other organizations, such as the Institute for Healthcare Improvement (IHI), have emerged to support quality improvement in health care. IHI's goals are improved health status, better clinical outcomes, reduced costs that do not compromise quality, greater access to care, an easier-to-use health care system, and improved satisfaction to patients and communities. IHI focuses on fostering collaboration, rather than competition, among health care organizations, and promotes the use of quality control tools that have proven to be beneficial in manufacturing. One early pilot project driven by IHI at 37 intensive care units resulted in huge drops in pneumonia and other complications, shorter patient stays, and cost reductions of up to 30 percent.

Although the national health care system as a whole may need a sweeping overhaul, many individual providers have turned toward quality as a means of achieving better performance and customer satisfaction.

In 1990, SSM Health Care became one of the first health care organizations in the United States to implement CQI throughout its entire system. Five years later, after visiting manufacturing recipients of the Baldrige Award and learning about their practices, SSM instituted a new leadership plan, improved strategic and financial planning processes, a new conference to share best practices among its hospitals, and an improved CQI model that permits rapid identification and correction of potential problems. In 2002, SSM became the first health care recipient of the Baldrige Award. Other examples include Boston's New England Deaconess Hospital, where teams identify problems that add unnecessary days to hospital stays, achieving a 10 percent overall decrease in length of hospital stay in two years; and Nash General Hospital in Rocky Mount, North Carolina, which examined processes within the emergency department and was able to reduce the length of stay by more than 50 percent.[16]

Technology has been important in health care quality improvement, For example, electronic medical record (EMR) systems allow doctors to type into a central database medical orders, prescriptions, diagnostic tests, and blood work results. The doctors' orders are matched against the patient's medical history, triggering red flags to prevent problems related to drug allergies, overdoses, and dangerous interactions with other drugs. Centralized records also allow nurses and pharmacists to find the information they need.

North Mississippi Medical Center

North Mississippi Medical Center's (NMMC) EMR is an important component of their performance improvement processes and has contributed to outstanding results.[17] Automated patient care and diagnostic systems such as laboratory, radiology, and admissions collect and feed patient data to the EMR as a product of daily operations. The foundation of the EMR is a unique, life-long identifier assigned to each patient upon his or her first contact with NMMC at any access point. This permanent identifier ensures that each record of every episode of care delivered at any setting within NMMC is consolidated and retained within the EMR. This "lifetime clinical record" system is available at all sites of care and provides real-time data and information to clinicians who use it every day. The EMR has built-in Provision of Care process protocols that alert caregivers to real-time in-process potential food–drug and drug–drug interactions, and drug allergies, as well as past due medications and treatments. The EMR's assessment database reduces errors by providing an up-to-date medication history and demographic data. NMMC is a role model for the federal government's initiative to make Electronic Health Records available to most Americans by 2015.

Although many health care organizations notice measurable improvements from their quality initiatives, they primarily occur in the areas of cost reduction and increased efficiency. A difficult challenge that most face is getting physicians involved in the quality process. Many are requiring their participation on teams and steering committees, creating a liaison role between management and physicians, using physicians as champions, and targeting training.[18]

QUALITY IN EDUCATION

Education represents one of the most interesting and challenging areas for quality improvement. Attacks on the quality of education in the United States, from kindergarten through the 12th grade (K–12) and at colleges and universities provided a rallying cry for education reform during the last decade.[19]

Mt. Edgecumbe High School

One of the earliest and most widely publicized stories of the successful use of quality in education is that of Mt. Edgecumbe High School in Sitka, Alaska.[20] Mt. Edgecumbe is a public boarding school with some 200 students, often from problem homes in rural Alaska. Many are Native Americans, who are struggling to keep their culture alive while learning to live and work in American society. David Langford, a teacher, brought the quality concepts to Mt. Edgecumbe after hearing about them at a meeting at McDonnell-Douglas Helicopter Company. After reading many books by quality gurus such as Deming, Juran, and Crosby, Langford took some students in a computer club on a trip to Gilbert (Arizona) High School. There, they observed how Delores Christiansen taught continuous improvement in her business classes. They also visited companies in the Phoenix area that were using quality principles. The students, with the coaching of Langford, began to use quality concepts to improve school processes. For example, the students tackled the problem of too many tardy classmates. By investigating the reasons for tardiness, the students persuaded the administration to drop the punishment for tardy students, and were able to reduce the average number of late occurrences per week from 35 to 5.

As an even more radical change, the school dropped the traditional grading system. Instead, students use statistical techniques to keep track of their own progress. No assignment is considered finished until it is perfect. Eliminating grades has had a positive effect. One student, James Penemarl reported, "I found myself learning a lot more. It's not the teacher having to check my progress, it's me having to check my progress. See, however much I learn is up to me, and if I want to learn, I'm going to go out and learn." What they call CIP, or the continuous improvement process, has been an obvious success (approximately 50 percent of students now go on to college), yet the messages that David Langford stresses in interviews about the school are (1) it takes time, effort, and persistence—it's not a "quick fix," and (2) there's always room for improvement.

Many other K–12 school districts such as Jenks Public Schools, which we highlighted in the opening Quality Profiles, have implemented TQ initiatives. In 2001, two K–12 schools were among the first Baldrige Education recipients: Chugach School District in Alaska, and Pearl River School District in New York.

Pearl River School District

The Pearl River School District (PRSD) is a 100-year-old school district located in Rockland County, 20 miles north of New York City on the west side of the Hudson River.[21] The district's mission is simple: *Every child can and will learn.* PRSD's quality approach is based on its core values:

- Our students are our customers, and the product we deliver is to allow them to achieve to their highest ability.
- Educational opportunity is for all students.
- Learning is an active process where students discover and create knowledge.
- Tracking academic performance is a consistent and constant practice.
- Active involvement from all stakeholders is integral to district operations.
- District employees are highly valued resources.
- The district recognizes the value it has in the community and the people it serves.
- Our business operations are cost-effective while maintaining quality and protecting program.

The chief reason the district is successful is that everything it does is aligned with its three strategic goals: (1) improve student academic achievement, (2) improve public perception of the district, and (3) maintain fiscal stability and improve cost-effectiveness.

More than 14 variables are considered in designing how to deliver curriculum and instruction to students. Faculty and staff development is integrated with the work system design so as to improve employee performance. Every one of the employees has annual goals and an evaluation, which support district goals. All faculty members participate in a minimum of 42 hours of professional development each year. All staff participate in a minimum of 21 hours of training.

PRSD uses a continuous improvement cycle to drive the performance improvement. A disciplined performance review process is used to collect and analyze data to evaluate whether the district goals, objectives, and projects are being accomplished. Throughout the school year, the district uses a number of formal and informal checkpoints to monitor and evaluate performance. Data are collected from student performance, environmental scanning, demographic and enrollment trends, student and stakeholder surveys, and national and state standardized tests. The district's continuous improvement cycle has been modified and customized so that the classroom teachers can use it. The process allows for curriculum alignment to meet federal and state standards, as well as faculty instructional delivery improvement so that all students learn.

In general, educators, educational institutions, political groups and leaders, and even the public have been slow to attack the problem of educational decline on a systematic basis. However, in 2002, President Bush signed into law the No Child Left Behind Act, which demanded accountability for results, tracking each student's accomplishments, and emphasizing teaching methods that have been proven to work. Essentially, states and districts are given an annual report card to measure school performance and rate progress. In addition, some encouraging evidence shows that educators at the K–12 level are beginning to recognize the need for quality improvement efforts. A national survey of 401 public school principals by Harris Interactive and sponsored by the American Society for Quality, found that U.S. elementary schools are more advanced than secondary schools in their use of quality tools and approaches.[22] The majority of the principals surveyed (70 percent) believe that U.S. schools will be more likely to adopt quality improvement programs in the future.

Some highlights of the research include the following:

- In 2002, approximately 58 percent of U.S. public schools had a formalized quality improvement approach in place; however, 63 percent of elementary schools had such a program. One explanation for this difference may be because of greater parental involvement at the elementary level.
- Nearly all principals (95 percent) report that their school has a school improvement plan that includes measurable outcomes.
- Eight in ten principals (81 percent) believe that improving standardized test score performance is extremely or very important.
- Nearly all of these schools (98 percent) measure their efforts in this area by regularly gathering quantifiable data.

Despite these findings, "principals are not as likely to measure their efforts in other areas that are important to them," according to a past ASQ president, Dr. Kenneth Case. "For example," Case continued, "the study showed that although 85 percent of principals believe that improving teacher satisfaction and morale is extremely or very important, only 71 percent of these schools are regularly gathering quantifiable data about their efforts in this area."

Koalaty Kid

The American Society for Quality (ASQ) has long promoted quality in elementary education through a program entitled *Koalaty Kid*.[23] It was an outgrowth of activities at Frederick C. Carder Elementary School in Corning, New York, where Fred the Koala appeared throughout the school on bulletin boards, at assemblies, in the cafeteria, and in the classrooms.

Carder Elementary School

In the 1980s, several teachers and the principal at Carder identified factors they deemed most important to student success and areas where they felt their students needed improvement. First, they believed that reading was the key to all other learning, and observed that students did not read much beyond what was required in the classroom. Second, they found that all too often, students were handing in homework with numerous errors. When asked to correct them, students could do so easily. They knew how to do it, but simply didn't habitually do it right the first time. Third, they observed that the most successful students were those who felt confident of their abilities and comfortable with themselves.

Having identified these critical issues, they developed a plan to bring about change throughout the whole school. Reading became a primary focus. Students were invited to read books of their own choosing. Reading at home was encouraged with a system of contracts. Students demonstrated that they understood what they read through book reports, and each book was recorded. Students who met their contracts were recognized at assemblies, and incentives helped to encourage the habit. Second, the teachers communicated the standard of work they expected in homework—best work the first time. When students handed in papers, they were asked to assess in their own minds, "Is this your best work?" Excellent papers were displayed on bulletin boards, and students were recognized for "Koalaty work." Third, teachers established schoolwide expectations for behavior, and made a point of "catching" students being good. This combination of efforts became known as "Koalaty Kid," and students eagerly strove to become "Koalaty Kids" to read more, do their best work the first time, and treat others with courtesy and respect.

In 1988, two ASQ members from Corning, Incorporated visited the school and learned about Koalaty Kid. They immediately saw the parallels to total quality: critical issues had been identified, a plan for improvement was developed and implemented, clear expectations were communicated, a measurement system was put in place, and a consistent system of recognition and reward reinforced student success. Excited by what they saw in Carder School, the businesspeople brought the Carder model to the attention of ASQ headquarters. The Society invested in a pilot program, providing incentives for reading and tracked increases in 26 pilot schools over two years. A Koalaty Kid steering committee, including educators, sponsors, and ASQ members, was formed to oversee the effort, and Koalaty Kid began to emphasize a broader and more rigorous use of total quality in schools. More than 800 U.S. schools and many overseas have adopted Koalaty Kid.

Because Koalaty Kid is an approach, not a prescribed program, schools can utilize it to achieve their own objectives.

The four key factors that make Koality Kid work are active involvement of the whole school community, committed leadership, a system for continuous improvement, and an environment that celebrates successes.

Active Involvement School administrators, teachers, sponsors, parents, and the students themselves work together on teams that are empowered to make decisions and implement change. This system does not mean that Koalaty Kid gives away the authority to run the schools. Rather, it means that everyone who is ultimately affected by a school has an opportunity to influence its success. Together, they represent a larger resource than the school's paid staff. And because they represent all constituencies, they can often create change more swiftly and lastingly. Teams might manage some of the school's ongoing operations. They might identify and tackle tough issues. Or, they might help the schools and students in any number of creative ways. It's up to the school leadership and the teams themselves to decide how they can best work toward achieving the school's goals.

Outside sponsoring organizations are vitally important to the success of Koalaty Kid schools. These businesses, institutions, community organizations, or ASQ sections participate on the school-based team. They may help the school in a variety of ways, depending on their own capabilities and the school's needs. Some provide funds for quality training, while others become a source of help for important school activities, expertise in troubleshooting quality processes, or enrichment for academic areas. Most important, their perspective as future employers or community representatives with a stake in the school's "output" helps to bring the school and its community closer together.

Parent involvement is critical to the success of Koalaty Kid schools. Parents work closely with their own children, monitoring homework assignments, reading aloud, identifying trouble spots, and communicating with students, teachers, and administrators about any factors that affect their children's success. In addition, they often serve as the core of the school's volunteer base. As volunteers, they may help the school in a variety of ways—supplementing the work of classroom teachers with one-on-one tutoring, raising funds for needed equipment, and participating actively in decision making on the school's teams.

Committed Leadership Schools can change only if their designated leaders are committed to improvement. Change occurs quickly if these administrators are also capable of inspiring the faculty, students, parents, sponsors, and other administrators to work with them. Because of their positions, these individuals can allocate resources, call meetings, and generally "make things happen." However, leadership from others can also be effective, provided it is accepted and endorsed by those with ultimate decision-making authority. Leaders inspire others in the school community because of the depth and sincerity of their belief and commitment. Part of their ability to persuade others also comes from articulating their own clear understanding of where they are headed and the process they will use to get there. They constantly listen and learn, and they draw others with skill and ideas into the process. School leaders often find that undertaking the Koalaty Kid process inspires them to new levels of their own professional growth and a more profound understanding of their own roles as leaders.

A System for Continuous Improvement Koalaty Kid uses total quality principles—establishing consistent standards of excellence, setting and communicating clear expectations, continuous improvement (as opposed to finding fault and blaming), looking at a work task as a process, involving all who have a stake in the outcome in the improvement process, measuring results, and recognizing and rewarding success—for bringing about change. Using a set of quality "tools," teams define a system, assess a situation, analyze causes, try out improvement theories, study results, standardize improvement, and plan continuous improvement.

Environment That Celebrates Successes Even though many schools are now using team-based management or employing total quality, the fourth distinguishing feature of Koalaty Kid schools is the excitement that permeates the school environment. This excitement is focused on celebrating student successes, large and small. Displays of papers that meet or exceed requirements, photos of students recognized for exemplary behavior, and rosters of student achievements adorn classroom bulletin boards and school hallways. At assemblies and pep rallies, students cheer for one another's accomplishments as they are recognized. In hundreds of ways, the teachers, staff, volunteers, and parents communicate their delight when students reach goals.

Among the success stories that have resulted from Koalaty Kid are Kingsley Elementary, a Sullivan County, Tennessee, Title 1 school, which has made a 58 percent gain in student writing performance over two years to the annual state mandated writing test administered every spring.[24] In developing a process to improve writing, two tools, The Kingsley Koalaty Kid steering team, with representation from each grade level, developed and implemented regular writing practice prompts using special improvement tools. These were used every week in the 2001–02 school year, and every other week in the 2002–03 school year throughout all classes. In addition, Kingsley students began charting their individual grades, which is a significant step toward students taking responsibility for their own learning. Students are recognized for writing accomplishments during school announcements, by the school Koalaty Kid Express, and twice during school assemblies. Teachers select students to receive recognition certificates for either writing excellence or writing improvement, and are congratulated by their ASQ Koalaty Kid mascot and business partner representative.[25]

Quality in Higher Education

Many colleges and universities have also made substantial commitments to quality efforts. However, the percentages of higher educational institutions engaged in long-term efforts to measure and improve quality have been relatively small. Between 2001 and 2008, only three higher education institutions have received the Baldrige Award. These are the University of Wisconsin-Stout, the University of Northern Colorado's Monfort College of Business, and Richland (Community) College.

Oregon State University

One of the early success stories at the university level is Oregon State University (OSU).[26] Following close study of the quality literature, a visit from Dr. W. Edwards Deming, company visits to Ford, Hewlett-Packard, and Dow, and attendance by the president and several top administrators at a seminar on problem-solving tools, administrators at OSU began the planning phase. The first pilot study at OSU was conducted in the physical plant area for a number of reasons: (1) quality was considered a high-priority issue; (2) it had a high probability of success; (3) management agreed that it was important; (4) no one else was working on it; and (5) it was also important to the customers of the organization. A multilevel team of 12 people chose to study the specific issue of ways to "decrease turnaround time in the remodeling process." The team made and implemented a number of recommendations. Among them were the development of a project manager position; installation of a customer service center to enhance work scheduling, control, and follow-up; implementation of customer surveys to assess communications; more consultation at the beginning of the process with customers; identification of equipment and materials that could be purchased during the design phase; and shop participation to identify potential problems during the design phase. The first pilot project reduced the remodeling project time by 10 percent. Using customer surveys, the team studied many other processes, such as those in recruitment and admissions. However, note that such early efforts focused on administrative systems—the manufacturing analogy of quality—and not in the core processes of teaching or research.

Business plays an important role in fostering quality improvement efforts in higher education by transferring knowledge and expertise on quality processes and implementation practices.

In 1989, Xerox Corporation hosted the first Quality Forum, a gathering of academic and business leaders. Business leaders urged academia to teach quality principles and to use them in managing their organizations. Many companies established partnerships with colleges and universities. For example, Motorola's partnership with Purdue University led to the formation of the university's continuous quality improvement approach called Excellence21, a system-wide effort by the university to explore the principles of continuous improvement and total quality management. Projects were developed in the areas of

1. Faculty and Staff Development and Worklife Enrichment
2. Assessment of Student Learning Outcomes
3. Undergraduate Education
4. Graduate Education
5. Student Related (Student services)
6. Administrative Processes
7. Technology

Other universities established similar partnerships with industry leaders. However, these efforts revolved around project approaches.

University of Wisconsin – Stout

One example of a university that has addressed quality within its overall management system is the University of Wisconsin–Stout, the first higher-education recipient of a Baldrige Award.[27] One of 13 publicly supported universities in the University of Wisconsin System, the University of Wisconsin–Stout, located in Menomonie, has about 1,200 faculty and staff and about 8,000 students. Operating on a $95 million annual budget, UW–Stout offers 27 undergraduate and 16 graduate degrees through three academic colleges: the College of Technology, Engineering and Management; the College of Human Development; and the College of Arts and Sciences.

Nearly half of UW–Stout's programs are unique within the University of Wisconsin system, and several are not offered anywhere else in the United States. This distinctive array of degree offerings stems from UW–Stout's "Mission Driven–Market Smart" focus aimed at developing students for careers in industry and education. This special mission guides all key processes, including strategic planning, program development, partnership building, and teaching and learning. In addition to its success in placing graduates in jobs and earning high satisfaction scores from students and alumni, UW–Stout has been described as a "hidden treasure" in a popular national catalog for high school guidance counselors. UW–Stout uses a comprehensive set of methods for listening to and learning from students throughout their academic careers and beyond. Student needs, expectations, attitudes, and performance are tracked through surveys, course and program evaluations, and a variety of "success measures" that link student performance to educational effectiveness.

The university began conducting student satisfaction surveys in the mid-1970s. Since then, it has supplemented its efforts through participation in state and national student surveys. Survey results and other student-related information are evaluated from numerous perspectives. The university's integrated relational database system permits almost unlimited segmentation of data. For example, student performance and satisfaction can be evaluated for standard categories, such as academic programs, diversity group, gender, or for unique segments of students. This ability supports efforts to determine the root causes of problems and to pin down the relationship between processes and outcomes.

The results of these and other analyses are helping UW–Stout to sharpen its "Mission Driven–Market Smart" focus to the benefit of students and employers alike. UW-Stout seniors exceeded the national peer averages of "active" learning—traditional instruction reinforced with real-life experience—by 13 percent in 2000. Since 1996, the job placement rate for graduates has been at or above 98 percent. Moreover, alumni earn salaries that exceed the national average from other institutions and the average for graduates from UW system schools.

Such results also lead to satisfaction. For example, more than 90 percent of graduate program alumni and almost 90 percent of undergraduate alumni say that, if they could do it all over again, they would choose to attend UW–Stout. Among employers, UW–Stout also earns consistently high marks. In the university's five most recent follow-up surveys to learn how employers view its graduates, 99 percent to 100 percent of respondents rated UW–Stout graduates as well prepared for their positions.

One of the particular efforts to encourage colleges and universities to engage in quality practices is the **Academic Quality Improvement Project (AQIP)**. The goals of AQIP are to help member organizations improve their performance and maximize their effectiveness; reshape the relationship with members of The Higher Learning Commission (an accreditation agency) into a partnership; and provide the public with credible quality assurance concerning higher education providers. Participation in AQIP is a voluntary alternative to traditional academic accreditation. It focuses on application of TQ principles to educational institutions to better understand their key processes, track performance, and understand students and other stakeholders; involves faculty more directly in the improvement process; and provides concrete feedback to enable institutions to raise performance levels. The criteria used for AQIP assessment are closely aligned with the Malcolm Baldrige Criteria for Performance Excellence that we will discuss in the next chapter.

AQIP criteria focuses on institutional practices for helping students learn, accomplishing other distinct objectives, understanding student and stakeholder needs, valuing people, leading and communicating, supporting institutional operations, measuring effectiveness, planning continuous improvement, and building collaborative relationships—all of which are key elements of performance excellence.

QUALITY IN SMALL BUSINESSES AND NOT-FOR-PROFITS

Small businesses and not-for-profits have generally been slow to adopt quality initiatives. In most cases, this lag is a result of a lack of understanding and knowledge of what needs to be done and how to do it, because managers are wrapped up in entrepreneurial activities that typically focus on sales strategies and market growth, day-to-day cash flow problems, and routine fire fighting. In addition, small firms and not-for-profits often lack the resources needed to establish and maintain more formal quality systems. However, in viewing the three principles of TQ, a focus on customers is clearly vital to small enterprises; the company president or founder is often the principal contact with key customers and knows them intimately. Most small businesses live or die from their customer relationship practices, but the other two TQ principles—employee engagement and teamwork, and a process focus and continuous improvement—are generally not well addressed. Small business executives, especially in family-owned enterprises, often have a "command-and-control" attitude that dominates decision making, leaving little discretion and empowerment to employees. In addition, processes tend to be highly unstructured and not based on adequate data and information. Simply getting by each day often takes precedence over long-term planning and improvement activities.

Many other characteristics of small firms adversely affect the implementation of TQ principles. These characteristics include the following:[28]

- The lack of market clout, which may impact a small firm's ability to get suppliers involved in quality efforts

- Not recognizing the importance of human resource management strategies in quality, and therefore experiencing lower levels of employee empowerment, involvement, and quality-related training
- Lack of professional management expertise and the short-term focus, which often results in inadequate allocation of resources to TQ efforts
- Lower technical knowledge and expertise, making it difficult for smaller firms to effectively use quality tools and improvement techniques
- The informal nature of communication and lack of structured information systems, which inhibit implementation

Perhaps the most important factor in successful quality initiatives in small businesses is the recognition by the CEO or president that a quality focus can be beneficial and lead to achieving organizational goals.

Nevertheless, many successful small businesses have shown that quality initiatives can be successfully accomplished. Small businesses often come to this conclusion as they grow or face critical market challenges; they simply cannot afford to be managed as they were in the past, and require a more systematic process-oriented infrastructure.

Texas Nameplate Company

One example is Texas Nameplate Company, Inc. (TNC), which manufactures and sells identification and information labels that are affixed to refrigerators, oil-field equipment, high-pressure valves, trucks, computer equipment, and other products made by more than 1000 customers throughout the United States and in nine foreign countries. With only about 43 employees, it is the smallest company to receive a Baldrige Award, which it did twice, in 1998 and again in 2004. Their quality journey began when a large customer threatened to cut them off if they did not begin applying quality control tools. However, it was the persistence of TNC's president, Dale Crownover, who made the difference and kept faith in his people. Not only did Crownover begin training his people, but he instituted profit-sharing and gainsharing incentives, along with higher-than-industry-average pay scales, to reinforce the workforce's commitment to quality and foster company loyalty. Customer contact employees are empowered to resolve customer complaints without consulting management, and production workers are responsible for tailoring processes to optimize contributions to company goals and to meet team-set standards.

To help workers identify opportunities for improvement, each process at TNC is mapped using a flow chart. The average employee receives 75 hours of training in the first two years, much of it delivered on a just-in-time basis. About one in 10 workers is a multipurpose employee, trained in three or more jobs, allowing them to be moved to any area of the company that needs assistance to meet fluctuating customer and market demands. As a result of these efforts, the company disbanded its quality control department, replaced it with a cross-functional team, and made quality the responsibility of all employees. Defects fell from 2.4 percent to less than 1 percent, employee turnover improved, and market share increased by 45 percent in just three years. Was it hard? In one interview, Crownover stated, "Yeah, it was hard. The last five years of my life doing this was very hard. But let me tell you about the first five years I was president of this company. We had legal issues, EEOC, customer complaints, people quitting . . . that was hard!" We will discuss the importance of leadership for implementing quality further in later chapters.

Similar comments hold true for not-for-profits, who, unlike their business counterparts, are not driven by the bottom line (although tight budgets can certainly be a driving factor in pursuing quality) and whose managers often lack the business acumen and technical expertise needed to make an organizational transformation. Little literature exists on how to apply quality principles to not-for-profits, and employees use a "language" different from business, making it challenging for them to translate business concepts into meaningful applications. Among the key challenges that not-for-profits face are overcoming the fear of change, changing the mindset that not-for-profits are different and cannot effectively apply quality principles, identifying a vision and customers, understanding work processes, dealing with limited resources, and understanding relationships with government and large corporations.[29] However, numerous not-for-profit organizations are adopting TQ principles because of their impact on the public and society—their major customers and stakeholders. The United Way of America, for example, began recognizing United Way organizations for quality achievements in 1994.

Quality Spotlight American Red Cross

The American Red Cross launched a multiyear, multimillion-dollar quality effort to enhance organizational effectiveness and improve its process of collecting, testing, and distributing blood. Their focus is to drive any variability, deviation, or error down to zero using initiatives such as the following:

- New technologies to reduce the potential for human error
- Restructuring and increasing the level of quality assurance staff
- Creating a more streamlined and comprehensive training system
- Reengineering the core manufacturing processes to make them more efficient and simplified so as to reduce and prevent errors
- Investing in facilities to enable more efficient and effective adoption of new technology[30]

Expansion of the Baldrige Award to not-for-profits in 2007 has spawned more interest in quality among these organizations.

QUALITY IN THE PUBLIC SECTOR

Like other not-for-profit organizations, quality in the public sector—federal, state, and municipal governments—has not achieved growth and momentum as rapidly as in the private sector. Nevertheless, many public sector entities have made remarkable strides to incorporate the principles of quality into their operations.

Quality in the Federal Government

The federal government has a surprisingly long history of quality improvement activities. Quality circle programs—a form of team participation—were developed in the late 1970s at several Department of Defense installations, such as the Norfolk Naval Shipyard and the Cherry Point Naval Air Station. NASA began its quality improvement efforts in the early 1980s, both internally and with its suppliers.[31] Quality caught the attention of a number of agencies and managers when President Ronald Reagan signed Executive Order 12637, "Productivity Improvement for the Federal Government," in 1988.[32] The order required senior managers to monitor and improve both quality and productivity. It also encouraged them to use employee involvement, training, and participation in decision making, along with the more traditional methods of incentives, recognition, and rewards, to enhance the process.

One of the mechanisms set up to promote quality during the 1980s was the Federal Quality Institute (FQI). The FQI was established within the U.S. Office of Personnel Management in Washington, D.C., as the "primary source of leadership, information, and consulting services on quality management in the federal government." The institute provides such products and services as seminars, start-up assistance, national and regional conferences, support of quality awards, research, a listing of private sector consultants, an information network, and publications. In 1990, the FQI was given responsibility for administering the President's Quality Award and the Quality Improvement Prototype Award.

During the Clinton administration, efforts toward the advancement of quality in the federal government continued. Under the direction of Vice President Al Gore, a series of awards, with the innovative title of "The Golden Hammer" Awards focused attention on the need for continuous improvement efforts to reduce government waste at the grassroots individual and organizational levels. In addition, a report entitled "Creating a Government That Works Better and Costs Less: Report of the National Performance Review" was published in the fall of 1993. The report outlined 384 recommendations and indicated 1,214 specific actions that the federal government should take to improve government operations and reduce costs.

The Presidential Award for Management Excellence—the President's Quality Award (PQA)—is the highest award given to Executive Branch agencies for management excellence. The award was established in 1988 to recognize excellence in quality and productivity, applying to the public sector similar criteria used for the Malcolm Baldrige National Quality Improvement Awards. In 2002, the PQA was redesigned to recognize Federal agencies that best achieve the objectives of the President's Management Agenda (PMA). There are three award categories:

1. **Category One Award—**For a specific practice, falling under one of the five government-wide Management Initiatives, that is innovative and exemplary.
2. **Category Two Award—**For agency performance in one of the five Government-wide Management Initiatives.
3. **Category Three Award—**For agency performance in integrating their management systems under the five Government-wide Management Initiatives.

The five management initiatives in the category two and three awards are:

1. Budget and Performance Integration
2. Strategic Management of Human Capital
3. Competitive Sourcing
4. Improved Financial Performance
5. Expanded Electronic Government

Descriptions of two PQA winners follow:[33]

- In 2005, the Department of Labor (DOL) was the first Executive Branch organization to receive the Award based on outstanding performance in all five government-wide President's Management Agenda (PMA) initiatives. The Department of Labor's approach to integrating all the President's Management Agenda initiatives throughout the Agency has resulted in sustainable and proven results. DOL's integration efforts began with Management Review Board to provide a Departmental forum for crosscutting management issues. Monthly executive Board meetings address topics ranging from annual Agency budget and performance to detailed results using internal PMA scorecards for 15 DOL agencies and components. Competitive sourcing competitions, a new managerial cost accounting system, and improved integration and enhancement of IT systems have made DOL more accessible to worker and employer clients of various agencies.

- The Environmental Protection Agency received the 2007 Presidential Award for Management Excellence. Through innovative new approaches, EPA continues to convert the Agency from a "reporting" organization to a "learning and doing" organization; from a "compliance" culture to one devoted to "performance." EPA developed a system for identifying its highest priority outcomes for streamlining and focusing its measurement systems, and for cascading from those long-term outcomes down to quarterly commitments and measures that can be used in the day-to-day management of the Agency. EPA also improved its operations and results through engaging Agency managers and staff across organizational units and at various management levels in performance management activities; facilitating the collection and accessibility of performance data; and improving the presentation and the use of performance measures to inform decisions. EPA's management activities emphasize continuous learning through participation, evaluation, information sharing, and replication.

State and Local Quality Efforts

State and local government agencies have gained momentum in developing their own quality programs and processes, albeit at a much slower rate than the private sector. Massachusetts, for example, formed a Quality Improvement Council to oversee and facilitate a broad quality program. State quality award programs, discussed in the next chapter, provide a basis for many state and local agencies to learn about quality and pursue performance excellence in the same manner as private business.

City of Madison, Wisconsin

One of the earliest examples of a successful public-sector quality initiative involved the city of Madison, Wisconsin. Joseph Sensenbrenner, mayor of Madison from 1983 to 1989, was one of the leaders in bringing quality principles to city government.[34] After a 1983 audit disclosed problems at the city garage, such as long delays in repair and equipment unavailability, Sensenbrenner attempted to apply quality improvement approaches, where the manager and mechanics were surprised to see "top management" personally visible and committed to their problems. Sensenbrenner obtained the cooperation of the union president and formed a team to gather data from individual mechanics and the repair process itself. The team found that many delays resulted from insufficient stocking of repair parts, which, in turn, was caused by having more than 440 different types, makes, models, and years of equipment—all obtained by purchasing from the lowest bidder.

Solving the problem required teamwork and breaking down barriers between departments. The concept of an internal customer was virtually unknown. When the 24-step purchasing policy was changed to 3 steps, employees were stunned and delighted that someone was listening to them. They studied the potential of a preventive maintenance program and discovered, for example, that city departments did not use truck-bed linings when hauling corrosive materials such as salt. Mechanics rode along on police patrols and learned that squad cars spent most of their time idling; this information was used to tune engines properly. Other departments helped

Quality concepts and principles are universal and can be applied in all types of organizations. The difficulty, of course, is developing an infrastructure to make it happen and the discipline to sustain efforts over time.

gather data. As a result, the average vehicle turnaround time was reduced from nine days to three with a net annual savings of about $700,000. The lessons learned in the city garage were expanded to other departments from painting to health. By the time Sensenbrenner left office in 1989, Madison's city departments each ran between 20 and 30 quality improvement projects at a time; five agencies focused on long-term commitment to new management practices, including continuous quality improvement skills and data-gathering techniques; the city provided training in quality to every employee; several state agencies eager to follow Madison's approach initiated joint efforts; and city workers continued to invent service improvements for internal and external customers.

BONUS MATERIALS

SUMMARY OF KEY POINTS AND TERMINOLOGY

The Bonus Materials folder on the Premium website, provides a summary of key concepts and terminology introduced in this chapter.

QUALITY IN PRACTICE

SERVICE QUALITY AT THE RITZ-CARLTON HOTEL COMPANY, L.L.C.[35]

Caesar Ritz defined the concept of a luxury hotel in the 1890s. In 1992, The Ritz-Carlton Hotel Company, L.L.C. became the first hospitality organization to receive the Malcolm Baldrige National Quality Award; in 1999 they became the second company to win the award a second time, a testament to their continuous journey of improvement. The hotel industry is a very competitive business, one in which consumers place great emphases on reliability, timely delivery, and value. The Ritz-Carlton focuses on the principal concerns of its main customers and strives to provide them with highly personalized, caring service. Attention to employee performance and information technology are two of the company's many strengths that helped it to achieve superior quality.

The Ritz-Carlton operates from an easy-to-understand definition of service quality that is aggressively communicated and internalized at all levels of the organization. Its Three Steps of Service, Motto, Employee Promise, Credo, and Service Values—collectively known as the Gold Standards—are shown in Figure 2.2, and instilled in all employees through extensive training approaches. They allow employees to think and act independently with innovation for both the benefit of the customer and the company. The company's approaches for selecting and training employees were discussed earlier in this chapter.

The Ritz-Carlton uses many sources of information to understand its customers. These include alliances with travel partners such as airlines and credit card companies; focus groups and customer satisfaction results; complaints, claims, and feedback from the sales force; customer interviews; travel industry publications and studies; and even special psychological studies to understand what customers mean, not what they say, and how to appeal to the customer in the language they most understand.

A formal strategic planning process sets business directions to achieve the company's long-term vision: "To Be the Premier Worldwide Provider of Luxury Travel and Hospitality Products and Services." Upper managers at the corporate and hotel level conduct monthly performance reviews of the strategic plan, focusing on key indicators that reflect employee pride and joy, customer loyalty, financial performance, and process performance. Quarterly reviews focus on opportunities for improvement and innovation. A variety of comparative data on competitors and other world-class organizations is used to evaluate and improve their practices. For example, data

Figure 2.2 The Ritz-Carlton Three Steps of Service, Motto, and Credo

THREE STEPS OF SERVICE

1
A warm and sincere greeting. Use the guest name, if and when possible.

2
Anticipation and compliance with guest needs.

3
Fond farewell. Give them a warm good-bye and use their names, if and when possible.

"We Are Ladies and Gentlemen Serving Ladies and Gentlemen"

THE RITZ-CARLTON®

CREDO

The Ritz-Carlton Hotel is a place where the genuine care and comfort of our guests is our highest mission.

We pledge to provide the finest personal service and facilities for our guests who will always enjoy a warm, relaxed yet refined ambience.

The Ritz-Carlton experience enlivens the senses, instills well-being, and fulfills even the unexpressed wishes and needs of our guests.

Source: Adapted from the Malcolm Baldridge National Quality Award Application Summaries of the Ritz-Carlton Hotel Company, L.L.C., 1998.

revealed that front desk turnover was higher than usual. The company found out that certain airlines were paying higher wages and attracting their employees. The Ritz-Carlton reevaluated its compensation policy to match the airlines and actually reduced its total costs by eliminating a supervisor who was required to constantly monitor new employees.

The Ritz-Carlton gathers and uses customer-satisfaction and quality-related data on a daily basis. Information systems involve every employee and provide critical, responsive data on guest preferences, quantity of error-free products and services, and opportunities for quality improvement. They track a set of service quality indicators (SQI), shown in Figure 2.3, which represent the 12 most serious defects that can occur during regular operations. Each day an index is computed and disseminated to the workforce and reviewed by hotel managers.

Each production and support process is assigned an "executive owner" at the corporate office and a "working owner" at the hotel level, who are responsible for the development and improvement of these processes. They have the authority to define the measurements and determine the resources needed to manage these processes. The "GreenBook," a handbook for employees, describes a nine-step quality improvement process to guide the design, control, and improvement of all processes, and is emphasized during new employee training and continual development. The Ritz-Carlton even has a process to overcome cultural resistance to change: stress the importance of the change, express confidence that the change can be made, provide a reason why people should make the change as a group, and allow time to find an accommodation to the change.

These examples show only a few of The Ritz-Carlton's quality practices and the results have been impressive. At the time of receiving its second Baldrige Award, overall "top box" customer satisfaction (using a scale of 1 to 5, with the "top

Figure 2.3 Ritz-Carlton Service Quality Indicators

SQI Defects	Points
1. Missing Guest Preferences	10
2. Unresolved Difficulties	50
3. Inadequate Guestroom Housekeeping	1
4. Abandoned Reservation Calls	5
5. Guestroom Changes	5
6. Inoperable Guestroom Equipment	5
7. Unready Guestroom	10
8. Inappropriate Hotel Appearance	5
9. Meeting Event Difficulties	5
10. Inadequate Food/Beverage	1
11. Missing/Damaged Guest Property/Accidents	50
12. Invoice Adjustment	3

Source: Adapted from the Malcolm Baldridge National Quality Award Application Summaries of the Ritz-Carlton Hotel Company, L.L.C., 1999.

box" being a 5) was 70 percent against 52 percent for its foremost competitor. Employee satisfaction on issues of decision-making authority, teamwork, communication, and empowerment exceeded service company norms by a significant margin. The time to process a new hire from walk-in to job offer dropped from 21 days to 1 day in three years. Total revenue per hour worked showed a steady upward trend, and pretax return on investment improved from 5.3 percent in 1995 to 12.9 percent in 1999. One lesson the hotel learned is not to underestimate the value of even one idea or quality improvement effort.

Key Issues for Discussion

1. What value does a focus on the Gold Standards have for The Ritz-Carlton?
2. What must a company do to reduce job offer processing times so dramatically?
3. How does information play a central role in everything that The Ritz-Carlton does?

Quality in Practice

Kenneth W. Monfort College of Business[36]

As a college within the University of Northern Colorado (UNC), the Kenneth W. Monfort College of Business (MCB) began in 1968 and quickly grew in step with the explosive growth of business school enrollments nationwide. Located on the university's 236-acre Greeley campus, MCB's 34 full-time faculty, 13 part-time adjunct faculty, and eight administrative staff graduate approximately 300 students a year, drawn from 32 states, primarily Colorado.

In 1984, the College took dramatic steps to make program quality its top priority. At the time, UNC's business program was generally regarded as average and largely overshadowed by a number of key competitors within a fifty-mile radius. With its competitors and most U.S. business programs opting for a growth strategy of degree program assortment and further proliferation of graduate programs, UNC's business administrators and faculty chose an opposite approach. A vision was cast for becoming Colorado's best undergraduate business program—a goal it was agreed would not be possible without making undergraduate business education the College's exclusive mission:

MCB's Mission

Our mission is to deliver excellent undergraduate business programs and related learning opportunities that prepare students for successful careers and responsible leadership in business.

MCB's Vision

Our vision is to build a reputation of excellence in Colorado and beyond for preparing future business leaders and professionals.

Within two years, a revolutionary plan commenced for eliminating all graduate programs, including a Ph.D. degree program and Colorado's largest MBA program. Additional changes were made at the undergraduate level, with the elimination of all but one degree program—the Bachelor of Science in business administration. Future business students would declare business as a major and choose from six emphasis areas: accounting, computer information systems, finance, management, marketing, or general business.

The College adopted two long-term strategies to guide its actions: a positioning strategy of high-quality and low-cost (i.e., exceptional value), and a program delivery framework of *high-touch, wide-tech*, and *professional depth*.

- *High-Touch*. Smaller class sizes are designed to facilitate faculty—student interaction in the classroom. No "mass sections" are permitted to ensure this interaction occurs across the entire curriculum. Smaller class sizes also allow for experiential, hands-on learning techniques to be employed and are designed to increase active learning levels within the student population. Each professor maintains student office hours to increase student access.
- *Wide-Tech*. MCB has invested millions of dollars in its technology infrastructure to support a curriculum that exposes students to a wide array of existing and emerging business technologies, enabling graduates to make a seamless transition into the workplace. The curriculum integrates technology within course content, and MCB prides itself on incorporating the most current versions of industry-standard technologies.
- *Professional Depth*. MCB values professional business experience as a selection trait for its instructors. The College also utilizes an innovative executive professor program to strengthen classroom currency and ties with the employment community for graduates. Many of these professors are regionally- or nationally-known executives teaching in-residence, while others are brought to campus as visiting lecturers. The College also has developed partnerships with the business community to provide students with additional opportunities to gain real-world experiences through course components (e.g., business plans, advertising campaigns, market research, and portfolio management).

MCB's value-based approach revolves around three sets of values—instructional, scholarship, and service. Each MCB value statement is held within an overall framework focused on the pursuit of excellence, and a philosophy of continuous improvement guides employee behavior. MCB's commitment to an overall organizational focus on continuous performance improvement and the significant progress made toward development and deployment of this systematic approach has been driven externally and internally. As a parent organization, UNC requires a regular cycle of program review and evaluation, and MCB's commitment to AACSB accreditation maintenance (which also requires continuous improvement) are both strong external drivers. Internally, drivers include the commitment of MCB leadership to performance improvement and a strategic planning system; Key Performance Indicator (KPI) goal sets; the Educational Testing Service and Educational Benchmarking, Inc. survey feedback, which measure achievement, satisfaction, and quality in areas ranging from recruitment, to curriculum, technology, financial resources, program reputation, and faculty and student performance; and the integration of a Malcolm Baldrige-based assessment system. Also included in this framework is the development of a student-centered process, the availability of emerging and existing technologies, the encouragement and support from university leadership, and a series of program accomplishments that have been contagious in creating expectations for continued performance improvement. Although basic processes were already in place during the last five years, MCB has formalized a set of mission-driven key success measures and a budgeting system to facilitate systematic improvement. MCB is proud of its broad set of relationships with key partners and the community and views them as critical to providing a quality education. Within the university, MCB works closely with UNC's admissions, college transition center, and career services offices to ensure that from the time students are enrolled until the time they graduate, they receive the support and guidance they need to be successful.

By most measures of success, MCB is fulfilling its mission of providing a top-quality education that prepares students for successful careers and leadership roles in business, and providing that education at an affordable price. In the results of national standardized tests and the ability of its students to attain jobs in their chosen career fields, MCB ranks among the nation's top undergraduate business programs. The College remains as one of just five undergraduate-only programs nationally to hold AACSB accreditations in business and accounting. MCB ranks in the top 10 percent on 10 of 16 student satisfaction factors measured on the 2004 Business Exit Survey by Educational Benchmarking, Inc. (EBI)—a performance comparison of 171 business schools nationwide. In 2003 and 2004, MCB scored in the top 1 percent for overall student satisfaction. Also, in 2003/04 MCB students scored in the top 10 percent on the major Field Achievement Test, a standardized exam administered by the Educational Testing Service of Princeton, NJ. The ETS exam is give to graduating seniors to measure their knowledge in core business areas. In 2003, nearly 25,000 students in 359 business schools nationwide took the exam. The 2005 numbers went up to 110,000 in 513 programs. As of 2005/06 academic year MCB seniors are scoring in the top 5 percent. Progress into the top 5 percent (the highest scoring band possible) reflects a sustained upward trend MCB has experienced over a 12-year span. EBI measures continued to be strong through the 2005/06 year. MCB received a Baldrige award in 2004.

Key Issues for Discussion

1. How does the mission and vision defined by MCB drive its organizational processes? Why is this important for any business?
2. How important is its continuous improvement philosophy in achieving its mission and vision?
3. Visit the Baldrige website (www.baldrige.nist.gov) and find and read MCB's application summary. Identify several "best practices" that MCB employs that might be useful to your own school for improving quality.

Additional Quality in Practice features can be found in the Bonus Materials folder on the Premium website.

BONUS MATERIALS

Review Questions

1. What is a system? Why is "systems thinking" important to quality management?
2. Explain how quality in manufacturing has moved beyond such technical issues as reliability, inspection, and process control.
3. Explain the quality concerns of each major function of a manufacturing system.
4. How can business support activities help to sustain quality in an organization? List the key business support activities and their role in quality.
5. What types of organizations fall under the definition of services? Why is service quality especially important in today's business environment?
6. How do service standards differ from manufacturing specifications? How are they similar?
7. Discuss the differences between manufacturing and service organizations. What are the implications of these differences for quality assurance?
8. Explain the roles of employees and information technology in providing quality service. How does The Ritz-Carlton Hotel Company, L.L.C. use employees and information technology for quality service?
9. Summarize the status of quality in the health care industry. How are professional organizations promoting quality improvement in health care?
10. How do the recommendations of the President's Advisory Commission on Consumer Protection and Quality in the Health Care Industry address the basic principles of TQ described in Chapter 1?

11. Summarize the major quality initiatives used in education. How are the approaches at K–12 institutions similar to yet different from those used in the colleges and universities?
12. Why have small businesses and not-for-profits been slow to adopt quality initiatives?
13. What must small businesses and not-for-profits do to successfully establish a total quality focus?
14. Describe some of the key quality initiatives that have been taken in the government sector, both federal and state.

Discussion Questions

1. In this chapter, we noted that much of the work performed in traditional manufacturing organizations now involve service. Provide some examples of this, drawing upon the functions illustrated in Figure 2.1.
2. Provide specific examples of how the differences between manufacturing and service organizations are evident in a school or a hospital.
3. Cite some examples from your own experience in which you felt service quality was truly top-notch and some in which it was not. What do you think might be some of the fundamental differences in the infrastructure and management practices of these organizations?
4. How is information technology used to improve service in your college or university?
5. What role has the Internet played in improving service quality? What barriers to service quality might it have?
6. Texas A&M University announced a pilot program whereby faculty members at three of the state system's universities could earn between $2,500 and $10,000 per year if they were rated in the top 18 percent of student evaluations in a voluntary pool of faculty who applied to be considered.[37] What are the quality implications, including advantages and limitations, of such a "customer focused" incentive program in an academic setting?
7. Discuss the implications of the following statements with respect to introducing TQ principles in a college classroom. Do you agree with them? How do they reflect TQ principles? What changes in traditional learning approaches would they require for both students and instructors?
   a. Embracing a customer focus doesn't mean giving students all As and abandoning standards.
   b. If students fail, the system has failed.
   c. Faculty members are customers of those who teach prerequisites.
   d. Treating students as customers means allowing students to choose not to come to class.
   e. Completing the syllabus is not a measure of success.
   f. New and tenured instructors should visit each other's classrooms.
   g. Eliminate performance appraisals based on classroom evaluations.
   h. No matter how good the test, luck will be involved.
8. Contrast the role of service quality at Amazon.com and Barnes and Noble (which operates traditional bookstores as well as an e-commerce site). What are the differences in their approaches? How might a company like Barnes and

Noble exploit its dual marketing focus (stores and e-commerce) in a complementary fashion to provide services that Amazon.com would not be able to offer?

9. Cite one or more examples of times when you received either high- or poor-quality service from a physician's office, dentist's office, or hospital. What do you think contributed most to your experience?
10. Review the Recommendations of the President's Advisory Commission on Consumer Protection and Quality in the Health Care Industry found in the Bonus Materials folder for this chapter on the Premium website, [Website icon] Discuss how they relate to the principles of total quality. Based on your knowledge of quality principles, can you think of any other recommendations that might be appropriate?
11. Thinking of your experiences at a post office, driver's license bureau, or other government agency, describe your perception of the quality of the service, and suggest some TQ approaches that might help the agency improve.

Projects, Etc.

1. Interview some key managers at a nearby manufacturing company and construct a diagram similar to Figure 2.1 showing the company's key functions and their relationships. Summarize the major quality concerns of each function.
2. Interview some managers at a local service organization and summarize the role of employees and information technology in providing quality service. How are employees and information technology integrated into long-range improvement plans and strategies?
3. Develop a Deming-type diagram of a college, university, or hospital as a production system. You might wish to talk with some faculty or administrators, or health care professionals to better understand the terminology and key issues.
4. Arrange a tour of a local hospital or clinic. How is quality managed in the organization? What individuals or groups spearhead quality improvement efforts? Is the entire workforce involved to any degree? What quality-related improvements have they made in the past two years?
5. Interview administrative officials at your college or university to determine what quality efforts have been made to improve both administrative functions and educational effectiveness.
6. Arrange an interview with a local high school principal or school district superintendent. Determine whether any quality initiatives have been adopted during the past two years. Have teachers been trained in quality improvement approaches? How does the school or district gather information from its stakeholders? Are the interviewees aware of the Koalaty Kid program?
7. Visit the quality in education case studies on the American Society for Quality website (http://www.asq.org/education/why-quality/case-studies.html) and write a report on the best practices that have been implemented and results that have been achieved.
8. Visit the AQIP website (http://www.aqip.org) and report on how AQIP is promoting quality in colleges and universities.
9. School boards provide a critical link between schools, parents, and the community. According to the National School Board Association, school boards must help to create a vision and structure for the school system while focusing on accountability to ensure results and advocacy for improved performance.

Interview members of a local school board or parents of children in a public school district that you know to determine how well the school board address the following tasks:

a. Focuses on issues related to student achievement
b. Sets a common vision for student achievement and a clear definition of student success
c. Uses reliable data to make informed decisions about how to support student achievement goals and how to measure progress
d. Brings diverse opinions to bear and create community consensus on student achievement goals
e. Sets benchmarks and discusses progress toward student achievement goals
f. Plays a leadership role in defining standards of achievement for all students
g. Develops a process for maintaining accountability within the schools and the school board itself
h. Models teamwork and partnership
i. Incorporates mechanisms for feedback from parents, administrators, teachers, and the greater community
j. Creates policies that clearly support student achievement goals

10. Have quality initiatives been adopted by your local government? Interview some local politicians and managers to answer this question: Can you, as a customer, obtain easy access to these people?
11. Talk to a local not-for-profit organization manager or small business owner about quality. How aware are they of quality principles and tools? What challenges do they see in trying to build quality into their organizations?

CASES

Additional cases are available in the Bonus Materials folder on the Premium website.

BONUS MATERIALS

THE NIGHTMARE ON TELECOM STREET[38]

H. James Harrington, a noted quality consultant, related the following story in *Quality Digest* magazine:

> *I called to make a flight reservation just an hour ago. The telephone rang five times before a recorded voice answered. "Thank you for calling ABC Travel Services," it said. "To ensure the highest level of customer service, this call may be recorded for future analysis." Next, I was asked to select from one of the following three choices: "If the trip is related to company business, press 1. Personal business, press 2. Group travel, press 3." I pressed 1.*
>
> *I was then asked to select from the following four choices: "If this is a trip within the United States, press 1. International, press 2. Scheduled training, press 3. Related to a conference, press 4." Because I was going to Canada, I pressed 2.*
>
> *Now two minutes into my telephone call, I was instructed to be sure that I had my customer identification card available. A few seconds passed and a very sweet voice came on, saying, "All international operators are busy, but please hold because you are a very important customer." The voice was then replaced by music. About two minutes later, another recorded message said, "Our operators are still busy, but please hold and the first available operator will take care of you." More music. Then yet another message: "Our operators are still busy, but please hold. Your business is important to us." More bad music. Finally the sweet voice returned, stating, "To speed up your service, enter your 19-digit customer service number." I frantically searched for their card, hoping that I could find it before I was cut off. I was lucky; I found it and*

entered the number in time. The same sweet voice came back to me, saying, "To confirm your customer service number, enter the last four digits of your social security number." I pushed the four numbers on the keypad. The voice said: "Thank you. An operator will be with you shortly. If your call is an emergency, you can call 1-800-CAL-HELP, or push all of the buttons on the telephone at the same time. Otherwise, please hold, as you are a very important customer." This time, in place of music, I heard a commercial about the service that the company provides.

At last, a real person answered the telephone and asked, "Can I help you?" I replied, "Yes, oh yes." He answered, "Please give me your 19-digit customer service number, followed by the last four digits of your social security number so I can verify who you are." (I thought I gave these numbers in the first place to speed up service. Why do I have to rattle them off again?)

I was now convinced that he would call me Mr. 5523-3675-0714-1313-040. But, to my surprise, he said: "Yes, Mr. Harrington. Where do you want to go and when?" I explained that I wanted to go to Montreal the following Monday morning. He replied: "I only handle domestic reservations. Our international desk has a new telephone number: 1-800-1WE-GOTU. I'll transfer you." A few clicks later a message came on, saying: "All of our international operators are busy. Please hold and your call will be answered in the order it was received. Do not hang up or redial, as it will only delay our response to your call. Please continue to hold, as your business is important to us."

Discussion Questions

1. Summarize the service failures associated with this experience.
2. What might the travel agency do to improve its customers' service experience?

U.S. Water Resource Agency—Flagstaff District:[39]

The Flagstaff District (FD) is one of 41 districts within the U.S. Water Resource Agency (USWRA—an Agency in the Department of Renewable Resources—DoRR) charged with the responsibility to develop, protect, and administer water resources within the United States. The Flagstaff District provides six major product lines of goods and services: (1) the development of new infrastructure and projects; (2) management of the operation and maintenance of existing infrastructure; (3) the performance of reimbursable work for others; (4) administration of regulatory requirements; (5) provision of emergency response and recovery; and (6) the delivery of defense, environmental, and restoration programs.

The Flagstaff District's purpose, vision, mission, and values are:

Purpose—To be effective stewards of the public trust.

Vision—The Flagstaff District embraces the Agency's vision as its own. This vision can be summed up in terms of our commitment to protect and promote our nation's water resources to be second to none.

Mission—To ensure and protect water resources for economic and recreation benefit to the nation, partner states, and local governments. FD's principal mission areas include

- development and management of projects and programs to provide for inland navigation, flood-damage reduction, environmental protection, recreation, water supply, and other public benefits
- protection of the region's waterways and wetlands
- support for emergency preparedness, natural-disaster relief, and recovery work worldwide
- provision of a broad range of engineering and technical support for other organizations

Values—The District achieves its mission by means of five core values that serve as the foundation of the organization's overall operations and the behavior of every employee.

- Honor and Respect
- Selfless Service and Courage
- Integrity
- Sharing Knowledge
- Working Safely

Field employees operate 24 multi-purpose dam projects and six lock-and-dam complexes, an equipment-repair station, and a fleet of maintenance vessels. Field offices are connected to the District Office by a radio network and Wide Area Network, or WAN. Computer-Aided Design (CAD) is used in all design projects, as well as Global Positioning System techniques and, most recently, Tele-engineering. Tele-engineering is a critically important advance in state-of-the- art engineering practices in that many projects support international efforts, such as mapping the hydrology of Iraq in just two weeks using a simultaneous combination of U.S.-based and on-site engineering capabilities.

One of the hardest concepts to translate from the private sector into the public sector is that of "competition." In many cases, the services provided to the public by an agency of the Federal Government can be obtained from only that Government agency. Historically, this has led to the unfortunate perception that Government service providers are "the only game in town," lessening the concern for, or need to understand, customer needs, desires, or drivers of satisfaction. In recent years, however, nothing could be further from reality. This realization has served to strengthen the USWRA commitment to providing exceptional value for its customers and continuously improving every aspect of its business. As a Government agency, FD "competes" in three major ways: (1) with private companies for projects or portions of projects; (2) with other districts for reimbursable work; and (3) through outsourcing studies that determine whether work will continue to be accomplished by Government employees or will be contracted to private companies.

Discussion Questions

1. As a public not-for-profit agency, who are Flagstaff District's customers?
2. How might the district define quality? How could it use this definition to evaluate its success in "competing" with other entities?

Walker Auto Sales and Service

Walker Auto Sales and Service (WASS) is a full service dealership for a major domestic automobile brand. Essentially, WASS provides three main services: new car sales, used car sales, and repair and maintenance service. Because of the competitive nature of the market, the firm's owner, Darren Walker, wants to take a more systematic approach to improving service and providing a high level of customer satisfaction. Through surveys, focus groups, and analysis of complaint data and information, he identified some important requirements for these services. Customers expect a favorable impression when they arrive at the dealership—a wide range of vehicles and options to evaluate, available salespeople, be greeted promptly, and feel comfortable and not pressured. They also expect salespersons to be courteous, knowledgeable about the cars, respect their time, and honor verbal promises. For repair and maintenance service, customers want to have the work explained appropriately, be fully informed of any additional necessary work, and have all work reviewed upon completion. They want good time estimates and communications with the service department.

Suppliers play an important role in the business and the entire value chain. The dealership needs quality parts, product availability when needed, timely delivery, and fair prices. WASS also receives corporate support for its employee benefits and certain training programs, information technology planning and intranet/Internet development, marketing and advertising, and strategic planning direction. WASS is facing increasing competition for skilled employee talent, changing customer demographics that are leading to growing demand, and more competition as a result of new foreign dealerships that are locating in its market area. Darren recognizes the need to "become the dealership of choice" in its market.

Drawing upon the principles of total quality discussed in Chapter 1, and the unique nature of services addressed in this chapter, describe some of the issues that Darren must consider in achieving his vision. Develop a list of action plans that he might consider.

NOTES

1. "Continuous Improvement Making Inroads in the Classroom," *Pittsburgh Post-Gazette (PA)*, February 18, 2008.

2. "Michigan Hospital Promises to Deliver," *Cincinnati Enquirer*, July 17, 1991, A2.

3. Ackoff, Russell L., Recreating the Corporation: A Design of Organizations for the 21st Century, Oxford, 1999.

4. "A Profile of Hershey Foods Corporation," Hershey Foods Corporation, Hershey, PA 17033, 7.

5. Jeff Sabatini, "Flawless (Nearly)," *Automotive Manufacturing & Production*, November 1999, 60–62.

6. D. A. Collier, "The Customer Service and Quality Challenge," *The Service Industries Journal* 7, no. 1 (January 1987), 79.

7. Frederick F. Reichheld and W. Earl Sasser, Jr., "Zero Defections: Quality Comes to Services," *Harvard Business Review* 68, no. 5 (September-October 1990), 105–112.

8. From John A. Byrne, *"Lessons From Our Customer Champions*," Letter from the Editor, *Fast Company*, October 16, 2004. Copyright © 2004 MANSUETO VENTURES LLC. Reprinted by permission. Permission via Copyright Clearance Center.

9. Ron Zemke, "Auditing Customer Service: Look Inside as Well as Out," *Employee Relations Today* 16 (Autumn 1989), 197–203.

10. Adapted from the Malcolm Baldrige National Quality Award application summaries of The Ritz-Carlton Hotel Company, L.L.C. © 1992 and 1999. All rights reserved. Reprinted with permission of The Ritz-Carlton Hotel Company, L.L.C.; Cheri Henderson, "Putting on the Ritz," *TQM Magazine* 2, no. 5 (November–December 1992), 292–296; and remarks by various Ritz-Carlton managers at the 2000 Quest for Excellence Conference, Washington, D.C.

11. "Quality '93: Empowering People with Technology," advertisement in *Fortune*, September 20, 1993.

12. "New JCAHO Standards Emphasize Continuous Quality Improvement," *Hospitals*, August 5, 1991, 41–44.

13. http://www.hcqualitycommission.gov

14. L. Kohn, J. Corrigan, and M. Donaldson, "To Err is Human: Building a Safer Health System," *National Academy Press*, 2000. The follow-up report cited is "Crossing the Quality Chasm: A New Health System for the 21st century," by the Committee on Quality Health Care in America, *National Academy Press*, 2001.

15. This information is adapted from NCQA's website, http://www.ncqa.org

16. Maureen Bisognano, "New Skills Needed in Medical Leadership," *Quality Progress*, June 2000, 32–41.

17. North Mississippi Medical Center, 2006 Malcolm Baldridge Application Summary. Reprinted with permission.

18. Nada R. Sanders, "Health Care Organizations Can Learn From the Experiences of Others," *Quality Progress*, February 1997, 47–49.

19. See, for example, Christina Del Valle, "Readin', Writin', and Reform," *Business Week/Quality* Special Issue, October 25, 1991, 140–142; Myron Tribus, "Quality Management in Education," *Journal for Quality and Participation* (January–February 1993), 12–21. See also Christopher W. L. and Paula E. Morrison, "Students Aren't Learning Quality Principles in Business Schools," *Quality Progress* 25, no. 1 (January 1992), 25–27; John A. Byrne, "Is Research in the Ivory Tower 'Fuzzy, Irrelevant, and Pretentious'?" *Business Week*, October 29, 1990, 62–66.

20. This section is adapted from an extensive account in Lloyd Dobyns and Clare Crawford-Mason, *Quality or Else* (Boston: Houghton-Mifflin, 1991), 221–230.

21. Adapted from *2001 Malcolm Baldrige National Quality Award Education Application*, courtesy of Pearl River School District, 275 East Central Avenue, Pearl River, NY 10965; http://www.pearlriver.k12.ny.us

22. http://www.asq.org/pub/qualityprogress/past/1102/16asqNEws1102.html, accessed September 22, 2006

23. Adapted from the http://www.koalatykid.org website. Permission to reprint is granted by the ASQ Koalaty Kid Alliance.

24. http://www.asq.org/edu/kkid/ (Education Division) Accessed 1/25/06.

25. Source: http://www.asq.org/edu/kkid/highlights.html (Education Division) Accessed 1/25/06.

26. L. Edwin Coate, "TQM at Oregon State University," reprinted with permission from *Journal for Quality and Participation* (December 1990), 56–65. See also L. Edward Coate, *Implementing Total Quality Management in a University Setting* (Corvallis, OR: Oregon State University, July 1990); Ralph G. Lewis and Douglas H. Smith, *Total Quality in Higher Education* (Delray Beach, FL: St. Lucie Press, 1994).

27. Adapted from *Baldrige Award Recipient Profile*, University of Wisconsin–Stout, National Institute of Standards and Technology, U.S. Department of Commerce. Courtesy of UW–Stout.

28. S. L. Ahire, D. Y. Golhar, "Quality Management in Large vs. Small Firms," *Journal of Small Business Management* 34, no. 2 (1996), 1–13.

29. Madhav N. Sinha "Helping Those Who Help Others," *Quality Progress*, July 1997; and Renee Oosterhoff Cox, "Quality in Nonprofits: No Longer Uncharted Territory," *Quality Progress*, October 1999, 57–61.

30. Kennedy Smith, "American Red Cross Undergoes Quality Transfusion," *Quality Digest*, March 2003, 6–7.

31. Ned Hamson, "The FQI Story: Today and Tomorrow," *Journal for Quality and Participation* (July–August 1990), 46–49.

32. Executive Order No. 12637, vol. 7. U.S. Code Congressional and Administrative News, 100th Congress—Second Session (St. Paul, MN: West Publishing Co.), B21–B23.

33. U.S. Office of Personnel Management, President's Quality Award Program www.opm.gov/pqa

34. Joseph Sensenbrenner, "Quality Comes to City Hall," *Harvard Business Review* (March–April 1991), 64–75.

35. See note 10.

36. Malcolm Baldrige National Quality Award 2004 Award Winner Profile, National Institute of Standards and Technology, Department of Commerce, and Kenneth W. Montfort College of Business Baldrige Award Application Summary. A good summary of Monfort's quality journey and approaches can also be found in Valerie Funk, "Narrow Focus Provides Widespread Benefits," *Quality Progress*, August 2005, 40-47. Information courtesy of Montfort College of Business.

37. Jeannie Kever. "Most of A&M Faculty Shun Cash Awards," *Houston Chronicle*, January 31, 2009. Accessed 2/3/09 at http://www.chron.com/disp/story.mpl/headline/metro/6240462.html

38. H. James Harrington, "Looking for a Little Service," *Quality Digest*, May 2000. Reprinted with permission.

39. Adapted from *Baldrige National Quality Program, 2006 Flagstaff Case Study*. This is a fictional agency and was used for training purposes for the not-for-profit Baldrige Award process.

CHAPTER 3

PHILOSOPHIES AND FRAMEWORKS

OUTLINE

QUALITY PROFILES: Texas Nameplate Company, Inc., and The Cedar Foundation
THE DEMING PHILOSOPHY
Foundations of the Deming Philosophy
Deming's 14 Points
THE JURAN PHILOSOPHY
THE CROSBY PHILOSOPHY
COMPARISONS OF QUALITY PHILOSOPHIES
OTHER QUALITY PHILOSOPHERS
A. V. Feigenbaum
Kaoru Ishikawa
Genichi Taguchi
QUALITY MANAGEMENT AWARDS AND FRAMEWORKS
THE MALCOLM BALDRIGE NATIONAL QUALITY AWARD
History and Purpose
The Criteria for Performance Excellence
Criteria Evolution
Using the Baldrige Criteria
Impacts of the Baldrige Program
Baldrige and Deming
INTERNATIONAL QUALITY AWARD PROGRAMS
The Deming Prize
European Quality Award
Canadian Awards for Business Excellence
Australian Business Excellence Award
Quality Awards in China
Baldrige and National Culture
ISO 9000:2000
Structure of the ISO 9000:2000 Standards
Factors Leading to ISO 9000:2000
Implementation and Registration
Benefits of ISO 9000
SIX SIGMA
Evolution of Six Sigma
Six Sigma as a Quality Framework
BALDRIGE, ISO 9000, AND SIX SIGMA
SUMMARY OF KEY POINTS AND TERMINOLOGY
QUALITY IN PRACTICE: ISO 9000 and Sears' Quality Management System
QUALITY IN PRACTICE: Integrating Quality Frameworks at Veridian Homes
REVIEW QUESTIONS
DISCUSSION QUESTIONS
PROJECTS, ETC.
CASES Santa Cruz Guitar Company
Can Six Sigma Work in Health Care?
Novel Connect: Understanding the Organizational Environment
Share Food Case Study: Understanding the Organizational Environment

In the 1890s, Caesar Ritz defined the standards for a luxury hotel; these evolved into the quality responsibilities of the employees—the "Ladies and Gentlemen Serving Ladies and Gentlemen"—of today's Ritz-Carlton Hotel Company: anticipating the wishes and needs of the guests, resolving their problems, and exhibiting genuinely caring conduct toward guests and each other. The Ritz-Carlton management recognized that the key to ensuring that these responsibilities are realized was to create a "Skilled and Empowered Work Force Operating with Pride and Joy." This quality-focused philosophy led the company to be a two-time recipient of the Malcolm Baldrige National Quality Award.

The concept of "pride and joy" in work—and its impact on quality—is one of the foundations of the philosophy of the late W. Edwards Deming. Deming, along with Joseph M. Juran and Philip B. Crosby, are regarded as true "management gurus" in the quality revolution. Their insights on measuring, managing, and improving quality have had profound impacts on countless managers and entire corporations around the world. The Quality Profiles in this chapter highlight two of the many companies around the world that reflect these philosophies.

This chapter presents the quality management philosophies of these three leaders, their similarities and differences, and also examines their individual contributions to modern practice. In addition, it discusses the contributions of other key individuals who have helped to shape current thinking in quality management. These philosophies became the cornerstone for quality management practice and frameworks, such as the Deming Prize, the Malcolm Baldrige National Quality Award, the ISO 9000 standards, and the Six Sigma philosophy, which we also introduce in this chapter, and which form the basis for much of the remainder of this book.

Quality Profiles

Texas Nameplate Company, Inc., and The Cedar Foundation

Founded in 1946, Texas Nameplate Company, Inc. (TNC), with only 43 employees, manufactures and sells identification and information labels that are affixed to refrigerators, oil-field equipment, high-pressure valves, trucks, computer equipment, and other products made by more than 1,000 customers throughout the United States and in nine foreign countries. TNC has honed the raw attributes inherent to its small size—from streamlined communications and rapid decision-making to shared goals and accessible leaders—into competitive advantages. It starts by changing the traditional, hierarchical leadership structure into a flatter, team-based structure built on mutual respect, and guided by the philosophy that "Fear is useless; what is needed is trust." The result is a closely knit organization that is finely tuned to the requirements of its customers. TNC aims to create a continuous learning environment that enables empowered teams of workers to take charge of processes and to deliver products and services with a "star quality." Through its "Customer Site Visit" program, a team of TNC employees visits customer facilities to identify opportunities for improving products and services. The results of these visits are shared with everyone at TNC. Customer contact employees are empowered to resolve customer complaints without consulting management, and production workers are responsible for tailoring processes to optimize contributions to company goals and to meet team-set standards. TNC reduced its defects from 3.65 percent to about 1 percent in four years. Customers consistently give the company an "excellent" rating (5 to 6 on a scale of 6) in 12 key business areas, including product quality, reliable performance, on-time delivery, and overall satisfaction, and in its employee survey, satisfaction rates in five areas employees say are the most important: fair pay, job content satisfaction, recognition, fairness/respect, and career development, exceed national norms by a significant margin. TNC was the first small business to receive the Baldrige Award twice.

The Cedar Foundation is a leading voluntary organization in Northern Ireland and is a chief contributor to delivering services to disabled people including people with brain injury. The organization delivers its mission by living and upholding its Values of Respect for the Individual; Equality of Opportunity; Pursuit of Excellence; Openness and Accountability; Teamwork and Partnership; and Commitment and Enthusiasm. In the 1990s, The Cedar Foundation went through a significant period of change in response to the changing expectations of disabled people and the sponsors. In order to respond to the changing market, the Foundation committed to a process of continuous improvement and the application of a range of quality management tools was central to the strategy. The organization adopted and has continued to use the Balanced Scorecard approach (see Chapter 8) to business planning. In 2005, ISO 9001:2000 registration was achieved by the whole organization. The Foundation was the first voluntary organization in Northern Ireland to use the European Federation for Quality Management (EFQM) Excellence Model and was a 2007 EFQM Award winner.

The Cedar Foundation has derived significant benefits from its journey towards excellence; the organization has enjoyed substantial financial growth, more than doubling its customer and service base in the last 10 years. By applying quality standards, the Foundation is able to identify and embrace best practice, thereby delivering better quality services, which achieve better results for Service Users and higher levels of customer satisfaction. At every level of the organization there is a clear understanding of and commitment to the Vision and Mission, which translates into a focus on the achievement of defined results. Strong leadership within the Foundation ensures that leaders are accessible to all stakeholders. The Foundation's comprehensive process management system ensures the effective execution and implementation of policy and strategy. Processes are reviewed and improved against factual information. There has also been a significant impact on the Foundation's people; staffs are expressing high levels of satisfaction, turnover is reducing, and retention and absenteeism has improved.

Source for Texas Nameplate: Texas Nameplate Company from Malcolm Baldrige Award Recipient Profiles, National Institute of Standards and Technology, U.S. Department of Commerce.
Source for The Cedar Foundation: EFQM 2007 Recognition Book (Ref: http://excellenceone.efqm.org/Default.aspx?tabid=381). Reprinted with permission.

THE DEMING PHILOSOPHY

No individual has had more influence on quality management than Dr. W. Edwards Deming (1900–1993). Deming received a Ph.D. in physics and was trained as a statistician, so much of his philosophy can be traced to these roots. He worked for Western Electric during its pioneering era of statistical quality control in the 1920s and 1930s. Deming recognized the importance of viewing management processes statistically. During World War II he taught quality control courses as part of the U.S. national defense effort, but he realized that teaching statistics only to engineers and factory workers would never solve the fundamental quality problems that manufacturing needed to address. Despite numerous efforts, his attempts to convey the message of quality to upper-level managers in the United States were ignored.

Shortly after World War II, Deming was invited to Japan to help the country take a census. The Japanese had heard about his theories and their usefulness to U.S. companies during the war. Consequently, he soon began to teach them statistical quality control. His thinking went beyond mere statistics, however. Deming preached the importance of top management leadership, customer/supplier partnerships, and continuous improvement in product development and manufacturing processes. Japanese managers embraced these ideas, and the rest, as they say, is history. Deming's influence on Japanese industry was so great that the Union of Japanese Scientists and Engineers established the Deming Application Prize in 1951 to recognize companies that show a high level of achievement in quality practices. Deming also received Japan's highest honor, the Royal Order of the Sacred Treasure, from the emperor. The former chairman of NEC Electronics once said, "There is not a day I don't think about what Dr. Deming meant to us."

Although Deming lived in Washington, D.C., he remained virtually unknown in the United States until 1980, when NBC telecast a program entitled "If Japan Can... Why Can't We?" The documentary highlighted Deming's contributions in Japan and his later work with Nashua Corporation. Shortly afterward, his name was frequently on the lips of U.S. corporate executives. Companies such as Ford, GM, and Procter & Gamble invited him to work with them to improve their quality. To their surprise, Deming did not lay out "a quality improvement program" for them. His goal was to change entire perspectives in management, and often radically. Deming worked with passion until his death in December 1993 at the age of 93, knowing he had little time left to make a difference in his home country. When asked how he would like to be remembered, Deming replied, "I probably won't even be remembered." Then after a long pause, he added, "Well, maybe . . . as someone who spent his life trying to keep America from committing suicide."[1]

Foundations of the Deming Philosophy

Unlike other management gurus and consultants, Deming never defined or described quality precisely. In his last book, he stated, "A product or a service possesses quality if it helps somebody and enjoys a good and sustainable market."[2] In Deming's view, variation is the chief culprit of poor quality. In mechanical assemblies, for example, variations from specifications for part dimensions lead to inconsistent performance and premature wear and failure. Likewise, inconsistencies in human behavior in service frustrate customers and hurt companies' reputations. To accomplish reductions in variation, Deming advocated a never-ending cycle of product/service design, manufacture/service delivery, test, and sales, followed by market surveys and then redesign and improvement. He claimed that higher quality leads to higher productivity, which in turn leads to long-term competitive strength. The **Deming Chain Reaction** theory (see Figure 3.1) summarizes this view. The theory is that improvements in quality lead to lower costs because they result in less rework, fewer mistakes, fewer delays and snags, and better use of time and materials. Lower costs, in turn, lead to productivity improvements. With better quality and lower prices, a firm can achieve a higher market share and thus stay in business, providing more and more jobs. Deming stressed that top management must assume the overriding responsibility for quality improvement.

The Deming philosophy focuses on continual improvements in product and service quality by reducing uncertainty and variability in design, manufacturing, and service processes, driven by the leadership of top management.

Deming's philosophy underwent many changes as he himself continued to learn. In his early work in the United States, he preached his **14 Points** (see Table 3.1), which are discussed later in the chapter. The 14 Points caused some confusion and misunderstanding among businesspeople, because Deming did not provide a clear rationale for them. Near the end of his life, however, he synthesized the underlying foundations of the 14 Points in what he called a **System of Profound Knowledge**. Understanding the elements of this "system" provides critical insights needed for designing effective management practices and making decisions in today's complex business environment.

Figure 3.1 The Deming Chain Reaction

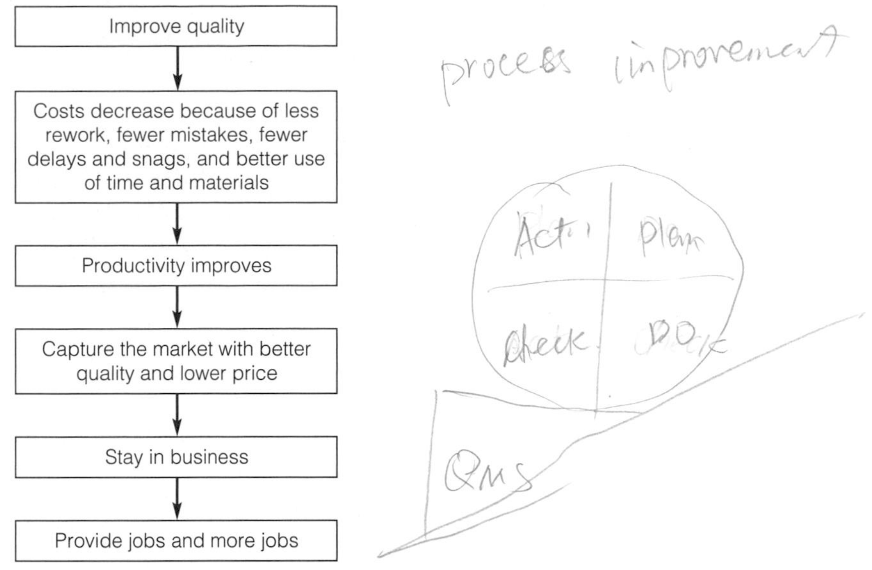

Source: Originally published in *Out of the Crisis*, pp.23–24, by W. Edwards Deming. Copyright © 1986 by The W. Edwards Deming Institute. Revised by W. Edwards Deming in January 1990. Reprinted with permission of MIT Press.

Table 3.1 Deming's 14 Points

1. Create and publish to all employees a statement of the aims and purposes of the company or other organization. The management must demonstrate constantly their commitment to this statement.
2. Learn the new philosophy, top management and everybody.
3. Understand the purpose of inspection, for improvement of processes and reduction of cost.
4. End the practice of awarding business on the basis of price tag alone.
5. Improve constantly and forever the system of production and service.
6. Institute training.
7. Teach and institute leadership.
8. Drive out fear. Create trust. Create a climate for innovation.
9. Optimize toward the aims and purposes of the company the efforts of teams, groups, staff areas.
10. Eliminate exhortations for the workforce.
11. (a) Eliminate numerical quotas for production. Instead, learn and institute methods for improvement.
    (b) Eliminate MBO [management by objective]. Instead, learn the capabilities of processes and how to improve them.
12. Remove barriers that rob people of pride of workmanship.
13. Encourage education and self-improvement for everyone.
14. Take action to accomplish the transformation.

Source: Originally published in *Out of the Crisis* by W. Edwards Deming. © 1986 by The W. Edwards Deming Institute. Revised by W. Edwards Deming in January 1990. Reprinted by permission of MIT Press, pp. 23–24.

Deming's Profound Knowledge system consists of four interrelated parts:

1. Appreciation for a system
2. Understanding variation
3. Theory of knowledge
4. Psychology

Each of these parts is explained here.

Systems We noted the importance of systems in Chapter 2. The components of any system must work together if the system is to be effective. Traditional organizations typically manage according to the functions in vertical organization charts. However, when interactions occur among the parts of a system (for instance, among functions and departments in an organization), managers cannot manage the system well by simply managing the parts in isolation; they must understand the processes that cross functional boundaries, align these processes toward a common vision or goal, and optimize their interactions. Suboptimization (doing the best for individual components) results in losses to everybody in the system. According to Deming, it is poor management, for example, to purchase materials or service at the lowest price or to minimize the cost of manufacturing if it is at the expense of the system. For instance, inexpensive materials may be of such inferior quality that they will cause excessive costs in scrap and repair during manufacturing and assembly. Minimizing the cost of manufacturing alone might result in products that do not meet designers' specifications and customer needs. Such situations lead to a win–lose effect. Purchasing wins, manufacturing loses; manufacturing wins, customers lose; and so on. To manage any system, managers must understand the interrelationships among the systems' components and among the people who work in it.

The aim of any system should be for all stakeholders—stockholders, employees, customers, community, and the environment—to benefit over the long term.

Deming stressed that systems must be focused toward a purpose. Stockholders can realize financial benefits, employees can receive opportunities for training and education that will enhance their joy in work, customers can receive products and services that meet their needs and create satisfaction, the community can benefit from business leadership, and the environment can benefit from responsible management.

Systems thinking applies to managing people also. Pitting individuals or departments against each other for resources is self-destructive to an organization. The individuals or departments will perform to maximize their own expected gain, not that of the entire firm. Therefore, optimizing the system requires internal cooperation. Similarly, using sales quotas or arbitrary cost-reduction goals will not motivate people to improve the system and customer satisfaction; the people will perform only to meet the quotas or goals and optimize their individual rewards. Traditional performance appraisals do not consider interactions within the system. Many factors affect an individual employee's performance, including the following:

- The training received
- The information and resources provided
- The leadership of supervisors and managers
- Disruptions on the job
- Management policies and practices

Few performance appraisals recognize such factors and often place blame on individuals who have little ability to control their environment. We will discuss this situation further in Chapter 6.

Variation The second part of Profound Knowledge is a basic understanding of statistical theory and variation. We see variation everywhere, from hitting golf balls to the meals and service in a restaurant. A device called a quincunx illustrates a natural process of variation. A computer-simulated quincunx is shown in Figure 3.2.[3] In a quincunx, small balls are dropped from a hole in the top and hit a series of pins as they fall toward collection boxes. The pins cause each ball to move randomly to the left or the right as it strikes each pin on its way down. Note that most balls end up toward the middle of the box. Figure 3.3 shows the frequency distribution of where the balls landed in one simulation. Note the roughly symmetrical bell shape of the distribution. A normal distribution is bell-shaped. Even though all balls are dropped from the same position, the end result shows variation.

The same kind of variation exists in any production and service process, generally due to factors inherent in the design of the system, which cannot easily be controlled. Today, modern technology has improved our ability to produce many physical parts with very little variation; however, the variation that stems from human behavior and performance continues to hamper quality efforts. Deming suggested that management first understand, and then work to reduce variation through improvements in technology, process design, and training. With less variation, both the producer and consumer benefit. The producer benefits by needing less inspection, experiencing less scrap and rework, and having more consistent human performance, resulting in higher productivity and customer satisfaction.

Figure 3.2 A Quincunx in Action

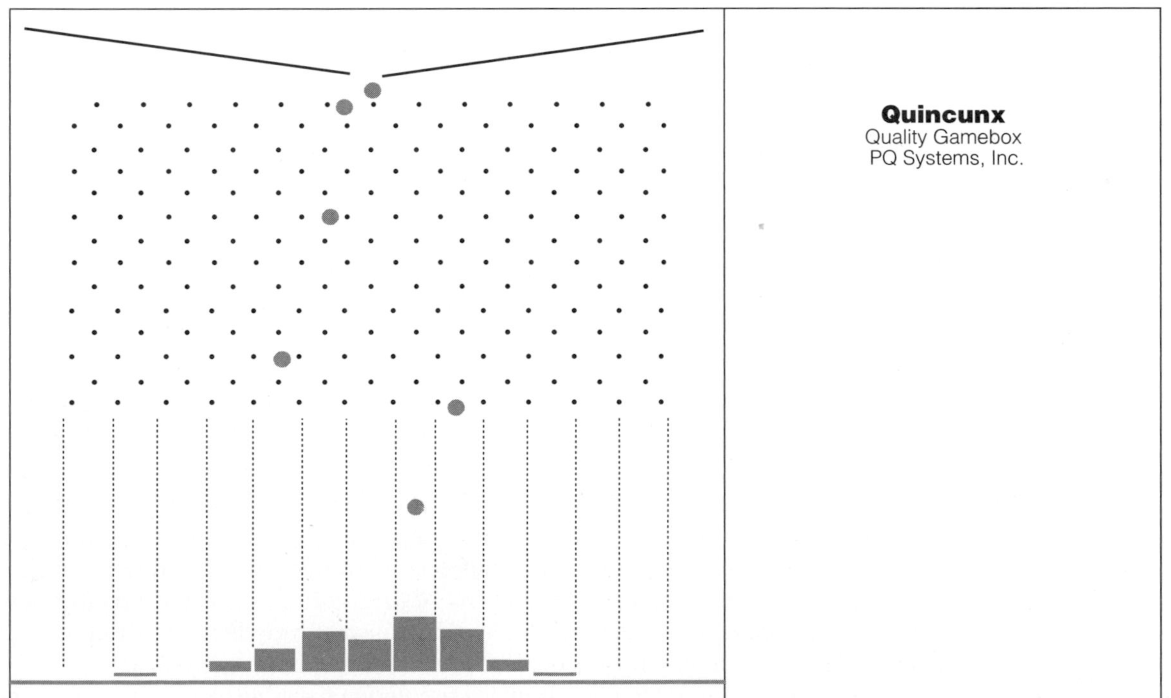

Source: From Quality Gamebox, a registered trademark of Productivity-Quality Systems, Inc. Reprinted with permission.

Figure 3.3 Results from a Quincunx Experiment

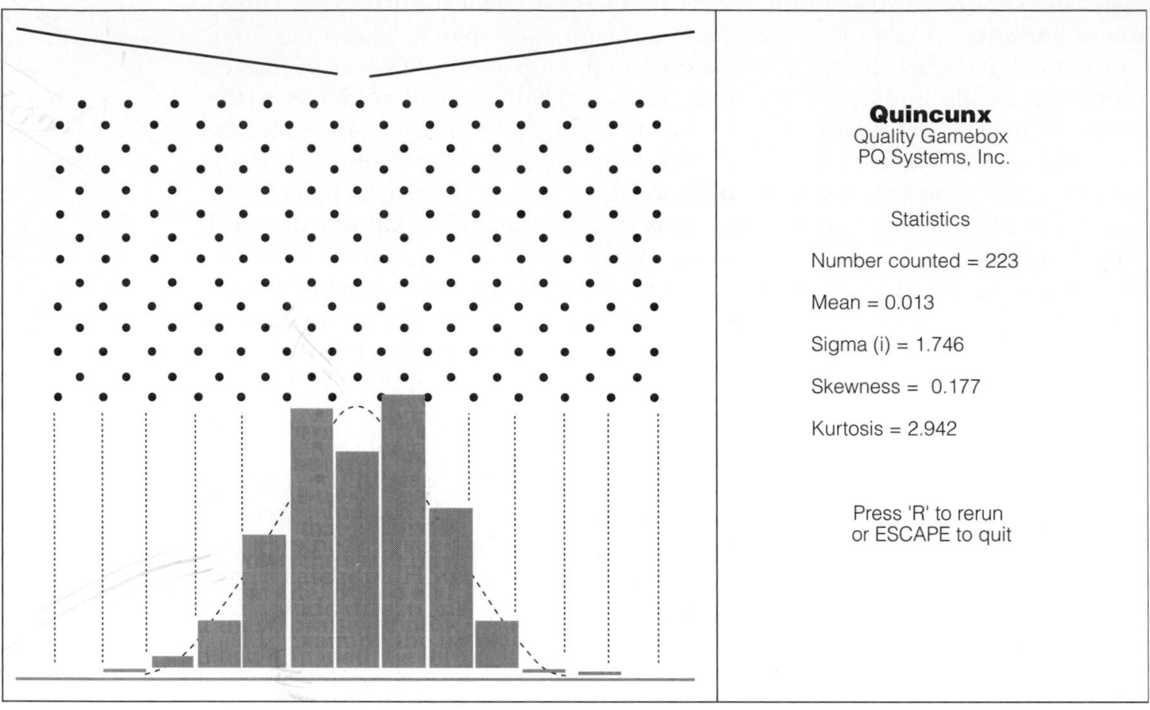

Source: From Quality Gamebox, a registered trademark of Productivity-Quality Systems, Inc. Reprinted with permission.

The consumer has the advantage of knowing that all products and services have similar quality characteristics and will perform or be delivered consistently. This advantage can be especially critical when the consumer is another firm using large quantities of the product in its own manufacturing or service operations.

Excessive variation results in products that fail or perform erratically and inconsistent service that does not meet customers' expectations.

Statistical methods are the primary tools used to identify and quantify variation. Deming proposed that every employee in the firm be familiar with statistical techniques and other problem-solving tools. Statistics can then become the common language that every employee—from top executives to line workers—uses to communicate with one another. Its value lies in its objectivity; statistics leaves little room for ambiguity or misunderstanding. We will explore issues of variation and statistics further in Chapter 10.

Theory of Knowledge The third part of Profound Knowledge is the "theory of knowledge," the branch of philosophy concerned with the nature and scope of knowledge, its presuppositions and basis, and the general reliability of claims to knowledge. Deming's system was influenced greatly by Clarence Irving Lewis, author of *Mind and the World*, who stated, "There is no knowledge without interpretation. If interpretation, which represents an activity of the mind, is always subject to the check of further experience, how is knowledge possible at all? . . . An argument from past to future at best is probable only, and even this probability must rest upon principles which are themselves more than probable."[4] Basically, managers need to understand how things work and why decisions that affect the future should be effective. Any rational plan, however simple, requires prediction concerning conditions, behavior, and comparison of performance, and such predictions should be grounded in theory.

For example, it is easy to learn a "cookbook" approach to statistics—being able to run a computer program or a Microsoft Excel procedure. Doing so, however, runs the risk of using the tools inappropriately. Understanding the assumptions and theory behind statistical tools and techniques is vital to applying them correctly. Countless managers use a similar cookbook approach to managing by reading the latest self-help book and blindly following the author's recommendations. Many companies jump on the latest popular approach advocated by business consultants, only to see the approach fail. Copying an example of success, without understanding it with theory, may lead to disaster.

Experience only describes—it cannot be tested or validated—and alone is no help in management. Theory, on the other hand, helps one to understand cause-and-effect relationships that can be used for prediction and rational management decisions.

Deming emphasized that knowledge is not possible without theory, and experience alone does not establish a theory. It is one reason why Deming never gave managers any "solutions" or prescriptions for achieving quality. He wanted them to learn and discover what works and what is appropriate for their individual organizations. The modern concept of organizational learning reflects the theory of knowledge. For example, many project managers conduct debriefings or postmortem reviews upon completion of projects. These reviews allow them to understand what went wrong and what went right, helping to develop a knowledge base and provide concrete information to improve in the future. Objective data and a systematic problem-solving process provide a rational basis for making decisions.

Psychology Psychology helps us understand people, interactions between people and circumstances, interactions between leaders and employees, and any system of management. It is critical to designing a work environment that promotes employee satisfaction and well-being. Much of Deming's philosophy is based on understanding human behavior and treating people fairly. People differ from one another. A true leader must be aware of these differences and work toward optimizing everybody's abilities and preferences. Most managers operate under the assumption that all people are alike. However, a true leader understands that people learn in different ways and at different speeds, and manages the system accordingly.

People are born with a need for love and esteem in their relationships with other people. Some circumstances provide people with dignity and self-esteem. Conversely, circumstances that deny people these advantages will smother intrinsic motivation. Fear does not motivate people; instead, it prevents the system from reaching its full potential. If people cannot enjoy their work, they will not be productive and focused on quality principles. Psychology helps us to nurture and preserve these positive innate attributes of people; otherwise, we resort to carrots and sticks that offer no long-term values.

People can be motivated intrinsically and extrinsically; however, the most powerful motivators are intrinsic.

One of Deming's more controversial beliefs is that pay is not a motivator, which industrial psychologists have been saying for decades. The chairman of General Motors once stated if GM doubled the salary of every employee, nothing would change. Monetary rewards are a way out for managers who do not understand how to manage intrinsic motivation. When joy in work becomes secondary to getting good ratings, employees are ruled by external forces and must act to protect what they have and avoid punishment.

Impacts of Profound Knowledge Peter Scholtes, a noted consultant, makes some salient observations about the failure to understand the components of Profound Knowledge:[5]

When people don't understand systems:

- They see events as individual incidents rather than the net result of many interactions and interdependent forces.
- They see the symptoms but not the deep causes of problems.
- They don't understand how an intervention in one part of [an organization] can cause havoc in another place or at another time.
- They blame individuals for problems even when those individuals have little or no ability to control the events around them.
- They don't understand the ancient African saying, "It takes a whole village to raise a child."

When people don't understand variation:

- They don't see trends that are occurring.
- They see trends where there are none.
- They don't know when expectations are realistic.
- They don't understand past performance so they can't predict future performance.
- They don't know the difference between prediction, forecasting, and guesswork.
- They give others credit or blame when those people are simply either lucky or unlucky, which usually occurs because people tend to attribute everything to human effort, heroics, frailty, error, or deliberate sabotage, no matter what the systemic cause.
- They are less likely to distinguish between fact and opinion.

When people don't understand psychology:

- They don't understand motivation or why people do what they do.
- They resort to carrots and sticks and other forms of induced motivation that offer no positive effect and impair the relationship between the motivator and the one being motivated.
- They don't understand the process of change and the resistance to it.
- They revert to coercive and paternalistic approaches when dealing with people.
- They create cynicism, demoralization, demotivation, guilt, resentment, burnout, craziness, and turnover.

When people don't understand the theory of knowledge:

- They don't know how to plan and accomplish learning and improvement.
- They don't understand the difference between improvement and change.
- Problems will remain unsolved, despite their best efforts.

Little of Deming's system of Profound Knowledge is original. Walter Shewhart developed the distinction between common and special causes of variation in the 1920s; business schools began to teach many of the behavioral theories to which

Deming subscribed in the 1960s; management scientists refined systems theory in the 1950s through the 1970s; and scientists in all fields have long understood the relationships among prediction, observation, and theory. Deming's major contribution was to tie these concepts together in the context of business. He recognized their synergy and developed them into a unified universal theory of management.

A group of Deming's associates and other quality-minded individuals have established the "In2:InThinking Network." Their mission is: "... to promote study and awareness of individual and collective thinking about sub-systems, psychology, variation, knowledge, and their interactions—elements recognized as the basis of W. Edwards Deming's 'System of Profound Knowledge.'" You can view their work and associated papers and blogs at their website: http://www.in2in.org/index.html.

Deming's 14 Points

Deming's 14 Points listed in Table 3.1 date back several decades to when many organizations were ruled by autocratic managers who were driven by short-term profits and who had little regard for engaging the workforce or interest in quality improvement. Deming was emphatic in his belief that these managerial practices needed a radical overhaul and proposed the 14 Points for achieving quality excellence. Although management practices today are vastly different from when Deming first began to preach his philosophy, the 14 Points still convey important insights and provide guidance for managing effective organizations. We will briefly consider the key lessons of each.

Point 1: *Create a Vision and Demonstrate Commitment* An organization must define its values, mission, and vision of the future to provide long-term direction for its management and employees. Deming believed that businesses should not exist simply for profit; they are social entities whose basic purpose is to serve their customers and employees. To fulfill this purpose, they must take a long-term view, invest in innovation, training, and research, and take responsibility for providing jobs and improving a firm's competitive position. This responsibility lies with top management, who must show commitment.

Making a commitment to drive improvement within an organization, perhaps through a Baldrige-based or Six Sigma approach that we will discuss later in this chapter, is still difficult for managers. Even when managers have conducted a thorough assessment of their organization and know what they need to change, many do not effectively follow up on opportunities.[6] Reasons range from denial ("We can't be that bad!") to excuses ("We have a lot of irons on the fire right now."). Effective leadership begins with commitment, and we will revisit this issue in Chapter 9.

Point 2: *Learn the New Philosophy* Historical methods of management built on early twentieth century practices, such as quota-driven production, work measurement, and adversarial work relationships, will not work in today's global business environment. Nevertheless, some organizations, such as call centers, are still managed like this. Deming recognized this problem a long time ago and sought to change the prevailing attitudes that ignored the importance of quality improvement. Specifically, companies cannot survive if products of poor conformance quality or poor fitness for use leave their customers dissatisfied. Instead, companies must take a customer-driven approach based on mutual cooperation between labor and management and a never-ending cycle of improvement. To effectively focus on the customers' needs, everyone, from the boardroom to the stockroom, must learn the principles of quality and performance excellence.

Today, many of these principles are indeed ingrained in managers and front-line employees through training and reinforcement of organizational values. However, people change jobs and organizations generally have a short memory—both need to continually renew themselves to learn new approaches and relearn many older ones. This concept of "organizational learning" will be addressed in Chapter 9.

Point 3: ***Understand Inspection*** Deming knew that inspection had been the principal means for quality control; companies employed dozens or even hundreds of people who inspected for quality on a full-time basis. Routine inspection acknowledges that defects are present, but does not add value to the product. Rather, it is rarely accurate, and encourages the production of defective products by letting someone else catch and fix the problem. The rework and disposition of defective material decreases productivity and increases costs. In service industries, rework often cannot be performed; external failures are the most damaging to business.

Deming encouraged workers to take responsibility for their work, rather than leave the problems for someone else down the production line. Simple statistical tools can be used to help control processes and eliminate mass inspection as the principal activity in quality control. Inspection should be used as an information-gathering tool for improvement, not as a means of "assuring" quality or blaming workers.

Today, this new role of inspection has been integrated into the quality management practices of most companies. However, few managers truly understand the concept of variation and how it affects their processes and inspection practices. By understanding and seeking to reduce variation, managers can eliminate many sources of unnecessary inspection, thus reducing non-value-added costs associated with operations.

Point 4: ***Stop Making Decisions Purely on the Basis of Cost*** Purchasing departments have long been driven by cost minimization and competition among suppliers without regard for quality. In 1931, Walter Shewhart noted that price has no meaning without quality.[7] (Think about the value based definition of quality from Chapter 1.) Yet, by tradition, the purchasing manager's performance has been evaluated by cost. Deming recognized that the direct costs associated with poor quality materials that arise during production or during warranty periods, as well as the loss of customer goodwill, can far exceed the cost "savings" perceived by purchasing. Thus, purchasing must understand its role as a supplier to production and its impact on the system.

Deming also urged businesses to establish long-term relationships with fewer suppliers, leading to loyalty and opportunities for mutual improvement. Management previously justified multiple suppliers for reasons such as providing protection against strikes or natural disasters, while ignoring "hidden" costs such as increased travel to visit suppliers, loss of volume discounts, increased setup charges resulting in higher unit costs, and increased inventory and administrative expense. Most importantly, constantly changing suppliers solely on the basis of price increases the variation in the material supplied to production, because each supplier's process is different. In contrast, a reduced supply base decreases the variation coming into the process, thus reducing scrap, rework, and the need for adjustment to accommodate this variation. A long-term relationship strengthens the supplier–customer bond, allows the supplier to produce in greater quantity, improves communication with the customer, and therefore enhances opportunities for process improvement. Suppliers know that only quality goods are acceptable if they want to maintain a long-term relationship.

Today's emphasis on supply chain management (SCM) reflects the achievement of Point 4. SCM focuses heavily on a system's view of the supply chain with the objective of minimizing total supply chain costs and developing stronger partnerships with suppliers.

Point 5: ***Improve Constantly and Forever*** Improvements are necessary in both design and operations. Improved design of goods and services comes from understanding customer needs and continual market surveys and other sources of feedback, and from understanding the manufacturing and service delivery process. Improvements in operations are achieved by reducing the causes and impacts of variation, and engaging all employees to innovate and seek ways of doing their jobs more efficiently and effectively. When quality improves, productivity improves and costs decrease, as the Deming chain reaction (Figure 3.1) suggests.

Traditionally, continuous improvement was not a common business practice; today it is recognized as a necessary means for survival in a highly competitive and global business environment. Quality improvement will be discussed extensively in Part III of this book. The tools for improvement are constantly evolving, and organizations need to ensure that their employees understand and apply them effectively, which requires training, the focus of the next Point.

Point 6: ***Institute Training*** People are an organization's most valuable resource; they want to do a good job, but they often do not know how. Management must take responsibility for helping them. Not only does training result in improvements in quality and productivity, but it adds to worker morale, and demonstrates to workers that the company is dedicated to helping them and investing in their future. In addition, training reduces barriers between workers and supervisors, giving both more incentive to improve further. For example, at Honda of America in Marysville, Ohio, all employees start out on the production floor, regardless of their job classification.

Training must transcend such basic job skills as running a machine or following the script when talking to customers. Training should include tools for diagnosing, analyzing, and solving quality problems and identifying improvement opportunities. Today, many companies have excellent training programs for technology related to direct production, but still fail to enrich the ancillary skills of their workforce. Here is where some of the most lucrative opportunities exist to make an impact on key business results.

Point 7: ***Institute Leadership*** Deming recognized that one of biggest impediments to improvement was a lack of leadership. The job of management is leadership, not supervision. Supervision is simply overseeing and directing work; leadership means providing guidance to help employees do their jobs better with less effort. Good managers are not police or paper-pushers, but rather leaders and coaches, helping workers to do a better job and develop their skills. Leadership can help to eliminate the element of fear from the job and encourage teamwork.

Leadership was, is, and will continue to be, a challenging issue in every organization, particularly as new generations of managers replace those who have learned to lead. Thus, this Point of Deming's will always be relevant to organizations.

Point 8: ***Drive Out Fear*** Driving out fear underlies many of Deming's 14 Points. Fear is manifested in many ways: fear of reprisal, fear of failure, fear of the unknown, fear of relinquishing control, and fear of change. No system can work without the mutual respect of managers and workers. Workers are often afraid to report quality problems because they might not meet their quotas, their incentive pay might be reduced, or they might be blamed for problems in the system. Managers are also afraid to cooperate with other departments, because the other managers might receive higher performance ratings and bonuses, or because they fear takeovers or reorganizations. Fear encourages short-term thinking.

Fear is a cultural issue for all organizations. Creating a culture without fear, as we will discuss in Chapter 9, is a slow process but can be destroyed in an instant with a transition of leadership and a change in corporate policies. Therefore, today's managers need to continue to be sensitive to the impact that fear can have on their organizations.

Point 9: ***Optimize the Efforts of Teams*** Teamwork helps to break down barriers between departments and individuals. Barriers between functional areas occur when managers fear they might lose power. Internal competition for raises and performance ratings contributes to building barriers. The lack of cooperation leads to poor quality because other departments cannot understand what their internal customers want and do not get what they need from their internal suppliers. Training and employee involvement are important means of removing such barriers. We will discuss these issues in greater detail in Chapter 6.

Point 10: ***Eliminate Exhortations*** Many early attempts to improve quality focused solely on behavioral change. However, posters, slogans, and motivational programs calling for Zero Defects, Do It Right the First Time, Improve Productivity and Quality, and so on, are directed at the wrong people. They assume that all quality problems are due to human behavior and that workers can improve simply through motivational methods. Workers become frustrated when they cannot improve or are penalized for defects.

Motivational approaches overlook the major source of many problems—the system. Causes of variation stemming from the design of the system are management's problem, not the workers'. If anything, workers' attempts to fix problems only increase the variation. Improvement occurs by understanding the nature of special and common causes. Thus, statistical thinking and training, not slogans, are the best routes to improving quality. Motivation can be better achieved from trust and leadership than from slogans and goals.

Point 11: ***Eliminate Numerical Quotas and Management by Objective (MBO)*** Many organizations manage by the numbers. Measurement has been, and often still is, used punitively. Standards and quotas are born of short-term perspectives and create fear. They do not encourage improvement, particularly if rewards or performance appraisals are tied to meeting quotas. Workers may short-cut quality to reach the goal. Once a standard is reached, little incentive remains for workers to continue production or to improve quality; they will do no more than they are asked to do.

Arbitrary management goals, such as increasing sales by 5 percent next year or decreasing costs next quarter by 10 percent, have no meaning without a method to achieve them. Deming acknowledged that goals are useful, but numerical goals set for others without incorporating a method to reach the goal generate frustration and resentment. Further, variation in the system year-to-year or quarter-to-quarter—a 5 percent increase or a 6 percent decrease, for example—makes comparisons meaningless. Management must understand the system and continually try to improve it, rather than focus on short-term goals.

Point 12: ***Remove Barriers to Pride in Workmanship*** People on the factory floor and even in management were often treated as, in Deming's words, "a commodity." Factory workers are given monotonous tasks, provided with inferior machines, tools, or materials, told to run defective items to meet sales pressures, and report to supervisors who know little about the job. How can these individuals take pride in their work?

Deming believed that one of the biggest barriers to pride in workmanship is performance appraisal. Performance appraisal destroys teamwork by promoting competition for limited resources, fosters mediocrity because objectives typically are driven by numbers and what the boss wants rather than by quality, focuses on the short term and discourages risk taking, and confounds the "people resources" with other resources. Although many companies will not eliminate performance appraisals completely, some have made substantial changes. Many now separate performance appraisal from annual salary reviews, using appraisal to recognize accomplishment of results and the use of quality processes. We will have more to say about this issue in Chapter 6.

Point 13: ***Encourage Education and Self-Improvement*** The difference between this Point and Point 6 is subtle. Point 6 refers to training in specific job skills; Point 13 refers to continuing, broad education for self-development. Organizations must invest in their people at all levels to ensure success in the long term. A fundamental mission of business is to provide jobs as stated in Point 1, but business and society also have the responsibility to improve the value of the individual. Developing the worth of the individual is a powerful motivation method.

Today, many companies understand that elevating the general knowledge base of their workforce—outside of specific job skills—returns many benefits. However, others still view this task as a cost that can be easily cut when financial trade-offs must be made.

Point 14: ***Take Action*** Any cultural change begins with top management and includes everyone. Changing an organizational culture generally meets with skepticism and resistance that many firms find difficult to deal with, particularly when many of the traditional management practices Deming felt must be eliminated are deeply ingrained in the organization's culture. We will discuss this challenge more in Chapter 9.

Many people have criticized Deming because his philosophy is just that: a philosophy. It lacks specific direction and prescriptive approaches and does not fit into the traditional American business culture. As we noted earlier, Deming did not propose specific methods for implementation because he wanted people to study his ideas and derive their own approaches. As he often stated, "There is no instant pudding." Despite the controversy, many firms organized their quality approaches around Deming's philosophy. Some companies, such as 1991 Baldrige Award winner Zytec Corporation, now a part of Artesyn Technologies, met with great success. Another example is Hillerich & Bradsby.

Hillerich & Bradsby Co. (H&B) has been making the Louisville Slugger brand of baseball bat for more than 115 years.[8] In the mid-1980s, the company faced significant challenges from market changes and competition. CEO Jack Hillerich attended a four-day Deming seminar, which provided the basis for the company's current quality efforts. Returning from the seminar, Hillerich decided to see what changes that Deming advocated were possible in an old company with an old union and a history of labor/management problems. Hillerich persuaded union officials to attend another Deming seminar with five senior managers. Following the seminar, a core group of union and management people developed a strategy to change the company. They talked about building trust and changing to system "to make it something you want to work in." Employees were interested, but skeptical. To demonstrate their commitment, managers examined Deming's 14 Points, and picked several they believed they could make progress on through actions that would demonstrate a serious intention to change. One of the first changes was the elimination of work quotas that were tied to hourly salaries and a schedule of warnings and penalties for failures to meet quotas. Instead, a team-based approach was initiated. Although only a few workers took advantage of the change, overall productivity actually improved as rework decreased because workers were taking pride in their work to produce things the right way first. H&B also eliminated performance appraisals and commission-based pay in sales. The company also focused its efforts on training and education, resulting in an openness for change and capacity for teamwork. Today, the Deming philosophy is still the core of H&B's guiding principles.

Deming's legacy lives on through the W. Edwards Deming Institute (http://deming.org).

THE JURAN PHILOSOPHY

Joseph Juran (1904–2008) was born in Romania and came to the United States in 1912. He joined Western Electric in the 1920s as it pioneered in the development of statistical methods for quality. He spent much of his time as a corporate industrial engineer and, in 1951, did most of the writing, editing, and publishing of the *Quality Control Handbook*. This book, one of the most comprehensive quality manuals ever written, has been revised several times and continues to be a popular reference.

Like Deming, Juran taught quality principles to the Japanese in the 1950s and was a principal force in their quality reorganization. Among the steps taken by Japanese organizations as a result of Juran's leadership were:

- Directing quality from the senior management level
- Training the entire management hierarchy in quality principles
- Striving to improve quality at a revolutionary rate
- Reporting progress on quality goals to executive levels
- Involving the workforce in quality
- Revising the reward and recognition structure to include quality[9]

These principles continue to be the backbone of modern quality culture (which we discuss further in Chapter 9).

During the quality revolution in the second half of the twentieth century, Juran echoed Deming's conclusion that U.S. businesses faced a major crisis in quality due to the huge costs of poor quality and the loss of sales to foreign competition. Both men felt that the solution to this crisis depends on new thinking about quality that includes all levels of the managerial hierarchy. Upper management in particular requires training and experience in managing for quality. Even into this century, Juran continued to warn the United States that it faces losing its status as an economic superpower unless it improves the quality of its goods and services.

Unlike Deming, however, Juran did not propose a major cultural change in the organization, but rather sought to improve quality by working within the system familiar to managers. Thus, his programs were designed to fit into a company's current strategic business planning with minimal risk of rejection. He argued that employees at different levels of an organization speak in their own "languages." (Deming, on the other hand, believed statistics should be the common language.) Juran stated that top management speaks in the language of dollars; workers speak in the language of things; and middle management must be able to speak both languages and translate between dollars and things. Thus, to get top management's attention, quality issues must be cast in the language they understand—dollars. Hence, Juran advocated the use of quality cost accounting and analysis to focus attention on quality problems. At the operational level, Juran focused on increasing conformance to specifications through elimination of defects, supported extensively by statistical tools for analysis. Thus, his philosophy fit well into existing management systems.

Juran proposed a simple definition of quality: "fitness for use."

Juran's definition of quality suggests that it should be viewed from both external and internal perspectives; that is, quality is related to (1) product performance that results in customer satisfaction; and (2) freedom from product deficiencies, which avoids customer dissatisfaction. How products and services are designed, manufactured and delivered, and serviced in the field all contribute to fitness for use. Thus, the pursuit of quality is viewed on two levels: (1) the mission of the firm as a whole is to achieve high design quality; and (2) the mission of each department in the firm is to achieve high-conformance quality. Like Deming, Juran advocated a never-ending spiral of activities that includes market research, product development, design, planning for manufacture, purchasing, production process control, inspection and testing, and sales, followed by customer feedback. The interdependency of these functions emphasizes the need for competent companywide quality management. Senior management must play an active and enthusiastic leadership role in the quality management process.

Juran's prescriptions focus on three major quality processes, called the **Quality Trilogy**: (1) *quality planning*—the process of preparing to meet quality goals; (2) *quality control*—the process of meeting quality goals during operations; and (3) *quality improvement*—the process of breaking through to unprecedented levels of performance. At the time he proposed this structure, few companies were engaging in any significant planning or improvement activities. Thus, Juran was promoting a major cultural shift in management thinking.

Quality planning begins with identifying customers, both external and internal, determining their needs, translating customer needs into specifications, developing product features that respond to those needs, and developing the processes capable of producing the product or delivering the service. Thus, like Deming, Juran wanted employees to know who uses their products, whether in the next department or in another organization. Quality goals based on meeting the needs of customers and suppliers alike at a minimum combined cost are then established. Next, the process that can produce the product to satisfy customers' needs and meet quality goals under operating conditions must be designed. Strategic planning for quality—similar to the firm's financial planning process—determines short-term and long-term goals, sets priorities, compares results with previous plans, and meshes the plans with other corporate strategic objectives.

As a parallel to Deming's emphasis on identifying and reducing sources of variation, Juran stated that quality control involves determining what to control, establishing units of measurement to evaluate data objectively, establishing standards of performance, measuring actual performance, interpreting the difference between actual performance and the standard, and taking action on the difference.

Unlike Deming, however, Juran specified a detailed program for quality improvement. According to Juran, all breakthroughs follow a commonsense sequence of discovery, organization, diagnosis, corrective action, and control, which he formalized as the **breakthrough sequence**, and which can be summarized as follows:

- *Proof of the need*: Managers, especially top managers, need to be convinced that quality improvements are simply good economics. Through data collection efforts, information on poor quality, low productivity, or poor service can be translated into the language of money—the universal language of top management—to justify a request for resources to implement a quality improvement program.
- *Project identification*: All breakthroughs are achieved project-by-project, and in no other way. By taking a project approach, management provides a forum for converting an atmosphere of defensiveness or blame into one of constructive action. Participation in a project increases the likelihood that the participant will act on the results.
- *Organization for breakthrough*: Organization for improvement requires a clear responsibility for guiding the project. The responsibility for the project may be as broad as an entire division with formal committee structures or as narrow as a small group of workers at one production operation. These groups provide the definition and agreement as to the specific aims of the project, the authority to conduct experiments, and implementation strategies. The path from problem to solution consists of two journeys: one from symptom to cause (the diagnostic journey) and the other from cause to remedy (the remedial journey), which must be performed by different individuals with the appropriate skills.
- *Diagnostic journey:* Diagnosticians skilled in data collection, statistics, and other problem-solving tools are needed at this stage. Some projects will require full-time, specialized experts (such as Six Sigma Black Belts) while the workforce can perform others. Management-controllable and operator-controllable problems require different methods of diagnosis and remedy.
- *Remedial journey*: The remedial journey consists of several phases: choosing an alternative that optimizes total cost (similar to one of Deming's points), implementing remedial action, and dealing with resistance to change.
- *Holding the gains*: This final step involves establishing the new standards and procedures, training the workforce, and instituting controls to make sure that the breakthrough does not die over time.

Juran's approaches are reflected in the practices of a wide variety of organizations today.

Many aspects of the Juran and Deming philosophies are similar. The focus on top management commitment, the need for improvement, the use of quality control techniques, and the importance of training are fundamental to both philosophies. However, they did not agree on all points. For instance, Juran believed that Deming was wrong to tell management to drive out fear. According to Juran, "Fear can bring out the best in people."[10] The Juran Institute, founded by Dr. Juran, provides substantial training in the form of seminars, videos, and other materials (http://www.juran.com).

THE CROSBY PHILOSOPHY

Philip B. Crosby (1926–2001) was corporate vice president for quality at International Telephone and Telegraph (ITT) for 14 years after working his way up from line inspector. After leaving ITT, he established Philip Crosby Associates in 1979 to develop and offer training programs. He also authored several popular books. His first book, *Quality Is Free*, sold about 1 million copies and was largely responsible for bringing quality to the attention of top corporate managers in the United States. The essence of Crosby's quality philosophy is embodied in what he calls the **Absolutes of Quality Management** and the **Basic Elements of Improvement**. Crosby's Absolutes of Quality Management include the following points:

- *Quality means conformance to requirements, not elegance.* Crosby quickly dispels the myth that quality follows the transcendent definition discussed in Chapter 1. Requirements must be clearly stated so that they cannot be misunderstood. Requirements act as communication devices and are ironclad. Once requirements are established, then one can take measurements to determine conformance to those requirements. The nonconformance detected is the absence of quality. Quality problems become nonconformance problems, that is, variation in output. Setting requirements is the responsibility of management. Crosby maintained that once the requirements are specified, quality is judged solely on whether they have been met. Therefore, these requirements must be clearly defined by management and not left by default to front-line personnel.
- *There is no such thing as a quality problem.* Problems must be identified by those individuals or departments that cause them. Thus, a firm may experience accounting problems, manufacturing problems, design problems, front-desk problems, and so on. In other words, quality originates in functional departments, not in the quality department, and therefore the burden of responsibility for such problems falls on these functional departments. The quality department should measure conformance, report results, and lead the drive to develop a positive attitude toward quality improvement. This Absolute is similar to Deming's third Point.
- *There is no such thing as the economics of quality; doing the job right the first time is always cheaper.* Crosby supports the premise that "economics of quality" has no meaning. Quality is free. What costs money are all actions that involve not doing jobs right the first time. The Deming chain reaction sends a similar message.
- *The only performance measurement is the cost of quality, which is the expense of nonconformance.* Crosby noted that most companies spend 15 percent to 20 percent of their sales dollars on quality costs. A company with a well-run quality management program can achieve a cost of quality that is less than 2.5 percent of sales, primarily in the prevention and appraisal categories. Crosby's program calls for measuring and publicizing the cost of poor quality. Quality cost data are useful to call problems to management's attention, to select opportunities for corrective action, and to track quality improvement over time. Such data provide visible proof of improvement and recognition of achievement. Juran supported this approach.
- *The only performance standard is "Zero Defects (ZD)."* Crosby felt that the Zero Defects concept is widely misunderstood and resisted. Many thought it to be a motivational program. It is described as follows:

  > *Zero Defects is a performance standard. It is the standard of the craftsperson regardless of his or her assignment . . . The theme of ZD is do it right the first time. That means concentrating on preventing defects rather than just finding and fixing them.*
  >
  > *People are conditioned to believe that error is inevitable; thus they not only accept error, they anticipate it. It does not bother us to make a few*

> *errors in our work . . . to err is human. We all have our own standards in business or academic life—our own points at which errors begin to bother us. It is good to get an A in school, but it may be OK to pass with a C.*
>
> *We do not maintain these standards, however, when it comes to our personal life. If we did, we should expect to be shortchanged every now and then when we cash our paycheck; we should expect hospital nurses to drop a constant percentage of newborn babies . . . We as individuals do not tolerate these things. We have a dual standard: one for ourselves and one for our work.*
>
> *Most human error is caused by lack of attention rather than lack of knowledge. Lack of attention is created when we assume that error is inevitable. If we consider this condition carefully, and pledge ourselves to make a constant conscious effort to do our jobs right the first time, we will take a giant step toward eliminating the waste of rework, scrap, and repair that increases cost and reduces individual opportunity.*[11]

Juran and Deming, on the other hand, would point out the uselessness, or even hypocrisy of exhorting a line worker to produce perfection because the overwhelming majority of imperfections stems from poorly designed manufacturing systems beyond the workers' control.

Crosby's Basic Elements of Improvement were *determination*, *education*, and *implementation*. Determination means that top management must take quality improvement seriously. Everyone should understand the Absolutes, which can be accomplished only through education. Finally, every member of the management team must understand the implementation process.

Unlike Juran and Deming, Crosby's approach was primarily behavioral. He emphasized using management and organizational processes rather than statistical techniques to change corporate culture and attitudes. Like Juran and unlike Deming however, his approach fit well within existing organizational structures.

COMPARISONS OF QUALITY PHILOSOPHIES

Despite their significant differences to implementing organizational change, the philosophies of Deming, Juran, and Crosby are more alike than different. Each views quality as imperative in the future competitiveness in global markets; makes top management commitment an absolute necessity; demonstrates that quality management practices will save, not cost money; places responsibility for quality on management, not the workers; stresses the need for continuous, never-ending improvement; acknowledges the importance of the customer and strong management/worker partnerships; and recognizes the need for and difficulties associated with changing the organizational culture.

The individual nature of business firms complicates the strict application of any one specific philosophy. Although each of these philosophies can be highly effective, a firm must first understand the nature and differences of the philosophies and then develop a quality management approach tailored to its individual organization. Any approach should include goals and objectives, allocation of responsibilities, a measurement system and description of tools to be employed, an outline of the management style that will be used, and a strategy for implementation. After taking these steps, the management team is responsible for leading the organization through successful execution. We address these issues further in Chapter 9.

OTHER QUALITY PHILOSOPHERS

Other notable figures in the quality arena include A. V. Feigenbaum and Kaoru Ishikawa. Feigenbaum and Ishikawa were both awarded the title of Honorary Members of the American Society for Quality in 1986.[12] At that time, the society had only four living honorary members, two of whom were W. Edwards Deming and Joseph M. Juran. Obviously, the title of "Honorary Member" is not given lightly by the ASQ. In this section we briefly review the accomplishments that made them part of this elite group, and also introduce another influential thinker in the quality movement, Genichi Taguchi.

A. V. Feigenbaum

A. V. Feigenbaum's career in quality began more than 50 years ago. For 10 years, he was the manager of worldwide manufacturing and quality control at General Electric. In 1968, he founded General Systems Company of Pittsfield, Massachusetts, and still serves as its president and CEO. Feigenbaum has traveled and spoken to various audiences and groups around the world over the years. He was elected as the founding chairman of the board of the International Academy of Quality, which has attracted active participation from the European Organization for Quality Control, the Union of Japanese Scientists and Engineers (JUSE), as well as the American Society for Quality.

Feigenbaum is best known for coining the phrase *total quality control*, which he defined as ". . . an effective system for integrating the quality development, quality maintenance, and quality improvement efforts of the various groups in an organization so as to enable production and service at the most economical levels which allow full customer satisfaction," and explained in his book *Total Quality Control*, which was first published in 1951 under the title *Quality Control: Principles, Practice, and Administration*. He viewed quality as a strategic business tool that requires involvement from everyone in the organization, and promoted the use of quality costs as a measurement and evaluation tool.

Feigenbaum's philosophy is summarized in his **Three Steps to Quality**:

1. *Quality Leadership*: A continuous management emphasis is grounded on sound planning rather than reaction to failures. Management must maintain a constant focus and lead the quality effort.
2. *Modern Quality Technology*: The traditional quality department cannot resolve 80 percent to 90 percent of quality problems. This task requires the integration of office staff as well as engineers and shop-floor workers in the process who continually evaluate and implement new techniques to satisfy customers in the future.
3. *Organizational Commitment*: Continuous training and motivation of the entire workforce as well as an integration of quality in business planning indicate the importance of quality and provide the means for including it in all aspects of the firm's activities.

Feigenbaum also popularized the term *hidden factory*, which described the portion of plant capacity wasted due to poor quality. Many of his ideas remain embedded in contemporary thinking, and have become important elements of the Malcolm Baldrige National Quality Award criteria. These aspects include the principles that the customer is the judge of quality; quality and innovation are interrelated and mutually beneficial; managing quality is the same as managing the business; quality is a continuous process of improvement; and customers and suppliers should be involved the process. In 2008, he received the prestigious National Medal of Technology and Innovation. More about Feigenbaum can be found on the General Systems Company website at http://www.gensysco.com/.

Kaoru Ishikawa

An early pioneer in the quality revolution in Japan, Kaoru Ishikawa was the foremost figure in Japanese quality until his death in 1989. He was instrumental in the development of the broad outlines of Japanese quality strategy, and without his leadership, the Japanese quality movement would not enjoy the worldwide acclaim and success that it has today. Dr. Ishikawa was a professor of engineering at Tokyo University for many years. As a member of the editorial review board for the Japanese journal *Quality Control for Foremen*, founded in 1962, and later as the chief executive director of the QC Circle Headquarters at the Union of Japanese Scientists and Engineers (JUSE), Dr. Ishikawa influenced the development of a participative, bottom-up view of quality, which became the trademark of the Japanese approach to quality management. However, Ishikawa was also able to get the attention of top management and persuade them that a companywide approach to quality control was necessary for total success.

Ishikawa built on Feigenbaum's concept of total quality and promoted greater involvement by all employees, from the top management to the front-line staff, by reducing reliance on quality professionals and quality departments. He advocated collecting and analyzing factual data using simple visual tools, statistical techniques, and teamwork as the foundations for implementing total quality. Like others, Ishikawa believed that quality begins with the customer and therefore, understanding customers' needs is the basis for improvement, and that complaints should be actively sought. Some key elements of his philosophy are summarized here.

1. Quality begins with education and ends with education.
2. The first step in quality is to know the requirements of customers.
3. The ideal state of quality control occurs when inspection is no longer necessary.
4. Remove the root cause, not the symptoms.
5. Quality control is the responsibility of all workers and all divisions.
6. Do not confuse the means with the objectives.
7. Put quality first and set your sights on long-term profits.
8. Marketing is the entrance and exit of quality.
9. Top management must not show anger when facts are presented by subordinates.
10. Ninety-five percent of problems in a company can be solved with simple tools for analysis and problem solving.
11. Data without dispersion information (i.e., variability) are false data.

Genichi Taguchi

A Japanese engineer, Genichi Taguchi—whose philosophy was strongly advocated by Deming—explained the economic value of reducing variation. Taguchi maintained that the manufacturing-based definition of quality as conformance to specification limits is inherently flawed. For example, suppose that a specification for some quality characteristic is 0.500 ± 0.020. Using this definition, the actual value of the quality characteristic can fall anywhere in a range from 0.480 to 0.520. This approach assumes that the customer, either the consumer or the next department

Figure 3.4 Traditional Economic View of Conformance to Specifications

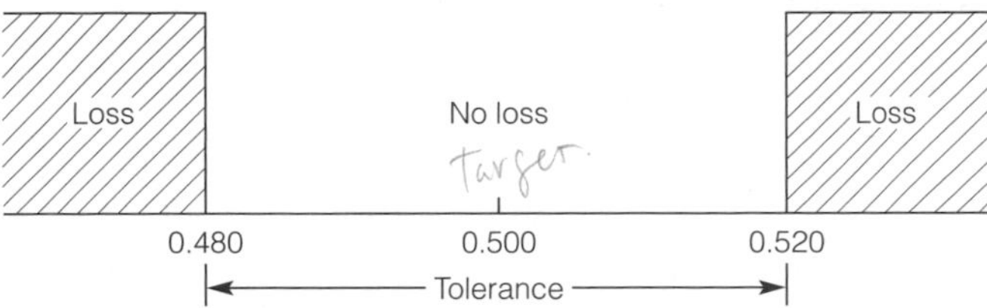

in the production process, would accept any value within the 0.480 to 0.520 range, but not be satisfied with a value outside this tolerance range. Also, this approach assumes that costs do not depend on the actual value of the quality characteristic as long as it falls within the tolerance specified (see Figure 3.4).

But what is the real difference between 0.479 and 0.481? The former would be considered as "out of specification" and either reworked or scrapped while the latter would be acceptable. Actually, the impact of either value on the performance characteristic of the product would be about the same. Neither value is close to the nominal specification 0.500. The nominal specification is the ideal target value for the critical quality characteristic. Taguchi's approach assumes that the smaller the variation about the nominal specification, the better is the quality. In turn, products are more consistent, and total costs are less. We will discuss the mathematics of this approach in Chapter 12.

Taguchi also contributed to improving engineering approaches to product design. By designing a product that is insensitive to variation in manufacture, specification limits become meaningless. He advocated certain techniques of experimental design to identify the most important design variables in order to minimize the effects of uncontrollable factors on product variation. Thus, his approaches attacked quality problems early in the design stage rather than reacting to problems that might arise later in production.

QUALITY MANAGEMENT AWARDS AND FRAMEWORKS

The philosophies of Deming, Juran, Crosby, and others provide much guidance and wisdom in the form of "best practices" to managers around the world, leading to the development of numerous awards and certifications for recognizing effective application of TQ principles. Although awards justifiably recognize only a select few, the award or certification criteria provide frameworks for managing from which every organization can benefit. The two frameworks that have had the most impact on quality management practices worldwide are the U.S. Malcolm Baldrige National Quality Award and international ISO 9000 certification process. Recently, the concept of Six Sigma has evolved into a unique framework for managing quality.

THE MALCOLM BALDRIGE NATIONAL QUALITY AWARD

In Chapter 1, we noted that the Malcolm Baldrige National Quality Award (MBNQA) has been one of the most powerful catalysts of total quality in the United States, and indeed, throughout the world. More importantly, the award's Criteria for Performance Excellence establish a framework for integrating total quality principles and practices in any organization. This framework provides the foundation for much of the next six chapters. In this section, we present an overview of the MBNQA, its criteria, and the award process.

History and Purpose

Recognizing that U.S. productivity was declining, President Reagan signed legislation mandating a national study/conference on productivity in October 1982. The American Productivity and Quality Center (formerly the American Productivity Center) sponsored seven computer networking conferences in 1983 to prepare for an upcoming White House Conference on Productivity. The final report on these conferences recommended that a National Quality Award, similar to the Deming Prize (discussed later in this chapter) in Japan, be awarded annually to those firms that successfully challenge and meet the award requirements. The report suggested that the award requirements and the accompanying examination process should be similar to the Deming Prize system. The Malcolm Baldrige National Quality Improvement Act was signed into law (Public Law 100-107) on August 20, 1987. The focus of the program was defined as follows:

- Helping to stimulate American companies to improve quality and productivity for the pride of recognition while obtaining a competitive edge through increased profits;
- Recognizing the achievements of those companies that improve the quality of their goods and services and providing an example to others;
- Establishing guidelines and criteria that can be used by business, industrial, governmental, and other enterprises in evaluating their own quality improvement efforts; and
- Providing specific guidance for other American enterprises that wish to learn how to manage for high quality by making available detailed information on how winning enterprises were able to change their cultures and achieve eminence.

The award is named after President Reagan's Secretary of Commerce, who was killed in an accident shortly before the Senate acted on the legislation. Malcolm Baldrige was highly regarded by world leaders, having played a major role in carrying out the administration's trade policy, resolving technology transfer differences with China and India, and holding the first Cabinet-level talks with the Soviet Union in seven years, which paved the way for increased access for U.S. firms in the Soviet market. Up to three companies can now receive an award in each of the original categories of manufacturing, small business, and service (prior to 1999, only two). Congress approved award categories in nonprofit education and health care in 1999. A final award category for other types of nonprofits was approved and implemented in 2007. This now allows any organization to apply for the Award. Table 3.2 shows the recipients through 2008.

The award has evolved into a comprehensive National Quality Program, administered through the National Institute of Standards and Technology in Gaithersburg, Maryland, of which the Baldrige Award is only one part. The National Quality Program is a public–private partnership, funded primarily through a private foundation. The program's website (at www.baldrige.nist.gov) provides current information about the award, the performance criteria, award winners, and a variety of other information.

Table 3.2 Malcolm Baldrige Award Recipients

Manufacturing
- Motorola, Inc. (1988)
- Westinghouse Commercial Nuclear Fuel Division (1988)
- Xerox Corp. Business Products and Systems (1989)
- Milliken & Co. (1989)
- Cadillac Motor Car Division (1990)
- IBM Rochester (1990)
- Solectron Corp. (1991)
- Zytec Corp. (now part of Artesyn Technologies) (1991)
- AT&T Network Systems (now Lucent Technologies, Inc. Optical Networking Group) (1992)
- Texas Instruments Defense Systems & Electronics Group (now part of Raytheon Systems Co.) (1992)
- Eastman Chemical Co. (1993)
- Armstrong World Industries Building Products Operations (1995)
- Corning Telecommunications Products Division (1995)
- ADAC Laboratories (1996)
- 3M Dental Products Division (1997)
- Solectron Corp. (1997)
- Boeing Airlift and Tanker Programs (1998)
- Solar Turbines, Inc. (1998)
- STMicroelectronics, Inc.–Region Americas (1999)
- Dana Corporation–Spicer Driveshaft Division (now Torque Traction Technologies, Inc.) (2000)
- KARLEE Company (2000)
- Clarke American Checks, Inc. (2001)
- Motorola, Inc. Commercial, Government and Industrial Solutions Sector (2002)
- Medrad, Inc. (2003)
- The Bama Companies, Inc. (2004)
- Sunny Fresh Foods, Inc. (2005)
- Cargill Corn Milling North America (2008)

Small Business
- Globe Metallurgical, Inc. (1988)
- Wallace Co., Inc. (1990)
- Marlow Industries (1991)
- Granite Rock Co. (1992)
- Ames Rubber Corp. (1993)
- Wainwright Industries, Inc. (1994)
- Custom Research, Inc. (1996)
- Trident Precision Manufacturing, Inc. (1996)
- Texas Nameplate Company, Inc. (1998)
- Sunny Fresh Foods (1999)
- Los Alamos National Bank (2000)
- Stoner, Inc. (2003)
- Texas Nameplate Company, Inc. (2004)
- Park Place Lexus (2005)
- MESA Products, Inc. (2006)
- PRO-TEC Coating Company (2007)

Service
- Federal Express (FedEx) (1990)
- AT&T Universal Card Services (now part of Citigroup) (1992)

continued

Table 3.2 Malcolm Baldrige Award Recipients (*Continued*)

- The Ritz-Carlton Hotel Co. (now part of Marriott International) (1992)
- AT&T Consumer Communication Services (now the Consumer Markets Division of AT&T) (1994)
- Verizon Information Services (formerly GTE Directories, Inc.) (1994)
- Dana Commercial Credit Corp. (1996)
- Merrill Lynch Credit Corp. (1997)
- Xerox Business Services (1997)
- BI (1999)
- The Ritz-Carlton Hotel Company, L.L.C. (1999)
- Operations Management International, Inc. (2000)
- Pal's Sudden Service (2001)
- Branch-Smith Printing Division (2002)
- Boeing Aerospace Support (2003)
- Caterpillar Financial Services (2003)
- DynMcDermott Petroleum Operations (2005)
- Premier Inc. (2006)

Education
- Chugach School District (2001)
- Pearl River School District (2001)
- University of Wisconsin–Stout (2001)
- Community Consolidated School District #15, Palatine, IL (2003)
- Robert W. Monfort College of Business (2004)
- Richland College (2005)
- Jenks Public Schools (2005)
- Iredell-Statesville Schools (2008)

Health Care
- SSM Health Care (2002)
- Baptist Hospital, Inc., Pensacola, FL (2003)
- Saint Luke's Hospital of Kansas City (2003)
- Robert Wood Johnson University Hospital Hamilton (2004)
- Bronson Methodist Hospital (2005)
- North Mississippi Medical Center (2006)
- Mercy Health System (2007)
- Sharp HealthCare (2007)
- Poudre Valley Health System (2008)

Nonprofit
- City of Coral Springs (2007)
- U.S. Army Armament Research, Development and Engineering Center (2007)

The Criteria for Performance Excellence

The award examination is based upon a rigorous set of criteria, called the Criteria for Performance Excellence, designed to encourage companies to enhance their competitiveness through an aligned approach to organizational performance management that results in:

1. Delivery of ever-improving value to customers, resulting in improved marketplace success;
2. Improvement of overall company performance and capabilities; and
3. Organizational and personal learning.

The criteria consist of a hierarchical set of categories, items, and areas to address. The seven categories are as follows:

1. *Leadership*: This category examines how an organization's senior leaders personal actions guide and sustain the organization. Also examined are an organization's governance system and how the organization fulfills its ethical, legal, and societal responsibilities, and supports its key communities.
2. *Strategic Planning*: This category examines how an organization develops strategic objectives and action plans. Also examined is how the chosen objectives and plans are deployed and changed if circumstances require, and how progress is measured.
3. *Customer Focus*: This category examines how an organization engages its customers for long-term marketplace success and builds a customer-focused culture. Also examined is how the organization listens to the voice of its customers and uses this information to improve and identify opportunities for innovation.
4. *Measurement, Analysis, and Knowledge Management*: This category examines how an organization selects, gathers, analyzes, manages, and improves its data, information, and knowledge assets, and how it manages its information technology. Also examined is how the organization reviews and uses reviews to improve its performance.
5. *Workforce Focus:* This category examines how an organization engages, manages, and develops its workforce to utilize its full potential in alignment with the organization's overall mission, strategy, and action plans. Also examined is the organization's ability to assess workforce capability and capacity needs and to build a workforce environment conducive to high performance.
6. *Process Management:* This category examines how an organization designs its work systems, and how it designs, manages, and improves its key processes for implementing those work systems to deliver customer value and achieve organizational success and sustainability. It also examines an organization's readiness for emergencies.
7. *Results:* This category examines an organization's performance and improvement in key business areas—product outcomes, customer-focused outcomes, financial and market outcomes, workforce-focused outcomes, process-effectiveness outcomes, and leadership outcomes. Performance levels are examined relative to those of competitors and other organizations providing similar products and services.

BONUS MATERIALS

The 2009–10 criteria can be found in the Baldrige Materials folder on the Premium website, and they will be used in various cases and exercises. We encourage you to read the entire document for clarifying notes and explanations. Also, slightly different versions of the criteria are written for education and health care, primarily to conform to unique language and practices in these sectors. Because the criteria are updated each year, we suggest that you obtain the latest version. A single free copy of the criteria can be obtained from the National Institute of Standards and Technology. Write to the Baldrige National Quality Program, National Institute of Standards and Technology (NIST), Administration Building, Room A600, 100 Bureau Drive, Stop 1020, Gaithersburg, MD 20899-1020; call 301-975-2036; send a fax to 301-948-3716; e-mail nqp@nist.gov; or download the criteria from the website http://www.baldrige.nist.gov.

Figure 3.5 Baldrige Criteria Framework

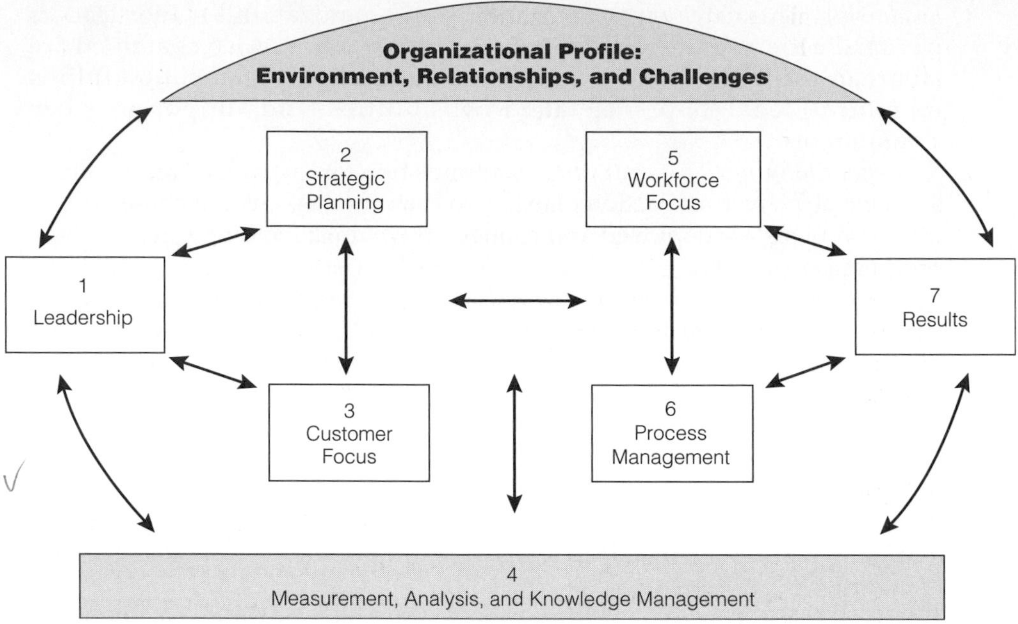

The seven categories form an integrated management system as illustrated in Figure 3.5. The umbrella over the seven categories reflect the fact that organizations must understand its competitive environment to drive their strategy and action plans as a basis for all key decisions. Leadership, Strategic Planning, and Customer Focus represent the "leadership triad," and suggest the importance of integrating these three functions. Workforce Focus and Process Management represent how the work in an organization is accomplished and leads to Business Results. These functions are linked to the leadership triad. Finally, Measurement, Analysis, and Knowledge Management support the entire framework by providing the foundation for a fact-based system for improvement.

Each category consists of several items (numbered 1.1, 1.2, 2.1, etc.) that focus on major requirements on which businesses should focus. Each item, in turn, consists of a small number of areas to address (e.g., 6.1a, 6.1b) that seek specific information on approaches used to ensure and improve competitive performance, the deployment of these approaches, or results obtained from such deployment.

For example, the Leadership category consists of two examination items, with a total of five areas to address:

1.1 Senior Leadership
  a. Vision, Values, and Mission
  b. Communication and Organizational Performance

1.2 Governance and Social Responsibilities
  a. Organizational Governance
  b. Legal and Ethical Behavior
  c. Societal Responsibilities and Support of Key Communities

The Vision, Values, and Mission area to address asks organizations to answer the following questions:

1. How do senior leaders set organizational vision and values? How do senior leaders deploy your organization's vision and values through your leadership system, to the workforce, to key suppliers and partners, and to customers and other stakeholders, as appropriate? How do senior leaders' personal actions reflect a commitment to the organization's values?
2. How do senior leaders promote an environment that fosters, requires, and results in legal and ethical behavior?
3. How do senior leaders create a sustainable organization? How do senior leaders create an environment for organizational performance improvement, the accomplishment of your mission and strategic objectives, innovation, competitive, or role-model performance leadership, and organizational agility? How do they create an environment for organizational and workforce learning? How do they develop and enhance their personal leadership skills? How do they personally participate in succession planning and the development of future organizational leaders?

To illustrate how an organization might address these questions, consider some of the information for the Leadership category provided by The Ritz-Carlton Hotel Company, L.L.C. (see the Quality in Practice in Chapter 2 for basic information about the company) in its 1992 and 1999 applications (with a caveat that the scope of the Leadership criteria changed substantially over the years). We will focus on the issues raised in question (1) above.

When Horst Schulze became president in 1983, he and his leadership team personally took charge of managing for quality because they realized that managing for quality could not be delegated. They personally established the Gold Standards, which are the foundation of The Ritz-Carlton quality philosophy. The Gold Standards, in their simplicity, represent an easy-to-understand definition of service quality, and are aggressively communicated and internalized at all levels of the organization.

The constant and continuous reinforcement techniques of the Gold Standards, led by senior leaders, include lectures at new employee orientation, developmental training, daily line-up meetings, administration of both positive and negative reinforcement, mission statements displayed, distribution of Credo cards, the Credo as first topic of internal meetings, and peer pressure. As a result, employees have an exceptional understanding and devotion to the company's vision, values, quality goals, and methods.

Since 1984, all members of senior leadership have personally ensured that each new hotel's goods and services are characteristic of The Ritz-Carlton on opening day. An important aspect of this quality practice takes place during the concentrated and intense "seven-day countdown" when senior leaders work side by side with new employees using a combination of hands-on behavior modeling and reinforcement. During these formative sessions, which all new employees must attend, the president and COO personally interacts with every new employee, both individually and in a group setting. He personally creates the employee-guest interface image and facilitates each department's first vision statement. Throughout the entire process, the senior leaders monitor work areas for "start-up," instill Gold Standards, model the company's relationship management, insist upon 100 percent compliance to customers' requirements, and recognize outstanding achievement.

Senior leaders set organizational vision and values through seven specific decisions:

10-Year Vision: To be the premier Worldwide Provider of Luxury Travel and Hospitality Products and Services
5-Year Mission: Product and Profit Dominance
3-Year Objectives: The Vital Few Objectives
1-Year Tactics: Key Production and Business Processes
Strategy: Customer and Market Focus Strategy with Action Plans
Methods: TQM—Application of Quality Sciences; Malcolm Baldrige National Quality Award Criteria; The GreenBook, 2nd Edition (the company's handbook of quality processes and tools)
Foundation: Values and Philosophy, The Gold Standards, Credo; Motto, Three Steps of Service, Service Value, Employee Promise

Leadership effectiveness is evaluated on key questions of a semiannual employee satisfaction survey and through audits on public responsibility. Gaps in leadership effectiveness are addressed with development/training plans and extensive use of developmental job assignments.

In the Baldrige criteria, areas to address that request information on approach or deployment begin with the word *how*. This wording means that the organization should be able to describe methods, measures and evaluation, learning, and improvement factors in explaining their approach for meeting the criteria requirements. It also implies that these approaches are performed on a regular basis and embedded in the practices of the organization, and are not simply ad hoc ways of doing business.

The Baldrige criteria define both an integrated infrastructure and a set of fundamental practices for a high-performance management system.

One thing the criteria do not do is prescribe specific quality tools, techniques, technologies, systems, or starting points, and are not associated with any one quality philosophy. Companies are encouraged to develop and demonstrate creative, adaptive, and flexible approaches to meeting basic requirements. Many innovative approaches have been developed by Baldrige recipients and are now commonly used by many other companies. We will see many examples of these in subsequent chapters. The Bonus Materials folder for this chapter on the Premium website provides a detailed description of the Baldrige Award application review and scoring process.

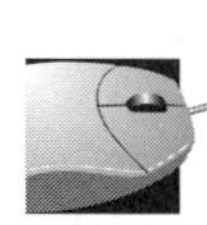
BONUS MATERIALS

The Baldrige criteria are based on a set of key principles, called the **Core Values and Concepts**:

- Visionary Leadership
- Customer-Driven Excellence
- Organizational and Personal Learning
- Valuing Workforce Members and Partners
- Agility
- Focus on the Future
- Managing for Innovation
- Management by Fact
- Societal Responsibility
- Focus on Results and Creating Value
- Systems Perspective

(They are described in detail in the Baldrige Criteria.) These values are embedded throughout the Criteria for Performance Excellence and in essence, provide a description of a culture of performance excellence. For example, if you review the criteria for Item 1.1, Senior Leadership, you can easily find direct or implied references to almost all of these values. The Core Values and Concepts represent the underlying philosophy of the criteria, similar to the principles of TQM we discussed in Chapter 1.

Criteria Evolution

As the important management practices of any organization should be, the award criteria are evaluated and improved each year. Over the years, the criteria have been streamlined and simplified to make them more easily understood and useful to organizations of all types and sizes, and its content revised to reflect the most relevant ate business practices and contemporary organizational thinking. For example, the initial set of criteria in 1988 had 62 items with 278 areas to address. Refinements over the next decade made the criteria more generic and user-friendly, and by 1997, resulted in 20 items and 30 areas to address. In 1999, the criteria were reworded in a question format that managers can easily understand. Most significantly, the word "quality" was judiciously dropped in the mid-1990s. For example, prior to 1994, the Strategic Planning category was titled "Strategic Quality Planning." The change to "Strategic Planning" signifies that quality should be a part of an organization's overall business planning, not a separate activity. Throughout the document, the term *performance* has been substituted for *quality* as a conscious attempt to recognize that the principles of total quality are the foundation for a company's entire management system, not just the quality system.

To this end, the most significant changes in the criteria reflect the maturity of business practices and total quality approaches. The criteria evolved from an initial emphasis on product and service quality assurance to a broad focus on performance excellence in a global marketplace. In addition, criteria updates are designed to address emerging and relevant issues facing business. In 2003, for example, the criteria strengthened its emphasis on organizational governance and ethics in the wake of the Enron, WorldCom, and Arthur Andersen scandals that occurred the year before. In 2005, Baldrige introduced the concept of **sustainability**—which refers to an organization's ability to address current business needs and to have the agility and strategic management to prepare successfully for the future, and to prepare for real-time or short-term emergencies—into the criteria. Recently, concepts of workforce and customer engagement have been integrated within the criteria.

Using the Baldrige Criteria

The Baldrige Award criteria form a model for business excellence in any organization—manufacturing, service, or not-for-profit; large or small; public or private. The former Texas Instruments Defense Systems and Electronics Group (now part of Raytheon), for example, used the criteria to provide focus and coherence to the activities across the corporation.[13] The company was able to tackle a part of total quality that previously had been unreachable: implementing quality efforts in staff, support, and nonmanufacturing areas. TI asked every business unit to prepare a mock award application as a way of measuring its progress. This task represented a radical change for some operations because, until that time, most staff functions were not required to measure their processes or their results. The Defense Systems & Electronics Group's self-assessment revealed that they were a long way from applying for and winning the Baldrige Award. But the group aggressively adopted the criteria as a blueprint for improving its business. Many executives did not believe that the criteria could be applied to defense contractors, but TI's experience clearly showed that it could.

Many other types of organizations have used the criteria. For example, although the legal profession in general has not adopted quality management practices, the Trial Division of Nationwide Insurance, which operates 56 law offices in 20 states, uses the Baldrige model as a key component of its business plan. Senior leaders introduced it to all of the company's managing trial attorneys and encouraged individual offices to apply for local or state Baldrige-based awards.[14] Many school districts now use the criteria, some states even mandate Baldrige assessment, and traditional accreditation bodies now allow Baldrige as an alternative means of preparing for accreditation. One large Chicago-area hospital applied for the Baldrige-based Lincoln Award for Excellence and prepared for its accreditation visit by JCAHO at the same time, recognizing the synergy and overlap of Baldrige principles and JCAHO standards.

Many small businesses (defined as those with 500 or fewer employees) believe that the Baldrige criteria are too difficult to apply to their organizations because they cannot afford to implement the same types of practices as large companies. This assumption is simply not true, as the Quality Profile on Texas Nameplate at the beginning of this chapter illustrates. For example, the ability to obtain customer and market knowledge through independent third party surveys, extensive interviews, and focus groups, which are common practices among large companies, may be limited by the resources of a small business. What is important, however, is whether the company is using appropriate mechanisms to gather information and use it to improve customer focus and satisfaction. Similarly, large corporations frequently have sophisticated computer/information systems for data management, while small businesses may perform data and information management with a combination of manual methods and personal computers. Also, systems for employee involvement and process management may rely heavily on informal verbal communication and less on formal written documentation. Thus, the size or nature of a business does not affect the appropriateness of the criteria, but rather the context in which the criteria are applied.

Approaches that organizations use to address the Baldrige criteria requirements need not be formal or complex, and can easily be implemented by small businesses.

Organizations use the Baldrige Criteria in different ways—for self-assessment or internal recognition programs, even if they do not intend to apply for the award. The benefits of using the criteria for self-assessment include accelerating improvement efforts, energizing employees, and learning from feedback—particularly if external examiners are involved. For instance, Honeywell, Inc., uses it as a companywide framework for understanding, evaluating, and improving their business. Honeywell's mandate is to use the model for managing the business and engaging senior management in an annual assessment process. This framework is used by general managers to exchange information, ask for help, and learn from each other.[15] Even the U.S. Postal Service decided to use the Baldrige Criteria as a basis to reestablish a quality system by identifying the areas that need the most improvement and providing a baseline to track progress. Using the award criteria as a self-assessment tool provides an objective framework, sets a high standard, and compares units that have different systems or organizations.

The approaches used for self-assessment vary. They may include simple questionnaires developed from the criteria, for which answers are compiled and used as a basis for an improvement plan; facilitated assessments in which key business leaders gather together to examine their organization against the criteria; and full written "applications" that are evaluated by trained internal or external examiners.[16] Assessments are often linked to the organization's strategic planning process, which serves as a means of implementing the opportunities for improvement that are identified through the process. The Baldrige Materials folder on the Premium website contains a brochure entitled "Why Baldrige?" that provides a simple overview of why the Baldrige approach is valuable to any organization.

BONUS MATERIALS

Impacts of the Baldrige Program

An economic evaluation study of the Baldrige program by the U.S. Department of Commerce concluded that a conservative estimate of the present value of the net social benefits associated with the program was $24.65 billion in constant 2000 dollars. This return was achieved by a $119 million investment in total social costs associated with the program, a 207:1 ratio. More importantly, the program changed the way in which many organizations around the world manage their operations, and helped significantly to bring the principles of TQ into the daily culture of these organizations. The true benefactors are the customers and other stakeholders who received better products and services.

Many U.S. states have developed award programs similar to the Baldrige Award (*Quality Digest* magazine publishes an annual directory of state quality award programs; see www.qualitydigest.com). State award programs generally are designed to promote an awareness of productivity and quality, foster an information exchange, encourage firms to adopt quality and productivity improvement strategies, recognize firms that have instituted successful strategies, provide role models for other businesses in the state, encourage new industry to locate in the state, and establish a quality-of-life culture that will benefit all residents of the state.[17] Each state is unique, however, and thus the specific objectives will vary. For instance, the primary objectives of Minnesota's quality award are to encourage all Minnesota organizations to examine their current state of quality and to become more involved in the movement toward continuous quality improvement, as well as to recognize outstanding quality achievements in the state. Missouri, on the other hand, has as its objectives to educate all Missourians in quality improvement, to foster the pursuit of quality in all aspects of Missouri life, and to recognize quality leadership. Other states, such as Tennessee and Ohio, use their award programs to provide developmental advice to organizations just starting on their quality journey. Information and links to state award programs can be found at the Alliance for Performance Excellence website, http://www.baldrigepe.org/alliance/. Jim Collins (author of *Good to Great: Why Some Companies Make the Leap . . . and Others Don't*) endorsed Baldrige with the following statement: "I see the Baldrige process as a powerful set of mechanisms for disciplined people engaged in disciplined thought and taking disciplined action to create great organizations that produce exceptional results."

Baldrige and Deming

It is no secret that W. Edwards Deming was not an advocate of the Baldrige Award.[18] (Joseph Juran, however, was highly influential in its development.) The competitive nature of the award is fundamentally at odds with Deming's teachings. However, many of Deming's principles are reflected directly or in spirit within the criteria.

BONUS MATERIALS

In fact, Zytec (now a part of Artesyn Technologies), which implemented its total quality system around Deming's 14 Points, received a Baldrige Award. We provide a discussion of how the Baldrige Criteria support each of Deming's 14 Points in the Bonus Materials folder for this chapter on the Premium website.

INTERNATIONAL QUALITY AWARD PROGRAMS

As we noted earlier, the Baldrige Award was inspired by Japan's Deming Prize, and the Baldrige Program has inspired many other national quality awards. We briefly discuss the Deming Prize and other award programs inspired by Baldrige here.

The Deming Prize

The Deming Application Prize was instituted in 1951 by the Union of Japanese Scientists and Engineers (JUSE) in recognition and appreciation of W. Edwards Deming's achievements in statistical quality control and his friendship with the Japanese people. The Deming Prize has three principal categories:

- The Deming Prize for Individuals – Given to those who have made outstanding contributions to the study of TQM or statistical methods used for TQM, or those who have made outstanding contributions in the dissemination of TQM.
- The Deming Application Prize – Given to organizations or divisions of organizations that have achieved distinctive performance improvement through the application of TQM in a designated year.
- The Quality Control Award for Operations Business Units – Given to operations business units of an organization that have achieved distinctive performance improvement through the application of quality control/management in the pursuit of TQM in a designated year According to JUSE,

> *"The Deming Prize examination does not require applicants to conform to a model provided by the Deming Prize Committee. Rather, the applicants are expected to understand their current situation, establish their own themes and objectives and improve and transform themselves company-wide. Not only the results achieved and the processes used, but also the effectiveness expected in the future are subjects for the examination. To the best of their abilities, the examiners evaluate whether or not the themes established by the applicants were commensurate to their situation; whether or not their activities were suitable to their circumstance and whether or not their activities are likely to achieve their higher objectives in the future.*
>
> *The Deming Prize Committee views the examination process as an opportunity for "mutual-development," rather than "examination." While in realty the applicants still receive the examination by a third party, the examiners' approach to evaluation and judgment is comprehensive. Every factor such as the applicants' attitude toward executing Total Quality Management (TQM), their implementation status and the resulting effects are taken into overall consideration. In other words, the Deming Prize Committee does not specify what issues the applicants must address, rather the applicants themselves are responsible for identifying and addressing such issues, thus, this process allows quality methodologies to be further developed."*

The Deming Prize is awarded to all companies that meet a prescribed standard. However, the small number of awards given each year is an indication of the difficulty of achieving the standard. The objectives are to ensure that a company has so thoroughly deployed a quality process that it will continue to improve long after a prize is awarded. The application process has no "losers." For companies that do not qualify, the examination process is automatically extended up to two times over three years. Deming Prize winners are also eligible for the Japan Quality Medal, which was established to encourage winners to continue practicing and enhancing their quality efforts.

The judging criteria for the Deming Prize establish a framework for TQ system. The criteria consist of a checklist of 6 categories:

1. Management policies and their deployment regarding quality management
2. New product development and/or work process innovation
3. Maintenance and improvement of product and operational qualities
4. Establishment of systems for managing quality, quantity, delivery, costs, safety, environment, etc.
5. Collection and analysis of quality information and utilization of information technology
6. Human resources development

Categories 2, 3, and 4 are considered the "core quality system" and are supported by the others. Each is reviewed and scored based on effectiveness to achieve objectives, consistency throughout the organization, continuity from mid- and long-term viewpoints, and thoroughness of implementation. The actual examination process is more complex than this, and we refer the reader to the Deming Prize website at http://www.juse.or.jp/e/index.html for further details.

European Quality Award

In October 1991, the European Foundation for Quality Management (EFQM) in partnership with the European Commission and the European Organization for Quality announced the creation of the European Quality Award (now called the European Excellence Award). EFQM was, and remains, a nonprofit organization. The award was designed to increase awareness throughout the European Community, and businesses in particular, of the growing importance of quality to their competitiveness in the increasingly global market and to their standards of life.

Figure 3.6 shows the integrated management framework for the European Excellence Award.[19] The model, which recognizes there are many approaches to achieving sustainable excellence in all aspects of performance, is based on the following premise: *Excellent results with respect to Performance, Customers, People and Society are achieved through Leadership driving Policy and Strategy, that is delivered through People, Partnerships and Resources, and Processes*. Results are driven by "Enablers" the means by which an organization approaches its business responsibilities, and a foundation of innovation and learning. The categories are roughly equivalent to those in Baldrige. However, the results criteria of people satisfaction, customer satisfaction, impact on society, and business results are somewhat different.[20] The impact on society results category focuses on the perceptions of the company by the community at large and the company's approach to the quality of life, the environment, and the preservation of global resources. The European Excellence Award criteria place greater emphasis on this category than is placed on the public responsibility item in the Baldrige Award criteria.

Like the Baldrige Core Values and Concepts, the EFQM framework is based on a set of "Fundamental Concepts of Excellence":

Figure 3.6 European Excellence Award Framework

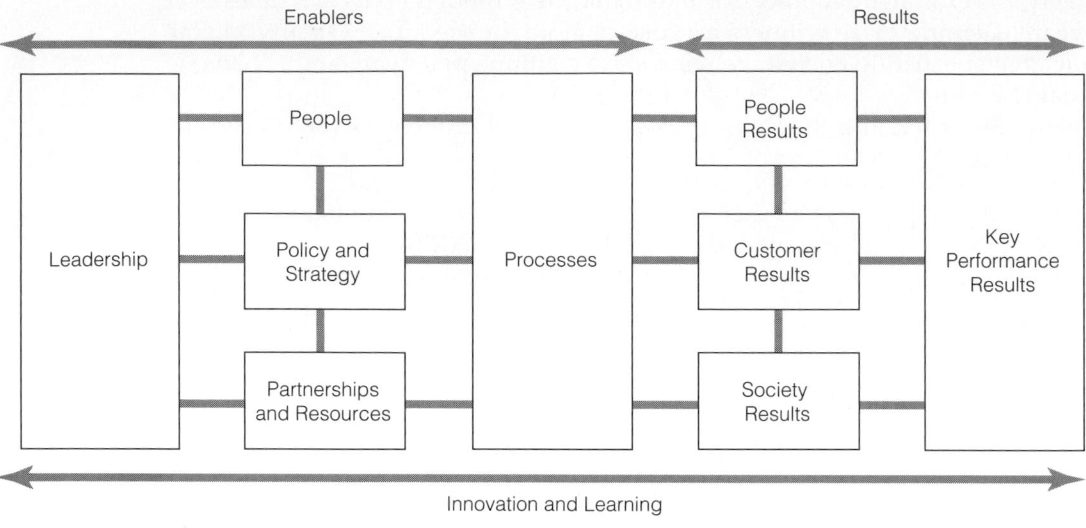

Source: Used with permission of EFQM. © EFQM, 1999. The EFQM Excellence Model is a registered trademark. Reprinted with permission.

Results Orientation
Excellence is achieving results that delight all the organization's stakeholders.

Customer Focus
Excellence is creating sustainable customer value.

Leadership and Constancy of Purpose
Excellence is visionary and inspirational leadership, coupled with constancy of purpose.

Management by Processes and Facts
Excellence is managing the organization through a set of interdependent and interrelated systems, processes and facts.

People Development and Involvement
Excellence is maximizing the contribution of employees through their development and involvement.

Continuous Learning, Innovation, and Improvement
Excellence is challenging the status quo and effecting change by utilizing learning to create innovation and improvement opportunities.

Partnership Development
Excellence is developing and maintaining value-adding partnerships.

Corporate Social Responsibility
Excellence is exceeding the minimum regulatory framework in which the organization operates and to strive to understand and respond to the expectations of their stakeholders in society.

The EFQM notes that if these Concepts are not fully understood and accepted, then progress with adopting the Excellence model will be difficult and potentially meaningless.

EFQM has three recognition levels. The EFQM Excellence Award is the highest form of recognition, similar to Baldrige. Previous Award winners include BMW, TNT Express, Yell, Bosch, Nokia, Volvo, as well as smaller progressive organizations, such as St Mary's College in Northern Ireland, Maxi Coco-Mat in Greece, and Schindlerhof Hotel in Germany. Two additional recognition levels have been added: (1) Recognized for Excellence, designed for organizations that are well along the journey to excellence, and (2) Committed to Excellence, for organizations that are at the beginning of the journey. Through the assessment process, these award levels provide feedback for further improvement.

Canadian Awards for Business Excellence

Canada's National Quality Institute (NQI) (http://www.nqi.ca) recognizes Canada's foremost achievers of excellence through the prestigious Canada Awards for Excellence. NQI is a nonprofit organization designed to stimulate and support quality-driven innovation within all Canadian enterprises and institutions, including business, government, education, and health care. The Canadian Awards for Business Excellence quality criteria are similar in structure to the Baldrige Award criteria, with some key differences. Separate, but similar, criteria are used for business organizations, public sector organizations, and "healthy workplace" organizations. The major categories and items within each category are:

1. *Leadership:* Strategic direction, leadership involvement, and outcomes
2. *Customer Focus*: Voice of the customer, management of customer relationships, measurement, and outcomes
3. *Planning for Improvement:* Development and content of improvement plan, assessment, and outcomes
4. *People Focus:* Human resource planning, participatory environment, continuous learning environment, employee satisfaction, and outcomes
5. *Process Optimization:* Process definition, process control, process improvement, and outcomes
6. *Supplier Focus:* Partnering and outcomes

These categories seek similar information as the Baldrige Award criteria. For example, the People Focus category examines the development of human resource planning and implementation and operation of a strategy for achieving excellence through people. It also examines the organization's efforts to foster and support an environment that encourages and enables people to reach their full potential. Recent recipients of Canada's top quality award include Delta Hotels Canada, Statistics Canada, The College of Physicians & Surgeons of Nova Scotia, College of Registered Nurses of Nova Scotia, Real Estate Board of Greater Vancouver, Toronto Transit Commission—Information Technology Services Department, and Ricoh Canada Inc.

Australian Business Excellence Award

The Australian Quality Awards (now called the Australian Business Awards) were developed independently from the MBNQA in 1988. The Awards were previously administered by the Australian Quality Awards Foundation, a subsidiary of the Australian Quality Council, a private, for-profit organization. In 2002, Standards Australia International [SAI] formally acquired a range of products and services previously owned by the Australian Quality Council [AQC]. SAI's Professional Services Division became the new home of the AQC and in recognition of the importance of business excellence to SAI, the division has been renamed Business Excellence Australia.

The Australian Business Excellence Prize is the pre-eminent award available for businesses in Australia. Only two organizations have achieved this level of excellence since the Awards' inception in 1988. In addition to the Australian Business Excellence Prize, four levels of awards are given:

1. *The Foundation in Business Excellence Level*—provides encouragement recognition for progress toward business excellence."
2. *The Bronze Award Level*—Bronze Award recipients will demonstrate Approach and Deployment that are well defined, planned, subject to review and show evidence of improvement over time.
3. *The Silver Award Level*—Organizations at this level should be able to demonstrate not only performance against the Framework at Bronze level, but also a philosophy of management that reflects the principles that underpin it and other Frameworks around the globe.
4. *The Gold Award Level*—Organizations at this level should meet Silver recognition plus be able to demonstrate superior performance in at least 5 of the Categories in the Framework and also have scored at least 50 percent in each Item.

The program also confers The Excellence Medal to the highest scoring applicant organization, and Category Awards to organizations that have achieved the highest evaluation score for that Category, above the benchmark set for a given year.

The Business Excellence Award Framework is based on eight Principles: leadership, customers, systems thinking, people, information and knowledge, corporate and social responsibility, and sustainable results. The assessment criteria address leadership, strategy and planning, information and knowledge, people, customer focus, process management, improvement and innovation, and success and sustainability within the framework shown in Figure 3.7. In this model, leadership and customer and market focus are the drivers of the management system and

Figure 3.7 Australia Business Excellence Award Framework

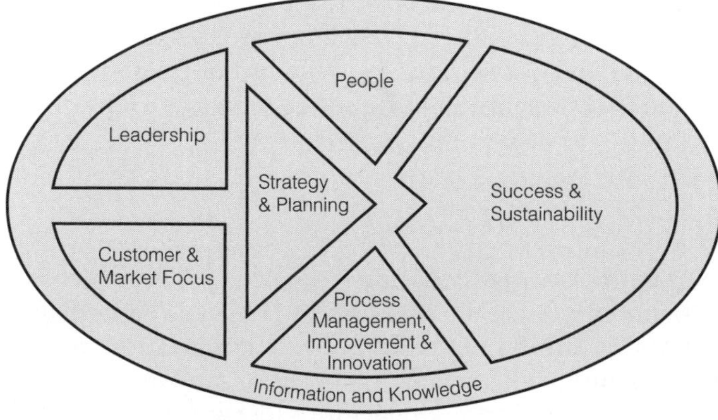

Source: Adapted from www.businessexcellenceaustralia.com/au.

enablers of performance. Strategy and planning, information and knowledge, and people are the key internal components of the management system. Quality of process management, improvement, and innovation are focused on how work is done to achieve the required results and obtain improvement. Success and sustainability is the outcome of the management system—a results category. As with Baldrige, the framework emphasizes the holistic and interconnected nature of the management process. The criteria are benchmarked with the Baldrige criteria and the European Business Excellence Model. One of the distinctive aspects of Australia's program is solid union support.

Quality Awards in China

In 2001, the China Association for Quality (CAQ) introduced the National Quality Award, which it recently renamed the Performance Excellence Award. To facilitate the emerging economy of China, the Chinese government has issued new quality standards that became effective on January 1, 2005, which are designed to encourage China's thriving business sector to strive for better quality.[21] The award criteria are based on components of the Malcolm Baldrige National Quality Award, and are geared toward China's unique business environment—especially in improving business credibility, brand-building strategy and sustainable development. The Chinese government used Representatives of the Shanghai Academy of Quality Management, who helped write the country's new quality standard, and invited Baldrige Award winners to Shanghai to report on their processes. At the same time, they held many seminars to study Baldrige criteria, learning to adapt those concepts to Chinese quality policy. Seventeen businesses have been awarded the Chinese National Quality Award during the first three years. Among them, Baosteel and Shanghai Dazhong Taxi won the World Class Organization Award and the Asia–Pacific Quality Award, in 2002 and 2004, respectively.

In 2004, Shenzhen became the first city to launch a local quality award, called the Mayor's Cup Quality Award. It is operated by the Shenzhen Bureau of Quality and Technical Supervision. The vice mayor leads an evaluation committee of local experts, which uses many of the Baldrige criteria, including international best practices, social factors, and governmental strategic initiatives issued by Shenzhen government leaders.

At the end of 2006, more than 55 organizations had applied for the award, and six firms had won, including Huawei in 2004, one of the first winners (see the Quality in Practice feature in Chapter 1). The 3 million RMB ($387,000 U.S.) prize is the highest among quality awards in China and has encouraged many organizations to participate and share best practices. Other cities and provinces, including Shanghai, have now set up local governmental quality awards to promote quality management systems and share experiences in various industries. There are over 200 locally applied district awards.[22]

China has also begun to embrace Six Sigma (described later in this chapter).[23] The Shanghai Association for Quality created the Six Sigma Excellent Organization Award in 2004 to recognize Chinese businesses for innovative and successful Six Sigma implementations. The first winners were Bao Shan Iron and Steel Co. Ltd., Shanghai Airlines Co. Ltd., Shanghai Turbine Generator Co. Ltd., Shanghai Jinting Automobile Harness Ltd., Shanghai Viva Ecology Electronics Technology Co. Ltd., Mettler-Toledo Instruments Co. Ltd. (Shanghai), Mettler-Toledo Instruments Weighing Equipment System Co. Ltd. (Changhzhou), and Ningbo Baoxin Stainless Steel Co. Ltd. Many enterprises report that the methodology solved problems they once thought were unsolvable. For example, winning company Baosteel decreased its oil consumption by a third after implementing Six Sigma.

Baldrige and National Culture

It is interesting to observe that although many countries substantially adopt the Baldrige criteria, some of them, such as the European Quality Award framework or the Chinese National Quality Award Criteria, use components of the Baldrige criteria, but customize them to reflect their unique business environment. International cultural differences can help to understand and explain these differences. A recent study found support for the notion that the Baldrige award is better suited with some national cultures than with others.[24] Receptiveness to change differs greatly among cultures, suggesting the need for countries to adapt their quality award programs to local conditions to ensure effectively implementing them. Perhaps surprisingly, Baldrige is a better fit to the national culture of Japan than it is to the United States. Some of the reasons for this are that the Baldrige framework was initially influenced heavily by Japanese quality management practices, and that changes to the criteria over the years are focused on *changing* U.S. management culture, not reflecting its current practice. These results provide even more validation of Deming's observation related to the Theory of Knowledge, that best practices cannot be copied blindly, but must be understood and adapted intelligently. This is an important lesson for managing in today's global environment.

ISO 9000:2000

As quality became a major focus of businesses throughout the world, various organizations developed standards and guidelines. Terms such as quality management, quality control, quality system, and quality assurance acquired different, sometimes conflicting meanings from country to country, within a country, and even within an industry.[25] When the Treaty on European Union, was signed at Maastricht, Germany, in 1992, free trade between member countries became the norm, and quality became a key strategic objective. To standardize quality requirements for European countries within the Common Market and those wishing to do business with those countries, a specialized agency for standardization, the International Organization for Standardization (IOS), founded in 1946 and composed of representatives from the national standards bodies of 91 nations, adopted a series of written quality standards in 1987. They were revised in 1994, and again (significantly) in 2000. The most recent version is called the **ISO 9000:2000** family of standards. (The core document of this family, ISO 9001, had a minor revision in 2008 as we discuss later.)

ISO 9000 defines quality system standards, *based on the premise that certain generic characteristics of management practices can be standardized, and that a well-designed, well-implemented, and carefully managed quality system provides confidence that the outputs will meet customer expectations and requirements.*

The IOS took a unique approach in adopting the "ISO" prefix in naming the standards. *ISO* is a scientific term for equal (as in isotherm lines on a weather map, which show equal temperatures). Thus, organizations certified under the ISO 9000 standard are assured to have quality equal to their peers. The standards have been adopted in the United States by the American National Standards Institute (ANSI) with the endorsement and cooperation of the American Society for Quality (ASQ). The standards are recognized by about 100 countries, including Japan.

The standards were created to meet five objectives:

1. Achieve, maintain, and seek to continuously improve product quality (including services) in relationship to requirements.
2. Improve the quality of operations to continually meet customers' and stakeholders' stated and implied needs.
3. Provide confidence to internal management and other employees that quality requirements are being fulfilled and that improvement is taking place.
4. Provide confidence to customers and other stakeholders that quality requirements are being achieved in the delivered product.
5. Provide confidence that quality system requirements are fulfilled.

The standards prescribe documentation for all processes affecting quality and suggest that compliance through auditing leads to continuous improvement. In some foreign markets, companies will not buy from suppliers who are not certified to the standards. For example, many products sold in Europe, such as telecommunication terminal equipment, medical devices, gas appliances, toys, and construction products require product certifications to assure safety. Often, ISO certification is necessary to obtain product certification. Thus, meeting these standards is becoming a requirement for international competitiveness.

Structure of the ISO 9000:2000 Standards

The ISO 9000:2000 standards focus on developing, documenting, and implementing procedures to ensure consistency of operations and performance in production and service delivery processes, with the aim of continual improvement, and supported by fundamental principles of total quality. The standards consist of three documents:

1. *ISO 9000—Fundamentals and vocabulary*. This document provides fundamental background information and establishes definitions of key terms used in the standards.
2. *ISO 9001—Requirements*. This document provides the specific requirements for a quality management system, to which users must conform in order to obtain third-party certification. An example of one of the requirements is "The supplier's management with executive responsibility shall define and document its policy for quality, including objectives for quality and commitment to quality. The quality policy shall be relevant to the supplier's organizational goals and the expectations and needs of its customers. The supplier shall ensure that this policy is understood, implemented, and maintained at all levels of the organization." Thus, the requirements state precisely what the organization needs to do. The requirements are organized into four major sections: Management Responsibility; Resource Management; Product Realization; and Measurement, Analysis, and Improvement.[26]
3. *ISO 9004—Guidelines for Performance Improvements*. This document provides guidelines to assist organizations in improving their quality management systems beyond the minimum requirements in ISO 9001, but does not prescribe any requirements that must be followed.

The requirements provide a structure for a basic quality assurance system. Management Responsibility addresses what top management must do to ensure an effective quality system, such as promoting the importance of quality throughout the organization, developing and implementing the quality management system, identifying and meeting customer requirements, defining an organizational quality policy and quality objectives, clearly defining responsibilities for quality, and controlling documents and records. Resource Management ensures that an organization provides sufficient people, facilities, and training resources. Product Realization refers to controlling the production/service process from receipt of an order or quote through design, materials procurement, manufacturing or service delivery, distribution, and subsequent field service. Measurement, Analysis, and Improvement focuses on control procedures for assuring quality in products and processes, analysis of quality-related data, and correction, prevention, and improvement planning activities.

In 2008, an amendment to the ISO 9001 standards was released, designed to clarify some of the language and concepts, and improve compatibility with ISO 14001:2004, the popular environmental standard. The result, ISO 9001:2008, does not introduce any additional requirements nor does it change the intent of ISO 9001:2000, but simply represents a fine-tuning of the standard. It is intended to clarify legal standards, outsourcing, internal audits, the concept of competence, design and development processes, monitoring and measuring processes, and controlling non-conforming products.[27] For example, one clarification regarding the control of nonconforming product was restructured to improve its ability to apply to all types of organizations, specifically service ones. Another on customer satisfaction was revised to include methods beyond the traditional customer survey an organization can use to monitor customer perception and show compliance to this requirement.

Although manufacturing is the largest adopter of ISO 9000, the standards are intended to apply to all types of businesses, including electronics and chemicals, and to services such as health care, banking, and transportation. The evolution of the standard has shed its manufacturing roots and made it easier for service companies to apply. For example, a software developer, Computer Associates of Islandia, New York, employs over 14,000 people in more than 40 countries. They used ISO 9001 to build a strong framework throughout all its sites (many of which were obtained through acquisitions of other software companies) to help standardize product development and support. Sears, Roebuck and Co. has registered almost 400 product repair centers and in-home services. As another example, in 1998, the Centers for Medicare and Medicaid Services began requiring ISO 9001 certification for all its new business contracts with claims processors.[28] Some professionals have argued that ISO 9000 can provide more effective management of public school systems.[29]

Factors Leading to ISO 9000:2000

The original ISO 9000:1994 series standards consisted of 20 fundamental elements of a basic quality system that included such things as management responsibility, design control, purchasing, product identification and traceability, process control, inspection and testing, corrective and preventive action, internal quality audits, training, and statistical techniques.

The original standards and the 1994 revision met with considerable controversy.[30] The standards only required that the organization have a documented, verifiable process in place to ensure that it consistently produces what it says it will produce. A company could comply with the standards and still produce a poor-quality product—as long as it did so consistently! Many never used the standards to drive improvement. Dissatisfaction with ISO 9000 resulted in the European Union calling for deemphasizing ISO 9000 registration, citing the fact that companies were more concerned with "passing a test" than on focusing their energies on quality processes. The Australian government stopped requiring ISO 9000 registration for government contracts. The Australian *Business Review Weekly* noted that "its reputation among small and medium businesses continues to deteriorate. Some small businesses have almost been destroyed by the endeavor to implement costly and officious quality assurance ISO 9000 systems that hold little relevance to their businesses."

The deficiencies in the old ISO 9000 standards led to a joint effort 1994 by the Big Three automobile manufacturers—Ford, Chrysler, and General Motors—as well as several truck manufacturers, to develop QS-9000, an interpretation and extension of ISO 9000 for automotive suppliers. The goal was to develop fundamental quality systems that provide for continuous improvement, emphasizing defect prevention and the reduction of variation and waste in the supply chain. QS-9000 is based on ISO 9000 and includes all ISO requirements. However, QS-9000 went well beyond ISO 9000 standards by including additional requirements such as continuous improvement, manufacturing capability, and production part approval processes. Now, even QS-9000 is considered inadequate and is being phased out.

ISO 9000:2000 is a response to the widespread dissatisfaction that resulted from the old standards. The new standards have a completely new structure, based on eight principles—"comprehensive and fundamental rules or beliefs for leading and operating an organization" that reflect the basic principles of total quality that we introduced in Chapter 1, and many of the core values and concepts of the Baldrige and European Quality Award criteria. These eight principles were voted on, and overwhelmingly approved, at a conference in 1997 attended by 36 representatives of countries that have delegates in the TC 176 technical committee, charged with the responsibility of revising the ISO 9000 standards.[31] The principles and their explanation as defined by the IOS are shown in Table 3.3.

Table 3.3 ISO 9000:2000 Quality Management Principles

Principle 1: Customer Focus
Organizations depend on their customers and therefore should understand current and future customer needs, should meet customer requirements, and strive to exceed customer expectations.

Principle 2: Leadership
Leaders establish unity of purpose and direction of the organization. They should create and maintain the internal environment in which people can become fully involved in achieving the organization's objectives.

Principle 3: Involvement of People
People at all levels are the essence of an organization and their full involvement enables their abilities to be used for the organization's benefit.

Principle 4: Process Approach
A desired result is achieved more efficiently when activities and related resources are managed as a process.

Principle 5: System Approach to Management
Identifying, understanding, and managing interrelated processes as a system contributes to the organization's effectiveness and efficiency in achieving its objectives.

Principle 6: Continual Improvement
Continual improvement of the organization's overall performance should be a permanent objective of the organization.

Principle 7: Factual Approach to Decision Making
Effective decisions are based on the analysis of data and information.

Principle 8: Mutually Beneficial Supplier Relationships
An organization and its suppliers are interdependent and a mutually beneficial relationship enhances the ability of both to create value.

Source: http://www.iso.org/iso/qmp. Reprinted with permission.

With this underlying philosophy, the ISO 9000:2000 revision aligns much closer to the performance excellence concept of Baldrige. For example,

- Organizations now need a process to determine customer needs and expectations, translate them into internal requirements, and measure customer satisfaction and dissatisfaction.
- Managers must communicate the importance of meeting customer and regulatory requirements, integrate ISO 9000 into business plans, set measurable objectives, and conduct management reviews. No longer can top management delegate the program to people lower in the organization. Organizations now must view work as a process and manage a system of interrelated processes. This approach is significantly different from the "document what you do" requirements of earlier versions.
- Analysis now needs to be done to provide information about customer satisfaction and dissatisfaction, products, and processes with the focus on improvement.
- Evaluation of training effectiveness and making personnel aware of the importance of their activities in meeting quality objectives are stressed.
- In the previous standards, organizations were required to perform corrective and preventive action, but now must have a planned process for improvement.

Implementation and Registration

Implementing ISO 9000 is not an easy task.[32] The ISO 9000 standards originally were intended to be advisory in nature and to be used for two-party contractual situations (between a customer and supplier) and for internal auditing. However, they quickly evolved into criteria for companies who wished to "certify" their quality management or achieve "registration" through a third-party auditor, usually a laboratory or some other accreditation agency (called a registrar). This process began in the United Kingdom. Rather than a supplier being audited for compliance to the standards by each customer, the registrar certifies the company, and this certification is accepted by all of the supplier's customers.

Recertification is required every three years. Individual sites—not entire companies—must achieve registration individually. All costs are borne by the applicant, so the process can be quite expensive. A registration audit may cost anywhere from $10,000 to more than $40,000, while the internal cost for documentation and training may exceed $100,000.

Benefits of ISO 9000

ISO 9001 has three principal benefits:[33]

- *It provides discipline.* The ISO 9001 requirement for third-party audits forces an organization to review its quality system on a routine basis. If it fails to maintain the quality system, audits should recognize this and call for corrective action.
- *It contains the basics of a good quality system.* ISO 9001 includes basic requirements for any sound quality system, such as understanding customer requirements, ensuring the ability to meet them, ensuring people recources capable of doing the work that affects quality, ensuring physical resources and support services needed to meet product requirements, and ensuring that problems are identified and corrected.
- *It offers a marketing program.* ISO certified organizations can use their status to differentiate themselves in the eyes of customers.

Many diverse organizations have realized significant benefits from ISO 9000 that range from higher customer satisfaction and retention, better quality products, and improved productivity. At DuPont, for example, ISO 9000 has been credited with increasing on-time delivery from 70 percent to 90 percent, decreasing cycle time from 15 days to 1.5 days, increasing first-pass yields from 72 percent to 92 percent, and reducing the number of test procedures by one-third. Sun Microsystems' Milpitas plant was certified in 1992, and managers believe that it helped deliver improved quality and service to customers.[34] In Canada, Toronto Plastics, Ltd. reduced defects from 150,000 per million to 15,000 per million after one year of ISO implementation.[35] The first home builder to achieve registration, Michigan-based Delcor Homes, reduced its rate for correctable defects from 27.4 to 1.7 in two years and improved its building experience approval rating from the mid-60s to the mid-90s on a 100-point scale.[36] Thus, using ISO 9000 as a basis for a quality system can improve productivity, decrease costs, and increase customer satisfaction. In addition, organizations have found that using ISO 9000 resulted in increased use of data as a business management tool, increased management commitment, more efficient management reviews, and improved customer communication.[37]

Current information can be obtained from the ISO website (http://www.iso.org).

SIX SIGMA

Six Sigma, which has garnered a significant amount of credibility over the last decade because of its acceptance at such major firms as Allied Signal (now part of Honeywell) and General Electric, is not as new a concept as it seems. Six Sigma incorporates many basic and advanced quality improvement and control tools that have found widespread application in fact-based management environments. However, the way it is practiced represents a departure from traditional management.

Six Sigma can be described as a business improvement approach that seeks to find and eliminate causes of defects and errors in manufacturing and service processes by focusing on outputs that are critical to customers and a clear financial return for the organization.

The term "six sigma" is based on a statistical measure that equates to 3.4 or fewer errors or defects per million opportunities. An ultimate "stretch" goal of all organizations that adopt a Six Sigma philosophy is to have all critical processes, regardless of functional area, at a six-sigma level of capability.

Evolution of Six Sigma

Motorola pioneered the concept of Six Sigma as an approach to measuring product and service quality. The late Bill Smith, a reliability engineer at Motorola, is credited with originating the concept during the mid-1980s and selling it to Motorola's CEO, Robert Galvin. Smith noted that system failure rates were substantially higher than predicted by final product test, and suggested several causes, including higher system complexity that resulted in more opportunities for failure, and a fundamental flaw in traditional quality thinking. He concluded that a much higher level of internal quality was required and convinced Galvin of its importance.[38] As a result, Motorola set the following goal in 1987:

> *Improve product and services quality ten times by 1989, and at least one hundred fold by 1991. Achieve six-sigma capability by 1992. With a deep sense of urgency, spread dedication to quality to every facet of the corporation, and achieve a culture of continual improvement to assure total customer satisfaction. There is only one ultimate goal: zero defects—in everything we do.*

The core philosophy of Six Sigma is based on some key concepts:[39]

1. Think in terms of key business processes and customer requirements with a clear focus on overall strategic objectives.
2. Focus on corporate sponsors responsible for championing projects, support team activities, help to overcome resistance to change, and obtain resources.
3. Emphasize such quantifiable measures as defects per million opportunities (dpmo) that can be applied to all parts of an organization: manufacturing, engineering, administrative, software, and so on.
4. Ensure that appropriate metrics are identified early in the process and that they focus on business results, thereby providing incentives and accountability.
5. Provide extensive training followed by project team deployment to improve profitability, reduce non-value-added activities, and achieve cycle time reduction.
6. Create highly qualified process improvement experts ("green belts," "black belts," and "master black belts") who can apply improvement tools and lead teams.
7. Set stretch objectives for improvement.

The recognized benchmark for Six Sigma implementation is General Electric. The efforts by General Electric in particular, driven by former CEO Jack Welch, brought significant media attention to the concept and made Six Sigma a popular approach to quality improvement. In the mid-1990s, quality emerged as a concern of many employees at GE. Jack Welch invited Larry Bossidy, then CEO of Allied Signal, who had phenomenal success with Six Sigma, to talk about it at a Corporate Executive Council meeting. The meeting caught the attention of GE managers and as Welch stated, "I went nuts about Six Sigma and launched it," calling it the most ambitious task the company had ever taken on.[40] To ensure success, GE changed its incentive compensation plan so that 60 percent of the bonus was based on financials and 40 percent on Six Sigma, and provided stock option grants to employees in Six Sigma training. In their first year, they trained 30,000 employees at a cost of $200 million and got back about $150 million in savings. From 1996 to 1997, GE increased the number of Six Sigma projects from 3,000 to 6,000 and achieved $320 million in productivity gains and profits. By 1998, the company had generated $750 million in Six Sigma savings over and above their investment, and would receive $1.5 billion in savings the next year.

GE had many early success stories. GE Capital, for example, fielded about 300,000 calls each year from mortgage customers who had to use voice mail or call back 24 percent of the time because employees were busy or unavailable. A Six Sigma team analyzed one branch that had a near perfect percentage of answered calls and applied their learning of their best practices to the other 41 branches, resulting in a 99.9 percent chance of customers' getting a representative on the first try. A team at GE Plastics improved the quality of a product used in CD-ROMs and audio CDs from a 3.8 sigma level to 5.7 level and captured a significant amount of new business from Sony.[41] GE credits Six Sigma with a 10-fold increase in the life of CT scanner X-ray tubes, a 400 percent improvement in return on investment in its industrial diamond business, a 62 percent reduction in turnaround time at railcar repair shops, and $400 million in savings in its plastics business.[42]

One of the key learnings GE discovered was that Six Sigma is not only for engineers. Welch observed the following:[43]

- Plant managers can use Six Sigma to reduce waste, improve product consistency, solve equipment problems, or create capacity.
- Human resource managers need it to reduce the cycle time for hiring employees.

- Regional sales managers can use it to improve forecast reliability, pricing strategies, or pricing variation.
- For that matter, plumbers, car mechanics, and gardeners can use it to better understand their customers' needs and tailor their service offerings to meet customers' wants.

After many years of implementation, Six Sigma has become a vital part of GE's company culture. In fact, as GE continues to acquire new companies, integrating Six Sigma into different business cultures is a significant challenge. Six Sigma is a priority in acquisitions and addressed early in the acquisition process.

Many other organizations such as Texas Instruments, Allied Signal (which merged with Honeywell), Boeing, 3M, Home Depot, Caterpillar, IBM, Xerox, Citibank, Raytheon, and the U.S. Air Force Air Combat Command have developed quality improvement approaches designed around the Six Sigma concept and also report significant results. Between 1995 and the first quarter of 1997, Allied Signal reported cost savings exceeding $800 million from its Six Sigma initiative. Citibank groups reduced internal callbacks by 80 percent, credit processing time by 50 percent, and cycle times of processing statements from 28 days to 15 days.[44]

Six Sigma as a Quality Framework

Six Sigma provides a blueprint for implementation of a total quality system. In many ways, Six Sigma is the realization of many fundamental concepts of "total quality management," notably, the integration of human and process elements of improvement.[45] Human issues include management leadership, a sense of urgency, focus on results and customers, team processes, and culture change; process issues include the use of process management techniques, analysis of variation and statistical methods, a disciplined problem solving approach, and management by fact. However, it is more than simply a repackaging of older quality approaches, such as the traditional notion of total quality management. Some of the contrasting features include:

- TQM is based largely on worker empowerment and teams; Six Sigma is owned by business leader champions.
- TQM activities generally occur within a function, process, or individual workplace; Six Sigma projects are truly cross-functional.
- TQM training is generally limited to simple improvement tools and concepts; Six Sigma focuses on a more rigorous and advanced set of statistical methods and a structured problem-solving methodology DMAIC—define, measure, analyze, improve, and control—which will be discussed in detail in Chapter 11.
- TQM is focused on improvement with little financial accountability; Six Sigma requires a verifiable return on investment and focus on the bottom line.

In addition, Six Sigma has elevated the importance of statistics and statistical thinking in quality improvement. Six Sigma's focus on measurable bottom-line results, a disciplined statistical approach to problem solving, rapid project completion, and organizational infrastructure make it a powerful methodology for improvement.

BALDRIGE, ISO 9000, AND SIX SIGMA

We examined three major frameworks for quality management systems: the Baldrige Criteria for Performance Excellence, ISO 9000, and Six Sigma. Although each of these frameworks is process-focused, data-based, and management-led, each offers a different emphasis in helping organizations improve performance and increase customer satisfaction. For example, Baldrige focuses on performance excellence for the entire organization in an overall management framework, identifying and tracking important organizational results; ISO focuses on product and service conformity for guaranteeing equity in the marketplace and concentrates on fixing quality system problems and product and service nonconformities; and Six Sigma concentrates on measuring product quality and driving process improvement and cost savings throughout the organization.

Although the 2000 revision of ISO 9000 incorporated many of the Baldrige criteria's original principles, it still is not a comprehensive business performance framework. Nevertheless, it is an excellent way to begin a quality journey. In fact, it provides more detailed guidance on process and product control than Baldrige, and provides systematic approaches to many of the Baldrige criteria requirements in the Process Management category. Thus, for companies in the early stages of developing a quality program, the standards enforce the discipline of control that is necessary before they can seriously pursue continuous improvement. The requirements of periodic audits reinforce the stated quality system until it becomes ingrained in the company.

ISO 9000 provides a set of good basic practices for initiating a quality system, and is an excellent starting point for companies with no formal quality assurance program.

Implementing Six Sigma fulfills in part many of the elements of ISO 9000:2000, including the Quality Management System, Resource Management, Product Realization, and Measurement, Analysis, and Improvement sections of the standards.[46] For instance, Six Sigma helps to demonstrate management commitment through periodic review of Six Sigma plans and projects, providing champions to sponsor projects, providing training resources, and communicating progress and achievements.

Because Baldrige and Six Sigma provide much more comprehensive views of quality management, we will focus on them throughout the remainder of this book. A critical question is whether an organization using Baldrige will be more successful if it also uses Six Sigma, and vice versa. If one views Six Sigma as only a small part of the Process Management category, one might believe that the impact would be marginal. However, let us examine the role of Six Sigma in each of the seven Baldrige categories. Six Sigma enhances the ability of leadership to focus on the critical factors that make a business successful—such as customer requirements and performance gaps—and select appropriate strategies and action plans. To implement Six Sigma effectively, leadership must allocate resources effectively, communicate with the workforce, and drive any necessary cultural changes. Therefore, Six Sigma can strengthen management practices in Leadership and Strategic Planning. Understanding customer requirements and linking them to processes and delivery systems is a principal focus of Baldrige. By focusing on critical to quality (CTQ) customer requirements—one of the important concepts in Six Sigma, organizations gain better knowledge about customer requirements, a key component of the Customer Focus category. Six Sigma methodology is driven by a management-by-fact methodology. This basis can improve an organization's ability to meet the requirements in the Measurement, Analysis, and Knowledge Management category. The role of people in championing projects and providing the technical and application-specific knowledge is vital. Six Sigma can improve work systems, training, and the work environment—all critical components of the Workforce Focus Baldrige category. With Six Sigma, process management is not a by-product, but it is one of the primary organizational goals. The DMAIC methodology provides a structured approach to category 6, Process Management. Finally, Six Sigma's focus on results leads organizations to track and monitor appropriate metrics, which mirrors Baldrige Category 7.

Taking a broad view, Six Sigma contributes to nearly 80 percent of the points available in a Baldrige assessment. Although no formal studies have investigated these synergies, many organizations have successfully married the two, including Texas Instruments, Motorola, Compaq, Solectron, Boeing, and others. In fact, Jack Swaim of Compaq Computer (now Hewlett-Packard) and a former Baldrige examiner, observed that Six Sigma can provide the impetus for change, while the Baldrige Core Values provide the keys to sustainability. He also suggests that pursuing Baldrige first can make it easier to implement Six Sigma. We also believe that Six Sigma can lay the foundation for a broader Baldrige perspective, and is reflected by a comment from another colleague, Cynthia Scribner at Raytheon, who noted that Six Sigma makes a great unifying story for a Baldrige application. Unfortunately, consultants and advocates appear to support their own perspectives, and such synergies are seldom exploited. The Bonus Materials folder for this chapter on the Premium website contains additional discussion of the synergies between Baldrige and Six Sigma.

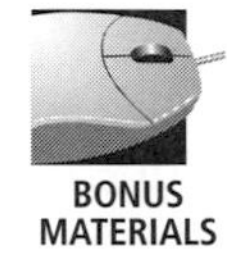
BONUS MATERIALS

Although different, Baldrige and Six Sigma are highly compatible and can each have a place in the management system of a successful organization.

So how should an organization choose? The correct answer is that it should not be either/or, but rather, any combination of these systems. One example of merging Baldrige with Six Sigma is Baxter Healthcare International.[47] The Business Excellence organization is a small group of people focused on helping internal clients improve their operations. Specific areas of responsibility in Business Excellence include:

- The Baxter Award for Operational Excellence (an internal Baldrige Award)
- Deployment of the Baxter Integrated Management System (the Baldrige model)
- The Corporate Quality Manual
- The Baxter Quality Institute (an internal quality training group)
- The Quality Leadership Process (a method of deploying performance excellence in manufacturing)
- Lean Manufacturing Initiative
- Six Sigma Initiatives

They rolled all of these areas together into a unified service offering. For example, consider the following fictitious scenario. The supply chain organization determined that their operating cost and cash flow contributions are not meeting the targets. Business Excellence would set out to help them in the following way. First, they work with members of the leadership team to develop an organizational profile of the supply chain organization. This initial assessment helps the team focus on who they are and what their specific challenges are. Next, they perform a simple Baldrige assessment online and then use the output to generate a feedback report of strengths and opportunities for improvement with strong emphasis on the integration of the model. Then they distill the feedback report down to 10–12 cross-cutting themes for the leadership team to focus on. These themes are built into an Excel spreadsheet for a "prioritization matrix" exercise, designed to identify the top two or three critical opportunities or issues that the group will focus on. Next, they bring in the Six Sigma approach and drill down into these opportunities to determine potential projects. When these projects have been identified and scoped sufficiently to make a decision to move forward, project charters are developed and assigned to Six Sigma specialists to implement them.

BONUS MATERIALS

SUMMARY OF KEY POINTS AND TERMINOLOGY

The Bonus Materials folder on the Premium website, provides a summary of key concepts and terminology introduced in this chapter.

QUALITY IN PRACTICE

ISO 9000 AND SEARS' QUALITY MANAGEMENT SYSTEM[48]

Sears, Roebuck and Co., a wholly owned subsidiary of Sears Holdings Corp., is one of the largest retailers in North America. Sears offers a range of home merchandise, apparel, and automotive products and services through more than 2,400 Sears-branded and affiliated stores in the United States and Canada, which includes about 926 full-line and 1,100 specialty stores in the United States alone. Sears is the largest national provider of product repair services, with more than 14 million repairs performed annually.

After an eight-year effort, the company registered its product repair centers' and in-home service's quality management systems (QMS) to ISO 9001. Sears has always maintained a strong commitment to quality in its products and services. In keeping with this commitment, in 1998 the company decided to register all of its product repair centers to the ISO 9002:1994 quality management system standard (which was subsequently replaced by ISO 9001:2000). By the end of 2002, all of the 32 carry-in service centers were registered to ISO 9001. Once the repair centers were registered, Sears turned to the in-home service side of its business. About 10,000 Sears' technicians repair one of every five appliances in America. By the end of 2005, Sears had 383 locations under the scope of its ISO 9001 registration, including all six in-home regions. The company's 48 districts have their own certificates.

Recognizing that ISO 9001 provides a framework for large organizations to implement a consistent, cohesive program across geographic lines and throughout a multifaceted business, Sears sought registration to enhance its organizational process compliance. The company wanted a consistent process for improving customer satisfaction and enhancing service capabilities. ISO 9001 implementation played a large role in assisting with process standardization across the company. ISO 9001 is often associated with the manufacturing industry, and one major hurdle Sears had to overcome was communicating the value of a QMS within a retail and service environment.

ISO 9001 became a fundamental tool that provides the company a safe base for continued improvements. For example, Sears has made dramatic improvements in calibrating the tools used for repairs and service calls. Although the company had calibrated some of its tools prior to implementing ISO 9001, the standard requires 100-percent tool calibration for safety purposes. Not only does Sears have an expansive program for calibrating its tools, but it has also opened and registered its own calibration lab to ISO/IEC 17025. This move minimizes calibration costs and expands third-party business opportunities.

Another significant benefit of ISO 9001 involves the company's handling of refrigerant. Sears works with Freon and other hazardous materials, which could pose a serious environmental violation if not handled properly. As part of its ISO 9001 efforts, Sears improved its existing hazardous-materials program by implementing a comprehensive program on refrigerant handling.

The standard also helped Sears' efficiency in completing repairs. For instance, in the Chattanooga, Tennessee, carry-in facility, the average daily completion rate for repairing lawn mowers or other items doubled from four or five to eight or nine per repairman as a result of ISO 9001 implementation.

Sears' district office in Houston has improved its technician recall rate because of the QMS. The recall rate is the percentage of times service technicians must return to customers' homes for a second time within 30 days. Before the SST, the recall rate in Houston was about 12 percent. In 2004, Houston service technicians made more than a quarter of a million service calls, with a 9.3-percent recall rate. In 2005, the rate dropped to 7.9 percent.

ISO 9001 has been instrumental in helping to standardize the manner in which technicians record field observations. This is important for solving certain types of problems, such as an appliance or part malfunction, customer abuse, or an accident. To ensure consistency, technicians use a special tool kit for recording the event, including a disposable camera and standardized forms.

Key Issues for Discussion

1. What issues do you think that a large company such as Sears had to face in implementing ISO 9000 across its vast organization?
2. How are the ISO 9000:2000 Quality Management Principles reflected in this example? How might these principles have helped Sears address the issues you identified in the first question?

Quality in Practice

Integrating Quality Frameworks at Veridian Homes[49]

Veridian Homes began in June 2003, when Don Simon Homes and Midland Builders, two of Wisconsin's oldest home builders, merged. The family owned and operated company dedicated itself to quality home building, community involvement and environmental stewardship. With 100 employees, Veridian Homes now builds 500 single-family and condominium homes each year in Madison, WI, and the surrounding area. The company has found the use of several quality methods, including a Baldrige self assessment system, is critical to the success of the company's improvement initiatives. Using best quality practices to increase customer focus and satisfaction, it has improved productivity while reducing impact on the environment.

The goal at Veridian Homes is to promote, educate on, and coordinate quality throughout the company. Specifically, the structure and systems employed to achieve this goal, from a strategic and operational mindset, include the National Housing Quality Award (NHQA), Malcolm Baldrige National Quality Award self assessment, builder certification and Six Sigma. The NHQA program is based on the Baldrige award, and provides applicants expert evaluation and feedback on their organizations' quality management practices. Unlike the Baldrige award, however, the NHQA process includes a third-party survey of the applicants' customers on their satisfaction with their homes and the home building process. The NHQA also includes a self-assessment, which helps identify opportunities for improvement (OFIs) and allows these efforts to be strategically implemented.

Self-assessments are conducted annually using Baldrige Express, an employee survey based on the Baldrige criteria. The National Council for Performance Excellence offers Baldrige Express surveys in association with state quality award organizations.

Employees rate the company on a Likert scale in each criterion and can provide detailed comments on strengths, weaknesses and OFIs. A report provides a detailed analysis for management to conduct annual measuring and monitoring and to identify and prioritize weaknesses. Veridian uses this analysis to drive its annual strategic planning process (SPP), placing Baldrige at the heart of the organizational strategy formation cycle (see Figure 3.8). Strategic goals are linked to each employee via the

Figure 3.8 Strategic Planning Cycle Driven By Baldrige Assessment

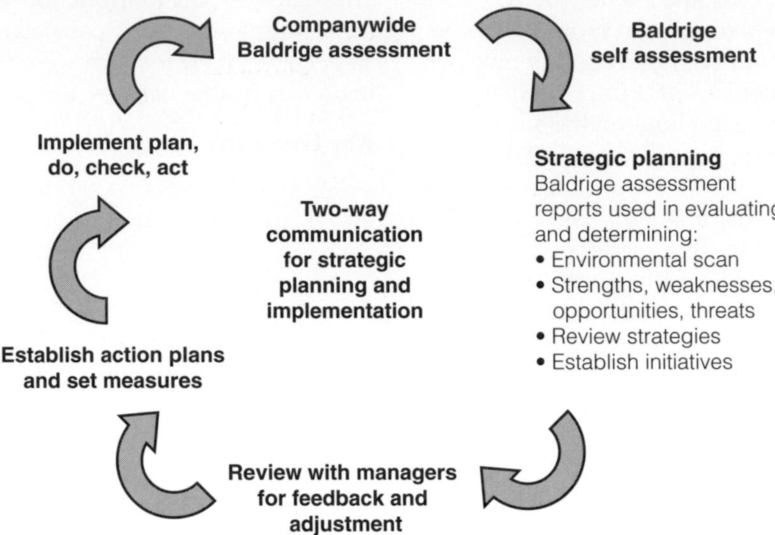

Source: Reprinted with permission From Denis Leonard," Building Quality at Veridian Homes," *Quality Progress*, October 2006, pp. 49–54. Copyright © 2006 American Society for Quality. No further distribution allowed without permission.

performance planning and development (PPD) process. This process helps an employee understand his or her role, priorities, resources, accomplishments, and professional development as they relate to the company's vision, mission, strategic drivers, and departmental strategic goals. The employees also take part in a profit sharing program, motivating and rewarding employees based on measured and sustained improvements in cost, quality, cycle times, customer service, and profits.

In fall 2004, Veridian Homes earned NAHBRC builder certification status for quality and safety management systems. The certification, based on ISO 9000, is third-party audited and included Veridian's construction, sales, and customer relations departments. Since earning certification, the land development, purchasing, estimating, and design departments have been incorporated into the certification. Veridian has also expanded its management system to include an environmental management system that focuses on improving activities such as erosion control and recycling. This has formed an integrated quality, environmental, health, and safety (QEHS) management system, which provides a tactical level methodology to structure, document, disseminate, implement, and manage Veridian's QEHS requirements.

Veridian uses various improvement tools and techniques to support quality implementation. On the Veridian intranet, which is available to all employees, a quality toolbox provides templates, PowerPoint based training, videos, and other materials covering topics such as trade partner certification, builder certification, NHQA criteria, Baldrige criteria, Six Sigma methodology, and other improvement tools and techniques.

Veridian uses numerous cross-functional improvement teams. Each team has a team leader, facilitator, and sponsor, and the company has one Six Sigma Black Belt and two Green Belts to provide support and expertise. The construction and customer relations departments have launched 10 improvement teams focusing on issues raised through warranty and customer feedback and directly linked to the strategy for the operations department.

Veridian's green building practices address the corporate social responsibility aspect of quality management and are reflected in the leadership criteria of the NHQA and the Baldrige award. In Wisconsin, green building practices are certified by Green Built Homes through the Wisconsin Environmental Initiative. Green Built certified builders undergo reviews of building plans, specifications and on-site visits to ensure the criteria are met. The criteria cover waste reduction, recycling and disposal of materials, energy efficient insulation and air sealing, storm water management and water conservation, landscape conservation, energy-efficient mechanical systems, and use of recycled materials and energy efficient materials and construction products.

Veridian's quality initiatives have resulted in several performance improvements, including:

- Model homes sold cycle times reduced from 32 days to 15 days
- Drafting time on models reduced by more than an hour
- Estimating time on model homes reduced by 32 percent
- Material variance (difference between ordered and required, perhaps due to damage on site) down by 20 percent for lumber, 24 percent for siding and 38 percent for trim
- Paperwork processing reduced by 208 hours per year, with a total estimated savings across Veridian of $200,000 through performance increases by implementing a production scheduler software system called Builder MT
- Person hours down by 200 per year through escrow and warranty process improvements
- Defects cut in half by using ten defect reduction teams in cooperation with trade partners

In national surveys conducted by NRS Corp., a consulting firm that specializes in research for the home building industry, Veridian customer satisfaction measures are consistently in the top 10 percent of the 333 builders reviewed. Satisfaction with Veridian's warranty is in the top 5 percent of all builders on the 30-day customer satisfaction survey and is in the top 15 percent of all builders on the annual customer satisfaction survey.

Key Issues for Discussion

1. What tools and approaches has Veridian used to integrate quality throughout the organization?
2. How have NHQA certification, the Baldrige process, and the Green Built certification process contributed to efficiency and cost effectiveness for Veridian?

Additional Quality in Practice features can be found in the Bonus Materials folder on the Premium website.

BONUS MATERIALS

Review Questions

1. Explain the Deming chain reaction.
2. How does Deming's definition of quality compare with the definitions discussed in Chapter 1?
3. Summarize the four components of Profound Knowledge. How do they mutually support each other?
4. Explain the implications of not understanding the components of Profound Knowledge as suggested by Peter Scholtes.
5. Summarize Deming's 14 Points. How does each point relate to the four components of Profound Knowledge?
6. Explain Juran's Quality Trilogy.
7. How is Juran's philosophy similar to or different from Deming's?
8. What are Crosby's Absolutes of Quality Management and Basic Elements of Improvement? How are they similar to or different from Deming's 14 Points?
9. Summarize the key contributions of Feigenbaum, Ishikawa, and Taguchi to modern quality thinking.
10. How does Taguchi's approach to measuring variation support the Deming philosophy?
11. Summarize the purposes of the Malcolm Baldrige National Quality Award.
12. Explain the Baldrige Award framework and why each element is important in any quality system.

13. Describe the key issues addressed in each of the seven categories of the Criteria for Performance Excellence.

BONUS MATERIALS

14. How do companies that do not apply for the award commonly use the Baldrige Award criteria?
15. How do the Baldrige criteria support Deming's 14 Points? (See the Bonus Materials folder on the Premium website.)
16. Explain the differences between the Baldrige framework and the EFQM framework.
17. What is the role of national culture in adapting the Baldrige framework to a particular country?
18. Briefly summarize the key elements of ISO 9000.
19. List the reasons companies pursue ISO 9000 registration. What benefits can registration provide?
20. Why has ISO 9000 been controversial? How has the 2000 revision addressed some of the controversial issues?

BONUS MATERIALS

21. Describe the evolution of Six Sigma. What impact has it had on General Electric?
22. What are the similarities and differences among Six Sigma, ISO 9000, and the Baldrige approaches? (See also the Bonus Materials folder on the Premium website).

Discussion Questions

1. Melissa Clare works for a software company as a technical support representative. Her duties include answering the telephone, providing information to customers, and troubleshooting technical problems. Her supervisor told her to be courteous and not to rush callers. However, the supervisor also told her that she must answer an average of 15 calls per hour so that the department's account manager can meet his or her budget. Melissa comes home each day frustrated because the computer is slow in delivering information that she needs, and sometimes provides the wrong information causing her to search for the information in complex manuals. She knows that she often cuts the call off prematurely or provides only the minimal information necessary. What is Melissa's job (not her job description)? What might Deming say about this situation? Drawing upon Deming's principles, outline a plan to improve this situation.
2. What implications might the Theory of Knowledge have for Wall Street analysts who react to daily news and government economic reports?
3. Discuss the interrelationships among Deming's 14 Points. How do they support each other? Why must they be viewed as a whole rather than separately?
4. The following themes form the basis for Deming's philosophy. Classify the 14 Points into these categories and discuss the commonalties within each category.
    a. Organizational purpose and mission
    b. Quantitative goals
    c. Revolution of management philosophy
    d. Elimination of seat-of-the-pants decisions
    e. Cooperation building
    f. Improvement of manager/worker relations
5. Think of a system with which you are familiar, such as your college, fraternity, or a student organization. What is the purpose of that system? What would it mean to optimize that system?

6. List some examples of variation that you observe in your daily life. How might they be reduced?
7. Suggest ways that management can recognize the existence of fear in an organization. What strategies might managers use to deal with and eliminate fear?
8. Discuss how Deming's 14 Points can apply to an academic environment. How can learning and classroom performance be improved by applying Deming's philosophy?
9. In a videotape made in 1993, Deming related a story of a woman executive who spent an entire day flying from city to city, changing planes several times, because her company's travel department received a cheaper fare than if she had taken a direct flight. How does this example violate the concepts of Profound Knowledge and the 14 Points, and what should the company do about it?
10. The original version of Deming's 14 Points (developed in the early 1980s) is given in Table 3.4. Contrast each of these with the revised version in Table 3.1

Table 3.4 Original Version of Deming's 14 Points

1. Create constancy of purpose toward improvement of product and service, with the aim of becoming competitive and to stay in business and to provide jobs.
2. Adopt the new philosophy. We are in a new economic age. Western management must awaken to the challenge, must learn their responsibilities, and take on leadership for change.
3. Cease dependence on inspection to achieve quality. Eliminate the need for inspection on a mass basis by building quality into the product in the first place.
4. End the practice of awarding business on the basis of price tag alone. Instead, minimize total cost. Move toward a single supplier for any one item, on a long-term relationship of loyalty and trust.
5. Improve constantly and forever the system of production and service to improve quality and productivity, and thus constantly decrease costs.
6. Institute training on the job.
7. Institute leadership. The aim of supervision should be to help people and machines and gadgets do a better job. Supervision of management is in need of overhaul, as well as the supervision of production workers.
8. Drive out fear so everyone can work effectively for the company.
9. Break down barriers between departments. People in research, design, sales, and production must work as a team, to foresee problems of production and those that may be encountered with the product or service.
10. Eliminate slogans, exhortations, and targets for the work force that ask for zero defects or new levels of productivity. Such exhortations only create adversarial relationships, as the bulk of the causes of low quality and low productivity belong to the system and thus lie beyond the power of the work force.

11a. Eliminate work standards (quotas) on the factory floor. Substitute leadership.

11b. Eliminate management by objective. Eliminate management by numbers, numerical goals. Substitute leadership.

12a. Remove barriers that rob hourly workers of their right to pride of workmanship. The responsibility of supervisors must be changed from sheer numbers to quality.

12b. Remove barriers that rob people in management and engineering of their right to pride in workmanship. This means, inter alia, abolishment of the annual or merit rating and of management by objective.

13. Institute a vigorous program of education and self-improvement.
14. Put everybody in the company to work to accomplish the transformation. The transformation is everybody's job.

Source: W. Edwards Deming, *Out of Crisis,* pp. 23–24.

early in the chapter. Explain the implications of the changes. Why might Deming have made these changes?

11. Refer to the example of how The Ritz-Carlton Hotel Company addresses some of the questions in the Senior Leadership category of the Baldrige criteria in this chapter. Explain what practices address each of the specific questions: How do senior leaders set organizational vision and values? How do senior leaders deploy your organization's vision and values through your leadership system, to the workforce, to key suppliers and partners, and to customers and other stakeholders, as appropriate? How do senior leaders' personal actions reflect a commitment to the organization's values?
12. Create a matrix diagram in which each row is a category of the Baldrige Award criteria and four columns correspond to a level of organizational maturity with respect to quality:
    - Traditional management practices
    - Growing awareness of the importance of quality
    - Development of a solid quality management system
    - Outstanding, world-class management practice

    In each cell of the matrix, list two to five characteristics that you would expect to see for a company in each of the four situations for that criteria category. How might this matrix be used as a self-assessment tool to provide directions for improvement?
13. Examine the questions in the Baldrige criteria and discuss which ones relate to the concept of sustainability as defined in this chapter? Why is sustainability an important issue in business?

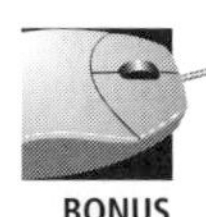
BONUS MATERIALS

14. Contrast the categories of the Baldrige Award with the Deming Prize (see the Materials folder on the Premium website). How are they similar? Different?
15. Discuss the implications of the Baldrige criteria for e-commerce. What are the specific challenges that e-commerce companies face within each category of the criteria?
16. Examine the following requirements from ISO 9001. Which directly help control or improve quality, and which do not? For those that do not, why do you think that they are part of the standard?
    a. "The organization shall determine requirements specified by the customer."
    b. "Records from management reviews shall be maintained."
    c. "...documentation shall include...documents needed...to ensure the effective planning, operation and control of its processes..."
    d. "...shall determine the monitoring and measurement to be undertaken...to provide evidence of conformity of product to determined requirements."
    e. "The quality management system...shall include a quality manual."
    f. "...establish and implement the inspection or other activities necessary for ensuring that purchased product meets specified requirements."
17. How might the principles of Six Sigma be used to improve a quality process in a school or university? What elements of the Six Sigma philosophy might be difficult to obtain support for in the educational environment? Why?

PROJECTS, ETC.

1. Study the annual reports of some major companies issued over a period of several years. Do you see evidence of implementation of the quality philosophies discussed in this chapter?
2. Design a questionnaire or survey instrument to determine the degree to which an organization is "Demingized." Explain how you developed the questions.
3. Visit the National Quality Program website (http://www.baldrige.nist.gov) and write a report on the information that can be found there.
4. Select a category from the Baldrige Education criteria found in the Baldrige Materials folder on the Premium website, and interview your school administrators using the criteria questions as a basis for the interview. Write a report assessing your school against the criteria.

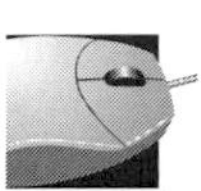

5. Carefully compare the 2009–10 Baldrige business, education, and health care criteria available in the Baldrige Materials folder on the Premium website. Evaluate the differences in the criteria categories among the sectors. What specific changes in the criteria were needed to meet their unique culture and requirements for not-for-profit organizations such as a United Way agency, or a government entity, such as a state department of taxation or a municipal government?

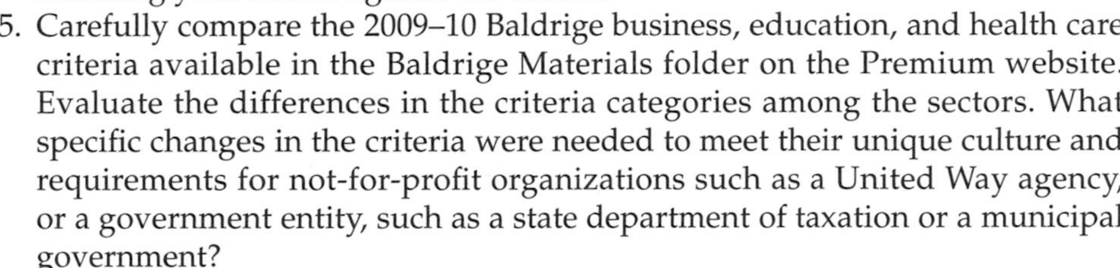

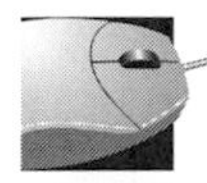

6. Does your state have a quality award program? If so, obtain some current information about the program and report on it. If not, contact your state representative to see why not.
7. Interview some managers at a local company that is pursuing or has pursued ISO 9000 registration. Report on the reasons for achieving registration, the perceived benefits, and the problems the company encountered during the process.
8. Search the Internet to find information about current registration trends for ISO 9000. How widespread is ISO 9000 in the United States as compared to Europe and other global regions?
9. Find a company that has implemented a Six Sigma process. What changes have they made in the organization in order to develop their Six Sigma approach?

CASES

Additional cases are available in the Bonus Materials folder on the Premium website.

SANTA CRUZ GUITAR COMPANY[50]

Santa Cruz Guitar Company (SCGC) is a small-scale manufacturing operation, producing fewer than 800 instruments a year. The company does not have a formal quality department nor has it consciously tried to apply the principles of TQM. Nevertheless, a tour of its facilities and operations suggest that many of the principles of TQM and Deming's 14 Points are evident.

Although modern computer numerical controlled (CNC) equipment is used to manufacture minor parts of the guitar, the secret of SCGC's success lies in the small staff of 14 craftsmen, known as luthiers, who apply care and attention to detail while hand-crafting the major components of each instrument. The shop floor is divided into six workstations at which the guitars are progressively assembled as they move from station to station. Experienced luthiers, who are empowered to make their own quality decisions, staff each station. The guitar does not move to the next station until the luthier and another more senior luthier are satisfied with the quality of the work. The manufacturing department inspects what it produces. The company recruits only those who desire to work in a team environment and have a passion for guitar making.

There are seven major steps in the process of making a guitar:

1. Selecting and drying the wood: The guitar making process starts with the selection of the highest grades of tonewoods. The wood is treated in an evaporative dehumidifying kiln that slowly and carefully removes bound cellular moisture from the wood. The target moisture level is 3 percent, but when exposed to the temperature/humidity conditions of the shop floor, the moisture content stabilizes at 6 percent. The shop floor is kept at a constant 47 percent humidity, which is optimum for maintaining the equilibrium of moisture conditions.
2. Rough cutting the wood: Once dried, the wood is worked down to rough usable forms using traditional woodworking tools. However, SCGC uses a CNC machine for creating the necks.
3. Bending the sides: To create the desired shapes, the guitar sides are first dipped into water for 10 minutes to condition the wood and then placed under gradual hand pressure on a hot bending template. At that point, the tension in the wood has been relaxed, and the wood eventually takes the shape of the template. This process is best performed by human hands because sides that are shaped by machines have a tendency to spring back when they are being forced into molds.
4. Cutting the top and back: The top and back of the guitars then are cut to shape, and braces are applied to each surface. The thicknesses of the top and braces have the most influence on the final sound of the guitar. As the luthier shaves off ribbons of wood from the top and braces, he will tap the top to hear the tone that results from each series of shavings until the tone is perfect. Because the true sound of the instruments will not be fully realized until they are assembled, the luthiers write down what they did while building the top. After final assembly, if a guitar produces a sound so special it knocks the player's socks off, the luthier who built the top will immediately be notified and asked to check his notes to see how this was accomplished so the sound can be duplicated in the future.
5. Cutting the neck: About 60 percent of the SCGC guitar necks are cut on the CNC machine. It is the only major part that is not hand-made. It is critical that the dimensions of the neck be consistent, and the CNC machine does that better than human hands. The 40 percent of necks that are hand-made are done that way because of a customer's specifications. Ebony fret boards, which are inlaid with mother-of-pearl, are then glued to the necks.
6. Applying the finish: The guitar body is finished with 12 protective layers of a specially formulated lacquer composed primarily of nitrocellulose and plasticizers to preserve the wood surfaces. But the lacquer is thin enough that the sound is not dampened.
7. Completing final assembly and setup: The neck is fitted to the body using a dovetail joint and glued in place. Then the bridge is glued to the body. In the next step, called the setup, the saddle and nut, which suspend the strings over the instrument and are made from bovine bones, are installed. Finally, the strings are placed on the guitar, and it is played for the first time. A technician then adjusts the neck or string height to optimize the feel and playability of the instrument.

SCGC has a web page where guitar owners can have questions about their guitars answered. At SCGC, workers are encouraged to further enhance their skills either by taking external courses or by a practice that allows them to build two instruments a year for personal use. These opportunities allow the craftsmen to explore new techniques in guitar building and become familiar with the entire guitar building process. SCGC workers are even encouraged to go out on their own to open a luthier business someday.

Based on this tour of SCGC, can you identify how the operations and quality practices reflect Deming's 14 points?

Can Six Sigma Work in Health Care?

Colin David is the CEO of Southwest Louisiana Regional Medical Center (SLRMC), a small nonprofit hospital with 150 beds and 825 employees, offering a wide range of outpatient and inpatient services. Colin had just returned from a health care conference during which one of the keynote speakers—from the financial services industry—discussed the philosophy and benefits of Six Sigma and urged health care organizations to consider moving toward a Six Sigma framework. Colin was quite excited. However, he knew that changing the culture in a hospital was indeed difficult. However, he felt that if he could accomplish that, SLRMC could truly become a nationally recognized leader in the industry. In discussing the concept, the executive management team was also excited about the possibilities. They identified four key areas where they thought that Six Sigma could lead to significant benefits: patient services, quality assessment, financial management, and human resources. As time was running short for the meeting, the team concluded with one major action item: The directors in charge of each of these four areas were to develop a set of strategic Six Sigma projects that would form the basis for the initiative. However, after the meeting broke up, Colin realized that in their initial euphoria over the potential of Six Sigma, they had not thought of how to introduce it to the hospital staff and physicians, or how to manage the initiative. Colin decided that it would be best to call in a consultant to help. Because you were highly recommended, you have a meeting scheduled with Colin in one week. What would be your agenda for this meeting? What questions would you need answered before proposing a Six Sigma implementation plan? How would you design an infrastructure to support Six Sigma at SLRMC?

Novel Connect: Understanding the Organizational Environment

BONUS MATERIALS

The complete Novel Connect case study, a fictitious example of a Baldrige application, can be found in the Baldrige Materials folder on the Premium website. (The case is based on the 2008 Baldrige criteria, which may have some key differences in the criteria questions as compared to later versions of the criteria, however these differences are not relevant for this case.) Read the Organizational Profile, which is a description of the organizational environment, relationships, and challenges that impact the company's performance excellence approaches. In examining the scope of the first six categories (excluding results) in the 2008 Baldrige criteria (also available in the Baldrige Materials folder on the Premium website), list the most relevant factors from the Organizational Profile that would affect your assessment of the management practices for this organization. For example, in considering the Customer Focus category, you might note that one of Novel Connect's strategic challenges is rapidly changing customer and market needs and volatility in niche markets. Therefore, you might expect to see that a key customer focus practice would be listening and learning about those needs. You might also note that a key success factor is a strong relationship with carriers; thus building relationships with them would be vital to this company. As a result, in your listing of the most relevant factors for the Customer Focus category, two of them might be:

- rapidly changing customer and market needs and volatility in niche markets
- strong relationship with carriers

Others might include basic characteristics of their customer base as identified in the Organizational Profile, such as:

- Key customer segments: personal consumers (students in Gen-Y, celebrities and sports stars, preteens, single adult females, the elderly, the disabled); personal/business consumers ("outdoors people"); business consumers (truckers, taxi drivers); business/government consumers (emergency services workers); and government consumers (the Department of Homeland Security)
- Key customer requirements: all—ease of use, reliability; personal consumers—trendiness, convenience, secure/encrypted data and transmission, personal/home safety and security, low cost, ruggedness; business consumers—ruggedness, personal safety and security, data and voice capability, sustained signal/strength across distances, secure/encrypted data and transmission; business/government consumers—security, data and voice capability, secure/encrypted data and transmission, sustained signal/strength across distances

Complete this list for each category and briefly justify why the factors you chose would be important.

SHARE FOOD CASE STUDY: UNDERSTANDING THE ORGANIZATIONAL ENVIRONMENT

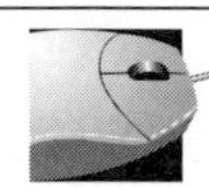

BONUS MATERIALS

The complete Share Food case study, a fictitious example of a Baldrige application based on the 2007 criteria (which is essentially the same as the 2008 criteria), can be found in the Baldrige Materials folder on the Premium website. Read the Organizational Profile and perform the same type of analysis as requested in the previous case for Novel Connect.

NOTES

1. John Hillkirk, "World-Famous Quality Expert Dead at 93," *USA Today*, December 21, 1993.
2. W. Edwards Deming, *The New Economics for Industry, Government, Education* (Cambridge, MA: MIT Center for Advanced Engineering Study, 1993).
3. The quincunx simulator is contained in the Quality Gamebox, a registered trademark of P-Q Systems, Inc., 10468 Miamisburg-Springboro Road, Miamisburg, OH 45342; 937-885-2255; 800-777-3020. It can be purchased and downloaded at: http://www.pqsystems.com/products/sixsigma/QualityGamebox/QualityGamebox.php
4. Clarence Irving Lewis, *Mind and the World* (Mineola, NY: Dover, 1929).
5. Reprinted with permission from Peter Scholtes, "Communities as Systems," *Quality Progress*, July 1997, 49–53. Copyright © 1997 American Society for Quality. No further distribution allowed without permission.
6. Matthew W. Ford and James R. Evans, "The Role of Follow-Up in Achieving Results from Self-Assessment Processes, *International Journal of Quality and Reliability Management*, Vol. 23, Issue 6, 2006.
7. Walter A. Shewhart, *Economic Control of Quality of a Manufactured Product* (New York: Van Nostrand, 1931).
8. Adapted from March Laree Jacques, "Big League Quality," *Quality Progress*, August 2001, 27–34.
9. "Juran Honors Japanese Quality at His 100th Birthday Event," *Quality Digest*, June 2004, 6.
10. Jeremy Main, "Under the Spell of the Quality Gurus," *Fortune*, August 18, 1986, 30–34.
11. Philip B. Crosby, *Quality Is Free* (New York: McGraw-Hill, 1979), 200–201.
12. Facts in this section were obtained from "Profile: the ASQC Honorary Members A. V. Feigenbaum and Kaoru Ishikawa," *Quality Progress* 19, no. 8 (August 1986), 43–45; and Bruce Brocka and M. Suzanne Brocka, *Quality Management: Implementing the Best Ideas of the Masters* (Homewood, IL: Business One Irwin, 1992).
13. Adapted from Jerry R. Junkins, "Insights of a Baldrige Award Winner," *Quality Progress* 27, no. 3 (March 1994), 57–58. Used with permission of Texas Instruments.
14. Nancy Blodgett, "Service Organizations Increasingly Adopt Baldrige Model," *Quality Progress*, December 1999, 74–78.
15. Paul W. DeBaylo, "Ten Reasons Why the Baldrige Model Works," *The Journal for Quality and Participation*, January/February 1999, 1–5.
16. DeBaylo, ibid.
17. Paul M. Bobrowski, and John H. Bantham, "State Quality Initiatives: Mini-Baldrige to Baldrige Plus,"

National Productivity Review 13, no. 3 (Summer 1994), 423–438.

18. Letter from W. Edwards Deming, *Harvard Business Review*, January–February 1992, 134.

19. See the EFQM website for a brief history and explanation of the model, found at: http://ww1.efqm.org/en/Home/aboutEFQM/Ourmodels/TheEFQMExcellenceModel/tabid/170/Default.aspx (accessed 7/20/09).

20. B. Nakhai, and J. Neves, "The Deming, Baldrige, and European Quality Awards," *Quality Progress*, April 1994, 33–37.

21. "China Issues New Quality Standard," *Quality Digest*, December 2004, http://www.qualitydigest.com/dec04/news.shtml#3, accessed 4/08/06.

22. Jack Pompeo "Living Inside China's Quality Revolution" *Quality Progress*, August 2007, 30–35.

23. "Chinese Businesses Receive Six Sigma Awards," *Quality Digest*, February 2005, http://www.qualitydigest.com/feb05/news.shtml accessed 4/08/06.

24. Barbara B. Flynn and Brooke Saladin, "Relevance of Baldrige constructs in an international context: A study of national culture," *Journal of Operations Management*, 2005.

25. Michael J. Timbers, "ISO 9000 and Europe's Attempts to Mandate Quality," *Journal of European Business*, March–April 1992, 14–25.

26. http://www.bsi.org.uk/iso-tc176-sc2/ "Transition Planning Guidance for ISO/DIS 9001:2000," ISO/TC 176/SC 2/N 474, December, 1999.

27. Dirk Dusharme, "ISO 9001: The Shift to Service," *Quality Digest*, July 2005, 33–36; John Scott, "ISO 9000 in Service: The Good, the Bad, and the Ugly," *Quality Progress*, September 2005, 42–48.

28. John E. "Jack" West. "Small Change, Big Payoff" *Quality Progress*, April 2009, 47–52.

29. William A. Stimson, "Better Public Schools With ISO 9000:2000," *Quality Progress*, September 2003, 38–45.

30. Amy Zuckerman, "ISO/QS-9000 Registration Issues Heating Up Worldwide," *The Quality Observer*, June 1997, 21–23.

31. Amy Zuckerman and Rosalind McClymont, "Tracking the Ongoing ISO 9000 Revisions," *Business Standards*, 2, no. 2 (March–April 2000), 13–15; Jack West, with Charles A. Cianfrani and Joseph J. Tsiakals, "A Breeze or a Breakthough? Conforming to ISO 9000:2000," *Quality Progress*, March 2000, 41–44. See also by West et al., "Quality Management Principles: Foundation of ISO 9000:2000 Family, Part 5," *Quality Progress*, February 2000, 113–116; and "Quality Management Principles: Foundation of ISO 9000:2000 Family, Part 6," *Quality Progress*, March 2000, 79–81.

32. Implementation guidelines are suggested by the case study by Steven E. Webster, "ISO 9000 Certification, A Success Story at Nu Visions Manufacturing," *IIE Solutions*, April 1997, 18–21.

33. Jack Dearing, "ISO 9001: Could It Be Better?" *Quality Progress*, February 2007, 23–27.

34. ISO 9000 Update, *Fortune*, September 30, 1996, 134[J].

35. Astrid L. H. Eckstein, and Jaydeep Balakrishnan, "The ISO 9000 Series: Quality Management Systems for the Global Economy," *Production and Inventory Management Journal* 34, no. 4 (Fourth Quarter 1993), 66–71.

36. "Home Builder Constructs Quality with ISO 9000," *Quality Digest*, February 2000, 13.

37. Sandford Liebesman and James Mroz, "ISO 9000:2000 Experiences: First Results Are In," *Quality Progress*, April 2002, 52–59.

38. "Origin of Six Sigma: Designing for Performance Excellence," *Quality Digest*, (May 2000), 30; and Harry, Mikel and Richard Schroeder. *Six Sigma* (New York: Currency, 2000), 9–11.

39. A composite of ideas suggested by Stanley A Marash, "Six Sigma: Business Results Through Innovation," *ASQ's 54th Annual Quality Congress Proceedings*, 2000, 627–630; and Dick Smith and Jerry Blakeslee, *Strategic Six Sigma: Best Practices from the Executive Suite* (New York: Wiley, 2002).

40. Jack Welch, *Jack: Straight from the Gut* (New York: Warner Books, 2001), 329–330.

41. Jack Welch, ibid, 333–334.

42. "GE Reports Record Earnings with Six Sigma," *Quality Digest*, December 1999, 14.

43. See note 39.

44. Rochelle Rucker, "Six Sigma at Citibank," *Quality Digest*, December 1999, 28–32.

45. Ronald D. Snee, "Guest Editorial: Impact of Six Sigma on Quality Engineering," *Quality Engineering* 12, no. 3 2000, ix–xiv.

46. Ronald D. Snee and Roger W. Hoerl, *Leading Six Sigma* (Upper Saddle River, NJ: Prentice-Hall, 2002).

47. The authors are grateful to Joe Sener, VP Business Excellence for Baxter International, for providing this information.

48. Text adapted from Pam Parry, "Sears Delivers a Better QMS," *Quality Digest*, January 10, 2007.

49. Adapted from Denis Leonard, "Building Quality at Veridian Homes," *Quality Progress*, October 2006, 49–54. Copyright © 2006 American Society for Quality. Text does not require permission.

50. Reprinted with permission from Luke T. Foo, "Good Vibrations: Ingrained Quality Practices Mirror Deming's 14 points," *Quality Progress*, February 2008, pp. 25–30. Copyright © 2008 American Society for Quality. No further distribution allowed without permission.

PART 2

THE MANAGEMENT SYSTEM

For quality to succeed in an organization, it must become a part of everyone's daily activities. A total quality system must be built on effective managerial practices that leverage an organization's strategic planning; focus on customers; involve and motivate everyone; control and continuously improve processes; provide useful information to maintain high performance; and provide leadership to build and sustain the organization. The Baldrige framework, introduced in Chapter 3, provides a structure for designing an organization around high-performance management practices. Part 2 of this book addresses the seven key elements of the Baldrige criteria on which a total quality foundation should be built.

Chapter 4 focuses on the importance of a strategic orientation for performance excellence, including strategic leadership, strategic planning, and organizational and work systems design. Chapter 5 examines the role and importance of customers and customer satisfaction in achieving performance excellence and describes various approaches for acquiring customer knowledge and measuring satisfaction. Chapter 6 examines the role of the workforce in achieving total quality, including designing, managing, and sustaining high-performance work systems. Chapter 7 discusses process management, including approaches for designing, controlling, and improving the processes by which work is accomplished. Chapter 8 deals with measurement and strategic information management, focusing on the importance of using a balanced set of performance measures and business results to guide organizational decisions and direction. In each of these chapters, we describe key practices that high-performance organizations, primarily Baldrige recipients, use in deploying the principles of total quality and examine how each topic is also addressed in ISO 9000 and Six Sigma initiatives. Finally, Chapter 9 focuses on the role of leadership in driving quality throughout an organization and addresses the all-important topic of how to build a true quality organization by developing a culture that promotes high performance and provides the motivation and direction for everyone to work toward the organization's vision. This chapter looks toward the future; as you read it, we hope that you will also look toward your future and what these principles will mean to the rest of your life.

Strategic Focus for Performance Excellence

Outline

Quality Profiles: Pal's Sudden Service and Premier, Inc.
Strategic Leadership
Understanding the Organizational Environment
Strategy Development
Strategy Deployment
Hoshin Kanri (Policy Deployment)
Linking Human Resource Plans and Business Strategy
The Seven Management and Planning Tools
Organizational Design for Performance Excellence
Core Competencies and Strategic Work System Design
Strategic Planning in the Baldrige Criteria, ISO 9000, and Six Sigma
Quality in Practice: Integrating Six Sigma with Strategic Planning at Cigna
Quality in Practice: Strategic Planning at Branch-Smith Printing Division
Review Questions
Discussion Questions
Problems
Projects, Etc.
Cases A Strategic Bottleneck
Clifton Metal Works
Novel Connect—Core Competencies and Work System Design
Novel Connect—Strategic Planning

In the executive suite at Best Buy's Minneapolis headquarters can be found a mock "retail hospital"—including a row of beds in which effigies of retailers like Kmart and Woolworth lie with their corporate logos propped up on pillows and awful financial results displayed on bedside charts.[1] A sign nearby reads: THIS IS WHERE COMPANIES GO WHEN THEIR STRATEGIES GET SICK. This provides a constant reminder that organizational success requires a clear, actionable, and effective strategy that must be kept current and fluid.

The concept of strategy holds different meanings for different people. One characterization of strategy is:

> *A strategy is a pattern or plan that integrates an organization's major goals, policies, and action sequences into a cohesive whole. A well-formulated strategy helps to marshal and allocate an organization's resources into*

a unique and viable posture based on its relative internal competencies and shortcomings, anticipated changes in the environment, and contingent moves by intelligent opponents.[2]

Essentially, **strategy** is the pattern of decisions that determines and reveals an organization's goals, policies, and plans to meet the needs of its stakeholders. **Strategic planning** is the process of envisioning the organization's future and developing the necessary goals, objectives, and action plans to achieve that future. For many firms, quality and performance excellence are essential elements of business strategy, as we saw in the case about Xerox in Chapter 1.

A strategy provides a roadmap to achieve a vision of what the organization should and could be three, five, or more years in the future. A good strategy should build a competitive posture that is so strong in selective ways that the organization can achieve its goals despite unforeseeable external forces.

Developing and implementing a strategy requires a robust and effective strategic planning and action plan deployment process. An effective strategic planning process requires that executives and managers understand the short- and longer-term factors that affect the organization and its marketplace, such as customers' expectations, new business and partnering opportunities, workforce development and hiring needs, the increasingly global marketplace, technological developments, the evolving e-business environment, changes in customer and market segments, evolving regulatory requirements, changes in community and societal expectations and needs, and strategic moves by competitors. However, while many organizations are quite proficient at strategic planning, executing plans is often a significant challenge. This is especially true in changing markets that require agility and preparation for unexpected change, such as disruptive technologies that can upset an otherwise fast-paced but more predictable marketplace.

The Baldrige Criteria maintain a strong focus on strategic thinking and organizational sustainability, and reflect much of Deming's philosophy regarding the need to plan for the long term. Pursuit of sustainable growth and market leadership requires a strong future orientation and a willingness to make long-term commitments to key stakeholders—customers, workforce, suppliers, partners, stockholders, the public, and the community. Thus, a focus on both customer- and stakeholder-driven quality and operational performance excellence, as opposed to simply financial and marketing goals, is essential to an effective strategy. To be competitive and profitable, an organization must focus on the drivers of customer satisfaction, customer retention, and market share; and build operational capability, including speed, responsiveness, and flexibility, to contribute to short- and longer-term productivity growth and cost/price competitiveness. Strategic planning also provides a framework for improvement and organizational learning. A key role of strategic planning is to align work processes and learning initiatives with an organization's strategic directions, thereby ensuring that improvement and learning prepare for and reinforce organizational priorities.

Organizations must also take a broad strategic focus in designing the organization and its work systems, and leveraging its core competencies—the things it does best. These include decisions regarding design of the organizational structure and leadership system, the structure of the supply chain, and outsourcing decisions. Table 4.1 summarizes key practices that organizations must address to achieve a strategic focus on performance excellence. The Quality Profiles highlight two organizations whose strategic focus has been vital to their success. We will expand upon these themes in the remainder of this chapter.

Table 4.1 Key Practices for a Strategic Focus on Performance Excellence

- Understand the organization's operating environment and its key relationships with customers, suppliers, partners, and stakeholders.
- Understand the competitive environment, the principal factors that determine success, the organization's core competencies, and strategic challenges—business, operational, and human resource-related—associated with organizational sustainability.
- Gather and analyze relevant data and information pertaining to such factors as the organizations strengths, weaknesses, opportunities, and threats; emerging trends in technology, markets, customer preferences, competitions, and the regulatory environment; long-term organizational sustainability; and the ability to execute strategic plans.
- Develop and refine a systematic approach for conducting strategic planning and setting strategic objectives, including identifying blind spots, leveraging strengths, and addressing challenges over appropriate time horizons.
- Develop and align short-term action plans with long-term strategic objectives, ensure adequate resources and the ability to sustain outcomes, assess financial and other risks associated with the plans, and communicate them throughout the organization.
- Derive human resource plans required to accomplish longer-term strategic objectives and shorter-term action plans that address the potential impacts on the workforce and potential changes to workforce capability and capacity needs.
- Identify key measures or indicators for tracking progress on action plans, ensure that the measurement system reinforces organizational alignment, and project performance of these key measures compared with competitors or comparable organizations to identify gaps and opportunities.
- Determine the organization's core competencies, and understand how they relate to the mission, competitive environment, and strategic objectives.
- View the work performed within the organization as a system, and make rational decisions about the mix of internal and external work processes that can best achieve the organization's mission.

Quality Profiles

Pal's Sudden Service and Premier, Inc.

A privately owned, quick-service restaurant chain, Pal's Sudden Service, serves hamburgers, hot dogs, chipped ham, chicken, French fries, and beverages as well as breakfast biscuits with country ham, sausage, and gravy to primarily drive-through customers at 17 locations, all within 60 miles of Kingsport, Tennessee. The company aims to distinguish itself from fast-food competitors by offering competitively priced food of consistently high quality, delivered rapidly, cheerfully, and without error. The company's Business Excellence Process is the key integrating element, a management approach to ensuring that customer requirements are met in every transaction, today and in the future. Carried out under the leadership of Pal's two top executives and its 17 store owner/operators, the Business Excellence Process spans all facets of the operation from strategic planning (done annually with two-year horizons) to online quality control. Every component process, including those for continual improvement and product introduction, is interactively linked, producing data that directly or indirectly inform the others. In customer satisfaction, including food quality, service, and order accuracy, Pal's is outperforming its primary competitor. Pal's order handout speed improved more than 30 percent since 1995, decreasing from 31 seconds to 20 seconds, almost four times faster than its top competitor. Errors in orders are rare, averaging less than one for every 2,000 transactions. In addition, Pal's consistently receives the highest health inspection scores in its market and in the entire state of Tennessee.

Serving 1,700 hospitals and more than 43,000 other health care sites, Premier Inc. is the largest health care alliance in the United States dedicated to improving patient outcomes while safely reducing the cost of care. Premier's three business units provide the following services: group purchasing and supply chain management, insurance and risk management, and informatics and performance improvement tools.

Premier's "Big Hairy Audacious Goal" is for its member hospitals to deliver the best, most cost-effective care in the nation and for the alliance to have a major influence on reshaping health care. The success of this strategy is evident:

- Hospitals that make up the Premier alliance have validated more than $2.5 billion in savings over the past three years achieved through cooperative purchasing and participation in Premier's other services.
- Premier's customer satisfaction levels of over 90 percent significantly exceed industry benchmarks.
- Premier is partnering with the Centers for Medicare and Medicaid Services (CMS) in a voluntary national demonstration project aimed at improving the quality of inpatient health care. Through the Premier Hospital Quality Incentive Demonstration, CMS is rewarding top performing hospitals for high quality care by increasing their payments for Medicare patients. The results show that participating hospitals have shown dramatic improvements in quality and performance.
- Operating margin grew from 35 percent in 2003 to 50 percent in 2006 and exceeded that of Premier's largest competitor in all years, while operating expenses have remained well below those of that competitor.

Premier has taken a leadership role in promoting best practices in ethical conduct, transparency, and accountability within its own organization and throughout the industry. In 1998, Premier instituted a Corporate Values Program and an employee Values Conference at which employees and senior leaders together discuss Premier's Core Values—focus on people, integrity, passion for performance, and innovation. The company's customers, who are also its owners, work closely with Premier and its employees to achieve their mutual goals. All of Premier's owners and other customers have ready access to the company's information, staff, resources, and services, particularly through Premier's field staff and its customer solution centers.

Source: Adapted from Malcolm Baldrige National Quality Award Profiles of Winners, National Institute of Standards and Technology, Department of Commerce.

STRATEGIC LEADERSHIP

Although we will discuss leadership in depth in Chapter 9, it is important to understand that strategy and leadership are inextricably linked. For a strategy to be successful, senior leaders must have extensive involvement in the planning process, create an environment for competitive success and performance leadership, and guide the design of the work and leadership systems that will ensure that the strategy is carried out.

Management theorists and practitioners have long recognized the differences between the work of senior leaders and those who perform supervisory roles at the operating levels. Senior leaders must think globally, while acting locally (in both a geographic and conceptual sense). This has been driven by the explosion in knowledge and complexity in the global business environment over the past several decades. In a study conducted by International Consortium for Executive Development Research,[3] 1,450 executives from 12 global companies were asked the question: "What are the key competencies that will emerge as critical for leadership effectiveness in the next three years?" Among 45 competencies that were suggested, the top one was: "articulate a tangible vision, values, and strategy." This was followed closely by: "be a catalyst/manager of strategic change;" and "get results—manage strategy to action."

These perspectives have led to the concept of **strategic leadership**, which can be defined as "a person's ability to anticipate, envision, maintain flexibility, think strategically, and work with others to initiate changes that will create a viable future for the organization, and its competitive advantage to the organization in this way."[4] Activities that strategic leaders perform generally include creating and communicating a vision of the future, sustaining an effective organization culture, making strategic decisions, developing key competencies and responsibilities, managing multiple constituencies, selecting and developing the next generation of leaders, and infusing ethical value systems into an organization's culture. Effective strategic leaders also have the capability to create and maintain what is termed absorptive capacity (the ability for an organization to learn) and adaptive capacity (the ability of an organization to change) in order to deal with increasingly hyper-turbulent environments.[5] Such leaders must also exhibit managerial wisdom, with the ability to perceive variation in their environment and understand the social actors and their relationship in the system.

Strategic leadership can also be viewed from three levels, similar to the way we viewed the three levels of quality in Chapter 1. From this perspective, senior leaders are involved in vision and strategy formulation, mid-level leaders develop executable action plans and projects that best use an organization's resources,[6] and supervisory leaders ensure that these action plans are deployed throughout the organization so that essential tasks and projects may be accomplished in support of the strategic vision.

The concept of strategic leadership has moved leadership perspectives away from the solitary "great leader" paradigm toward a team- and system-based "great group" concept.[7] Thus, the characteristics of effective strategic leadership include

- Serving as both leaders and team members;
- Demonstrating the importance of integrity through actions rather than simply articulating it;
- Thinking in terms of processes rather than outcomes;
- Leveraging the collective knowledge of everyone in the organization;
- Designing work that reflects relationships rather than the organizational hierarchy;
- Anticipating environmental change rather than reacting to it;
- Viewing employees as organizational citizens rather than resources; and
- Operating with a global mindset rather than a domestic mindset.

Many of these notions of strategic leadership are reflected in the Baldrige criteria, which recognize the value of strategic leadership in driving performance excellence.

UNDERSTANDING THE ORGANIZATIONAL ENVIRONMENT

An organization cannot make good strategic decisions without a solid understanding of its internal and external environments. Yet, you would be amazed at how few senior executives truly grasp these characteristics and their impact on strategic decisions.

The Baldrige Criteria provides a list of key questions called the **Organizational Profile**, which addresses the basic characteristics of the organization, organizational relationships, the competitive environment, the advantages an organization has and the challenges that it faces, and its approach to performance improvement. The Organizational Profile provides the "big picture" of the organization and sets the context for good strategic decisions. These questions are shown in Table 4.2.

These characteristics, such as the mission, vision, values, competitive environment, core competencies, and strategic challenges, impact the way an organization is run and the decisions that are made. Why is this important? The simple answer is that understanding these factors helps to better focus strategic thinking within the organization. For example, knowledge of an organization's strengths, vulnerabilities, and opportunities for both improvement and growth helps an organization to identify those products, service and program offerings, processes, competencies, and performance attributes that are unique; those that set it apart from other organizations; and those that help to sustain a competitive advantage.

The Organizational Profile provides a frame of reference to help an organization better understand the internal and external factors that shape its operating environment, the key requirements for current and future business success, and organizational sustainability; and the needs, opportunities, and constraints placed on the organization's performance management system.

The first set of questions, under the heading "Organizational Environment," help to provide a clear understanding of the essence of the organization, why it exists, and where senior leaders want to take the organization in the future. An organization's main goods and services, how it provides them to customers, and its organizational culture are often reflected in formal mission, vision, and values statements (think back to Deming's point on defining the purpose of an organization).

A mission statement might include a definition of products and services the organization provides, technologies used to provide these products and services, types of markets, important customer needs, and distinctive competencies or the expertise that sets the firm apart from others. For example, the mission of Pal's Sudden Service and Premier, Inc. (see the Quality Profiles in this chapter) are respectively, *To deliver excellence in food service while providing a menu focused on exceptional quality*, and *To improve the health of communities*.

*The **mission** of a firm defines its reason for existence; it answers the question "Why are we in business?"*

A firm's mission guides the development of strategies by different groups within the firm. It establishes the context within which daily operating decisions are made and sets limits on available strategic options. In addition, it governs the trade-offs among the various performance measures and between short- and long-term goals. Finally, it can inspire employees to focus their efforts toward the overall purpose of the organization.

*The **vision** describes where the organization is headed and what it intends to be; it is a statement of the future that would not happen by itself.*

The vision articulates the basic characteristics that shape the organization's view of the future and its strategy. A vision should be brief, focused, clear, and inspirational to an organization's employees. It should be linked to customers' needs and convey a general strategy for achieving the mission. For example, Premier's vision is stated as its "Big Hairy Audacious Goal"—

Table 4.2 Baldrige Organizational Profile Questions

1. Organizational Description
   a. Organizational Environment
      (1) What are your organization's main product offerings? What are the delivery mechanisms used to provide your products to your customers?
      (2) What are the key characteristics of your organizational culture? What are your stated purpose, vision, values, and mission? What are your organization's core competencies and their relationship to your mission?
      (3) What is your workforce profile? What are your workforce or employee groups and segments? What are their education levels? What are the key factors that motivate them to engage in accomplishing your mission? What are your organization's workforce and job diversity, organized bargaining units, key benefits, and special health and safety requirements?
      (4) What are your major facilities, technologies, and equipment?
      (5) What is the regulatory environment under which your organization operates? What are the applicable occupational health and safety regulations; accreditation, certification, or registration requirements; relevant industry standards; and environmental, financial, and product regulations?
   b. Organizational Relationships
      (1) What are your organizational structure and governance system? What are the reporting relationships among your governance board, senior leaders, and parent organization, as appropriate?
      (2) What are your key market segments, customer groups, and stakeholder groups, as appropriate? What are their key requirements and expectations for your products, customer support services, and operations? What are the differences in these requirements and expectations among market segments, customer groups, and stakeholder groups?
      (3) What are your key types of suppliers, partners, and collaborators? What role do these suppliers, partners, and collaborators play in your work systems and the production and delivery of your key products and customer support services? What are your key mechanisms for communicating and managing relationships with suppliers, partners, and collaborators? What role, if any, do these organizations play in your organizational innovation processes? What are your key supply chain requirements?

2. Organizational Situation
   a. Competitive Environment
      (1) What is your competitive position? What is your relative size and growth in your industry or markets served? What are the numbers and types of competitors for your organization?
      (2) What are the principal factors that determine your success relative to your competitors? What are any key changes taking place that affect your competitive situation, including opportunities for innovation and collaboration, as appropriate?
      (3) What are your key available sources of comparative and competitive data from within your industry? What are your key available sources of comparative data from outside your industry? What limitations, if any, are there in your ability to obtain these data?
   b. Strategic Context
      What are your key business, operational, and human resource strategic challenges and advantages? What are your key strategic challenges and advantages associated with organizational sustainability?
   c. Performance Improvement System
      What are the key elements of your performance improvement system, including your evaluation and learning processes?

Premier's Owners will be the leading health care systems in their markets, and, with them, Premier will be a major influence in reshaping health care. Pal's Sudden Service vision statement is somewhat more detailed:

> *To be the preferred quick service restaurant in our market achieving the largest market share by providing:*
>
> - *The quickest, friendliest, most accurate service available*
> - *A focused menu that delights customers*
> - *Daily excellence in our product, service, and systems execution*
> - *Clean, organized, sanitary facilities*
> - *Exceptional value*
> - *A fun, positive, and profitable experience for all stakeholders*

A vision must be consistent with the culture and values of the organization, which are often stated formally to provide guidance to all employees and leaders in the organization.

Pal's Sudden Service Values and Code of Ethics are stated as:

> ***Values**, or **guiding principles**, guide the journey to a vision by defining attitudes and policies for all employees, which are reinforced through conscious and subconscious behavior at all levels of the organization.*

> ***Positive Energy*** *We will always nurture a positive, enthusiastic atmosphere, which will foster mutual trust and respect among employees, customers, and suppliers. Further, we will always operate with open agendas, positive interactions, and genuine motives.*
>
> ***Honesty and Truthfulness*** *We will always be honest and truthful in all relationships, respecting and relying on each other.*
>
> ***Employee Well Being*** *We will always provide a safe, healthy, and desirable workplace.*
>
> ***Citizenship*** *We will always provide community involvement through personal and company contributions of time, effort, and resources. Through our best effort and consideration, we will always protect public health, safety, and the environment.*
>
> ***Golden Rule*** *We will always do unto others as we would have them do unto us.*

For Premier, the core values are

> ***Integrity*** *of the individual and the enterprise.*
>
> ***A passion for performance*** *and a bias for action, creating real value for all stakeholders, and leading the pace.*
>
> ***Innovation:*** *Seeking breakthrough opportunities, taking risks, and initiating meaningful change.*
>
> ***Focus on people:*** *Showing concern and respect for all with whom we work, building collaborative relationships with the community, our customers, co-workers, and business associates.*

The mission, vision, and guiding principles serve as the foundation for strategic planning. Top management and others who lead, especially the CEO, must articulate them. They also have to be transmitted, practiced, and reinforced through symbolic and real action before they become "real" to the employees and the people, groups, and organizations in the external environment that do business with the firm.

Most organizations have a very diverse workforce from the perspective of job descriptions and responsibilities. In a manufacturing firm, for example, the workforce might be comprised of skilled labor, white-collar knowledge workers, and different levels of management; a health care system has physicians, nurses, general labor, managers, and so on. Some groups may be unionized and others not. Each of these groups may differ in terms of their requirements for training and safety, compensation and rewards, and motivation, for instance. This can impact the strategic decisions that the organization makes. Similarly, the mix of facilities, technologies, and equipment used in operations may limit strategic choices and affect how key processes are managed. Finally, the regulatory environment in which an organization operates places specific requirements on the organization. Understanding this environment is vital to making effective operational and strategic decisions. Further, it allows one to identify whether the organization is merely complying with the minimum requirements of applicable laws, regulations, and standards of practice or exceeding them, a hallmark of leading organizations.

The second group of questions, listed under "Organizational Relationships," addresses the organizational structure, governance system, differences among customer and stakeholder groups, and supplier and partnering relationships. Leading organizations have well-defined governance systems with clear reporting relationships. It is important to clearly identify which functions are performed by senior leaders and, as applicable, by the governance board and the parent organization. Board independence and accountability frequently are key considerations in the governance structure.

Customer groups and market segments might be based on product or service lines or features, distribution channels, business volume, geography, or other factors that are important to your organization to define related market characteristics. Requirements might include on-time delivery, low defect levels, safety, security, ongoing price reductions, electronic communication, rapid response, after-sales service, socially responsible behavior, and community service. Understanding these can help design the most appropriate products and service delivery systems.

In supplier-dependent organizations, suppliers play critical roles in processes that are important to running the business and to maintaining or achieving a sustainable competitive advantage. Supply chain requirements might include on-time or just-in-time delivery, flexibility, variable staffing, research and design capability, and customized manufacturing or services.

The remaining questions in the Organizational Profile address key organizational challenges. Understanding who the competitors of an organization are, how many an organization has, and their key characteristics is essential for determining what competitive advantage an organization may have in its industry and marketplace. Leading organizations have an in-depth understanding of their current competitive environment, including the factors that affect day-to-day performance and factors that could impact future performance. Sources of comparative and competitive data might include industry journals and other publications, benchmarking activities, annual reports for publicly traded companies and public organizations, conferences, local networks, and industry associations.

Strategic challenges frequently are driven by an organization's future competitive position relative to other providers of similar products or services. They might include operational costs (e.g., materials, labor, or geographic location); expanding or decreasing markets; mergers or acquisitions both by the organization and by its competitors; economic conditions, including fluctuating demand and local and global economic downturns; the cyclical nature of the industry; the introduction of new or substitute products or services; rapid technological changes; or new competitors entering the market. In addition, an organization may face challenges related to the recruitment, hiring, and retention

*The term **strategic challenges** refers to those pressures that exert a decisive influence on an organization's likelihood of future success.*

of a qualified workforce. For example, like most health care organizations today, North Mississippi Medical Center faces strategic challenges such as shortages of health care providers and unique challenges in their community such as a high poverty level, poor health status, and lack of health care insurance. Their most significant strategic challenges are organized by their five critical success factors:[8]

PEOPLE—Maintain and enhance our employees' satisfaction, skills, and engagement. Recruit and retain skilled staff. Develop staff and physician leaders.

SERVICE—Increase our patients' and physicians' satisfaction. Enhance our patient–customer loyalty.

QUALITY—Provide high level, evidence-based, quality care and maintain patient safety.

FINANCIAL—Generate the financial resources necessary to support the organization in an environment of reimbursement pressures and increasing charity care.

GROWTH—Continue to expand in areas consistent with our Mission.

A particularly significant challenge that some organizations face is being unprepared for a disruptive technology that threatens its competitive position or its marketplace. In the past, such technologies have included personal computers replacing typewriters, cell phones challenging land lines and pay phones, fax machines capturing business from overnight delivery services, and e-mail challenging all other means of correspondence. Today, organizations need to be scanning the environment inside and outside their immediate industry to detect such challenges at the earliest possible point in time.

One of the many issues facing organizations today is how to manage, use, evaluate, and share their ever-increasing organizational knowledge. Leading organizations already benefit from the knowledge assets of their workforce, customers, suppliers, collaborators, and partners, who together drive organizational learning and improve performance. To leverage this knowledge, organizations need a performance improvement approach that can systematically drive organizational change. Overall approaches to performance improvement might include implementing a Lean Enterprise System, applying Six Sigma, using the ISO 9000:2000 or Baldrige frameworks, or employing other process improvement approaches that we will discuss throughout this book.

STRATEGY DEVELOPMENT

The goal of strategy development is envisioning the future for purposes of decision making and resource allocation. Henry Mintzberg, an unconventional thinker when it comes to management and organizational structures, describes strategy development as

> *. . . . capturing what the manager learns from all sources (both soft insights from his or her personal experiences and the experiences of others throughout the organization and the hard data from market research and the like) and then synthesizing that learning into a vision of the direction that the business should pursue.*[9]

In many organizations, strategy development is nothing more a group of managers sitting around in a room and proposing ideas. Clearly this is not an effective approach. Using a systematic process helps to optimize the use of resources, ensure the availability of trained employees, and ensure bridging between short- and longer-term requirements that may entail capital expenditures or supplier development, for example. Caterpillar Financial Services Corporation uses a structured six-step strategic planning process that yields both a one-year tactical

Effective strategy development requires a systematic process that involves participation by all necessary stakeholders, ensures that relevant and important data and information are captured and analyzed, addresses both short- and long-term time horizons, addresses key strategic challenges, and leads to innovation and sustainability.

plan and a four-year strategic plan. The process starts with an annual retreat where strategic direction is revised by the top senior leaders, followed by a four-month strategy development period; an annual leadership conference where the top 45 leaders and managers develop preliminary division strategies and support department requirements; a cycle for developing action plans and goals for divisions, support departments, and Six Sigma projects; a plan review and resource allocation step; and, the final step of developing unit action plans/goals and individual employee performance and development plans.

Although specific approaches vary from one organization to another, all generally follow the basic model that Eastman Chemical Company uses as shown in Figure 4.1. This model begins with gathering critical information about the organization and its environment, developing a strategy, translating that strategy into specific action plans or projects, and reviewing performance for improvement opportunities. In some organizations, strategic planning might involve participation by key suppliers, distributors, partners, and customers. It is not unusual for customers and suppliers to be involved in strategic planning efforts because of their importance in the supply chain and their knowledge of markets and technology.

Figure 4.1 Strategic Planning Process at Eastman Chemical Company

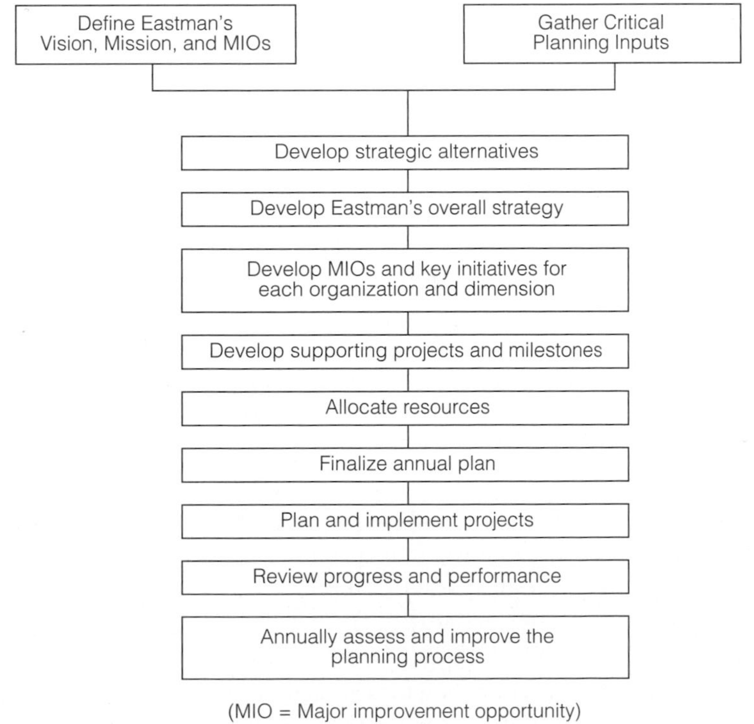

Source: Used with permission of Eastman Chemical Company.

Figure 4.2 Strategic Planning Process at Park Place Lexus

Corporate Direction
Mission
Vision
Values
Lexus Direction
Ongoing Market and Environment Analysis
• Client inputs
• Member inputs
• Competitive info
• Market analysis
• Operational capabilities
• Operational opportunities
PPL Alignment and Planning
Store Alignment and Planning
Department Alignment and Planning
Ongoing Review and Tracking
Organization Action Plans and Goals
Department Action Plans and Goals
Store Action Plans and Goals
Key Operational Measures and Targets

Adapted from public domain material—*Source:* 2005 Malcolm Baldridge Application Summary, NIST U.S. Department of Commerce. Courtesy Park Place Lexus.

Figure 4.2 shows the strategic planning process for Park Place Lexus, which shows the alignment of action plans and goals throughout the organization, and which is supported by ongoing review and tracking. Good strategy development processes often include active participation of top management, employees, and even customers or suppliers. Employees represent an important resource in strategic planning. Not only can the company capitalize on employee knowledge of customers and processes, but also employee involvement greatly enhances the effectiveness of strategy implementation. Such "bottom-up" planning facilitates better understanding and assessment of customer needs. At Solar Turbines, Inc., the strategy development process involves people from all parts of its worldwide organization, customers, and suppliers. Sales, marketing, service, engineering, and manufacturing people in functional and cross-functional teams perform information gathering, analysis, and conclusions. This information is carried forward to the leadership system committees and the Operations Council where it is integrated and synthesized into strategies and critical success factor goals.

Many strategic planning processes begin with the organization's leaders first exploring and agreeing upon (or reaffirming) the mission, vision, and guiding principles of the organization, which form the foundation for the strategic plan. Although an organization's mission, vision, and values rarely change, the environment in which the organization exists usually does. Thus, strategy development requires an **environmental assessment** of key factors which typically include

- The organization's strengths, weaknesses, opportunities, and threats (SWOT)
- Early indications of major shifts in technology, markets, customer preferences, competition, or the regulatory environment
- Long-term organizational sustainability
- The ability to execute the strategic plan

A SWOT analysis should address all factors that are key to an organization's future success, and might include customer and market needs, expectations, and opportunities; opportunities for innovation and role model performance; core competencies; competitive environment and performance relative to competitors and comparable organizations; product life cycles; technological and other key innovations or changes that might affect products, services, and operations; human and other resource needs; ability to capitalize on diversity; opportunities to redirect resources to higher-priority products, services, or areas; financial, societal, ethical, regulatory, technological, security, and other potential risks; ability to prevent and respond to emergencies, including natural or other disasters; changes in the national or global economy; partner and supply chain needs, strengths, and weaknesses; and other factors unique to the organization. Solar Turbines, Inc., for instance, looks at six external factors that affect its business: customer needs and wants, market trends and opportunities, industry trends, competitive dynamics, governmental and regulatory issues, and technological innovations that can change the nature of products and services. The ability to execute a strategic plan should address how the organization is capable of mobilizing the necessary resources and knowledge and should also address how the organization might react to circumstances that require a shift in plans and rapid execution of new or changed plans.

All this information is usually analyzed using various types of forecasts, projections, options, scenarios, or other approaches. Strategic planning teams use the results of these analyses to develop strategies, objectives, and action plans that address strategic challenges and opportunities and balance the needs of all stakeholders.

A strategy might be directed toward becoming a preferred supplier, a low-cost producer, a market innovator, or a high-end or customized service provider. Strategic objectives set an organization's longer-term directions and guide resource allocation decisions. They are typically focused externally and relate to customer, market, product, service, or technological opportunities and challenges. Strategic objectives set an organization's long-term direction and guide resource allocation decisions. For example, a strategic objective for a supplier in a highly competitive industry might be to develop and maintain a price leadership position. Action plans include details of resource commitments and time horizons for accomplishment. For the supplier seeking to develop a price leadership position, action plans might include the design of efficient processes and creation of an accounting system that tracks activity-level costs. Action plans form the basis for effective implementation, or what is called *deployment*, of a strategy.

Strategies *are broad statements that set the direction for the organization to take in realizing its mission and vision.* ***Strategic objectives*** *are what an organization must change or improve to remain or become competitive.* ***Action plans*** *are things that an organization must do to achieve its strategic objectives.*

Strategy deployment *involves developing specific action plans to achieve strategic objectives, ensuring that adequate financial and other resources are available to accomplish the action plans, developing contingencies should circumstances require a shift in plans and rapid execution of new plans, aligning work unit, supplier, or partner activities as necessary, and identifying performance measures for tracking progress.*

STRATEGY DEPLOYMENT

Essentially, strategy deployment links the planners (who focus on "doing the right thing") with the doers (whose focus is on "doing things right"). At The Ritz-Carlton, teams at all levels—corporate, management, and employee—set objectives and devise action plans. Each hotel designates a quality leader who serves as a resource and advisor to teams for developing and implementing plans.

Action plan development represents the critical stage in planning when strategic objectives and goals are made specific so that effective, organization-wide understanding and deployment are possible. Action plans typically include details of resource commitments and time horizons for their accomplishment. Deployment also might require specialized training for some employees or recruitment of personnel. An example of a strategic objective for a supplier in a highly competitive industry might be to develop and maintain a price leadership position. Action plans could entail designing efficient processes and creating an accounting system that tracks activity-level costs, aligned for the organization as a whole. Deployment requirements might include work unit and team training in setting priorities based on costs and benefits. Organizational-level analysis and review likely would emphasize productivity growth, cost control, and quality.

Many organizations simply do a poor job of deployment, despite having elegant and comprehensive strategy development approaches. Poor deployment often results from one of three reasons:[10]

1. *Lack of alignment across the organization.* Good deployment aligns resources and policies. For example, a strategic objective of increasing the number of patents generated might require hiring more engineers, developing a creativity training program, and changing its financial incentive approaches. Organizational goals should be linked, or aligned, with division, department, team, and individual goals. Everyone should be able to answer the question: What does strategy mean in terms that I can act on?
2. *Misallocation of resources.* Good strategic planning dedicates resources to making improvements or changes in those areas that are critical to an organization's strategic advantage. Spreading resources too thin to make a real difference in key areas of the business or allocating them to projects that have no real impact on strategy is ineffective.
3. *Insufficient operational measures.* Organizations need appropriate measurement systems at the operational level to track progress and know if action plans are really accomplishing their objectives. These measurement systems often include projections into the future based on accomplishment of action plans and might also compare to competitors' projections. Measures and indicators of projected performance might include changes resulting from new ventures; organizational acquisitions or mergers; new value creation; market entry and shifts; new legislative mandates, legal requirements, or industry standards; and significant anticipated innovations in products, services, and technology. Projections of key performance measures and comparisons with competitors, benchmarks, and past performance help an organization evaluate its performance in achieving its objectives, strategies, and ultimately, its vision. Organizations might use a variety of modeling, scenario, or other techniques and judgments to project the competitive environment. Medrad, for example, aligns strategic directions through a corporate scorecard, which measures performance on five short- and long-term goals: (1) exceed the financial objectives; (2) grow the company; (3) improve quality and productivity; (4) improve customer satisfaction; and (5) improve employee growth and satisfaction.

SSM Health Care and BI

Many examples of effective deployment can be found among Baldrige recipients. SSM Health Care identified three specific action plans during one year to help meet its strategic objective of "Exceptional patient, employee, and physician satisfaction": improve patient satisfaction with pain management, implement Nursing Shared Accountability model, and increase diversity representation within leadership. Key indicators to track the success of these actions plans, such as nurse turnover rate and the number of minorities in managerial professional ranks, were developed and monitored. Communication ensures that strategies will be deployed effectively at the "three levels of quality"—the organization level, process level, and individual job level. At BI, the Strategic Business and Quality Plan (SBQP) is communicated to all BI leaders and then all vice presidents facilitate division planning with their teams. The result is a divisional SBQP with measurable objectives and action plans, which is communicated to all associates within the division. Each director, regional sales manager, and team leader then facilitates a planning session with his or her individual team, which results in a department, region, or team plan with objectives and action plans of its own. The Strategic Planning Team meets quarterly to report progress of each action plan against its timeline and reviews results measurements against corporate objectives.

Hoshin Kanri (Policy Deployment)

The traditional approach to deploying strategy has been top-down. However, taking a total quality perspective, subordinates are both customers and suppliers, and therefore their input and involvement is necessary. An iterative process in which senior management asks what lower levels of the organization can do, what they need, and what conflicts may arise can avoid many of the implementation problems that managers typically face.

Japanese firms introduced a deployment process known as **hoshin kanri**, or *hoshin planning*. In the United States, this process is often referred to as **policy deployment**, or *management by planning*. Many organizations, notably Florida Power and Light, Hewlett-Packard, and AT&T among many others, have adopted this process. The literal Japanese translation of hoshin kanri is "pointing direction."[11] The idea is to point, or align, the entire organization in a common direction. Florida Power and Light defines policy deployment as "the executive deployment of selected policy-driven priorities and the necessary resources to achieve performance breakthroughs." Hewlett-Packard calls it "a process for annual planning and implementation which focuses on areas needing significant improvement." AT&T's definition is "an organization-wide and customer-focused management approach aimed at planning and executing breakthrough improvements in business performance." Regardless of the particular definition, policy deployment emphasizes organization-wide planning and setting of priorities, provides resources to meet objectives, and measures performance as a basis for improving performance. Policy deployment is essentially a quality-based approach to executing a strategy by ensuring that all employees understand the business direction and are working according to a plan to make the vision a reality.

M. Imai provides an example of policy deployment:

> *To illustrate the need for policy deployment, let us consider the following case: The president of an airline company proclaims that he believes in safety and that his corporate goal is to make sure that safety is maintained throughout the company. This proclamation is prominently featured in the company's quarterly report and its advertising. Let us further suppose that the department managers also swear a firm belief in safety. The catering manager says he believes in safety. The pilots say they believe in safety. The flight crews say they believe in safety. Everyone in the company practices safety. True? Or might everyone simply be paying lip service to the idea of safety?*
>
> *On the other hand, if the president states that safety is company policy and works with his division managers to develop a plan for safety that defines their responsibilities, everyone will have a very specific subject to discuss. Safety will become a real concern. For the manager in charge of*

> *catering services, safety might mean maintaining the quality of food to avoid customer dissatisfaction or illness.*
>
> *In that case, how does he ensure that the food is of top quality? What sorts of control points and checkpoints does he establish? How does he ensure that there is no deterioration of food quality in flight? Who checks the temperature of the refrigerators or the condition of the oven while the plane is in the air?*
>
> *Only when safety is translated into specific actions with specific control and checkpoints established for each employee's job might safety be said to have been truly deployed as a policy. Policy deployment calls for everyone to interpret policy in light of his own responsibilities and for everyone to work out criteria to check his success in carrying out the policy.*[12]

Figure 4.3 provides a simplified description of the policy deployment process.[13] With policy deployment, top management is responsible for developing and communicating a vision, then building organization-wide commitment to its achievement.[14] The long-term strategic plan forms the basis for shorter-term planning. This vision is deployed through the development and execution of annual objectives and plans. All levels of employees actively participate in generating strategy and action plans to attain the vision. At each level, progressively more detailed and concrete means to

Figure 4.3 The Policy Deployment Process

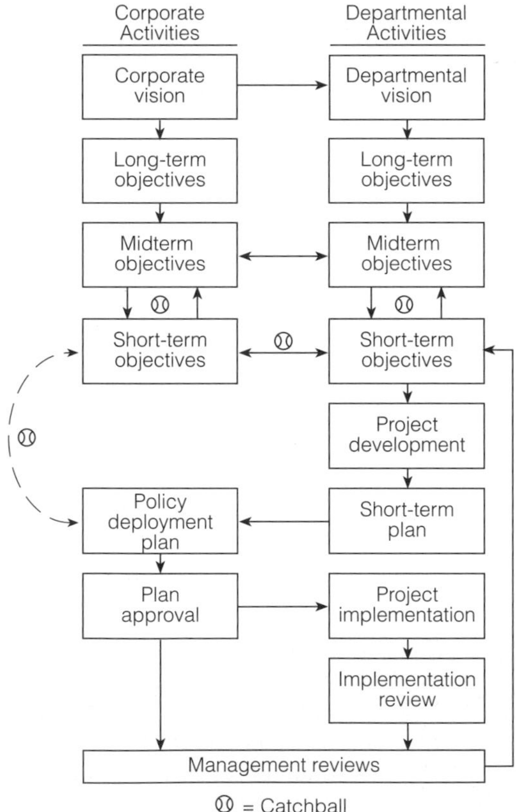

Source: Reprinted with permission from Kersi F. Munshi, "Policy Deployment: A Key to Long-Term TQM Success," *ASQC Quality Congress Transactions* (Boston, 1993), pp. 236–244.

accomplish the objectives are determined. Objectives should be challenging, but people should feel that they are attainable. To this end, middle management negotiates with senior management regarding the objectives that will achieve the strategies, and what process changes and resources might be required to achieve those objectives. Middle management then negotiates with the implementation teams the final short-term objectives and the performance measures that are used to indicate progress toward accomplishing the objectives.

Management reviews at specific checkpoints ensure the effectiveness of individual elements of the strategy. The implementation teams are empowered to manage actions and schedule their activities. Periodic reviews (monthly or quarterly) track progress and diagnose problems. Management may modify objectives on the basis of these reviews, as evidenced by the feedback loop in the figure. Top management evaluates results as well as the deployment process itself through annual reviews, which serve as a basis for the next planning cycle.

Note, however, that top management does not develop action plans; it sets overall guidelines and strategies. Departments and functional units develop specific implementation plans. Hence, the process in Figure 4.3 includes both corporate and departmental activities. In practice, policy deployment entails a high degree of detail, including the anticipation of possible problems during implementation. The emphasis is on the improvement of the process, as opposed to a results-only orientation.

The negotiation process is called *catchball* (represented by the baseball symbol in Figure 4.3). Leaders communicate midterm objectives and measures to middle managers who develop short-term objectives and recommend necessary resources, targets, and roles/responsibilities. These issues are discussed and debated until agreement is reached. The objectives then cascade to lower levels of the organization where short-term plans are developed. Catchball is an up, down, and sideways communication process as opposed to an autocratic, top-down management style. It marshals the collective expertise of the whole organization and results in realistic and achievable objectives that do not conflict. In the spirit of Deming, the process focuses on optimizing the system rather than on individual goals and objectives. Clearly, this process can only occur in a culture that nourishes open communication.

Linking Human Resource Plans and Business Strategy

Whenever an organization seeks to do something different, people are invariably impacted. Thus, it is important to consider organizational change and plan for necessary human resource changes that may be needed. These changes might include new training initiatives, work reorganization, or compensation and incentive approaches. For example, to address a national nursing shortage, Baptist Hospital's strategy for nurse recruitment and retention required numerous human resource changes, such as revamping the clinical ladder program, pay adjustments to recruit graduate nurses, increasing the number of scholarships to nursing students, and involving experienced nurses to speak to high school students to raise interest in the field. Motorola's Commercial, Government, and Industrial Solutions Sector ties the following human resource plans into its strategic planning

Strategic objectives and action plans often require significant changes in human resource requirements, such as redesigning the work organization or jobs to increase employee empowerment and decision making, promoting greater labor/management cooperation, modifying compensation and recognition systems, or developing new education and training initiatives.

process: breakthrough changes in work design, team member development, education, and training; compensation, recognition, and benefits; and human resources needs identification and recruitment. When GE decided to adopt a Six Sigma framework for the organization, it was necessary to train 12,000 black-belt leaders to implement the plan. Incentives for project champions in upper management were restructured to account for 40 percent of their bonuses.[15]

Strategic human resource plans often include one or more of the following:

- Redesign of the work organization to increase empowerment and decision-making or team-based participation;
- Initiatives for promoting greater labor/management cooperation, such as union partnerships;
- Initiatives to foster knowledge sharing and organizational learning; and
- Partnerships with educational institutions to help ensure the future supply of well-prepared employees.

Whatever the choices, it is vital that they support the organization's overall strategy. For example, suppose that a firm identifies its critical success factors as customer satisfaction, employee satisfaction, market growth, and world-class performance. Each critical success factor will have one or more strategic objectives defined through the firm's strategic planning process. Because successful accomplishment of these strategic objectives will depend on execution by the firm's workforce, it is important that key human resource plans, such as enhancing skills, knowledge, and motivation, be identified to support these strategic objectives. Without proper alignment, the work that people do can be focused in an entirely different direction than the organization intends to go. Some generic examples are shown in Table 4.3.

Table 4.3 Alignment of Human Resource Plans With Critical Success Factors and Strategic Objectives

Critical Success Factor and Strategic Objectives	Human Resource Plans
Customer Satisfaction	
Strengthen customer relationships by improving responsiveness	Implement new training program for front-line staff
Employee Satisfaction	
Encourage employee development and career planning to capitalize on workforce diversity	Develop, implement, and deliver online training courses
	Require leadership rotation in team projects
Market Growth	
Pursue new and expanded market opportunities	Actively participate on marketing teams to determine HR requirements
	Develop a hiring plan for new product development and marketing initiatives
World Class Performance	
Improve process quality	Support Six Sigma training initiatives
Reduce costs to world-class benchmark levels	Develop lean expertise throughout the workforce

THE SEVEN MANAGEMENT AND PLANNING TOOLS

Managers may use a variety of tools and techniques, known as the **Seven Management and Planning Tools**, to implement policy deployment.

1. *Affinity diagram*: A tool for organizing a large number of ideas, opinions, and facts relating to a broad problem or subject area
2. *Interrelationship diagraph*: A tool for identifying and exploring causal relationships among related concepts or ideas
3. *Tree diagram*: A tool to map out the paths and tasks necessary to complete a specific project or reach a specified goal
4. *Matrix diagram*: "Spreadsheets" that graphically display relationships between ideas, activities, or other dimensions in such a way as to provide logical connecting points between each item
5. *Matrix data analysis*: A tool to take data and arrange them to display quantitative relationships among variables to make them more easily understood and analyzed
6. *Process decision program chart*: A method for mapping out every conceivable event and contingency that can occur when moving from a problem statement to possible solutions
7. *Arrow diagrams*: A tool for sequencing and scheduling project tasks

These tools are particularly useful in structuring unstructured ideas, making strategic plans, and organizing and controlling large, complex projects. Thus, they can benefit all employees involved in quality planning and implementation.

The Seven Management and Planning Tools had their roots in post–World War II operations research developments in the United States, but were combined and refined by several Japanese companies over the past several decades as part of their planning processes. They were popularized in the United States by the consulting firm GOAL/QPC, and have been used by a number of firms since 1984 to improve their quality planning and improvement efforts. Many organizations formally integrated these tools into policy deployment activities. These management and planning tools are described in detail in the Bonus Materials folder for this chapter on the Premium website, along with examples of how they can be used in strategic planning and deployment. These seven tools provide managers with improved capability to make better decisions and facilitate the implementation process. With proper planning, managers can use their time more effectively to continuously improve and innovate.

BONUS MATERIALS

ORGANIZATIONAL DESIGN FOR PERFORMANCE EXCELLENCE

The effectiveness of an organization depends in part on its **organizational structure**—the clarification of authority, responsibility, reporting lines, and performance standards among individuals at each level of the organization. It is also true that effective strategy deployment is dependent upon, and tends to shape, organizational structure because the organizational structure must be aligned with and support the accomplishment of strategic initiatives. Thus, organizational design is an important strategic decision.

Traditional organizations tend to develop structures that help them to maintain stability. They tend to be highly structured, both in terms of rules and regulations, as well as the height of the "corporate ladder," sometimes with seven or more layers of managers between the CEO and the first-line worker. In contrast, organizations in the rapidly changing environments characteristic of modern organizations have to build flexibility into their organization structures. Hence, they tend to have fewer written rules and regulations and flatter organizational structures.

Several factors having to do with the context of the organization affect how work is organized. They include the following:[16]

1. *Operational and organizational guidelines.* Standard practices that have developed over the firm's history often dictate how an organization organizes and operates.
2. *Management style.* The management team operates in a manner unique to a given organization. For example, management style might be formal or informal, or democratic or autocratic. If the organization operates in a highly structured, formal atmosphere, organizing a quality effort around informal meetings would probably meet with little success.
3. *Customer influences.* Customers, particularly governmental agencies, may require formal specifications or administrative controls. Thus, the organization needs to understand and respond to these requirements.
4. *Size.* Large organizations have the ability to maintain formal systems and records, whereas smaller ones may not.
5. *Diversity and complexity of product line.* An organization suitable for the manufacture of a small number of highly sophisticated products may differ dramatically from an organization that produces a high volume of standard goods.
6. *Stability of the product line.* Stable product lines generate economies of scale that influence supervision, corrective action, and other quality-related issues. Frequent changes in products necessitate more control and commensurate changes to the quality system.
7. *Financial stability.* Quality managers need to recognize that their efforts must fit within the overall budget of the firm.
8. *Availability of personnel.* The lack of certain skills may require other personnel, such as supervisors, to assume duties they ordinarily would not be assigned.

An organization chart shows the *apparent structure* of the formal organization. However, some organizations refuse to be tied down by a conventional organization chart, even to the extent that employees make a running joke of titles. For example, Semco S/A, a radically unconventional manufacturer of industrial equipment (mixers, washers, air conditioners, bakery plant units) located in São Paulo, Brazil, has what is called a "circular" organization chart with four concentric circles. They avoid the use of the term *levels*. The titles that go with these are Counselors (CEO and the equivalent of vice presidents), Partners (business unit heads), Coordinators (supervisory specialists and functional leaders), and Associates (everyone else). If anyone desires, he or she can think up a title for external use that describes his or her area or job responsibility. As owner and CEO Ricardo Semler explains:

> *Consistent with this philosophy, when a promotion takes place now at Semco we simply supply blank business cards and tell the newly elevated individual: "Think of a title that signals externally your area of operation and responsibility and have it printed." If the person likes "Procurement Manager," fine. If he wants something more elegant, he can print up cards saying, "First Pharaoh in Charge of Royal Supplies." Whatever he wants. But inside the company, there are only four options. (Anyway, almost all choose to print only their name.)*[17]

Although many different organizational structures exist, most are variations or combinations of three basic types: (1) the line organization, (2) the line and staff organization, and (3) the matrix organization.

The line organization is a functional form, with departments that are responsible for marketing, finance, and operations. In the traditional organization, the quality department ("Quality Control," "Quality Assurance," or some similar name) is generally distinct from other departments. In a TQ organization, the role of quality should be invisible in the organization chart, because quality planning and assurance are part of the responsibility of each operating manager and employee at every level. In theory, this organizational form could exist in a fairly large organization if all employees were thoroughly indoctrinated in the philosophy of quality and could be counted on to place quality as the top priority in all aspects of their daily work. In practice, this particular structure is not generally successful except when used in small firms. One example is Texas Nameplate Company, which trained all of its approximately 50 employees in quality management and assurance and effectively eliminated a formal quality control function.

The line and staff organization is the most prevalent type of structure for medium-sized to large firms. In such organizations, line departments carry out the functions of marketing, finance, and production for the organization. Staff personnel, including quality managers and technical specialists, assist the line managers in carrying out their jobs by providing technical assistance and advice. Variations on the basic line and staff organization can include geographic or customer organizations. In this traditional form of organization structure, instead of technical experts who assist line managers and workers in attaining quality, quality managers and inspectors may take on the role of guardians of quality. This guardian-type role also happens when the quality assurance function is placed too low in the organization or when pressure from higher levels of the organization forces quality inspectors to ease up on quality so that more products can be shipped. The major cause of this problem is too much responsibility with insufficient authority.

The matrix-type organization was developed for use in situations where large, complex projects are designed and carried out, such as defense weapons systems or large construction projects. Firms that do such work have a basic need to develop an organizational structure that will permit the efficient use of human resources while maintaining control over the many facets of the project being developed. In a matrix-type organization, each project has a project manager and each department that is providing personnel to work on the various projects has a technical or administrative manager. Thus, a quality assurance technician might be assigned to the quality assurance department for technical and administrative activities but would be attached to Project A for day-to-day job assignments. The technician would report to the project manager of Project A and to his or her "technical boss" in the quality assurance department. When Project A is completed, the technician might be reassigned to Project B under a new project manager. He or she would still be reporting to the "technical boss" in quality assurance, however.

As more and more organizations accept the process view, they are structuring the quality organization around functional or cross-functional teams.

The matrix type of organization for project work has a number of advantages. It generally improves the coordination of complex project work as well as improving the efficiency of personnel use. Its major drawback is that it requires split loyalty for people who report to two supervisors. This division of loyalty can be especially troublesome or even dangerous in a quality assurance area. For example, in a nuclear power plant

Figure 4.4 Customer-Focused Team-Based Organizational Chart

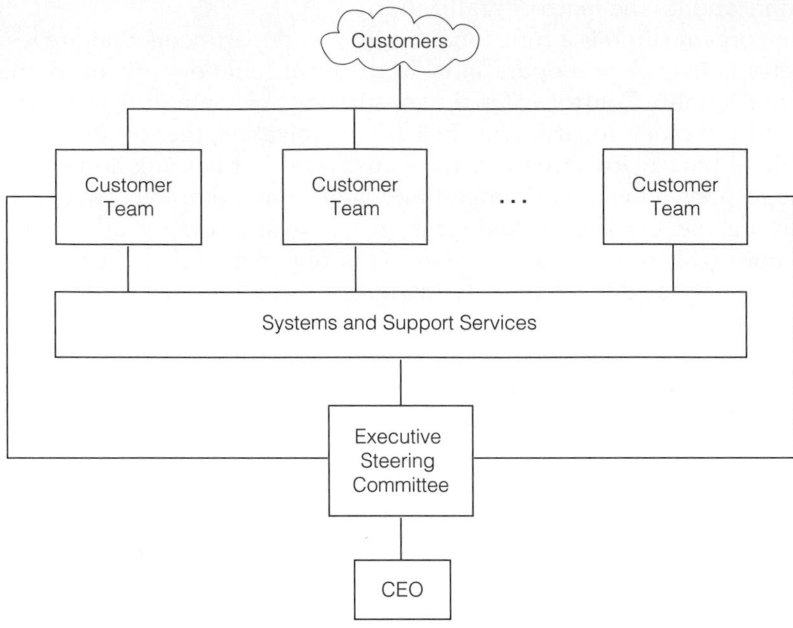

project, a project manager who is under pressure to complete a project by a certain deadline might try to influence quality assurance personnel to take shortcuts in completing the inspection phase of the project. The quality manager, who might be hundreds of miles away from the site, would often not have the influence over the inspectors that the project manager would have. One example that revolves around customer teams is shown in Figure 4.4. Such an organizational structure would be appropriate for a marketing research firm, for instance, which may work with a small number of large corporate clients. Another example is shown in Figure 4.5. In this example, the management board leads the quality effort, meeting twice each month to discuss and review management and quality issues. Quality is implemented through various teams: core business process team, cross-functional coordinating committee, regional management councils, major business process management teams (PMTs), Malcolm Baldrige National Quality Award (MBNQA) teams, and quality improvement teams. The regional management councils identify and address key regional issues; the cross-functional coordinating committee reviews major proposals for consistency with the strategic plan and business priorities. Such team-based organization structures spread the ownership and the accountability for quality throughout the organization. The "quality department" serves as an internal consulting group, providing advice, training, and organizational development to the teams.

We see that a "one-size-fits-all" quality organization is inappropriate. The organization must be tailored to reflect unique differences and provide the flexibility and the ability to change. What is important, however, is that senior leaders drive quality and performance excellence concepts throughout the organization through effective communication and as role models, and ensure that strategic planning focuses all key stakeholders in achieving the organization's mission and vision.

Figure 4.5 Cross-Functional Team-Based Organizational Chart

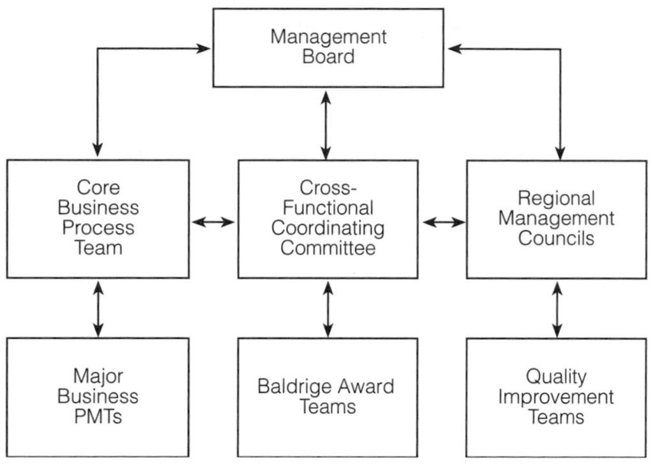

Source: Courtesy of GTE Directories Corporation (now Verizon Information Services). Reprinted with permission.

CORE COMPETENCIES AND STRATEGIC WORK SYSTEM DESIGN

*The term **work systems** refers to how the work of an organization is accomplished.*

Work systems coordinate the internal work processes and the external resources necessary to develop, produce, and deliver products and services to customers and to succeed in the marketplace. Work systems involve the workforce, key suppliers and partners, contractors, collaborators, and other components of the supply chain needed to produce and deliver products, services, and business and support processes. For example, Henry Ford's early factories did everything from steel-making to final assembly; today's automobile companies are characterized by complex networks of suppliers that are much more decentralized.

***Core competencies** refer to an organization's areas of greatest expertise that provide a sustainable competitive advantage in the marketplace or service environment.*

Decisions about work systems are strategic. These decisions involve protecting and capitalizing on *core competencies* and deciding what should be procured or produced outside the organization in order to be efficient and sustainable in the marketplace.

Gary Hamel and C.K. Prahalad suggested that a core competency meets three conditions:[18]

It contributes significantly to customer benefits.

It provides access to many products and markets.

It is difficult for competitors to imitate.

Core competencies may involve technology expertise, unique service offerings, a marketplace niche, or a particular business acumen (e.g., business acquisitions). Some examples of core competencies might be quality and productivity practices (e.g., Toyota), superior customer relationship management (e.g. Nordstrom's), innovation in design and new product development (e.g., Apple), supply chain management (e.g., Dell), or marketing/branding expertise (e.g., Procter & Gamble). An organization needs to understand its core competencies and how they support the organization's mission, enable it to compete against its competitors, and help drive strategic objectives and action plans.

Mercy Health System's (MHS) core competencies are stated as 1) partnering with physicians to create and maintain an effective integrated health care delivery system; and 2) engaging employees and physicians using the Servant Leadership Philosophy and the Culture of Excellence model, which provide a balanced approach to patient-focused care. The integrated delivery system model has enabled growth and diversification of business lines, supporting the ability to effectively coordinate quality health care delivery across the continuum of care and supporting the mission, "to provide exceptional healthcare services resulting in healing in the broadest sense." Partnering with physicians supports a collaborative focus on quality health care and information sharing across the organization's core services. The integrated delivery model supports coordinated transitions between departments, providers, and care settings to ensure efficient, effective, and patient-focused care. Through the use of the Servant Leadership Philosophy, leaders provide excellent service to partners, and partners provide excellent service to customers. Applying this philosophy, leaders are facilitators whose role is to serve those who provide value to patients. Caregivers provide patient-focused care by offering consideration for personal preferences, cultural traditions and family situations, and involving patients and their loved ones in care decisions to support healing in the broadest sense. These competencies drive action plans designed to achieve MHS's visionary strategic goals.[19]

Some contemporary theories suggest that business activities that do not comprise an organization's core competency should be outsourced. **Outsourcing** refers to the practice of transferring the operations of a business function to an outside supplier. Many organizations have done this; for example, outsourcing manufacturing or assembly, information technology operations, human resource management, or customer service telephone support operations. Much outsourcing is done through offshoring, in which the outsourced function is relegated to foreign shores. The opposite of outsourcing is **vertical integration**, by which certain business functions are acquired and consolidated within a firm. For example, a firm may purchase a key supplier to strengthen its value chain.

The decision to outsource or vertically integrate should be examined relative to all factors that can affect organizational performance. In many cases, the decision is based solely on costs without considering the impact on other business priorities such as quality and customer satisfaction or risks associated with protecting intellectual property. For instance, the toy industry faced serious issues with toxic chemicals found in toys manufactured in China. Dell had moved a customer call center to India to lower costs, but later closed that center and moved it back to the United States because of dissatisfaction with the level of technical support that customers were receiving. Because outsourcing can have significant impacts on an organization's work system effectiveness, it must be dealt with strategically.

The City of Coral Springs, Florida, bases decisions to operate a process with internal resources on two criteria: whether the process is a key work process and whether an external resource can do it cheaper while sustaining quality standards. Key work processes are central to public trust and therefore are operated with internal resources. The City needs to directly manage these areas to monitor the quality of outputs on a daily basis and to have the agility needed to adapt to changing customer requirements and civic emergencies. Occasionally, processes that are not fundamental to local government are subject to an RFP (request for proposal) process to determine if City staff can perform the function better and at a lower cost than the private sector. Fleet maintenance, operation of the Tennis Center, and water billing are examples of functions assessed through an RFP process. External resources are used for the operation of the Center for the Arts because a company called Professional Facilities Management can take advantage of economies of scale (they run several facilities in Florida) to get better prices on shows; Waste Management provides trash removal and recycling services for many south Florida municipalities; Charter School USA uses one management staff for several facilities and specializes in customer-driven education.[20]

STRATEGIC PLANNING IN THE BALDRIGE CRITERIA, ISO 9000, AND SIX SIGMA

Our discussion of strategy development and deployment follows closely with the Baldrige Criteria. Category 2, *Strategic Planning*, examines how an organization develops strategic objectives and action plans, how they are deployed and changed if circumstances require, and how progress is measured. Item 2.1, *Strategy Development*, examines how an organization determines its strategic challenges and advantages, how it conducts strategic planning, how it uses external and internal information in the strategic planning process, and how it establishes strategy and strategic objectives to address its strategic challenges.

Item 2.2, *Strategy Deployment*, looks at how an organization converts strategic objectives into action plans to accomplish the objectives, how resources are allocated, and how changes resulting from action plans are sustained. It also addresses human resource plans and key measures and indicators for tracking progress and how the measures help to align all important work units and stakeholders in meeting objectives. It also seeks projections of key performance measures as a basis for comparing past performance and performance relative to competitors and benchmarks.

Although it appears in the *Process Management* category, Item 6.1a deals with key strategic issues of work systems design, specifically how the organization designs and innovates its overall work systems, particularly regarding decisions related to outsourcing. We have discussed work systems design in this chapter because of its strategic nature.

ISO 9000 does not address strategic planning as broadly as in the Baldrige criteria; however, the ISO 9000 standards do require that top management ensure that quality objectives are established at relevant functions and levels within the organization, that they be measurable and consistent with the quality policy, that planning be carried out in order to meet quality system requirements and the quality objectives, and that the integrity of the quality management system is maintained when changes are planned and implemented.

Six Sigma is a way to turn performance improvement needs into reality. To be effective, it must be integrated into strategic planning processes. In many organizations there are three levels of strategy: corporate, strategic business unit (SBU), and competitive.[21] At the corporate strategy level, the key question facing planners is, "How do we, as an organization, grow?" At the SBU or divisional level, the strategic question is, "Where does the organization focus its resources to enhance its value offering?" An organization's competitive strategy is its plan for enhancing its capacity to deliver value, thus increasing market share. Competitive strategy that focuses on value enhancement addresses key questions such as: "Where are the organization's best opportunities for widening a value advantage or closing a disadvantage? On what basis does the organization widen or close the value gap? How does the organization get its best return on investment for these efforts?"

The competitive strategy level is where organizational strategy and Six Sigma must align, because it is at this level that the tools of Six Sigma can be most effectively applied. Effective competitive strategies are necessarily focused on value gaps and are either designed to extend value leadership or to close the gap with a value leader. In either case, the deployment of that strategy will require a focus on the organization's business processes. The tools of Six Sigma are particularly effective for improving business processes. The challenge lies in directing those tools toward improvements that will have a direct impact on value gaps. That requires aligning Six Sigma with the organization's competitive strategy.

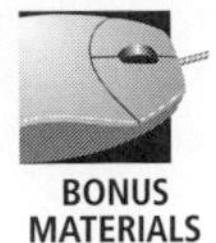
BONUS MATERIALS

SUMMARY OF KEY POINTS AND TERMINOLOGY

The Bonus Materials folder on the Premium website, provides a summary of key concepts and terminology introduced in this chapter.

QUALITY IN PRACTICE

INTEGRATING SIX SIGMA WITH STRATEGIC PLANNING AT CIGNA[22]

At Cigna Corp., a 28,000-employee provider of employee health care and related insurance benefits, the vice president of Six Sigma business excellence is just two levels below the CEO on the organizational chart. The woman who holds this title, Leslie Behnke, reports directly to a member of the corporation's management team. This simple fact helps to explain the rapid growth, holistic use, and impressive results of Six Sigma at Cigna.

Cigna has five strategic imperatives:

1. Establish a meaningful cost advantage relative to the competition.
2. Help improve the health and well-being of members and the people Cigna insures.
3. Bring innovative products and services to market.
4. Become the partner of choice to its customers.
5. Create a winning environment in the organization.

Strategic planning is an absolute necessity in a company like Cigna that competes in a tough, volatile marketplace. Six Sigma is viewed as a means to execute the strategic plan effectively and to do so in a way that enhances quality, reduces costs and makes the company a stronger competitor. Executives and managers learn the basics of Six Sigma, lean tools, continuous improvement and the basics of design for Six Sigma (which we will learn in subsequent chapters). Managers also learn what behaviors are required to ensure the following:

- There is continuous improvement.
- The right projects are selected with the right people to lead them.
- There is ongoing assessment of projects.
- People have time to serve on projects.
- Managers ask the right questions during each phase of a project.

Strategic planning has become increasingly important as Six Sigma has matured at Cigna. When Six Sigma was launched at Cigna, leadership made it clear the approach would be holistic and would not just be productivity improvement, but would require behavioral changes and a focus on customers. Figure 4.6 shows the conceptualization of how Six Sigma supports a strategic focus at Cigna. One project involved one of Cigna's largest clients, which was dissatisfied with errors and how long it was taking to pay claims accurately. This customer got its own Six Sigma professionals to work with Cigna. The Six Sigma project exceeded the customers' expectations from both timeliness and quality standpoints.

Figure 4.6 Cigna's Holistic Six Sigma Model

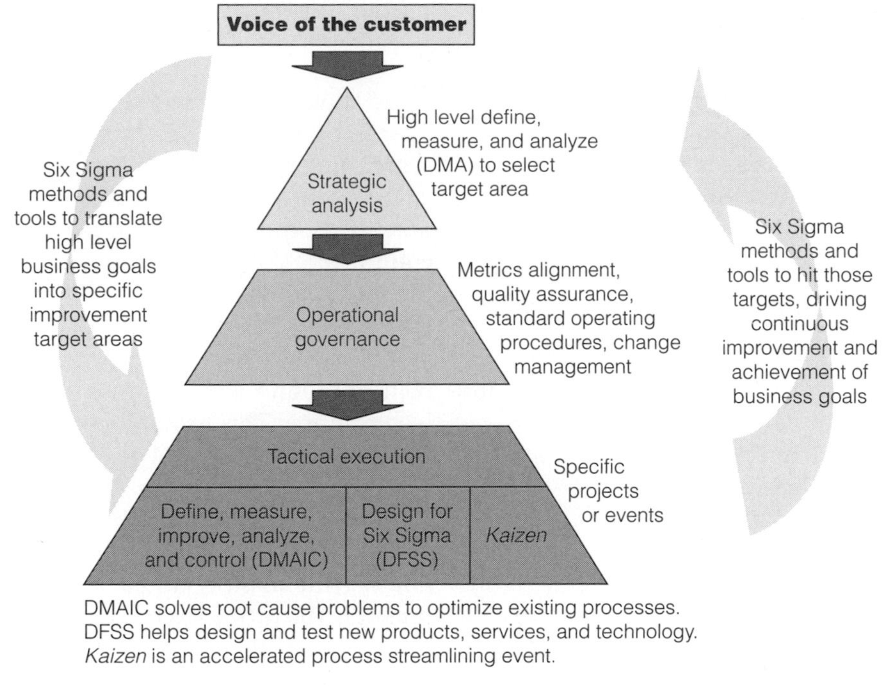

Source: Reprinted with permission from Susan E. Daniels, "Six Sigma at Cigna," *Quality Progress*, pp. 43–48, May 2007. Copyright © 2007 American Society for Quality. No further distribution allowed without permission.

In fact, the customer was so satisfied, it gave Cigna additional business.

Cigna looks at the cost of doing nothing differently, figures how much improvement it can make, and then comes up with a dollar differential. A 0.1 percent improvement can save millions. While initial concentration was on efforts that would bring quick and significant results, Six Sigma at Cigna has matured, and it has increasingly focused on impacting goals of the most strategic importance to the organization. The challenges of the huge cost of care and quality of care facing the U.S. health care industry have led Cigna managers to wonder whether they could extend its improvement methodology to the industry as a whole to address some of the key challenges in the U.S. health care marketplace, including:

- A shift away from cost based models of health care toward a value based system
- Medical care cost inflation
- Demographic changes that necessitate the need for more care availability
- Inconsistent quality of care
- The growing number of Americans who use emergency rooms for primary care because they lack health insurance
- Rising consumer expectations fueled by greater transparency of quality

As one of them noted, "Six Sigma is about quality, continuous improvement, and sustained excellence—all of which should be basic to the mission of every organization that's in the business of providing access to health care."

Key Issues for Discussion

1. Suggest how Six Sigma might be used to help Cigna address its five strategic imperatives? Is their approach consistent with the discussion of Six Sigma and competitive strategy at the end of this chapter?
2. Can you think of specific types of Six Sigma projects that might support Cigna's strategic imperatives?

Quality in Practice

Strategic Planning at Branch-Smith Printing Division[23]

Branch-Smith, Inc., is a fourth-generation family business founded by Aaron Smith in 1910. The Branch-Smith Printing Division in Ft. Worth, Texas, has only 70 full-time employees and specializes in creating multipage, bound materials with services ranging from design to mailing for specialty customers. The company produces publications, magazines, catalogs, directories, and books, as well as some general commercial printing, typically in quantities generally less than 20,000. It offers a complete array of turnkey services to customers, including design, image scanning, electronic and conventional prepress work, printing, binding, and mailing/delivery.

Within the Printing Division, the context of the business is set through their Vision Statement: *"Market Leading Business Results through an Expert Team providing Turnkey Solutions to Customer Partners."* This vision expresses the desire to produce strong and sustainable results through balanced performance improvement. It creates success for long-term customers and rewards for their employees who bring solutions to bear on our opportunities. The mission is stated as: *"The mission of the Branch-Smith Printing Division is to provide expert solutions for publishers."* This purpose guides Branch-Smith Printing in meeting customers' needs on its own terms. Publishers work with them because Branch-Smith focuses on serving publishers' niche requirements for printing as well as offering the vertically integrated value-added services that result in lower costs, reduced cycle times, and on-time delivery. An important component of the solution is easy accessibility for the customer, and timely and appropriate information. It is also expressed in its Quality Policy, which states: *"Branch-Smith Printing will seek to continuously improve results for all stakeholders through the application of its Innovating Excellence Process."*

The printing industry is very competitive with numerous companies seeking market share. Branch-Smith Printing stands out among competitors based on its approach for identifying and serving a specific niche, focusing on development of long-term relationships, partnering with suppliers, and involvement in standard defining industry associations. To ensure a competitive position, it focuses on serving a select market niche that most other printers have difficulty serving well. Many competitors focus on attracting jobs with greater quantity outputs because of the limitations of their equipment. They charge much higher prices for the shorter runs, thus giving Branch-Smith an advantage in this market. Its equipment and technologies are directed to cost-effectively serve this niche through sheet-fed press versus the popular web printing. This technology allows for faster changeovers from one type of print to another and process automation offers cost savings.

Although Branch-Smith is a small family business, they engage in a formal planning process annually with monthly updates during management reviews. The process is built around a continuous learning cycle that begins with lessons learned from previous years to determine and implement improvements. The strategic planning process (SPP) is a key tool the company uses to visualize the ideal future and create strategies and plans to achieve it, and to incorporate improvement opportunities into prioritized action plans. Strategic planning occurs formally each year with updates and tracking conducted monthly during management reviews. Ongoing updates throughout the year allow the company to correct direction or to proactively respond to risks and opportunities.

Figure 4.7 represents the full strategic planning, deployment, and review process. A month prior to strategic planning, assignments are made to PLT members to research information needed for strategic decision making. The assignment list includes 28 specific areas for understanding organizational and supplier/partner capabilities, market conditions, stakeholder input and requirements, competitive information, industry issues, and risks. Branch-Smith gathers information through a customer survey, lost revenues, and complaints to identify customer needs and their importance, trends and directions of the printing industry, and market requirements from industry association networking. Involvement in professional associations provides industry knowledge and benchmarks concerning customer needs and competitor

Figure 4.7 Branch-Smith Strategic Planning Process

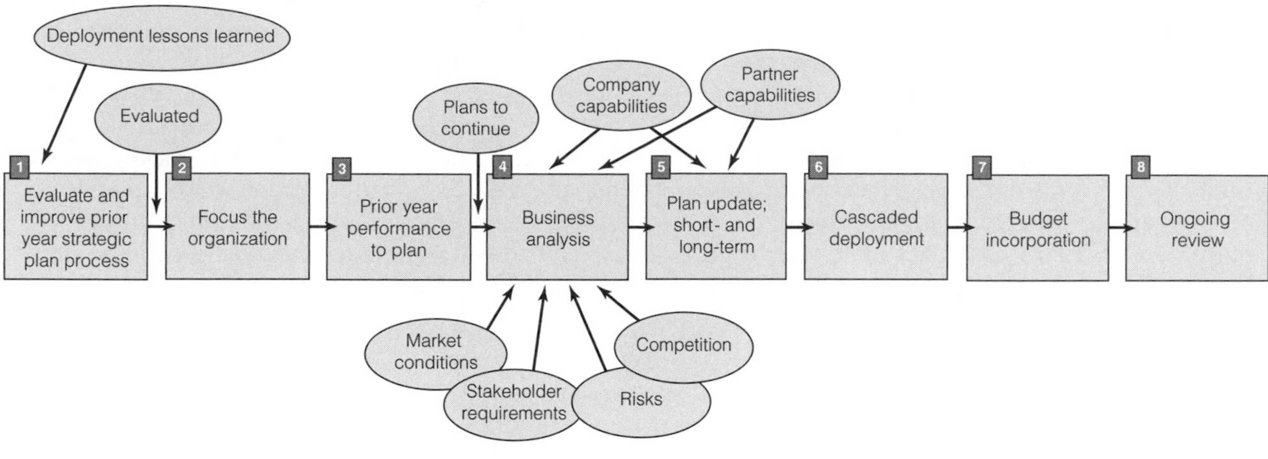

Source: Used with permission of AIM, Inc.

actions, including emerging tools and competitors. Trade magazines and discussions with key suppliers provide additional input about customer needs, competitor directions, and supplier capabilities. Trends and directions in technology and other environmental changes are also identified through involvement with trade associations and external benchmarking groups, and through general understanding of the business climate gained through newspapers, journals, and periodicals.

One important source of information for strategic planning regarding human resource needs and capability is an annual employee survey. Human resource and operational capabilities are identified through review of aggregate measures of performance and productivity, which are enhanced with feedback from scheduled ISO audits that identify processes in need of improvement. Primary inputs on process efficiency and capability come from in-process productivity measures, revenue lost due to complaints, and other measures, which include spoilage cost, frequency, and reason. These measures are recorded daily through electronic, shop-floor data collection. Strategic partnerships with key suppliers help to gather information about availability of materials and supplier growth plans to help determine their capability to meet Branch-Smith's changing needs. Finally, part of the annual operational review involves understanding suppliers' current financial position and trends in profitability and utilization, which is compared to external economic conditions to identify areas of potential risk and opportunity over the short- and longer-term.

The formal planning activity is conducted during the fall of each year by the Print Leadership Team (PLT) through a series of meetings on and off site. Step 1 of Figure 4.7 ensures that lessons learned and improvement cycles are built into the SPP. The PLT analyzes the effectiveness of the overall planning and deployment process to determine and implement improvements. The effectiveness of the leadership system is also evaluated and areas for improvement for the coming year are determined. These improvements are documented as potential actions for the strategic plan. In Step 2, the company reviews its vision, mission, and values to ensure they still reflect the current environment. Next, management reviews and revises objectives, which are intended to communicate to employees and all stakeholders what the company expects to accomplish in the next three to five years.

In Step 3, the company conducts an operational review to analyze the results of the organization's key performance measures for the prior year. They then review and incorporate information into the plan from annual Baldrige-based self-evaluation or from external review feedback. This analysis provides an understanding of key strengths and weaknesses for the SWOT (strengths, weaknesses, opportunities, and threats) analysis in Step 5. Step 4 involves a business analysis to evaluate the external environment to forecast changing trends and gain market requirements. PLT members bring forward defined inputs, including literature and studies for scanning the environment and identifying new opportunities for products, services, competitive advantage, marketing, and technology approaches. From the review of this information, the PLT develops a list of potential opportunities and threats for each environmental element. In Step 5, a SWOT analysis is conducted based upon the issues identified in Steps 1, 3, and 4. SWOT elements are used to identify and prioritize key areas to address.

Based upon the SWOT review, the PLT develops short- and longer-term strategies and actions to move the company toward its vision and objectives. They add in action plans that are still in process from the prior year to allow them to also be prioritized, set appropriate measures and goals for objectives and strategies, and sort and prioritize the action plans. Action plans are assigned to PLT members to develop (or update) steps, timelines, resources, costs, and measures of success. These plans are then entered into the Quality Improvement Database (QID) for review and tracking. A final balancing meeting is held to review the plan as a whole and make needed adjustments to timing of plans and financial and human resource requirements to balance the plan to resource constraints. In Step 6, the company creates documents and methods to support deployment of the plan.

Results of strategic planning are first communicated to employees through a deployment meeting. Leaders, with their departmental teams or other appropriate members, then discuss the plans during follow-up sessions. Teams and individuals update goals and mission statements for their departments that support the division plans, thus aligning actions, measures, and goals throughout the organization. Other stakeholders receive a variety of communications to detail our plans and strategies for informational and planning purposes. For example, a supplier appreciation luncheon is held to provide a more direct opportunity to present plans to key supplier partners and receive feedback on plans and needs. In Step 7, financial resource requirements to accomplish the action plans are rationalized into short- and longer-term budget projections. Then, in Step 8, ongoing tracking of action plans is conducted through monthly management review of overall progress to plans and key measures. Throughout the year as needed, the strategic plan is updated with new or modified action plans to reflect the changes to the environment.

Key Issues for Discussion

1. Compare Branch-Smith's approach to the generic strategic planning process described in this chapter. What are some of its unique features?
2. Branch-Smith's current objectives are "1) To continuously improve business results through a process improvement focus, partnership with our suppliers, and strong financial performance. 2) To become the partner of choice for our customers through: a targeted marketing plan, excellent execution to customer requirements, and relationship development. To become the partner of choice, our value package must be continually improved. 3) To become the employer of choice through: a caring, involved culture; continually improving training systems; providing growth opportunities; and industry leading compensation, benefits, and reward and recognition systems. We extend the same quality environment to coworkers as we extend to customers." How do these objectives address the strategic challenges cited in the case? What types of activities might the company deploy to achieve these objectives?

Review Questions

1. What is a strategy? What elements do most strategies contain?
2. Summarize the key practices for a strategic focus on performance excellence.
3. Explain the concept of strategic leadership.

4. Describe the information sought in the Baldrige Organizational Profile. What value does it provide to an organization?
5. Explain the basic strategic planning process.
6. Define mission, vision, and guiding principles. What is the purpose of each?
7. What is hoshin kanri? Provide a simplified description of this process.
8. How does catchball play an important role in policy deployment?
9. List and explain the major uses for the seven management and planning tools.
10. Describe the key contextual factors that affect organizational structure. What implications do they have for quality?
11. Describe the types of organizational structure commonly used. What are the advantages or disadvantages of each?
12. What types of organizational structures are common in TQ-based organizations today?
13. What are core competencies? Why is it important to understand them?
14. Explain the strategic role of work systems design. How should outsourcing and vertical integration decisions be made from a strategic context?
15. Explain how strategic planning is addressed in the Baldrige, ISO 9000:2000, and Six Sigma frameworks.

Discussion Questions

1. The Johnson & Johnson credo was written in 1943 by its chairman Robert Wood Johnson: "We believe our first responsibility is to the doctors, nurses, and patients, to mothers and fathers, and all others who use our products and services. In meeting their needs, everything we do must be of high quality." What would you expect to see in Johnson & Johnson's strategic planning approaches that reflect this philosophy?
2. Examine the following mission statements. Do you think they have a true purpose or are they merely cosmetic devices because someone felt that no major organization can be seen without one?[24]
   a. Our single focus will continue to be helping customers all over the world succeed in their businesses. When we do that—when we make them winners—then employees, dealers, and stockholders win as well.
   b. XYZ strives to understand and fulfill the needs of all our customers by providing the highest level of reliability and service at all times.
   c. XYZ creates value by providing transportation-related products and services with superior quality, safety, and environmental care to demanding customers in selected segments.
   d. We are dedicated to being the world's best at bringing people together—giving them easy access to each other and to the information and services they want and need—anytime, anywhere.
   e. To serve the most vulnerable.
3. Try to match the following companies with their actual mission statement in question 2. Could you think of more appropriate mission statements for any of these organizations?
   a. Volvo
   b. AT&T
   c. The International Red Cross
   d. Caterpillar
   e. DHL Worldwide Express

4. Contrast the following vision statements in terms of their usefulness to an organization.
   a. To become the industry leader and achieve superior growth and market share.
   b. To become the best-managed electric utility in the United States and an excellent company overall and be recognized as such.
   c. Being the best at everything we do, exceeding customer expectations; growing our business to increase its value to customers, employees, shareowners, and communities in which we work.
5. Propose three applications for each of the seven management and planning tools discussed in the chapter (see the Bonus Materials folder on the Premium website, for detailed information and examples). You might consider some applications around school, such as in the classroom, studying for exams, and so on.

6. What are the core competencies of your college? How are they leveraged from a strategic perspective?
7. Discuss how each of the following quality values (which are the core values and concepts underlying the Baldrige criteria) are reflected in each item of the Baldrige criteria for Strategic Planning (i.e., Item 2.1 Strategy Development, and Item 2.2 Strategy Deployment): customer-driven, visionary leadership, organizational and personal learning, valuing employees and partners, agility, managing for innovation, focus on the future, management by fact, social responsibility, focus on results and creating value, and systems perspective.

Projects, Etc.

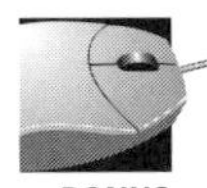

1. Use the Baldrige Organizational Profile questions to prepare an organizational profile for your college or a local organization that would be willing to provide you with the information. Use the format of the Novel Connect case study in the Baldrige Materials folder on the Premium website as a guide for writing the profile.
2. Interview managers at some local organizations to determine whether they have well-defined missions, visions, and guiding principles. If they do, how are these translated into strategy? If not, what steps should they take?
3. Find several examples of mission and vision statements for *Fortune* 500 companies. Critique these statements with respect to their usefulness, relevance to the organization, and ability to inspire and motivate employees.
4. Does your university or college have a mission and strategy? How might policy deployment be used in a university setting? Discuss with a senior executive administrator at your college or university (such as the VP of administration or the VP of academic affairs/provost) how policy deployment is, or might be, done.
5. Research the strategic planning practices of recent Baldrige Award winners. Discuss different approaches that these firms use and why they seem appropriate for their organizations. How do they reflect the leading practices described in this chapter?
6. In your role as a student, develop your own statements of mission, vision, and guiding principles. How would you create a strategy to achieve your mission and vision?

7. Compare the organizational structures of several manufacturing or service firms. What differences are reflected in their quality approaches and results?
8. Try to identify and contrast the core competencies of two different organizations within the same industry, such as Dell and Apple, Toyota and General Motors, or Sears and Wal-Mart, for example. Does your research suggest that these competencies are reflected in their supply chain or strategic directions?

CASES

Additional cases are available in the Bonus Materials folder for this chapter on the Premium website.

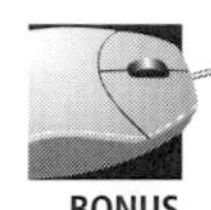
BONUS MATERIALS

A STRATEGIC BOTTLENECK[25]

An international bottle manufacturer produces glass containers for customers that include condiment producers, breweries, and wineries. The growing demand for plastic containers, and a history of higher production costs due to high scrap and return rates drove the business to focus its improvement efforts on cost and customer performance. However, the unique characteristics of the bottle manufacturing process and the way in which the company measured and motivated its workforce's performance made these improvements difficult to accomplish.

Bottle plants are traditionally organized around two primary functions: forming and selecting. Forming is where raw materials are melted in furnaces and molten glass is cut and formed by fast-moving, noisy, and dangerous machines that turn out thousands of bottles each minute. The workforce is primarily older males. In the selecting department, the work is relatively quiet and clean. The majority of workers are female, and the work is focused on spotting and removing bottles that fail to meet height, weight, dimension, centricity, and thickness specifications.

The principal performance measure in the forming department is the pack-to-melt ratio, calculated by dividing the total weight of bottles shipped by the total weight of the raw materials used. Individual and team performance goals are typically tied to this measure. The focus is on throughput and getting the highest percentage of produced bottles packed and shipped to customers. In the selecting department, customer satisfaction is the key measure of work performance, and compensation is based on how much product is accepted by the customer. As you can imagine, relations between the two departments were quite strained.

To achieve its strategic goals of lower cost and improved customer performance, what could this company do to align the goals of the forming and selecting departments?

CLIFTON METAL WORKS[26]

Clifton Metal Works (CMW) was founded in the mid-1940s by Donald Chalmer in a 3,000-square-foot building with nine people as a small family business to produce custom machined parts. In the 1960s, as business grew, the company expanded its facilities and its capability to develop its own tooling patterns, eventually moving into a 40,000-square-foot building.

However, as technology advanced, small family businesses like CMW met stiff competition. To survive, the company knew it had to listen more to its customers. From surveys and focus groups, the firm discovered that customers were not happy with the quality of the products they had been receiving. In 1985, CMW made a commitment to quality by hiring a quality assurance manager, Paul Levitt. Driven by the Deming philosophy, the company developed a variety of quality approaches and eventually became ISO 9000 certified in 1998. CMW made some substantial improvements in the quality of its products, particularly reducing scrap and reject rates.

Paul worked closely with the factory workers directly responsible for the products, asking them what they needed to get the job done and ensuring management commitment to provide the necessary resources. For example, CMW invested in computer-based statistical process control technology, which enabled workers to monitor their processes and adjust them as needed. The success of this project led the company to empower employees to control many other aspects of the system.

Business remained steady, but after hearing presentations from some Baldrige winners, Chalmer realized that a lot more could be done. In 2005, he hired a senior executive for performance excellence, James Hubbard. Hubbard saw an opportunity to change the company's culture and introduce many Baldrige principles he had learned in his previous job at a manufacturing firm that had applied the Baldrige criteria for many years. One of the first things he did was to review the current mission statement, which had remained relatively untouched since 1985:

> *Our mission at CMW is to improve the return on investment. We can accomplish this by changing attitudes and incorporating a quality/team environment. This will improve the quality of our products, enhance our productivity (which in turn will allow us to quote competitive prices), and elevate our service and response level to our customers. There are several factors which make positive change imperative.*
>
> *The standards for competitive levels of quality and service are becoming more demanding. The emergence of the "World Market" has brought on new challenges. We are in a low-growth, mature market. In order for CMW to improve return on investment, we must develop a strategy to improve quality and responsiveness in all areas of the company. We need to have all employees recognize the importance of product quality and service and move toward more favorable pricing. We need to change thinking throughout the organization to get employees involved, to encourage teamwork, to develop a more flexible workforce and adaptable organization. We need to instill pride in the workplace and the product.*
>
> *We believe that we can best achieve the desired future state by study of and adherence to the teachings of W. Edwards Deming.*

Hubbard did not feel that this mission statement provided a clear and vivid direction, especially in the 21st century. Consequently, he set up a planning retreat for senior management (including Chalmer) to develop a new strategic vision.

Discussion Questions

1. Comment on the current mission statement. Does it provide the strategic direction necessary for success for this company?
2. How can the mission statement be improved? Suggest a better statement of mission, vision, and guiding principles.

Novel Connect—Core Competencies and Work Systems Design

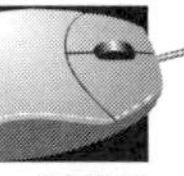

BONUS MATERIALS

The complete Novel Connect case study, a fictitious example of a Baldrige application, can be found in the Baldrige Materials folder on the Premium website. If you have not read the Organizational Profile yet (see the related case in Chapter 3), please do so first. Read the information provided in 6.1a(1) and 6.1a(2) on page 28 of the case study; these responses address the Baldrige criteria questions:

(1) How does your organization determine its core competencies? What are your organization's core competencies, and how do they relate to your mission, competitive environment, and action plans?

(2) How do you design and innovate your overall work systems? How do you decide which processes within your overall work systems will be internal to your organization (your key work processes) and which will use external resources?

How would you assess the company's approaches used to address these questions? Are they effective? Can you identify any opportunities for improvement?

Novel Connect—Strategic Planning

BONUS MATERIALS

The complete Novel Connect case study, a fictitious example of a Baldrige application, and the 2008 Baldrige criteria on which it is based can be found in the Baldrige Materials folder on the Premium website. If you have not read the Organizational Profile yet (see the related case in Chapter 3), please do so first. What factors in the Organizational Profile would be most important in evaluating their strategic planning and deployment approaches? Examine their response in Category 2 to the 2008 Baldrige criteria questions for this category). What are their strengths? What are their weaknesses and opportunities for improvement? What specific advice, including useful tools and techniques that might help them, would you suggest?

NOTES

1. Matthew Boyle, "Best Buy's Giant Gamble," *Fortune* April 3, 2006, 69–75.
2. James Brian Quinn, *Strategies for Change: Logical Incrementalism* (Homewood, IL: Richard D. Irwin, 1980).
3. Michael Hitt and Duane Ireland. "Achieving and Maintaining Strategic Competitiveness in the 21st Century: the Role of Strategic Leadership," *Academy of Management Executive*, [reprinted from February, 1999]. 19, No. 4, November 2005, 63.
4. Meryl Davids. "Where Style Meets Substance," *Journal of Business Strategy*, 16, No. 1, January/February 1995, 49.
5. Kimberly B. Boal and Robert Hooiberg. "Strategic Leadership Reasearch: Moving On," *Leadership Quarterly*, 11, 4, 2000, 516–518.
6. Mike Freeman with Benjamin B. Tregoe. *The Art and Discipline of Strategic Leadership* (New York: McGraw-Hill, 2003), 22–23.
7. Hitt and Ireland, pp. 65–67.
8. 2007 North Mississippi Medical Center Malcolm Baldrige Application Summary.
9. Henry Mintzberg, "The Fall and Rise of Strategic Planning," *Harvard Business Review*, January–February 1994, 107–114.
10. Victor Cvascella, "Effective Strategic Planning," *Quality Progress*, November 2002, 62–67.
11. Bob King, *Hoshin Planning: The Developmental Approach* (Methuen, MA: GOAL/QPC, 1989).
12. M. Imai, *Kaizen: The Key to Japan's Competitive Success* (New York: McGraw-Hill, 1986), 144–145.
13. Adapted from Kersi F. Munshi, "Policy Deployment: A Key to Long-Term TQM Success," *ASQC Quality Congress Transactions* (Boston, 1993), 236–244.
14. The Ernst & Young Quality Improvement Consulting Group, *Total Quality: An Executive's Guide for the 1990s*, (Homewood, IL: Dow Jones–Irwin, 1990).
15. Noel Tichy and Nancy Cardwell, *The Cycle of Leadership* (New York: HarperCollins, 2002), 185; and James M. Lucas. "The Essential Six Sigma," *Quality Progress*, January, 2002, 28.
16. Kermit F. Wasmuth, "Organization and Planning," in Loren Walsh, Ralph Wurster, and Raymond J. Kimber (eds.), *Quality Management Handbook* (Wheaton, IL: Hitchcock Publishing Company, 1986), 9–34.
17. Ricardo Simler, *Maverick* (New York: Warner Books, 1993), 196.
18. Gary Hamel and C. K. Prahalad, "The Core Competence of the Corporation", *Harvard Business Review*, vol. 68, no. 3, May–June 1990, pp. 79–93.
19. Adapted from Mercy Health System Malcolm Baldrige 2007 National Quality Program Application.
20. Adapted from: Malcolm Baldridge Award application, printed courtsey of Liz Kolodney, Director of Communications and Marketing, City of Coral Springs, Florida.
21. R. Eric Reidenbach and Reginald W. Goeke, "Six Sigma, Value, and Competitive Strategy," *Quality Progress*, July 2007, 45–49. Copyright © 2007 American Society for Quality. Reprinted with permission.
22. Reprinted with permission from Susan E. Daniels, "Six Sigma at Cigna," *Quality Progress*, May 2007, pp. 43–48. Copyright © 2007 American Society for Quality. No further distribution allowed without permission.
23. Branch-Smith Printing, Application Summary, 2002. Courtesy of David Branch, President.
24. "Missions for All Seasons," *Across the Board*, April, 2000, 12.
25. Adapted material—Reprinted with permission from Victor Cascella, "Effective Strategic Planning," *Quality in Progress*, November 2002, pp. 62–67. Copyright © 2002 American Society for Quality. No further distribution allowed without permission.
26. This fictitious case stems from ideas suggested by the author's former students John P. Rosiello and David Seilkop.

FOCUSING ON CUSTOMERS

OUTLINE

QUALITY PROFILES: Park Place Lexus and Mercy Health System
THE IMPORTANCE OF CUSTOMER SATISFACTION AND ENGAGEMENT
  The American Customer Satisfaction Index
IDENTIFYING CUSTOMERS
  Customer Segmentation
UNDERSTANDING CUSTOMER NEEDS
  Gathering and Analyzing the Voice of the Customer
LINKING CUSTOMER INFORMATION TO DESIGN, PRODUCTION, AND SERVICE DELIVERY
BUILDING A CUSTOMER-FOCUSED CULTURE
  Commitments and Customer Support
  Selecting and Developing Customer Contact Employees
  Customer Contact Requirements
  Complaint Management and Service Recovery
  Strategic Partnerships and Alliances
  Customer-Focused Technology
MEASURING CUSTOMER ENGAGEMENT
  Designing Satisfaction Surveys
  Analyzing and Using Customer Feedback
  Why Many Customer Satisfaction Efforts Fail
  Customer Perceived Value
CUSTOMER FOCUS IN THE BALDRIGE CRITERIA, ISO 9000, AND SIX SIGMA
SUMMARY OF KEY POINTS AND TERMINOLOGY
QUALITY IN PRACTICE: Understanding the Voice of the Customer at LaRosa's Pizzerias
QUALITY IN PRACTICE: Customer Focus at Amazon.com
REVIEW QUESTIONS
DISCUSSION QUESTIONS
PROJECTS, ETC.
Cases Pauli's Restaurant and Microbrewery
  First Internet Reliable Bank
  Gold Star Chili: Customer and Market Knowledge
  Novel Connect: Customer Focus

Feargal Quinn is the executive chairman of Superquinn, a 5,600-employee, 19-store chain of supermarkets in Ireland. In every deed, the focus is on persuading the customer to return.[1] Quinn calls it the "boomerang principle." His tireless and inventive exploration of this principle earned him the reputation as Ireland's "pope of customer service." Superquinn inspires such intense devotion that many customers say that they drive out of their way—and past several of its biggest competitors—to shop there. At Superquinn, you don't have to pay for broccoli stalks and carrot tops you never use; the store provides scissors to cut off what you don't want. The checkout technology provides a running tab on a screen that faces the customer, and then organizes the final receipt by product category, rather than the order in which products were scanned. Every store features a professionally staffed playhouse where mothers can leave young children while they shop. The program costs the company a bundle, but it has earned even more in loyal customers and reputation. Kindergarten teachers around the country (Ireland doesn't have preschool) recognize "Superquinn kids" as the most socialized and school-ready of each new class. Superquinn's fresh produce, butchers, and fishmongers are mixed in with futuristic flat screen displays, digital shelf labels, and kiosks that link customers to their bank, their SuperClub account, as well as to wine recommendations and interactive recipe planners. Quinn notes that "What seems reasonable or even valuable from the perspective of the company is often glaringly wrong from the point of view of the customer." Each month, Superquinn managers are required to spend time in customers' shoes, shopping, asking questions, lodging complaints, waiting in line. In fact, Mr. Quinn himself regularly packs bags for customers and holds weekly panels to listen to shoppers who tell him how they think the store can serve them better.

Don Peppers and Martha Rogers sum up the importance of customers eloquently:

> *The only value your company will ever create is the value that comes from customers—the ones you have now and the ones you will have in the future. Businesses succeed by getting, keeping, and growing customers. Customers are the only reason you build factories, hire employees, schedule meetings, lay fiber-optic lines, or engage in any business activity. Without customers, you don't have a business.*[2]

In Japanese, a single word, *okyakusama*, means both "customer" and "honorable guest." World-class organizations are obsessed with meeting and exceeding customer expectations. Many organizations such as The Ritz-Carlton Hotel Company, Disney, and Toyota's Lexus division were built on the notion of satisfying the customer.

To create satisfied customers, the organization needs to identify customers' needs, design the production and service systems to meet those needs, and measure the results as the basis for improvement.

Other firms, however, have to break old habits and *learn* to be customer-focused. Many entrepreneurial start-ups, for example, create new markets with innovative products; however, this process essentially tells customers what they want. As customers become more sophisticated and competition increases, these firms often face a competitive crisis and must begin to listen more closely to customers. Many organizations do not view customer focus as a key business process. Organizations must use customer focus as a key driver for their strategic planning activities.

This chapter focuses on this concept of customer-driven excellence. Table 5.1 summarizes the key practices for performance excellence in this area. We will discuss these issues in the remainder of the chapter. The Quality Profiles provide two examples of organizations that focus considerable attention on their customers.

Table 5.1 Key Customer Focused Practices for Performance Excellence

- Identify the most important customer groups and markets, considering competitors and other potential customers, and segment the customer base to better meet differing needs.
- Understand both near-term and longer-term customer needs and expectations (the "voice of the customer") and employ systematic processes for listening and learning from customers, potential customers, and customers of competitors to obtain actionable information about products and customer support.
- Understand the linkages between the voice of the customer and design, production, and delivery processes; and use voice-of-the-customer information to identify and innovate product offerings and customer support processes to meet and exceed customer requirements and expectations, to expand relationships, and to identify and attract new customers and markets.
- Create an organizational culture and manage customer relationships to ensure a consistently positive customer experience that contributes to customer engagement, the ability to meet and exceed their expectations, and the ability to acquire new customers.
- Develop effective complaint management processes that ensure that customers receive prompt resolution of their concerns and that lead to recovery of their confidence, and enhance their satisfaction and engagement, and that enable aggregation and analysis of complaints to facilitate improvement.
- Measure customer satisfaction, engagement, and dissatisfaction; compare the results relative to competitors and industry benchmarks; and use the information to evaluate and improve organizational processes.

Quality Profiles

Park Place Lexus and Mercy Health System

With two locations in the Dallas, Texas area, Park Place Lexus (PPL) sells new Lexus vehicles and pre-owned luxury vehicles, services Lexus and other vehicles, and sells Lexus parts to the wholesale and retail markets. PPL has committed substantial resources to ensuring that client relationships, once established, can be maintained in a way that contributes value to both parties. This includes the development and deployment of a Client-relationship management database that tracks all aspects of the PPL-Client interaction and provides the resulting information to members (the term used by PPL to refer to company employees). PPL uses its Client Concern Resolution (CCR) process to address any problems that might occur in any area of the client experience. CCR empowers the individual member to resolve client complaints on the spot by allowing each member to spend up to $250 to resolve a complaint, or up to $2,000 by committee.

PPL has identified eight key value creation processes that have direct interface with clients, significantly contribute to the delivery of service to its clients, or provide opportunity for business growth. For all of these key processes, PPL has identified process requirements as well as process measures to help them track progress toward meeting these requirements. PPL has extensive training programs and career development planning for its workforce. A focus on personal and organizational learning is the key to PPL's efforts to motivate members, which then results in exceptional understanding of client's needs and the ability to deliver service to meet those needs.

As a result of these focused efforts, Park Place Lexus Grapevine location had a New Car Client Satisfaction Index (CSI) of 99.8 percent in 2004, making it the highest rated Lexus dealership in the nation. PPL's continued client focus has reduced the number of complaints that promises were not met from 130 in 2002 to 3 in 2005, that clients were misled by staff from 22 in 2002 to 1 in 2005, and about discourteous treatment from 28 in 2002 to 1 in 2005.

In 1989, Mercy Hospital was a single standalone community hospital primarily serving Janesville, Wisconsin. Today, Mercy Health System (MHS) is a fully integrated health care system with three hospitals and a network of 64 facilities consisting of 39 multi-specialty outpatient centers located in six counties throughout southern Wisconsin and northern Illinois. Mercy has a unique W2 Physician Partnership Model with 285 primary and specialty physicians. To further its mission of providing "exceptional health care services, resulting in healing in the broadest sense," MHS has created a culture of high quality care, customer focus, partner cooperation, innovation, and cost consciousness.

The entire organization is aligned according to its Culture of Excellence Four Pillars—quality, service, partnering, and cost—and its values—healing in its broadest sense, patients come first, treat each other like family, and strive for excellence. Every MHS partner is committed to exceeding patient expectations by making quality care a top priority. Best-practice benchmarks are used to measure clinical care and ensure continuous improvement and patient safety. At MHS, an engaged, empowered workforce and advanced medical and information technology are key to high quality patient care.

MHS focuses on patient and customer satisfaction, timely resolution of problems, and expanding and improving services. Continuous benchmarking, tracking of quality indicators, and surveying patients and customers help MHS ensure excellence in patient care. MHS's "Take the **L.E.A.D**" program—**L**isten to the customer; **E**mpathize with the customer; **A**ccept the customer's perspective, **A**pologize, **A**cknowledge concern and take **A**ction to recover; **D**irect to the person able to recover the situation—is used to turn negative experiences into positive ones. The Mercy Health Mall is a one-stop superstore offering a number of services, including acupuncture, massage therapy, a vision center, a pharmacy, durable medical equipment and supplies, an urgent care clinic, a cardiac rehabilitation and fitness center, outpatient diabetic treatment, an entire array of health products, and more. MHS is the leader in market share for inpatient services and outpatient surgery in its Wisconsin service area. In 2006, about 84 percent of hospital customers and about 90 percent of multi-specialty outpatient center customers would recommend MHS to others, a key indicator of customer loyalty and a reflection of overall satisfaction.

Source: Adapted from Malcolm Baldrige National Quality Award, Profiles of Winners, National Institute of Standards and Technology, Department of Commerce.

THE IMPORTANCE OF CUSTOMER SATISFACTION AND ENGAGEMENT

Avis recognizes two ways to increase market share in the rental car business: (1) by buying large volumes of corporate business with extremely low rates, and (2) by improving customer satisfaction levels, thereby increasing repurchase intent and repeat business. Avis stated that it will not buy business at low rates for the sole purpose of increasing market share. Avis's marketing department uses a full range of research and analysis to keep pace with changing market trends and develops programs that respond to customers' needs. Through information technology, Avis queries all customers at car return to monitor trends and levels of customer satisfaction. It also calls 1,500 customers each month to assess in detail satisfaction levels in each of nine service delivery areas.[3]

Customer wants and needs drive competitive advantage, and statistics show that growth in market share and financial success are strongly correlated with customer satisfaction.

Customer satisfaction is an important factor for the bottom line. Statistics show that the typical company gets 65 percent of its business from existing customers, and it costs five times more to find a new customer than to keep an existing one happy.[4] One study found that businesses with a 98 percent customer retention rate are twice as profitable as those at 94 percent. Johnson Controls, Inc. (JCI), discovered that 91 percent of contract renewals came from customers who were either satisfied or very satisfied. A percentage point increase in the overall satisfaction score was worth $13 million in service contract renewals annually. JCI also learned that those customers who gave a "not satisfied" rating had a much higher defection rate. After seeing the financial impact of customer satisfaction, JCI made improving customer satisfaction a key initiative.[5]

Although satisfaction is important, modern firms need to look further. First, they must avoid creating dissatisfied customers because of product or service failures. Studies have shown that dissatisfied customers tell at least twice as many friends about bad experiences than they tell about good ones. For example, customers of mass merchandisers shared negative experiences with an average of six people during a recent Christmas shopping season, and people told about the experiences were up to five times as likely to avoid the store as the original unhappy customer.[6] Second, they must try to develop *loyal* customers—those who stay with a company and make positive referrals. Satisfaction and loyalty are very different concepts. To quote Patrick Mehne, former chief quality officer at The Ritz-Carlton Hotel Company: "Satisfaction is an attitude; loyalty is a behavior." Customers who are merely satisfied may often purchase from competitors because of convenience, promotions, or other factors. Loyal customers place a priority on doing business with a particular organization, and will often go out of their way or pay a premium to stay with the company. Loyal customers spend more, are willing to pay higher prices, refer new clients, and are less costly to do business with. As an example, Carl Sewell, owner of Sewell Cadillac in Dallas, calculated that the average lifetime value of a loyal customer for his dealership was $332,000.[7]

***Customer engagement** refers to customers' investment in or commitment to a brand and product offerings.*[8]

Customer engagement is an important outcome of a customer-focused culture and the organization's listening, learning, and performance-excellence strategy. Characteristics of customer engagement include customer retention and loyalty, customers' willingness to make an effort to do business with the organization, and customers' willingness to actively advocate for and recommend the brand and product offerings. Customer engagement is influenced by an organization's integrity and the relationships it builds with its customers.[9] As one small business owner stated, "We build customer loyalty by telling our customers the truth, whether it is good or bad news."[10]

Value, as defined in Chapter 1, is quality related to price. Consumers no longer buy solely on the basis of price. They compare the quality of the total package of goods and services that a business offers (sometimes called the **customer benefit package**) with price and with competitive offerings. The customer benefit package includes the physical product and its quality dimensions; presale support, such as ease of ordering; rapid, on-time, and accurate delivery; and post-sale support, such as field service, warranties, and technical support. If competitors offer better choices for a similar price, consumers will rationally select the package with the highest perceived quality. If a competitor offers the same quality package of goods and services at a lower price, customers would generally choose the one having the lower price. The ability to keep prices low requires a strong internal focus on efficiency and quality, as quality improvements in operations generally reduce costs. Thus, organizations must focus on continually improving both the consumer benefit package and the quality of their internal operations.

Customer satisfaction results from an organization's ability to meet and exceed expectations and deliver higher value than competitors.

The American Customer Satisfaction Index[11]

In 1994, the University of Michigan Business School and the American Society for Quality (ASQ) released the first American Customer Satisfaction Index (ACSI), an economic indicator that measures customer satisfaction at the national level. It was the first cross-industry benchmark in the United States to measure customer satisfaction. Similar indexes previously existed in Sweden and Germany. One of the goals of the ACSI is to raise the public's perception and understanding of quality, as do the consumer price index and other economic indicators. This increased awareness will help to interpret price and productivity measures and promote customer-driven quality.

The ACSI is based on customer evaluations of the quality of goods and services purchased in the United States and produced by both domestic firms and foreign firms with a substantial U.S. market share. The 1994 ACSI provides a baseline against which customer satisfaction levels can be tracked over time. It is designed to answer the questions: Are customer satisfaction and evaluations improving or declining for the nation's output of goods and services? Are they improving or declining for particular organizations, sectors of industry, or specific industries? The index quantifies the value that customers place on products, and thus drives quality improvement. Organizations can use the data to assess customer loyalty, identify potential barriers to entry within markets, predict return on investments, and pinpoint areas in which customer expectations are not being satisfied.

The index uses a tested, multi-equation econometric model to produce four levels of indexes: a national customer satisfaction index and indexes for seven industrial sectors, 40 specific industries, and 203 organizations and agencies within those industries. ACSI is based on results of telephone interviews conducted in a national sample of 46,000 consumers who recently bought or used a company's product or service. This model is summarized in Figure 5.1.

The econometric model used to produce ACSI links customer satisfaction to its determinants: customer expectations, perceived quality, and perceived value. Customer satisfaction, in turn, is linked to customer loyalty, which has an impact on profitability.

The initial 1994 results showed that nondurable manufacturing scored relatively high in customer satisfaction, whereas public administration and government services scored relatively low. However, the overall national index declined continually until 1997, but has generally improved overall since. Some of the largest improvements occurred in the retail, finance, and e-commerce sectors.

The ACSI is updated on a rolling basis with one to three sectors of the economy measured each quarter. Magazines and newspapers such as *Fortune* and *The Wall Street Journal* generally report current ACSI results; a question later in this chapter will ask you to research recent trends. Results and other information are available from the ACSI website, www.theacsi.org/

Figure 5.1 ACSI Model

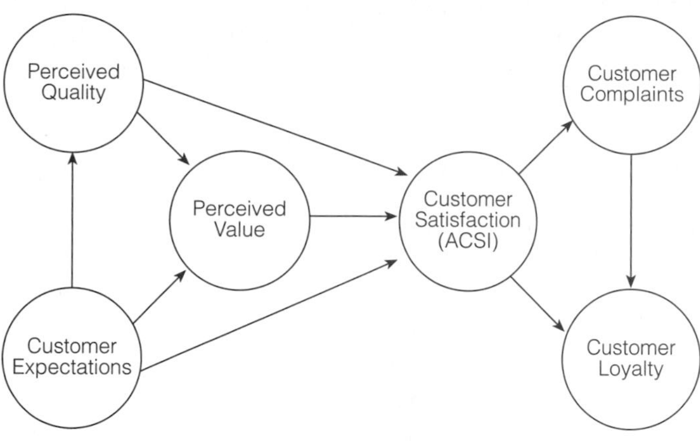

Source: Courtesy of National Quality Research Center (see endnote 11).

IDENTIFYING CUSTOMERS

The first step in being customer focused is to understand who your customers are. While this sounds obvious, the concept of "customer" may mean many different things. Most employees think that "customers" are those people who ultimately purchase and use a company's products. These end users, or **consumers**, certainly are an important group. However, consumers are not the only customer group of concern. The easiest way to identify customers is to think in terms of customer–supplier relationships.

AT&T uses a customer–supplier model as shown in Figure 5.2. Every process receives inputs from suppliers and creates outputs for customers. The feedback loops suggest that suppliers must also be considered as customers. They need appropriate information about the requirements they must meet. This model can be applied at the organization level, the process level, and the performer level (see the discussion of the "Three Levels of Quality" in Chapter 1).

At the organization level, a business has various **external customers** who may fall between the organization and the consumer, and who have distinct needs and expectations. For example, manufacturers of consumer products distribute to retail stores such as Wal-Mart and grocery stores. The retail stores are external customers

Figure 5.2 AT&T's Customer–Supplier Model

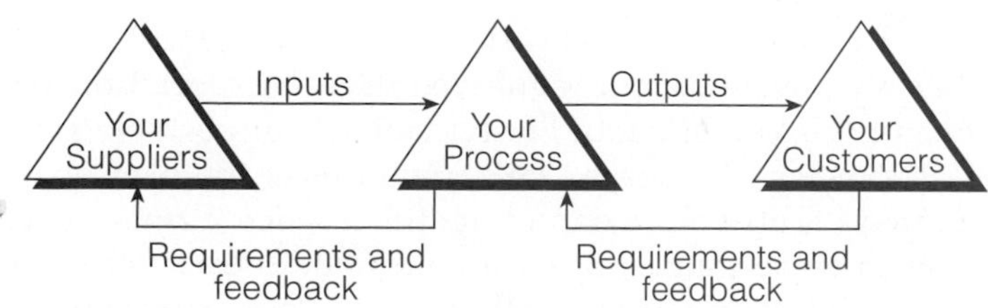

Source: Reproduced with permission from AT&T © 1988. All rights reserved.

of the manufacturers. They have specific needs for timely delivery, appropriate product displays, accurate invoicing, and so forth. Because these stores allocate shelf space for the manufacturers' products, they represent important customers. The manufacturers are customers of the chemical companies, printing companies, and other suppliers of such things as materials and packaging materials.

At the process level, departments, and key cross-functional processes within a company have **internal customers** whose work ultimately serves consumers and external customers. These internal customers are other departments or processes within the organization. For instance, manufacturing is a customer of purchasing, a nursing unit is a customer of the hospital laundry, and the reservations department is a customer of the information systems department for an airline or hotel. Figure 2.1 in Chapter 2 is a good example of the internal customer–supplier relationships within a typical manufacturing firm.

At the performer level, each employee receives inputs from others and produces some output for individual internal customers. Examples of such internal customers are the assembly line worker at the next station, an executive's secretary, the order taker who passes along orders to the kitchen staff at McDonald's, or an X-ray technician who must meet a physician's timely request.

Identifying customer–supplier relationships begins with asking some fundamental questions:

1. What goods or services are produced by my work?
2. Who uses these products and services?
3. Who do I call, write to, or answer questions for?
4. Who supplies the inputs to my process?

Eventually, everyone can better understand their role in satisfying not only their internal customers, but also the external customers.

The natural customer–supplier linkages among individuals, departments, and functions build up the "chain of customers" throughout an organization that connect every individual and function to the external customers and consumers, thus characterizing the organization's value chain.

At the organization level, a firm should also recognize that its customers include employees and the public at large. Viewing employees as customers, an organization then must consciously strive to build and maintain a work environment conducive to the well-being and growth of all employees by paying attention to health, safety, and ergonomics (the study of physical capabilities of people in the design of workplaces, tools, instruments) issues. An organization must also anticipate public concerns and assess the possible impacts on society of its products, services, and operations, such as safety and environmental concerns. These issues will be addressed further in Chapters 6 and 9.

Customer Segmentation

Customers generally have different requirements and expectations. For example, Macy's department stores defines four lifestyles of its core customers: "Katherine"—traditional, classic dresser who doesn't take a lot of risks and likes quality; "Julie"—neo-traditional and slightly more edgy but still classic; "Erin"—a contemporary customer who loves newness and shops by brand; and "Alex"—the fashion customer who wants only the latest and greatest (there's a male version too!).[12] A company usually cannot satisfy all customers with the same products or services. This issue is particularly important for those that do business globally (just think of the differences in regulations for automobiles in various countries or the differences in electrical power systems in the United States versus Europe). Therefore, organizations that segment customers into natural groups and customize the products or services are better able to respond to customers' needs.

Customer segmentation might be based on geography, demographic factors, ways in which products are used, volumes, or expected levels of service.

There are many different ways to approach customer segmentation. Motorola's Commercial, Government, and Industrial Solutions Sector segments its customers in two ways, first by world region, and second by sales distribution channel (direct and indirect). The Ritz-Carlton Hotel Company ranks potential and current customers by volume, geography, and profit. The Royal Bank of Canada (RBC) identified a key customer segment, "snowbirds," Canadians who spend the winter in Florida or Arizona. These individuals want to borrow in the United States for condos or houses and want to be served by employees who know Canada as well as the United States and even speak French when necessary. So, RBC opened a branch in Florida, which achieved exceptional results.[13]

Juran suggests classifying customers into two main groups: the vital few and the useful many.[14] For example, organizers of conventions and meetings book large blocks of hotel rooms and have large catering needs. They represent the vital few and deserve special attention on an individual basis. Individual travelers and families are the useful many and typically need only standardized attention as a group.

Another way of segmenting customers with an eye toward business results is by profitability. Many businesses spend a lot of money trying to acquire customers who are not profitable and probably will never be. Profit potential can be measured by the net present value of the customer (NPVC).[15] NPVC is the total profits (revenues associated with a customer minus expenses needed to serve a customer) discounted over time. For instance, the profit associated with customers at an automobile dealer consist of the profit from the sale of a car plus the profit from service visits. The number of transactions associated with repeat customers can easily be estimated. As another example, frequent fliers represent high NPVC customers to an airline. By segmenting them according to their frequency, an airline can determine the net value of offering increasing levels of benefits to fliers at higher frequency levels as a means of retaining current customers or enticing potential customers. Firms can also use NPVC to eliminate customers with low or negative values that represent a financial liability. For example, the Fleet Financial Group dropped its basic savings account interest rate, hoping to lose customers who had only savings accounts.[16]

Segmentation allows a company to prioritize customer groups, for instance by considering for each group the benefits of satisfying their requirements and the consequences of failing to satisfy their requirements.

Segmentation allows the company to align its internal processes according to the most important customer expectations or their impact on shareholder value. For instance, Fidelity Investments realized that some customers who were doing limited business with Fidelity were using costly resources of service representatives too frequently. They began teaching those customers how to use the company's lowest cost channels: its automated phone lines and its website, which was made friendlier and easier to use. They could still talk to service reps, but the phone system identified their calls and routed them into longer queues as a disincentive to call, so the most profitable

customers could be served more quickly. Fidelity was willing to lose some of these customers, because their profitability would increase; however, 96 percent of them stayed and most switched to lower-cost channels.[17]

UNDERSTANDING CUSTOMER NEEDS

At Ideo, one of the world's leading design firms (which designed Apple's first mouse, standup toothpaste tubes, and the Palm V), design doesn't begin with a far-out concept or a cool drawing. It begins with a deep understanding of the people who might use whatever product or service that eventually emerges from its work, drawing from anthropology, psychology, biomechanics, and other disciplines.[18] Organizations first need to understand the drivers of customer satisfaction—what do customers want or expect from our goods and services? For example, credit card users might have the following expectations for four key business activities associated with the card:

1. *Applying for an account:* Accessible, responsive, accurate, and professional
2. *Using the card:* Easy to use and hassle free, features, reasonable fees, and credit limits
3. *Billing:* Accurate, timely, and easy to understand
4. *Customer service*: Accessible, responsive, and professional

Perhaps one of the best examples of understanding customer needs and using this information effectively is Frank Perdue's chicken business.[19] Perdue learned what customers' key purchase criteria were; these criteria included a yellow bird, high meat-to-bone ratio, no pinfeathers, freshness, availability, and brand image. He also determined the relative importance of each criterion, and how well the company and its competitors were meeting each one. By systematically improving his ability to exceed customers' expectations relative to the competition, Perdue gained market share even though his chickens were premium-priced. Among Perdue's innovations was using a jet engine that dried the chickens after plucking, allowing the pinfeathers to be singed off.

Considerable marketing efforts go into correctly identifying customer needs. Ford, for instance, identified about 90 features that customers want in sales and service, including a ride to their next stop when they drop off a car for service and appointments within one day of a desired date. Ford then trimmed the list to seven service standards and six sales standards against which dealers have begun to measure themselves.[20]

David A. Garvin suggested that products have multiple dimensions of quality:[21]

1. *Performance:* A product's primary operating characteristics. Using an automobile as an example, characteristics would include such things as acceleration, braking distance, steering, and handling.
2. *Features:* The "bells and whistles" of a product. A car may have power options, a CD player, iPod® connections, satellite radio, and antilock brakes.
3. *Reliability:* The probability of a product's surviving over a specified period of time under stated conditions of use. A car's ability to start on cold days and frequency of failures are reliability factors.
4. *Conformance:* The degree to which physical and performance characteristics of a product match pre-established standards. A car's fit and finish and freedom from noises and squeaks can reflect this dimension.
5. *Durability:* The amount of use one gets from a product before it physically deteriorates or until replacement is preferable. For a car it might include corrosion resistance and the long wear of upholstery fabric.

Table 5.2 Quality Dimensions of a Manufactured Product and Service

Quality Dimension	Manufactured Product (Stereo Amplifier)	Service Product (Checking Account)
Performance	Signal-to-noise ratio; power	Time to process customer requests
Features	Remote control	Automatic bill paying
Conformance	Workmanship	Accuracy
Reliability	Mean time to failure	Variability of time to process requests
Durability	Useful life	Keeping pace with industry trends
Serviceability	Ease of repair	Resolution of errors
Aesthetics	Oak cabinet	Appearance of bank lobby

Source: Adapted from Paul E. Pisek, "Defining Quality at the Marketing/Development Interface," *Quality Progress*, Vol. 20, No. 6, pp. 28–36. Copyright © 1987 American Society for Quality. Reprinted with permission.

6. *Serviceability:* The speed, courtesy, and competence of repair work. An automobile owner might be concerned with access to spare parts, the number of miles between major maintenance services, and the expense of service.
7. *Aesthetics:* How a product looks, feels, sounds, tastes, or smells. A car's color, instrument panel design, control placement, and "feel of the road," for example, may make it aesthetically pleasing.

Table 5.2 gives some examples of these dimensions for both a manufactured product and a service product. They form the basis for what customers want. A driver seeking performance, for example, might look to BMW, while one who values reliability might prefer a Toyota. Others who want different features might choose Chrysler or Lincoln.

Customers today pay more attention to service issues than to the physical goods themselves. One study found that customers are five times more likely to switch because of perceived service problems than for price concerns or product quality issues.[22] For services, research identified five principal dimensions that contribute to customer perceptions of service quality:

1. *Reliability:* The ability to provide what was promised, dependably and accurately. Examples include customer service representatives responding in the promised time, following customer instructions, providing error-free invoices and statements, and making repairs correctly the first time.
2. *Assurance:* The knowledge and courtesy of employees, and their ability to convey trust and confidence. Examples include the ability to answer questions, having the capabilities to do the necessary work, monitoring credit card transactions to avoid possible fraud, and being polite and pleasant during customer transactions.
3. *Tangibles:* The physical facilities and equipment, and the appearance of personnel. Tangibles include attractive facilities, appropriately dressed employees, and well-designed forms that are easy to read and interpret.
4. *Empathy:* The degree of caring and individual attention provided to customers. Some examples might be the willingness to schedule deliveries at the customer's convenience, explaining technical jargon in a layperson's language, and recognizing regular customers and calling them by name.

5. *Responsiveness:* The willingness to help customers and provide prompt service. Examples include acting quickly to resolve problems, promptly crediting returned merchandise, and rapidly replacing defective products.

A Japanese professor, Noriaki Kano, suggested segmenting customer requirements into three groups:

1. *Dissatisfiers:* Requirements that are expected in a product or service. In an automobile, a radio, heater, and required safety features are examples, which are generally not stated by customers but assumed as given. If these features are not present, the customer is dissatisfied.
2. *Satisfiers:* Requirements that customers say they want. Many car buyers want a sunroof, satellite radio, or antilock brakes. Although these requirements are generally not expected, fulfilling them creates satisfaction.
3. *Exciters/delighters:* New or innovative features that customers do not expect, such as separate rear-seat video controls that allow children to watch DVD movies, or even wi-fi capabilities.

Meeting customer expectations (that is, providing satisfiers) is often considered the minimum required to stay in business. To be truly competitive, organizations must surprise and delight customers by going beyond the expected. Hospitals, for example, are introducting numerous innovations in patient care services that are designed to change traditions. These not only include significant improvements in food services—Doyleston Hospital in Philadelphia started an "At Your Request" program offering gourmet selections—as well as other amenities such as in-room massages, video-on-demand, wireless access, and even champagne in maternity wards.[23] Thus, successful organizations continually innovate and study customer perceptions to ensure that needs are being met.

As customers become familiar with them, exciters/delighters become satisfiers over time. Eventually, satisfiers become dissatisfiers.

For instance, antilock brakes and traction control certainly were exciters/delighters when they were first introduced. Now, many car buyers expect them and look for them when buying a new car. Satellite navigational systems for automobiles are a more-recent example of exciters/delighters that are becoming more commonplace and are probably viewed as satisfiers today. As technology evolves, consumer expectations continually increase.

In the Kano classification system, dissatisfiers and satisfiers are relatively easy to determine through routine marketing research. For example, the hot-selling Ford F-150 pickup truck relied on extensive consumer research at the beginning of the redesign process. However, traditional market research efforts may not be effective in understanding exciters/delighters, and may even backfire. For example, Ford listened to a sample of customers and asked whether they wanted a fourth door on one of its minivans. Only about one-third thought it was a great idea, so Ford scrapped the idea. Chrysler, on the other hand, spent a lot more time living with owners of vans and observing their behavior, watching them wrestle to get things in and out, noting all the occasions where a fourth door would really be convenient, and was very successful after introducing a fourth door.[24] Thus, a company must make special effort to identify exciters/delighters.

Besides consumers, organizations must also pay attention to the needs of external customers. In designing its Icy Rider sled, Rubbermaid used a combination of field research, competitive product analysis, and consumer focus groups. It also listened to major retailers, such as Wal-Mart, who wanted such products to be stackable and save space.[25] Sometimes, attention to the needs of external customers even extends to exciters/delighters. General Electric (which makes aircraft engines for the airline industry) provided Six Sigma specialists to Southwest Airlines at no cost to work on problems that had nothing to do with GE products. GE also offers training in its management techniques, shares its expertise in working globally, and allows customers to tap into market information and basic research developed by its business units. As one GE executive noted, "The more successful our customers are, the more successful we will be."[26]

Understanding the needs of internal customers is as important as understanding those of consumers and external customers. This point is reflected in the AT&T customer–supplier model in Figure 5.2, which the company uses to help employees comprehend internal customer–supplier issues. For example, in many service industries, customer-contact employees depend on a variety of information and support from internal suppliers, such as the information systems department, warehousing and production scheduling, and engineering and design functions. Failure to meet the needs of customer-contact employees will have a detrimental effect on external customers. A division of the former General Telephone and Electronics Corporation (now Verizon), GTE Supply, negotiated contracts, purchased products, and distributed goods for internal telephone operations customer groups at each GTE local telephone company. In response to complaints from its internal customers, GTE Supply began to survey its internal customers to identify needs and information for improvement. This approach dramatically improved satisfaction levels, reduced costs, and decreased cycle times.[27]

Gathering and Analyzing the Voice of the Customer

Customer requirements, as expressed in the customer's own terms, are called the **voice of the customer**. However, the customer's meaning is the crucial part of the message. As the vice president of marketing at Whirlpool stated, "The consumer speaks in code."[28] Whirlpool's research showed that customers wanted clean refrigerators, which could be interpreted to mean that they wanted easy-to-clean refrigerators. After analyzing the data and asking more questions, Whirlpool found out what most consumers actually wanted was refrigerators that looked clean with minimum fuss. As a result, Whirlpool designed new models to have stucco-like fronts and sides that hide fingerprints.

Organizations use a variety of methods, or "listening posts," to collect information about customer needs and expectations, their importance, and customer satisfaction with the company's performance on these measures.

When former Disney executive Paul Pressler assumed the CEO position at Gap, he met with each of Gap's top 50 executives, asking them such standard questions as "What about Gap do you want to preserve and why?" "What about Gap do you want to change and why?" and so on. But he also added one of his own: "What is your most important tool for figuring out what the consumer wants?"[29]

Some of the key approaches to gathering customer information include comment cards and formal surveys, focus groups, direct customer contact, field intelligence, complaint analysis, and Internet monitoring.

Comment cards and formal surveys: Comment cards and formal surveys are easy ways to solicit customer information. These approaches typically concentrate on measuring customer satisfaction, which is discussed later in this chapter, and often include questions pertaining to the customers' perception of the importance of particular quality dimensions as well as open-ended questions. However, few customers generally will respond to comment cards placed at restaurant tables or in hotel rooms, and those who do may not represent the typical customer. Formal surveys can be designed to scientifically sample a customer base, but can also suffer from nonresponse bias. However, some organizations find that they work well.

Focus groups: A focus group is a panel of individuals (customers or non-customers) who answer questions about a company's products and services as well as those of competitors. This interview approach allows a company to carefully select the composition of the panel and probe panel members about important issues, such as comparing experiences with expectations, in depth. Key questions that one might ask include: What do you like about the product or service? What pleases or delights you? What do you dislike? What problems have you encountered? If you had the ability, how would you change the product or service? Binney & Smith, maker of Crayolas, conducts focus groups with the ultimate customer: young children. Focus groups offer a substantial advantage by providing the direct voice of the customer to an organization. A disadvantage of focus groups is their higher cost of implementation compared to other approaches.

Direct customer contact: In customer-driven organizations, top executives commonly visit with customers personally. Hearing issues and complaints firsthand is often an eye-opening experience. For example, Black & Decker executives have gone to homeowners' workshops to watch how customers used their tools, asked why they liked or disliked certain ones, and even observed how they cleaned up their work space when they finished.

Field intelligence: Any employee who comes in direct contact with customers, such as salespeople, repair technicians, telephone operators, and receptionists, can obtain useful information simply by engaging in conversation and listening to customers. The effectiveness of this method depends upon a culture that encourages open communication with superiors. As another approach, employees simply observe customer behavior. One hotel noticed that customers did not use the complimentary bath crystals, so they eliminated the crystals (saving costs) and added other features that customers wanted. Field intelligence is perhaps one of the least-exploited approaches to listening and learning.[30] To do it well, organizations need to build awareness of the need to gather information, develop a system to feed information to a central collecting place for analysis and dissemination, train employees who have frequent direct customer contact to actively listen to the voice of the customer and feed information back through the system, make review of the information a standard part of the company's management review process, and ensure that the right individuals take action and follow up.

Study complaints: Complaints, although undesirable from a service point of view, can be a key source of customer information. Complaints allow an organization to learn about product failures and service problems, particularly the gaps between expectations and performance. Hewlett-Packard, for example, assigns every piece of customer feedback to an "owner" in the company who must act on the information and report back to the person who called. If a customer complains about a printer, someone will check the company's database to see if the complaint is widespread and what the company is doing about it.

Monitor the Internet:[31] The growth of the Internet is offering organizations a fertile arena for finding out what consumers think of their products. Internet users frequently seek advice from other users on strengths and weaknesses of products, share experiences on service quality, or pose specific problems they need to resolve. By monitoring the conversations on discussion groups and blogs, for example, managers can obtain valuable insights on customer perceptions and product or service quality problems. In open forums, customer comments can often be translated into creative product improvements. In addition, the Internet can be a good source of information about competitors' products. The cost of monitoring Internet conversations is minimal compared to the costs of other types of survey approaches, and customers are not biased by any questions that may be asked. However, the conversations may be considerably less-structured and unfocused, and thus may contain less usable information. Also, unlike a focus group or telephone interview, inaccurate perceptions or factual errors cannot be corrected.

Many leading organizations use a combination of multiple listening posts to gather customer information, and then cross-check the results for validity and synthesize the information. Figure 5.3 shows the wide variety of listening and learning approaches used by North Mississippi Medical Center for different customers segments.

Some organizations use unconventional and innovative approaches to understand customers. Texas Instruments created a simulated classroom to understand

Figure 5.3 North Mississippi Medical Center Listening and Learning Approaches

Current Patients	
Outpatient, inpatient, home care, LTC, ESD, wellness, behavioral health	
Structured	Ongoing patient satisfaction surveys per service, discharge phone calls, nurse manager rounds
Spontaneous	Careline, personal contacts, DH/SLA rounds
Current & Potential Patients (Community)	
Structured	CHA, market research, focus groups, quarterly survey of Nurse Link Customers, health care boards (e.g., home health, HIV), task forces (e.g., Women's health), CRF, Health Link members
Spontaneous	Feedback cards from mailings, health fairs, Internet web site, Community Advocate Helpline, Appointment Desk calls analysis, civic organizations, community and church involvement, CRF
Physicians	
Structured	Satisfaction survey, manpower studies, survey of and quarterly visits with Health Link PPO providers
Spontaneous	Medical staff committees, physician support services
Payers	
Structured	Quarterly employer roundtable discussions, bi-annual survey of Health Link employers, bi-annual survey of Acclaim customers, senior leaders, visit key employers bimonthly
Spontaneous	Helpline, database, quarterly visits with Health Link employer clients

Source: North Mississippi Medical Center, 2007 Malcolm Baldridge Application Summary. Reprinted with permission.

how mathematics teachers use calculators; and a manager at Levi Strauss used to talk with teens who were lined up to buy rock concert tickets. The president of Chick-fil-A, and all other corporate employees, spend at least one day each year behind the counter. The president has camped out overnight with customers at over a dozen store openings in just one year. At Whirlpool, when customers rate a competitor's product higher in satisfaction surveys, engineers take it apart to find out why. They also have hundreds of consumers fiddle with computer-simulated products while engineers record the users' reactions on videotape.[32]

Information gathered from the listening and learning activities usually is collected and analyzed using a customer relationship management database to identify the key requirements for each customer group and as input into strategic planning, service design, and its performance improvement process. Because voice of the customer data typically consists of a large number of verbal comments or other textual information, it needs to be sorted and consolidated into logical groups so that managers can understand the key issues. One useful tool for organizing large volumes of information efficiently and identifying natural patterns or groupings in the information is the **affinity diagram**. An affinity diagram is a main ingredient of the KJ method, developed in the 1960s by Kawakita Jiro, a Japanese anthropologist, which is a technique for gathering and organizing a large number of ideas or facts.[33]

To illustrate, suppose that a banking team determined that the most important requirement for mortgage customers is timely closings.[34] Through focus groups and other customer interviews, customers listed the following as key elements of timely closings:

1. Expeditious processes
2. Reliability
3. Consistent and accurate information
4. Competitive rates
5. Notification of industry changes
6. Prior approvals
7. Innovation
8. Modem link between computers
9. Buyer orientation
10. Diversity of programs
11. Mutual job understanding
12. Flexibility
13. Professionalism
14. Timely and accurate status reports

The company's team would group these items into logical categories (Post-It® notes are often used because they can be easily moved around on a wall) and provide a descriptive title for each category. The result is an affinity diagram, shown in Figure 5.4, which indicates that the key customer requirements for timely closings are communication, effective service, and loan products. Through organization of an affinity diagram, information can be used to better design a company's products and processes to meet customer requirements.

Affinity diagrams can be used for many other applications. For example, they can be used to organize any large group of complex ideas or issues, such as potential reasons for quality problems, or things a company must do to successfully market a product.

Figure 5.4 Affinity Diagram

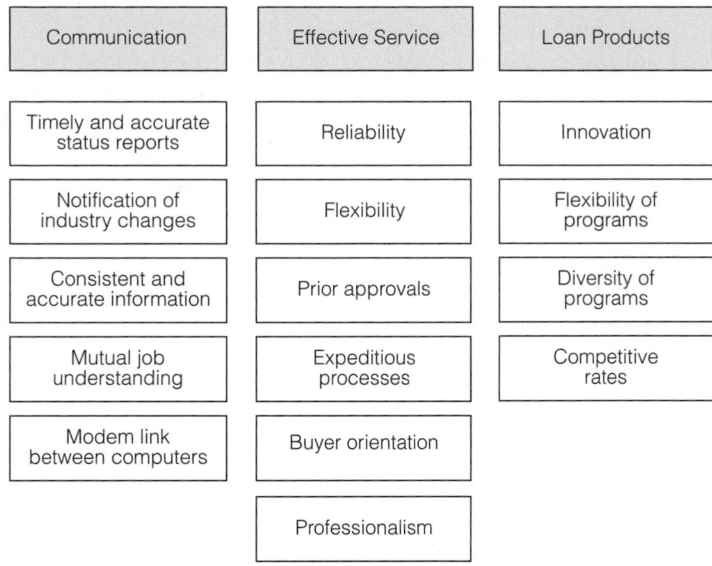

LINKING CUSTOMER INFORMATION TO DESIGN, PRODUCTION, AND SERVICE DELIVERY

As we noted in Figure 1.1 in Chapter 1, providing customers with a quality good or service requires that customer needs and expectations be linked to design and subsequent production and delivery processes. Here are but a few examples.

- Every week, employees from Seven-Eleven Japan stores from all over the country meet to discuss specific hypotheses tested and verified in its stores about customer offerings and service; a good example is changing the noodle order for the next day's lunch based on the weather forecast. A cold day? Serve warm noodles![35]
- Recognizing that many of its customers must drive hundreds of miles to one of less than 200 Lexus dealerships in the United States, the corporation designed a new service—they converted a truck into a mobile service station that can go to the customer's home.
- Ames Rubber Corporation uses a closed-loop communication system, called Continuous Supplier and Customer Involvement. New products begin with a series of customer meetings to create a product brief, which outlines technical, material, and operational requirements. The product brief is then forwarded to internal departments to select materials, processes, and procedures as approved by the customer. The customer evaluates prototypes until completely satisfied. Finally, a trial production run is made. Not until the customer approves the results does full-scale production commence.

The Quality in Practice case, Software Support Center, in the Chapter 5 Bonus Materials folder on the Premium website is an example of building operational improvements to increase customer satisfaction.

Producers must look at design, production, and service delivery processes through the eyes of the customer, not the organization. A good example of one company that viewed its processes synergistically with customer needs and exciter/delighters is Advanced Circuits, a small Denver manufacturer of printed circuit boards.[36] In struggling to compete with off-shore competitors, Advanced Circuits took a close look at its customers and their needs, and redesigned their processes enabling them to cut prices by 50 percent, triple production capacity, and double profitability. They began with a clear customer segmentation strategy: while they couldn't compete for production orders with long lead times, they could compete successfully where delivery time was critical—generally three days or fewer—or when orders were too small to interest big manufacturers with large production setup costs. They combined different jobs in the same production run, thus minimizing the material used in each batch, reducing production costs, and increasing capacity. They also discovered that customers need prototypes for boards quickly during the design process, often in two or three days, they need only a very small quantity, and they often need to communicate directly with the fabricator about design specifications.

To support this strategy, they mailed brochures describing a fixed pricing matrix. This in itself was revolutionary in the industry. Prior to that time, all quotes were individually requested and delivered. They also added credit card capability and the promise that prototype orders would be delivered on time or they'd be free. The Internet was used to provide better and faster service, such as enabling engineers to enter design parameters online, which allowed them to return quotes instantly. (Even today, many competitors take up to a week to return a quote.) Customers began to use the quote engine as a design tool. Because they could get quotes so fast, they were able to experiment with different board designs, densities, and geometries. As the company founder noted, "Customer focus is a great device for motivating employees because it removes all ambiguity from the decision-making process. Our view is, if it's good for our customers, it's probably good for us."

An organization's focus is often reflected by the measures that it uses to evaluate its performance. When an organization's principal focus is on such things as production schedules and cost, productivity, or output quantity rather than ease of product use, availability, or cost of ownership, it is difficult to create a customer-focused culture.

Many organizations still focus on measuring processes and products from an internal perspective, rather than from the perspective of the external customer.

Organizations must understand how to minimize the potential gaps between what customers want and what they actually get. To do this, they must take great care to ensure that customer needs are met or exceeded both by design and production processes. Figure 5.5 provides a view of the process in which customer needs and expectations are translated into perceptions during the design, production, and delivery processes. True customer needs and expectations might be called **expected quality**. Expected quality is what the customer assumes will be received from the product. The producer identifies these needs and expectations and translates them into specifications for products and services. **Actual quality** is the outcome of the production process and what is delivered to the customer. However, actual quality may differ considerably from expected quality if information gets lost or is misinterpreted from one step to the next in Figure 5.5. For instance, ineffective market research efforts may incorrectly assess the true customer needs and expectations. Designers of products and services may develop specifications that inadequately reflect these needs.

Figure 5.5 Customer-Driven Quality Cycle

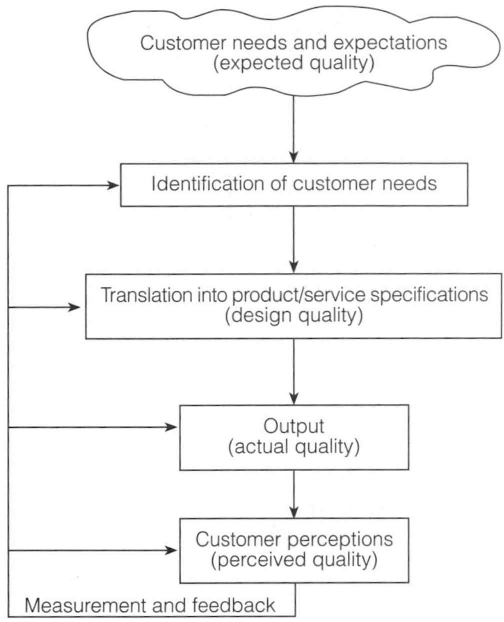

Manufacturing operations or customer-contact personnel may not deliver according to the specifications.

Customers will assess quality and develop perceptions (**perceived quality**) by comparing their expectations (expected quality) with what they receive (actual quality). If expected quality is higher than actual quality, then the customer will probably be dissatisfied. On the other hand, if actual quality exceeds expectations, then the customer will be satisfied or even surprisingly delighted. Because perceived quality drives consumer behavior, producers should make every effort to ensure that actual quality conforms to expected quality. One complication comes from the customer who sees and believes that the quality of the product is considerably different from what he or she actually receives (actual quality), which might be shaped by advertising or prior negative experiences. Thus, perceptions are not always accurate, and may even change over time, for example, when a customer finds that the initial quality of an automobile is high, but begins to experience problems in the long run.

Figure 5.5 suggests that organizations have good internal communication among all design and production activities to minimize the difference between expected and actual quality, and indeed, to strive to ensure that actual quality exceeds expected quality. This includes recognizing that many causes of dissatisfaction are not attributable to production or service defects or employee mistakes.[37] Customers may not use the product correctly or may have unreasonable expectations about what it can do, marketing sometimes makes promises it cannot keep, or advertising is misleading. Thus, organizations need to pay greater attention to overall customer experiences that impact perceptions. Such attention might include better user manuals or information on product packaging as well as unambiguous advertising.

A great way of exploiting customer knowledge in service delivery is through empowered employees (see Chapter 6 for more detailed discussion of this concept).

Employees at the specialty grocery chain Trader Joe's talk and listen extensively to customers and are empowered to take action to meet their needs. For example, employees can open any product a customer wants to taste and are encouraged to recommend products they like and be honest about items they don't. All store employees can email buyers directly with ideas or feedback from customers. Trader Joe's store design and inventory stems directly from listening to its customers.[38]

Although we have said much about the importance of listening to customers, producing breakthrough goods or services often requires that businesses ignore consumer feedback and take risks. Henry Ford was quoted as saying "If I had asked people what they wanted, they would have said faster horses." Thus, creativity and innovation are necessary for "breakthrough" products such as the PDAs, iPhones®, and many other products that we take for granted.

BUILDING A CUSTOMER-FOCUSED CULTURE

An organization fosters customer engagement by developing trust, communicating with customers, and effectively managing the interactions and relationships with customers through its processes and its people.

Truly excellent organizations foster close relationships with customers that lead to high levels of satisfaction and loyalty. For example, Lexus owners who become accustomed to the at-home pickup of their vehicles for service, free loaners, and other special dealer touches such as concierge service may find it difficult to give up these services when it is time to purchase a new car. In Bank of Montreal's Private Client Services group, bankers provide services according to the preferences of their clients who value convenience and time, not the traditions of the bank. These preferences might mean meeting in the client's home or office instead of the bank.[39] Dell offers a variety of customer-friendly services that includes loading all of the customer's software, even proprietary applications, at the factory and configuring it the way it is going to be used, saving hours of work by highly paid computer technicians.[40]

Customer satisfaction or dissatisfaction takes place during ***moments of truth****—every interaction between a customer and the organization.*

Moments of truth may be direct contacts with customer representatives or service workers, interactions with an organization's website, or when customers read letters, invoices, or other company correspondence. Problems result from unkept promises, failure to provide full service, service not provided when needed, incorrectly or incompletely performed service, or failure to convey the correct information. At moments of truth, customers form perceptions about the quality of the service by comparing their expectations with the actual outcomes.

Consider an airline, for example. (The phrase "moment of truth" was popularized by the CEO of Scandinavian Airlines System, Jan Carlzon.) Moments of truth occur when a customer makes a reservation, buys tickets, checks baggage, boards a flight, orders a beverage, requests a magazine, deplanes, and picks up baggage. Multiply these instances by the number of passengers and the number of daily flights, and it is easy to see that hundreds of thousands of moments of truth occur each day. Each occurrence influences a positive or negative image about the company.

Southwest Airlines recognizes the power of customer focus.[41] Known for its legendary service, the Southwest culture ensures that it serves the needs of its Customers (with a capital C) in a friendly, caring, and enthusiastic manner. Every one of the approximately 1,000 customers who write to the airline get a personal response (not a form letter) within four weeks, and frequent fliers get birthday cards. The airline even moved a flight up a quarter-hour when five medical students who commuted weekly to an out-of-state medical school complained that the flight got them to class 15 minutes late. To quote the CEO, "We dignify the Customer." This statement applies to internal customers also; it is not unusual to find pilots helping ground crews unload baggage. As one executive stated, "We are not an airline with great customer service. We are a great customer service organization that happens to be in the airline business." Southwest's customer commitment was apparent in the hours after the September 11 terrorist attacks. The top executives swiftly agreed to grant refunds to all customers who asked for them, regardless of ticket restrictions, despite the fact that it might have cost them several hundred million dollars. Refund claims never came; in fact, one loyal customer sent in $1,000 to support Southwest after the attacks. Southwest has consistently been the most profitable U.S. airline.

A customer-focused culture depends on several management practices:

1. Making sincere commitments and providing appropriate customer support
2. Selecting and developing customer contact employees
3. Establishing relevant customer contact requirements
4. Managing complaints and service recovery
5. Leveraging strategic partnerships and alliances
6. Using effective technology

Each of these is addressed in the following sections.

Commitments and Customer Support

Organizations that truly believe in the quality of their products make sincere commitments to their customers. Effective commitments address the principal concerns of customers, are free from conditions that might weaken customers' trust and confidence, and are communicated clearly and simply to customers. A customer commitment might be as simple as guaranteeing that your call or e-mail inquiry will be returned promptly. (Have you ever encountered a website with a disclaimer "We cannot always answer every question that we receive"?) Many commitments take the form of explicit guarantees and warranties. Extraordinary guarantees that promise exceptional, uncompromising quality and customer satisfaction, and back that promise with a payout intended to fully recapture the customer's goodwill with few if any strings attached are one of the strongest actions a company can take to improve itself.[42] L.L. Bean's guarantee is a good example: "Everything we sell is backed by a 100 percent unconditional guarantee. We do not want you to have anything from L.L. Bean that is not completely satisfactory. Return anything you buy from us at any time for any reason it proves otherwise."

Customer support is often a sore point for many consumers. Customer-focused organizations make it easy for customers to do business. Procter & Gamble was the first company to install a toll-free number for its products in 1974. Today, e-mail and website access are the media of choice for many consumers. For example, Premier, Inc. provides a wide variety of avenues for customers to seek assistance, conduct business, and make complaints or suggestions. These include toll-free telephone, Internet, a Customer Solution Center, customer advisory committee meetings, product user group meetings, field staff site visits, technical assistance fax, regional performance improvement forums, and product support centers. The City of Coral Springs provides a website, CityTV, CityRadio, CityBlog, Customer Care Center, a quarterly magazine, annual report, neighborhood and business meetings, and advisory boards and committees.

Selecting and Developing Customer Contact Employees

Customer-contact employees are particularly important. They are the people whose main responsibilities bring them into regular contact with customers—in person, by telephone, or through other means. Procter & Gamble calls its consumer relations department the "voice of the company." A staff of more than 250 employees handles in excess of 3 million contacts each year. Their mission is stated as "We are a world-class consumer response center. We provide superior service to consumers who contact Procter & Gamble, encourage product repurchase, and help build brand loyalty. We protect the Company's image and the reputation of our brands by resolving complaints before they are escalated to government agencies or the media. We capture and report consumer data to key Company functions, identify and share consumer insights, counsel product categories on consumer issues and trends, and manage consumer handling and interaction during crises."

Businesses must carefully select customer contact employees, train them well, and empower them to meet and exceed customer expectations.

Many businesses begin with the recruiting process, selecting those employees who show the ability and desire to develop good customer relationships; for example Procter & Gamble seeks people with excellent interpersonal and communication skills, strong problem-solving and analytical skills, assertiveness, stress tolerance, patience and empathy, accuracy and attention to detail, and computer literacy. Job applicants often go through rigorous screening processes that might include aptitude testing, customer-service role-playing exercises, background checks, credit checks, and medical evaluations.

Organizations committed to customer relationship management ensure that customer-contact employees understand the products and services well enough to answer any question, develop good listening and problem recovery skills, and feel able to handle problems. Effective training not only increases employees' knowledge, but improves their self-esteem and loyalty to the organization. Fairmont Hotels created an orientation program to help new employees understand what it feels like to be a guest, even having their cars valet-parked and staying in the hotel for a night. The Ritz-Carlton Hotel Company follows orientation training with on-the-job training and, subsequently, job certification. The company reinforces its values daily, recognizes extraordinary achievement, and appraises performance based on expectations explained during the orientation, training, and certification processes. For many organizations, customer relationship training involves every person who comes in contact with customers, including receptionists.

Customer-focused organizations empower their front-line people to do whatever is necessary to satisfy the customer. At The Ritz-Carlton, all employees are empowered to do whatever it takes to provide "instant pacification." No matter what their normal duties are, other employees must assist if aid is requested by a fellow worker who is responding to a guest's complaint or wish. Ritz-Carlton employees can spend up to $2,000 to resolve complaints with no questions asked. However, the actions of empowered employees should be guided by a common vision; that is, employees require a consistent understanding of what actions they may or should take.

Many organizations rely on call centers as their primary means of customer contact. Call centers can be a means of competitive advantage by serving customers more efficiently and personalizing transactions to build relationships; however, they can also be a source of frustration if not designed and managed correctly. Customer-contact employees need access to the right technology and company information to do their jobs. FedEx, for example, furnishes employees with the information and technology they need to continually improve their performance. The Digitally Assisted Dispatch System (DADS) communicates to all couriers through screens in their vans, enabling quick response to pickup and delivery dispatches; it allows couriers to manage their time and routes with high efficiency. Information technology improves productivity, increases communication, and allows customer contact employees to handle almost any customer issue.

Customer Contact Requirements

Front-line personnel who come in daily contact with customers have a significant amount of responsibility for customer satisfaction. **Customer contact requirements** are measurable performance levels or expectations that define the quality of customer contact with representatives of an organization. These expectations might include technical requirements such as response time (answering the telephone within two rings), or behavioral requirements (using a customer's name whenever possible). St. Luke's Hospital has translated its understanding of how patients want to be treated and involved and has established a clear set of 12 Customer Contact Requirements (see Figure 5.6). The Quality in Practice case about Florida Power and Light in the Chapter 5 Bonus Materials folder on the Premium website provides a good example of how customer expectations determine contact requirements.

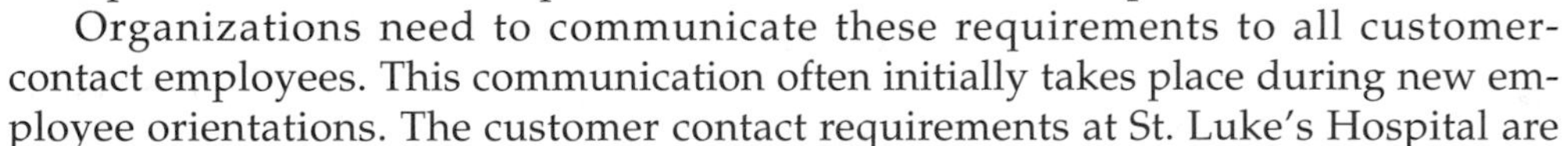

Organizations need to communicate these requirements to all customer-contact employees. This communication often initially takes place during new employee orientations. The customer contact requirements at St. Luke's Hospital are

Figure 5.6 St. Luke's Hospital of Kansas City Customer–Contact Requirements

Saint Luke's Hospital of Kansas City
Customer Contact Requirements

1. Greet patients/guests by introducing myself, address patients/guests by last name unless otherwise told.
2. Ask sincerely, "How may I help you?"
3. Knock, request permission to enter the room, and explain what I am going to do.
4. Complete initial assessment on all patients within eight hours.
5. Acknowledge all patient/guests requests, and be accountable for follow-up.
6. Address all complaints within 24 hours or less.
7. Introduce any replacement caregiver.
8. Promote family-centered care: listen thoughtfully to all patients/guests, and provide timely communication to the appropriate person(s) for action.
9. Respect and acknowledge diversity, culture, and values of my patients, their family, visitors, and my co-workers.
10. Maintain confidentiality of all information.
11. Know, or have access to, legal and regulatory requirements and standards of care related to my specific responsibilities.
12. Thank my customers for choosing Saint Luke's Hospital.

Source: Malcolm Baldrige National Quality Award Application Summary, 2003, National Institute of Standards and Technology, Department of Commerce, Courtesy of St. Luke's Health System.

incorporated into a new patient-focused care delivery model and all health care team members are trained in these contact requirements. All employees receive a VIP (Very Important Principles) card with these requirements and they are posted throughout the hospital.

However, to maintain the consistency and effectiveness of these standards, they must continually be reinforced. Additionally, many customer-contact employees depend on internal customers for support, who also must understand the role they play in meeting the requirements. The key to satisfying external customers is to satisfy internal customers first. At Southwest Airlines, for example, the philosophy is that if employees can provide the same service to one another as they do to passengers, the airline will benefit.[43] Each operating division identifies an internal customer. Mechanics who service planes target the pilots who fly them, and marketers treat reservation agents as customers. Departments even provide free ice cream or pizza as tokens of customer appreciation or for a job well done. Use of the customer–supplier model approach effectively communicates the importance of these relationships.

Finally, a company should implement a process for tracking adherence to the requirements and providing feedback to the employees to improve their performance.  Information technology supplies the data for effectively tracking conformance to customer contact requirements.

Complaint Management and Service Recovery

Despite all efforts to satisfy customers, every business experiences unhappy customers. Complaints can adversely affect business if not dealt with effectively. A company called TARP, formerly known as Technical Assistance Research Programs, Inc., conducted studies that revealed the following information:[44]

1. The average company never hears from 96 percent of its unhappy customers. Dissatisfied individual and business customers tend not to complain. For every complaint received, the company has 26 more customers with problems, six of whom have problems that are serious.
2. Of the customers who make a complaint, more than half will again do business with that organization if their complaint is resolved. If the customer feels that the complaint was resolved quickly, the figure jumps to 95 percent. On the other hand, experiences of customers who remain unsatisfied after complaining result in substantial amounts of negative word of mouth.
3. The average customer who has had a problem will tell nine or ten others about it. Customers who have had complaints resolved satisfactorily will only tell about five others of the problem resolution.
4. With the advent of the Internet, TARP also found that 4 percent of satisfied customers post their feelings on the Web, while 15 percent of unsatisfied customers do the same.[45]

Customer-focused organizations consider complaints as opportunities for improvement. Encouraging customers to complain, making it easy for them to do so, and effectively resolving complaints increases customer loyalty and retention. A compelling story was related by a Wal-Mart customer in a letter to *Fortune* magazine. He had telephoned Wal-Mart's headquarters to complain about its store in La Plata, Argentina. The switchboard immediately rang the vice president of international operations, who thanked him for calling, asked detailed questions, and inquired whether he was willing to repeat his story to the Latin American VP, to whom he was transferred immediately. He was then asked if he would be willing to talk to the Argentinean store manager; 10 minutes later he received the call from La Plata. The customer observed, "On my next trip to Argentina, a year later, the store had been transformed. No wonder Wal-Mart is the world's largest retailer."

The Ritz-Carlton uses Guest Incident Action forms, which are aggregated on a monthly basis at each hotel, to ensure that complaints were handled effectively and steps taken to eliminate the cause of the problem. Customer service or sales reps who receive a complaint at Branch-Smith Printing are responsible for providing resolution options within 48 hours, recording the complaint, and delivering it to the quality manager who must determine the cause and modify work instructions or conduct retraining as necessary. Medrad uses its Field Force Automation system and InSITE database to capture customer information and complaints, to share that information throughout the organization, and to analyze and improve customer satisfaction, product performance, and sales.

Many customers do not complain because they feel it wouldn't do any good or they are uncomfortable with the process. Retail, field sales, and service systems filter and discourage complaints. TARP also found that brand loyalty can be retained by merely getting customers to articulate their problems.[46] Thus, leading firms actively solicit complaints. Nissan, for instance, telephones each person who buys a new car or brings one in for significant warranty work. Its objective is to resolve all dissatisfaction within 24 hours.[47]

Service recovery is a vital element to maintaining customer relationships. Studies in the service management literature suggest that customers who rated service quality highly also had the highest expectations for service recovery. Loyal customers are most likely to lose loyalty when problems are not resolved but are most likely to increase or maintain loyalty whenever the problem is deemed to have been resolved successfully. However, non-loyal customers show the greatest likelihood of decreasing their loyalty even when a failure is resolved. This suggests that there is much to gain from responding to service failures to non-loyal customers, but it also highlights how difficult this may be to accomplish.[48] An example of the impact of service recovery on customer satisfaction was reported in a *Fortune* magazine article:

> *A global hotel chain was stunned to discover a perverse consequence of its customer-centric Six Sigma quality initiative. Apparently guests were mildly pleased by the chain's sincere efforts to provide a hassle-free stay. But what really moved the customer-satisfaction needle was how well the hotel responded when something went wrong. Guests who had experienced a problem that was quickly and politely resolved rated the hotel service higher than guests who had had no problems at all. What's more, more guests with happy resolution of their hassle said they were likely to recommend the hotel than did the trouble-free guests.*[49]

Organizations involved in customer relationship management train customer-contact personnel to deal with complaints. Customer service workers need to listen carefully to determine the customer's feelings and then respond sympathetically, ensuring that the complaint is understood. They should make every effort to resolve the problem quickly. This should include first acknowledging that a customer had a problem ("We're sorry you had a problem") to express empathy for the inconvenience that the customer encountered; willingly accepting the complaint ("Thanks for letting us know about it")' describe corrective action concisely and clearly ("Here's what we're going to do about it"); and appealing to the customer for continued loyalty ("We'd appreciate you giving us another chance"). The objective is to leverage the complaint into long-term customer loyalty.[50]

Figure 5.7 BI Service Recovery Process

Apologize for customer inconvenience
↓
Listen, empathize, ask clarifying questions
↓
Solve problem quickly in partnership with customer
↓
Offer atonement
↓
Keep the promise
↓
Follow up
↓
Prevent recurrence

Source: Courtesy of Guy Schoenecker, president and chief quality officer.

Many organizations have well-defined processes for dealing with complaints. For example, at BI, all complaints, regardless of where they come from, are forwarded directly to the business unit manager related to the complaint.[51] The manager follows the Service Recovery Process (see Figure 5.7), and contacts the customer directly for clarification of the issue and additional information. Findings are then communicated to the account executive, sales manager, account manager, and all involved business unit associates via e-mail. This process enables the BI team to work in conjunction with the customer to address the failure and provide a solution that meets the customer's needs. A written follow-up of the resolution is shared with all BI team members working with the customer.

Complaints provide a source of product and process improvement ideas. Leading-edge organizations encourage employees to bring complaints to the surface in a variety of formal and informal ways, such as a response center to encourage employees to call with ideas and process improvements as well as complaints, and rewards and recognition for employees involved in the processes. Costs associated with complaints can be significant, and include lost business, complaint handling costs, and claims and compensation. Typically, cross-functional teams study the information, determine the real source of the complaints, and make recommendations. Technology is often used to capture, analyze, and report complaint data. Eastman Chemical, for example, discovered that most complaint investigations stopped after learning who caused the problem, and corrective actions did not address the true causes. After developing a process to drill down to the actual sources of complaints and prevent their occurrence, Eastman nearly halved the level of customer complaints in three years, resulting in improved customer satisfaction, increased sales, reduced waste, and lower costs.[52] Finally, the complaint process itself needs to be

To improve products and processes effectively, organizations must do more than simply fix the immediate problem. They need a systematic process for collecting and analyzing complaint data and then using that information for improvements.

monitored, evaluated, and improved. Organizations typically track the percentage of customers who are satisfied with complaint resolution, the cost of resolving complaints, and the time required to resolve them.

Strategic Partnerships and Alliances

Today's suppliers are being asked to take on greater responsibilities to help their customers. As organizations focus more on their core competencies—the things they do best—they are looking outside their organizations for assistance with noncritical support processes. **Customer–supplier partnerships**—long-term relationships characterized by teamwork and mutual confidence—represent an important strategic alliance in achieving excellence and business success. Benefits of such partnerships include access to technology or distribution channels not available internally, shared risks in new investments and product development, improved products through early design recommendations based on supplier capabilities, and reduced operations costs through better communications. For example, FedEx and Jostens formed a strategic partnership that enabled both to benefit from new sales of scholastic jewelry and yearbooks.[53] They took advantage of each other's strengths: Jostens provided a high-quality product with superior service, and FedEx provided reliable high-volume, short-interval delivery for these time-critical products.

Many organizations work closely with suppliers that share common values. This close relationship improves supplier capabilities by teaching them quality-related tools and approaches. Although many businesses have formal supplier certification programs (discussed in Chapter 7) in which they rate their suppliers, some ask suppliers to rate them as customers. Motorola uses a 15-member council of suppliers that rates Motorola's practices and offers suggestions for improving, for example, the accuracy of production schedules or design layouts that Motorola provides.[54] Some typical questions that might be asked of their suppliers include:[55] What expectations do you have that are not being met? What type of technical assistance would you like from us? What type of feedback would you like from us? What benefits are you looking for in a partnership? Better two-way communication can improve both products and relationships.

Customer-Focused Technology

Technology can greatly enhance an organization's ability to leverage customer-related information and provide improved customer service. For instance, Continental Airlines' online system alerts the company when planes arrive late and assesses passengers' needs, delaying departures of other flights or sending carts to make connections easier; the BT Group revamped its self-service Web portal used by customers to manage telecom accounts and linked it to the system used by the company's customer support staff to improve consistency.[56] Another company that exploits technology in developing customer relationships is Tsutaya, Japan's largest video, book, and CD chain.[57] Using a point-of-sale system that facilitates real-time inventory tracking between headquarters and franchises and a Web and wireless site called Tsutaya Online (TOL), Tsutaya tracks purchases, demographic data, spending behavior, and by implication, lifestyles, and interests. This system enables them to offer personalized product recommendations. For example, if you bought a CD by a certain artist, TOL will e-mail a digital music clip when the next album debuts. Tsutaya also

Tsutaya

developed a sophisticated recommendation engine to match a customer's video rental history and mood to the ideal movie selection. Many other organizations, such as Netflix, Blockbuster, and Amazon.com, use technology in similar ways.

The use of the Internet for purchasing goods and services has exploded. Millions of people—called virtual customers—perform transactions online rather than engaging in traditional "face-to-face" transactions. In many cases, customer service and understanding of the voice of the customer have not kept up with the expanding technological capabilities to advertise and deliver products. Thus, customers who are hoping to experience quick, easy, reliable transactions that will reduce stress and save time and money, are finding that the opposite is happening. Recent studies have shown the importance of customer focus and the limitations of poor website design and inadequate service to these customers. One study investigated service quality at 23 Internet banks in the United States, surrounding seven characteristics and capabilities of:

- Opening an account;
- Deposits and withdrawals;
- Rates and fees;
- Navigation and ease of use;
- Bill paying;
- Security; and
- Customer service.

Most of the sampled banks showed an unsatisfactory level of service quality.[58] Another study by Accenture found that only 5 percent of respondents strongly agree and 33 percent somewhat agree that technology has improved the quality of service in the past five years; 62 percent don't think that technology has helped at all. They also found that some 12% of bank customers switched providers during the past year, due to poor customer service.[59] A third study of Internet bank service focused on identifying quality characteristics that customers found to be most important.[60] The researchers found that customers perceived quality along three broad categories: customer service quality, banking service product quality, and online systems quality. Dimensions of quality that were important to customers included:

- Customer service quality: reliability, responsiveness, competence, courtesy, credibility, access, communication, understanding the customer, collaboration, and continuous improvement;
- Banking service product quality: product variety/diverse features; and
- Online systems quality: content, accuracy, ease of use, timeliness, aesthetics, and security.

Interestingly, there were no significant differences in the dimensions that were derived for "pure" Internet banks and traditional banks with Internet services.

Technology is a key enabler of **customer relationship management (CRM)** software, which is designed to help organizations increase customer loyalty, target their most profitable customers, and streamline customer communication processes. More than $11 billion was spent on CRM-related U.S. sales at the turn of the century and is growing significantly.[61] A typical CRM system includes market segmentation and analysis, customer service and relationship building, effective complaint resolution, cross-selling goods and services, order processing, and field service.

CRM helps firms gain and maintain competitive advantage by:

- Segmenting markets based on demographic and behavioral characteristics
- Tracking sales trends and advertising effectiveness by customer and market segment

- Identifying which customers should be the focus of targeted marketing initiatives with predicted high customer response rates
- Forecasting customer retention (and defection) rates and providing feedback as to why customers leave a company
- Studying which goods and services are purchased together, leading to good ways to bundle them
- Studying and predicting which Web characteristics are most attractive to customers and how the website might be improved

CRM systems provide a variety of useful operational data to managers, including the average time spent responding to customer questions, comments, and concerns; average order tracking (flow) time; total revenue generated by each customer (and sometimes their family or business) from all goods and services bought by the customer; and the total picture of economic value of the customer to the firm, cost per marketing campaign, and price discrepancies.

MEASURING CUSTOMER ENGAGEMENT

Customer feedback is vital to a business. Through feedback, a company learns how satisfied its customers are with its products and services and sometimes about competitors' products and services. Measurement of customer engagement completes the loop shown in Figure 5.5. It allows an organization to do the following:

1. Discover customer perceptions of how well the organization is doing in meeting customer needs, and compare performance relative to competitors.
2. Identify causes of dissatisfaction and failed expectations as well as drivers of delight to understand the reasons why customers are loyal or not loyal to the company.
3. Identify internal work process that drive satisfaction and loyalty and discover areas for improvement in the design and delivery of products and services, as well as for training and coaching of employees.
4. Track trends to determine whether changes actually result in improvements.

BI uses three approaches to track customer satisfaction: a Transactional Customer Satisfaction Index for immediate feedback, an annual Relationship Customer Satisfaction Index to learn about specific attributes of satisfaction and intent for repeat business, and a competitive study to see how it performs relative to competitors. SSM Health Care uses standardized patient satisfaction surveys that are customized to its five major patient segments, informal discussions with patients and families, and focus groups to understand satisfaction and dissatisfaction. They use online analytical processing software to drill down to a particular nursing unit, for example, to examine inpatient loyalty and compare those to other units within a hospital or across the corporation. Then, they distribute results electronically that identify specific improvements that will give the greatest gains in patient satisfaction to executives and patient satisfaction coordinators.

An effective customer satisfaction measurement system results in reliable information about customer ratings of specific product and service features and about the relationship between these ratings and the customer's likely future market behavior.

Customer satisfaction measures may include product attributes such as product quality, product performance, usability, and maintainability; service attributes such as attitude, service time, on-time delivery, exception handling, accountability, and technical support; image attributes such as reliability and price;

and overall satisfaction measures. Comparisons with key competitors can be especially insightful. Businesses often rely on third parties to conduct blind surveys to determine who key competitors are and how their products and services compare. Competitive comparisons often clarify how improvements in quality can translate into better customer satisfaction or whether key quality characteristics are being overlooked. For example, the city of Portland, Oregon, mails a survey annually to about 10,000 of its citizens, asking them to rate the performance of the police department, water bureau, environmental services, and public transportation. The city also asks them if they feel safe walking at night in their neighborhoods, parks, and downtown; whether the streets are clean enough, how they feel about recreation services offered, and how they rate the livability of the city. The results are benchmarked against six other cities, and if Portland is not doing as well, the mayor tries to find out why.[62]

It is important to understand that customer satisfaction is a psychological attitude. It is not easy to measure, and can only be observed indirectly. The ACSI model in Figure 5.1 shows that customer satisfaction is influenced by customer expectations and perceptions of quality and value. Thus, it is difficult to reduce these complex relationships into a single measure.

Designing Satisfaction Surveys

The first step in developing a customer satisfaction survey is to determine its purpose. Surveys should be designed to clearly provide the users of the survey results with the information they need to make decisions. A critical question to consider is "Who is the customer?" Managers, purchasing agents, end users, and others all may be affected by a company's products and services. Xerox, for instance, sends specific surveys to buyers, managers, and users. Buyers provide feedback on their perceptions of the sales processes, managers provide input on billing and other administrative processes, and users provide feedback on product performance and technical support. Customer satisfaction measurement should not be confined to external customers. Information from internal customers also contributes to the assessment of the organization's strengths and weaknesses. Often the problems that cause employee dissatisfaction are the same issues that cause dissatisfaction in external customers. Many organizations use employee opinion surveys or similar vehicles to seek employee feedback on the work environment, benefits, compensation, management, team activities, rewards and recognition, and company plans and values. However, other indicators of employee satisfaction are absenteeism, turnover, grievances, and strikes, which can often supply better information than surveys that many employees may not take seriously.

The next question to address is who should conduct the survey. Independent third-party organizations often have more credibility to respondents and can ensure objectivity in the results. After these preliminary steps are completed, it is necessary to define the sample frame; that is, the target group from which a sample is chosen. Depending on the purpose of the survey, it might be the entire customer base or a specific segment. For example, a manufacturer of commercial lawn tractors might design different surveys for golf course superintendents who purchase the tractors and another for end users who ride them daily.

The next step is to select the appropriate survey instrument. Formal written surveys are the most common means of measuring customer satisfaction, although other techniques, such as face-to-face interviews, telephone interviews, and focus groups are used. Written surveys have the advantage of low data collection costs, self-administration, and ease of analysis; when used, they should be kept short and simple. In addition, they can probe deeply into the issues. However, they suffer from high nonresponse bias, require large sample sizes, and generally measure predetermined perceptions of what is important to customers, thus reducing the scope of qualitative information that can be obtained. Face-to-face interviews and focus groups, on the other hand, require much smaller sample sizes and can generate a significant amount of qualitative information, but incur high costs and participant time commitments. Telephone interviews fall somewhere in between these extremes. Telephone interviews appear to be the preferred approach for companies with a limited number of business customers; mail-based surveys are used to track routine transactions, where key attributes are stable over time. For example, Toyota uses mail surveys to identify unhappy customers and then telephones them for more details. This approach is cost-effective when the majority of customers are satisfied.[63]

Customer satisfaction surveys are difficult to design properly, and you can find many examples of poor and ineffective surveys at many restaurants and retailers. Some surveys are too long; others are too short. It is important to choose carefully the questions that matter the most to customers. Many survey questions lack reliability—that is, they often do not reflect the attribute being measured, or different customers interpret the questions differently. One should avoid leading questions, compound questions that address more than one issue or idea, ambiguous questions, acronyms and jargon that the respondent may not understand, and double negatives. For example, the question "How would you rate our service?" is too ambiguous and provides little actionable information. A better question would be "How would you rate the response time of our technical support desk?" Another poor example is "Should Burger Mart increase its food portions at a higher price?" This question addresses two different issues. Open-ended questions such as "If this were your business, what would you do differently?" often lead to honest opinions and provide more useful information. Most surveys also ask for basic demographic information to stratify the data.

*The types of questions to ask in a survey must be properly worded to achieve **actionable** results. By actionable, we mean that responses are tied directly to key business processes, so that what needs to be improved is clear; and information can be translated into cost/revenue implications to support the setting of improvement priorities.*

A "Likert" scale is commonly used to measure the response (see Table 5.3). Likert scales allow customers to express their degree of opinion. Five-point scales have been shown to have good reliability and are often used, although 7- and even

Table 5.3 Examples of Likert Scales Used for Customer Satisfaction Measurement

Very Poor	Poor	Neither Poor nor Good	Good	Very Good
1	2	3	4	5
Strongly Disagree	Disagree	Neither Agree nor Disagree	Agree	Strongly Agree
1	2	3	4	5
Very Dissatisfied	Dissatisfied	Neither Satisfied nor Dissatisfied	Satisfied	Very Satisfied
1	2	3	4	5

10-point scales are common. Responses of "5" tell a company what it is doing very well. Responses of "4" suggest that customer expectations are being met, but that the company may be vulnerable to competitors. Responses of "3" mean that the product or service barely meets customer expectations and that much room for improvement exists. Responses of "1" or "2" indicate serious problems. However, most scales like these exhibit response bias; that is, people tend to give either high or low values. If responses are clustered on the high side, it is difficult to discriminate among responses, and the resulting skewness in the distribution causes the mean value to be misleading.

Many customer satisfaction measures evaluate service characteristics. Developing measurable service quality characteristics can be difficult. For instance, a quality characteristic such as "availability" is ambiguous and not as easy to measure as the accuracy of order filling. Typically, such quality characteristics are translated into specific statements that clearly describe the concept. For example, any of the following statements could be used to describe "availability."

1. The doctor was available to schedule me at a good time.
2. I could get an appointment with the doctor at a time I desired.
3. My appointment was at a convenient time.

Commonly used factors to measure customer loyalty are:[64]

- Overall satisfaction
- Likelihood of a first-time purchaser to repurchase
- Likelihood to recommend
- Likelihood to continue purchasing the same products or services
- Likelihood to purchase different products or services
- Likelihood to increase frequency of purchasing
- Likelihood to switch to a different provider

One example of a simple satisfaction survey for Hilton Hotels is shown in Figure 5.8. The survey asks direct and detailed questions about the guest bathroom, including such potential dissatisfiers as shower water pressure and temperature and bathtub/sink drainage, assesses measures of loyalty, identifies and specifies problems the customer may have encountered and provides space for open-ended comments.

The final task is to design the reporting format and the data entry methods. Modern technology, such as computer databases in conjunction with a variety of statistical analysis tools, assists in tracking customer satisfaction and provides information for continuous improvement. As a final note, surveys should always be pretested to: determine whether instructions are understandable, identify questions that may be misunderstood or poorly worded, determine how long it takes to complete the survey, and determine the level of customer interest.

Graniterock Company is a California manufacturer of high-quality construction materials for road and highway construction and maintenance, and for residential and commercial building construction. Its major product lines include rock, sand, and gravel aggregates, ready-mix concrete, blacktop, and other products. Surveying its principal customer groups is one of the key approaches Graniterock uses to improve customer satisfaction. The surveys ask respondents to rate factors in buying concrete, not only from Graniterock, but from competitors as well. (Figure 5.9 shows such a survey.) Through information obtained from the surveys, Graniterock determined that the most important factors to customers in order of importance are on-time delivery, product quality, scheduling (ability to deliver products on short notice), problem resolution, price, credit terms, and salespeople's skills. Annually,

Figure 5.8 Hilton Hotel Guest Survey

Completely fill in your response ● Correct **GUEST**Scope

Hilton

Please rate your satisfaction with the comfort level of your accommodations.

	Level of Satisfaction Low 1	2	3	Avg. 4	5	6	High 7	N/A
Accommodations look and smell clean and fresh:	○	○	○	○	○	○	○	○
Clean and comfortable linens:	○	○	○	○	○	○	○	○
Comfort level of pillow:	○	○	○	○	○	○	○	○
Comfort level of mattress:	○	○	○	○	○	○	○	○
Easily regulated room temperature:	○	○	○	○	○	○	○	○
Housekeeping during stay:	○	○	○	○	○	○	○	○
Overall Satisfaction with this Hilton:	○	○	○	○	○	○	○	
Likelihood you would recommend Hilton:	○	○	○	○	○	○	○	
Likelihood, **if returning to the area**, you would return to this Hilton:	○	○	○	○	○	○	○	
Value of accommodations for price paid:	○	○	○	○	○	○	○	

Primary purpose of visit? ○ Individual business ○ Convention/Meeting ○ Pleasure

How many times have you been a guest at this Hilton? ○ 1 ○ 2 ○ 3 ○ 4 ○ 5+

Did you have a hotel product or service problem during your stay? ○ Yes ○ No

If yes - did you report it to the staff? ○ Yes ○ No

If yes - was it resolved to your satisfaction? ○ Yes ○ No

If yes - what was the nature of the problem? ______________________

Please share any thoughts on any other aspects of your visit; including the names of any staff members who made your stay more enjoyable: ______________________

Name: *Daytime Phone:*

Date of Stay: *Room:*

PLEASE DO NOT WRITE BELOW LINE FD2

Figure 5.9 Graniterock Customer Importance Survey

What is important to *YOU*?

Please rate each of the following on a scale from 1 to 5 with 5 being most important in your decision to purchase from a supplier.

Importance	Concrete Least . . . Most	Building Materials Least . . . Most
Responsive to special needs	1 2 3 4 5	1 2 3 4 5
Easy to place orders	1 2 3 4 5	1 2 3 4 5
Consistent product quality	1 2 3 4 5	1 2 3 4 5
On-time delivery	1 2 3 4 5	1 2 3 4 5
Accurate invoices	1 2 3 4 5	1 2 3 4 5
Lowest prices	1 2 3 4 5	1 2 3 4 5
Attractive credit terms	1 2 3 4 5	1 2 3 4 5
Salespeople's skills	1 2 3 4 5	1 2 3 4 5
Helpful dispatchers	1 2 3 4 5	1 2 3 4 5
Courteous drivers	1 2 3 4 5	1 2 3 4 5
Supplier resolves problems fairly and quickly	1 2 3 4 5	1 2 3 4 5

Please write in any other items not listed above which are very important to you in making your purchase decision:

____

____

Source: Reprinted with permission of Graniterock.

the company surveys customers and noncustomers to obtain a "report card" on their service (see Figure 5.10). Graniterock repeats the survey every three or four years as priorities change, particularly if the economy changes. The surveys also ask open-ended questions about what customers like and dislike.[65]

Analyzing and Using Customer Feedback

Appropriate customer satisfaction measurement identifies processes that have high impact on satisfaction and distinguishes between low performing processes low performance and those that are performing well.

Deming stressed the importance of using customer feedback to improve a company's products and processes (refer to Figure 1.3 in Chapter 1). By examining trends in customer satisfaction measures and linking satisfaction data to its internal processes, a business can see its progress and areas for improvement. As the next step, the company assigns to an employee or group of employees the responsibility and accountability for developing improvement plans based on customer satisfaction results. Many businesses, for example, tie managers' annual bonuses to customer satisfaction results. This practice acts as an incentive for managers and a direction for their efforts.

One way to evaluate customer satisfaction and use it effectively is to collect information on both the importance and the performance of key quality characteristics. For example, a hotel might ask how important check-in speed, check-out speed, staff attitude, and so on, are, as well as how the customer rates the hotel on these attributes. Evaluation of such data can be accomplished using a grid similar to the one shown in Figure 5.11, on which mean performance and importance scores for individual attributes are plotted.[66] Results in the diagonal quadrants (the shaded areas) are good. A firm ideally wants to achieve high performance on important characteristics, and not to waste resources on characteristics of low importance. Results off the diagonal indicate that the firm either is wasting resources to achieve

Figure 5.10 Graniterock Customer Report Card

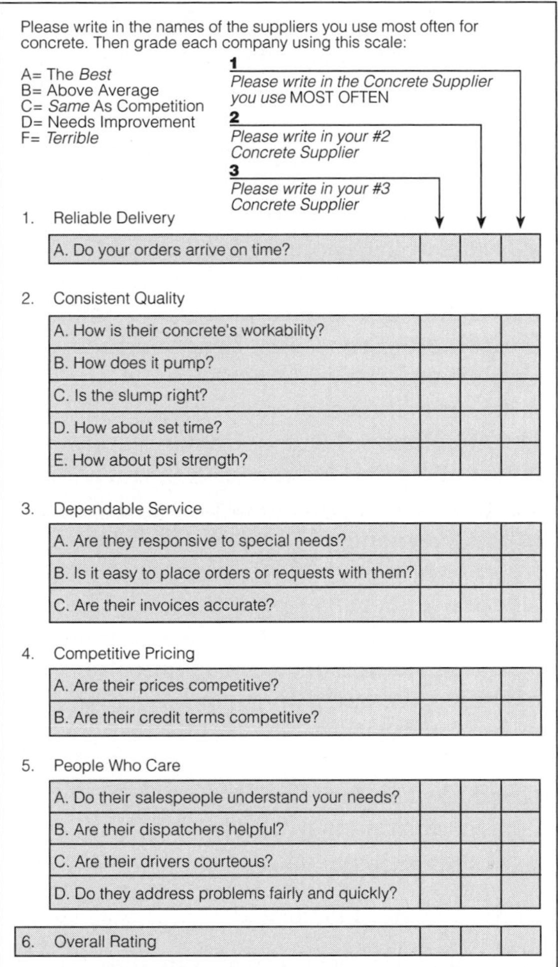

Please write in the names of the suppliers you use most often for concrete. Then grade each company using this scale:

A= The *Best*
B= Above Average
C= *Same* As Competition
D= Needs Improvement
F= *Terrible*

1 *Please write in the Concrete Supplier you use* MOST OFTEN
2 *Please write in your #2 Concrete Supplier*
3 *Please write in your #3 Concrete Supplier*

	3	2	1
1. Reliable Delivery			
A. Do your orders arrive on time?			
2. Consistent Quality			
A. How is their concrete's workability?			
B. How does it pump?			
C. Is the slump right?			
D. How about set time?			
E. How about psi strength?			
3. Dependable Service			
A. Are they responsive to special needs?			
B. Is it easy to place orders or requests with them?			
C. Are their invoices accurate?			
4. Competitive Pricing			
A. Are their prices competitive?			
B. Are their credit terms competitive?			
5. People Who Care			
A. Do their salespeople understand your needs?			
B. Are their dispatchers helpful?			
C. Are their drivers courteous?			
D. Do they address problems fairly and quickly?			
6. Overall Rating			

Source: Reprinted with permission of Graniterock.

high performance on unimportant customer attributes (overkill), or is not performing acceptably on important customer attributes, leaving the firm vulnerable to competition. The results of such an analysis can help target areas for improvement and cost savings, as well as provide useful input for strategic planning. Often, competitor data are also plotted, providing a comparison against the competition. Graniterock Company, featured in

Figure 5.11 Performance-Importance Comparison

Importance	**Performance** Low	High
Low	Who cares?	Overkill
High	Vulnerable	Strengths

the last section, uses this approach. The results of their importance survey and competitive performance survey are summarized and plotted on an importance/performance graph to assess the strengths and vulnerabilities of the company and its competitors. The scales are chosen so that each axis represents the industry average. Graniterock looks at the distance between its ratings and those of the competitors. If the ratings are close, customers cannot differentiate Graniterock from its competitors on that particular measure. By posting these graphs on bulletin boards at each plant, the company ensures that all employees, particularly salespeople, are fully informed of the survey results.

Many organizations have integrated customer feedback into their continuous improvement activities and in redesigning products and services. For example, Skilled Care Pharmacy (see Case Study in Chapter 1), located in Mason, Ohio, is a $25 million dollar privately held regional provider of pharmaceutical products delivered within the long-term care, assisted living, hospice, and group home environments. Skilled Care developed a Customer Grade Card, benchmarked from Baldrige winner Wainwright Industries, to measure customer satisfaction. The Grade Card uses a school-like A-B-C-D scoring system shown in Figure 5.12. The scores from the four questions covering Quality, Responsiveness, Delivery, and Communication are converted from letters to numbers and averaged. Any questions that were graded C or below generate an immediate phone call or personal visit to the customer by the Customer Care Team to investigate and resolve the issue. An example of how the feedback was used for improvement involved some low scores received for "Delivery." Management determined there was potential risk of losing valuable customers. Upon investigation, it became evident that the issue was not timely delivery, but their system of cut-off times for ordering medications for same-day delivery. If the customer missed the cut-off time, then they did not receive their order until the next day, and, Skilled Care was considered to be "late." Their response to this customer need was to extend pharmacy ordering hours and to aggressively modify staff schedules for the order processing and pharmacy departments. In turn, they were able to offer an additional five hours for customers to phone or fax medication orders for receipt the same day. As a result, satisfaction scores for "Delivery" rose dramatically.

Why Many Customer Satisfaction Efforts Fail[67]

Determining and using customer satisfaction information should be viewed as a key business process. Just going through the motions can often lead to failure. A. Blanton Godfrey suggests several reasons why customer satisfaction efforts fail to produce useful results.

1. Poor measurement schemes. Just tracking the percentage of "satisfied and very satisfied" customers on a 5-point Likert scale provides little actionable information. Many surveys provide biased results because few dissatisfied customers respond, or the surveys lack adequate sample sizes or randomization. Survey designers need appropriate understanding of statistical concepts.

Figure 5.12 Skilled Care's Customer Grade Card Scoring System

A = Customer Totally Satisfied	100 points
B = Customer Generally Satisfied	90 points
C = Customer Generally Dissatisfied	50 points
D = Customer Totally Dissatisfied	0 points

Source: Reprinted with permission of Skilled Care.Inc.

2. Failure to identify appropriate quality dimensions. Many surveys address issues the company thinks are important, not what customers think. This error results from a lack of capturing reliable information about customer needs and expectations.
3. Failure to weight dimensions appropriately. Even if organizations measure the right things, they may not understand which dimensions are important. As a result, they spend too much effort on dimensions with the lowest scores that may not be important to the customers. Use of techniques such as importance/performance analysis can help focus attention to the key dimensions.
4. Lack of comparison with leading competitors. Quality and perception of quality is relative. Without appropriate comparative data, competitors may be improving much faster than an organization realizes.
5. Failure to measure potential and former customers. Without an understanding of why non-customers do not do business with a company, or more importantly, why customers leave, an organization risks losing market share to competitors and may be headed for demise.
6. Confusing loyalty with satisfaction. As we noted at the beginning of this chapter, these two concepts are different. Customer retention and loyalty provide an indication of the organization's future.

CPV measures how customers assess benefits—such as product performance, ease of use, or time savings—against costs, such as purchase price, installation cost or time, and so on, in making purchase decisions.

Customer Perceived Value[68]

Measuring **customer perceived value (CPV)** is an alternative to traditional customer satisfaction measurement that focuses more on customer loyalty than on satisfaction.

Sellers that provide the greatest CPV at the time of the purchasing decision always win the sale. CPV measurement includes potential buyers rather than just existing customers, is forward-looking rather than retrospective, and examines choices relative to alternatives rather than relative to expectations. Typical questions that are asked include "What benefits are important to you?" and "How well do you believe that each product or supplier will deliver those benefits?" and focus on perceptions of future value rather than past experiences.

CPV methodology identifies the most important product attributes that prospective customers use to compare one offering against another, and their relative importance and performance. One approach for assessing importance is to ask the customer to place a percentage value of importance on each attribute so the total sums to 100 percent, thus eliminating the common problem of giving high ratings to each factor. Asking customers to rate the performance of different offerings on each attribute on a 10-point scale can assess relative performance; the difference in ratings is the relative performance. For example, in comparing two casual dining restaurants, A and B, we might find the following:

Attribute	Relative Importance	Relative Performance (A–B rating)
Menu variety	30	−2
Food quality	20	+3
Atmosphere	10	0
Value	40	+1

By multiplying the relative importance values by relative performance and summing, we see that overall, restaurant A has a higher perceived value but could improve its perceived value by improving its menu variety. Such information becomes the basis for strategic decisions.

CUSTOMER FOCUS IN THE BALDRIGE CRITERIA, ISO 9000, AND SIX SIGMA

Category 3 of the 2009–10 Malcolm Baldrige National Quality Award Criteria for Performance Excellence (available in the Baldrige Materials folder on the Premium website) is titled *Customer Focus*. Item 3.1, *Customer Engagement*, examines an organization's processes for determining product offerings and mechanisms to support customers' use of products, and how an organization builds a customer-focused culture. The criteria ask how an organization identifies and innovates its product offerings to meet customer needs and how it determines key means of customer support and customer support requirements. The item also asks how an organization creates a customer-focused culture that contributes to customer engagement and builds and manages customer relationships. Finally, the item asks how an organization improves its customer-focused approaches so that it can keep current with changing business needs and directions. Continuous improvement of business processes is a core concept of the Baldrige criteria.

Item 3.2, *Voice of the Customer*, examines an organization's processes for listening to customers and acquiring satisfaction and dissatisfaction information, and using this information to improve marketplace success. It addresses how organizations listen to customers to obtain actionable feedback, manage complaints and service recovery processes, determine customer satisfaction and engagement and compare results with competitors and industry benchmarks, and measure customer dissatisfaction for use in improvement.

Customer focus is a key requirement of ISO 9000:2000. For example, in the Management Responsibility section, one requirement is "Top management shall ensure that customer requirements are determined and are met with the aim of enhancing customer satisfaction." This puts the responsibility for customer focus on senior leadership. In the Product Realization section, the standards require that the organization determine customer requirements, including delivery and post-delivery activities, and any requirements not stated by the customer but necessary for specified or intended use. In addition, the organization must establish procedures for communicating with customers about product information and other inquiries, and for obtaining feedback, including complaints. In the Measurement, Analysis, and Improvement sections, the standards require that the organization monitor customer perceptions as to whether the organization has met customer requirements; that is, customer satisfaction. Note that even though some basic customer-focused processes are required, the scope is not as broad as in Baldrige.

Customers are sometimes a "hidden" part of Six Sigma efforts, because the focus tends to be on the improvement projects and measurement issues. However, a focus on the customer is vital at every stage of Six Sigma projects. For instance, product design (and design of associated manufacturing or service delivery processes) will be far more successful if the "voice of the customer," is included. A fundamental aspect of Six Sigma methodology is identification of critical to quality (CTQ) characteristics that are vital to customer satisfaction.

During the process of producing a product or service, it is important to gather information needed by internal customers for process control activities to ensure that the product is meeting the CTQs. If the CTQs are not being met, then the organization needs to develop a better measurement and control system.[69] Often, internal data that can improve control processes—such as whether materials arrived on time, how often an accounting report had incorrect data, or how many employees were absent from work—are kept in departmental records, where they are difficult to access. The solution may require a Six Sigma study to determine the types of data and information that are needed to provide necessary monitoring and control, and how the information gap (if one exists) can be closed.

Finally, at the delivery stage, customer satisfaction measures can provide clear information about the success of Six Sigma efforts. In fact, many common Six Sigma projects revolve around developing appropriate customer satisfaction measurement processes, as well as trying to improve the design and delivery of CTQs identified through voice of the customer processes.

SUMMARY OF KEY POINTS AND TERMINOLOGY

BONUS MATERIALS

The Premium website for this chapter provides a summary of key concepts and terminology introduced in this chapter.

QUALITY IN PRACTICE

UNDERSTANDING THE VOICE OF THE CUSTOMER AT LAROSA'S PIZZERIAS[70]

"All business is the same, it just looks different" is a favorite quote of T. D. Hughes, CEO of LaRosa's, Inc. LaRosa's is a privately held chain of neighborhood pizzerias with 54 locations in Cincinnati, Ohio, northern Kentucky, and southeast Indiana, that offers full-service dine-in, carryout, and home delivery. LaRosa's competes against such national chains as Pizza Hut, Papa John's, Uno's, and other local restaurants, yet holds a 45 to 50 percent share in its market area. LaRosa's has been a leader among local businesses in adopting and promoting total quality principles. Hughes' quote provides a foundation for learning from other organizations and adopting high-performance practices that have proven successful, no matter what business they come from. One of these is the Voice of the Customer process.

In 1997, as part of a new strategic planning process, LaRosa's identified growth as a key strategic goal. Because the local market was essentially saturated, however, the executive management team worked on strategies for growing the company for three years and produced no tangible results. One of the reasons for the impasse was the lack of sound, factual data. The executive management team had developed three growth strategies, but could not agree on which one to follow because of a lack of a fact-based foundation for the decision.

In 2000, a project team was formed to tackle this issue, and was given complete latitude to make any recommendation for an Italian/pizzeria concept based on customer needs and expectations. The team consisted of the marketing director (team leader), two executive vice presidents, the director of operations, two franchise owners, an external strategic business partner, and the CEO, who was the team sponsor. The key tool that successfully led to an understanding of their customers and to a new and innovative restaurant design was Voice of the Customer (VOC). VOC is a structured methodology for listening to customers that is promoted by the Center for Quality of Management (CQM), an industrial consortium based in Boston (http://www.cqm.org). The basis for VOC is asking customers to express their needs and expectations through their experiences. LaRosa's completed 16 in-depth, one-on-one interviews with current and potential customers both inside and outside of their current market area to provide examples of dining incidents these individuals had experienced, seeking "the good, the bad, and the ugly." Here are some responses from customers of current competitors and potential competitors in other markets.

1. "So there I was, like herded cattle, standing on the hard concrete floor, cold wind blasting my ankles every time the door opened, waiting and waiting for our name to be called."
2. "And then I saw a dirty rag being slopped around a dirty table!"

3. "The manager said, 'That's not a gnat, that's black pepper,' so I said I know the difference between black pepper and a gnat, black pepper doesn't have little wings on it!"
4. "When they're that age, going to the bathroom is a full-contact sport—they're reaching and grabbing at everything, and you're trying to keep them from touching anything because the bathroom is so dirty."

What were the customers actually saying? One of the challenges that LaRosa's faced was to translate the "customer voices" into actionable terms. In these examples, LaRosa's understood the customers as saying that restaurant design should consider the diverse comfort needs of all guests, that it provide a facility that customers implicitly trust, that customers feel cared for by service staff, and that restroom cleanliness affirms guests' trust in restaurant cleanliness. In analyzing all the responses gathered, LaRosa's was able to prioritize the most important customer requirements: (1) assurance that the kitchen is clean (which is reflected by the cleanliness of the restrooms), (2) prompt service, (3) food and drinks at their proper temperature, (4) fresh food, (5) meeting the unique needs of adult guests as well as families, (6) exceeding service expectations, (7) an easy to read and understand menu, and (8) caring staff.

The experience of using VOC changed the company focus from a "product-out" to a "market in" mentality. It gave them a decision-making tool based on factual data and broke down communication silos within the company, and eliminated the age-old sales and marketing versus operations conflict. The executive management team and directors were able to agree on a growth strategy that had eluded them for three years. The result was a new restaurant design concept that explicitly addressed the voice of the customer. To meet the diverse needs of customers, for example, LaRosa's developed a larger waiting area, a casual bar area with more of an adult atmosphere in addition to the family dining areas, both table and booth seating, and a private dining area for parties. LaRosa's also initiated an improved kids' program highlighted by Luigi's Closet, a small area in which children can select a toy or activity to keep them busy and crackers to eat while waiting for dinner. The Chapter 5 Bonus Materials folder on the Premium website includes a PowerPoint presentation of LaRosa's Restaurant Design.

BONUS MATERIALS

The new restaurant jumped to second in sales behind LaRosa's flagship location. The dining room check average is 25 percent higher than the market average, profitability as a percent of gross sales is well above the chain average, and secret shopper satisfaction results show that it is performing at the top of the chain.

Key Issues for Discussion

1. How does VOC differ from other forms of market research into customer needs and expectations? What advantages and possible disadvantages does it have?
2. What impact did the VOC process have for LaRosa's?
3. Conduct a mock VOC for your school or college. What did you learn?

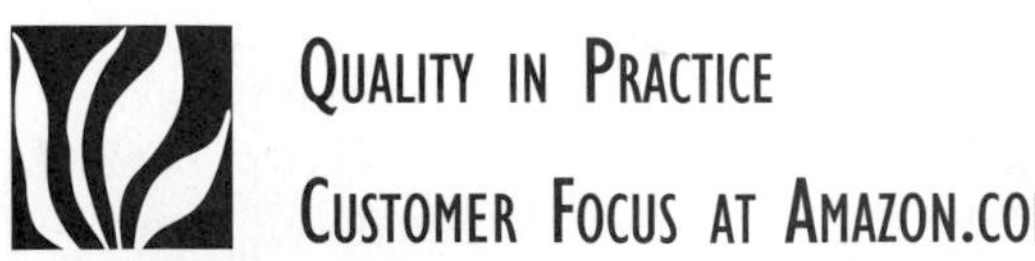

Quality in Practice
Customer Focus at Amazon.com

Warren Buffett, the well-known financier and CEO of Berkshire Hathaway, has never been a big backer of technology businesses.[71] However, he owns $459 million worth of Amazon.com's bonds, making him one of Amazon's biggest debt holders. Buffet observes, "I've been using a computer for eight or ten years now and I still really pay for only three things on the Internet: The Wall Street Journal, online bridge, and books from Amazon.com. That they are one of only three companies online that have gotten money out of my pocket tells me they are doing something right."

The concept of Amazon began in 1994 when Jeff Bezos, its founder and CEO, read a study that predicted the Internet would explode in popularity. He settled on selling books online because almost every book was already catalogued electronically, yet no physical bookstore could carry them all. Bezos has a rare talent for a relentless focus on the customer, and a studied disregard for short-term pressures to show results on the "bottom line." The original Amazon model envisioned giving customers access to a gigantic selection without the time, expense, and hassle of opening stores and warehouses and dealing with inventory. However, Bezos quickly discovered that the only way to make sure customers get a good experience and that Amazon gets inventory at good prices was to operate his own warehouses so he could control the transaction from start to finish. In its 2008 Annual Report, a letter from the 1997 Annual Report was reproduced, explaining Amazon's customer-focused philosophy in these words:

> *From the beginning, our focus has been on offering our customers compelling value. We realized that the Web was, and still is, the World Wide Wait. Therefore, we set out to offer customers something they simply could not get any other way, and began serving them with books. We brought them much more selection than was possible in a physical store (our store would now occupy 6 football fields), and presented it in a useful, easy-to-search, and easy-to-browse format in a store open 365 days a year, 24 hours a day. We maintained a dogged focus on improving the shopping experience, and in 1997 substantially enhanced our store. We now offer customers gift certificates, 1-Click^{SM} shopping, and vastly more reviews, content, browsing options, and recommendation features. We dramatically lowered prices, further increasing customer value. Word of mouth remains the most powerful customer acquisition tool we have, and we are grateful for the trust our customers have placed in us. Repeat purchases and word of mouth have combined to make Amazon.com the market leader in online bookselling.*[72]

Bezos's letter made numerous points to explain how that vision of customer service had developed and expanded, including:

- We have deep selection that is unconstrained by shelf space.
- We turn our inventory 19 times in a year.
- We personalize the store for each and every customer.
- We trade real estate for technology (which gets cheaper and more capable every year).
- We display customer reviews critical of our products.
- You can make a purchase with a few seconds and one click.
- We put used products next to new ones so you can choose.
- We share our prime real estate, our product detail pages, with third parties, and, if they can offer better value, we let them.
- Customer experience costs that remain variable, such as the variable portion of fulfillment costs, improve in our model as we reduce defects. Eliminating defects improves costs and leads to better customer experience.[73]

Many of the customer-pleasing features of Amazon's operations are not noticed, or even known, by Amazon's customers. These fall into the categories of technology, order fulfillment, and retailing strategies. In technology, the company's website has been, and remains, leading edge. In an effort to serve customer needs, Amazon was one of the early pioneers to develop software for collaborative filtering of customer data. Basically, the filter is used to suggest similar or related products to a customer after he or she has focused on a product or product category. For example, if a customer browses or purchases *Managing for Quality and Performance Excellence*, other books in quality management would then be suggested on the viewer's Web browser. These suggestions are based on what other readers of the text had purchased, in addition to the target text. Web features and capabilities have expanded over the years, to include features such as "look inside the book" for a chapter preview, in-store pickup of orders, shipping choices (priority vs. regular), and affinity group selections (Wedding Registry, Baby Registry, personal Wish List, etc.).

In order fulfillment, the capabilities of its high-tech warehouses continue to drive costs down, as mentioned earlier. For example, Amazon has a nearly perfect process for sorting multiple item orders. As it expands its offerings and adds more retail partners, Amazon's fulfillment capabilities pay dividends to its partners, as well as adding revenues to Amazon. By reducing the time it takes to get all the items in an order into the sorting system, Amazon shipped 35 percent more units with the same number of people than it had in earlier years.[74]

Its retailing strategy is based more and more on partnerships with those who, in most businesses, would be considered competitors. Amazon proclaims that it seeks "to offer Earth's Biggest Selection℠ and to be Earth's most customer-centric company, where customers can find and discover anything they might want to buy online." However, at any time, its competitor–partners may be offering the same item through their linked websites at a different price. For example, when a book is being viewed, the web page will also permit the viewer to go to a linking web page of a partner's book company, where the same title used (or even new) book is being sold for a lower price. Its partners include well-known retailers such as Borders Books, Waldenbooks, Waterstone, Target Stores, Lands' End, and thousands of other lesser-known organizations, large and small. In fact, through what is called their Associates Program, Amazon.com provides a link to 900,000 websites carrying specialty items and where online auctions are taking place every day.

With millions of customers and potential customers accessing its global sites in the United States, the United Kingdom, Germany, Japan, and Canada daily, Amazon.com's sophisticated technology allows it to build an in-depth and potentially valuable database of many of its customers. In 1999, Amazon.com experimented with a highly controversial feature on its website. It started featuring thousands of individual bestseller lists categorized by Zip codes, workplaces, and colleges—wherever its customers were ordering from. With a mouse click on its website, browsers could peek behind the scenes at the books that specific groups were reading, the compact discs they were listening to, and the videos they were watching. Amazon described it as "fun," happily announcing the feature, Purchase Circles, in a press release. Soon, however, citing customer complaints, the company began backtracking. Customers were allowed to opt out of having their data collected, as long as they were savvy enough to read the fine print and send an e-mail to the company. Companies could choose not to be included by sending a fax.[75] Despite the controversy, Amazon.com retained Purchase Circles on its website for a number of years. They were removed in mid-2009 in order to undergo "a major renovation," with promises to return soon.

Key Issues for Discussion

1. How does Amazon.com's CRM software help it to gain market share and maintain its competitive advantage?
2. How are operating efficiencies realized in order fulfillment activities of Amazon.com? Will costs continue to fall, given that their warehouses are currently operating at less than 50% of capacity? (Note: This measure is expected to change over time, depending on the state of the economy.)
3. What are the customer privacy risks, besides the ones mentioned in the case, that Amazon.com must guard against in order to continue to grow its business?

Additional Quality in Practice features can be found in the Chapter 5 Bonus Materials folder on the Premium website.

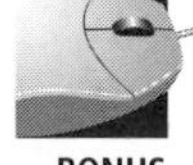

BONUS MATERIALS

Review Questions

1. Summarize the key customer focused practices for performance excellence. Which of these are reflected in Park Place Lexus and Mercy Health System?
2. Explain the difference between satisfaction and loyalty. Why is loyalty more important?
3. What does customer engagement mean? How does it differ from satisfaction?
4. What is a consumer benefit package? Why is it important in understanding satisfaction and loyalty?
5. Describe the model used in computing the American Customer Satisfaction Index. How might a business use the information from the ACSI database?

6. Define the types of customers that an organization encounters at the three levels of quality.
7. Explain the AT&T customer–supplier model.
8. Why is it important to segment customers? Describe some ways of defining customer segments.
9. Explain the different dimensions of quality defined by David Garvin and the key dimensions of service quality. How are these dimensions similar and different?
10. What is the Kano model, and what are its implications for quality management?
11. What is the voice of the customer? Why is it important to understand it?
12. List the major listening and learning approaches to gather information about customer needs and expectations. What are the advantages and disadvantages of each?
13. Describe how affinity diagrams and tree diagrams are used to organize and work with customer-related information.
14. Explain the customer-driven quality cycle. What do expected quality, actual quality, and perceived quality mean, and how do they relate with one another?
15. Explain the concept of moments of truth.
16. Explain the importance of commitments and customer support to building customer relationships.
17. Who are customer contact employees? Why are they critical to an organization?
18. Explain the role of training and empowerment of customer-contact employees in achieving customer satisfaction.
19. Define the term customer contact requirements. Why are they important?
20. Why should a company make it easy for customers to complain? How should complaint information be used? Outline a generic complaint management process.
21. What is the importance of service recovery?
22. Why are strategic partnerships and alliances useful to an organization?
23. Summarize the issues associated with customer focus in e-commerce.
24. How can customer relationship management (CRM) software help organizations develop and improve a focus on customers?
25. Why should an organization measure customer satisfaction? Describe the key steps that must be addressed in designing customer satisfaction surveys.
26. What types of questions should be included in customer satisfaction surveys?
27. Explain the concept of importance-performance analysis and its benefit to an organization.
28. Why do many customer satisfaction efforts fail?
29. What is customer perceived value, and how can an organization benefit from measuring it?
30. What specific issues of customer focus are addressed in the Baldrige Award criteria, ISO 9000, and Six Sigma frameworks?

Discussion Questions

1. Can you describe a customer-focused organization similar to Superquinn with which you have had personal experience? What aspects of the organization impressed you the most?

2. A service representative of a major U.S. airline told a customer about an internal memo that had been circulated called "No Waivers, No Favors," which promises significant and negative consequences to any employee giving a customer special treatment outside of the airline's strict policies. As the employee noted, "Now, nobody is doing anything until we find out what happens to us if we are a little lenient about enforcing a rule. People are scared." Why do you think that management adopted this policy? What implications will it probably have for customers?
3. Construct a list of at least 10 different names for a "customer," for example, buyer, client, and so on.
4. Thinking about organizations that you encounter in your daily life (your college, bookstores, restaurants, and so on) identify examples of customer focused practices from Table 5.1 that are evident in these organizations.
5. Are you loyal to any particular businesses? Why or why not?
6. Consider a fraternity or other student organization and make a list of all of its customers.
7. Think about the "supply chain" for filling a doctor's prescription. Describe the different types of customers involved in the process.
8. Recall the AT&T customer–supplier model in Figure 5.2. For each of the following departments in a typical company, discuss who are their internal or external customers and suppliers.
   a. Operations
   b. Information Systems
   c. Human Resources
   d. Mailroom
   e. Payroll
9. How might a college or university segment its customers? What specific needs might each of these customer groups have?
10. You might be familiar with the electronics superstore Best Buy. Like the Macy's example in the chapter, Best Buy has segmented its customer base into fictitious people: Barry—an affluent tech enthusiast, Jill—a busy suburban mom, Buzz—a young gadget fiend, Ray—a price-conscious family guy, and Mr. Storefront—a small business owner.[76] How might this segmentation help the company to better design its stores and train its employees? Suggest some things that the company might do to customize its stores and service to these customer segments.
11. Choose a product other than an automobile and explain how Garvin's dimensions of quality are reflected in that product.
12. Which of the five key dimensions of service quality—reliability, assurance, tangibles, empathy, or responsiveness—would the following items from a retail banking customer survey address?
    a. Following through on promises
    b. Offering convenient banking hours
    c. Providing prompt customer service
    d. Properly handling any problems that arise
    e. Maintaining clean and pleasant branch office facilities
    f. Demonstrating knowledge of bank products and services
    g. Giving undivided attention to the customer
    h. Never being too busy to respond to customer requests
    i. Charging reasonable service fees

j. Maintaining a professional appearance
k. Providing error-free bank statements
l. Keeping customer transactions confidential

13. Deer Valley Resort in Park City, Utah, is viewed by many as the Ritz-Carlton of ski resorts, providing exceptional services and a superior ski vacation experience.[77] The resort offers curbside ski valet service to take equipment from vehicles, parking lot attendants to ensure efficient parking, and a shuttle to transport guests from the lot to Snow Park Lodge. Guests walk to the slopes on heated pavers to prevent the pavement from freezing and assist in snow removal. The central gathering area by the base lifts is wide and level, allowing plenty of room to put on equipment and easy access to the lifts. At the end of the day, guests can store their skis without charge at each lodge. The resort limits the number of skiers on the mountain to reduce lines and congestion, and offers complimentary mountain tours for both expert and intermediate skiers. Everyone is committed to ensuring that each guest has a wonderful experience, from "mountain hosts" stationed at the top of the lifts to answer questions and provide directions, to the friendly workers at the cafeterias and restaurants, whose food is consistently rated number one by ski enthusiast magazines. "Our goal is to make each guest feel like a winner," says Bob Wheaton, vice president and general manager. "We go the extra mile on the mountain, in our ski school, and throughout our food-service operation because we want our guests to know they come first." What dimensions of quality—as described by David Garvin and specific to services that are described in this chapter—are evident at Deer Valley?
14. Give several examples of dissatisfiers, satisfiers, and exciters/delighters in products or services that you recently purchased. Why did you classify them into these categories?
15. Consider the following customer expectations for a fast-food (quick-service) restaurant. Would you classify them as dissatisfiers, satisfiers, and exciters/delighters?
    a. Special prices on certain days
    b. Food is safe to eat
    c. Hot food is served hot
    d. Service is friendly
    e. Background music
    f. Playland for children
    g. Restaurant is clean inside
    h. Food is fresh
    i. A "one-bite" money-back guarantee
    j. Orders can be phoned in for pickup at a separate window
16. In the context of a fast-food restaurant, make a list of different characteristics that might describe "freshness." Classify them by means of an affinity diagram or tree diagram. What does your response mean for measuring satisfaction of this attribute?
17. How might your school use the customer-driven quality cycle in Figure 5.5?
18. Prepare a list of moments of truth that you encounter during a typical quarter or semester at your college or university.
19. Write a generic customer satisfaction policy that a firm might use to convey trust to its customers and as a means of determining employee values, policies, and training initiatives.

20. Discuss the lessons that organizations can learn about customer relationships and customer contact employees from the following experiences:[78]
    a. In shopping for a cell phone, a customer met a salesperson who introduced herself, asked her name, went through the features that related to her needs, and didn't try to sell her the most expensive phone.
    b. A woman encountered a sales person in a home improvement store who commented "Oh, shopping for your husband?"
    c. A couple stranded in a restaurant booth with no waiter or silverware made eye contact with a waitress who quickly replied "Your waiter is late. I can't take your order because this isn't my station."
    d. While shopping for a TV antenna, a customer asked the difference between various models. The salesperson replied "Some cost more because they look better."
21. If you were the manager of a small pizza restaurant (dine-in and limited delivery), what customer contact requirements might you specify for your employees who take phone orders, work the cash register, and serve as waiters? How would you train them?
22. Choose some e-commerce site with which you are familiar. Analyze how "customer-focused" the organization appears to be and provide specific examples to justify your opinions.
23. One of our former students discovered a way to receive great service: Ask for a satisfaction survey before the end of the transaction. In one experience, the student observed an instant change in how she was treated. What does such an experience tell you about the company?
24. If you were to design satisfaction surveys for high school students, colleges where they attend, or businesses who might hire them directly out of high school, what questions would you ask and why?
25. Comment on the following questions that you might see on customer satisfaction surveys. Discuss some of the problems with these questions and how they might be improved.
    a. The staff is professional.
    b. ETAs are adequate.
    c. Waiting time was reasonable.
    d. Food safety is important to my purchase decision.
    e. The service representative was friendly and helpful.
26. A local franchise of a national car rental firm conducted a survey of customers to determine their perceptions of the importance of key product and service attributes as well as their perceptions of the company's performance.[79] The results are given in Tables 5.4 and 5.5. In Table 5.4, importance

Table 5.4 Importance Ratings of Product/Service Attributes

Attribute	Rating
Mechanical condition of car	4.00
Cleanliness of vehicle	3.93
Friendliness of staff	3.86
Check-out speed/efficiency	3.80
Getting reserved car or better	3.80
Check-in speed/efficiency	3.79
Cleanliness of facility	3.66
Employee appearance	3.45
Getting nonsmoking car	3.45
Speed of coach service	3.24

Table 5.5 Customer Ratings of Performance

	Personal use	Business use
Mechanical condition of car	4.815	4.750
Cleanliness of vehicle	4.893	4.563
Friendliness of staff	4.929	4.688
Check-out speed/efficiency	4.759	4.688
Getting reserved car or better	96%	100%
Check-in speed/efficiency	4.821	4.750
Cleanliness of facility	4.893	4.500
Employee appearance	100%	100%
Getting nonsmoking car	86%	100%
Speed of coach service	100%	100%

was measured on a four-point scale ranging from "not at all important" to "very important." Note that Table 5.5 is segmented by personal and business use, and that two different scales were used (the percentage values are based on the percentage of "yes" responses; all others are on a 5-point scale from "poor" to "excellent"). What conclusions might you make from these data? What possible improvements can you suggest?

27. Analyze the following customer satisfaction results (on a 5-point scale) for a fast-food restaurant. What recommendations would you make to the managers?

Attribute	**Importance**	**Performance**
Fresh buns	4.83	4.80
Cheese is melted	4.26	4.82
Drink is not watery	4.88	4.64
Fries are crisp	4.85	4.80
Fries are salty	4.12	4.48
Service is fast	4.93	4.61
Open 24 hours	3.91	4.81
Good variety of food	4.46	3.87
Nutritional data displayed	3.76	4.65
Children's menu available	4.80	3.97
Tables kept clean	4.91	4.89
Low-fat items available	3.62	4.55

28. How might a bank quantify the value of a loyal customer? Try to develop a quantitative model.
29. How does the Baldrige criteria address the issues raised in the discussion of the reasons why many customer satisfaction efforts fail? How can using the criteria help to mitigate these reasons?

Projects, Etc.

1. Perform some research to examine recent trends in the American Customer Satisfaction Index. What economic sectors show improvement? Which don't? How has the overall index changed?
2. Based on the information in this chapter, propose new approaches for measuring customer satisfaction for your faculty and instructors that go beyond the traditional course evaluation processes that your school may use.

Table 5.6 Airline Customer Requirements

- Quality food
- Ability to solve problems and answer questions during flight
- Efficient boarding procedures
- Appealing interior appearance
- Well-maintained seats
- Reservation calls answered promptly
- Timely and accurate communication of information prior to boarding
- Good selection of magazines and newspapers
- Efficient and attentive flight attendants
- Good beverage selection
- Clean lavatories
- Efficient ticket line and waiting procedures
- Convenient ground transportation
- Courteous reservations personnel
- Good-quality audio/visual system
- Sufficient quantity of food
- Interesting in-flight magazine
- Courteous and efficient gate personnel
- In-flight telephone access
- Good variety of audio/visual programming
- Flight attendants knowledgeable of airline programs and policies
- Correct explanation of fares and schedules
- Efficient seat-selection process
- Courteous and efficient sky cap
- Timely and accurate communication of flight information (in-flight)
- Convenient baggage check-in
- Timely baggage check-in
- Comfortable seating and leg room
- Assistance for passengers with special needs
- Courteous ticket counter personnel
- Convenient parking close to terminal
- Ability to solve baggage claim problems
- Ability of reservation agents to answer questions

3. You may have visited or purchased items from large computer and software retail stores. In a group brainstorming session, identify those characteristics of such a store that would be most important to you, and design a customer survey to evaluate customers' importance and the store's performance.
4. Table 5.6 is a hypothetical list of customer requirements as determined through a focus group conducted by an airline. Develop an affinity diagram, classify these requirements into appropriate categories, and design a questionnaire to survey customers. Be sure to address any other pertinent issues/questions as well as customer information that would be appropriate to include in the questionnaire.
5. Interview some managers of small businesses to determine how they respond to complaints and use complaint information in their organizations.
6. Describe some ways that organizations can improve websites and make them more customer-focused. You might consider examining a variety of websites and identifying "best practices."
7. Gather several customer satisfaction surveys or comment cards from local establishments. Analyze them as to their ability to lead to actionable

information that will help the organization, and propose any improvements or redesign you deem appropriate.

8. This exercise provides an experience with developing an affinity diagram for analyzing complaints and would best be performed by the class as a whole.[80] Each student writes one or more descriptions of personal experiences of frustration and dissatisfaction with products and services. Two examples might be: "Every time I purchase a CD, the seal is difficult and time-consuming to remove. I have even cracked the case a few times while trying to remove it." "I purchased a new pair of running shoes, and the laces were too long." These experiences should be written on large sticky notes and posted on the classroom wall. Students then group the responses in to logical categories and develop descriptive headers for each group that explain the causes of dissatisfaction and then create the affinity diagram. For instance, the shoe example might fall into a group titled "Product components are incompatible." An alternative project is to use positive comments about products and services.
9. A number of pizza chains or restaurants are undoubtedly located around your college campus. Using a focus group of students, conduct an interview to determine what factors are important in selecting a traditional or pizza restaurant. Once you have identified these factors, design a satisfaction survey to compare perceptions among the most popular restaurants in your area. Ask a sample of students who visited at least to two of them to complete the survey. Analyze the results and draw conclusions in a written report.
10. Design customer satisfaction questionnaires for high school students and their parents who take a campus visit and are considering applying to your school.

CASES

Additional cases are available in the Chapter 5 Bonus Materials folder on the Premium website.

BONUS MATERIALS

PAULI'S RESTAURANT AND MICROBREWERY

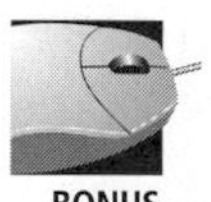

BONUS MATERIALS

The Case of the Missing Reservation in the Chapter 5 Bonus Materials folder on the Premium website is a good companion case to this one.

You have been appointed General Manager of Pauli's Restaurant and Microbrewery, a popular downtown pub in a major city, after working there for several years as a waiter and recently a shift manager. Pauli's has locations in six regional cities and operates a corporate website. One of the features of the website is a customer feedback section that is sent directly to the corporate VP and to the appropriate General Manager. After your first weekend on the job, you received the following comment:

> *We had a lousy service experience last Saturday at your restaurant. We eat there several times a year before the theater and had 6:15 reservations, with which we are usually done eating—including dessert—by 7:30 or 7:40 the latest to get to the theater in time. Service was ridiculously slow. We finally ordered dessert around 7:20–7:25 and it took at least 10 minutes for the waitress to come back and tell us they didn't have the coconut key lime pie that was listed on special; we ordered something else and waited and waited. Eventually, we had to find the waitress and tell her to forget it because we didn't have time. My wife tried to flag her down for half an hour to get her coffee refilled. To top it off, we didn't even receive an apology; the only thing she did quickly was to process the check. She was clearly over-committed to too many tables to*

provide us with adequate service. Very disappointing for what we considered one of our favorite places, especially as we were bringing friends with us who had never been there before.

Draft a response to this customer. Analyze the responses of your classmates. What makes a good "service recovery" response? Develop some general guidelines.

First Internet Reliable Bank

First Internet Reliable (FIR) Bank was started in 1994 by Mimi Livingstone, the daughter of a prominent banker in Redmond, Washington, and two men. Livingstone had worked for five years at Washington Mutual Bank and then quit to earn her MBA at the University of Washington. She teamed up with two "techies"—Marvin Arbol and Nick Sistemas—who had gone to the same Seattle suburban high school as Bill Gates, who graduated from there some ten years earlier. Arbol and Sistemas worked at Microsoft in the late 1980's after they had graduated from prestigious universities with degrees in software engineering, and had led teams that pioneered in the development of some of Microsoft's most popular products. Having accumulated a substantial amount in Microsoft stock options, they decided to leave Microsoft and do something different by helping Livingstone start her bank.

With their combination of skills and excellent insights into technology, Livingstone, Abol, and Sistemas foresaw that the Internet could be used to deliver innovative banking services, beginning at the local level, and expanding regionally, nationally, and internationally as growth and technological maturity permitted.

The goals of FIR Bank were to:

- To pioneer banking over the Internet, locally, nationally, and internationally
- To develop a network to initially provide loan services and stock trading, but later to add additional products such as individual and commercial accounts, as the business growth warranted
- To provide customer service that reached or exceeded service found at a "bricks and mortar" bank at a lower cost than was traditionally expected
- To make financial information about loans, investing and financial services available online through such downloadable materials as a quarterly newsletter, booklets, audio-visual and other "state of the art" media, as web technology permitted
- To avoid the temptation, that was becoming evident among other Internet companies, to "grow like crazy," burn through the cash of venture capitalists and other investors, take the company public, and sell out

Internet Banking 1995–2000

At the time that Livingstone, Arbol, and Sistemas started FIR, they were both visionary and practical. They understood that, initially, customers of Internet banks come from innovation-minded, busy people who are technologically advanced. They also knew that there were many limitations to this form of enterprise that included:

- Internet banks don't have "bricks and mortar" offices and branches open to customers
- The "product" is intangible, unlike books or flowers
- Security is a major concern
- Customer expectations vary widely
- Regulation is heavy in the banking industry
- Profit margins are narrow

However, many advantages existed for starting an Internet bank in 1995, including:

- There is no direct competition in the banking sector
- The costs of "bricks and mortar" can be avoided
- Many of the transactions that bank clerks and tellers do can be automated
- Electronic infrastructure available at reasonable costs is rapidly being built
- If volumes can be "ramped up" costs per transaction will rapidly decrease
- Reliable operations can be built electronically for high volumes of transactions

FIR Bank grew and prospered in the last years of the twentieth century and survived growing competition from copycat Internet banks and later from the "bricks and mortar" banks that saw the growing threat and promise of Internet banking. Many banks got in too late to make it a profitable business, but it became something that a bank had to do because of competition. FIR Bank stuck to their strategy, and Livingstone, Arbol, and Sistemas matured in their ability to grow with a constant eye on customer and market needs.

Internet Banking 2001–Present

After the September 11, 2001 attack on the World Trade Center and the Dot.Com Internet bust that occurred almost simultaneously, there were fewer banks of every variety, but the Internet banking competition got tougher.

A nationwide survey, done in 2004, showed the team at FIR that some of the key characteristics of online bank customers were:[81]

- *Broadband and online experience.* 63 percent of those with broadband Internet capability at home have tried online banking, compared with 32 percent of those with dial-up connections. And 51 percent of those who have more than six years of internet experience have tried banking online, compared to 27 percent of those with three years or less of online experience.
- *The rise of GenX.* People with Internet connections between the ages of 28 and 39 to have tried online banking. Some 60 percent have done so, compared to 38 percent of wired GenY members (those 18–27) and 25 percent of those with Internet connections over the age of 60.
- *Men.* In the past two years, online men are notably more likely to perform online banking activities than online women. Half of men with Internet connections (49 percent) have tried online banking, compared to 39 percent of online women. This is a change from the situation two years ago when internet-connected men and women were equally as likely to be banking online.
- *Higher socio-economic status.* Online banking, like many other Internet activities, is most likely to be performed by those living in well-off households (households with more than $75,000 in income), those who have college and graduate degrees, and those who live in suburbs. It is important to note, though, that there has been an across-the-board increase in online banking that has brought more of those who are working class, those who don't have college degrees, and those in rural areas into the online banking population.

By 2005, there were fewer than 20 viable autonomous Internet banks (those without traditional bank facilities and operations). FIR found that their Internet customers were more profitable than "ordinary" banking customers, were more likely to remain loyal to their bank if treated well, and provided excellent "word-of-mouth" advertising to friends, family members, and acquaintances. In short, they were worth competing for.

FIR did a customer survey over the Internet in 2005 consisting of a random sample of 1,000 customers. Responses showed that there were a number of things that customers liked about the online banking experience, but a number of things that they did not like. The survey provided for both closed-ended and open-ended responses.

One of the most important questions involved customer service perceptions. Customers were asked to name the dimension of customer service that gave them the most satisfaction. Interestingly, these responses centered around personal contact with customer service representatives. The top responses included: the accessibility provided by FIR to discuss problems with customer service representatives (CSR's) (16 percent); the relatively short time it takes to resolve most problems (15 percent); the quality of the response provided by CSR's (14 percent); and the manner and approach of CSR's (11 percent).

The closed-ended responses, when matched with customer demographics, confirmed that FIR customers were generally "typical" of Internet banking customers, as suggested by the Pew survey. Most had high-speed Internet connections, were men, and were in medium to high socio-economic categories. As might be expected, because of their location in the northwest United States, approximately 50 percent of their customers were in technical occupations.

The open-ended questions showed other areas, some of which were unexpected. Some typical responses included:

- Respondent 13: I relly luv the convience of being abl to bank online 24/7. The Web page is EZ to use.
- Respondent 889: I can easily check my balance and pay bills from my FIR account. It's a little inconvenient to have to mail my deposits. However, I have recently requested that my company direct-deposit my paycheck, so that will make things easier.
- Respondent 557: When I looked around to determine where I could get the best deal on a home equity loan, FIR beat the competition by a mile! Not only did they have the best interest rate, but my CSR, Veena, was really helpful. She used the online application information that I submitted to get preliminary approval the same day. Then she "locked in" the rate. By the end of the week, she had the appraisal done by a local appraiser, and had e-mailed the forms to me to sign. I printed them, signed, and had my signature notarized the same day. All the signed forms were sent and returned in three days, via package express. Total elapsed time was 6 working days. GREAT WORK!!
- Respondent 235: I really like your website, where I frequently pay bills, check my balances, and transfer money between my accounts. Since I do some business overseas, your recent addition of the capability to transfer funds electronically has been a Godsend. That's why I'm frustrated and puzzled. Why can't you add one OBVIOUS capability—the ability to get my money from an ATM? I have to keep a local account open, just for that!
- Respondent 3: I've been satisfied with my FIR account, but I'm considering closing my account and opening a traditional account with my local bank. I've received three PHISHING-type e-mails that used the FIR Bank name and looked just like those that you send out, right down to your logo! The first time, I actually went to the website in the e-mail, but when it asked for my social security number, as well as my account number, I got suspicious. I logged off and called your security office. They told me that you'd never send out an e-mail asking for the social security number. They were very nice and took down the information about the PHISH'er. They followed up with an e-mail, saying that they were getting close to finding and "closing down" the crook. Still, I'm very concerned about identity theft. What are you doing to increase security and guard my information against hackers?
- Respondent 137: I have been delighted with the features and functionality of my commercial FIR account until now. However, I'm forced to close my account and open one with one of the traditional "bricks and mortar" banks that has become more competitive in Internet and commercial customer service. As you know, businesses don't have the protection that retail customers have, when it comes to identity theft/hackers. Individuals are protected, so if anyone steals their credit card, they bear a maximum risk of $50. We businesspeople are open to any kind of bank fraud, and must bear all the risk if someone swipes our card number. However, XYA Bank has now set a policy to protect small businesses in the same way as individual clients. I'm going with them.

After reviewing the survey results, Livingstone, Abol, and Sistemas wondered if their business model simply needed tweaking or a major overhaul, which might even require building brick and mortar offices to meet customer needs.

Discussion Questions

1. Even though the complete survey is not included in the case, summarize how the closed-ended and open-ended questions provided valuable customer insights for FIR.
2. What customer segments are targeted by FIR? On what issues should FIR focus in order to build relationships with its varied customer segments?
3. Can you recommend specific activities and practices that they might engage in order to improve customer service quality and retain customers such as Respondents 3 and 137?

GOLD STAR CHILI (A)[82]

Gold Star Chili, Inc., based in Cincinnati, Ohio, was founded in 1965 as a family-owned system of franchised and company-owned restaurants. Gold Star operates over 100 regional locations (most of which are franchised, with a few being company restaurants or are co-owned). The Gold Star menu is based on a unique, "Cincinnati-style" chili recipe, flavored with a proprietary blend of spices from around the world. The chili is prepared in a central commissary, designed to reduce equipment needs at individual restaurants, promote consistency, and reduce labor costs. Most locations have both in-store dining and a drive-through. Gold Star operates in a highly competitive market against other multi-location chili firms and traditional fast-food competitors such as McDonald's, Taco Bell, and Kentucky Fried Chicken. It trails its major competitor, Skyline, which has a larger advertising budget, in market share. Gold Star Chili is an active participant with the Cincinnati Restaurant Association and the National Restaurant Association. These connections help maintain awareness of business trends, and advances in new technology. Changing business needs are assessed by reviewing the annual reports of competing restaurants, and an annual market research study that permits benchmarking against the restaurant/convenience food industry in general.

Gold Star Chili defines two key customer groups: direct customers who use Gold Star products and services, and indirect customers with whom Gold Star has other relationships. Direct customers are divided into six customer segments, determined by product use: restaurant customers, franchisees, franchise applicants, retail customers, retail wholesalers, and mail-order customers. Indirect customers include product suppliers, service suppliers, co-packers, brokers/consultants, shareholders, and regulatory agencies.

Gold Star's mission is to create lasting relationships based upon respect, trust, and support given to customers. More than 70 percent of customers eat in a Gold Star restaurant at least once a month, and 20 to 30 percent eat at least once per week. The loyalty of the customer base permits servers and store managers to get to know customers personally and learn much about consumer needs.

Franchisees are attracted by the relatively low investment required to join the Gold Star family of restaurants, the opportunity to operate a profitable business, and to benefit from the strong brand equity built into the Gold Star name. All department heads treat franchisees as internal customers, and have signed a pledge guaranteeing to return calls within 24 hours. If a franchisee reports a problem with product quality, Gold Star often hand-delivers replacement product the same day. Many franchisees build relationships through local store marketing. Many owner/managers are active in the community with sponsorships of teams or school programs. Gold Star provides owners with school achievement awards they can distribute to local schools.

Visit the company's website at www.goldstarchili.com to gain a perspective about the company, its menu, activities, and culture. Click the "About Us" link to read about the history and mission of the company. Using the information provided in the case and concepts developed in this chapter, answer the following:

1. What would be some moments of truth in Gold Star's environment?
2. What implications would the segmentation of Gold Star's customers have on their customer-focused practices?
3. What types of approaches should Gold Star consider to listen and learn from these customer groups?
4. Which approaches might be more effective with the different segments?
5. How would you design customer satisfaction surveys for Gold Star consumers and for franchisee (who are customers of the corporation)? What types of questions would you ask?

NOVEL CONNECT: CUSTOMER FOCUS

The complete Novel Connect case study, a fictitious example of a Baldrige application, can be found in the Baldrige Materials folder on the Premium website accompanying this book. If you have not read the Organizational Profile yet (see the case in Chapter 3), please do so first. Examine their response to Category 3 in the context of the Baldrige criteria for Category 3. What are their strengths? What are their weaknesses and opportunities for improvement? What specific advice, including useful tools and techniques that might help them, would you suggest?

BONUS MATERIALS

NOTES

1. Adapted from the article on Feargal Quinn by Polly Labarre in "Who's Fast in 2002," *Fast Company*, November 2001, 88–94.

2. Don Peppers & Martha Rogers, Customers "Don't Grow on Trees," Fast Company, July 2005, pp. 19–20. Fast Company by Feargal Quinn by Polly Labarre. Copyright © 2005 Mansueto Venturers LLC. Reprinted by permission.

3. AVIS 1992 Annual Report and *Quality Review*.

4. Jane Norman, "Royal Treatment Keeps Customers Loyal," *Cincinnati Enquirer*, May 31, 1998, E3, E5.

5. Steve Hoisington and Earl Naumann, "The Loyalty Elephant," *Quality Progress*, February 2003, 33–41.

6. "Revenge of the Irate Shopper," *Business Week*, April 17, 2006, 14.

7. Carl Sewell and Paul B. Brown, *Customers for Life* (New York: Doubleday-Currency, 1990).

8. Customer engagement was introduced in the 2009–10 Baldrige Criteria for Performance Excellence as a recognition of its increasing importance to organizations that compete in a global marketplace and in competitive local markets.

9. J. M. Juran, *Juran on Quality by Design* (New York: The Free Press, 1992), 7.

10. The Forum Corporation, "Customer Focus Research," executive briefing, Boston, 1988.

11. Model developed by National Quality Research Center, University of Michigan Business School for the American Customer Satisfaction Index, (ACSI). Cosponsored with American Society for Quality Control, 1994.

12. "Here's Mr. Macy," *Fortune*, November 28, 2005, 139–142.

13. Larry Selden and Geoffrey Colvin, "5 Rules for Finding the Next Dell," *Fortune*, July 12, 2004, 103–107.

14. J. M. Juran, *Juran on Quality by Design* (New York: The Free Press, 1992), Chapter 3.

15. Michael J. Stahl, William K. Barnes, Sarah F. Gardial, William C. Parr, and Robert B. Woodruff, "Customer-Value Analysis Helps Hone Strategy," *Quality Progress*, April 1999, 53–58.

16. "Time to Put Away the Checkbook: Now Fleet Needs to Bring Order to Its Furious Expansion," *Business Week*, June 10, 1996, 100.

17. Larry Selden and Geoffrey Colvin, "Will This Customer Sink Your Stock?" *Fortune*, September 30, 2002, 127–132.

18. Daniel H. Pink, "Out of the Box," *Fast Company*, October 2003, 104–106.

19. Robert D. Buzzell and Bradley T. Gale, *The PIMS Principles: Linking Strategy to Performance* (New York: The Free Press, 1987).

20. Rahul Jacob, "Why Some Customers Are More Equal Than Others," *Fortune*, September 19, 1994, 215–224.

21. David A. Garvin, "What Does Product Quality Really Mean?" *Sloan Management Review* 26, no. 1 (1984), 25–43.

22. The Forum Corporation, "Customer Focus Research," Executive briefing, Boston, 1988.

23. Dawn Fallik, "Hospitals Try to woo patients with amenities," *The Cincinnati Enquirer*, October 9, 2005, A28.

24. "Getting an Edge," *Across the Board*, February 2000, 43–48.

25. Bruce Nussbaum, "Designs for Living," *Business Week*, June 2, 1997, 99.

26. Diane Brady, "Will Jeff Immelt's New Push Pay Off for GE?" *Business Week*, October 13, 2003, 94–98.

27. James H. Drew and Tye R. Fussell, "Becoming Partners with Internal Customers," *Quality Progress* 29, no. 10 (October 1996), 51–54.

28. "How to Listen to Consumers," *Fortune*, 11 January, 1993, 77.

29. Patricia Sellers, "Gap's New Guy Upstairs," *Fortune*, April 14, 2003, 110–116.

30. Russ Westcott "Your Customers Are Talking, But Are You Listening?" *Quality Progress*, February 2006, 22–27.

31. Byron J. Finch, "A New Way to Listen to the Customer," *Quality Progress* 30, no. 5 (May 1997), 73–76.

32. "How to Listen to Consumers," *Fortune*, January 11, 1993, 77.

33. "KJ" is a registered trademark of the Kawayoshida Research Center.

34. This example is adapted from Donald L. McLaurin and Shareen Bell, "Making Customer Service More Than Just a Slogan," *Quality Progress* 26, no. 11 (November 1993), 35–39.

35. Larry Selden and Geoffrey Colvin, "5 Rules for Finding the Next Dell," *Fortune*, July 12, 2004, 103–107.

36. Ron Huston, "Made in the U.S.A," *Quality Digest*, December 2004, 22–25.

37. John A Goodman, Dianne Ward, and Scott Broetzmann, "It Might Not Be Your Product," *Quality Progress*, April 2002, 73–78.

38. "2004 Fast Company Customers First Awards," *Fast Company*, October 2004, 79–88.

39. Jane Carroll, "Mickey's Not for Everybody," *Across the Board*, February 2000, 11.

40. "Making Customer Loyalty Real: Lessons from Leading Manufacturers," Special Advertising Section, *Fortune*, June 21, 1999.

41. Richard S. Teitelbaum, "Where Service Flies Right," *Fortune*, August 24, 1992, 117–118; Southwest Airlines, available at http://iflyswa.com; Kevin Freiberg and Jackie Freiberg, *NUTS! Southwest Airlines' Crazy Recipe for Business and Personal Success* (Austin, TX: Bard Press, 1996); "Holding Steady," *Business Week*, February 3, 2003, 86.

42. Christopher Hart, "What Is an Extraordinary Guarantee?" *The Quality Observer* 3, no. 5 (March 1994), 15.

43. Teitelbaum (see note 41).

44. Karl Albrecht and Ronald E. Zemke, *Service America* (Homewood, IL: Dow Jones-Irwin, 1985), and John Goodman and Steve Newman, "Understanding customer behavior and complaints," *Quality Progress*, January 2003, 51–55.

45. John Goodman, Pat O'Brien, and Eden Segal, "Turning CFOs Into Quality Champions—Show Link to Enhanced Revenue and Higher Margins," *Quality Progress* 33, no. 3 (March 2000), 47–56.

46. John Goodman and Steve Newman, "Understanding customer behavior and complaints," *Quality Progress*, January 2003, 51–55

47. "Focusing on the Customer," *Fortune*, June 5, 1989, 226.

48. Christopher W. Craighead, Kirk R. Karwan, and Janis L. Miller. "The Effects of Severity of Failure and Customer Loyalty on Service Recovery Strategies," *Production and Operations Management*, Vol. 13, No. 4, Winter 2004, pp. 307–321.

49. Michael Schrage "Make No Mistake?" *Fortune*, December 11, 2001.

50. Craig Cochran, "Leveraging Customer Complaints into Customer Loyalty," *Quality Digest*, December 2004, 26–29.

51. BI 1999 Malcolm Baldrige National Quality Award Application Summary.

52. Gary Hallin and Robert J. Latino, "Eastman Chemical's Success Story," *Quality Progress*, June 2003, 50–54.

53. AT&T Corporate Quality Office, *Supplier Quality Management: Foundations* (1994), 52.

54. Myron Magnet, "The New Golden Rule of Business," *Fortune*, February 21, 1994, 60–64.

55. Patricia C. La Londe, "Surveys As Supplier Relationship Tool" ASQ's 54th Annual Quality Congress proceedings, Indianapolis, IN, 2000, 684–686.

56. "Pacesetters – Customer Service" *Business Week*, November 21, 2005, 85.

57. Eric Almquist and Carla Heaton, "Customers Are Disappearing," *Across the Board*, July–August, 2002, 61–63.

58. S. Rose, "The truth about online banking," *Money*, 29, 4, 2000, 114–122.

59. Robert Wollan. "CIOs and the battle for consumers," *Bank Systems & Technology*, January 31, 2006, http://www.banktech.com/news/showArticle.jhtml?articleID=177103806&pgno=2.

60. Minjoon Jun and Shaohan Cai, "The key determinants of Internet banking service quality: a content analysis," *International Journal of Bank Marketing*. 19, 7, 2001, 276–291.

61. "Behind the Numbers," *CIO Magazine*, November 2, 2000, available at http://www2.cio.com/.

62. Lucy McCauley, "How May I Help You?" *Fast Company*, March 2000, 93.

63. John Goodman, David DePalma, and Scott Breetzmann, "Maximizing the Value of Customer Feedback," *Quality Progress* 29, no. 12 (December 1996), 35–39.

64. Bob E. Hayes, "The True Test of Loyalty," *Quality Progress*, June 2008, 20–26.

65. Malcolm Baldrige National Quality Award Profiles of Winners, 1988–1993; and materials provided by Graniterock, including the 1992 Malcolm Baldrige Application Summary; Edward O. Welles, "How're We Doing?" *Inc.*, May 1991; Martha Heine, "Using Customer Report Cards Ups Service," undated reprint from Concrete Trader; and "Customer Report Cards at Graniterock," available at http://www.baldrigeplus.com.

66. Importance-performance analysis was first introduced by J.A. Martilla and J.C. James, "Importance-Performance Analysis," *Journal of Marketing*, 41, 1977, 77–79.

67. A. Blanton Godfrey, "Beyond Satisfaction," *Quality Digest*, January 1996, 15.

68. David C. Swaddling and Charles Miller, "Don't Measure Customer Satisfaction," *Quality Progress*, May 2002, 62–67.

69. Mike Carnell, "Gathering Customer Feedback," *Quality Progress*, 36, no. 1 (January 2003), 60.

70. Our thanks go to Brian Cundiff of LaRosa's Inc. for providing this case.

71. Fred Vogelstein. "Mighty Amazon," *Fortune*, May 26, 2003, 64.

72. 1997 Amazon.com, Inc. Annual Report, as quoted in the 2008 Amazon.com, Inc. Annual Report, 5.

73. 2002 Amazon.com, Inc. Annual Report, 1–2.

74. Robert D. Hof and Heather Green, "How Amazon Cleared the Profitability Hurdle," *Information Technology*, February 4, 2002, available at http://www. businessweek .com/magazine/content/02_05/b3768079.htm.

75. David Streitfeld, "Amazon.com's Data-Mining Technology Stirs Internet Privacy Controversy," *Washington Post*, as quoted by http://www.onlineathens.com/stories/082899/new_0828990006.shtml.

76. Matthew Boyle, "Best Buy's Giant Gamble," *Fortune*, April 3, 2006, 69–75.

77. Courtesy of Deer Valley Resort.

78. "Getting to very satisfied," *Fast Company*, February 2004, 32.

79. Adapted from Ralph F. Altman and Marilyn M. Helms, "Quantifying Service Quality: A Case Study of a Rental Car Agency," *Production and Inventory Management* 36, no. 2 (Second Quarter 1995), 45–50. Reprinted with permission of APICS—The Educational Society for Resource Management, Falls Church, VA.

80. Edna White, Ravi Behara, and Sunil Babbar, "Mine Customer Experiences," *Quality Progress*, July 2002, 63–67.

81. Susannah Fox, "The state of online banking, Pew Internet & American Life Project," November 2004. http://www.pewinternet.org/PPF/r/149/report_display.asp Accessed 2/8/06.

82. We thank Kim Olden of Gold Star Chili for providing basic company information; and Gold Star Chili, Inc., for granting permission to use this material.

High Performance Workforce Management

Outline

Quality Profiles: Sunny Fresh Foods and PRO-TEC Coating Company

The Evolution of Workforce Management

Principles of Engagement and Motivation
- Workforce Engagement
- Motivation

Designing High-Performance Work Systems
- Work and Job Design
- Empowerment
- Teamwork
- Developing and Empowering Teams
- Workplace Environment
- Engaging the Workforce in Process Excellence
- Skills for Team Leaders
- Skills for Team Members

Managing High-Performance Work Systems
- Compensation and Recognition
- Performance Management
- Assessing Workforce Engagement, Satisfaction, and Effectiveness

Sustaining High-Performance Work Systems
- Workforce Capability and Capacity
- Workforce Learning and Development

Workforce Focus in the Baldrige Criteria, ISO 9000, and Six Sigma

Summary of Key Points and Terminology

Quality in Practice: Training for Improving Service Quality at Honda

Quality in Practice: Improving Employee Retention Through Six Sigma

Review Questions

Discussion Questions

Projects, Etc.

Cases Golden Plaza Hotel
- The Hopeful Telecommuter
- Nordam Europe, Ltd.
- Novel Connect: Workforce Focus

Toyota's Georgetown, Kentucky, plant has been a multiple winner of the J. D. Power Gold Plant Quality Award. When asked about the "secret" behind the superior Toyota paint finishes, one manager replied, "We've got nothing, technology-wise, that anyone else can't have. There's no secret Toyota Quality Machine out there. The quality machine is the workforce—the team members on the paint line, the suppliers, the engineers—everybody who has a hand in production here takes the attitude that we're making world-class vehicles."[1] Deming emphasized that no organization can survive without good people; people who are improving. The human resource is the only one that competitors cannot copy, and the only one that can synergize, that is, produce output whose value is greater than the sum of its parts. In the words of Walter Wriston, former CEO of Citibank, "The person who figures out how to harness the collective genius of the people in his or her organization is going to blow the competition away."

Organizations are learning that to satisfy customers, they must first satisfy the workforce.

Aside from leadership, people are the most important component of performance excellence. FedEx, for instance, has found direct statistical correlation between customer and workforce satisfaction; a drop in workforce satisfaction scores precedes a drop in customer satisfaction by about two months. Researchers in service operations in industries ranging from communications to banking to fast food, have observed similar relationships.[2] They found that as workforce satisfaction increased, so did customer satisfaction and loyalty to the organization. If people were satisfied with their working conditions and jobs, they stayed with the company, became familiar with customers and their needs, had the opportunity to correct errors because the customers knew and trusted them, and had outcomes of higher productivity and high service quality. Customers of these firms became more loyal, thus providing more repeat business, were willing to complain about service problems so that employees could fix them, and benefited from the relationship by seeing lower costs and better service, thus leading to a new cycle of increased customer satisfaction. An extensive research study by the Gallup Organization of 7,939 business units in 36 companies showed that employee satisfaction and engagement were positively related to not only to customer satisfaction and loyalty, but also to productivity, profit, turnover, and safety.[3]

The Alliance for Work-Life Progress found that companies that provide job autonomy, challenging work and continuous learning opportunities, involvement in decision-making, supervisors support of workers' success on the job, and flexible work options have a happier and more effective workforce. One need only look at *Fortune* magazine's annual list of the "100 Best Companies to Work For" to support these findings. Although this list changes each year, Google has been at the top of the list. As *Fortune* noted,

> *At Google you can do your laundry; drop off your dry cleaning; get an oil change, then have your car washed; work out in the gym; attend subsidized exercise classes; get a massage; study Mandarin, Japanese, Spanish, and French; and ask a personal concierge to arrange dinner reservations. Naturally you can get haircuts onsite. Want to buy a hybrid car? The company will give you $5,000 toward that environmentally friendly end. Care to refer a friend to work at Google? Google would like that too, and it'll give you a $2,000 reward. Just have a new baby? Congratulations! Your employer will reimburse you for up to $500 in takeout food to ease your first four weeks at home. Looking to make new friends? Attend a weekly TGIF party, where there's usually a band playing. Five onsite doctors are available to give you a checkup, free of charge.*[4]

Fortune noted that among those factors that characterize a great place to work, two that have never changed and never will are trust and recognition. "Employees treasure the freedom to do their job as they think best, and great employers trust them. . . . Telling employees they're doing a great job costs nothing but counts big."[5] A survey by Annandale, Virginia-based MasteryWorks Inc. concluded that employees leave their organizations because of trust, observing that "Lack of trust was an issue with almost every person who had left an organization."[6]

The focus on customer satisfaction and flexibility to meet ever-changing customer demands new approaches to workforce management. By "workforce,"

Table 6.1 Key Workforce-Focused Practices for Performance Excellence

- Understand the key factors that drive workforce engagement, satisfaction, and motivation.
- Design and manage work and jobs to promote effective communication, cooperation, skill sharing, empowerment, innovation, and the ability to benefit from diverse ideas and thinking of employees and develop an organizational culture conducive to high performance and motivation.
- Create an environment that ensures and improves workplace health, safety, and security, and supports the workforce via policies, services, and benefits.
- Develop a performance management system based on compensation, recognition, reward, and incentives that supports high performance work and workforce engagement.
- Assess workforce engagement and satisfaction and use results for improvement.
- Assess workforce capability and capacity needs and use the results to capitalize on core competencies, address strategic challenges, recruit and retain skilled and competent people, and accomplish the work of the organization.
- Make appropriate investments in development and learning, both for the workforce and the organization's leaders.
- Manage career progression for the entire workforce and succession planning for management and leadership positions.

we mean everyone who is actively involved in accomplishing the work of an organization. This includes paid employees as well as volunteers and contract employees, and includes all team leaders, supervisors, and managers at all levels. In this chapter, we address key issues that organizations must focus on in order to build a workforce environment conducive to high performance. Table 6.1 summarizes key workforce-related practices for performance excellence. The Quality Profiles describe how Sunny Fresh Foods and PRO-TEC leverage these practices to achieve outstanding results.

Quality Profiles

Sunny Fresh Foods and PRO-TEC Coating Company

Sunny Fresh Foods (SFF) manufactures and distributes more than 160 different types of egg-based food products to more than 2,000 customers, such as quick service restaurants, schools, hospitals, convenience stores, and the military. A subsidiary of Cargill, Inc., SFF operates five manufacturing facilities with 620 employees. At SFF, a satisfied, motivated workforce is a vital ingredient of the company's successful operational and business performance. As measured in annual surveys, employees' rising level of satisfaction and their nearly complete awareness of how their jobs affect customers correlate directly with increasing customer satisfaction. From 2001 to 2004, more than 90 percent of employees answered "yes" to the following questions: "I understand the goals of Sunny Fresh." "I understand how my job affects the customer." and "My managers demonstrate and communicate focus on the customer." This far exceeds the national Hewitt engagement database of 82.5 percent, and is comparable to levels at several Baldrige Award recipients. SFF refers to its workers as "stakeholders" and ensures that they share in the benefits of continuous improvement. For example, although the base pay is set slightly below the industry midpoint for salaried workers, incentives can increase earnings above the 75th percentile. In addition, extensive reward and recognition systems, including monetary rewards for exemplary safety performance to extra vacation days for quality achievements, also help to motivate employees to contribute to the company's progress toward its improvement goals.

Innovations and a near perfect record for on-time delivery, which improved from 98.1 percent in 2001 to 99.8 percent in 2005, helped SFF earn sole-supplier status from several major national restaurant chains. Product rejections for SFF at all four plants have continuously declined. Reducing rework can provide significant productivity improvements: SFF's rework reduction percentage was measured at 15 percent from 2001 to 2002, 61 percent from 2002 to 2003, and 75 percent from 2003 to 2004. SFF was a 1999 and 2005 Baldrige Award recipient.

Established in 1990 as a joint venture between United States Steel Corporation and Kobe Steel Ltd. of Japan, PRO-TEC Coating Company provides coated sheet steel primarily to the U.S. automotive industry for use in manufacturing cars, trucks, and sport utility vehicles. PRO-TEC's 236 employees, called Associates, work in a state-of-the-art 730,000-square-foot facility in the small rural town of Leipsic, Ohio. With its heritage from U.S. Steel and Kobe Steel, PRO-TEC has developed its own unique culture centered around three fundamental concepts—ownership, responsibility, and accountability. From the beginning, the company incorporated numerous best-management practices, including lean manufacturing and continuous improvement, and relied on a well-trained, self-directed, empowered workforce to help the company become an industry leader. PRO-TEC routinely scores better than its competition in product quality, on-time delivery, service, product development, and overall quality.

PRO-TEC's Associates work in self-directed teams and are empowered, innovative leaders who fix problems as they are identified and use a continuous improvement process called "**I-to-I**" to **I**nitiate and **I**mplement process and product improvements. New Associates go through three weeks of orientation and training, followed by six months of mentoring. The company's commitment to Associate quality of life through safety, education and training, and an above-average compensation and "cafeteria-style" benefits package reflects the value PRO-TEC places on attracting and retaining its workforce. All Associates are salaried and participate in a profit sharing plan that has provided an average payout of approximately 15 percent of annual base pay. In a survey, Associates agreed or strongly agreed with the following statements: "The people I work with cooperate and work as a team," "I know what is expected of me at work," "I am supported when responding to customers' questions or problems," and "I am satisfied with my job." PRO-TEC has a turnover rate of less than 2 percent and has never had a layoff.

In a manufacturing environment that poses potential hazards, PRO-TEC's facility was designed with safety, health, and security in mind, along with minimizing environmental impacts. During an emergency, PRO-TEC's hierarchy of priorities are to first, preserve human life and the safety of Associates, responders, and the public; second, minimize impact to the environment; and, third, minimize property damage and disruption of operations. Since 2004, PRO-TEC has shown a 1.65 recordable injury frequency or below per 200,000 man-hours. PRO-TEC was a 2007 Baldrige recipient.

Source: Malcolm Baldrige National Quality Award, Profiles of Winners, National Institute of Standards and Technology, Department of Commerce.

THE EVOLUTION OF WORKFORCE MANAGEMENT

The role of people at work certainly changed as business and technology evolved over the years. Prior to the Industrial Revolution, skilled craftspeople had a major stake in the quality of their products because their families' livelihoods depended on the sale of those products. They were motivated by pride in their work as well as the need for survival. Frederick W. Taylor promulgated the departure from the craftsmanship concept. Taylor concluded that a factory should be managed on a scientific basis. So he focused on work methods design, the establishment of standards for daily work, selection and training of workers, and piecework incentives. Taylor separated planning from execution, concluding that foremen and workers of those days lacked the education necessary to plan their work. The foreman's role was to ensure that the workforce met productivity standards. Other pioneers of scientific management, such as Frank and Lillian Gilbreth and Henry Gantt, further refined the Taylor system through motion study, methods improvement, ergonomics, scheduling, and wage incentive systems.

The Taylor system dramatically improved productivity. However, it also changed many manufacturing jobs into a series of mundane and mindless tasks. Without a systems perspective and a focus on the customer, the responsibility for quality shifted from workers to inspectors, and as a result, quality eroded. The Taylor philosophy also contributed to the development of labor unions and established an adversarial relationship between labor and management that has yet to be completely overcome. Nevertheless, the Taylor system was the key force behind the explosive economic development of the twentieth century.

On the other hand, the Taylor system failed to exploit an organization's most important asset—the knowledge and creativity of the workforce. As executives at The Ritz-Carlton Hotel Company have stated, human beings don't serve a function, they have a purpose, and the role of the human resources function is to unleash the power of the workforce to achieve the goals of the organization.[7] Studies show that this new philosophy results in higher quality, lower costs, less waste, better utilization, increased capacity, reduced turnover and absenteeism, faster implementation of change, greater human skill development, and better individual self-esteem.[8] It also requires more attention to the psychological aspects of work—one of the key principles of the Deming philosophy.

Workforce management (which has also been widely known as **human resource management,** or **HRM**) consists of those activities designed to provide for and coordinate the people of an organization.[9] These activities include determining the organization's workforce needs; assisting in the design of work systems; recruiting, selecting, training and developing, counseling, motivating, and rewarding employees; acting as a liaison with unions and government organizations; and handling other matters of employee well-being. Human resource professionals need to foster competence and commitment among employees, develop the capabilities that allow managers to execute on strategy, help build relationships with customers, and create confidence among investors in the future value of the firm.[10] Many modern practices evolved from research at the Hawthorne Works of the Western Electric Company in the late 1920s. Interestingly, both Deming and Juran were working for Western Electric at the time, which may have influenced their views on quality and the workforce. Many other individuals contributed to understanding motivation, employee development, and effective job design.

The objectives of an effective workforce management system are to build a high-performance workplace and maintain an environment for quality excellence to enable employees and the organization to achieve strategic objectives and adapt to change.

Workforce management has assumed a strategic leadership role in modern organizations. For example, its importance at a company such as BI, a Baldrige recipient, is reflected in the fact that a senior vice president within the Office of the President leads the human resource function. Its principles have permeated the daily job responsibilities of managers at all levels. Developing skills through training and coaching, promoting teamwork and participation, motivating and recognizing employees, and providing meaningful communication are important human resource skills that all managers must practice to achieve performance excellence. At Xerox, for instance, managers are directly accountable for the development and implementation of workforce plans that support the quality goals of the company. Thus, understanding both the theory and practice of workforce management is a vital task for all managers.

PRINCIPLES OF ENGAGEMENT AND MOTIVATION

The foundation of high performance workforce management practices is built on understanding the principles of workforce engagement and motivation. As we have seen, workforce satisfaction is strongly related to customer satisfaction and ultimately, to business performance. A survey of 55,000 workers by the Gallup Organization found that four key employee attitudes, taken together, correlate strongly with higher profits:

- Workers feel they are given the opportunity to do what they do best every day.
- They believe their opinions count.
- They sense their fellow workers are committed to quality.
- They've made a direct connection between their work and the company's mission.

Workforce Engagement

One way is to create more satisfied employees is to engage them in their work and make them a part of the "fabric" of the organization. **Workforce engagement** refers to the extent of workforce commitment, both emotional and intellectual, to accomplishing the work, mission, and vision of the organization.

Organizations with high levels of workforce engagement are often characterized by high-performing work environments in which people are motivated to do their utmost for the benefit of their customers and for the success of the organization.

Engagement is manifest in Deming's concept of "pride and joy" in work that was reflected in his 14 Points. Engagement means that workers find personal meaning and motivation in their work, have a strong emotional bond to their organization, are actively involved in and committed to their work, feel that their jobs are important, know that their opinions and ideas have value, and often go beyond their immediate job responsibilities for the good of the organization. A compelling example occurred in 2002 when former Southwest Airlines CEO Herb Kelleher sent a letter concerning the current fuel cost crisis to the home of every employee. "Jet fuel costs three times what it did one year ago. Southwest uses 19 million gallons a week. Our profitability is in jeopardy," he wrote. He asked each worker to help by identifying a way to save $5 a day. That would, he explained in the letter, save Southwest $51 million annually. The response was immediate. A group of mechanics figured out how to reduce the costs of heating the aircraft. Another department offered to do its own janitorial work. Within six weeks of the letter being sent to the employees, this large organization found ways to save more than $2M.[11] Studies have shown that engagement leads to greater levels of satisfaction among the workforce and improves organizational performance.[12]

Organizations that provide an environment in which workers can do their best every single day foster engagement. Key factors contributing to engagement include performing meaningful work; having organizational direction, performance accountability, and an efficient work environment; and having a safe, trusting, and cooperative environment. In many nonprofit organizations, employees and volunteers are drawn to and derive meaning from their work because the work is aligned with their personal values. As the president of a successful travel agency once stated, "By maintaining an enjoyable, bureaucracy-free work environment, one that encourages innovative thinking . . . and honest communication, people are freed to concentrate solely on the needs of the clients."[13]

Workforce engagement is rooted in the psychology of human needs and supported by the motivation models of Maslow, Herzberg, and McGregor that we will discuss shortly. Employees are motivated through exciting work, responsibility, and recognition. Engagement provides a powerful means of achieving the highest order individual needs of self-realization and fulfillment. Employee engagement offers many advantages over traditional management practices as it:

- Replaces the adversarial mentality with trust and cooperation
- Develops the skills and leadership capability of individuals, creating a sense of mission and fostering trust
- Increases employee morale and commitment to the organization
- Fosters creativity and innovation, the source of competitive advantage
- Helps people understand quality principles and instills these principles into the corporate culture
- Allows employees to solve problems at the source immediately
- Improves quality and productivity[14]

Engagement begins with involvement. **Employee involvement (EI)** refers to any activity by which employees participate in work-related decisions and improvement activities, with the objectives of tapping the creative energies of all employees and improving their motivation. Tom Peters suggested involving everyone in everything, in such activities as quality and productivity improvement, measuring and monitoring results, budget development, new technology assessment, recruiting and hiring, making customer calls, and participating in customer visits.[15] Pete Coors, CEO of Coors Brewing, explained it simply, "We're moving from an environment where the supervisor says, 'This is the way it is going to be done and if you don't like it, go someplace else,' to an environment where the supervisor can grow with the changes, get his troops together and say, 'Look, you guys are operating the equipment, what do you think we ought to do?'"[16]

EI approaches can range from simple sharing of information or providing input on work-related issues and making suggestions to self-directed responsibilities such as setting goals, making business decisions, and solving problems, often in cross-functional teams.

EI initiatives are by no means new.[17] Many programs and experiments have been implemented over more than 100 years by industrial engineers, statisticians, and behavioral scientists. Early attempts influenced modern practices considerably. Unfortunately, these approaches lacked the complementary elements of TQ, such as a customer orientation, top management leadership and support, and a common set of tools for problem solving and continuous improvement.

The continuum of EI approaches is summarized in Table 6.2. As total quality matures in an organization, higher levels of employee involvement are evident. One of the most prominent employee involvement processes has been GE's "Work-Out" program.[18] Employees are encouraged to get together in a series of meetings to discuss reports, meetings, measurements, and approvals in their work area or department. The meetings are facilitated by an outside leader, but supervisors

Table 6.2 Levels of Employee Involvement

Level	Action	Primary Outcome
1. Information sharing	Managers decide, then inform employees	Conformance
2. Dialogue	Managers get employee input, then decide	Acceptance
3. Special problem solving	Managers assign a one-time problem to selected employees	Contribution
4. Intragroup problem solving	Intact groups meet weekly to solve local problems	Commitment
5. Intergroup problem solving	Cross-functional groups meet to solve mutual problems	Cooperation
6. Focused problem solving	Intact groups deepen daily involvement in a specific issue	Concentration
7. Limited self-direction	Teams at selected sites function full time with minimum supervision	Accountability
8. Total self-direction	Executives facilitate self-management in an all-team company	Ownership

Source: Jack D. Osborne, Linda Moran, Ed Musselwhite, and John H. Zenger, *Self-Directed Work Teams* (Burr Ridge, IL: Business One Irwin), p. 34.

are forbidden to attend, except for a brief opening appearance, until the last day of a three-day session. At the final Work-Out session, the supervisor, and often, his or her boss, are at the front of the room, with no idea of what has been discussed during the previous two days. The supervisor can only respond to items that the employees recommend in one of three ways:

1. Agree on the spot to implement the proposal.
2. Say no to the proposal.
3. Ask for more information.

Typically, more than 80 percent of the Work-Out recommendations received an immediate answer. For example, Armand Lauzon, head of plant services at GE Aircraft Engines factory in Lynn, Massachusetts, was confronted with 108 proposals at the end of a Work-Out session by his employees. He said yes to 100 recommendations on the spot, including one in which an employee had sketched a design for protective shields for machines on a brown paper bag. The employee asked whether his group could bid on the work. They got the bid when they quoted a cost of $16,000 versus an outside vendor's proposed cost of $96,000!

One of the easiest ways to involve employees on an individual basis is the **suggestion system**. An employee suggestion system is a management tool for the submission, evaluation, and implementation of an employee's idea to save cost, increase quality, or improve other elements of work such as safety. Companies typically reward employees for implemented suggestions. At Toyota, for instance, employees generate nearly 3 million ideas each year—an average of 60 per employee—of which 85 percent are implemented by management. Suggestion systems are often tied to incentives. Baldrige recipient Wainwright Industries developed a unique and effective approach that has been benchmarked extensively.[19] Suggestion programs were viewed as neither systematic nor continuous, and not woven into the fabric of daily operations. Their approach was designed to overcome these shortcomings in the following ways:

- Focusing employees on small, incremental improvements within their own areas of responsibility and control
- Recognizing all employees for their level of participation regardless of the value of the improvement
- Scaling team-based improvement efforts in a way that minimizes downtime and provides people with the tools and techniques to produce successful outcomes
- Positioning supervisors as the catalyst for cultural change through a coaching and support role in the employee involvement and improvement process

The process contains two main components: individual implemented improvements and team-based system improvements. Rather than submitting suggestions for someone else to approve and implement, employees are provided with training and given the responsibility to take the initiative to make improvements on their own without prior approval within the scope of their main job responsibilities. Upon making improvements, they complete a form to document what they have done and present it to the supervisors, whose role is not to approve or disapprove, but to acknowledge the improvement and to point out any issues that the employee needs to understand. All forms submitted during the week are placed into a random drawing for some type of award determined by the individual unit. At the end of each quarter, every individual who met his or her goal of implemented improvements receives some type of valued recognition. The team-based approach breaks large initiatives into smaller manageable projects. Breaking down large tasks allows employees to understand how their individual jobs fit into the big picture and maximizes participation reduces time requirements for any particular employee. Wainwright was able to cite more than 50 implemented improvements per employee per year, far exceeding those of most American and Japanese companies.

Fostering employee creativity has many benefits. Thinking about solutions to problems at work makes even routine work enjoyable; writing down the suggestions improves workers' reasoning ability and writing skills. Satisfaction is the by-product of an implemented idea and a job made easier, safer, or better. Recognition for suggestions leads to higher levels of motivation, peer recognition, and possible monetary rewards. Workers gain an increased understanding of their work, which may lead to promotions and better interpersonal relationships in the workplace. Table 6.3 summarizes strategies that can foster the success of suggestion systems.

Motivation

Understanding human behavior and motivation are major elements of Deming's Profound Knowledge discussed in Chapter 3. Deming spoke of motivation as being primarily intrinsic (internal), and was suspicious of external forms of motivation, such as incentives and bonuses. Although thousands of studies have been performed over the years on human and animal subjects in attempts to define and refine the concept of motivation, it remains an extremely complex phenomenon that still is not fully understood. As managers in a high performance environment take on the roles of coaches and facilitators, their skills in motivating employees become even more crucial.

Table 6.3 Success Factors for Suggestion Systems

1. Ensure that management, first and foremost, is involved in the program. Involvement should begin at the top and filter down through all levels until all employees participate.
2. Push decision making regarding suggestion evaluation to lower levels.
3. Gain union support by pledging no layoffs due to productivity gains from adopted suggestions.
4. Train everyone in all facets of the suggestion system. Improve problem-solving capability by promoting creative problem solving through the use of the seven basic statistical tools.
5. Resolve all suggestions within one month.
6. Encourage all suggestors to personally describe their idea to a supervisor, engineer, or manager.
7. Promote pride in work, and quality and productivity gains from suggestions, rather than the big cash awards if possible.
8. Remove ceilings on intangible suggestion awards. Revise evaluations of intangible suggestions to value them more on par with tangible suggestions.
9. Eliminate restrictions prohibiting suggestions regarding a worker's immediate work area.
10. Continuously promote the suggestion program, especially through supervisor support.
11. Trust employees enough to make allowances for generation, discussion, and submittal of suggestions during work hours.
12. Keep the program simple.

Source: From Muse and Finster, "A Comparison of Employee Suggestion Systems in Japan and the USA," University of Wisconsin Working Paper (1989). Reprinted with permission.

Saul W. Gellerman defined **motivation** as "the art of creating conditions that allow every one of us, warts and all, to get his work done at his own peak level of efficiency."[20] A more formal definition of motivation is *an individual's response to a felt need*. Thus, some stimulus, or activating event, must spur the need to respond to that stimulus, generating the response itself. For example, an individual worker given the goal or quality task of achieving zero defects on the parts that he or she produces may feel a need to keep his or her job. Consequently, the worker is motivated by the stimulus of fear and responds by carefully producing parts to achieve the goal. Another less insecure worker may feel the need for approval of his or her work by peers or superiors and be motivated by the stimulus of pride. The worker then responds to that need and that stimulus by producing high-quality parts.

There is no such thing as an unmotivated employee, but the system within which people work can either seriously impede motivation or enhance it.

Researchers have proposed many theories and models to describe how and why people are motivated. A theory is a way to describe, predict, and control what is observed in the world. Models graphically or symbolically show what a theory is saying in words. Often a model is so closely associated with a theory that the terms are used interchangeably. For example, Herzberg's Two-Factor theory describes two categories of factors in his model, called "maintenance" and "motivational" factors. Maintenance factors are conditions that employees have come to expect, such as a safe working environment, a reasonable level of job security, supervision, and even adequate pay. Workers in a situation with these conditions will not be dissatisfied, but maintenance factors generally do not provide any motivation to work harder. Motivational factors, such as recognition, advancement, achievement, and the nature of the work itself are less tangible, but do motivate people to be more committed to and satisfied with their work. From Herzberg's theory arose the concept of job enrichment. With job enrichment, employees gain a sense of fulfillment (satisfaction) from completion of every cycle of a task.

Table 6.4 A Classification of Motivation Theories

Motivation Theory	Pioneer/Developer	Type of Theory
Content Theories		
Hierarchy of Needs	Abraham Maslow	Need
Motivation and Maintenance	Frederick Herzberg	Need/satisfaction
Theory X-Y	Douglas McGregor	Managerial expectations
n-Ach, n-Aff, n-Pow	David McClelland	Acquired need
Process Theories		
Preference–Expectancy	Victor H. Vroom	Expectancy
Contingency	Porter and Lawler	Expectancy/reward
Goal Setting	Edward Locke	Goal
Path–Goal Theory of Leadership	Robert J. House	Goal
Environmentally Based Theories		
Operant Conditioning	B. F. Skinner	Reinforcement
Equity	J. Stacy Adams	Equity
Social Learning/Self-Efficacy	A. Bandura; Snyder and Williams	Social learning/self-efficacy

Acquiring cross-functional skills, working in teams, and increased empowerment are forms of job enrichment.

Theories and models are often classified according to common themes. James L. Bowditch and Anthony F. Buono categorize motivation theories as *content*, *process*, and *environmentally based* theories.[21] These theories are often studied in traditional management courses and are summarized in Table 6.4. In the behavioral sciences, as well as in the pure sciences, the originator of a theory is becoming more and more difficult to determine because many researchers' ideas often overlap. Thus, the information in Table 6.4 is merely suggestive of one or more names that have been associated with the development of the theory. The Bonus Materials folder for this chapter on the Premium website contains detailed descriptions of some of these key theories, and we suggest that you review them.

BONUS MATERIALS

Motivation theories can be applied to support high performance in any organization. For example, Herzberg's theory suggests that ignoring maintenance factors such as supervision, working conditions, salary, peer relations, status, and security will produce dissatisfaction and negatively impact the work environment, while enhancing the motivating factors will produce a positive effect. Thus, understanding and applying the theories should result in more effective designs of work systems and the work environment.

A rather puzzling situation exists in the theoretical and practical development of the concept of motivation. Very little new research has been performed on new concepts or approaches to motivation in recent years. Yet, the workplace has been the scene of constant and chaotic change that has spawned new motivational challenges, as Steers, et al. noted:

- Companies are both downsizing and expanding (often at the same time, in different divisions or levels of the hierarchy);
- The workforce is characterized by increased diversity with highly divergent needs and demands;

- Information technology has frequently changed both the manner and location of work activities;
- New organizational forms (such as those found in e-commerce) are now commonplace;
- Teams are redefining the notion of hierarchy, as well as traditional power distributions;
- The use of contingent workers is on the rise;
- Managing knowledge workers continues to perplex experienced managers across divergent industries; and
- Globalization and the challenges of managing across borders are now the norm instead of the exception.[22]

It is apparent that the chaotic content, process, and environment of motivation will make new demands on both workers and leader/managers. To the extent that any of the factors of motivation can be controlled, it is important to tailor motivation approaches to the needs and culture of the organization as well as to individual employees. Nucor, for instance, motivates employees through its innovative compensation structure. American Express focuses on helping employees reach a development goal using an approach called "label and link" (their employee surveys indicate that learning and development is a high priority). When managers give someone an assignment, they should label what they are doing and link it to what's important to that person.[23] Thus, by allowing employees to achieve their own unique levels of excellence and valuing them for what they contribute, they will be motivated to work towards meeting common organizational goals.

DESIGNING HIGH-PERFORMANCE WORK SYSTEMS

High-performance work *refers to work approaches used to systematically pursue ever-higher levels of overall organizational and human performance.*

Performance simply means the extent to which an individual contributes to achieving the goals and objectives of an organization. High-performance work is characterized by flexibility, innovation, knowledge and skill sharing, alignment with organizational directions, customer focus, and rapid response to changing business needs and marketplace requirements. The design and organization of work and jobs directly impacts quality, productivity, and effectiveness. Moreover, the wealth of knowledge and experience of the workforce is a strategic asset that should be leveraged.

Leading companies view the design of work systems in a fashion similar to the design of their key products and processes. For example, Sunny Fresh Foods designs its work systems to emphasize safety, quality, compensation and recognition, and employee development in support of individual development and SFF's long-term goals. Many of its work systems are unique to the industry. Examples are a "ramp-in" schedule in which new employees are allowed to work for only a specified number of hours to learn their jobs and minimize the potential for repetitive stress injuries; and a rotation system by which employees rotate to another workstation every 20 minutes. This format ensures that workers can understand and respond to product quality issues at any stage of the process and understand their internal customers; it also fights boredom, reduces repetitive stress injuries, and promotes learning. In addition, SFF uses a "buddy" system in which new employees are matched with high-performing experienced employees who serve as role models for operational excellence and behavioral competencies.

Work and Job Design

Work design refers to how employees are organized in formal and informal units, such as departments and teams. **Job design** refers to responsibilities and tasks assigned to individuals. Both work and job design are vital to organizational effectiveness and personal job satisfaction. Unfortunately, managers often do not understand workers' needs. One research study found that the top five employee needs in the workplace are (1) interesting work, (2) recognition, (3) feeling "in" on things, (4) security, and (5) pay. Managers, however, believed pay to be number one. Many companies understand that the best way to influence job satisfaction and motivate workers is to make jobs more rewarding, which can entail introducing variety into work, emphasizing the importance and significance of the job, providing more autonomy and empowerment, and giving meaningful feedback.

The design of work should provide individuals with both the intrinsic and extrinsic motivation to achieve quality and operational performance objectives.

An integrating theory that helps us understand how job design impacts motivation, satisfaction, and organizational effectiveness was proposed by Hackman and Oldham.[24] Their model, which has been validated in numerous organizational settings, is shown in Figure 6.1. The model contains four major segments:

1. Critical psychological states
2. Core job characteristics
3. Moderating variables
4. Outcomes

Figure 6.1 Hackman and Oldham Work Design Model

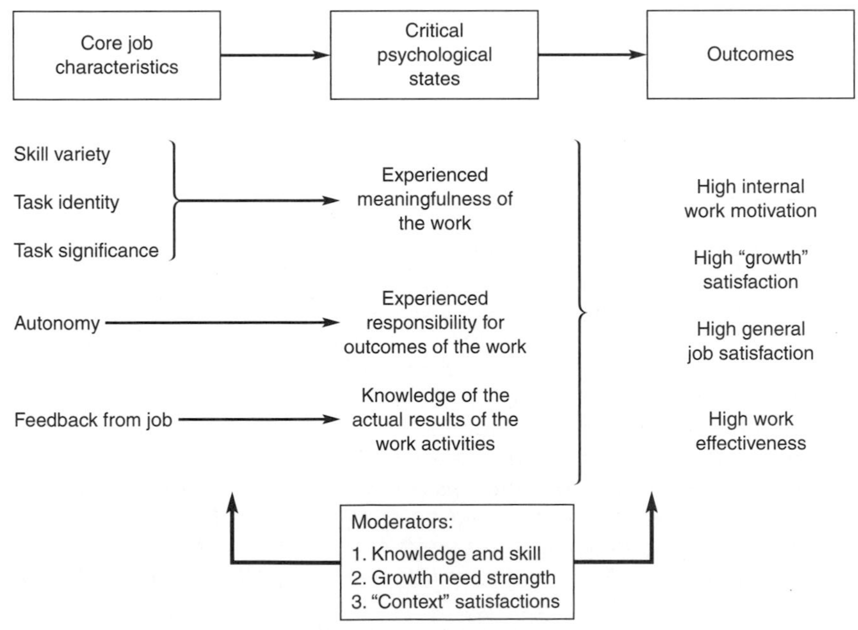

Source: From J. Richard Hackman and Greg R. Oldham, *Work Redesign*, Figure 4.6, p. 90. Copyright © 1980 by Addison-Wesley Publishing Co., Inc. Reprinted by permission of Addison Wesley Longman.

Three critical psychological states drive the model. *Experienced meaningfulness* is the psychological need of workers to have the feeling that their work is a significant contribution to the organization and society. *Experienced responsibility* indicates the need of workers to be accountable for the quality and quantity of work produced. *Knowledge of results* implies that all workers feel the need to know how their work is evaluated and the results of their evaluation.

Five core job characteristics have been identified as having an impact on the critical psychological states:

1. *Task significance:* The degree to which the job gives the participants the feeling that they have a substantial impact on the organization or the world, for example, solving a customer's problem rather than simply filing papers
2. *Task identity:* The degree to which the worker can perceive the task as a whole, identifiable piece of work from start to finish, for example, building an entire component rather than performing a small repetitive task
3. *Skill variety:* The degree to which the job requires the worker to use a variety of skills and talents, for example, physical skills in machining a part and mental skills in using a computer to track quality measurements
4. *Autonomy:* The degree to which the task permits freedom, independence, and personal control to be exercised over the work, for example, being able to stop a production line to solve a problem
5. *Feedback from the job:* The degree to which clear, timely information about the effectiveness of performance of the individual is available, not only from supervisors, but also from measurements that the worker might take directly

Quality is related in a primary or secondary sense to all five of these core job characteristics. Quality of a product or service is undoubtedly increased by a worker's dedicated application of skills, which is enhanced by task identity and a feeling of task significance. More directly, quality of work is enhanced by a job design that incorporates autonomy and feedback relating to quality characteristics. The key outcomes of high general job satisfaction and high work effectiveness can then be seen as results that define and reinforce excellent quality.

An example illustrating the Hackman and Oldham model stems from the experiences of one of the authors' students. She was a liberal arts major in college, and had worked at the art museum in the city where she attended college.

> *"After I'd been there for three years, I was able to work more autonomously, troubleshooting problems, taking steps to resolve those problems, and taking the initiative to improve my job. Guided by the museum's mission statement and my department's mission statement, I felt empowered to make changes or take steps to achieve the museum's strategic goals. After a while, I learned that my job wasn't entirely about following strict procedures. It was a real epiphany for me to figure out that I could make decisions and think on my feet to benefit a visitor, a volunteer, a co-worker, etc. For example, every year in May, the museum experiences a rush of school tours. It's the busiest time of year with school groups touring every day, Tuesday through Friday, on the hour or half-hour. The more years I worked through this crunch, the better equipped I was to promote positive changes for the "spring rush." Two years ago, the museum had a spring exhibit of Egyptian artifacts that was expected to attract many school tours. Working with many other departments like Security and Marketing, I was able to help implement school tours on Mondays when we were normally closed to the public and relieve some of the problems associated with the high demand."*[25]

Her comments show autonomy facilitated by empowerment. Her example of benefiting customers, volunteers, and coworkers demonstrate task significance and task identity, along with evidence of skill variety. She clearly experienced meaningfulness of the work and experienced responsibility. Although feedback is not addressed directly, it can be implied that she received feedback from the stakeholders regarding their experiences and her contribution to achieving them. This example particularly shows the importance of work design in jobs that have much direct customer contact, but it also applies to other types of jobs such as manufacturing where it can be more difficult to convey the significance of the task.

Several common approaches to work design—job enlargement, job rotation, and job enrichment—are supported by this model. IBM was apparently the first user of **job enlargement**, in which workers' jobs were expanded to include several tasks rather than one single, low-level task. This approach reduced fragmentation of jobs and generally resulted in lower production costs, greater worker satisfaction, and higher quality, but it required higher wage rates and the purchase of more inspection equipment. Job rotation is a technique by which individual workers learn several tasks by rotating from one to another. The purpose of job rotation is to renew interest or motivation of the individual and to increase his or her complement of skills. However, several studies showed that the main benefit was to increase workers' skills but that little, if any, motivational benefit could be expected.[26] Finally, **job enrichment** entails "vertical job loading" in which workers are given more authority, responsibility, and autonomy rather than simply more or different work to do.

Garvin presents an interesting example of how Japanese managers in the air-conditioning industry view job enrichment as important to quality.[27] In Japan, newly hired workers are trained so that they can do every job on the line before eventually being assigned to only one job. Training frequently requires 6–12 months, in contrast to the standard training time of one to two days for newly hired production workers in U.S. air-conditioning companies. The advantage of this "enriched" training is that workers are better able to track a defect to its source and can frequently suggest remedies to problems because they understand the entire process from start to finish. Job enrichment has been used successfully in a number of firms, notably AT&T, which experienced better employee attitudes and performance, as well as Texas Instruments, IBM, and General Foods.

In today's technology-dominated world, the nature of work is constantly changing. Today's entry-level workers are accustomed to new ways of interacting such as blogs and wikis (editable websites). For instance, about 1,500 employees of the financial firm Dresdner Kleinwort Wasserstein use wikis and blogs as virtual workspaces to create, edit, comment, and revise projects in real time. Another example is Basecamp®, a collaborative project-management service that lets groups of people post messages and files, create to-do lists, and set milestones for a project, all on simple private Web pages. One firm cut the time to complete a massive redesign project from at least two years to about eight months. New capabilities to use Basecamp® for interactive collaboration anywhere and anytime are available now via an i-Phone® application.[28] Thus, managers will constantly face new challenges to design work and jobs that are effective in meeting organizational goals and objectives as well as motivating and satisfying to the people in their organizations.

Empowerment

Empowerment is a shift of decision responsibility downward within an organization—from management to workers on the production floor or to service workers on the front lines. Empowerment requires employees to step outside their traditional roles and make decisions previously made by managers.[29]

Empowerment simply means giving people authority—to make decisions based on what they feel is right, have control over their work, take risks and learn from mistakes, and promote change.

The need to empower the entire workforce in order for quality to succeed has long been recognized. Juran wrote that "ideally, quality control should be delegated to the workforce to the maximum extent possible."[30] Five of Deming's 14 Points relate directly to the notion of empowerment:

Point 6: Institute training.
Point 7: Teach and institute leadership.
Point 8: Drive out fear. Create trust. Create a climate for innovation.
Point 10: Eliminate exhortations for the workforce.
Point 13: Encourage education and self-improvement for everyone.[31]

These points suggest that managers need to involve workers more directly in decision-making processes, thus giving them the security and confidence to make decisions, and providing them with the necessary tools and training.

Empowerment requires, as the management philosophy of Wainwright Industries states, *a sincere belief and trust in people*. Examples of empowerment abound. At AT&T, design engineers have the authority to stop a design, and line operators can stop the production line if they detect a quality problem. In Ritz-Carlton hotels, each employee can "move heaven and earth" and spend up to $2,000 to satisfy a customer. Because of the high level of empowerment given to individuals and teams at Texas Nameplate, the company disbanded its quality control department, assigning its activities to various people who do the work. Workers in the Coors Brewery container operation give each other performance evaluations, and even screen, interview, and hire new people for the line. A Corning Glass plant replaced 21 different jobs with one "specialist" job and gave employee teams broad authority over production scheduling and division of labor.

Empowerment can benefit customers who buy the organization's products and services. For instance, empowered employees can often reduce bureaucratic red tape that customers encounter—such as seeking a supervisor's signature—which makes customer transactions speedier and more pleasant. At Motorola, for instance, sales representatives have the authority to replace defective products up to six years after purchase, a decision that used to require top management approval. Anne Mulcahy, CEO of Xerox, describes the benefits of empowerment using an example about service representatives who handle customers' calls and take orders for supplies:

> *It's a demanding job that traditionally hasn't included much flexibility. Well, we had real issues in one of our call centers a few years ago. Effectiveness and morale were down; absenteeism and turnover were up. And when managers got tough, things only got worse. So we tried something radically different—we asked the reps to set their own schedules. After we did this, all our measures started heading in the right direction.*[32]

Empowered employees must have the wisdom to know what to do and when to do it, the motivation to do it, and the right tools to accomplish the task.[33] These requirements may mean significant changes in work systems, specifically, the following:

- Employees be provided education, resources, and encouragement
- Policies and procedures be examined for needless restrictions on the ability of employees to serve customers
- An atmosphere of trust be fostered rather than resentment and punishment for failure

- Information be shared freely rather than closely guarded as a source of control and power
- Workers feel their efforts are desired and needed for the success of the organization
- Managers be given the required support and training to adopt a "hands-off" leadership style
- Employees be trained in the amount of latitude they are allowed to take. Formulating decision rules and providing role-playing scenarios are excellent ways of teaching employees[34]

Empowerment also means that leaders and managers must relinquish some of the power that they previously held. This power shift often creates management fears that workers will abuse this privilege. However, experience shows that frontline workers generally are more conservative than managers. For example, companies that have empowered employee groups to evaluate performance and grant pay raises to their peers have found that they are much tougher than managers were.

Empowerment gives managers new responsibilities. They must hire and develop people capable of handling empowerment, encourage risk taking, and recognize achievements. Giving employees information about company finances and the financial implications of empowered decisions is also important. At DuPont's Delaware River plant, management shares cost figures with all workers.[35] By sharing this information, management believes that workers will think more for themselves and identify with company goals. To help employees make decisions on issues affecting production, a department manager at the Eastman Chemical plant in Texas supplied operators with a daily financial report that showed how their decisions affected the bottom line. As a result, department profits doubled in four months and quality improved by 50 percent as employees began suggesting cost-saving improvements.[36]

David Geisler suggests that what traditionally passes for empowerment does not allow employees to use their skills and talents to the maximum.[37] He promotes the concept of **self-determination** as an extension of empowerment (see Table 6.5 for contrasts) and argues that: 1) individual and organizational effectiveness result when employees are allowed to achieve their own unique levels of excellence; and 2) personal power arises when employees are certain that the organization is free of barriers, they are valued for what they contribute, and they are allowed to express themselves.

Teamwork

Perhaps one of the most significant organizational changes that has been facilitated by total quality is teamwork. A single person rarely has enough knowledge or experience to understand all aspects of the most important work processes; thus, team approaches are essential for achieving performance excellence. Teams, and the need for such team skills as cooperation, communication, and group decision making, represent a fundamental shift in how the work is performed in the United States and most countries in the Western world. Although organizations traditionally were formed around task or work groups, the focus of teams and teamwork has taken on a new meaning in today's work environment. Teamwork breaks down barriers among individuals, departments, and line and staff functions, an action prescribed by one of Deming's 14 Points. Teams provide opportunities to individuals to solve problems that they may not be able to solve on their own. Employees who participate in team activities feel more empowered, are

*A **team** is a small number of people with complementary skills who are committed to a common purpose, set of performance goals, and an approach for which they hold themselves mutually accountable.*[38]

Table 6.5 Employee Empowerment Versus Self-Determination

Employee Empowerment	Employee Self-Determination
1. The employee is hired with technical skills to do a specific job within organizational parameters.	1. The employee is hired with personal power to self-determine his or her own unique level of personal excellence.
2. The employee is given specific duties and tools to do a job.	2. The employee is given work processes and individual objectives to achieve alignment with the organization's mission, vision, and goals.
3. The organization provides the culture and work processes with which the employee is to perform a job.	3. The organization provides the opportunity within the culture and work processes for the employee to meet objectives.
4. The organization identifies expected behavior and performance for the employee.	4. The organization expects unique behavior and performance from the employee in work processes and individual objectives.
5. The organization facilitates and mentors desired behavior and level of power, including practices and techniques to instill a feeling of power, so expected performance is reached.	5. The organization does not have barriers that hinder self-assurance, self-worth, and opportunity, allowing the employee to use personal power and the need for self-determination to choose what allows him or her to achieve a unique level of personal excellence.
6. The employee meets, does not meet, or exceeds the expected performance of a job.	6. The employee's unique level of personal excellence meets, does not meet, or exceeds the objectives of the job aligned with the organization's mission, vision, and goals.
7. The organization responds to the employee's performance by reacting neutrally, negatively, or positively to the level of excellence achieved. The employee reacts to the organization's response to the level of excellence achieved neutrally, negatively, or positively.	7. The organization and employee respond to the level of employee performance by considering the unique level of excellence achieved and the impact of the work on the organization's mission, vision, and goals.
8. The organization decides to keep the employee in a job, terminate the employee, or promote the employee. The employee decides to keep the job, separate from the organization while keeping the job, or be promoted inside or outside the organization.	8. The organization and employee identify where the employee's unique level of excellence will be most mutually beneficial to the organization and the employee, enhancing self-assurance, self-worth, and opportunity.
9. The cycle of jobs continues.	9. The journey of excellence continues.

Source: Reprinted with permission from David Geisler, "The Next Level in Employment Empowerment," *Quality Progress*, Vol. 38, No. 6, pp.48–52.

more satisfied with the rate of improvement in quality in their companies, and receive better training in both job-related and problem-solving skills. Teams also help organizations to capitalize on diverse ideas, cultures, and thinking of employees.

Teams encourage free-flowing participation and interaction among its members. FedEx has thousands of Quality Action teams; Boeing Airlift and Tanker Division has more than 100 integrated product teams (IPTs) that are typically made up of engineering, work-team, customer, and supplier representatives. Granite Rock, with fewer than 400 employees, has about 100 functioning teams, ranging from 10 corporate quality teams to project teams, purchasing teams, task forces, and function teams composed of people who do the same job at different locations.

Teams often perform a variety of problem-solving activities, such as determining customer needs, developing a flowchart to study a process, brainstorming to discover opportunities for improvement, selecting projects, recommending corrective

Figure 6.2 Teams at Baptist Hospital, Inc.

People	Service	Quality	Financial	Growth
Baptist University Board Education Planning Committee Employee Benefits Team Bright Ideas Diversity Council Faith in Action Operation Teen	Patient Loyalty Teams: • Culture • Communication • Customer Loyalty • Physician Loyalty • Employee Loyalty	Clinical Excellence Teams: • Acute Myocardial • Congestive Heart Failure • Pneumonia Skin Care Integrity Team Medication Event Team Environment of Care Committee	Revenue Cycle Teams: • Payment Compliance • Patient Registration • Billing and Collections • Managed Care Pricing • Documentation & Coding • Late/Lost Charges • Charge Master	Service Lines: • Oncology • Cardiology • Orthopedics

Source: Malcolm Baldridge National Quality Award Application Summary. National Institue of Standards and Technology, U.S. Department of Commerce, 2003. Courtsey of Ava Abney, VP Quality & Safety, Baptist Health Care. Reprinted with permission.

actions, and tracking the effectiveness of solutions. Teams may also assume many traditional managerial functions. For example, an assembly team at GM's Saturn plant interviews and hires its own workers, approves parts from suppliers, chooses its equipment, and handles its own budget.

Many types of teams exist in different companies and industries (see Figure 6.2 for an example of teams at Baptist Hospital, Inc.). Among the most common are the following:

- *Management teams:* Teams consisting mainly of managers from various functions, such as sales and production that coordinate work among teams
- *Natural work teams:* Teams organized to perform entire jobs, rather than specialized, assembly line-type work
- *Self-managed teams (SMTs):* Specially empowered work teams defined as "a highly trained group of employees, from 6 to 18, on average, fully responsible for turning out a well-defined segment of finished work—also known as **self-directed work teams**. The segment could be a final product, like a refrigerator or ball bearing; or a service, like a fully processed insurance claim. It could also be a complete but intermediate product or service, like a finished refrigerator motor, an aircraft fuselage, or the circuit plans for a television set."[39] More information on the evolution and activities of SMTs can be found in the Bonus Materials folder for this chapter on the Premium website for this chapter.

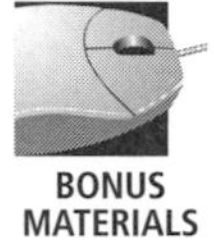
BONUS MATERIALS

- *Virtual teams:* A relatively new format in which team members communicate by computer, take turns as leaders, and jump in and out as necessary.[40] These types of teams use a combination of Internet, e-mail, phone, fax, video conferencing, PC-to-PC connections, and shared computer screen technologies to get their jobs done.
- *Quality circles:* Teams of workers and supervisors that meet regularly to address work-related problems involving quality and productivity.[41]
- *Problem-solving teams:* Teams whose members gather to solve a specific problem and then disband (The difference between these and quality circles is that quality circles usually remain in existence for a much longer period of time.)
- *Project teams:* Teams with a specific mission to develop something new or to accomplish a complex task (Project teams have been in use since World War II, and probably before that. However, project teams recently gained a new measure of importance and respect in the context of Six Sigma.)

Management teams, natural work teams, self-managed teams, and virtual teams typically work on routine business activities—managing an organization, building a product, or designing an electronic system—and are an integral part of how work is organized and designed. Quality circles, problem-solving teams, and project teams, on the other hand, work more on an ad-hoc basis to address specific tasks or issues, often relating to quality improvement. Also, natural work teams, self-managed teams, and quality circles typically are *intraorganizational;* that is, members usually come from the same department or function. Management teams, problem-solving teams, virtual teams, and project teams, are usually *cross-functional;* they work on specific tasks or processes that cut across boundaries of several different departments regardless of their organizational home. An example of a cross-functional team is the platform team approach to automotive vehicle development introduced by Chrysler.[42] This cross-functional team approach brings together professionals from engineering, design, quality, manufacturing, business planning, program management, purchasing, sales, marketing, and finance to work together to get a new vehicle to market. Today, all automobile manufacturers develop products using similar cross-functional team approaches.

Virtual teams present special challenges to managers.[43] Virtual teaming requires special attention to communication, technology, sponsorship, and leadership issues. For example, the team leader needs to be able to tackle issues that he or she might not have encountered with traditional teams. One of the biggest disadvantages is the lack of experience members have working with one another. They are not aware of each other's work standards and cannot scrutinize these ethics as consistently as traditional teams. This issue can be overcome by developing operating agreements by all team members, spelling out what they commit to do or not to do. Another factor is that communication is more complex because body language, voice inflection, and other communication cues are eliminated. Thus, virtual team members must be able to excel in relating their own ideas, and also understand the information others are trying to convey.

Quality Circles Quality circles were one of the first types of teams to focus specifically on quality. Although quality circles were popularized and implemented on a widespread basis in Japan beginning around 1960 and are often attributed to Kaoru Ishikawa of the University of Tokyo, history suggests that the concept was first implemented by Daniel Willard at the Baltimore and Ohio Railroad as part of "The Cooperative Plan," which began from joint worker-management meetings designed to raise and evaluate service-quality-related issues and suggestions.[44] The Union of Japanese Scientists and Engineers (JUSE) estimated that registration in quality circles in Japan grew from 400 members in 1962 to 200,000 members in 1968 to more than 700,000 members in 1978. Today, millions of workers are involved. Toyota, for example, uses the problem-solving skills of circles and engineers to their advantage. When the firm found that 50 percent of its warranty losses were caused by 120 large problems and 4,000 small problems, the set of large problems were assigned to their engineers. The set of small problems were given to their quality circles.[45]

Quality circle concepts were not only known but also used by some U.S. firms in the late 1960s, according to existing evidence.[46] However, the concept received widespread publicity when a team of managers for Lockheed Missiles and Space Division in California made a trip to Japan in 1973 to view quality circles in action, and subsequently established them at Lockheed. After the success of the Lockheed program became known, many other manufacturing firms—including Westinghouse, General Electric, Cincinnati Milacron, Ford Motor Company, Dover Corporation, and Coors Brewing Company—established quality circle programs or began using similar team problem-solving approaches. Later, service organizations such as hospitals, school systems, and state and federal governmental units started quality circle programs.[47] After about five or six years of use in the United States, however, quality circles were labeled a "fad." Much of the feeling of disappointment in their promise resulted from management's failure to understand how to implement and manage them successfully. Still, they represented a starting point for many U.S. companies to develop and test out ideas on teamwork and participative management, and many are still active today. More importantly, they paved the way for more progressive kinds of teams.

Internationally, quality control circles are still alive and well. In fact, the 2005 International Convention on Students' Circles, held in Lucknow, India, drew approximately 2,500 attendees from 20 countries. The program featured contests such as a poster competition to illustrate quality concepts, and other quality-related activities. The participants came from various industries, business houses, organizations and student delegates from 99 educational institutions. Annual conventions continue to be held, and there is no indication that student enthusiasm is waning.[48]

Six Sigma Project Teams Teams are vital to Six Sigma projects because of the interdisciplinary nature of such projects. Six Sigma projects require a diversity of skills that range from technical analysis, creative solution development, and implementation. Thus, Six Sigma teams not only address immediate problems, but also provide an environment for individual learning, management development, and career advancement. Six Sigma teams are comprised of several types of individuals:

- *Champions:* Senior-level managers who promote and lead the deployment of Six Sigma in a significant area of the business. Champions understand the philosophy and tools of Six Sigma, select projects, set objectives, allocate resources, and mentor teams. Champions own Six Sigma projects and are responsible for their completion and results; typically they also own the process that the project is focused on improving. They select teams, set strategic direction, create measurable objectives, provide resources, monitor performance, make key implementation decisions, and report results to top management. More importantly, champions work toward removing barriers—organizational, financial, personal—that might inhibit the successful implementation of a Six Sigma project.
- *Master Black Belts:* Full-time Six Sigma experts who are responsible for Six Sigma strategy, training, mentoring, deployment, and results. Master Black Belts are highly trained in how to use Six Sigma tools and methods and provide advanced technical expertise. They work across the organization to develop and coach teams, conduct training, and lead change, but are typically not members of Six Sigma project teams.
- *Black Belts:* Fully-trained Six Sigma experts with up to 160 hours of training who perform much of the technical analysis required in Six Sigma projects, usually on a full-time basis. They have advanced knowledge of tools and DMAIC methods, and can apply them either individually or as team leaders. They also mentor and develop Green Belts. Black Belts need good leadership and communication skills in addition to technical skills and process knowledge. They should be highly motivated, eager to gain new knowledge, and well-respected among their peers. As such, Black Belts are often targeted by the organization as future business leaders.
- *Green Belts:* Functional employees who are trained in introductory Six Sigma tools and methodology and work on projects on a part-time basis, assisting Black Belts while developing their own knowledge and expertise. Typically, one of the requirements for receiving a Green Belt designation is to successfully complete a Six Sigma project. Successful Green Belts are often promoted to Black Belts.
- *Team Members:* Individuals from various functional areas who support specific projects.

The roles of the Six Sigma champion and the Master Black Belt leader are similar to those of the champion and sponsor described in Table 6.6. The role of a Black Belt is

Table 6.6 Team Member Roles, Responsibilities, and Performance Attributes

Role Name	Responsibility	Definition	Attributes of Good Role Performance
Champion	Advocate	The person initiating a concept or idea for change/improvement	• Is dedicated to seeing it implemented • Holds absolute belief it is the right thing to do • Has perseverance and stamina
Sponsor	Backer; risk taker	The person who supports a team's plans, activities, and outcomes	• Believes in the concept/idea • Has sound business acumen • Is willing to take risk and responsibility for outcomes • Has authority to approve needed resources • Will be listened to by upper management
Team leader	Change agent; chair; head	A person who • Staffs the team or provides input for staffing requirements • Strives to bring about change/improvement through the team's outcomes • Is trusted by followers to lead them • Has the authority for, and directs the efforts of, the team • Participates as a team member • Coaches team members in developing or enhancing necessary competencies • Communicates with management about the team's progress and needs • Handles the logistics of team meetings • Takes responsibility for team records	• Is committed to the team's mission and objectives • Has experience in planning, organizing, staffing, controlling, and directing • Is capable of making and maintaining channels that enable members to do their work • Is capable of gaining the respect of team members; serves as a role model • Is firm, fair, and factual in dealing with a team of diverse individuals • Facilitates discussion without dominating • Actively listens • Empowers team members to the extent possible within the organization's culture • Supports all team members equally • Respects each team member's individuality
Facilitator	Helper; trainer; adviser; coach	A person who • Observes the team's processes and team members' interactions and suggests process changes to facilitate positive movement toward the team's goals and objectives • Intervenes if discussion develops into multiple conversations • Intervenes to skillfully prevent an individual from dominating the discussion or to engage an overlooked individual in the discussion the team as a whole	• Is trained in facilitating skills • Is respected by team members • Is tactful • Knows when and when not to intervene • Deals with the team's process, not content • Respects the team leader and does not override his or her responsibility • Respects confidential information shared by individuals or within the team • Will not accept facilitator role if expected to report to management information that is proprietary to the team

Facilitator		• Assists the team leader in bringing discussions to a close • May provide training in team building, conflict management, and so forth	• Will abide by the ASQ Code of Ethics
Timekeeper	Gatekeeper; monitor	A person designated by the team to watch the use of allocated time and remind the team members when their time objective may be in jeopardy	• Is capable of assisting the team leader in keeping the team meeting within the predetermined time limitations • Is sufficiently assertive to intervene in discussions when the time allocation is in jeopardy • Is capable of participating as a member while still serving as a timekeeper
Scribe	Recorder; note taker	A person designated by the team to record critical data from team meetings (Formal "minutes" of the meetings may be published and distributed to interested parties.)	• Is capable of capturing on paper, or electronically, the main points and decisions made in a team meeting and providing a complete, accurate, and legible document (or formal minutes) for the team's records • Is sufficiently assertive to intervene in discussions to clarify a point or decision in order to record it accurately • Is capable of participating as a member while still serving as a scribe
Team members	Participants: subject matter experts	The persons selected to work together to bring about a change/improvement, achieving this goal in a seated environment of mutual respect, sharing of expertise, cooperation, and support	• Are willing to commit to the purpose of the team • Are able to express ideas, opinions, and suggestions in a nonthreatening manner • Are capable of listening attentively to other team members • Are receptive to new ideas and suggestions • Are even-tempered and able to handle stress and cope with problems openly • Are competent in one or more fields of expertise needed by the team • Have favorable performance records • Are willing to function as team members and forfeit "star" status

Source: John E. Bauer, Grace L. Duffy and Russell T. Wescott, eds. *The Quality Improvement Handbook*, 2006, Table 3.1, pp.43–44. Copyright © 2002 American Society for Quality Press, Milwaukee, WI. Reprinted by permission.

similar to a staff quality expert, while Green Belts are typically given the team leadership role.

More than any other type of organizational structure, the team structure depends on cooperation, communication, and clarity. Eckes estimates that 60 percent of failures of Six Sigma teams are due to failures in the "mechanics" of team operations, as opposed to poor project selection or improper use of tools.[49] He cites contributing factors such as lack of application of meeting skills, improper use of agendas, failure to determine team member roles and responsibilities, lack of setting and keeping ground rules, and lack of appropriate facilitative behaviors. Electronic communications, virtual teams, and motivation were discussed earlier, but they must also be used effectively if teams are to be successful.

Developing and Empowering Teams

Jumping into team approaches without adequate planning is an invitation to disaster. Robbins and Finley list 14 reasons why teams fail, although they are quick to point out that no one reason, and often multiple reasons, explain why it happens.[50] Their list includes organizational problems (bad policies, stupid procedures, bleary vision, ill-conceived reward system, confused goals, unresolved roles, antiteam culture), leadership problems (bad leadership, insufficient feedback and information, the wrong tools), and individual/team barriers (mismatched needs, hidden agendas, personality conflicts, lack of team trust, unwillingness to change). Thus, managers need to carefully evaluate how teams are introduced in their organizations and address team building as a critical work process.

Team implementation should always begin with a period of investigation, reflection, and soul searching. Many companies rush out and form the wrong kind of teams for a specific job. For example, quality circle-type teams cannot achieve the same type of results as a cross-functional problem-solving team or a self-managed team. Managers should examine their organization's goals, objectives, and culture to evaluate its readiness to develop and support team-based initiatives. This step may be the most difficult portion of the process, because it demands a hard self-appraisal of the organization as a whole. One enthusiastic manager can often get teams going, but solid support at a number of managerial levels is necessary to keep them going. Managers should then analyze the work required. Teams take a lot of maintenance, and if the work can be done faster and better by a single person, a team should not be used.

Self-managed teams (SMTs) represent the greatest challenge. Organizations that use SMTs typically arrive at them through one of two routes: organizational start-up with SMTs in place, or transformations from more limited team structures. The second is often a next logical step after other types of employee involvement programs reach maturity. Figure 6.3 shows the approach used by Boeing Airlift and Tanker Programs to develop self-managed teams, a result of a historic agreement between the company and union to support employee participation and empowerment. Some evidence of the effectiveness of this process is that the work of the Boeing C-17 Stuffed Tailcone team earned it a first place finish in the 2007 International Team Excellence Competition, sponsored by ASQ's Team and Workplace Excellence Forum.[51]

The key stages of a team's life cycle are called forming, storming, norming, performing, and adjourning.[52]

Teams go through a fairly predictable cycle of formation and growth, regardless of their charge and goals. Teams are generally formed in organizational settings by direction from a manager, leader, or governing body. They are typically given a broad objective (operate this

Figure 6.3 Boeing A&T Team Development Process

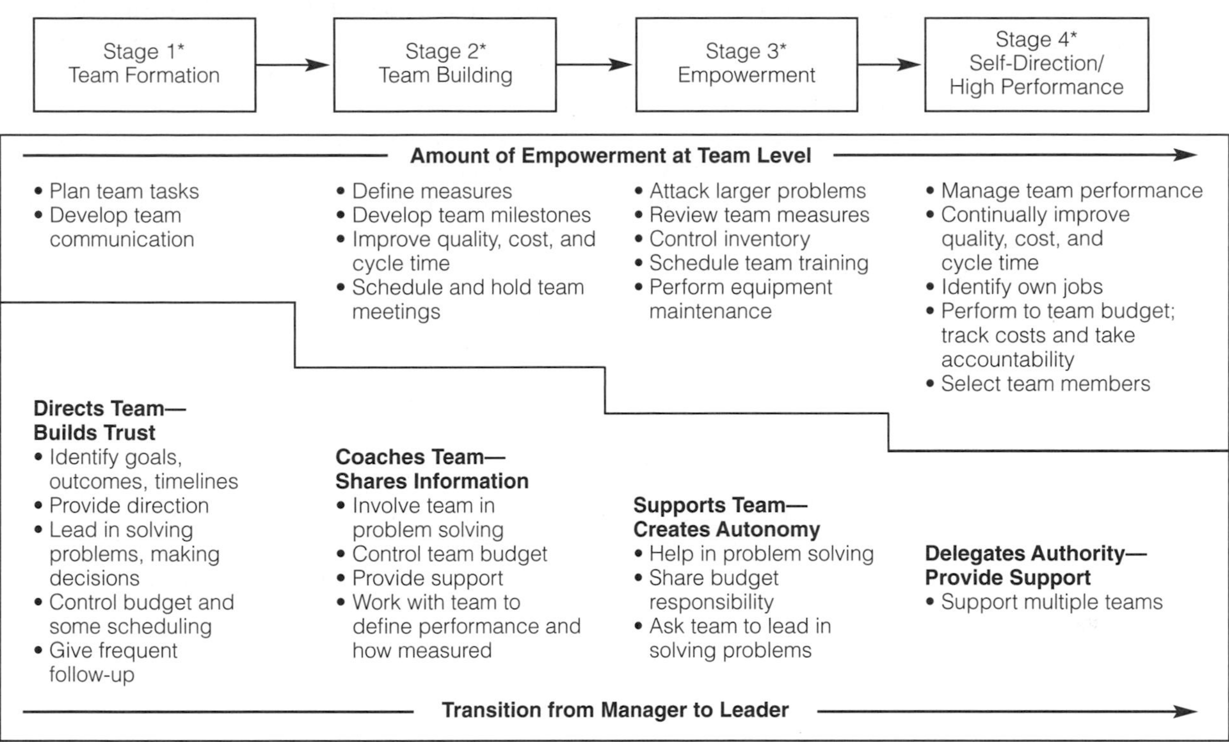

* Stages may overlap under certain conditions. Team maturity and level of process improvement already in place may impact stage application.

Source: Courtesy of Boeing Airlift and Tanker Programs.

process according to certain guidelines, put a man on the moon in this decade, design a process to make cookies using elves as workers, etc.). The team may also be given a time frame and resource limits, if it is a project team.

Forming takes place when the team is introduced, meets together, and explores issues of their new assignment. *Storming* occurs when team members disagree on team roles and challenge the way that the team will function. The third stage, *norming*, takes place when the issues of the previous stage have been worked out, and team members agree on roles, ground rules, and acceptable behavior when doing the work of the team. Stage four, *performing*, characterizes the productive phase of the life cycle when team members cooperate to solve problems and complete the goals of their assigned work. In the *adjourning* phase, the team wraps up the project, satisfactorily completes its goals, and prepares to disband or move on to another project.

Peter Scholtes, a leading authority on teams for quality improvement, suggested 10 ingredients for a successful team. These items provide some guidance during the forming stage and can mitigate issues that might lead to "storming":

1. *Clarity in team goals.* As a sound basis, a team agrees on a mission, purpose, and goals.
2. *An improvement plan.* A plan guides the team in determining schedules and mileposts by helping the team decide what advice, assistance, training, materials, and other resources it may need.

3. *Clearly defined roles.* All members must understand their duties and know who is responsible for what issues and tasks.
4. *Clear communication.* Team members should speak with clarity, listen actively, and share information.
5. *Beneficial team behaviors.* Teams should encourage members to use effective skills and practices to facilitate discussions and meetings.
6. *Well-defined decision procedures.* Teams should use data as the basis for decisions and learn to reach consensus on important issues.
7. *Balanced participation.* Everyone should participate, contribute their talents, and share commitment to the team's success.
8. *Established ground rules.* The group outlines acceptable and unacceptable behaviors.
9. *Awareness of group process.* Team members exhibit sensitivity to nonverbal communication, understand group dynamics, and work on group process issues.
10. *Use of the scientific approach.* With structured problem-solving processes, teams can more easily find root causes of problems.[53]

Teams require various leadership and maintenance activities, especially if the team is large and the project or work assignment is complex. Typical roles that members must assume are the champion, sponsor, team leader, facilitator, timekeeper, scribe, and team member.

Workplace Environment

Because employees are key stakeholders of any organization, their health, safety, and overall well-being are important factors in the work environment. Health and safety have always been priorities in most companies, but working conditions now extend beyond basic issues of keeping the work area safe and clean. For example, as we learn more about ergonomic-related disorders such as carpal tunnel syndrome, employers have an even greater responsibility to incorporate health and safety factors into human resource plans. Ames Rubber Corporation, for example, has nine major long-range plans in effect, covering such areas as affirmative action, health benefits and safety, and accident reduction. FedEx teaches employees how to handle dangerous goods, lift heavy packages correctly, and drive safely. Johnson & Johnson's Ethicon Endosurgery Division, in Blue Ash, Ohio, has a Wellness Center with exercise rooms and equipment to support employees in their manufacturing and R&D facility. Employees can use the center before or after working hours or during their breaks. In addition, those workers who are assembling products get regular, programmed "ergonomic" breaks every few hours, where they are required to do exercises designed to prevent repetitive motion injuries. Texas Instruments uses safety, environmental, and ergonomic experts to institute preventive actions, investigate accidents, and provide training. At The Ritz-Carlton Hotel Company, L.L.C., project teams configure the best combination of technology and procedures to eliminate causes of safety and security problems. Other responsibilities include providing reasonable accommodations to workers with disabilities or ensuring that male and female employees are protected from sexual harassment from fellow workers and others.

Most companies provide many opportunities that contribute to the quality of working life. They can provide personal and career counseling, career development and employability services, recreational or cultural activities, day-care, special leave for family responsibilities or for community services, flexible work hours, outplacement services, and extended health care for retirees. Texas Instruments, for example, has a company-sponsored employee association called "Texins" that provides fitness activities, recreational clubs, and family events; the company also offers free counseling for personal and relationship problems. Granite Rock sponsors company picnics and parties at regular intervals. Solectron provides American culture and citizenship classes, wellness committees to communicate health information programs, employee assistance programs, sports and recreation programs, and tuition reimbursement. All of these opportunities contribute to creating a more productive, safer, and more enjoyable work environment.

SAS Institute, Inc., consistently one of *Fortune*'s "100 Best Companies to Work For," is a high-tech software development company based in Cary, North Carolina. SAS has a people-focused founder and CEO in the person of James Goodnight. Perhaps the most eye-opening policy of the firm is its mandated seven-hour workday. No "all-nighters" are expected of SAS employees. The multibillionaire Goodnight sets the example by leaving the office at 5 P.M., sharp. Many of the lavish employee perks at the sprawling corporate campus are family and lifestyle-oriented, from daycare centers, lactation rooms, a Montessori school, and a college prep private high school, to a 55,000-square-foot athletic facility, free massages, free car washes, and end-of-year bonuses. The payoff? SAS has about 4 percent turnover in an industry where 20 percent is the norm.[54]

How can organizations determine what types of programs and benefits are best for their workforce? The answer is simple: Ask them! Genencor, a joint venture between Genentech and Corning based in Palo Alto, California, regularly polls its employees about what benefits they enjoy and which they would like the company to offer. Many of them go beyond the expected, such as free train and bus passes, and bikes and cars that can be signed out by employees who rely on public transportation and need to run errands during the day. They also provide on-site services such as dry cleaning, photo processing, eyeglass repair, a travel agency, and even an oil change service. While these programs might seem expensive, the HR director notes that it represents "a drop in the bucket" compared with the cost of recruiting and training new employees.[55]

Engaging the Workforce in Process Excellence

People are key to process excellence. They create innovative ideas, initiate and implement improvement projects, and apply tools and techniques to solve problems. It is not so much a question of what things people need to know as it is a question of what things they need to know *how* to do. One team or one team member can make or break an improvement project or a Six Sigma initiative. People skills can be learned, but often take more time than is available for a single project; thus, they should be a routine part of every employee's educational program.

Compared to the technical tools for gathering and analyzing data, the "soft skills"—those that involve people—such as project management and team facilitation, are more difficult to teach and learn.

Some of the essential elements for effective process excellence from a people perspective are a *shared vision* and *behavioral skills*. A shared vision can unify a team and provide the motivation for successfully implementing a project or change initiative. Developing one generally requires team discussions early on; unfortunately, inexperienced project leaders frequently bypass these discussions in an effort to get the project underway. People who are technically oriented often neglect behavioral skills, thinking that such skills are unnecessary in order to solve technical problems. Behavioral skills require both knowledge and practice. Part of Deming's foundation for "profound knowledge" (Chapter 3) was the requirement to study, learn, and use psychology to improve quality.

Skills for Team Leaders

As we discussed, team members often assume the role of project leaders and project managers and yet must defer to superior knowledge of other team members and take on roles as followers. In an insightful book on team-based project management, James Lewis observed that people skills needed by project managers could also be easily applied to team members.[56] These skills include the following:

- Conflict management and resolution
- Team management
- Leadership skills
- Decision making
- Communication
- Negotiation
- Cross-cultural training

Conflict management involves dealing proactively with disagreements that may occur when two or more technical experts get together. Team management involves ensuring that project members remain focused on the goals, time frame, and costs of their part of the project. Leadership skills require that the project leader guide the work of the team, including team development, while managing upward to the project champion and outward to other project teams and team leaders. Decision making requires that good decisions be made in a timely fashion. Communication channels must be established and maintained throughout the course of the project. Negotiation is needed in order to secure the resources required for successful project completion. Cross-cultural training may involve team members of other nationalities, or it may simply involve people from different functional areas with divergent points of view. In either case, it is extremely important for team members to be able to listen and learn about different perspectives on shared project goals from team and nonteam people who may have widely differing thoughts about issues under consideration.

Skills for Team Members

Perhaps the two areas of greatest importance in team functioning for project team members are meetings and shared decision making. Meetings are important because they consume considerable valuable time of team members. Shared decision making is important because most individuals in organizations have more practice in receiving direction from a supervisor, or making an individual decision in their own workplace. Shared decisions are new territory for many individuals.

Peter Scholtes provides some rules for effective meetings:[57]

- Use agendas.
- Have a facilitator.
- Take minutes.
- Draft the next agenda.
- Evaluate the meeting.
- Adhere to the "100-mile" rule.

Scholtes suggests the use of detailed agendas that include topics, a sentence about the importance of each, who will present them, the estimated time for each topic, and the type of item, such as discussion, decision, or information topics. A facilitator can keep the discussion on time and on target, prevent anyone from dominating or being overlooked, and help bring the discussion to a close. A scribe who takes minutes can record subjects, decisions, and who will be responsible for actions taken. Drafting the next agenda at the end of the meeting serves to set a plan of action for going forward. Evaluating the meeting incorporates a continuous improvement step. Adhering to the "100-mile" rule requires a commitment to focus on the meeting so clearly that "no one should be called from the meeting unless it is so important that the disruption would occur even if the meeting was 100 miles away from the workplace."[58]

Decision-making techniques abound in quality improvement literature. One of the most powerful is called the nominal group technique (NGT), developed to provide a way to prioritize and focus on important project objectives in the project definition stage.[59] One of the major advantages of the technique is that it balances the power of each individual involved in the decision process. Key steps in the process include the following:

1. Request that all participants (usually 5–10 persons) write or say which problem or issue they feel is most important.
2. Record all problems or issues.
3. Develop a master list of problems or issues.
4. Generate and distribute to each participant a form that numbers the problems or issues in no particular order.
5. Request that each participant rank the top five problems or issues by assigning five points to their most important perceived problem and one point to the least important of their top five.
6. Tally the results by adding the points for each problem or issue.
7. The problem or issue with the highest number is the most important one for the team as a whole.
8. Discuss the results and generate a final ranked list for process improvement action planning.[60]

This approach provides a more democratic way of making decisions and helps individuals to feel that they have contributed to the process.

MANAGING HIGH-PERFORMANCE WORK SYSTEMS

Workers want to be treated with respect, have their basic needs addressed, understand the goals of their work, and have managers recognize their unique individual differences. They want to be given challenging, meaningful work in which they can experience pride of ownership, personal learning and growth, and be rewarded fairly and equitably when they perform.

Individuals are motivated both intrinsically and extrinsically. The design of interesting work and jobs, empowerment, teamwork, and a great work environment can provide intrinsic motivation, but invariably the question "What's in it for me?" ultimately gets asked. In managing high-performance work systems, managers need to provide fair and motivating compensation and recognition, evaluate performance and coach employees for improvement, and understand the workforce's attitudes about engagement and satisfaction in order to continually improve work systems and the work environment.

Compensation and Recognition

> ***Compensation and recognition*** *refer to all aspects of pay and reward, including promotions, bonuses, and recognition, either monetary and nonmonetary or individual and group.*

Compensation is always a sticky issue, closely tied to the subject of motivation and employee satisfaction. Although money can be a motivator, it often causes employees to believe they are being treated unfairly, and forces managers to deliver negative messages. Eventually, it diminishes intrinsic motivation and creates win–lose situations. The objectives of a good compensation system should be to attract, retain, and not demotivate employees. Other objectives include reducing unexplainable variation in pay (think about Deming's principles) and encouraging internal cooperation rather than competition. Most companies still use traditional financial measures, such as revenue growth, profitability, and cost management, as a basis for compensation; more progressive organizations use quality measures such as customer satisfaction, defect prevention, and cycle time reduction to make compensation decisions.

Many progressive companies now base compensation on the market rate for an individual with proven capabilities, and then make adjustments as capabilities are increased, along with enhanced responsibilities, seniority, and business results. Medrad, for example, bases its pay range on market pricing rather than on an internally focused job-evaluation process. A cross-functional project team developed a market-based compensation system that reinforced the goals and objectives of the company and pays base pay in the top quartile of similar positions in the market. The team redesigned the pay structure to:

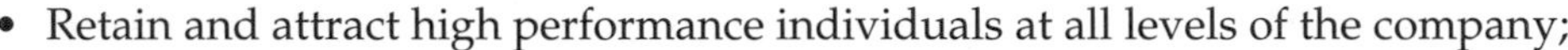

- Retain and attract high performance individuals at all levels of the company;
- Align individuals and teams with corporate goals;
- Support Medrad's culture and employee growth and development; and,
- Maintain the view of base pay as one component of total compensation that also includes variable incentive pay, gainsharing, benefits, and other rewards and programs.

Medrad uses role profiles to match all jobs to market salary data. The new pay equation combines market value for a given job with the unique qualities of the individual. Every job now has a market range with a target zone. Medrad's goal is to move employees to their target zone over time, based on their performance and experience.

Many companies link compensation to company track records, unit performance, team success, or individual achievement.[61] At Kaiser Aluminum, such performance-based compensation incentives led to an 80 percent improvement in productivity and 70 percent decrease in poor quality costs over five years.[62] Team-based pay and **gainsharing**, an approach in which all employees share savings equally, is gaining in popularity and importance. Compensation for individuals is sometimes tied to the acquisition of new skills, often within the context of a continuous improvement program in which all employees are given opportunities to broaden their work-related competencies. STMicrolectronics' compensation system rewards employees through pay increases and promotions as skills are developed and demonstrated. A variable pay program encourages individual, team, unit, and company goal achievement for all employees.

Nucor Corporation, one of the nation's largest steel producers, is well-known for having succeeded in attacking quality, productivity, participation, and compensation issues.[63] Nucor has more than 11,000 employees in plants in the United States and is the nation's largest steel recycler. The company's management philosophy is clearly described on the company's website:[64]

> *The company's success comes from its more than 11,000 employees. Nucor seeks to hire and retain highly talented and productive people. Nucor has a simple, streamlined organizational structure to allow employees to innovate and make quick decisions. The company is highly decentralized, with most day-to-day operating decisions made by the division general managers and their staff. The organizational structure at a typical division is made up of only three management layers:*
>
> *General Manager*
> *Department Manager/Supervisor/Professional*
> *Hourly Employee*
>
> *Employee relations at Nucor are based on four clear-cut principles:*
>
> 1. *Management is obligated to manage Nucor in such a way that employees will have the opportunity to earn according to their productivity.*
> 2. *Employees should be able to feel confident that if they do their jobs properly, they will have a job tomorrow.*
> 3. *Employees have the right to be treated fairly and must believe that they will be.*
> 4. *Employees must have an avenue of appeal when they believe they are being treated unfairly.*

By implementing these four basic principles within a relatively simple organizational structure, Nucor has been able to attract and retain highly talented and productive employees.

To emphasize the importance of employees as a vital part of the corporate culture and its ongoing success, the cover of the company's Annual Report contains the individual names of every single employee. All employees, from the president on down, have the same benefits; the only differences in individual pay are related to responsibilities. The corporate website states: "Nucor takes an egalitarian approach to providing benefits to its employees. That is, the upper levels of management do not enjoy better insurance programs, vacation schedules, or holidays. In fact, certain benefits such as Nucor's Profit Sharing, Scholarship Program, Employee Stock Purchase Plan, Extraordinary Bonus, and Service Awards Program are not available to Nucor's officers. Senior executives do not enjoy traditional perquisites such as company cars, corporate jets, executive dining rooms, or executive parking places."[65]

Workers at Nucor's nonunion steel mills earn base hourly rates that are less than half of the going rate for unionized steelworkers. Nucor uses pay incentives designed around groups of 40 to 50 workers, including secretaries and senior managers. They offer four basic compensation plans:

1. *Production:* Employees involved directly in manufacturing are paid weekly bonuses based on the production of their work groups. Most Nucor employees are covered under this system. Typically, these bonuses are based upon anticipated production time or tonnage produced, depending upon the type of facility. The formulas are non-discretionary, based upon established production goals. This plan creates peer pressure for everyone to perform well and, in some facilities, is tied to on-time attendance. No bonus is paid if equipment is not operating, creating strong emphasis on maintaining equipment in top

operational condition at all times. Maintenance personnel are assigned to each shift, and they participate in the bonus along with the other bonus groups. Production supervisors are part of the bonus group and receive the same bonus as the employees they supervise. The bonus can average 80–170 percent of the base wage and has no set limit.

2. *Department Manager:* Department managers earn incentive bonuses paid annually based primarily on the return on investment of their facility. These bonuses can be as much as 100 percent of base salary. All facilities have a common and clear goal because these bonuses are based on easily understood plans.
3. *Non-Production and Non-Department Manager:* This group includes accountants, engineers, clerks, receptionists, and others. Their bonus is based primarily on their facility's return on investment. The bonus is based on a written plan that is clear and accessible to employees. Each operation receives a monthly report showing its year-to-date return on investment. This chart is posted in the employee cafeteria or break area together with a chart of the bonus payments. This bonus can be as much as 28 percent of their salary.
4. *Senior Officer:* Nucor senior officers do not have employment contracts. They receive no profit sharing pension or retirement plan. Their base salaries are set at less than what executives at comparable companies receive. A significant part of senior officer compensation is based on Nucor's return on stockholder's equity, above certain minimum earnings. A portion of pre-tax earnings is placed into a pool that is divided among the officers in bonuses that are about 60 percent cash and 40 percent stock. If Nucor does well, the officers' pay is well above average, as much as several times base salary. If not, the officers' compensation is only base salary.

In addition to these established bonus plans, Nucor has periodically issued an extraordinary bonus to all employees, except officers, in years of particularly strong company performance. This bonus has been as high as $2,000 for each employee. During downturns, managers at Nucor frequently find that their bonuses are cut, even while hourly workers continue to receive theirs, based on production rates. However, despite the tough times, it maintained their policy of no layoffs as it had throughout the history of the current company. More about the Nucor story can be found on its website at http://www.nucor.com.

Recognition and Reward Recognition and rewards can be monetary or nonmonetary, formal or informal, individual or group. Rewards might include trips, promotional gifts, clothing, time off, plaques and certificates, or simple recognition ceremonies. In many cases, sincere nonmonetary recognition is valued more by employees than money or gifts, which can often create resentment. Whatever the recognition, it should have symbolic value that employees can inspire employees in the future. A great example was related in an article in *Fast Company* magazine.[66]

> *When the chicken strips at a KFC sold out that day, a customer had to wait while employees cooked up a fresh batch. Latoya Gardner, working the lunch shift, apologized for the delay and offered the man a free side item so he wouldn't go hungry. She and her team members "were just so attentive to me," the customer recalls. It was no ordinary customer experience—and*

the man, it turned out, was no ordinary customer. As senior VP of public affairs at Yum Brands Inc. (formerly Tricon Global Restaurants), KFC's parent company, Jonathan Blum was in a position to recognize employees going the extra mile. Blum hurried back to nearby Yum headquarters, grabbed one of his signature awards—a seat belt on a plaque, symbolizing the "roller coaster" nature of the restaurant business—and returned to the KFC to fete Gardner. "In front of all her peers, I said, 'You didn't know that I work at Yum. I want you to know how proud I am of you.' " Today, a photo of a beaming Gardner hangs in Blum's office. In Yum parlance, they call it "catching people doing things right"—taking time to notice and publicly reward employees who exceed expectations. "People innately want to be recognized for their hard work," says Yum chairman and CEO David Novak.

Recognition has important benefits to both employees and their organizations. Employees understand that their efforts make a difference, that the organization values its people and cares about their success, thus reinforcing their pride and self-esteem (remember Deming's focus on "pride and joy" in work). Organizations receive greater motivation, loyalty, and effort from recognized employees along with increased performance, thereby improving their advantages over competitors.[67]

Recognition provides a visible means of promoting quality efforts and telling employees that the organization values their efforts, which stimulates their motivation to improve.

Not everyone values the same types of recognition and reward. A Conference Board study found that a combination of cash and noncash recognition works better for clerical and hourly workers than for managers and professional/technical employees; for these groups, compensation-based incentives such as stock options are more successful.[68] Thus, any recognition and reward initiative should be tailored to the specific needs and wants of the employee segment.

Certain key practices lead to effective recognition and rewards:

- *Give both individual and team awards.* At The Ritz-Carlton, individual awards include verbal and written praise and the most desirable job assignments. Team awards include bonus pools and sharing in the gratuity system. Many companies have formal corporate recognition programs, such as the Xerox President's Award and Team Excellence Award.
- *Tie rewards to measurable performance.* A Monsanto Company chemical plant ties worker bonuses to results at individual units and rewards workers for helping to prevent accidents.[69] When Custom Research, Inc. attains a specific corporate goal, the entire company is taken on a trip to destinations such as San Francisco and Disney World!
- *Involve everyone.* Recognition programs should be available to everyone in the organization, including both front-line employees and senior management, and employees should participate in their design. Solectron rewards groups by buying lunch for entire divisions and bringing in ice cream for everyone in the plant. At Monsanto, different programs exist in different plants—all developed with the participation of workers. Bonus plans that failed had been ones decreed by corporate headquarters, rather than those formulated in cooperation with employees.
- *Drive behaviors that support organizational values and high performance.* Leading companies recognize and reward behavior, not just results. Figure 6.4 shows the different types of recognition and reward mechanisms used by Premier, Inc.

Figure 6.4 Premier, Inc. Recognition and Reward Mechanisms

Award	Recognition
The Premier Award	Value-based high performance
The Premier Team Award	Team-based high performance
Cash Spot Bonus	Project/Goal achievement
Premier "Turtle" Award	Innovation "sticking your neck out"
Employee Choice Award	Spontaneous values behavior
Service Recognition (5, 10, 15, 20, 25, 30 yr)	Service years with Premier
Commission Programs	Sales objectives
Unit Recognition programs	Behaviors and achievement

Source: Premier, Inc. Recognition and Reward Mechanisms; Premier Preformance Management Process, 2007 Malcolm Baldridge Application Summary, NIST, U.S. Department of Commerce. Reprinted with permission.

- *Publicizing extensively*. Many companies recognize employees through newsletters, certificates and pins, special breakfasts or luncheons, and annual events such as competitions. Motorola, for example, developed a worldwide Total Customer Satisfaction (TCS) team competition. Teams compete locally, regionally, and internationally to attend the final one-day, corporate-wide competition held at a resort each year. Teams are scored on such criteria as project selection, teamwork, analysis techniques, remedies, results, institutionalization (permanence, deployment, and team growth from the project), and presentation. Corporate-wide results over eight years have been impressive, with an estimated savings of $2.4 billion per year.[70] Making recognition public reinforces its significance, and having top managers preside in giving recognition sends an important message that they really understand and appreciate employees' efforts.
- *Making recognition fun*. Domino's Pizza stages a national Olympics, in which teams from the company's three regions compete in 15 events based on 15 job categories, such as doughmaking, driving, answering the telephone, and delivery. Winners, standing on platforms while the Olympic theme is played, receive medals, checks, and other forms of recognition. The finals are broadcast live to commissaries around the country. Domino's Olympics provides an excellent way to benchmark efforts throughout the corporation; winners attend three days of discussion with upper management to talk about what's good about the company, what needs improvement, and how those improvements can be made.[71]

Performance Management

Considerable truth can be found in the statement, "How one is evaluated determines how one performs." This reality can be dangerous. Analog Devices, a successful Massachusetts analog and digital equipment manufacturer, embraced TQ but found its stock price steadily declining. One of its key measures (on which managers were rewarded) was new product introduction time, with an objective of reducing it from 36 to 6 months. The product development team focused on this objective; as a result, engineers turned away from riskier new products and designed mundane derivatives of old products that no longer met customers' needs. The company subsequently scrapped that goal.[72]

Performance appraisal is a process for evaluating and generating information about employees' effectiveness and efficiency at work.[73] However, performance appraisal is an exceedingly difficult activity. Organizations typically use performance appraisals for a number of reasons: to provide feedback to employees who can then recognize and build on their strengths and work on their weaknesses, to determine salary increases, to determine training needs, to identify people for promotion, and to deal with human resource legalities. As such, they can provide a paper trail to fight wrongful-discharge suits and act as a formal warning system to marginal employees.[74] Many leading organizations use performance appraisal for changing corporate culture.

Conventional appraisal processes typically involve setting objectives for a certain period of time (typically for the year ahead), either unilaterally or jointly by the manager with his or her subordinate. Objectives might focus on development of knowledge or skills, results such as output and productivity, or behavior. Objective setting is followed by a supervisory review of accomplishments, strengths and weaknesses, or personal characteristics of the subordinate related to the job at the end of the review period. Often, the form used for performance rating has 10 to 15 tangible and intangible categories, such as quantity of work, quality of work, works well with others, takes initiative, and so on, to be rated on a five- or seven-point scale from "excellent" to "unsatisfactory" or "poor." The performance appraisal interview may be accompanied by announcements of raises, bonuses, or promotions. In some cases, company policy dictates a certain distribution of results, such as "no more than 10 percent of any department's employees may be rated as excellent" or "merit raises or bonuses will only be paid to employees who are rated as excellent or very good."

Dissatisfaction with conventional performance appraisal systems is common among both managers, who are the appraisers, and workers, who are appraised. General Motors, for example, discovered that 90 percent of its people believed they were in the top 10 percent. How discouraging is it to be rated lower? Many managers are inclined to give higher ratings because of potential negative impacts. Numerous research studies over the past several decades have pointed out the problems and pitfalls of performance appraisals.[75] Many legitimate objections can be made:[76]

- They tend to foster mediocrity and discourage risk taking.
- They focus on short-term and measurable results, thereby discouraging long-term planning or thinking and ignoring important behaviors that are more difficult to measure.
- They focus on the individual and therefore tend to discourage or destroy teamwork within and between departments.
- The process is detection-oriented rather than prevention-oriented.
- They are often unfair, as managers frequently do not possess observational accuracy.
- They fail to distinguish between factors that are within the employees' control and system-determined factors that are beyond their control.

One approach that has overcomes many of these objections is called **360-degree feedback**.[77] In an ideal 360-degree approach, a group of individuals who interact with the employee (or team) on a frequent basis participate in both the goal-setting process and the performance appraisal process. This group might include suppliers, clients, peers, internal customers, managers, and subordinates. The process involves two-way communication in which both parties discuss such needs as service levels, response times, accuracy of work and so on, which are often expressed as written service contracts. At the end of the performance period, selected representatives who participated in the goal setting evaluate how well the goals of the service contracts have been met, and provide feedback. The final performance appraisal consists of discussing an aggregation of the comments and ratings with

Figure 6.5 Premier Performance Management Process

Step	Process
1	Establish Expectation (Define expected outcomes & behaviors)
2	Manage Performance (Provide performance feedback and support)
3	Measure and Reward Performance (Assess performance (Performance Appraisals), Reward appropriate outcomes/behaviors)
4	Improve Performance (Provide development and growth (IDP) for continued improvement and growth)

Source: Premier Performance Management Process, 2007 Malcolm Baldridge Application Summary, NIST, U.S. Department of Commerce. Reprinted with permission.

the employee, and serves as a process for setting goals for the next period and for employee development. Because the approach is new, little systematic research has been performed on its effectiveness; however, user feedback has been positive.

Performance appraisals are most effective when they are based on the objectives that support the strategic directions of the organization, best practices, and continuous improvement.

An effective performance management process should focus on feedback and improvement. Figure 6.5 shows a typical process that is used at Premier, Inc. It begins with a clear picture of employee expectations in Step 1. As part of the strategic planning process, all goals and actions are cascaded to units and employees through Deployment Grids that outline employee performance goals to ensure line of sight to Corporate and BU Goal achievement. Managers meet individually with each employee to review and agree upon expectations and to identify support needed to accomplish goals. Plans are developed by managers and employees to support Unit Goal achievement. In Step 2, managers provide on-going feedback, coaching, and redirection, as appropriate, to individuals and teams to encourage goal achievement and Core Values based behaviors. Both informal and formal interaction and review takes place throughout the year, with a minimum of two formal review meetings with each employee. Step 3 takes place at the end of each fiscal year, with managers meeting each employee to provide required formal evaluation. The first part of the evaluation measures Corporate Goal achievement and individual contribution against fiscal year goals documented on the Deployment Grid. The second part is based on three dimensions: individual performance, Premier Core Values-based competencies, and leadership and team support skills.[78]

Today, many leading organizations are focusing on identifying a small number of core competencies that are critical to the organization's success.[79] These core competencies are the behaviors, skills, and attributes every member is expected to have. They also use **mastery descriptions**, narratives of behavior that one who has mastered it would likely engage in. For example, a mastery description of *Customer Focus* might be:

> *Dedicated to meeting the expectations and requirements of internal and external customers. Knows who every one of his/her customers is and can state what that individual's expectations are. Gets firsthand customer information and uses it for improvements in products and services. Speaks and acts with customers in mind. Takes the client's side in well-founded complaints. Is skilled at managing customer expectations. Establishes and*

maintains effective relationships with customers and gains their trust and respect. Actively seeks customers' feedback on the quality of service he/she provides.

A behavioral frequency scale, in which appraisers indicate how frequently the appraisee does the things listed in the mastery descriptions (rarely, occasionally, frequently, or regularly, for example) is often used. This avoids numerical judgments of performance, defensive reactions, and provides a guide of what to do to improve.

In the spirit of Deming, many companies are replacing performance evaluation altogether with workforce development and learning systems that provide feedback for improvement. Granite Rock, for example, does not emphasize past performance, but sets professional development goals in conjunction with the company's needs. No stigma is attached to failure; the thrust of the process is to develop each individual to the fullest.

Assessing Workforce Engagement, Satisfaction, and Effectiveness

Measurement of engagement and satisfaction are useful to determine the effectiveness of work systems in contributing to an organization's strategic objectives and also to provide a foundation for improvement. In fact, research has suggested that organizations that use people measures as part of a balanced set of measures to manage the business achieve significantly higher return on investment and return on assets than those that don't. The same holds true for organizations that say their employee surveys provide valuable information to guide decision making. Nevertheless, few organizations have well-defined people measures or use them to predict key business outcomes.[80]

Measures of employee engagement and satisfaction allow companies to predict customer satisfaction, identify those issues that have the greatest impact on business performance, and provide a foundation for improvement.

Both outcome and process measures provide data by which to assess workforce effectiveness. Outcome measures might include "hard" measures such as number of teams, rate of growth, percentage of employees involved, number of suggestions implemented, time taken to respond to suggestions, employee turnover, absenteeism, and grievances; as well as "soft" measures such as perceptions of teamwork and management effectiveness, engagement, satisfaction, and empowerment. Typical process measures include the number of suggestions that employees make, the numbers of participants in project teams, and participation in educational programs. Team process effectiveness can be assessed by tracking the average time it takes to complete a process improvement project, and determining whether teams are getting better, smarter, and faster at performing improvements. Organizations should also look for other indicators of performance, such as improvements in team selection and planning processes, frequency of use of quality improvement tools by employees, employee understanding of problem-solving approaches, and senior management involvement. Many companies also ask employees to rate their supervisors on leadership, communication, and support.

Data can be gathered in many ways. For example, at Saint Luke's Hospital, factors that determine employee well-being, satisfaction, and motivation are uncovered through formal surveys, open forums with senior leaders, targeted focus groups, senior leader "walk rounds," "staying" and "exit" interviews, and the Peer Review Grievance Process. Employee satisfaction results are segmented by unit level, job type, shift assignments, and ethnicity, to provide hospital leadership with information that can be acted upon to enhance satisfaction and motivation.

A formal survey is the most common approach to assessing workers' attitudes. Questions in a typical survey might be grouped into such basic categories as quality of worklife, teamwork, communications, opportunities and training, facilities, leadership, compensation, benefits, and the company. Surveys might also address important team and individual behaviors, such as unity for a common purpose, listening effectively and acknowledging others' contributions, obtaining the participation of all members of the team, gathering and analyzing relevant data and information, sharing responsibility, using problem-solving processes and tools, and meeting company objectives for quality improvement. Many research-based and commercial survey instruments are available.[81] Like the customer satisfaction surveys we discussed in Chapter 5, many employee surveys also seek feedback on the importance of key issues.

Employee surveys also help organizations better understand the "voice of the employee," particularly with regard to employee satisfaction, management policies, and their internal customers and suppliers. Such feedback helps organizations improve their human resource management practices. For example, Marlow Industries uses a survey that addresses a broad variety of issues, including management support, the company's total quality system, organizational effectiveness, training, and continuous improvement. Table 6.7 shows most of the questions included in their survey. All responses are made on a five-item scale ranging from *totally disagree* to *very much agree*. Xerox produces its survey in 25 languages. Fifty-four questions are grouped into eight categories: Directions/communications, Valuing people, Trust, Learning, Feedback, Recognition, Participation/involvement, and Teamwork. Xerox compares results against similar companies such as Allied Signal, Honeywell, Sun Microsystems, Texas Instruments, and others.

Results provide a basis for evaluation and improvement. For instance, Sunny Fresh Foods identifies its key factors for employee well-being from performance reviews, exit interviews, and individual discussions. Results are segmented and analyzed by plant and employee group, which allows management at each plant to tailor initiatives for their employees. In evaluating results, trends and long-term results should be emphasized, and they should be communicated to employees. A good system should report results on a regular basis, perhaps monthly or quarterly, with a summary year-end report, using graphical aids wherever possible. Detailed reports should go to lower-level managers, showing results at their level. Summary reports should go to higher management levels. Specific action, such as training, changes in reward or recognition, or improvements to support employee well-being should be taken based on results.

SUSTAINING HIGH-PERFORMANCE WORK SYSTEMS

Organizations must take a long-term view of its work systems, and take the necessary steps to ensure that high performance is sustained. This requires a regular assessment of workforce capability and capacity needs; hiring, training and retention of employees, and career progression and succession planning.

Workforce Capability and Capacity

Workforce capability refers to an organization's ability to accomplish its work processes through the knowledge, skills, abilities, and competencies of its people. Capability may include the ability to build and sustain relationships with customers;

Table 6.7 Employee Quality Survey—Marlow Industries

Management Support

1. The president is an active supporter of quality at Marlow Industries.
2. Senior management (VPs) are active supporters of quality at Marlow Industries.
3. My supervisor is an active supporter of quality at Marlow Industries.
4. My supervisor is concerned more about the quality of my work than the quantity of my work.
5. My supervisor can help me to do my job better.
6. My supervisor encourages good housekeeping efforts.
7. I receive recognition for a top quality job done.

Total Quality System

1. Marlow Industries' Total Quality System is not a fad. It will be active long into the future.
2. The Total Quality system has made an improvement in the performance of my work.
3. The Total Quality system has made an improvement in my ability to do my job right the first time.
4. I understand the meaning of the Quality Policy.
5. I believe in the meaning of the Quality Policy.
6. I understand the meaning of the Quality Pledge.
7. I believe in the meaning of the Quality Pledge.
8. All departments within Marlow Industries support the Total Quality system.
9. My co-workers support quality first.
10. My co-workers believe in the Quality Pledge.
11. My "supplier" co-worker treats me as his/her "customer" and meets my needs.
12. I know who my internal "customer" is.
13. I am able to meet the requirements of my internal customer.
14. I believe that improving quality is the key to maintaining Marlow Industries' success.

Organizational Effectiveness

1. I receive feedback that helps me perform my job better.
2. I am encouraged to stop and ask questions if something does not seem right.
3. There is a high level of quality in the products we ship to our external customers.
4. Marlow Industries provides reliable processes and equipment so that I can do my job right the first time.
5. I do not use defective materials.
6. I am provided proper procedures to do my job right.
7. My fellow workers have a high level of enthusiasm about Marlow Industries' quality.
8. I believe control charts will help us improve quality.
9. I believe Marlow Industries offers a high quality working environment.
10. I enjoy my job.

Training

1. I have received training to be able to do my job right the first time.
2. I have received training on how to determine if the work I do conforms to Marlow Industries' workmanship standards, and other requirements of the customer.
3. I receive adequate safety training so that I am aware of the safety and health requirements of my job.
4. My supervisor has received adequate training to be able to do his/her job right the first time.
5. My co-worker has received adequate training to be able to do his/her job right the first time.
6. I have received ongoing training.
7. The training I have received has been very helpful to me in my job.

Job Satisfaction and Morale

1. I have a high level of personal job satisfaction.
2. My morale is high.
3. The morale of my work group is high.

Involvement

1. I feel involved at Marlow Industries.
2. I would like to be more involved at Marlow Industries.

Source: Reprinted with permission of Marlow Industries.

to innovate and transition to new technologies; to develop new products, services, and work processes; and to meet changing business, market, and regulatory demands. **Workforce capacity** refers to an organization's ability to ensure sufficient staffing levels to accomplish its work processes and successfully deliver products and services to customers, including the ability to meet seasonal or varying demand levels.

Workforce capability and capacity should consider not only current needs but also future requirements based on strategic objectives and action plans. That is why we emphasized the importance of human resource planning in conjunction with strategic planning in Chapter 4. For example, to assess its workforce capability, Consolidated District 15 school system asks its department staff a series of audit questions to clarify how they contribute to the accomplishment of the school's mission. The answers to these questions drive the development of determining the work that needs to be done and school improvement plans. To manage its workforce capacity, Saint Luke's Hospital has a workforce planning system responsive to both current and changing health care needs. The system includes a "Workforce Planning and Assessment Tool," a detailed staffing analysis for all departments supporting patient care, and human resource action plans that are created based upon the strategic plan.

Meeting and exceeding customer expectations begins with hiring the right people whose skills and attitudes will support and enhance the organization's objectives.

An important aspect of meeting workforce capability and capacity needs is an organization's process for hiring the right people. First, one must identify what skills and competencies they need. At Medrad, for example, the Human Resources department, working with senior staff, came up with a list of core behavioral/management competencies through an analysis of future leadership requirements based on Medrad's vision and an assessment of the company's current capabilities. Then, Medrad hired a consulting company to help refine and expand the definition and use of core competencies. The consultants worked with the HRAB and senior staff, conducted extensive interviews of high potential, high performing companies, and made recommendations based on their analysis and industry experience. Table 6.8 shows the key competencies they expect in their employees.

The next step is to identify job candidates based on the skills and competencies during the hiring process. Branch-Smith Printing specifies the set of skills required

Table 6.8 Key Employee Competencies at Medrad

- Performance development
- High performance orientation
- Adaptability
- Sound judgment
- Detail orientation
- Planning organizing
- Communications (written, verbal, professional)
- Motivation and empowerment
- Cross-functional teamwork and collaboration
- Customer focus
- Values driven (respect for others, integrity, etc.)
- Continuous innovation and improvement (creativity process orientation, etc.)
- Change implementation
- Persuasion and consensus building
- Medrad/market/industry knowledge
- Global perspective
- Building partnerships
- Strategic visioning
- Project management

Source: Reprinted with permission of Medrad.

to perform a job. Candidates are screened with a set of questions designed to assess their skills to perform the job functions as defined in the job descriptions. They use behavior-based questions to assess whether candidates have the characteristics to excel in their team-based, quality-focused environment. Two additional assessments are given to candidates who meet the first criteria. One is a pre-employment screening tool for assessing the attitudes of job candidates regarding integrity, responsibility, and work ethic. The second uses advanced technology to predict job suitability and matches people with the job for which they are applying.

Customer-contact employees make up a large segment of today's workforce. Limited availability of people with the skills to perform complex, rapidly changing jobs is forcing workforce managers to rethink their selection criteria. Traditional hiring practices have been based on cognitive or technical rather than interpersonal skills. The criterion is now shifting to attributes such as enthusiasm, resourcefulness, creativity, and the flexibility to learn new skills rapidly. The internal customer concept suggests that every employee needs good interpersonal skills. Even technical skill requirements are changing; to apply quality principles on the job, all workers must have basic mathematics and logical-thinking abilities. To ensure that job candidates have the requisite skills, new approaches, such as psychological testing and situational role playing, are now being used in the hiring process.

Some organizations are using highly innovative approaches to recruit employees. Health care, for example, has long faced severe shortages of key personnel such as nurses. North Mississippi Medical Center has a unique recruiting process that begins with Let's Pretend Hospital, a tool to educate first graders in health care careers. Other programs, such as the Summer Health Academy and the Advanced Health Academy are designed for middle school students. High school and vocational students can participate in Medical Explorers, Job Shadowing, and facility tours. High school seniors pursuing a medical career are candidates for annual medical scholarships. The Nurse Mentorship Academy provides 16 hours of lecture, guest speakers, job shadowing, and volunteering for exploring a career in nursing.

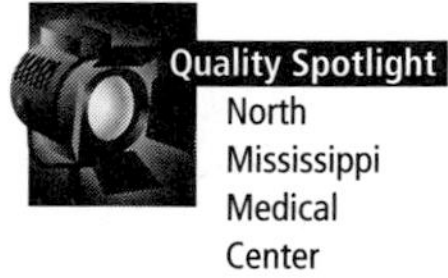

An important part of workforce capability and capacity planning for long-term sustainability is succession planning for leadership and management positions. Many companies have formal processes to identify, develop, and position future leaders to assume key responsibilities. Many managers are required to identify successors and create formal succession plans that include development objectives and activities such as mentoring and coaching, or job rotation. The City of Coral Springs, Florida, for example, formalizes succession planning through its Leadership Development Program, which proactively identifies and develops employees who have the potential to hold future leadership and key individual contributor positions. Through the program, two development paths have been created to support individual growth and guide the timing of leadership development: Senior Leadership path and Management Leadership path. Participants in the Senior Leadership path participate in designated strategic learning events including Leadership Coral Springs, the Florida International University Strategic Management Program, joint senior management team/participant meetings, quarterly Supervisory Forums, 360-degree assessments, attendance at one City Commission meeting per quarter, and attendance at all strategic planning and budget workshops. In addition to the strategic learning events, participants complete a career development profile and are paired with a mentor from the senior management team. Participants in the Management Leadership path participate in designated activities including quarterly Supervisory Forums, Request for Proposal (RFP) processes, focus groups and cross-functional teams, and a personality profile.

Workforce Learning and Development

Training can be one of the largest costs in an organization. Not surprisingly, it is one in which many companies are reluctant to invest. However, research indicates that companies that spend heavily on training their workers outperform companies that spend considerably less, as measured on the basis of overall stock market returns.

Organizations committed to quality and performance excellence invest heavily in training and education, recognizing that such investments add value to organizational capabilities.

The leaders in quality—Deming, Juran, and Crosby—actively promoted quality training and education. Two of Deming's 14 Points, for example, are devoted to these issues. Customer service representatives at FedEx receive five weeks of training before they ever speak unsupervised with a customer. Even an 18-employee digital printing company in Reykjavik, Iceland—Umslag, ehf—spends 4 percent of total wages on training, which includes training in equipment repair to reduce the need to bring in expertise from Holland, languages to support growth in international business, and personal interests, such as computer programming, that can benefit the business.[82]

These investments include ensuring that training addresses key organizational needs and contributes to the organizational mission and vision, is delivered effectively, evaluated, and reinforced on the job. For example, Baptist University, the internal education and training arm of Baptist Hospital, Inc. (BHI), is used as the primary source for training all employees at BHI. All BHI employees are required to receive 60 hours of learning per year. All leaders and employees get together in a "daily line-up" to communicate important operational information and reinforce values. BHI's return on learning tracking and investment research led to its being named as a "Top 50" learning organization by *Training* magazine in 2003. Before starting their job, every new employee at Stoner, Inc., a small, family-owned business with less than 50 employees, completes a two-week orientation program. In addition to ethics and safety training, new employees spend one day shadowing every job in the company including spending time with the company president. With almost 13 percent of its workforce being minorities, Sunny Fresh Foods has translated training materials into Spanish and uses interpreters to facilitate understanding, and offers English as a Second Language classes during work hours.

In a culture of performance excellence, employees need to understand the importance of customer satisfaction, to be given the training and responsibilities to achieve it, and to feel that they do indeed make a difference.

At the Coors Brewing Company in Golden, Colorado, the customer satisfaction improvement program is focused on giving employees the appropriate skills, and on creating the environment in which employees have one responsibility and one hoped-for result: to satisfy and delight their customers, especially internal customers. Coors engaged in a massive training program to learn quality principles, and then restructured its organization systems (compensation, evaluation, and so on) to support the new effort. The company succeeded in developing in its employees a passion for their jobs and pride in their work, which translated into measurable improvements in productivity, a remarkably low turnover rate, and the delivery of quality products and service throughout the system.[83]

Training specific to performance excellence generally includes quality awareness, leadership, project management, communications, teamwork, problem solving, interpreting and using data, meeting customer requirements, process analysis, process simplification, waste reduction, cycle time reduction, error-proofing, and other issues that affect employee effectiveness, efficiency, and safety. For example, employees at Xerox learn a range of techniques, from the basic quality improvement tools through benchmarking, and Motorola employees learn statistical methods and defect reduction approaches. Education needs might also include basic skills, such as reading, writing, language, mathematics, or computer skills.

Many large companies have formal training departments, whose systems and approaches evolved along with their overall quality systems. Identifying training opportunities and implementing them is a key business process; Figure 6.6 shows how Medrad uses a systematic process to design, deliver, and evaluate education and training.

Education and training can be delivered in a variety of ways, including on-the-job or traditional classroom environments. Today, computer-based and distance learning education are becoming increasingly popular. Capitalizing on today's technology and the demographics of its younger employees, fast-food chains such as Pal's Sudden Service and Chuck E. Cheese are using or testing video iPods for training. Their advantage is rapid updating and easy downloading of content.[84] Training can also be accomplished through developmental assignments within or outside the organization. Specific approaches vary by company. In some, managers train their workers directly in a top-down fashion; this approach was pioneered by Xerox, beginning with the CEO, David Kearns himself, during their transition to total quality. Others use self-paced methods employing advanced technology. The FedEx Quality Academy, established in 1991, uses a television network that broadcasts courses in a just-in-time fashion at the employees' work site. It also has a network of interactive video instruction, and more than 2,000 course titles are available for self-paced instruction. The Quality Academy tracks test scores, pass

Figure 6.6 Medrad Learning and Development Process

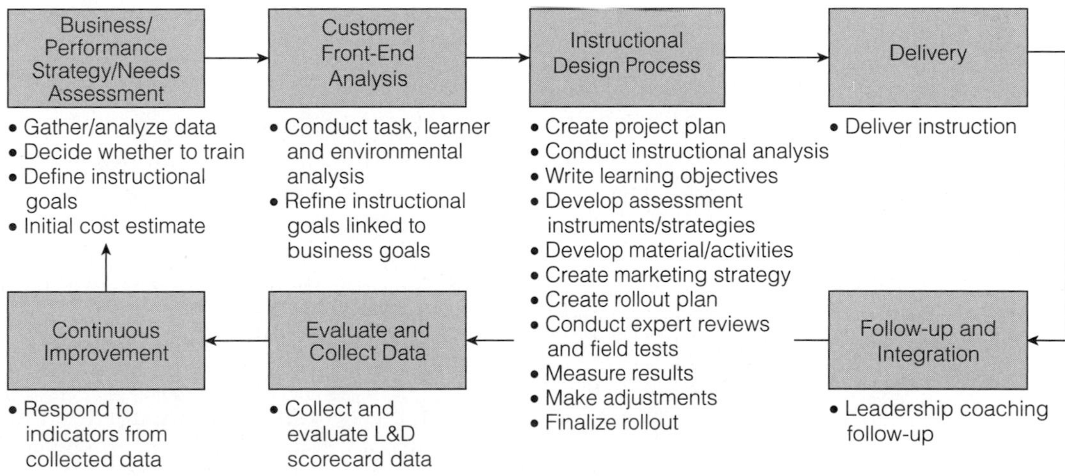

Source: MEDRAD, Malcolm Baldridge Application Summary, 2003, National Institue of Standards and Technology, U.S. Department of Commerce. Repritned with permission.

rates, and time spent online.[85] Honda of America uses interactive computer-based training modules on dedicated workstations in the plant.[86] Smaller companies often use outside consultants. The content should be customized to the company's needs; "packaged" seminars are often a waste of time.

Continual reinforcement of knowledge learned is essential. Many companies send employees to courses, but then allow the knowledge to slip away. New knowledge can be reinforced in several ways. Motorola uses on-the-job coaching to reinforce training; The Ritz-Carlton has follow-up sessions to monitor instructional effectiveness. The Ritz-Carlton holds a "quality lineup" briefing session each day in every work area. During these sessions, employees receive instructions on achieving quality certification within the company. Work area teams set the quality certification performance standards of each position. Finally, companies need an approach for evaluating training effectiveness. The Ritz-Carlton requires employees to pass written and skill demonstration tests. Other companies use on-the-job evaluation or tests in simulated work environments. Many measure behavior and attitude changes. However, the true test of training effectiveness is results. By establishing a link between training and results (see the discussion of interlinking in Chapter 8), companies can show the impact on customer satisfaction and also identify gaps in training.

Career development is also changing because of a focus on quality and high performance. As managerial roles shift from directing and controlling to coaching and facilitating, managers, who must deal with cross-functional problems, benefit more from horizontal movement than from upward movement in narrow functional areas. Flatter organizations limit promotion opportunities. Thus, career development expands learning opportunities and creates more challenging assignments rather than increasing spans of managerial control. At Pal's Sudden Service, employees advance on a planned basis to fill process team roles as they learn more job skills and operational positions. The most capable team members are selected to back up assistant managers and are put on a path for advancement to assistant manager, and possibly to owner/operator succession.

WORKFORCE FOCUS IN THE BALDRIGE CRITERIA, ISO 9000, AND SIX SIGMA

Category 5 of the 2009–10 Malcolm Baldrige National Quality Award Criteria for Performance Excellence is *Workforce Focus.* This category examines how an organization engages, manages, and develops the workforce to utilize its full potential in alignment with the organization's mission, strategy, and action plans. It also addresses the ability to assess workforce capability and capacity needs and to build a high-performance work environment. Item 5.1, *Workforce Engagement*, focuses on how an organization, engages, compensates, and rewards the workforce to achieve high performance, how its employees and leaders are developed, how workforce engagement is assessed, and how the results are used to achieve higher performance. Item 5.2, *Workforce Environment*, focuses on how an organization manages its workforce capability and capacity to accomplish the work of the organization and maintains a safe, secure, and supportive work climate.

The focus of people in ISO 9000:2000 revolves primarily around training and the work environment, but does not address the subject as comprehensively as Baldrige does. The standards require that "Personnel performing work affecting product quality shall be competent on the basis of appropriate education, training, skills, and experience." The standards further require that organizations determine the level of competence that employees need, provide training or other means to ensure competency, evaluate the effectiveness of training or other actions taken, ensure that employees are aware of how their work contributes to quality objectives, and maintain appropriate records of education, training, and experience. The standards also address the work environment from the standpoint of providing buildings, workspace, utilities, equipment, and supporting services needed to achieve conformity to product requirements, as well as determining and managing the work environment, including safety, ergonomics, and environmental factors.

Workforce focus is essential to Six Sigma. We discussed the role of project teams in Six Sigma earlier in this chapter. One quality professional noted that "Six Sigma actually owes its success to all the quality efforts that have come before it, and teams are an integral part of Six Sigma implementation."[87] In addition to teams, selecting the right people to serve on teams, training and skill development, and reward and recognition approaches to drive behavior are vital to Six Sigma efforts. Six Sigma efforts often result in significant change recommendations to the organization; work processes change and employees need to do things differently. Understanding how changes affect people is a necessary issue that organizations must address after Six Sigma projects are completed; project champions, in particular, need to apply the principles discussed in this chapter to their organizations.

SUMMARY OF KEY POINTS AND TERMINOLOGY

The Premium website for this chapter provides a summary of key concepts and terminology introduced in this chapter.

QUALITY IN PRACTICE

TRAINING FOR IMPROVING SERVICE QUALITY AT HONDA[88]

American Honda Motor Co. is part of Honda's North American operations. Based in Torrance, CA, American Honda provides information services, purchasing, financial services, leasing support, and a host of sales and marketing-related services to Honda's business and manufacturing units throughout North America. In 2001, American Honda's associate learning and organizational development group undertook a broad assessment of its approach to training, looking at what was offered, why, to whom, and how. One focus of this initiative was to deepen the emphasis on quality, which has long permeated Honda's manufacturing operations, within the internal support and service portions of the organization. "The Honda philosophy encourages every individual to continuously expand his or her ability to identify and impact both internal and supplier quality," says Lou Juneman, manager of associate learning and organizational development for American Honda. "Innovation, branding, customer satisfaction, and efficiency are central to our success; therefore, quality is at the core of everything we do."

The challenge laid out for the development group was to improve and extend the delivery of training for employees, reduce their time away from the job for training, take advantage of expanding technology capabilities and infrastructure and, above all, ensure a tangible transfer of skills that would take internal service quality to an entirely new level. Honda's approach to service quality improvement through e-learning was focused and disciplined. First, the company began to use a learning management system (LMS) to schedule, administer, and track training. The system was applied not only to instructor-led offerings but also to pure online training, blended learning (a unique mix of online and instructor-led training), and other offerings. Using a customized LMS, Honda employees and their managers learned to define and manage individual training plans as well as enroll in, complete, and track their progress in courses and curricula through a learner-specific Web portal.

Decisions also had to be made about which programs to offer and which formats would best support the overall emphasis on growth and quality. Their approach, called blended learning, is to provide the best mix of electronic, instructor-led, and self-paced learning to employees. One of the programs to which the blended learning approach was applied problem solving and decision making. This program sharpens an individual's ability to separate and clarify issues, identify those that need immediate attention, and resolve them using a systematic, rational problem-solving, decision-making or action-planning process. These rational thinking skills have been successfully taught at American Honda for many years in a purely instructor-led workshop version. The skills have been critical to establishing and sustaining quality throughout Honda, in both the manufacturing and service/support areas. American Honda worked closely with several vendors to shorten the time spent at the workshop, produce online learning elements, and document results electronically. The blended learning approach also enabled American Honda to capture and measure detailed, useful data about how the problem-solving and decision-making processes are used to impact and improve quality in critical service and support areas.

American Honda realized from the beginning that training, by itself, wouldn't lead to quality improvements. Applying the skills you learn during a training experience regularly and accurately requires a great deal of practice and support. This led to American Honda's three-phase learning model (see Figure 6.7). The first phase takes place online. For two to three weeks, learners access a series of online modules that introduce the logical processes for effective problem solving and decision making. Learner progress is essentially self-paced, but because the content is driven from a Web server, the instructor can follow the progress

Figure 6.7 American Honda's Three-Phase Learning Model

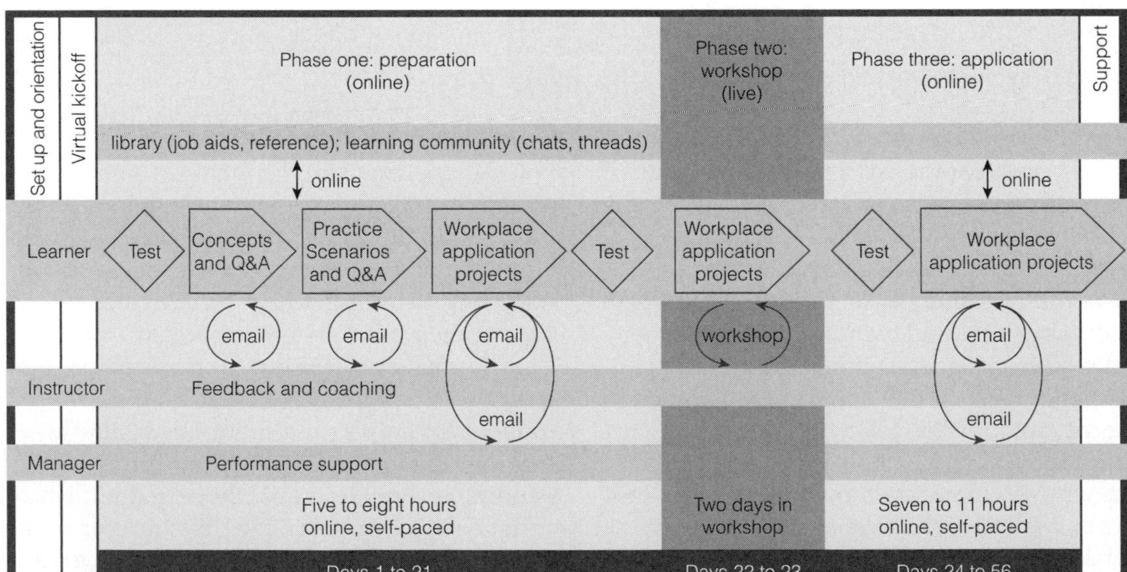

Source: Reprinted with permission from Wayne Stottler, "Improving Service Quality at Honda," *Quality Progress*, October 2004, pp. 33–38.

of each learner and provide ongoing encouragement and support. During phase one, learners are also asked to identify situations to which they intend to apply the techniques so they can focus on these situations when they attend the workshop. This powerful combination of initial learning and preparation for applying the concepts to real-life issues ensures the following phase will not only be efficient but will also build deep understanding and significant motivation to use the ideas on the job after training.

The second phase takes place at the workshop. Guided by the instructor, learners spend two days deepening their understanding of the concepts, discussing best practices and additional techniques for problem solving and decision making, and practicing on detailed case scenarios. Because skill transfer—and results—occur most rapidly when you start with the learner's on-the-job issues, a significant portion of the session is spent working on the problems, decisions and plans identified in phase one. Simultaneously, learners receive coaching and feedback from the instructor and one another. Learners leave the session ready to fully apply the concepts and with a plan in hand to move successfully from the workshop to consistent use of the concepts back on the job.

The final phase takes place back online. In the three weeks following the session, learners resolve the on-the-job issues they began to work on during the workshop. They document for instructor review, feedback, and approval the specific techniques they used to resolve the issues. During phase three, learners have access to a host of online support tools and information. They can contact the instructor with questions at any time. The goal of this phase is to ensure use of the learned concepts, build confidence, get results, and capture information about how the problem-solving and decision-making tools impact American Honda's business; how they create quality and value through their use.

Honda managers learned a lot about electronic learning. As one observed, "True online learning requires culture change, and like any change, it requires planning, communication, and persistence." While online learning displaces some workshop time—the session was pared from three days to two—learners must take time to go online and learn. This requires new behaviors on the part of learners (who have to find the time and resist distractions), managers (who have to encourage and protect the time necessary for online learning), and instructors (who become performance partners and must be available to coach and support learners).

To promote and support the success rate of online learners, American Honda now kicks off each training session with a Web conference to clarify expectations and provide participants with practical tips for online learning. In addition, learners' managers are brought into the loop and asked for input into the choice of high priority problems, decisions, and plans to be tackled during the workshop. Instructors at American Honda have also received additional training to help them effectively coach online learners and act quickly to intervene with anyone experiencing difficulties. The company has also created an extensive online library of reference and support materials on which instructors can draw.

Because instructors can track phase one learning progress in real time, they can provide direct support to individual learners even before they come to the workshop. As a result, the instructor can tailor the learning experience, minimizing the one-size-fits-all approach that frustrates many people in traditional training. After the session, the instructor becomes an on-call coach—tracking progress, providing pointers, and answering questions so learners get personalized support during the critical days following the workshop, when traditional learners often stumble and give up in frustration.

This adds up to a higher quality learning experience that produces the motivation and support Juneman believes are key to setting the stage for integrating learned concepts into daily use long-term. Because learners now submit online documentation of the issues they have resolved, it is much easier to see how and where the concepts are being used and evaluate the impact of the training on the bottom line of the organization. They have identified five indicators that support the success of this initiative:

1. Increased learner readiness for workshop learning
2. Better identification of relevant application topics
3. Increased volume of completed applications

4. Increased dollar value of after workshop applications
5. Greater ongoing use of skills

With more than 300 learners taking advantage of the blended learning opportunity in the last couple of years, American Honda is happy with the results. Juneman offers an example: "When someone in our dealer support function uses these rational-thinking processes to systematically find and resolve the cause of a longstanding computer systems issue, I know he or she and a number of other people across the organization will be able to work more efficiently. The quality of individual output is improved, customers are happier and more efficient, and learners are very likely to use the problem-solving process again and again to achieve similar results."

Key Issues for Discussion

1. Why did Honda use a blended learning approach rather than, for example, a pure virtual online learning approach?
2. What were the benefits of the three-phase learning model? How does it support the achievement of high performance?
3. What lessons might other organizations learn from Honda's experience?

Quality in Practice

Improving Employee Retention Through Six Sigma[89]

Hewitt Associates, based in Lincolnshire, IL, is a human resources (HR) outsourcing and consulting company. The customer service (CS) role at Hewitt—and many other companies that rely heavily on CS to deliver outsourced processes—requires significant training on the proprietary systems used to handle data from client organizations. The organization was losing CS talent at an annual turnover rate close to 100 percent, which is common in this line of work. When the company determined it could save millions of dollars through stronger retention of its CS representatives, senior leaders ask the HR department to make it happen. Consequently, HR embarked on as Six Sigma project.

The first step was to quantifying the cost of turnover for CS representatives—to defend the required investment and realize the proposed return on investment (ROI). The cost of turnover includes both hard and soft costs: separation processing costs, replacement hiring costs, new hire training costs, and lost productivity. HR brought together the statisticians, workforce engineers, and line leaders responsible for coordinating and managing the costs of a 2,500-plus person CS center. The team focused on hiring and training hard costs, but spent the bulk of time on measuring lost productivity in the CS environment—the biggest cost in any turnover model. The model resulted in an average hard dollar cost savings figure of about $24,000 for each avoided separation. Based on the annualized turnover rate for the current year, the cost of lost CS productivity for the HR outsourcing segment of Hewitt's business was estimated as approximately $14.5 million. Layering in the hard dollar costs for training and recruiting brought the total to nearly $16 million, or about 13 percent of Hewitt's overall net operating income in that year.

Based on the work Hewitt does with its HR consulting clients, the company knows there is a strong positive relationship between engagement and organizational performance. Specifically, companies with higher levels of engagement are likely to have greater sales growth and higher total shareholder return. Hewitt conducts an annual associate engagement survey that measures not only all the standard employee opinion survey components, such as satisfaction with opportunities, but also intent to display certain behaviors known to have an impact on business results (see Figure 6.8). One of those survey items asked: "How likely is it that you will be working at Hewitt one year from now?" Predictive analysis has shown that of the representatives who respond it is unlikely they will be working at Hewitt, about half actually leave within one year, making this item an important leading indicator of retention.

Hewitt also uses regression analysis to determine the most important drivers of retention

Figure 6.8 Hewitt's Employee Engagement Framework

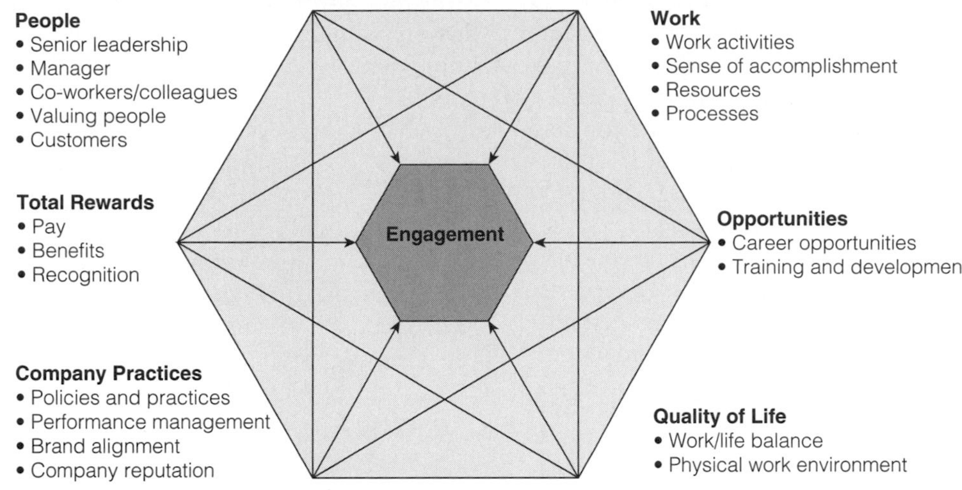

Source: Reprinted with permission from Jon Leatherbury, "Talent Show," *Quality Progress*, Vol. 41, No. 11, November 2008. Copyright © 2008 American Society for Quality. No further distribution allowed without permission.

for the CS representatives. Elements of the work environment in which satisfaction is low but the relationship to retention is high were identified as opportunities for growth and training and rewards (pay and recognition). Elements of the work environment in which satisfaction is high but the threat to retention is high if the area is neglected were work activities and managers and leadership.

The team focused on solutions aligned to the retention driver areas, specifically rewards. A careful review of recent market data then revealed total compensation rates had dropped slightly below market average. A targeted group of proficient CS representatives received a market correction in their base pay. The retention rate for the group of representatives receiving the adjustment was significantly higher than the retention rate of those not receiving adjustments (96 percent vs. 83 percent).

Based on this intervention, the resulting analysis revealed Hewitt was able to avoid losing an additional 80 proficient CS representatives, assuming retention among these proficient CS representatives would have been on par with the overall group who did not receive the intervention. At $24,000 for each separation avoided, the benefit associated with the pay increase equaled $1.9 million—or a return on investment of 217 percent.

At first, senior leaders were reluctant to make further investments in the rewards strategy for a population of associates who historically come and go frequently. But hard data, involvement from line management and, eventually, a bold proposal from HR helped them to see the business problem differently. In the end, the annualized ROI bought credibility with senior leaders and highlighted the importance of HR being in a position to make and defend data-based decisions that yield a strong ROI.

Fixing competitive pay was only part of the solution. The company began to implement additional solutions aimed at the other top drivers of retention for the CS population. HR developed a realistic job profile targeted at explicitly showing candidates up front what the first few months of the role—when turnover is highest—entail. Additionally, HR has implemented a role-based capability assessment to measure job fit at the time of application. The data will aid in understanding how well incoming job fit is predictive of future performance. The goal is to further impact attrition within the first six months that is due to job abandonment, inability to meet basic productivity requirements, or dislike of day-to-day responsibilities.

HR redesigned technical training to ensure associates become productive more quickly and better understand the link between performance and growth opportunity, which is based on productivity results. A formal career path tool is also being constructed to help CS representatives navigate the career journey more effectively. The goal is to decrease time to proficiency and attrition in the 6–12 month timeframe—a period when CS representatives become more productive but often leave for better-perceived career and development opportunities elsewhere. Finally, HR developed a formal manager effectiveness curriculum for managers and local leaders, focusing this training on interaction management, team leading, and conflict resolution. Manager interaction sessions also will be delivered to improve one-on-one coaching opportunities between managers and CS representatives. This should lead to stronger engagement and retention of CS representatives and managers. Enhanced interactions and coaching opportunities will lead to enhanced productivity.

The Six Sigma method has helped HR professionals at Hewitt think differently about business problems, addresses root causes quicker and demonstrate the ROI of the talent solutions they implement.

Key Issues for Discussion

1. Explain the importance and benefit of using data-driven analytical tools and Six Sigma methodology to address a human resource management issue.
2. Discuss how the solutions that the company identified support its employee engagement framework and should improve engagement and ultimately retention.

Review Questions

1. Explain why there is a logical relationship between customer satisfaction and employee satisfaction.
2. Summarize the key workforce-focused practices for performance excellence.
3. Describe the impact of the Taylor system on quality, productivity, and workforce management. How do TQ principles differ from the Taylor system?
4. Define workforce management. Explain its role from a strategic perspective.
5. Explain the concept of workforce engagement. What advantages does it provide to an organization?
6. What is employee involvement? Discuss different approaches to employee involvement.
7. Define the term *motivation*. Why is motivation critical for performance excellence?
8. List the key factors that characterize high performance work.
9. Explain the difference between *work design* and *job design*. How does the Hackman and Oldham model enhance understanding of how job design affects motivation, satisfaction, and organizational effectiveness?
10. Contrast job enlargement with job enrichment. How do they support the Hackman and Oldham model?
11. What is *empowerment*? How does it benefit both the organization and employees?
12. Explain the concept of self-determination and how it differs from empowerment.
13. What is a *team*? Define the major types of teams found in organizations today.
14. Contrast the differences between quality circles and self-managed teams. What are the key characteristics of self-managed teams not found in quality circles?
15. How are the roles in Six Sigma teams similar to and different from traditional project teams?
16. Discuss the four phases that teams typically go through during their life cycle.

17. Explain the important issues an organization must consider in developing successful teams.
18. What issues must organizations consider with respect to health, safety, and employee well-being in the work environment?
19. List and describe the tools needed for running an effective meeting.
20. What are the steps required to perform the nominal group technique (NGT)?
21. What types of compensation practices support a performance excellence philosophy?
22. Explain the key practices that lead to effective recognition and reward approaches?
23. Briefly summarize traditional performance appraisal processes. From a performance excellence perspective, what objections have been raised concerning these processes? Describe some modern practices.
24. What is *360-degree feedback*? How does it differ from traditional performance appraisal approaches? How does it address the major criticisms of traditional performance appraisal processes and support TQ efforts?
25. Why is it important to assess workforce engagement and satisfaction? Describe some common approaches.
26. Why is it important to consider workforce capability and capacity in designing and sustaining high performance work systems?
27. Explain some modern practices for hiring, workforce learning, and career development.
28. Summarize the workforce management issues addressed in the Malcolm Baldrige National Quality Award criteria, ISO 9000:2000, and the Six Sigma philosophy.

Discussion Questions

1. What is your reaction to the quote about Toyota in the opening paragraph of the chapter? Would such an observation be true of most other organizations? Is it really true that competitors cannot copy the human resources of an organization? Why or why not?
2. The late Peter Drucker, arguably the most respected and influential writers on management in the 20th Century, observed:

   Whatever his limitations and shortcomings—and he had many—no other American, not even Henry Ford (1863–1947), had anything like Taylor's impact. "Scientific Management" (and its successor, "Industrial Engineering") is the one American philosophy that has swept the world—more so even than the Constitution and the Federalist Papers. In the last century there has been only one worldwide philosophy that could compete with Taylor's: Marxism. And in the end Taylor has triumphed over Marx.[90]

   Comment on Drucker's observations about the Taylor system. Do you agree with his statement about Taylor versus Marx? Why or why not?
3. How can a fraternity or student organization use the workforce-focused practices in Table 6.1 to improve the organization? If you are involved in such an organization, develop a strategic "workforce" plan that supports performance excellence.
4. What things might you observe in an organization that has high levels of workforce engagement? What might you observe in one that has low levels of engagement?

5. What motivates *you* to study and perform in the classroom? How do motivation theories apply to you personally? Discuss how these theories might lead to new ways of teaching and learning.

6. When simple theories such as those of Maslow, Herzberg, and McGregor explain motivation, why does the search continue for more complex ones or for ones that integrate several different theories, such as Porter and Lawler's theory? What implications do they have for quality? (Refer to the Bonus Materials folder for this chapter on the Premium website for the document on Theories of Motivation to answer this question.)
7. Think of a job you have had. Apply the Hackman and Oldham model to evaluate how the job design impacted your motivation and satisfaction, as well as organizational effectiveness.
8. Describe some examples of job enlargement or job enrichment that you have either seen or personally encountered in a job.
9. Cite some examples of empowerment or lack of empowerment from your own experiences.
10. How might the concept of empowerment be employed in a classroom?
11. How might a jazz quartet be viewed as a metaphor for a team in a business situation?
12. How should teams deal with "slackers"? How would you deal with it in the context of a student project team?
13. How might Kano's model of customer needs (see Chapter 5) be applied to employee needs and the work environment? Can you relate it to Maslow's Hierarchy of Needs?
14. Consider the statement, "How one is evaluated determines how one performs." What does this notion mean for your classes? Would your performance change if grades were abolished (as Deming strongly advocated)?
15. Discuss the conditions under which team incentives, gainsharing, and "pay for increased skills" reward systems may work. When is it a poor idea to install such systems?
16. Students in early grades often receive many kinds of recognition: stickers, candy, and so on, for good work. As we discussed, similar forms of recognition are common in the workplace. Yet little daily recognition is given at the high school and college level. Discuss possible reasons for this difference and design a recognition program that might be appropriate in your class.
17. Discuss the controversy over performance appraisal. Do you agree with Deming's approach, or do you take the more traditional viewpoint toward performance review? Why?
18. Most colleges and universities use a course/instructor evaluation system. If your school has one, how is it used? Does it support continuous improvement or is it used strictly for performance appraisal? How might the evaluation instrument or process be modified to better reflect qualtiy principles?
19. Jack Welch, former CEO of General Electric, stated his passion for making people GE's core competency. He used a system in which executives in the bottom 10 percent of a forced performance ranking were eliminated. What do you think of this approach? How does it fit with a total quality philosophy? How would you respond to someone who says, "I think all my people are pretty good. If I fire the bottom 10 percent, that would just give me a new bottom 10 percent. Where does it end?"
20. Recently, new "employee performance software" has been developed to track individual output. For example, British Airways uses it to ensure that

customer service reps' time in the break room or on personal calls doesn't count on the clock. The technology can keep track so that extra incentive dollars are eventually directed in to the paychecks of those whose digital records merit them. It can also help managers understand how to assemble the most effective teams or who to lay off.[91] Discuss the implications of such technology from a quality and high performance perspective.

21. Many companies today seek the best available applicants and train them in quality principles. What implications does this practice have for designing college curricula and choosing elective courses in a given program?
22. What can an organization do about individuals who "aren't good with numbers" if they have a policy that they become Green Belts, and later, Black Belts, as a prerequisite for promotion to higher levels of management?
23. Undoubtedly you have received a recorded message prior to a call to company that says something like "For quality purposes, this call may be recorded." What do you think the real purpose of such an approach is? Is it to improve quality or to monitor poorly trained employees or catch them deviating from company scripts? Would an empowered organization need to use this method?
24. The training strategy that Xerox used is summarized as follows:
    a. The training is uniform—common tools and processes are taught across all of Xerox, to all employees, creating a "common language within Xerox" that fosters cohesive team functioning.
    b. Training is conducted in family groups, with all members starting and finishing training at the same time to facilitate the change process.
    c. Training starts at the top of the organization with the CEO and cascades downward to all employees.[92]

    What advantages does such strategy have? Do you see any possible disadvantages? Would this approach work in any business?
25. Labor relations between unions and management can make it difficult to establish TQ-oriented HRM practices within organizations. The National Labor Relations Board (NLRB) ruled on two cases in 1993 and 1994 that complicate a company's determination of how far it can go legally to set up and use employee participation programs (EPPs) to make improvements in the workplace. The two cases involved a small, nonunion company, Electromation, and a large company, DuPont. These case decisions by a five-person board were based on interpretations of the 58-year-old National Labor Relations Act (NLRA, or Wagner Act) that prohibits unfair labor practices. The rulings are found in the NLRB proceedings as Electromation vs. International Brotherhood of Teamsters (309 NLRB-No. 163), and E. I. duPont de Nemours and Company vs. Chemical Workers Association, Inc. (311 NLRB-No. 88). In the Electromation case, the nonunion company's management set up five employee action committees to deal with policies concerning absenteeism, smoking, communications, pay for premium positions, and attendance bonuses. In DuPont's case, management unilaterally (without bargaining with the union) changed the composition of safety and fitness committees to include nonmanagerial employees (where the committees had previously been composed only of management) at a unionized New Jersey plant. Stated briefly, the cases specified that "employer-dominated labor organizations" are prohibited. In both cases, the employee teams/committees were ruled to be "labor organizations" and to be "management dominated." Discuss the implications of these cases, particularly in the context of high performing organizations. You might wish to conduct further research on these cases.

Projects, Etc.

1. Review the most recent list of *Fortune's* "100 Best Companies to Work For" and summarize the best practices of these companies, classifying them into themes such as engagement, work environment, training, and so on. Have any of these companies or their business units have received a Baldrige Award?
2. Search some current business periodicals (e.g., *Fortune, Fast Company, Business Week*) for articles dealing with workforce-management issues. Explain how they relate to the material in this chapter. Are any new approaches or practices emerging?
3. Interview managers at a local organization about their workforce-management practices, focusing on engagement and work and job design issues. Report on your perceptions of how well their practices support a high-performance workplace.
4. Survey local companies to determine if and how they use suggestion systems. What levels of participation do they have? Are suggestions tied to rewards and recognitions?
5. Investigate the extent of team participation at some local companies. What kinds of teams do you find? Do managers believe these teams are effective?
6. Find a small to medium-sized company that is using Six Sigma teams. Have they changed the GE/Motorola model in the way that they train and use team leaders and resource people (Green, Black, and Master Black Belts)? Are they using those roles for management development purposes?
7. Interview some managers at a local company on their approaches to motivation. Summarize their responses and analyze them in the context of motivation theories. Can you provide any suggestions for improving their practices?
8. Research the impacts of the Internet on workforce management practices in an actual firm. One possible approach would be to interview an HR manager at a company that is building e-commerce capability. Another approach might be to visit the websites of several firms, examine practices that may be described, and compare and contrast your findings.
9. Does your school survey its faculty and staff to assess issues of engagement, satisfaction, and the work environment? If so, obtain a copy of the survey and analyze it relative to the concepts in this chapter; if not, design one that might be used.

Cases

Additional cases are available on the Premium website for this chapter.

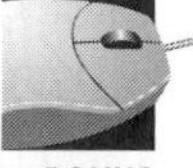
BONUS MATERIALS

Golden Plaza Hotel

Sandra Wilford was recently promoted to General Manager of the Golden Plaza Hotel, San Francisco. She had previously been an assistant manager at the corporation's hotel in Denver. The Denver hotel was truly a team-based organization. Sandra had seen the benefits from teamwork that propelled the hotel to the top of the corporation in customer satisfaction ratings. In fact, it was one of the reasons she was asked to take over the San Francisco property. The previous General Manager's policies had created large turnover among the staff and continuing loss of market share that led to his firing.

Sandra was reviewing her notes from a meeting with all the hotel's supervisors and assistant managers. The meeting tried to identify why many employees were reluctant to be "team players" or even to participate on teams that she was trying to initiate based on her experiences in Denver. Among the reasons that surfaced were the following

- Child care obligations, classes, and other outside commitments made it difficult for some associates to meet before or after shifts.
- Many of the custodial workers who were functionally illiterate seemed to be uncomfortable in interaction with other associates.
- Several associates feel that their current jobs are simply too demanding to take on the additional meetings that would be necessary.
- One assistant manager felt that some of her people preferred to work alone and usually disrupted meetings in which they were involved.
- Because of the previous general manager, there was a lot of cynicism among the associates and many didn't trust management. They felt that teams were simply a political ploy to get support for unpopular decisions. The previous general manager had established some teams that had failed miserably and many associates were bitter and had conflicts with other departments. There seemed to be a widespread attitude of "What's in it for me?"
- Some associates thought that the expectations of team processes would be overwhelming and were afraid if the team fails, they would be held personally responsible and their careers would be in jeopardy. Others thought that their jobs might be eliminated.

Sandra stared at this list and wondered what she got herself into. What recommendations would you make to her to address these issues?

The Hopeful Telecommuter

Jennifer Smith was pregnant, and she was happy about it. She and her husband, Jim, had been planning to start a family for some time. However, she was concerned about her job as a Northeast Zone supply chain manager for health and beauty products for Big Bear Stores. Big Bear was a large, multibillion dollar food store chain that had stores in 47 states. It was a conventionally organized retailer divided into three geographic regions (Atlantic, Mid-American, and Western) with 12 zones (4 per region).

Zone supply chain managers, such as Jennifer, were the link between the store managers and their product-line suppliers. Jennifer had been ranked number one in customer and in supplier satisfaction surveys for health and beauty product lines for the last two years. She knew that she was eligible for six months of maternity leave under the federal Family Leave Act, and that the company would have to provide a job for her upon her return. What she didn't like was the thought that they did not have to, and probably would not, give her the same job that she was now holding so well.

Jennifer had talked with Jim, at length, about what to do. They agreed that she should approach her regional manager, Sarah Strong, the Zone VP, about the possibility of "telecommuting" to her job after the baby came. Jennifer thought that she could do 85–90 percent of the job at home on her own schedule. A large part of her job consisted of verbal and fax contacts with store managers and suppliers, as well as extensive use of a computer for manipulating databases, preparing spreadsheet reports, and sending and responding to e-mail. The other 10–15 percent of the time, when she had to be in the office for face-to-face meetings or had to take brief trips, her parents and Jim could keep the baby and cover for her at home.

When Jennifer approached Sarah Strong, Sarah was interested, but would not commit herself to supporting Jennifer's request to telecommute. She said that the company had never done that before, and it might pose a number of difficulties. She did say that she would take her request forward to the two VP's who could approve or disapprove it. Both senior managers would have to approve Jennifer's request, however. Sarah asked Jennifer to prepare some "talking points" concerning the benefits versus the limitations of the arrangement that she could present to the vice president of human resources, and the senior vice president of operations, Sarah's manager. Sarah also asked Jennifer to prepare a cost estimate, in consultation with the Zone information systems manager.

The following was what Jennifer prepared for the estimated costs:

Laptop computer and docking station	$3,500.00
Setup DSL dedicated phone line	250.00
Fax machine	250.00
Computer desk and chair	375.00
Telephone line charges (6 months)	240.00
Total	$4,615.00

Discussion Questions

1. You are Jennifer. What "talking points" would you prepare to support your case? Include both the strengths and limitations of telecommuting. Keep in mind the needs of your "customers," the human resources VP, as well as Sarah, and the VP of operations.
2. What issues do you think that the VP of human resources might raise? What issues do you think the senior VP of operations might raise?
3. How does your answer demonstrate the principles of empowerment? How might it fit the components of the Hackman–Oldham Job Characteristics model?

Nordam Europe, Ltd.[93]

Nordam Europe, Ltd. is a joint venture between The Nordam Group, Inc., and GE. Aircraft Engine Services, Ltd. The Nordam group is an acknowledged leader in aircraft component manufacturing and repair with facilities on three continents, and is the largest privately held FAA-approved repair station in the world for composite, aircraft structures. Some of its customers include: General Electric, British Airways, FedEx, DHL, and Air France. The Blackwood, Wales facility's primary role is the overhaul and repair of jet engines. The Blackwood division employs 180 workers, 16 of whom are aged 50 and over.

The company has a strong, though brief, history of adoption and practice of equal opportunity in its hiring and HR practices. The company's Equal Opportunities policy prohibits hiring, placement, or dismissal based on gender, race, religion, or age. The HR Department is currently in the process of reviewing most of the company's HR policies in order to develop a Staff Handbook containing all employee related policies. The policies were originally set up in 1997, when the company was formed. Approval of the revised policies will be done by the managing director and the Head of Support Services. A systematic process is also being set up to review all HR policies annually.

The company's early HR policies were developed in a period of rapid expansion. The internal promotion of the Head of Support Services as the senior HR manager has resulted in development of a new, systematic approach towards upgrading all aspects of employee relations management. With a non-discriminatory HR process, the company will continue to judge all employees on the basis of their ability, attitude, skills, commitment, and general approach to work.

Recruitment

In the past, Nordam Europe had used an employment agency for recruitment, but recently it has set a policy to place all recruitment advertising for operative staff with the local JobCentre, a government supported agency. Nordam continues to use some employment agents to fill certain positions, and at the senior management level, the company has made use of a headhunting agency. The HR department has been vigilant in avoiding the use of direct or indirect reference to age or other bias in advertising. In addition, it develops both job and person profiles, again ensuring that there are no age-related or other discriminatory descriptions.

Selection and Retention

Nordam Europe's business is heavily dependent on a high level of safety, quality, and working to precise standards in order to maintain aircraft jet engine nacelles and thrust reversers. Nordam continues to work on policies that will provide stability in its workforce. The following is a brief summary of the company's selection process.

1. Applicant's résumés are received.
2. Screening of applicants is performed by a departmental manager and a personnel officer to develop a short list of those they would like to interview. Suitability for the job is assessed by reviewing the individuals' background and relevant job or technical experience. The process avoids any consideration of race, gender, nationality, disability, religion, or age.
3. The short-listed applicants are invited for interview with the departmental manager and personnel officer. The latter is a trained, experienced interviewer who provides consistency within the interviewing process, ensuring that equal opportunity issues are taken into consideration where appropriate. The company is clear that all decisions relating to job offers are made on the basis of suitability for the post and that age, or other non-job related factors, are irrelevant.

Nordam Europe's Head of Support Services was voluntarily separated from his previous job after 30 years in the automotive industry, where he worked primarily in finance, administration, and operational areas. He sought alternative work in those areas. He circulated his résumé to numerous companies, but was concerned that his age (50) would count against him. The individual was pleased to be asked to visit Nordam Europe for an informal chat. He was later surprised to be offered a role in the production-engineering department. Although new to production engineering, Nordam felt that he would be able to make a valuable contribution to the business, because of his previous experience and administrative skills. He began in production engineering on a three-month temporary contract, but after approximately four weeks, Nordam recognized his capabilities and offered him a permanent position within the company, which he accepted.

Training and Development

Nordam Europe engages in extensive training and development. Because of the industry's need to maintain safety and precision standards in aircraft components, there are ongoing training requirements. These are related to technological advances in the context of repairs to aircraft engine nacelle and thrust reversers. All new employees receive a copy of Training and Development Policy Statement upon company induction. The annual staff appraisal system includes performance measurement and provides an opportunity to identify training and development needs in line with the company's business objectives. Shop floor workers are expected to take training, particularly where training is required to maintain their technical approvals to work on jet engines. All workers have been found to be eager to receive the training made available.

Promotion

Because of the newness of the company, a formal promotion structure has not been developed, although a few individuals have been promoted to fill key posts, when vacated. Age is never a factor in selection for promotion. The post of Head of Support Services was created in 1999. As mentioned, the individual who was hired for the position in production engineering had broad experience in finance, administration, and operational areas in the automotive industry. He was promoted to Head of Support Services. Later, the Head of Support Services was invited by the new managing director to take responsibility for the company's Human Resource Department. Despite him not being an HR specialist, the company felt that his previous experience would provide a good core competence, particularly in the area of "managing people." Thus, the previous experiences of an older worker was recognized by a company and used to good effect in filling a variety of posts. As the Head of Support Services said, "I was able to offer a range of experiences and a high degree of flexibility to an organization that was developing and growing."

Redundancy (Layoff) Policy

Recently, the company faced the situation of having to make several employees redundant (British term for layoffs). The company's redundancy policy had several options including seeking volunteers, a reduction in the scale of working and the application of objective selection criteria.

The objective selection criteria were used in this situation. No worker was selected for redundancy on the basis of their age.

Discussion Questions

1. How do the approaches used by Nordam Europe seem to support high performance work, drawing upon the ideas presented in this chapter?
2. How do employee education, training, and development address the organizational needs associated with new employee orientation, diversity, ethical business practices, and management and leadership development?
3. What are some possible leadership and motivation advantages of using older workers for the type of work done by Nordam Europe?
4. How are the problems of age discrimination in hiring and layoffs in the United States and the U.K. similar and different? (You may want to research the issue on the Internet.) Why is this important, and how does it tie to the social responsibility issues discussed in Chapter 5?

NOVEL CONNECT: WORKFORCE FOCUS

BONUS MATERIALS

The complete Novel Connect case study, a fictitious example of a Baldrige application, can be found in the Baldrige materials folder on the Premium website that accompanies this book. If you have not read Landmark's Organizational Profile yet (see the case in Chapter 3), please do so first. Examine their response to Category 5 in the context of the Baldrige criteria. What are their strengths? What are their weaknesses and opportunities for improvement? What specific advice, including new approaches that might help them, would you suggest?

NOTES

1. Robin Yale Bergstrom, "People, Process, Paint," *Production*, April 1995, 48–51.
2. James L. Heskett, W. Earl Sasser, Jr., and Leonard A. Schlesinger, *The Service Profit Chain* (New York: The Free Press, 1997), 101.
3. James K. Harter, Frank L. Schmidt, and Theodore L. Hayes "Business-Unit-Level Relationship Between Employee Satisfaction, Employee Engagement, and Business Outcomes: A Meta-Analysis," *Journal of Applied Psychology*, Vol. 87, No. 2, 2002, 268–279.
4. Adam Lashinski, "Google is No. 1: Search and enjoy" *Fortune,* January 8, 2007. http://money.cnn.com/magazines/fortune/fortune_archive/2007/01/22/8397996/index.htm accessed on 4/9/09.
5. "The 100 Best Companies to Work for 2006," *Fortune* 1/11/2006, 71–108.
6. "It's My Manager, Stupid," *Across the Board,* January 2000, 9.
7. Town Hall discussion at the Quest for Excellence Conference, Washington D.C., March 2000.
8. Richard E. Walton, "From Control to Commitment in the Workplace," *Harvard Business Review* 63, no. 2 (March/April 1985), 77–84. © by the President and Fellows of Harvard College; all rights reserved.
9. Lloyd L. Byars and Leslie W. Rue, *Human Resource Management*, 6th ed. (New York: Irwin/McGraw-Hill, 2000), 6.
10. "How to DO HR Right," *Fast Company*, August 2005, 46.
11. The Employee Involvement Association's e-newsletter *Ideas & Inspirations*, which gave credit to: *The CEO Refresher* by Freda Turner, PhD. The Web link is no longer active.
12. Lawler, Mohrman, and Ledford, *Employee Involvement,* p. 60; and Linda Grant, "Happy Workers, High Returns," *Fortune,* January 12, 1998, p. 81. A formal research study of the relationship between employee engagement and business outcomes is reported in James K. Harter, Frank L. Schmidt, and Theodore L. Hayes, "Business-Unit-Level Relationship Between Employee Satisfaction, Employee Engagement, and Business Outcomes: A Meta-Analysis," *Journal of Applied Psychology,* 87, 2, 2002, pp. 268–279.
13. Hal F. Rosenbluth, "Have Quality, Will Travel," *The TQM Magazine,* November/December 1992, pp. 267–270.
14. Joseph J. Gufreda, Larry A. Maynard, and Lucy N. Lytle, "Employee Involvement in the Quality Process," in Ernst & Young Quality Improvement Consulting Group, *Total Quality!: An Executive's Guide for the 1990s* (Homewood, IL: Richard D. Irwin, 1990).
15. Tom J. Peters, *Thriving on Chaos: Handbook for a Management Revolution* (New York: Alfred A. Knopf, 1988).

16. Alan Wolf, "Golden Opportunities," *Beverage World*, February 1991.

17. A more comprehensive review of history and the forerunners of quality circles from the early 1900s can be found in William M. Lindsay, "Quality Circles and Participative Work Improvement: A Cross-Disciplinary History," in Dennis F. Ray (ed.), *Southern Management Association Proceedings* (Mississippi State, MS: Mississippi State University, 1987), 220–222.

18. Robert Slater, *Jack Welch and the GE Way* (New York: McGraw-Hill, 1999), 153–155, 158–159.

19. From materials provided by Mike Simms, former plant manager.

20. Saul W. Gellerman, *Motivation in the Real World* (New York: Dutton, 1992).

21. James L. Bowditch and Anthony F. Buono, *A Primer on Organizational Behavior*, 2d ed. (New York: John Wiley & Sons, 1990), 52.

22. Richard M. Steers, Richard T. Mowday, and Debra L. Shapiro, "Introduction to special topic forum: the future of work motivation theory," *Academy of Management Review*, 2004, Vol. 29, No. 3, 379–387.

23. "Making the Job Meaningful All the Way Down the Line," *Business Week* May 1, 2006, 60.

24. Portions adapted from Chapter 4, "Motivation Through the Design of Work," in J. R. Hackman and G. R. Oldham, *Work Redesign* (Reading, MA: Addison-Wesley, 1980).

25. Our appreciation goes to Ms. Gretchen Faulkner for providing this example.

26. Hackman and Oldham, 25 (see note 24).

27. David A Garvin, *Managing Quality* (New York: The Free Press, 1988), 202–203.

28. Robert D. Hof, "Teamwork, Supercharged," *Business Week*, November 21, 2005, 90–94.

29. Douglas K. Miscikowski and Eric W. Stein, "Empowering Employees to Pull The Quality Trigger," *Quality Progress*, October 2008, 43–48.

30. J. M. Juran, *Juran on Leadership for Quality: An Executive Handbook* (New York: The Free Press, 1989), 264.

31. Phillip A. Smith, William D. Anderson, and Stanley A. Brooking, "Employee Empowerment: A Case Study," *Production and Inventory Management* 34, no. 3 (1993), 45–50.

32. "Leader of the Pack," insert in special advertising feature "Work Life," *Fortune*, 9/19/2005, S4.

33. John Troyer, "Empowerment," Guest Editorial, *Quality Digest*, October 1996, 64.

34. AT&T Quality Steering Committee, *Great Performances* (AT&T Bell Laboratories, 1991), 39; and William Smitley and David Scott, "Empowerment: Unlocking the Potential of Your Work Force," *Quality Digest* 14, no. 8 (August 1994), 40–46.

35. "Changing a Culture: DuPont Tries to Make Sure That Its Research Wizardry Serves the Bottom Line," *The Wall Street Journal*, March 27, 1992, A5.

36. Robert S. Kaplan, "Texas Eastman Company," Harvard Business School Case, No. 9-190-039.

37. David Geisler, "The next level in employee empowerment," *Quality Progress*, Vol. 38, No. 6, 48–52, 2005. Copyright © 2001, American Society for Quality. Reprinted with permission.

38. Jon R. Katzenback and Douglas K. Smith, "The Discipline of Teams," *Harvard Business Review* (March/April 1993), 111–120.

39. Jack D. Orsburn, Linda Moran, Ed Musselwhite, and John H. Zenger, *Self-Directed Work Teams* (Homewood, IL: Business One-Irwin, 1990), 8.

40. Brian Dumaine, "The Trouble with Teams," *Fortune*, 5 September, 1994, 86–92.

41. For an historical pespective, see J. M. Juran, "The QC Circle Phenomenon," *Industrial Quality Control*, January 1967, 329–336.

42. "Platform Approach at Chrysler," *Quality '93: Empowering People with Technology*, *Fortune* Advertisement, September 20, 1993.

43. Mark R. Hagen, "Teams Expand into Cyberspace," *Quality Progress*, June 1999, 90–93.

44. David M. Vrooman, *Daniel Willard and Progressive Management on the Baltimore and Ohio Railroad*, Ohio State University Press, Columbus (1991).

45. Jeremy Main. *Quality Wars* (New York: The Free Press, 1994), 62.

46. Sidney P. Rubinstein, "QC Circles and U.S. Participative Movements," *1972 ASQC Technical Conference Transactions*, Washington, D.C., 391–396.

47. For more about the history and impact of quality circles in the early 1980s in the United States, see William M. Lindsay, *Measurement of Quality Circle Effectiveness: A Survey and Critique*, unpublished M.S. thesis, University of Cincinnati, College of Engineering (May 1986), 72, 117–120.

48. *Quality Digest*, "Quality circles still big in India," http://www.qualitydigest.com/currentmag/news.shtml#7; and http://www.cmseducation.org/icsqcc/. Flyer for Twelth International Convention on Students' Quality Control Circles 2009. Accessed on 1/13/09.

49. George Eckes, *The Six Sigma Revolution* (New York: John Wiley & Sons, 2001), 251–254.

50. Harvey A. Robbins and Michael Finley, *Why Teams Don't Work: What Went Wrong and How to Make it Right* (Princeton, NJ: Peterson's/Pacesetter Books, 1995), 14–15.

51. Nicole Adrian, "A Gold Medal Solution," *Quality Progress*, March 2008, 44–50.

52. Samuel C. Certo, *Modern Management*, 9th ed. (Upper Saddle River, NJ: Prentice Hall, 2003), 389.

53. Peter R. Scholtes et al., *The Team Handbook: How to Use Teams to Improve Quality* (Madison, WI: Joiner Associates, Inc., 1988) 6-10–6-22.

54. Michelle Conlin and Kathy Moore, "Photo Essay—SAS," *Business Week*, June 19, 2000, 192–202.

55. Fiona Haley, "Mutual Benefit," *Fast Company*, October 2004, 98–99.

56. James P. Lewis, *Team-Based Project Management* (New York: Amacom, 1998).

57. Peter R. Scholtes, *The Team Handbook,* 3rd ed. Madison, WI: Oriel, Inc., 2003, 4-2 through 4-5.

58. Scholtes (see note 57), 4–5.

59. Andre L. Delbecq, Andre H. Van de Ven, and David H. Gustafson, *Group Techniques for Program Planning* (Glenview, IL Scott Foresman and Co., 1975).

60. John E. Bauer, Grace L. Duffy, and Russell T. Westcott (eds.), *The Quality Improvement Handbook* (Milwaukee, WI: ASQ Quality Press, 2002), 108–109.

61. "Bonus Pay: Buzzword or Bonanza?" *Business Week*, November 14, 1994, 62–64.

62. Woodrumm Imberman, "Pay for Performance Boosts Quality Output," *IIE Solutions*, October 1996, 34–36.

63. Nancy J. Perry, "Here Come Richer, Riskier Pay Plans," *Fortune*, December 19, 1988, 50–58; "The Nucor Story," available at http://www.nucor.com.

64. http://www.nucor.com/index.aspx?=about us. Reprinted with permission.

65. ibid.

66. Curtis Sittenfeld, "Great Job! Here's a Seat Belt!" *Fast Company* January 2004, p. 29. Copyright © 2004 FAST COMPANY. Reprinted by permission. Permission obtained via Copyright Clearance Center.

67. Craig Cochran, "The Sound of All Hands Clapping," *Quality Digest*, September 2003, 38–40.

68. Bruce N. Pfau and Steven E. Gross, *Innovative Reward and Recognition Strategies in TQM*, The Conference Board, Report Number 1051, 1993.

69. "Bonus Pay: Buzzword or Bonanza?" *Business Week*, November 14, 1994, 62–64.

70. Leigh Ann Klaus, "Motorola Brings Fairy Tales to Life," *Quality Progress,* June 1997, 25–28.

71. "Domino's Pizza, Inc.," *Profiles in Quality* (Boston: Allyn and Bacon, 1991), 90–93.

72. Jeremy Main, *Quality Wars* (New York: The Free Press, 1994), 130.

73. Khalid A. Aldakhilallah and Diane H. Parente, "Redesigning a Square Peg: Total Quality Management Performance Appraisals," *Total Quality Management* 13, no. 1 (2002), 39–51.

74. George Eckes, "Practical Alternatives to Performance Appraisals," *Quality Progress* 27, no. 11 (November 1994), 57–60.

75. Douglas McGregor, "An Uneasy Look at Performance Appraisal," *Harvard Business Review*, September–October 1972; Herbert H. Meyer, Emanuel Kay, and John R. P. French, Jr., "Split Roles in Performance Appraisal," *Harvard Business Review*, January–February 1965; Harry Levinson, "Appraisal of What Performance?" *Harvard Business Review*, January–February 1965; A. M. Mohrman, *Deming Versus Performance Appraisal: Is There a Resolution?* (Los Angeles: Center for Effective Organizations, University of Southern California, 1989).

76. John F. Milliman and Fred R. McFadden, "Toward Changing Performance Appraisal to Address TQM Concerns: The 360-Degree Feedback Process," *Quality Management Journal* 4, no. 3 (1997), 44–64.

77. Milliman and McFadden (see note 70).

78. Adapted from: 2007 Malcolm Baldridge Application Summary, National Institute of Standards and Technology, U.S. Department of Commerce. Reprinted with permission.

79. Dick Grote, "The Secrets of Performance Appraisal: Best Practices from the Masters," *Across the Board,* May 2000, 14–20.

80. Brian S. Morgan and William A. Schiemann, "Measuring People and Performance: Closing the Gaps," *Quality Progress,* January 1999, 47–53.

81. See John D. Cook, Susan J. Hepworth , Toby D. Wall, and Peter B. Warr, *The Experience of Work* (London, Academic Press, 1981); and Dale Henderson and Fess Green, "Measuring Self-Managed Workteams," *Journal for Quality and Participation*, January–February 1997, 52–56.

82. "Small Company's Training Policy Yields Big Results," *The Human Element* (a publication of the Human Development and Leadership Division of the American Society for Quality), 20, no. 1 (Spring 2003).

83. Alan Wolf, "Coors' Customer Focus," *Beverage World,* March 1991.

84. "The Boss is Watching – So Watch Your iPod," *Business Week*, April 24, 2006, 16.

85. Bill Wilson, "Quality Training at FedEx," *Quality Digest* 15, no. 1 (January 1995), 40–43.

86. "Honda of America Launches Computerized Quality Assurance Training," *Quality Progress* 30, no. 10 (October 1997), 19–20.

87. Nancy Page Cooper and Pat Noonan, "Do Teams and Six Sigma Go Together?" *Quality Progress,* June 2003, 25–28.

88. Text adapted from Wayne Stottler, "Improving Service Quality at Honda," *Quality Progress*, October 2004, 33–38. Copyright © 2001, American Society for Quality. Reprinted with permission.

89. Reprinted with permission from Jon Leatherbury, "Talent Show," *Quality Progress*, Vol. 41, No. 11, November 2008, 48–55. Copyright © 2008, American Society for Quality. No further distribution allowed without permission.

90. Peter F. Drucker. *Management Challenges for the 21st Century*. (New York: HarperBusiness, 1999), 139.

91. Michelle Conlin, "The Software Says You're Just Average," *Business Week,* February 25, 2002, 126.

92. Xerox Business Products and Systems, Malcolm Baldrige National Quality Award application, 1989.

93. Adapted from http://www.dwp.gov.uk/age-positive/ by permission of Age Positive/Department for Work and Pensions.

Process Management

Outline

Quality Profiles: DynMcDermott Petroleum Operations Company and Boeing Aerospace Support

Business Processes
- Process Requirements

Process Management Frameworks

Designing Work Processes
- Process Design Approaches
- Mistake-Proofing Processes

Process Control
- Quality Control in Manufacturing
- Quality Control in Services

Process Improvement
- Kaizen
- Improvement Opportunities

Process Improvement Methodologies
- The Deming Cycle
- Creative Problem Solving
- Custom Methodologies

Breakthrough Improvement
- Benchmarking
- Reengineering

Process Management in the Baldrige Criteria, ISO 9000, and Six Sigma

Summary of Key Points and Terminology

Quality in Practice: Gold Star Chili: Process Management

Quality in Practice: Building Japanese Quality in North America

Review Questions

Discussion Questions

Projects, Etc.

Cases The State University Experience
- The PIVOT Initiative at Midwest Bank, Part I
- Novel Connect: Process Management

Netflix turned the DVD rental industry on its ear by offering an all-DVD library of more than 15,000 titles sent through the mail, with no due dates and no late fees. Netflix's Worcester, Massachusetts, hub is a former shoe warehouse that stocks more than 90,000 DVDs, and yet has no shelves. Each morning at 8:00, the U.S. Postal Service (cheaper and quicker than the alternatives, incredibly) drops off "pumpkin carts," orange bins with thousands of returned DVDs from all over New England. Instead of cataloging titles at fixed shelf locations and retrieving them to satisfy a customer order, operators scan the returned discs, collecting data, which computers at Netflix's San Jose headquarters match to new orders. After lunch, the Worcester operators rescan every disc in their inventory; with each scan, they act on instructions from San Jose to "Ship Disc," if a customer wants the film, or "Scan Tomorrow," if not. The Scan Tomorrows move faster, set aside by the handful. Ship Discs get an

Table 7.1 Key Process Management Practices for Performance Excellence

- Identify vital work processes that relate to core competencies and deliver customer value, profitability, organizational success, and sustainability.
- Determine key work process requirements, incorporating input from customers, suppliers, partners, and collaborators.
- Design and innovate work processes to meet all requirements, incorporating new technology, organizational knowledge, cycle time, productivity, cost control, and other efficiency and effectiveness factors.
- Minimize overall costs associated with inspections, tests, and process or performance audits, and seeking to prevent defects, service errors, and rework and minimize warranty costs or customers' productivity losses, as appropriate.
- Implement work processes and control their day-to-day operation to ensure that they meet design requirements, using appropriate performance measures along with customer, supplier, partner, and collaborator input as needed.
- Improve work processes to achieve better performance, reduce variability, improve products and services, and keep processes current with business needs and directions, and share improvements with other organizational units and processes to drive organizational learning and innovation.

envelope and a pair of stickers. Outgoing discs pass through the Omega, a 40-foot-long machine that can organize more than 20,000 outgoing rentals an hour into bins specified by zip codes. Presorting saves Netflix six to seven cents per DVD, as well as providing faster shipping times to customers.[1]

The importance of designing and managing effective processes—such as product design, order entry, manufacturing, distribution, and customer service—throughout the value chain is vital to customer satisfaction and competitive success. Process design and management activities help to prevent defects and errors, eliminate waste and redundancy, and thereby lead to better quality and improved company performance through shorter cycle times, improved flexibility, and, in the case of Netflix, faster and more consistent customer response.

Deming and Juran observed that the overwhelming majority of quality problems are associated with processes; few are caused by the workers themselves. Rather, management is responsible to design the processes and continuously improve them with the help of the workforce. The former president of Texas Instruments Defense Systems & Electronics Group (now part of Raytheon) had a sign in his office that sums up these issues nicely: *"Unless you change the process, why would you expect the results to change?"*

In this chapter, we focus on process management activities that support high performance. Table 7.1 summarizes the key process management practices for performance excellence. The Quality Profiles in this chapter describe two organizations that leverage process management for the benefit of their customers.

Quality Profiles

DynMcDermott Petroleum Operations Company and Boeing Aerospace Support

DynMcDermott Petroleum Operations Company (DM) is the sole management and operations contractor for the Department of Energy's Strategic Petroleum Reserve. The SPR is the United States' emergency oil stockpile and is the largest emergency petroleum supply in the world. As the operations and maintenance contractor, DM performs all tasks to ensure the availability of oil upon order of the President during a supply disruption. DM uses numerous exercises and drills to identify potential needs and challenges in the operating environment and assess its ability to rapidly respond to changing needs and conditions. Twenty-one measures have been identified by DOE as being critical to the readiness of the SPR. Drawdown systems availability has sustained a 98 percent or better performance level and has exceeded DOE expectations in each year and at each site since 2001. Drawdown, providing crude oil to U.S. refineries by order of the President during severe disruptions of foreign supply, is the primary mission of the SPR. Drawdown readiness shows a steadily improving trend from 95 percent in 1999 to 99 percent or better from 2002 through 2005, exceeding DOE's 95 percent drawdown target. Days to Commence Drawdown, as a measure of performance, has been reduced from 15 in 2002 to 13 in 2005.

Several of DM's sites were directly impacted by hurricanes Katrina and Rita in 2005, resulting in the majority of employees being displaced from their homes and worksites. DM was able to restore operations immediately and begin the Oil Exchange Program (providing oil to refiners in order for them to continue operations) in less than five days after Hurricane Katrina. To conduct these operations in the face of Hurricane Katrina, the primary SPR computer network was re-routed and deployed to an Emergency Operation Center in Texas. Hurricane Rita forced another evacuation and DM deployed its mobile emergency operations center according to plan. During this period, President Bush declared a drawdown from the SPR, an action that has occurred only twice in 30 years. Even though the Emergency Operation Center had to be relocated over 200 miles, DM made its first drawdown oil delivery three days after Rita. DM received a Baldrige Award in 2005.

Boeing Aerospace Support (AS) is part of the Boeing Company, the largest aerospace company in the world. Boeing AS provides products and services, including aircraft maintenance, modification, and repair, and training for aircrews and maintenance staff, to reduce life-cycle costs and increase the effectiveness of aircraft. Ninety-seven percent of Boeing AS' business comes from military customers. Carefully planned and well-managed processes combined with a culture that encourages knowledge sharing and working together have been essential to Boeing AS' ability to deliver high-quality products and services. Boeing AS has developed a seven-step approach for defining, managing, stabilizing, and improving processes. This process-based management, or PBM, methodology also is used to set goals and performance metrics and requires interaction and agreement among process owners, users, suppliers, and customers. Teams of employees who "own" and are responsible for the company's complex operations and processes are the core of the company's high-performance work environment. A highly structured process known as the "AS People System" helps to ensure that employees who comprise these teams understand priorities and expectations; have the knowledge, training, and tools they need to do the job and to assess performance against goals and objectives; and are rewarded and recognized for their accomplishments.

Since 1999, on-time delivery of maintenance and modification products and services, significant hardware, and other products has been between 95 and 99 percent. Quality ratings for the maintenance of C-17 aircraft has been near 100 percent since 1998 compared to AS' competitors, which trail at 70 percent in 2002 and 90 percent in 2003.

The Supplier On-Time Delivery Rate has improved from about 68 percent in 1999 to about 95 percent in 2003, matching best-in-Boeing results. Quality of Supplier Deliverables has been above 99.5 percent for the last three years and was at 99.7 percent for 2003, the year in which it received a Baldrige Award.

Source: DynMcDermott Petroleum Operations Company, Malcolm Baldridge Application Summary, 2005. National Institute of Standards and Technology, U.S. Department of Commerce. Reprinted with permission.

BUSINESS PROCESSES

Common business processes include acquiring customer and market knowledge, strategic planning, research and development, purchasing, developing new products or services, fulfilling customer orders, managing information, measuring and analyzing performance, and training employees, to name just a few.

Leading companies identify important business processes throughout the value chain that affect their ability to deliver customer value. These processes typically fall into two categories: value-creation processes and support processes.

Value-creation processes (sometimes called *core processes*) are those most important to "running the business" and maintaining or achieving a sustainable competitive advantage. These processes frequently relate to an organization's core competencies and strategic objectives, which we discussed in Chapter 4. They drive the creation of products and services, are critical to customer satisfaction, and have a major impact on the strategic goals of an organization. Value-creation processes typically include product design and production/delivery processes. Product design processes involve all activities that are performed to incorporate customer requirements, new technology, and organizational knowledge into the functional specifications of a product (i.e., a manufactured good or service). We will discuss product design in depth in Chapter 12. Production/delivery processes create or deliver the actual product; examples are manufacturing, assembly, dispensing medications, teaching a class, and so on. In addition, value-creation processes include other critical business processes such as research and development, technology acquisition, supply chain management, mergers and acquisitions, and project management. In non-profit organizations, value-creation processes might include fundraising, media relations, and public policy advocacy.

Support processes are those that are most important to an organization's value-creation processes, employees, and daily operations. They provide infrastructure for value-creation processes, but generally do not add value directly to the product or service. Support processes might include processes for finance and accounting, facilities management, legal services, human resource services, public relations, and other administrative services. A process such as order entry that might be thought of as a value-creation process for one company (e.g., a direct mail distributor), might be considered as a support process for another (e.g., a custom manufacturer). In general, value-creation processes are driven by external customer needs, whereas support processes are driven by internal customer needs. Because value-creation processes do add value to products and services, they require a higher level of attention than do support processes.

For many organizations, supply chains are among the most important business processes and can be viewed as encompassing many key value-creation and support processes. They help companies create competitive advantage in delivery, flexibility, and cost reduction. A report from AMR Research, Inc. suggests that companies that excel in supply chain operations also perform better in other financial measures of success. As one executive at AMR Research stated ". . . value chain performance translates into productivity and market-share leadership. . . . supply chain leadership means more than just low costs and efficiency—it requires a superior ability to shape and respond to shifts in demand with innovative products and services."[2] An important part of supply chain management is managing supplier relationships (e.g., how performance requirements are communicated and ensured, mutual assistance and training, etc.); this is often viewed as an important support process.

We may view processes according to the three levels of quality discussed in Chapter 1. Major value-creation and support processes are generally defined at the organizational level; these activities require attention by senior managers. Each major process consists of many subprocesses that are managed by functional managers or cross-functional teams. Finally, each subprocess consists of many specific work steps performed by individuals at the performer level. As an example, Boeing Airlift

In many companies, value-creation processes take the form of ***projects****—temporary work structures that start up, produce products or services, and then shut down.*[3]

and Tanker (A&T) Programs have developed an "enterprise process model" that views the entire business as eight interconnected process families. These major groupings range from enterprise leadership and new business development to production and post-delivery product support. Each family encompasses up to 10 major processes, which, in turn, are made up of several tiers of supporting subprocesses. A&T manages cross-cutting relationships as "mega-processes" that extend to suppliers and customers.

Some organizations are project-focused because of the nature of their work. They tend to deliver unique, one-of-a-kind products or services tailored to the specific needs of an individual customer. Examples include performing clinical trials for pharmaceutical companies, market research studies, consulting, and systems installation. **Project management** involves all activities associated with planning, scheduling, and controlling projects. Project management is particularly important for Six Sigma, because typical projects generally cut across organizational boundaries and require the coordination of many different departments and functions.

Although every project is unique, many projects have similar underlying processes, viewing them from a process management perspective can improve the overall quality of the project effort. To illustrate, consider Custom Research Incorporated (CRI), which conducts unique market research studies for many different organizations. A Cycle Time Task Force identified nine common processes for all marketing research studies: identification of client requirements/expectations, questionnaire design, questionnaire programming, sampling, data collection, data tabulation, report and analysis, internal communication, and client communication. A Process Task Force was formed to map and improve each process. For example, CRI developed a "one-entry system" that eliminates the need to enter data into its computer system more than once, and allows questionnaires to be tested for validity and reliability, eliminating several programming steps and helping to reduce cycle time. An account team is in charge of every research project. Project-related problems anywhere in the process are recognized and reported by the team. Team members use their problem-solving skills to determine whether the variation is due to common or special causes, analyze the reasons for the occurrence, and implement changes that will prevent it from recurring. When each project is completed, the account team completes a Project Quality Recap documenting problems and solutions and rating the performance of internal departments. Teams refer to the Recaps on file when they have similar projects or subsequent projects from the same client.[4]

Organizations such as Custom Research use a pure-project organizational structure whereby team members are assigned exclusively to projects and report only to a project manager. This approach makes it easier to manage projects, because project teams can be designed for efficiency by including the right mix of skills; however, it can result in inefficiencies because of duplication of resources across the organization, for example, having a different information technology support person on each project. However, in a typical manufacturing or service firm, projects are not the major value-creation process, but such projects are chartered to meet infrequent needs, such as a new facility layout or technology rollout. In these cases, a matrix organizational structure, which "loans" people and other resources to projects while still maintaining functional control over them, is often used. Matrix organizational structures have proven to be effective in Six Sigma organizations. The importance of the project management life cycle for Six Sigma projects will be discussed in more detail in Chapter 11.

Process Requirements

Understanding the requirements that processes should meet is vital to designing them. One of the fundamental questions asked by SSM Health Care during their process design activities is "What are the customer's expected outcomes from the process?" Reviewing patient/customer feedback data, conducting specialized surveys or focus groups, and including customers on design teams help them answer this question.

Given the diverse nature of value-creation processes, the requirements and performance characteristics might vary significantly for different processes. Value-creation process requirements usually depend significantly on product and service characteristics. For example, if hotel customers expect fast, error-free check-in, then the check-in process must be designed for speed and accuracy. Support process requirements, on the other hand, usually depend on internal requirements, and they must be coordinated and integrated to ensure efficient and effective linkage and performance. For example, information technology processes at a hotel must support the check-in process requirements of speed and accuracy; this would require real-time information on room availability.

Table 7.2 shows the value-creation processes and their requirements defined by Pal's Sudden Service, a regional chain of fast-food restaurants in the southeastern United States. Their support processes include accounting/finance, human resources, maintenance, management information systems, ordering, and stocking. Other critical support processes that lead to business success and growth might be research and development, technology acquisition, supply chain management and supplier partnering, mergers and acquisitions, project management, or sales and marketing. These processes will differ greatly among organizations, depending on the nature of products and services, customer and market requirements, global focus, and other factors. For example, a hospital might define its key value-creation processes as pre-admission screening, admission and registration, assessment and diagnosis, treatment, discharge and follow up; support services might include workforce management, medical records and information technology, financial planning, supply chain management, environmental services, and physical plant operations.

Table 7.2 Value-Creation Processes for Pal's Sudden Service

Process	**Principal Requirements**
Order taking	Accurate, fast, friendly
Cooking	Proper temperature
Product assembly	Proper sequence, sanitary, correct ingredients and amounts, speed, proper temperature, neat
Cash collection	Accurate, fast, friendly
Slicing	Cut/size, freshness/color
Chili preparation	Proper temperature, quantity, freshness
Ham/chicken preparation	Proper temperature, quantity, freshness
Supply chain management	Price/cost, order accuracy
Property acquisition	Sales potential, adherence to budget
Construction	On time, within budget
Marketing and advertising	Clear message, brand recognition

Source: Reprinted with permission of Pal's Sudden Service.

Process management involves planning and administering the activities necessary to achieve a high level of performance in key business processes, and identifying opportunities for improving quality and operational performance, and ultimately, customer satisfaction.

PROCESS MANAGEMENT FRAMEWORKS

As we noted in Chapter 1, essentially all work in an organization is performed by some process. The goal of process management is to achieve the highest level of process performance. Nearly every leading company views process management as a fundamental business activity. AT&T, for example, bases its methodology on the following principles:

- Process improvement focuses on the end-to-end process.
- The mind-set of quality is one of prevention and continuous improvement.
- Everyone manages a process at some level and is simultaneously a customer and a supplier.
- Customer needs drive process improvement.
- Corrective action focuses on removing the root cause of the problem rather than on treating its symptoms.
- Process simplification reduces opportunities for errors and rework.
- Process improvement results from a disciplined and structured application of the quality management principles.[5]

Individuals or groups, known as **process owners**, are accountable for process performance and have the authority to manage and improve their process. Process owners may range from high-level executives who manage cross-functional processes to workers who run a manufacturing cell or an assembly operation on the shop floor. Assigning process owners ensures that someone is responsible to manage the process and optimize its effectiveness. For example, processes that support learning-centered processes at a Baldrige-recipient school system—Community Consolidated School District 15—include transportation, custodial, central stores, technology infrastructure, and maintenance. These processes are aligned with the learning-centered processes to help achieve student performance targets. Owners of these processes collect student and stakeholder requirement data through both formal and informal means, and use these data to design, implement, and evaluate processes that will both improve organizational efficiency and contribute to student learning results.

Process management consists of three important activities: *design*, *control*, and *improvement*.[6] *Design* focuses on ensuring that the inputs to the process, such as materials, technology, work methods, and people are adequate, and that the process steps are well-defined, mistake-proofed, sequenced properly, lean, and understood for consistent and effective execution. *Control* focuses on assessing whether the process performed as planned and the process output is on target. If not, then the cause must be determined and corrected. *Improvement* focuses on continually seeking to achieve higher levels of performance in the process, such as reduced variation, higher yields, fewer defects and errors, and so on.

Many companies use an integrated framework for their process management activities. For instance, Boeing Aerospace Support developed a process-based management (PBM) framework that consists of three phases: *define the process* (design), *measure the process* (control), and *improve the process*. The framework begins with a design phase by defining the process and establishing customer-centric metrics by which to measure performance. The control phase monitors the metrics and stabilizes the process to lead to predictable performance. Finally, an improvement phase sets improvement goals, develops an implementation plan, and implements it.

This phase uses Six Sigma, lean tools, and other classic methods. After improvements are implemented, the approach goes back to the control phase to monitor the new improvement. Note that all three elements of process management—design, control, and improvement—are integrated into this framework.

To apply the techniques of process management, processes must be, (1) repeatable, and (2) measurable. Repeatability means that the process must recur over time. The cycle may be long, as with product development processes or patent applications; or it may be short, as with a manufacturing operation or an order entry process. Measurement provides the ability to capture important quality and performance indicators to reveal patterns about process performance. Each measurement should aim for a standard or target that is driven by customer requirements. Meeting these two conditions ensures that sufficient data can be collected to reveal useful information for evaluation and control, as well as learning that leads to improvement and maturity.

DESIGNING WORK PROCESSES

Process design can have a significant impact on cost (and hence profitability), flexibility (the ability to produce the right types and amounts of products as customer demand or preferences change), and the quality of the output. A good process design ensures that goods and services meet both external and internal customer requirements, and that the process is capable of achieving the requisite level of performance. Other factors that might need to be considered in process design include safety, process performance and variability, productivity, environmental impact, "green" manufacturing, measurement capability, and maintainability of equipment.

The goal of process design is to develop an efficient procedure to satisfy both internal and external customer requirements.

As customer needs and expectations change, organizations must design processes that are increasingly agile. **Agility** is a term that is commonly used to characterize flexibility and short cycle times. Electronic commerce, for instance, requires more rapid, flexible, and customized responses than traditional market outlets. Flexibility might demand special strategies such as modular designs, sharing components, sharing manufacturing lines, and specialized training for employees. It also involves outsourcing decisions, agreements with key suppliers, and innovative partnering arrangements. Enablers of agility include close relationships with customers to understand their emerging needs and requirements, empowering employees as decision makers, effective manufacturing and information technology, close supplier and partner relationships, and breakthrough improvement.

***Flexibility** refers to the ability to adapt quickly and effectively to changing requirements. It might mean rapid changeover from one product to another, rapid response to changing demands, or the ability to produce a wide range of customized services.*

One example of agility is the Stockholm-based fashion retailer, Hennes & Mauritz (H&M). While traditional clothing retailers design their products at least six months in advance of the selling season, H&M can rush items into stores in as little as 3 weeks. By monitoring consumer trends and identifying hot-selling items, its designers immediately start to sketch new styles, which are then developed by pattern makers, often using employees as live models. Designs are sent electronically to factories in Europe and Asia that can handle the jobs quickly, and in less than two months, most H&M stores will have the new styles in stock. One of the company's enablers is empowered employees who can dream up and produce new fashions without formal approval.[7]

Agility is crucial to such customer-focused strategies as *mass customization*—providing personalized, custom-designed products to meet individual customer preferences at prices comparable to mass-produced items. Lands' End customers can take simple shirt and pants size measurements at home and answer a series of questions on its website. Then, using a series of algorithms, Lands' End translates the information into a customized pattern that is sent to one of five contracted manufacturers in the United States and overseas, where the plants cut and sew the garment and ship it directly to the customer. The data are saved on the website, making reordering a breeze.[8] Mass customization requires significant changes to traditional manufacturing processes that focus on either customized, crafted products or mass-produced, standardized products.[9] These processes incorporate flexible manufacturing technologies, just-in-time systems, information technology, and emphasize cycle time reduction.

Process Design Approaches

In manufacturing, process design usually involves detailed technical analysis of product characteristics, technology capabilities, production sequences, assembly methods, and so on, using tools such as flow-process charts, assembly charts, and work methods analysis, which are often conducted by industrial or manufacturing engineers. Fast-food restaurants, for example, have carefully designed their food preparation and delivery processes for a high degree of accuracy and fast response time.[10] New hands-free intercom systems, better microphones that reduce ambient kitchen noise, and screens that display a customer's order are all focused on these requirements. Timers at Wendy's count every segment of the order completion process to help managers identify problem areas. Kitchen workers wear headsets to hear orders as they are placed. Even the use of photos on drive-through order boards make it more likely for customers to select these items; less variety means faster order fulfillment.

Most cross-functional business value-creation processes and all support processes are primarily service-oriented. Thus, it is important to understand the fundamental differences between manufacturing and service processes. First, the outputs of service processes are not as well defined, as are manufactured products. For example, even though all banks offer similar tangible goods such as checking, loans, automatic tellers, and so forth, the real differentiating factor among banks is the service they provide. Second, most service processes involve a greater interaction with the customer, often making it easier to identify needs and expectations. On the other hand, customers often cannot define their needs for service until after they have some point of reference or comparison.

Service processes often involve both internal and external activities, a factor that complicates design for quality. In a bank, for example, poor service can result from the way that tellers treat customers and also from poor quality of computers and communications equipment beyond the control of the tellers. Internal activities are primarily concerned with efficiency (quality of conformance), while external activities—with direct customer interaction—require attention to effectiveness (quality of design). All too often, workers involved in internal operations do not understand how their performance affects the customers they do not see. The success of the process depends on everyone—workers involved in internal as well as external activities—understanding that they add value to the customer.

Designing any process begins with identifying and documenting it. For example, Corning Telecommunications Products Division (TPD) has identified and documented more than 800 processes in all areas of its business, of which 50 are designated as "core business processes" that merit special emphasis in continuous improvement efforts. Each core process is owned and managed by a key business leader. Documenting a process involves describing how it is performed. It will likely include developing a process "map" or flowchart, and writing standard operating procedures and work instructions. Many companies use ISO 9000 to assist in this effort. Branch-Smith Printing, for example, identified more than 40 processes as part of the process of converting to ISO 9000.

Because processes generally cut across traditional organizational functions, accurately defining a process may take some investigation and thought. A process flowchart (see Chapter 11 for further discussion) helps in doing this as it lists in detail the sequence of steps—value-adding activities and specific tasks—involved in producing a product or delivering a service. Such a graphical representation provides an excellent communication device for visualizing and understanding the process. Flowcharts can become the basis for job descriptions, employee-training programs, and performance measurement. They help managers to estimate human resources, information systems, equipment, and facilities requirements. As design tools, they enable management to study and analyze processes prior to implementation in order to improve quality and operational performance. Figure 7.1 shows The Ritz-Carlton's Three Steps of Service process. The process is highly structured and defines the procedures for anticipating and complying with customer needs. All employees who come in contact with customers are trained to follow this process.

A basic approach to process design is suggested by Motorola:

1. *Identify the product or service:* What work do I do?
2. *Identify the customer:* Who is the work for?
3. *Identify the supplier:* What do I need and from whom do I get it?
4. *Identify the process:* What steps or tasks are performed? What are the inputs and outputs for each step?

Figure 7.1 The Ritz-Carlton Hotel Company: Three Steps of Service Process

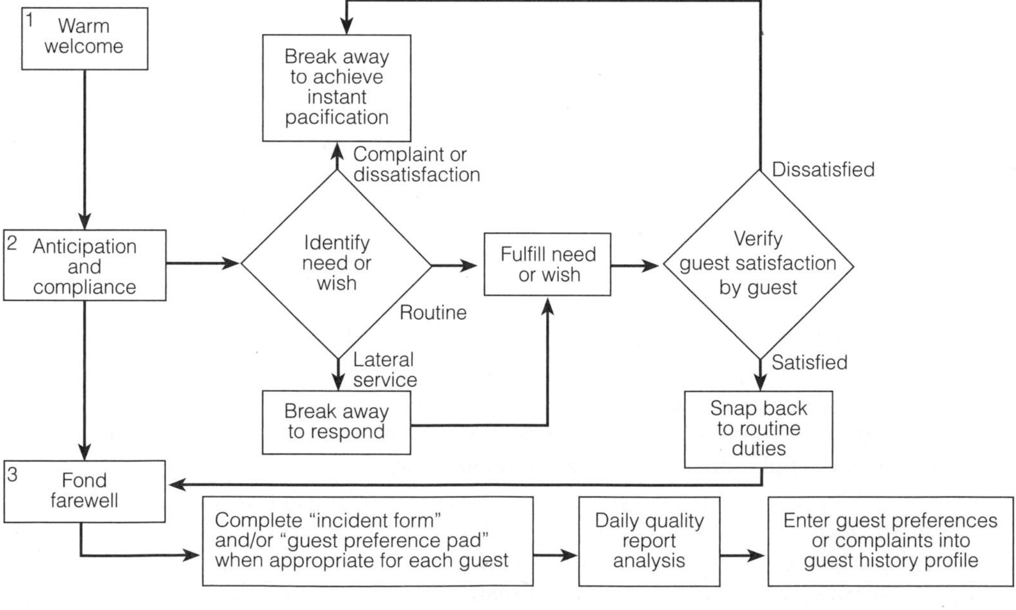

Source: Adapted from the Malcolm Baldridge National Quality Award Application Summaries of the Ritz-Carlton Hotel Company, L.L.C., copyright © 1992.

5. *Mistake-proof the process:* How can I eliminate or simplify tasks? What "poka-yoke" (i.e., mistake-proofing) devices (see discussion later in this chapter) can I use?
6. *Develop measurements, controls, and improvement goals*: How do I evaluate the process? How can I improve further?

Steps 1 through 3 address such questions as "What is the purpose of the process?", "How does the process create customer satisfaction?", and "What are the essential inputs and outputs of the process?" Step 4 focuses on the actual process design by defining the specific tasks performed in transforming the inputs to outputs. Step 5 focuses on making the process efficient and capable of delivering high quality. Step 6 ensures that the process will be monitored and controlled to the level of required performance. This monitoring involves gathering in-process measurements and/or customer feedback on a regular basis and using this information to control and improve the process.

Pure-service processes are often designed around the five key service dimensions that we introduced in Chapter 5: reliability, assurance, tangibles, empathy, and responsiveness. For example, the City of Coral Springs, Florida, clearly understands its customer requirements and incorporates them into the design of its processes. The city's building permit work process is designed to be responsive, professional, consistent, and accessible; and its fleet maintenance work process is designed to be reliable, convenient, and responsive. Processes are designed to meet all key requirements through multiple phases of testing and revision before a process or signifiant process change is fully implemented and through involvement of customers in the design. Teams develop innovations when existing processes fail to meet changing requirements or research on best practices shows that exiting approaches are inadequate to meet new requirements. New technology is incorporated into processes through Information Services staff who serve on all development teams. They research best practices, and scout and critique new technology through professional associations, user groups, and networks of local governments. Coral Springs has incorporated web-enabled applications into the building permit process, the employment process, and water bill payment.[11]

Services have three basic components: physical facilities, processes, and procedures; employee behavior; and employee professional judgment.[12]

Designing a service essentially involves determining an effective balance of physical facilities, process, and procedures; employee behavior; and employee professional judgement. The goal is to provide a service whose elements are internally consistent and directed at meeting the needs of a specific target market segment. Too much or too little emphasis on one component will lead to problems and poor customer perceptions. For example, too much emphasis on procedures might result in timely and efficient service, but might also suggest insensitivity and apathy toward the customer. Too much emphasis on behavior might provide a friendly and personable environment at the expense of slow, inconsistent, or chaotic service. Too much emphasis on professional judgment might lead to good solutions to customer problems but also to slow, inconsistent, or insensitive service.

A useful approach to designing effective services is first to recognize that services differ in the degree of customer contact and interaction, the degree of labor intensity, and the degree of customization. For example, a railroad is low in all three dimensions. On the other hand, an interior design service would be high in all three dimensions. A fast-food restaurant would be high in customer contact and labor intensity, but low in customization.

Services low in all three dimensions of this classification are more similar to manufacturing organizations. The emphasis on quality should be focused on the physical facilities and procedures; behavior and professional judgment are relatively unimportant. As contact and interaction between the customer and the service system increases, two factors must be taken into account. In services low in labor intensity, the customer's impression of physical facilities, processes, and procedures is important. Service organizations must exercise special care in choosing and maintaining reliable and easy-to-use equipment. With higher levels of contact and interaction, appropriate staff behavior becomes increasingly important.

As labor intensity increases, variations between individuals become more important; however, the elements of personal behavior and professional judgment will remain relatively unimportant as long as the degrees of customization and contact and interaction remain low. As customization increases, professional judgment becomes a bigger factor in the customer's perception of service quality. In services that are high in all three dimensions, facilities, behavior, and professional judgment must be equally balanced.

In services, quality standards take the place of the dimensions and tolerances applicable in manufacturing. Examples of standards set by one of the airline industry leaders, Swissair, include:

- Ninety percent of calls are answered within 30 seconds.
- Ninety percent of passengers are checked in within three minutes of arrival.
- Baggage claim time is only 10 minutes between the first and last customer.

However, service standards are inherently more difficult to define and measure than manufacturing specifications. They require extensive research into customer needs and attitudes regarding timeliness, consistency, accuracy, and other service requirements, as discussed in previous chapters. Even though many product specifications developed for manufactured products are focused on meeting a target, such as a product dimension, service targets typically are "smaller is better." Thus, the true service standard is zero defects, and any other standards (such as those of Swissair) should be construed as interim standards and targets only.

In designing high-quality service processes, consider the following questions:[13]

- What service standards are already in place?
- Which of these standards have been clearly communicated to all service personnel?
- Have these standards been communicated to the public?
- Which standards require refinement?
- What is the final result of the service provided? What should it ideally be?
- What is the maximum access time that a patron will tolerate without feeling inconvenienced?
- How long should it take to perform the service itself?
- What is the maximum time for completion of service before the customer's view of the service is negatively affected?
- At what point does service begin, and what indicator signals the completion of the service?
- How many different people must the consumer deal with in completing the service?
- What components of the service are essential? Desirable? Superfluous?

- What components or aspects of service must be controlled in order to deliver a service encounter of equal quality each time one occurs?
- Which components can differ from encounter to encounter while still leading to a total service encounter that meets standards?
- What products that affect its service performance does a service organization obtain from other sources?

As you can see, service process design is not a trivial exercise!

Mistake-Proofing Processes

Human beings tend to make mistakes inadvertently.[14] Typical mistakes in production are omitted processing, processing errors, setup errors, missing parts, wrong parts, and adjustment errors. Such errors can arise from the following factors:

- Forgetfulness due to lack of concentration
- Misunderstanding because of the lack of familiarity with a process or procedures
- Poor identification associated with lack of proper attention
- Lack of experience
- Absentmindedness
- Delays in judgment when a process is automated
- Equipment malfunctions

Blaming workers not only discourages them and lowers morale, but also does not solve the problem.

The poka-yoke concept was developed and refined in the early 1960s by the late Shigeo Shingo, a Japanese manufacturing engineer who developed the Toyota production system.[15] Shingo visited a plant and observed that the plant was not using any type of measurement or statistical process control system for tracking defects. When asked why, the manager replied that they did not make any defects to track! His investigation led to the development of a mistake-proofing approach called Zero Quality Control, or ZQC. ZQC is driven by simple and inexpensive inspection processes, such as successive checking, in which operators inspect the work of the prior operation before continuing, and self-checking, in which operators assess the quality of their own work. Poka-yokes are designed to facilitate this process or remove the human element completely.

***Poka-yoke** (POH-kah YOH-kay) is an approach for mistake-proofing processes using automatic devices or methods to avoid simple human error.*

Poka-yoke is focused on two aspects: (1) prediction, or recognizing that a defect is about to occur and providing a warning, and (2) detection, or recognizing that a defect has occurred and stopping the process. Many applications of poka-yoke are deceptively simple, yet creative. Usually, they are inexpensive to implement. One of Shingo's first poka-yoke devices involved a process at the Yamada Electric plant in which workers assemble a switch having two push buttons supported by two springs.[16] Occasionally, the worker would forget to insert a spring under each button, which led to a costly and embarrassing repair at the customer's facility. In the old method, the worker would take two springs out of a large parts box and then assemble the switch. To prevent this mistake, the worker was instructed first to place two springs in a small dish in front of the parts box, and then assemble the switch. If a spring remains in the dish, the operator knows immediately that an error has occurred. The solution was simple, cheap, and provided immediate feedback to the operator. Many other examples can be cited:

- Machines have limit switches connected to warning lights that tell the operator when parts are positioned improperly on the machine.
- A device on a drill counts the number of holes drilled in a work piece; a buzzer sounds if the work piece is removed before the correct number of holes has been drilled.
- Computer programs display a warning message if a file that has not been saved is to be closed. Computers are also designed so that the correct cord can only be plugged into the correct socket.
- Passwords used for Web accounts are often entered twice.

From this discussion and examples, we see three levels of mistake-proofing with increasing costs associated with them:

1. *Designing potential errors out of the process.* Clearly, this approach is the most powerful form of mistake-proofing because it eliminates any possibility that the error or defect might occur and has no direct cost in terms of time or rework and scrap.
2. *Identifying potential defects and stopping a process before the defect is produced.* Although this approach eliminates any cost associated with producing a defect, it does require the time associated with stopping a process and taking corrective action.
3. *Finding defects that enter or leave a process.* This approach eliminates wasted resources that would add value to nonconforming work, but clearly results in scrap or rework.

Richard B. Chase and Douglas M. Stewart suggest that the same concepts can be applied to services.[17] The major differences are that service mistake-proofing must account for the customers' activities as well as those of the producer, and for interactions between the customer and provider. Chase and Stewart classify service poka-yokes by the type of error they are designed to prevent: server errors and customer errors. Server errors result from the task, treatment, or tangibles of the service. Customer errors occur during preparation, the service encounter, or during resolution. The following list summarizes the typical types of service errors and related poka-yokes.

Task errors include doing work incorrectly, work not requested, work on the wrong order, or working too slowly. Some examples of poka-yoke devices for task errors are computer prompts, color-coded cash register keys, measuring tools such as a French-fry scoop, and signaling devices. Hospitals use trays for surgical instruments that have indentations for each instrument, preventing the surgeon from leaving one of them in the patient. Simple checklists are often used; for example, LifeWings, a company that applies flight-tested safety lessons from the aviation industry to medicine, works with medical teams to create standardized lists of activities for every procedure.[18]

Treatment errors arise in the contact between the server and the customer, such as lack of courteous behavior, and failure to acknowledge, listen, or react appropriately to the customer. A bank encourages eye contact by requiring tellers to record the customer's eye color on a checklist as they start the transaction. To promote friendliness at a fast-food restaurant, trainers provide the four specific cues for when to smile: when greeting the customer, when taking the order, when telling about the dessert special, and when giving the customer change. They encourage employees to observe whether the customer smiled back, a natural reinforcer for smiling.

Tangible errors are those in physical elements of the service, such as unclean facilities, dirty uniforms, inappropriate temperature, and document errors. Hotels wrap paper strips around towels to help the housekeeping staff identify clean linen and show which ones should be replaced. Spell-checkers in word processing software help reduce document misspellings (provided they are used!).

Customer errors in preparation include the failure to bring necessary materials to the encounter, to understand their role in the service transaction, and to engage the correct service. A computer manufacturer provides a flowchart to specify how to place a service call. By guiding the customers through three yes-or-no questions, the flowchart prompts them to have the necessary information before calling.

Customer errors during an encounter can be due to inattention, misunderstanding, or simply a memory lapse, and include failure to remember steps in the process or to follow instructions. Poka-yoke examples include height bars at amusement rides that indicate rider size requirements, beepers that signal customers to remove cards from ATM machines, and locks on airplane lavatory doors that must be closed to turn on the lights. Some cashiers at restaurants fold back the top edge of credit card receipts, holding together the restaurant's copies while revealing the customer's copy.

Customer errors at the resolution stage of a service encounter include failure to signal service inadequacies, to learn from experience, to adjust expectations, and to execute appropriate post-encounter actions. Hotels might enclose a small gift certificate to encourage guests to provide feedback. Strategically placed tray-return stands and trash receptacles remind customers to return trays in fast-food facilities.

PROCESS CONTROL

A British Airways Boeing B-777 was forced to make an emergency landing in Houston after an engine caught fire. The cause was traced to the fact that the wrong engine blade had been processed and shipped to the customer, and that inspections to prevent such an error were inadequate. GE's "quality notice" on the incident stated that employees failed to detect that the blade casting was misidentified when it arrived at the plant or after they processed and cleared it for installation. The notice recommended adding verification requirements at several stages of the process, which the company has done. The incident cost GE $8 million.[19] Although GE acted swiftly to resolve the problems, this case demonstrates the importance of *process control*.

Control is the activity of ensuring conformance to the requirements and taking corrective action when necessary to correct problems and maintain stable performance. The distinction between control and improvement is illustrated in Figure 7.2. Any process performance measure naturally fluctuates around some average level. Abnormal conditions or unusual events may cause a departure from this pattern. Removing the causes of such abnormalities and maintaining consistent performance is the essence of control. However, even a controlled process that has too much variation can be detrimental to customer satisfaction and financial performance. For example, research in the airline industry has shown that lack of service consistency (with respect to arrival times) has a definite impact on customer dissatisfaction. Process consistency was found to be at least as important as average performance for better-performing firms, where customer expectations are high.[20] Thus, improvement can mean changing the average performance to a new level or reducing variation around the current average performance. Control charts, which will be discussed thoroughly in Chapter 13, are an important tool for controlling processes.

Process control is important for two reasons. First, process control methods are the basis for effective daily management of processes. Second, long-term improvements cannot be made to a process unless the process is first brought under control.

Any control system has four elements: (1) *a standard or goal*, (2) *a means of measuring*

Figure 7.2 Control versus Improvement

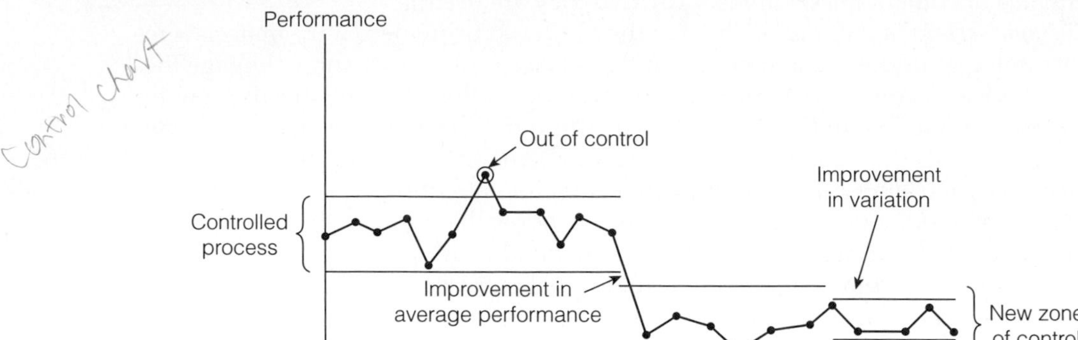

accomplishment, (3) *comparison of results with the standard to provide feedback,* and (4) *the ability to make corrections as appropriate.* Goals and standards are defined during planning and design processes. They establish what is supposed to be accomplished. These goals and standards are reflected by measurable quality characteristics, such as product dimensions, service times, or employee behavior. For example, golf balls must meet five standards to be considered as conforming to the Rules of Golf: minimum size, maximum weight, spherical symmetry, maximum initial velocity, and overall distance.[21] In some call centers, employees must follow a specific script or ask certain questions of every customer. Measuring quality characteristics may be accomplished through some sort of inspection activity. For instance, golf balls are measured for size by trying to drop them through a metal ring—a conforming ball sticks to the ring while a nonconforming ball falls through; digital scales measure weight to one-thousandth of a gram; and initial velocity is measured in a special machine by finding the time it takes a ball struck at 98 mph to break a ballistic screen at the end of a tube exactly 6.28 feet away. Call centers might record conversations between customers and employees. By comparing results with the standards or goals, one can determine whether corrective action is needed. Many companies use statistical process control (see Chapter 13) as a means of signaling when deviations from standards require corrective action. Corrective action might entail adjusting the processes that make golf balls or retraining call center employees. Proper corrective action involves changes at the source of the deviation. Such corrective action should minimize the likelihood of this type of variation occurring again or elsewhere in the organization.

Many different mechanisms are used in manufacturing facilities to control quality. For example, DaimlerChrysler manufactures the PT Cruiser at the company's Toluca Assembly Plant in Mexico. The Toluca plant verifies parts, processes, fit, and finish every step of the way, from stamping and body to paint and final assembly. The control practices include visual management through quality alert systems, which are designed to call immediate attention to abnormal conditions. The system provides visual and audible signals for each station for tooling, production, maintenance, and material flow.[22] In many cases, control processes are automated. For instance, in the production of plastic sheet stock, thickness depends on temperature. Sensors monitor the sheet thickness; if it begins to go out of tolerance, the system can adjust the temperature in order to change the thickness.

Table 7.3 SSM Health Care Process Requirements and Measures

Process	Key Requirements	Key Measures
Admit		
Admitting/ registration	Timeliness	• Time to admit patients to the setting of care • Timeliness in admitting/registration rate on patient satisfaction survey questions
Assess		
Patient assessment	Timeliness	• % of histories and physicals charted within 24 hours or prior to surgery • Pain assessed at appropriate intervals, per hospital policy
Clinical laboratory and radiology services	Accuracy and Timeliness	• Quality control results/repeat rates • Turnaround time • Response rate on medical staff satisfaction survey
Care Delivery/Treatment		
Provision of clinical care	Nurse responsiveness, pain management, successful clinical, outcomes	• Response rate on patient satisfaction and medical staff survey questions • Wait time for pain medications • % CHF patients received medication instructions/weighing • % Ischemic heart patients discharged on proven therapies • Unplanned readmits/returns to ER or Operating Room • Mortality
Pharmacy/ medication use	Accuracy	• Use of dangerous abbreviations in medication orders • Med error rate or adverse drug events resulting from medication errors
Surgical services/ anesthesia	Professional skill, competence/ communication	• Clear documentation of informed surgical and anesthesia consent • Perioperative mortality • Surgical site infection rates
Discharge		
Case management	Appropriate utilization	• Average length of stay (ALOS) • Payment denials • Unplanned readmits
Discharge from setting of care	Assistance and clear directions	• Discharge instructions documented and provided to patient • Response rate on patient satisfaction survey

Source: Reprinted with permission of SSM Health Care.

Measures and indicators are the basis for controlling processes. The key measures used by SSM Health Care to monitor their processes are shown in Table 7.3. Daily, weekly, monthly, and quarterly performance assessments provide the opportunity to review and manage these measures and identify ways of preventing potential errors before they affect the patient. Measurements should occur at the earliest points possible in processes to minimize problems and costs that may result from deviations from expected performance.

In many industries, in-process measures are collected through some type of manual inspection process. Such processes that rely on visual interpretation of product characteristics or manual reading of gauges and instruments may encounter error rates of from 10 to 50 percent. These high rates occur for several reasons:

- *Complexity:* The number of defects caught by an inspector decreases with more parts and less orderly arrangement.
- *Defect rate:* When the product defect rate is low, inspectors tend to miss more defects than when the defect rate is higher.
- *Inspection rate:* The inspector's performance degrades rapidly as the inspection rate increases.[23]

These factors can be mitigated by using automated technology, or at the very least, minimizing the number of quality characteristics that must be inspected, reducing time pressures, using repeated inspections (if the same item is inspected by several people, a higher percentage of total defects will be caught), and improving the design of the workspace to facilitate the inspection task.

Short-term corrective action generally should be taken by those who own the process and are responsible for doing the work, such as machine operators, order-fulfillment workers, and so on. Long-term remedial action is the responsibility of management. The responsibility for control can be determined by checking the four elements of control systems. If any of these are not available to the process owner (for instance, lack of standards or goals, or inability to take corrective action), then the process is the responsibility of management, not the process owner.

Control should be the foundation for organizational learning. Many companies have adopted an approach that has been used in the U.S. military, called **after-action review**, or **debrief**. This review consists of asking four basic questions:

1. What was supposed to happen?
2. What actually happened?
3. Why was there a difference?
4. What can we learn?

Thus, rather than simply correcting unacceptable events, the focus is on preventing them from occurring again in the future.

Quality Control in Manufacturing

In manufacturing, control is usually applied to incoming materials, key processes, and final products and services.

Quality control in manufacturing starts with incoming materials. Clearly, if incoming materials are of poor quality, then the final product will certainly be no better. In a TQ environment, customers should not have to rely on heavy inspection of purchased items. The burden of supplying high-quality product should rest with the suppliers themselves. Occasional inspection might be used to audit compliance, but suppliers should be expected to provide documentation and statistical evidence that they are meeting required specifications. Many firms have formal supplier management programs that deal with quality issues. For example, STMicroelectronics developed an annual Supplier Quality & Service Plan, which sets goals for suppliers and specifies how ST will review performance, share data, and carry out other responsibilities in the relationship. Long-term partnerships with quality-minded suppliers enabled Texas Nameplate Company to nearly eliminate inspections of incoming materials. These "ship-direct-to-stock" suppliers are required to be defect-free for at least two years and meet all requirements specified on purchase orders. The Bonus Materials folder for this chapter on the Premium website contains additional material on supplier and partnering process management.

BONUS MATERIALS

Because unwanted variation can arise during production, in-process control is needed throughout the production process. At Hyundai, for example, optical sensors are used to measure tolerances to ensure tight welds and minimal gaps between panels, and cars are put through high-pressure water chambers to test the integrity of door seals. When the process owner assumes the role of inspector for manual manufacturing work or assembly, the occurrence of unwanted variation can quickly be recognized and immediate adjustments to stabilize the process can be made. Done properly, this activity can eliminate the need for independent inspection after the fact.

Final inspection represents the last point in the manufacturing process at which the producer can verify that the product meets customer requirements, and avoid external failure costs. For many consumer products, final inspection consists of functional testing. At Hyundai, every vehicle produced at its Alabama plant is road tested on a special test track. In many industries such as electronics, computerized test equipment allows for 100 percent inspection to be conducted rapidly and cost-effectively.

Documented control procedures are usually written down in a **process control plan**. Cincinnati Fiberglass, a small manufacturer of fiberglass parts for trucks, uses a control plan for each production process that includes the process name, tool used, standard operating procedure, tolerance, inspection frequency, sample size, person responsible, reporting document, and reaction plan. Of particular importance is the ability to trace all components of a product back to process equipment, operators, and to the original material from which it was made. Process control also includes monitoring the accuracy and variability of equipment, operator knowledge and skills, the accuracy of measurement results and data used, and environmental factors such as time and temperature. An example of process control in the food industry—the HACCP approach—is discussed in the Bonus Materials folder on the Premium website.

Effective quality control systems include documented procedures for all key processes; a clear understanding of the appropriate equipment and working environment; methods for monitoring and controlling critical quality characteristics; approval processes for equipment; criteria for workmanship, such as written standards, samples, or illustrations; and maintenance activities.

BONUS MATERIALS

Quality Control in Services

Many people think that quality control applies only to manufacturing. This assumption could not be further from the truth. The approach used by The Ritz-Carlton Hotel Company to control quality is proactive because of their intensive personalized service environment.[24] Systems for collecting and using quality-related measures are widely deployed and used extensively throughout the organization. Each hotel tracks service quality indicators on a daily basis. The Ritz-Carlton recognizes that many customer requirements are sensory, and thus, difficult to measure. However, by selecting, training, and certifying employees in their knowledge of The Ritz-Carlton Gold Standards of service, they are able to assess their work through appropriate sensory measurements—taste, sight, smell, sound, and touch—and take appropriate actions.

The company uses three types of control processes to deliver quality:

1. Self-control of the individual employee based on their spontaneous and learned behavior.
2. Basic control mechanisms, which are carried out by every member of the workforce. The first person who detects a problem is empowered to break

away from routine duties, investigate and correct the problem immediately, document the incident, and then return to their routine.

3. Critical success factor control for critical processes. Process teams use customer and organizational requirement measurements to determine quality, speed, and cost performance. These measurements are compared against benchmarks and customer satisfaction data to determine corrective action and resource allocation. The Ritz-Carlton conducts both self-audits and outside audits. Self-audits are carried out internally at all levels, from one individual or function to an entire hotel. Process walk-throughs occur daily in hotels, while senior leaders assess field operations during formal reviews at various intervals. Outside audits are performed by independent travel and hospitality rating organizations. All audits must be documented, and any findings must be submitted to the senior leader of the unit being audited. They are responsible for action and for assessing the implementation and effectiveness of recommended corrective actions.

An example of a structured quality control process in the service industry is the "10-Step Monitoring and Evaluation Process" set forth by the Joint Commission on Accrediting Health Care Organizations. This process, shown in Table 7.4, provides a detailed sequence of activities for monitoring and evaluating the quality of health care in an effort to identify problems and improve care. Standards and goals are defined in steps 2 through 5; measurement is accomplished in step 6; and comparison and feedback is performed in the remaining steps.

The most common quality characteristics in services, time (waiting time, service time, delivery time) and number of nonconformances, can be measured rather easily. Insurance companies, for example, measure the time to complete different transactions such as new issues, claim payments, and cash surrenders. Hospitals measure the percentage of nosocomial (health care-associated) infections and the percentage of unplanned re-admissions to the emergency room, intensive care, or operating room within, say, 48 hours.[25] Other quality characteristics are observable. They include the types of errors (wrong kind, wrong quantity, wrong delivery date, etc.) and behavior (courtesy, promptness, competency, and so on). Hospitals might monitor the completeness of medical charts and the quality of radiology readings, measured by a double-reading process.

Simple data collection procedures capture the measurements for service quality control. Time is easily measured by taking two observations: starting time and finishing time. Many observed data assume only "yes" or "no" values. For example, a survey of pharmaceutical operations in a hospital might include the following questions:

- Are drug storage and preparation areas within the pharmacy under the supervision of a pharmacist?
- Are drugs requiring special storage conditions properly stored?
- Are drug emergency boxes inspected on a monthly basis?
- Is the drug emergency box record book filled out completely?

Even though human behavior is easily observable, the task of describing and classifying the observations is far more difficult. The major obstacle is developing operational definitions of behavioral characteristics. For example, how does one define courteous versus discourteous, or understanding versus indifference? Defining such distinctions is best done by comparing behavior against understandable standards.

Table 7.4 10-Step Monitoring and Evaluation Process for Health Care Organizations

- *Step 1: Assign Responsibility.* The emergency department director is responsible for, and actively participates in, monitoring and evaluation. The director assigns responsibility for the specific duties related to monitoring and evaluation.
- *Step 2: Delineate Scope of Care.* The department considers the scope of care provided within emergency services to establish a basis for identifying important aspects of care to monitor and evaluate. The scope of care is a complete inventory of what the emergency department does.
- *Step 3: Identify Important Aspects of Care.* Important aspects of care are those that are high-risk, high-volume, and/or problem-prone. Staff identify important aspects of care so that monitoring and evaluation focuses on emergency department activities with the greatest impact on patient care.
- *Step 4: Identify Indicators.* Indicators of quality are identified for each important aspect of care. An indicator is a measurable variable related to a structure, process, or out-come of care. Examples of possible indicators (all of which would need to be further defined) include insufficient staffing for sudden surges in patient volume (structure), delays in physicians reporting to the emergency room (process), and transfusion errors (outcome).
- *Step 5: Establish Thresholds for Evaluation.* A threshold for evaluation is the level or point at which intensive evaluation of care is triggered. A threshold may be 0% or 100% or any other appropriate level. Emergency department staff should establish a threshold for each indicator.
- *Step 6: Collect and Organize Data.* Appropriate emergency department staff should collect data pertaining to the indicators. Data are organized to facilitate comparison with the thresholds for evaluation.
- *Step 7: Evaluate Care.* When the cumulative data related to an indicator reach the threshold for evaluation, appropriate emergency department staff evaluate the care provided to determine whether a problem exists. This evaluation, which in many cases will take the form of peer review, should focus on possible trends and performance patterns. The evaluation is designed to identify causes of any problems or methods by which care or performance may be improved.
- *Step 8: Take Actions to Solve Problems.* When problems are identified, action plans are developed, approved at appropriate levels, and enacted to solve the problem or take the opportunity to improve care.
- *Step 9: Assess Actions and Document Improvement.* The effectiveness of any actions taken is assessed and documented. Further actions necessary to solve a problem are taken and their effectiveness is assessed.
- *Step 10: Communicate Relevant Information to the Organization-wide Quality Assurance Program.* Findings from and conclusions of monitoring and evaluation, including actions taken to solve problems and improve care, are documented and reported monthly through the hospital's established channels of communication.

Source: "Medical Staff Monitoring and Evaluation—Departmental Review," Chicago. Copyright by the Joint Commission on Accreditation of Health Care Organizations, Oakbrook Terrace, IL. Reprinted with permission.

For instance, a standard for "courtesy" might be to address the customer as "Mr." or "Ms." Failure to do so is an instance of an error. "Promptness" might be defined as greeting a customer within five seconds of entering the store, or answering letters within two days of receipt. These behaviors can easily be recorded and counted. Figure 7.3 shows some behavioral questions used in a patient survey by a group of Southern California hospitals.[26]

Figure 7.3 Sample Hospital Staff Behavior Questions

Admissions

11. Altogether, how long did you have to wait to be admitted?
    More than 1 hour: ______ (1) 1 hour: ______ (2) 30 min.: ______ (3) 15 min.: ______ (4)
12. If you had to wait 30 minutes or longer before someone met with you, were you told why?
    YES: ______ (1) NO: ______ (2) Did not wait 30 minutes: ______ (3)

Nursing Staff

21. Did a nurse talk to you about the procedures for the day?
    Never: ______ (1) Sometimes: ______ (2) Often: ______ (3) Always: ______ (4)
22. Were you on IV fluids?
    YES: ______ (1) NO: ______ (2)
    A. If YES, did the IV fluids ever run out?
    YES: ______ (1) NO: ______ (2)

Medical Staff

28. Did the doctor do what he/she told you he was going to do?
    Never: ______ (1) Sometimes: ______ (2) Often: ______ (3) Always: ______ (4)

Housekeeping

36. Did the housekeeper come into your room at least once a day?
    YES: ______ (1) NO: ______ (2)
39. Was the bathroom adequately supplied?
    Always: ______ (1) Often: ______ (2) Sometimes: ______ (3) Never: ______ (4)

X-Ray

When you received services from the X-ray technician, were the procedures explained to you?
Always: ______ (1) Often: ______ (2) Sometimes: ______ (3) Never: ______ (4)

Food

34. Generally, were your meals served at the same time each day?
    Always: ______ (1) Often: ______ (2) Sometimes: ______ (3) Never: ______ (4)

Source: Adapted from K. M. Casarreal, J. L. Mill, and M. A. Plant, "Improving Service Through Patient Surveys in a Multihospital Organization," Hospital & Health Services Administration, Health Administration Press, Ann Arbor, MI, March/April 1986, 41–52. © 1986, Foundation of the American College of Health Care Executives.

PROCESS IMPROVEMENT

Continuous improvement is one of the foundation principles of total quality that we introduced in Chapter 1. It is an important business strategy in competitive markets because

- Customer loyalty is driven by delivered value.
- Delivered value is created by business processes.
- Sustained success in competitive markets requires a business to continuously improve delivered value.
- To continuously improve value-creation ability, a business must continuously improve its value-creation processes.[27]

The concept of continuous improvement dates back many years. One of the earliest examples in the United States was at National Cash Register Company (NCR).

After a shipment of defective cash registers was returned in 1894, the company's founder, John Patterson, discovered unpleasant and unsafe working conditions. He made many changes, including better lighting, new safety devices, ventilation, lounges, and lockers. The company offered extensive evening classes to improve employees' education and skills, and instituted a program for soliciting suggestions from factory workers. Workers received cash prizes and other recognitions for their best ideas; by the 1940s the company was receiving an average of 3,000 suggestions each year.

Over the years, many other companies such as Lincoln Electric and Procter & Gamble developed innovative and effective improvement approaches. However, many of these focused almost exclusively on productivity and cost. Toshiba in 1946, Matsushita Electric in 1950, and Toyota in 1951 initiated some of the earliest formal continuous improvement programs. Toyota, in particular, pioneered just-in-time (JIT), which showed that companies could make products efficiently with virtually zero defects. JIT established a philosophy of improvement, which the Japanese call **kaizen** (pronounced kī-zen).

Kaizen[28]

Kaizen is a Japanese word that means gradual and orderly continuous improvement. The kaizen philosophy encompasses all business activities and everyone in an organization. In this philosophy, improvement in all areas of business—cost, meeting delivery schedules, employee safety and skill development, supplier relations, new product development, or productivity—serve to enhance the quality of the firm. Thus, any activity directed toward improvement falls under the kaizen umbrella. Activities to establish traditional quality control systems, install robotics and advanced technology, institute employee suggestion systems, maintain equipment, and implement just-in-time production systems all lead to improvement.

Kaizen focuses on small, gradual, and frequent improvements over the long term with minimum financial investment, and participation by everyone in the organization.

The Kaizen Institute (http://www.kaizen-institute.com) suggests some basic tips for implementing kaizen. These suggestions include not seeking perfection; discarding conventional fixed ideas; thinking of how to do something, not why it cannot be done; not making excuses, but questioning current practices; and seeking the "wisdom of ten people rather than the knowledge of one." By instilling kaizen into people and training them in basic quality improvement tools, workers can build this philosophy into their work and continually seek improvement in their jobs. This process-oriented approach to improvement encourages constant communication among workers and managers.

Kaizen is so ingrained in employees at Toyota that one manager was quoted saying "When I'm mowing the grass, I'm trying different turns to see if I can do it faster."[29] An example at the Georgetown, Kentucky, plant shows the power of kaizen. A workstation used for installing visors and seat belts used to consist of eight racks of parts. The racks crowded the workstation, giving the worker ready access to all possible parts. The operator would eyeball the car coming up the line, step to the racks of visors and seat belts, and grab the right parts and run to the car. He or she would step into the slowly advancing car, bolt belts and visors in place, step back onto the factory floor, and do it again—all in 55 seconds, the unvarying time each slowly moving car spends at each workstation. The problem was, there were 12 possible combinations of sun visors and nine variations of seat belts. So just deciding which parts to snatch had become a job in itself. In every shift, 500 cars passed the racks, each car needing four specific parts: 2,000 opportunities to make an error. Even with 99 percent perfection, five cars per shift got the wrong sun visors or seat belts. So a team of assembly employees came up with a solution. Don't make the worker pick the parts; let the worker focus on installation. Deliver a kit of presorted visors and seat belts—one kit per car, each containing exactly the right parts. The team applied the simplest technology available, a Rubbermaid caddy.

Three things are required for a successful kaizen program: operating practices, total involvement, and training.[30] First, operating practices expose new improvement opportunities. Practices such as just-in-time reveal waste and inefficiency as well as poor quality. Second, in kaizen, every employee strives for improvement. Top management, for example, views improvement as an inherent component of corporate strategy and provides support to improvement activities by allocating resources effectively and providing reward structures that are conducive to improvement. Middle management can implement top management's improvement goals by establishing, upgrading, and maintaining operating standards that reflect those goals; by improving cooperation between departments; and by making employees conscious of their responsibility for improvement and developing their problem-solving skills through training. Supervisors can direct more of their attention to improvement rather than "supervision," which, in turn, facilitates communication and offers better guidance to workers. Finally, workers can engage in improvement through suggestion systems and small group activities, self-development programs that teach practical problem-solving techniques, and enhanced job performance skills. All these improvements require significant training, both in the philosophy and in tools and techniques.

The kaizen philosophy has been widely adopted and is used by many firms in the United States and around the world. For example, at ENBI Corporation, a New York manufacturer of precision metal shafts and roller assemblies for the printer, copier, and fax machine markets, kaizen projects have resulted in a 48 percent increase in productivity, a 30 percent reduction in cycle time, and a 73 percent reduction in inventory.[31] Kaizen has been successfully applied in the Mercedes-Benz truck factory in Brazil, resulting in reductions of 30 percent in manufacturing space, 45 percent in inventory, 70 percent in lead time, and 70 percent in set-up time over a three-year period. Sixteen employees have full-time responsibility for kaizen activities.[32]

Kaizen, however, requires a significant cultural change from everyone in the organization, from top management to front-line employees. In many organizations, this is difficult to achieve. As a result, and also because of the typical business focus on short-term results and the search for the "silver bullet" solution, kaizen is not always properly implemented.[33]

Quality Spotlight
The Ritz-Carlton Hotel Company

The kaizen philosophy is reflected in many organizations. For example, Motorola's Commercial, Government, and Industrial Solutions Sector uses continuous improvement teams that meet regularly to proactively evaluate and improve processes. The Ritz-Carlton Hotel Company has eight mechanisms devoted solely to the improvement of process, product, and service quality:

- *New hotel start-up improvement process:* A cross-sectional team from the entire company works together to identify and correct problem areas.
- *Comprehensive performance evaluation process:* The work area team mechanism that empowers people who perform a job to develop the job procedures and performance standards.

- *Quality network:* A mechanism of peer approval through which an individual employee can advance a good idea.
- *Standing problem-solving team:* A standing work area team that addresses any problem it chooses.
- *Quality improvement team:* Special teams assembled to solve an assigned problem identified by an individual employee or leaders.
- *Strategic quality planning:* Annual work area teams identify their missions, primary supplier objectives and action plans, internal objectives and action plans, and progress reviews.
- *Streamlining process:* The annual hotel evaluation of processes, products, or services that are no longer valuable to the customer.
- *Process improvement:* The team mechanism for corporate leaders, managers, and employees to improve the most critical processes.

*A **kaizen blitz** is an intense and rapid improvement process in which a team or a department throws all its resources into an improvement project over a short time period, as opposed to traditional kaizen applications, which are performed on a part-time basis.*

Although kaizen is meant to be a part of daily work, many organizations are faced with quality or performance issues that require immediate attention. As a result, kaizen concepts have been incorporated into a team- and project-driven rapid improvement initiative called a *kaizen blitz*.

Blitz teams are generally comprised of employees from all areas involved in the process who understand it and can implement changes on the spot. Improvement is immediate, exciting, and satisfying for all those involved in the process.

Some examples of using kaizen blitz at Magnivision include the following:[34]

- The molded lens department ran two shifts per day, using 13 employees, and after 40 percent rework, yielded 1,300 pieces per day. The production line was unbalanced and work piled up between stations, which added to quality problems as the work-in-process was often damaged. After a three-day blitz, the team reduced the production to one shift of six employees and a balanced line, reducing rework to 10 percent and increasing yield to 3,500 pieces per day, saving more than $179,000.
- In Retail Services, a blitz team investigated problems that continually plagued employees, and discovered that many were related to the software system. Some of the same customer information had to be entered in multiple screens, sometimes the system took a long time to process information, and sometimes it was difficult to find specific information quickly. Neither the programmers nor the engineers were aware of these problems. By getting everyone together, some solutions were easily determined. Estimated savings were $125,000.

Improvement Opportunities

Many opportunities for improvement exist, the most obvious being reductions in manufacturing defects or service errors. One example occurred at Dell. Although it has had some of the highest quality ratings in the PC industry, CEO Michael Dell became obsessed with finding ways to reduce machine failure rates. He concluded that failures were related to the number of times a hard drive was handled during assembly, and insisted that the number of "touches" be reduced from an existing level of more than 30 per drive. Production lines were revamped and the number was reduced to fewer than 15. Soon after, the reject rate of hard drives fell by 40 percent and the overall failure rated dropped by 20 percent.[35]

Another important business metric is cycle time. **Cycle time** refers to the time it takes to accomplish one cycle of a process (e.g., the time from when a customer orders a product to the time that it is delivered, or the total time needed to introduce a new product). Reductions in cycle time serve two purposes. First, they speed up work processes so that customer response is improved. Second, reductions in cycle time can only be accomplished by streamlining and simplifying processes to eliminate non-value-added steps such as rework. This approach forces improvements in quality by reducing the potential for mistakes and errors. By reducing non-value-added steps, costs are reduced as well. Thus, cycle time reductions often drive simultaneous improvements in organization, quality, cost, and productivity. Significant reductions in cycle time cannot be achieved simply by focusing on individual subprocesses; cross-functional processes must be examined all across the organization. Through these activities, the company comes to understand work at the organizational level and to engage in cooperative behaviors.

One example of cycle time reduction is Procter & Gamble's over-the-counter (OTC) clinical division, which conducts clinical studies that involve testing drugs, health care products, or treatments in humans.[36] Such testing follows rigorous design, conduct, analysis, and summary of the data collected. P&G had at least four different ways to perform a clinical study and needed to find the best way to meet its research and development needs. They chose to focus on cycle time reduction. Their approach built on fundamental TQ principles: focusing on the customer, fact-based decisions, continual improvement, empowerment, the right leadership structure, and an understanding of work processes. An example is shown in Figure 7.4. The team found that final reports took months to prepare. Only by mapping the existing process did they fully understand the causes of long production times and the amount of rework and recycling during review and sign-off. By restructuring the activities from sequential to parallel work and identifying critical measurements to monitor the process, they were able to reduce the time to less than four weeks.

Improvement should be a proactive task of management and be viewed as an opportunity, not simply as a reaction to problems and competitive threats.

In addition to reducing defects, errors, and cycle times, organizations should also consider improving employee morale, satisfaction, and cooperation; improving managerial practices; improving the design of products with features that better meet customers' needs, and that can achieve higher performance, higher reliability, and other market-driven dimensions of quality; and improving the efficiency of manufacturing systems by reducing workers' idle time and unnecessary motions, and by eliminating unnecessary inventory, unnecessary transportation and material handling, and scrap and rework.

PROCESS IMPROVEMENT METHODOLOGIES

Successful quality and business performance improvement depends on the ability to identify and solve problems; this ability is fundamental to the Six Sigma philosophy. Many nonquantitatively inclined managers (which may include 75 or 80 percent of the population) have difficulty in grasping the concept of a systematic, fact-based, and often statistical problem-solving approach. Yet, using such an approach is vital to effectively identifying sources of problems, understanding their causes, and

Figure 7.4 Final Report "Is" and "Should" Process Map Example

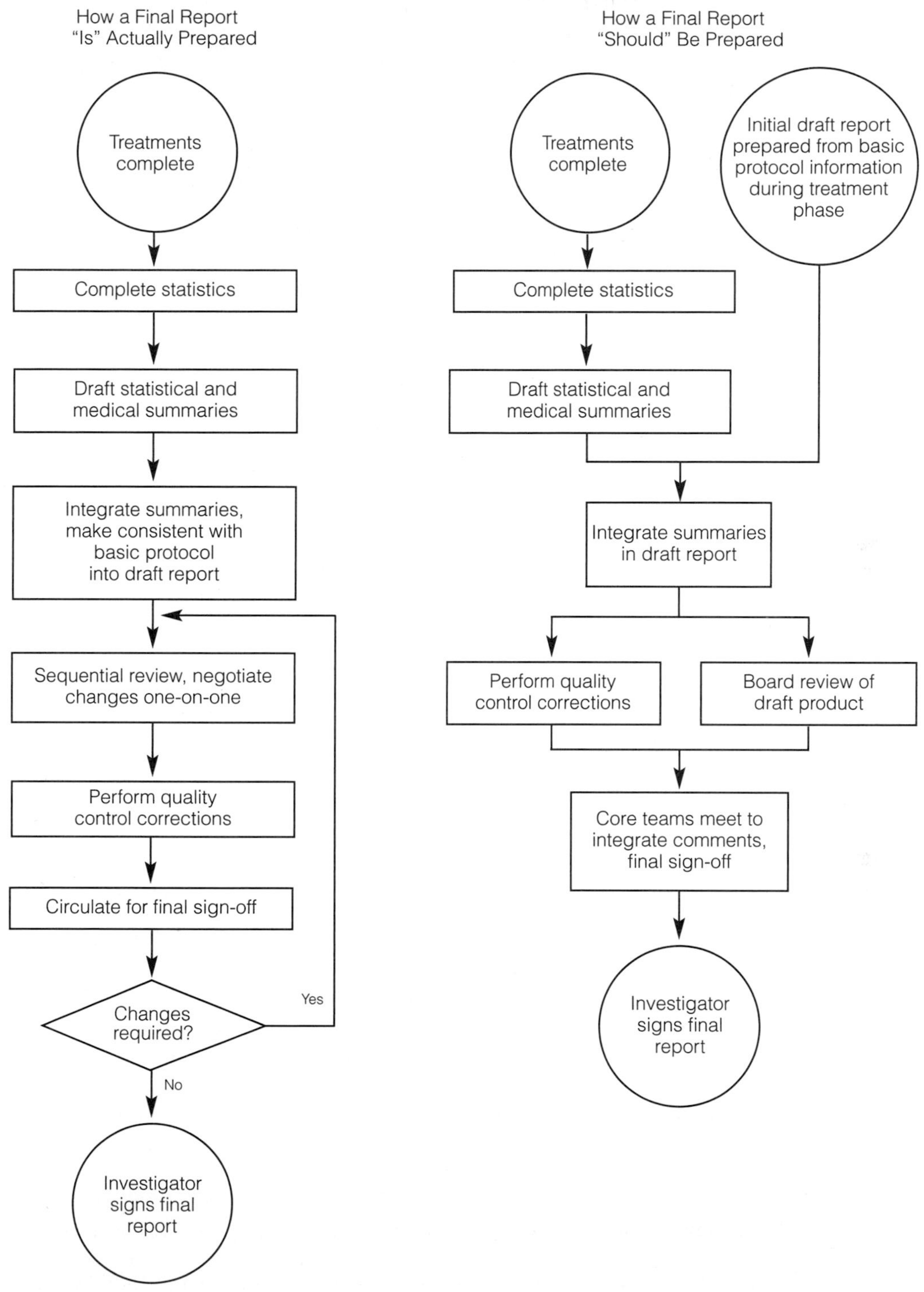

Source: Reprinted with permission from David A. McCamey, Robert W. Bogs, and Linda M. Bayuk, "More, Better, Faster From Total Quality Effort," Quality *Improvement Handbook*, 2nd edition, August 1999, pp. 43–50. http://www.asq.org/quality-press/display-item/index=H1289&xvl=76BK H1289.

Figure 7.5 QIP Process at Branch-Smith Printing

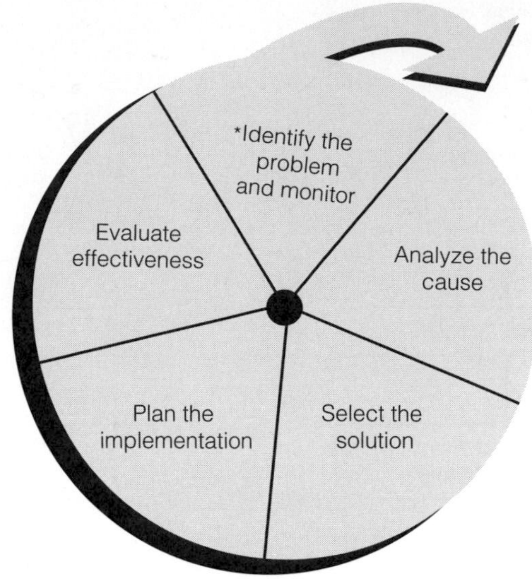

Reprinted with permission from AIM, Inc.

A structured problem-solving process provides all employees with a common language and a set of tools to communicate with each other, particularly as members of cross-functional teams.

developing improvement solutions. "Speaking the same language" builds confidence and assures that solutions are developed objectively, rather than by intuition. Branch-Smith Printing, for example, uses a simple quality improvement process (QIP) shown in Figure 7.5 to evaluate and improve all production and delivery processes, using performance data and complaints to prioritize opportunities for process improvement.

Numerous methodologies for improvement have been proposed over the years. Although each methodology is distinctive in its own right, they share many common themes:[37]

1. *Redefining and analyzing the problem:* Collect and organize information, analyze the data and underlying assumptions, and reexamine the problem for new perspectives, with the goal of achieving a workable problem definition.
2. *Generating ideas:* "Brainstorm" to develop potential solutions.
3. *Evaluating and selecting ideas:* Determine whether the ideas have merit and will achieve the problem solver's goal.
4. *Implementing ideas:* Sell the solution and gain acceptance by those who must use them.

We will review some of the more prominent approaches here. We also note that they are supported by numerous analytical tools, most of which are discussed in Chapter 11.

The Deming Cycle

The **Deming cycle** is a simple methodology for improvement that was strongly promoted by W. Edwards Deming. It was originally called the *Shewhart cycle* after its original founder, Walter Shewhart, but was renamed the Deming cycle by the Japanese in 1950. The Deming cycle is composed of four stages: *plan, do, study,* and *act* (PDSA) as illustrated in Figure 7.6. (The third stage—Study—was formerly called *check*, and the Deming cycle was known as the *PDCA cycle*. Deming made the change in 1990. "Study" is more appropriate; with only a "check," one might miss something. However, many people still use "check.")

The Plan stage consists of studying the current situation and describing the process: its inputs, outputs, customers, and suppliers; understanding customer expectations; gathering data; identifying problems; testing theories of causes; and developing solutions and action plans. In the Do stage, the plan is implemented on a trial basis, for example, in a laboratory, pilot production process, or with a small group of customers, to evaluate a proposed solution and provide objective data. Data from the experiment are collected and documented.

The Study stage determines whether the trial plan is working correctly by evaluating the results, recording the learning, and determining whether any further issues or opportunities need be addressed. Often, the first solution must be modified or scrapped. New solutions are proposed and evaluated by returning to the Do stage. In the last stage, Act, the improvements become standardized and the final plan is implemented as a "current best practice" and communicated throughout the organization. This process then leads back to the Plan stage for identification of other improvement opportunities.

The Deming cycle focuses on both short-term continuous improvement and long-term organizational learning.

Table 7.5 summarizes the steps in the Deming Cycle in more detail. The fundamental premise is that improvement comes from the application of knowledge.[38] This knowledge may be knowledge of engineering, management, or how a process operates that can make a job easier, more accurate,

Figure 7.6 The Deming Cycle

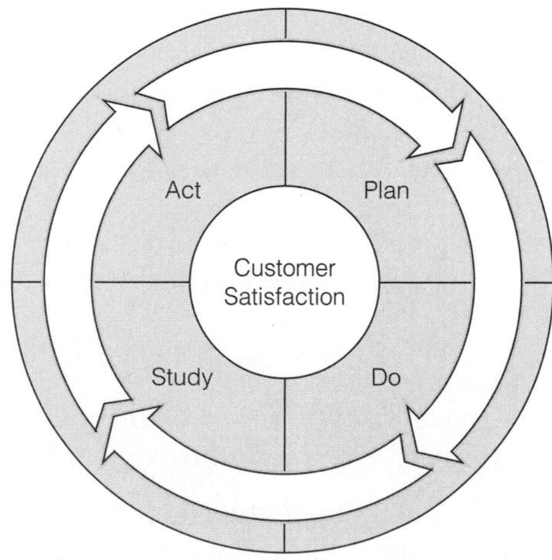

Table 7.5 Detailed Steps in the Deming Cycle

Plan

1. Define the process: its start, end, and what it does.
2. Describe the process: list the key tasks performed and sequence of steps, people involved, equipment used, environmental conditions, work methods, and materials used.
3. Describe the players: external and internal customers and suppliers, and process operators.
4. Define customer expectations: what the customer wants, when, and where, for both external and internal customers.
5. Determine what historical data are available on process performance, or what data need to be collected to better understand the process.
6. Describe the perceived problems associated with the process; for instance, failure to meet customer expectations, excessive variation, long cycle times, and so on.
7. Identify the primary causes of the problems and their impacts on process performance.
8. Develop potential changes or solutions to the process, and evaluate how these changes or solutions will address the primary causes.
9. Select the most promising solution(s).

Do

1. Conduct a pilot study or experiment to test the impact of the potential solution(s).
2. Identify measures to understand how any changes or solutions are successful in addressing the perceived problems.

Study

1. Examine the results of the pilot study or experiment.
2. Determine whether process performance has improved.
3. Identify further experimentation that may be necessary.

Act

1. Select the best change or solution.
2. Develop an implementation plan: what needs to be done, who should be involved, and when the plan should be accomplished.
3. Standardize the solution, for example, by writing new standard operating procedures.
4. Establish a process to monitor and control process performance.

Source: Adapted from *Small Business Guidebook to Quality Management*, Office of the Secretary of Defense, Quality Management Office, Washington, DC. Copyright © 1998.

faster, less costly, safer, or better meet customer needs. Three fundamental questions to consider are:

- What are we trying to accomplish?
- What changes can we make that will result in improvement?
- How will we know that a change is an improvement?

Through a process of learning, knowledge is developed. From this perspective, many organizations use the Deming cycle as the basis for their organizational performance improvement activities. For example, Mercy Health Systems, a 2007 Baldrige

Figure 7.7 Mercy Health System Application of the Deming Cycle`

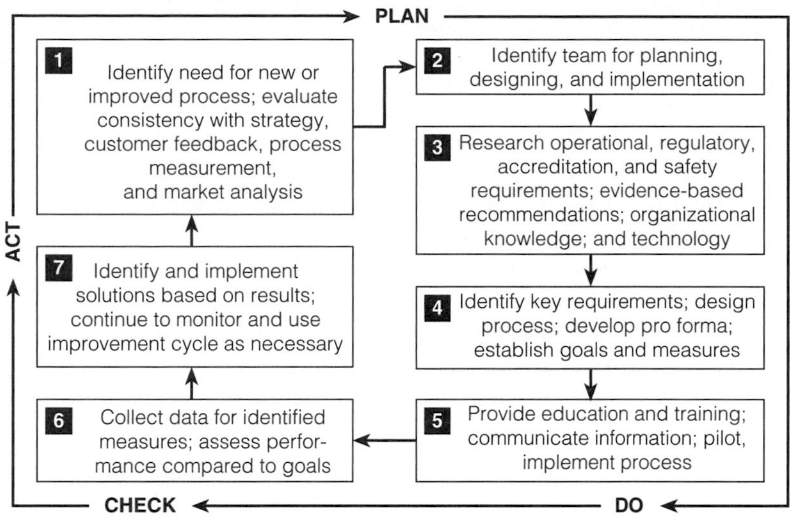

Source: Mercy Health Systems 2007 Baldrige National Quality Award application Summary. Reprinted with permission.

recipient, uses the Deming cycle as its process management framework as shown in Figure 7.7.

The following example demonstrates how the Deming cycle can be applied in practice. The co-owners of a diner decided to do something about the long lines that occurred every day in their place of business.[39] After discussions with their employees, several important facts came to light:

- Customers waited in line for up to 15 minutes.
- Usually, tables were available.
- Many of their customers were regulars.
- People taking orders and preparing food were getting in each other's way.

To measure the improvement that might result from any change they made, they decided to collect data on the number of customers in line, the number of empty tables, and the time until a customer received the food ordered.

In the Plan stage, the owners wanted to test a few changes. They decided on three changes:

1. Provide a way for customers to fax their orders in ahead of time (rent a fax machine for one month).
2. Construct a preparation table in the kitchen with ample room for fax orders.
3. Devote one of their two cash registers to handling fax orders.

Both the length of the line and the number of empty tables were measured every 15 minutes during the lunch hour by one of the owners. In addition, when the 15-minute line check was done, the last person in line was noted, and the time until that person got served was measured.

In the Do phase, the owners observed the results of the three measures for three weeks. In the study phase, they detected several improvements. Time in line went down from 15 minutes to an average of 5 minutes. The line length was cut to a peak average of 12 people, and the number of empty tables decreased slightly. In the Act phase, the owners held a meeting with all employees to discuss the results. They decided to purchase a fax machine, prepare phone orders in the kitchen with the fax orders, and use both cash registers to handle walk-up and fax orders.

Creative Problem Solving

Solving quality problems often involves a high amount of creativity. Creativity is seeing things in new or novel ways. Many creativity tools are designed to help you change the context in which you view a problem or opportunity, thereby leading to fresh perspectives. The brilliant and creative mathematician John Nash, whose life was profiled in the book and movie *A Beautiful Mind*, was described by one of his colleagues in the following way: "Everyone else would climb a peak by looking for a path somewhere on the mountain. Nash would climb another mountain altogether and from a distant peak shine a searchlight back on the first peak."[40]

In Japanese, the word *creativity* has a literal translation as "dangerous opportunity." In the Toyota production system, which has become the benchmark for world-class efficiency, a key concept is *soikufu*—creative thinking or inventive ideas, which means capitalizing on worker suggestions. The chairman of Toyota once observed, "One of the features of Japanese workers is that they use their brains as well as their hands. Our workers provide 1.5 million suggestions a year, and 95 percent of them are put to practical use. There is an almost tangible concern for improvement in the air at Toyota."[41]

While many creative ideas seemingly come at moments of inspiration, systematic approaches can refine your thinking and help prepare for those moments. An effective problem-solving process that can easily be adapted to quality improvement stems from creative problem-solving (CPS) concepts pioneered by Osborn and refined by Parnes.[42] This strategy consists of the following steps:

- Understanding the "mess"
- Finding facts
- Identifying specific problems
- Generating ideas
- Developing solutions
- Implementing solutions

The CPS literature provides many tools and approaches to facilitate each of these steps and develop more creative results.

Custom Methodologies

Numerous variations of the Deming Cycle and creative problem-solving process exist. In Chapter 11, we will discuss in detail the Six Sigma methodology for improvement known as DMAIC—*define, measure, analyze, improve,* and *control*. Many organizations incorporate lean tools (also discussed in Chapter 11) that focus on the elimination of waste and non-value-added activities within their process improvement approaches. For example, MESA, Inc., a Baldrige recipient, uses lean as its primary improvement approach and integrated within the framework of the Deming cycle.

Some organizations align process-improvement methodologies with their unique organizational culture. For example, some organizations embed the Deming cycle within a broader framework. An example from a health care organization is shown in Figure 7.8. The left side of the figure incorporates the essential elements of CPS. Once a solution is proposed, the Deming cycle is then used to test and evaluate the solution prior to implementation. Not every approach is appropriate for all organizations; one must be chosen or designed to fit the organization's culture and people.

Figure 7.8 Incorporating the Deming Cycle in a Process Improvement Model

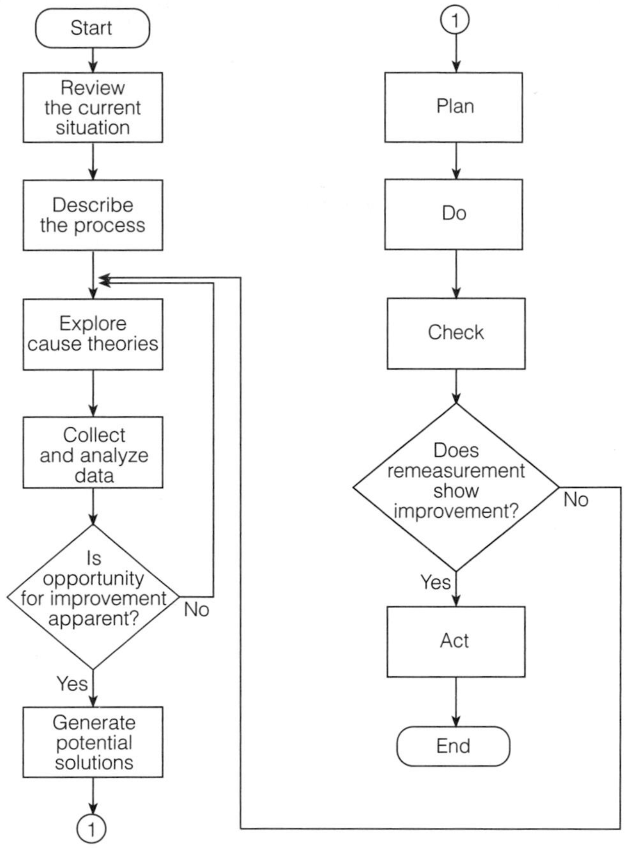

Source: Reprinted with permission of Bethesda Hospital, Inc., 619 Oak Street, Cincinnati, OH 45241.

One approach used by some hospitals and the U.S. Coast Guard, is known by the acronym FADE: *focus, analyze, develop,* and *execute.* In the Focus stage, a team selects the problem to be addressed and defines it, characterizing the current state of the process, why change is needed, what the desired result should be, and the benefits of achieving that result. In the Analyze stage, the team works to describe the process in detail, determine what data and information are needed, and develop a list of root causes for the problem. The Develop stage focuses on creating a solution and implementation plan along with documentation to explain and justify recommendations to management who must allocate the resources. Finally, in the Execute stage, the solution is implemented and a monitoring plan is established. As another example, Park Place Lexus, the first automobile dealer to receive the Baldrige Award, developed a process known as DRIVE—*Define* the problem, *Recognize* the cause, *Identify* the solution, *Verify* the actions, and *Evaluate* the results. Clearly this acronym has meaning for the organization and is easy for employees to remember.

How one approaches problem solving is not as critical as doing it in a systematic fashion, whether one uses the Deming cycle, CPS, or some other variation.

Recently, particularly in the context of Six Sigma, organizations have been applying an approach called **TRIZ**, which is a Russian acronym for the *Theory of Inventive Problem Solving*. TRIZ was developed by a Russian patent clerk who studied thousands of submissions, and observed patterns of innovation common to the evolution of scientific and technical advances. He recognized that these concepts could be taught and developed some 200 exercises to foster creative problem solving. TRIZ has been used by such companies as Samsung, Ford, Motorola, Procter & Gamble, 3M, Phillips, LG, and many others. It has been useful in increasing the yield of semiconductor factories, designing new motors for washing machines, and increasing the viewing angle of LCD televisions.[43]

BREAKTHROUGH IMPROVEMENT

Breakthrough improvement refers to discontinuous change, as opposed to the gradual, continuous improvement philosophy of kaizen. Breakthrough improvements result from innovative and creative thinking; often these are motivated by **stretch goals**, or **breakthrough objectives**.

Stretch goals force an organization to think in a radically different way, and to encourage major improvements as well as incremental ones.

When a goal of 10 percent improvement is set, managers or engineers can usually meet it with some minor improvements. However, when the goal is 1,000 percent improvement, employees must be creative and think "outside of the box." The seemingly impossible is often achieved, yielding dramatic improvements and boosting morale. Motorola's Six Sigma thrust was driven by a goal of improving product and services quality ten times within two years, and at least 100-fold within four years.

For stretch goals to be successful, they must derive unambiguously from corporate strategy. Organizations must not set goals that result in unreasonable stress to employees or punish failure. In addition, they must provide appropriate help and tools to accomplish the task. Two approaches for breakthrough improvement that help companies achieve stretch goals are *benchmarking* and *reengineering*.

Benchmarking

The development and realization of improvement objectives, particularly stretch objectives, is often aided through the process of benchmarking. **Benchmarking** is defined as "measuring your performance against that of best-in-class companies, determining how the best-in-class achieve those performance levels, and using the information as a basis for your own company's targets, strategies, and implementation,"[44] or more simply, "the search of industry best practices that lead to superior performance."[45]

*The term **best practices** refers to approaches that produce exceptional results, are usually innovative in terms of the use of technology or human resources, and are recognized by customers or industry experts.*

Through benchmarking, a company discovers its strengths and weaknesses and those of other industry leaders and learns how to incorporate the best practices into its own operations. Benchmarking can provide motivation to achieve stretch goals by helping employees to see what others can accomplish. For example, to meet a stretch target of reducing the time to build new 747 and 767 airplanes at Boeing from 18 months (in 1992) to 8 months, teams studied the world's best producers of everything from computers to ships. By 1996, the time had been reduced to 10 months.[46]

The concept of benchmarking is not new.[47] In the early 1800s, Francis Lowell, a New England industrialist, traveled to England to study manufacturing techniques at the best British mill factories. Henry Ford created the assembly line after taking a tour of a Chicago slaughterhouse and watching carcasses, hung on hooks mounted on a monorail, move from one workstation to another. Toyota's just-in-time production system was influenced by the replenishment practices of U.S. supermarkets. Modern benchmarking was initiated by Xerox and has since become common practice among leading firms.

An organization may decide to engage in benchmarking for several reasons. It eliminates "reinventing the wheel" along with associated wasted time and resources. It helps identify performance gaps between an organization and competitors, leading to realistic goals. It encourages employees to continuously innovate. Finally, because it is a process of continuous learning, benchmarking emphasizes sensitivity to the changing needs of customers.[48]

Three major types of benchmarking have emerged in business. **Competitive benchmarking** involves studying products, processes, or business performance of competitors in the same industry to compare pricing, technical quality, features, and other quality or performance characteristics of products and services. For example, a television cable company might compare its customer satisfaction rating or service response time to other cable companies; a manufacturer of TVs might compare its unit production costs or field failure rates against competitors. Significant gaps suggest key opportunities for improvement. Competitive benchmarking was refined into a science by Xerox during the 1970s and 1980s.

Process benchmarking emerged soon after. It centers on key work processes such as distribution, order entry, or employee training. This type of benchmarking identifies the most effective practices in companies that perform similar functions, no matter in what industry. For example, when Graniterock could not find any company that was measuring on-time delivery of concrete, it talked with Domino's Pizza, a worldwide leader in on-time delivery of a rapidly perishable product (a characteristic shared with freshly mixed concrete) to acquire new ideas for measuring and improving its processes. Xerox adapted the warehousing and distribution practices of L.L. Bean for its spare parts distribution system. Texas Instruments studied the kitting (order preparation) practices of six companies, including Mary Kay Cosmetics, and designed a process that captured the best practices of each of them, cutting kitting cycle time in half. A General Mills plant in Lodi, California, had an average machine changeover time of three hours. Then somebody said, "From three hours to 10 minutes!" Employees went to a NASCAR track, videotaped the pit crews, and studied the process to identify how the principles could be applied to the production changeover processes. Several months later, the average time fell to 17 minutes.[49] Thus, companies should not aim benchmarking solely at direct competitors or similar organizations; in fact, they would be mistaken to do so. If a company simply benchmarks within its own industry, it may merely be competitive and have a slight edge in those areas in which it is the industry leader. However, if benchmarks are adopted from outside the industry, a company may learn ideas and processes as well as new applications that allow it to surpass the best within its own industry and to achieve distinctive superiority.

Finally, **strategic benchmarking** examines how companies compete and seeks the winning strategies that have led to competitive advantage and market success. The typical benchmarking process can be described by the process used at AT&T.

1. *Project conception:* Identify the need and decide to benchmark.
2. *Planning:* Determine the scope and objectives, and develop a benchmarking plan.
3. *Preliminary data collection:* Collect data on industry companies and similar processes as well as detailed data on your own processes.
4. *Best-in-class selection:* Select companies with best-in-class processes.

5. *Best-in-class collection:* Collect detailed data from companies with best-in-class processes.
6. *Assessment:* Compare your own and best-in-class processes and develop recommendations.
7. *Implementation planning:* Develop operational improvement plans to attain superior performance.
8. *Implementation:* Enact operational plans and monitor process improvements.
9. *Recalibration*: Update benchmark findings and assess improvements in processes.[50]

Reengineering

The process of **reengineering** has been defined as "the fundamental rethinking and radical redesign of business processes to achieve dramatic improvements in critical, contemporary measures of performance, such as cost, quality, service, and speed."[51] Such questioning often uncovers obsolete, erroneous, or inappropriate assumptions. Radical redesign involves tossing out existing procedures and reinventing the process, not just incrementally improving it. The goal is to achieve quantum leaps in performance. Successful reengineering requires fundamental understanding of processes, creative thinking to break away from old traditions and assumptions, and effective use of information technology. Consider the following examples:

Reengineering involves asking basic questions about business processes: Why do we do it? and Why is it done this way?

- IBM Credit Corporation cut the process of financing IBM computers, software, and services from seven days to four hours by rethinking the process. Originally, the process was designed to handle difficult applications and required four highly trained specialists and a series of handoffs. The actual work took only about 1.5 hours; the rest of the time was spent in transit or delay. By questioning the assumption that every application was unique and difficult to process, IBM Credit Corporation was able to replace the specialists by a single individual supported by a user-friendly computer system that provided access to all the data and tools that the specialists would use.
- Intel Corporation had previously used a 91-step process costing thousands of dollars to purchase ballpoint pens—the same process used to purchase forklift trucks! The improved process was reduced to eight steps.
- In rethinking its purpose as a customer-driven, retail service company rather than a manufacturing company, Taco Bell eliminated the kitchen from its restaurants. Meat and beans are cooked outside the restaurant at central commissaries and reheated. Other food items such as diced tomatoes, onions, and olives are prepared off-site. This innovation saved about 11 million hours of work and $7 million per year over the entire chain.[52]

Benchmarking can greatly assist reengineering efforts. Reengineering without benchmarking probably will produce 5 to 10 percent improvements; benchmarking can increase this percentage to 50 or 75 percent. When GTE reengineered eight core processes of its telephone operations, it examined the best practices of some 84 companies from diverse industries. By studying outside best practices, a company can identify and import new technology, skills, structures, training, and capabilities.[53]

PROCESS MANAGEMENT IN THE BALDRIGE CRITERIA, ISO 9000, AND SIX SIGMA

Category 6 of the 2009–10 Malcolm Baldrige National Quality Award Criteria for Performance Excellence is *Process Management*. Item 6.1, *Work Systems Design*, examines how an organization determines its core competencies and designs its work systems and key processes to deliver customer value, prepare for potential emergencies, and achieve organizational success and sustainability. Because some of these issues are more strategic in nature, we have addressed them in Chapter 4. However, Item 6.1b specifically addresses the identification of key work processes, their requirements, and how they are designed for efficiency and effectiveness. Item 6.2, *Work Process Management and Improvement*, deals with control and improvement activities in process management. It addresses how processes are managed on a day-to-day basis; how stakeholder input and performance measures are used for control and improvement; how costs are minimized and how prevention of defects, errors, and rework are accomplished; and how processes are improved and learnings shared across the organization. This might include lean tools, Six Sigma approaches, use of ISO 9000:2000, or the Deming cycle.

Many aspects of ISO 9000:2000 deal with process management activities. (In fact, the entire set of standards is focused on an organization's ability to understand, define, and document its processes.) For example, one of the requirements is that organizations plan and control the design and development of products and manage the interfaces between different groups involved in design and development to ensure effective communication and clear assignment of responsibility. The standards also address the management of inputs and outputs for design and development activities, and use of systematic reviews to evaluate the ability to meet requirements, identify any problems, and propose necessary actions; purchasing processes; control of production and service, including measurement and process validation; control of monitoring and measuring devices used to evaluate conformity; analysis and improvement; monitoring and measurement of quality management processes; and continual improvement, including preventive and corrective action. The standards require that an organization use its quality policy, objectives, audit results, data analysis, corrective and preventive actions, and management reviews to continually improve its quality management system's effectiveness.

Six Sigma is based on understanding and improving processes on a project-by-project basis. Two of the advantages of Six Sigma are that projects are clearly linked to strategic needs and organizational objectives, and that projects are managed under a common framework. This linkage enables projects to be timely and relevant, and ensures that controls are put in place to leverage the improvements that are identified.

The Six Sigma team-project approach provides a natural fit with the requirements of product and process design, control, and improvement. A good system for process management is a prerequisite to Six Sigma. Obviously, to effectively design or improve a process you first need to understand it. If an organization does not have an ongoing system of process management, it will be quite difficult to implement Six Sigma. Some key processes that are necessary to implement Six Sigma include the following:

- Project selection and definition
- Financial review
- Training
- Leadership for project leaders

- Project leader mentoring
- Certification for Six Sigma specialists
- Project tracking and reporting
- Information management and dissemination

It is important to note that Six Sigma is not a substitute for continuous improvement. Because of its reliance on specialists—the "Black Belts" who lead the high-profile projects—it becomes quite easy to ignore simple improvements that can be achieved at the process owner level. In fact, it can easily alienate process owners who, instead of seeking continuous improvements, leave them to the specialists. Thus, the objectives are somewhat different, yet both approaches can easily support one another. Process owners should be trained in Six Sigma methods and be involved in formal Six Sigma projects, but still have responsibility for continuous improvement on a daily basis.

BONUS MATERIALS

SUMMARY OF KEY POINTS AND TERMINOLOGY

The Bonus Materials folder for this chapter on the Premium website provides a summary of key concepts and terminology introduced in this chapter.

QUALITY IN PRACTICE

GOLD STAR CHILI: PROCESS MANAGEMENT[54]

(We encourage you to read the Gold Star Chili case in Chapter 5 first for background information about the company.) Gold Star Chili, a chain of chili restaurants in the greater Cincinnati area, views process management activities as critical to its business success. Quality improvement teams, technology, and strong relationships with suppliers ensure that their chili is produced in a consistent fashion with respect to taste, viscosity, and general quality.

Figure 7.9 shows a process-based organization of the company. Three major value-creation processes link the operation of the company to its customers and other stakeholders:

1. Franchising
2. Restaurant operations
3. Manufacturing/distribution

Sustaining these processes are various support processes, such as research and development, human resources, accounting, purchasing, operations, training, marketing, and customer satisfaction, as well as design processes for new products, menus, and facilities. Production/delivery processes are coordinated at the corporate office and documented in manuals provided to each store. Internal customer needs are addressed in quality improvement team meetings.

The franchising process, outlined in Figure 7.10, is designed to ensure a smooth and successful start-up that meets company objectives. The process has been refined over time and includes extensive interaction with prospective and approved franchises. New technology has been introduced to facilitate the process. For example, a site-selection software package is used to evaluate market potential using a variety of demographic data. Computer-aided design is also used for site development. Because franchise process delays are costly, the process helps to eliminate variability, reduce cycle time, and cut down on problems that might occur during development and introduction. Procedure manuals have been developed to provide each store with the necessary information and training to ensure that they operate efficiently.

Restaurant processes include Cash Register, Steam Table, Drive-Thru, Tables, Bussers, and Management. These processes are designed to

Figure 7.9 Gold Star Chili, Inc. Organization

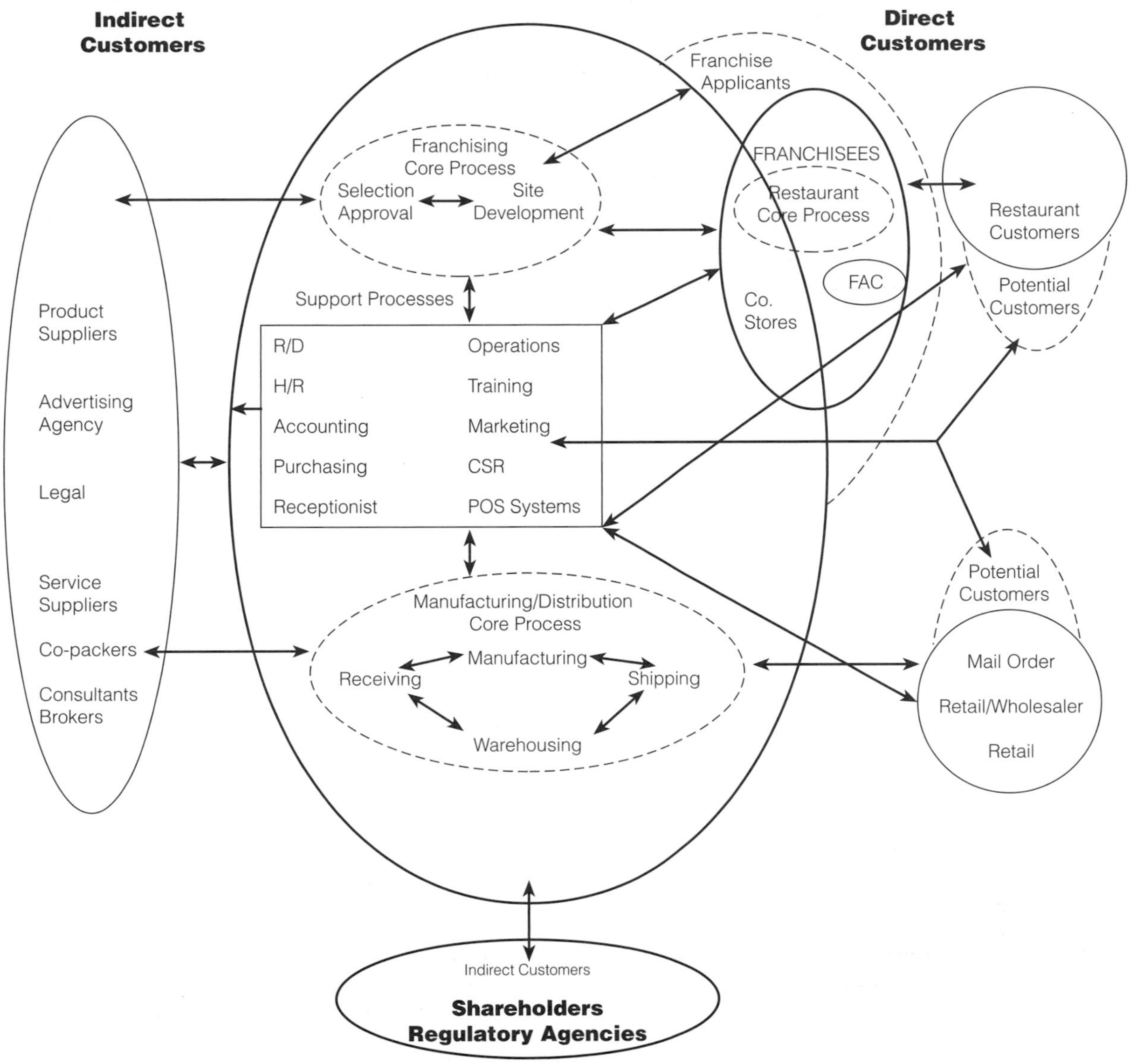

Source: Reprinted with permission of Gold Star Chili.

ensure that the principal requirements of all customers, such as being served in a timely manner and receiving their order accurately, are met. Prior to the opening of each restaurant, training sessions ensure that these processes are performed correctly and according to company standards. Each employee is cross-trained to perform each function.

Chili production is performed at the Gold Star Commissary. A nine-member team, cross-trained to perform each process, is responsible for adding beef, spices, tomatoes, and water during production. The chili must pass a series of strict tests before being shipped to restaurants. Control of chili production is assisted by various pieces of equipment for precise measurement. For example,

Figure 7.10 Gold Star Chili Franchising Process

GOLD STAR CHILI, INC.

650 Lunken Park Drive
Cincinnati, Ohio 45226
(513) 231-4541

Steps to a Gold Star Chili Franchise

1. Submit a fully completed franchise application. We will respond to you within 15 business days of your application.
2. You will receive for your review our Uniform Franchise Offering Circular and Exhibits. At this time you will sign and date the Receipt of Offering Circular.
3. Ten days after we receive your Receipt of Offering Circular, you will be sent a Confidentiality Agreement which you must hold for 5 days, then sign, date, and return to us.
4. Schedule and complete a meeting with support staff of Gold Star Chili in our Cincinnati location.
5. Attend a two-day orientation in Cincinnati. You will work with our Operations and Training personnel who will review your qualifications and objectives.
6. You will then be notified of your approval or disapproval of your request to become a Gold Star Chili Franchisee.
7. Gold Star personnel will begin the process of identifying and approving a restaurant location. A scope of work per Gold Star standards will be completed.
8. Sign Gold Star Chili Franchise Agreement and pay initial fee.
9. Begin construction.
10. Complete the training program.
11. Develop an opening plan.
12. Open your Gold Star Chili Restaurant.

Source: Reprinted with permission of Gold Star Chili.

a Bostwick Viscosity Meter determines the consistency of the chili, determining whether it is too thick or thin, and a flow meter adds the proper amount of water. Other equipment analyzes the fat content of the ground beef used in the chili. The final taste test is performed by members of the commissary to ensure that each batch meets established standards.

The commissary team also serves as a quality improvement team. Since July 1996, they have met informally on a daily basis to discuss processes and feedback from internal and external customers; they use a formal improvement process in reporting their activities. They use information from customer comment cards, measurements of waiting time for drive-through service, and feedback from restaurant managers to analyze and adjust processes as necessary. Store performance and quality are measured quarterly through visits by corporate employees. Monthly meetings of key process leaders and daily team meetings analyze processes for improvement opportunities, such as changes in procedures or the introduction of new technology. For example, several restaurants discovered large clumps of beef in the chili. The team determined that a new beef pump was not grinding the meat correctly.

The selection of suppliers is driven by two criteria: quality and price. Gold Star partners with key product suppliers for restaurant equipment and food products. They seek out local companies and educate them in their business needs and practices. For example, they have invited suppliers to attend a seminar on the Gold Star Chili total quality philosophy and suppliers' role in the process. To ensure that raw materials meet Gold Star specifications, potential and current suppliers visit the commissary to be informed about what Gold Star requires and what technologies the company expects them to have. Suppliers are required to meet or exceed quality standards and provide products at reasonable prices. Gold Star recently embarked on establishing a supplier scorecard to measure and monitor supplier performance. The scorecard includes ratings on on-time delivery or service, accuracy of invoicing and shipping documents, customer service, cost and value, technical expertise, and supplier quality initiatives, and seeks to identify strengths and targeted areas for improvement in each key area.

Gold Star attempts to establish long-term relationships with its suppliers. Company managers visit suppliers' facilities on a regular basis to solicit comments and complaints, and to discuss areas for improvement. During these discussions, suppliers often provide Gold Star with information about new technologies, suggestions for process improvements, and other helpful knowledge. For example, by sharing information with one key paper supplier, the supplier was able to redesign Gold Star's purchasing process, enabling the supplier to increase minimum order levels for deliveries, which reduced Gold Star's overall costs. The company conducts annual cost audits to determine whether costs might be lowered without sacrificing quality. If an alternative supplier is found with similar quality, service, and lower costs, Gold Star will approach its current supplier with the opportunity to lower costs.

Key Issues for Discussion

1. How does the organization structure in Figure 7.9 reflect Deming's view of a production system as discussed in Chapter 1?
2. As a small, privately held company, Gold Star is relatively new at applying total quality management approaches to its process management. Based on the information provided here, what suggestions might you provide in the process management area as the company matures in its journey to total quality?

Quality in Practice

Building Japanese Quality in North America[55]

Lexus automobiles have consistently led the industry in quality. In 2000, Cambridge, Ontario was chosen as the site of the first Lexus plant outside Japan, designated to build the RX 330 SUV. The assistant general manager for manufacturing observed, "We understood from the beginning that to be accepted we had to be not just as good as but better than Kyushu [the location of the Lexus plant in Japan]."

Teamwork at Cambridge starts with teaching workers about every stage of the production process, and about the duties of other team members. Not only does this reinforce the idea that each job is important, but it increases motivation: Each team member does his or her job better if he or she understands how other jobs are done and how one job affects another. This is all part of the *kaizen* philosophy, which at Cambridge is all about the many small inventions masterminded by team members on the line. Most are simple ideas that would occur only to a person doing the job—a clip to hold a part, say, or a jig or template to protect a part from damage, or the replacement of several parts by one. (These inventions are themselves called *kaizens.*)

In order to foster this mindset, engineers and managers created an environment like a clean room, brightly lit like a pharmaceutical laboratory, with a place for everything and everything in its place. Traditional automobile factories are dark and noisy places, filled with flying sparks and the pounding of metal stamping machines. The Cambridge plant, by contrast, is painted in light colors (coordinated by an interior designer) and boasts a spotless floor—the result of constant sweeping up with small brooms and dustpans. These come from "5s" stations, a key element of lean production (see Chapter 11). Cleanliness plays such a large role because at a typical automobile plant most defects are caused by the process of manufacturing itself, by bumps and scrapes from workers. That's why there are no rings or watches on the line at Cambridge, no jeans with rivets to scratch bodies, and why fragments of metal are swept up before they can infiltrate the paint system. The Lexus philosophy is based on the fundamental insight that quality must be built into each part of the production process, not applied as an afterthought through inspections or fixes. Each worker is also a quality control inspector of his or her own work and that of his or her fellow team members—entrusted with the task of eliminating defects before they move down the line.

In the service of this ideal, computer monitors high above the plant's floor display the status of production at each point. Pulling a cord allows team members to stop the line entirely if necessary. When this happens, the news is indicated by towers of lights, and by characteristic brief musical tones unique to each station, like personal cell phone rings. At the Cambridge plant, Lexus has taken this quality control to a new level, with the introduction of "quality gates": checkpoints where items found to be of particular concern to customers (such as flawless vertical paint surfaces and the fit of headlights into the body of the vehicle) are noted and evaluated. At the welding area's quality gate, for example, welds are tested with hammer and chisel and alignments measured with jigs. Team members certify each vehicle's weld integrity by applying their initials in bright colors. These personal testimonials to care and quality will ride with the vehicles for their lifetimes, albeit under coats of paint or hidden away from the customer's eye. Then, at the end of the welding process, the bodies receive an even closer inspection, distinguished by that special human touch that makes Lexus so rare among car companies. Under an angled roof made up of light tubes, team members sweep their hands carefully across every inch of the vehicles' exteriors. With small, black abrasive squares in their gloved hands, they smooth out any remaining spots or irregularities.

Once welded, vehicle bodies move to the paint shop, more spotless than any other part of the plant. It has the air of a Silicon Valley clean room. Team members wear special antistatic suits. Two sets of doors make an airlock to the paint area. Down-drafts and grated walkways with water beneath catch particles of lint and dust. No cardboard is allowed anywhere in the area. Each vehicle body is vacuumed to remove metal shavings. And the basecoats themselves—the key paint layers that give vehicles their colors—are made of a water-soluble paint, not environmentally hazardous solvents. Spraying is carried out by robotic arms grasping cartridges of measured paint. The cartridges hold just enough paint for one vehicle and are refilled. This allows for mixing colors on the line—no longer must a batch of blue or red vehicles be run together. Finally, a machine called a Perceptron, which measures the changing reflection of light on the vehicle's surface, a rippling effect called "orange peel"—tests for gloss and smoothness.

After painting comes assembly. Here the focus is on the fit and finish of doors, windows, and other key items, such as interior accent pieces. Doors are removed early in the assembly process and make their own course through the plant before rejoining the body—always the same body, of course. This affords access to the inside of the vehicle and protects the door leather and wood from damage. To install the headliner—the large single piece in the ceiling—a team member is swung inside the vehicle in a clever little seat on an arm, called a Raku. Then there are the interior detail items, such as wood paneling. Each vehicle comes with sets of wooden parts that are cut from the same log, and then stained and finished together. If a wood component is damaged in assembly, all the other pieces from its set are replaced as well.

At the end of the line, on a typical day, one vehicle sits in a steady rainstorm, undergoing weatherproof testing. Two others are installed in bays for what are known as "shipping quality audits"—where random vehicles are chosen for an extra-close, no-holds-barred, semi-surgical inspection. The finished RX 330s then run through a test track with bumps and curves. A driver speeds, then brakes, then takes his hands off the wheel to be sure the new vehicles don't pull to one side or the other. Eventually, they'll board the railcars ready to carry them off to a distant city and a new owner. As for Cambridge surpassing Japan, so far they're on track: They're even sending kaizens back to Kyushu.

Key Issues for Discussion

1. Discuss how the processes designed into the Cambridge plant support the achievement of high product quality. What specific aspects of the process relate to design, control, and improvement?
2. What lessons or best practices might be learned and applied to other companies (outside of the automotive industry)?

Review Questions

1. Explain the differences between value-creation and support processes and provide some examples of each.
2. Describe some organizations that use projects as their primary value-creation processes. Why is project management important for managing Six Sigma projects?
3. Define process management and its key activities. Why is process management important to any business?
4. Why is agility important for processes in today's business environment?
5. Explain the differences between designing processes for manufactured goods and services. How should the design of service processes be approached?
6. Summarize the principles on which AT&T bases its process management methodology.
7. How can one check whether process owners have true responsibility for controlling a process?
8. Why is it important that processes be repeatable and measurable?
9. Why do people make inadvertent mistakes? How does poka-yoke help prevent such mistakes?
10. Describe the types of errors that service poka-yokes are designed to prevent.
11. Describe the three components of any control system.
12. Explain the concept of after-action review.
13. Explain the Japanese concept of kaizen. How does it differ from traditional Western approaches to improvement?
14. How can reductions in cycle time lead to improvements in processes?
15. What is the Deming cycle? Explain the four steps.
16. Describe the Creative Problem-Solving (CPS) process.
17. What is a stretch goal? How can stretch goals help an organization?
18. Define benchmarking and list its benefits.
19. What is reengineering? How does it relate to TQ practices?
20. Why is it important to establish strong relationships with suppliers? What are some good supplier management practices? (See the Bonus Materials for this chapter on the Premium website.)

BONUS MATERIALS

21. What is the purpose of supplier certification? Explain some of the common practices for supplier certification. (See the Bonus Materials for this chapter on the Premium website.)
22. What is the importance of using projects for Six Sigma improvements and what are the advantages of using the Six Sigma approach to projects?
23. Discuss how process management is addressed in the Baldrige criteria, ISO 9000:2000, and Six Sigma.

Discussion Questions

1. A. Blanton Godfrey notes that many organizations are "wired for failure;" that is, their processes are not designed effectively or aligned with each other.[56] He cites several examples. One is overscheduling at airports. During the 4:15 to 4:30 p.m. time slot, 35 arrivals are scheduled in Atlanta, even though in optimal weather conditions the airport can handle only 25 in 15 minutes; with bad weather, this number drops to 17. Another company celebrated its largest sales contract in history only to discover that all qualified suppliers for critical materials were at capacity. A third example is the unwillingness of departments to work together. When products fail in the plant or in service, it isn't because designers choose components they know will fail; they often have insufficient information about the problems that result from their choices. Such problems can be mitigated by good process management. Discuss his observations and cite examples of your own to illustrate each of the three issues.
2. Identify some of the key processes associated with the following business activities for a typical company: sales and marketing, supply chain management, managing information technology, and managing human resources.
3. Provide some examples of processes that are repeatable and measurable and some that are not.
4. List some of the common processes that a student performs. How can these processes be improved?
5. Are classroom examinations a means of control or improvement? What should they be?
6. Why are modern products more difficult to manufacture than traditional products such as bicycles or hand tools?
7. How can kaizen be applied in a classroom?
8. The kaizen philosophy seeks to encourage suggestions, not to find excuses for failing to improve. Typical excuses are "If it's not broken, don't fix it," "I'm too busy to work on it," and "It's not in the budget." Think of at least five other excuses why people don't try to improve.
9. How might Six Sigma projects be applied to course design?
10. What is the "product development process" a school might use for designing and introducing a new course? How might it be improved to reduce "time-to-market"?
11. How can a manager effectively balance the three key components of a service system design?
12. In a true story related by our colleague Professor James W. Dean, Jr., the general manager of an elevator company was frustrated with the lack of

cooperation between the mechanical engineers who designed new elevators and the manufacturing engineers who determined how to produce them.[57] The mechanical engineers would often completely design a new elevator without consulting with the manufacturing engineers, and then expect the factory to somehow figure out how to build it. Often, the new products were difficult or nearly impossible to build, and their quality and cost suffered as a result. The designs were sent back to the mechanical engineers (often more than once) for engineering changes to improve their manufacturability, and customers sometimes waited for months for deliveries. The general manager believed that if the two groups of engineers would communicate early in the design process, many of the problems would be solved. At his wits' end, he found a large empty room in the plant and had both groups moved into it. The manager relaxed a bit, but a few weeks later he returned to a surprise. The two groups of engineers had finally learned to cooperate—by building a wall of bookcases and file cabinets right down the middle of the room, separating them from each other! What would you do in this situation?

13. Legal Sea Foods operates several restaurants and fish markets in the Boston area and other East Coast locations. The company's standards of excellence mandate that it serves only the freshest, highest-quality seafood. It guarantees the quality by buying only the "top of the catch" fish daily. Although Legal Sea Foods tries to make available the widest variety every day, certain species of fish are subject to migratory patterns and are not always present in New England waters. Weather conditions may also prevent local fishermen from fishing in certain areas.

    Freshly caught fish are rushed to the company's quality control center where they are cut and filleted in an environmentally controlled state-of-the-art facility. All shellfish come from government-certified beds and are tested in an in-house microbiology laboratory for wholesomeness and purity. There are even special lobster storage tanks so that all lobsters are held under optimum conditions, in clean, pollution-free water. Every seafood item is inspected for quality eight separate times before it reaches the table.

    At Legal Sea Foods' restaurants, each meal is cooked to order. Even though servers make every effort to deliver all meals within minutes of each other, they will not jeopardize the quality of an item by holding it beneath a heat lamp until the entire order is ready. The service staff is trained to work as a team for better service. More than one service person frequently delivers food to a table. When any item is ready, the closest available person serves it. Customer questions can be directed to any employee, not just the person who took the initial order.

    a. What are the major processes performed by Legal Sea Foods? How does the process design support its goal of serving only the freshest, highest-quality seafood?
    b. Where would Legal Sea Foods fall on the three-dimensional classification of service organizations? Is its process design consistent with this classification?

14. The president of Circle H assigned you to perform a complete investigation to determine the causes of certain quality problems and to recommend appropriate corrective action. You have authority to talk to any other person within the company.

    The early stages of your investigation establish that the three reasons most often cited by customers are symptomatic of some major quality problems in the company's operations. In proceeding with the audit, you decide to review all available data, which may yield indications of the root causes of these problems.

Further investigation reveals that, over a recent four-month period, a procedural change was made in the order approval process. You wish to find out whether this change caused a significant difference in the amount of time required to process an order from field sales through shipping. You therefore decide to investigate this particular situation.

On completion of your investigation into the problems with order processing, you determine that the change in procedures for order approval led to an increase in the amount of time required restocking goods in the customers' stores. You want to recommend corrective action for this problem, but you first do additional investigation as to why the change was made. You learn that, because of large losses on delinquent accounts receivable, the change was made to require that the credit manager approve all restock orders. This approval requirement added an average of three hours to the amount of internal processing time needed for a restock order.

On review of your report, the president of Circle H takes note of administrative problems whose existence he had never suspected. To assure that corrective action will be effective and sustained, the president assigns you to take charge of the corrective action program.[58]

a. What types of data would be most useful to review for clues as to why the three major customer complaints occurred?
b. How would you investigate whether the change in the order approval process had a significant effect on order processing time?
c. Given your knowledge of problems in both order processing and accounts receivable, what should you do?

15. McDonald's used to make food to stock, storing sandwiches in a large tray used to fulfill customer orders. When sales went flat in the mid 1990s and independent market testing showed a widening gap with competition in food quality, McDonald's recognized that the make-to-stock process was not meeting customer demands. After five years of lab and market testing, McDonald's rolled out the new "Just for You" system, which began in March 1998, to create a make-to-order environment. This shift required a massive change in technology with computers to coordinate orders; food production equipment using "rapid toasters" and temperature-controlled "launching zones" to replace the old heat lamps and holding bins; new food preparation tables, and retraining efforts for the entire domestic food production organization of more than 600,000 crew members. However, this system has apparently backfired. Sales did not improve as expected and customers complained about slow service. The new system increased the average service time 2 to 3 minutes per order, and 15-minute waits were not uncommon. McDonald's stock price decreased, and rivals such as Wendy's captured additional market share.[59] What lessons does this experience suggest for process management? What might McDonald's have done differently?
16. The Cincinnati Water Works (CWW) serves approximately 1 million customers.[60] Its billing system allows customer service representatives (CSRs) to retrieve information from customer accounts quickly using almost any piece of data such as customer name, address, phone number, social security number, and so on. Besides a customer's account history, the system contains everything that was said in a call, including documentation of past problems

and their resolution. An integrated voice response system provides automated phone support for bill paying and account balances, tells customers of the approximate wait time to speak to a CSR, and allows the customers to leave a message for a CSR to return a call. An information board in the department shows the number of customers waiting, average length of time waiting, and the number of CSRs that are busy and doing post-call work. A pop-up screen provides CSRs with customer data before the phone rings so that he or she will have the customer's information before they even say hello. Work orders taken by CSRs, such as a broken water main or leaking meter, are routed automatically to a field service supervisor for immediate attention. This system is also used internally to allocate maintenance workers when a problem arises at a pumping station or treatment facility. A geographic information system is used for mapping the locations of water mains and fire hydrants, and provides field service employees, meter readers, and contractors exact information to accomplish their work. Handheld meter readers are used to locate meters and download data into computers. Touch pad devices provide exterior connections to inside meters, eliminating the necessity to enter a house or building. CWW is also investigating automated meter readers and radio frequency devices that simply require a company van to drive by the building to automatically obtain readings. Discuss how technology has affected the processes of CWW. What specific types of improvements (quality, cycle time, etc.) were these applications designed to address? Can you think of similar uses of these technologies in other service applications?

17. A hospital developed a design process consisting of the following steps: Plan, Design, Measure, Assess, and Improve. Below is a list of specific activities that comprise these five steps in random order. Place the activities in the most appropriate order within the correct step of the design process.
    Pilot or test design
    Submit proposal
    Define measures to assess design performance
    Implement design
    Identify potential solutions to reduce out of control conditions
    Develop business plan
    Disseminate improvements throughout the organization
    Monitor process performance
    Select the best solution to improve control
    Identify out of control conditions
    Propose new concept
    Create design to meet requirements
    Identify new improvement opportunities
    Monitor the new process design
    Implement the best solution to improve control
    Verify proposal alignment with strategic objectives
    Establish design team
    Identify causes of out of control conditions
    Analyze causes
    Identify and validate customer requirements
    Identify and evaluate best practices
18. Table 7.6 shows the Pepsi-Cola Company's three-step method for customer-valued process improvement. Discuss its differences and similarities to the Deming cycle.

Table 7.6 Pepsi-Cola Process Improvement Methodology

Steps	Actions
1. Start with the customer	a. Understand and prioritize customer needs b. Establish customer measures and success criteria c. Select a process with most impact on customer needs
2. Understand ourselves and plan improvements	a. Analyze the current process involving the performers in each step b. Design improved process c. Establish process measures
3. Do it	a. Pilot-test improved process b. Implement improved process c. Stabilize process d. Go to Step 1 (continuously improve)

Source: Courtesy of Pepsi-Cola Co. Reprinted with permission of The Forum Corporation.

19. What types of defects or errors might the following organizations measure and improve as part of a Six Sigma initiative?
    a. A metropolitan bus company
    b. A local department store
    c. An electric power company
    d. Walt Disney World or a regional amusement park, such as Paramount or Six Flags
    e. Your college or university
20. The following summary of a quality improvement project performed by an employee team at Siemens Energy and Automation.[61] Discuss how the approach used can be viewed in the context of (1) the Deming cycle, and (2) the creative problem solving process.

The Makin' Waves team is a Continuous Improvement team from the Siemens facility located in Urbana, Ohio. The Urbana facility is a supplier plant to the Siemens plant in Bellefontaine. We supply molded plastic, stamping, and plating support to the Bellefontaine plant. The Makin' Waves team is from the Plastics Department. Our team has been functioning for four years and has completed many highly successful projects. The team consists of two press operators, one product repairperson, one janitor, and one Quality Assurance person, all from the Plastics Department. We also included a supervisor from the E-Frame circuit breaker line in Bellefontaine who was added at the beginning of this project as a representative of our stakeholders and to provide valuable input.

Our team began this project by looking into ideas for a project from the Corrective Action System and the Value Improvement Program. Our project started out as a way to reduce the negative effect caused by the poor appearance of the E-Frame breaker. Upon investigating the problem, we discovered that we could actually eliminate the operation that was causing the negative appearance. We decided to make our project the elimination of the washing operation station in the production of the E-Frame plastic case.

The E-Frame breaker case is molded in a compression press. The problem begins during the trimming and filing processes that are done after the part is removed from the mold. The plastic contains fiberglass, which becomes a fine dust that adheres to the part. To eliminate the dust, the parts are put through a washing operation. This process uses a conveyor system to carry the parts through a water spray cleaning system. The problem with this process is that the finish comes out looking spotty and with some fiberglass particles still adhering to the parts themselves.

Our customers on the E-Frame breaker line had written Corrective Actions against this procedure because of the poor appearance and the dust still being present on the parts. They were experiencing problems with the fiberglass and had to wear gloves to protect their hands.

Through data collection we realized that this operation takes 6,831 labor-hours a year at a cost of over $96,000. Yet after the washing process the parts still were not clean and had a negative appearance that was not acceptable. We took the top five part numbers and charted the clean versus the dirty parts. We found that 97 percent of the parts did not meet customer standards and that our customers had to add a rework operation to keep the E-Frame line going!

We set a goal to eliminate the washing operation by May 1997. In order to have this happen we needed to find a better process to take its place. We did a fishbone analysis to outline the causes of the problem, and followed up with a root cause analysis to eliminate any causes that did not pertain.

We brainstormed for possible solutions, producing five possible alternatives to the washing operation. They were:

- *Constant air flow*
- *Shop vacuum*
- *Deflashing parts*
- *Ionizer (mouse trap)*
- *Air hose at press*

We tested and evaluated each solution, working with both the operators in the Plastics department and our customers on the breaker line. As a result of our evaluation, we found that an air hose at the press was the best solution. We instructed the operators that after the parts were filed, they should be blown free of all fiber particles. Because they were not being washed with water, this would eliminate the spotty appearance of the parts. We set up direct communication with our customers to make sure that this process was eliminating the problem permanently. Their feedback showed that they were satisfied with the new process and that there was not a problem with either the fiberglass or the appearance of the parts. We then took the findings and recommended that the washing operation be eliminated and replaced by an air hose at the press. We communicated to Quality Assurance that the job instructions should be updated to include our new process so that supervisors and operators would be trained on the new process at the end of their safety meetings. We then went to the scheduler and had the washing process eliminated from the system. After this was accomplished and there was still favorable feedback from the customers, we pulled the plug on the washing operation altogether.

Our goal as a team was to eliminate the washing operation and we accomplished this goal. There were other benefits attached to the project:

- *$98,000 cost reduction in labor and maintenance*
- *Additional 136 square feet of valuable floor space freed up*
- *Improved delivery to customer*
- *Improved teamwork between customer and supplier*
- *Open communication with customer*
- *Elimination of a rework operation*
- *Improved quality to the consumer*
- *Improved safety and health of operators*

21. Maintaining accuracy of books on the shelves in a college library is an important task. Consider the following problems that are often observed.
    a. Books are not placed in the correct shelf position, which includes those books that have been checked out and returned, as well as those taken off the shelves for use within the library by patrons.
    b. New or returned books are not checked in and consequently, the online catalog does not show their availability.

    What procedures or poka-yokes might you suggest for mitigating these problems? You might wish to talk to some librarians or administrators at your college library to see how they address such problems.
22. Rick Hensley owns an automotive dealership. Service is a major part of the operation. Rick and his service team spent considerable time in analyzing the service process and developed a flowchart, shown in Figure 7.11, which

Figure 7.11 Automobile Service Flowchart (Problem 11)

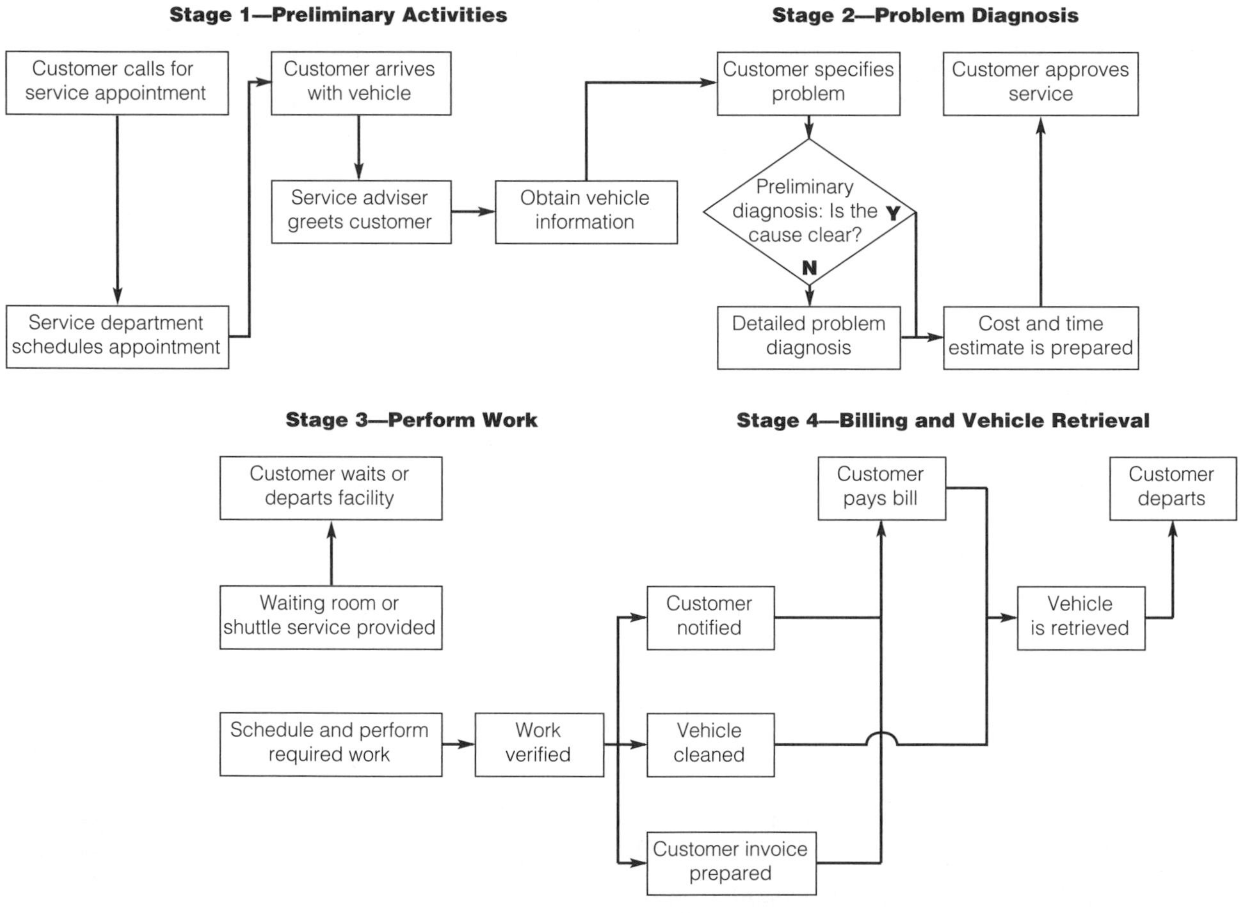

Source: Richard B. Chase and Douglas M. Stewart, "Make Your Service Fail-Safe," *Sloan Management Review*, pp. 40–41.

Figure 7.12 Medical Administration Process

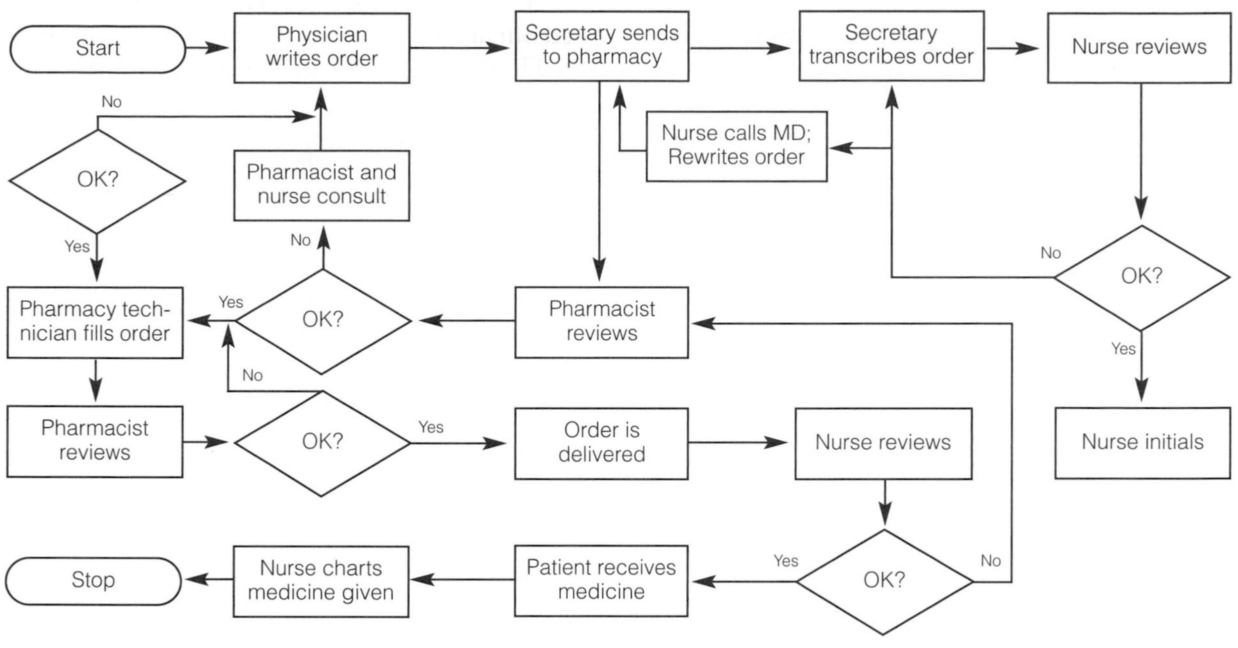

Source: Ellen Williams and Ray Tailey, "The Use of Failure Mode Effect and Criticality Analysis in a Medication Error Subcommittee," *ASQC Health Care Division Newsletter*, Winter 1996, 4. Copyright © 1996 ASQC. Reprinted with permission.

describes the typical activities in servicing a customer's automobile. Rick wants to ensure that customers receive superior service and are highly satisfied; thus, he wants to establish poka-yokes for any possible failures that may occur. Your assignment is to identify any possible failure in the service process that may be detrimental to customer satisfaction and suggest poka-yokes to eliminate these failures.

23. Figure 7.12 shows a medication administration process in a hospital. The administrative staff of the hospital is concerned about frequent medication errors. After examining this flowchart, discuss possible sources of errors, the types of individuals responsible (e.g., physicians, nurses, pharmacists, other), and poka-yokes that might be used to mitigate these errors.
24. The process for depositing a check at a local bank begins with the teller determining if the customer wants to receive any cash back. If not, the teller checks to see if the payee's name is on the account, stamps the deposit slip, and gives the customer a receipt. If there is cash back, the teller adds the checks and subtracts the net deposit to verify the cash amount on the deposit slip, checks and verifies the customer's account, makes a "cash out" ticket for bank accounting, and gives the customer back the cash and receipt. Draw a flowchart for this process and identify potential sources of error and poka-yokes that might be used to mitigate these errors.

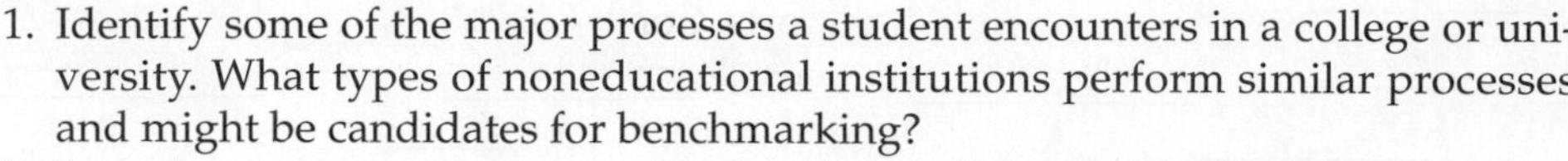

Projects, Etc.

1. Identify some of the major processes a student encounters in a college or university. What types of noneducational institutions perform similar processes and might be candidates for benchmarking?
2. Interview a plant manager at a local factory to determine his or her philosophy on process management. What techniques does the company use?
3. Investigate design-for-environment practices in some of your local industries. Describe company policies and the methods and techniques that they use to address environmental concerns in product design.

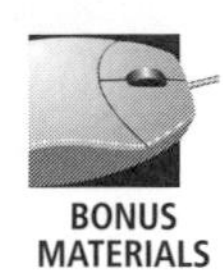

BONUS MATERIALS

4. Christina Clark works at a food service operation for a large amusement park. She has been charged with developing a process control plan based on HACCP principles for meeting food safety requirements (see the Bonus Materials for this chapter on the Premium website). For example, the requirements for hot dogs include:
   - *Receiving:* Refrigerated hot dogs should be between –40 and 34 degrees Fahrenheit when received.
   - *Storage:* Storage temperature should be between –40 and 34 degrees Fahrenheit.
   - *Cooking:* Hot dogs should be heated to a temperature of 145 ± 5°F within 30 minutes of placing on the grill.
   - *Cooked Storage:* Leftover hot dogs must be covered and placed in refrigeration immediately and reach a temperature of 40°F or lower within 4 hours.
   - *Reheating:* Hot dogs must be reheated to an internal temperature of 165 ± 5°F within 20 minutes, one time only.

   Develop a process control plan for ensuring that these requirements are met. Design any forms or "standard operating procedures" that you think would be helpful in implementing your plan.
5. Design a process for the following activities:
   a. Preparing for an exam
   b. Writing a term paper
   c. Planning a vacation
   d. Making breakfast for your family
   e. Washing your car

   Discuss ways in which both quality and cycle time might be improved.
6. Design an instrument for evaluating the "process orientation" of an organization. For example, what characteristics would you look for in firms that have a strong process orientation?
7. Barker is a small custom producer of equipment used in various process industries such as chemicals and beverages. Each piece of equipment is customer designed from customer specifications. The process generally consists of five steps:
   1. Customer quote creation
   2. Pre-production planning (if awarded the contract)
   3. Quality assurance plan
   4. Manufacturing
   5. Inspection and delivery

   Develop a process manual for this company that outlines specific activities that should be performed within each of these process steps. Be sure to clearly describe how design, control, and improvement are integrated into this process, and also consider other issues discussed in this chapter, such as the project nature of this process.

8. Research several companies to identify the type of problem-solving approach they use in their improvement efforts. Compare and contrast their approaches. Which, if any, of the approaches described in the chapter are they most similar to?
9. Work with your school administrators to identify an important quality-related problem they face. Outline a plan for improvement.
10. Describe a personal problem you face and how you might use the Deming cycle to address it.
11. Work with teachers at a local high school or grade school to identify some students who are having difficulties in school. Apply quality tools to help find the source of the problems and create an improvement plan.
12. Identify several sources of errors as a student or in your personal life. Develop some poka-yokes that might prevent them.
13. Interview a plant manager or quality professional at one or more local companies to see whether they use any poka-yoke approaches to mistake-proof their operations.
14. Search the Internet for websites that contain descriptions and examples of quality improvement methodologies approaches. How do they compare with the ones described in this chapter?
15. Search the Internet for John Grout's Poka-Yoke website. Read several of the interesting articles available there and write a report on the information you discover.

Cases

Additional cases are available in the Bonus Materials Folder on the Premium website.

BONUS MATERIALS

The State University Experience

Wow! That State University video was really cool. It has lots of majors; it's close to home so I can keep my job; and Mom and Dad loved it when they visited. I wish I could know what it's really like to be a student at State. Hmmm, I think I'll ask Mom and Dad to take a campus tour with me . . .

I'm sure that we took our tour on the hottest day of the summer. The campus is huge—it took us about two hours to complete the tour and we didn't even see everything! I wasn't sure that the tour guide knew what he was doing. We went into a gigantic lecture hall and the lights weren't even on. Our tour guide couldn't find them so we had to hold the doors open so the sunlight could come in. About three-fourths of the way through the tour, our guide said, "State University isn't really a bad place to go to school; you just have to learn the system." I wonder what he meant by that?

This application is really confusing. How do I let the admissions office know that I am interested in physics, mechanical engineering, and industrial design? Even my parents can't figure it out. I guess I'll call the admissions office for some help . . .

I'm so excited! Mom just handed me a letter from State! Maybe they've already accepted me. What? What's this? They say I need to send my transcript. I did that when I mailed in my application two weeks ago. What's going on? I hope it won't affect my application. I'd better check with Admissions . . .

You can't find my file? I thought you were only missing my transcript. I asked my counselor if she had sent it in yet. She told me that she sent it last week. Oh, you'll call me back when you locate my file? O.K. . . .

Finally, I've been accepted! Wait a minute. I didn't apply to University College; that's a two-year program. I wanted physics, M.E., or industrial design. Well, because my only choice is U. College and I really want to go to State, I guess I'll send in the confirmation form. It really looks a lot like the application. In fact, I know I gave them a lot of the same information. I wonder why they need it again? Seems like a waste of time . . .

Orientation was a lot of fun. I'm glad they straightened out my acceptance at U. College. I think I will enjoy State after all. I met lots of other students. I saw my advisor and I signed up for classes. All I have left to do is pay my tuition bill. Whoops. None of my financial aid is on this bill. I know I filled out all of the forms because I got an award letter from State. There is no way my parents and I can pay for this without financial aid. It says at the bottom, I'll lose all of my classes if I don't pay the bill on time . . .

I'm not confirmed on the computer? I sent in my form and the fee a long time ago. What am I going to do? I don't want to lose all of my classes. I have to go to the admissions office or my college office and get a letter that says I am a confirmed student. O.K. If I do that tomorrow, will I still have all of my classes? . . .

I can't sleep; I'm so nervous about my first day . . .

Discussion Questions

1. What breakdowns in service processes has this student experienced?
2. What types of process management activities should State University administrators undertake?

The PIVOT Initiative at Midwest Bank, Part I[62]

Midwest, a bank holding company, is located in Ohio. Its main subsidiary provides a diverse line of banking and financial products and services regionally; and selected business activities are conducted nationally. Consumer, small business, and investment products and services are offered through a network of retail banking centers located primarily within Ohio and Kentucky. Midwest Bank also has a growing presence in Florida with 13 retail banking centers. Commercial banking products and services are offered through nine regional offices. Customers can also access this Midwest's financial and banking products and services 24-hours per day via its network of ATMs, a 24-hour telephone customer service center, or online. This bank has served the financial needs of its customers for 100 years, and currently 3,200 associates serve approximately 600,000 customers.

The PIVOT Initiative

The PIVOT initiative, the name that Midwest gave its Six Sigma process improvement approach, started with the selection of three pilot projects, one of which was in the Commercial Processing Department (CPD) that works as Midwest Bank's cash vault. CPD already operated at a high level of sigma (4.26) as found early in Yellow Belt Six Sigma training. CPD processes a high dollar volume of transactions. One costly error in the previous year resulted in a loss of over a quarter million dollars and brought the department to the forefront of change initiatives. Once the project was chosen, the bank selected six associates to run the first PIVOT project.

A project coordinator working from the project office was selected as project manager for the Six Sigma functions of the project. An operations financial manager was in charge of financial impact analysis and equipment purchasing. The assistant vice president and team supervisor, were subject matter experts from within CPD. Another project coordinator was brought on board for her bankwide knowledge and overall project support. The project analyst for CPD and five other areas was in charge of the departmental project management and was the Six Sigma analyst for the team. The Six Sigma analyst was responsible for data integrity, graphical analysis, and data stratification. After their weeklong Six Sigma course, the six team members followed the Six Sigma DMAIC process steps (*define, measure, analyze, improve,* and *control*) to define the project and get it underway.

DMAIC Define Stage

The senior vice president and vice president over CPD were the champions for this project and initially worked to establish the problem definition statement. These champions were responsible for the process every day and also held accountable for the errors in the department.

Because the two largest potential sources of errors (strapping and deposit processing) did not influence each other in the process and had separate causes for creating errors, the champions separated them. The problem statement defined the number of errors the department was accountable for during the previous year and the dollar losses of these errors. In this case study, the number of errors and the actual dollar losses are only approximate. The (disguised) problem statement was:

In (the previous year) the number of internal and external defects for the CPD was 150, resulting in Bank losses of $400,000 as well as significant potential risk exposure. Included in the losses is an anomaly of $280,000. The remainder represents a gap of $120,000 versus the goal of $0 of total losses due to Commercial Processing Department operations. Our objective is to reduce the internal error ratio by December of the current year and the total amount of losses by over 50 percent in the following 12 months. Projects from this business case will reduce loss expense and risk exposure, while increasing customer satisfaction.

Much debate centered on whether to include the anomaly loss since it skewed the numbers considerably. However, the decision was finally made to include it. Support for the CPD PIVOT project centered on risk mitigation, which is difficult to quantify, and on dollar losses required to carry the project. Based on the potential reduction of approximately $400,000 in losses and the future risk mitigation, the steering committee approved the project launch, and the CPD PIVOT team moved onto the Measure stage.

Discussion Questions

1. What conclusions can you reach on the importance of team preparation and member selection to the "Define" stage, and eventual success of Six Sigma projects, such as the PIVOT project?
2. How did the roles of the PIVOT team members, described in the case, potentially contribute knowledge or skill necessary to carry out each stage of the DMAIC process? *Hint: Refer back to the team member roles and responsibilities in Chapter 6, Table 6.1.*
3. What factors do you think weighed in the decision to include the $280,000 "anomaly" in the project justification? If you were the project champion, how would you assess this justification in deciding on whether the project was significant enough to move forward.

Novel Connect: Process Management

BONUS MATERIALS

The complete Novel Connect case study, a fictitious example of a Baldrige application, can be found in the Baldrige Materials folder on the Premium website accompanying this book. If you have not read the Organizational Profile yet (see the case in Chapter 3), please do so first. Examine their response to Category 6 in the context of the Baldrige criteria for Category 6. What are their strengths? What are their weaknesses and opportunities for improvement? What specific advice, including useful tools and techniques that might help them, would you suggest?

NOTES

1. Lucas Conley, "90,000 DVDs. No Shelves." *Fast Company*, September 2003, p. 38. FAST COMPANY by LUCAS CONLEY. Copyright 2003 by MANSUETO VENTURES LLC. Reprinted with permission.
2. "Supply Chain Excellence," Special Advertising Section, *Business Week*, April 25, 2005.
3. Paula K. Martin and Karen Tate, "Projects That Get Quality Treatment," *The Journal for Quality and Participation*, November/December 1998, 58–61.
4. Custom Research Incorporated, "Highlights of CRI's Best Practices," 1996 *Baldrige Application Abstract*, 13–14.
5. AT&T Quality Steering Committee, *Process Quality Management & Improvement Guidelines*, AT&T Publication Center, AT&T Bell Laboratories (1987).
6. In his article, "Beyond PDCA—A New Process Management Model," *Quality Progress*, July 2006, 45–52, Praveen Gupta proposes a variation of these activities: prepare, perform, perfect, and progress, as an easily understood and implementable framework for process management.
7. "It's the Latest Thing – Really," *Business Week*, March 27, 2006, 70–71.

8. Julie Schlosser, "Cashing in on the new world of me," *Fortune*, December 13, 2004, 245–250.

9. Rebecca Duray and Glenn W. Milligan, "Improving Customers Satisfaction Through Mass Customization," *Quality Progress*, August 1999, 60–66.

10. Sarah Anne Wright, "Putting Fast-Food to the Test," *The Cincinnati Enquirer*, July 9, 2000, F1, 2.

11. City of Coral Springs 2007 Baldrige Application.

12. John Haywood-Farmer, "A Conceptual Model of Service Quality," *International Journal of Operations and Production Management* 8, no. 6 (1988), 19–29.

13. Charles D. Zimmerman, III, and John W. Enell, "Service Industries," Sec. 33 in J. M. Juran (ed.), *Juran's Quality Control Handbook*, 4th ed. (New York: McGraw-Hill, 1988).

14. For an interesting, albeit academic discussion of the psychology of human error and its relationship to mistake-proofing, see Douglas M. Stewart and Richard B. Chase, "The Impact of Human Error on Delivering Service Quality," *Production and Operations Management* 8, no. 3 (Fall 1999), 240–263; and Douglas M. Stewart and John R. Grout, "The Human Side of Mistake Proofing," *Production and Operations Management* 10, no. 4 (Winter 2001), 440–459.

15. From *Poka-Yoke: Improving Product Quality by Preventing Defects*. Edited by NKS/Factory Magazine, English translation copyright ©1988 by Productivity Press, Inc., P.O. Box 3007, Cambridge, MA 02140, 800-394-6868. Reprinted by permission.

16. Harry Robinson, "Using Poka-Yoke Techniques for Early Defect Detection," Paper presented at the Sixth International Conference on Software Testing and Analysis and Review (STAR '97).

17. Excerpts reprinted from Richard B. Chase and Douglas M. Stewart, "Make Your Service Fail-Safe," *Sloan Management Review* 35, no. 3 (Spring 1994), 35–44. © 1994 by the Sloan Management Review Association. All rights reserved.

18. Michael A. Prospero, "Top Scalpel," Fast *Company*, April 2006, 31.

19. "GE errors linked to plane fire," *The Cincinnati Enquirer*, December 14, 2004, F1,2.

20. N. Tsikriktsis and J. Heineke, "The Impact of Process Variation on Customer Dissatisfaction: Evidence from the U.S. Domestic Airline Industry," *Decision Sciences*, 35, 1, Winter 2004, 129–142.

21. "Testing for Conformity: An Inside Job," *Golf Journal*, May 1998, 20–25.

22. "DaimlerChrysler's Quality Practices Pay Off for PT Cruiser," News and Analysis, *Metrologyworld.com*, (accessed March 23, 2000).

23. Douglas H. Harris and Frederick B. Chaney, *Human Factors in Quality Assurance* (New York: John Wiley & Sons, Inc., 1969).

24. Adapted from the Malcolm Baldridge National Quality Award Application Summaries of the Ritz-Carlton Hotel Company, L.L.C., 1992 and 1999.

25. The Centers for Disease Control [CDC] have developed a national system, called NNIS for tracking such infections. (See http://www.cdc.gov/ncidod/dhqp/nnis.html for details.)

26. Adapted from K. M. Casarreal, J. I. Mills, and M. A. Plant, "Improving Service Through Patient Surveys in a Multihospital Organization," *Hospital & Health Services Administration*, Health Administration Press, Ann Arbor, MI (March/April 1986), 41–52. © 1986, Foundation of the American College of Health Care Executives.

27. Robert A. Gardner, "Resolving the Process Paradox," *Quality Progress*, March 2001, 51–59.

28. Masaaki Imai, *KAIZEN—The Key to Japan's Competitive Success* (New York: McGraw-Hill, 1986).

29. "No Satisfaction at Toyota," *Fast Company*, December 2006, p. 82.

30. Alan Robinson (ed.), *Continuous Improvement in Operations* (Cambridge, MA: Productivity Press, 1991).

31. Lea A. P. Tonkin, "Kaizen BlitzSM 5: Bottleneck-Bashing comes to Rochester, NY," *Target* 12, no. 4 (September–October 1996), 41–43.

32. Mark Oakeson, "Makes Dollars & Sense for Mercedes-Benz in Brazil," *IIE Solutions* (April 1997), 32–35.

33. For a perspective on this and related issues from Japan's "Father of Continuous Improvement," see Laura Smith, "Profiles in Quality With Masaaki Imai," *Quality Digest*, October 2005, 54–56.

34. Eleanor Chilson, "Kaizen Blitzes at Magnivision: $809,270 Cost Savings," *Quality Management Forum* 29, no. 1 (Winter 2003).

35. Andrew E. Serwer, "Michael Dell Turns the PC World Inside Out," *Fortune*, September 8, 1997, 76–86.

36. David A. McCamey, Robert W. Bogs, and Linda M. Bayuk, "More, Better, Faster From Total Quality Effort," *Quality Progress*, August 1999, 43–50.

37. A. VanGundy, "Comparing 'Little Known' Creative Problem-Solving Techniques," in *Creativity Week III, 1980 Proceedings* (Greensboro, NC: Center for Creative Leadership, 1981). The reader is also referred to James R. Evans, *Creative Thinking in the Decision and Management Sciences* (Cincinnati, OH: South-Western Publishing Co., 1991), for a thorough treatment of creative problem solving.

38. Gerald Langley, Kevin Nolan, and Thomas Nolan, "The Foundation of Improvement," Sixth Annual International Deming User's Group Conference, Cincinnati, OH (August 1992).

39. Langley et al. (see note 38).

40. Sylvia Nasar, "What Makes Beautiful Minds," *Fast Company*, December 2004, 50–52.

41. Masaaki Imai, *Kaizen: The Key to Japan's Competitive Success* (New York: McGraw-Hill, 1986), 15.

42. A. F. Osborn, *Applied Imagination,* 3rd ed. (New York: Scribner's, 1963); S. J. Parnes, R. B. Noller, and A. M. Biondi (eds.), *Guide to Creative Action* (New York: Scribner's, 1977).

43. Peter Lewis, "A Perpetual Crisis Machine," *Fortune*, September 19, 2005, 57–76.

44. Lawrence S. Pryor, "Benchmarking: A Self-Improvement Strategy," *Journal of Business Strategy,* November/December 1989, 28–32.

45. Robert C. Camp, *Benchmarking: The Search for Industry Best Practices That Lead to Superior Performance* (Milwaukee. WI: ASQC Quality Press and UNIPUB/Quality Resources, 1989).

46. Shawn Tully, "Why to Go for Stretch Targets," *Fortune,* November 14, 1994, 45–58.

47. Christopher E. Bogan and Michael J. English, "Benchmarking for Best Practices: Winning Through Innovative Adaptation," *Quality Digest,* August 1994, 52–62.

48. Cathy Hill, "Benchmarking and Best Practices," The 54th Annual Quality Congress *Proceedings of the American Society for Quality*, 2000.

49. John Hackl, "New Beginnings: Change is Here to Stay," *Quality Progress,* February 1998, 5.

50. AT&T Consumer Communication Services Summary of 1994 Application for the Malcolm Baldrige National Quality Award.

51. Michael Hammer and James Champy, *Reengineering the Corporation* (New York: HarperBusiness, 1993), 177–178.

52. ibid.

53. Bogan and English (see note 47).

54. Reprinted with permission of Gold Star Chili.

55. Adapted from Phil Patton, "Northern Exposure," *Lexus Magazine*, Quarter 1, 2004, 39–42.

56. A. Blanton Godfrey, "Planned Failures," *Quality Digest*, March 2000, 16.

57. This story was first published in James W. Dean, Jr. and James R. Evans *Total Quality: Management, Organization, and Strategy*, Minneapolis/St. Paul: West Publishing Company, 1994, p. 143.

58. Adapted from ASQ Quality Auditor Certification Brochure, July 1989.

59. John E. Ettlie, "What the Auto Industry Can Learn from McDonald's," *Automotive Manufacturing & Production*, October 1999, 42; David Stires, "Fallen Arches," *Fortune*, April 29, 2002, 74–76.

60. Adapted from a student project by one of the author's students, Tim Planitz, December 2001.

61. Courtesy of Siemens Energy and Automation Distribution Products Division.

62. Appreciation is expressed to one of the author's students, Michael Wolf, who wrote the paper on which this case is based, as part of the requirements for MGT 699, *Total Quality Management*, 2002, at Northern Kentucky University, and Cathy Ernst, senior vice president at the bank.

Chapter 8 Performance Measurement and Information Management

Outline

Quality Profiles: Wainwright Industries, Inc. and Baptist Hospital, Inc.
The Scope of Performance Measurement
The Balanced Scorecard
Product Outcomes
Customer-Focused Outcomes
Financial and Market Outcomes
Workforce-Focused Outcomes
Process Effectiveness Outcomes
Leadership Outcomes
Designing Effective Performance Measurement Systems
Selecting Measures and Indicators
Linking Measures to Strategy
Process-Level Measurements
Identifying and Selecting Process Measures
Aligning Strategic and Process-Level Measurements
Analyzing and Using Performance Data
The Role of Comparative Data
Performance Review
The Cost of Quality
Quality Cost Classification
Capturing and Using Quality Costs
Quality Costs in Service Organizations
Measuring the Return on Quality
Managing Information Resources
Knowledge Management
Knowledge Transfer
Measurement and Information Management in the Baldrige Criteria, ISO 9000, and Six Sigma
Summary of Key Points and Terminology
Quality in Practice: Using the Balanced Scorecard at the United States Postal Service
Quality in Practice: Knowledge Management for Continuous Improvement at Convergys
Review Questions
Discussion Questions
Problems
Projects, Etc.
Cases Skyhigh Airlines
Coyote Community College
Novel Connect: Identifying Key Performance Measures
Novel Connect: Measurement, Analysis, and Knowledge Management

In the early 1990s, Boeing's assembly lines were morasses of inefficiency. A manual numbering system dating back to World War II bomber days was used to keep track of an airplane's four million parts and 170 miles of wiring; changing a part on a 737's landing gear meant renumbering 464 pages of drawings. Factory floors were covered with huge tubs of spare parts worth millions of dollars. In an attempt to grab market

share from rival Airbus, the company discounted planes deeply and was buried by an onslaught of orders. The attempt to double production rates, coupled with implementation of a new production control system, resulted in Boeing being forced to shut down its 737 and 747 lines for 27 days in October 1997, leading to a $178 million loss and a shakeup of top management. Much of the blame was focused on Boeing's financial practices and lack of real-time data. With a new CFO and finance team, the company created a "control panel" of vital measures such as material costs, inventory turns, overtime, and defects using a color-coded spreadsheet. For the first time, Boeing was able to generate a series of bar charts showing which of its programs were creating value and which were destroying it. The results were eye-opening; not only did they help improve operations, but they also helped formulate a growth plan. As one manager noted, "The data will set you free."[1]

Considerable value lies in using objective data to support strategic planning and daily operating decisions. Osborne and Gaebler make three insightful observations:

1. If you don't measure results, you can't tell success from failure.
2. If you can't see success, you can't reward it—and if you can't reward success, you are probably rewarding failure.
3. If you can't recognize failure, you can't correct it.[2]

As one notable example, when Dr. Noriaki Kano consulted with Florida Power and Light (FPL), the company told him that lightning was the principal cause of service interruptions. Kano asked why groundings or arresters had not prevented the interruptions; FPL replied that these would not work with Florida's severe lightning. Kano asked for the data to back up this conclusion, but FPL could not produce any. About 18 months later, when Kano next visited the company, they had collected data and found that interruptions occurred even when strong lightning was not present. In addition, they discovered that many utility poles did not have sufficient groundings, a situation they had not recognized until they collected the data.[3]

A supply of consistent, accurate, and timely data across all functional areas of business provides real-time information for the evaluation, control, and improvement of processes, products, and services to meet both business objectives and rapidly changing customer needs.

Although Deming believed in using data as a basis for problem solving, he was highly critical of overemphasizing measurement. He often stated that the most important figures, such as the value of a loyal customer, are unknown and unknowable. However, as our understanding of measurement and the use of technology to support it has improved, many "intangibles" that were once thought to be impossible to measure can be measured economically.[4]

Data are simply representations of facts that come from some type of measurement process. **Measurement** is the act of quantifying the performance dimensions of products, services, processes, and other business activities. **Measures and indicators** refer to the numerical results obtained from measurement. **Information** is derived from the analysis of data and measurements and expressed in the context of a business or organization. For example, the presence or absence of surface defects for a brass sink fixture might be assessed by visual inspection. A useful measure of quality that might be derived from such data is the percentage of fixtures that have surface defects. Further analysis might provide information about the type and location of the defects that can be used to determine the source. As another example, the diameters of machined ball bearings might be measured with a micrometer. Statistics such as the mean diameter and standard deviation provide information to evaluate the ability of the production process to meet specifications. For services, some examples of quality measurements would be the percentage of orders filled accurately and the time taken to fill a customer's order. The term *indicator* is often used for measurements that are not a direct or exclusive measure of performance. For instance, you cannot directly measure dissatisfaction, but you can use the number of complaints or lost customers as indicators of dissatisfaction.

Despite the fact that more than half of the workforce in the United States is engaged in the generation, processing, or dissemination of data and/or information, many organizations do a poor job of systematically collecting appropriate data, getting it to the right people, and analyzing it properly. Organizations ignore measurement for a variety of reasons: They don't know what to measure; they don't want to spend the time or effort to do it; they don't see the value of measurement; or they are afraid to uncover problems.

Measurements and indicators provide a scorecard of business performance that can be used at all levels of the organization. This chapter focuses on the design and use of measurement systems and information management to guide an organization toward the achievement of high performance and meeting its strategic objectives. Table 8.1 summarizes the key measurement and information management practices to meet these goals. The Quality Profiles in this chapter describe two organizations that have exploited these practices to their advantage.

Table 8.1 Key Measurement and Information Management Practices for Performance Excellence

- Select, collect, align, and integrate data and information for tracking daily operations and for tracking overall organizational performance, including progress relative to strategic objectives and action plans, and using data and information to support organizational decision making and innovation.
- Select and ensure the effective use of comparative data and information.
- Review organizational performance and capabilities using effective methods of analysis to assess organizational success, competitive performance, and progress relative to strategic objectives and action plans, and using these reviews to assess the organization's ability to respond rapidly to changing organizational needs and challenges.
- Translate organizational review findings into priorities for continuous and breakthrough improvement and into opportunities for innovation, and deploy them to work group and functional-level operations to support for decision making?
- Make needed data and information available and accessible to the workforce, suppliers, partners, collaborators, and customers as needed.
- Ensure that hardware and software are reliable, secure, and user-friendly, and that information systems support the continued availability of data and information in the event of an emergency.
- Ensure that organizational data, information, and knowledge are accurate, reliable, timely, secure, and confidential.
- Manage organizational knowledge to accomplish the collection and transfer of workforce knowledge; knowledge from and to customers and other stakeholders; rapid identification, sharing, and implementation of best practices; and the assembly and transfer of relevant knowledge for use in strategic planning.
- Keep performance measurement systems, hardware, and software current with business needs and directions, and changes in the organizational or external environment.

Quality Profiles

Wainwright Industries, Inc. and Baptist Hospital, Inc.

Wainwright Industries, Inc., headquartered in St. Peters, Missouri, is a family-owned business that manufactures stamped and machined parts for U.S. and foreign customers in the automotive, aerospace, home security, and information-processing industries. The company employs 275 associates. Craftsmanship, teamwork, and innovation have been commitments at Wainwright since its inception in 1947. Delivering products and services of unequaled quality that generate total customer satisfaction is Wainwright's principal objective. This commitment led the company to a Malcolm Baldrige National Quality Award in the small business category in 1994.

Wainwright Industries aligns the company's business objectives with customers' critical success factors: price, line defects, delivery, and partnership. This alignment process prompted the development of five key strategic indicator categories: safety, internal customer satisfaction, external customer satisfaction, defect rate, and business performance. Within each category, Wainwright developed specific indicators and goals. For instance, for external customer satisfaction, they measure a satisfaction index and compile complaints each month; for business performance, they track sales, capital expenditure, and market share for drawn housings.

Wainwright constantly looks for ways to improve, searching inside and outside the organization for ideas and examples on how to streamline processes, cut delivery times, make training programs more effective, or enhance any other facet of its customer-focused operations. Its empowered workforce provides a rich source of ideas; each associate averages more than one implemented improvement per week. Ninety-five percent of all purchase orders are processed within 24 hours. The lead time for making one of Wainwright's principal products—drawn housings for electric motors—was reduced to 15 minutes from its former level of 8.75 days.

Baptist Hospital, Inc. (BHI) is a subsidiary of Baptist Health Care with about 2,252 employees and includes two hospitals and an ambulatory care complex that delivers an array of outpatient and diagnostic services. Continuous improvement is an important aspect of BHI's culture, driven by peer, employee, physician, and patient surveys, as well as Baldrige-based processes to gather information and identify opportunities for improvement.

BHI uses a variety of listening and learning approaches to determine customer needs, including surveys and Customer Value Analysis to determine patient loyalty attributes. Information gathered from the listening and learning activities is collected and analyzed using a customer relationship management database to identify the key requirements for each customer group and as input into strategic planning, service design and FOCUS-PDCA (a performance improvement process). BHI's information and knowledge management systems enable it to collect and integrate data from clinical systems, employees, patients, financial systems, decision support systems, and physicians for tracking overall organizational performance and for identifying opportunities for improvement. BHI has developed CARE (Clinical Accountability Report of Excellence) and BAR (Budget Accountability Report) reports, which allow it to aggregate and compare clinical quality improvement results, customer satisfaction data, financial information, and trends. Reports are generated to support organizational performance and learning, clinical outcomes improvement, team activities, and continuous improvement.

Overall satisfaction for inpatients, outpatients, ambulatory surgery, and home health care for services provided by BHI has been consistently near the 99th percentile of the national Press Ganey survey each quarter. BHI received a Baldrige Award in 2003.

Source: Malcolm Baldrige National Quality Award, Profiles of Winners, National Institute of Standards and Technology, Department of Commerce.

THE SCOPE OF PERFORMANCE MEASUREMENT

Organizations need good measures for three reasons:[5]

1. To lead the entire organization in a particular direction; that is, to drive strategies and organizational change.
2. To manage the resources needed to travel in this direction by evaluating the effectiveness of action plans.
3. To operate the processes that make the organization work and continuously improve.

Effective information systems provide the right information to the right people at the right time. As a result, individuals in manufacturing can have input on product design and sales; designers can obtain immediate feedback about manufacturing and financial implications of decisions; and everyone can share information for solving problems. Empowered individuals with the right information can make more timely decisions and can take action to better serve customers.

Data and information support process management activities at the "three levels of quality"—individual, process, and organization—as discussed in Chapter 1. At the individual level, such information about quality performance, adherence to schedules, and costs of operations provide real-time information for feedback and process control. These might be obtained from inspection activities, laboratory analyses, or automated capture of part dimensions to provide the foundation for taking corrective action. At the process level, operational performance data such as yields, cycle times, and productivity measures help middle managers determine whether their processes are accomplishing their objectives, whether they are using resources effectively, and where improvement might be necessary. Information at this level generally is aggregated; for example, daily or weekly scrap reports, customer complaint data obtained from customer service representatives, or monthly sales and cost figures faxed in from field offices. At the organization level, product and service quality and operational performance data from all areas of the firm, along with relevant customer, financial, human resource, and other organizational effectiveness data, form the basis for strategic planning and design of products, services, and processes. Such information is highly aggregated and obtained from many different sources throughout the organization.

Measurement-managed organizations are more likely to be in the top third of their industry financially, complete organizational changes more successfully, reach clear agreement on strategy among senior managers, enjoy favorable levels of cooperation and teamwork among management, undertake greater self-monitoring of performance by employees, and have a greater willingness by employees to take risks.[6]

Traditionally, most organizations have relied on performance data based almost solely on financial or accounting-based factory productivity considerations, such as return on investment, earnings per share, direct labor efficiency, and machine utilization.[7] Unfortunately, many of these indicators stress quantity over quality.[8] They reward the wrong behavior; lack predictive power; do not capture key business changes until it is too late; reflect functions, not cross-functional processes; and give inadequate consideration to difficult-to-quantify resources such as intellectual capital.[9] For example, financial measures reflect past decisions; they do not focus on factors that create value and predict financial success. Measurements such as direct labor efficiency promote building unnecessary inventory and lead to over-control of direct labor, thus preventing workers from assuming responsibility for process control and from focusing on process improvement. An emphasis on machine utilization encourages having fewer, but larger, general-purpose machines, which results in more complex material flows and increased inventory and throughput time. To achieve a high level of performance excellence requires a much broader set of performance measures that are aligned to an organization's strategy.

The Balanced Scorecard

Robert Kaplan and David Norton pose the following scenario:[10]

> *Imagine entering the cockpit of a modern jet airplane and seeing only a single instrument there. How would you feel about boarding the plane after the following conversation with the pilot?*
>
> *Q: I'm surprised to see you operating the plane with only a single instrument. What does it measure?*
>
> *A: Airspeed. I'm really working on airspeed this flight.*
>
> *Q: That's good. Airspeed certainly seems important. But what about altitude? Wouldn't an altimeter be helpful?*
>
> *A: I worked on altitude for the last few flights and I've gotten pretty good at it. Now I have to concentrate on proper airspeed.*
>
> *Q: But I notice you don't even have a fuel gauge. Wouldn't that be useful?*
>
> *A: You're right; fuel is significant, but I can't concentrate on doing too many things well at the same time. So on this flight I'm focusing on airspeed. Once I get to be excellent at airspeed, as well as altitude, I intend to concentrate on fuel consumption on the next set of flights.*

Clearly, you would be a bit uneasy about taking this flight. However, the analogy with business is not that far-fetched. Many organizations still manage by concentrating primarily on financial measures.

Art Schneiderman at Analog Devices first developed the concept of a balanced scorecard in 1987.[11] Analog Devices established and openly published a set of nonfinancial performance goals as part of its five-year strategic plan. A one-page summary that combined these performance goals with the key financial goals was originally referred to as the "Quarterly Performance Audit," but quickly became known as the "Scorecard." Robert Kaplan and David Norton of the Harvard Business School studied Analog Devices and promoted the concept in *Harvard Business Review* articles and a book. The purpose of the balanced scorecard is "to translate strategy into measures that uniquely communicate your vision to the organization." Their version of the balanced scorecard consists of four perspectives:

To make decisions that further the overall organizational goals of meeting, or exceeding, customer expectations and making productive use of limited resources, organizations need good data and information about customers and markets, human resource effectiveness, supplier performance, product and service quality, and other key factors, in addition to traditional financial performance and accounting measures.

- *Financial Perspective:* Measures the ultimate results that the business provides to its shareholders. They include profitability, revenue growth, return on investment, economic value added (EVA), and shareholder value.
- *Internal Perspective:* Focuses attention on the performance of the key internal processes that drive the business. They include such measures as quality levels, productivity, cycle time, and cost.

- *Customer Perspective:* Focuses on customer needs and satisfaction as well as market share. This includes service levels, satisfaction ratings, and repeat business.
- *Innovation and Learning Perspective:* Directs attention to the basis of a future success—the organization's people and infrastructure. Key measures might include intellectual assets, employee satisfaction, market innovation, and skills development.

Organizations need to know what is happening now and what might happen in the future. For example, customer survey results about recent transactions might be a leading indicator for customer retention (a lagging indicator); employee satisfaction might be a leading indicator for turnover, and so on.

A good balanced scorecard contains both leading and lagging measures and indicators. ***Lagging measures*** *(outcomes) tell what has happened;* ***leading measures*** *(performance drivers) predict what will happen.*

Pearl River School District uses a modified balanced scorecard that includes leading and lagging indicators relative to strategic objectives under each of its three district goals (Figure 8.1). Lagging indicators represent long-term results and leading indicators are either short-term or line-of-sight predictors for lagging indicators. For example, stakeholder satisfaction rates are key factors in the level of support the district can expect in their annual budget vote. The fourth and eighth grade New York State exams are designed to be predictors of student success on the Regents examinations.

Leading and lagging measures and indicators can help to establish cause-and-effect relationships across perspectives. Figure 8.2 shows the causal relationships among the key measures in IBM Rochester's balanced scorecard. This model suggests that improving internal capabilities such as people skills, product/service quality, and products and

Figure 8.1 Pearl River School District Balanced Scorecard

Strategic Objectives	Lag Indicators (long-term)	Lead Indicators (predictive)
	Academic Performance	
Academic Achievement	Regents Diploma Rate	Achievement on 4th and 8th grade NYS exams CTPIII Reading and Math Achievement
College Admissions	AP Participation Rate AP Performance Rate	Special Education Opportunity Passing rate on Regents exams SAT I and II Participation Rate Scholar Athlete Teams
	Perception	
Parent/Community Satisfaction	Maintain 2:1 Plurality on Budget Votes Market Share	Stakeholder Satisfaction Surveys Adult Education Enrollment Student Satisfaction Surveys Prospective Homeowner Requests New Resident Survey
	Fiscal Stability	
Cost-Effective Fiscal Management	Contain Per-Pupil Expenditure	Reduce Costs in Noninstructional Areas

Source: Reprinted with permission of Pearl River School District.

Figure 8.2 Causal Relationships Among Categories of IBM Rochester's Balanced Scorecard

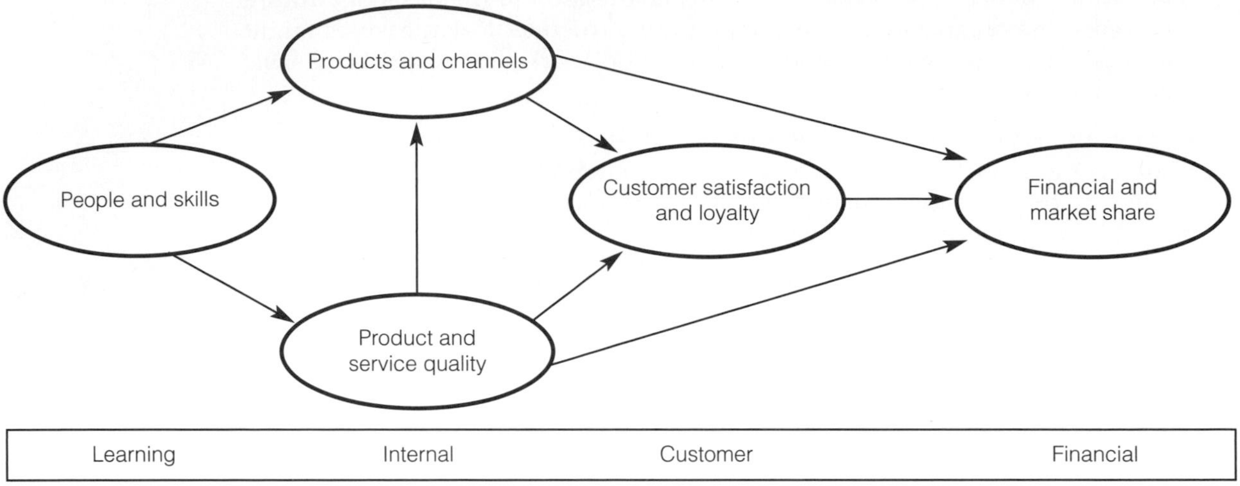

Source: Reprinted with permission of IBM Rochester, MN.

channels, will lead to improved customer satisfaction and loyalty, which in turn, lead to improved financial and market share performance. Understanding such relationships is important in using data and information for strategic and operational decisions.

Kaplan and Norton's balanced scorecard is only one version of performance measurement systems that have emerged as organizations recognized the need for a broad set of performance measures that provide a comprehensive view of business performance. For instance, Raytheon's version defines customer, shareholder, process, and people perspectives. The Malcolm Baldrige Criteria for Performance Excellence Results category groups performance measures into six sets:

- Product outcomes
- Customer-focused outcomes
- Financial and market outcomes
- Workforce-focused outcomes
- Process effectiveness outcomes
- Leadership outcomes

These categories are summarized in Figure 8.3, along with examples of measures in each category. This set is quite similar to the balanced scorecard, and in fact, any measure in the balanced scorecard can easily be assigned to one of these categories. We will briefly discuss each of these categories. As we describe specific examples, note that the specific measures an organization chooses are tied to the key factors that make it competitive in its industry.

Product Outcomes

Measures and indicators of product and service performance that have strong correlation with customer satisfaction and decisions relative to future purchases and relationships are important for organizations to track. They might include internal quality measurements, field performance of products, defect levels, service errors, response times, data collected from customers or third parties on ease of

Figure 8.3 Organizational Performance Measures and Indicators

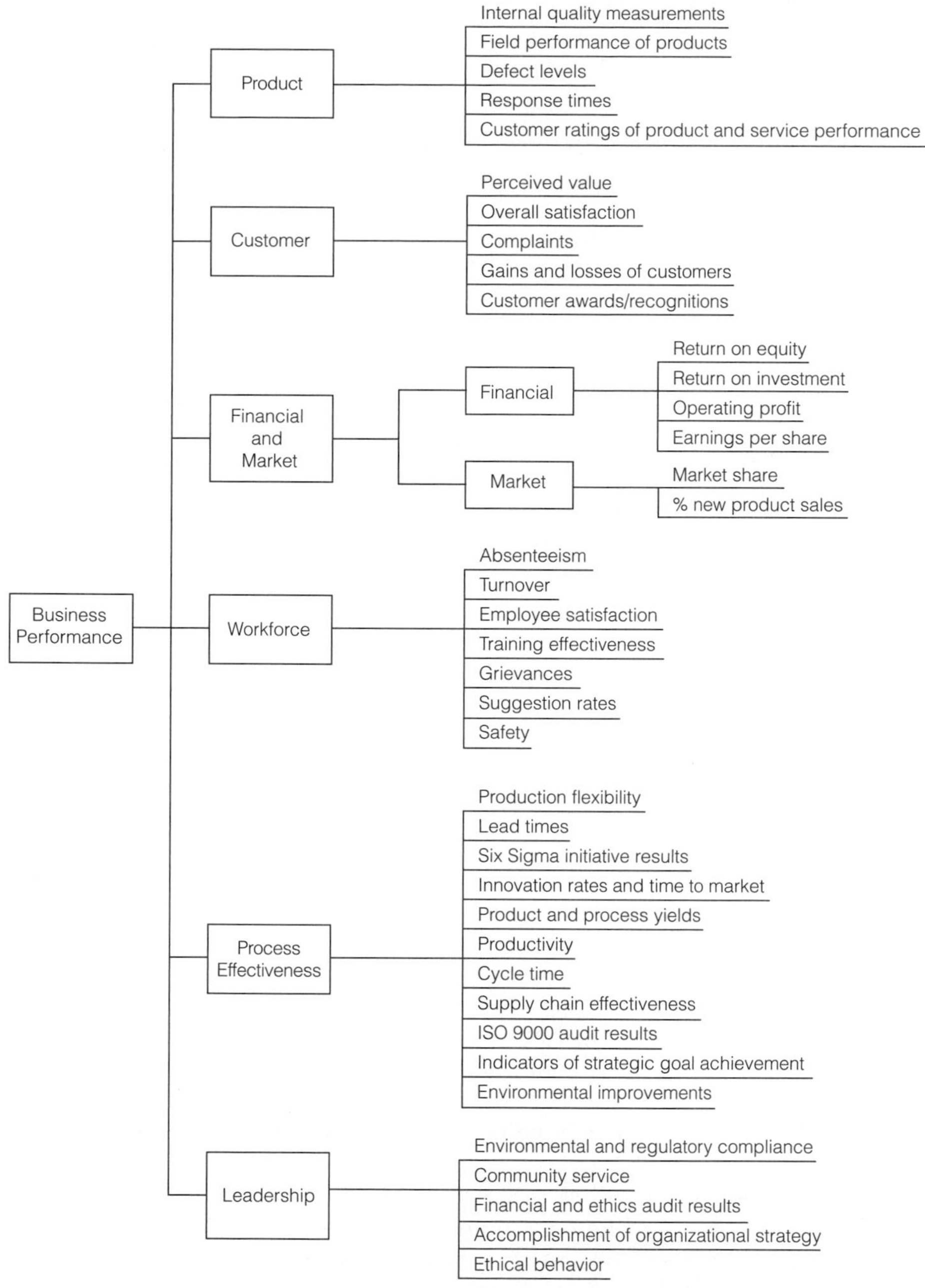

use or other attributes, and customer surveys on product and service performance. STMicroelectronics, for example, tracks the number of nonconforming production lots, which play a significant role in complaints received by their customers. They also track different measures for different customer segments. For instance, the telecommunications industry has a very short cycle-to-market requirement; key measures that address this factor are delivery time, flexibility, response delay, early warning, quality/reliability, and response quality.

Customer-Focused Outcomes

Relevant measures and indicators of an organization's performance as viewed by customers include direct measures of customer satisfaction and dissatisfaction, customer retention, gains and losses of customers and customer accounts, customer complaints, and warranty claims. Other indicators of customer satisfaction include measures of perceived value, loyalty, positive referral, and customer relationship building. Service quality measures often revolve around the dimensions of reliability, assurance, tangibles, empathy, and responsiveness that we discussed in Chapter 5. As an example, 3M's automotive trades business has as its direct customers automotive distributors, while end users are the secondary group. Service quality and cycle times are key satisfaction measures for distributors, while product quality is the principal satisfaction indicator for end users. 3M's measurements include the following:

- In-stock service levels
- On-time delivery
- Order completeness
- Emergency response time
- Ease of dealing with supplier
- Ease of contact with customer service department
- Complaint handling
- Accuracy of shipment
- Order cycle time
- Product quality and performance[12]

Financial and Market Outcomes

Financial measures are generally tracked by senior leadership to gauge overall organizational performance and are often used to determine incentive compensation for senior executives. Measures of financial performance might include revenue, return on equity, return on investment, operating profit, pretax profit margin, asset utilization, earnings per share, and other liquidity measures. In a capital-intensive industry such as airplane production, key financial measures at Boeing Airlift and Tanker Programs are return on sales, return on net assets, and net asset turnover. The Ritz-Carlton Hotel Company, on the other hand, monitors earnings before taxes, depreciation, and amortization, administrative costs, and gross profit among its key financial indicators. A useful financial performance indicator is the *cost of quality*, which managers use to prioritize improvement projects and gauge the effectiveness of total quality efforts and which we will discuss later in this chapter. It is one of Solar Turbine's key measures.

Marketplace performance indicators could include market share, measures of business growth, new product and geographic markets entered, and percentage of new product sales as appropriate. In a commodity market in which Sunny Fresh Foods competes, its performance drivers include their share of the U.S. market and total pounds of egg products sold. In the highly competitive semiconductor industry, STMicroelectronics looks not only at sales growth, but at differentiated product sales.

Workforce-Focused Outcomes

Workforce-focused outcomes show how well the organization has created and maintained a productive, engaging, and caring work environment. One outcome measure might be increased workforce retention resulting from a peer recognition program or the number of promotions that have resulted from the organization's leadership development program. Other examples include safety, absenteeism, turnover, training effectiveness, engagement, and employee satisfaction. Texas Nameplate Company measures the percent of net earnings for its risk-based compensation (gain sharing) program, because it significantly impacts employee productivity, motivation, and satisfaction. Because of the important relationship that Boeing Airlift and Tanker Programs has with its unions, A&T tracks grievance backlog reduction as a way of quantifying improving relationships. The Ritz-Carlton tracks percent turnover closely, because this measure is a key indicator of employee satisfaction and the effectiveness of their selection and training processes.

Process Effectiveness Outcomes

Measures and indicators of process effectiveness and efficiency might include work system performance that demonstrates improved cost savings or higher productivity by using internal and/or external resources; reduced emission levels, waste stream reductions, by-product use, and recycling; internal responsiveness indicators, such as cycle times, production flexibility, lead times, set-up times, and time to market; and improved performance of administrative and other support functions. They also might include business-specific indicators, such as innovation rates and increased use of product and process yields, Six Sigma initiative results, and acceptable product performance at the time of delivery; supply chain indicators, such as reductions in inventory and incoming inspections, increases in quality and productivity, improvements in electronic data exchange, and reductions in supply chain management costs; and third-party assessment results, such as ISO 9001 audits.

Boeing A&T, for instance, tracks the mean time between corrective maintenance of its aircraft; increasing this time indicates improved quality of the aircraft systems. Other examples are reduced emission levels and waste stream reductions, Six Sigma initiative results, and ISO 9000 assessment audits. STMicroelectronics tracks key indicators of strategic goal achievement, such as R&D investment and number of patents granted. American Express analysts monitor telephone conversations for politeness, tone of voice, accuracy of the transaction, and other customer service aspects. Comparisons between judgments of the analysts and judgments of customers in post-transaction interviews determine the relevance of specific internal measurements. Because of the importance of hiring skilled people, The Ritz-Carlton embarked on a major project to improve the cycle time from when a potential new-hire walks in the door until a job offer is tendered; it became one of their key measures in this category. With the increased focus on supply chain management, many organizations are now reviewing cost savings; total supply chain management costs; reductions in inventory and cycle time; and indicators of better communication, such as those achieved via electronic commerce. Solar Turbines, for example, monitors supplier lead times for two critical components—forgings and castings.

Leadership Outcomes

With an increased focus on issues of governance, ethics, and leadership accountability, it is important for organizations to practice and demonstrate high standards of overall conduct. Relevant performance measures can help organizations monitor these issues.

They might include measures of regulatory/legal compliance, results of oversight audits, and financial and ethics review results. Leadership outcomes also include measures of social responsibility and community service, such as volunteer hours and presentations to educational or civic groups, and outcomes that relate to accomplishment of organizational strategy and action plans. Measuring progress in accomplishing their strategic objectives is also a key challenge. Frequently, these progress measures can be determined by first defining the results that would indicate end-goal success in achieving the strategic objective and then using that end-goal to define intermediate measures.

DESIGNING EFFECTIVE PERFORMANCE MEASUREMENT SYSTEMS

The purposes of a performance measurement system include the following:

- Providing a perspective of the past, present, and future
- Identifying trends and progress
- Facilitating understanding of cause-and-effect relationships
- Providing direction and support for continuous improvement
- Allowing performance comparison to benchmarks

In addition, they should be intelligible to a majority of employees, provide real-time information for decisions, and support personal and organizational learning.[13] Balanced scorecards often fail for a variety of reasons, including not identifying the real drivers of customer satisfaction; not defining measures appropriately to focus attention on the areas having the greatest impact on organizational performance; negotiating goals rather than basing them on customer requirements, process limitations, and improvement capabilities; or not linking nonfinancial and financial results in a quantitative fashion.[14] Thus, organizations must carefully design their performance measurement systems.

Selecting Measures and Indicators

In designing a performance measurement system, organizations must consider how the measures will support senior executive performance review and organizational planning to address the overall health of the organization, and how the measures will support daily operations and decision making.

An organization must align its measurement system to its vision and strategy and select meaningful process-level measurements. Many organizations make two fundamental mistakes: (1) not measuring key characteristics critical to organizational performance or customer behavior, and (2) taking irrelevant or inappropriate measurements. In the first case, the organization often fails to meet customer expectations or performance goals. In the second, the organization cannot isolate the meaningful data and usually wastes considerable time and resources. Measurement systems often become unwieldy simply because of the lack of monitoring and assessment. Most measures have probably been around for a long time, and few managers can probably say where, when, and why they were developed. In most cases, somebody just decided they were good to have. When Ford studied Mazda's management approaches, former CEO Donald Peterson observed, "Perhaps, most important, Mazda had been able to identify the types of information and records that were truly useful. It didn't bother with any other data. [At Ford] we were burdened with mountains of useless data and stifled by far too many levels of control over them."[15]

Mark Graham Brown suggests some practical guidelines for designing a performance measurement system:[16]

- Fewer is better. Concentrate on measuring the vital few key variables rather than the trivial many.
- Measures should be linked to the factors needed for success, namely, the key business drivers.
- Measures should include a mix of past, present, and future to ensure that the organization is concerned with all three perspectives.
- Measures should be based around the needs of customers, shareholders, and other key stakeholders.
- Measures should start at the top and flow down to all levels of employees in the organization.
- Measures should be changed or at least adjusted as the environment and strategy changes.

Leading organizations select appropriate measures and indicators using well-defined criteria. IBM Rochester, for example, asks the following questions:

- Does the measurement support our mission?
- Will the measurement be used to manage change?
- Is it important to our customers?
- Is it effective in measuring performance?
- Is it effective in forecasting results?
- Is it easy to understand/simple?
- Are the data easy/cost-efficient to collect?
- Does the measurement have validity, integrity, and timeliness?
- Does the measure have an owner?

Boeing A&T uses five criteria to select data: important to customers, effective in measuring performance, effective in forecasting results, actionable, and easily collected with integrity. As another example, Clarke American structures its performance measurements along two dimensions: how they are used—to either *change the business* or *run the business*—and whether they are predictive (leading) or diagnostic (lagging). "Change the business" measures are those most critical to the achievement of strategic objectives and evaluate organizational performance, such as total order cycle time and implemented ideas. "Run the business" measures are those used for daily operations and include measures of accuracy, responsiveness, and timeliness for deliveries.

Linking Measures to Strategy

Kaplan and Norton note that inappropriate measures lead to actions incongruent with strategies, even if they are well formulated and communicated, while appropriate measures lead to attainment of strategic goals and impact the goals and strategies needed to achieve them. A balanced scorecard approach helps in identifying the right measures by aligning them with the organization's vision and strategy. With a balanced scorecard, organizations have a means of setting targets and allocating resources for short-term planning, communicating strategies, aligning departmental and personal goals to strategies, linking rewards to performance, and supplying feedback for organizational learning.

Effective performance measures that are aligned with business strategy should be driven by internal and external factors that shape an organization's operating environment. These factors are reflected in the Baldrige Organizational Profile that we described in Chapter 4 (see Table 4.2). In particular, performance measures should strongly align with the principal factors that determine competitive success and the strategic challenges the organization faces. For example, the First National Bank of Chicago asked its customers what they considered as good-quality features of a product and the delivery of those features.[17] Responses included timeliness, accuracy, operations efficiency, economics, and customer responsiveness. These responses initiated the development of performance indicators such as lockbox processing time, bill keying accuracy, customer service inquiry resolution time, and money transfer timeliness. A computer software company might not need to collect extensive data on environmental quality issues, whereas a chemical company certainly would. A pizza franchise that delivers bulk orders to fraternities and parties around a college campus would have a different set of performance measures and indicators than one in a quiet suburban residential neighborhood. Thus, an organization first needs to fully understand its internal capabilities and external environment.

Measures should logically be tied to key business drivers. MBNA, the Wilmington, Delaware, credit card company that markets custom cards to "affinity groups" such as professional associations, universities, and sports team fans, views speed of service as one of its key business drivers. Thus, it measures the time to process customer address changes, the percentage of times phones are picked up within two rings, and the times taken to transfer calls from the switchboard.[18] Armstrong Building Products Operations identified five components of value that drive its business strategy: customer satisfaction, sales growth, operating profit, asset management, and high-performance organization. Each of these components is supported by key measurements and analysis approaches. For example, product quality, a key driver of customer satisfaction, is measured by dimensions and squareness, fire performance, acoustics and color, dimensional stability, competitor product quality analysis, and claims. Likewise, service quality is measured by on-time delivery and missed-item promises, pricing and billing, and information support for customers. Another key business driver, operating profit, is measured by process effectiveness, units per employee, scrap and downtime, and cost of quality. Organizational performance measures include recordable injury rate, number of improvements/work orders, percentage of employees recognized, gainsharing savings, and employee satisfaction trends and turnover rate.

Quality Spotlight
Mercy Health System

Key performance measures should be aligned with strategies and action plans. Setting targets for each measure provides the basis for strategy deployment as discussed in Chapter 5. Mercy Health System has a formal performance measurement system that is shown in Figure 8.4. System measures are driven by strategic objectives and action plans and aligned with departmental measures. The Information Management Advisory Committee ensures proper infrastructure and technology are in place for gathering, reporting, analyzing, and integrating data and information. The Process Improvement process further ensures data integration through the committee reporting structure.

Process-Level Measurements

Good measures and indicators are ***actionable****; that is, they provide the basis for decisions at the organizational level at which they are applied.*

What makes a good process measurement? Many organizations use the acronym *SMART* to characterize good measures and indicators: *simple, measurable, actionable, related* (to customer requirements and to each other), and *timely*. Process measures should also clearly align with customer requirements. For example, product reliability might be measured by the number of repair calls, billing accuracy by the percentage of billing inquiries or

Figure 8.4 Mercy Health System Performance Measurement Process

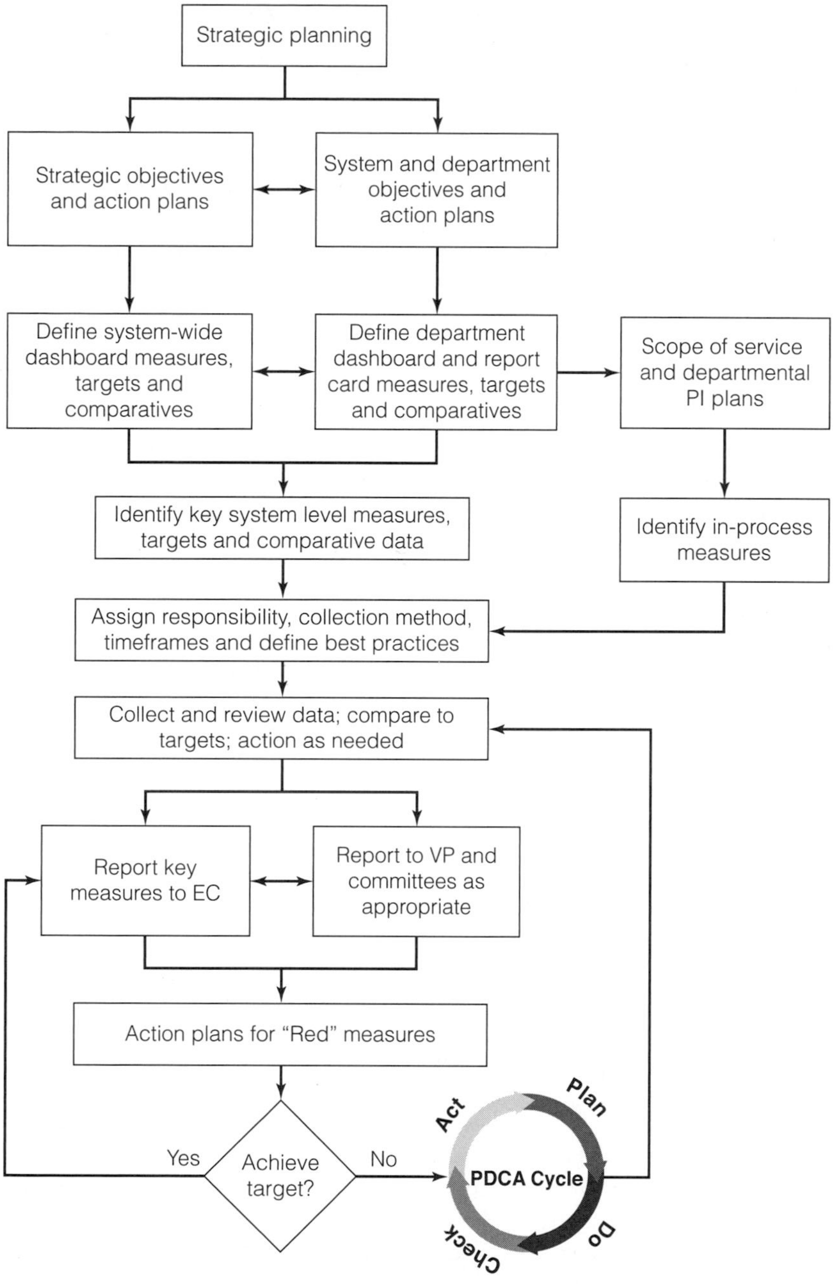

Strategic planning

Strategic objectives and action plans

System and department objectives and action plans

Define system-wide dashboard measures, targets and comparatives

Define department dashboard and report card measures, targets and comparatives

Scope of service and departmental PI plans

Identify key system level measures, targets and comparative data

Identify in-process measures

Assign responsibility, collection method, timeframes and define best practices

Collect and review data; compare to targets; action as needed

Report key measures to EC

Report to VP and committees as appropriate

Action plans for "Red" measures

Achieve target?

Yes

No

PDCA Cycle

Plan

Do

Check

Act

Source: Mercy Health System Malcolm Baldrige National Quality Award Application Summary, 2007. Reprinted with permission.

complaints, knowledgeable customer representatives by supervisor observations or analysis of recorded calls, ease of use by number of calls to a help desk, and so on.

At the process level, product and service quality measures focus on the outcomes of manufacturing and service processes. Six Sigma began by stressing a common measure for quality. In Six Sigma terminology, a **defect**, is any mistake or error that is passed on to the customer. A **unit of work** is the output of a process or an individual process step. A measure of output quality is **defects per unit (DPU)**:

$$\text{Defects per unit} = \text{Number of defects discovered}/\text{Number of units produced}$$

(Because of the negative connotation of "defect" and its potential implications in liability suits, many organizations use the term *nonconformance*; however, quite a few still use the term *defect*. In this book, both terms are used interchangeably to be consistent with current literature and practice.)

DPU tends to focus on the final product, not the process that produces the product. In addition, it is difficult to use for processes of varying complexity, particularly service activities. Two different processes might have significantly different numbers of opportunities for error, making appropriate comparisons difficult. To account for this, Six Sigma uses as **defects per million opportunities (dpmo)**:

$$\text{dpmo} = (\text{Number of defects discovered})/\text{opportunities for error} \times 1{,}000{,}000$$

Thus, a defect rate of 2 per 1,000 is equivalent to 2,000 dpmo. For example, suppose that an airline wishes to measure the effectiveness of its baggage handling system. A DPU measure might be lost bags per customer. However, customers may have different numbers of bags; thus the number of opportunities for error is the average number of bags per customer. If the average number of bags per customer is 1.6, and the airline recorded 3 lost bags for 8000 passengers in one month, then

$$\text{dpmo} = 3/[(8{,}000)(1.6)] \times 1{,}000{,}000 = 234.375$$

In services, the term often used is **errors per million opportunities (epmo)**. The use of dpmo and epmo allows us to define quality broadly. In the airline case, a broad definition might mean every opportunity for a failure to meet customer expectations from initial ticketing until bags are retrieved.

Many organizations classify defects into three categories:

1. *Critical defect:* A critical defect is one that judgment and experience indicate will surely result in hazardous or unsafe conditions for individuals using, maintaining, or depending on the product and will prevent proper performance of the product.
2. *Major defect:* A major defect is one not critical but likely to result in failure or to materially reduce the usability of the unit for its intended purpose.
3. *Minor defect:* A minor defect is one not likely to materially reduce the usability of the item for its intended purpose, nor to have any bearing on the effective use or operation of the unit.[19]

Critical defects may lead to serious consequences or product liability suits; thus, they should be monitored and controlled for carefully. On the other hand, minor defects might not be monitored as closely, because they do not affect fitness for use. For many products, however, even minor defects can lead to customer dissatisfaction. To account for each category, organizations often create a composite index in which major and critical defects are weighted more heavily than minor defects. For example, FedEx has an extensive quality measurement system that includes a composite measure, called the service quality indicator (SQI), which is a weighted sum of 10 factors that reflect customers' expectations of organizational performance. FedEx's SQI is shown in Table 8.2. Different weights reflect the importance of each failure; losing a package, for instance, is more serious than delivering it a few minutes late. The index is reported weekly and summarized on a monthly basis.

Another common process-level measurement, extensively used in Six Sigma environments, is **rolled throughput yield (RTY)**—the probability that a unit can

Table 8.2 FedEx Service Quality Indicator and Factors

Error Type	Description	Weight
1. *Complaints reopened*	—customer complaints (on traces, invoices, missed pickups, etc.) reopened after an unsatisfactory resolution	3
2. *Damaged packages*	—packages with visible or concealed damage or spoilage due to weather or water damage, missed pickup, or late delivery	10
3. *International*	—a composite score of performance measures of international operations	
4. *Invoice adjustments*	—customer requests for credit or refunds for real or perceived failures	1
5. *Late pickup stops*	—packages that were picked up later than the stated pickup time	3
6. *Lost packages*	—claims for missing packages or with contents missing	10
7. *Missed proof of delivery*	—invoices that lack written proof of delivery information	1
8. *Right date late*	—delivery past promised time on the right day	1
9. *Traces*	—package status and proof of delivery requests not in the COSMOS IIB computer system (the FedEx "real time" tracking system)	3
10. *Wrong day late*	—delivery on the wrong day	5

Source: Service Quality Indicators at FedEx (Internal company document).

pass through a series of process steps without defects; equivalently, the percentage yield of good parts from a series of process steps. The RTY is analogous to the efficiency of a bucket brigade—a chain of people working to put out a fire by passing buckets of water from person to person. Imagine there are five people in the chain and each one spills 10 percent of the water from the bucket as he or she passes it to the next person. In other words, each person is 90 percent efficient at transporting the water. At the end of the chain, the bucket will have lost quite a bit of water. The efficiency of the bucket brigade is calculated by multiplying the efficiencies of each member of the team:

$$0.90 \times 0.90 \times 0.90 \times 0.90 \times 0.90 = 0.591$$

Even though each individual is 90 percent effective, the team is collectively only 59 percent efficient; 41 percent of the water is wasted.[20] RTY is a useful measure for analyzing process efficiencies and understanding the implications of improvement strategies.

Identifying and Selecting Process Measures

To generate useful process performance measures a systematic process is required.[21]

1. *Identify all customers of the system and determine their requirements and expectations.* Organizations need answers to key questions: Who are my customers? and What do they expect? Many of the "customer listening" approaches introduced in Chapter 5 can be used in this step. Customer expectations change over time; thus, regular feedback must be obtained.
2. *Define the work process that provides the product or service.* Key questions include: What do I do that affects customer needs? and What is my process? The use of flowcharts for process mapping can stimulate the definition of work processes and internal customer-supplier relationships.
3. *Define the value-adding activities and outputs that comprise the process.* This step—identifying each part in the system in which value is added and an

intermediate output is produced—weeds out activities that do not add value to the process and contribute to waste and inefficiency. Analysis performed in this step identifies the internal customers within the process along with their needs and expectations.

4. *Develop specific performance measures or indicators.* Each key activity identified in step 3 represents a critical point where value is added to the output for the next (internal) customer until the final output is produced. At these checkpoints, performance can be measured. Key questions include: What factors determine how well the process is producing according to customer requirements? What deviations can occur? What sources of variability can occur?
5. *Evaluate the performance measures to ensure their usefulness.* Questions to consider include: Are measurements taken at critical points where value-adding activities occur? Are measurements controllable? Is it feasible to obtain the data needed for each measure? Have operational definitions for each measurement been established? Operational definitions are precise definitions of measurements that have no ambiguities. For example, when measuring "invoice errors," a precise definition of what is an error and what is not is needed. Does an error include an omission of information, wrong information, or misspelling? Operational definitions provide a common understanding and enhance communication throughout the organization.

To illustrate this approach, consider the process of placing and filling a pizza order. Customer expectations include a quick response and a fair price. The process that provides this service is shown in Figure 8.5. To begin, the order taker is an (internal) customer of the caller (who provides the pizza order). Later, the caller is a customer of the deliverer (either at the pickup window or the caller's home). Also, the cook is a customer of the order taker (who prepares the documentation for the ordered pizza).

Some possible performance measures include:

- *Number of pizzas, by type per hour.* If this number is high relative to the kitchen's capacity, then perhaps cooking time and/or preparation is being short-cut or delivery times are stretched out.
- *Order accuracy (as transmitted to the kitchen).* This measure can indicate a lack of attention or knowledge on the part of the order taker.
- *Number of pizzas rejected per number prepared.* A high number for this measure can indicate a lack of proper training of cooks, resulting in poor products and customer complaints.
- *Time to delivery.* This measure might indicate a problem within the restaurant or inadequate training of the driver. (Of course, as happened with Domino's Pizza, measuring delivery time could encourage drivers to drive too fast and lead to safety problems.)
- *Number of errors in collections.* Errors here can result in lost profits and higher prices.
- *Raw materials (dough, etc.) or finished pizzas inventory.* A high number might result in spoilage and excess costs. Low inventory might result in lost orders or excessive customer waiting time.

Notice that these measures—only a few among many possible measures—are related to customer expectations and business performance.

Many organizations use **dashboards**, which typically consist of a small set of measures (five or six) that provide a quick summary of process performance

Figure 8.5 Example of a Pizza Ordering and Filling Process for Home Delivery

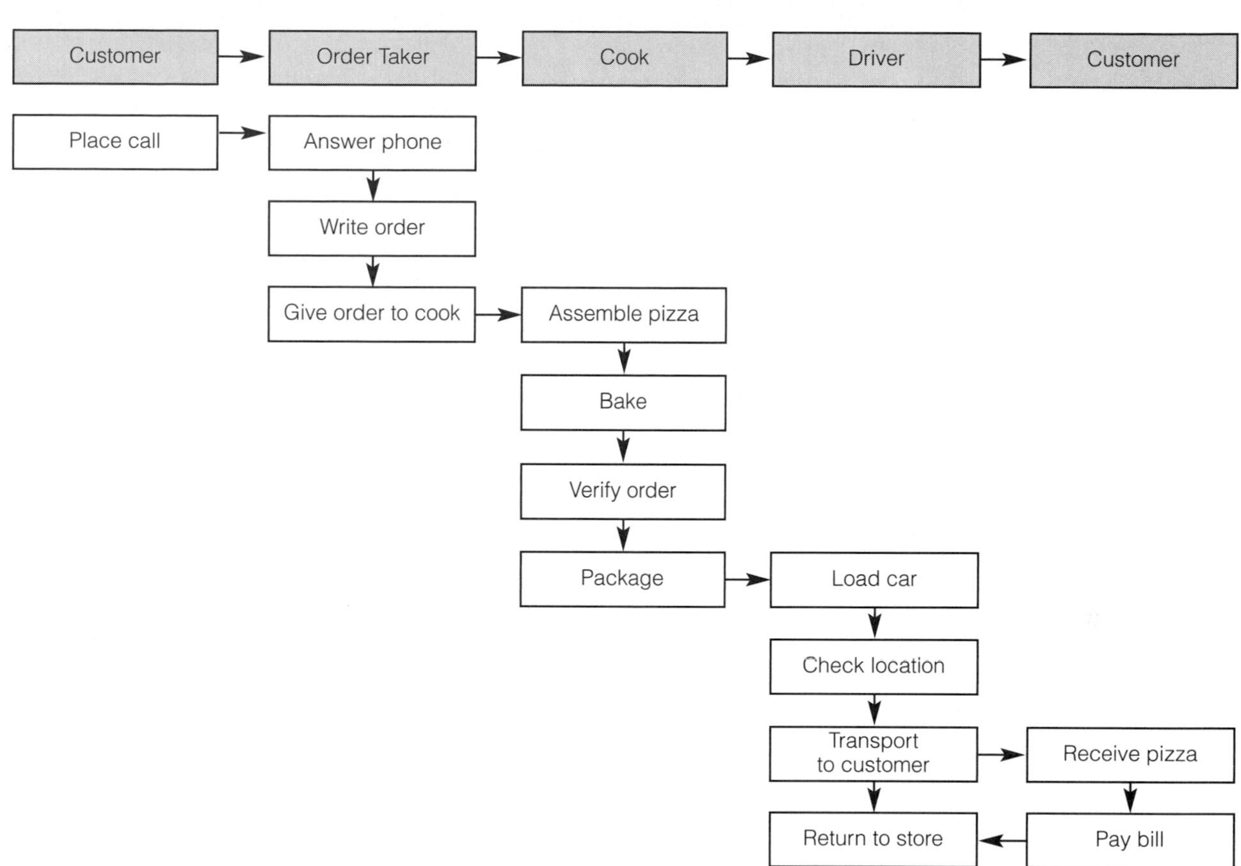

(this term is sometimes also used to describe a balanced scorecard at the organizational level). This preference stems from the analogy to an automobile's dashboard—a collection of indicators (speed, RPM, oil pressure, temperature, etc.) that summarize performance. Dashboards often use graphs, charts, and other visual aids to communicate key measures and alert managers when performance is not where it should be.

Aligning Strategic and Process-Level Measurements[22]

It is possible that all work processes could be meeting their requirements while the organization is not achieving its longer-term goals. Thus, aligning strategic and process-level measurements is vital to a high-performing organization, and can be viewed as an approach for strategy deployment (see Chapter 4). Figure 8.6 illustrates how goals and measures might be aligned for a hypothetical retail manufacturer. Alignment might even go further, down to the team and individual levels. Note that alignment is tied fundamentally to the performance goals; the measures support goal attainment. The organization does not have to have one set of performance measures that everyone produces and reports, but rather, measures are used where they are most appropriate. Production line data, for example, might be reviewed only at the line level for daily operations control, while some data might be integrated at the next level for process improvement. Information that supports review of organizational-level performance is passed on to the corporate level.

Figure 8.6 An Example of Aligning Strategic and Process-Level Performance Measures

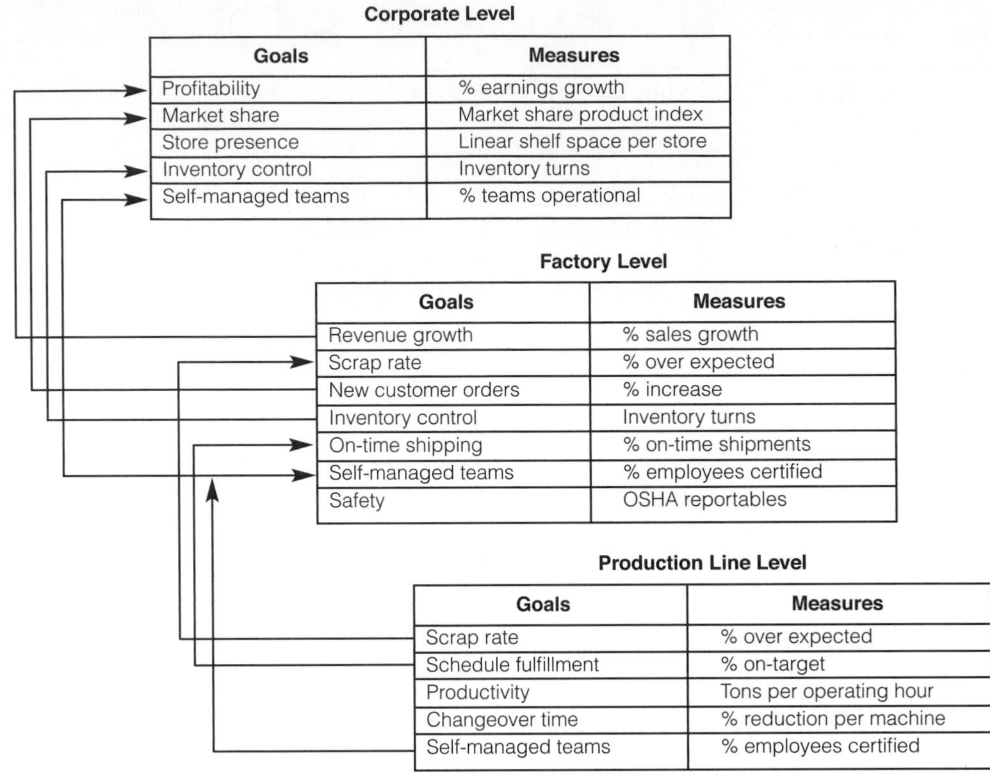

Corporate Level

Goals	Measures
Profitability	% earnings growth
Market share	Market share product index
Store presence	Linear shelf space per store
Inventory control	Inventory turns
Self-managed teams	% teams operational

Factory Level

Goals	Measures
Revenue growth	% sales growth
Scrap rate	% over expected
New customer orders	% increase
Inventory control	Inventory turns
On-time shipping	% on-time shipments
Self-managed teams	% employees certified
Safety	OSHA reportables

Production Line Level

Goals	Measures
Scrap rate	% over expected
Schedule fulfillment	% on-target
Productivity	Tons per operating hour
Changeover time	% reduction per machine
Self-managed teams	% employees certified

Source: R. I. Wise, "A Method for Aligning Process-Level and Strategy-Level Performance Metrics," *The Quality Management Forum*, 25, no. 1, pp. 4–6, (Spring 1999), Copyright © 1999 American Society for Quality, 11th Annual Quality Management Conference. Reprinted with permision.

Enterprise Resource Planning (ERP)—systems are software packages that integrate organizational information systems and provide an infrastructure for managing information across the enterprise.[23] They integrate key aspects of a business—accounting, customer relationship management, supply chain management, manufacturing, sales, and human resources—into a unified information system, and provide timely analysis and reporting of sales, customer, inventory, manufacturing, human resource, and accounting data. The three most prominent vendors for ERP software are SAP, Oracle, and PeopleSoft. For example, when a salesperson fills an order, the system can check the customer's credit and their own manufacturing capacity, record the order, schedule the shipment, log the order on the production schedule, order parts from suppliers, and update financial and accounting records. ERP systems allow organizations to share databases in a networking environment and store and process key data in a unique database, and distribute it to a large group of users. Typical ERP applications span financial, human resource, operations and supply chain, and sales and marketing data. Many ERP systems now offer performance measurement system modules that are focused on helping manage the wide scope of data that are collected in the system.

ANALYZING AND USING PERFORMANCE DATA

Analysis refers to an examination of facts and data to provide a basis for effective decisions. Examples of possible analyses include the following:

- Examining trends and changes in measures and indicators using charts and graphs
- Calculating a variety of statistical measures such as means, proportions, and standard deviations
- Applying sophisticated statistical tools such as correlation and regression analysis to help understand relationships among different measures
- Comparing results relative to other business units, competitors, or best-in-class benchmarks

At a basic level, measures should be charted over time to show levels, trends, and variation. Pal's Sudden Service uses an automated data collection, integration, and analysis system, SysDine, to generate store-level and companywide reports on sales, customer count, product mix, ideal food and material cost, and turnover rates, and also has an automated correlation routine available for analyzing key data to support organizational performance reviews and strategic planning. As a result, they are able to identify how changes in one performance area affect all other areas, make accurate performance projections, and understand how to optimize their management system.

Some organizations use creative ways to convey information to facilitate understanding and decision making. At Mercy Health System, for example, the Dashboard Alert System color codes each dashboard indicator relative to progress made toward targets: green (99 percent of target or higher); yellow (94–98 percent of target); and red (93 percent or less of target). Red dashboard measures prompt 90-day Dashboard Alert action plans and the Executive Council mobilizes Performance Improvement teams or the Leadership Group to redirect resources toward underperforming areas. Green indicators showing sustained success assist in identifying areas for best practice.

As we noted in our discussion of the balanced scorecard, managers must also understand the linkages between key measures of business performance. Examples of such analyses are:

- How product and service quality improvement correlates with key customer indicators such as customer satisfaction, customer retention, and market share
- Financial benefits derived from improvements in employee safety, absenteeism, and turnover
- Benefits and costs associated with education and training
- Relationships between product and service quality, operational performance indicators, and overall financial performance
- Profit impacts of customer satisfaction and retention
- Market share changes as a result of changes in customer satisfaction
- Impacts of employee satisfaction on customer satisfaction

Interlinking is the term that describes the quantitative modeling of cause-and-effect relationships between performance measures, such as the customer satisfaction and product quality or employee performance.[24] For example, the controls group of Johnson Controls Inc. examined the relationship between satisfaction levels and contract renewal rates. They found that 91 percent of contract renewals came from customers who were either satisfied or very satisfied, and customers who gave a "not satisfied" rating had a much higher defection rate. By examining the data, they found that a one percentage point increase in the overall satisfaction score was worth $13 million in service contract renewals annually. As a result, Johnson Controls made improving customer satisfaction a key strategic initiative.[25]

A more compelling example was found at IBM Rochester.[26] IBM's AS/400 Division in Rochester, Minnesota, winner of the 1990 Malcolm Baldrige National Quality Award, struggled with understanding which factors have the greatest impact on overall business performance. IBM initiated a study to determine whether any relationships existed among the numerous measurements such as market share, overall customer satisfaction, employee morale, job satisfaction, warranty costs, inventory costs, product scrap, and productivity. Using 10 years of data, the researchers identified a strong correlation among market share, customer satisfaction, productivity, warranty cost, and employee satisfaction. Figure 8.7 shows a model that describes the cause-and-effect relationship among the key factors (those with a correlation factor equal to or greater than 0.7 are shown). This model suggests that to improve employee satisfaction, a manager must focus on improving job satisfaction, satisfaction with management, and satisfaction with having the right skills for the job. To improve job satisfaction, a manager must focus on improving satisfaction with management and satisfaction with having the right skills for the job. Improving satisfaction with having the right skills for the job will improve employee satisfaction and job satisfaction and will positively impact productivity, market share, and customer satisfaction. Improving employee satisfaction will directly impact productivity and customer satisfaction and will decrease warranty costs. Decreasing warranty costs will directly impact customer satisfaction and market share. Improving customer satisfaction will directly impact market share.

Not all interlinking models need to be based on sophisticated statistical and computer models.

Figure 8.7 The Relationship Between Market Share, Customer Satisfaction, Productivity, Cost of Quality, and Employee Satisfaction

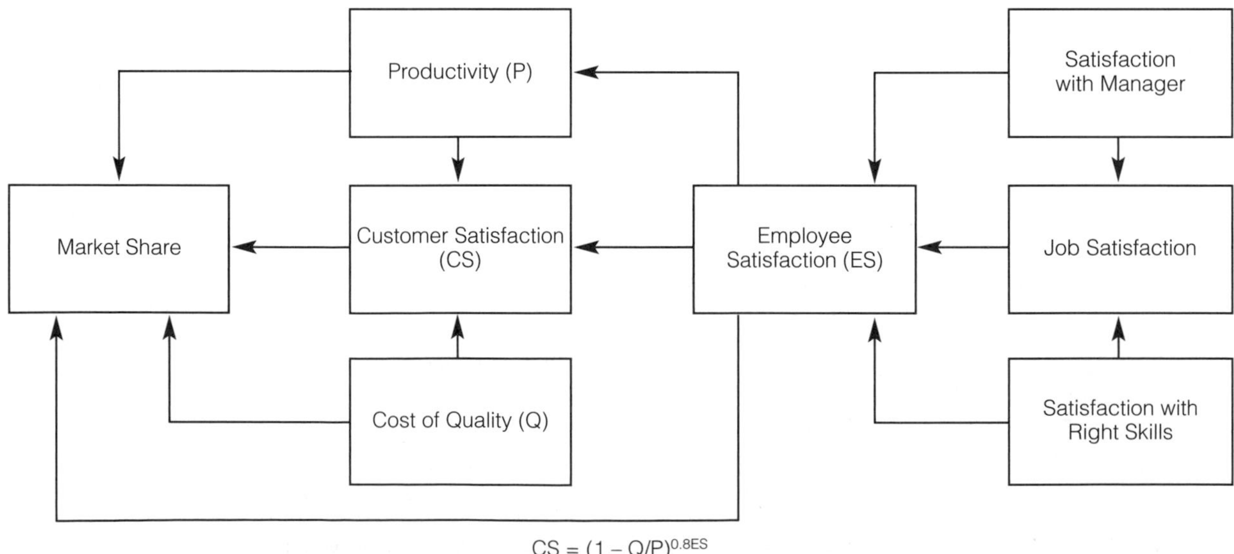

Ames Rubber Corporation found that simple charts help to understand important correlations among measures that impact business decisions and strategy. It discovered that internal yields increase as employee turnover decreases, and that lost time accidents decrease with increasing training hours, leading to new initiatives for training and HR policies. North Mississippi Medical Center (NMMC) developed an innovative format for presenting the relationships between process and outcome measures, allowing clear understanding of cause-and-effect relationships. For example, Figure 8.8 shows that improvements in various in-process interventions for acute myocardial infarction (heart attack) patients result in improved outcomes.

Strong analytical capability supports good analysis. For example, Fuji-Xerox, a Japanese subsidiary of Xerox, uses a variety of statistical techniques such as regression and analysis of variance to develop mathematical models relating such factors as copy quality, machine malfunctions, and maintenance time to customer satisfaction results. Correlation analysis of product and service performance and customer indicators is a critical management tool for defining and focusing on key quality and customer requirements, identifying product and service differentiators in the marketplace, and determining cause-effect relationships between product and service attributes and measures of customer satisfaction and loyalty, as well as positive referrals. Caterpillar uses correlation analyses for its scoring and credit decision models to predict profitability, and segmentation analysis to compare satisfaction of origination processes versus termination processes, success in meeting varying requirements of differing industries, or describing employee salary ranges by job category.

The capabilities of today's spreadsheet and database software, such as Microsoft Excel and Access, make analysis simple to do by nearly any employee. Also, some evidence suggests that organizations that use more sophisticated statistical tools for analysis tend to have better business results. The fact that effective analysis requires more advanced statistical thinking might explain the lack of good approaches in most organizations. Thus, organizations are advised to develop improved statistical expertise among their employees, which is one of the key benefits of Six Sigma.

New technology for analyzing data, such as data mining, is improving organizational ability to develop good information. **Data mining** is the process of searching

Figure 8.8 Example of NMMC Process-Outcome Linkages

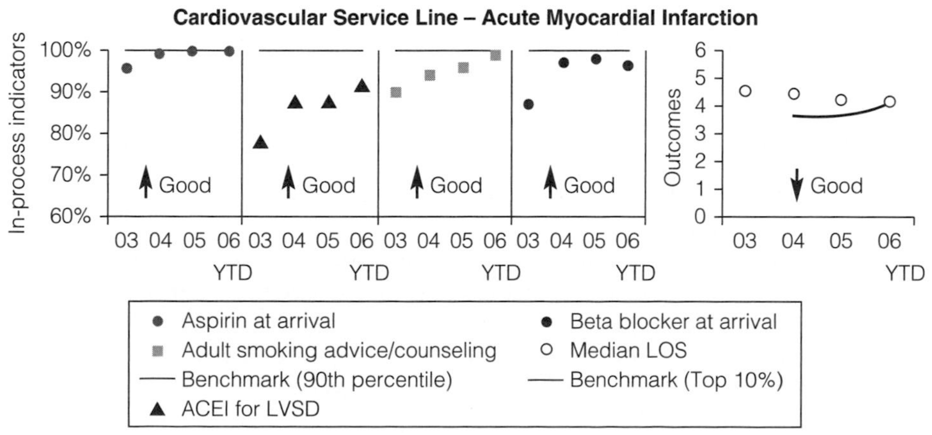

Source: NMMC Malcolm Baldrige National Quality Award Application Summary, 2007. Reprinted with permission.

large databases to find hidden patterns in data, using analytical approaches and technologies such as cluster analysis, neural networks, and fuzzy logic. Data mining computer programs can sort through millions of pieces of information and identify subtle correlations between many variables, which is far more than the human mind is capable of doing. For example, data mining might discover that a particular supplier has a higher defect rate on parts costing less than $5, or that consumers who purchase a backup disk drive also tend to purchase a software utility package. Using data mining, MCI developed a set of 22 detailed and highly secret statistical profiles to identify potential customers who might leave for a rival company.[27] Data mining is relatively inexpensive and can provide new competitive knowledge. However, it requires clean data, even though it establishes correlations among variables, it cannot necessarily establish cause and effect. Also, it can easily lead to useless insights or overlook insights that are important. Nevertheless, the technology holds considerable promise.

The Role of Comparative Data

The use of comparative data and information is important to all organizations. Comparative data are needed because an organization needs to know where it stands relative to competitors and to best practices; comparative information and information obtained from benchmarking often provide the impetus for significant ("breakthrough") improvement or change; and comparing performance information frequently leads to a better understanding of processes and their performance. Looking at data without a basis for comparison can easily lead to a false sense of achievement. For example, a performance measure may be improving, but at a rate slower than its competition. Without that information, it would be difficult for an organization to recognize the need for further improvements or an accelerated pace of change to close the gap.

The effective selection and use of comparative data and information require the determination of needs and priorities, criteria for seeking appropriate sources for comparisons—from within and outside an organization's industry and markets, and the use of data and information to set stretch goals and to promote breakthrough improvements in areas most critical to the organization's competitive strategy.

Organizations need comparative data, such as industry averages, best competitor performance, and world-class benchmarks to gain an accurate assessment of performance and know where they stand relative to competitors and best practices.

Comparative data may be obtained in many ways and include third-party surveys and benchmarking approaches. The Ritz-Carlton Hotel Company, for instance, uses ratings and awards from travel industry publications and salesforce reports to assess its competitive status. Boeing A&T seeks information from three sources:

1. *Best-in-Boeing:* High-performing processes identified through various company-level councils
2. *Best-in-Industry:* Organizations identified through various benchmarking centers, the International Benchmarking Clearinghouse, and their internal Business Environmental Assessment group
3. *World Class:* Leading-edge organizations, winners of national awards, or those cited by customers, suppliers, and industry experts

Figure 8.9 shows an example from Mercy Hospital in Janesville, Wisconsin. The average length of stay performance is compared to other hospitals in the state, a specific peer group of hospitals, and a best practice (BP) benchmark for a competitor. A good source of comparative benchmarks is often the performance of Baldrige recipients.

Figure 8.9 An Example of Comparative Data from Mercy Hospital, Janesville

Source: Mercy Health Systems Malcolm Baldrige National Quality Award Application Summary, 2007.

Performance Review

The analysis of data provides the foundation for management review. Managers review performance results for several reasons:

- To assess organizational success and performance relative to competitors
- To understand how well progress on strategic objectives and action plans is being achieved
- To identify priorities for improvement and opportunities for innovation for products, services, and processes

Performance reviews are usually conducted on a daily or weekly basis for short-term control decisions, and periodically throughout the year for longer-term decisions and improvement. Figure 8.10 shows a summary of the performance reviews by which organizational decision-making and innovation are achieved at PRO-TEC Coating Company. Decisions regarding breakthrough innovations are decided at meetings with "change-the-business" aspects to them (Monday-Wednesday-Friday morning meeting, Departmental, and Management Committee and Leadership meetings). At the lower levels of the organization, PRO-TEC expects individual Associates and workgroups to review operational "run-the-business" metrics and provide most of the ideas for continuous improvement.

At Mercy Health System, senior leaders participate in performance review as members of interdisciplinary committees.[28] Standing system-wide committees, such as the Quality Council, Safety Committee, IMACinformation Management Advisory Committee, and Pharmacy and Therapeutics Committee, review in-process, trended performance, and create action plans to achieve goals. Key performance indicators are compared to best-practice measures during analysis to assess organizational success and competitive performance. Data summaries are integrated and reported to appropriate committees, company leadership, and physicians. MHS uses the results of organizational performance reviews to evaluate achievement of system-wide goals, on both an annual and ongoing basis. During the Strategic Planning Process and budgeting process, the Executive Committee identifies opportunities and priorities for improving key processes, sets targets for organizational performance, and defines system-level action plans to achieve those targets.

Figure 8.10 Performance Review Summary at PRO-TEC Coating Company

	Operational	Mon.-Wed.-Fri.	Departmental	Monthly	Others
Who	Value creation personnel	Value creation personnel, support processes	Each department personnel	Leadership Team and stakeholders	PRO-TEC Mgmt. Committee, Leadership Team (strategic planning), Departmental planning
When	Daily	3 times weekly	1–2 per month	Monthly	3 times a year, annual
What	Run Balanced Scorecard (BSC)—quality, volume, uptime	Run BSC—Interdepartmental cooperative efforts, corrective actions; Change BSC—current issues driving change	Run BSC—review projects, departmental issues, plan versus actual; Change BSC—support of tactical and strategic planning	Run BSC—review departmental performance, action items	Run BSC—review company performance; Change BSC—develop change strategy for long-term viability (update Change BSC)
Analysis	Trending, process logs	Review of operations, pareto, correlation, statistical	Statistical, uptime metrics, correlation, pareto	Statistical, uptime metrics, correlation, pareto	Roll-up of measures done at lower levels
Decisions made	Production, operational, equipment	Safety, business direction, operational	Innovation	Resourcing	Strategic planning, Change BSC items

Source: PRO-TEC Malcolm Baldrige Application Summary, 2007. Reprinted with permission.

THE COST OF QUALITY

In most firms, cost accounting is an important function. All organizations measure and report costs as a basis for control and improvement. The concept of the **cost of quality (COQ)** emerged in the 1950s. Traditionally, the reporting of quality-related costs had been limited to inspection and testing; other costs were accumulated in overhead accounts. As managers began to define and isolate the full range of quality-related costs, a number of surprising facts emerged.[29] First, quality-related costs were much larger than previously reported, generally in the range of 20 to 40 percent of sales. Second, quality-related costs were not only related to manufacturing operations, but to ancillary services such as purchasing and customer service departments as well. Third, most of the costs resulted from poor quality and were avoidable. Finally, while the costs of poor quality were avoidable, no clear responsibility for action to reduce them was assigned, nor was any structured approach formulated to do so. As a result, many firms began to develop cost of quality programs. The "costs of quality"—or specifically, the costs of *poor* quality—are those costs associated with avoiding poor quality or those incurred as a result of poor quality.

COQ approaches have numerous objectives, but perhaps the most important one is to translate quality problems into the "language" of upper management—the language of money.

Juran noted that workers and supervisors speak in the "language of things"—units, defects, and so on. Unfortunately, quality problems expressed as the number of defects typically have little impact on top managers who are generally more concerned with financial performance. But if the magnitude of quality problems can be translated into monetary terms, such as "How much would it cost us to run this business if there were no quality problems?" the eyes of upper managers are opened. Dollar figures can be added meaningfully across departments or products, and compared to other dollar measures. Middle managers, who must deal with workers and supervisors as well as top management, must have the ability to speak in both languages. Quality cost information serves a variety of other purposes, too. It helps management evaluate the relative importance of quality problems and thus identify major opportunities for cost reduction. It can aid in budgeting and cost control activities. Finally, it can serve as a scoreboard to evaluate the organization's success in achieving quality objectives.

To establish a cost of quality approach, one must identify the activities that generate cost, measure them, report them in a way that is meaningful to managers, and analyze them to identify areas for improvement. The following sections discuss these activities in greater detail.

Quality Cost Classification

Quality costs can be organized into four major categories: prevention costs, appraisal costs, internal failure costs, and external failure costs. **Prevention costs** are investments made to keep nonconforming products from occurring and reaching the customer, including the following specific costs:

- *Quality planning costs*, such as salaries of individuals associated with quality planning and problem-solving teams, the development of new procedures, new equipment design, and reliability studies
- *Process control costs*, which include costs spent on analyzing production processes and implementing process control plans
- *Information systems costs* expended to develop data requirements and measurements
- *Training and general management costs*, including internal and external training programs, clerical staff expenses, and miscellaneous supplies

Appraisal costs are those associated with efforts to ensure conformance to requirements, generally through measurement and analysis of data to detect nonconformances. Categories of appraisal costs include the following:

- *Test and inspection costs* associated with incoming materials, work-in-process, and finished goods, including equipment costs and salaries
- *Instrument maintenance costs* due to calibration and repair of measuring instruments
- *Process measurement and control costs*, which involve the time spent by workers to gather and analyze quality measurements

Internal failure costs are incurred as a result of unsatisfactory quality found before the delivery of a product to the customer; some examples include the following:

- *Scrap and rework costs*, including material, labor, and overhead
- *Costs of corrective action*, arising from time spent determining the causes of failure and correcting production problems
- *Downgrading costs*, such as revenue lost when selling a product at a lower price because it does not meet specifications
- *Process failures*, such as unplanned machine downtime or unplanned equipment repair

External failure costs occur after poor-quality products reach the customer, specifically:

- *Costs due to customer complaints and returns,* including rework on returned items, cancelled orders, and freight premiums
- *Product recall costs* and *warranty claims,* including the cost of repair or replacement as well as associated administrative costs
- *Product liability costs,* resulting from legal actions and settlements

Capturing and Using Quality Costs

Quality has had a major impact on the role of accounting systems in business.[30] Standard accounting systems are generally able to provide quality cost data for direct labor, overhead, scrap, warranty expenses, product liability costs, and maintenance, repair, and calibration of test equipment. However, most accounting systems are not structured to capture important cost-of-quality information. Costs such as service effort, product design, remedial engineering effort, rework, in-process inspection, and engineering change losses must usually be estimated or collected through special efforts. Some costs due to external failure, such as customer dissatisfaction and future lost revenues, are impossible to estimate accurately. Although prevention costs are the most important, appraisal costs, internal failure, and external failure (in that order) are usually easier to collect. **Activity-based costing** organizes information about the work (or activity) that consumes resources and delivers value in a business. Examples of activities might be moving, inspecting, receiving, shipping, and order processing. Activity-based costing allocates overhead costs to the products and services that use them, making it easier to assign costs to proper quality cost categories and facilitate continuous improvement activities.

A convenient way of reporting quality costs is through a breakdown by organizational function as shown in Figure 8.11. Such a report can be implemented easily on a spreadsheet. This matrix serves several purposes. First, it allows all departments to recognize their contributions to the cost of quality and participate in a cost of quality program. Second, it pinpoints areas of high quality cost and directs attention toward improvement efforts. For instance, if we rank internal failure costs from largest to smallest, chances are that 70 or 80 percent of all internal failure costs are due to only one or two manufacturing problems. Identifying these "vital few," as they are called, leads to corrective action that has a high return for a low dollar input. This technique, which we will study formally in a later chapter, is called *Pareto analysis.*

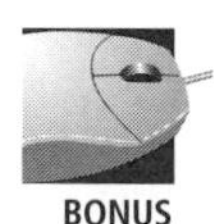
BONUS MATERIALS

Quality costs are often reported as an *index,* that is, the ratio of the current value to a base period. The Bonus Materials folder for this chapter on the Premium website contains further information about computing and using quality cost indexes.

Quality costs in different categories are rarely distributed evenly.

Experts estimate that 60 to 90 percent of total quality costs are the result of internal and external failure and are the responsibility of management. Managers typically react to high failure costs by increasing inspection. Such actions, however, only increase appraisal costs. The overall result is little, if any, improvement in overall quality or profitability. In practice, an increase in prevention usually generates larger savings in all other cost categories. In a typical scenario, the cost of replacing a poor-quality component in the field might be $500; the cost of replacement after assembly might be $50; the cost of testing and replacement during assembly might be $5; and the cost of changing the design to avoid the problem might be only 50 cents. Thus, organizations

Figure 8.11 Cost of Quality Matrix

	Design Engineering	Purchasing	Production	. . .	Finance	. . .	Accounting	Totals
Prevention costs Quality planning Training . . .								
Appraisal costs Test and inspection Instruments . . .								
Internal failure costs Scrap Rework . . .								
External failure costs Returns Recall costs . . .								
Totals								

should first attempt to reduce external failure costs to zero by investing in appraisal activities to discover the sources of internal failures and take corrective action. As quality improves, failure costs will decrease, and the amount of appraisal can be reduced with the shift of emphasis to prevention activities. However, because many organizations focus on the short term, they fail to understand that investment in prevention will reduce overall system costs.

Quality Costs in Service Organizations

The nature of quality costs differs between service and manufacturing organizations. Traditional external failure costs such as warranty and field support are less relevant to services than to manufacturing. Process-related costs, such as customer-service and complaint-handling staff and lost customers are more critical.

Internal failure costs might not be as evident in services as in manufacturing. For example, a small distributor focused a great deal of attention on minimizing inventories while trying to improve service. The company knew that backorders existed, but believed that they were simply the nature of the business. Further analysis revealed nearly one backorder for every five orders. After examining the process, the cost of backorders was determined to be $30 per transaction, for an annual cost of $200,000. The reasons included suppliers not meeting delivery dates, errors in sales orders, and other

In manufacturing, quality costs are primarily product-oriented; for services, however, they are generally labor-dependent, with labor often accounting for up to 75 percent of total costs.

non-value-added operations.[31] Internal failure costs tend to be much lower for service organizations with high customer contact, which have little opportunity to correct an error before it reaches the customer. By that time, the error becomes an external failure.

Work measurement and sampling techniques are often used to gather quality costs in service organizations. For example, work measurement can be used to determine how much time an employee spends on various quality-related activities. The proportion of time spent multiplied by the individual's salary represents an estimate of the quality cost for that activity. Consumer surveys and other means of customer feedback are also used to determine quality costs for services. In general, however, the intangible nature of the output makes quality cost accounting for services difficult.

MEASURING THE RETURN ON QUALITY

Total Quality efforts should lead to the achievement of outstanding business results. However, a successful quality initiative does not guarantee financial success. (Many argue that without it, however, the organization will eventually be doomed to failure.) Many organizations fail to pay enough attention to the financial returns on quality-related investments. Financial returns not only demonstrate when the efforts are going in the right direction, but can help identify changes and improvements that need to be made before staying on the wrong path too long. For example, AT&T's chairman receives a quarterly report from each business unit that describes quality improvements and their financial impacts.

Traditionally, measuring reductions in quality-related costs through COQ was the principal method of documenting the benefits of quality. However, this approach only focuses on the internal view of quality. More attention is being paid to the external view and accounting for increases in revenues associated with improved quality and customer satisfaction. Balancing quality costs against expected revenue gains has become known as **return on quality (ROQ)**. ROQ is based on four main principles:[32]

- *Quality is an investment*. Thus, it is not fundamentally different from investing in equipment or buildings.
- *Quality efforts must be made financially accountable*. Because businesses evaluate other investments in this way, quality efforts should be subject to the same types of financial justification.
- *It is possible to spend too much on quality*. Customers might not be willing to pay the premiums associated with higher levels of quality, or the process improvement benefits might not justify the expense.
- *Not all quality expenditures are equally valid*. An improvement in product design or customer response might be much more important from a strategic point of view than improving the capability of a minor process in the manufacturing plant.

The foundation for the approach stems from the model shown in Chapter 1 (Figure 1.4) relating quality and profitability, which proposes that quality improvement leads to financial returns through improvements in customer satisfaction and loyalty. Sophisticated statistical methods are often used to estimate these effects and the financial implications. Thinking of quality as a financially justifiable investment in this fashion is fundamental to project selection in Six Sigma.

ROQ was applied to evaluating a training program to improve customer service skills of branch staff at Chase Manhattan Bank.[33] The intended outcomes of the program included the ability of the branch staff to identify behavior that creates a positive memorable customer experience, analyze interactions with customers, identify what customers want, and understand the nature of caring customer service. By using a test and control group, estimating the net present value of the loss avoided from customers not becoming dissatisfied as a result of the training program, $471,000, and comparing this figure to the net present value of training costs, $326,000, the return on investment was computed to be 44.4 percent. This analysis showed that a system-wide training program would likely be profitable. Results were circulated among Chase managers and the company moved forward with expansion of the training program.

MANAGING INFORMATION RESOURCES

Simply collecting data is not enough. Organizations must ensure that both data and information and the hardware and software systems that process them are reliable, accurate, user-friendly, and secure, and that data and information are available to all who need them in a timely fashion.

Reliability of a measurement *refers to how well the measuring instrument—manual instruments, automated equipment, or surveys and questionnaires—consistently measures the "true value" of the characteristic.*

The familiar computer cliché, "Garbage in, garbage out," applies equally well to organizational performance data. Any measurement is subject to error, and hence the credibility of data can be suspect. Measurement reliability in manufacturing demands careful attention to metrology, the science of measurement. This topic is discussed in Chapter 12 in the context of Six Sigma. A useful approach to ensuring data reliability is for internal cross-functional teams or external auditors to conduct periodic audits of the processes used to collect the data. Standardized forms, clear instructions, and adequate training lead to more consistent performance in data collection. An AT&T division, for example, used standard data entry templates and procedures to facilitate the consistency and uniform editing of manually input data. Data collected automatically from interfaces with other systems use standard record formats and edits, and are reconciled at each handoff. Also, a central data dictionary defined critical data elements according to source, meaning, format, and valid content of each. AT&T followed stringent guidelines and standards for developing, maintaining, documenting, and managing data systems.

Like any business process, information creation should be managed with total quality principles.[34] The quality of information can be improved by capturing data only once, and as close to the origin of the data as possible; eliminating human error by capturing data electronically where possible; using a single database whenever feasible; eliminating all unnecessary handling of data by intermediaries, such as data entry clerks; placing accountability on the creators of data and information; ensuring proper training; and defining targets and measures of data quality. Maintaining computer systems, backing up databases, and building error-checking capabilities into software provides added measures for ensuring data and information validity and availability. Frequent computer crashes or network problems can wreak havoc on operations and customer responsiveness.

An organization's efforts are wasted if collected data are not available to the right employees when needed. A customer service representative who tells a customer that he or she needs to find some information and will call back the next day cannot satisfy that customer in a timely fashion. At Milliken, all databases, including product specifications, process data, supplier data, customer requirements, and environmental data are available to every associate throughout the computer network. Electronic charts displayed throughout the plant and in business support departments show key quality measures and trends. Data accessibility empowers employees and encourages their participation in quality improvement efforts. Wainwright Industries posts all business information—quality, customer satisfaction, and financial performance—in a room accessible to all employees, customers, suppliers, and visitors. Organizations that share results often exhibit better performance because information provides the basis for better decisions, and employees understand why certain decisions are made. Figure 8.12 shows how a wide variety of data is made accessible to all stakeholders at Pearl River School District. Sharing data is becoming increasingly important in business networks and supply chains.

Modern information technology plays a critical role in data accessibility. Many organizations have state-of-the-art online computer networks supplemented by local processing capabilities. Prudential Insurance Company agents take portable computers to customer's homes or places of business.[35] This practice reduces the time needed to answer a client's questions and increases the accuracy and reliability of the answers. Sales and service offices are connected electronically. Each can obtain information about the current status of contracts being serviced by another office, and thus can be of assistance to customers who contact them directly. They can also electronically forward requests for action to the appropriate office. The Hospital Information System (HIS) at Baptist Hospital is used to gather, connect, and integrate data from clinical systems, employees, patients, financial systems, decision support

Figure 8.12 Data Accessibility at Pearl River School District

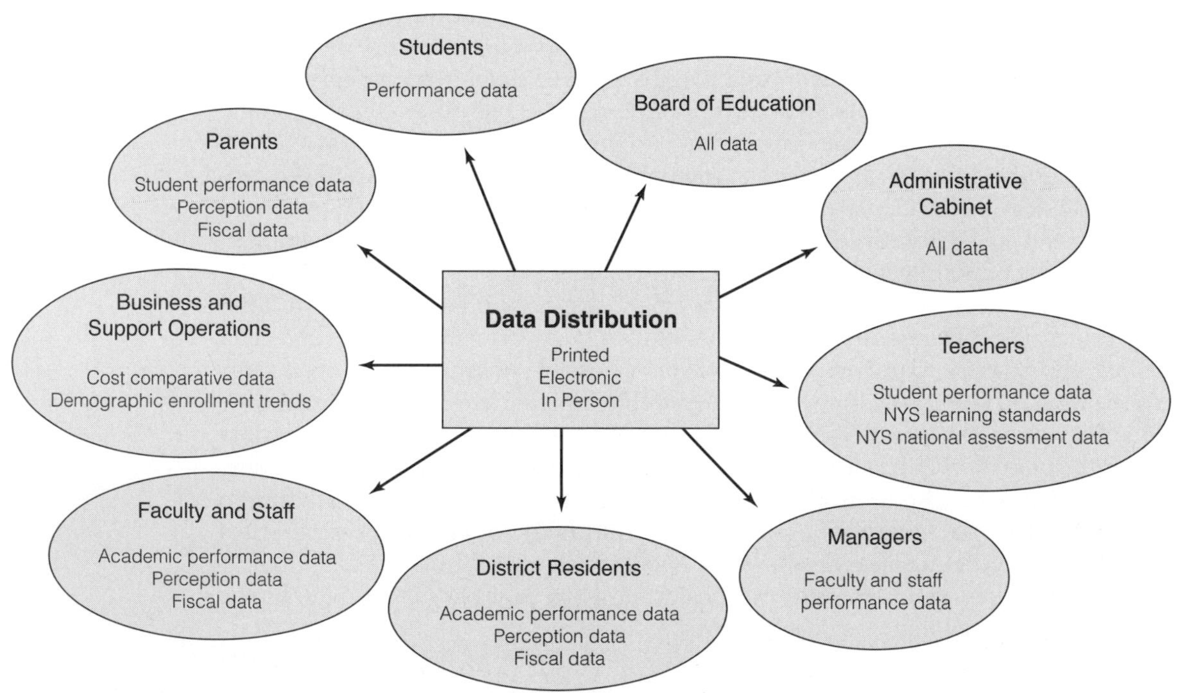

Source: Pearl River School District Malcolm Baldrige Application Summary, 2001. Reprinted with permission.

systems, and physicians. The HIS is accessed through mobile terminals, through the Medical Information Data Access System for physicians, and through kiosks located throughout the organization.

The reliability of hardware and software is crucial to ensure the integrity of performance measurement systems. At Branch-Smith Printing, server uptime is protected with redundant power supplies and hard drives. Two servers have two identical mirrored drives so that if a device on the primary fails, we can remove one of the drives and install it in the sister machine, and have the server operating again in just minutes. At Motorola, special interest groups or technical advisory boards and working groups have been formed across the corporation to involve users in establishing and updating desktop hardware and software standards to reduce costs, ensure reliability, and improve ease of use.

Confidentiality and security are critical in managing data, particularly with the increasing use of electronic data transfer. Using firewalls to prevent external systems attacks and passwords to ensure that only authorized users have access to sensitive data such as customer records and financial information are vital in an information management system. At Clarke American, for instance, when an associate leaves the company, the Termination Identification Process System (TIPS) automatically notifies Systems Assurance to remove access to all facilities and systems.

Finally, data and information must be kept current. Antiquated measurements lead to poor decisions. Leading organizations continually improve their performance measurement systems, staying abreast of new techniques. They conduct ongoing review and update their sources and uses of data, shorten the cycle time from data gathering to access, and broaden access to everyone who requires data for management and improvement. For example, ADAC Laboratories hosted quarterly "measurement summits" that included representatives from all departments to review the types of data collected according to three criteria: whether the data support key business drivers; address one of the "five evils"—waste, defects, delays, accidents, or mistakes; or support objective analysis for improvement. Teams at Corning TPD brainstorm and research new measurements, consult with experts, and test the measurements for three to six months before full implementation.

KNOWLEDGE MANAGEMENT

One Hewlett-Packard manager noted, "The fundamental building material of a modern corporation is knowledge." Process improvement requires new knowledge to result in better processes and procedures. Increasing the knowledge of the organization, both in an individual sense as well as for the organization as a whole, is the essence of learning and ties closely to Deming's concept of the theory of knowledge (see Chapter 3). H. James Harrington observed, "All organizations have it, but most don't know what they know, don't use what they do know, and don't reuse the knowledge they have."[36] Knowledge assets have become more important than financial and physical assets in many organizations. For example, Skandia, a large Swedish financial services company, internally audits its intellectual capital every year for inclusion in its annual report.

Chevron CEO Kenneth Derr has stated:

> *Of all the initiatives we've taken at Chevron... few have been as important or as rewarding as our efforts to build a learning organization by sharing and managing knowledge throughout our company. In fact, I believe this priority was one of the keys to reducing our operating costs by more than $2 billion per year... over the last seven years.*[37]

Unfortunately, as compared with money, labor, and capital equipment, knowledge is probably the most difficult to manage. It can easily be lost if information is not documented or when individuals are promoted or leave the organization. Knowledge is perishable and if it is not renewed and replenished, it becomes worthless.

***Knowledge assets** refer to the accumulated intellectual resources that an organization possesses, including information, ideas, learning, understanding, memory, insights, cognitive and technical skills, and capabilities.*

Knowledge assets consist of two types: explicit knowledge and tacit knowledge. **Explicit knowledge** includes information stored in documents or other forms of media such as databases, policies and procedures, and technical drawings. Explicit knowledge is easily captured, stored, and disseminated using computer technology (think Google!). **Tacit knowledge** is information that is formed around intangible factors resulting from an organization's or individual's experience, and is content-specific. Intellectual assets such as patents, software, or a unique understanding of customer requirements that differentiates an organization from its competitors are some examples, as are knowledge resulting from research or job experience, cross-functional teamwork, or after action reviews. These two aspects represent the "know-how" that an organization has available to use, invest, and grow. Customers, suppliers, and partners may also hold key knowledge assets.

Knowledge management involves the process of identifying, capturing, organizing, and using knowledge assets to create and sustain competitive advantage. A knowledge management system allows intangible information to be managed as an organizational asset in a manner similar to tangible assets. A benchmarking study co-sponsored by the American Productivity and Quality Center reported that 79 percent of managers from the 70 responding companies felt that managing organizational knowledge is central to the organization's strategy, but 59 percent stated that their firm was performing this management function poorly or not at all.[38] Also, 88 percent believed that a climate of openness and trust is important for knowledge sharing, but 32 percent of the respondents believed that their organization did not have such a climate. In many organizations, the gap was attributed to a lack of commitment to knowledge management on the part of top managers.

Managing information and knowledge can require a significant commitment of resources as the sources of information grow dramatically each year. Information from internal operations, from the Internet, and from business-to-business (B2B) and business-to-consumer (B2C) communications challenges organizational abilities to provide the information that people need to do their work, keep current, and improve. Clarke American, for example, has an automated information collection and distribution system that provides a central repository for information for partners, customers, and associates. Caterpillar Financial Services Corporation manages organizational knowledge through several mechanisms, including e-mail; an Intranet; shared network drives; public folders which store knowledge by subject, department, and other customized formats; Caterpillar's Knowledge Network which is a web-based tool that provides for collaboration at many levels; and a searchable database called eTracker, which captures learning from over 1,000 Six Sigma projects. Best practices are identified through annual state quality conferences, the Quest for Excellence conference, which features recipients of the Malcolm Baldrige National Quality Award, and Peer Learning Network meetings.

An effective knowledge management system should include the following:

- A way of capturing and organizing explicit as well as tacit knowledge of how the business operates, including an understanding of how current business processes function
- A systems-approach to management that facilitates assimilation of new knowledge into the business system and is oriented toward continuous improvement/innovation
- A common framework for managing knowledge and some way of validating and synthesizing new knowledge as it is acquired
- A culture and values that support collaborative sharing of knowledge across functions and encourages full participation of all employees in the process[39]

Knowledge Transfer

The transfer of knowledge within organizations and the identification and sharing of best practices often set high-performing organizations apart from the rest. Many organizations perform similar activities at different locations or by different people. For example, consider a sales organization with district managers spread out over the country, or a clinical research organization that performs research studies for drug companies in a project environment, or a school district with teachers teaching the same subjects at different locations throughout the district. Suppose that an individual develops an innovative practice. How is this knowledge shared among others performing similar jobs? In many organizations, the answer is that knowledge is probably never shared.

High-performance organizations use many different mechanisms to share and transfer knowledge. For example, Premier, Inc. uses a team-oriented approach to transfer knowledge, which is accomplished using various tools, technologies, and processes to fill needs or gaps identified through proactive research. Teams use standardized tools for collection and transfer, which occurs regularly to support continuous cycles of improvement. Methods for collecting and transferring knowledge include large group meetings, work groups, surveys/market, publications, technology systems that are available 24/7, and functions to answer questions at any time. Special activities within key events (e.g., Values Conferences, Breakthroughs Conferences, as well as project team and staff meetings) include the transfer of best practices among employees and customers.[40]

The ability to identify and transfer best practices within the organization is sometimes called **internal benchmarking**. In this area, the most mature organizations may falter, even those that are adept at benchmarking other organizations. The American Productivity and Quality Center (APQC) noted that executives have long felt frustrated by their inability to identify or transfer outstanding practices from one location or function to another. They know that some facilities have superior practices and processes, yet operating units continue to reinvent or ignore solutions and repeat mistakes.[41] Research identified three categories of barriers:

1. Lack of motivation to adopt the practice
2. Inadequate information about how to adapt the practice and make it work
3. Lack of "absorptive capacity," the resources and skill to make and manage the change

APQC suggests that although most people have a natural desire to learn and share their knowledge, organizations have a variety of logistical, structural, and cultural hurdles to overcome, including the following:

- Organizational structures that promote "silo" thinking in which locations, divisions, and functions focus on maximizing their own accomplishments and rewards, or, as Deming called it, "suboptimization"
- A culture that values personal technical expertise and knowledge creation over knowledge sharing
- The lack of contact, relationships, and common perspectives among people who don't work side by side
- An overreliance on transmitting "explicit" rather than "tacit" information—the information that people need to implement a practice that cannot be codified or written down
- Not allowing or rewarding people for taking the time to learn and share and help each other outside of their own small corporate village

Technology, culture, leadership, and measurement are enablers that can help or hinder the process. Many organizations create internal databases by which employees can share their practices and knowledge. For example, Texas Instruments has a Best Practices Knowledgebase delivered via Lotus Notes, Intranet, and TI's network systems. Information is often organized around business core and support processes. Cultural issues include how to motivate and reward people for sharing best practices and establishing a supportive culture. As with any TQ effort, senior leadership must take an active role by tying initiatives to the organization's vision and strategy, communicating success stories at executive meetings, removing implementation barriers, reinforcing and rewarding positive behaviors, leading by example, and communicating the importance of best-practice sharing with all employees. Finally, measuring the frequency of use and satisfaction with best-practice databases, linking practices to financial and customer satisfaction, focusing on cycle time to implement best practices, and measuring the growth of virtual teams that share information are ways in which the organization can monitor the effectiveness of their approaches.

Internal benchmarking requires a process: first, identifying and collecting internal knowledge and best practices; second, sharing and understanding those practices; and third, adapting and applying them to new situations and bringing them up to best-practice performance levels.

Quality Spotlight
Royal Mail

One example of an internal best-practice learning process is Royal Mail, the largest business unit within the Post Office Group in the United Kingdom (UK), which handles an average of 64 million letters per day using approximately 160,000 people at 1,900 operational sites throughout the UK.[42] Each potential good practice (a term used to recognize that a practice may not be the best, but is good enough to provide significant performance gains) requires formalized documentation that includes a description of the practice; names and telephone numbers of the contacts; date; process diagram; description of the major steps, who performs them, and what is needed to do the work; implementation resources; and risks and barriers. These good practice descriptions are scrutinized by a panel for evaluation of their potential for transferability to other parts of the business. The panel characterizes the good practice as either mandatory, where all units and staff are required to adopt it, or recommended, where application is optional, depending on local conditions. Royal Mail uses six measurements for evaluating its approach:

1. The number of potential national good practices reaching national process groups
2. The proportion of national good practices becoming confirmed good practices
3. The extent of implementation
4. The cycle time from first submission to entry in the national database
5. The benefit gained compared to the anticipated benefit
6. Satisfaction from members of the national and business unit process groups

Organizations such as Raytheon and Texas Instruments are beginning to exploit the concept of **rapid knowledge transfer (RKT)**.[43] Rapid knowledge transfer involves the discovery, learning, creation, and reuse of knowledge that eventually becomes intellectual capital—knowledge that can be converted into value and profits. Four global phenomena have increased the importance of RKT in organizations:

1. Driven by high-speed bandwidth, PC microchip improvements, digital technology, and the growth of the Internet, speed has become critical to every facet of business, giving an edge to organizations that rapidly transfer knowledge. These gains in speed have turned knowledge transfer into a race.
2. Intellectual capital (IC) has become a prominent concept that now overshadows physical capital. Knowledge is the main ingredient of IC, and human capital—the tacit knowledge in the minds of employees consisting of know-how, experiences, skills, and creativity—is the source of it all and must be nurtured and protected.
3. The upcoming record retirement of 77 million baby boomers, born between 1946 and 1964, will account for huge losses of vital tacit knowledge. The first group will turn 65 in 2011. By 2030, the 65-plus segment will account for about 20 percent of the U.S. population—double what it was in 2000. When these workers retire, they will take their tacit knowledge with them. Why not capture and transfer the most vital knowledge before it is lost?
4. A growing reservoir of proven, valuable and profitable best-practice business knowledge is currently available for transfer, and most of it is free. The worldwide quality and productivity improvement revolution has produced business excellence models that replicate successes, including the Baldrige criteria, the EFQM European Award, the Shingo Prize for Excellence in Manufacturing, ISO 9000, Lean, and Six Sigma.

A knowledge-enabled culture is created when an organization employs a system of aligned human resource policies, tactics, processes, and practices that ensure knowledge is created, captured, used, and reused to achieve superior organizational results as a sustainable advantage. RKT combines knowledge management and systematic improvement in an integrated process framework that consists of a knowledge-enabled culture and four key steps (see Figure 8.13):

1. Search for and import best practices.
2. Learn, understand, and share.
3. Create intellectual capital.
4. Convert knowledge into value and profits.

RKT has proven capable of replicating the successes of Baldrige winning organizations such as Texas Instruments (TI) at other geographical locations inside and outside of TI.

Figure 8.13 Rapid Knowledge Transfer Framework

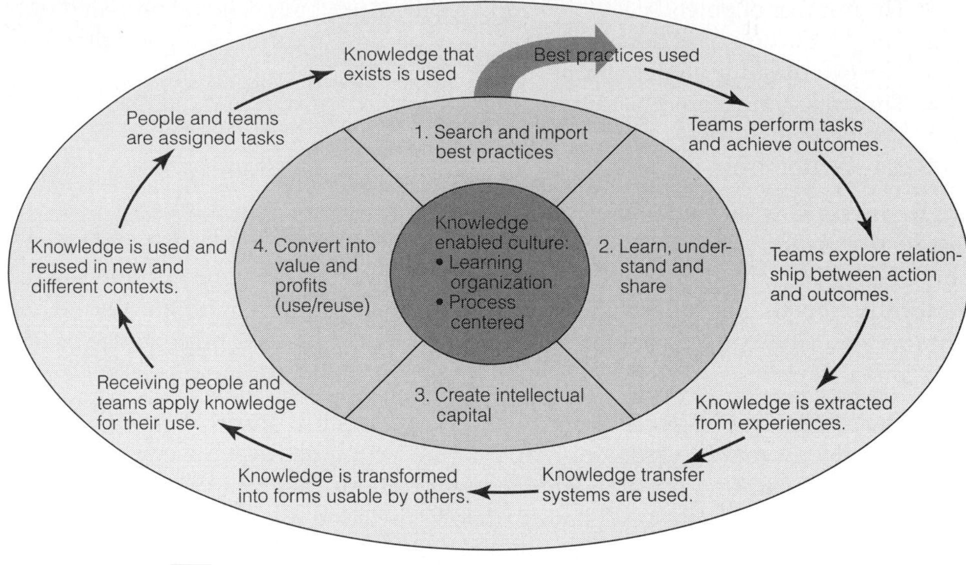

Source: Reprinted with permission from Michael J. English and William H. Baker, Jr. "Rapid Knowledge Transfer: The Key to Success," *Quality Progress*, February 2006, pp. 41–48. Copyright © 2006 American Society for Quality. No further distribution allowed without permission.

MEASUREMENT AND INFORMATION MANAGEMENT IN THE BALDRIGE CRITERIA, ISO 9000, AND SIX SIGMA

Category 4 of the 2009–10 Malcolm Baldrige National Quality Award Criteria for Performance Excellence is titled *Measurement, Analysis, and Knowledge Management.* This category is positioned as the foundation for all other categories in the systems framework that underlies the Baldrige philosophy and provides a key feedback structure linking business results. This category examines how an organization selects, gathers, analyzes, manages, and improves its data, information, and knowledge assets, and how it manages information technology and uses organizational reviews to improve performance. Item 4.1, *Measurement, Analysis, and Improvement of Organizational Performance*, focuses on the major components of an effective performance measurement system. It addresses an organization's selection, management, and use of data and information for performance measurement and analysis in support of organizational planning and performance improvement. The criteria ask how an organization gathers and integrates data and information for monitoring daily operations and supporting organizational decision making, how it selects and uses comparative data and information, and how the performance measurement system is kept current with changing business needs and directions. In addition, the criteria asks what analyses are used to support senior leaders' review of overall organizational performance and strategic planning, and how results are translated into improvement opportunities and communicated throughout the organization.

Item 4.2, *Management of Information, Knowledge, and Information Technology,* looks at how an organization ensures the quality and availability of needed data and information for all key users—the workforce, suppliers and partners, collaborators, and customers. This process includes ensuring that data, information, and organizational knowledge possess all the characteristics that users expect: accessibility, integrity, reliability, accuracy, timeliness, and appropriate levels of security and confidentiality. In addition, the criteria ask how an organization ensures that hardware systems and software are reliable, secure, and user-friendly and how they are maintained in the event of an emergency. It also addresses how an organization manages organizational knowledge to accomplish effective collection and transfer of workforce knowledge; transfer of relevant knowledge from and to customers, suppliers, partners, and collaborators; the rapid identification, sharing, and implementation of best practices; and the transfer of knowledge for use in strategic planning.

ISO 9000:2000 provides a basic framework for managing data and information. The document and data control requirements of ISO 9000 require organizations to define a process for ensuring that any critical information that is required for the performance of a business process is accurate, up-to-date, and effective for its intended purpose. Because ISO 9000 places an emphasis on processes that, in many cases are cross-functional, it forces companies to break down some of the organizational and functional silos that inhibit effective sharing of information.[44]

The measurement, analysis, and improvement requirements of ISO 9000:2000 deal with the measurement of product and process characteristics, performance of the quality system, and search for continuous improvement, requiring that management make decisions based on analysis and trends of product and process performance indicators, internal auditing, and customer feedback. Specific requirements include the following:

- Establishing, planning, and implementing measurement, monitoring, and improvement activities
- Monitoring information about customer satisfaction as a performance metric
- Establishing measurement and monitoring methods to assure that product and process requirements are attained
- Acquiring and analyzing data to determine improvement effectiveness
- Promoting continuous improvement using auditing reports, data analysis, and management reviews

Using a balanced scorecard approach or the Baldrige measurement framework can clearly provide the foundation for meeting these requirements for firms that pursue ISO 9000.

Six Sigma emphasizes fact-based decisions and provides organizations with tools to generate measurable results from Six Sigma projects. Six Sigma methodology requires measuring and reporting performance goals, and using performance indicators to control and sustain improvements. Project selection is based on understanding the financial as well as the nonfinancial benefits to the organization, such as cost savings, increased sales, reduced cycle times, or improved customer satisfaction. Thus, measurements are vital in "selling" Six Sigma projects to top management.

Six Sigma can have a significant impact on the cost of quality because of its focus on financial return; in fact, one survey observed that the top three measures used to quantify Six Sigma success are cost takeout, productivity, and revenue generation.[45] Many Six Sigma projects focus on reducing the costs of poor quality that result from low sigma levels of performance, and improved designs that will increase customer satisfaction and hence, revenue. The different categories of the cost of quality described earlier in this chapter provide many opportunities for Six Sigma projects. For example, an organization might identify all costs that would vanish if sigma performance levels were increased. The list might include costs associated with credits given to customers because of late delivery, billing errors, scrap and rework, unplanned downtime, extra inventory to buffer against defects, errors in specifications and drawings, and accounts payable mistakes. Quantifying these costs establishes the justification for Six Sigma projects. Six Sigma projects can also be categorized in different levels, based upon their impact on results:[46]

1. Level 1 projects directly affect an organization's profit margin (projects have a clear, hard dollar impact on profitability).
2. Level 2 projects result in redeployment of resources inside an organization to increase operating efficiency or productivity.
3. Level 3 projects directly affect operations by avoiding expenditures or increasing the chances of obtaining higher future revenues.

SUMMARY OF KEY POINTS AND TERMINOLOGY

The Premium website for this chapter provides a summary of key concepts and terminology introduced in this chapter.

QUALITY IN PRACTICE

USING THE BALANCED SCORECARD AT THE UNITED STATES POSTAL SERVICE[47]

The U.S. Postal Service (USPS) employs roughly 700,000 workers, with a fleet of over 200,000 vehicles driven about a billion miles a year to deliver more than 206 billion pieces of mail to over 142 million delivery points. It operates one of the largest facilities networks in the nation, with about 38,000 retail offices. Like most organizations, the Postal Service has multiple stakeholders. However, the scope and scale of postal operations makes balancing the interests of its stakeholders somewhat more complex, especially as there are no direct "shareholders" that command precedence in determining organizational priorities. As a public institution, the Postal Service has numerous responsibilities and accountabilities not shared by typical private sector organizations.

The Postal Service had traditionally been able to depend on the growth of the economy to drive mail volume and revenue increases in a protected environment. By the late 1980's it was becoming clear that this planning assumption could no longer be taken for granted. The Postal Service had fairly sophisticated operational planning, and in fact successfully deployed a massive automation program (Corporate Automation Plan) to reduce the number of manual processes in mail processing. The Postal Service also developed a rigorous financial planning process, including rate case and capital investment planning, but something more was needed because service performance and customer satisfaction were declining.

Anticipating the need for substantial change, the Board of Governors appointed Marvin Runyon as the nation's 70th postmaster general in July 1992. Formerly a senior executive with Ford Motor Company, and the first president and CEO of Nissan America, Runyon had successfully applied quality management principles. He established a quality group at the senior management level of the Postal Service.

Runyon began an assessment of the Postal Service in 1993 using the Baldrige criteria. The results of that process led to the creation of what was called CustomerPerfect!, now known simply as the management cycle. One of the critical features that emerged was the development of strategic goal areas of emphasis called "voices": Voice of the Customer, Voice of the Employee, and Voice of the Business. This was the beginning of the balanced scorecard approach in the Postal Service and served as a major focal point toward developing a quality approach. A senior management committee was established to set goals and improvement targets, and to develop specific performance indicators and measurement systems.

One of the first areas of emphasis was the "Voice of the Employee," which focused on providing a safe and secure workplace in response to instances of violence and poor employee relations. A second major initiative, the "Voice of the Business," focused on the "Breakthrough Productivity Initiative," while the third area, the "Voice of the Customer," focused on providing timely, reliable delivery. In their balanced scorecard work, Kaplan and Norton advocated a well-connected mapping that leads from an organization's main strategy to the four perspectives of the balanced scorecard: Financial, Customer Satisfaction, Internal Process, and Learning and Growth. Each element works to support the strategic objectives in a linked process. Learning and Growth ("Voice of the Employee" in postal terms) supports improved Internal Processes ("Voice of the Business"), which support Customer Satisfaction ("Voice of the Customer"). Customer satisfaction leads to the desired Financial outcome, which in the case of the Postal Service is sufficient revenue to support the universal delivery service mission.

Most organizations adapt the balanced scorecard to their own conditions, which is why it is difficult to assess the effectiveness of the approach across organizations. At USPS, they were responding to performance gaps in three specific and critical areas. One of the critical areas that needed improvement in the labor-intensive Postal Service was the workplace environment (Voice of the Employee). A strategic goal was established and indicators were developed to measure annual improvements. The primary indicators of performance in this category of the scorecard were safety, based on the requirements of the Occupational Safety and Health Administration, and employee satisfaction. Employee satisfaction is measured by a survey of all employees that is conducted annually but can be tracked monthly by each unit. The Voice of the Business was separated into two areas—one represented by a productivity measure and the other by a revenue generation measure. The last major area of strategic emphasis, "Voice of the Customer," is owned by the chief marketing officer in partnership with the chief operating officer. The primary indicator was a set of delivery service measurement systems.

The organization's efforts were focused on achieving specific, measurable results in each area. A balanced scorecard was constructed, as shown in Figure 8.14. As demonstrated by the arrows, there is an implied alignment from the performance-driven culture reflected in human capital improvements, to operational efficiency, to improvements in customer satisfaction, all of which will improve financial stability. The Postal Service drove the concept throughout the organization by deploying specific goals relevant to the functional and operational units involved.

The Postal Service developed a rigorous performance review process tied to achieving the targets set. Ann Wright, then-manager of performance assessment, stated, "USPS has developed a National Performance Assessment (NPA) system, which provides detailed measures for each of the corporate-level indicators, that provides a line-of-sight link to unit and individual performance down to the frontline supervisor. These are consistent across operating areas and job categories within the operating units. Each of the indicators is objective and measurable, and focuses on results or outcomes rather than activities or processes." Individual and unit performance within organizations ares driven, in large part, by the focus given to specific activities and by the incentives associated with achievement of the specific goals. The NPA system provides a systematic approach more akin to the private sector, and, in fact, the Postal Service has been a forerunner of "pay-for-performance" approaches now being implemented elsewhere in the federal government.

The results of these initiatives have delivered impressive results. The Postal Service has improved its performance on those measures assessing a safe and secure environment. USPS has been recognized as one of the best places for minorities to work. The Postal Service's implementation of the REDRESS (Resolve Employment Disputes Reach Equitable Solutions Swiftly) program has received national recognition. The USPS Occupational Safety and Health Administration OSHA Illness and Injury rate improved to 6.3 in 2004 from 8.7 in 2000. The results of the annual employee satisfaction survey, expressed as an index for six key questions (where a larger index indicates improvement), have advanced from 57.5 in 2000 to 62.1 in 2004. The improvements in the workplace, along with aggressive implementation of automation and

Figure 8.14 U.S. Postal Service's Balanced Scorecard

Building a Balanced Scorecard: The Postal Experience

Goals	Strategies	Measures
Generate revenue	Financial stability	Total revenue
Improve service	Customer focus	% Mail delivered to standard
Manage costs	Operational efficiency	Total factor productivity
Performance-driven culture	Human capital	Employee attitudes and safety
Structural modifications	President's management agenda	Increased flexibility

other management investments, have led to a remarkable growth in postal productivity that has outpaced the growth of productivity in the U.S. economy. The result is that the Postal Service is delivering more mail to more places, with fewer employees. Postal delivery service also has improved significantly. First-class mail performance has improved to over 95 percent of overnight mail being delivered on time, with improvements in other categories of first-class mail.

One way to summarize the effectiveness of the postal implementation of the balanced scorecard approach is to refer to the assessment of the American Society for Quality in their annual American Customer Service Index, where they described the Postal Service in their 2004 survey as "the most improved organization" since the comparative measurement program began in 1994. In an overall comparison to industry ratings of customer satisfaction, the Postal Service ranked above the Transportation, Telecommunications, and Utilities averages, and about equaled the Services industry.

Key Issues for Discussion

1. Explain how the Voice of the Employee supports improved internal processes (Voice of the Business), and how the Voice of the Business supports customer satisfaction (Voice of the Customer).
2. While Figure 8.14 shows only representative measures associated with the balanced scorecard, suggest some other measures that might be included, using your knowledge of postal operations.

Quality in Practice

Knowledge Management for Continuous Improvement at Convergys[48]

Convergys Corporation (NYSE: CVG), a member of the S&P 500 and the *Forbes* Platinum 400, is the global leader in integrated billing, employee care, and customer care services provided through outsourcing or licensing. Convergys serves top companies in telecommunications, Internet, cable and broadband services, technology, financial services, and other industries in more than 40 countries, and also provides integrated, outsourced, human resource services to leading companies across a broad range of industries. Convergys software processes more than 1.5 million individual bills each day to support more than 120 million subscribers, and manages more than 1.7 million separate customer and employee contacts, both live and via electronic interaction. Convergys employs more than 48,000 people in 48 customer contact centers, data centers, and other offices in the United States, Canada, Latin America, Europe, the Middle East, and Asia. Convergys is on the Internet at http://www.convergys.com, and has world headquarters in Cincinnati.

The outsourced customer service industry is maturing rapidly, extremely dynamic, and the environment continues to become more and more complex. Some factors contributing to this situation include consolidation of providers, stiff price competition, and new competition from both the expansion to offshore markets such as India and the Philippines, as well as traditional systems integrators who are further penetrating the business process outsourcing (BPO) market. In addition, Convergys is a fairly young organization, having grown through a series of acquisitions that number more than 20 in the last 20 years. This high number of mergers created a unique challenge as cultures collided and as employees were challenged to integrate the myriad of processes, procedures, and systems. With this environment and the expectations of clients, shareholders, and employees to constantly improve, Convergys developed a vision: "To establish a high-performance culture focused on continuously improving the value we provide to our clients, shareholders, and employees."

To deploy continuous improvement (CI) as a key part of the company's culture and achieve this vision, Convergys followed a two-step approach:

1. Establish leadership support and financial relevance.
2. Support and encourage total participation—establish CI as part of everyone's job.

First, they built leadership support by linking CI to important business initiatives in a highly visible way. With this strong foundation, they turned more attention to getting all employees involved in improving the business. To accomplish this goal, Convergys needed a tool to help facilitate sharing and accelerating improvement efforts. The tool they chose was a web-based employee intranet that called the CI Portal (see Figure 8.15).

The CI Portal provides an infrastructure for companywide knowledge management activities. One of the primary ways employees use it is to submit, track, and manage improvement efforts (see Figure 8.16). Additionally, all improvement efforts and success stories from throughout the organization can be assessed through the CI Portal. Since its inception in the fourth quarter of

Figure 8.15 Convergys CI Portal

Source: Reprinted with permission of Convergys, Inc.

Figure 8.16 Process for Submitting and Managing Improvement Efforts

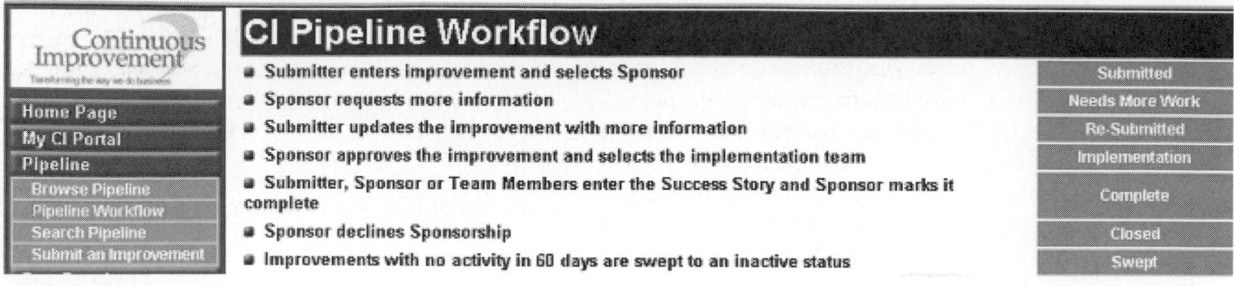

Source: Reprinted with permission of Convergy's Inc.

2000, more than 2,400 improvement efforts have been submitted in the pipeline, 300 of which were completed, successful improvements by mid-2003.

Convergys also introduced a Best Practices Knowledgebase to the CI Portal (see Figure 8.17). The purpose of the knowledge base is to encourage and facilitate the sharing of best practices that improve the value of services provided to their clients. Furthermore, through this knowledge base, best practices can be adopted and leveraged across the organization. To facilitate the sharing of knowledge across the organization, the knowledge base was designed to make it easy to record a best practice in a consistent format that makes it understood by others with little difficulty. Additionally, best practices are categorized in a way that makes it easy to find those that are relevant to a diverse set of needs. To ensure the ongoing credibility of the Best Practices Knowledgebase, a potential best practice is reviewed and endorsed before it can be designated as a best practice. Once the proper documentation is in place, the potential best practice is forwarded to a vice president deemed to be a subject matter expert in the area of the idea. The VP is asked to review the practice and decide whether its use should be encouraged across the organization. The VP then designates the practice as a Best Practice.

Figure 8.17 Example of Best Practice Knowledgebase

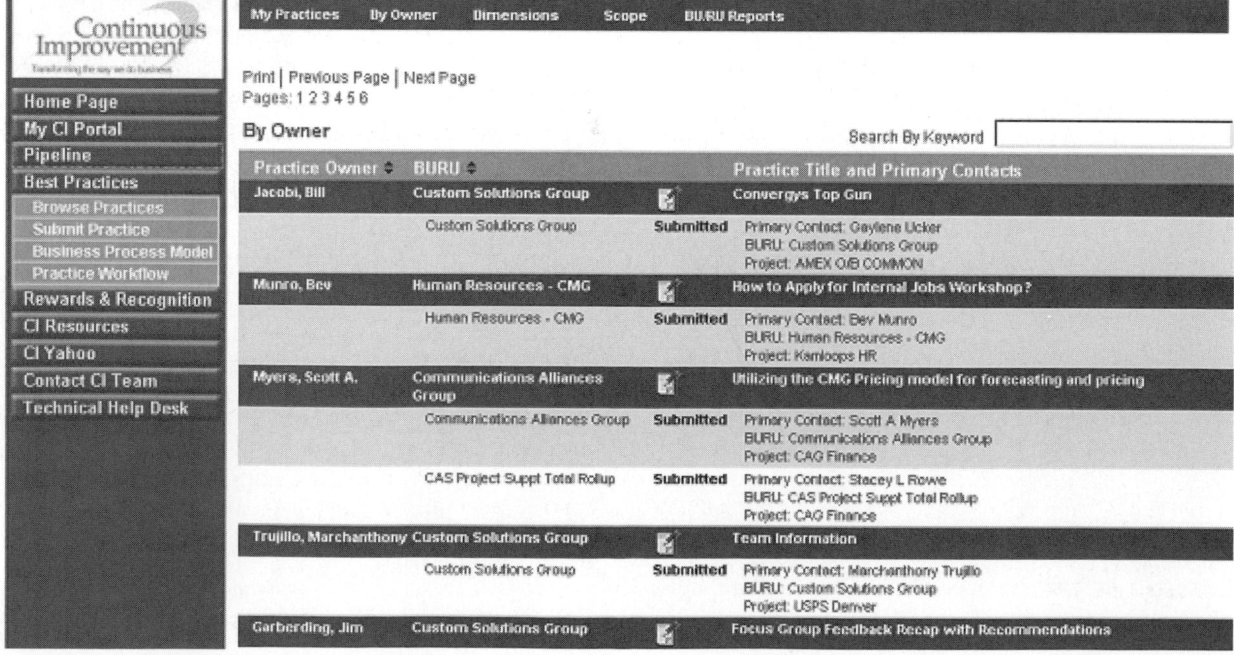

Source: Reprinted with permission of Convergys, Inc.

Figure 8.18 The Improvement Process (TIP)

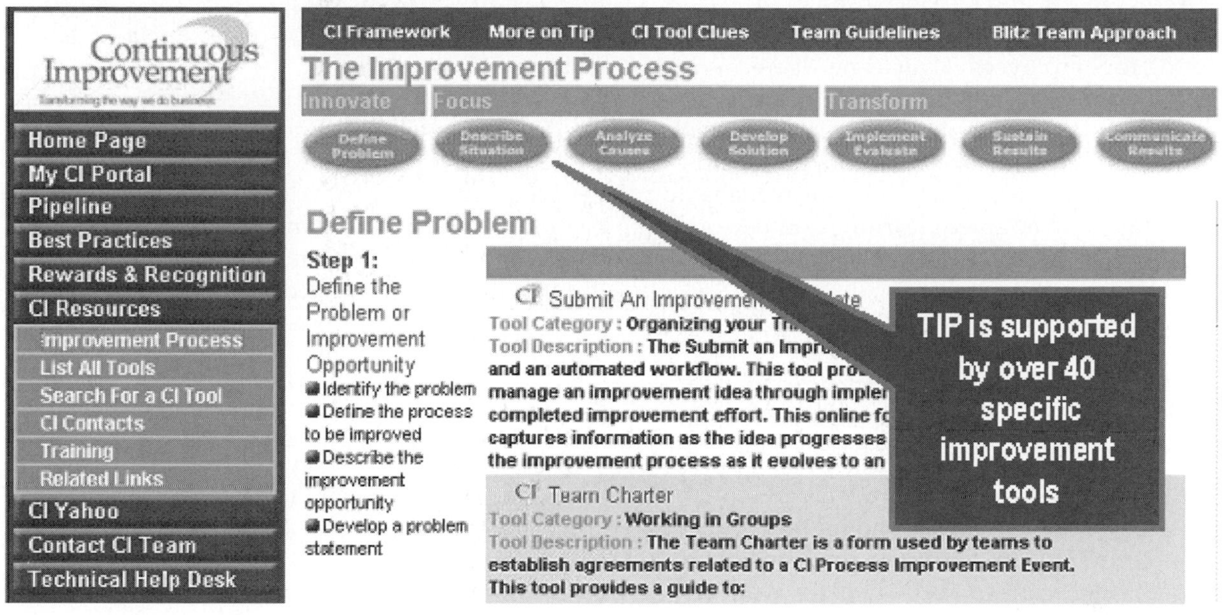

Source: Reprinted with permission of Convergys, Inc.

Another reason employees go to the CI Portal is to access resources to help them facilitate or accelerate improvement efforts. More than 40 specific improvement tools that are accessible through the CI Portal support their standard improvement methodology, which is referred to as The Improvement Process or TIP. Figure 8.18 shows TIP as accessed in the CI Portal. For each step of TIP, CI Tools are identified that support that step.

CI Tools are approaches, tips, and techniques that facilitate problem solving and making improvements. CI Tools are basically proven methods that assist in making fact-based decisions. CI Tools can be used in a variety of ways. Independently, each tool can help to solve a common business issue. CI Tools also support a structured improvement effort. CI Tools are documented in the CI Portal in a simple, consistent, easy-to-use format. Figure 8.19

Figure 8.19 CI Tools

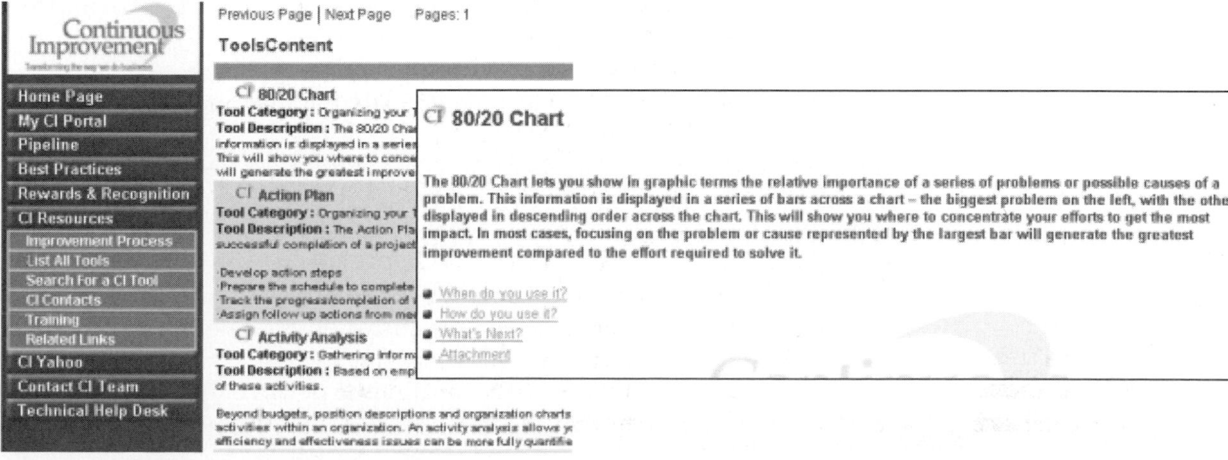

Source: Reprinted with permission of Convergys, Inc.

shows a short list of the types of tools included in the CI Portal as well as the consistent format.

Access to TIP and CI tools through the CI Portal provides an ongoing source of continual training for employees on an as-needed basis and a way to refresh and reinforce continuous improvement approaches. Additionally, self-paced training modules have been developed specifically for CI and the CI Portal and are available to all employees to augment learning and personal development. Examples of the self-paced courses including the following:

- Driving Improvements with the CI Portal
- Accelerating Improvements with TIP and CI Tools
- Improving Business Processes

Continuous improvement (CI) is an integral part of Convergys's culture and its value proposition. Through CI, Convergys has been able to generate significant financial benefits, such as maintaining higher profit margins than its competition. In 2002 alone, more than 2,000 management employees (or 45 percent of management) were directly involved in CI activities. In a 24-month period, more than 2,400 improvement ideas were submitted. Furthermore, thousands more embraced the CI culture. Several clients also acknowledged their approach to continuous improvement as a point of differentiation.

CI and the uses of the CI Portal keep expanding. The focus will continue to be on how employees can be better equipped to facilitate making their own improvements. Additionally, Convergys continues to learn how to most effectively leverage the knowledge and experience of its employees through the sharing of success stories and best practices, and, in the process, strengthen CI as a competitive advantage.

Key Issues for Discussion

1. How does Convergys's CI Portal help to align improvement ideas and projects with the firm's strategic goals?
2. What is the specific process used to take employees' ideas from the concept stage to the "best practice" stage?
3. How are the best practices and tools used to promote learning and develop a knowledge-based organization via the CI Portal?

Review Questions

1. Define measurement.
2. Explain the difference between measures and indicators.
3. Why do organizations need performance measures?
4. Explain the use of data and information at the "three levels of quality" in an organization.
5. What are the benefits of good data and information systems?
6. Summarize the leading practices related to data and information management.
7. What is the balanced scorecard? Describe its four components.
8. Explain the difference between leading and lagging measures. How are they used within a balanced scorecard?
9. What are the six key categories of results measures in the Malcolm Baldrige Criteria? Provide examples of measurements and indicators in each category.
10. Explain the types of measures commonly used for product and service quality.
11. What is the role of comparative data in a performance measurement system?
12. What two fundamental mistakes do organizations frequently make about measurement?
13. Explain the importance and utility of linking performance measures to strategy.

14. What do we mean by the term *actionable* in reference to measures and indicators?
15. Describe the process of defining process-level measurements.
16. Why are cost of quality programs valuable to managers?
17. List and explain the four major categories of quality costs. Give examples of each.
18. Discuss how index numbers are often used to analyze quality cost data.
19. How do quality costs differ between service and manufacturing organizations?
20. How does activity-based costing facilitate the acquisition of quality cost data?
21. What do we mean by validity and reliability of data? Why are these concepts important?
22. What is return on quality (ROQ)? Why is it a useful approach for organizations?
23. Why is accessibility of data important? How does information technology improve accessibility?
24. Describe ways by which data can be analyzed to generate useful managerial information?
25. What is interlinking? Provide an example.
26. How is information and analysis addressed in the Baldrige criteria, ISO 9000:2000, and Six Sigma?

Discussion Questions

1. Classify the measurements described in Figure 8.3 into one of the "three levels of quality": organization, process, and individual performer.
2. Under which perspective of the balanced scorecard would you classify each of the following measurements?
   a. On-time delivery to customers
   b. Time to develop the next generation of products
   c. Manufacturing yield
   d. Engineering efficiency
   e. Quarterly sales growth
   f. Percent of products that equal 70 percent of sales
   g. Cash flow
   h. Number of customer partnerships
   i. Increase in market share
   j. Unit cost of products
3. How might a SWOT (strengths, weaknesses, opportunities, and threats) analysis be of use for identifying measures in a balanced scorecard? What types of questions might you ask?
4. Many "course and instructor evaluation" systems consist of inappropriate or ineffective measurements. Discuss how the principles in this chapter can be used to develop an effective measurement system for instructor performance.
5. How can measurement be used to control and improve the daily operations of your college or university?
6. What types of performance measurements might be used by a fraternity or student organization?

7. In making cheese, companies test milk for somatic cell count to prevent diseases. They also test for bacteria to determine how clean the milk is, and perform a freezing-point test to see whether the milk was diluted with water (milk with water in it freezes at a lower temperature, which increases production costs because all the excess water must be extracted). Final cheese products are subjected to tests for weight, presence of foreign elements or chemicals, and for taste and smell. What customer-related measures might interlink with these internal measures?
8. What information would you need to fully answer the questions that IBM Rochester uses for selecting measures and indicators (p. 375)? Where would you get this information?
9. Discuss what the different categories of quality costs might mean to your college and university. How can they be measured?
10. Many quality experts such as Joseph Juran and Philip Crosby advocate cost-of-quality evaluations. Deming, however, states that "the most important figures are unknown and unknowable." How can these conflicting opinions be resolved?
11. Should a quality department have to cost-justify an expensive piece of measuring equipment based on a return on quality argument, or should the department manager simply point to "increased competition" as justification?
12. Using information you learned in prior courses in statistics or quantitative methods, discuss some analytical approaches that organizations can use for analyzing performance data.
13. How does the adoption of a Six Sigma approach within an organization change the amount and types of data that may be gathered routinely, as well as for specific projects?
14. A large hospital identified the following strategic priorities:

    Patient accessibility
    Patient safety
    Clinical excellence
    Few hassles for patients and families
    Workforce well-being
    Family-centered care
    Operational efficiency

    Suggest some measures that link to these strategic priorities. You might wish to do some research on how hospitals measure patient safety and clinical excellence.

Problems

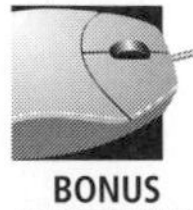

Note: Data sets for many problems in this chapter are available in the Excel workbook *C8Data* on the Premium website that accompanies this chapter. Click the appropriate worksheet tab as noted in the problem (e.g. *Prob. 8-2, etc.*) to access the data. Also, see the Bonus Materials folder for this chapter for information about analyzing quality costs.)

1. The rate of baggage mishandling reported by the Department of Transportation in the United States was 3.75 per 1,000 passengers. If the average number of checked bags per passenger is now 1.3, how many defects per million

opportunities (DPMO) does this represent? How does this compare with the rate given in the chapter—better or worse?

2. Analyze the cost data in the Excel workbook *C8Data* for the Costcutin Co. What percent of sales are represented by each category of cost? What are the implications of these data for management?
3. Imagimatrix, which designs prototype components for the computer gaming industry, has begun a quality program. About a year ago, for the first time, they began to measure quality costs. They were so shocked by their initial figure of 60 percent internal and external failure costs that they immediately launched a Six Sigma quality improvement effort. The percentage of total quality costs recently, after six months of improvements for the firm, are distributed as follows:

Prevention	20%
Appraisal	33%
Internal failure	32%
External failure	15%

   What conclusions can you reach from these data?
4. Analyze the quality cost information by computing a sales dollar base index for Farwest Sales, Inc., in the Excel workbook *C8Data*. Prepare a memo to management explaining your findings and conclusions.
5. Analyze the cost data in the Excel workbook *C8Data* for Product B. What are the implications of these data for management? Chart these data. Calculate the quality indices as a relationship to the cost of sales. How do these data differ from those given in Problem 2?
6. Analyze the cost data from ABEC Corp in the Excel workbook *C8Data*. What are the implications of these data for management? How do these data differ from those in problem 5?
7. D.B. Smith Company recycles computers. It buys them and salvages parts and materials from the obsolete systems. It considers that it has done a "quality" job if it can salvage 60 percent of the "book value" of equipment that it buys. The book value of a particular lot that it bought was $1,700,000. What conclusions can be drawn from the cost data incurred in processing the lot, as found in the Excel workbook *C8Data*? Customer returns are simply scrapped and replaced. Be sure and specify your assumptions about categories of quality costs.
8. Prepare a chart showing the different quality cost categories and percentages for the Great Press Printing Company. See the data in the Excel workbook *C8Data*.
9. Compute a labor cost base index for Miami Valley Aircraft Service Co. to analyze the quality cost information and prepare a memo to management explaining your conclusions. See the data in the Excel workbook *C8Data*.
10. The cost of quality data collected at the installment loan department of the McCutcheon Bank can be found in the Excel workbook *C8Data*. Classify these data into the appropriate cost of quality categories and analyze the results. What suggestions would you make to management?
11. Repack Solutions, Inc. has a distribution center in Cincinnati where it receives and breaks down bulk orders from suppliers' factories, and ships out products to retail customers. Prepare a chart showing the different quality cost categories and percentages for the company's quality costs that were incurred over the past year. See the Excel workbook *C8Data* for the data.
12. Use Pareto analysis to investigate the quality losses at Nosoco Paper Mill. What conclusions do you reach? See the Excel workbook *C8Data* for the data.

13. Given the cost elements in the Excel workbook *C8Data*, determine the total percentage in each of the four major quality cost categories for the HiTeck Tool Company.
14. Worldwide Metrology Repairs, Inc. has a thriving business repairing and upgrading high-technology measuring instruments. The costs of quality that they have collected over the past year can be found in the Excel workbook *C8Data*. Use Pareto analysis to investigate their quality losses and to suggest which areas they should address first in an effort to improve their quality.
15. Use Pareto analysis to investigate the quality losses at Beechcom Software Corp. using the data in the Excel workbook *C8Data*. What conclusions do you reach?
16. The Hausburg Company has collected information about customer behavior and lost sales as a result of service problems. They estimate that, given the current level of service and historical data on complaints, the company will lose a total of 900,000 sales from customers who experience problems over a five-year period.
    a. At an average of $20 profit per sale, what is the average lost profit per year?
    b. Suppose the company can reduce its annual number of lost sales by 10 percent by investing $300,000 to enhance its service through training and better technology. How much profit can be earned as a result? What is the return on this quality investment?
17. Excelsior Inn, a medium-sized hotel (approximately 450 rooms) has gathered a considerable amount of data and is trying to estimate its return on quality. The site manager is interested in determining what the return would be if she invested in additional service. She has evidence that additional effort in making sure that rooms (in particular, the bathroom) are clean will result in increases in market share, which can easily be translated into dollars of profit. In the table, found in the Excel workbook *C8Data*, are data taken from a pilot study where various amounts of additional labor, above the present standard, were applied to room cleaning. These have been expressed in annual dollar amounts, based on wages and fringe benefits of current employees servicing the rooms. Customers who stayed in those rooms were then surveyed to determine their levels of satisfaction/dissatisfaction. Percentages of dissatisfied customers have been matched with the annual dollars of improvement efforts from the study.
    a. Using linear regression (for example, the Data Analysis tool or Add Trendline option in Excel), determine the equation that can be used to estimate the reduction in customer dissatisfaction, based on additional cleaning effort. What would be the appropriate level of effort to apply, based on your calculations?
    b. If each point of market share increase brings in approximately $600,000 of profit per year, and the cost per year is your suggested investment in improvement (from part a above). What would be the return on quality (improvement), based on a three year discounted cash flow at 10 percent of the investment costs, if the site manager estimated that she could realize a 2.5 percent increase in market share?

Projects, Etc.

1. Interview managers at a local airline, hospital, governmental agency, or police department to determine what types of performance measures or indicators they use. Can you construct a balanced scorecard for them?
2. Many restaurants and hotels use "tabletop" customer satisfaction surveys. Find several of these from local businesses. What internal performance indicators might be good leading indicators for the customer satisfaction items in the surveys?
3. Interview managers at a local company to identify the key factors that drive their business. What performance measures or indicators does the company use? Are these indicators consistent with their business factors?
4. Interview managers at a local company to determine which, if any, of the leading practices described in this chapter they follow. What advice would you give them?
5. Using as many measures in Figure 8.3 as you can, draw a diagram similar (but with more detail) to the IBM Rochester model in Figure 8.2 showing leading/lagging and cause-and-effect relationships among these measures.
6. Interview some local quality or production managers to determine whether their companies conduct cost-of-quality evaluations. If they do, how do they use the information? What types of quality costs do they measure?
7. Design a spreadsheet template for conducting quality cost analyses and apply it to problems in this chapter.
8. Interview Black Belts or Project Champions in an organization that has adopted a Six Sigma approach. Discuss their requirements for data and find out how easy or difficult it is to gather the data needed to support their teams and recommendations to management.

Cases

Additional cases, including Baldrige assessment cases, are available in the Bonus Materials Folder for this chapter on the Premium website.

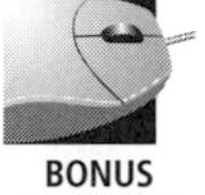

Skyhigh Airlines

Skyhigh Airlines is a small regional airline that was started by Tex Weston in West Texas in the 1980s. Tex was the first regional airline CEO to come up with the idea of developing a strategic partnership with a major carrier, which provided stability and a guaranteed market. In turn, Skyhigh developed a reputation for high reliability, on-time arrivals and departures, and safety.

Like all domestic air carriers, Skyhigh's fleet must be certificated by the Federal Aviation Agency (FAA), in order to fly domestic airline routes. There are required avionic systems on board all their airplanes, which must be inspected periodically, according to FAA regulations. An avionic system normally includes several electronic "boxes" containing components essential to safe navigation of the aircraft. Some of these boxes are located in the cockpit, whereas other parts of the system are located in the tail of the plane, with cables connecting the components. There are five components in the avionic system on the typical airplane in Skyhigh's fleet.

A critical avionics maintenance procedure at Skyhigh Airlines requires the assignment of five workers on each avionics crew for a full eight hours per day. All crew members are cross-trained and can work on any tasks necessary to complete the procedure. There are five tasks (A through E) that must be carried out, sequentially, in order to complete the procedure. Each task requires five labor hours to complete.

Because of tight spaces in the aircraft, only three people can work on task A at the same time, while the remaining two are idle; four people can work on task B, with one idle; all five people can work on task C at the same time; two people can work on task D, with three idle; and four people can work on task E, with one idle.

Assignment

Address the questions below, and after doing so, state the general conclusions you can reach, and what advice would you give to management in a brief report.

1. Because each task requires five person hours to complete, determine how much elapsed time will it take to complete the entire procedure, considering that work on the next task cannot begin until work on the previous task is completed?
2. What percent of time will be productive and what percent will be wasted on each task?
3. What is the rolled throughput yield (RTY) of the procedure?
4. If a tool could be developed which would allow all five workers to work on task D at the same time, how would that effect the RTY of the procedure?

Coyote Community College

Coyote Community College is a comprehensive, two-year public college that serves and strengthens the greater Albuquerque, New Mexico, community by providing postsecondary education and learning opportunities to all who want to identify and develop their abilities and interests. Since 1968, Coyote's programs and services have been providing accessible, affordable, high-quality higher education opportunities in a learning environment that encourages challenging, innovative teaching methods and delivery systems that enhance student learning. Coyote is a commuter college with a main campus in downtown Albuquerque and two branch campuses: one located in Bernalillo, 20 miles north of Albuquerque, and the other in Armijo, southeast of downtown Albuquerque. The campus in Albuquerque accounts for 44 percent of Coyote's enrollment, the Bernalillo campus accounts for 25 percent, and the Armijo campus accounts for 31 percent.

Coyote's innovative, community-centered educational programs are designed to meet a variety of academic, career, and personal educational goals. Program offerings fall into one of three general areas: (1) General Education, University Transfer Education, and Developmental Education; (2) Workforce Development, Certificate Programs, and Continuing Education; and (3) Community Education and Outreach. The majority of these programs lead to the award of diplomas, degrees, or certificates. Coyote also provides high-quality student support services and resources in collaboration with community agencies to enable students to formulate their goals and pursue them realistically. These services include academic and occupational counseling, job and educational placement services, assistance in obtaining financial aid, and special needs programs.

Programs and offerings in the area of General Education, University Transfer Education, and Developmental Education enable students to achieve academic and personal goals, enter the job market, or, in some cases, to successfully transfer to four-year colleges and universities. Coyote offers Associate of Arts (AA) degrees in liberal arts, business administration, education, hotel and restaurant management, computer science, pre-engineering, and biological sciences. AA degrees are intended for students transferring to four-year colleges and universities such that no remedial coursework is required upon transfer. Occupational programs in technical, vocational, and paraprofessional fields lead to an Associate of Science (AS) degree or a certificate. Occupational programs also provide retraining and upgrading of skills in these fields so that students are qualified to meet current needs of the labor market. AS degrees are generally not intended for transfer to four-year institutions. Students who do transfer with AS degrees are required to take additional remedial courses as required by each specific degree program. Students may select from 30 occupational programs, including computer technology, computer applications, day care management, nursing, retailing, computer-aided design/computer-aided manufacturing (CAD/CAM), graphic design technology, biotechnology, heating-ventilating-air conditioning (HVAC), hydrological technology, and contract administration.

In the area of Developmental Education, Coyote offers General Education Development (GED) preparation courses, courses in English as a Second Language (ESL), and strong remedial courses in math, reading, and writing. Sixty percent of all Coyote students enrolled in traditional college courses enroll in at least one remedial course, and 15 percent enroll in an ESL course.

In the area of Workforce Development, Certificate Programs, and Continuing Education, Coyote provides custom-designed, on-site training courses and services that meet the needs of local businesses. In partnership with several local employers, Coyote offers contract training for computer networking technicians, water management specialists, office managers, contract administrators, and prison guards. Coyote also offers intensive ESL and remedial English and math courses under contract. In addition, Coyote offers a wide variety of short-term certification courses, such as Network Administrator, Network Engineer, Advanced Office Automation, Systems Engineer, Quality Auditor, Purchasing Manager, and Certified Nursing Assistant, to the general public and by contract. Continuing Education programs address those students who wish to improve professional skills, acquire new skills, or expand their fields of knowledge and general interest.

In the area of Community Education and Outreach, Coyote provides programs and community services that offer multicultural, recreational, and community development activities to meet the needs of lifelong learners. These activities, which include a Women in Transition program, the Coyote Cultural Center, an Elder Learning Center, and a day care center, also encourage the use of community college facilities and services by all citizens of the community for educational and cultural purposes.

Students at Coyote are divided among (1) those enrolled in traditional college credit degree curricula, (2) those enrolled in noncredit contract training and in short-term certificate courses, and (3) those involved in the community outreach programs. Because of demands placed on their resources and time by employers, family, and others, students tend to pursue the education intermittently, and approximately 75 percent of students attend part-time.

Coyote employs 280 full-time faculty, 830 adjunct (part-time) faculty, 40 administrators, and 150 support staff. The faculty are members of the National Education Association union. Fifty percent of full-time faculty hold a master's degree, 40 percent hold doctoral degrees, and 10 percent hold bachelor's degrees. Adjunct faculty, many of whom are working in the field in which they teach, hold at least a bachelor's degree. Seventy-five percent of the administrators hold a master's degree or higher.

Although Coyote's primary stakeholders are its students, key stakeholders also include college faculty and staff, four-year colleges and universities to which Coyote's students transfer, local employers, the New Mexico State Board of Community Colleges, Coyote's Board of Governors (BOG), and the surrounding community at large, including local taxpayers. The requirements of the primary stakeholders are shown in Figure 8.20.

Coyote's oversight body is the BOG. The members of Coyote's BOG are elected by voters in seven geographical districts within the two-county region the college serves. Funding for programs and for most construction and equipment comes from a property tax levy in the two-county region and annual appropriations by the New Mexico legislature. Coyote's BOG approves spending over $50,000, intergovernmental agreements, bond spending, building improvements, and construction. The BOG also provides continuous evaluation and assessment of Coyote's policies, procedures, and practices to ensure that the college is fulfilling its mission and achieving its purposes. In addition, Coyote has a private nonprofit foundation for private contributions, which are increasing every year.

Figure 8.20 Stakeholders and Requirements

Stakeholder	Requirements
Students	Acquisition of needed skills and knowledge, learning skill development, accessibility, flexibility in scheduling, affordability, increased capacity for self-directed learning, responsive services, effective curriculum
Faculty/Staff	Receive professional development, feedback, support, recognition
Four-year colleges and universities	Strong student academic foundations compatible with higher learning
Employers	Current/future employees' acquisition of needed skills/knowledge/ attitude, cost-efficient learning, innovative problem-solving and team skills, leadership skills, computer proficiency, professional proficiency
SBCC and BOG	Return for dollar
Taxpayers and community	Fulfillment of education needs that are not met by other institutions, support to region/state, efficient expenditure of funding

Coyote is accredited by the North Central Association of Colleges and Schools (NCACS), and 12 individual programs are certified or accredited by other appropriate organizations. Coyote was reviewed by the NCACS in 1998 and is scheduled for another review in 2008. Coyote is also responsive to a variety of federal, state, and local regulations, including the Occupational Safety and Health Administration (OSHA) requirements, Environmental Protection Agency (EPA) regulations, federal and state financial aid regulations, and affirmative action guidelines. Coyote complies with the Americans with Disabilities Act (ADA). Coyote is also proud of its partnerships with the colleges and universities to which the majority of its credit students transfer. Faculty members from these universities serve on Coyote's Curriculum Advisory Teams. In addition, articulation agreements with all four-year institutions in the region are in place for all of Coyote's university transfer programs (AA degrees), as well as for more than 50 percent of the occupational degree programs.

A key differentiator of online programs offered by out-of-state colleges is convenience. Students can attend online courses any time of the day or night to accommodate their busy and sometimes changing schedules. Coyote is responding to this need by developing both online and video-based programs. In addition, Coyote's key differentiator is that it focuses on preparing graduates to be successful in the local community. Input of local employers in the planning process, new program design, and student internships enables Coyote's graduates to find desirable jobs in the local community more easily and to succeed at those jobs. Coyote's growing, individualized, technology-based delivery of educational programs with related support services (individualized program design and certification), which is targeted to employed adult students with needs for specific skill development, is another important competitive advantage. Planning is focused on providing learning excellence through use of state-of-the-art learning technologies to expand the off-campus student population while retaining the current levels of on-campus students.

The principal factors that determine competitive success include accessibility, flexibility in scheduling, affordability, ability to offer high value at a low cost, the effectiveness of the curriculum, the time to complete programs, and the range of programs offered. Dr. Gayle Brooks, who previously served as Deputy Provost at McMoto Industrial University, was selected as Coyote's president in 1992, with a mandate to reverse a six-year-long trend of declining enrollment and diminishing student success. In the last eight years, Coyote has shown steady increases in enrollment and in student success as judged by student employment rates and acceptance rates by four-year colleges and universities. The foundation of this turnaround was the establishment of a common mission, vision, and values. These provide continuing direction for the college and drive specific goals to stretch Coyote's capabilities. In 1994, under the direction of Dr. Brooks, Coyote developed and adopted LEARN, a three-point philosophy of education. These points are:

- *Learning Excellence:* All aspects of the education process are learner-centered, and the needs of the learner are paramount. Recognition of the diversity of learning styles and rates of learning is fundamental. Technology is used as a tool to facilitate learning.
- *Assessment:* Assessment of learning is ongoing for both learners and learning facilitators. Technology is a tool to facilitate the assessment of processes associated with learning.
- *Recognizing Needs:* It is imperative to identify and respond to the needs of all of Coyote's stakeholders. Needs vary by stakeholder, as shown in Figure 8.20.

As a result of implementing LEARN, Coyote recently identified the following three key technology-based strategies designed to improve student learning and meet learner requirements. Each of these strategies is currently at different levels of implementation within the college:

1. *Incorporation of technologies into the traditional classroom:* In order to enhance student learning, instructors are being encouraged to incorporate multimedia into traditional delivery techniques.
2. *Technology mediation allowing individually paced learning:* Computer-based instruction allows learners to begin precisely at their current level of knowledge and progress through structured materials at their own pace. Monthly start dates of sequenced courses allow students to proceed to the next course when ready, with no delays or potential loss of learning due to waiting.
3. *Distance learning delivery methods:* A variety of technologies allow Coyote to meet learner needs. An interactive video system (teleclasses) ties the three campuses together to decrease the need for students to drive from one campus to another. This system also allows Coyote to offer some traditionally low enrollment courses that meet specific student needs, including upper-level foreign language and math classes. Online courses offered via the Internet and video-based courses (telecourses) offered via cable television and video cassette checkout will meet the needs of students with difficult schedules and geographic constraints.

The leadership at Coyote wants to develop a balanced scorecard. To customize it for the educational environment, they renamed the categories as

1. Funder/Financial Perspective
2. Student/Participant Perspective
3. Internal Process Perspective
4. Innovation and Resource Perspective

Based on the description of this college and its environment, what specific types of measures should they include in each of these perspectives of the balanced scorecard? How would they be measured?

Novel Connect: Identifying Key Performance Measures

BONUS MATERIALS

The complete Novel Connect case study, a fictitious example of a Baldrige application, can be found in the Baldrige Materials folder on the Premium website accompanying this book. Review the Organizational Profile for Novel Connect and then their response to Category 7 of the Baldrige criteria (Business Results). After carefully analyzing the measures used in tracking their performance results in comparison with their vital organizational factors and strategic challenges, identify gaps in their performance measurement system. For example, what other measures might be relevant to managing their business that they have not reported? Are all measures reported appropriately segmented (for instance, by location, type of employee, type of customer, and so on)? Summarize your findings as a consultant to the organization in a well-written report to the company president.

Novel Connect: Measurement, Analysis, and Knowledge Management

The complete Novel Connect case study, a fictitious example of a Baldrige application, can be found in the Baldrige Materials folder on the Premium website accompanying this book. If you have not read the Organizational Profile yet, please do so first.

Examine their response to Category 4 in the context of the leading practices described in this chapter (you need not consider the actual Baldrige criteria for this activity). What are their strengths? What are their weaknesses and opportunities for improvement? What specific advice, including useful tools and techniques that might help them, would you suggest?

NOTES

1. Jerry Useem, "Boeing Versus Boeing," *Fortune,* October 2, 2000, 148–160.
2. D. Osborne and T. Gaebler, *Reinventing Government: How the Entrepreneurial Spirit Is Transforming the Public Sector* (Reading, MA: Addison-Wesley Publishing Co., 1992).
3. Noriaki Kano, "A Perspective on Quality Activities in American Firms," *California Management Review,* Spring 1993, 12–31.
4. Douglas W. Hubbard, *How to Measure Anything,* Hoboken, NJ: John Wiley & Sons, 2007.
5. Kicab Casteñeda-Méndez, "Performance Measurement in Health Care," *Quality Digest,* May 1999, 33–36.
6. Laura Struebing, "Measuring for Excellence," *Quality Progress,* December 1996, 25–28.
7. Robert S. Kaplan and David P. Norton, "The Balanced Scorecard—Measures That Drive Performance," *Harvard Business Review,* January/February 1992, 71–79. © 1992 by the President and Fellows of Harvard College; all rights reserved.
8. Ernest C. Huge, "Measuring and Rewarding Performance," in Ernst & Young Quality Consulting Group, *Total Quality: An Executive's Guide for the 1990s* (Homewood IL: Irwin, 1990).
9. New Corporate Performance Measures, A Research Report, Report Number 1118-95-RR, New York: The Conference Board, 1995.
10. Robert S. Kaplan and David P. Norton, *The Balanced Scorecard* (Boston, MA: Harvard Business School Press, 1996), 1.
11. Consult Schneiderman's website, http://www.schneiderman.com for many interesting papers about the history, design, and use of balanced scorecards and other aspects of measurement.
12. John Geanuracos and Ian Meiklejohn, *Performance Measurement: The New Agenda; Using Non-Financial Indicators to Improve Profitability* (London: Business Intelligence, 1993).
13. Roberto Antonio Martins, "Use of Performance Measurement Systems: Some Thoughts Toward a Comprehensive Approach," Second International Conference on Performance Measurement, University of Cambridge, July 2000.
14. Arthur M. Schneiderman, "Why Balanced Scorecards Fail," *Journal of Strategic Performance Measurement* 3, no. 1 (January 1999), 6–11.
15. Blan Godfrey, "Future Trends: Expansion of Quality Management Concepts, Methods, and Tools to All Industries," *Quality Observer* 6, no. 9 (September 1997) 40–43, 46.
16. Mark Graham Brown, *Keeping Score: Using the Right Metrics to Drive World-Class Performance* (New York: Quality Resources, 1996).
17. "First National Bank of Chicago," *Profiles in Quality* (Boston, MA: Allyn and Bacon, 1991).
18. Justin Martin, "Are You as Good as You Think You Are?" *Fortune,* September 30, 1996, 142–152.
19. Glenn E. Hayes and Harry G. Romig, *Modern Quality Control* (Encino, CA: Benziger, Bruce & Glencoe, Inc., 1977).
20. Michael S. Pestorius, "Applying Six Sigma to Sales and Marketing," *Quality Progress,* January 2007, 19–24.
21. U.S. Office of Management and Budget, "How to Develop Quality Measures That Are Useful in Day-to-Day Measurement," U.S. Department of Commerce, National Technical Information Service (January 1989).
22. Robert I. Wise, "A Method for Aligning Process Level and Strategy Level Performance Metrics," American Society for Quality, 11th Annual Quality Management Conference.
23. Marcelo Telles de Menezes and Roberto Antonio Martins, "Performance Measurement After ERP Implementation: Some Empirical Evidences," *Proceedings,* Third World Congress on Intelligent Manufacturing Processes & Systems, Cambridge, MA, June 2000, 146–151.
24. David A. Collier, *The Service/Quality Solution* (Milwaukee, WI: ASQC Quality Press, and Burr Ridge, IL: Richard D. Irwin, 1994).
25. Steve Hoisington and Earl Naumann, "The Loyalty Elephant," *Quality Progress,* February 2003, pp. 33–41.
26. Reprinted with permission from Steven H. Hoisington and Tse-Hsi Huang, "Customer Satisfaction and Market Share: An Empirical Case Study of IBM's AS/400 Division," in Earl Naumann and Steven H. Hoisington (eds.) *Customer-Centered Six Sigma.* Copyright © 2001 American Society for Quality, Quality Press, Milwaukee, WI. No further distribution allowed without permission.
27. "Coaxing Meaning Out of Raw Data," *Business Week,* February 3, 1997, 134–138.
28. Mercy Health System 2007 Malcolm Baldrige National Quality Program Application.

29. Frank M. Gryna, "Quality Costs," in *Juran's Quality Control Handbook*, 4th ed. (New York: McGraw-Hill, 1988).

30. The reader is referred to the text by Cooper and Kaplan (1991) cited in the bibliography for a thorough treatment of this topic.

31. ASQ Quality Costs Committee, "Profiting from Quality in the Service Arena," *Quality Progress*, May 1999, 81–84.

32. R. T. Rust, A. J. Zahorik, and T. L. Keiningham, "Return on Quality (ROQ): Making Service Quality Financially Accountable," *Journal of Marketing* 59, no. 2 (April 1995), 58–70.

33. Roland T. Rust, Timothy Keiningham, Stephen Clemens, and Anthony Zahorik, "Return on Quality at Chase Manhattan Bank," *Interfaces* 29, no. 2 (March/April 1999), 62–72.

34. Larry English, "Data Quality: Meeting Customer Needs," *Data Management Review*, November 1996, 44–51, 86.

35. Ethan I. Davis, "Quality Service at The Prudential," in Jay W. Spechler, *When America Does It Right* (Norcross, GA: Industrial Engineering and Management Press, 1988), 224–232.

36. H. James Harrington, "Creating Organizational Excellence—Part Four," *Quality Digest*, April 2003, 14.

37. Comment made at the Knowledge Management World Summit, San Francisco, January 11, 1999; cited in R. Sabherwal and S. Sabherwal, "Knowledge Management Using Information Technology: Determinants of Short-Term Impact on Firm Value," *Decision Sciences*, 36, 4, 2005, 531–567.

38. Robert J. Heibeler, "Benchmarking Knowledge Management," *Strategy and Leadership* 24, no. 2 (March/April, 1996), as cited in Verna Allee, *The Knowledge Evolution: Expanding Organizational Intelligence* (Boston: Butterworth-Heinemann, 1997), 8.

39. Chuck Cobb, "Knowledge Management and Quality Systems," The 54th Annual Quality Congress *Proceedings*, 2000, American Society for Quality, 276–287.

40. 2007 Premier Baldrige Application Summary.

41. Carla O'Dell and C. Jackson Grayson, "Identifying and Transferring Internal Best Practices," APQC White Paper, 2000; http://www.apqc.org/free/whitepapers/cmifwp/index.htm.

42. Mohamed Zairi and John Whymark, "The transfer of best practices: How to build a culture of benchmarking and continuous learning—Part 1," *Benchmarking: An International Journal* 7, no. 1 (2000), 62–78.

43. This discussion is adapted from Michael J. English and William H. Baker, Jr. "Rapid Knowledge Transfer: The Key to Success," *Quality Progress*, February 2006, pp. 41–48.

44. Cobb (see note 39).

45. Brian Swayne and Brent Harder, "Where Has All the Magic Gone?" *Six Sigma Forum Magazine* 2, no. 3 (May 2003), 22–32.

46. George Byrne and Bob Norris, "Drive Baldrige Level Performance," *Six Sigma Forum Magazine* 2, no. 3 (May 2003), 13–21.

47. Adapted from Nicholas J. Mathys and Kenneth R. Thompson, "Using the Balanced Scorecard: Lessons Learned from the U.S. Postal Service and the Defense Finance and Accounting Service."

48. We wish to gratefully acknowledge Ms. Julie Coughlin of Convergys for providing this case.

Chapter 9

Leading, Building, and Sustaining Performance Excellence

Outline

Quality Profiles: Saint Luke's Hospital of Kansas City and American Electric Power
Leadership for Performance Excellence
- Leadership Systems
- Leadership, Governance, and Societal Responsibilities

Leadership Theory and Practice
- Contemporary and Emerging Leadership Theories
- New Perspectives on the Practice of Leadership

Building Performance Excellence in Organizations
- Implementing ISO 9000, Baldrige, and Six Sigma
- Organizational Culture and Performance Excellence
- Changing Organizational Culture
- Barriers to Change
- Best Practices

The Journey Toward Performance Excellence
- The Life Cycle of Quality Initiatives
- Organizational Learning
- Self-Assessment

Leadership in the Baldrige Criteria, ISO 9000, and Six Sigma
A View Toward the Future
Summary of Key Points and Terminology
Quality in Practice: Leadership Changes at Alcoa
Quality in Practice: Merging Divergent Quality Systems at Honeywell
Review Questions
Discussion Questions
Projects, Etc.
Cases Distinguished Ad Agency
Novel Connect—Leadership
The Parable of the Green Lawn
The Yellow Brick Road to Quality

Although Hyundai Motor Co. dominated the Korean car market in its early days, it had a poor reputation for quality overseas, with doors that didn't fit properly, frames that rattled, and engines that delivered puny acceleration. And the company was losing money. When Chung Mong Koo became CEO in 1999, he visited Hyundai's plant at Ulsan. To the shock of his employees, who had rarely set eyes on a CEO, Chung strode onto the factory floor and demanded a peek under the hood of a Sonata sedan. He didn't like what he saw: loose wires, tangled hoses, bolts painted four different colors—the kind of sloppiness you'd never see in a Japanese car. On the spot, he instructed the plant chief to paint all bolts and screws black and ordered workers not to release a car unless all was orderly under the hood. "You've got to get back to basics. The only way we can survive is to raise our quality to Toyota's level," he fumed. In addition to investing heavily in research and development, he created a quality control czar, who studied quality manuals of U.S. and Japanese automakers and developed one for the company, making it clear who is responsible for each manufacturing step, what outcome is required, and who checks and confirms performance levels. The next year, U.S. sales rose by 42 percent, and Hyundai is now recognized as one of the leading auto companies in the world.[1]

Building and sustaining performance excellence requires effective leadership, a commitment to change and long-term sustainability, the adoption of sound practices and implementation strategies, and continual organizational learning.

The principles of total quality we introduced in Chapter 1—focus on the customer, involve everyone, and continuously improve—are simple to understand and represent common sense. Yet many organizations have experienced great difficulty in implementing them. As the example from Hyundai suggests, building quality and performance excellence into an organization requires strong and committed leadership and the adoption of the right tools and approaches. It may also require significant changes in organizational design, processes, and culture. Change has always been a stumbling block for many organizations, and researchers have noted that upwards of 70 percent of all change initiatives fail.

One of the most important roles of leadership is to build and sustain the organization for the long run. Recall Deming's Chain Reaction (Figure 3.1) that argued that quality leads to keeping companies in business and creating more jobs. As one professional observed, managers manage for the present; leaders lead for the future. To sustain performance excellence demands continual learning and adaption to the changing global business landscape. An important element of sustainability is ensuring future leadership; thus the development of future leaders and a formal succession plan are vital.

We emphasize that the journey is not easy, yet many organizations—large and small, for-profit and not-for-profit—do it successfully (see the *Quality Profiles*). In this chapter, we focus on the role of leadership for guiding organizations through the process of creating a culture for performance excellence, and discuss effective approaches for managing change and long-term sustainability.

Sustainability *refers to an organization's ability to address current needs and have the agility and management skills and structure to prepare successfully for the future, including preparedness for emergencies.*

Quality Profiles: Saint Luke's Hospital of Kansas City and American Electric Power

Saint Luke's Hospital (SLH) is the largest hospital in the Kansas City, Mo., metropolitan area, employing 3,186 staff and 500 physicians. It is a not-for-profit comprehensive teaching and referral health care organization that provides 24-hour coverage in every health care discipline. SLH is driven by its vision, "The Best Place to Get Care, The Best Place to Give Care," and its core values of Quality/Excellence, Customer Focus, Resource Management, and Teamwork.

Saint Luke's "Leadership for Performance Excellence + Model" captures all of the elements that drive its focus on performance improvement and excellence, including the strategic planning and performance management process, process improvement model, and a commitment to excellence assessment model based on the seven Baldrige performance excellence categories. Saint Luke's vision, mission, core values, and strategy sit at the top of the model and influence all of the organization's plans and processes. A robust strategic planning approach consists of three phases and seven steps that integrate direction setting, strategy development and deployment, financial planning, and plan management. At a series of retreats, the leadership team develops strategy and uses a 90-day action planning process to deploy the strategy to all departments. The balanced scorecard process produces a measurement system that aligns all departments with the strategy and ensures the proper focus in key performance areas throughout the organization.

A highly empowered, high-performing workforce is key to Saint Luke's success. To ensure that everyone is in tune with the hospital's focus, all employees take part in the Performance Management Process. The process helps employees develop action plans and goals that are aligned with the organization's strategy and core values and identify personal commitments which contribute to SLH's values. An independent study by the National Research Corporation shows that patients believe SLH delivers the best quality health care and has the best doctors and the best nurses of the 21 facilities in the market area. In 2002, Consumer's Checkbook, a consumer education organization, ranked SLH 35th in the nation out of 4,500 hospitals evaluated. Saint Luke's received a Baldrige Award in 2003.

The Conesville, Ohio, plant of American Electric Power (AEP) was a recipient of Ohio's Governor's Award for Excellence, the state equivalent of the Baldrige Award, in 2001. The plant is one of the largest in Ohio and one of the most complex in the United States. The plant's difficult journey to performance excellence began with a major reorganization when the plant was forced to cut 25 percent of its workforce. In a two-day meeting in 1995, amidst a tense and emotional atmosphere, new leaders outlined a mission, vision, and goals for the first time, making trust and caring the principal core values. The old culture that was characterized by a conservative, top-down leadership style, functional silos, an adversarial unionized workforce, and a highly political atmosphere, had to be dismantled.

A leadership team, which included union representatives, was established, new employee development programs were created in an atmosphere of empowerment and learning, all with a new focus on external and internal customers. The cultural changes included an employee-developed behavior-based safety program, weekly newsletters, systems thinking, opening the books to all, improved manager communications, and solving problems internally rather than escalating grievances. In a few short years, the plant received the AFL-CIO National Labor-Management Award, grievances fell from 37 to zero, and it received national recognition for its school-to-work program. Coupled with a new performance management program, a balanced scorecard, and a process-focused management approach, the plant achieved record high production, a more than 100 percent increase in employee productivity, a 45 percent reduction in operation and maintenance costs, and greater than $5 million in process improvement savings.

Sources: Ohio Award for Excellence Governor's Award Winner presentation, and the Malcolm Baldrige National Quality Award, Profiles of Winners, National Institute of Standards and Technology, Department of Commerce.

LEADERSHIP FOR PERFORMANCE EXCELLENCE

***Leadership** is the ability to positively influence people and systems under one's authority so as to have a meaningful impact and achieve important results.*

The one thing that all quality experts agree on is that strong leadership, especially from senior managers, is absolutely necessary to develop and sustain a culture of quality and excellence.

Leadership for quality dates back to the early writings of Deming, Juran, and Crosby. Several of Deming's 14 Points (see Chapter 3) address leadership; for instance:

Point 1. Create and publish to all employees a statement of the aims and purposes of the company or other organization. The management must demonstrate constantly their commitment to this statement.

Point 7. Teach and institute leadership.

Point 12. Remove barriers that rob people of pride of workmanship.

Point 14. Take action to accomplish the transformation.

Leadership is the first category in the Baldrige framework, signifying its importance. As we pointed out in Chapter 4, strategy and leadership are closely linked. Strategic planning, providing a motivating environment in which work can take place in a productive and meaningful way, and assuring that performance excellence is continuously pursued are the essential tasks of organizational leaders. Nevertheless, a co-director of the Juran Center for Leadership in Quality at the University of Minnesota observed:

- Despite substantial efforts, only a few U.S. organizations have reached world-class excellence.
- Even fewer companies have sustained such excellence during changes in leadership.
- Most corporate quality failures rest with leadership.[2]

Clearly, leadership is not an easy task.

The Human Development and Leadership Division of the American Society for Quality has summarized six competencies for leadership based on more than 50 authors' thoughts on leadership.[3] These are:

- *Navigator:* Creates shared meaning and provides direction towards a vision, mission, goal or end-result. This competency may entail risk taking and requires constant evaluation of the operating environment to ensure progress in the appropriate direction is achieved.
- *Communicator:* Effectively listens and articulates messages to provide shared meaning. This competency involves the creation of an environment that reduces barriers and fosters open, honest and honorable communication.
- *Mentor:* Provides others with a role to guide their actions. This competency requires the development of personal relationships that help others develop trust, integrity, and ethical decision making.
- *Learner:* Continuously develops personal knowledge, skills, and abilities through formal study, experience, reflection, and recreation.
- *Builder:* Shapes processes and structures to allow for the achievement of goals and outcomes. This competency also entails assuming responsibility for ensuring necessary resources are available and the evaluation of processes to ensure effective resource use.
- *Motivator:* Influences others to take action in a desirable manner. This competency also includes the evaluation of people's actions to ensure they are performing consistently with the mission, goal, or end-result.

A collection of personal leadership characteristics underlie these six competencies:

1. *Accountability:* Taking responsibility for the organization, community, or self that the leader serves. This provides the means for measuring performance and dealing with performance that is not good.
2. *Courage:* The mental or moral strength to venture, persevere, and withstand danger, fear, or difficulty with a firmness of mind and will, allowing leaders to navigate into the unknown.
3. *Humility:* What gives excellent leaders their ability to mentor, communicate, and learn, and understand that they are servants of those that follow.

4. *Integrity:* The ability to discern what is right from wrong and commit to the right path.
5. *Creativity:* The ability to see possibilities, horizons, and futures that don't yet exist, enabling the leader to help create a shared vision.
6. *Perseverance:* Sticking to a task or purpose, no matter how hard or troublesome. This is vital to overcoming obstacles and motivating subordinates.
7. *Well-being:* The ability to stay healthy in both work and play, demonstrating the importance of being ready to implement leadership competencies when needed.

These characteristics provide the foundation for exercising the competencies. Many notable leaders, from presidents to CEOs have exhibited these characteristics.

These leadership competencies are reflected in the Leadership category of the Baldrige criteria, which are summarized in Table 9.1. Many examples demonstrate how these practices are accomplished. For example, senior leaders at Baptist Hospital, Inc. (BHI) organize all formal meeting agendas around or in reference to the expectations set forth its core strategies: People, Service, Quality, Financial, and Growth; and lead around the clock employee forums at least three times per year at each facility. These meetings reinforce its Mission, Values, and Vision as well as addressing goals and results. Senior leaders serve as role models and are held accountable for organizational performance excellence through a "No Excuses" policy. BHI's culture provides "open-door" access to everyone, including access to the president to discuss work design and improvement opportunities.

Table 9.1 Key Practices for Performance Excellence Leadership

- Set organizational vision and values and deploy them through the organization's leadership system, to the workforce, to key suppliers and partners, and to customers and other stakeholders as appropriate.
- Demonstrate a commitment to organizational values through personal actions.
- Promote an organizational environment that fosters, requires, and leads to legal and ethical behavior.
- Create a sustainable organization.
- Create an environment for organizational performance improvement, the accomplishment of the organization's mission and strategic objectives, innovation, competitive or role-model performance leadership, and organizational agility.
- Create an environment for organizational and workforce learning.
- Personally participate in succession planning and the development of future organizational leaders.
- Communicate with and engage the entire workforce.
- Encourage frank, two-way communication throughout the organization.
- Communicate key decisions.
- Take an active role in reward and recognition programs to reinforce high performance and a customer and business focus.
- Create a focus on action to accomplish the organization's objectives, improve performance, and attain the organization's vision.
- Review performance measures to inform them on needed actions.
- Create and balance value for customers and other stakeholders in their organizational performance expectations.
- Evaluate their own performance and use the results to improve their personal leadership effectiveness and that of the organization's leadership system.
- Contribute to supporting and strengthening key communities such as charitable organizations, education, and others.

In many organizations, CEOs lead quality training sessions, serve on quality improvement teams, work on projects that do not usually require top-level input, and personally visit customers. Senior managers at the former Texas Instruments Defense Systems & Electronics Group, for example, led 150 of 1,900 cross-functional teams. In small businesses, such as Marlow Industries, CEO and president Raymond Marlow chairs the TQM Council and has daily responsibility for quality-related matters. To help accomplish its goals, General Electric redefined its promotion standards around quality. In the new standards, managers are not considered for promotions, but face dismissal, unless they visibly demonstrate support for the company's Six Sigma quality strategy.[4]

Successful leaders continually promote their vision throughout the organization using many forms of communication: personal interaction, talks, newsletters, seminars, e-mail, and video. For example, senior leaders communicate Medrad's values, direction, and expectations to all employees through the President's monthly highlights, a memorandum that summarizes trends and performance on each of the five goals listed above and provides special recognition for teams and individuals. Other key communication methods include Quarterly Business Reviews (QBR), Quarterly Management Interaction (QMI) sessions, Quality Forums, advisory board and function leadership, cross-functional team participation, staff meetings, the performance management system, participation in training for new and existing employees, and the annual "all-employee" meetings.

At Park Place Lexus, a 2005 Baldrige recipient, senior leaders receive feedback through employee surveys, committee findings, self-assessments, external consultant input, and Organizational Excellence department input, and use it to create training and development plans such as better business skills or team building.

Leadership Systems

The ability to successfully perform the activities listed in Table 9.2 requires an effective leadership system. The **leadership system** refers to how leadership is exercised, formally and informally, throughout an organization. These elements include how key decisions are made, communicated, and carried out at all levels. The leadership system includes structures and mechanisms for decision making, selection and development of leaders and managers, and reinforcement of values, directions, and performance expectations. It builds loyalties and teamwork based upon shared values, encourages initiative and risk taking, and subordinates organization to purpose and function. An effective leadership system also includes mechanisms for leaders' self-examination and improvement.

An effective leadership system respects the capabilities and requirements of employees and other stakeholders, and sets high expectations for performance and performance improvements.

To illustrate these themes, the leadership system at Solar Turbines, Inc., shown in Figure 9.1, operates in three distinct, yet highly integrated modes. First, through a functional organizational structure led by the president's staff ("1" in Figure 9.1), Solar maintains a focus on functional excellence through the recruitment, hiring, development of critical skills, and the application of tools and common processes to continuously improve functional effectiveness. Second, three cross-functional leadership structures ("2" in the figure), comprised of managers and technical experts selected from multiple levels of the organization, facilitate companywide teamwork and decision making. This Expanded

Table 9.2 SolarTurbines, Inc., Committee Structure

Committee	Purpose	Conducted
Operations Council	Communicate business status, develop strategies and business plans	Biannually
Quality Council	Customer satisfaction, operational quality	Monthly
Sales and Operations Planning	Current and future performance to plan, supplier performance	Monthly
MRP II Steering Committee	Process improvement, benchmarking, teams, employee satisfaction, internal Baldrige assessments	Monthly
Products Committee	New product development, product strategy	Monthly
Education Steering Committee	Training and education, human resource development	Quarterly
Environmental Council	Environmental health, safety, products and processes	Quarterly
ERP/IT Council	Information technology planning and deployment, enterprise resource planning	Monthly
Audit Committee	Internal/external policy, regulatory compliance, and business controls	Quarterly
Ethics and Compliance Committee	Contract review, ethics, legal compliance, and oversight	Quarterly

Source: Reprinted with permission of SolarTurbines, Inc.

Figure 9.1 SolarTurbines, Inc. Leadership System

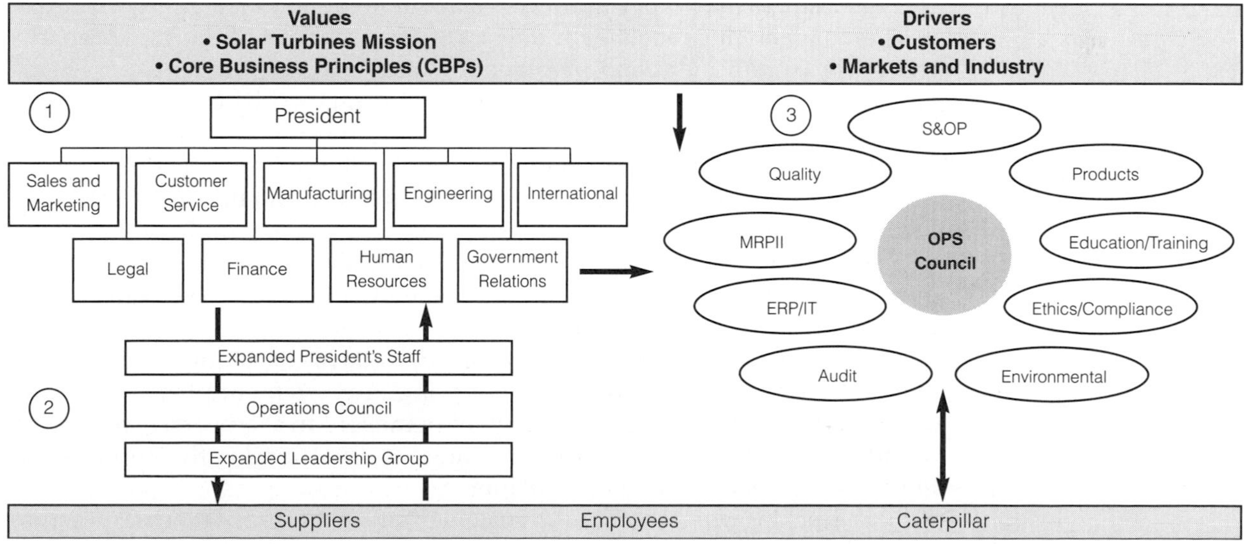

Source: Repritned with permission of SolarTurbines, Inc.

Leadership Team, consisting of the Operations Council (74 leaders from across the business) and the Expanded Leadership Group (more than 400 managers and supervisors), enables Solar to develop the next generation of business leaders. It also promotes rapid, effective communication among employees with cross-functional teaming occurring at all levels of the organization. The third leadership structure is the set of 10 interlocking committees ("3" in the figure) that coordinate and integrate all business areas. These committees, listed in Table 9.2, provide a mechanism to strengthen organizational learning through cross-functional sharing, company-wide communication, and strategic direction setting. Members of the president's staff chair key committees and, along with other senior business leaders, actively participate to provide guidance, learn, share, and support each other's decisions as a leadership team.[5]

In contrast to the large manufacturing environment at Solar, Stoner Incorporated (a very small chemical specialty manufacturing and sales company with less than 50 employees) has a six member senior leadership team empowered by the owner to manage and lead the company. The leadership team created and refined the Stoner Excellence System to define and communicate to all team members how the business is run. This is depicted by the diagram in Figure 9.2. The system is based on Leadership, Strategy, and Process, which are combined with an Assess/Improve/Implement continuous improvement approach. Stakeholder value is at the center of the system to characterize the main focus on the customer. Stoner's leadership approach is built on (1) leadership at all levels, (2) worker leaders, and (3) strong fundamental leadership skills based on Stephen Covey's Seven Habits of Highly Effective People.

The use of steering teams of senior managers is prevalent in many leadership systems. Such teams assume many responsibilities such as incorporating total quality principles into the company's strategic planning process and coordinating the overall effort. At AT&T, the steering team is characterized by several essential elements.[6]

- *Leadership:* Promoting and articulating the quality vision, communicating responsibilities and expectations for management action, aligning the business management process with the quality approach, maintaining high visibility for commitment and involvement, and ensuring that business-wide support is available in the form of education, consulting, methods, and tools.
- *Planning:* Planning strategic quality goals, understanding basic customer needs and business capabilities, developing long-term goals and near-term priorities, formulating human resource goals and policies, understanding employees' perceptions about quality and work, ensuring that all employees have the opportunity and skills to participate, and aligning reward and recognition systems to support the quality approach.
- *Implementation:* Forming key business process teams, chartering teams to manage and improve these processes, reviewing improvement plans, providing resources for improvement, enlisting all managers in the process, reviewing quality plans of major organizational units, and working with suppliers and business partners in joint quality planning.
- *Review:* Tracking progress through customer satisfaction and internal measures of quality, monitoring progress in attaining improvement objectives, celebrating successes, improving the quality system through auditing and identifying improvement opportunities, planning improvements, and validating the impact of improvements.

Figure 9.2 Stoner Business Excellence System

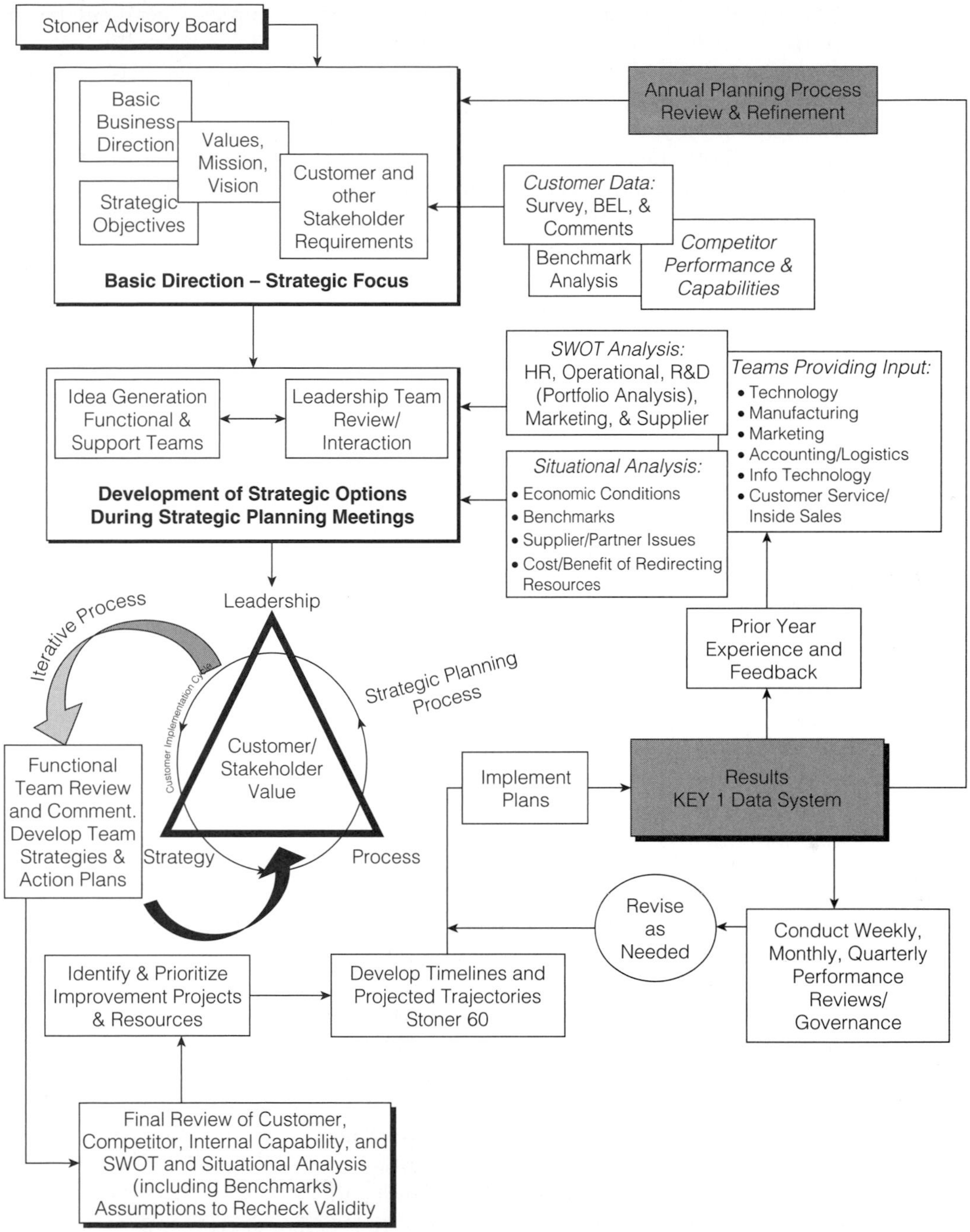

Stoner Advisory Board

Basic Business Direction

Values, Mission, Vision

Strategic Objectives

Customer and other Stakeholder Requirements

Basic Direction – Strategic Focus

Annual Planning Process Review & Refinement

Customer Data: Survey, BEL, & Comments

Benchmark Analysis

Competitor Performance & Capabilities

Idea Generation Functional & Support Teams

Leadership Team Review/ Interaction

Development of Strategic Options During Strategic Planning Meetings

SWOT Analysis: HR, Operational, R&D (Portfolio Analysis), Marketing, & Supplier

Teams Providing Input:

- Technology
- Manufacturing
- Marketing
- Accounting/Logistics
- Info Technology
- Customer Service/ Inside Sales

Situational Analysis:

- Economic Conditions
- Benchmarks
- Supplier/Partner Issues
- Cost/Benefit of Redirecting Resources

Iterative Process

Leadership

Customer Implementation Cycle

Strategic Planning Process

Customer/ Stakeholder Value

Strategy

Process

Prior Year Experience and Feedback

Functional Team Review and Comment. Develop Team Strategies & Action Plans

Implement Plans

Results KEY 1 Data System

Revise as Needed

Conduct Weekly, Monthly, Quarterly Performance Reviews/ Governance

Identify & Prioritize Improvement Projects & Resources

Develop Timelines and Projected Trajectories Stoner 60

Final Review of Customer, Competitor, Internal Capability, and SWOT and Situational Analysis (including Benchmarks) Assumptions to Recheck Validity

Source: Malcolm Baldridge National Quality Award Application Summary, 2005. Reprinted with permission of Stoner, Inc., www.moreshine.com.

Leadership, Governance, and Societal Responsibilities

An important aspect of an organization's leadership is its responsibility to the public and practice of good citizenship. General Electric's CEO Jeffrey Immelt noted, "Good leaders give back . . . It's up to us to use our platform to be a good citizen. Because not only is it a nice thing to do, it's a business imperative."[7]

Corporate social responsibility has become a strategic imperative and a competitive or marketplace necessity, particularly in the wake of corporate scandals that have occurred. Evidence suggests a positive relationship between CSR and business performance.[8] An ethical business environment creates trust from customers and employees, resulting in higher customer satisfaction, stronger employee commitment, and improved quality, all of which lead to higher profits. The International Organization for Standardization is developing a voluntary social responsibility standard, ISO 26000 which is scheduled for release in 2010, attesting to the importance of this issue. The standard will broaden awareness of CSR; assist organizations in addressing their social responsibilities while respecting cultural, societal, environmental and legal differences, and economic development conditions; provide practical guidance to operationalize social responsibility practices, and emphasize performance results and improvement.

__Corporate social responsibility (CSR)__ includes ethics, corporate governance, and protection of public health, safety, and the environment. These factors are becoming increasingly important to the workforce, to customers, and even to investors.

Senior management is responsible for creating an environment in which employees' decisions and actions and stakeholder interactions conform to the organization's moral and professional principles. Senior leaders must build stakeholders' and **employees'** trust in the governance of their organizations and ensure legal compliance and ethical behavior. For any organization, large or small, public or private, ethics should mean going beyond profit or loss considerations, beyond simply distributing a code of conduct, to creating an organizational culture that values sound governance, transparency, integrity, and social responsibility.

SSM Health Care and Medrad

SSM Health Care, for example, implemented a system-wide organizational ethics effort called the Corporate Responsibility Process (CRP). The CRP aligns with the elements of the national Office of Inspector General's model compliance plan, but goes beyond compliance to ensure that corporate values are reflected in all work processes. Employees, physicians, volunteers, and suppliers can use a confidential help line to raise questions, and any reported issues are investigated and acted upon. KPMG identified the CRP as a best practice nationwide. At Medrad, a Code of Conduct defines ethical behavior in all transactions and interactions and has been deployed to all employees worldwide as well as to Medrad's suppliers. Code of Conduct training is part of the company's employee orientation program, and the training is reinforced through a quarterly Code of Conduct Challenge distributed by email to all employees. In addition, Medrad has an anonymous ethics hotline and email address, a Business Ethics Committee, and a Legal Advisory Board.

An important aspect of the leadership system is __governance__, which refers to the system of management and controls exercised in the stewardship of an organization.

Corporate charters, bylaws, and policies document the rights and responsibilities of owners/shareholders, board of directors, and the CEO, and describe how the organization is managed to ensure accountability, transparency of operations, and fair treatment of all stakeholders. Governance processes may include approving strategic direction, monitoring and evaluating CEO performance, succession planning, financial auditing, executive compensation, disclosure, and shareholder reporting. Effective governance processes can mitigate the types of problems manifested by stock manipulations, financial misreporting, and corporate and personal greed that have occurred in the past. In fact, evidence indicates that good governance and integrity are important ingredients for success;

for example, organizations with the best corporate governance practices have also generally outperformed the major stock indexes.

The Public Company Accounting Reform and Investor Protection Act of 2002, commonly known as the *Sarbanes-Oxley Act*, was passed as a result of the corporate financial scandals at firms such as Enron. As a result of the legislation, all publicly-traded companies are required to submit an annual report of the effectiveness of their internal accounting controls to the SEC. The Sarbanes-Oxley Act imposes criminal and civil penalties for noncompliance, and requires certification of internal auditing, and increased financial disclosure.

In 2002, about the same time the Sarbanes-Oxley legislation was passed, The Business Roundtable, a respected group of CEO's from many of the *Fortune* 500 corporations, developed a set of Principles of Corporate Governance to provide guidelines for compliance.[9] These principles describe the responsibilities of the board of directors in overseeing senior managers and the ethical operation of the company, of management to operate in an effective and ethical manner, of producing fair and timely financial disclosures, of using an independent auditing firm to audit financial statements, of the independent accounting firm to avoid conflicts of interest and work in accordance with Generally Accepted Auditing Standards, of dealing with employees in a fair and equitable manner, of the board to respond to shareholders' concerns, and of the corporation to deal with all its stakeholders in a fair and equitable manner.

Caterpillar Financial Services

As one example, Caterpillar Financial Services Corporation (CFSC) has established strong internal financial control mechanisms. Segregation of duties and authorities prevents abuse, and systems are audited internally and externally. CFSC's Business Excellence Council monitors portfolio quality, and, as an issuer of publicly traded debt, CFSC's financial and portfolio practices and results are evaluated and made public by external rating agencies and analysts. The Caterpillar Executive Office and Audit Committee of the Board of Directors provide oversight to CFSC. Although not required by law, Caterpillar also established share ownership requirements for recipients of stock option grants more than a decade ago, and shareholders approve all equity programs.

Corporate social responsibility includes safety in product design and manufacturing. Planning activities such as product design should anticipate adverse impacts from production, distribution, transportation, use, and disposal of a company's products to protect the welfare of consumers and society. Another responsibility is the management and security of sensitive information. For example, State Farm Insurance put in place physical, electronic, and organizational safeguards to protect customer information. They continually review their policies and practices, monitor computer networks, and test the strength of security in order to help ensure the safety of customer information. Finally, organizations have a responsibility to protect the environment. Research has suggested that superior environmental performance and superior quality are complementary. Firms that improve quality in goods and services can easily transfer their knowledge and learning to environmental processes. In addition, there is evidence that achieving superior environmental performance can be a significant driver of higher quality.[10]

Solar Turbines

At Solar Turbines, a wholly owned subsidiary of Caterpillar Inc. and the world's largest supplier of mid-range industrial gas turbine systems, its Social Responsibility Core Business Principle and Environmental, Health, and Safety Policy guide the company's responsibility and citizenship actions. Solar's environmental health and safety strategy for its internal operation is to surpass compliance and strive for industry leadership. Products and services must comply with local, state, and federal standards in each locale as well as country-specific and governing body standards for emissions and effluent discharge. Solar's strategy has yielded significant reduction in the use of hazardous raw materials and production of hazardous waste, increased recycling and reuse, improved energy efficiency, and reduced water consumption. Solar and one of its key suppliers partnered with Cal-Poly State University to establish a Vibration and Rotor Dynamics Laboratory. Organizations should not only meet all local, state, and federal laws and regulatory requirements, but should treat these as opportunities for continuous improvement beyond mere compliance.

Practicing good citizenship refers to leadership and support—within the limits of an organization's resources—of publicly important purposes, including improving education, community health, environmental excellence, resource conservation, community service, and professional practices.

Consolidated School District 15

Corporate social responsibility also entails leading efforts to help define the obligations of the industry to its communities. Consolidated School District 15 supports the community in a variety of ways. It is one of the largest contributors to the local United Way, contributions increased by more than 50 percent from 1998–99 to 2002–03; it established the Al Hoover/PTA Health fund, which partners with local health providers to serve D15 students who otherwise would be unable to obtain needed medical care; and its administrators contribute more than 1,500 volunteer hours on 48 local committees. In addition, D15 has established numerous community service opportunities for its students, such as providing labor to repair homeless shelters, donating clothing and books to needy families, making quilts for children in hospitals, and supporting food drives.[11]

Many businesses partner with educational institutions for mutual benefit. Businesses bring to schools, colleges, and universities sound quality operational practices and processes, leadership and management skills and training, volunteers as mentors and tutors, and school-to-work opportunities. In return, the education community supplies businesses with potential employees who not only have traditional skills associated with academic subjects, but also have the new basic skills, such as problem solving, critical thinking, decision making, teaming, and creativity. By recognizing the business community as an important customer, business needs are factored into curriculum, and the end product, the graduate, is better prepared to enter the employment world.

LEADERSHIP THEORY AND PRACTICE

To understand how leadership is developed and practiced, it is important to understand its foundations in management theory. Dozens of leadership theories have been derived from literally thousands of leadership studies. Unlike some areas of quality management that are only a few decades old, leadership theories can often be traced back 50–75 years or more. Despite this extensive body of research, the precise nature of leadership and its relationship to key variables such as subordinate satisfaction, commitment, and performance is still uncertain. Fred Luthans observed that "it [leadership] does remain pretty much of a 'black box' or unexplainable concept."[12]

The purpose of leadership theories is to explain differences in leadership styles and contexts.

A comprehensive review of leadership theories is well beyond the scope of this text. However, the theories are quite important within the context of quality and performance excellence; therefore, we provide a brief summary of the most popular leadership approaches and discuss their implications for performance excellence. Table 9.3 summarizes some of the key theories that have influenced today's leadership styles.

Table 9.3 Classification of Leadership Theories[13]

Leadership Theory	Pioneer/Developer	Type of Theory
"Great man" model	Ralph Stogdill	Trait
Ohio State Studies	E. A. Fleishman, E. F. Harris et al.	Leader behavior
Michigan Studies	Rensis Likert	
Theory X-Theory Y model	Douglas MacGregor	
Managerial Grid model	Robert Blake; Jane S. Mouton	
Leadership effectiveness model	Fred E. Fiedler	Contingency (situational)
Supervisory contingency decision model	V. H. Vroom & P. W. Yetton V. H. Vroom and A. G. Jago	
Situational	Hersey and Blanchard	
Managerial roles	Henry Mintzberg	Role approach
Leader-Member Exchange	George Graen et al.	Emerging theories
Charismatic theory	R. J. House; J. A. Conger	
Transformational theory	James M. Burns; N. M. Tichy and D. O. Ulrich; B. M. Bass	
Substitutes for leadership	Jon P. Howell et al.	
Emotional intelligence	Daniel Goleman et al.	

Because many of the traditional and contingency leadership theories are developed more fully in principles of management and organizational behavior courses, their characteristics will not be explored in detail here. Instead, a summary of the concepts of these theories is included in the Bonus Materials folder for this chapter on the Premium website, and we will focus on characteristics of the "emerging" leadership theories that are generating active discussion in academic settings and being applied in practice today.

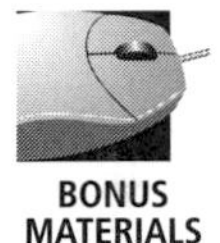
BONUS MATERIALS

Contemporary and Emerging Leadership Theories

Emerging leadership theories build on or enlarge traditional theory by attempting to answer questions raised, but not answered, by earlier approaches.

Many of the theories we classify as "emerging" were proposed in the 1970's and 1980's and have been around for many years, but are still considered "emerging" because of the difficulty that researchers encounter in testing social science theories. It often takes decades to establish empirical evidence as to a theory's value; for example, theories of team participation that originated in the 1930's were not researched adequately until the 1950's, and for the most part, have only recently found substantial application in practice.[14]

Situational Leadership Situational leadership, one of the better-known contingency theories of leadership offers important insights into the interaction between subordinate ability and leadership style and is taught in many executive management seminars. The theory was initially introduced in 1969 and revised in 1977 by Hersey and Blanchard. The major proposition of situational leadership theory is that the effectiveness of task and relationship-oriented leadership behaviors depends upon the maturity of a leader's subordinates. It suggests that the key contingency factor affecting leaders' choice of leadership style is the task-related maturity of the subordinates. Subordinate maturity is defined in terms of the ability of subordinates to accept responsibility for their own task-related behavior. The theory classifies leader behaviors into the two broad classes of task-oriented and relationship-oriented behaviors.[15]

According to situational leadership, leadership styles might vary from one person to another, depending on the "readiness" of subordinates, which is characterized by their skills and abilities to perform the work, and their confidence, commitment, and motivation to do it. The model defines four levels of follower maturity (readiness):

1. Unable and unwilling
2. Unable but willing
3. Able but unwilling, and
4. Able and willing

Blanchard and Hersey defined four leadership styles that best address these four levels of maturity (readiness):

1. *Directing.* In this style of leadership, managers define tasks and roles, and closely supervise work. Communication is generally one way—top down. This style of leader-initated "task-oriented" behavior applies best to followers who lack the skills and knowledge to perform a job and lack confidence or commitment to their work (unable and unwilling). Little time or effort is spent on developing relationships with followers.
2. *Coaching.* In this style, leaders set the overall approach and direction but work with subordinates and allow them to manage the details. Leaders might need to provide some direction, based on experience (a task-oriented behavior), or support (relationship-oriented behavior) to individual followers having the drive and motivation to do a good job, but who might lack some experience or skills (unable but willing).
3. *Supporting.* Here, leaders allocate tasks and set direction, but the subordinate has full control over the performance of the work. These individuals do not need much supervision or direction (task-oriented behavior), but may require leadership to assist them in building motivation and confidence (relationship-oriented behavior), particularly if the task is new (able but unwilling).
4. *Delegating.* In this style, subordinates can do their work with little supervision or support (minimal task-oriented behavior). Once the work is delegated, leaders take a hands-off approach (minimal relationship-oriented behavior), except when asked to provide assistance by the subordinate. The followers can work on a project by themselves with little supervision or support (able and willing).

A leader might also apply different styles to the same person at different times. This can be difficult, as many leaders seem to be more comfortable in one style. However, the choice should not be driven by personal preference, but rather the needs of the subordinates. In fully empowered TQ organizations and those with strong self-directed teams, you would probably find the delegating style to be most prevalent. However, when introducing new skills, such as Six Sigma, into an organization, it may be necessary to provide more direct control, coaching, or support while individuals are learning and practicing new skills or are transitioning into new job responsibilities. As managers work with different individuals in different stages of careers and maturity, it is their responsibility to adapt the leadership style to the individual and the situation.[16]

Although situational leadership theory is often used in practice, it has been criticized on both theoretical and methodological grounds, including ambiguity, a lack of consistency and incompleteness, as well as mixed empirical validation.[17] One author summarizes the controversy and contributions of situational leadership as follows:

> *"A few studies found support for the proposition that more directive supervision is needed for subordinates who have low ability and confidence. However, there was little evidence that using the contingent pattern of task and relations behavior prescribed by the theory will make leaders more effective... Despite its deficiencies, the theory has made some positive contributions to our understanding of dyadic leadership. One contribution was the emphasis on flexible adaptive behavior, which has become a central tenet of some recent theory and research."*[18]

Transactional and Transformational Leadership Theory According to the various contemporary leadership theories developed over the last 20 or 30 years, leadership effectiveness can be improved with the correct mix of the leader's style of management, the characteristics of those who are led, and the situation. Two of the most popular are transactional and transformational theory.

Transactional Leadership Theory assumes that certain leaders may develop the ability to inspire their subordinates to exert extraordinary efforts to achieve organizational goals, through behaviors that may include contingent rewards, and active and passive management by exception. Contingent reward behavior includes clarification of the work required to obtain rewards to influence motivation. Passive management by exception includes use of contingent punishments and other corrective actions in response to deviations from acceptable performance standards. Active management by exception is defined in terms of looking for mistakes and enforcing rules to avoid mistakes.

Transformational Leadership Theory[19] was first developed by James M. Burns, and later extended by Bernard M. Bass and his colleagues. According to this theory, leaders adopt many of the behaviors discussed earlier in this chapter: idealized influence, individualized consideration, inspirational motivation, and intellectual stimulation.[20] Leaders who take on a transformational style have a long-term perspective, focus on customers, promote a shared vision and values, work to stimulate their organizations intellectually, invest in training, take some risks, and treat employees as individuals.

Bass differentiated transformational from transactional leadership behavior, stating: "Transformational leaders have greater interest in continuous organizational change and improvement transcending or aligning self-interests for the longer-range greater good of the organization and its members. This is in contrast to transactional leaders, who are more focused on the satisfaction of self-interests and the maintenance of the organization's status quo."[21] In practice, however, it is often difficult to distinguish between the two theories, and research has discovered that they are distinct, but related processes. While transactional leaders may increase follower motivation and performance more than transactional leaders, effective leaders use a combination of both types, depending on the situation.[22]

Transformational leadership is more aligned with organizational change required by total quality and Baldrige-like performance excellence models.

The CEOs and executive team members of nearly every Malcolm Baldrige Award recipient have generally modeled this leadership behavior, and some empirical evidence found in research suggests that transformational leadership behavior is strongly correlated with lower turnover, higher productivity and quality, and higher employee satisfaction than other approaches. However, not all managers in TQ organizations need be transformational leaders. An organization pursuing TQ needs both those who establish visions and those who are effective at the day-to-day (transactional) tasks needed to achieve them.[23] In fact, Avolio and Bass extended the concept of transformational leadership by developing a hybrid of transactional and transformational leadership, which they labeled the Full Range of Leadership™ approach.[24] They noted that "Transformational leadership adds to transactional leadership in its effects on follower satisfaction and performance. Transformational leadership does not replace transactional leadership . . . Transactional leadership, particularly contingent rewards, provides a broad basis for leadership, but a greater amount of effort, innovation, effectiveness, risk taking, and satisfaction can be achieved by transactional leadership if it is augmented by transformational leadership."

Another emerging concept of leadership is called the **Substitutes for Leadership theory**.[25] This research takes the intriguing view that in many organizations, if characteristics of subordinates (team members), the nature of the tasks that they perform, and the guidance and incentives provided by the organization are aligned, then formal leadership tends to be unproductive or counterproductive. It is suggested that this leadership approach may be useful in cases of low leadership effectiveness where the leader cannot be removed for various political or other reasons (the owner's incompetent son or daughter is the "leader"), or where team member training or competence is especially high (a surgical team), or where the situation is particularly dynamic (battling oil well fires in the desert). In such situations, self-management, professional education, or even computer technology can be developed or built in to substitute for leadership. The implication for a TQ-focused organization is that each situation calls for just the right amount of leadership (not too much and not too little) in order to attain high-quality results.

One of the more recent emerging leadership theories is called the **Emotional Intelligence theory**.[26] Goleman defines five components of emotionally intelligent leaders: (1) self-awareness, (2) self-regulation, (3) motivation, (4) empathy, and (5) social skill. His premise is that too much reliance was placed on the rational side of leadership in leadership research studies and training done over the years. He argues that expectations for emotional intelligence are generally not captured in performance evaluation systems, but that the self-management (components 1 through 3) and interpersonal skills (components 4 and 5) represented by the five components are as essential for executive-level leaders as "traditional" intelligence (measured by IQ tests) and technical competence. The significance of emotional intelligence for effective total quality lies in translating the "vision" of an integrated leadership system and long-range planning process into action. Without credible self-management, represented by the first three components, it will be difficult for subordinates within the organization to "buy into" the vision of the leader. Without mature empathy and social skills, represented by the last two components, it will be difficult for the leader to work effectively with customers, suppliers, and others outside the organization in order to build rapport needed for long-term enterprise effectiveness, which is critical for a TQ-focused organization.

Quality Spotlight
The Ritz Carlton Hotel Company

Chapter 3 describes how senior leadership at The Ritz-Carlton Hotel Co. modeled many of the behaviors of effective leaders within the context of the Baldrige criteria.

(You might wish to review this material before continuing.) By examining characteristics of several of the emerging leadership theories, we can see how they are applied in practice at The Ritz-Carlton.

Horst Schulze, the retired CEO of The Ritz-Carlton, and his senior leadership team take care that leaders' judgments on how to deal with subordinates in a specific situation are based on positive attributions (attribution theory). The assumption of worker competency is a given at Ritz-Carlton, even extending to the company motto of "We are ladies and gentlemen serving ladies and gentlemen."

Aspects of Transformational Leadership theory are evident during the new hotel start-up process, when senior leaders are visible, doing what transformational leaders do. These activities include taking a long-term perspective, focusing on customers, promoting a shared vision and values, working to stimulate their organizations intellectually, investing in training, taking some risks, and treating employees as individuals.

Can it be that The Ritz-Carlton's staff is expected to be like a team of oil-well firefighters? The Substitutes for Leadership theory provides some support for this notion. As outlined earlier, if characteristics of subordinates (team members), the nature of the tasks that they perform, and the guidance and incentives provided by the organization are aligned, then formal leadership tends to be unproductive or counterproductive. The Ritz-Carlton's leadership model incorporates a high level of team member training (focusing on the Gold Standards) and competence (often seen in highly professional jobs, such as surgical teams), and the situation is often very dynamic. Thus, workers must often be self-led. They "substitute for leadership" and are empowered to take action without waiting for supervisory approval.

By empowering employees as leaders at every level, The Ritz-Carlton provides an environment that will lead to the development and use of greater emotional intelligence, as outlined in Emotional Intelligence theory. Thus, the employee–guest interface and relationship management approaches that The Ritz-Carlton teaches every employee, provide interpersonal skills and supplement self-management. The components of emotionally intelligent leaders—self-awareness, self-regulation, motivation, empathy, and social skill—are regularly seen in employees' ability to be self-managed (components 1 through 3) and in their use of interpersonal skills (components 4 and 5).

New Perspectives on the Practice of Leadership[27]

The Center for Creative Leadership (CCL) has been studying the "changing nature of leadership" (CNL). CNL studies have engaged survey, interactive classroom, archival, and competitive benchmarking research. Subjects in the studies were U.S. and international top and middle managers, many of whom participated in CCL's widely-respected leadership training sessions. Two aspects of the research stand out—evidence that in an increasingly complex and chaotic business environment, critical leadership skills are trending away from "hard" analysis to "soft," collaborative ones, and that academic research journal articles are not mirroring that trend.

The research classified the types of challenges facing present and future management into three categories—technical, adaptive, and critical. Technical challenges were those that leaders and their organizations had faced in the past and built competence in solving. Adaptive challenges were those where current leadership skills had to be extended and adapted to new environments. Critical leadership skills were those required to meet discontinuous or crisis conditions, never before faced by the leader or the organization.

The research suggests that leadership skills will have to change from:

- A position to a process
- A functional orientation to a boundary-less orientation
- A focus at the top to a focus throughout the organization
- Independent decision making to interdependent decision making
- Developing via individual competencies to developing via groups and networks
- Power resulting from position to power resulting from knowledge
- Competition to collaboration
- Logical and rational to feeling and emotional
- Staying the course strategy to emergent/flexible strategy
- Selling opinions to inquiring for buy-in

Many of these changes are already evident in many organizations, particularly those that embrace quality principles, except for possibly feeling/emotional, as this conflicts with the management by fact philosophy of quality management. In the future, respondents believe organizations will continue to move towards viewing leadership as a process that happens throughout the organization through interdependent decision making, and that organizations should continue to seek more of a balance between developing leadership through individual competencies and groups/network competencies, and between a functional versus a boundary-less orientation.

BUILDING PERFORMANCE EXCELLENCE IN ORGANIZATIONS

Whatever approach or combination of approaches an organization uses should make the most sense—and work—in the organization.

Organizations can take many routes to performance excellence, but none of them represents the "one best way." Joshua Hammond of the American Quality Foundation urges business leaders in the United States to develop approaches that maximize their own strengths. A successful strategy needs to fit within the existing organization culture and capabilities, which is the reason the Baldrige Award criteria are nonprescriptive. One study of Baldrige Award winners concluded that each has a unique "quality engine" that drives the quality activities of the organization.[28] Some examples are summarized in Table 9.4. This table does not suggest that all other aspects of performance excellence are ignored; they are not. The quality engine simply customizes the quality effort to the organizational culture and provides focus.

Implementing ISO 9000, Baldrige, and Six Sigma

Many organizations start with ISO 9000 because of its prescriptive nature and process orientation. One of the first things to do is to establish a **quality policy** that identifies key objectives of products and services such as fitness for use, performance, safety, and dependability; and basic procedures for such key activities as process control, inspection, testing, control of nonconforming product, corrective action, control of measuring and test equipment, and maintenance of essential records and documentation.

Management must also identify and provide appropriate resources to achieve the objectives set forth in their quality policy. These resources might include people

Table 9.4 Some Examples of Quality Engines

Company	Quality Engine	Focus
Pal's Sudden Service	Process focus	Everything—from new product introduction to hiring to work systems—viewed as process that affects customer satisfaction.
Clarke American Checks	Strategic planning	Involving all stakeholders in a "First in Service" strategy focused on running and changing the business
Sharp Health Care	Customer focus	The Sharp Experience aimed at transforming the health care experience
North Mississippi Medical Center	Measurement and knowledge management	Award-winning management information system and electronic medical records
PRO-TEC Coating Co.	Workforce engagement	Safety as a first priority; leadership and communication throughout the organization
MESA Products	Technology	Manufacturing equipment and design center unique to the industry

with special skills, manufacturing equipment, inspection technology, and computer software. Individuals must be given the responsibility to initiate actions to prevent the occurrence of defects and errors, to identify and solve quality-related problems, and to verify the implementation of solutions. The system should also include an audit program to determine if the activities and results of the quality system comply with plans.

ISO 9000 requires that all the elements required for a quality system, such as control processes, measuring and test equipment, and other resources needed to achieve the required quality of conformance, be documented in a **quality manual**, which serves as a permanent reference for implementing and maintaining the system. A quality manual need not be complex; a small company might need only a dozen pages while a large organization might need manuals for all key functions. Sufficient records should be maintained to demonstrate conformance to requirements and verify that the quality system is operating effectively. Typical records that might be maintained are inspection reports, test data, audit reports, and calibration data. They should be readily retrievable for analysis to identify trends and monitor the effectiveness of corrective actions. Other documents, such as drawings, specifications, inspection procedures and instructions, work instructions, and operation sheets are vital to achieving quality and should likewise be controlled.

Finally, the system needs to be maintained and kept up to date. This maintenance can be facilitated through **internal audits**, which focus on identifying whether documented procedures are being followed and are effective, and reporting the issues to management for corrective action. Internal audits generally include a review of process records, training records, complaints, corrective actions, and previous audit reports. A typical internal audit begins by asking those who perform a process regularly to explain how it works.[29] Their statements are compared to written procedures, and compliance and deviations are noted. Next, the trail of paperwork or other data are examined to determine whether the process is consistent with the intent of the written procedure and the worker's explanation. Internal auditors also need to analyze whether the process is meeting its intent and objectives, thus focusing on continuous improvement.

ISO 9000 can be implemented in an organization that has not fully embraced TQ and result in significant benefits. In fact, it may even be redundant in a mature organization that has used Baldrige or Six Sigma as a framework for some time. These organizations most likely do all the things required by the standards, and perhaps the only thing missing is the formal documentation. Implementation of ISO 9000 requires the resources and support of top management, but the details fall mainly within the province of operating managers, supervisors, and employees to identify, develop, and document critical work processes. Meeting the registration standards can be a painstaking and costly undertaking, often requiring organizations to develop and institute many new procedures and train many people.

Perhaps the best way to understand the process of building the Baldrige framework into an organization is to review lessons learned by St. Luke's Hospital in their quality journey:

- Leadership drives and sustains the process
- Leadership at all levels is important
- More difficult to change the culture than to learn the tools
- Valuable team building experience
- Trust is extremely important
- There are no "quick fixes"
- Must always focus on the customer
- Should never be satisfied with the present level of quality
- Decisions must be driven by data and compared to "best"
- Employees make it happen!

These observations clearly indicate the challenge that Baldrige presents. Implementing Baldrige requires repetitive cycles of self-assessment, priority-setting, action planning to address gaps and opportunities for improvement, and reflection of results, all driven by an organization's vision, strategic challenges, and capabilities.

A major benefit of Baldrige is that it naturally provides a framework for organizational learning, and therefore, helps to enhance and sustain an organization, no matter what its current level of maturity. For example, the requirement of Performance Analysis and Review in Category 4 focuses organizations to provide a picture of their "state of health" and examine how well they are currently performing and also how well they are moving toward the future. This review capitalizes on the information generated from the measurement and analysis of business results and is intended to provide a reliable means to guide both improvement and change at the strategic planning level.

As we indicated throughout the preceding chapters, a fully implemented Six Sigma process is a strategic approach that is driven and supported by top management, but is deployed throughout the organization at every level. Several key principles are necessary for effective implementation of Six Sigma:[30]

- *Committed leadership from top management.* Managers at GE participate in hands-on approaches such as personally spending time in every Six Sigma training wave, speaking to and answering questions from students, dropping in (usually unannounced) on weekly and monthly Six Sigma reviews, and making site visits at the manufacturing and call-taking operations to observe firsthand the degree to which Six Sigma in ingrained in the culture.

- *Integration with existing initiatives, business strategy, and performance measurement.* Six Sigma should have a clear justification in terms of an organization's mission and strategic direction. However, with its focus on customers and the bottom line, this integration usually is not too difficult. At companies like GE and Allied Signal, Six Sigma has been extended to all areas of the company, such as product development and financial services. For example, GE first identifies all critical customer performance features and subjects them to a rigorous statistical design process, thus designing products for Six Sigma levels.
- *Process thinking.* As one of the foundation principles of total quality, a process focus is, not surprisingly, a necessary prerequisite. Mapping business processes is one of the key activities in Six Sigma efforts, as is a disciplined approach to the information gathering, analysis, and problem solving.
- *Disciplined customer and market intelligence gathering.* The ultimate goal is to improve those characteristics that are most important to customers; thus knowledge of customer needs is vital. Approaches that we discussed in Chapter 4 are essential to help focus Six Sigma projects on customers.
- *A bottom-line orientation.* Six Sigma projects must produce real savings or revenues in both the short term and long term. Most Six Sigma projects are designed to be completed within three to six months. GE has a financial analyst certify the results of every project.
- *Leadership in the trenches.* Within GE, Six Sigma includes a diverse population of technical and nontechnical people, managers, and others from key business areas who work together as a team to attack a problem using the DMAIC approach. All employees participate, not just those that hold the "belts."
- *Training.* Six Sigma organizations train nearly everyone in rigorous statistical and problem-solving tools. GE's Green Belt training is delivered to all GE employees and is available in strategic locations across the world. It is typically rolled out over a four-month period and is scheduled to help facilitate the trainee in leading a "Green Belt project" to not only yield savings but also practice in a real-life situation what is being learned in the training.
- *Continuous reinforcement and rewards.* Six Sigma organizations have significantly changed performance measurement and reward systems. At GE, 40 percent of executive incentives are tied to Six Sigma goals and progress. Before any savings are credited to an individual, the Black Belt overseeing the project must show that the problems are fixed permanently. All employees, even executives, who want to be considered for promotion must be trained in Six Sigma and complete a project. Some organizations also pool the savings at the business unit level and share the savings with the Six Sigma team members.

Many organizations integrate Baldrige, ISO 9000, and Six Sigma in some way.[31] For example, the performance improvement system at Mesa Products, Inc. is embedded and managed through its quality management system (QMS), primarily through ISO 9001 certification. The company uses several improvement processes built around methods such as the plan-do-check-act (PDCA) cycle, lean and Six Sigma's define, measure, analyze, improve, and control strategy. The ISO 9001 based

Figure 9.3 Mesa's Quality Management System

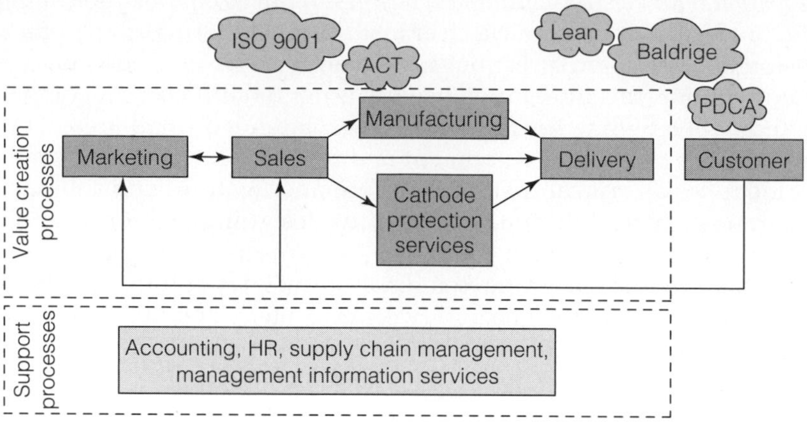

ACT = accurate, continuous improvement and timely
PDCA = plan-do-check-act

Source: Mesa Products, Inc. 2006 Malcolm Baldrige Quality Award Application Summary.

QMS combines with the Baldrige criteria at Mesa to bind business processes in an integrated, aligned direction, resulting in performance excellence (see Figure 9.3).

Organizational Culture and Performance Excellence

Culture (specifically, *corporate culture*) is an organization's value system and its collection of guiding principles. Culture is an important factor for sustainability and long-term success of any organization. Strong corporate cultures are evident in firms such as Disney, Procter & Gamble, and IBM. A survey conducted by the Wyatt Company, a Washington, D.C., consulting firm, found that the barriers to change cited most often were employee resistance and "dysfunctional corporate culture"—one whose shared values and behavior are at odds with its long-term health.[32] An example of a dysfunctional culture is a high-tech company that stresses individual rewards while innovation depends on teamwork.

For quality and performance excellence to truly succeed in an organization, it must define and drive the culture of the organization.

Culture is driven by leadership.[33] In an entrepreneurial venture, for instance, the founder's behavior is often reflected in the behavior of the organization's workforce. During the formative years, the leader's behavior and personality are showcased to the employees through day-to-day interactions. For example, one entrepreneur might establish a culture based on the timely delivery of products and honoring of promises to clients. Another might be more tolerant of delays in client deliveries, and be sending a dubious message to the workforce that negatively influences the firm's performance. Such values eventually can become the values of the workforce.

As the firm grows, the process of creating and disseminating the desired culture tends to become increasingly difficult because the entrepreneur is no longer involved in the day-to-day activities of the organization. At this stage, it becomes necessary to formally define the firm's cultural values and the behavior expected from the workforce. This is typically done through organizational policies and practices.[34] For example, cultural values are often seen in the mission and vision statements of organizations as we saw in Chapter 4. It is not unusual to see statements such as, "We will continuously strive to improve the level of quality in all our products" or "Teamwork is essential to our mutual success" in corporate mission and vision statements.

Culture is a powerful influence on behavior because it is shared widely and because it operates without being talked about, and indeed, often without being thought of. Therefore, organizations that believe in the principles of performance excellence are more likely to implement the practices successfully. Conversely, actions set culture in motion. As performance excellence practices are used routinely within an organization, its people learn to believe in the underlying principles of total quality, and cultural changes can occur.

Changing Organizational Culture

It is important to differentiate between organizational changes resulting from strategy development and implementation (i.e., "strategic change"), and organizational changes resulting from operational assessment activities (i.e., "process change").[35] Strategic change stems from strategic objectives, which are generally externally focused and relate to significant customer, market, product/service, or technological opportunities and challenges. An organization must change these aspects to remain or become competitive. Strategic change is broad in scope, is driven by environmental forces, and is tied closely to the organization's ability to achieve its goals. Some examples are General Electric's implementation of Six Sigma throughout the corporation, and Hewlett-Packard's decision to merge with Compaq. In contrast, process change deals with the operations of an organization. Some examples of process change are a health care organization that discovered weaknesses in the organization's ability to collect and analyze information, followed by a $50 million information system upgrade; or an AT&T division that found that many employees did not recall the division's strategic vision, which prompted managers to increase meetings and interactions with employees to improve communication.

Although change to a business process tends to have lasting effects, the change tends to be narrow in scope. Unlike strategic change, which motivates organization-wide changes in behavior, process change is often confined to a particular unit, division, or function of the organization. For example, changing an organization's process for measuring customer satisfaction usually requires substantive adjustment to a limited number of functional areas, such as marketing or information systems. In Table 9.5, we describe the characteristics of strategic change in contrast with process change. Strategic changes are the ones that impact culture the most rapidly. However, an accumulation of continuously improving process changes can also lead to a positive and sustainable culture change.

Organizations contemplating change must answer some tough questions, such as, Why is the change necessary? What will it do to my organization (department, job)? What problems will I encounter in making the change? and perhaps the most important one—What's in it for me?

Change makes people uncomfortable, thus, managing change is seldom pleasant.[36] Managing change usually requires a well-defined process, just like any other business process. Thinking of change management as a process helps to define the steps necessary to achieve the desired outcomes. It also forces the organization

Table 9.5 Strategic versus Process Change

	Strategic Change	**Process Change**
Theme of change	Shift in organizational direction	Adjustment of organizational processes
Driving force	Usually environmental forces—market, rival, technological change	Usually internal—"How can we better align our processes?"
Typical antecedent	Strategic planning process	Self-assessment of management system
How much of the organization changes?	Typically widespread	Often narrow—divisional or functional
Examples	Entering new markets Seeking low-cost position Mergers and acquisitions	Improving information systems Establishing hiring guidelines Developing improved customer satisfaction measures

Adapted from Matthew W. Ford and James R. Evans, "Baldrige Assessment and Organizational Learning: The Need For Change Management," *Quality Management Journal*, 8, 3, 2001, 9–25.

to think of its employees as customers who will be affected by the change. Most change processes include three basic stages. The first stage involves questioning the organization's current state and dislodging accepted patterns of behavior. The second stage is a state of flux, where new approaches are developed to replace suspended old activities. The final period consists of institutionalizing the new behaviors and attitudes. American Express, for example, views its change process as consisting of five steps:[37]

1. *Scope the change:* Why are we doing this?
2. *Create a vision:* What will the change look like?
3. *Drive commitment:* What needs to happen to make the change work?
4. *Accelerate the transition:* How are we going to manage the effort on an ongoing basis?
5. *Sustain momentum:* What have we learned and how can we leverage it?

The motivation to adopt a performance excellence philosophy usually stems from one of two basic reasons—either a firm reacts to competition that poses a threat to its survival, or it recognizes that performance excellence practices represent an opportunity to improve and grow the business.

The first question an organization must ask is "Why change?" Most firms—even Baldrige Award winners—have changed their cultures because of threats to their survival. Xerox, for example, watched its market share fall from 80 percent to 13 percent in a little more than a decade (see the *Quality in Practice* feature in Chapter 1); and Boeing Airlift and Tanker Programs was on the verge of having its contract with the U.S. government canceled. Although not facing dire crises, perceived future threats were the impetus for FedEx, Solectron, and Wainwright Industries. When faced with a threat to survival, an organization implements change more quickly and smoothly. However, an organization will generally have more difficulty in gaining support for any significant change when not facing a crisis. This reluctance is a reflection of the attitude "If it ain't broke, don't fix it." Unfortunately, complacency today often leads to crises tomorrow. Leaders with foresight view Baldrige as an opportunity to get better, and to maintain or enhance existing market leadership positions. In such cases, one might even attempt to manufacture a crisis mentality to effect change.[38]

In many situations, middle managers recognize the need for change, but gaining commitment from top executives is not easy. As one quality director noted, "It's a hard sell if management is not predisposed." Dale Crownover, CEO of Texas Nameplate Company, believes the best way to sell quality to top executives is to show them where money is being lost due to absenteeism, downtime, not having procedures in place, lack of job descriptions, and poor training. Demonstrating the return on quality investments that we discussed in Chapter 8 is a powerful motivator.

Management must understand what needs to change. A culture of performance excellence is very different from a traditional management culture. Many traditional practices stem from the fundamental structure of U.S. business, which derives from the Adam Smith principles of division of labor in the eighteenth century and their reinforcement during Frederick Taylor's scientific management era.[39] These include autocratic leadership, internal competition, functional silos, and rigid procedures. The Bonus Materials folder for this chapter on the Premium website, elaborates on the key differences between traditional practices and TQ. Although they were quite appropriate in their time and contributed to past economic success, those practices no longer suffice. Julia Graham has summarized characteristics of a culture of performance excellence:[40]

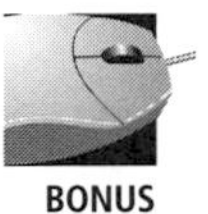

BONUS MATERIALS

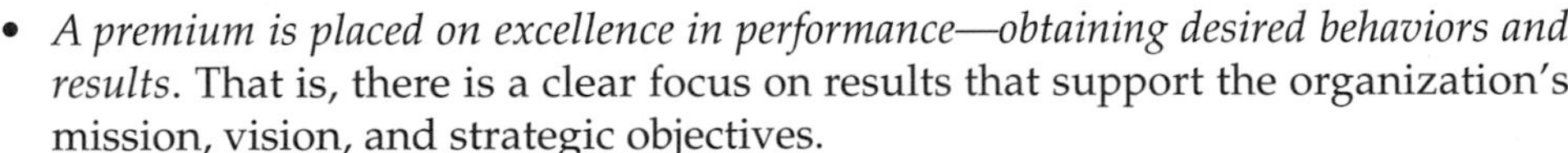

- *A premium is placed on excellence in performance—obtaining desired behaviors and results.* That is, there is a clear focus on results that support the organization's mission, vision, and strategic objectives.
- *Organizations acknowledge that their success is contingent upon the successful performance of their employees.* People are the most important driver of performance.
- *Strategic outcomes drive the work.* There is clear alignment at the three levels of quality—organization, process, and individual—that we discussed in Chapter 1.
- *Management is strongly committed to creating conditions and consequences that support and sustain strong performance.* Finally, leadership is vital to success.

To drive change, organizations must change behavior as well as policies and procedures. Juran and others suggest that an organization must foster five key behaviors to develop a positive quality culture:[41]

1. It must create and maintain an awareness of quality by disseminating results throughout the organization.
2. It must provide evidence of management leadership, such as serving on a quality council, providing resources, or championing quality projects (Six Sigma, for example).
3. It must encourage self-development and empowerment through the design of jobs, use of empowered teams, and personal commitment to quality.
4. It must provide opportunities for employee participation to inspire action, such as improvement teams, product design reviews, or Six Sigma training.
5. It must provide recognition and rewards, including public acknowledgment for good performance as well as tangible benefits.

It is interesting to note that these suggestions generally revolve around people, and as we have emphasized, people are the most important element in a successful organization.

All employees play a critical role in achieving performance excellence. We have already discussed extensively the role of senior leadership. Middle managers provide the leadership by which the vision of senior management is translated into the operations of the organization. Middle management has been tagged by many as a direct obstacle to creating a supportive environment for performance excellence.[42] Because of their position in the organization, middle managers have been accused of feeding territorial competition and stifling information flow. They have also been blamed for not developing or preparing employees for change. Unwilling to take initiatives that contribute to continuous improvement, middle managers appear to be threatened by continuous improvement efforts. Often, they are left out of the equation, with attention being paid to top management and the front-line workforce. However, middle management's role in creating and sustaining a culture of performance excellence is critical. Middle managers improve the operational processes that are the foundation of customer satisfaction. They can make or break cooperation and teamwork; and they are the principal means by which the remaining workforce prepares for change.

Middle managers must exhibit behaviors that are supportive of performance excellence, as they act as role models for first-level managers and employees. Such behaviors include listening to employees as customers, creating a positive work environment, being role models for first-level managers and supervisors, implementing quality improvements enthusiastically, challenging people to develop new ideas and reach their potential, encouraging supervisors to empower their people, setting challenging goals and providing positive feedback, and following through on promises. These changes are often difficult for many middle managers to accept.

In the end, the workforce delivers quality and, for a performance excellence strategy to succeed, must be granted not only empowerment, but ownership. Ownership goes beyond empowerment; it gives the employee the right to have a voice in deciding what needs to be done and how to do it.[43] At Westinghouse, workers defined ownership as "taking personal responsibility for our jobs . . . for assuring that we meet or exceed our customers' standards and our own. We believe that ownership is a state of mind and heart that is characterized by a personal and emotional commitment to approach every decision and task with the confidence and leadership of an owner." Self-managed teams, discussed in Chapter 6, represent one form of ownership.

Organizational policies and procedures such as reward systems often must be adjusted for the new culture to take hold. For instance, customer service representatives in many firms are rewarded for the speed with which they process calls, rather than for how completely they satisfy the customers who call. Unless this type of reward system is changed, management's pleas to increase customer satisfaction will fall upon deaf ears.

Wainwright Industries

One powerful example of cultural change is the case of Wainwright Industries, which has been cited several times in previous chapters.[44] During the 1970s and 1980s, Wainwright lost millions of dollars in sales; operations slowed to three days a week; and tensions grew between employees and management. Recognizing that the problem lay with management, the CEO made some radical changes. Workers were called "associates," and everyone was put on salary. Associates are paid even if they miss work and still receive time-and-a-half for overtime. The company has maintained better than 99 percent attendance since this change. Managers shed their white shirts and ties, and everyone from the CEO down wears a common uniform, embroidered with the label Team Wainwright. A team of associates developed a profit-sharing plan, whereby everyone receives the same bonus every six months. Everyone has access to the privately held company's financial records. In addition, all reserved parking spaces were removed; walls—including those for the CEO's office—were replaced with glass. Customers, both external and internal, are treated as partners, with extensive communication. The most striking example occurred when one worker admitted having accidentally damaged some equipment, even though most workers were afraid to report such incidents. The CEO called a plantwide meeting and explained what had happened. Then he called the man up, shook his hand, and thanked him for reporting the accident. Reporting of accidents increased from zero to 90 percent, along with suggestions on how to prevent them. As we noted in Chapter 6, Wainwright's culture can be summed up as a *sincere belief and trust in people.*

Barriers to Change

Numerous barriers exist to successfully transform organizations to a sustained culture of performance excellence. Understanding these barriers can help significantly in managing change processes.

One reason for failure of quality initiatives is a lack of what Deming called "constancy of purpose" in his original version of the 14 Points. The people who implement quality initiatives often have conflicting goals and priorities and simply do not not follow through with the initiative. In most cases, this is a failure to understand the benefits that can result. A new CEO may ignore or dismantle a successful quality initiative. Such behaviors can cause an incredible amount of cynicism on the part of the workforce who lose their motivation to participate.

Another reason for failure is the lack of a holistic systems perspective—one of the Core Values and Concepts of the Baldrige criteria. Many approaches to "implementing quality" are one-dimensional and are consequently prone to failure. For example, some firms might emphasize the use of Six Sigma, but may only deploy them in a narrow part of the organization, such as manufacturing. These firms will see some improvement, but because the entire organization is not involved success will be limited. Others might focus on reducing defects in production and customer service but ignore product design and customer relationship management processes. Achieving performance excellence requires a comprehensive effort that encompasses all of the elements discussed in this book thus far and span across the "three levels of quality"—individual, process, and organization—that we have discussed. Even though it is easy to focus on process improvement, it is certainly more difficult to establish cross-functional cooperation and to build the entire organization around a framework such as Baldrige.

__Alignment__ is defined as consistency of plans, processes, actions, information, decisions, results, analysis, and learning to support key organization-wide goals. __Integration__ refers to the harmonization of plans, processes, information, resource decisions, actions, results, and analyses to support key organization-wide goals.

Perhaps the most significant failure encountered in most organizations is a lack of alignment and integration with the organizational system. The Baldrige criteria emphasize these concepts. Effective alignment requires common understanding of purposes and goals and use of complementary measures and information for planning, tracking, analysis, and improvement at each of the three levels of quality. Integration goes beyond alignment and is achieved when the individual components of a performance management system operate as a fully interconnected unit.

A well-aligned organization has its processes focused on achieving a shared vision and strategy. Aligning the organization is a challenging task that is accomplished through a sound strategy and effective deployment.

Best Practices

The organizational infrastructure, as evidenced by an organization's management systems and practices, is vital to successful quality implementation. **Best practices** are simply those that are recognized by the business community (and often verified through some type of research) to lead to successful performance. Such organizations as Disney, Microsoft, and many Baldrige winners have recognized best practices that are adopted by other organizations.

Research performed by H. James Harrington with Ernst & Young and the American Quality Foundation, called the International Quality Study (IQS), suggested that trying to implement all the best practices of world-class organizations may not be a good strategy.[45] In fact, implementing the wrong practices can actually hurt the organization. The study indicated that only five best practices are "universal," and the chances are only 5 percent that they may not improve performance. They are:

1. Cycle-time analysis
2. Process value analysis
3. Process simplification
4. Strategic planning
5. Formal supplier certification programs

Beyond these five, best practices depend on an organization's current level of performance. That is, organizations must build their capability slowly and methodically. For example, organizations starting out on the road to performance excellence can reap the highest benefits by concentrating on fundamentals. These fundamentals include departmental and cross-functional teamwork, training in customer relationships, problem solving and suggestion systems, using internal customer complaint systems for new product and service ideas, emphasizing cost reduction when acquiring new technology, using customer satisfaction measures in strategic planning, increased training for all levels of employees, and focusing quality strategy on "building it in" and "inspecting it in." Once these fundamentals are in place, they can move on to practices such as department-level improvement teams, training employees in problem solving and other specialized topics, listening to supplier suggestions about new products, emphasizing the role of enforcement for quality assurance, making regular and consistent measurements of progress and sharing quality performance information with middle management, and emphasizing quality as a key to an organization's reputation. Finally, organizations that have a solid quality system in place can gain the most from providing customer-relationship training for new employees, emphasizing quality and teamwork for senior management assessment, encouraging widespread participation in quality meetings among non-management employees, using world-class benchmarking, communicating strategic plans to customers and suppliers, conducting after-sales service to build customer loyalty, and emphasizing competitor-comparison measures and customer satisfaction measures when developing plans. The study also showed that certain practices could have a negative impact on performance if applied inappropriately. For example, organizations at the early stages of the quality journey do not benefit from process benchmarking while those that have solid systems in place attain no benefit from increased training.

Strangely, the IQS Best Practices Report was interpreted by some news media as a criticism of the quality management philosophies that were advocated at that time.[46] They translated the report as simply saying that many quality practices are a waste of time and ineffective. On the contrary, the results were the first significant effort to develop a prescriptive theory (back to Deming again) of implementing quality and performance excellence, rather than relying on intuition and anecdotal evidence.

Impatient managers often seek immediate results by adopting off-the-shelf quality programs and practices, or by imitating other successful organizations. In most cases, this approach is setting themselves up for failure.

Best practices, however, cannot be blindly benchmarked and adopted. Unfortunately, many organizations seek the magic quick fix for quality.[47] In a famous anecdote, a person once wrote a letter to W. Edwards Deming and asked for the formula to quality improvement, offering to pay whatever price Deming required. This led to what has become one Deming's most famous quotes: "There is no instant pudding." We have seen similar behavior with Six Sigma. Many firms rushed to benchmark GE. However, GE already had a culture of quality improvement and extensive experience when Six Sigma began. The other firms were unable to copy the GE Method without the GE culture.

Rather, organizations advance in stages along a learning curve in their development of a quality culture and must carefully design their programs to optimize its effect. A good example is the Toyota Production System. It has never been a secret, yet many companies have tried and failed to duplicate it. Toyota's approach can be summarized as follows:

- They stayed the course and developed, implemented, and tweaked that system until it fit the organization like a glove.
- They did not spend their time looking for a prefabricated answer to all their problems that might or might not work in their organization.
- They took the time to understand their organization and their business and created a system that delivered the things they knew would make them a force in their industry.

As one professional observed: "The closest we will come to a silver bullet is innovative leadership. Courageous leaders have vision, take time to comprehend their own organizations, and create an indigenous strategy to fit their organization."[48]

THE JOURNEY TOWARD PERFORMANCE EXCELLENCE

Sustaining performance excellence requires the ability to overcome barriers and frustration, to view performance excellence as a journey, not an end, and the ability to develop into a "learning organization."

Successful organizations realize that quality and performance excellence is a never-ending journey. As an old Chinese proverb says, a journey begins with a single step. Getting started often seems easy by comparison with sustaining a performance excellence focus. Numerous organizational barriers and challenges get in the way. New efforts usually begin with much enthusiasm, in part because of the sheer novelty of the effort. After awhile, reality sets in and doubts surface. Real problems develop as early supporters begin to question the process. At this point, the organization can resign itself to inevitable failure or persist and seek to overcome the obstacles.

The Life Cycle of Quality Initiatives

To help understand these issues, it is useful to recognize that quality initiatives—as well as most any business initiative—follows a natural life cycle.[49] Leonard and McAdam suggest that understanding the life cycle "provides a strategic mechanism to chart and sustain quality while proactively countering shortcomings of its implementation, such as stagnation and limited application, which can ultimately result in failure." The six stages of a quality life cycle are

1. *Adoption:* The implementation stage of a new quality initiative.
2. *Regeneration:* When a new quality initiative is used in conjunction with an existing one to generate new energy and impact
3. *Energizing:* When an existing quality initiative is refocused and given new resources
4. *Maturation:* When quality is strategically aligned and deployed across the organization
5. *Limitation or stagnation:* When quality has not been strategically driven or aligned
6. *Decline:* When a quality management system (QMS) has had a limited impact, initiatives are failing, and the QMS is awaiting termination

The following example serves to illustrate the implications of this life cycle model.

One organization began adopting quality by introducing team building and establishing problem-solving teams. However, after four years the quality management initiative failed. Initial training had been limited, and implementation was unfocused and not directly related to the strategic objectives of the organization. As a result, the new teamwork approach came as a culture shock to the organization, and its quality initiative began a decline. The organization was determined to continue with quality management and subsequently adopted a second initiative. This involved new training and teams provided with improvement kits based on problem solving tools and techniques. In addition, senior management focused on the coordination of improvement efforts with strong links to the organization's strategic goals. Structured performance assessments monitored progress. The quality manager cited "management commitment and leadership from the top" as the key to its successful second quality initiative. The quality life cycle of this second initiative reflects its progress from adoption to maturity. This approach created strong quality dynamics, which achieved strategic alignment and deployment throughout the organization. From this example, we observe two things:

1. Awareness that separate initiatives create a cumulative impact leads to an appreciation that selection of new quality initiatives must be based on where an organization is in the quality life cycle.
2. Understanding that the quality life cycle elements enable an organization to apply energizing or regenerating actions proactively to successfully sustain its quality journey.

An awareness of such impacts on the dynamics of quality, in particular on the characteristics of the quality life cycle, provides the capability to sustain successful quality management by strategically adopting responses based on energizing and regenerating elements.

In studying Baldrige recipients in the health care sector, a group of former Baldrige examiners and judges proposed a similar model that describes the Baldrige journey, shown in Figure 9.4.[50] At Stage 0, organizations opt to wait for mandates and regulations, and they implement change when required to maintain compliance.

Figure 9.4 Baldrige Roadmap to Performance Excellence

Stage 0
"Status Quo"
Regulatory compliance only

Stage 1
"False Starts"
Project mentality, characterized by various tactical improvement activities

Stage 2
"Traction"
Alignment of projects to strategy, attention to leadership and management processes

Stage 3
"Integration"
Clear linkage of process management and improvement to operational results

Stage 4
"Sustaining"
Continued improvement as methodologies are embedded into the organization's culture

Baldrige recipient

Baldrige start

- OR
Give up on the process when managed as a delegated project

?

- OR
Decline, as the organization loses discipline and changes course

Progress

Time

3–8 Years

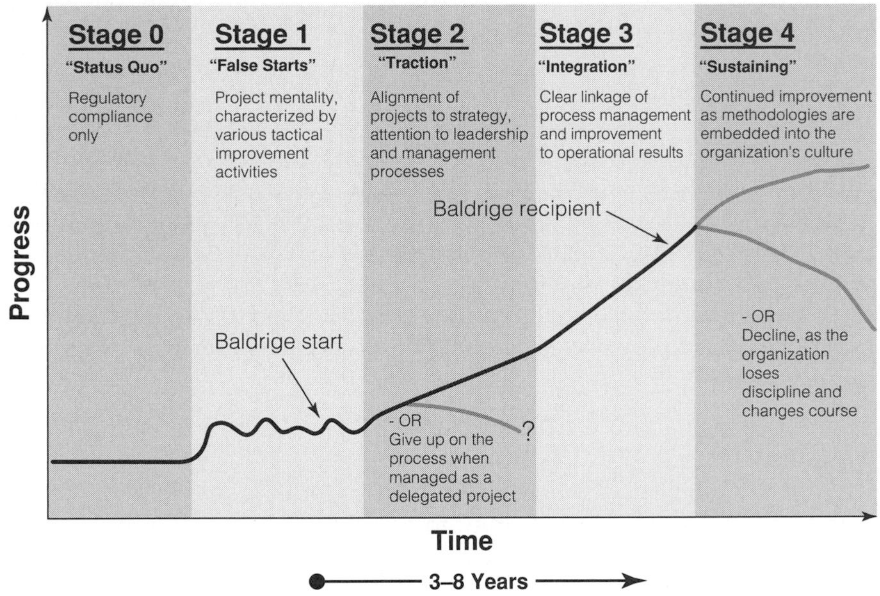

Source: Reprinted with permission from Kathleen J. Goonan, Joseph Muzikowski & Patricia K. Stoltz, "Journey to Excellence: Healthcare Baldridge Leaders Speak Out," *Quality in Healthcare*, January 2009, pp. 11–15. Copyright © 2009 American Society for Quality, Quality Press. No further distribution without permission.

While they may experience occasional "random acts of improvement," there is no overarching impetus to drive the organization to higher levels of performance. In Stage 1, organizations commit to a proactive approach to improvement. Initial steps tend to include learning and implementing quality improvement tools and methods. Often this project-focused phase brings new capabilities to execute initiatives that change routine practices and processes for the better. However, organizations at this stage typically reach a plateau. Leaders became frustrated with the overall impact of their continuous improvement efforts and the pace of change. For most of these organizations, projects succeed often enough, but the overall culture does not change and system-wide performance excellence is elusive. Visionary leaders recognize the inherent limitations of a project-based approach to performance improvement: slow pace of change, incremental gains, and depleted organizational energy. They seek an approach to build system integration across silos and departments in order to create a high-performance, results-oriented culture throughout their organizations.

When senior leaders became personally and actively engaged with the criteria and feedback—whether through simply answering the questions, conducting a self-assessment, or writing an application for a state or national award program—they begin to experience traction on their organizational transformation strategies (Stage 2). This phase marks the transition from the singular focus on change through projects, however well executed, to systematic evaluation and improvement of leadership approaches. Projects become more focused and aligned to organizational strategy while leadership and management processes receive attention as well, shoring up capability to spread improvements and hardwire sustainability. As organizations become more skillful at these approaches, integration (Stage 3) begins to occur. Approaches and processes of leadership, such as values deployment and culture building, begin to link and align with strategic planning and action planning, scorecards and dashboards, job descriptions and performance review methods, and other operational processes. Nonaligned improvement initiatives are dropped or postponed as focused effort replaces frenetic activity. The Integration phase is characterized by action on the feedback, usually by incorporating it into the strategic planning process.

Finally, the Sustaining stage (Stage 4) can result in two outcomes: continued improvement or decline as organizations lose focus or become distracted. While Baldrige Award recognition might appear to carry with it the potential for loss of momentum, many organizations renew their commitment to achieving even higher levels of performance. This may occur through continuing annual participation in a Baldrige-based award process, or through internal assessment processes, often as a first step in annual strategic planning.

One example that reflects this roadmap is St. Luke's Hospital, which began its journey around 1988.[51] Key organizational milestones are summarized below:

1988–1991:

- Limited focus Patient Care Committee to a broader organizational quality assurance concept
- Hierarchal nursing governance to a shared governance model
- Decreased focus on the "bad apple" to process improvement activities
- Specialty-specific committees reconfigured to organizational cross-functional multidisciplinary teams

1992–1993:

- Development of an organization-wide customer satisfaction research program
- Individual care plans to formal clinical care pathways
- Cultural shift to organizational empowerment
- Board, medical staff, and administration retreat to implement Total Quality Management

1994:

- Organizational learning in statistical process control techniques
- Patient focused work redesign initiated
- Adopted Baldrige framework
- Participated on health care criteria design team for Missouri Quality Award

1995–1996:

- Embraced corporate culture of external performance review
- Received Missouri Quality Award (MQA)
- Began voluntarily reporting outcome data to the community
- Shared best practices across Missouri
- Used MQA feedback to improve performance

1997–1999:

- Deployed "Commitment to Excellence" initiative: an internal Baldrige-based assessment
- Received second Missouri Quality Award
- Quality was elevated to vice president status
- Restructured metrics architecture and developed Balanced Scorecard

2000–2001

- Used 1999 Baldrige and MQA feedback to improve organizational processes and share best practices
- Prepared internal Baldrige assessment and had it scored externally

- Focused on multiple action-oriented process teams
- Medical staff and senior leaders joined to drive organizational performance via Performance Improvement Steering Committee (PISC)

2002:
- Received third Missouri Quality Award
- Site visit by MBNQA
- Third refinement of the Balanced Scorecard
- Deployed 90-Day Action Planning Process

2003:
- Began preparation to achieve Nursing Magnet designation
- Created the role of Chief Learning Officer
- Developed and deployed process level scorecards in key areas
- Selected as a Malcolm Baldrige National Quality Award recipient

As you can clearly see, such a journey takes persistence and commitment.

Organizational Learning

Organizations are dynamic entities. Managers must consider the dynamic component in order to deal with instability in the environment, imperfect plans, the need for innovation, and the common human desire for variety and change.

Sustainability requires continual learning. Therefore, both the culture and the organizational structure should be designed to support the established direction in which the organization is moving, and modified whenever that direction changes significantly. Managers, especially those who do not understand the nature of leadership, are often hesitant to make needed organizational changes as the organization grows, even when the need for change becomes obvious. This need to change is embodied in a concept called the *learning organization.*

The concept of organizational learning is not new. It has its roots in general systems theory[52] and systems dynamics[53] developed in the 1950s and 1960s, as well as theories of learning from organizational psychology. Peter Senge, a professor at the Massachusetts Institute of Technology (MIT), defines the **learning organization** as:

> *. . . an organization that is continually expanding its capacity to create its future. For such an organization, it is not enough merely to survive. "Survival learning" or what is more often termed "adaptive learning" is important—indeed it is necessary. But for a learning organization, "adaptive learning" must be joined by "generative learning," learning that enhances our capacity to create.*[54]

The conceptual framework behind this definition requires an understanding and integration of many of the concepts and principles that are part of the TQ philosophy. Senge repeatedly points out, "Over the long run, superior performance depends on superior learning." What he means is that organizations cannot count on being successful in the long run if they merely have committed leaders who use TQ principles for strategic planning and policy deployment, practice TQ in daily operations, and use it for continuous improvement of the current process.

Learning organizations have become skilled in creating, acquiring, and transferring knowledge and in modifying the behavior of their employees and other contributors to their enterprises. A good example of a learning organization (and a learning individual!) is General Electric and its former CEO Jack Welch. In his first letter to

GE shareholders in 1981, he noted, "This commitment to the utmost in quality and personal excellence is our surest path to continued business success. Quality is our best assurance of customer allegiance. It is our strongest defense against foreign competition and the only path to sustained growth and earnings." Welch's approach to business improvement has gone through three cycles of learning:

1. In the first cycle (early 1980s to late 1980s), he focused GE on the elimination of variety in its portfolio of businesses by reducing the nonperforming business units as judged by market performance. The elimination of unprofitable businesses permitted a better use of working capital. However, only so much gain can result from trimming the organization or eliminating bureaucracy, which led to the next phase of learning.
2. During the late 1980s to mid-1990s, he focused the company on simplifying and eliminating non-value-added activities through creative efforts of teams using Work-Outs and the Change Action Process (later renamed the Change Acceleration Process). Work-Out is a tool for involving all people from all ranks, levels, and functions of the organization in problem solving and improvement. Work-Out demolished the artificial barriers and walls within the organization and fostered the idea of "boundary-less learning."
3. Throughout his learning journey, Welch challenged his people to keep looking for creative ways to apply new learning from any source to improve the business. In 1995, Welch discovered Six Sigma and studied its implementation at both Motorola and Allied Signal. This phase of discovery focused on the elimination of variation from already lean business operations to drive gains in productivity and financial performance with a better focus on the customer.

Welch's process for continuous learning led to the discovery that business must simplify first, then automate best practices that have been designed for robust performance in the face of variation in business conditions. As Welch noted, "It is this passion for learning and sharing that forms the basis for the unrelenting optimism with which we view the future, and for the conviction that our greatest days lie ahead." The emphasis on quality and improvement through Six Sigma has been continued by Jeffrey Immelt, who succeeded Jack Welch as CEO at GE in 2001. Immelt's "Letter to Stakeholders" in the 2004 annual report stated:

> *We have a new area of focus that we call **Lean Six Sigma**. We have leveraged Lean manufacturing's classic tools for reducing cycle time with the problem-solving capability of Six Sigma. In the last two years, Transportation improved inventory turns from seven to nine, and Advanced Materials improved receivables by six turns. We achieved $2.7 billion of improvements in working capital in 2003–04 and intend to continue this progress.*
>
> *We have a broad operating initiative called **Simplification**. We are targeting a reduction in "non-growth cost" of $3 billion over three years. We are measuring reductions in legal entities, headquarters, "rooftops," computer systems... anything that is not directly linked with customer satisfaction and growth. We are creating "Centers of Excellence" to share best practices and reduce cost.*[55]

The 2007 annual report describes the results of a new initiative called "Growth as a Process," and its approaches to operational excellence that include using Lean Six Sigma, quality, and simplification to enhance value.

The key to developing learning organizations, according to Senge, is a new approach to leadership. Leaders must develop the capability to integrate creative thinking and problem solving throughout the organization. Instead of the traditional focus on reacting to events and responding to historical trends, leaders must encourage and model decision making based on understanding the causes of events and the behavior behind the trends in order to make positive changes to the system.

Researchers have suggested that both transactional and transformational leadership support organizational learning; in times of change, organizational learning benefits more from transformational leadership while in times of stability, organizational learning processes serve to refresh and reinforce current learning—a task best suited to transactional leadership. The ideal leader needs to identify and exercise the leadership behaviors appropriate to the circumstances.[56]

Learning organizations have to become good at performing five main activities, including systematic problem solving, experimentation with new approaches, learning from their own experiences and history, learning from the experiences and best practices of others, and transferring knowledge quickly and efficiently throughout the organization.[57]

Virtually all of these skills are central to the philosophy of performance excellence. For example, systematic problem solving is reflected in Six Sigma and other improvement methodologies; experimentation is the basis for Deming's plan-do-study-act cycle; learning from experiences and history is often termed Santayana review[58] and is basic to Deming's philosophy; learning from the experiences and best practices of others is reflected in benchmarking practices; and transferring knowledge quickly and efficiently throughout the organization is the basis for modern knowledge management practices that we discussed in Chapter 8.

Cole has called for "continuous innovation" as an evolutionary step for extending "continuous improvement."[59] He pointed out that market pressures for better and cheaper products, delivered faster to the marketplace than ever before, require a new strategy that he advocates as a "probe and learn" process. Probe-and-learn is described as a non-linear, discontinuous, experimental, back-and-forth process that is needed in order to develop products and services to compete in the existing turbulent business environment. It requires methods such as rapid prototyping, beta testing with intentional generation of errors if they contribute to learning, learning from failure (and successes), and rapidly making decisions through peer and customer review.

You need only go back to the relationship between quality and profitability (Figure 1.6 in Chapter 1) to understand the importance of continuous innovation. From this argument, it is evident that the need for innovation has been known all along; however, most efforts (TQM, ISO 9000, Six Sigma, for example) have focused mainly on the quality of conformance rather than innovative design. Businesses are now closing the loop on a more complete performance excellence system with increasing emphasis on design and innovation.

Leaders in twenty-first-century organizations are finding that not only must they create learning organizations, but they must also create teaching organizations. For example, GE developed the concept of the virtuous teaching cycle (VTC) that guides their entire leadership development process, of which the Six Sigma approach is a vital part. The VTC includes some of the following concepts and assumptions, as well as others:[60]

- Leadership at all levels [as opposed to leadership at the top]
- Teamwork [as opposed to passive-aggressive behavior]
- Teachable point of view (TPOV) throughout [as opposed to a rigid, top-down process]

- Organizational knowledge grows [as opposed to organizational knowledge being depleted]
- Boundarylessness [as opposed to a boundary-laden, turf-oriented organization]

Self-Assessment

One way for organizations to build accomplish organizational learning is to conduct self-assessments of where it stands relative to best practices and key requirements. **Self-assessment** is the holistic evaluation of processes and performance.[61] It helps managers answer essential questions such as "How are we doing?," "What are our strengths?," and "What areas require improvement?" The *self* part of the term means that it should be conducted internally rather than simply relying on an external consultant, which promotes greater involvement of the organization's people, yielding a higher level of understanding and buy-in.

Self-assessment should identify both strengths and opportunities for improvement, creating a basis for evolving toward higher levels of performance. Thus, a major objective of most self-assessment projects is the improvement of organizational processes based on opportunities identified by the evaluation.

At a minimum, a self-assessment should address the following:

- *Management involvement and leadership*. To what extent are all levels of management involved?
- *Product and process design*. Do products meet customer needs? Are products designed for easy manufacturability?
- *Product control*. Is a strong product control system in place that concentrates on defect prevention before the fact, rather than defect removal after the product is made?
- *Customer and supplier communications*. Does everyone understand who the customer is? To what extent do customers and suppliers communicate with each other?
- *Quality improvement*. Is a quality improvement plan in place? What results have been achieved?
- *Employee participation*. Are all employees actively involved in quality improvement?
- *Education and training*. What is done to ensure that everyone understands his or her job and has the necessary skills? Are employees trained in quality improvement techniques?
- *Quality information*. How is feedback on quality results collected and used?

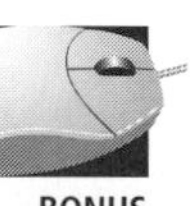

BONUS MATERIALS

Many self-assessment instruments that provide a picture of the state of quality in the organization are available.[62] The Baldrige National Quality Program provides two simple instruments called *Are We Making Progress?* (one for employees and one for leaders). They provide a way of capturing the voice of the employee and the perspective of leadership to develop baseline measurements of an organization's progress using the Baldrige criteria. The *Are We Making Progress?* surveys are available in the Baldrige Materials folder on the Premium website. Most self-administered surveys, however, can only provide a rudimentary assessment of an organization's strengths and weaknesses. The most complete way to assess the level of performance excellence maturity in an organization is to evaluate its practices and results against the Malcolm Baldrige National Quality Award criteria by using trained internal or external examiners, or by actually applying for the Baldrige or a similar state award and receiving comprehensive examiner feedback. Of course, many organizations, especially smaller ones, that are just starting on a quality journey should begin with the basics, for example, a well-documented and consistent quality assurance system such as ISO 9000.

Assessment findings often identify specific processes and activities that require extensive modification.[63] A Baldrige assessment, for example, might find that the organization lacks a systematic approach for determining customer satisfaction relative to its competitors. A number of actions might be taken to address this opportunity. The organization might consider instituting a competitive analysis program, sponsoring an industry-wide customer satisfaction research program, benchmarking best-in-class organizations, or undertaking some other initiatives to improve its intelligence gathering practices. Although interventions of such scope commonly involve many employees, involvement of senior management in direction setting, resource provision, and subsequent monitoring is usually necessary for effective implementation.

Because the Baldrige process is based on self-assessment against the criteria, it is not surprising that some of the best examples of learning organizations are Baldrige winners. In pursuing their improvement efforts that eventually led to the award, they have continually and systematically translated the examiner feedback into improvements in their management practices. A vice president at Texas Instruments Defense Systems & Electronics (DS&E) Group noted that "participating in the Baldrige Award process energized improvement efforts."[64] By 1997, just before its purchase by Raytheon, DS&E had reduced the number of in-process defects to one-tenth of what they were at the time it won the Baldrige. Production processes that took four weeks several years before were reduced to one week, with 20 to 30 percent less cost. As another example, the superintendent of Iredell-Statesville Schools, a 2008 recipient, noted "The big [opportunity for improvement provided by the Baldrige feedback report] that kept us from achieving recognition in 2007 was that we had a well-deployed Baldrige criteria at the classroom level, but were so focused on meeting the requirements of the No Child Left Behind Act in student learning that we missed opportunities for improvement on the operation side, for example, in maintenance, transportation, and child nutrition. We were using Deming's plan-do-study-act cycles, and once we got into the operation side of the house we found all kinds of expenses that could be reduced, with the savings then used in the academic side of the house. So, it was a great feedback report. It gave us the impetus to go to the next level."[65]

Although some research suggests a positive relationship between the conduct of self-assessment and performance outcomes, other evidence suggests that many organizations derive little benefit from conducting self-assessment and achieve few of the process improvements suggested by self-study.

It is not uncommon for organizations to spend considerable time and effort on assessing their organizations, only to seemingly ignore the results.[66] This lack of follow-through might seem a bit surprising. Why would organizations take the time to conduct a self-assessment and then not follow up on the results? After all, improvement opportunities usually offer significant gains in organizational effectiveness and competitive performance. Some managers may not follow up because they truly do not sense a problem—despite information suggesting otherwise. Often, however, managers get the message but choose not to respond. Many managers react negatively or by denial: "These are wrong," "This is not how it is here," and "These [examiners] missed the boat" are often heard. Such remarks are particularly likely when the report suggested that the organization was a less-than-stellar performer in areas perceived as strengths by senior managers.

Other mangers may not know what to do with the information. Managers possessing little understanding of how the organization operates may not know which levers to pull in order to effect change or simply do it to appease their superiors. Typical comments include, "There's some good stuff here, but I have no idea where to go from here," and "It's hard for me to understand how to turn this [assessment report] into action." After reading his copy of the feedback report, the head of one manufacturing company manager muttered, "Well, we've satisfied [the boss's demand for conducting the self-assessment] for another year. Now we can put this all away and get back to business."

Following up requires senior leaders to engage in two types of activities: action planning and subsequently tracking implementation progress.

Managers must take a positive approach to self-assessment findings, no matter how unpleasant they might appear—"OK, what should we do to improve these areas?" Positive reactions often reinforce long-held but suppressed views about how the organization functioned. For example, at a meeting where results were being presented to the top management team, the chief engineering manager, upon hearing of low evaluations related to the organization's communications processes, exclaimed, "I've been telling you guys this for years! Maybe now you'll believe me that we need to do something."

The action plan identifies particular activities necessary to address the improvement opportunities. Effective action plans share some common characteristics. First, key actions to address the opportunities must be identified. A meeting to discuss the findings with key employees is often an excellent way to begin. Once identified, action plans should be documented and the who, what, when, where, and how of each action item specified. A draft version of the action plan should be communicated to inform those directly affected and gain their cooperation. Finally, the action plan should be reviewed to ensure that it effectively addresses the key opportunities identified by the self-assessment findings.

Many managers consider their job finished when action plans are set in motion. However, planned changes are rarely implemented as initially intended. Moreover, people responsible for implementing the plans may need to use encouragement or involvement in order to effectively execute their portions of the intended change. Change implementation demands a second component of effective follow-up—tracking the progress of action plan execution—to provide managers with crucial feedback on whether the intervention is effective.

To leverage self-assessment findings, managers must do four things:

1. *Prepare to be humbled.* "Humbling" is a word we often hear from managers who have recently digested assessment findings. Many of them have trouble believing that the performance levels of the organization are as low as they appear. Managers can temper their expectations by learning about the self-assessment activities and experiences of other organizations. Hearing it from peers, through phone calls to colleagues, and attending conferences, permit managers to learn firsthand about the self-assessment experiences of others.
2. *Talk though the findings.* Follow-up can be enhanced when the top management team discusses the self-assessment findings. Discussing the issues, concerns, and ideas can generate greater shared perspective among executives and improve consensus.
3. *Recognize institutional influences.* Managers should be sensitive to the institutional forces working on their self-assessment activities, such as pressures from customers. Institutional influence can be **covertly** transmitted through the

literature, presentations, and conversation that managers encounter. During the planning phase of the assessment, frank discussion about the environmental motivators of the project can sensitize managers to these outside influences.

4. *Grind out the follow-up.* Even though follow-up activities may not be as exciting as plotting competitive strategy or entertaining customers, they provide infrastructure for realizing the process improvements possible from self-assessment.

LEADERSHIP IN THE BALDRIGE CRITERIA, ISO 9000, AND SIX SIGMA

Category 1 of the Malcolm Baldrige National Quality Award Criteria for Performance Excellence is *Leadership*. As the first of the seven categories, it signifies the critical importance of leadership to business success. Item 1.1, *Senior Leadership*, examines how senior leaders guide and sustain an organization by setting and deploying its vision and values; creating an environment for performance improvement, role-model performance leadership, organizational agility, workforce learning, and legal and ethical behavior; communicate with the workforce and take an active role in reward and recognition programs; and create a focus on action to accomplish objectives, improve performance, and attain the vision.

Item 1.2, *Governance and Societal Responsibilities*, addresses how the organization's governance system addresses management and fiscal accountability and protection of stakeholder interests; how performance of senior leaders is evaluated; and how senior leaders use performance reviews to improve leadership effectiveness and the leadership system. It also addresses how an organization fulfills its public responsibilities, ensures ethical behavior, and practices good citizenship. These responsibilities include how the organization addresses impacts and risks of products, services, and operations on society in a proactive manner; how it ensures ethical business practices in all stakeholder interactions; and how the organization, its senior leaders, and employees identify, support, and strengthen key communities as part of good citizenship practices.

Leadership underlies many of the requirements of ISO 9000:2000. The entire section on Management Responsibility is concerned with the role of leadership in driving a quality system. For example, the standards require that "Top management shall provide evidence of its commitment to the development and implementation of the quality management system and continually improving its effectiveness by a) communicating to the organization the importance of meeting customer as well as statutory and regulatory requirements, b) establishing the quality policy, c) ensuring that quality objectives are established, d) conducting management reviews, and e) ensuring the availability of resources." More specific responsibilities are spelled out in detail in other clauses of the standards.

Leadership is a fundamental value of Six Sigma. Driving organizational change to create and sustain a Six Sigma culture simply cannot be done without strong leadership. In other words, Six Sigma cannot be an add-on or a "flavor of the month." It must become the way business is done in organizations that adopt it.

A VIEW TOWARD THE FUTURE

As we close this part of the book, it is a good exercise to try to look into the future and think about how things will be. In reflecting on quality in the past century, A.V. Feigenbaum and Donald S. Feigenbaum observed:

> *[Quality] has become one of the 20th century's most important management ideas. It has exorcised the traditional business and graduate management school notion that a company's success means making products and offering*

services quicker and cheaper, selling them hard and providing a product service net to try to catch those that don't work well. It has replaced this notion with the business principle that making products better is the best way to make them quicker and cheaper and that what is done to make quality better anywhere in an organization makes it better everywhere in the organization.[67]

What the future will hold is never predictable. We face a serious challenge in sustaining the principles of quality amidst the continuing emergence of short-lived management fads, changing leadership driven by pressures of the stock market, e-commerce, and a myriad of other factors. In the January 2000 issue of *Quality Progress,* the American Society for Quality invited 21 individuals to provide comments on quality in the 21st century.[68] We conclude this chapter with a sample of those comments, and invite you to reflect on what they mean for you as you continue your education and embark on your future careers.

"Those who understand that quality is derived from effectively managing systems will provide leadership in the new millennium. How many CEOs do you know who arise from the ranks of quality? Few, if any. Yet, I believe tomorrow's business leaders will have deep roots in quality and advanced understanding of how it nourishes their organizations' broader management systems."—Alexander Chong

"The new millennium presents us with some fundamental challenges:

- *Altered labor markets with higher skill levels, a greater gender balance, and increasing diversity.*
- *Competitive demands for continuous improvement, customer responsiveness, and levels of business excellence that are not price prohibitive.*

These can only be met through an emphasis on quality with equality." —Eileen Drew

"The 21st century will see leading edge companies apply to information the quality principles successfully applied to manufacturing. This will usher in the next economic revolution—the 'realized' Information Age, created by applying information quality management to information and knowledge processes."—Larry P. English

"Quality is necessary for public education to thrive in the future. We have a moral imperative to use quality to make a difference in the lives of our children." —Diane Rivers

"The quality perspective will shape the redefinition of the role of government. This new role will mean serving as a facilitator of relationships and innovative partnerships across all sectors, with less focus on direct delivery of service. Those who understand this context will thrive." —Tina Sung

Finally, Miles Maguire, Editor of *Quality Progress* noted:

In the first 10 seconds of the new century... the world will witness the birth of 44 infants... by the time a year has passed almost 140 million children will have been born... Consider all the new technologies and products and concepts and ideologies that have taken hold in the last decade: flip phones, fax machines, hiphop, SUVs, global markets, cyberschooling, eco-tourism, eco-terrorism, extreme sports, e-commerce, gene therapy, streaming media, and digital encryption—to name just a few. And now consider how the next decade, the first 1 percent of the new millennium, will bring at least as great a proliferation of ideas, innovations, and improvements. These developments will set a higher

> *standard of expectations, creating a marketplace with a dizzying diversity of demands that can scarcely be imagined. What will the voice of the 21st century customer be telling us? We'll have to listen carefully to find out.*[69]

Time will tell how whether or not these predictions will be realized. How do you see the organizations that you are familiar with addressing them?

SUMMARY OF KEY POINTS AND TERMINOLOGY

The Bonus Materials folder for this chapter on the Premium website provides a summary of key concepts and terminology introduced in this chapter.

QUALITY IN PRACTICE

LEADERSHIP CHANGES AT ALCOA[70]

Alcoa, ranked as the 79th largest firm in the 2005 *Fortune* 500, employs approximately 129,000 people worldwide and had 2004 annual sales of $23.96 billion. Alcoa has been known for progressive, innovative management. It treats its employees well, tries to avoid layoffs and plant closures unless forced to make changes as a result of continued negative results, and has unions at only about 15 of its 47 locations. Nevertheless, at Alcoa's industrial magnesium plant in Addy, Washington, a crisis of epic proportions rocked the plant and rattled the company, leading to some key leadership changes that ultimately resulted in dramatic improvements in safety, productivity, and profits.

At the time of this case (in the late 1980's) the plant was facing two severe problems: an unacceptable rate of serious injuries that averaged 12.8 per year, and five years of unprofitable operations. No clear, easily-implemented solutions were apparent for the first problem, but corporate management had suggested that layoffs of 100 or more employees were all but inevitable in order to stem the tide of red ink. Operating statistics bore out the depth and breadth of the problem. Prices of magnesium had dropped, and units selling for $1.45 on the open market cost $1.48 to make at Alcoa's plant. Quality control was below what was needed to counteract market forces, with magnesium recovery at only 72 percent of the raw material being processed.

The apparent causes of plant problems consisted of a complex mix of lack of accountability, poor quality control, inadequate leadership, and low morale, especially among hourly employees. Corporate management stressed safety above all, and profitability second. The death of an employee, who was related to seven other employees, and the unacceptable financial losses led senior corporate management to decide that a change in plant management was essential. Don Simonic, a former college football coach, with Alcoa experience, was tapped for the job of plant manager. His turnaround team members included the then-personnel manager, Tom McCombs and outside consultants Robert and Patricia Crosby. If the new leadership team could not turn the plant around, plant closure or sell-off were the only remaining options.

Since its construction, the plant had been designed with an open-systems, team-based culture, adapted from socio-technical systems theory. It was structured similar to the way that Procter and Gamble had set up its soap plants, and was considered a leading-edge organizational design. The process for producing the industrial magnesium was highly advanced and technical, and the innovative work team structure seemed to fit the technical systems characteristics. The plant attracted visitors from inside and outside the company who wanted to benchmark the operation and talk to team members. The organizational structure included:

- Autonomous, self-directed teams with no immediate supervisors. Teams were responsible for their own work areas.
- Hourly employee leadership that consisted of a team coordinator, safety person, training person, and team resource (internal facilitator) on each team.

- Supervisors, called shift coordinators, with four or five teams reporting to them, who were connected to the team coordinators. Shift coordinators generally stayed at arm's length, because if they intervened in team operations, they would get in trouble. The teams would say, "Leave us alone. We know what we're doing." If they didn't intervene, upper management would say that the teams weren't doing what they should be. The supervisors were caught in the middle.

Employees were empowered, but unable to face critical decisions that needed to be made to stem the crisis. The Crosbys identified lack of clarity in decision making and authority as the main culprit in the plant's environment. The new leadership model, conceived by the Crosbys and the plant leaders, involved major changes in goal-setting and decision-making practices. It required:

- New clarity in goal-setting
- A consultative, instead of a pure consensus approach to decision making
- Coming to grips with the need to cut costs pragmatically

As the turnaround proceeded, Simonic decided that cutting staff was essential to meeting the new goals. First, all temporary and contract workers were laid off. As leaders were explaining the facts that had led to a decision to lay off an additional 100 workers, an hourly worker revealed a breakthrough that his team had made to significantly reduce the downtime required to turn a magnesium smelting furnace around. This process involved switching over to a new crucible once the other was filled (a form of the Japanese manufacturing technique called SMED—single minute exchange of dies). The new team approach required more labor, but cut the downtime from the usual one-and-a-half-hour turnaround time to just one hour. Simonic called off the impending layoffs. When the new process was implemented on all nine furnaces in the plant, the savings reached $10 million. This was more than the wages of the 100 employees, who were allowed to keep their jobs.

Simonic held strategic meetings where he engaged salaried and non-salaried employees in intensive dialogue. His objective was to align all parts of the system, clarify who would be making what decisions, explain how decisions could be influenced, and communicate why decisions were made. Simonic then set the goals. Simonic made clear statements like, "These are the goals. You and all our employees have firsthand knowledge of how things work around here. I don't care how you get there. I will support you in making choices about how to get there. And, if you can't get there, I will step in and decide how we will get there." McCombs, the personnel manager, remembered how they developed a matrix reflecting what kind of decisions team members and supervisors would make. Supervisors would still retain authority over all decisions, if needed. Before Simonic's arrival, decisions had been made largely by consensus.

As a result of this process, one person was made responsible for every project or task, known as single-point accountability. This proved to be a critical change that was used instead of the consensus (team) approach, which was previously the only way to perform projects. McCombs and Simonic believed that for single-point accountability to succeed, it was necessary to establish the "by whens"—when particular tasks would be accomplished. After making clear to the teams and employees what was expected, they started achieving goals better.

Eighteen months after Alcoa's brought Simonic in as plant manager, the change efforts had produced impressive results: Unit costs had been reduced from $1.48 to $1.18, recovery of magnesium increased by 5 percentage points (worth $1.3 million per point), and the serious-injury frequency fell from 12.8 to 6.3 per year. Although positive signs appeared throughout the process, the incident in which the layoffs were averted proved to be the most critical, because employees subsequently had taken responsibility for applying their own creativity to meeting plant goals. Over the next two years, the plant became the lowest-cost producer in the world, and shortly afterward had boosted productivity by 72 percent. The president of Alcoa even asked all of the plant managers to visit the site and learn from Addy's turnaround.

One decision-making technique that was practiced at Addy and several other Alcoa plants was consultative decision-making, where the manager makes the final decision but consults with the team first. For example, McCombs recalls an incident requiring disciplinary action on several teams: "The teams would have 24 hours to give their recommendations to management on how the discipline should be handled-up to and including termination and management would administer the discipline. At least 95 percent of the time we took the team's recommendation and moved on," says McCombs.

The consultative method was also used to make hiring decisions. For example, the boundaries laid out for a team might concern Alcoa's desire to hire minorities. Typically, "the team would present their selection of who to hire to the manager, and often they would do such a good job the decision was just "'rubber-stamped,'" explains McCombs.

Another successful approach was called the "cadre." During the turnaround, Simonic and the Crosbys would work with the cadre, a group of key people, chosen from a vertical slice of the employees, who engaged in two specific roles: (1) observing and evaluating the change process as it played out while (2) simultaneously participating in the process. The cadre became a skilled resource for the plant on leadership development, change management, conflict management, quality, and work processes.

In reflecting on Simonic's impact on the organization, McCombs noted: "Don had a dynamic personality and was very charismatic. He possessed a very strong leadership style and was very clear. But you also must work with the intact families in the organization—one of Simonic's own beliefs. That's where change happens—in the small groups. You must work with that supervisor and that crew and get them aligned with the organization and work out any conflict." According to McCombs, Simonic was guided by four clear principles: "Leaders have to lead, make decisions, have a clear vision, and set direction. Once leaders set direction and get a breakthrough goal in mind that people can rally around, then people can tell the leader how they are going to get it done. A leader shouldn't tell how to do it, but he or she needs to set that direction. And that's what Simonic did very well," insists McCombs.

Unfortunately, Addy didn't sustain the momentum of the turnaround. In 1992, Simonic and McCombs left to help turn around other Alcoa plants. Corporate management continued to reduce the workforce. They eliminated all the department heads and everybody ended up reporting to the shift supervisor or plant manager. This caused lack of clarity about leadership and authority in decision making all over again, and as McCombs explained, "They stripped away the leadership that could have supported the change efforts afterwards."

Perhaps because of the previous successes and the skills gained in the previous turnaround, Crosby believed that the second recovery that occurred some time after Simonic and McCombs left, was going to be much easier. The plant appeared to be back on track and headed for success again, but the fortunes of business intervened. There was another drop in the price of magnesium, and the Addy plant lost its competitive edge. In fall of 2001, the plant was closed down and approximately 350 employees lost their jobs.[71]

Key Issues for Discussion

1. From a strategic management standpoint, why do you think that corporate management at Alcoa delayed taking action for five years as the plant continued to lose money and deteriorate in other operational measures?
2. What type of leadership style did Simonic seem to follow? Does it fit any of the leadership theories that were developed in the chapter?
3. How easy or difficult would it be for other organizations to duplicate the leadership style of Simonic and the organizational systems practiced at Addy, prior to, and after Simonic's tenure?

QUALITY IN PRACTICE

MERGING DIVERGENT QUALITY SYSTEMS AT HONEYWELL[72]

AlliedSignal and Honeywell each had years invested in their quality management systems (QMSs) when they merged in 1999 into Honeywell International. AlliedSignal was a leading supporter of, and participant in, the Six Sigma movement. By the time of the merger, AlliedSignal was five years into its Six Sigma program, which was key to the company's effort to capture growth and productivity opportunities more rapidly and efficiently. Meanwhile, Honeywell had developed its own Baldrige-based QMS—the Honeywell Quality Value (HQV) program. The merger between AlliedSignal and Honeywell required merging and reshaping these two diverse approaches, which was renamed Six Sigma Plus. Six Sigma Plus combines the characteristics of the former AlliedSignal's Six Sigma program and the former Honeywell's HQV method, including lean enterprise, a lean manufacturing component; and activity-based management (ABM), which aids in analyzing customer profitability and targeting future costs for new product development.

Key to making Six Sigma Plus universal in each of Honeywell International's businesses was committing to a strategy of approaching every improvement project with the same logical method, the DMAIC process. Their leadership criteria were also logical and rigorous. Candidates for Six Sigma Plus leadership positions were expected to possess an aptitude for learning, the ability to lead, the ability to mentor others, and the desire to continue to progress through the organization.

Honeywell International's CEO Michael R. Bonsignore made clear the future of Six Sigma at the new company: "As a new organization, our challenge is to continue the performance improvements of our predecessors, delight customers, and achieve aggressive growth. Six Sigma Plus will drive growth and productivity by energizing all of Honeywell International's 120,000 employees worldwide—providing the skills and tools to create more value for our customers, improve our processes, and capitalize on the power of the Internet through e-business. I am determined to make it a way of life at Honeywell International."

Edward M. Romanoff, Honeywell International's communications director for Six Sigma Plus and productivity, stated: "Lean helps us to reengineer a process to focus only on customer value-added elements. ABM helps us to understand the profitability of our products and services and to tailor our business models appropriately. The HQV process is being streamlined, timed to affect our annual operating plans, and geared to help our businesses prioritize remedial process improvements that affect customers and the financial well-being of the business. These two pieces—Six Sigma and HQV—come together nicely in that the latter provides the framework for how one should run a business in total, and Six Sigma gives you the quantitative specifics of what and how to improve."

"The Baldrige criteria might mandate that a company measure a given product's performance from a customer's perspective," explains Ray Stark, VP of Six Sigma and Productivity. "And if no such reporting mechanism existed, the Baldrige examiner would suggest that best-performing companies have this kind of system and that your company should put one in place. With a Six Sigma QMS, we would not only say you should put something in place, but we would give you the specific measurements that would help you understand the capability of the product. And it would be done in a way that would allow you to index its quality against a yardstick that we call Six Sigma."

Being able to effectively use Stark's yardstick meant training. Employees of the former AlliedSignal needed to learn about the HQV elements added to their Six Sigma program to create Six Sigma Plus, but the bigger challenge was training employees of the former Honeywell in Six Sigma methodology, a program that had not been developed or implemented there.

But "training" didn't accurately characterize Honeywell International's project based educational system. "Our program is not about training, it's about learning," explains Romonoff. "You can put people in a classroom and give them statistical training. You can give them hypothetical examples to make your point and people do learn, some faster than others. But the part that's unique here is that people come into this mentored environment with a project beforehand. It's something that they or their business particularly needs done. And they're given that project and asked to go and learn about these tools and how they can apply them to get a desired result or 'outcome.' It's very much results-orientated." Management expects this newly gained knowledge to trickle down the corporate structure as soon as the training is completed. Employees who complete the program are expected to go back to their business and complete two to three Six Sigma projects per year. Additionally, they are to mentor as many as 10 groups of employees a year in their Six Sigma Plus learning curve.

"So if that's 10 teams at 10 people each, you've got 100 employees that can be potentially impacted by this one individual," explains Stark. "So it's very important that these people have the team-dynamic skills to deal with different types of people, behaviors and situations. At the end of the day, what we want is at least a simple understanding of the applications of these tools by every employee."

Honeywell International employees who become skilled in Six Sigma Plus tools can earn certification in the following core areas of proficiency:

- Green Belt—A person with working knowledge of Six Sigma Plus methodology and tools, who has completed training and a project to drive high-impact business results.
- Black Belt—A highly skilled Six Sigma Plus expert who has completed four weeks of classroom learning and, over the course of four to six months, demonstrated mastery of the tools through the completion of a major process improvement project.
- Master Black Belt—The Six Sigma Plus expert most highly skilled in the methodologies of variation reduction. After a year-long, project-based certification program, Master Black Belts train and mentor Black Belts, help select and lead high-value projects, maintain the integrity of the sigma measurements, and develop and revise Six Sigma Plus learning materials.
- Lean Expert—A person who has completed four weeks of lean training and one or more projects that have demonstrated significant, auditable business results and the appropriate application of Six Sigma Plus lean tools.
- Lean Master—A person highly skilled in implementing lean principles and lean tool utilization in diverse business environments. Certification involves one year of intense study and practice in advanced lean tools, teaching, and mentoring.
- ABM Expert—A person who has demonstrated proficiency in activity-based management (ABM) through a business application involving product costing, process costing, or customer profitability analysis. Certification involves attending an ABM training course, defining a meaningful project, displaying knowledge of the ABM tools, and using the data for key decision making. ABM experts frequently link Six Sigma Plus tools to projected and actual financial results.
- ABM Master—A person who has the skills of an expert plus the ability to develop and deliver ABM learning courses. Certification typically takes one year and involves demonstrating the use of ABM data for multiple purposes with repeatable and sustainable results. ABM Masters are proficient in the use of advanced cost management tools and have the ability to tailor cost data and analysis to a business's vision and strategy.
- TPM Expert—A person who applies total productive maintenance (TPM) and reliability methodologies and tools to assist or lead teams in optimizing asset capacity-productivity at minimum life cycle cost. A TPM Expert is responsible for determining critical equipment and measuring its overall effectiveness, thus enabling growth and productivity through optimum asset utilization.
- TPM Master—A highly skilled individual experienced in the use of TPM and reliability tools and methodologies. TPM Masters' responsibilities include assisting leadership in identifying high-leverage asset improvement opportunities; leading critical, high-leverage improvement projects in a business; and leading cultural paradigm shifts from reactive to proactive asset management.

This commitment to training and expansion of Six Sigma Plus around the world has paid significant dividends. One of Honeywell's European divisions, Aerospace Services, merged activity-based management and lean manufacturing techniques at its Raunheim, Germany, facility. The site repairs auxiliary power units, propulsion engines, and components that provide air conditioning and other power-related features aboard aircraft. The site impressed customers over a recent two-year period with a 43 percent reduction in component repair time. It helped Honeywell achieve a $47 million increase in revenue and was a major factor in $900,000 worth of productivity improvements. An Industrial Control team developed a reliable, cost-effective family of chips and assembled components for the burgeoning data communications market. As a result, Industrial Control achieved a 500 percent increase in revenue growth, resulting in a year-over-year increase in operating profits of several million dollars. Cycle time was reduced 35 percent, and yields increased from 75 percent to 93 percent.

Key Issues for Discussion

1. Trace the development of Six Sigma, the Honeywell Quality Value (HQV) program, and Six Sigma Plus, before and after the AlliedSignal and Honeywell merger. What role did the corporate culture of each organization play in the results from the Six Sigma Plus initiative?
2. How does top management show its support of Six Sigma Plus? Do you believe that an adequate structure exists to continue building and sustaining the quality effort at Honeywell for the foreseeable future?
3. What are the unique features of Six Sigma Plus that are not part of the standard Six Sigma process discussed in earlier chapters?

Additional Quality in Practice features are available in the Bonus Materials folder for this chapter on the Premium website.

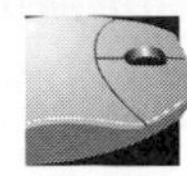

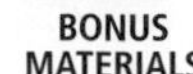

Review Questions

1. Discuss what organizations must do to build and sustain performance excellence. Why is it important?
2. Define leadership. Why is it necessary for a culture of performance excellence?
3. List and explain the key competencies and personal characteristics that strong leaders possess.
4. Summarize the key leadership practices for performance excellence.
5. Define the term *leadership system*. What elements should an effective leadership system have?
6. What is the role of steering teams in many leadership systems?
7. What is corporate social responsibility and why is it important for organizations?
8. Explain the traditional theories of leadership and their implications for quality and performance excellence. (See the Bonus Materials folder for this chapter on the Premium website.)

9. How do emerging leadership theories differ from traditional theories? Summarize them and their importance in leadership for performance excellence.
10. What are some approaches that organizations should employ to successfully implement ISO 9000, Baldrige, and Six Sigma?
11. What is *culture*? How are cultural values reflected in organizations?
12. Explain the difference between strategic change and process change.
13. Discuss the role of middle management and the workforce in achieving quality and performance excellence.
14. What lessons can be learned from Wainwright Industries about changing an organization's culture?
15. Define the terms *alignment* and *integration*. Why are they important?
16. What are best practices? What are the major conclusions and implications of the Best Practices report of Ernst & Young and the American Quality Foundation? How do they relate to Deming's philosophy?
17. Describe the typical life cycle of a quality initiative and the Baldrige "Roadmap." Why are they important for senior leaders to understand?
18. Explain the notion of organizational learning and why it is important for sustaining performance excellence.
19. What is self-assessment? Why is it valuable? What issues should self-assessment address?

20. Why is follow-up important as a part of self-assessment processes? What two key activities should comprise follow-up? What advice should managers heed to leverage self-assessment?

Discussion Questions

1. We emphasized that leadership is the "driver" of a total quality system. What does this statement imply and what implications does it have for future CEOs? Middle managers? Supervisors?
2. Provide examples from your own experiences in which leaders (not necessarily managers—consider academic unit heads, presidents of student organizations, and even family members) exhibited one or more of the six key leadership competencies described in this chapter. What impacts did these competencies have on the organization?
3. Explain how leaders can demonstrate each of the seven personal leadership characteristics cited in this chapter.
4. State some examples in which leaders you have worked for exhibited some of the leading practices described in this chapter. Can you provide examples for which they have not?
5. Referring to the Traditional Leadership Theories document in the Bonus Materials folder for this chapter on the Premium website, give examples of different "situational conditions" that would affect leadership styles according to Fiedler's model. As an organization moves from a little to a high degree of adoption of performance excellence principles, how do the situational conditions change? What do these changes mean for leadership?

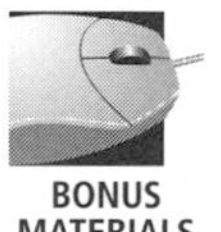

BONUS MATERIALS

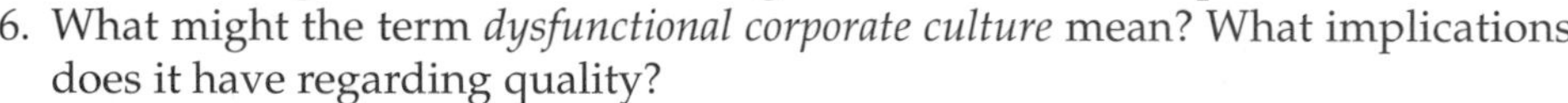

6. What might the term *dysfunctional corporate culture* mean? What implications does it have regarding quality?
7. Discuss how each of the Baldrige Core Values and Concepts are explicitly or implicitly reflected in each of the first six categories of the Baldrige criteria.
8. For each of the Baldrige Core Values and Concepts, discuss things that you might observe in a site visit to a Baldrige recipient and one that has never used the criteria.
9. What might the learning organization concept mean to a college or university?
10. You have undoubtedly seen a flock of geese flying overhead. How do the following behaviors of this species provide some insight for organizations wishing to pursue performance excellence?
    a. As each bird flaps its wings, it creates uplift for the bird behind. By using a "V" formation, the whole flock adds 71 percent more flying range than if each bird flew alone.
    b. Whenever one falls out of formation, it suddenly feels the resistance of trying to fly alone, and quickly gets back into formation to take advantage of the lifting power of the birds immediately in front.
    c. When the lead bird gets tired, it rotates back into formation and another flies at the point position.
    d. The birds in formation honk from behind to encourage those up front to maintain their speed.
    e. When one gets sick or wounded or shot down, two birds drop out of formation and follow their fellow member down to help or provide

protection. They stay with this member of the flock until it can fly again or dies. Then they launch out on their own, with another formation or to catch up with their own flock.

11. What is your opinion on the future of quality? Do you agree with the comments made in the concluding section of this chapter? Why or why not?

Projects, Etc.

1. Using the information in this chapter, design a questionnaire that might be used to understand leadership effectiveness in an organization.
2. Interview someone you know about the leadership characteristics of their supervisor. What leadership style does he or she appear to reflect?
3. Joseph Conklin proposes 10 questions for self-examination to help you understand your capacity for leadership.[73] Answer the following questions, and discuss why they are important for leadership.
   a. How much do I like my job?
   b. How often do I have to repeat myself?
   c. How do I respond to failure?
   d. How well do I put up with second guessing?
   e. How early do I ask questions when making a decision?
   f. How often do I say "thank you"?
   g. Do I tend to favor a loose or strict interpretation of the rules?
   h. Can I tell an obstacle from an excuse?
   i. Is respect enough?
   j. Have I dispensed with feeling indispensable?
4. Examine some corporate websites and comment on the cultural values that are reflected by the information you find. How important do these organizations view quality to their success?
5. Talk to individuals that you know from some local organizations (companies, schools, government agencies) about the organization's commitment to quality and performance excellence principles. What factors do they attribute to either the success or failure of their organization's approaches?
6. For each numbered set of questions in Categories 1–6 of the Baldrige criteria, determine whether each of the core values and concepts are reflected (a) strongly, (b) moderately, or (c) little to not at all. Summarize your results in a matrix (rows represent core values and columns represent the item questions).
7. Interview your fellow students to identify a set of "best learning practices." Develop a plan for sharing these throughout your school.
8. Find an organization that has implemented ISO 9000, Baldrige, or Six Sigma. Prepare a report on the implementation issues and challenges that the organization faced. How did they address them, and what was the result of their efforts?
9. Create a matrix diagram in which each row is a category of the Baldrige criteria and four columns correspond to the following:
   - Traditional management practices
   - Growing awareness of the importance of quality
   - Development of solid quality management system
   - Outstanding, world-class management practice

In each cell of the matrix, list two to five characteristics that you would expect to see for an organization in each of the preceding four situations for that category. How might this matrix be used as a self-assessment tool to provide directions for improvement?

10. Develop a hierarchy of the questions within the Baldrige Award criteria that would guide an organization starting to pursue performance excellence toward world-class performance. In other words, what key issues within the criteria would be more appropriate for organizations just starting out to concentrate on, and how should they progress toward fully meeting the Baldrige criteria?

CASES

Additional cases are available in the Bonus Materials folder on the Premium website.

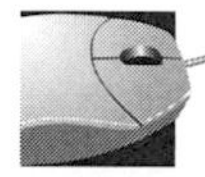

BONUS MATERIALS

DISTINGUISHED AD AGENCY[74]

Distinguished Ad Agency (DAA) had been in business for about 10 years. It had a strong regional reputation, and counted divisions of five *Fortune* 500 firms among its clients. Manuel Novedad, co-founder and president, had built the firm on a foundation of client focus, adherence to a quality system, and rapid response.

One of their largest customers, a *Fortune* 500 consumer products company, required compliance to jointly developed protocols and a mature quality management system, but not to registration under ISO. A documented system was in place, and Novedad chaired an active steering committee. Members were department heads, including the quality manager, and the union president. System upgrades were made on a routine basis. However, this valued customer, Megaproducts Incorporated, had missed a scheduled launch date for a new, potentially important mega-product because of miscommunications with DAA's project team and faulty ad copy, which had to be revised after being sent to the printer. These problems could have been prevented if DAA's protocols had been followed and required quality checks had been performed.

Time was a factor because noncompliant product had been reaching the customer despite DAA's assurances that protocols were being followed. Much of the documentation had been written by the quality manager and edited by the president. Review by managers and supervisors, who were asked to implement applicable elements in their departments, was minimal. Consequently, many of the procedures and instructions did not reflect work realities. They depicted an ideal and were ultimately challenged as supervisors and process operators tried to implement them. But, since the clock was ticking and Megaproducts was threatening to cancel orders, implementation proceeded with promises of a complete quality management system revision once improvements were in place.

Making the quality system operable was chaotic. Managers, not wanting to appear unsure of their changed responsibilities and authority, clung to the status quo. Training—when done—focused on lower level employees, which left supervisors without a good understanding of new requirements. They were caught saying one thing but doing another. Interfaces between departments and individuals, although described in an organizational chart and statements of authority and responsibility, were not truly functional. System workflow faltered because new relationships and interdependencies encountered old departmental barriers. Audit reports and corrective actions languished because the president periodically overrode the quality manager's authority, fearing delivery promises might be compromised. However, early implementation steps were handled well. Gaps and shortfalls were identified, and proposed solutions recommended. But, because of time, it was assumed that acceptance and adoption would be automatic. Steering committee members rationalized that everyone knew what needed to be done because solution finding had been such a fervent effort. However, like many improvement projects, concluding steps were inadequately thought through and poorly managed. Proposed solutions were not completely integrated into daily activities.

Eventually the Steering Committee realized that they lacked a comprehensive plan that would make system changes truly operational. The Committee understood that this created indecision at supervisory levels, plus inadequate coordination and dissatisfaction by those trying to make the changes workable. They saw that first-line design project managers, writers, and artists were trying to maintain a sense of order and get their work done by falling back on customary routines. Amazingly, their "stopgap" actions allowed them to get some of the Megaproducts projects back on schedule, but they realized that they must go back to the drawing board to develop a comprehensive plan. Time was running out.

Discussion Questions

1. What mistakes did Novedad and the Steering Committee make in the initial development of the protocols and documentation and the early implementation stage?
2. What were the early indications that the system was not working as planned, and why were they ignored? Why weren't improvement efforts more effective?
3. Now that Novedad and the Steering Committee have received their "wake-up" call, what steps should be taken to revise and implement an improved, workable quality management system?

NOVEL CONNECT—LEADERSHIP

BONUS MATERIALS

The complete Novel Connect case study, a fictitious example of a Baldrige application, and the 2008 Baldrige criteria on which it is based can be found in the Baldrige Materials folder on the Premium website. If you have not read the Organizational Profile yet (see the related case in Chapter 3), please do so first. What factors in the Organizational Profile would be most important in evaluating their leadership approaches? Examine their response in Category 1 to the 2008 Baldrige criteria questions for this category). What are their strengths? What are their weaknesses and opportunities for improvement? What specific advice, including useful tools and techniques that might help them, would you suggest?

THE PARABLE OF THE GREEN LAWN[75]

A new housing development has lots of packed earth and weeds, but no grass. Two neighbors make a wager on who will be the first to have a lush lawn. Mr. Fast N. Furious knows that a lawn will not grow without grass seed, so he immediately buys the most expensive seed he can find because everyone knows that quality improves with price. Besides, he'll recover the cost of the seed through his wager. Next, he stands knee-deep in his weeds and tosses the seed around his yard. Confident that he has a head start on his neighbor, who is not making much visible progress, he begins his next project.

Ms. Slo N. Steady, having grown up in the country, proceeds to clear the lot, till the soil, and even alter the slope of the terrain to provide better drainage. She checks the soil's pH, applies weed killer and fertilizer, and then distributes the grass seed evenly with a spreader. She applies a mulch cover and waters the lawn appropriately. She finishes several days after her neighbor, who asks if she would like to concede defeat. After all, he does have some blades of grass poking up already.

Mr. Furious is encouraged by the few clumps of grass that sprout. While these small, green islands are better developed than Ms. Steady's fledgling lawn, bare spots and weeds surround them. If he maintains these footholds, he reasons, they should spread to the rest of the yard. He notices that his neighbor's lawn is more uniform and is really starting to grow. He attributes this progress to the Steady children, who water the lawn each evening. Not wanting to appear to be imitating his neighbor, Mr. Furious instructs his children to water his lawn at noon.

The noon watering proves to be detrimental, so he decides to fertilize the remaining patches of grass. Because he wants to make up for the losses the noon watering caused, he applies the fertilizer at twice the recommended application rate. Most of the patches of grass that escape being burned by the fertilizer, however, are eventually choked out by the weeds.

After winning the wager with Mr. Furious, Ms. Steady lounges on the deck enjoying her new grill, which she paid for with the money from the wager. Her lawn requires minimal maintenance, so she is free to attend to the landscaping. The combination of the lawn and landscaping also results in an award from a neighborhood committee that determines that her lawn is a true showplace. Mr. Furious still labors on his lawn. He blames the poor performance on his children's inability to properly water the lawn, nonconforming grass seed, insufficient sunlight, and poor soil. He claims that his neighbor has an unfair advantage and her success is based on conditions unique to her plot of land. He views the loss as grossly unfair; after all, he spends more time and money on his lawn than Ms. Steady does.

He continues to complain about how expensive the seed is and how much time he spends moving the sprinkler around to the few remaining clumps of grass that continue to grow. But Mr. Furious thinks that things will be better for him next year, because he plans to install an automatic sprinkler system and make a double-or-nothing wager with Ms. Steady.

Discussion Questions

1. Within the context of the continual struggles to create a "world-class" lawn and "world-class" business, draw analogies between the events when total quality is implemented.
2. Specifically, translate the problems described here into business language. What are the implementation barriers to achieving total quality?

THE YELLOW BRICK ROAD TO QUALITY[76]

In the film *The Wizard of Oz*, Dorothy learned many lessons. Surprisingly, managers can learn a lot also. For each of the following summaries of scenes in the film, discuss the lessons that organizations can learn in pursuing change and a TQ culture.

1. Dorothy was not happy with the world as she knew it. A tornado came along and transported her to the Land of Oz. Dorothy's house was dropped by the tornado on the Wicked Witch of the East, killing the witch. "Ding, dong, the witch is dead!" rang throughout Munchkinland, but Dorothy had enraged the dead witch's sister. Dorothy only temporarily lost her home support provided by family back in Kansas. All is not good, however, in the Land of Oz. Dorothy's problem is to find her way home to Kansas. Her call to action was precipitated by a crisis—the tornado that transported her to an alien land.
2. In the throes of a Kansas tornado, Dorothy is transported to an unfamiliar land. Immediately, she realizes her world is different and the processes and people she encounters are different, yet bear some similarity to her Kansas existence. She is lost and confused and uncertain about the next steps to take. She realizes she is in a changed state—the Land of Oz—and must devise a plan to get home.
3. Dorothy is a hero for killing the Wicked Witch of the East. Glinda, the Good Witch, sends Dorothy on her way to meet the Wizard of Oz who will help her get back to Kansas. The Wicked Witch of the West tries to get Dorothy's newly acquired ruby slippers, but to no avail. Dorothy and Toto leave for Oz via the Yellow Brick Road. Along the way, they are joined by Scarecrow, Tin Man, and Lion. Through their teamwork, they provide mutual support to endure the vexing journey. They overcome many risks and barriers, including the sleeping poppy field, flying monkeys, and a haunted forest on the way to Oz.
4. Dorothy and her entourage finally reach Oz and meet the Wizard. Rather than instantly granting their wishes, the Wizard gives them an assignment—to obtain the Wicked Witch's broom. They depart for the West.

5. Charged with the task of obtaining the broom, Dorothy and company experience several encounters with near disaster, including Dorothy's incarceration in the witch's castle while an hourglass counts the time to her death. In a struggle to extinguish the Scarecrow's fire (incited by the Wicked Witch), Dorothy tosses a bucket of water, some of which hits the Witch and melts her. Dorothy is rewarded with the broomstick and returns to Oz.
6. Returning to Oz, the group talks with the Wizard, expecting him to help Dorothy return to Kansas. After defrocking the Wizard, they find out he does not know how. The Wizard tries to use a hot air balloon to return and accidentally leaves Dorothy and Toto behind upon takeoff. Glinda arrives and helps Dorothy realize she can return to Kansas on her own with the help of the ruby slippers.
7. Dorothy awakens from her dream and experiences a new understanding and appreciation for her home and family in Kansas. "Oh, Auntie Em, there's no place like home."

Discussion Questions

1. In examining the process that Dorothy used to manage the development and implementation of this project, what factors contributed to her success?
2. Try to develop a model in the form of a flowchart that characterizes an effective change process based on this case.

NOTES

1. "Hyundai Gets Hot," *Business Week*, December 17, 2001, 84–85; J.D. Power and Associates, "The Power Report, Special Power Report on Hyundai," June 2004; "Hyundai: Kissing Clunkers Goodbye," *Business Week*, May 17, 2004, 45.

2. Debbie Phillips-Donaldson, "On Leadership," *Quality Progress*, August 2002.

3. Rudolph C. Hirzel, "Leadership Characteristics for Quality Performance," *The Quality Management Forum*, Winter 2004, Vol. 30, No. 1, 3–4.

4. Robert Slater, *Jack Welch and the GE Way* (New York: McGraw-Hill, 1999), 219.

5. Solar Turbines, Inc., Malcolm Baldrige National Quality Award Application Summary, 1999, 4.

6. AT&T Quality Steering Committee, *Leading the Quality Initiative*, AT&T Bell Laboratories, 1990, 13–14.

7. Marc Gunther, "Money and Morals at GE," *Fortune*, November 15, 2004, 176–182.

8. Bjorn Andersen, "A Framework for Business Ethics," *Quality Progress*, March 2000, 22–28.

9. n.a. The Business Roundtable. *Principles of Corporate Governance* (May 2002, revised in November, 2005), http://www.businessroundtable.org/pdf/CorporateGovPrinciples.pdf (accessed 3/2/06).

10. Frits K. Pil and Sandra Rothenberg, "Environmental Performance as a Driver of Superior Quality," *Production and Operations Management*, 12, 3, 2003, 404–415.

11. Consolidated School District 15, Malcolm Baldrige National Quality Award Application Summary, 2003.

12. http://www.referenceforbusiness.com/management/Int-Loc/Leadership-Theories-and-Studies.html. This and all documents under and extending from the group *Encyclopedia of Management—Int-Loc* are Copyright © 2006 by Thomson Gale, a part of the Thomson Corporation (accessed 2/17/06).

13. The following references provide additional information about each of the leadership theories cited in Table 9.1.

"Great man" model: R. M. Stogdill, *Handbook of Leadership* (New York: The Free Press, 1974).

Ohio State Studies: E.A. Fleishman and E.F. Harris "Patterns of Leadership Behavior Related to Employee Grievances and Turnover." *Personnel Psychology* (1962), 15, 43–56.

Michigan Studies: Rensis Likert, *The Human Organization: Its Management and Value* (New York: McGraw-Hill, 1967).

Theory X – Theory Y Model: Douglas McGregor, *The Human Side of Enterprise* (New York: McGraw-Hill, 1960).

Managerial Grid model: R. R. Blake and J. S. Mouton, *The Managerial Grid* (Houston: Gulf Publishing, 1965).

Leadership effectiveness model: Frederick E. Fiedler, *A Theory of Leadership Effectiveness* (New York: McGraw-Hill, 1967).

Supervisory contingency decision model: V. H. Vroom and A. G. Jago, *The New Leadership* (Englewood Cliffs, NJ: Prentice-Hall, 1988).

Managerial roles: Henry Mintzberg, *Mintzberg on Management: Inside Our Strange World of Organizations* (New York: The Free Press, 1989). Also, *The Nature of Managerial Work* (New York: Harper & Row, 1973); "The Manager's Job: Folklore and Fact," *Harvard Business Review* (July/August 1975).

Leader-Member exchange: Graen, G. B., & Uhl-Bien, M. (1995). Relationship-based approach to leadership: Development of leader-member exchange (LMX) theory of leadership over 25 years: Applying a multi-level multi-domain perspective: Special Issue: Leadership: The multiple-level approaches (Part 1). *Leadership Quarterly*, 6, 219–247.

Charismatic theory: R.J. House "A 1976 Theory of Charismatic Leadership" in J.G. Hunt and L.L. Larson (Eds.) *Leadership: The Cutting Edge*. (Carbondale, IL: Southern Illinois University Press, 1977), 189–207. Also, J.A. Conger *The Charismatic Leader: Behind the Mystique of Exceptional Leadership* (San Francisco: Jossey-Bass, 1989).

Transformational theory: op cit. James M. Burns; N. M. Tichy and D. O. Ulrich, etc.

Substitutes for leadership: op cit. Jon P. Howell, David E. Bowen, Peter W. Dorfman, Steven Kerr, Phillip M. Podsakoff.

Emotional Intelligence: op cit. Daniel Goleman.

14. Bass, Bernard M. and Bruce J. Avolio. (1994) *Improving Organizational Effectiveness through Transformational Leadership*, Thousand Oaks, CA: Sage Publications, 2.

15. http://www.referenceforbusiness.com/management/Int-Loc/Leadership-Theories-and-Studies.html. Encyclopedia of Management—Int-Loc are Copyright © 2006 by Thomson Gale, a part of the Thomson Corporation (accessed 2/17/06).

16. For further discussion of this model, see Richard A. Grover and H. Fred Walker, "Changing from Production to Quality: Application of the Situational Leadership and Transtheoretical Change Models," *Quality Management Journal*, 10, 3, 2003, pp. 8–24 and Gary Yukl. *Leadership in Organizations*, 6th Ed., Upper Saddle River, NJ: Prentice-Hall, 2006, 223–224.

17. Claude F. Graeff. Evolution Of Situational Leadership Theory: A Critical Review, *Leadership Quarterly*, Summer 1997, Vol. 8, No. 2; Warren Blank, John R. Weitzel, Stephen G. Green. A Test of the Situational Leadership Theory, *Personnel Psychology*, Autumn 1990, Vol. 43, Issue 3.

18. Gary Yukl. *Leadership in Organizations*, 6th Ed., Upper Saddle River, NJ: Prentice-Hall, 2006, 224–225.

19. The term *transformational leadership* has been attributed to James M. Burns. See his book, *Leadership* (New York: Harper & Row, 1978). Other sources are N. M. Tichy and D. O. Ulrich, "The Leadership Challenge: A Call For the Transformational Leader," *Sloan Management Review* 26 (1984), 59–68; N. M. Tichy and M. A. Devanna, *The Transformational Leader* (New York: John Wiley & Sons, 1986); B. M. Bass, *Leadership and Performance Beyond Expectations* (New York: The Free Press, 1985).

20. B. M. Bass. *A New Paradigm of Leadership: an Inquiry into Transformational Leadership*. Alexandria, VA: US Army Research Institute for Behavioral and Social Sciences, 1996 cited in Yukl (Note 15), 263.

21. Bruce J. Avolio and Bernad M. Bass (2002) *Developing Potential Across a Full Range of Leadership*, 117–118.

22. Yukl (citing Bass, 1985), p. 262 (see Note 9).

23. Philip Atkinson, "Leadership, Total Quality and Cultural Change," *Management Services*, June 1991, 16–19.

24. Bruce J. Avolio and Bernad M. Bass (2002) *Developing Potential Across a Full Range of Leadership*, p. 6.

25. Jon P. Howell, David E. Bowen, Peter W. Dorfman, Steven Kerr, and Phillip M. Podsakoff "Substitutes for Leadership: Effective Alternatives for Ineffective Leadership" *Organizational Dynamics*, Summer 1990. Also see Steve Kerr and John Jermier, "Substitutes for Leadership: Their Meaning and Measurement" *Organizational Behavior and Human Performance*, December, 1978; and Jon P. Howell, Peter W. Dorfman, and Steven Kerr, "Moderator Variables in Leadership Research," *Academy of Management Review*, January, 1986.

26. Daniel Goleman, "What Makes a Leader?" *Harvard Business Review*, November–December, 1998, 93–102; and Daniel Goleman, *Working with Emotional Intelligence* (New York: Bantam Books, 1998).

27. http://www.ccl.org/leadership/pdf/research/NatureLeadership.pdf. (accessed 2/9/06). André Martin. *2005 Changing Nature of Leadership Report*. Center for Creative Leadership, 2005.

28. James H. Davis, *Who Owns Your Quality Program? Lessons from Baldrige Award Winners* (New York: Coopers & Lybrand, undated).

29. Tom Taormina, "Conducting Successful Internal Audits," *Quality Digest*, June 1998, 44–47.

30. Source: Repritned with permission of Jermone A. Blakeslee Jr., "Implementing the Six Sigma Solution", *Quality Progress*, July 1999, pp. 77–85. Copyright © 1999 American Society for Quality. No further distribution allowed without permission.

31. Susan E. Daniels, "From One-Man Show to Baldrige Recipient," *Quality Progress*, July 2007, 50–55.

32. Thomas A. Stewart, "Rate Your Readiness to Change," *Fortune*, February 7, 1994, 106–110.

33. Savio Capelossi Filho, "Creating and Preserving a Business Culture," *Quality Progress*, August 2007, 36–41.

34. James R. Evans and Matthew W. Ford, "Value-Driven Quality," *Quality Management Journal*, 4, no. 4 (1997), 19–31.

35. Matthew W. Ford and James R. Evans, "Baldrige Assessment and Organizational Learning: The Need for Change Management," *Quality Management Journal*, 8, no. 3 (2001), 9–25.

36. Much of this section and Table 9.5 are adapted from Matthew W. Ford and James R. Evans,

"Baldrige Assessment and Organizational Learning: The Need For Change Management," *Quality Management Journal*, 8, 3, 2001, 9–25.

37. Janet Young, "Driving Performance Results at American Express," *Six Sigma Forum Magazine* 1, no. 1 (November 2001), 19–27.

38. Brian Dumaine, "Times Are Good? Create a Crisis," *Fortune,* June 28, 1993, 123–130.

39. Paul R. Keck, "Why Quality Fails," *Quality Digest,* November 1995, 53–55.

40. Julia Graham, "Developing a Performance-Based Culture," *The Journal for Quality and Participation*, Spring 2004, 4–8.

41. Joseph M. Juran and A. Blanton Godfrey (eds.), *Juran's Quality Handbook* 5th ed. (New York: McGraw-Hill, 1999); and Frank M. Gryna, *Quality Planning and Analysis,* Fourth ed. (New York: McGraw-Hill, 2001). This concept is summarized in Mary Anne Watson and Frank M. Gryna "Quality Culture in Small Business: Four Case Studies," *Quality Progress,* January 2001, 41–48.

42. Mark Samuel, "Catalysts for Change," *The TQM Magazine* 2, no. 4 (1992), 198–202.

43. Davis (see Note 28).

44. Gregory P. Smith, "A Change in Culture Brings Dramatic Quality Improvements," *The Quality Observer,* January 1997, 14–15, 37.

45. "Special Report: Quality," *Business Week,* November 30, 1992, 66–75; and H. James Harrington, "The Fallacy of Universal Best Practices," Report TR 97-003, Ernst & Young, 1997.

46. Cyndee Miller, "TQM's Value Criticized in New Report," *Marketing News,* 1992; Gilbert Fuchsberg, "'Total Quality' Is Termed Only Partial Success," *The Wall Street Journal,* October 1, 1992, B1, B7.

47. Mike Carnell, "Forget Silver Bullets and Instant Pudding," *Quality Progress*, January 2008, 72–73.

48. Ibid.

49. This discussion and examples are adapted from Denis Leonard and Rodney McAdam, "Quality's Six Life Cycle Stages," *Quality Progress*, August 2003, 50–55.

50. Kathleen J. Goonan, Joseph Muzikowski, and Patricia K. Stoltz, "Journey to Excellence: Healthcare Baldrige Leaders Speak Out," *Quality in Healthcare*, American Society for Quality publication, January 2009, pp. 11–15, www.asq.org/qhc. Copyright © 2009 American Society for Quality. Reprinted with permission.

51. Adapted from presentation notes at the 2004 Baldrige National Quality Program Quest for Excellence XVI conference.

52. L. von Bertalanffy, "The Theory of Open Systems in Physics and Biology," *Science,* 111 (1950), 23–29.

53. J. W. Forrester, *Industrial Dynamics* (New York: John Wiley & Sons, 1961).

54. Peter M. Senge, *The Fifth Discipline: The Art and Practice of the Learning Organization* (New York: Doubleday Currency, 1990), 14.

55. Letter to Stakeholders p. 4; source: http://www.ge.com/ar2004/letter3.jsp, accessed 3/03/06.

56. Dusya Vera and Mary Crossan, "Strategic Leadership and Organizational Learning," *Academy of Management Review*, 29, 2, 2004, 222–240.

57. David A. Garvin, *Learning in Action: A Guide to Putting the Learning Organization to Work* (Boston: Harvard Business School Press, 2000), 11.

58. This intriguing label deserves a special explanation. It was coined by Joseph Juran in *Juran on Quality by Design* (New York: The Free Press, 1992), 409–413. It refers to the remark once made by philosopher George Santayana, who said, "Those who cannot remember the past are condemned to repeat it."

59. Robert Cole, "From continuous improvement to continuous innovation," *Quality Management Journal*, 8, No. 4, 7–21, 2001.

60. Sim B. Sitkin, Kathleen M. Sutcliffe, and Roger G. Schroeder. "Distinguishing Control from Learning in Total Quality Management: A Contingency Perspective," *Academy of Management Review,* 19, no. 3 (1994), 537–564.

61. Matthew W. Ford and James R. Evans, "Models for Organizational Self Assessment," *Business Horizons*, November–December 2002, 25–32.

62. See, for example, Mark Graham Brown, "Measuring Up Against the 1997 Baldrige Criteria," *Journal for Quality and Participation* 20, no. 4 (September 1997), 22–28.

63. Many examples of these interventions and of management's involvement in them have been documented in the popular literature. See, for example, D. H. Myers, and J. Heller, "The Dual Role of AT&T's Self-Assessment Process," *Quality Progress,* January 1995, 79–83; D. Zaremba, and T. Crew, "Increasing Involvement in Self-Assessment: The Royal Mail Approach," *TQM Magazine*, February 1995, 29–32; and M. Blazey, "Insights into Organizational Self-Assessments," *Quality Progress*, October 1998, 47–52.

64. Ann B. Rich, "Continuous Improvement: The Key to Success," *Quality Progress* 30, no. 6 (June 1997).

65. "Speaking About the Baldrige: Terry Holliday Interview," *Quality Digest,* January 2009, 6.

66. Matthew W. Ford and James R. Evans, "Managing Organizational Self-Assessment: Follow-up and Its Influencing Factors," Working Paper, College of Business, Northern Kentucky University and College of Business, University of Cincinnati. See also Matthew W. Ford, "A Model of Change Process and Its Use in Self Assessment," Doctoral Dissertation, University of Cincinnati, 2000.

67. A.V. Feigenbaum and Donald S. Feigenbaum, "New Quality for the 21st Century," *Quality Progress,* December 1999, 27–31.

68. "21 Voices for the 21st Century," *Quality Progress,* January 2000, 31–39.

69. Miles Maguire, "The Voice of the 21st Century Customer," *Quality Progress,* January 2000, 41.

70. Adapted from Sara R. Olberding, "Turnaround drama instills leadership," The Journal for Quality and Participation, Jan/Feb 1998. Source: http://www.findarticles.com/

71. http://www.uswa329.org/June_2001/june22a.htm

72. Reprinted with permission of Robert Green, "Dedicated Teams Successfully Merge Two Divergent Quality Systems," *Quality Digest*, December 2000, pp. 24–28. Copyright © 2000 American Society for Quality. No further distribution allowed without permission.

73. Joe Conklin, "What It Takes to Be a Leader," *Quality Progress,* November 2001, 83.

74. This case was inspired by the article by John R. Schultz "Eight Steps to Sustain Change," *Quality Progress,* November 2007, 25–31.

75. Adapted from James A. Alloway, Jr., "Laying Groundwork for Total Quality," *Quality Progress,* 27, no. 1 (January 1994), 65–67. © 1994 American Society for Quality. Reprinted with permission.

76. David M. Lyth and Larry A Mallak, "'We're Not in Kansas Anymore, Toto' or Quality Lessons from the Land of Oz," *Quality Engineering,* 10, no. 30 (1998), 579–588.

PART 3

SIX SIGMA AND THE TECHNICAL SYSTEM

Even though a strong foundation of managerial practices is absolutely essential for success, quality is made in the trenches—on the factory floor and by service workers who interact with customers on a daily basis. Assuring quality of products and services is accomplished primarily by the appropriate use of effective analytical tools and techniques for analyzing data, solving problems, improving and controlling processes, and reducing the potential for failure. In this part of the book, we focus on these issues, using the philosophy and structure of Six Sigma to guide the organization of these chapters.

Chapter 10 builds on the Deming philosophy introduced in Chapter 3, particularly the role of statistics and statistical thinking in evaluating process effectiveness and making informed decisions. These topics are the foundation for many Six Sigma applications. Chapter 11 expands on the concepts of Six Sigma that were introduced in Chapter 3, focusing on the DMAIC methodology, project management, and tools for process improvement. In Chapter 12, we focus on Design for Six Sigma (DFSS), an emerging philosophy supported by a collection of tools and methodologies for building quality and reliability into products and services. Finally, in Chapter 13, we address statistical process control, focusing on the construction and use of the most common types of control charts. Each chapter in this section of the book provides numerous problems for practice in developing these technical skills.

CHAPTER 10

STATISTICAL THINKING AND APPLICATIONS

OUTLINE

STATISTICAL THINKING
QUALITY PROFILES: Graniterock Company and Branch-Smith Printing Division
Deming's Red Bead and Funnel Experiments
STATISTICAL FOUNDATIONS
Random Variables and Probability Distributions
Sampling
STATISTICAL METHODOLOGY
Descriptive Statistics
Statistical Analysis with Microsoft Excel
Statistical Inference
Enumerative and Analytic Studies
Design of Experiments
Analysis of Variance (ANOVA)
Regression and Correlation
SUMMARY OF KEY POINTS AND TERMINOLOGY
QUALITY IN PRACTICE: Improving Quality of a Wave Soldering Process Through Design of Experiments
QUALITY IN PRACTICE: Applying Statistical Analysis in a Six Sigma Project at GE Fanuc
REVIEW QUESTIONS
PROBLEMS
PROJECTS, ETC.
Cases The Disciplinary Citation
The Quarterly Sales Report
The HMO Pharmacy Crisis

Brian Joiner, a noted quality management consultant, relates the following case:

> *Ed was a regional VP for a service company that had facilities around the world. He was determined that the facilities in his region would get the highest customer satisfaction ratings in the company. If he noticed that a facility had a major drop in satisfaction ratings in one month or had "below average" ratings for three months in a row, he would call the manager and ask what had happened—and make it clear that next month's rating had better improve. And most of the time, it did!*[1]

As the average satisfaction score dropped from 65 to 60 between February and March, Ed's memo to his managers read:

> *Bad news! We dropped five points! We should all focus on improving these scores right away! I realize that our usage rates have increased faster than*

anticipated, so you've really got to hustle to give our customers great service. I know you can do it!

As Joiner observed, "Do you look at data this way? This month versus last month? This month versus the same month last year? Do you sometimes look at the latest data point? The last two data points? I couldn't understand why people would only want to look at two data points. Finally, it became clear to me. With any two data points, it's easy to compute a trend: 'Things are down 2 percent this month from last month. This month is 30 percent above the same month last year.' Unfortunately, we learn nothing of importance by comparing two results when they both come from a stable process . . . and most data of importance to management are from stable processes."

Many managers who do not understand how to use statistics effectively make similar mistakes. Statistical concepts are crucial to good quality management and are the key in dealing with processes and their inherent variation. They are fundamental to Six Sigma practice and studies; in fact, Six Sigma has elevated the importance of statistics in business analysis. Statistical methods have applications in many other areas of quality management, including product and market analysis, product and process design, process control, testing and inspection, identification and verification of process improvements, and reliability analysis. All managers, supervisors, and production and clerical workers should have some knowledge of the technical aspects of statistical methods. Companies large and small need to understand statistical aspects of data analysis to make good decisions (see the *Quality Profiles* for Graniterock and Branch-Smith).

Readers of this text are assumed to have prior knowledge of elementary statistics. This chapter provides a brief review of some important statistical concepts and applications in Six Sigma and other quality control and improvement activities, but the chapter is not intended to replace a rigorous treatment of statistical methods. However, we have found that statistics is a subject for which you learn something new every time you review the concepts, so we encourage you to do so. A complete treatment of statistical methods for Six Sigma can be found in Breyfogle's book found in the Bibliography at the end of this book.

STATISTICAL THINKING

Statistics is a science concerned with "the collection, organization, analysis, interpretation, and presentation of data."[2] Measurement processes provide data. The data may be dimensions of bolts being produced on a production line, order entry errors per day in an order entry department, or numbers of flight delays per week at an airport.

Raw data collected from the field do not provide the information necessary for quality control or improvement. Data must be organized, analyzed, and interpreted. Statistics provide an efficient and effective way of obtaining meaningful information from data, allowing managers and workers to control and improve processes.

The importance of statistical concepts in quality management cannot be overemphasized. Indeed, statistics is essential in implementing a continuous improvement philosophy. The use of statistical methods in quality dates back to 1903, when the Bell System faced a problem designing its central offices.[3] A telephone subscriber takes the phone off the hook and gets a dial tone, meaning that he is connected to a trunk line that goes to the central office. The question was, "How many of those lines do you need?" Theoretically, every subscriber could use the phone at the same time, but in reality only a few percent actually do. Analysts collected and analyzed statistical information on the demand day-by-day, hour-by-hour, and identified the peak periods to determine how

Quality Profiles

Graniterock Company and Branch-Smith Printing Division

Founded in 1900, Graniterock produces rock, sand, and gravel aggregates; ready-mix concrete; asphalt; road treatments; and recycled road-base material. It also retails building materials made by other manufacturers and runs a highway-paving operation. It competes in a six-county area extending from San Francisco southward to Monterey. Most of its major competitors are firms owned by multinational construction-material companies.

Charts for each product line help executives assess Graniterock's performance relative to competitors on key product and service attributes, ranked according to customer priorities. After annual improvement targets are set, the executive committee expects branches and divisions to develop their own implementation plans. Coordination across divisions is fostered by 10 Corporate Quality Teams that oversee and help align improvement efforts across the entire organization.

As part of Graniterock's effort to reduce process variability and increase product reliability, many employees are trained in statistical process control, root-cause analysis, and other quality-assurance and problem-solving methods. This workforce capability helps the company exploit the advantages afforded by investments in computer-controlled processing equipment. Its newest batch plant features a computer-controlled process for mixing batches of concrete, enabling real-time monitoring of key process indicators. With the electronically controlled system, which Graniterock helped a supplier design, the reliability of several key processes has reached the 6-sigma level.

Applying statistical process control to all product lines has helped the company reduce variable costs and produce materials that exceed customer specifications and industry- and government-set standards. For example, Graniterock's concrete products consistently exceed the industry performance specifications by 100 times.

Branch-Smith, Inc., is a fourth-generation family business. The Branch-Smith Printing Division (BSPD) specializes in creating multi-page, bound materials with services ranging from design to mailing for specialty customers. The company took the time to find out precisely what niche it could most successfully fill in the ultra-competitive printing arena. Aware that more than 1,000 printing firms crowd the Dallas/Fort Worth market, Branch-Smith used a study of the industry to determine a primary customer base. This careful, data-driven approach—typical of how the company operates—pointed toward clients with printing needs too small for larger shops, but that fit well with what BSPD did best, providing expert solutions and leveraging cost advantages normally associated with web press operations while capitalizing on its specialized sheet-fed printing capabilities. Every Branch-Smith function is geared toward providing the best possible customer service at the lowest possible cost. To that end, databases and software tools are used extensively to gather information about, and to improve, processes involving customer service, all phases of production, continuous improvement, and decision making. An important tool called the Quality Information Database, or QID, places key data dealing with suppliers, opportunities for improvement, customer complaints, and internal nonconformance in a central location. The company's Management Review Team—responsible, among other things, for establishing and monitoring the organization's direction—uses this data to document and track progress. BSPD experienced a 72 percent growth over four years and held that gain in 2002, when the industry declined 6.6 percent. Even though BSPD is a small business in a highly fragmented industry, its market share in the Dallas/Fort Worth area has almost tripled, increasing from 0.50 percent in 1997 to 1.46 percent in 2002.

Source: Adapted from Malcolm Baldrige National Quality Award, Profiles of Winners, and 2002 Quest for Excellence video script, National Institute of Standards and Technology, Department of Commerce.

many lines were required to meet a service standard (the probability of not getting a dial tone). In the 1920s, Bell Labs thought that statistical tools would have applications in the factory, and began to experiment with statistical sampling, eventually leading to the development of control charts. Joseph Juran was involved in trying to sell this new technology in the factories, but had little success until World War II, when the push to improve quality in the military began with the implementation of statistical methods in factories in earnest. The rest, as they say, is history.

Simply knowing statistical tools and methods is not enough; one must understand the role that the science of statistics plays in managerial decisions. Managers need to *think* statistically. **Statistical thinking** is a philosophy of learning and action based on these principles:

1. All work occurs in a system of interconnected processes.
2. Variation exists in all processes.
3. Understanding and reducing variation are keys to success.[4]

Understanding processes provides the context for determining the effects of variation and the proper type of managerial action to be taken. By viewing work as a process, we can apply statistical tools to establish consistent, predictable processes; study them; and improve them. While variation exists everywhere, many business decisions do not often account for it, and managers frequently confuse common and special causes of variation. We must understand the nature of variation before we can focus on reducing it.

Any production process contains many sources of variation, as illustrated in Figure 10.1. Different lots of material vary in strength, thickness, or moisture content, for example. Cutting tools have inherent variation in their strength and composition. During manufacturing, tools experience wear, vibrations cause changes in machine settings, and electrical fluctuations cause variations in power. Operators do not position parts on fixtures consistently, and physical and emotional stress affect operators' consistency. In addition, measurement gauges and human inspection capabilities are not uniform. Even when measurements of several items by the same instrument are the same, it is due to a lack of precision in the measurement instrument; extremely precise instruments always reveal slight differences.

The complex interactions of these variations in materials, tools, machines, operators, and the environment are not easily understood. Variation due to any of these individual sources appears at random; individual sources cannot be identified or explained. However their combined effect is stable and can usually be predicted statistically. These factors are present as a natural part of a process and are referred to as **common causes** of variation. Common causes are a result of the design of the product and production system and generally account for about 80 to 95 percent of the

Figure 10.1 Sources of Variation in a Production Process

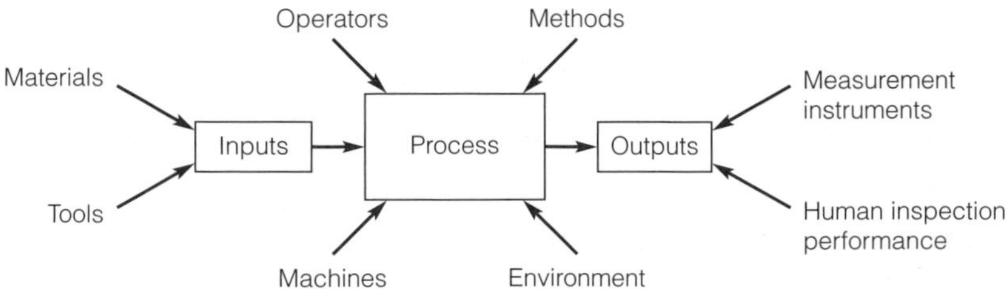

observed variation in the output of a production process. Therefore, common cause variation can only be reduced if the product is redesigned, or if better technology or training is provided for the production process. For example, Wilson Sporting goods acknowledged that small irregularities in golf balls can cause the heavier core of golf balls to be off center, resulting in balls that don't roll straight, with up to 1 in 12 high-end balls having this problem. To solve the problem, Wilson introduced a new ball design, with a lighter core and heavier cover.[5] As an example of common cause variation in a process, suppose that boards are to be cut to the precise length of 55 inches. If the worker is provided with only a handsaw, a table, and a 12-inch ruler, it will be virtually impossible for him or her to cut lengths of this precision consistently, and a significant amount of measurable variation will exist. However, suppose that a 60-inch metal tape measure, a fixture for holding the boards, and an electric saw are available, and workers are trained in how to use them properly. Clearly, the output from this system will have less variability and more consistent quality.

The remaining variation in a production process is the result of **special causes**, often called **assignable causes** of variation. Special causes arise from external sources that are not inherent in the process. They appear sporadically and disrupt the random pattern of common causes. Hence, they tend to be easily detectable using statistical methods and are usually economical to correct. For instance, the worker cutting boards may be distracted by a supervisor and mark the boards incorrectly before cutting, resulting in several pieces that may be an inch too short. Common factors that lead to special causes are a bad batch of material from a supplier, a poorly trained substitute machine operator, a broken or worn tool, or miscalibration of measuring instruments. Unusual variation that results from such isolated incidents can be explained or corrected.

A system governed only by common causes is called a ***stable system****. Understanding a stable system and the differences between special and common causes of variation is essential for managing any system.*

Some of the operational problems created by variation include the following:[6]

- *Variation increases unpredictability:* If we don't understand the variation in a system, we cannot predict its future performance.
- *Variation reduces capacity utilization:* If a process has little variability, then managers can increase the load on the process because they do not have to incorporate slack into their production plans.
- *Variation contributes to a "bullwhip" effect:* This well-known phenomenon occurs in supply chains; when small changes in demand occur, the variation in production and inventory levels becomes increasingly amplified upstream at distribution centers, factories, and suppliers, resulting in unnecessary costs and difficulties in managing material flow.
- *Variation makes it difficult to find root causes:* Process variation makes it difficult to determine whether problems are due to external factors such as raw materials or reside within the processes themselves.
- *Variation makes it difficult to detect potential problems early:* Unusual variation is a signal that problems exist; if a process has little inherent variation, then it is easier to detect when a problem actually does occur.

Management can make two fundamental mistakes in attempting to improve a process:

1. To treat as a special cause any fault, complaint, mistake, breakdown, accident, or shortage when it actually is due to common causes.

2. To attribute to common causes any fault, complaint, mistake, breakdown, accident, or shortage when it actually is due to a special cause.

In the first case, tampering with a stable system can increase the variation in the system. In the second case, the opportunity to reduce variation is missed because the amount of variation is mistakenly assumed to be uncontrollable.

How often do managers make decisions based on a single data point or two, seeing trends when they don't exist, or manipulating financial figures they cannot truly control? The lack of broad and sustained use of statistical thinking in many organizations is due to two reasons.[7] First, statisticians historically functioned as problem solvers in manufacturing, research, and development and thereby focused on individual clients rather than on organizations. Second, statisticians focused primarily on technical aspects of statistics rather than emphasizing process definition, measurement, control, and improvement—the key activities that lead to bottom-line results.

Senior management needs to champion the use of statistical thinking by defining the strategy and goals of the approach, clearly and consistently communicating the benefits and results, providing the necessary resources, coaching others, and recognizing and rewarding the desired behavior. To help managers work in this fashion, many organizations are creating core groups of highly trained professionals who are skilled in statistical thinking tools and can help others to use them effectively. This task requires an environment conducive to learning new behaviors and concepts.

Statistical thinking can be applied at all levels of an organization.[8] At the organizational level, it helps executives understand the business system and its core processes, use data from the entire organization to assess performance, develop useful measurement systems, and encourage employees to experiment to improve their work. At the process level, it can motivate managers to develop and assess standardized project management systems, set realistic goals, keep employees better informed, and focus on the process without blaming employees for variation. Finally, at the individual or personal level, statistical thinking can help employees be knowledgeable about variation, analyze work data better, and identify important measures and improvement opportunities. Thus, every manager and employee can benefit from statistical thinking and using total quality tools. Technology, such as today's powerful PCs and user-friendly software for data analysis and visualization such as Microsoft Excel and other spreadsheet packages, has greatly facilitated the ability to use statistics and quality tools in daily work.

Deming's Red Bead and Funnel Experiments[9]

Statistical thinking is at the heart of the Deming philosophy and his principles of Profound Knowledge (see Chapter 3). Frank H. Squires, a well-known expert on quality, credited W. Edwards Deming with keeping statistics in the forefront of the worldwide quality improvement movement. Squires stated:

> *The triumph of statistics is the triumph of Dr. Deming. When others have wavered or been lukewarm in their support for statistics, Dr. Deming has stood firm in his conviction that statistics is the heart of quality control. Indeed, he goes further and makes statistical principles central to the whole production process.*[10]

In his four-day management seminars, Deming used two simple, yet powerful experiments to educate his audience about statistical thinking. The first is the "Red Bead" experiment, which proceeds as follows. A Foreman (usually Deming) selects several volunteers from the audience: Six Willing Workers, a Recorder, two Inspectors, and a Chief Inspector. The materials for the experiment include 4,000 wooden beads—800 red and 3,200 white—and two Tupperware boxes, one slightly smaller than the other. Also, a paddle with 50 holes or depressions is used to scoop up 50 beads, which is the prescribed workload. In this experiment, the company is "producing" beads for a new customer who needs only white beads and will not take red beads. The Foreman explains that everyone will be an apprentice for three days to learn the job. During apprenticeship, the workers may ask questions. Once production starts, however, no questions are allowed. The procedures are rigid; no departures from procedures are permitted so that no variation in performance will occur. The Foreman explains to the Willing Workers that their jobs depend on their performance and if they are dismissed, many others are willing to replace them. Furthermore, no resignations are allowed.

The company's work standard, the Foreman explains, is 50 beads per day. The production process is simple: Mix the raw material and pour it into the smaller box. Repeat this procedure, returning the beads from the smaller box to the larger one. Grasp the paddle and insert it into the bead mixture. Raise the paddle at a 44-degree angle so that every depression will hold a bead. The two Inspectors count the beads independently and record the counts. The Chief Inspector checks the counts and announces the results, which are written down by the Recorder. The Chief Inspector then dismisses the worker. When all six Willing Workers have produced the day's quota, the Foreman evaluates the results.

Figure 10.2 shows the results of the first day's production generated with the Quality Gamebox computer simulation software.[11] The Foreman is disappointed. He reminds the Willing Workers that their job is to make white beads, not red ones. The company is on a merit system, and it rewards only good performance. Marty only made 7 red beads and deserves a pay increase. The data do not lie; he is the best worker. Dennis made 14 red beads. Everyone likes him, but he must be placed on probation. The Foreman announces that management has set a goal of no more than 7 red beads per day per worker, and sees no reason why everyone cannot be as good as Marty.

Figure 10.2 First Day's Production (The paddle shows the result of the last Willing Worker, Ann)

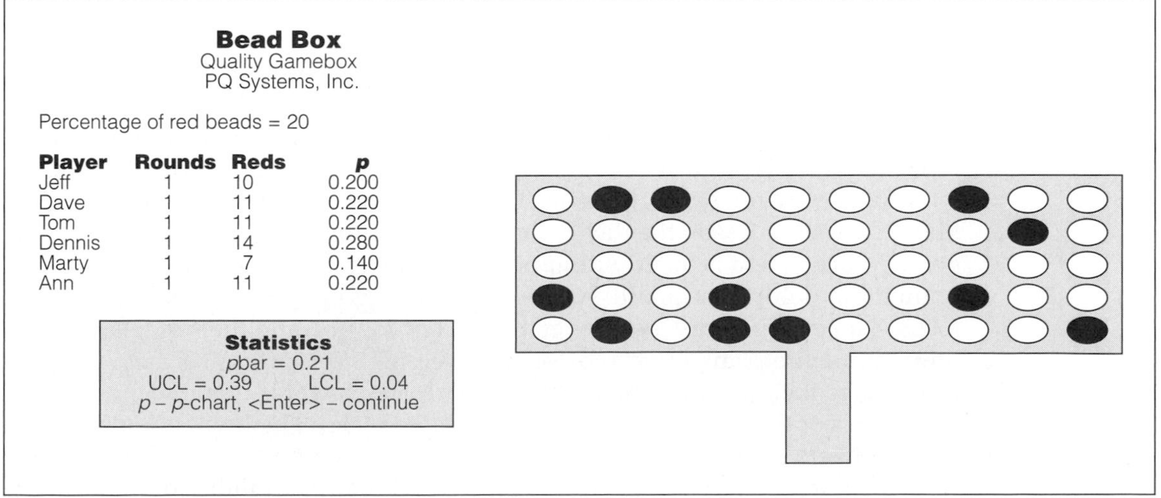

Source: Reprinted with permission of PQ Systems.

Figure 10.3 Second Day's Cumulative Results

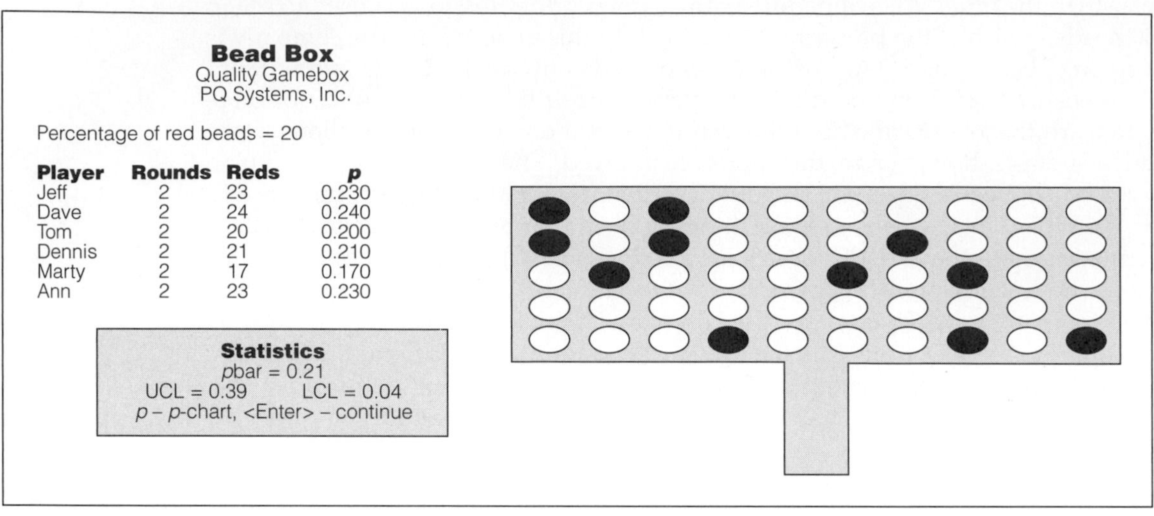

Source: Reprinted with permission of PQ Systems.

Figure 10.3 shows the cumulative results for the second day. We see that after two days, Jeff had produced 23 red beads, Dave 24, Tom 20, Dennis 21, Marty 17, and Ann 23. (The second day's results can be found by subtraction: Jeff produces 13 beads, Dave 13, Tom 9, Dennis 7, Marty 10, and Ann 12.) The overall performance was not good. Management is watching carefully. The Foreman reminds them again that their jobs depend on performance. Marty is a big disappointment. The merit increase obviously went to his head. The Foreman chastises him in front of the other workers. Dennis, on the other hand, showed remarkable improvement; probation and the threat of losing his job made him a better worker—only 7 red beads—a 50 percent reduction in defects! He met the goal; if he can do it, anyone can. Dennis gets a special commendation from the plant manager.

At the beginning of the third day, management announces a Zero Defects Day. Everyone will do their best on this last day of the apprenticeship program. The Foreman is desperate and he tells the Willing Workers again that their jobs are their own responsibility. From Figure 10.4, production figures can be determined (by computing the difference between the cumulative output of day 3 and day 2), and show that Jeff produces 12 red beads, Dave 18, Tom 17, Dennis 9, Marty 6, and Ann 11. Clearly, Marty learned a lesson the day before, but the group's overall performance is not good. Management is bitterly disappointed at the results. The Zero Defect Day program did not improve quality substantially; in fact, more red beads were produced today than ever before. Costs are getting out of control, and there is talk of shutting down the entire plant. Dave and Tom receive pink slips informing them that tomorrow will be their last day; their work is clearly much worse than the others. But the Foreman is optimistic. He puts up a poster saying "Be a Quality Worker!" to encourage the others to reach the goal.

On the fourth day (see Figure 10.5), we find that the number of red beads produced by the six Willing Workers is 8, 11, 8, 9, 8, and 9. The production is still not good enough. The Foreman announces that management has decided to close the plant after all.

Figure 10.4 Third Day's Cumulative Results

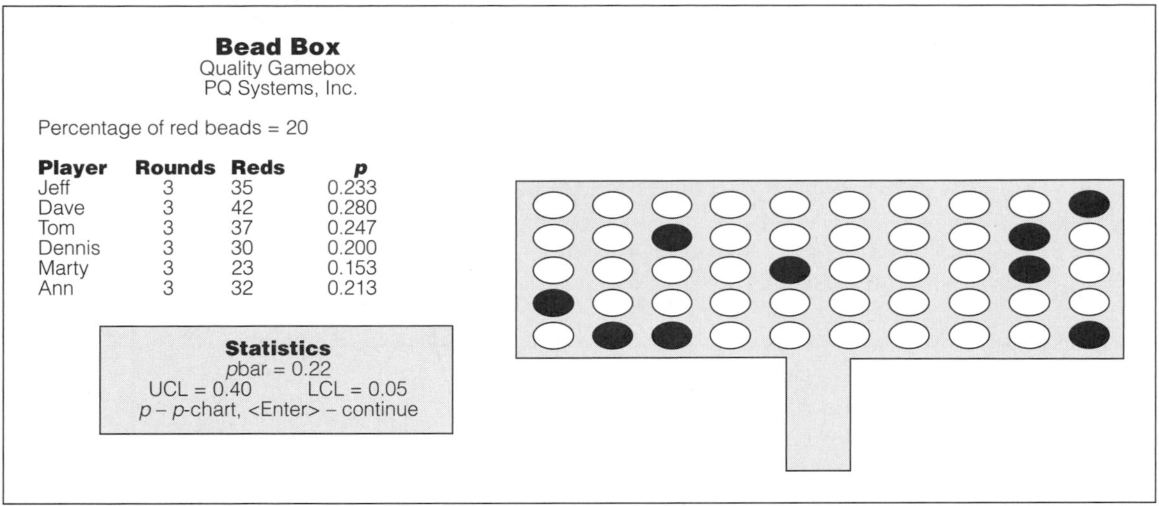

Source: Reprinted with permission of PQ Systems.

The Red Bead experiment offers several important lessons for managers:

- *Variation exists in systems and, if stable, can be predicted.* If we plot the fraction of red beads produced by each worker each day, we can observe this variation easily. Figure 10.6 is a plot of the fraction of red beads produced over time. All points fluctuate about the overall average, which is 0.21, falling roughly between 0.10 and 0.40. In Chapter 13, we will learn to calculate *statistical limits of variation* (0.04 and 0.38)—limits between which we would expect results from a stable system to fall. This variation shows that that the system of production is indeed stable; that is, the variation arises from common causes. Although the

Figure 10.5 Fourth Day's Cumulative Results

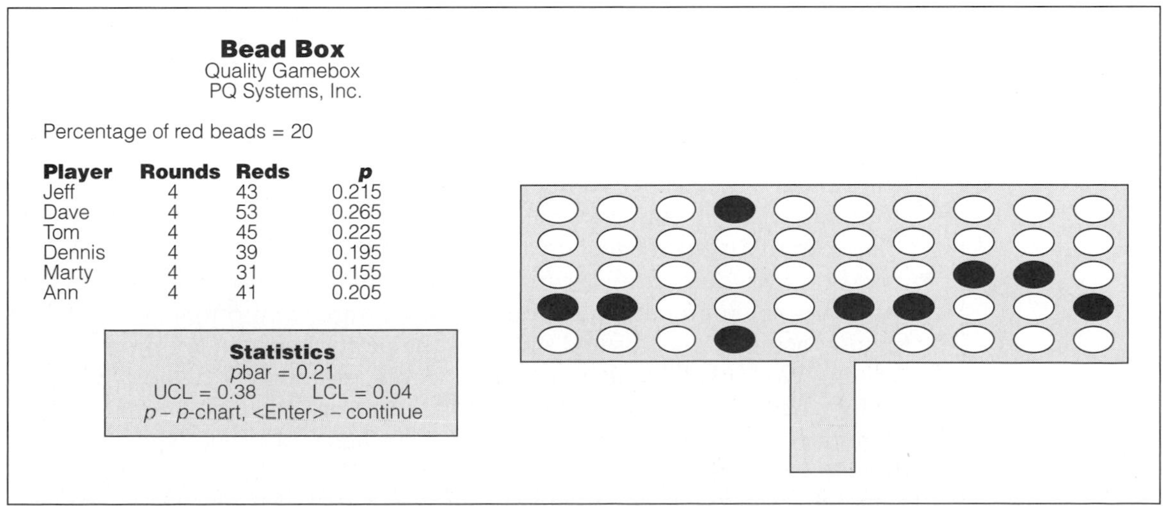

Source: Reprinted with permission of PQ Systems.

Figure 10.6 Run Chart of Fraction of Red Beads Produced

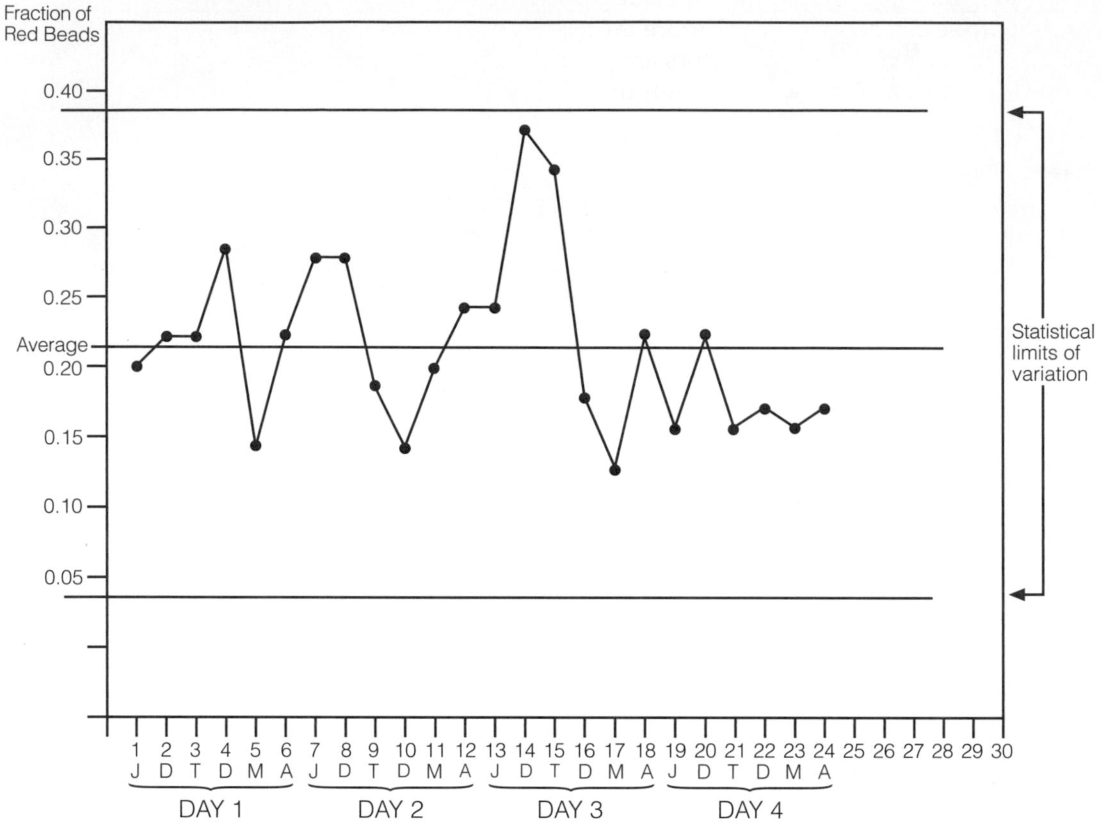

Fraction of Red Beads

0.40
0.35
0.30
0.25
Average
0.20
0.15
0.10
0.05

Statistical limits of variation

1 2 3 4 5 6 7 8 9 10 11 12 13 14 15 16 17 18 19 20 21 22 23 24 25 26 27 28 29 30
J D T D M A J D T D M A J D T D M A J D T D M A
DAY 1 DAY 2 DAY 3 DAY 4

Source: Reprinted with permission of Marcel Dekker, Inc.

exact number of red beads in any particular paddle is not predictable, we can describe statistically what we expect from the system.

- *All the variation in the production of red beads, and the variation from day to day of any Willing Worker, came entirely from the process itself.* In this experiment, Deming deliberately eliminated the source of variability that managers usually believe is the most significant: people. Each worker was basically identical, and no evidence showed that any one of them was better than another. They could not control the number of red beads produced and could do no better than the system would allow. Neither motivation nor threats had any influence. Unfortunately, many managers believe that all variation is controllable and place blame on those who cannot do anything about it.
- *Numerical goals are often meaningless.* A Foreman who gives out merit pay and puts people on probation, supposedly as rewards and punishment of performance, actually rewards and punishes the performance of the process, not the Willing Workers. To rank or appraise people arbitrarily is demoralizing, especially when workers cannot influence the outcomes. No matter what the goal is, it has no effect on the actual number of red beads produced. Exhorting workers to "Do their best" only leads to frustration. Management has no basis to assume that the best Willing Workers of the past will be the best in the future.
- *Management is responsible for the system.* The experiment shows bad management. Procedures are rigid. The Willing Workers have no say in improving the

process. Management is responsible for the incoming material, but does not work with the supplier to improve the inputs to the system. Management designed the production system and decided to rely on inspection to control the process. These decisions have far more influence on the outcomes than the efforts of the workers. Three inspectors are probably as costly as the six workers and add practically no value to the output.

Deming's second experiment is the Funnel Experiment. Its purpose is to show that people can and do affect the outcomes of many processes and create unwanted variation by "tampering" with the process, or indiscriminately trying to remove common causes of variation. In this experiment, a funnel is suspended above a table with a target drawn on a tablecloth. The goal is to hit the target. Participants drop a marble through the funnel and mark the place where the marble eventually lands. Rarely will the marble rest on the target. This variation is due to common causes in the process. One strategy is to simply leave the funnel alone, which creates some variation of points around the target. This may be called *Rule 1*. However, many people believe they can improve the results by adjusting the location of the funnel. Three possible rules for adjusting the funnel are:

Rule 2. Measure the deviation from the point at which the marble comes to rest and the target. Move the funnel an equal distance in the opposite direction from its current position [Figure 10.7(a)].

Rule 3. Measure the deviation from the point at which the marble comes to rest and the target. Set the funnel an equal distance in the opposite direction of the error from the target [Figure 10.7(b)].

Rule 4. Place the funnel over the spot where the marble last came to rest.

Figure 10.8 shows a computer simulation of these strategies using the Quality Gamebox. Clearly the first rule—leave the funnel alone—results in the least variation.

People use these rules inappropriately all the time, causing more variation than would normally occur. An amateur golfer who hits a bad shot tends to make an immediate adjustment. If the last manufactured part is off-specification, adjust the machine. If a schedule was not met last month, change the process. If the last quarter's earnings report was less than expected, dump the stock. If an employee's performance last week was subpar (or exceptional), punish (or reward) the employee. In all of these cases, the error is usually compounded by an inappropriate reaction. All of these policies stem from a lack of understanding of variation, which originates from not understanding the process.

Figure 10.7 Two Rules for Adjusting the Funnel

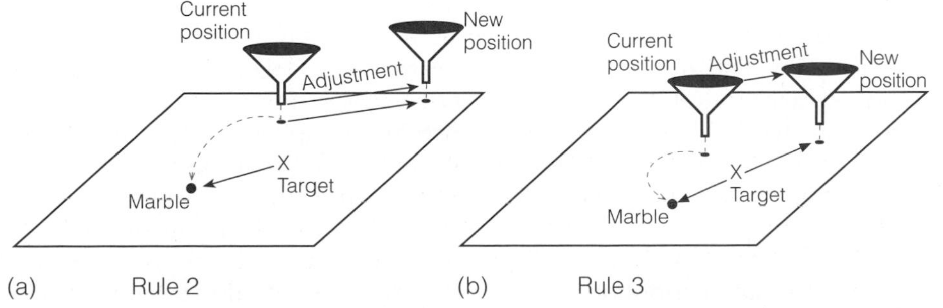

Source: Reprinted with permission of Marcel Dekker, Inc.

Figure 10.8 Results of the Funnel Experiment

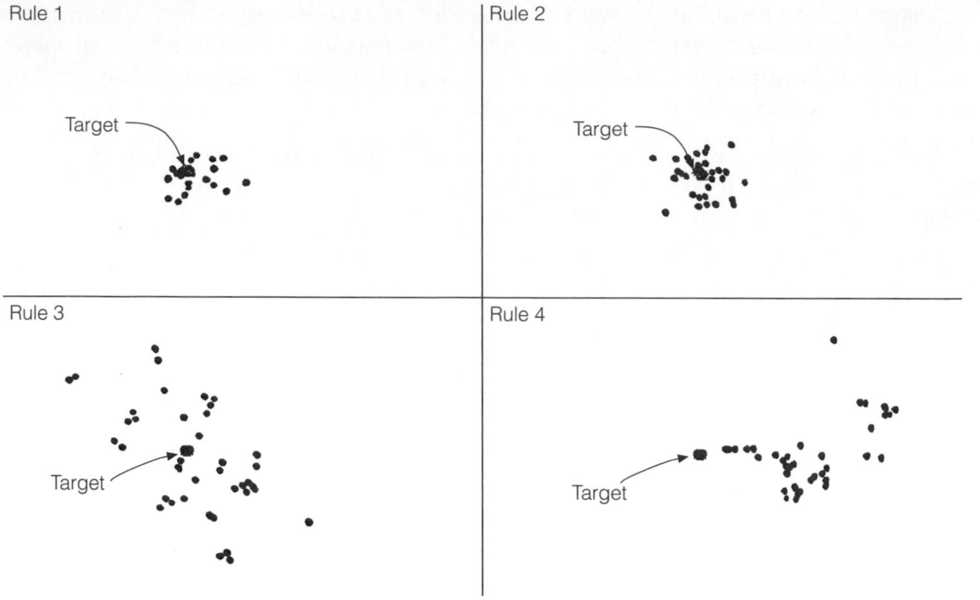

Rule 1 — Target
Rule 2 — Target
Rule 3 — Target
Rule 4 — Target

Source: Reprinted with permission by Marcel Dekker Inc.

STATISTICAL FOUNDATIONS

To apply statistics properly, you need to have a basic understanding of probability distributions and sampling. These concepts are the focus of this section.

Random Variables and Probability Distributions

Random variables and probability distributions are the foundation for understanding statistical methods. The collectively exhaustive set of outcomes from an experiment makes up a *sample space*. A mathematical function that assigns numerical values to every possible outcome in a sample space is called a **random variable**. A random variable can be either discrete or continuous, depending on the specific numerical values it may assume. A *discrete random variable* can take on only finite values. An example would be the number of defects observed in a sample. A *continuous random variable* can take on any real value over a specified interval of real numbers. An example would be the diameters of bearings being manufactured in a factory. Of course, the actual observed values for the variable are limited by the precision of the measuring device. Hence, only a finite number of actual observations would occur. In theory, this result would still be a continuous random variable. Random variables are the key component used in the development of probability distributions.

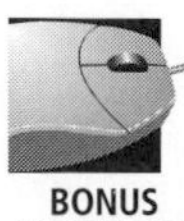

A **probability distribution** represents a theoretical model of the relative frequency of a random variable. Relating probability distributions to the random variables that they represent allows a classification of the distributions as either discrete or continuous. The Bonus Materials folder for this chapter on the Premium website contains a review of the more useful probability distributions in quality applications. You are undoubtedly quite familiar with the normal distribution and its use as a common assumption in statistical models. Unfortunately, most business processes do not produce normal distributions.[12] Lack of a normal distribution often results from the tendency to control processes tightly, which eliminates many sources of natural variation, as well as from human behavior, physical laws, and inspection practices. For example, data on the number of days customers take to pay bills typically show that many customers like to prepay; others send payments that arrive just after the due date. This behavior causes spikes in the distribution that do not conform to normality. In a hot-dip galvanizing process, a zinc layer forms when the base material reaches the temperature of molten zinc. However, if the part is removed before the critical temperature is reached, no zinc will adhere at all. Thus, all parts will have some minimum zinc thickness and the left side of the distribution will not tail off gradually as does a normal distribution. Measuring perpendicularity as the absolute deviation from 90 degrees instead of the actual angle can easily lead to nonnormality. Therefore, it is important to fully understand the nature of your data before applying statistical theory that depends on normality assumptions.

Sampling

Sampling forms the basis for applications of statistics. Suppose that you worked in a 1,000-bed hospital and wanted to determine the attitudes of a certain group of patients about the quality of care they received while in the hospital. Several factors should be considered before making this study:

1. What is the objective of the study?
2. What type of sample should be used?
3. What possible error might result from sampling?
4. What will the study cost?

One approach to tackling this problem would be to take a complete census—a survey of every person in the entire population. However, the objective of the study will dictate which method should be used to perform the study in the most effective and efficient manner. This decision requires sensitivity to the needs of the user and an understanding of the strengths and weaknesses of the specific techniques being used. Would sampling work just as well? If the user needs the results next week to make a decision involving the expenditure of $1,000, the study will require a different design from one in which the results influence a decision that will be made in six months and has a $1 million expenditure. Sampling provides a distinct advantage over a complete census in that much less time and cost are required to gather the data. In many cases, such as inspection, sampling may be more accurate than 100 percent inspection because of reduction of inspection errors. However, sampling is frequently subject to a higher degree of error.

The second issue relates to different methods of sampling. The following are some of the most common:

1. *Simple random sampling:* Every item in the population has an equal probability of being selected.
2. *Stratified sampling:* The population is partitioned into groups, or strata, and a sample is selected from each stratum.
3. *Systematic sampling:* Every *n*th (4th, 5th, etc.) item is selected.
4. *Cluster sampling:* A typical group (e.g., division of the company) is selected, and a random sample is taken from within the group.
5. *Judgment sampling:* Expert opinion is used to determine the location and characteristics of a definable sample group.

In choosing the appropriate type of sampling method, an analyst must consider what the sample is designed to do.

Suppose that your objective is to provide a report to top management of the hospital to help them decide whether to expand the use of quality control measures within the hospital. Some issues that would have to be considered before choosing a sample would be the time frame for completing the study, the size and cost limitations of the sample, the accessibility of the population of patients, and the desired accuracy. Assume that you have six weeks to complete the study, a limited operating budget of $1,500, and a population of 800 maternity patients (the category in which you are interested) who could be involved in the quality study. Further assume that the accuracy of your study requires a sample of at least 400 patients and that the cost of each response would vary from $2 to $4, depending on how the survey is administered. Obviously, you would have to select a sample, because a complete census of all patients would not be feasible because of the budget limitation. Time limitations would make travel to conduct face-to-face interviews virtually impossible. Thus, the only feasible alternatives would be mailed questionnaires, telephone interviews, or a combination of the two.

A good sampling plan should select a sample at the lowest cost that will provide the best possible representation of the population, consistent with the objectives of precision and reliability that have been determined for the study.

Given this information, what type of sample should be chosen? Each type has advantages and disadvantages. A simple random sample would be easy to select but might not include sufficient representation by floor or ward. If a list of the patients, perhaps in alphabetical order, was available, a systematic sample of every fourth name could easily be selected. It would have the same disadvantages as the random sample, however. On the other hand, a cluster sample or judgment sample could be selected to include more representatives from floors or wards. However, cluster and judgment samples frequently take more time to identify and select appropriate sampling units. Also, because more subjective judgment is involved, a biased, nonrepresentative sampling plan is more likely to be developed.

The third issue in sampling relates to error. Sampling error occurs naturally and results from the fact that a sample may not always be representative of the population, no matter how carefully it is selected. The only way to reduce sampling error is to take a larger sample from the population. Systematic errors, however, can be reduced or eliminated by design.

*Errors in sampling generally stem from two causes: **sampling error** and **systematic error** (often called nonsampling error).*

Sources of systematic error include the following:

1. *Bias:* The tendency to systematically over- or underestimate true values
2. *Noncomparable data:* Data that come from two populations but are erroneously considered to have come from one
3. *Uncritical projection of trends:* The assumption that what has happened in the past will continue into the future
4. *Causation:* The assumption that because two variables are related, one must be the cause of changes in the other
5. *Improper sampling:* The use of an erroneous method for gathering data, thus biasing results (e.g., using electronic mail surveys to get opinions from a population having few individuals with electronic mail services)

These sources of error can be overcome through careful planning of the sampling study. Bias can be reduced by frequent interaction with end users of the study as well as cross-checking of research designs with knowledgeable analysts. Noncomparable data can be avoided by a sensitivity to conditions that could contribute to development of dissimilar population segments. In the hospital example, data gathered from different floors, wards, or shifts could prove to be noncomparable. In production firms, different shifts, machines, or products may define different populations, even though the characteristics being measured are the same for each. Uncritical projection of trends can be avoided by analysis of the underlying causes of trends and a constant questioning of the assumption that tomorrow's population will be the same as yesterday's. Reasons for causation must be investigated. Relationships between variables alone are not sufficient to conclude that causality exists. Causation can often be tested by holding one variable constant while changing the other to determine effects of the change. Finally, improper sampling can be avoided by a thorough understanding of sampling techniques and a determination of whether the method being used is capable of reaching any unit in the population in an unbiased fashion. This section concludes with some examples of sampling applications in quality.

Simple Random Sampling A **simple random sample** is a small sample of size n drawn from a large population of size N in such a way that every possible sample of size n has an equal chance of being selected. For example, if a box of 1,000 plastic components for electrical connectors is thoroughly mixed and 25 parts are selected randomly without replacement, the random aspect of this definition has been satisfied. Simple random sampling forms the basis for most scientific statistical surveys, such as auditing, and is a useful tool for quality assurance studies. Many statistical procedures depend on taking random samples. If random samples are not used, bias may be introduced. For instance, if the items are rolled in coils, sampling only from the exposed end of the coil (a convenience sample) can easily result in bias if the production process that produced the coils varies over time.

Simple random samples can be selected by using a table of random numbers (see Appendix C). A unique number is assigned to each element of the population by using serial numbers, by placing the items in racks or trays with unique row and column numbering, or by associating with each item a physical distance (such as depth in a card file). Numbers are then chosen from the table in a systematic fashion. A sample is formed by selecting the items that correspond to the chosen random numbers. The selection may begin at any point in the table and move in any direction, using any set of digits that serves the sampler's purpose. An illustration of the use of the random number table for simple random sampling follows.

A particular nursing unit has 30 patients. Five patient records are to be sampled to verify the correctness of a medical procedure. To determine which patients to select, assign numbers 1 through 30 to the 30 patients. Select, for example, the first row in Appendix C and examine consecutive two-digit integers until five different numbers between 01 and 30 are found. (Any two-digit number greater than 30 is rejected because it does not correspond to an item in the given population.) Thus, the following sequence of random numbers and decisions occurs.

Number	Decision
63	Reject
27	Select
15	Select
99	Reject
86	Reject
71	Reject
74	Reject
45	Reject
11	Select
02	Select
15	Duplicate
14	Select

Based on the preceding sequence, 2, 11, 14, 15, and 27 are selected.

Simple random sampling is generally used to estimate population parameters such as means, proportions, and variances. To use simple random sampling effectively, you must also determine the appropriate sample size. The Bonus Materials folder for this chapter on the Premium website addresses issues of sample size determination.

Other Types of Sampling Procedures Alternatives to simple random sampling are available and are discussed briefly here. These methods have distinct advantages over simple random sampling in many situations.

1. **Stratified random sampling:** A stratified random sample is one obtained by separating the population into nonoverlapping groups, and then selecting a simple random sample from each group. The groups might be different machines, wards in a hospital, departments, and so on. For example, suppose a population of 28,000 items is produced on three different machines:

Machine	Group Size
1	20,000
2	5,000
3	3,000

   Assume that a specific confidence level requires a sample of 525 units in this case. We could draw these units randomly from the entire population. Under stratified random sampling, a simple random sample of 250 units from machine 1, 150 units from machine 2, and 125 units from machine 3 might be taken. Formulas are available for combining the results of individual samples into an overall estimate of the population parameter of interest. This technique will demonstrate quality differences that may exist among machines.

   Stratified random sampling will provide results similar to simple random sampling but with a smaller total sample size. It produces a smaller bound on the error of the estimation than would be produced by a simple random sample of the same size. These statements are particularly true if measurements within each group are homogeneous, that is, if the units within strata are alike.

2. **Systematic sampling:** In some situations, particularly with large populations, selecting a simple random sample using random number tables and searching through the population for the corresponding element is impractical. With systematic sampling, the population size is divided by the sample size required, yielding a value for n. The first item is chosen at random from among the first n items. Thereafter, every nth item is selected. For example, suppose that a population has 4,000 units and a sample of size 50 is required. Select the first unit randomly from among the first 80 units. Every 80th (4,000/50) item after that would be selected.

   Systematic sampling is based on the assumption that if the first element is chosen at random, the entire sample will have the properties of a simple random sample. This method should be used with caution because quality characteristics may vary in some periodic fashion with the length of the sampling interval and thus bias the results.

3. **Cluster sampling:** In cluster sampling, the population is first partitioned into groups of elements called clusters. A simple random sample of the clusters is selected. The elements within the clusters selected constitute the sample. For example, suppose that products are boxed in groups of 50. Each box can be regarded as a cluster. We would draw a sample of boxes and inspect all units in the boxes selected.

Cluster sampling tends to provide good results when the elements within the clusters are not alike (heterogeneous). In this case, each cluster would be representative of the entire population.

4. **Judgment sampling:** With judgment sampling, an arbitrary sample of pertinent data is examined and the percentage of nonconformances is calculated. Because judgment sampling is not random, the risks associated with making an incorrect conclusion cannot be quantified. Thus, it is not a preferred method of sampling.

STATISTICAL METHODOLOGY

Figure 10.9 summarizes the basic statistical methodology used in quality applications. The first major component of statistical methodology is the efficient collection, organization, and description of data, commonly referred to as **descriptive statistics**. Frequency distributions and histograms are used to organize and present data. Measures of central tendency (means, medians, proportions) and measures of dispersion (range, standard deviation, variance) provide important quantitative information about the nature of the data. For example, an airline might investigate the problem of lost baggage and determine that the major causes of the problem are lost or damaged identification tags, incorrect tags on the bags, and misrouting to baggage claim areas. An examination of frequencies for each of these categories might show that lost or damaged bags accounted for 50 percent of the problems,

Figure 10.9 Basic Statistical Methodology for Quality

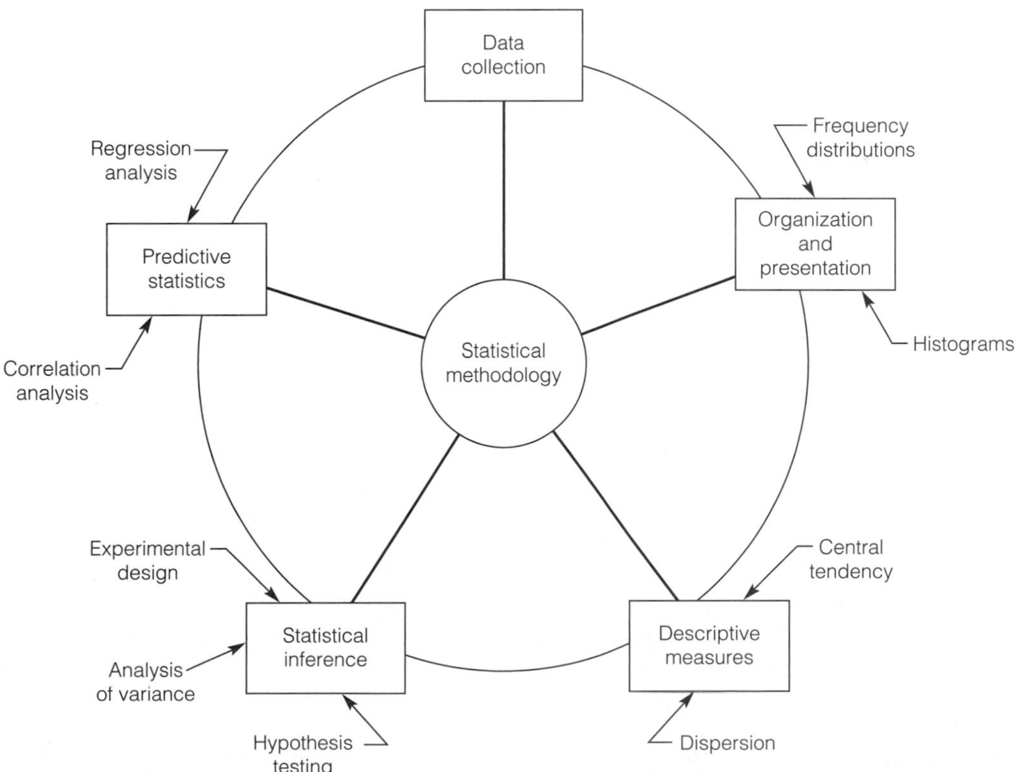

incorrect tags for 30 percent, and misrouting for only 20 percent. The airline might also compute the average number of baggage errors per 1,000 passengers each month. Such information is useful in identifying quality problems and as a means of measuring improvement.

The second component of statistical problem solving is **statistical inference**. Statistical inference is the process of drawing conclusions about unknown characteristics of a population from which data were taken. Techniques used in this phase include confidence intervals, hypothesis testing, and experimental design. For example, a chemical manufacturer might be interested in determining the effect of temperature on the yield of a new manufacturing process. Because of variation in yields, a confidence interval might be constructed to quantify the uncertainty of sample data. In a controlled experiment, the manufacturer might test the hypothesis that the temperature has an effect on the yield against the alternative hypothesis that temperature has no effect. If the temperature is, in fact, a critical variable, steps will be required to maintain the temperature at the proper level and to draw inferences as to whether the process remains under control, based on samples taken from it. Experimental design is important for helping to understand the effects of process factors on output quality and for optimizing systems.

The third component in statistical methodology is **predictive statistics**, the purpose of which is to develop predictions of future values based on historical data. Correlation analysis and regression analysis are two useful techniques. Frequently, these techniques can clarify the characteristics of a process as well as predict future results. For example, in quality assurance, correlation is frequently used in test instrument calibration studies. In such studies, an instrument is used to measure a standard test sample that has known characteristics. The actual results are compared to standard results, and adjustments are made to compensate for errors.

Descriptive Statistics

A *population* is a complete set or collection of objects of interest; a *sample* is a subset of objects taken from the population. Characteristics of a population, such as the mean μ, standard deviation σ, or proportion π, are generally known as *parameters* of the population. In statistical notation, they are written as follows:

$$\text{Population mean: } \mu = \frac{1}{N}\sum_{i=1}^{N} x_i$$

$$\text{Population standard deviation: } \sigma = \sqrt{\frac{\sum_{i=1}^{N}(x_i - \mu)^2}{N}}$$

$$\text{Population proportion: } \pi = \frac{Q}{N}$$

where x_i is the value of the ith observation; N is the number of items in a population; and Q is the number of items exhibiting a criterion of interest, such as manufacturing defects or on-time departures of aircraft.

The sample mean, sample standard deviation, and sample proportion are computed as follows:

$$\text{Sample mean: } \bar{x} = \frac{1}{n}\sum_{i=1}^{n} x_i$$

$$\text{Sample standard deviation: } s = \sqrt{\frac{\sum_{i=1}^{n}(x_i - \bar{x})^2}{n - 1}}$$

$$\text{Sample proportion: } p = \frac{q}{n}$$

where n is the number of items in a sample and q is the number of items in a sample exhibiting a criterion of interest.

The purpose of sampling is to gain knowledge about the characteristics of the population from the information contained in a sample. For instance, the sample statistic $\bar{x}$ is generally used as a point estimator for the population parameter μ, s as a point estimator for σ, and p as a point estimator for π. The actual numerical values of $\bar{x}$, s, and p, which represent the single "best guess" for each unknown population parameter, are called *point estimates.* Other useful statistics to describe a set of data include the median, range, and coefficient of skewness.

Statistical Analysis with Microsoft Excel

BONUS MATERIALS

Spreadsheets are the most useful tools for managers and analysts. In this part of the book, we will use Microsoft Excel whenever appropriate to perform statistical calculations and display graphs or charts. The Bonus Materials folder on the Premium website accompanying this book contains all of the major spreadsheets used in examples in this book that will help you in working many end-of-chapter problems. The files available on the disk are identified by their name (NAME.XLS) in the text.

Microsoft Excel provides data analysis tools, called the *Analysis ToolPak,* that are useful in complex statistical analyses. You provide the data and parameters for each analysis; the tool uses the appropriate statistical functions and then displays the results in an output table. Some tools generate charts in addition to output tables. To view a list of available analysis tools in Excel 2007, click on *Data Analysis* in the *Analysis* group under the *Data* tab in the Excel menu bar. If this is not present, then you must install the add-in. To do so, click the *Office* button at top left of the toolbar. Click on *Excel Options* button at the bottom of the pop-up and choose *Add-Ins* from the left column. At the bottom of the dialog, make sure *Excel Add-ins* is selected in the *Manage:* box and click *Go*. In the *Add-Ins* dialog, if *Analysis Toolpak, Analysis Toolpak VBA,* and *Solver Add-in* are not checked, simply check the boxes and click OK. In Excel 2003, *Data Analysis* will be found on the *Tools* menu. Excel also provides many worksheet functions for statistical, applications. The easiest way to locate a particular function is to select a cell and click on the *Insert function* button which looks like [f_x] on the toolbar. We strongly encourage you to learn how to use the capabilities of Excel for quality assurance applications. Much more information can be found in the Help files available with Excel.

We will assume that the sample of U-bolt measurements in Table 10.1 is representative of the population from which they were drawn. These data were entered into an Excel spreadsheet in the range A2:A121. Figure 10.10 shows the Descriptive

Table 10.1 Measurements of U-Bolts (U-bolt Data.XLS)

10.65	10.70	10.65	10.65	10.85
10.75	10.85	10.75	10.85	10.65
10.75	10.80	10.80	10.70	10.75
10.60	10.70	10.70	10.75	10.65
10.70	10.75	10.65	10.85	10.80
10.60	10.75	10.75	10.85	10.70
10.60	10.80	10.70	10.75	10.75
10.75	10.80	10.65	10.75	10.70
10.65	10.80	10.85	10.85	10.75
10.60	10.70	10.60	10.80	10.65
10.80	10.75	10.90	10.50	10.85
10.85	10.75	10.85	10.65	10.70
10.70	10.70	10.75	10.75	10.70
10.65	10.70	10.85	10.75	10.60
10.75	10.80	10.75	10.80	10.65
10.90	10.80	10.80	10.75	10.85
10.75	10.70	10.85	10.70	10.80
10.75	10.70	10.60	10.70	10.60
10.65	10.65	10.85	10.65	10.70
10.60	10.60	10.65	10.55	10.65
10.50	10.55	10.65	10.80	10.80
10.80	10.65	10.75	10.65	10.65
10.65	10.60	10.65	10.60	10.70
10.65	10.70	10.70	10.60	10.65

Figure 10.10 Microsoft Excel Descriptive Statistics Dialog Box

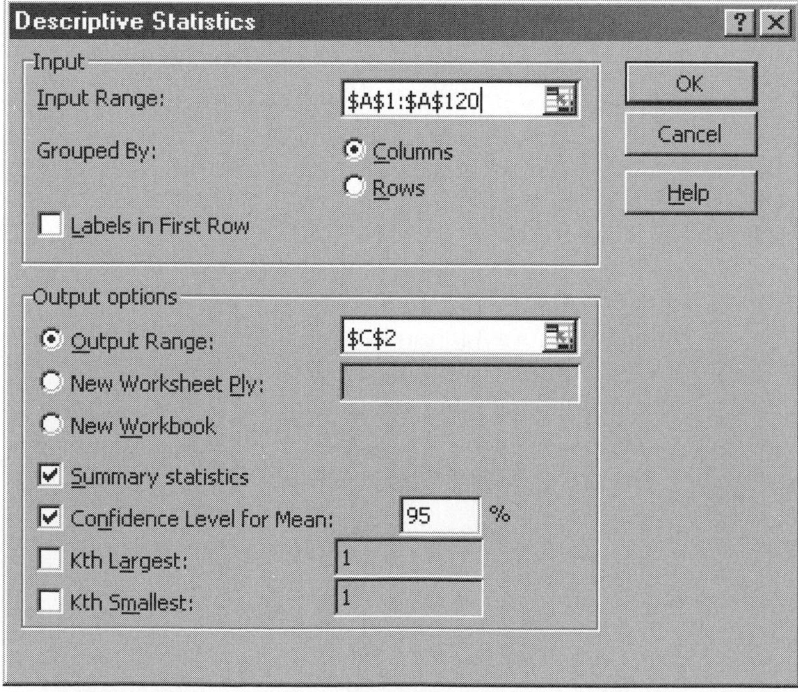

Statistics dialog box that is displayed after selecting the Descriptive Statistics tool. An explanation of the items in this dialog box follows. (This information can also be obtained from the Help files in Excel.)

Input Range: Enter the cell reference for the range of data you want to analyze. The reference must consist of two or more adjacent ranges of data arranged in columns or rows. Excel will compute individual statistics for each row or column; thus, all data in Table 10.1 are entered in a single column.

Grouped By: To indicate whether the data in the input range are arranged in rows or in columns, click *Rows* or *Columns.*

Labels in First Row/Labels in First Column: If the first row of the input range contains labels, select the Labels in First Row check box. If the labels are in the first column of the input range, select the Labels in First Column check box. This check box is clear if the input range has no labels; Microsoft Excel generates appropriate data labels for the output table.

Confidence Level for Mean: Select this option to include a row in the output table for the confidence level of the mean. In the box, enter the desired confidence level. For example, a value of 95 percent calculates the confidence level of the mean at a significance of 5 percent.

Kth Largest: Select this option to include a row in the output table for the *k*th largest value for each range of data. In the box, enter the number to use for *k*. If you enter 1, this row contains the maximum of the data set.

Kth Smallest: Select this option to include a row in the output table for the *k*th smallest value for each range of data. In the box, enter the number to use for *k*. Enter 1 and this row will contain the minimum of the data set.

Output Range: Enter the reference for the upper-left cell of the output table. This tool produces two columns of information for each data set. The left column contains statistics labels and the right column contains the statistics. Microsoft Excel writes a two-column table of statistics for each column or row in the input range, depending on the Grouped By option selected.

New Worksheet Ply: Click to insert a new worksheet in the current workbook and paste the results starting at cell A1 of the new worksheet. To name the new worksheet, type a name in the box.

New Workbook: Click to create a new workbook and paste the results on a new worksheet in the new workbook.

Summary Statistics: This option commands Microsoft Excel to produce one field for each of the following statistics in the output table: Mean, Standard Error (of the mean), Median, Mode, Standard Deviation, Variance, Kurtosis, Skewness, Range, Minimum, Maximum, Sum, Count, Largest (#), Smallest (#), and Confidence Level. Figure 10.11 shows the results obtained.

A second useful data analysis tool is the *Histogram* tool, which is described as follows. Figure 10.12 shows the Excel dialog box for this option.

Input Range: Enter the reference for the range of data to be analyzed.

Bin Range (optional): Enter the cell reference to a range that contains an optional set of boundary values that define bin ranges. These values should be in ascending order. Microsoft Excel counts the number of data points between the current bin number and the adjoining higher bin, if any. A number is counted in a particular bin if it is equal to or less than the bin number down to the last bin. All values below the first bin value are counted together, as are the values above the last bin value. If the bin range is omitted, Microsoft Excel creates a set of evenly distributed bins

Figure 10.11 Microsoft Excel Descriptive Statistics Results

	A	B	C	D
1	10.65			
2	10.75		*Column1*	
3	10.75			
4	10.60		Mean	10.71708333
5	10.70		Standard Error	0.007927716
6	10.60		Median	10.7
7	10.60		Mode	10.65
8	10.75		Standard Deviation	0.086843778
9	10.65		Sample Variance	0.007541842
10	10.60		Kurtosis	-0.53752485
11	10.80		Skewness	-0.0420018
12	10.85		Range	0.4
13	10.70		Minimum	10.5
14	10.65		Maximum	10.9
15	10.75		Sum	1286.05
16	10.90		Count	120
17	10.75		Confidence Level(95.0%)	0.015697649

between the data's minimum and maximum values. In this example, we defined the bin range in cells F3:F11.

Labels: Select if the first row or column of the input range contains labels. Clear this check box if the input range has no labels; Microsoft Excel generates appropriate data labels for the output table.

Figure 10.12 Microsoft Excel Histogram Dialog Box

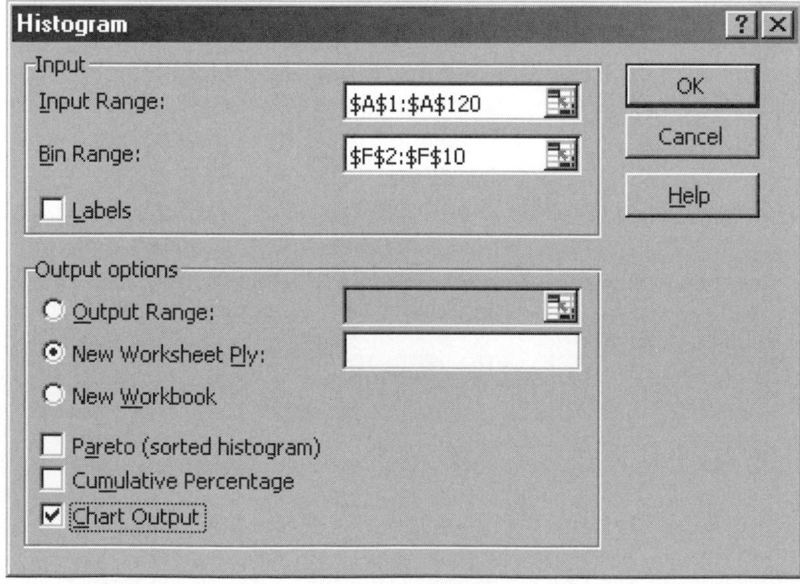

Output Range: Enter the reference for the upper-left cell of the output table. Microsoft Excel automatically determines the size of the output area and displays a message if the output table will replace existing data.

Pareto (sorted histogram): Select to present data in the output table in descending order of frequency. If this check box is cleared, Microsoft Excel presents the data in ascending order and omits the three rightmost columns that contain the sorted data.

Cumulative Percentage: Select to generate an output table column for cumulative percentages and to include a cumulative percentage line in the histogram chart. Clear to omit the cumulative percentages.

Chart Output: Select to generate an embedded histogram chart with the output table.

Figure 10.13 shows the frequency distribution and histogram generated. We will use these results in another example later in this chapter.

Statistical Inference

Statistical inference is concerned with drawing conclusions about populations based on sample data. To be able to make probability statements about the relationship between sample statistics and population parameters and draw inferences, we first need to understand sampling distributions.

Sampling Distributions Different samples will produce different estimates of the population parameters. Therefore, sample statistics such as $\bar{x}$, s, and p are random variables that have their own probability distribution, mean, and variance. These probability distributions are called sampling distributions. In quality, the sampling distributions of $\bar{x}$ and p are of the most interest.

When using simple random sampling, the expected value of $\bar{x}$ is the population mean μ, or

$$E(\bar{x}) = \mu$$

Figure 10.13 Histogram and Frequency Distribution

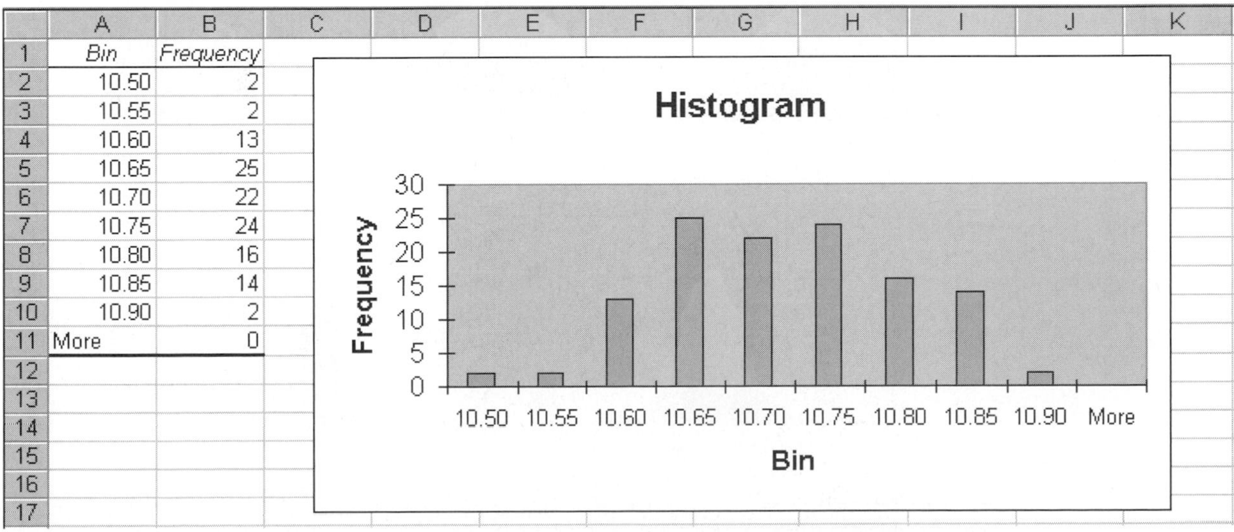

Bin	Frequency
10.50	2
10.55	2
10.60	13
10.65	25
10.70	22
10.75	24
10.80	16
10.85	14
10.90	2
More	0

The standard deviation of $\bar{x}$ (often called the **standard error of the mean**) is given by the formula

$$\sigma_{\bar{x}} = \frac{\sigma}{\sqrt{n}} \quad \text{for infinite populations or sampling with replacement from an infinite population}$$

$$\sigma_{\bar{x}} = \sqrt{\frac{N-n}{N-1}}\frac{\sigma}{\sqrt{n}} \quad \text{for finite populations}$$

When $n/N \leq 0.05$, $\sigma_{\bar{x}} = \sigma/\sqrt{n}$ provides a good approximation for finite populations.

The last step is to characterize the form of the probability distribution of $\bar{x}$. If the true population distribution is unknown, the Central Limit Theorem (CLT) can provide some useful insights:

> *If simple random samples of size* n *are taken from any population having a mean* μ *and a standard deviation of* σ*, the probability distribution of the sample mean approaches a normal distribution with mean* μ *and standard deviation (standard error)* $\sigma_{\bar{x}} = \sigma/\sqrt{n}$ *as n becomes very large. In more precise mathematical terms: As* $n \rightarrow \infty$ *the distribution of the random variable* $z = (\bar{x} - \mu)/(\sigma/\sqrt{n})$ *approaches that of a standard normal distribution.*

The power of the central limit theorem can be seen through computer simulation using the *Quality Gamebox* software. Figure 10.14 shows the results of sampling from a triangular distribution for sample sizes of 1, 2, 5, and 10. For samples as small as five, the sampling distribution begins to develop into the symmetric bell-shaped form of a normal distribution. Also observe that the variance decreases as the sample size increases. The approximation to a normal distribution can be assumed for sample

Figure 10.14 Illustration of the Central Limit Theorem

Theoretical Distribution

Actual Distribution

Sample size = 1

Actual Distribution

Sample size = 2

Actual Distribution

Sample size = 5

Actual Distribution

Sample size = 10

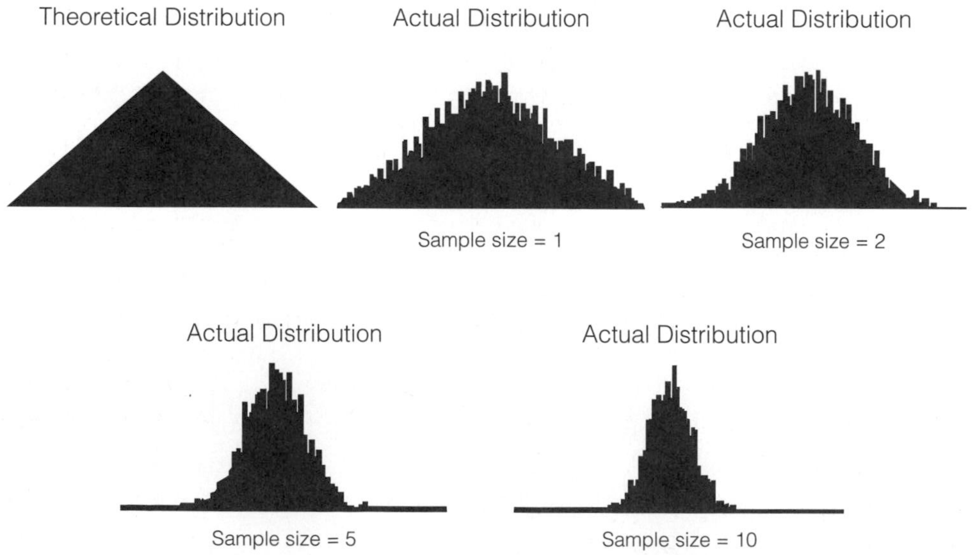

Source: Reprinted with permission of P–Q Systems, Inc.

sizes of 30 or more. If the population is *known* to be normal, the sampling distribution of $\bar{x}$ is normal for any sample size.

Next, consider the sampling distribution of p, in which the expected value of p, $E(p) = \pi$. Here π is used as the population parameter and is not related to the *number* $\pi \approx 3.14159$. The standard deviation of p is

$$s_p = \sqrt{\frac{\pi(1-\pi)}{n}}$$

for infinite populations.

For finite populations, or when $n/N > 0.05$, modify s_p by

$$s_p = \sqrt{\frac{N-n}{N-1}}\sqrt{\frac{\pi(1-\pi)}{n}}$$

In applying the central limit theorem (CLT) to p, the sampling distribution of p can be approximated by a normal distribution for large sample sizes.

This and subsequent chapters explore various applications of the CLT to statistical quality control in the areas of process capability determination and control charting. Consider the following example as we illustrate an application of sampling distributions.

The mean length of shafts produced on a lathe has historically been 50 inches, with a standard deviation of 0.12 inch. If a sample of 36 shafts is taken, what is the probability that the sample mean would be greater than 50.04 inches?

The sampling distribution of the mean is approximately normal with mean 50 and standard deviation of $0.12/\sqrt{36}$. Thus,

$$z = \frac{\bar{x}-\mu}{\sigma/\sqrt{n}} = \frac{50.04-50}{0.12/\sqrt{36}} = 2.0$$

In the standard normal table, the value of 2.0 yields the probability of 0.4772 between the mean and this value. The area for $z \geq 2.0$ then is found by

$$P(z \geq 2.0) = 0.5000 - 0.4772 = 0.0228$$

Thus, the probability of a value equal to or greater than 50.04 inches as the mean of a sample of 36 items is only 0.0228 if the population mean is 50 inches. The applicability of sampling distributions to statistical quality is that "shifts" in the population mean can quickly be detected using small representative samples to monitor the process.

Similarly, if a sample size of 64 is used, $\sigma/\sqrt{n} = 0.12/8 = 0.015$ and

$$z = \frac{\bar{x}-\mu}{\sigma/\sqrt{n}} = \frac{50.04-50}{0.015} = 2.67$$

and $P(z \geq 2.67) = 0.5000 - 0.4962 = 0.0038$. As the sample size increases, it is less likely that a mean value of at least 50.04 will be observed purely by chance. If it did, some special cause would likely be present.

Confidence Intervals A confidence interval (CI) is an interval estimate of a population parameter that also specifies the likelihood that the interval contains the true population parameter. This probability is called the level of confidence, denoted by $1 - \alpha$, and is usually expressed as a percentage. For example, we might state that "a 90 percent CI for the mean is 10 ± 2." The value 10 is the point estimate calculated from the sample data, and 2 can be thought of as a margin for error. Thus, the interval estimate is [8, 12]. However, this interval may or may not include the true population mean. If we take a different sample, we will most likely have a different point estimate, say 11.4, which determines the interval estimate [8.4, 12.4]. Again, this interval may or may not include the true population mean. If we chose 100 samples, leading to 100 different interval estimates, we would expect that 90 percent of them—the level of confidence—would contain the true population mean. We would say we are 90 percent confident that the interval we obtain from sample data contains the true population mean. Commonly used confidence levels are 90, 95, and 99 percent; the higher the confidence level, the more assurance we have that the interval contains the true population parameter. As the confidence level increases, the confidence interval becomes larger to provide higher levels of assurance.

Some common confidence intervals are

- Confidence interval for the mean, standard deviation known, sample size = n:

  $$\bar{x} \pm z_{\alpha/2}\sigma/\sqrt{n}$$

- Confidence interval for the mean, standard deviation unknown, sample size = n:

  $$\bar{x} \pm t_{\alpha/2,\, n-1}(s/\sqrt{n})$$

- Confidence interval for a proportion, sample size = n:

  $$p \pm z_{a/2}\sqrt{\frac{p(1-p)}{n}}$$

- Confidence interval for difference between two means, independent samples, equal variance, sample sizes = n_1 and n_2:

  $$x_1 - x_2 \pm (t_{a/2,\, n_1+n_2-2})s_p\sqrt{\frac{1}{n_1} + \frac{1}{n_2}}$$

- Confidence interval for differences between two proportions, sample sizes = n_1 and n_2:

  $$p_1 - p_2 \pm z_{a/2}\sqrt{\frac{p_1(1-p_1)}{n_1} + \frac{p_2(1-p_2)}{n_2}}$$

Hypothesis Testing Hypothesis testing involves drawing inferences about two contrasting propositions (hypotheses) relating to the value of a population parameter, one of which is assumed to be true in the absence of contradictory data. For instance, suppose that a company is testing out a prototype process that is designed to reduce manufacturing cycle time. They can evaluate the proposed process by testing a hypothesis that the mean cycle time is the same as the current process.

A hypothesis test involves the following steps:

1. Formulate the hypotheses to test.
2. Select a level of significance that defines the risk of drawing an incorrect conclusion about the assumed hypothesis that is actually true.
3. Determine a decision rule on which to base a conclusion.
4. Collect data and calculate a test statistic.
5. Apply the decision rule to the test statistic and draw a conclusion.

To illustrate hypothesis testing, let us examine a producer of computer-aided design software for the aerospace industry that receives numerous calls for technical support. Tracking software is used to monitor response and resolution times. The company has a service standard of four days for the mean resolution time. However, the manager of the technical support group has been receiving some complaints of long resolution times. During one week, a sample of 44 customer calls resulted in a sample mean of 5.23 and standard deviation of 13.5. Even though the sample mean exceeds the four-day standard, does the manager have sufficient evidence to conclude that the mean service time exceeds four days, or is this particular sample mean simply a result of sampling error?

The hypothesis tested is

H_0: Mean response time ≤ 4

H_1: Mean response time > 4

The appropriate test statistic is

$$t = \frac{\bar{x} - 4}{s/\sqrt{n}}$$

The decision rule is to reject H_0 if $t > t_{n-1,\,\alpha}$. We compute the value of the test statistic as

$$t = \frac{\bar{x} - 4}{s/\sqrt{n}} = \frac{5.23 - 4}{13.5/\sqrt{44}} = \frac{1.24}{2.035} = 0.609.$$

Because $t_{43,\,.05} = 1.6811$, we cannot reject the null hypothesis. Therefore, the manager finds no sufficient statistical evidence that the mean response time exceeds 4.

Enumerative and Analytic Studies

A static population, such as employees in a company or its customer base, can be analyzed to estimate population parameters such as the mean, variance, or proportion. Confidence intervals and hypothesis tests can be applied. However, the purpose of sampling from a process is generally to predict the future. The characteristics of the population may change over time as a plot of sample means or variances might show. In such cases, confidence intervals and hypothesis tests are not appropriate *unless the time series can be shown to be stationary,* that is, have a constant mean and variance over time. Examining a trend chart of the data over time can usually provide insight as to whether or not a time series is stationary. Deming called the analysis of a static population an **enumerative study**, and the analysis of a dynamic time series an **analytic study**. Applying classical statistical inferences to an analytic study is not appropriate because they provide no basis for prediction. Thus, it is important to understand how to apply statistical tools properly.

One of the biggest mistakes that people make in using statistical methods is confusing data that are sampled from a static population (cross-sectional data) with data sampled from a dynamic process (time series data).

In the hypothesis testing example, for instance, we need to assume that the data are stationary during the week over which they were collected to apply this tool correctly. If we sampled the data over a long period of time and the characteristics of the population (mean or variance) changed over that time, then conducting a hypothesis test would not be appropriate.

Design of Experiments

Design of experiments (DOE), developed by R. A. Fisher in England, dates back to the 1920s. A designed experiment is a test or series of tests that enables the experimenter to compare two or more methods to determine which is better or determine levels of controllable factors to optimize the yield of a process or minimize the variability of a response variable.[13] DOE differs from observational statistical studies in that the factors of interest are controlled by the experimenter, rather than simply observed through the selection of random samples. For example, a paint company might be interested in determining whether different additives have an effect on the drying time of paint in order to select the additive that results in the shortest drying time. As another example, suppose that two machines produce the same part. The material used in processing can be loaded onto the machines either manually or with an automatic device. The experimenter might wish to determine whether the type of machine and the type of loading process affect the number of defectives and then select the machine type and loading process combination that minimizes the number of defectives.

As a practical tool for quality improvement, experimental design methods have achieved considerable success in many industries. In a celebrated case, Ina Tile Company, a Japanese ceramic tile manufacturer, had purchased a $2 million kiln from West Germany in 1953.[14] Tiles were stacked inside the kiln and baked. Tiles toward the outside of the stack tended to have a different average size and more variation in dimensions than those further inside the stack. The obvious cause was the uneven temperatures inside the kiln. Temperature was an uncontrollable factor, a noise factor. To try to eliminate the effects of temperature would require redesign of the kiln itself, a very costly alternative. A group of engineers, chemists, and others who were familiar with the manufacturing process brainstormed and identified seven major controllable variables that could affect the tile dimensions:

1. Limestone content
2. Fineness of additive
3. Content of agalmatolite
4. Type of agalmatolite
5. Raw material quantity
6. Content of waste return
7. Content of feldspar

The group designed and conducted an experiment using these factors. The experiment showed that the first factor, the limestone content, was the most significant factor; the other factors had smaller effects. By increasing the limestone content from 1 percent to 5 percent and choosing better levels for other factors, the percentage of size defects was reduced from 30 percent to less than 1 percent. Limestone was the cheapest material in the tile. In addition, the experiment revealed that a smaller amount of agalmatolite, the most expensive material in the tile, could be used without adversely affecting the tile dimension. Both the effect of the noise factor and the cost of the product were reduced at the same time! This discovery was a breakthrough in the ceramic tile industry.

As another example, ITT Avionics Division, a leading producer of electronic warfare systems, experienced a high defect rate when using a wave solder machine to solder assemblies on printed circuit boards.[15] The wave solder machine, developed to eliminate hand soldering, transports printed circuit boards through a wave of solder under computer control. A brainstorming session identified 14 process variables. From three sets of designed experiments, the subsequent data resulted in decisions that lowered the defect rate from 7 or 8 to 1.5 per board. With 2,500 solder connections per board, this translated to a defect rate of 600 defects per million connections. Another division, ITT's Suprenant Company, an electrical wire and cable manufacturer and a supplier to Ford, saved an estimated $100,000 per year in scrap, reduced product variability by a factor of 10, and improved the run rate of an extruding operation by 30 percent.

Historically, experimental design was not widely used in industrial quality improvement studies because engineers had trouble working with the large number of variables and their interactions on many different levels in industrial problems. However, improved computer software and more sophisticated training have shown experimental design to be an important tool for quality improvement. In particular, it is one of the most important tools in Six Sigma projects, and employees at all levels are receiving training in this subject.

Factorial Experiments One of the most common types of experimental designs is called a **factorial experiment**. In a factorial experiment, all combinations of levels of each factor are considered. For example, suppose that temperature and reaction time are identified as important factors in the yield of a chemical process. Currently the process operates at a temperature of 100°C and a 60-minute reaction time. In an effort to reduce costs and improve yield, the plant manager wants to determine if changing the temperature and reaction time will have any significant effect on the percent yield and, if so, to identify the best levels of these factors to optimize the yield.

A simple designed experiment to analyze the effect of two levels of each factor (for instance, temperature at 100° and 120° and time at 60 and 75 minutes) would result in $2^2 = 4$ possible combinations to test. In general, an experiment with m factors at k levels would have k^m combinations. The different levels of each factor are commonly called *treatments;* hence, there are four different treatment combinations:

Treatment	Temperature	Time
A	100°	60 minutes
B	120°	60 minutes
C	100°	75 minutes
D	120°	75 minutes

For instance, treatment A corresponds to setting the temperature at 100° and the reaction time at 60 minutes.

Often the factor levels are designated as "high" or "low." For example, a temperature of 100° would be designated as the low level, whereas a temperature of 125° would correspond to the high level. In this fashion, treatment A corresponds to both factors at their low levels, treatment D corresponds to both factors at their high levels, and treatments B and C correspond to one factor at the low level and the other factor at the high level. Usually, multiple observations are taken for each treatment combination to account for sampling error. Each combination should be performed in a random fashion to eliminate any potential systematic bias.

The purpose of a factorial experiment is to estimate the effects of each factor and any possible interaction. A **main effect** measures the difference that a factor has on the response. For instance, what is the effect of a 20-degree change in temperature? Of a 15-minute change in reaction time? These questions are answered easily by finding the differences of the averages at each level. For instance, suppose we obtained the following results (with two observations for each treatment):

Treatment	Temperature	Time	Yield (%)
A	100°	60 minutes	85, 83
B	120°	60 minutes	90, 91
C	100°	75 minutes	88, 89
D	120°	75 minutes	80, 82

The average yields for each treatment combination are summarized as follows:

Treatment	Temperature	Time	Average Yield
A (low, low)	100°	60 minutes	84
B (high, low)	120°	60 minutes	90.5
C (low, high)	100°	75 minutes	88.5
D (high, high)	120°	75 minutes	81

The main effects are calculated as follows:

$$\begin{aligned}\text{Temperature effect} &= (\text{Average yield at high level}) - (\text{Average yield at low level})\\ &= (B + D)/2 - (A + C)/2\\ &= (90.5 + 81)/2 - (84 + 88.5)/2\\ &= 85.75 - 86.25 = -0.5 \text{ percent}\end{aligned}$$

$$\begin{aligned}\text{Reaction effect} &= (\text{Average yield at high level}) - (\text{Average yield at low level})\\ &= (C + D)/2 - (A + B)/2\\ &= (88.5 + 81)/2 - (84 + 90.5)/2\\ &= 84.75 - 87.25 = -2.5 \text{ percent}\end{aligned}$$

Thus, we might conclude that increasing either the temperature or reaction time decreases the yield of the process and that increasing both from their low to high levels would decrease yield by 0.5 + 2.5 = 3.0 percent. However, we cannot draw this conclusion until we determine whether any interactions are present.

In many situations, the effect of changing one factor depends on the level of other factors. For example, the effect of temperature may depend on the reaction time. In this example, we see that if the temperature is held constant at 100°, an increase in reaction time results in a higher yield. However, when the temperature is 120°, an increase in reaction time decreases the yield. This *interaction* is easy to determine by graphing the results as shown in Figure 10.15. If the lines are nearly parallel, then no interaction exists. If the lines are somewhat, but not quite, parallel, then we have a mild interaction. If the lines cross, then a strong interaction exists. In this case, we observe a strong interaction. When interactions are present, we *cannot* estimate response changes by simply adding main effects; the effect of one factor must be interpreted relative to levels of the other factor.

We may quantify the interaction by taking the average of difference of the response (yield) when the factors are both at the high or low levels and subtracting the average difference of the response when the factors are at opposite levels:

Figure 10.15 Interaction Effects

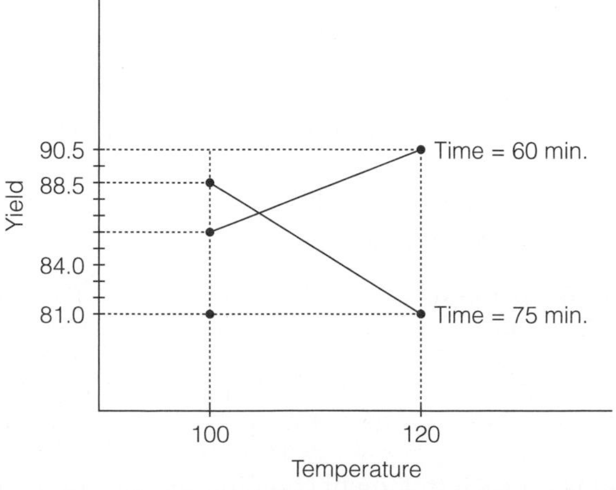

Temperature × Time interaction
= (Average yield, both factors at same level)
− (Average yield, both factors at opposite levels)
= (A + D)/2 − (B + C)/2
= (84 + 81)/2 − (90.5 + 88.5)/2 = −7.0 percent

The closer this quantity is to zero, the smaller the interaction effect. In this case, a significant interaction is apparent. Interaction measures how much influence the reaction time has on temperature. For example, the main effect of temperature was found to be −0.5 percent. Because the interaction is −7.0 percent, the effect of temperature will vary from its average value of −0.5 percent by plus or minus −7 percent as the level of reaction time changes. Thus, if we examine the results where time is fixed at its high level (treatments B and D), the average difference in yield by increasing the temperature is 81 − 88.5 = −7.5 percent—that is, the main effect of −0.5 percent plus the interaction of −7.0 percent. If we look at the results where reaction time is fixed at its low level, the average difference in yield by increasing the temperature is 90.5 − 84 = 6.5 percent. This is the same as subtracting the interaction effect from the main effect—that is, −0.5 − (−7.0) = 6.5 percent. Our conclusion is that a combination of higher temperature and lower time appear to optimize the yield.

The following example shows a simple application of a three-factor experiment not unlike those used in industrial and business settings. Many one-tenth scale remote control (RC) model car racing enthusiasts believe that spending more money on high-quality batteries, using expensive gold-plated connectors, and storing batteries at low temperatures will improve battery life performance in a race.[16] To test this hypothesis, an electrical test circuit was constructed to measure battery discharge under different configurations. Each factor (battery type, connector type, and temperature) was evaluated at two levels, resulting in $2^3 = 8$ experimental conditions, shown in Table 10.2. In this case, there is only one observation per treatment, simplifying the calculations.

Calculations of the main effects are as follows:

Battery cost
Low = (72 + 93 + 75 + 94)/4 = 83.5 minutes
High = (612 + 490 + 493 + 489)/4 = 521 minutes
Main effect = High − Low = 437.5 minutes

Table 10.2 Experimental Design for Testing Battery Performance

Experimental Run	Battery Type	Connector Type	Battery Temperature	Discharge Time (minutes)
1	High cost	Gold-plated	Ambient	493
2	High cost	Gold-plated	Cold	490
3	High cost	Standard	Ambient	489
4	High cost	Standard	Cold	612
5	Low cost	Gold-plated	Ambient	94
6	Low cost	Gold-plated	Cold	75
7	Low cost	Standard	Ambient	93
8	Low cost	Standard	Cold	72

Source: Reprinted with permission from Eric Wasilof & Curtis Hargitt, "Using DOE to Determine AA Battery Life," *Quality Progress*, March 1999, pp. 67–71.

Connector type

Gold-plated = (94 + 75 + 490 + 493)/4 = 288 minutes
Standard = (72 + 93 + 612 + 489)/4 = 316.5 minutes
Main effect = Standard – Gold-plated = 28.5 minutes

Temperature

Cold = (72 + 75 + 490 + 612)/4 = 312.25 minutes
Ambient = (93 + 489 + 493 + 94)/4 = 292.25 minutes
Main effect = Ambient – Cold = 20 minutes

These results suggest that high-cost batteries do have a longer life, but that the effects of gold plating or battery temperature do not appear to be significant. Because only one factor appears to be significant, calculation of interaction effects are not required. These conclusions can be tested more rigorously using analysis of variance, which will be discussed briefly next. Indeed, an analysis of variance confirms that the battery cost factor is statistically significant, whereas the other factors are indistinguishable from experimental error.

Classical design of experiments can require many, often costly, experimental runs to estimate all main effects and interactions. A Japanese engineer, Dr. Genichi Taguchi, proposed another approach to DOE. He developed an approach to designing experiments that focused on the critical factors while deemphasizing their interactions, which greatly reduced the number of required experiments. However, Taguchi's approach violates some traditional statistical principles and has been criticized by the statistical community.[17] To add to the shortcomings of his approach, Taguchi introduced some statistically invalid and misleading analyses, ignored modern graphical approaches to data analysis, and failed to advocate randomization in performing the experiments. Even though many of these issues are subject to debate, numerous companies have used Taguchi's approaches effectively.

Analysis of Variance (ANOVA)

Because of Six Sigma, practitioners have "rediscovered" such techniques as **analysis of variance**, or **ANOVA**, which has long been an important tool in statistical analysis. ANOVA is a methodology for drawing conclusions about equality of means of multiple populations. In its simplest form—one-way ANOVA—we are interested in comparing means of observed responses of several different levels of a single factor. ANOVA tests the hypothesis that the means of all populations are equal against the alternative hypothesis that at least one mean differs from the others. To conduct an ANOVA, we need to

1. Carefully define the purpose and assumptions of the experiment.
2. Gather data related to the factor levels of interest.
3. Compute ANOVA statistics.
4. Interpret the meaning of the data.
5. Take action.

Let us suppose that the model race car enthusiasts in the previous example were interested in determining whether any significant differences exist between various brands of batteries (the factor levels). Understanding possible differences in battery performance could be a first step in examining whether connection or temperature has an effect on performance. Table 10.3 shows discharge times for three different brands of batteries, gathered through a measurement process.

Microsoft Excel provides a simple procedure to conduct a one-way ANOVA. Select *ANOVA: Single Factor* from the *Tools/Data Analysis* options. In the dialog box that pops up, enter the input range of the data in your spreadsheet and check whether it is stored in rows or columns. Table 10.4 shows the results of applying this tool. What does it tell us?

Table 10.3 Battery Discharge Time Data by Brand

	Brand		
Observation	**A**	**B**	**C**
1	493	108	94
2	490	95	75
3	489	115	93
4	612	82	72

The objective of ANOVA is to statistically test the differences between the means of the groups (the time to discharge for the various brands of batteries) to determine whether they are the same or at least one mean is different. To make this determination, ANOVA partitions the total variability of the data into two parts, the variation between groups and the variation within groups. If the total variation between groups is relatively small compared with the variation within groups, it suggests that the populations are essentially the same. A relatively large variation between groups, however, suggests that differences exist in the unknown population means. The variation in the data is computed as a sum of squared (SS) deviations from the appropriate sample mean, and scaled as a variance measure, or "mean square" (MS). By dividing the mean square between groups by the mean square within groups, an F statistic is computed. If this value is larger than a critical value, F_{crit}, then the data suggest that a difference in means exist.

An examination of the SUMMARY section in Table 10.4 shows that Group A's mean value and variance are considerably larger than the others. In the ANOVA part of the table, the mean square between groups is significantly larger than the mean square within groups, resulting in an F statistic of 183.0412. When this value is compared to the critical F-value (4.256), for 2 and 9 degrees of freedom at a 0.05 level of significance (from an F-table, available in any statistics text), we can reject the hypothesis that the means for the three battery types are the same. In fact, $F = 183$ is

Table 10.4 Results of Microsoft Excel ANOVA Procedure

Summary

Groups	Count	Sum	Average	Variance
A	4	2084	521	3683.333
B	4	400	100	212.6667
C	4	334	83.5	135

ANOVA

Source of Variation	*SS*	*df*	*MS*	*F*	*P*-value	*F* crit
Between Groups	491892.67	2	245946.33	183.0412	5.13E-08	4.256492
Within Groups	12093	9	1343.6667			
Total	503985.67	11				

so much larger than 4.256, that we only have a 5.13×10^{-8} probability (the p-value in the output) that we could be wrong and should have failed to reject the hypothesis!

The model race car enthusiasts could conclude that a significant difference exists between the battery types. Other statistical tests are available to demonstrate what factor levels differ from the others (although in this case, it is fairly obvious). The next step might be to explore other variables (connector type, battery temperature) to see how they might affect battery discharge time. It would require more sophisticated ANOVA methods. We encourage you to consult more complete statistics books, such as Montgomery or Lipson and Sheth.[18]

You can probably identify many applications of ANOVA in Six Sigma projects, when differences among critical quality characteristics must be explored. However, ANOVA requires that some statistical assumptions be satisfied for proper interpretation of the results, namely that the populations from which the samples are drawn are normally distributed and have equal variances, and that the data are randomly and independently obtained. These assumptions should be validated if possible.

Regression and Correlation

Regression analysis is a tool for building statistical models that characterize relationships between a dependent variable and one or more independent variables, all of which are numerical. The relationship may be linear, one of many types of nonlinear forms, or there may be no relationship at all. A regression model that involves a single independent variable is called *simple regression*. A regression model that involves several independent variables is called *multiple regression*. To develop a regression model, you first must specify the type of function that best describes the data. This step is important, because using a linear model for data that are clearly nonlinear, for instance, would probably lead to poor business decisions and results. The type of relationship can usually be seen in a scatter diagram, and we always recommend that you create one first to gain some understanding of the nature of any potential relationship.

Correlation is a measure of a linear relationship between two variables, X and Y, and is measured by the (population) correlation coefficient. Correlation coefficients will range from -1 to $+1$. A correlation of 0 indicates that the two variables have no linear relationship to each other. Thus, if one changes, we cannot reasonably predict what the other variable might do using a linear equation (we might, however, have a well-defined nonlinear relationship). A correlation coefficient of $+1$ indicates a perfect positive linear relationship; as one variable increases, the other will also increase. A correlation coefficient of -1 also shows a perfect linear relationship, except that as one variable increases, the other decreases.

To illustrate regression, we will use a common issue in quality that we will discuss again in a later chapter—ensuring that instruments are properly calibrated. In principle, it is a simple matter to check calibration. One connects the instrument to a known source, such as an extremely accurate voltage generator to check a voltmeter or a precision gauge block to check a micrometer. A reading is then obtained to determine whether the instrument is capable of accurately measuring the known variable. In practice, numerous sources of variation in the process may make calibration difficult.

The data in Figure 10.16 represent actual readings obtained from the calibration of a voltmeter versus the standard source readings from an accurate voltage generator. The source readings were purposely not set in even integer increments so as to minimize possible bias of the inspector taking the actual readings. To determine whether the instrument is accurate, we can develop a regression equation for the data. Using the Regression tool in Microsoft Excel, we obtain the results shown in Figure 10.16. The estimated regression equation is

$$Y = 0.0265 + .9914X$$

Figure 10.16 Microsoft Excel Regression Results

	A	B	C	D	E	F	G	H	I	J
1	**Voltmeter Calibration**									
2				SUMMARY OUTPUT						
3	Actual (Y)	Source (X)								
4	1.09	1.05		*Regression Statistics*						
5	2.12	2.15		Multiple R	0.999967043					
6	3.08	3.12		R Square	0.999934087					
7	4.09	4.08		Adjusted R Square	0.999925848					
8	5.11	5.11		Standard Error	0.027282724					
9	6.08	6.07		Observations	10					
10	7.2	7.23								
11	8.3	8.34		ANOVA						
12	9.59	9.66			*df*	*SS*	*MS*	*F*	*Significance F*	
13	10.41	10.49		Regression	1	90.33725522	90.33726	121364.4	5.16118E-18	
14				Residual	8	0.005954776	0.000744			
15				Total	9	90.34321				
16										
17					*Coefficients*	*Standard Error*	*t Stat*	*P-value*	*Lower 95%*	*Upper 95%*
18				Intercept	0.02648404	0.018447595	1.435636	0.189028	-0.016056219	0.069024299
19				Source (X)	0.991364042	0.002845689	348.374	5.16E-18	0.984801867	0.997926217

The value of R^2 is 0.9999, indicating an excellent fit. Note also that the value of the intercept is close to 0 and the slope is close to 1, which is where they should be. We would conclude that the instrument is in near perfect calibration, as the scatter chart in Figure 10.17 also indicates.

Figure 10.17 Scatter Chart of Voltmeter Calibration Readings

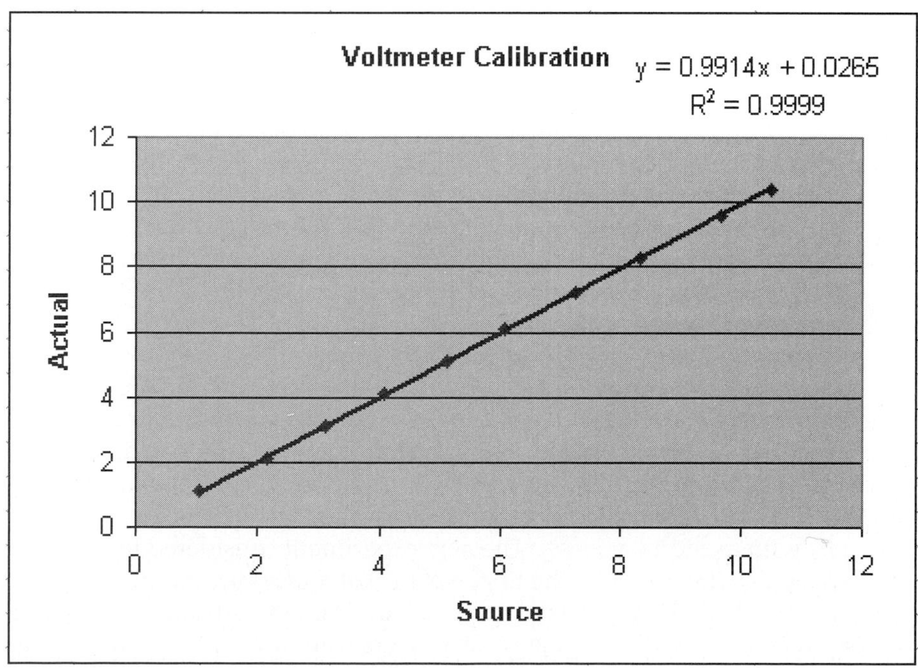

SUMMARY OF KEY POINTS AND TERMINOLOGY

The Premium website for this chapter provides a summary of key concepts and terminology introduced in this chapter.

Quality in Practice

Improving Quality of a Wave Soldering Process Through Design of Experiments[19]

A Printed Circuit Assembly—Encoder (PCA-Encoder) is a critical component for the base carriage assembly for a printer. The PCA-Encoder is produced by putting the electronic components on printed circuit boards (panels) that contain eight small boards, and then soldering the components using a wave soldering process. Any defect in any of the solder joints will lead to the failure of the circuit. Thus, it is important to ensure that soldering is defect-free. Typical soldering defects are blowholes (insufficient solder) and bridges (solder between two joints). At a Hewlett-Packard India, Ltd., plant in Bangalore, India, a high level of soldering defects was observed, necessitating 100 percent inspection for all circuit boards. Any defects identified required manual rework, which consumed much time.

A study was undertaken to optimize the wave soldering process for reducing defects, thereby eliminating the inspection stage after the process. The quality engineers conducted a detailed study on the solder defects to understand what aspects of the wave soldering process might affect the resulting quality. These were identified as

1. Conveyor speed
2. Conveyor angle
3. Solder bath temperature
4. Solder wave height
5. Vibration of wave
6. Preheater temperature
7. Air knife
8. Acid number (solid content in the flux), which is difficult to control because of environmental conditions

The engineers decided to use experimental design because of the long time frame required to adjust process parameters by trial and error, and the lack of insight into the possible joint effects of different parameters. Based on discussions with technical personnel, seven factors at three levels were selected for the experiment, as shown in Table 10.5. Conveyor speed and conveyor angle were fixed. A full factorial experiment would take 1,458 trials to conduct, which was not deemed to be practical. From statistical theory in the design of experiments, the seven main effects could be estimated by conducting only 18 trials as shown in Table 10.6. The experimental outcomes (response) were the number of defective solder joints in a frame (352 joints). Each experiment was repeated three times.

Table 10.5 Factors and Levels for Experimentation

		Level		
Factor	**Code**	**1**	**2**	**3**
Bath temperature (°C)	A	248[a]	252	
Wave height[b]	B	4.38	4.40[a]	4.42
Overheated preheater (OH-PH) (PH-1)	C	340	360[a]	380
Preheater-1 (PH-1) (°C)	D	340	360[a]	380
Preheater (PH-2) (°C)	E	340	360[a]	380
Air knife	F	0	3[a]	6
Omega[c]	G	0	2[a]	4

[a]Existing level.
[b]The wave height is measured as the rpm of the motor pumping the solder.
[c]Omega refers to the vibration of the solder wave.

Source: Kalyan Kumar Chowdhury, E.V. Gigo, and R. Raghavan, "Quality Improvement Through Design of Experiments: A Case Study," *Quality Engineering* 12, no. 3 (2000), 4072416. Copyright 2000 by Marcel Dekker, Inc. Reprinted with permission.

Using analysis of variance, it was observed that bath temperature, wave height, and omega had a significant effect on the soldering defects. By setting the factors at the optimum levels identified through the experiments, the predicted defect level was 1,670 ppm as opposed to the current rate of more than 6,000 ppm. However, the predicted average and the result of a confirmatory experiment were not sufficient to eliminate inspection completely, so additional experimental designs were conducted to reduce defects.

The next experiment considered the results of the first experiment and some of the uncontrollable factors. However, the different levels of the significant factors from the first experiment were selected in such a way that the new levels were allowed to vary around the optimum level of the first experiment. Based on the results of these additional experiments, new optimum levels of factors were identified and implemented with significant improvements. Figure 10.18 shows the

Table 10.6 Data Corresponding to the First Experiment

Exp. No.	(1) Bath Temp. (°C)	(2) Wave Height	(3) OH-PH (°C)	(4) PH-2 (°C)	(5) PH-1 (°C)	(6) Air Knife	(7) Omega	Response		
								1	2	3
1	248	4.38	340	340	340	0	0	1	2	1
2	248	4.38	360	360	360	3	2	0	2	0
3	248	4.38	380	380	380	6	4	0	1	0
4	248	4.40	340	340	360	3	4	1	0	1
5	248	4.40	360	360	380	6	0	4	2	0
6	248	4.40	380	380	340	0	2	8	1	6
7	248	4.42	340	360	340	6	2	2	4	3
8	248	4.42	360	380	360	0	4	4	1	0
9	248	4.42	380	340	380	3	0	2	2	4
10	252	4.38	340	380	380	3	2	1	3	1
11	252	4.38	360	340	340	6	4	1	2	1
12	252	4.38	380	360	360	0	0	6	3	2
13	252	4.40	340	360	380	0	4	3	3	4
14	252	4.40	360	380	340	3	0	4	3	8
15	252	4.40	380	340	360	6	2	2	1	1
16	252	4.42	340	380	360	6	0	2	7	3
17	252	4.42	360	340	380	0	2	2	1	3
18	252	4.42	380	360	340	3	4	4	2	1

Source: Kalyan Kumar Chowdhury, E.V. Gigo, and R. Raghavan, "Quality Improvement Through Design of Experiments: A Case Study," *Quality Engineering* 12, no. 3 (2000), 4072416. Copyright 2000 by Marcel Dekker, Inc. Reprinted with permission.

Figure 10.18 Solder Defects After Experimental Design Optimization

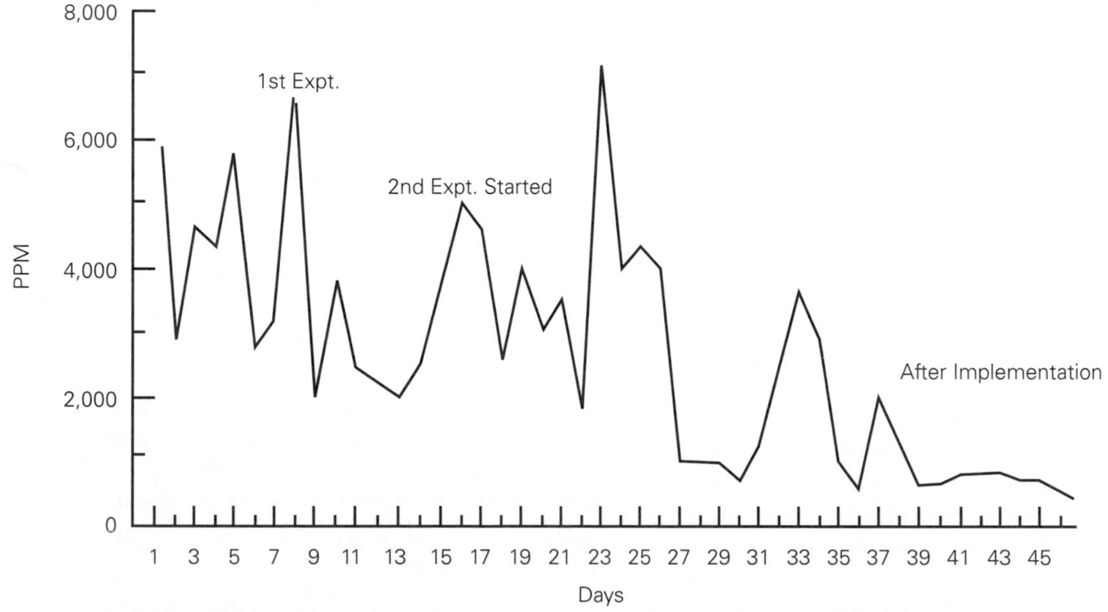

Source: Kalyan Kumar Chowdhury, E.V. Gigo, and R. Raghavan, "Quality Improvement Through Design of Experiments: A Case Study," *Quality Engineering* 12, no. 3 (2000), 4072416. Copyright 2000 by Marcel Dekker, Inc. Reprinted with permission.

parts per million level during the course of the experimentation, which took only 45 days.

Key Issues for Discussion

1. Why did the first experimental design not find the true optimum combination of factors to achieve the maximum reduction of defects?
2. What were some of the advantages of using experimental design over a traditional trial-and-error approach?

Quality in Practice

Applying Statistical Analysis in a Six Sigma Project at GE Fanuc[20]

(This Quality in Practice features another project performed at the GE Fanuc plant. We encourage you to read the related case in Chapter 11 for some additional background.)

In mid-2002 a team at the GE Fanuc manufacturing plant in Charlottesville, Virginia, led by Six Sigma Black Belt Donald Splaun was given the go-ahead to investigate Black Belt Project #P52320. The objective of the project was to evaluate Printed Wire Board (PWB) Fabricated Board Finishes to determine if the high-priced nickel-gold (Ni-Au) finished boards that were being used were necessary as mounting platforms for fine pitch surface-mounted devices (SMDs) or for fine-pitched Ball Grid Array (BGA) electronic controller boards. SMDs are electronic components, such as microprocessors, that are placed on the top of electronic circuit boards (fabricated boards) and then have their electrical wire leads soldered into place. Fine pitch SMDs don't have much space between their electrical wire leads, making it difficult to put just the right amount of solder on them to make the proper electrical connect to the circuit boards on which they are mounted. The completed boards with all components properly mounted on them are then used in electrical assemblies to control the operations of industrial machinery.

Splaun had seven people on his analysis team, plus a financial representative to verify the dollar costs and savings; a Master Black Belt reviewer, who would evaluate the project to prevent obvious gaps in the analysis; and perhaps most importantly from a managerial standpoint, a Champion/Sponsor, who would ensure project visibility and that resources were allocated to complete the project. Team members and their job functions were:

Team Members, Titles, and Functions

Team Leader and Black Belt
Process engineer and fabricated board expert
Advanced manufacturing engineer responsible for SMD board assembly
Sourcing agent who purchases the boards
Test engineer who tests and evaluates boards
Producibility engineer who works with design teams
Production line operator who runs boards
Supplier quality analysis technician responsible for incoming board quality

Outside Resources

Financial representative to assist in cost calculations
Champion/Sponsor
Reviewer and Master Black Belt

After being formed, the team used a 12-step DMAIC process developed by GE Fanuc, to guide them through the project (see Table 10.7). The first three pre-project definition substeps (A, B, and C) required them to identify project CTQs, develop a team charter and have it approved, and define a process map.

Project team members identified the CTQs by using a standard cause-and-effect matrix, and weighted rankings of CTQ factors to prioritize them. The team determined there were three CTQs, two of which were business factors and the other a project factor:

- *Business CTQ factors*: Variable cost productivity (VCP) improvement, composed of the

Table 10.7 GE Fanuc 12-Step DMAIC Process

Step	Description	Tools	Deliverables
Define			
A	Identify project CTQs		Project CTQs (1)
B	Develop team charter		Approved charter (2)
C	Define process map		High-level process map (3)
Measure			
1	Select CTQ characteristics	Customer, QFD, FMEA	Project Y (4)
2	Define performance standards	Customer, Blueprints	Performance standard for Project Y (5)
3	Measurement system analysis	Continuous Gage R&R, Test/Retest, Attribute R&R	Data collection plan and MSA (6), Data for Project Y (7)
Analyze			
4	Establish process capability	Capability indices	Process capability—Project Y (8)
5	Define performance objectives	Team, Benchmarking	Improvement goal for Project Y (9)
6	Identify variation sources	process and graphical Analysis, Hypothesis tests	Prioritized list of all Xs (10)
Improve			
7	Screen potential causes	DOE-screening	List of vital few Xs (11)
8	Discover variable relationships	Factorial designs	Proposed solution (12)
9	Establish operating tolerances	Simulation	Piloted solution (13)
Control			
10	Define and validate measurement system on Xs (independent variables) in actual application	Continuous Gage R&R, MSA Test/Retest, Attribute R&R	
11	Determine process capability	Capability indices	Process capability Y, X (14)
12	Implement process control	Control charts, Mistake proof, FMEA	Sustained solution (15), Documentation (16)

CTQs of internal cost reduction and contribution margin improvement

- *Project CTQ factor*: Benefits associated with additional Ni-Au cost of $190,000 per year, suspected to be unnecessary

The team developed their charter to define the problem and working relationships. The problem clearly and succinctly stated as: *GE Fanuc currently specifies Ni-Au on fine-pitch SMD and BGA boards. The purpose of this project is to evaluate if this specification is necessary.*

The team also identified tools and databases that were to be used in the study, not only to ensure that everyone was working from a common source, but also to take advantage of the training that had been provided to team members. The tools included two statistical/spreadsheet software packages (Minitab and Excel) and a plantwide integrated database (SAP) that contained information on board characteristics, usage, specifications, costs, and so on.

Based on a 29-step process flow chart, it was decided that the analysis would require the use of a moderately complex experimental design. This design was required to determine the effects of supplier differences and finishes, because relatively few defects were being observed in manufacturing the boards. Data would have to be gathered from the experiment and from supplier surveys to help the team track potential causes that could have a bearing on the functionality and cost of each of the alternative boards or board materials being considered.

The experiment was designed to sample and test 288 CX3A1 boards:

- 96 hot air solder leveled (HASL) boards, 32 from each supplier
- 96 nickel-gold (Ni-Au) boards, 32 from each supplier
- 96 silver (Ag) boards, 32 from each supplier and to evaluate three suppliers.

The three suppliers were:

- Vendor G, Singapore/China (one or two GE Fanuc production suppliers)
- Vendor P, Taiwan/China (second major GE Fanuc supplier)
- Vendor D, USA (current prototype/fast turn supplier)

The cause-and-effect matrix identified 13 characteristics (Xs, or independent variables) that were considered important to measure during the experiment for each of the three finish types (Ys, or dependent variables). The primary hypothesis was that no significant differences in numbers of defects would be incurred, regardless of finish. In addition, a hypothesis that no significant interaction effects existed between suppliers, coatings, and any of the 13 characteristics considered essential for quality board functioning was investigated. The data collection and analysis process consisted of eight carefully defined steps conducted over a six-day period, involving almost $37,500 worth of boards and hard-to-measure production delays while the test boards were run on what is normally high speed, highly automated production machines.

After the data were collected, numerous ANOVA computer runs were made to pinpoint problem areas and test hypotheses. It was especially important to test the capabilities of each of the three types of board finishes to determine whether they were equivalent to the current, and very expensive, Ni-Au finished boards. It was also necessary to get some data to prove or disprove hypotheses about supplier capabilities as well. Table 10.8 shows a typical computer printout and analysis of one of the 13 variables that was tested, called "Wave Solder Skips."

Of 15 ANOVA analysis runs performed on the 13 experimental variables that were measured, eight showed no significance, primarily because those variables had zero defects. Other findings included:

- Ni-Au boards are not significantly different from or better than horizontally processed HASL or Silver Boards for fine pitch SMD processing, therefore the firm can save money by switching from Ni-Au to HASL or Silver.
- The company should not use Vendor D for production. Results and suggestions for improvement of their prototype quality should be discussed with them.
- Ni-Au is worse for wave soldering, based on a defect measure of "insufficient solder fill."
- Vendor G was found to have an issue with a defect measure of "GR False Failures" (to be reviewed with the supplier).
- The GE Fanuc PWB Fab Specifications should be changed to reflect these conclusions.

From these analyses, the summary conclusion was that GE Fanuc did not need nickel-gold boards for fine pitch SMD.

The estimated savings from this project ranged from 7.1 percent on two-layer boards to 22.8 percent on four-layer boards, with an average of 14.3 percent savings on these 89 board types, and total estimated savings of $190,000 per year.

Key Issues for Discussion

1. Why did the experimental design have to be so complex? Why were so many individuals involved in this project?
2. What might have been some contributing factors that caused the company to select the Ni-Au over the cheaper boards in the past?
3. For Table 10.8, what can you conclude, given the *F* values and the *p*-values in the table? What steps should the team take, regarding use of vendors and further testing for this particular independent variable?

Table 10.8 Typical ANOVA Output for Vendor and Finish Analysis

Solder Skips, Analysis All
Two-Way Analysis of Variance
Analysis of Variance for Wave Solder Skips

Source	DF	SS	MS	F	P
Vendors	2	36.55	18.27	15.27	0.000
Finish	2	16.44	8.22	6.87	0.001
Interaction	4	23.39	5.85	4.89	0.001
Error	279	333.94	1.20		
Total	287	410.32			

Process Variable Averages

Manufacturers	**Mean Number of Defects**
Vendor C	0.03
Vendor D	0.80
Vendor G	0.06

Finish

HASL	0.271
Ni-Au	0.021
Silver	0.604

REVIEW QUESTIONS

1. What is statistical thinking? Why is it important to managers and workers at all levels of an organization?
2. Explain the difference between common and special causes of variation.
3. Explain the two fundamental mistakes that managers make when attempting to improve a process. Can you cite any examples in your personal experience in which such mistakes were made?
4. What are the lessons of the red bead and funnel experiments? Can you cite any examples in your experience where someone acted counter to these lessons?
5. Discuss the differences among the three major components of statistical methodology (descriptive statistics, statistical inference, and predictive statistics). Why might this distinction be important to a manager?
6. Provide some examples of discrete and continuous random variables in a quality management context.
7. Define a population and a sample. What are their major characteristics?
8. Explain the difference between the standard deviation and the standard error of the mean. How are they related?
9. State the meaning of the central limit theorem in your own words. How important is it to the development and use of statistical quality control techniques?

10. What two factors influence sampling procedures?
11. Discuss the basic questions that must be addressed in a sampling study.
12. Describe the different methods of sample selection and provide an example in which each would be most appropriate.
13. What are the sources of systematic error in sampling? How can systematic error be overcome?
14. What is the purpose of design of experiments?
15. Describe a factorial experiment. Provide some examples of factorial experiments that you might use to solve some type of quality-related problem.
16. What limitations of simple factorial experiments can be overcome by using ANOVA?
17. What is the statistical basis for ANOVA; that is, what is it designed to test, statistically?

PROBLEMS

Note: Data sets for many problems in this chapter are available in the Excel workbook *C10Data* on the Premier website accompanying this text. Click on the appropriate worksheet tab as noted in the problem (e.g., Prob. 10-1) to access the data.

1. Use the data for Twenty First Century Laundry for the weights of loads of clothes processed through their washing department in a week. (See the worksheet *Prob. 10-1* in the Excel file *C10Data* on the Premier website). Apply the Descriptive Statistics and Histogram tools in Excel to compute the mean, standard deviation, and other relevant statistics, as well as a frequency distribution and histogram for the following data. From what type of distribution might you suspect the data are drawn?
2. The times for carrying out a blood test at Rivervalley Labs were studied in order to learn about process characteristics. Apply the Descriptive Statistics and Histogram analysis tools in Excel to compute the mean, standard deviation, and other relevant statistics, as well as a frequency distribution and histogram, for the data taken from 100 tests and found in the worksheet *Prob. 10-2* in the Excel file *C10Data* on the Premier website. From what type of distribution might you suspect the data are drawn?
3. The data in the worksheet *Prob. 10-3* in Excel file *C10Data* on the Premier website represent the weight of castings (in kilograms) from a production line in the Fillmore Metalwork foundry. Based on this sample of 100 castings, compute the mean, standard deviation, and other relevant statistics, as well as a frequency distribution and histogram. What do you conclude from your analysis?
4. The data in the worksheet *Prob. 10-4* in the Excel file *C10Data* on the Premier website show the weight of castings (in kilograms) being made in the Fillmore Metalwork foundry and were taken from another production line. Compute the mean, standard deviation, and other relevant statistics, as well as a frequency distribution and histogram. Based on this sample of 100 castings, what do you conclude from your analysis?
5. San Juan Green Tea is sold in ½ liter (500 milliliter) bottles. The standard deviation for the filling process is 10 milliliters. If the process requires a 1 percent, or smaller, probability of over-filling, defined as over 495 milliliters, what must the target mean for the process be?

6. Texas Punch was made by Frutayuda, Inc. and sold in 12-ounce cans to benefit victims of Hurricane Ike. The mean number of ounces placed in a can by an automatic fill pump is 11.8 with a standard deviation of 0.12 ounce. Assuming a normal distribution, what is the probability that the filling pump will cause an overflow in a can, that is, the probability that more than 12 ounces will be released by the pump and overflow the can?
7. Kiwi Blend is sold in 900 milliliter (ml) cans. The mean volume of juice placed in a can is 876 ml with a standard deviation of 12 ml. Assuming a normal distribution, what is the probability that the filling machine will cause an overflow in a can, that is, the probability that more than 900 ml will be placed in the can?
8. Wayback Beer bottles have been found to have a standard deviation of 5 ml. If 95 percent of the bottles contain more than 250 ml, what is the average filling volume of the bottles?
9. The mean filling weight of salt containers processed by the Piedra Salt Co. is 15.5 ounces. If 2 percent of the containers contain more than 16 ounces, what is the standard deviation of the filling weight of the containers?
10. In filling bottles of E&L Cola, the average amount of over- and under-filling has not yet been precisely defined, but should be kept as low as possible. If the mean fill volume is 11.9 ounces and the standard deviation is 0.05 ounce:
    a. What percentage of bottles will have more than 12 ounces (overflow)?
    b. Between 11.9 and 11.95?
    c. Less than 11.83 ounces?
11. The frequency table in the worksheet *Prob. 10-11* in the Excel file *C10Data* on the Premier website shows the weight of castings (in kilograms) being made in the Fillmore Metalwork foundry (also see the worksheet *Prob. 10-3* for raw data).
    a. Based on this sample of 100 castings, find the mean and standard deviation of the sample. (Note: If only the given data are used, it will be necessary to research formulae for calculating the mean and standard deviations using grouped data from a statistics text.)
    b. Prepare and use an Excel spreadsheet, if not already done for Problem 10-3, to plot the histogram for the data.
    c. Plot the data on normal probability paper to determine whether the distribution of the data is approximately normal. (Note: The Regression tool in Excel has a normal probability plot that may be used here.)
12. The frequency table in the worksheet *Prob. 10-12* in the Excel file *C10Data* on the Premier website shows the weight of another set of castings (in kilograms) being made in the Fillmore Metalwork foundry (also see the worksheet *Prob. 10-4* for the raw data).
    a. Based on this sample of 100 castings, find the mean and standard deviation of the sample. (Note: If only the given data are used, it will be necessary to research formulae for calculating the mean and standard deviations using grouped data from a statistics text.)
    b. Prepare and use an Excel spreadsheet, if not already done for Problem 10-4, to plot the histogram for the data.
    c. Plot the data on normal probability paper to determine whether the distribution of the data is approximately normal. (Note: The Regression tool in Excel has a normal probability plot that may be used here.)
13. In a filling line at A & C Foods, Ltd., the mean fill volume for rice bubbles is 325 grams and the standard deviation is 20 grams. What percentage of containers will have less than 295 grams? More than 345 grams (assuming no overflow)?

14. Tessler Electric utility requires service operators to answer telephone calls from customers in an average time of 0.1 minute or less. A sample of 30 actual operator times was drawn, and the results are given in the following table. In addition, operators are expected to determine customer needs and either respond to them or refer the customer to the proper department within 0.5 minute. Another sample of 30 times was taken for this job component and is also given in the table. If these variables can be considered to be independent, is the average time taken to perform each component statistically different from the standard?

Component	Mean Time	Standard Deviation
Answer	0.1023	0.0183
Service	0.5290	0.0902

Note: Problems 15–19 address sample size determination and refer to theory covered in the Bonus Materials document on the Premier website regarding Sample Size Determination.

15. You are asked by the owner of the Moonbow Motel to develop a customer satisfaction survey to determine the percentage of customers who are dissatisfied with service. In the past year, 10,000 customers were serviced. She desires a 95 percent level of confidence with an allowable statistical error of ± 0.01. From past estimates, the manager believes that about 3.5 percent of customers have expressed dissatisfaction. What sample size should you use for this survey?
16. Determine the appropriate sample size needed to estimate the proportion of sorting errors at the Puxatawney Post Office at a 99 percent confidence level. Historically, the sorting error rate is 0.015, and you wish to have an allowable statistical error of 0.02.
17. A management engineer at Country Squire Hospital determined that she needs to make a work sampling study to see whether the proportion of idle time in the diagnostic imaging department had changed since being measured in a previous study several years ago. At that time, the percentage of idle time was 8 percent. If the engineer can only take a sample of 850 observations due to cost factors, and can tolerate an allowable error of 0.02, what percent confidence level can be obtained from the study?
18. Localtel, a small telephone company, interviewed 200 customers to determine their satisfaction with service. Nineteen expressed dissatisfaction. Compute the sample size needed to ensure that they can be 90 percent confident of correctly estimating the proportion dissatisfied with an allowable error of 0.04.
19. Using the Discovery Sampling table in the bonus materials folder for this chapter on the Premier website, suppose that a population consists of 2,000 units. The critical rate of occurrence is 1 percent, and you wish to be 99 percent confident of finding at least one nonconformity. What sample size should you select?
20. The process engineer at Sival Electronics was trying to determine whether three suppliers would be equally capable of supplying the mounting boards for the new "gold plated" components that she was testing. The table found in the worksheet *Prob. 10-20* in the Excel file *C10Data* on the Premier website shows the coded defect levels for the suppliers, according to the finishes that were tested. Lower defect levels are preferable to higher levels. Using one-way ANOVA, analyze these results. What conclusion can be reached, based on these data?

21. The process engineer at Sival Electronics is also trying to determine whether a newer, more costly design involving a gold alloy in a computer chip is more effective than the present, less expensive silicon design. She wants to obtain an effective output voltage at both high and low temperatures, when tested with high and low signal strength. She hypothesizes that high signal strength will result in higher voltage output, low temperature will result in higher output, and the gold alloy will result in higher output than the silicon material. She hopes that the main and interaction effects with the expensive gold will be minimal. The data found in the worksheet *Prob. 10-21* in the Excel file *C10Data* on the Premier website were gathered in testing of all $2n$ combinations. What recommendation would you make, based on these data?

PROJECTS, ETC.

1. A computer version of Deming's Funnel Exercise is available (free) at http://www.symphonytech.com/funnelexp.htm. Download and run the funnel simulation. Does it simulate the same rules as described in this chapter?
2. Devise an experiment similar to the battery performance test example to test different levels of some factor and conduct a statistical analysis of the results. Write up your experiment and results in a report along with the conclusions that you reach from the analysis. You might wish to consult the following paper: "101 Ways to Design an Experiment, or Some Ideas About Teaching Design of Experiments" by William G. Hunter, Technical Report No. 413 dated June 1975 at http://curiouscat.com/bill/101doe.cfm for some ideas.
3. Using one sheet of paper, design and build a helicopter. Some methods of making a paper helicopter can be found at: http://www.exploratorium.edu/science_explorer/roto-copter.html and http://www.faa.gov/education/student_resources/kids_corner/ages_13/paper_helicopter/

   Use design of experiments to develop a design that keeps the helicopter airborne for as long as possible.

CASES

I. THE DISCIPLINARY CITATION[21]

A local delivery service has 40 drivers who deliver packages throughout the metropolitan area. Occasionally, drivers make mistakes, such as entering the wrong package number on a shipping document, failing to get a signature, and so on. A total of 240 mistakes were made in one year as shown in the *Excel file Ch10Data* in the Bonus materials folder on the Premier website. The manager in charge of this operation has issued disciplinary citations to drivers for each mistake.

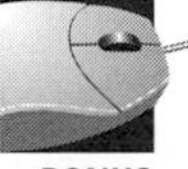

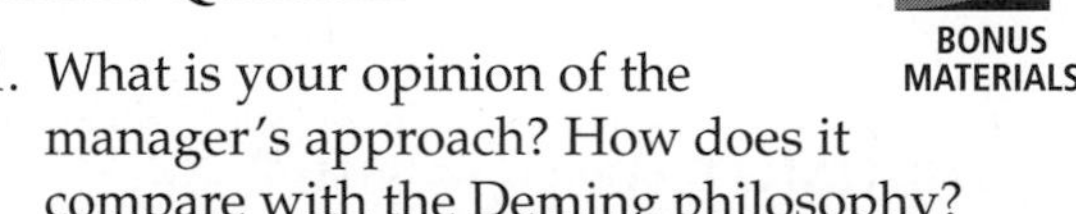

Discussion Questions

1. What is your opinion of the manager's approach? How does it compare with the Deming philosophy?
2. How might the analysis of these data help the manager to understand the variation in the system? (Plot the data to obtain some insight.) How can the data help the manager to improve the performance of this system?

II. The Quarterly Sales Report[22]

BONUS MATERIALS

Ron Hagler, the vice president of sales for Selit Corp., had just received a report on the past five years of quarterly sales data for the regions under his authority (see sales data shown in the Ch10Data.xls spreadsheet in the Bonus materials folder on the Premier website). Not happy with the results, he got on the phone to his secretary. "Marsha, tell the regional managers I need to speak with them this afternoon. Everyone must attend."

Marsha had been Hagler's secretary for almost a decade. She knew by the tone in his voice that he meant business, so she contacted the regional managers about the impromptu meeting at 2 P.M. At 1:55 P.M., the regional managers filed into the room. The only time they were called into a meeting together was when Hagler was unhappy.

Hagler wasted no time. "I just received the quarterly sales report. Northeast sales were fantastic. Steve, you not only improved 17.6 percent in the fourth quarter, but you also increased sales a whopping 20.6 percent over the previous year. I don't know how you do it!" Steve smiled. His philosophy to end the year with a bang by getting customers to stockpile units had paid off again. Hagler had failed to notice that Steve's first quarter sales were always sluggish.

Hagler continued: "Terry, Southwest sales were also superb. You showed an 11.7 percent increase in the fourth quarter and an 11.8 percent increase over the previous year." Terry also smiled. She wasn't sure how she did so well, but she sure wasn't going to change anything.

"Jan, Northwest sales were up 17.2 percent in the fourth quarter, but down 8.2 percent from the previous year," said Hagler. "You need to find out what you did previously to make your sales go through the roof. Even so, your performance in the fourth quarter was good." Jan tried to hide his puzzlement. Although he had received a big order in November, it was the first big order he had received in a long time. Overall, sales for the Northwest were declining.

Hagler was now ready to deal with the "problem" regions. "Leslie, North Central sales were down 5.5 percent in the fourth quarter, but up 4.7 percent from the previous year. I don't understand how your sales vary so much. Do you need more incentive?" Leslie looked down. She had been working very hard the past five years and had acquired numerous new accounts. In fact, she received a bonus for acquiring the most new business in 1998.

"Kim, Mid-Atlantic sales were down 3.2 percent in the fourth quarter and down 2.6 percent from the previous year. I'm very disappointed in your performance. You were once my best sales representative. I had high expectations for you. Now, I can only hope that your first quarter results show some sign of life." Kim felt her face get red. She knew she had sold more units in 2003 than in 2002. "What does Hagler know anyway," she thought to herself. "He's just an empty suit."

Hagler turned to Dave, who felt a surge of adrenaline. "Dave, South Central sales were the worst of all! Sales were down 19.7 percent in the fourth quarter and down 22.3 percent from the previous year. How can you explain this? Do you value your job? I want to see a dramatic improvement in this quarter's results or else!" Dave felt numb. It was a tough region, with a lot of competition. Sure, accounts were lost over the years, but those lost were always replaced with new ones. How could he be doing so badly?

How can Ron improve his approach by applying principles of statistical thinking? Use any analyses of the data that you feel are appropriate to fully explain your thinking and help him.

III. The HMO Pharmacy Crisis[23]

John Dover had just completed an intensive course, "Statistical Thinking for Continuous Improvement," that was offered to all employees of a large health maintenance organization (HMO). There was no time to celebrate, however. Dover worked as a pharmacy assistant in the HMO's pharmacy and he was under a lot of pressure, because his manager, Juan de Pacotilla, was about to be fired. Pacotilla's dismissal appeared imminent because of numerous complaints and even a few lawsuits over inaccurate prescriptions. Pacotilla now was asking Dover for his assistance in trying to resolve the problem.

"John, I really need your help," said Pacotilla. "If I can't show some major improvement or at least a solid plan by next month, I'm history."

"I'll be glad to help," replied Dover, "but what can I do? I'm just a pharmacy assistant."

"Your job title isn't important. I think you're just the person who can get this done," said Pacotilla. "I realize that I've been too far removed from day-to-day operations in the pharmacy, but you work there every day. You're in a much better position to find out how to fix the problem. Just tell me what to do, and I'll do it."

"But what about the statistical consultant you hired to analyze the data on inaccurate prescriptions?" asked Dover.

"To be honest, I'm really disappointed with that guy. He has spent two weeks trying to come up with a new modeling approach to predict weekly inaccurate prescriptions. I tried to explain to him that I don't want to predict the mistakes; I want to eliminate them. I don't think I got through, however, because he said we need a month of additional data to verify the model before he can apply a new method he just read about in a journal to identify 'change points in the time series,' whatever that means. But get this, he will only identify the change points and send me a list. He says it's my job to figure out what they mean and how to respond. I don't know much about statistics. The only thing I remember from my course in college is that it was the worst course I ever took. I'm becoming convinced that statistics really doesn't have much to offer in solving real problems. Because you've just gone through the statistical thinking course, maybe you can see something I can't. I realize it's a long shot, but I was hoping you could use this as the project you need to officially complete the course."

"I used to feel the same way about statistics, too," replied Dover. "But the statistical thinking course was interesting because it didn't focus on crunching numbers. I have some ideas about how we can approach making improvements in prescription accuracy. I think it would be a great project. But we might not be able to solve this problem ourselves. As you know, there is a lot of finger pointing going on. Pharmacists blame the doctors' sloppy handwriting and incomplete instructions for the problem. Doctors blame the pharmacy assistants, who do most of the computer entry of the prescriptions, claiming that they are incompetent. Pharmacy assistants blame the pharmacists for assuming too much about their knowledge of medical terminology, brand names, known drug interactions, and so on."

"It sounds like there's no hope," said Pacotilla.

"I wouldn't say that at all," replied Dover. "It's just that there might be no quick fix we can do by ourselves in the pharmacy. Let me explain what I'm thinking about doing and how I would propose attacking the problem using what I just learned in the statistical thinking course."

How do you think John should approach this problem, using what he has just learned? Assume that he really did pick up a solid understanding of the concepts and tools of statistical thinking in the course.

NOTES

1. Adapted from Brian L. Joiner, *Fourth Generation Management* (New York: McGraw-Hill, 1994), 129.

2. J. M. Juran and Frank M. Gryna, Jr., *Quality Planning and Analysis,* 2nd ed. (New York: McGraw-Hill, 1980), 35.

3. Scott M. Paton, "Juran: A Lifetime of Quality: An Exclusive Interview with a Quality Legend," *Quality Digest,* August 2002, 19–23.

4. Reprinted with permission from Galen Britz, Don Emerling, Lynne Hare, Roger Hoerl, and Janice Shade, "How to Teach Others to Apply Statistical Thinking," *Quality Progress,* June 1997, 67–79. © 1997, American Society for Quality. No further distribution allowed without permission.

5. Kimberly Weisul, "So Your Lie May Always Be True," *BusinessWeek,* February 25, 2002, 16.

6. Steven A. Melnyk and R. T. Christensen, "Variance is Evil," *APICS The Performance Advantage,* June 2002, 19.

7. Ronald D. Snee, "Getting Better Business Results: Using Statistical Thinking and Methods to Shape the Bottom Line," *Quality Progress,* June 1998, 102–106.

8. Britz, et al. (see Note 4).

9. Based on descriptions given in W. Edwards Deming, *The New Economics For Industry, Government, Education* (Cambridge, MA: MIT Center for Advanced Engineering Study, 1993).

10. Frank H. Squires, "The Triumph of Statistics," *Quality,* February 1982, 75.

11. Quality Gamebox is a product of PQ Systems; further information is available at http://www.pqsystems.com/products/sixsigma/QualityGamebox/QualityGamebox.php

12. Thomas Pyzdek, "Non-Normal Distributions in the Real World," *Quality Digest*, December 1999, 36–41.

13. Johannes Ledolter, and Claude W. Burrill, *Statistical Quality Control* (New York: John Wiley & Sons, 1999).

14. N. Raghu Kackar, "Off-Line Quality Control, Parameter Design, and the Taguchi Method," *Journal of Quality Technology* 17, no. 4 (October 1985), 176–188.

15. Bruce D. Nordwall, "ITT Uses Process Control Methods to Increase Plant Productivity," *Aviation Week & Space Technology*, May 11, 1987, 69–74.

16. Eric Wasiloff and Curtis Hargitt, "Using DOE to Determine AA Battery Life," *Quality Progress*, March 1999, 67–71. © 1999, American Society for Quality. Reprinted with permission.

17. Joseph J. Pignatiello, Jr., and John S. Ramberg, "The Top 10 Triumphs and Tragedies of Genichi Taguchi," presented at the 35th ASQC/ASA Fall Technical Conference, Lexington, KY, 1991.

18. Douglas C. Montgomery, *Design and Analysis of Experiments* (New York: John Wiley & Sons, 1996); Charles Lipson and Narendra J. Sheth. *Statistical Design and Analysis of Engineering Experiments* (New York: McGraw-Hill, 1973).

19. Kalyan Kumar Chowdhury, E.V. Gigo, and R. Raghavan, "Quality Improvement Through Design of Experiments: A Case Study," *Quality Engineering* 12, no. 3 (2000), 407–416. Copyright 2000 by Marcel Dekker, Inc.

20. Courtesy of Donald B. Splaun, Jr., Manager, Advanced Manufacturing Technology, GE-Fanuc, Inc.

21. Based on an anecdote in W. Edwards Deming, *Out of the Crisis* (Cambridge, MA: MIT Center for Advanced Engineering Study, 1986).

22. Reprinted with permission from Galen Britz, Don Emerling, Lynn Hare, Roger Hoerl, and Janice Shade, "How to Teach Others to Apply Statistical Thinking," *Quality Progress*, June 1997, pp. 67–79. Copyright © 1997 American Society for Quality. No further distribution allowed without permission.

23. Ibid.

CHAPTER 11

SIX SIGMA AND PROCESS IMPROVEMENT

OUTLINE

QUALITY PROFILES: KARLEE Company and Caterpillar Financial Services Corporation
THE STATISTICAL BASIS OF SIX SIGMA
SIX SIGMA DMAIC METHODOLOGY
PROJECT MANAGEMENT FOR SIX SIGMA
Six Sigma Project Selection
TOOLS FOR PROCESS IMPROVEMENT
The "Seven QC Tools"
Lean Tools
Lean Six Sigma
SIX SIGMA IN SERVICES AND SMALL ORGANIZATIONS
QUALITY IN PRACTICE: An Application of Six Sigma to Reduce Medical Errors
SUMMARY OF KEY POINTS AND TERMINOLOGY
QUALITY IN PRACTICE: Applying Quality Improvement Tools to an Order Fulfillment Process
REVIEW QUESTIONS
DISCUSSION QUESTIONS
PROBLEMS
PROJECTS, ETC.
Cases LT, Inc.
Janson Medical Clinic
Readilunch Restaurant

When former Cincinnati City Manager Valerie Lemmie started her job, she asked building inspectors whether the city had a "one-stop shop" for building permits. They said, "Sure. You stop here once, you stop there once, and you stop there once." What she found out was that a permit stops 473 times on its way from the initial application to the printer! After spending a week at City Hall and taking notes on every step of the process, a consultant hired to analyze the Department of Buildings and Inspections ended up with about 30 feet of flowcharts that depicted the building permit process. Although Ms. Lemmie conceded that improvement wouldn't be easy, an assistant noted that a lot of people wanted to know how they could do their jobs better. "They know everything that's wrong with it probably more than anyone else. And more than anyone else, they need to be part of the solution."[1]

Improving such a complex process takes a lot of work, as companies such as KARLEE and Caterpillar Financial Services (see the Quality Profiles) certainly understand. Having the right tools is important and can make the task considerably easier. We introduced basic concepts of process improvement in Chapter 7. However, the focus in that chapter was on the philosophy of improvement in the broader context of process management. In this chapter, we focus on Six Sigma methodology and process improvement tools that support it.

Many years ago, Juran defined *breakthrough* as the accomplishment of any improvement that takes an organization to unprecedented levels of performance. Breakthrough attacks chronic losses or, in Deming's terminology, common causes of variation. The objectives of Six Sigma often focus on breakthrough improvements that add value to the organization and its customers through systematic approaches to problem solving. By incorporating a wide variety of statistical, traditional quality improvement tools, and concepts from lean manufacturing, Six Sigma and Lean Six Sigma have become powerful approaches to help organizations achieve breakthrough improvements.

Quality Profiles

KARLEE Company and Caterpillar Financial Services Corporation

KARLEE Company is a contract manufacturer of precision sheet metal and machined components for the telecommunications, semiconductor, and medical equipment industries. It provides a full range of manufacturing services from initial component design to assembled, integrated products. Located in Garland, Texas, KARLEE's 550 team members have met or exceeded sales growth goals every year since 1994, while continuing to improve customer satisfaction and operational performance. Serving four major customers, KARLEE's customer focus is exemplified by constant, scheduled communications. Each primary customer is assigned a three-person customer service team to provide ongoing and proactive support. KARLEE leadership and team members actively support the community. Activities include tutoring at a local elementary school, coaching a high school team for a national robotics competition, and adopting needy families in the Garland community. To improve the work environment and production processes, KARLEE uses manufacturing cells, consisting of state-of-the-art computer numerical control equipment, machining centers, and robotic loading systems as well as concepts, such as lean manufacturing principles and statistical process control, which are not often used by smaller companies. Continued mastery of these techniques has helped the company to improve efficiency and productivity and, as a result, benefit customers by reducing delivery times and controlling costs. In 2000, KARLEE went from lead-time assemblies of two to three weeks to quick turn assemblies of one to two days. These increased turns remained consistent in the presence of sales growth of 49 percent for these products.

With total U.S. assets exceeding $14 billion and managing more than 100,000 contracts monthly, Caterpillar Financial Services Corporation U.S. (CFSC) is the second-largest captive-equipment lender in the United States. With a U.S. workforce of nearly 750 employees, CFSC has more than $1 billion in revenues as the financial services business unit within Caterpillar Inc. True to its mission of "helping Caterpillar and our customers succeed through financial service excellence," CFSC maintains a constant focus on process improvement. Tools such as Six Sigma, help CFSC prioritize and manage projects, design products, and improve processes. Ninety-seven percent of employees are trained in Six Sigma procedures for designing new processes, called DMEDI (Define, Measure, Explore, Develop, Implement), and for improving existing ones, called DMAIC (Define, Measure, Analyze, Improve, Control). Specially trained employees called Black Belts, experts in the Six Sigma process and team facilitation; Green Belts, subject matter experts; and Yellow Belts, trained in basics of Six Sigma, comprise teams of employees that implement these procedures.

Handling over 100,000 contracts monthly and working with customers and equipment dealers who demand accurate, timely, complete, and responsive service have led CFSC to invest in leading-edge information-management systems and hardware. Investments in technology along with a continuing focus on excellence and process improvements are helping CFSC achieve its corporate vision: "to be a significant reason why customers select Caterpillar worldwide." Seventy-nine percent of customers considering the purchase of Cat equipment say that CFSC products and services favorably influenced their decision. Research also verified that CFSC exceeded customers' expectations twice as often as competitors. Satisfaction levels of performance exceed industry and ACSI (American Customer Satisfaction Index) world-class benchmarks. CFSC received a Baldrige Award in 2003.

Source: Malcolm Baldrige National Quality Award Winners' Profiles, U.S. Department of Commerce, National Institute of Standards and Technology.

THE STATISTICAL BASIS OF SIX SIGMA

Six Sigma began as a manufacturing focus to reduce defect levels to only a few parts per million. It has evolved into a formal business strategy designed to accelerate improvements in every facet of an organization.[2]

Six Sigma represents a quality level of at most *3.4 defects per million opportunities,* or 3.4 dpmo (the calculation of dpmo was explained in Chapter 8). Figure 11.1 explains the theoretical basis for Six Sigma in the context of manufacturing specifications. Motorola chose this figure because field failure data suggested that Motorola's processes drifted by this amount on average. The allowance of a shift in the distribution is important, because no process can be maintained in perfect control. As will be discussed in Chapter 13, many common statistical process control (SPC) plans are based on sample sizes that only allow detection of shifts of about two standard deviations. Thus, it would not be unusual for a process to drift this much and not be noticed. The area under the shifted curves *beyond* the Six Sigma ranges (the tolerance limits) is only 0.0000034, or 3.4 parts per million. Thus, if the process mean can be controlled to within 1.5 standard deviations of the target, a maximum of 3.4 defects per million can be expected. If it is held

A six sigma quality level *corresponds to a process variation equal to half of the design tolerance while allowing the mean to shift as much as 1.5 standard deviations from the target.*

Figure 11.1 Theoretical Basis for Six Sigma

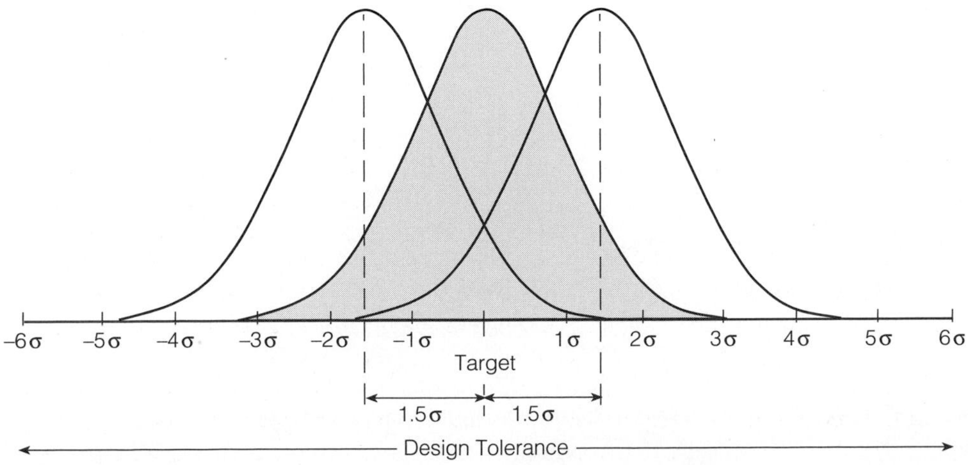

exactly on target (the shaded distribution in Figure 11.1), only 2.0 defects per billion would be expected.

In a similar fashion we could define three sigma quality, five sigma quality, and so on. The easiest way to understand it is to think of the distance from the target to the upper or lower specification (half the tolerance), measured in terms of standard deviations of the inherent variation, as the sigma level. A k sigma quality level satisfies the equation:

$$k \times \text{process standard deviation} = \text{tolerance}/2$$

Note that in Figure 11.1, if the design specification limits were only 4 standard deviations away from the target, the tails of the shifted distributions begin to exceed the specification limits by a significant amount.

Table 11.1 shows the number of defects per million for different sigma quality levels and different amounts of off-centering. Note that a quality level of 3.4 defects per million can be achieved in several ways, for instance;

- with 0.5 sigma off-centering and 5 sigma quality
- with 1.0 sigma off-centering and 5.5 sigma quality
- with 1.5 sigma off-centering and 6 sigma quality[3]

In many cases, controlling the process to the target is less expensive than reducing the process variability. This table can help assess these trade-offs.

The sigma level can easily be calculated on an Excel spreadsheet using the formula

$$= \text{NORMSINV}(1 - \text{Number of Defects}/\text{Number of Opportunities}) + \text{SHIFT}$$

or equivalently,

$$= \text{NORMSINV}(1 - \text{dpmo}/1{,}000{,}000) + \text{SHIFT}$$

SHIFT refers to the off-centering as used in Table 11.1. In Chapter 8, we presented a simple example involving lost airline baggage to illustrate calculating dpmo. In that example, we assumed 3 lost bags for 8,000 customers with an average of 1.6 bags per customer, which resulted in dpmo = 234.375. Using the formula

Table 11.1 Number of Defectives (Parts per Million) for Specified Off-Centering of the Process and Quality Levels

	Sigma Quality Levels						
Off-Centering	**3.00**	**3.50**	**4.00**	**4.50**	**5.00**	**5.50**	**6.00**
0.00	1,350	233	32	**3.4**	0.29	0.019	0.001
0.25	2,980	577	88	11	1.02	0.076	0.004
0.50	6,210	1,350	233	32	**3.4**	0.29	0.019
0.75	12,224	2,980	577	88	11	1.02	0.076
1.00	22,750	6,210	1,350	233	32	**3.4**	0.29
1.25	40,059	12,224	2,980	577	88	11	1.02
1.50	66,807	22,750	6,210	1,350	233	32	**3.4**
1.75	105,650	40,059	12,224	2,980	577	88	11
2.00	158,655	66,807	22,750	6,210	1,350	233	32

Source: Pandu R. Tadikamalla, "The Confusion over Six-Sigma Quality," *Quality Progress* 27, no. 11 (November 1994).

above, the sigma level is calculated as =NORMSINV(1 − 234.375/1000000) + 1.5 = 4.99828 or about a 5-sigma level. The truth is less impressive. It was reported that 3.67 mishandled baggage reports per 1,000 passengers were filed in May 2003, which was up from 3.31 per 1,000 a year earlier.[4] This result yields a sigma level of only 4.33, assuming 1.6 bags per passenger.

Six Sigma has been applied in product development, new business acquisition, customer service, accounting, and many other business functions. For example, suppose that a bank tracks the number of errors reported in customers' checking account statements. If they find 12 errors in 1,000 statements, it is equivalent to an error rate of 12,000 per million, somewhere between 3.5 and 4 sigma levels. The difference between a 4- and 6-sigma quality level can be surprising. Put in practical terms, if your cellular phone system operated at a 4-sigma level, you would be without service for more than four hours each month, whereas at 6-sigma, it would only be about 9 seconds a month; a 4-sigma process would result in 1 nonconforming package for every three truckloads, whereas a 6-sigma process would have only one nonconforming package in more than 5,000 truckloads. And, if you play 100 rounds of golf each year, you would only miss one putt every 163 years at a 6-sigma level! What may be more surprising to realize is that a change from 3 to 4 sigma represents a 10-fold improvement; from 4 to 5 sigma, a 30-fold improvement; and from 5 to 6 sigma, a 70-fold improvement—difficult challenges for any organization.

Although originally developed for manufacturing in the context of tolerance-based specifications, the Six Sigma concept has been operationalized to any process and has come to signify a generic quality level of at most 3.4 defects per million opportunities.

However, not all processes should operate at a six sigma level.[5] The appropriate level should depend on the strategic importance of the process and the cost of improvement relative to the benefit. It is generally easy to move from a 2 or 3-sigma level to a 4-sigma level, but moving beyond that requires much more effort and sophisticated statistical tools.

At Motorola, Six Sigma became part of the common language of all employees. To them, it means near perfection, even if they do not understand the statistical details. (Some tell their coworkers, "Have a six-sigma weekend!") Since stating its goal, Motorola has made great strides in meeting this goal, achieving six-sigma capability in many processes and 4- or 5-sigma levels in most others. Even in those departments that have reached the goal, Motorola employees continue their improvement efforts in order to reach the ultimate goal of zero defects.

In addition to a focus on defects, Six Sigma seeks to improve all aspects of operations. Thus, other key metrics include cycle time, process variation, yield, and throughput. Selecting the appropriate metric depends on the scope and objectives of the project, making Six Sigma a universal approach for improvement in all aspects of a business.

SIX SIGMA DMAIC METHODOLOGY

The principal problem solving methodology used by Six Sigma is **DMAIC**—define, measure, analyze, improve, and control. This is one of the first things that a Green Belt in training learns.

1. **Define** After a Six Sigma project is selected, the first step is to clearly define the problem. This activity is significantly different from project selection. Project selection generally responds to symptoms of a problem and usually

results in a rather vague problem statement. One must describe the problem in operational terms that facilitate further analysis. For example, a firm might have a history of poor reliability of electric motors it manufactures, resulting in a Six Sigma project to improve motor reliability. A preliminary investigation of warranty and field service repair data might suggest that the source of most problems was brush wear, and more specifically, suggest a problem with brush hardness variability. Thus, the problem might be defined as "reduce the variability of brush hardness." This process of drilling down to a more specific problem statement is sometimes called **project scoping**.

A good problem statement should also identify customers and the CTQs that have the most impact on product or service performance, describe the current level of performance or the nature of errors or customer complaints, identify the relevant performance metrics, benchmark best performance standards, calculate the cost/revenue implications of the project, and quantify the expected level of performance from a successful Six Sigma effort. The Define phase should also address such project management issues as what will need to be done, by whom, and when.

2. **Measure** This phase of the DMAIC process focuses on how to measure the internal processes that impact CTQs. It requires an understanding of the causal relationships between process performance and customer value. These concepts were discussed in Chapter 8. However, once they are understood, procedures for gathering facts—collecting good data, observation, and careful listening—must be defined and implemented. Data from existing production processes and practices often provide important information, as does feedback from supervisors, workers, customers, and field service employees. Many of the technical issues of measurement and statistics that must be considered in a Six Sigma project were discussed in Chapter 10.

Data collection should not be performed blindly. One must first ask some basic questions:

- What questions are we trying to answer?
- What type of data will we need to answer the question?
- Where can we find the data?
- Who can provide the data?
- How can we collect the data with minimum effort and with minimum chance of error?

The first step in any data collection effort is to develop **operational definitions** for all performance measures that will be used. For example, what does it mean to have "on-time delivery"? Does it mean within one day of the promised time? One week? One hour? What is an error? Is it wrong information on an invoice, a typographical mistake, or either? Clearly, any data are meaningless unless they are well defined and understood without ambiguity.

The Juran Institute suggests 10 important considerations for data collection:

1. Formulate good questions that relate to the specific information needs of the project.
2. Use appropriate data analysis tools and be certain the necessary data are being collected.
3. Define comprehensive data collection points so that job flows suffer minimum interruption.
4. Select an unbiased collector who has the easiest and most immediate access to the relevant facts.

5. Understand the environment and make sure that data collectors have the proper experience.
6. Design simple data collection forms.
7. Prepare instructions for collecting the data.
8. Test the data collection forms and the instructions and make sure they are filled out properly.
9. Train the data collectors as to the purpose of the study, what the data will be used for, how to fill out the forms, and the importance of remaining unbiased.
10. Audit the data collection process and validate the results.[6]

These guidelines can greatly improve the process of uncovering relevant facts necessary to identify and solve problems.

Six Sigma uses the notion of a function in mathematics to portray the relationship between process performance and customer value:

$$Y = f(X)$$

Where Y is the set of CTQs and X represents the set of critical input variables that influence Y. For example, Y might represent the time to deliver bags from an airplane to baggage handling and the number of lost bags, X might include the number of baggage handlers, number of trucks, time they are dispatched, bar code scanning accuracy, and so on. Figure 11.2 shows a visual example of how one might "drill down" from Y to identify the critical X-factors. This functional relationship helps in defining the experiments that need to be conducted to confirm how input variables affect response variables. It also sets the stage for the Control phase by defining those factors that requiring monitoring and control.

3. **Analyze** A major flaw in many problem-solving approaches is a lack of emphasis on rigorous analysis. Too often, we want to jump to a solution

Figure 11.2 Visual Mapping of $Y = f(X)$

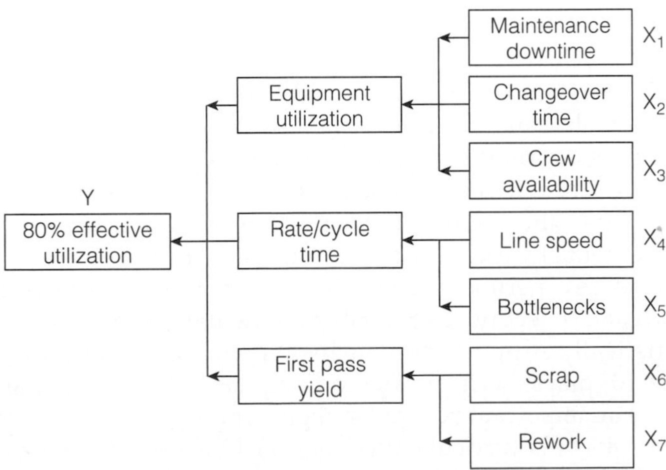

Source: Reprinted with permission from Thomas Bertels and George Patterson, "Selecting Six Sigma Projects that Matter," Six Sigma Forum Magazine, November 2003, pp. 13–15. Copyright © 2003 American Society for Quality. No further distribution allowed without permission.

without fully understanding the nature of the problem and identifying the source of the problem. The Analyze phase of DMAIC focuses on *why* defects, errors, or excessive variation occur, which often result from one or more of the following:

- A lack of knowledge about how a process works, which is particularly critical if different people perform the process. Such lack of knowledge results in inconsistency and increased variation in outputs.
- A lack of knowledge about how a process *should* work, including understanding customer expectations and the goal of the process
- A lack of control of materials and equipment used in a process
- Inadvertent errors in performing work
- Waste and complexity, which manifest themselves in many ways, such as unnecessary steps in a process and excess inventories
- Hasty design and production of parts and assemblies; poor design specifications; inadequate testing of incoming materials and prototypes
- Failure to understand the capability of a process to meet specifications
- Lack of training
- Poor instrument calibration and testing
- Inadequate environmental characteristics such as light, temperature, and noise

Finding the answers requires identifying the key variables that are most likely to create errors and excessive variation—the root causes. NCR Corporation defines **root cause** as "that condition (or interrelated set of conditions) having allowed or caused a defect to occur, which once corrected properly, permanently prevents recurrence of the defect in the same, or subsequent, product or service generated by the process."[7] As with a medical analogy, eliminating symptoms of problems usually provides only temporary relief; eliminating root causes provides long-term relief.

One useful approach for identifying the root cause is the "5 Why" technique.[8] This approach forces one to redefine a problem statement as a chain of causes and effects to identify the source of the symptoms by asking why, ideally five times. In a classic example at Toyota, a machine failed because a fuse blew. Replacing the fuse would have been the obvious solution; however, this action would have only addressed the symptom of the real problem. Why did the fuse blow? Because the bearing did not have adequate lubrication. Why? Because the lubrication pump was not working properly. Why? Because the pump axle was worn. Why? Because sludge seeped into the pump axle, which was the root cause. Toyota attached a strainer to the lubricating pump to eliminate the sludge, thus correcting the problem of the machine failure.

After potential variables are identified, experiments are conducted to verify them. These experiments generally consist of formulating some hypothesis to investigate, collecting data, analyzing the data, and reaching a reasonable and statistically supportable conclusion. Statistical thinking and analysis (Chapter 10) plays a critical role in this phase. It is one of the reasons why statistics is an important part of Six Sigma training (and one that engineering and many business curricula often ignore). Other experiments might employ computer simulation techniques.

4. **Improve** Once the root cause of a problem is understood, the analyst or team needs to generate ideas for removing or resolving the problem and improve the performance measures and CTQs. This idea-gathering phase is a highly

creative activity, because many solutions are not obvious. One of the difficulties in this task is the natural instinct to prejudge ideas before thoroughly evaluating them. Most people have a natural fear of proposing a "silly" idea or looking foolish. However, such ideas may actually form the basis for a creative and useful solution. Effective problem solvers must learn to defer judgment and develop the ability to generate a large number of ideas at this stage of the process, whether practical or not.

A number of processes and tools to facilitate idea generation can be used. One of the most popular is brainstorming. Brainstorming, a useful group problem-solving procedure for generating ideas, was proposed by Alex Osborn "for the sole purpose of producing checklists of ideas" that can be used in developing a solution to a problem.[9] With brainstorming, no criticism is permitted, and people are encouraged to generate a large number of ideas through combination and enhancement of existing ideas. Wild ideas are encouraged and frequently trigger other good ideas from somewhere else.

Checklists are often used as a guide for generating ideas. Osborn proposed about 75 fundamental questions based on the following principles:

- Put to other uses?
- Adapt?
- Modify?
- Magnify?
- Minify?
- Substitute?
- Rearrange?
- Reverse?
- Combine?

By consciously seeking ideas based on this list, one can generate many unusual and often useful ideas.

After a set of ideas have been proposed, it is necessary to evaluate them and select the most promising. This process includes confirming that the proposed solution will positively impact the key process variables and the CTQs, and identifying the maximum acceptable ranges of these variables.

Problem solutions often entail technical or organizational changes. Often some sort of decision or scoring model is used to assess possible solutions against important criteria such as cost, time, quality improvement potential, resources required, effects on supervisors and workers, and barriers to implementation such as resistance to change or organizational culture. To implement a solution effectively, responsibility must be assigned to a person or a group who will follow through on what must be done, where it will be done, when it will be done, and how it will be done. Project management techniques are helpful in implementation planning.

5. **Control** The Control phase focuses on how to maintain the improvements, which includes putting tools in place to ensure that the key variables remain within the maximum acceptable ranges under the modified process. These improvements might include establishing the new standards and procedures, training the workforce, and instituting controls to make sure that improvements do not die over time. Controls might be as simple as using checklists or periodic status reviews to ensure that proper procedures are followed, or employing statistical process control charts (see Chapter 13) to monitor the performance of key measures.

The following example shows how DMAIC was used at American Express to improve the number of customers who received renewal cards.[10] (In this example, data have been masked to protect confidentiality.)

Define and Measure: On average in one year, American Express received 1,000 returned renewal cards each month. Of these renewals, 65 percent are due to the fact that the card members changed their addresses and did not tell the company. The U.S. Post Office calls these forwardable addresses. Amex does not currently notify a card member when they receive a returned plastic card.

Analyze: Analysis of the data noted significant differences in the causes of returned plastics between product types. Optima, the revolving card product, had the highest incidence of defects, but was not significantly different from other card types in the percentage of defects. Renewals had by far the highest defect rate among the three areas of replacement, renewal, and new accounts. After additional testing, returns with forwardable addresses were overwhelmingly the largest percentage and quantity of returns.

Improve: An experimental pilot study was run on all renewal files issued, comparing records against the National Change of Address database. As a result, they were able to reduce the dpmo rate by 44.5 percent, from 13,500 to 6,036 defects per million opportunities. This action enabled over 1,200 card members who would not have automatically received their credit cards to receive them, increasing revenue and customer satisfaction.

Control: Amex began tracking the proportion of returns over time as a means of monitoring the new process to ensure that it remains in control.

PROJECT MANAGEMENT FOR SIX SIGMA

Projects are the vehicles that are used to organize team efforts and to implement the DMAIC process. One of the requirements for achieving Green Belt status (see Chapter 6) is to successfully complete a basic Six Sigma project by solving a meaningful business problem that positively impacts customers or business performance. Often Green Belt projects address small problems within a department or work function. As employees develop their skills, become Black Belts, and start applying Six Sigma on a routine basis, they begin to address larger and more complex issues, such as problems associated with key value-creation or cross-functional processes, such as supply chains.

Although projects are set up as temporary organization structures, their flexibility allows cross-functional teams to complete significant work in minimum time, if well managed. One of the challenges of implementing Six Sigma projects is to coordinate them with normal work activities. Some slack time, as well as physical and financial resources, must be allocated to project teams in order for them to achieve their objectives. Team members and project leaders cannot be expected to carry a full load of routine work and still participate fully and effectively on Six Sigma project teams.

Projects fail for a variety of reasons, including not adhering to schedules, poor planning, and "scope creep" when the nature of the project gradually loses its focus and becomes unwieldy, mismatching of skills, and insufficient knowledge transfer.[11] Being able to manage a large portfolio of projects, as would be found in Six Sigma environments, is vital to organizational success. The Project Management Body of Knowledge (PMBOK),[12] developed by the Project Management Institute, defines 69 tools that a project manager should master, but few have done so. Achieving professional certification in project management can significantly assist Six Sigma efforts.

Six Sigma Project Selection

One of the more difficult challenges in Six Sigma is the selection of the most appropriate problems to attack. According to Kepner and Tregoe, a **problem** is a deviation between what should be happening and what actually is happening that is important enough to make someone think the deviation ought to be corrected.[13] Research using more than 1,000 published cases describing quality problem solving activities suggests that virtually every instance of quality problem-solving falls into one of five categories:[14]

1. *Conformance problems* are defined by unsatisfactory performance by a well-specified system. Users are not happy with system outputs, such as quality or customer service levels. Traditional quality improvement tools and Six Sigma methods are often used here.
2. *Efficiency problems* result from unsatisfactory performance from the standpoint of stakeholders other than customers. Typical examples are cost and productivity issues. Lean tools are often used to address such problems.
3. *Unstructured performance problems* result from unsatisfactory performance by a poorly specified system. That is, the task is nonstandardized and not fully specified by procedures and requirements. Unstructured problems require more creative approaches to solving them.
4. *Product design problems* involve designing new products that better satisfy user needs—the expectations of customers that matter most to them. For such problems, Design for Six Sigma (see Chapter 12) tools and methods are applicable.
5. *Process design* problems involve designing new processes or substantially revising existing processes. The challenge here is determining process requirements, generating new process alternatives, and linking these processes to customer needs. Work systems design approaches discussed in Chapter 7 are typically used.

Lynch and colleagues point out two ways to generate projects: top-down and bottom-up.[15] Top-down projects generally are tied to business strategy and are aligned with customer needs. Their major weakness is that they are often too broad in scope to be completed in a timely manner. In addition, top managers may underestimate the cost and overestimate the capabilities of the team or teams to which the project is assigned. In a bottom-up approach, Black Belts (or Master Black Belts) choose the projects that are well-suited to the capabilities of teams. However, a major drawback of this approach is that the projects may not be tied closely to strategic concerns of top management, thus receiving little support and low recognition from the top. Perhaps the best way to ensure success is for executive champions, who understand the impact of projects from a strategic perspective, to work closely with the technical experts in choosing the most relevant projects that fit within the capabilities of Six Sigma teams.

Classifying quality- and performance-related problems by problem type can help identify potential Six Sigma projects and the most appropriate tools to address them.

A Six Sigma project might span an entire division or be as narrow as a single production operation. Factors that should be considered when selecting Six Sigma projects include the following:

- Financial return, as measured by costs associated with quality and process performance, and impacts on revenues and market share
- Impacts on customers and organizational effectiveness
- Probability of success

- Impact on employees
- Fit to strategy and competitive advantage

As we noted several times in earlier chapters, Six Sigma projects are driven by expected financial returns. Reducing costs associated with poor quality, such as scrap, rework, excessive cycle times, delays, and lost customers often provide an obvious justification for pursuing a project. A Cost of Quality process (discussed in Chapter 8) often facilitates identifying opportunities and measuring results.

One of the pitfalls experienced in organizations new to Six Sigma is a lack of ability of senior managers to estimate what the resources they allocate (or fail to allocate) to Six Sigma projects will "buy" in the way of bottom-line returns. Thus, it becomes important to be able to differentiate between, and to estimate fairly accurately, the differences in resources required to bring a $250,000 project versus a $50,000 project to a successful conclusion. Six Sigma projects should lead to improved customer satisfaction and organizational performance. Such improvements can lead directly to higher sales or market share, thus providing financial justification for selecting a project.

Projects chosen should have a high likelihood of success. Considerable risk comes in choosing problems that can best be compared with "solving world hunger." At the outset of a Six Sigma initiative, it is beneficial to pick the "low-hanging fruit"—projects that are easy to accomplish, or even can be completed by a single individual in order to show early successes. This visible success helps to build momentum and support for future projects. Studies show that many projects are significantly overbudget, behind schedule, or do not result in desired outcomes.[16] Thus, good project management, as we discussed in Chapter 7, is essential.

Six Sigma projects should fit within the capabilities of the people and teams that work on them. Many indirect benefits accrue. The training received as Green or Black Belts improves employee and organizational knowledge, and participating in Six Sigma projects improves team and leadership skills, as pointed out in Chapter 6. Six Sigma can motivate employees to innovate and improve their work environment, and ultimately their satisfaction on the job and personal self-esteem. Many projects offer opportunities to reduce frustration with inadequate work processes or to provide increased value to customers; these types of projects are certainly important candidates for selection.

Finally, Six Sigma projects should support the organization's vision and competitive strategy. In Chapter 4, we stressed the importance of creating action plans that help an organization achieve its chosen strategies. At GE, for example, business goals work their way down the organization, helping employees to distinguish between projects that will not have a significant effect on business performance and those that do.[17]

Of course, most organizations probably have more opportunities for Six Sigma projects than available resources to do them. In many cases, project selection is often political in nature. Senior executives who champion Six Sigma projects might exercise political influence to get their pet projects recognized and accepted. However, taking a more objective viewpoint is more effective. Prioritizing and selecting projects using some rational criteria can contribute to greater effectiveness. Project steering committees that include at least a portion of the organization's senior leadership often guide these decisions. This group can act as a filter for the voices of both the external and internal customers in evaluating and prioritizing projects. At Xerox, the management teams identify Six Sigma projects based on customer experience improvement opportunities, alignment of strategic plans, ability to close business gaps, and key areas for process improvement. Potential projects are assessed based on their potential business impact and estimated effort; projects with relatively high benefits compared to effort requirements are the ones selected.[18]

Simple scoring models may be used to evaluate and prioritize potential projects. An example of a project selection matrix is shown in Figure 11.3. The top box shows the customer importance ratings on a set of key *critical to quality* (CTQ) characteristics using the scale at the bottom left. The numbers in the main table are based on the scale on the bottom right, and are determined by the steering committee. By multiplying these rankings by the customer importance ratings, we can arrive at a total score in the right-hand column (Project ranking metric). The higher the number,

Figure 11.3 Example of a Project Selection Matrix

Customer Issues	Missing parts ordered	Late delivery	Damaged orders	Wrong orders	More parts than ordered	On hold too long
Customer importance	8	5	7	10	3	3

Project	*Project ranking based on correlation to customer issues*						**Project ranking metric**
Order fill process flow optimization	5	8	3	3	5	0	146
Replenishment cycle time reduction project	5	8	5	0	0	0	115
Customer service feedback reporting	5	3	3	8	0	5	171
Delivery vendor certification	0	10	8	0	0	0	106
IT upgrade process integration	7	5	0	8	8	3	194

Customer importance	Relationship to customer importance
0	Not important
3	Slightly important
5	Important
8	Very important
10	Critical

Project rank	Relationship to customer issue
0	No correlation
3	Very little correlation
5	Some correlation
8	High correlation
10	Complete correlation

Source: Reprinted with permission from William Michael Kelly, "Three Steps to Project Selection," *Six Sigma Forum Magazine* 2, no. 1 (November 2002), 29–32.

the more the project affects customer issues. This process takes the guesswork and opinions out of the project selection process and focuses on the important issues to the customer and the organization.

TOOLS FOR PROCESS IMPROVEMENT

Two of the unique features of DMAIC are its emphasis on customer requirements and the disciplined use of statistical and other types of improvement tools. Most of the tools used in DMAIC have been around for a long time. For example, both Deming and Juran promoted using statistics and simple visual tools in quality improvement activities. Thomas Pyzdek, a noted quality consultant, states that more than 400 tools are now available in the "TQM Toolbox."[19] However, most organizations rarely go beyond the basic improvement tools and fail to recognize the benefits from more sophisticated statistical tools such as design of experiments. Early practitioners of Six Sigma recognized the power of advanced statistical methods and took them beyond the realm of engineering. Table 11.2 shows a list of the most popular tools used in DMAIC. Some of these have already been introduced in previous chapters; others will be described in this or subsequent chapters.

Although we view process improvement tools and techniques from the perspective of Six Sigma, it is important to understand that they are simply a collection of methods that have been used successfully in all types of quality management and improvement initiatives, from generic TQM efforts, to ISO 9000, and in Baldrige processes.

These tools are integrated into standard Six Sigma curricula, which typically involve a blend of technical topics and project management and leadership topics. Figure 11.4 shows a typical Six Sigma Black Belt training curriculum. The topics covered may be categorized into seven general groups:[20]

- *Elementary statistical tools* (basic statistics, statistical thinking, hypothesis testing, correlation, simple regression)
- *Advanced statistical tools* (design of experiments, analysis of variance, multiple regression)

Table 11.2 Common Six Sigma Tools Used in DMAIC

Define:
Project charter
Cost of quality analysis
Pareto analysis
High level process mapping

Analyze:
Detailed process mapping
Statistical inference
Cause-and-effect diagrams
Failure mode and effects analysis
Root cause analysis

Control
Statistical process control
Standard operating procedures

Measure:
Check sheets
Descriptive statistics
Measurement system evaluation
Process capability analysis
Benchmarking

Improve:
Design of experiments
Mistake proofing
Lean production
Deming cycle
Seven management and planning tools

Figure 11.4 Six Sigma Black Belt Training

Week 1	Week 2	Week 3	Week 4
• Overview • Process improvement planning • Process mapping • Quality function deployment • Failure mode and effects analysis • Organizational effectiveness concepts • Basic statistics • Process capability • Measurement systems analysis	• Statistical thinking • Hypothesis testing • Correlation • Simple regression • Team assessment	• Design of experiments • Analysis of variance • Multiple regression • Facilitation tools	• Control plans • Statistical process control • Mistake-proofing • Team development

Source: Reprinted with permission from Roger W. Hoerl, "Six Sigma and the Future of the Quality Profession," *Quality Progress*, June 1998, 35–48. © 1998. American Society for Quality. No further distribution allowed without permission.

- *Product design and reliability* (quality function deployment, failure mode, and effects analysis)
- *Measurement* (process capability, measurement systems analysis)
- *Process control* (control plans, statistical process control)
- *Process improvement* (process improvement planning, process mapping, mistake proofing)
- *Implementation and teamwork* (organizational effectiveness, team assessment, facilitation tools, team development)

A more complete list of the "Six Sigma Body of Knowledge" as advocated by the American Society for Quality can be found in the Bonus Materials for this chapter on the Premium website.

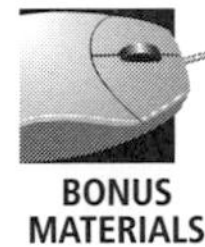
BONUS MATERIALS

The "Seven QC Tools"

Among the many tools that comprise the Six Sigma toolbox are seven simple tools: flowcharts, check sheets, histograms, Pareto diagrams, cause-and-effect diagrams, scatter diagrams, and control charts. The Japanese called them the **Seven QC** (quality control) **Tools**, and they have been used for decades to support quality improvement efforts. Table 11.3 shows the primary applications of each tool in DMAIC. You can easily see how they also apply in the Deming cycle and other methods, such as Creative Problem Solving, which we discussed in Chapter 7. They are designed simply so that workers at all levels can use them easily. We will briefly review each tool to explain its role in quality improvement.

Flowcharts To clearly define a Six Sigma or any process improvement project, one must first understand the process that creates the outputs that internal or external customers receive. This understanding sets the foundation for identifying critical to quality (CTQ) issues, selecting measurements, and identifying root causes of

Table 11.3 Application of the Seven QC Tools in Six Sigma

Tool	DMAIC Steps
Flowcharts	Define, Control
Check sheets	Measure, Analyze
Histograms	Measure, Analyze
Cause-and-effect diagrams	Analyze
Pareto diagrams	Analyze
Scatter diagrams	Analyze, Improve
Control charts	Control

problems, identifying non-value-added steps, and reducing variation.

*A **flowchart** or **process map** identifies the sequence of activities or the flow of materials and information in a process. Flowcharts help the people involved in the process understand it much better and more objectively by providing a picture of the steps needed to accomplish a task.*

Flowcharts are best developed by having the people involved in the process—employees, supervisors, managers, and customers—construct the flowchart. A facilitator provides objectivity in resolving conflicts. The facilitator can guide the discussion through questions such as "What happens next?" "Who makes the decision at this point?" and "What operation is performed at this point?" Quite often, the group does not universally agree on the answers to these questions due to misconceptions about the process itself or a lack of awareness of the "big picture." Flowcharts can easily be created using Microsoft Excel using the features found on the drawing toolbar.[21]

Flowcharts help all employees understand how they fit into a process and who are their suppliers and customers. This realization then leads to improved communication among all parties. By participating in the development of a flowchart, workers feel a sense of ownership in the process, and hence become more willing to work on improving it. If flowcharts are used in training employees, more consistency will be achieved. Flowcharts also help to pinpoint places where quality-related measurements should be taken. Once a flowchart is constructed, it can be used to identify quality problems as well as areas for productivity improvement. Questions such as "How does this operation affect the customer?" "Can we improve or even eliminate this operation?" or "Should we control a critical quality characteristic at this point?" trigger the identification of opportunities.

The AT&T customer–supplier model that we introduced in Chapter 4 provides a way of building a detailed process flowchart. Start with the outputs, or customer requirements, and move backward through the process to identify the key steps needed to produce each output; stop when the process reaches the supplier input stage. AT&T calls this technique backward chaining.[22] AT&T suggests the following steps:

1. Begin with the process output and ask, "What is the last essential subprocess that produces the output of the process?"
2. For that subprocess, ask, "What input does it need to produce the process output?" For each input, test its value to ensure that it is required.
3. For each input, identify its source. In many cases, the input will be the output of the previous subprocess. In some cases, the input may come from external suppliers.

4. Continue backward, one subprocess at a time, until each input comes from an external supplier.

This technique can be applied to each subprocess to create a more detailed process description.

After a flowchart is constructed, several fundamental questions can be asked to analyze the process:

- Are the steps in the process arranged in logical sequence?
- Do all steps add value? Can some steps be eliminated and should others be added in order to improve quality or operational performance? Can some be combined? Should some be reordered?
- Are capacities of each step in balance; that is, do bottlenecks exist for which customers will incur excessive waiting time?
- What skills, equipment, and tools are required at each step of the process? Should some steps be automated?
- At which points in the system might errors occur that would result in customer dissatisfaction, and how might these errors be corrected?
- At which point or points should quality be measured?
- Where interaction with the customer occurs, what procedures and guidelines should employees follow to present a positive image?

These types of questions are fundamental to lean Six Sigma thinking. For example, to determine if a process step has value, more detailed questions may be asked, such as:

- Would the customer notice a loss of value if this step were eliminated?
- Would the product or service be obviously incomplete without this step?
- If you were forced to complete the product or service on an emergency basis, is this step too important to skip?
- If you owned the business and could pocket the savings from skipping this step, would you include it?
- If the step is a review or inspection, is the reject rate significant? Are the consequences of an error at this step significant?

If any of these answers is no, then the value of the step is suspect and should be investigated more thoroughly.[23]

Process mapping and analysis is a powerful tool. Using process mapping as a basis for improvement, Motorola reduced manufacturing time for pagers from 40 days to less than one hour. Citibank adopted this approach and reduced internal callbacks in its Private Bank group by 80 percent and the credit process time by 50 percent. Its Global Equipment Finance division, which provides financing and leasing services to Citibank customers, lowered the credit decision cycle from three days to one. Copeland Companies, subsidiaries of Travelers Life & Annuity, reduced the cycle time of processing statements from 28 days to 15 days.[24] The following example shows in more detail how Boise exploited process mapping.[25]

The Timber and Wood Products Division of Boise Cascade (now Boise) formed a team of 11 people with diverse backgrounds from manufacturing, administration, and marketing to improve a customer claims processing and tracking system that affected all areas and customers in its six divisions. Although external customer surveys indicated that the company was not doing badly, internal opinions of the operation were far more critical.

The first eye-opener came when the process was flowcharted and the group discovered that more than 70 steps were performed for each claim. Figure 11.5 shows the original flowchart from the marketing and sales department. Combined division

Figure 11.5 Original Flowchart from the Marketing and Sales Department

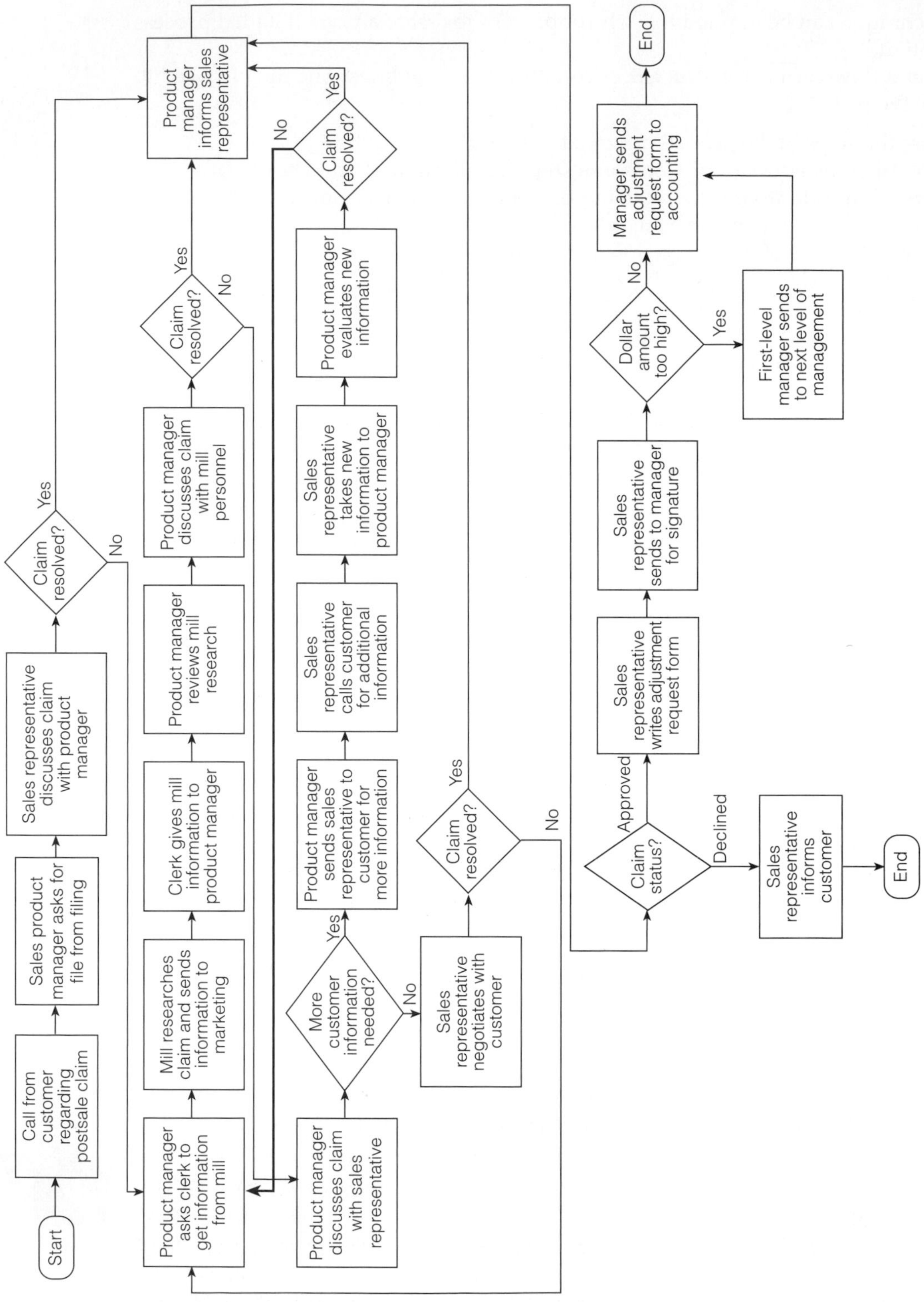

Source: Process Improvement at Boise Casade. Reprinted with permission.

Figure 11.6 New Small Adjustment Request Form Process Flowchart for Marketing and Sales Department

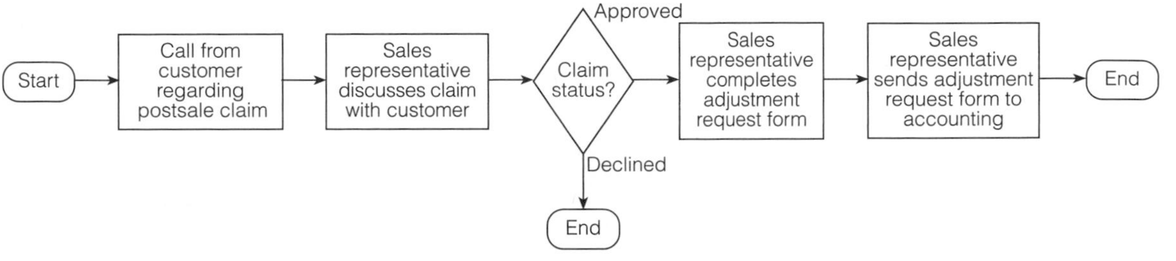

Source: Reprinted with permission from Lakshmi U. Tatikonda, " A Less Costly Billing Process," *Quality Progress*, January 2008, pp. 31–39.

tasks numbered in the hundreds for a single claim; the marketing and sales portion of the flowchart alone consisted of up to 20 separate tasks and seven decisions, which sometimes took months to complete. Most of these steps added no value to the settlement outcome. The flowchart accomplished much more than just plotting Boise's time and efforts; it also helped build team members' confidence in each other and foster mutual respect. When they saw how each member was able to chart his or her part of the process and state individual concerns, everyone's reason for being on the team was validated. The group eliminated 70 percent of the steps for small claims in the original flowchart, as shown in Figure 11.6.

Run Charts and Control Charts A **run chart** is a line graph in which data are plotted over time. The vertical axis represents a measurement; the horizontal axis is the time scale. The daily newspaper usually includes several examples of run charts, such as the Dow Jones Industrial Average. They can be used to track such things as production volume, costs, and customer satisfaction indexes.

Run charts show the performance and the variation of a process or some quality or productivity indicator over time in a graphical fashion that is easy to understand and interpret. They also identify process changes and trends over time and show the effects of corrective actions.

The first step in constructing a run chart is to identify the measurement or indicator to be monitored. In some situations, one might measure the quality characteristics for each individual unit of process output. For low-volume processes, such as chemical production or surgeries, this approach would be appropriate. However, for high-volume production processes or services with large numbers of customers or transactions, it would be impractical. Instead, samples taken on a periodic basis provide the data for computing basic statistical measures such as the mean, range or standard deviation, proportion of items that do not conform to specifications, or number of nonconformances per unit.

Constructing the chart consists of the following steps:

Step 1. Collect the data. If samples are chosen, compute the relevant statistic for each sample, such as the average or proportion.

Step 2. Examine the range of the data. Scale the chart so that all data can be plotted on the vertical axis. Provide some additional room for new data as they are collected.

Step 3. Plot the points on the chart and connect them. Use graph paper if the chart is constructed by hand; a spreadsheet program is preferable.

Step 4. Compute the average of all plotted points and draw it as a horizontal line through the data. This line denoting the average is called the center line (CL) of the chart.

Figure 11.7 Structure of a Control Chart

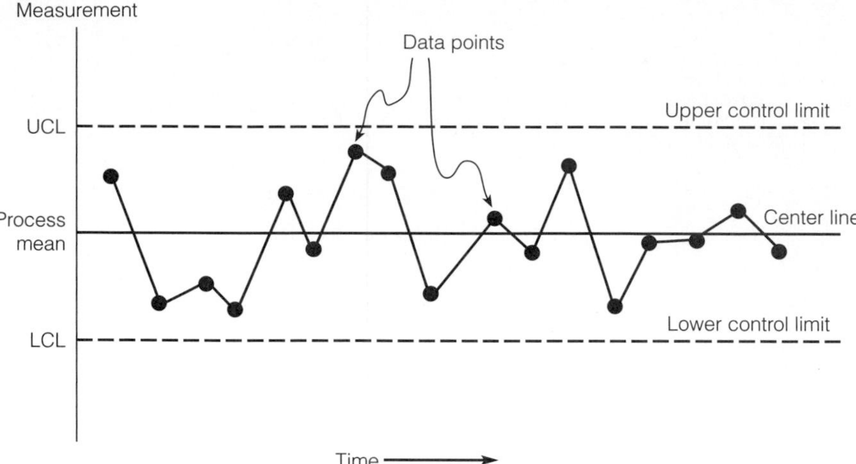

If the plotted points fluctuate in a stable pattern around the center line, with no large spikes, trends, or shifts, they indicate that the process is apparently under control. If unusual patterns exist, then the cause for lack of stability should be investigated and corrective action should be taken. Thus, run charts can identify messes caused by lack of control.

A **control chart** is simply a run chart to which two horizontal lines, called **control limits** are added: the **upper control limit (UCL)** and **lower control limit (LCL)**, as illustrated in Figure 11.7. Control charts were first proposed by Walter Shewhart at Bell Laboratories in the 1920s and were strongly advocated by Deming. Control limits are chosen statistically to provide a high probability (generally greater than 0.99) that points will fall between these limits if the process is in control. Control limits make it easier to interpret patterns in a run chart and draw conclusions about the state of controi. These issues will be discussed in more detail in Chapter 13.

If sample values fall outside the control limits or if nonrandom patterns occur in the chart, then special causes may be affecting the process; the process is not stable. The process should be examined and corrective action taken as appropriate. If evaluation and correction are done in real time, then the chance of producing nonconforming product is minimized. Thus, as a problem-solving tool, control charts allow operators to identify quality problems as they occur. Of course, control charts alone cannot determine the source of the problem. Operators, supervisors, and engineers may have to resort to other problem-solving tools to seek the root cause.

Consider the following example. The Joint Commission Accreditation of Health Care Organizations (JCAHO) monitors and evaluates health care providers according to strict standards and guidelines. Improvement in the quality of care is a principal concern. Hospitals are required to identify and monitor important quality indicators that affect patient care and establish "thresholds for evaluation" (TFEs), which are levels at which special investigation of problems should occur. TFEs provide a means of focusing attention on nonrandom errors (that is, special causes of variation). A logical way to set TFEs is through control charts.

For instance, a hospital collects monthly data on the number of infections after surgeries. These data are shown in Table 11.4. Hospital administrators are concerned about whether the high percentages of infections (such as 1.76 percent in month 12) are caused

Table 11.4 Monthly Data on Infections After Surgery

Month	Surgeries	Infections	Percent
1	208	1	0.48
2	225	3	1.33
3	201	3	1.49
4	236	1	0.42
5	220	3	1.36
6	244	1	0.41
7	247	1	0.40
8	245	1	0.41
9	250	1	0.40
10	227	0	0.00
11	234	2	0.85
12	227	4	1.76
13	213	2	0.94
14	212	1	0.47
15	193	2	1.04
16	182	0	0.00
17	140	1	0.71
18	230	1	0.43
19	187	1	0.53
20	252	2	0.79
21	201	1	0.50
22	226	0	0.00
23	222	2	0.90
24	212	2	0.94
25	219	1	0.46
26	223	2	0.90
27	191	1	0.52
28	222	0	0.00
29	231	3	1.30
30	239	1	0.42
31	217	2	0.92
32	241	1	0.41
33	220	3	1.36
34	278	1	0.36
35	255	3	1.18
36	225	1	0.44
	7,995	55	

by factors other than randomness. A control chart constructed from these data is shown in Figure 11.8. (Note that if the control limits are removed, it becomes a simple run chart.) The average percentage of infections is 55/7995 = 0.688 percent. Using formulas described in Chapter 13, the upper control limit is computed to be 2.35 percent. None of the data points fall above the upper control limit, indicating that the variation each month is due purely to chance and that the process is stable. To reduce the infection rate, management would have to attack the common causes in the process. The upper control limit would be a logical TFE to use, because any value beyond this limit is unlikely to occur by chance. Management can continue to use this chart to monitor future data.

Check Sheets Check sheets are simple tools for data collection. Nearly any kind of form may be used to collect data. **Data sheets** use simple columnar or tabular forms

Figure 11.8 Control Chart for Surgery Infections

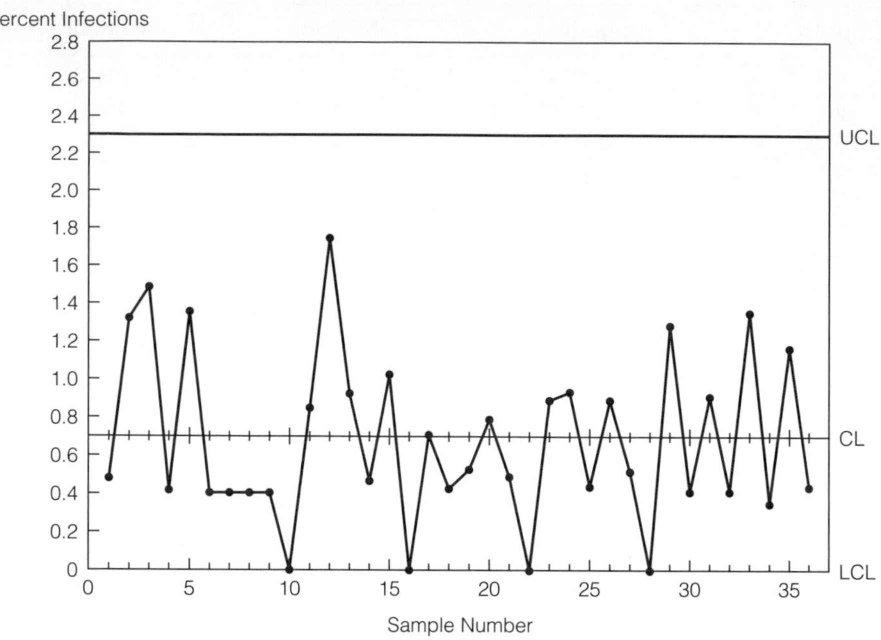

to record data. However, to generate useful information from raw data, further processing generally is necessary.

In manufacturing, check sheets similar to Figure 11.9 are simple to use and easily interpreted by shop personnel. Including information such as specification limits makes the number of nonconforming items easily observable and provides an immediate indication of the quality of the process. For example, in Figure 11.9 a significant proportion of dimensions are clearly out of specification, with a larger number on the high side than the low side.

> ***Check sheets*** *are special types of data collection forms in which the results may be interpreted on the form directly without additional processing.*

A second type of check sheet for defective items is illustrated in Figure 11.10, which shows the type of defect and a tally in a resin production plant. Such a check sheet can be extended to include a time dimension so that data can be monitored and analyzed over time, and trends and patterns, if any, can be detected.

Figure 11.11 shows an example of a defect location check sheet. Kaoru Ishikawa relates how this check sheet was used to eliminate bubbles in laminated automobile windshield glass.[26] The location and form of bubbles were indicated on the check sheet; most of the bubbles occurred on the right side. Upon investigation, workers discovered that the pressure applied in laminating was off balance—the right side was receiving less pressure. The machine was adjusted, and the formation of bubbles was eliminated almost completely.

Histograms A **histogram** is a basic statistical tool that graphically shows the frequency or number of observations of a particular value or within a specified group. The check sheet in Figure 11.9, for example, was designed to provide the visual

Figure 11.9 Check Sheet for Data Collection

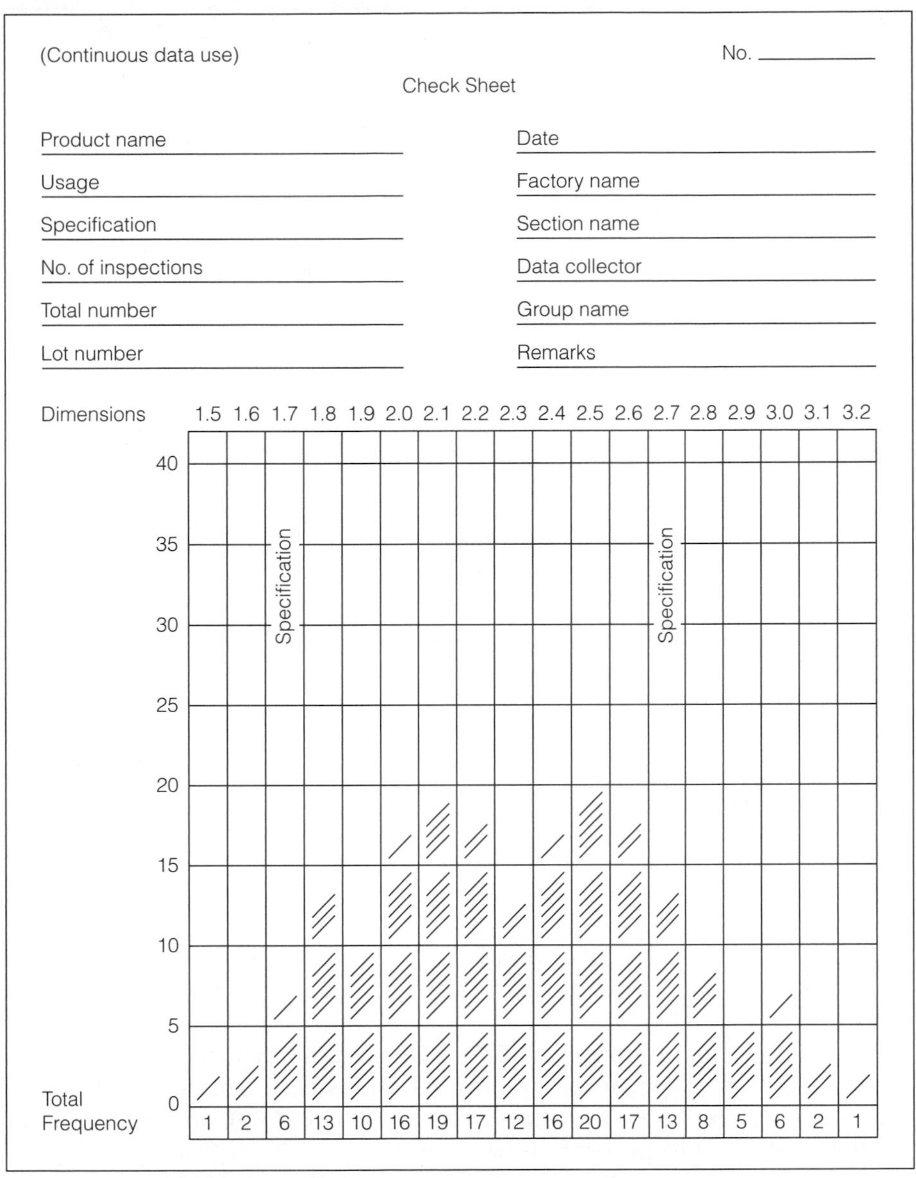

(Continuous data use) No. ______

Check Sheet

Product name ______ Date ______

Usage ______ Factory name ______

Specification ______ Section name ______

No. of inspections ______ Data collector ______

Total number ______ Group name ______

Lot number ______ Remarks ______

Dimensions	1.5	1.6	1.7	1.8	1.9	2.0	2.1	2.2	2.3	2.4	2.5	2.6	2.7	2.8	2.9	3.0	3.1	3.2
Total Frequency	1	2	6	13	10	16	19	17	12	16	20	17	13	8	5	6	2	1

Source: K. Ishkawa ed., Guide to Quality Control, 2nd rev., 1982, p. 31 Copyright © 1982 Asian Productivity Organization, Tokyo. Reprinted by permission.

appeal of a histogram as the data are tallied. For these data, one can easily determine the proportion of observations that fell outside the specification limits.

Histograms provide clues about the characteristics of the parent population from which a sample is taken. Patterns that would be difficult to see in an ordinary table of numbers become apparent.

Some cautions should be heeded when interpreting histograms. First, the data should be representative of typical process conditions. If a new employee is now operating the equipment, or some aspect of the equipment, material, or method has changed, then new data should be collected. Second, the sample size should be large

Figure 11.10 Defective Item Check Sheet

Check Sheet

Product:

Manufacturing stage: final insp.

Type of defect: scar, incomplete, misshapen

Total no. inspected: 2530

Remarks: all items inspected

Date:

Factory:

Section:

Inspector's name:

Lot no.

Order no.

Type	Check	Subtotal
Surface scars	~~////~~ ~~////~~ ~~////~~ ~~////~~ ~~////~~ ~~////~~ //	32
Cracks	~~////~~ ~~////~~ ~~////~~ ~~////~~ ///	23
Incomplete	~~////~~ ~~////~~ ~~////~~ ~~////~~ ~~////~~ ~~////~~ ~~////~~ ~~////~~ ~~////~~ ///	48
Misshapen	////	4
Others	~~////~~ ///	8
	Grand total	115
Total rejects	~~////~~ ~~////~~ ~~////~~ ~~////~~ ~~////~~ ~~////~~ ~~////~~ ~~////~~ ~~////~~ ~~////~~ ~~////~~ ~~////~~ ~~////~~ ~~////~~ ~~////~~ ~~////~~ ~~////~~ /	86

Source: K. Ishkawa ed., Guide to Quality Control, 2nd rev., 1982, p. 33. Copyright © 1982 Asian Productivity Organization, Tokyo. Reprinted by permission.

enough to provide good conclusions; the larger, the better. Various guidelines exist, but a suggested minimum of at least 50 observations should be drawn. Finally, any conclusions drawn should be confirmed through further study and analysis.

Pareto Diagrams Joseph Juran popularized the Pareto principle in 1950 after observing that a high proportion of quality issues resulted from only a few causes. He named this technique after Vilfredo Pareto (1848–1923), an Italian economist who determined that 85 percent of the wealth in Milan was owned by only 15 percent of the people. For instance, in analyzing costs in a paper mill, Juran found that 61 percent of total quality costs were attributable to one category—"broke," which is paper mill terminology for paper so defective that it is returned for reprocessing. In an analysis of 200 types of field failures of automotive engines, only five accounted for one-third of all failures; the top 25 accounted for two-thirds of the failures. In a textile mill, three of fifteen weavers were found to account for 74 percent of the defective cloth produced. Pareto analysis clearly separates the vital few from the trivial many and provides direction for selecting projects for improvement.

*A **Pareto distribution** is one in which the characteristics observed are ordered from largest frequency to smallest. A **Pareto diagram** is a histogram of the data from the largest frequency to the smallest.*

Figure 11.11 Defect Location Check Sheet

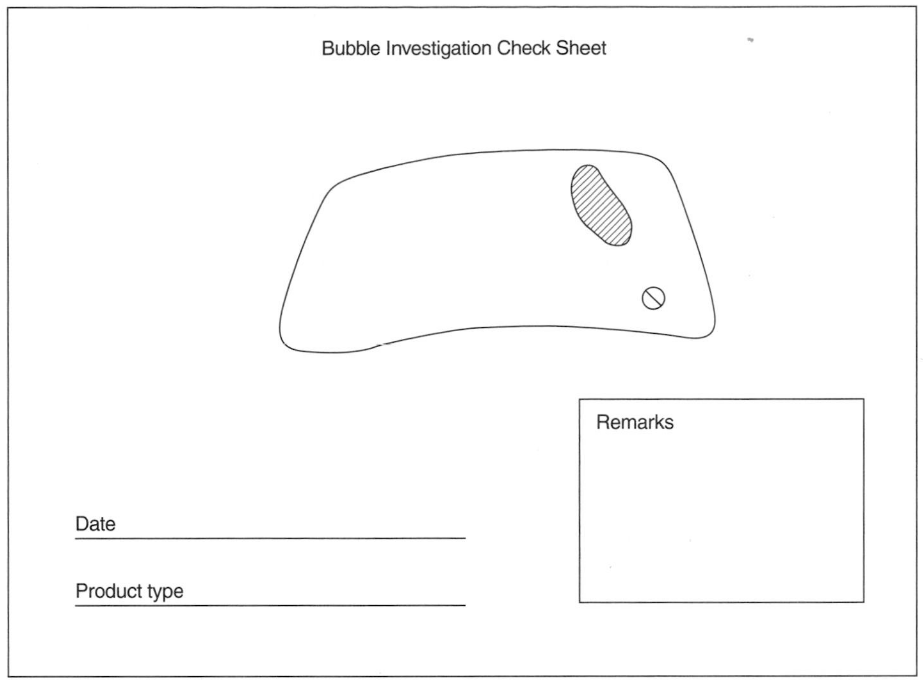

Source: K. Ishkawa ed., *Guide to Quality Control*, 2nd rev., 1982, p. 34. Copyright © 1982 Asian Productivity Organization, Tokyo. Reprinted by permission.

Pareto analysis is often used to analyze data collected in check sheets. One may also draw a cumulative frequency curve on the histogram, as shown in Figure 11.12. Such a visual aid clearly shows the relative magnitude of defects and can be used to identify opportunities for improvement. The most costly or significant problems stand out. Pareto diagrams can also show the results of improvement programs over time. They are less intimidating to employees who are fearful of statistics.

A good example of Pareto analysis is found at Rotor Clip Company, Inc., of Somerset, New Jersey, a major manufacturer of retaining rings and self-tightening hose clamps, and a believer in the use of simple quality improvement tools.[27] One application involved the use of a Pareto diagram to study rising premium freight charges for shipping retaining rings. The study covered three months in order to collect enough data to draw conclusions. The Pareto diagram is shown in Figure 11.13. The results were startling. The most frequent cause of higher freight charges was customer requests. The decision was made to continue the study to identify which customers consistently expedited their shipments and to work closely with them to find ways of reducing costs. The second largest contributor was the lack of available machine time. Once a die was installed in a stamping press, it ran until it produced the maximum number of parts (usually a million) before it was removed for routine maintenance. Although this policy resulted in efficient utilization of tooling, it tied up the press and ultimately accounted for rush shipments. The policy was revised to limit die runs to fill orders more efficiently.

Pareto diagrams help analysts to progressively focus in on specific problems. Figure 11.14 shows one example. At each step, the Pareto diagram stratifies the data

Figure 11.12 Pareto Diagram

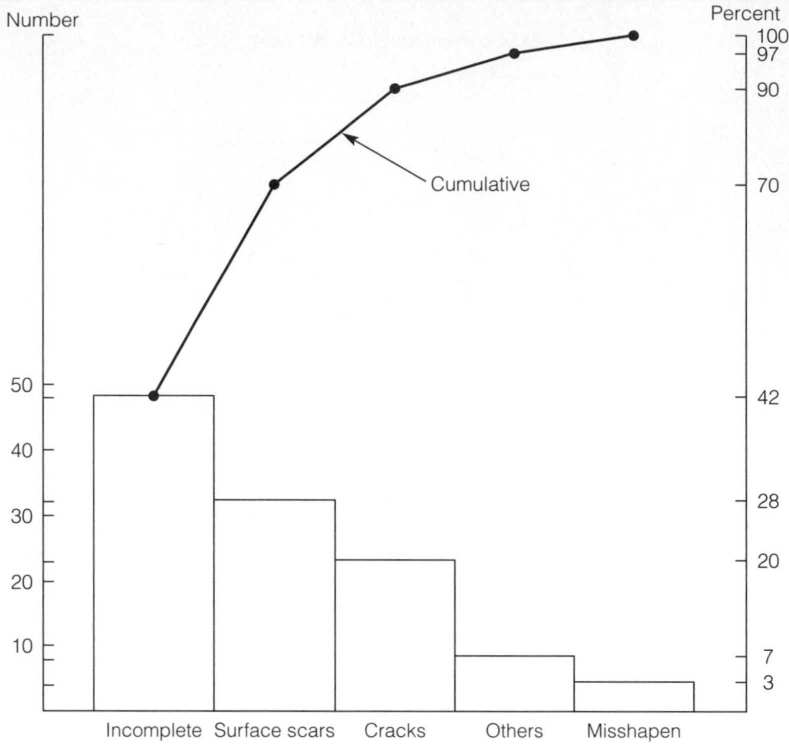

Source: Adapted from Bruce Rudin, "Simple Tools Solve Complex Problems," *Quality*, April 1990. Copyright © 1990 Hitchcock Publishing Company, a Capital/ABC, Inc., Company.

Figure 11.13 Pareto Diagram of Customer Calls

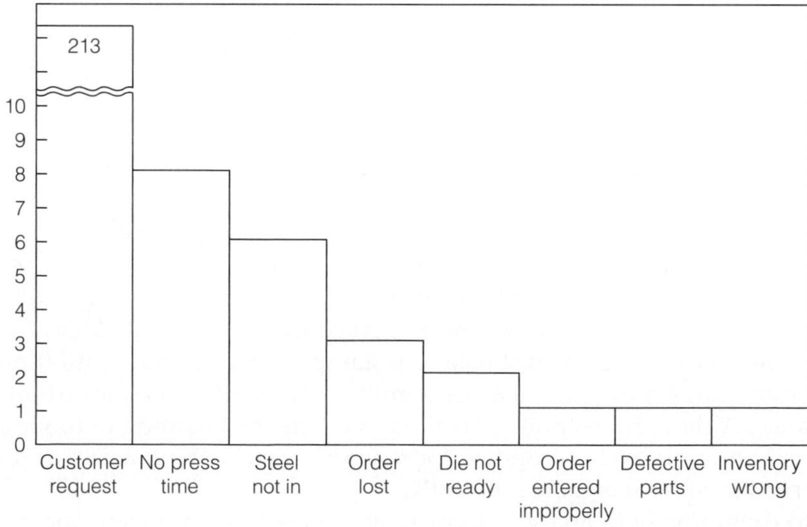

Figure 11.14 Use of Pareto Diagrams for Progressive Analysis

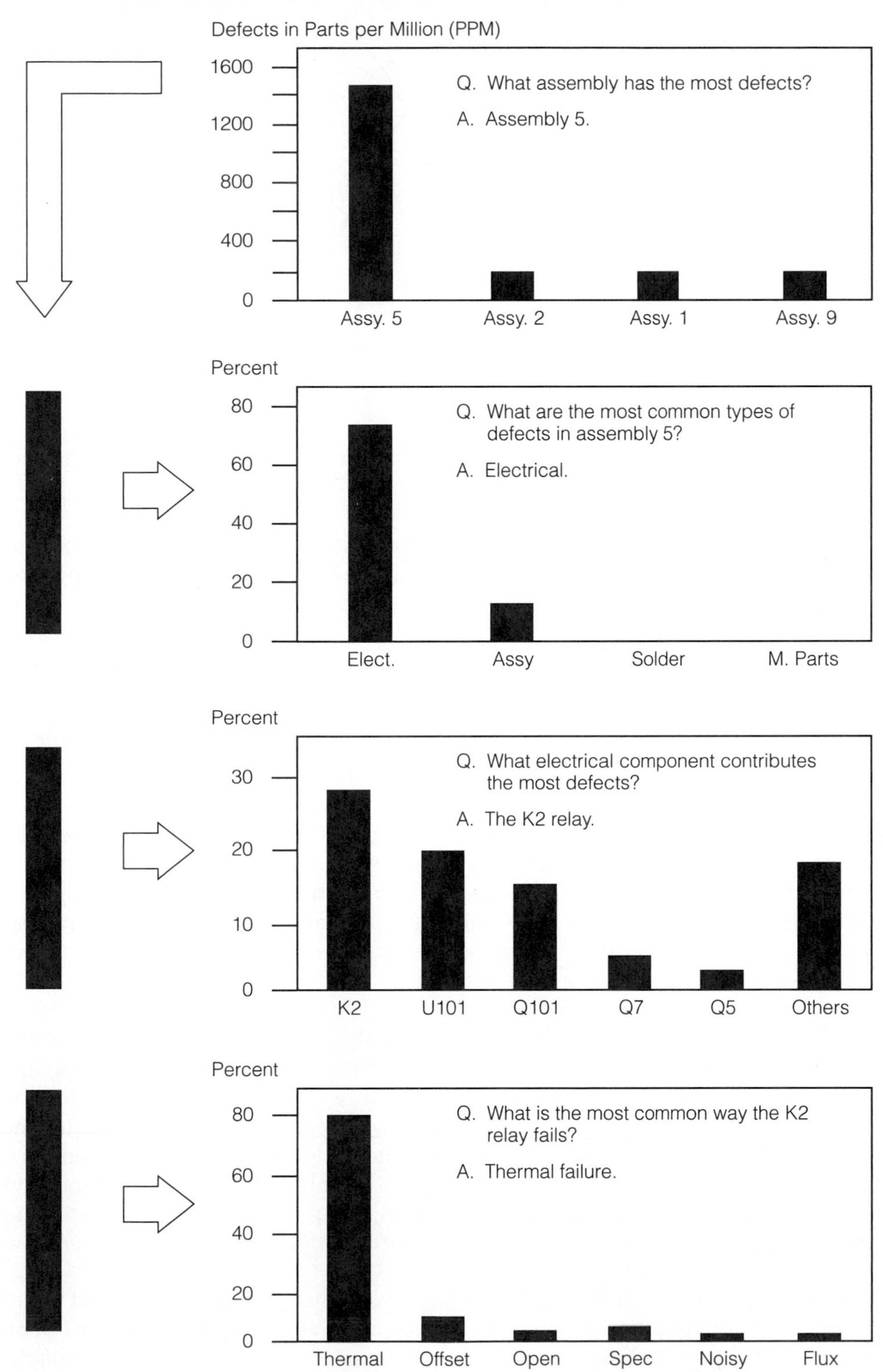

Source: Small Business Guidebook to Quality Management, Office of the Secretary of Defense, Quality Management Office, Washington, D.C.

Figure 11.15 General Structure of Cause-and-Effect Diagram

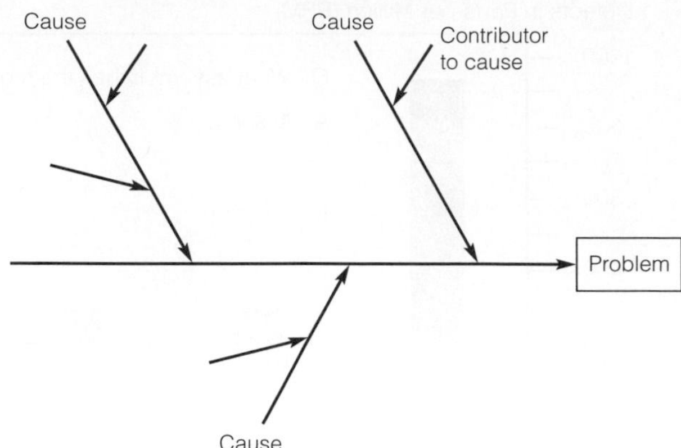

to more detailed levels (or it may require additional data collection), eventually isolating the most significant issues.

Cause-and-Effect Diagrams Variation in process output and other quality problems can occur for a variety of reasons, such as materials, machines, methods, people, and measurement. The goal of problem solving is to identify the causes of problems in order to correct them. The cause-and-effect diagram is an important tool in this task; it assists the generation of ideas for problem causes and, in turn, serves as a basis for solution finding.

*A **cause-and-effect diagram** is a simple graphical method for presenting a chain of causes and effects and for sorting out causes and organizing relationships between variables.*

Kaoru Ishikawa introduced the cause-and-effect diagram in Japan, so it is also called an Ishikawa diagram. Because of its structure, it is often called a *fishbone diagram*. The general structure of a cause-and-effect diagram is shown in Figure 11.15. At the end of the horizontal line, a problem is listed. Each branch pointing into the main stem represents a possible cause. Branches pointing to the causes are contributors to those causes. The diagram identifies the most likely causes of a problem so that further data collection and analysis can be carried out.

Cause-and-effect diagrams are constructed in a brainstorming type of atmosphere. Everyone can get involved and feel they are an important part of the problem-solving process. Usually small groups drawn from operations or management work with a trained and experienced facilitator. The facilitator guides attention to discussion of the problem and its causes, not opinions. As a group technique, the cause-and-effect method requires significant interaction between group members. The facilitator who listens carefully to the participants can capture the important ideas. A group can often be more effective by thinking of the problem broadly and considering environmental factors, political factors, employee issues, and even government policies, if appropriate.

To illustrate a cause-and-effect diagram, a major hospital was concerned about the length of time required to get a patient from the emergency department to an inpatient bed. Significant delays appeared to be caused by beds not being available. A quality improvement team tackled this problem by developing a cause-and-effect diagram. They identified four major causes: environmental services, emergency

Figure 11.16 Cause-and-Effect Diagram for Hospital Emergency Admission Problem

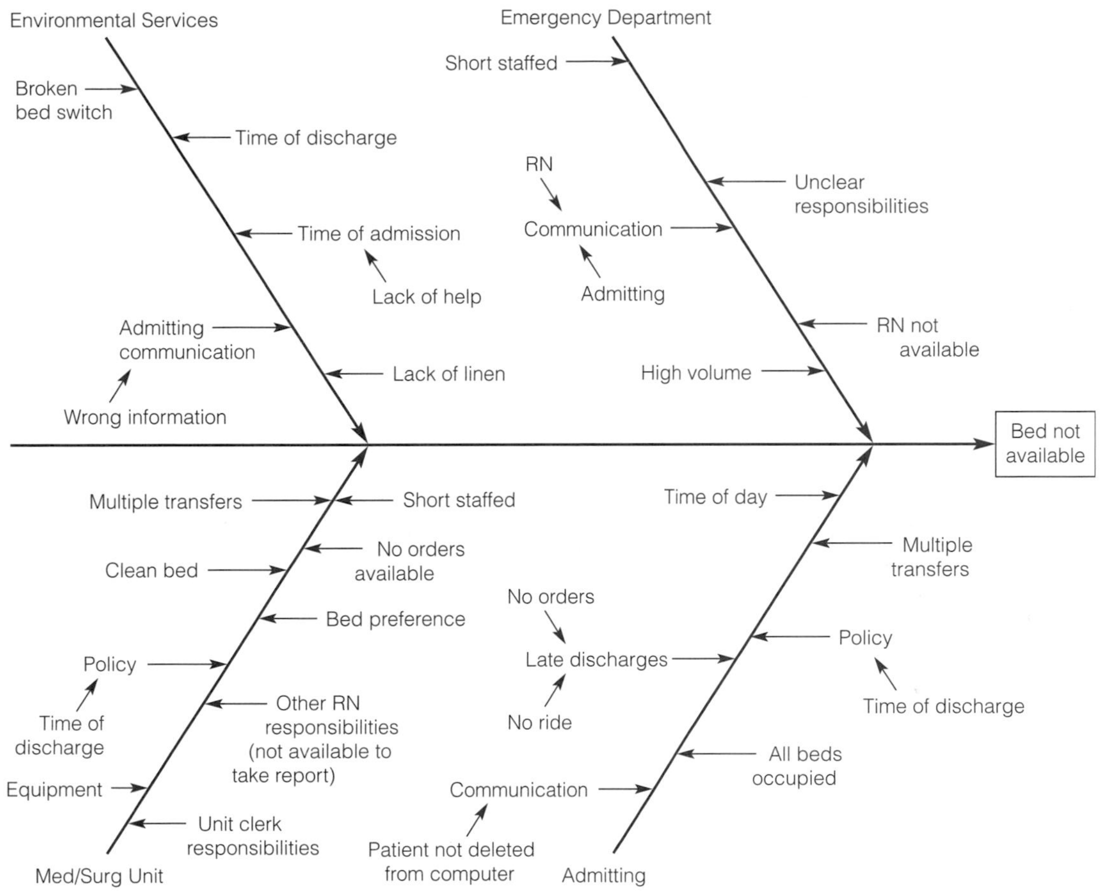

department, medical/surgery unit, and admitting. Figure 11.16 shows the diagram with several potential causes in each category. It served as a basis for further investigations of contributing factors and data analysis to find the root cause of the problem.

Scatter Diagrams **Scatter diagrams** are the graphical component of regression analysis. Even though they do not provide rigorous statistical analysis, they often point to important relationships between variables, such as the percentage of an ingredient in an alloy and the hardness of the alloy. Typically, the variables in question represent possible causes and effects obtained from Ishikawa diagrams. For example, if a manufacturer suspects that the percentage of an ingredient in an alloy is causing quality problems in meeting hardness specifications, an employee group might collect data from samples on the amount of ingredient and hardness and plot the data on a scatter diagram.

Statistical correlation analysis is used to interpret scatter diagrams. Figure 11.17 shows three types of correlation. If the correlation is positive, an increase in variable x is related to an increase in variable y; if the correlation is negative, an increase in x is related to a decrease in y; and if the correlation is close to zero, the variables have no linear relationship.

Figure 11.17 Three Types of Correlation

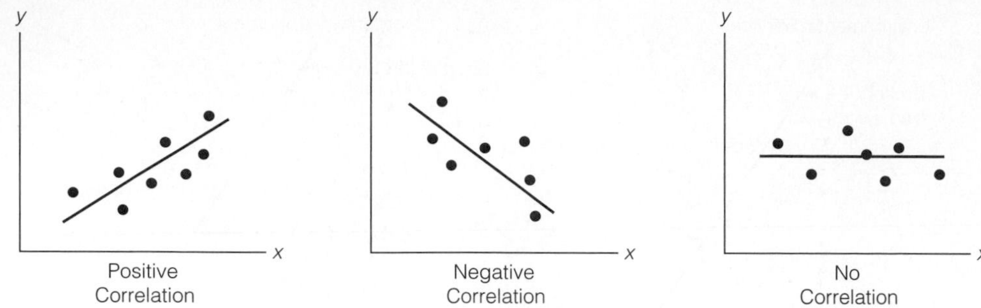

At Rotor Clip, which we highlighted earlier, the effect of advertising expenditures on the bottom line had been difficult to assess.[28] Management wanted to learn whether the number of advertising dollars spent correlated with the number of new customers gained in a given year. Advertising dollars spent by quarter were plotted against the number of new customers added for the same period for three consecutive years (see Figure 11.18). The positive correlation showed that heavy advertising was related to new customers. The results were fairly consistent from year to year except for the second quarter of the third year, in which an outlier clearly stood out from the rest. Advertising checked the media schedule and discovered that experimental image ads dominated that particular period. This discovery prompted the advertising department to eliminate image ads from its schedule.

Lean Tools

Lean production refers to approaches that originated at the Ford Motor Company in the early 1900s, but which were refined and modernized by the Toyota Motor Corporation later in the century. Lean approaches focus on the elimination of waste in all forms, including defects requiring rework, unnecessary processing

Figure 11.18 Scatter Diagram of New Customers Versus Advertising Dollars

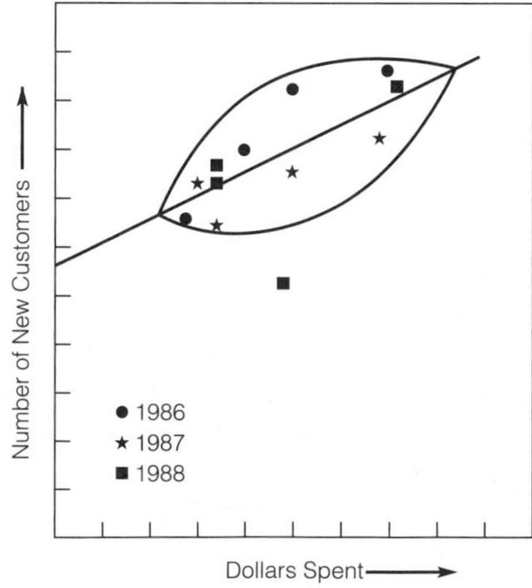

A Toyota assembly plant fairly hums: Every movement has a purpose, and there is no slack. Tour a typical auto plant, and you see stacks of half-finished parts, assembly lines halted for adjustment, workers standing idle. At Toyota the workers look like dancers in a choreographed production: retrieving parts, installing them, checking the quality, and doing it all in immaculate surroundings.[29]

steps, unnecessary movement of materials or people, waiting time, excess inventory, and overproduction. A simple way of defining it is "getting more done with less."[30] It involves identifying and eliminating non-value-added activities throughout the entire value chain to achieve faster customer response, reduced inventories, higher quality, and better human resources. As one article about Toyota observed, to see the Toyota production system in action is to "behold a thing of beauty."

Lean production is facilitated by a focus on measurement and continuous improvement, cross-trained workers, flexible and increasingly automated equipment, efficient machine layout, rapid setup and changeover, just-in-time delivery and scheduling, realistic work standards, worker empowerment to perform inspections and take corrective action, supplier partnerships, and preventive maintenance. Some of the benefits claimed by proponents of lean production include the following:

- At least 60 percent reduction in cycle times
- 40 percent improvement in space utilization
- 25 percent greater throughput
- 50 percent reduction in work-in-process and finished goods inventories
- 50 percent improvement in quality
- 20 percent improvements in working capital and worker productivity

However, as one industry expert observed, it takes "an incredible amount of detailed planning, discipline, hard work, and painstaking attention to detail." Surveys have noted that midsized and large companies are likely to be familiar with lean principles and have systems in place; however, few small manufacturing shops have much familiarity with the principles. Thus, considerable opportunity exists for this important economic sector.

Some of the key tools used in lean production include:

- *The 5S's*. The 5S's are derived from Japanese terms: *seiri* (sort), *seiton* (set in order), *seiso* (shine), *seiketsu* (standardize), and *shitsuke* (sustain). They define a system for workplace organization and standardization. Sort refers to ensuring that each item in a workplace is in its proper place or identified as unnecessary and removed. Set in order means to arrange materials and equipment so that they are easy to find and use. Shine refers to a clean work area. Not only is this important for safety, but as a work area is cleaned, maintenance problems such as oil leaks can be identified before they cause problems. Standardize means to formalize procedures and practices to create consistency and ensure that all steps are performed correctly. Finally, sustain means to keep the process going through training, communication, and organizational structures.
- *Visual controls*. Visual controls are indicators for tools, parts, and production activities that are placed in plain sight of all workers so that everyone can understand the status of the system at a glance. Thus, if a machine goes down, or a part is defective or delayed, immediate action can be taken.
- *Efficient layout and standardized work*. The layout of equipment and processes is designed according to the best operational sequence, by physically linking and arranging machines and process steps most efficiently, often in a cellular

arrangement. Standardizing the individual tasks by clearly specifying the proper method reduces wasted human movement and energy.

- *Pull production.* In this system (also described as kanban or just-in-time), upstream suppliers do not produce until the downstream customer signals a need for parts.
- *Single minute exchange of dies (SMED).* SMED refers to rapid changeover of tooling and fixtures in machine shops so that multiple products in smaller batches can be run on the same equipment. Reducing setup time adds value to the operation and facilitates smoother production flow.
- *Total productive maintenance.* Total productive maintenance is designed to ensure that equipment is operational and available when needed.
- *Source inspection.* Inspection and control by process operators guarantees that product passed on to the next production stage conforms to specifications.
- *Continuous improvement.* Continuous improvement provides the link to Six Sigma. In order to make lean production work, one must get to the root causes of problems and permanently remove them. Teamwork is an integral part of continuous improvement in lean environments. Many techniques that we discuss in subsequent chapters are used.

Sunset Manufacturing

One example of the application of lean concepts is found at Sunset Manufacturing, Inc., of Tualatin, Oregon, a 35-person, family-owned machine shop.[31] Because of competitive pressures and a business downturn, Sunset began to look for ways to simplify operations and cut costs. They established a lean steering committee to coordinate and drive the process. The committee chartered a kaizen team to reduce setup time on vertical milling machines by 50 percent. The team used SMED and the 5S's approach as their basic tools. Several actions were taken, including (1) standardizing parts across milling machines, (2) reorganizing the tool room, (3) incorporating the SMED approach in machine setups, and (4) and implementing what was termed "dance cards," which gave operators the specific steps required for the SMED of various machines and products. The results were impressive. Tool preparation time dropped from an average of 30 minutes to less than 10 minutes, isolation and identification of worn tools was improved, safety enhancement and orderliness in the tool room due to 5S's application was apparent, and machine setup time was reduced from an average of 216 minutes to 36 minutes (an 86 percent improvement). Estimated savings were $33,000 per year, with an implementation cost of less than half of that amount. The net impact was to allow smaller lots to be run, a 75 percent reduction in setup scrap, emergence of a more competitive organization, and a morale boost for team members.

Lean tools can easily be applied to nonmanufacturing environments. Pure service firms such as banks, hospitals, and restaurants have benefited from lean principles. In these contexts, lean production is often called **lean enterprise**. For example, banks require quick response and efficiency to operate on low margins, making many of their processes, such as check sorting and mortgage approval, natural candidates for lean enterprise solutions. Handling of paper checks and credit card slips, for instance, involves a physical process not unlike an assembly line. The faster a bank moves checks through its system, the sooner it can collect its funds and the better its returns on invested capital.

One North American financial institution applied lean enterprise principles to check processing operations.[32] They followed one check as it made its way through the bank's systems, documenting the time spent in actual processing and in waiting, rework, and handling. They found that almost half of the bank's processing capacity was consumed by nonprocessing activities such as fixing jams and setting up machines. Further investigation revealed wide variations in productivity between individual operators on a single shift. When the work practices of the least and most productive operators were compared, it became evident that although all were engaged in the same task, differences in the way they performed it were creating huge swings in productivity.

To adopt a lean manufacturing approach, the bank first matched the flow of incoming checks to processing capacity. At the end of each business day, the check processing operation was swamped with more checks than it could handle; this bottleneck created the false impression that capacity was constrained. The bank applied just-in-time principles to the processing of incoming checks and spread the check flow evenly through the day. A second bottleneck occurred at the beginning of the day; standard practice dictated that all checks presented for morning processing were sorted three times. This process prevented the processing operation from handling the morning check volume in time to meet the account posting deadline. However, many of the checks did not need to be completed by the morning deadline, and once the sorting of these low-priority items was shifted to later in the day when volumes were lower, capacity increased by 122 percent.

By uncovering and freeing up "phantom" capacity that had previously been taken up by waiting time, maintenance, and rework, they could increase actual capacity by more than 25 percent without investing in additional equipment. The bank was able to both sell its services to other banks at an attractive price and to expand capacity during the most time-sensitive period of the day, when its services could be priced at a premium. In all, these one-off improvements resulted in a more than doubling of the margin contributed by the operation.

Metro Health Hospital[33]

Metro Health Hospital in Grand Rapids, Michigan, has successfully applied lean principles in its pharmacy services. The Metro pharmacy started with a modest goal of reducing the lead time for getting the first dose of a medication to a patient. The lead time was measured from the time an order arrived at the pharmacy to its delivery on the appropriate hospital floor. Using lean, the Metro pharmacy carefully laid out all the process steps involved in getting the first dose of the correct medication to the right patient. The pharmacy found that it had a 14-stage process with some unnecessary steps, resulting in a total lead time of 166 minutes. During the evaluation process, the pharmacy calculated that it took technicians an average of 1.5 minutes to locate a product. For a pharmacy operating around-the-clock and delivering more than 100,000 doses a month, time wasted in searching was costly to the organization. In fact, technicians were spending 77.4 percent of their time locating products; when a pharmacist needed a technician for clinical activities, the technician was usually off searching for a drug.

The lean teams outlined several non-value-added steps in the process, only one of which was out of the pharmacy's control (i.e., the time it took to transport the ordered medication, once filled, to the appropriate floor). Standardization was a key component of the redesign, especially with the process flow as it moved through the department. As a part of the standardization process, the pharmacy implemented two new counters: a "check" counter and a "to-go" counter. They put in a simple color system in which red indicated the check counter and green indicated the to-go counter. They decreased the number of distractions by implementing a "safe zone" where a pharmacist could check medications without being disturbed. Product no longer sits on the counter without a pharmacist knowing it's there, nor are there redundant steps between the delivery baskets and delivery carts. After the checkpoint, the medication automatically goes in the "to-go" area delivery bin. Overall, the pharmacy at Metro realized a 33-percent reduction in time to get medications to patients, and reduced the number of process steps from 14 to nine simply by removing non-value-added steps. Patients have experienced a 40-percent reduction in pharmacy-related medication errors, and the severity of those errors has decreased.

Lean Six Sigma

Six Sigma is a useful and complementary approach to lean production. For example, a cycle time reduction project might involve aspects of both. Lean tools might be applied to streamline an order entry process. This application leads to the discovery that significant rework occurs because of incorrect addresses, customer numbers, or shipping charges and results in high variation of processing time. Six Sigma tools might then be used to drill down to the root cause of the problems and identify a solution. Because of these similarities, many practitioners have begun to focus on **Lean Six Sigma**, drawing upon the best practices of both approaches. Both are driven by customer requirements, focus on real dollar savings, have the ability to make significant financial impacts on the organization, and can easily be used in non-manufacturing environments. Both use basic root cause, process, and data analysis techniques. An executive search firm, Avery Point Group, noted that more companies are looking for candidates who demonstrate a mix of lean and Six Sigma skills, even for companies that may not have a full-blown Six Sigma or lean deployment underway.[34]

However, some differences clearly exist between lean production and Six Sigma. First, they attack different types of problems. Lean production addresses visible problems in processes, for example, inventory, material flow, and safety. Six Sigma is more concerned with less visible problems, for example, variation in performance. In essence, lean is focused on efficiency by reducing waste and improving process flow, whereas Six Sigma is focused on effectiveness by reducing errors and defects. Another difference is that lean tools are more intuitive and easier to apply by anybody in the workplace, whereas many Six Sigma tools require advanced training and expertise of Black Belt or Master Black Belt specialists, or consultant equivalents. For example, the concept of the 5S's is easier to grasp than statistical methods. Thus, organizations might be well advised to start with basic lean principles and evolve toward more sophisticated Six Sigma approaches. However, it is important to integrate both approaches with a common goal—improving business results.

SIX SIGMA IN SERVICES AND SMALL ORGANIZATIONS

Although Six Sigma was developed in the manufacturing sector, it can easily be applied to a wide variety of transactional, administrative, and service areas.[35] In fact, it is generally agreed that 50 percent or more of the total savings opportunity in an organization lies outside of manufacturing. General Electric was one of the early organizations that understood that Six Sigma could be applied to any process that created defects, and introduced Six Sigma in GE Financial. Within the service sector, Six Sigma is beginning to be called **transactional Six Sigma**.

All Six Sigma projects have three key characteristics: a problem to be solved, a process in which the problem exists, and one or more measures that quantify the gap to be closed and can be used to monitor progress.

However, while Six Sigma applies equally well in service areas, it is true that services have some unique characteristics relative to manufacturing processes. First, the culture is usually less scientific and service employees typically do not think in terms of processes, measurements, and data. The processes are often invisible, complex, and not well defined or well documented. Also, the work typically requires considerable human intervention, such as customer interaction, underwriting or approval decisions, or manual report generation. These differences make opportunities difficult to identify, and projects difficult to define. Finally, similar service activities are often done in different ways. If you have three people doing the same job, perhaps in three different locations, it is unlikely that they will do the job in the same way.

Because service processes are largely people-driven, measurements are often nonexistent or ill-defined, because many believe that defects cannot be measured. Therefore, one must create measurement systems before collecting any data. Applying Six Sigma to services requires examination of four key measures of the performance:

- *Accuracy*, as measured by correct financial figures, completeness of information, or freedom from data errors
- *Cycle time*, which is a measure of how long it takes to do something, such as pay an invoice
- *Cost*, that is, the internal cost of process activities (in many cases, cost is largely determined by the accuracy and/or cycle time of the process; the longer it takes, and the more mistakes that have to be fixed, the higher the cost)
- *Customer satisfaction*, which is typically the primary measure of success

Fortunately, important similarities can be shown between manufacturing and nonmanufacturing processes. First, both types of processes have "hidden factories," those places where the defective "product" is sent to be reworked or scrapped (revised, corrected, or discarded in nonmanufacturing terms). Find the hidden factory and you also find opportunities to improve the process. Performing manual account reconciliation in accounting, revising budgets repeatedly until management will accept them, and making repeat sales calls to customers because all the information requested by the customer was not available are all examples of the hidden factory.

Consider how a janitorial service company might use DMAIC. In the Define stage, a key question would be to define what a defect represents. One might first create a flowchart of the cleaning process, specifying what activities are performed. One example of a defect might be leaving streaks on windows because it is a source of customer dissatisfaction, a CTQ. In the Measure stage, not only would the firm want to collect data on the frequency of defects, but also information about what products and tools employees use. The Analyze stage might include evaluating differences among employees to determine why some appear better at cleaning than others. Developing a standard operating procedure might be the focus of the Improve stage. Finally, Control might entail teaching employees the correct technique and measuring improvement over time.

In one application at CNH Capital, Six Sigma tools were applied to decrease asset management cycle time in posting repossessions to a bid list and remarketing website.[36] Cycle time was reduced 75 percent, from 40 days to 10 days, resulting in significant ongoing dollar savings. A facility management company had a high level of "days sales outstanding." Initially, they tried to fix this issue by reducing the term of days in its billing cycle, which, however, upset customers. Using Six Sigma, they found that a large percentage of accounts with high days sales outstanding received invoices having numerous errors. After understanding the source of the errors and making process changes, the invoice process improved and days sales outstanding was reduced. At DuPont, a Six Sigma project was applied to improve cycle time for an employee's application for long-term disability benefits.[37]

Some examples of financial applications of Six Sigma include the following:[38]

- Reduce the average and variation of days outstanding of accounts receivable.
- Close the books faster.
- Improve the accuracy and speed of the audit process.
- Reduce variation in cash flow.
- Improve the accuracy of journal entries (most businesses have a 3–4 percent error rate).
- Improve accuracy and cycle time of standard financial reports.

One large banking and financial services company, facing increasing customer dissatisfaction because of inefficiencies in international wire-transfer operations that increased the bank's costs—some of which were passed on to customers as transaction fees—applied Six Sigma to redesign the process, greatly reducing errors, customer callbacks, transfer delays, and transfer fees. Transfer cycle time was reduced 46 percent and the cost-per-payment order was reduced by more than 50 percent, enabling the bank to waive its transaction fees and improve customer satisfaction.[39]

Six Sigma is widely used in health care, but predominantly in nonmedical areas. Some of these include increasing capacity in the X-ray or surgical departments, reducing discharge delays, decreasing patient waiting time, reducing defects in billing or patient records, and so on. Medical professionals often ignore the potential of Six Sigma for improving what matters most—the quality of medical treatment and reduction of life-threatening errors.[40] Like other aspects of quality management, it is generally more difficult to engage professionals like physicians than support staff in such activities.

Government and other public agencies have been exploring the potential of Six Sigma in such services as water quality and distribution, electricity production, education, military operations, and even intelligence gathering. Because of the non-profit nature of government, the focus is not on increasing profits, but often revolves around improving cycle time and supply chain efficiency, which generally also lead to reduced costs. The city of Fort Wayne, Indiana, for example, began a Six Sigma initiative in 2000 and began training division and department managers. A Black Belt was appointed as the city's first quality enhancement manager, and soon other city employees received Black Belt training. The first projects included pothole repair and permitting. Using simple tools, the time to fix potholes was reduced from as much as four days to four hours, and the time to issue a permit was cut from 50 days to around 12. In the first five years, the city completed 60 Six Sigma projects and saved $10 million.[41]

Small organizations are often confused and intimidated by the size, costs, and extensive technical training they see in large organizations that implement "formal" Six Sigma processes. For this reason, they often don't even try to adopt these approaches. Small organizations are usually lean by necessity, but not always effectively so. Their processes often operate at quality levels of two to three sigma, and they are not even aware of it. Spanyi and Wurtzel provide some sage advice to small organizations thinking about adopting Six Sigma or lean production:[42]

- Obtain management commitment.
- Identify key processes and goals.
- Prioritize the improvement projects.
- Be systematic.
- Don't worry about training Black and Green Belts.
- Use just-in-time practices to learn the Six Sigma tools necessary to successfully carry out specific projects.
- Communicate successes and reward and recognize performers.

Small companies often need to bring in consultants for training or improvement initiatives in the early stages of learning. These types of initiatives can help to develop in-house expertise and put them on the right track.

SUMMARY OF KEY POINTS AND TERMINOLOGY

The Bonus Materials folder on the Premium website provides a summary of key concepts and terminology introduced in this chapter.

BONUS MATERIALS

QUALITY IN PRACTICE

AN APPLICATION OF SIX SIGMA TO REDUCE MEDICAL ERRORS[43]

Medication administration and laboratory processing/results reporting are examples of complex systems in health care that are known to be error prone. As described in the report of the National Academy of Sciences/Institute of Medicine, medication errors are a substantial source of preventable errors in hospitals, but result in part from poorly designed complex systems. At Froedtert Hospital in Milwaukee, Wisconsin, errors with IV medication drips and laboratory processing and results reporting were well documented. Additionally, errors in ordering, transporting, analyzing, and reporting clinical laboratory tests were known to be a significant source of error at the hospital. It is for these reasons that these two areas were targeted for initial study.

A consortium was created by four Milwaukee-based organizations committed to the development of an approach to reduce errors and improve patient safety. The consortium members include the Medical College of Wisconsin, Froedtert Memorial Lutheran Hospital, the American Society for Quality, and SecurTrac, a company formed specifically to develop technologies to improve patient safety. The consortium is currently addressing three major efforts: (1) improved identification and reporting of health care errors, (2) deployment of the Six Sigma methodology to reduce errors, and (3) testing and implementation of technical solutions to improve patient safety. At the center of this approach is the effort to determine whether the Six Sigma error reduction methodology can be successfully applied in health care.

Using Six Sigma methods and selected statistical tools, Froedtert Hospital's processes for medication delivery were evaluated with the goal of designing an approach that would decrease the likelihood of errors. The design employed the classic Six Sigma process steps. A multidisciplinary group of physicians, nurses, pharmacists, and administrators identified medication delivery by continuous IV infusions as a process subject to substantial error. Continuous IV infusions are used in many clinical settings and errors can severely impact patient well-being. Initially, the focus was on five specific IV medications. Soon it was realized that the number was too small to permit quantification of error rates. The scope of the project was expanded to 22 medications delivered by continuous IV infusion. Team members developed a process map (flowchart) to delineate each step in the procedure for continuous IV medication infusion. The process map revealed nine steps: (1) physician order, (2) order review, (3) pharmacist order entry, (4) dose preparation, (5) dose dispensing, (6) infusion rate calculation, (7) IV pump setup, (8) pump programming, and (9) pump monitoring.

Each of the steps was subjected to a failure modes and effect analysis (FMEA—see Chapter 12) and scored on a scale of 1 to 10 for three categories: frequency of occurrence, detectability, and severity. The scores were multiplied together to yield a risk priority number (RPN) for each step. Eighteen months of retrospective medication error reports were reviewed to provide additional data for the RPN calculation. This review confirmed the FMEA results that IV rate calculations and IV pump setup were the two most error-prone steps in the IV infusion process. Initial efforts to delineate and reduce errors focused on these two steps.

Because it was not known how often errors went unrecognized or unreported, an audit was conducted to determine whether the prescribed dose rate matched the actual infusion rate.

Two weeks of audit data were collected and the resulting 124 data points were rated on a discrepancy scale of 1 to 3 (1 for a ≤1 ml/hr discrepancy, 2 for a 1–5 ml/hr discrepancy, 3 for a ≥5ml/hr discrepancy). Ten of the audits were rated at level 2 and four were rated at level 3. Root cause analysis was employed to determine the cause of the discrepancies. Work was then begun to affect the accuracy of infusion rates.

Using Six Sigma methods and statistical tools, the team also examined the hospital's clinical laboratory process. Key elements in the acquisition, laboratory analysis, and reporting of patient specimens were identified. The steps included (1) physician order, (2) order entry, (3) matching the order to the patient, (4) collecting the specimen, (5) labeling the specimen, (6) transporting the specimen, (7) analyzing the specimen, (8) reporting the results, and (9) entering the results into the patient's chart. Each of these steps is subject to error. Applying Six Sigma analysis, the steps subject to the most errors were identified. These steps were: order entry by the unit clerical staff, transportation of the specimens to the lab, and analysis of specimens in the lab. To identify, define, and reduce these errors, a laboratory error reduction task force was established. It included members from administration, lab, nursing, clerical staff, information systems, and quality management. The task force first developed a process map so that all members could appreciate the complexity and vulnerability of the entire process. The process map provided the task force with the tools to analyze the clinical laboratory problem in depth. The FMEA technique was employed to arrive at a risk priority number (RPN) so that steps in the laboratory analysis process could be prioritized in terms of their vulnerability to error. Again, order entry, transportation, and analysis of specimens were identified. Statistical tools, including correlation and regression, analysis of variance, confidence intervals, and hypothesis testing, were employed to evaluate the laboratory process further.

The analysis of medication delivery by IV infusions served as a good example of deployment of Six Sigma methodology to reduce error and improve patient safety in a health care setting. Significant variability in the ordering and processing of IV drips was identified. Lack of standardization in many steps of the process posed the greatest risk for system failure. Those steps with the highest degree of variability and the greatest chance for error were

1. MD ordering practices (i.e., lack of standardization in medication description, dosage, concentration, etc.)
2. IV drip preparation (lack of standardization by pharmacy and nursing of IV bag concentrations)
3. RN labeling and documentation of IV concentrations

In these three areas, a multidisciplinary task force created standards to reduce variation. Specific interventions included implementation of standardized physician order sheets, a policy requiring preparation of all IV medications in a standard concentration, and use of color-coded labels when nonstandard concentrations were in use. Thirty days after implementation, measurable improvement was evident. Level 1 discrepancies fell from 47.4 percent to 14 percent. Level 2 discrepancies fell from 21.1 percent to 11.8 percent and level 3 discrepancies fell from 15.8 percent to 2.9 percent. Though far from achieving a six sigma level of performance, substantial efforts continue to move toward that goal.

The laboratory project proved to be more complex. It was evident early on that the scope of this complex system was too broad for an initial effort. The project was broken down into smaller individual steps of the larger process. Once refocused, the appointed task force identified opportunities to reduce variation in select steps of the laboratory process. Alternate means of identifying specimens, changes in the approach to "point of care" laboratory analysis, decentralization of some laboratory tests, and a revised system to order and process stat lab tests was put into place. Effectiveness monitoring continues as does measurement of sustainable error reductions. These efforts marked the beginning of a long laboratory redesign process aimed at driving out error, reducing turnaround time, and improving patient safety.

Key Issues for Discussion

1. How did the team use process mapping as a key part of the Six Sigma process? What value did process mapping have?
2. Why were the teams and task forces multidisciplinary in nature? What benefits does this approach have?

QUALITY IN PRACTICE

APPLYING QUALITY IMPROVEMENT TOOLS TO AN ORDER FULFILLMENT PROCESS[44]

This case study involves a large automotive parts distribution center in Europe. Car dealerships and repair garages from several countries call in orders for replacement parts needed to repair various types of motor vehicles. When an order is received, the distribution center must quickly locate the requested parts and ship them to the repair facility. Time is of the essence because car owners typically become increasingly upset the longer their vehicles are out of service.

Because the distribution center was having trouble shipping orders on time, many of its customers were unhappy and threatening to switch to other part distributors. To appease these customers, the manager of the center promised all orders would be delivered within 24 hours or the customer would get the parts at no charge. The manager then assembled a team to discover ways to reduce order processing time so at least 98 percent of orders would meet the 24-hour deadline.

To better understand the situation, the team decided to draw a map showing how an order was received, filled, checked, packed, and finally shipped to the customer. After discussing the required steps and actually following an order from start to finish, the team created a flowchart of the entire order fulfillment process. The diagram, which is shown in Figure 11.19, identifies those activities the team had the power to change and, it was hoped, improve. This type of layout also encouraged every team member to focus on the big picture rather than on only the particular activity in which he or she worked.

To determine where the longest time delays were occurring, the team randomly chose 50 orders from those received during a one-week period. As members tracked these selected orders through the distribution center, they noted the time each entered and left the various activity areas appearing on the flowchart. To ensure these times were accurately and consistently recorded, the team designed the check sheet shown in Figure 11.20. One sheet was used per order, with the completion time for a given activity computed by subtracting its in time from its out time. For example, order XR-03018 began the "pack parts" activity at 2:16 P.M. and finished at 2:34 P.M. Therefore, the time to complete this particular activity was 18 minutes (2:34–2:16). At the end of the week, the average completion time for each activity was calculated by adding its 50 completion times—one for each of the 50 orders tracked—and dividing this total by 50. When these average times were analyzed with the Pareto diagram in Figure 11.21, picking time was identified as the largest contributor to order processing delays, representing about 52 percent of the total time needed to process an order.

Figure 11.19 Flowchart for the Order Fulfillment Process

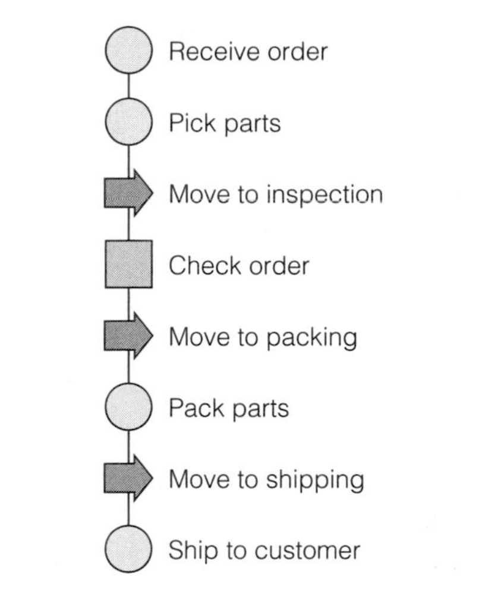

Source: Reprinted with permission from Davis R. Bothe, "Improve Service and Administration," *Quality Progress*, September 2003, pp. 53–57. Copyright © 2003. No further distribution allowed without permission.

Based on this new information, the team refined its original mission statement, "Reduce the time for processing an order," to the more specific, "Reduce the time for picking parts." With the scope of the search narrowed to just the picking operation, members invited some of the part pickers to join the team because these personnel were the local experts in picking parts and possessed the most knowledge about the function.

To provide a more detailed analysis of the picking operation, the 50 individual times recorded for picking orders (one from each of the 50 check sheets collected during the team's earlier study) were plotted on the histogram in Figure 11.22. The shape of

Figure 11.20 Check Sheet for Recording Times

Order # XR=03018 Recorder Robert
Date 16 Dec Comments

Activity	In	Out	Completion
Receive order	1:24	1:31	7
Pick parts	1:32	1:51	19
Move to inspection	1:52	2:03	11
Check order	2:04	2:10	6
Move to packing	2:11	2:15	4
Pack parts	2:16	2:34	18
Move to shipping	2:35	2:38	3

Source: Reprinted with permission from Davis R. Bothe, "Improve Service and Administration," *Quality Progress*, September 2003, pp. 53–57.

the histogram—having three humps—was an initial surprise because it implied the existence of three distinct clusters of picking times. With this valuable clue in mind, the team now concentrated on what could be responsible for these three separate time groups.

During a brainstorming session, a part picker suggested the three humps of the histogram reflected the number of trips made to the parts storage area of the distribution center to complete an order.

Figure 11.21 Pareto Diagram for Average Time of Each Activity

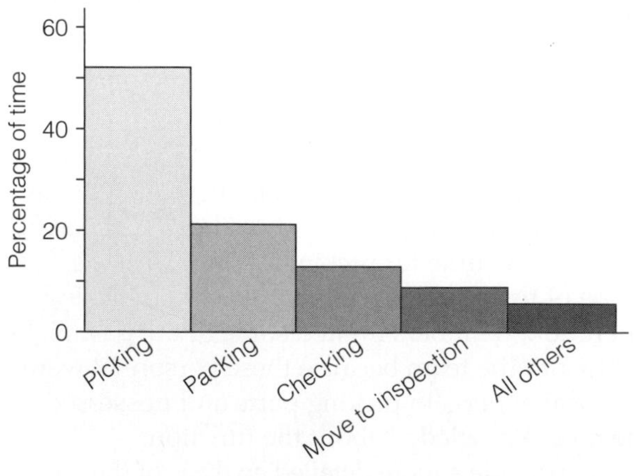

Source: Reprinted with permission from Davis R. Bothe, "Improve Service and Administration," *Quality Progress*, September, 2003, pp. 53–57.

Figure 11.22 Histogram of Picking Times

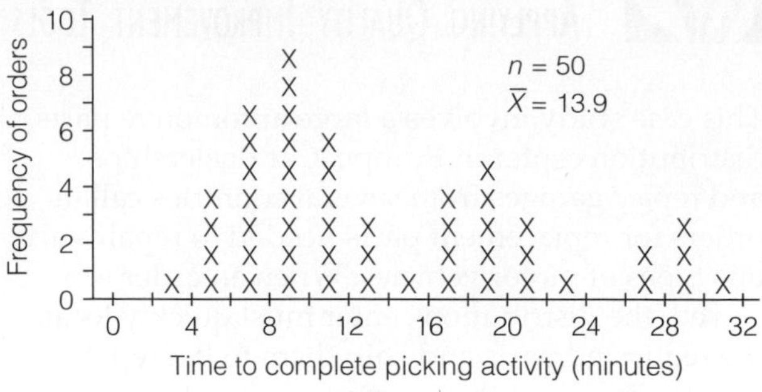

Source: Reprinted with permission from Davis R. Bothe, "Improve Service and Administration," *Quality Progress*, September 2003, pp. 53–57.

He explained that many orders were filled with just one trip, but two were sometimes required and, on occasion, even three. Thus, the left hump could consist of times an order was completed with only one trip, the middle could represent those requiring two, whereas the third could be those in which three trips were needed. By watching the part picking activity for two days, the team members could verify the part picker's theory was indeed correct.

Armed with this additional insight, the team brainstormed reasons multiple trips were needed to complete an order and then organized these ideas on the cause-and-effect diagram in Figure 11.23. After discussion, the team eventually decided the push carts used by the part pickers to carry the parts were too small (see the equipment branch of Figure 11.23). When part pickers were gathering parts to fill a large order, the cart became full long before all the needed parts were gathered. The picker had to travel to the inspection area to empty the cart and make a return trip to the warehouse to retrieve the remainder of the order.

As a pilot study, a few wider push carts were ordered and put into service for a one-week trial run. Although more parts could fit into these new carts, the pickers complained they were so wide two of them could not pass each other in the narrow aisles, causing traffic jams and thereby actually increasing picking times. The team then tried using longer carts, which were found to take care of both problems. By watching the part picking activity over the next several days, the team was able to verify the switch to longer carts greatly reduced the number of multiple trips needed. In

Figure 11.23 Cause-and-Effect Diagram of Potential Causes of Multiple Trips

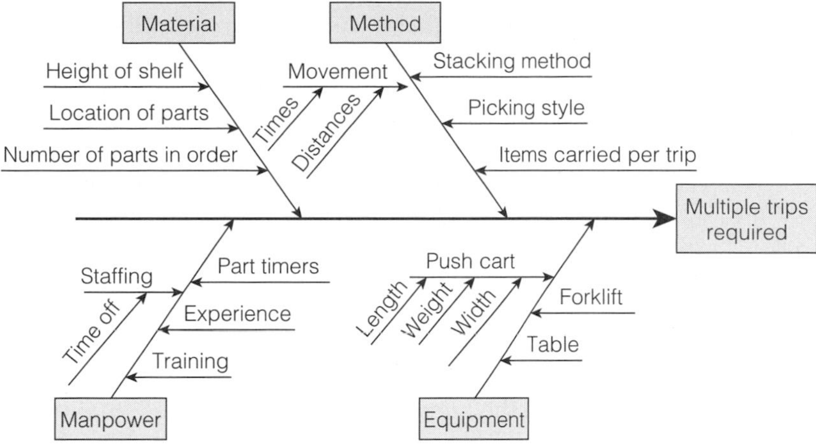

Source: Reprinted with permission from Davis R. Bothe, "Improve Service and Administration," Quality Progress, September 2003, pp. 53–57. Copyright © 2003 American Society for Quality. No further distribution allowed without permission.

fact, with the new push carts, a picker could often complete two small orders during the same trip.

To estimate the decrease in part picking time, the team constructed a histogram of 30 picking times associated with the longer carts (see Figure 11.24). This example has a unimodal distribution, with an average picking time of only 8.3 minutes vs. the original average of 13.9 minutes.

Although a reduction of 5.6 minutes (13.9–8.3) per trip doesn't seem like much of a time savings, consider that on an eight-hour shift, a part picker spends about seven hours—420 minutes—actually gathering parts. Using the old push carts, a picker would complete an average of 30.2 orders (420/13.9) per shift. With the longer carts, that same picker could now complete 50.6 orders (420/8.3) per shift. This increase of 20.4 orders (50.6–30.2) per worker meant the four part pickers could fulfill an additional 81 orders (20.4 x 4) during their shift. Thus, the seemingly small reduction in average trip time translated into a fairly significant increase in the throughput of this bottleneck operation.

Figure 11.24 Histogram of Picking Times with Longer Carts

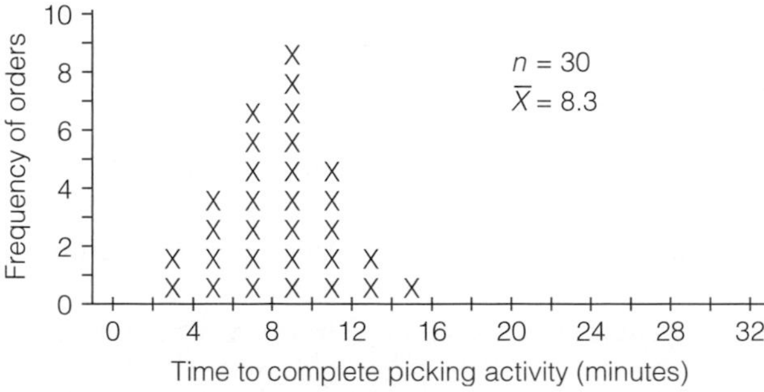

Source: Adapted from Davis R. Bothe, "Improve Services and Administration," *Quality Progress*, September 2003, pp. 53–57. Copyright 2003 American Society for Quality. Reprinted by permission.

Key Issues for Discussion

1. Explain how the process the team followed might align with DMAIC, the Deming Cycle, and the creative problem solving process described in Chapter 7.
2. What might the team do if the reduction in order processing time resulting from the introduction of the longer carts was not large enough to achieve the goal of having 98 percent of the orders meet the 24-hour deadline?
3. Suppose packing parts is now the activity responsible for the greatest delays in processing an order. How might this affect the project organization and next steps?

Additional Quality in Practice features can be found in the Bonus Materials folder for this chapter on the Premium website.

Review Questions

1. Explain the theoretical basis for Six Sigma quality. How does it relate to the natural variation in a process and manufacturing specifications?
2. Describe the Six Sigma problem-solving approach (DMAIC). How is it similar to or different from the other problem-solving approaches discussed in Chapter 7?
3. What is the difference between project selection and problem definition?
4. What is a root cause? How does the "5 Why" technique help uncover the root cause?
5. What are the key principles for effective implementation of Six Sigma?
6. What are the major types of tools used in Six Sigma projects?
7. What is Kepner and Tregoe's definition of a problem? How does this definition apply to quality issues? Provide some examples.
8. List and explain the five categories into which all quality problem solving can be classified.
9. List and explain the Original Seven QC Tools. In what phases of the CPS process, described in Chapter 7, might each be most useful?
10. What types of questions might one ask to identify opportunities for improvement with a process flowchart?
11. Describe a control chart. How does it differ from a run chart?
12. Describe different types of check sheets that are useful in quality improvement.
13. Explain the difference between a histogram and a Pareto diagram. Do they apply to the same types of data?
14. Describe the structure of a cause-and-effect diagram.
15. How do scatter diagrams assist in finding solutions to quality problems?
16. List and explain some of the tools and approaches used in "lean" organizations. How does the lean operating concept relate to Six Sigma?
17. What are some reasons why the lean approach appeals to small organizations?

Discussion Questions

1. The January 22, 2001, issue of *Fortune* contained an article "Why You Can Safely Ignore Six Sigma," that was highly critical of Six Sigma. Here are some of the criticisms levied against Six Sigma:
   a. The results often don't have any noticeable impact on company financial statements. Thus, Six Sigma success doesn't correlate to higher stock value. This criticism applies to 90 percent of the companies that implement Six Sigma.
   b. Only early adopters can benefit.
   c. Six Sigma focuses on defects, which are hard to objectively determine for service businesses.
   d. Six Sigma can't guarantee that your product will have a market.

   How would you respond to these statements?
2. Some of the key processes associated with business activities for a typical company include sales and marketing, supply chain management, managing information technology, and managing human resources. What types of Six Sigma projects might be considered in order to improve each of these activities?

3. Suggest a set of CTQs that might influence overall service satisfaction for service at an automobile dealership.
4. "Resistance to change" is a common theme in the behavioral sciences. What part do you believe that resistance to change plays in management's fostering of successful versus unsuccessful adoptions of Six Sigma approaches? What impact does workers' resistance or lack of resistance have?
5. List some of the common processes that a student performs. How can these processes be improved using a Six Sigma approach?
6. Why are modern products that often require high tolerances, short production runs, and heavy customer input difficult to manufacture in order to meet Six Sigma specifications?
7. Discuss what would be the most appropriate tool to use to attack each of these quality issues:
   a. A copy machine suffers frequent paper jams and users are often confused as to how to fix the problem.
   b. The publication team for an engineering department wants to improve the accuracy of its user documentation but is unsure of why documents aren't error-free.
   c. An office manager has experienced numerous problems with a laser printer: double-spaced lines, garbled text, lost text, and blank pages. She is trying to figure out which is the most significant problem.
   d. A military agency wants to evaluate the weight of personnel at a certain facility.
   e. A bank needs to determine how many teller positions, drive-through stations, and ATM machines it needs for a new branch bank in a certain busy location. Its information includes the average numbers and types of customers served by other similar facilities, as well as demographic information to suggest the level of customer traffic in the new facility.
   f. A contracting agency wants to investigate why they had so many changes in their contracts. They believe that the number of changes may be related to the dollar value of the original contract or the days between the request for proposal and the contract award.
   g. A travel agency is interested in gaining a better understanding of how call volume varies by time of year in order to adjust staffing schedules.
8. How can lean concepts be applied in a classroom?
9. The Six Sigma philosophy seeks to develop technical leadership through "Belt" training, then use it in team-based projects designed to improve processes. To what extent are these two concepts (technical experts versus team experts) at odds? What must be done to prevent them from blocking success in improvement projects?
10. How might a Six Sigma project be done to improve a registration process in a university? An admission process?
11. How can a manager effectively balance the key components of a Six Sigma implementation design related to who, what, where, when, why, and how it could be done?
12. In 1995, Jack Welch sent a memo to his senior managers telling them that they would have to require every employee to have started Six Sigma training to be promoted. Furthermore, 40 percent of the managers' bonuses were to be tied to the successful introduction of Six Sigma. Do you believe that this directive was a motivational action, or did it violate W. Edwards Deming's maxim that managers and leaders must "cast out fear"? Why or why not?

13. A consultant told the story of two Six Sigma teams that made separate presentations on how they would improve processes in their own areas. At the end of the second presentation, the consultant asked a basic question that stopped both Black Belt team leaders in their tracks: "Haven't you both just proposed making improvements based on eliminating parts of processes in the other group's areas? It seems that the implementation costs in one area will cancel out the savings in the other area!" What had the Black Belts failed to recognize? What would you recommend to prevent this situation from happening in other organizations?
14. In manufacturing, the concept of a "hidden factory" describes the necessity of repair and rework of defective products. List some places where the "hidden factory" can exist in service businesses.

PROBLEMS

BONUS MATERIALS

Note: Data sets for many problems in this chapter are available in the Excel workbook *C11Data* on the Premium website that accompanies this chapter. Click the appropriate worksheet tab as noted in the problem (e.g. *Prob. 11-11, etc.*) to access the data.

1. Wellplace Insurance Company set a standard that policy applications should be processed within three days of receipt. If, out of a sample of 1,000 applications, 65 fail to meet this requirement, at what sigma level is this process operating?
2. During one month, 35 preflight inspections were performed on an airplane at Southstar Airlines. Nine nonconformances were noted. Each inspection checks 30 items. What sigma level does Southstar maintain if this incidence of nonconformance is typical of their entire fleet of airplanes?
3. Over the last year 1,054 injections were administered at the Fairhealth clinic. Quality is measured by the proper amount of dosage as well as the correct drug. In two instances, the incorrect amount was given, and in one case, the wrong drug was given. At what sigma level is Fairhealth's process?
4. A few years back, the Wall Street Journal reported that about 750,000 airplane components are manufactured, machined, or assembled for Boeing Co. by workers from the Seattle Lighthouse for the Blind. A Boeing spokeswoman noted that the parts have an "exceptionally low" rejection rate of one per thousand. At what sigma level is this process operating?
5. Broadwork Electronics manufactures 500,000 circuit boards per month. A random sample of 5,000 boards is inspected every week for five characteristics. During a recent week, two defects were found for one characteristic, and one defect each was found for the other four characteristics. If these inspections produced defect counts that were representative of the population, what is the overall sigma level for this Broadwork process? What is the sigma level for the characteristic that showed two defects?
6. Outsource Microprocessor Corporation (OMC) sells 1500 specialized computer processing chips each month at a price of $1,200 each.[45] Variable costs amount to $1,000,000, and fixed costs are $400,000. Currently the company has a defect rate of 8 percent (which are chips returned by customers, scrapped by OMC, and replaced). Note that the variable costs include the cost of producing the defective chips.

Figure 11.25 Flowchart for a Fast-Food Drive-Through Window (Problem 7)

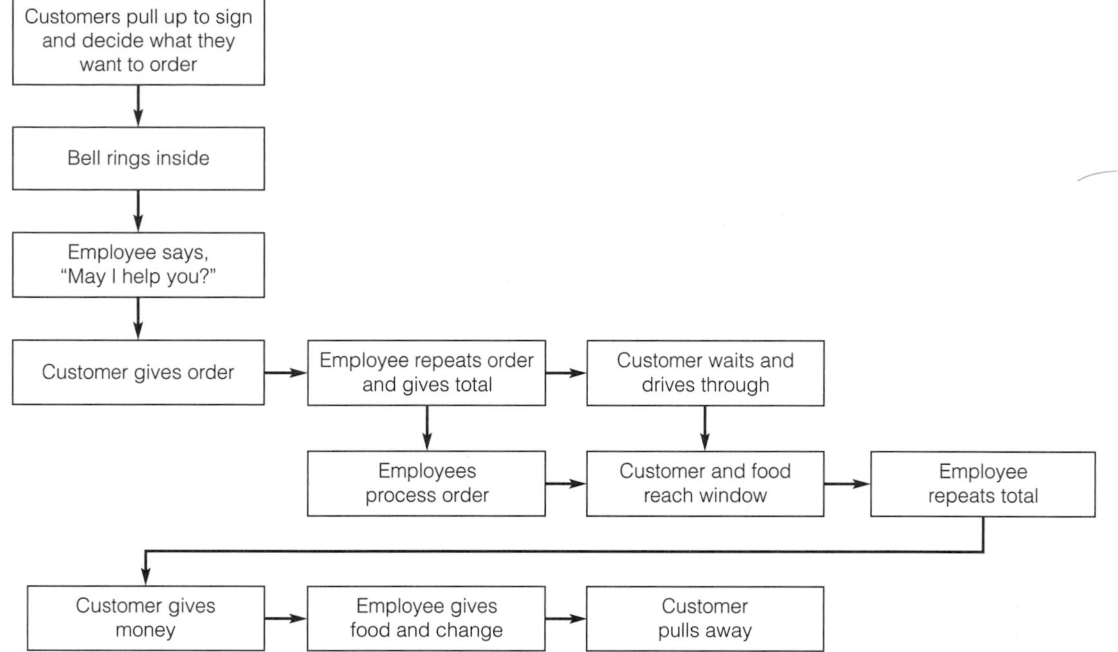

a. What is the hidden cost to the company of making this rate of defectives instead of 1500 good chips each month?
b. Suppose a Six Sigma effort can reduce the defects to a six-sigma level (assume for simplicity that the defective rate is essentially zero). What is the impact on profitability?

7. A flowchart for a fast-food drive-through window is shown in Figure 11.25. Determine the important quality characteristics inherent in this process and suggest possible improvements.
8. The current process for fulfilling a room service request at the Luxmark hotel can be described as follows. After the tray is prepared at the room service station, the server proceeds to the room, knocks on the door, sets up the meal, has the customer sign the check, asks if anything else is needed, and then returns to the room service station.
   a. Draw a flowchart that describes this process.
   b. From the perspective of creating a high level of customer satisfaction from this experience, what improvements might you suggest to enhance this process? Think creatively!
9. Placewrite, Inc., an independent outplacement service, helps unemployed executives find jobs. One of the major activities of the service is preparing resumes. Three word processors work at the service typing resumes and cover letters. Together they handle about 120 individual clients. Turnaround time for typing is expected to be 24 hours. The word-processing operation begins with clients placing work in the assigned word processor's bin. When the word processor picks up the work (in batches), it is logged in using a time clock stamp, and the work is typed and printed. After the batch is completed,

the word processor returns the documents to the clients' bins, logs in the time delivered, and picks up new work. A supervisor tries to balance the workload for the three word processors. Lately, many of the clients have been complaining about errors in their documents—misspellings, missing lines, wrong formatting, and so on. The supervisor has told the word processors to be more careful, but the errors still persist.

a. Develop a cause-and-effect diagram that might clarify the source of errors.
b. What tools might the supervisor use to study ways to reduce the number of errors?

10. A catalog order-filling process at Cats Catalog Company for personalized printed products for pet owners can be described as follows:[46] Telephone orders are taken over a 12-hour period each day. Orders are collected from each person at the end of the day and checked for errors by the supervisor of the phone department, usually the following morning. The supervisor does not send each one-day batch of orders to the data processing department until after 1:00 P.M. In the next step—data processing—orders are invoiced in the one-day batches. Then they are printed and matched back to the original orders. At this point, if the order is from a new customer, it is sent to the person who did the customer verification and setup of new customer accounts. This process must be completed before the order can be invoiced. The next step—order verification and proofreading—occurs after invoicing is completed. The orders, with invoices attached, are given to a person who verifies that all required information is present and correct to permit typesetting. If the verifier has any questions, they are checked by computer or by calling the customer. Finally, the completed orders are sent to the typesetting department of the print shop.
    a. Develop a flowchart for this process.
    b. Identify opportunities for improving the quality of service in this situation.
11. A Six Sigma analyst at Riverside United Bank suspected that errors in counting and manually strapping cash into bundles were related to the number of weeks that employees had been employed on that job. The data available in the Excel file *C11Data* for Prob. 11-11 on the Premier website for this chapter were gathered from the process. What do you conclude from your analysis? What do you recommend?
12. The times required for trainees in an electronics course at Elecktronica Tech to assemble a component used in a computer were measured. These are provided in the Excel file *C11Data* for Prob. 11-12 on the Premier website for this chapter. Construct a histogram to graphically show the data. What recommendations for improvement would you give the course instructor, based on your findings?
13. The times required to prepare standard-size packages for shipping at Packman Shipping Company were measured. The packers were divided into two equal groups of 20 people, each, having similar experience in packing. These data are provided in the Excel file *C11Data* for Prob. 11-13 on the Premier website for this chapter. Construct a scatter diagram for these data. What recommendations for improvement would you give the section leader, based on your findings?
14. The data available in the Excel file *C11Data* for Prob. 11-14 on the Premier website for this chapter were gathered from a process used to make PrintGear, Inc.'s plastic gears for a computer printer. The gears were designed to be 2.75 ± 0.05 centimeters (cm) in diameter. Construct a histogram based on the data given. What can you observe about the shape of the distribution? What would you recommend to the production manager, based on your analysis?

15. Ace Printing Company realized that they were losing customers and orders due to various delays and errors. In order to get to the root cause of the problem, they decided to track problems that might be contributing to customer dissatisfaction. The list of the problems provided in the Excel file *C11Data* for Prob. 11-15 on the Premier website for this chapter shows their frequencies of occurrence over a six-month period. What technique might you use to graphically show the causes of customer dissatisfaction? What recommendations could you make to reduce errors and increase customer satisfaction?
16. In an AcmeWidget, Inc. process, the production rate (parts/hour) was thought to affect the number of defectives found during a subsequent inspection. To test this theory, the production rate was varied and the numbers of defects were collected for the same batch sizes. The results are available in the Excel file *C11Data* for Prob. 11-16 on the Premier website for this chapter. Construct a scatter diagram for these data. What conclusions can you reach?
17. The number of defects found in 25 samples of 100 Gamma Candy Company lemon drops taken on a daily basis from a production line over a five-week period is given in the Excel file *C11Data* for Prob. 11-17 on the Premier website for this chapter. Plot these data on a run chart, computing the average value (center line), but ignoring the control limits. Do you suspect that any special causes are present? Why?
18. Analysis of customer complaints at DOT.COM Apparel Company revealed errors in five categories, such as billing, shipping, etc. Data are provided in the *C11Data* file for Prob. 11-18 on the Premier website for this chapter. Construct a Pareto diagram for these data. What conclusions can you reach?
19. A pharmaceutical company that manufactures individual syringes is conducting a process capability study (see Chapter 13). The data provided in the Excel file *C11Data* for Prob. 11-19 on the Premier website for this chapter represent the lengths of 35 consecutive samples.[47] Plot these data on a run chart. Do the data appear to come from a stable system so that a process capability study may be conducted appropriately?
20. The Monterey Fiesta Mexican Restaurant is trying to determine whether sales of its popular Pan Con Mucho Sabor breadsticks are correlated with the sales of margaritas. It has data on sales of breadstick baskets and margaritas for 25 weeks, provided in the Excel file *C11Data* for Prob. 11-20 on the Premier website for this chapter. Use the correlation utility, along with a scatter diagram, in Microsoft Excel to analyze these data. What do they indicate?

Projects, Etc.

1. Three popular Web sites for Six Sigma are http://www.ge.com/sixsigma, http://www.isixsigma.com, and http://www.sixsigmaformum.com. Explore these sites and consider the following questions.
   a. How does GE use Six Sigma to enhance customer perception of its products and services?
   b. What is the apparent purpose of the isixsigma website?
   c. Who are the customers of the sixsigmaforum website?
   d. Do the three websites reach basic agreement about the concept of Six Sigma? How do they differ?

2. Identify an important problem around your school or in some related function, such as a student organization, and apply the DMAIC process to develop an improved solution. You might wish to use some of the Seven QC Tools.
3. Find a local company that is using Six Sigma or lean principles. Write a case study of their experiences, focusing on the challenges they faced during their implementation efforts.
4. Develop a flowchart of the process you use to study for an exam. How might you improve this process?
5. In small teams, develop cause-and-effect diagrams for the following problems:
   a. Poor exam grade
   b. No job offers
   c. Late for work or school

CASES

Additional cases are available in the Bonus Materials folder for this chapter on the Premium website.

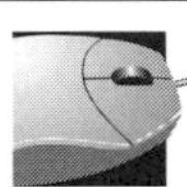

BONUS MATERIALS

LT, INC.[48]

LT, Inc. started as a small, family-owned company. For a long time, owners managed most of the operations, including billing, and customers were happy. Over time, the company grew steadily and acquired plants in the United States and many other countries. Most of its operations were departmentalized, and the accounting systems varied among the many companies LT acquired. While LT successfully dealt with most of the problems caused by rapid growth, it remained unable to get a grip on billing errors. The customer service and billing departments were often flooded with complaints about erroneous bills.

The billing process at LT evolved over time, resulting in a lack of consistency among billing personnel. Customer order taking and billing procedures were confusing, inadequate and obsolete. Not all billing clerks had the same level of knowledge and training. A lack of documentation added to the confusion and aggravated the situation. Billing personnel followed the policies and procedures they thought were reasonable and did things the way they felt was right.

To get a handle on its billing problem, LT appointed a Six Sigma team comprised of employees with various interdisciplinary backgrounds and expertise. The team discussed the problem, researched Six Sigma and lean tools and techniques, learned from other companies and consulted with experts in the field.

The first thing the team did was study the billing process and prepare a flow chart (see Figure 11.26). The team then reviewed how billing errors were resolved. Most scenarios followed a similar path: A customer calls to inquire about a bill and listens to a pre-recorded message with menu options. The customer listens to several options that don't describe their particular problem and gets frustrated when the system only deals with select inquiries. After several minutes, the customer finally gets to speak to a customer service representative, but only after being put on hold or bounced from one representative to another, forcing the customer to repeat the problem several times. Finally, the customer is assured the problem will be corrected, only to have the next month bring the same bill, the same error, the same complaint, the same aggravation and, in the end, the loss of an annoyed customer.

A further study revealed many different types of billing errors:

- Bills with wrong prices and charges
- Bills sent to the wrong customer
- Bills sent to the wrong address
- Double billing and late billing
- Billing for unordered goods
- Billing for returned goods
- Billing before the goods were shipped

Using cause-and-effect diagrams, the Six Sigma team brainstormed potential causes and

Figure 11.26 Flowchart of LT Billing Process

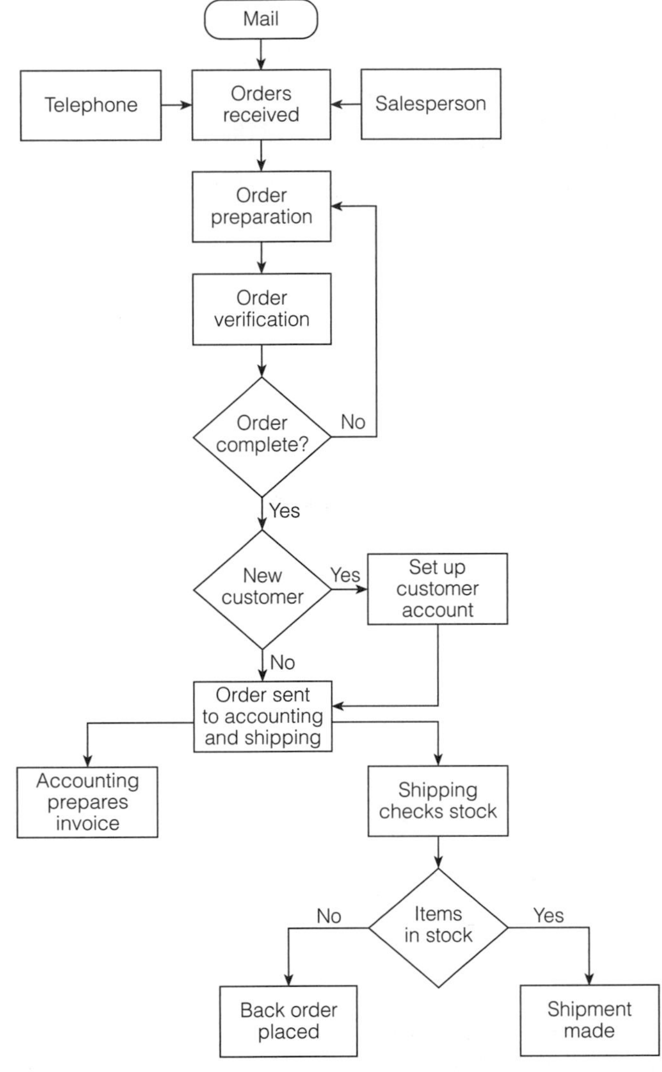

Source: Reprinted with permission from Lakshmi U. Tatikonda, "A Less Costly Billing Process," *Quality Progress*, January 2008, pp. 31–39.

explored them in depth (see Figure 11.27). A Pareto analysis showed that 70 percent of the errors were due to an incorrect amount on the bill or billing for unordered goods.

To gain a better understanding of the sources of communication errors, the team members decided to walk through the billing activities. Customer orders arrived via mail, fax and phone. At each step, they were batched and queued for processing. The main steps included: order taking (folders made for each customer), order preparation (current and new customers sorted, information added), order pricing, shipping, and billing. Table 11.5 provides a detailed description of the activities.

Using the information provided, outline specific steps that you would recommend to improve the process. Include a list of performance metrics that you would recommend that the company monitor in the future to track the efficiency and effectiveness of the process. Summarize your results in a formal report the company's management.

Figure 11.27 Cause-and-Effect Diagram for Billing Errors

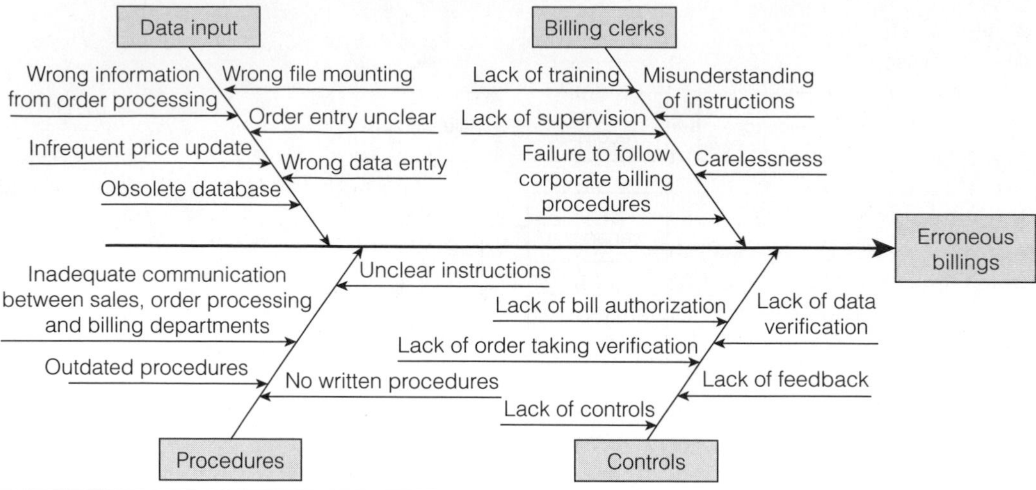

Source: Adapted from Lakshmi U. Tatikonda, "A Less Costly Billing Process," *Quality Progress*, January 2008, pp. 31–39. Copyright © 2008 American Society for Quality. Reprinted by permission.

Table 11.5 Data and activities included in the billing process

Customer	Order Preparation	Billing
• Orders via mail, fax, phone, and e-mail. • Average daily orders: 200/day Central mailroom • Receive outside mail. • Sort according to departments. • Put in boxes. • Deliver to departments. • Stamp postage and send outgoing mail. Order taking • Receive orders from customers and central mailroom, • Open customer mail orders. • Record customer phone orders on paper. • Sort all orders by customer name and stamp date. • Prepare folders with customer order information. • Move batch of customer orders to order preparation once a day. Credit check • Check customer credit once a week. • Add credit status to folders. • Sort customers according to acceptable and not acceptable credit. • Batch and move the sorted folders to billing.	• Receive folders with customer order information. • Sort folders according to new and current customers. • Send new customer folders to data processing. • Receive new customer folders from data processing. • Move customers order folders to order verification. • Receive folders from order verification. • Make two copies of customer order folders. • Send one copy of the order to shipping and one copy to billing. Data processing • Receive new customer folders from order taking. • Batch the folders, assign a customer number and create customer record. • Add new customer number and other information to customer folders. • Batch customer folders to order preparation once a day. Order verification • Receive customer order folders from order preparation. • Check stock availability. • Make price estimates. • Add price estimates to customer order folder. • Move the folders to order preparation once a day.	• Receive copy of customer order folders from order preparation. • Send new customer folders to credit check. • Receive customer folders from credit check with credit status. • Sort the customer folders according to acceptable and not acceptable credit. • Send the customer folders with not acceptable status back to order takers. • Send the acceptable customer folders to sales tax department. • Receive customer folders from sales tax. • Calculate the total amount (purchases, taxes) to bill. • Enter all the necessary data into computer and print invoices twice a month. • Address envelopes, fold, insert invoices and close. Move the envelopes to central mailroom twice a day. Shipping • Receive customer order folders from other preparation. • Pick and pack the items in the order. • Print and paste address labels on the boxes. • Ship the packages twice a day.

Source: Reprinted with permission from Lakshmi U. Tatikonda, "A Less Costly Billing Process," *Quality Progress*, January 2008, pp. 31–39. Copyright © 2008 American Society for Quality. No further distribution allowed without permission.

JANSON MEDICAL CLINIC

The Janson Medical Clinic recently conducted a patient satisfaction survey of 100 patients. Using a scale of 1–5, with 1 being "very dissatisfied" and 5 being "very satisfied," the clinic compiled a check sheet for responses that were either 1 or 2, indicating dissatisfaction with the performance attributes. This check sheet is shown in Table 11.6.

Doctors have extremely busy schedules. They have surgeries to perform, and many are teaching faculty at the local medical school. Many surgeries are emergencies or take longer than expected, resulting in delays of getting back to the clinic.

In the clinic, one or two telephone receptionists answer calls for three different departments, which include 20 or more doctors. Their job is basically to schedule appointments, provide directions, and transfer calls to the proper secretaries, which generally requires putting the patient on hold. Often, the receptionist must take a handwritten message and personally deliver it to the secretary because the secretary's phone line is busy. However, the receptionist cannot leave her desk without someone else to cover the phones.

A student intern examined the processes for answering phone calls and registering patients. The flowcharts she developed are shown in Figures 11.28 and 11.29.

Discussion Questions

1. Construct a Pareto diagram for dissatisfaction. What conclusions do you reach?

Table 11.6 Check Sheet of Dissatisfied Responses

Making an Appointment
- Ease of getting through on the phone—10
- Friendliness of the telephone receptionist—5
- Convenience of office hours—7
- Ease of getting a convenient appointment—12

Check-in/Check-out
- Courtesy and helpfulness of the receptionist—7
- Amount of time to register—1
- Length of wait to see a physician—13
- Comfort of registration waiting area—4

Care and Treatment
- Respect shown by nurses/assistants—0
- Responsiveness to phone calls related to care—5
- How well the physician listened—3
- Respect shown by the physician—2
- Confidence in the physician's ability—1
- Explanation of medical condition and treatment—2

2. Select the top three sources of patient dissatisfaction and propose cause-and-effect diagrams for the possible reasons behind them.
3. Propose some process improvements to the flowcharts in Figure 11.28 and develop redesigned processes along with new flowcharts. How will your suggestions address the sources of dissatisfaction in Table 11.6?

Figure 11.28 Current Process for Answering Phone Calls

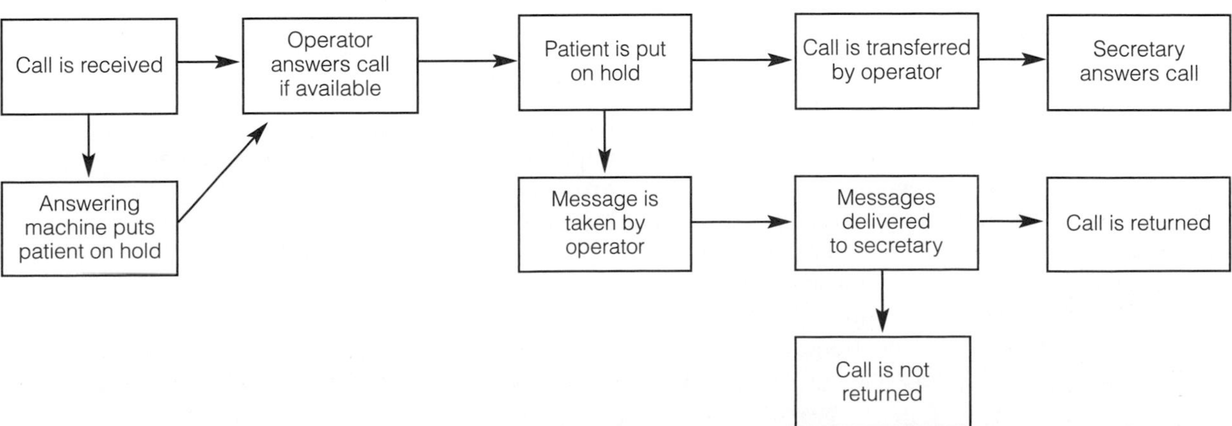

Figure 11.29 Current Patient Registration Process

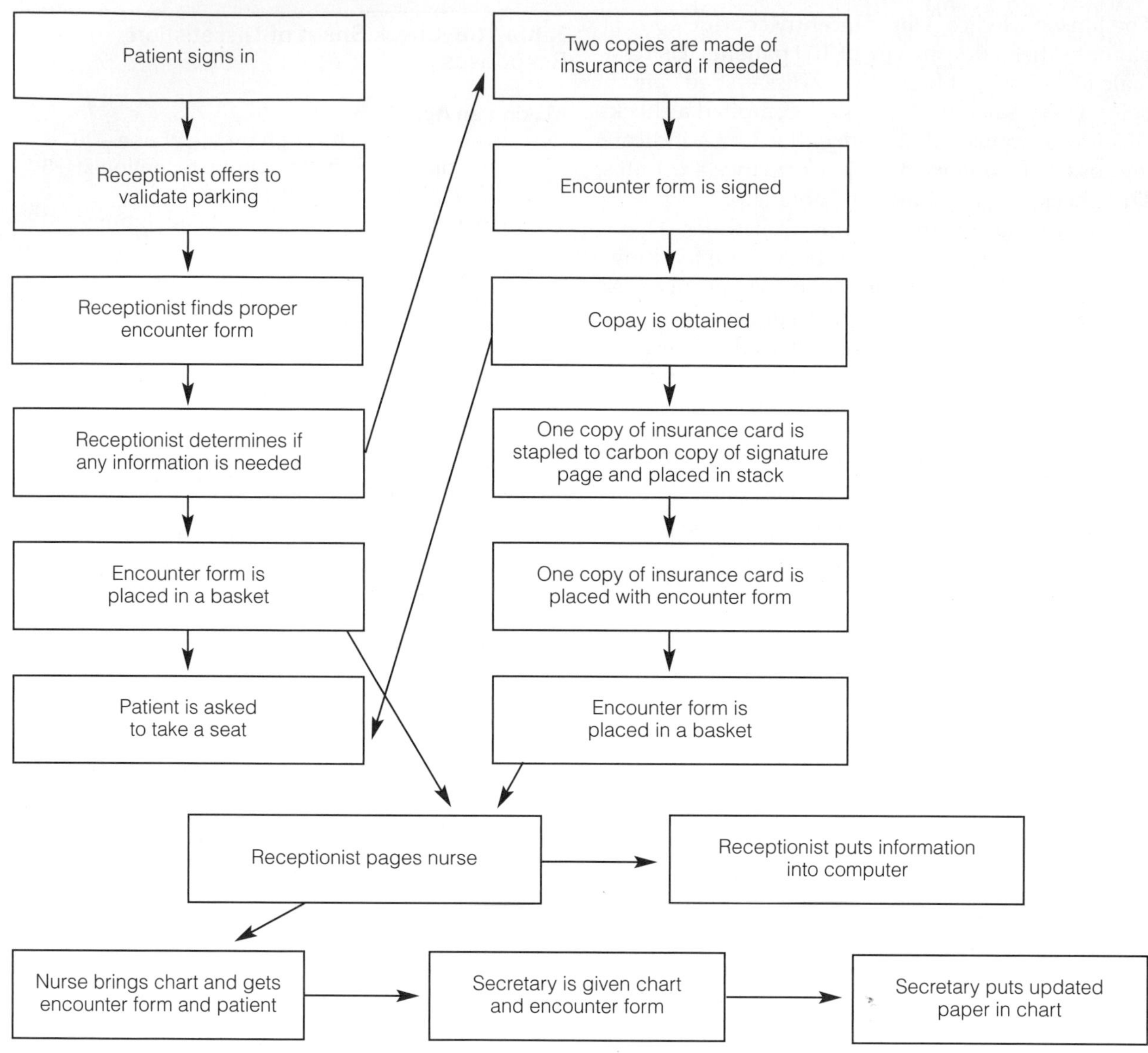

Readilunch Restaurant

BONUS MATERIALS

Carole Read, the owner of the Readilunch Restaurant, a downtown, quick service restaurant, was concerned about the loss of several regular customers. She measured the number of empty lunch tables from 11 A.M. until 2 P.M. over a four-week period. To better understand the reasons for the loss of customers, long lines, and dissatisfied patrons, Carol talked to several regular customers. She found that they liked the food and atmosphere of the restaurant, but felt that there were opportunities for improvement based on the lack of capability to quickly handle take-out orders (they had to be phoned in, not faxed), excessive time spent waiting for tables, inefficient service, surly waiters on certain days, and long lines at the cash register. She puzzled over how to sort out possible causes that led to these perceived problems. Carol also decided to design a check sheet to systematically gather data and determine which of these problems were the most significant.

Note: Data for the check sheet information gathered for "Vacant Tables" and for "Customer Concerns" can be found in the *Readilunch 1* and *Readilunch 2* tabs in the Excel file *C11Data* on the Premier website for this chapter.

Discussion Questions

1. Plot the average number of empty tables on a run chart, computing the average value (center line), but ignoring the control limits. What do these data show?
2. Use one of the seven Tools to come up with possible causes to explain customer dissatisfaction, based on the reasons described in the case.
3. Analyze the check sheet data on the student Premier website for this chapter. What conclusions do you reach?
4. What do you recommend that Carol do to overcome these problems?

NOTES

1. Gregory Korte, "473 Steps," *The Cincinnati Enquirer*, October 30, 2002, A1, A10.
2. Ronald D. Snee, "Why Should Statisticians Pay Attention to Six Sigma?" *Quality Progress*, September 1999, 100–103.
3. Pandu R. Tadikamalla, "The Confusion over Six-Sigma Quality," *Quality Progress* 27, no. 11, November 1994, 83–85. Reprinted with permission of Pandu R. Tadikamalla and *Quality Progress*.
4. "Up, Up, and Away?" *Fortune*, July 21, 2003, 149.
5. Kervin Linderman, Roger G. Schroeder, Srilata Zaheer, and Adrian S. Choo, "Six Sigma: A Goal-Theoretic Perspective," *Journal of Operations Management* 21, (2003), 193–203.
6. "The Tools of Quality Part V: Check Sheets," *Quality Progress* 23, no. 10 (October 1990), 53.
7. "NCR Corporation," in *Profiles in Quality* (Needham Heights, MA: Allyn and Bacon, 1991).
8. Howard H. Bailie, "Organize Your Thinking with a Why-Why Diagram," *Quality Progress* 18, no. 12 (December 1985), 22–24.
9. A. F. Osborn, *Applied Imagination*, 3rd ed. (New York: Scribners, 1963); S. J. Parnes, R. B. Noller, and A. M. Biondi (eds.), *Guide to Creative Action* (New York: Scribners, 1977).
10. Reprinted with permission of Chris Bott, Elizabeth Keim, Sai Kim, and Lisa Palser, "Service Quality Six Sigma Case Studies," *ASQ's 54th Annual Congress Proceedings*, 2000, 225–231. No further distribution allowed without permission.
11. H. James Harrington, "Creating Organizational Excellence—Part Two," *Quality Digest*, February 2003, 14.
12. *A Guide to the Project Management Body of Knowledge* (PMBOK® Guide)—Fourth Edition (Newtown Square, PA: Project Management Institute), 2008.
13. Charles H. Kepner and Benjamin B. Tregoe, *The Rational Manager* (New York: McGraw-Hill, 1965).
14. Gerald F. Smith, "Too Many Types of Quality Problems," *Quality Progress*, April 2000, 43–49.
15. Donald P. Lynch, Suzanne Bertolino, and Elaine Cloutier, "How to Scope DMAIC Projects," *Quality Progress* 36, no. 1 (January 2003), 37–44.
16. Jeffrey K. Pinto, "The Power of Project Management," *Industry Week*, August 18, 1997, 138–140.
17. "Six Sigma at GE-Lunar, Manufacturing and Technology Matters," Erdman Center for Manufacturing and Technology Management, University of Wisconsin-Madison School of Business, Fall/Winter 2002, 1–3.
18. Arthur Fornari and George Maszle, "Lean Six Sigma Leads Xerox," *Six Sigma Forum Magazine*, August 2004, 11–16.
19. Thomas Pyzdek, *The Six Sigma Handbook* (Tuscon, AZ: McGraw-Hill/Quality Publishing, 2001), 301.
20. Roger W. Hoerl, "Six Sigma and the Future of the Quality Profession," *Quality Progress*, June 1998, 35–42. © 1998, American Society for Quality. Reprinted with permission.
21. Daniel R. Heiser and Paul Schikora, "Flowcharting with Excel," *Quality Management Journal* 8, no. 3 (2001), 26–35.
22. AT&T Quality Steering Committee, *Reengineering Handbook*, AT&T Bell Laboratories (1991), 45.
23. Gary Vansuch, "Improving the 'Improve' Step in Six Sigma DMAIC Projects: Lean Enterprise and Process Streamlining Tools—Part 1," *Competitive Advantage*, 12, 2, Spring 2004, 1, 4–5, www.asq-sqd.com. Site is no longer active.
24. Rochelle Rucker, "Six Sigma at Citibank" was found at http://www.insidequality.wego.net. Site is no longer active.
25. Adapted from Dwight Kirscht and Jennifer M. Tunnell, "Boise Cascade Stakes a Claim on Quality," *Quality Progress* 26, no. 11 (November 1993), 91–96. With permission of Dwight M. Kirscht, Timber and Wood Products Division, Boise Cascade Corporation.
26. Kaoru Ishikawa, *Guide to Quality Control*, 2nd rev. ed. (Tokyo: Asian Productivity Organization, 1986).

Available from UNIPUB/Quality Resources, One Water Street, White Plains, NY 10601.

27. Adapted from Bruce Rudin, "Simple Tools Solve Complex Problems." Reprinted with permission from *Quality*, April 1990, 50–51; a publication of Hitchcock Publishing, a Capital Cities/ABC, Inc.

28. Adapted from Rudin (see Note 27).

29. Alex Taylor III, "How Toyota Defies Gravity," *Fortune*, December 8, 1997, 100–108.

30. Gary Conner, "Benefitting from Six Sigma," *Manufacturing Engineering*, February 2003, 53–59.

31. Ibid.

32. Anthony R. Goland, John Hall, and Devereaux A. Clifford, "First National Toyota," *The McKinsey Quarterly* no. 4 (1998), 58–66.

33. Patricia Houghton, "Improving Pharmacy Service," *Quality Digest*, October 18, 2007.

34. "Study Shows Six Sigma, Lean are Merging," *Industry Week*, March 7, 2008.

35. This discussion of the applicability of Six Sigma to services is adapted from Soren Bisgaard, Roger W. Hoerl, and Ronald D. Snee, "Improving Business Processes With Six Sigma," *Proceedings of ASQ's 56th Annual Quality Congress*, 2002 (CD-ROM), and Kennedy Smith, "Six Sigma for the Service Sector," *Quality Digest*, May 2003, 23–28.

36. Adapted from Elizabeth Keim, LouAnn Fox, and Julie S. Mazza, "Service Quality Six Sigma Case Studies," *Proceedings of the 54th Annual Quality Congress of the American Society for Quality*, 2000 (CD-ROM).

37. Lisa Palser, "Cycle Time Improvement for a Human Resources Process," *ASQ's 54th Annual Quality Congress Proceedings*, 2000 (CD-ROM).

38. Roger Hoerl, "An Inside Look at Six Sigma at GE," *Six Sigma Forum Magazine* 1, no. 3 (May 2002), 35–44.

39. Zachery Brice, "Six Sigma Sharpens Services," *Quality Digest*, May 2004, 37–42.

40. Greg Brue, "The Elephant in the Operating Room," *Quality Digest*, June 2005, 49–55.

41. Laura Smith, "Six Sigma Goes to Washington," *Quality Digest*, May 2005, 20–24.

42. Andrew Spanyi and Marvin Wurtzel. "Six Sigma for the Rest of Us," *Quality Digest* 23, no. 7 (July 2003), 26.

43. Reprinted with permission from Cathy Buck, "Application of Six Sigma to Reduce Medical Errors," *Proceedings of the 55th Annual Quality Congress of the American Society for Quality*, 2001 (CD-ROM). © 2001, American Society for Quality. No further reproduction allowed without permission.

44. Reprinted with permission from Davis R. Bothe, "Improve Service and Administration," *Quality Progress*, September 2003, 53–57. Copyright © 2003 American Society for Quality. No further distribution allowed without permission.

45. Modeled after an example in Soren Bisgaard and Johannes Freiesleben. "Six Sigma and the Bottom Line," *Quality Progress*, Vol. 37, No. 9, September 2004, 57–62.

46. Adapted from Ronald G. Conant, "JIT in a Mail Order Operation Reduces Processing Time from Four Days to Four Hours," *Industrial Engineering* 20, no. 9 (September 1988), 34–37.

47. Leroy A. Franklin and Samar N. Mukherjee, "An SPC Case Study on Stabilizing Syringe Lengths," *Quality Engineering* 12, no. 1 (1999–2000), 65–71.

48. Reprinted with permission from Lakshmi U. Tatikonda, "A Less Costly Billing Process," *Quality Progress*, January 2008, 31–39. Copyright © 2008 American Society for Quality. No further distribution allowed without permission.

Design for Quality and Product Excellence

Outline

Quality Profiles: Spicer Driveshaft and 3M Dental Products Division

Product Design Processes
- Concurrent Engineering
- Design for Six Sigma

Concept Development
- Concept Engineering

Design Development
- Quality Function Deployment
- Design for Manufacturability
- Design and Environmental Responsibility
- Design for Excellence
- Target and Tolerance Design

Design Optimization
- The Taguchi Loss Function
- Design Failure Mode and Effects Analysis
- Reliability Prediction and Optimization

Design Verification
- Design Reviews
- Reliability Testing
- Measurement System Evaluation
- Calibration
- Process Capability Evaluation

Summary of Key Points and Terminology

Quality in Practice: Testing Audio Components at Shure, Inc.

Quality in Practice: Applying QFD in a Managed Care Organization

Review Questions

Problems

Projects, Etc.

Cases Applying Quality Function Deployment to a University Support Service

Black Elk Medical Center

Despite remarkable advances in manufacturing and service technology, as well as the attention to process improvement and approaches like Six Sigma, businesses and consumers are still plagued with product failures or service upsets. Consumers don't receive the products they ordered, or are given inaccurate information. Thousands of people die from medical errors each year. Software that controls most modern products are prone to failure.[1] Most of these problems fundamentally result from poor design or inadequate design processes. Noted quality consultant H. James Harrington recently made the case that U.S. automakers should concentrate less on lean and more on design quality:

> *In 2000, about two-thirds of all cars purchased in North America were bought from U.S. companies. That figure has now [in 2008] dropped to 54 percent.*

Detroit sales keep falling while Japanese and Korean auto companies gain ground in the U.S. market. Consumer Reports *recommends a much smaller percentage of autos manufactured by U.S. companies than by their Japanese counterparts—37 percent to 80 percent, respectively . . . But what's causing U.S. companies to lose market share isn't incoming quality; rather, it's outgoing reliability. The problem is neither the suppliers nor the production workers in U.S. plants; it's automotive design . . . Another culprit sharing the blame is long-term reliability. It's not the small percentage of bad parts that are found in manufacturing; it's the good parts that fail before customers are through using them . . . Why is Toyota winning the market? Because, during a 10-year period, the average Toyota vehicle's total number of problems are fewer than a four-year-old U.S.-brand vehicle. When you compare first-year performance, Japanese and South Korean automakers make the most reliable cars, with 11 problems per 100 vehicles on average. U.S. automakers record 16 problems per 100 cars, and European automakers lag far behind with 19 problems per 100 cars.*[2]

Effective design processes are vital to meeting customer requirements, achieving quality, and innovation, as the Quality Profiles in this chapter suggest. In this chapter, we introduce some of the more important practices and tools that support quality design efforts.

Quality Profiles

Spicer Driveshaft and 3M Dental Products Division

Spicer Driveshaft (a former division of Dana Corporation when they received the Baldrige Award in 2000), now Torque Traction Technologies, Inc., is North America's largest independent manufacturer of driveshafts and related components for light, medium, heavy duty, and off-highway vehicles. The company has 17 manufacturing, assembly, and administrative facilities around the United States, employing more than 3,400 people.

Customer Platform Teams are one of the focal points for identifying customer requirements and building and maintaining new business, product offerings, and customer relationships. These teams include sales, engineering, quality, and warranty personnel that use a variety of formal and informal methods to listen and learn from customers. All senior leaders are involved in a two-phase strategic planning process that addresses long-term direction and short-term objectives, which are linked and aligned from headquarters to the individual manufacturing plants. A comprehensive diversity plan is used to help develop candidates for promotion from within the organization, improve community involvement efforts, and establish a mentoring program.

From 1997 to 1999, sales increased by nearly 10 percent; economic value added increased from $15 million to $35 million; inventory as a percentage of sales decreased from 6.8 percent to 6.3 percent; and working capital decreased from 13 percent to 10.2 percent of sales. Internal defect rates decreased more than 75 percent from 1996 to 2000 and are approaching best-in-class levels. Employees are encouraged to develop and implement changes and innovative ideas and evaluate their results. Ideas submitted by employees average about three per month, which is approaching best-in-class. In 1999, almost 80 percent of ideas were implemented. The employee turnover rate is below 1 percent, which is better than the best competitor; and the attendance rate has remained above 98 percent for the last six years.

Launched in 1964, 3M Dental Products Division (DPD), a Baldrige recipient in 1997, is a business unit of 3M Corporation, manufacturing and marketing more than 1,300 products used by dentists around the world, including restorative and crown and bridge materials and dental adhesive and infection control products. Innovation is a key success factor enabling the company to be a leader in the competitive dental products marketplace. Insights into changing customer requirements—combined with knowledge of technological, societal, and environmental trends—are the starting point for product and process innovations. Dentists, distributors, and major suppliers are involved in the division's systematic approach to translating key customer requirements into design requirements, prototypes, and, ultimately, reliable, quality products. Examples of customer involvement include simulated operations on "Fletchers," mannequins with human-like mouth features and conditions. Dentists use these mannequins to evaluate variations of prototype material or hardware products. Through this and other methods, customer feedback is received at least three times during the development cycle. The company's business performance management matrix provides a systematic and comprehensive tool for aligning key business drivers and goals down, through, and across all business and functional units. More than 40 cross-functional teams arrange new product introduction, solve problems, and manage and improve business processes.

In 1997, new product sales accounted for 45 percent of total sales, accelerating from 12 percent in 1992. Additionally, the number of patents per employee, an indicator of innovation, is better than twice the rate of its closest competitor. 3M DPD has been the industry leader in overall satisfaction of its U.S. distributors since 1989 and in overall satisfaction of dentists since 1987.

Source: Adapted from Malcolm Baldrige National Quality Award, Profiles of Winners, National Institute of Standards and Technology, Department of Commerce.

PRODUCT DESIGN PROCESSES

Companies today face incredible pressures to continually improve the quality of their products while simultaneously reducing costs, to meet ever-increasing legal and environmental requirements, and to shorten product life cycles to meet changing consumer needs and remain competitive. The ability to achieve these goals depends on a large extent on product design (by which we also imply *redesign*). Better designs not only reduce costs, but improve quality. For example, simpler designs have fewer components, which mean fewer points of failure and less chance of assembly error.[3] Although we tend to equate product design with manufactured goods, it is important to realize that design processes apply to services as well. For example, in the late 1980s, Citibank designed a new mortgage approval procedure that reduced turnaround times from 45 to less than 15 days; FedEx has consistently developed new variations of its package delivery services.[4]

Most companies have some type of structured product development process. The typical product development process, shown in Figure 12.1, consists of six phases:

1. *Idea Generation*. New or redesigned product ideas should incorporate customer needs and expectations. However, true innovations often transcend customers' expressed desires, simply because customers may not know what they like until they have it. Thus, idea generation often focus on exciters and delighters as described in the Kano model in Chapter 5. A good example is Chrysler's decision to develop the minivan, despite research that showed that people balked at such a non-traditional vehicle at the time.[5]
2. *Preliminary Concept Development*. In this phase, new ideas are studied for feasibility, addressing such questions as: Will the product meet customers' requirements? Can it be manufactured economically with high quality? Objective criteria are required for measuring and testing the attributes associated with these questions.

Figure 12.1 Structured Product Development Process

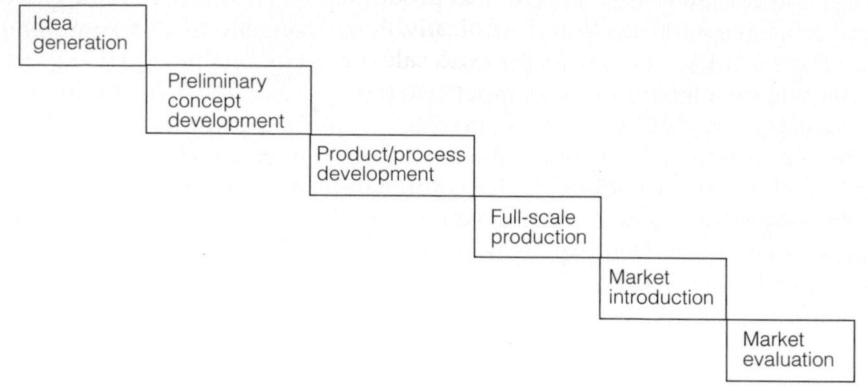

Source: Reprinted with permission from D. Daetz, "The Effect of Product Design on Product Quality and Product Cost," *Quality Progress*, Vol. 20, no. 6, pp. 63–67, June 1987. Copyright © 1987 American Society for Quality. No further distribution allowed without permission.

3. *Product/Process Development*. If an idea survives the concept stage—and many do not—the actual design process begins by evaluating design alternatives and determining engineering specifications for all materials, components, and parts. This phase usually includes prototype testing, in which a model (real or simulated) is constructed to test the product's physical properties or use under actual operating conditions, as well as consumer reactions to the prototypes. For example, Boeing's 777 jet was built using digital prototypes. Design reviews are frequently conducted to identify and eliminate possible causes for manufacturing and marketing problems. In addition to the actual product design, companies develop, test, and standardize the processes used in manufacturing, which include selecting the appropriate technology, tooling, and suppliers, and performing pilot runs to verify results.
4. *Full-Scale Production*. If no serious problems are found, the company releases the product to manufacturing or service delivery teams.
5. *Market Introduction*. The product is distributed to customers.
6. *Market Evaluation*. Deming and Juran both advocated an ongoing product development process that relies on market evaluation and customer feedback to initiate continuous improvements. In fact, Deming's view of the production system (see Figure 1.3 in Chapter 1) promoted the use of market evaluation to improve designs of products and processes.

An example of how this generic process is implemented is Caterpillar's DMEDI (*define, measure, explore, design, implement*) process:

1. *Define Opportunities:* Understand the purpose of the process to be developed by goal statements, generation plans, and resource identification.
2. *Measure Customer Needs:* Understand the outputs required of the new process by examining customer needs and competitive analysis.
3. *Explore Design Concepts:* Use creative techniques to develop alternative concepts and evaluate those ideas by validating customer requirements.
4. *Develop Detailed Design:* Turn the concept into reality by the use of process and product designs, pilot programs, and testing.
5. *Implement Detailed Design:* Fully deploy the new process and assess its value against the desired outcome.

Many companies view customers as significant partners in product development, thus integrating market evaluation throughout the process. Ames Rubber Company, for example, uses a four-step approach to product development that maintains close communication with the customer.[6] Typically, Ames initiates a new product through a series of meetings with the customer and sales/marketing or the technical services group. From these meetings, management prepares a product brief listing all technical, material, and operational requirements. The brief is forwarded to internal departments, such as engineering, quality, and manufacturing. The technical staff then selects materials, processes, and procedures, and submits its selections to the customer. Upon the customer's approval, a prototype is made. Ames delivers the prototype to the customer, who evaluates and tests it and reports results to the company. Ames makes the requested modifications and returns the prototype for further testing. This process continues until the customer is completely satisfied. Next, Ames makes a limited preproduction run. Data collected during the run are analyzed and shared with the customer. Upon approval, full-scale production commences.

Concurrent Engineering

The importance of speed in product development cannot be overemphasized. To succeed in highly competitive markets, companies must churn out new products quickly. Nearly every industry is focused on reducing product development cycles. Whereas automakers once took four to six years to develop new models, most are striving to do it within 24 months or less. Rapid product development demands the involvement and cooperation of many different functional groups within an organization, such as marketing, engineering, and manufacturing.

Unfortunately, the product development process often is performed without good cooperation. In many large firms product development is accomplished in a serial fashion, as suggested in Figure 12.1. In the early stages of development, design engineers dominate the process. Later, the prototype is transferred to manufacturing for production. Finally, marketing and sales personnel are brought into the process. This approach has several disadvantages. First, product development time is long. Second, up to 90 percent of manufacturing costs may be committed before manufacturing engineers have any input to the design. Third, the final product may not be the best one for market conditions at the time of introduction.

One of the most significant barriers to efficient product development is poor intraorganizational cooperation.

An approach that alleviates these problems is called **concurrent engineering**, or **simultaneous engineering**. Concurrent engineering involves multifunctional teams, usually consisting of 4 to 20 members and including every specialty in the company. The functions of such teams are to develop the concept and decide what design methods and production methods are appropriate; analyze product functions so that all design decisions are focused on the customer; determine whether the design can be improved without affecting performance; and develop efficient manufacturing processes. Boeing A&T has more than 100 integrated product teams (IPTs) that oversee the design, production, and delivery of the C-17 aircraft's more than 125,000 parts and supporting services. Developing a unique approach, AT&T established nine expert breakthrough teams—called Achieving Process Excellence Teams—that identify process improvements for developing and deploying products faster in the market. They establish standards, procedures, and training for cross-functional communication that prevents problems from occurring. At The Ritz-Carlton Hotel Company, customized hotel products and services, such as meetings and banquet events, receive the full attention of local hotel cross-functional teams. These teams involve all internal and external suppliers, verify production and delivery capabilities before each event, critique samples, and assess results.

Typical benefits of concurrent engineering include 30 to 70 percent less development time, 65 to 90 percent fewer engineering changes, 20 to 90 percent less time to market, 200 to 600 percent improvement in quality, 20 to 110 percent improvement in white collar productivity, and 20 to 120 percent higher return on assets.[7] Among U.S. automakers, Chrysler has been an innovator in fast product development.[8] Chrysler's adoption of simultaneous engineering enabled it to develop and introduce the celebrated Viper sports car in just two years.

Concurrent engineering is a process in which all major functions involved with bringing a product to market are continuously involved with product development from conception through sales. Such an approach not only helps achieve trouble-free introduction of products and services, but also results in improved quality, lower costs, and shorter product development cycles.

Design for Six Sigma

Design for Six Sigma (DFSS) represents a set of tools and methodologies used in the product development process for ensuring that goods and services will meet customer needs and achieve performance objectives, and that the processes used to make and deliver them achieve six sigma capability.

DFSS consists of four principal activities:[9]

1. *Concept development:* In which product functionality is determined based upon customer requirements, technological capabilities, and economic realities
2. *Design development:* Which focuses on product and process performance issues necessary to fulfill the product and service requirements in manufacturing or delivery
3. *Design optimization:* Which seeks to minimize the impact of variation in production and use, creating a "robust" design
4. *Design verification:* Which ensures that the capability of the production system meets the appropriate sigma level

These activities are often incorporated into a variation of the DMAIC process, known as **DMADV**, which stands for *define, measure, analyze, design,* and *verify.* The Define step focuses on identifying the opportunity and clearly defining the issue to be addressed. Measure gathers the voice of the customer and identifies the vital CTQs. The Analyze step is focused on concept development. Design focuses on detailed specifications, design reviews, and approvals. Finally, Verify involves prototype development and testing and implementation planning. The key differences with DMAIC is that DMAIC focuses on existing processes and internal customers, whereas DMADV focuses on goods and services and external customers and generally requires more focus on the voice of the customer and creativity.

Like Six Sigma itself, most tools for DFSS have been around for some time; its uniqueness lies in the manner in which they are integrated into a formal methodology, driven by the Six Sigma philosophy, with clear business objectives in mind.

General Electric was an early adopter of DFSS. For example, back in its 1998 annual report, GE stated that "Every new product and service in the future will be DFSS . . . They were, in essence, designed by the customer, using all of the critical-to-quality performance features (CTQs) the customer wanted in the product and then subjecting these CTQs to the rigorous statistical Design for Six Sigma Process."

One of the early applications of DFSS was at GE's Medical Systems Division. The Lightspeed Computed Tomography (CT) System was the first GE product to be completely designed and developed using DFSS. Lightspeed allows doctors to capture multiple images of a patient's anatomy simultaneously at a speed six times faster than traditional scanners. As a result, productivity doubled while the images had much higher quality.[10]

The remainder of this chapter introduces various tools and approaches that support the four stages of DFSS.

CONCEPT DEVELOPMENT

Concept development is the process of applying scientific, engineering, and business knowledge to produce a basic functional design that meets both customer needs and manufacturing or service delivery requirements. Concept development is a highly creative activity that can be enhanced by such techniques as brainstorming and Brainwriting—a written form of brainstorming—and is focused first on identifying potential ideas. After potential ideas have been identified, they are evaluated using cost/benefit analysis, risk analysis, and other techniques. Finally, the best concept is selected, often using some type of scoring matrix to weight the selection criteria.

The first question one must ask during concept development is: What is the product (good or service) intended to do? In Chapter 5, we stressed the importance of understanding the voice of the customer. It is the starting point for concept development.

How the voice of the customer is translated into physical or operational specifications and production processes for a product or service can mean the difference between a successful product and an outright failure. Other design considerations include a product's weight, size, appearance, safety, life, serviceability, and maintainability. When decisions about these factors are dominated by engineering considerations rather than by customer requirements, poor designs that fail in the market are often the result. A structured approach for concept development is called concept engineering.

Concept Engineering

Concept engineering (CE) emerged from a consortium of companies affiliated with the Center for Quality of Management (http://www.cqm.org) that included Polaroid and Bose along with researchers at MIT. CE is a focused process for discovering customer requirements and using them to select superior product or service concepts that meet those requirements. It employs various techniques to ensure effective processing of qualitative data. Five major steps comprise the process:

1. *Understanding the customer's environment*. This step involves first project planning activities such as team selection, identifying fit with business strategy, and gaining team consensus on the project focus. It also includes collecting the voice of the customer to understand the customer's environment—physical, psychological, competitive, and so on.
2. *Converting understanding into requirements*. In this step, teams analyze the customer transcripts to translate the voice of the customer into more specific requirements using the KJ method we introduced in Chapter 4. Essentially, this step focuses on identifying key design requirements, selecting the most significant ones, and "scrubbing" the requirements to refine them into clear and insightful statements.

3. *Operationalizing what has been learned*. This step involves determining how to measure how well a customer requirement is met by the design concept. For example, a requirement developed for a project at Polaroid was "Document photographer delivers document photo quickly while the customer waits." The principal requirement is about throughput time, so the concept of "quickly" needs to be operationalized and measured.[11] Once potential metrics are defined, they are evaluated to reduce the number of metrics that need to be used while ensuring that they cover all key requirements. This evaluation usually requires some sort of customer questionnaire to identify the importance of the requirements and prioritize them.
4. *Concept generation*. This step focuses on generating ideas for solutions that will potentially meet customers' needs. One unique approach is to brainstorm ideas that might resolve each individual customer requirement, select the best ones, and then classify them under the more traditional functional product characteristics. This approach helps to develop a "market in" rather than a "product out" orientation. Creative thinking techniques are applied here to increase the number and diversity of potential ideas.
5. *Concept selection*. Finally, the potential ideas are evaluated with respect to meeting requirements, trade-offs are assessed, and prototyping may begin. The process ends with reflection on the final concept to test whether the decision "feels right" based on all the knowledge acquired.

As an example, Bose Corporation, a leader in high-end audio products, used concept engineering to improve its European delivery system while decreasing overhead cost to the company.[12] The delivery system included every activity from the time a dealer realizes that he or she needs a product from Bose until the product is delivered. In personal visits to dealers in France, Germany, Holland, Spain, Belgium, and the United Kingdom, Bose developed an interview guide that addressed the following:

1. How do you describe the perfect supplier?
2. Please describe your process of ordering.
3. Where does customer service fit into your business?
4. General questions about your impressions of Bose.

In processing the qualitative data obtained from the interviews, Bose focused on the question, "What scenes or images come to mind when you visualize a supplier's delivery system?" From an analysis of more than 100 customer requirements, 24 were selected as key requirements for a world-class delivery system. This analysis led the team to the conclusion that supplier reliability and system efficiency build confidence and create trusting relationships. Next, these requirements were stated in measurable terms and questionnaires were developed to ensure that the requirements truly reflected the opinions of the dealers. For example, a requirement might be "Have a simple and swift return policy for faulty or damaged products." This requirement might then be measured by the amount of information required to process a product return. The team spent nearly three days generating potential solutions for each customer requirement. As they discussed the strengths of each idea, new ones often emerged, even from seemingly bizarre ideas. The four strongest ideas were chosen, and the team wrote a story or scenario with specific changes that needed to be made to the delivery system as a way of presenting the solution; this form of presentation would enable those outside of the team to understand how the new systems would work in delighting the customer. Although the process was quite tedious, the team members agreed that it was an excellent approach for arriving at an effective solution and turned them "into believers."

DESIGN DEVELOPMENT

After a concept is selected, the detailed design process begins, with a focus on establishing technical requirements and specifications, which represent the transition from a designer's concept to a producible design, while also ensuring that it can be produced economically, efficiently, and with high quality.

Developing a basic functional design involves translating the design concept and customer requirements into measurable technical requirements and, subsequently, into detailed design specifications.

A major problem with the traditional product development process is that customers and engineers speak different languages. Technical requirements, sometimes called design characteristics, translate the voice of the customer into technical language that provides a basis for design specifications such as dimensions and tolerances. A customer might express a requirement for a car as "easy to start." The translation of this requirement into technical language might be "car will start within 10 seconds of continuous cranking." Or, a requirement that "soap leaves my skin feeling soft" demands translation into pH or hardness specifications for the bar of soap. Such specifications provide manufacturing with actionable information for designing and controlling processes.

A powerful tool for establishing technical design requirements that meet customer needs is *quality function deployment.*

Quality Function Deployment

The Japanese developed an approach called **quality function deployment (QFD)** to meet customers' requirements throughout the design process and also in the design of production systems. The term, a translation of the Kanji characters used to describe the process, can sound confusing. QFD is a planning process to guide the design, manufacturing, and marketing of goods by integrating the voice of the customer throughout the organization. Through QFD, every design, manufacturing, and control decision is made to meet the expressed needs of customers. It uses a type of matrix diagram to present data and information.

QFD originated in 1972 at Mitsubishi's Kobe shipyard site. Toyota began to develop the concept shortly thereafter, and has used it since 1977 with impressive results. Between January 1977 and October 1979, Toyota realized a 20 percent reduction in start-up costs on the launch of a new van. By 1982, start-up costs had fallen 38 percent from the 1977 baseline, and by 1984, were reduced by 61 percent. In addition, development time fell by one-third at the same time that quality improved.

Xerox and Ford initiated the use of QFD in the United States in 1986. (At that time, more than 50 percent of major Japanese companies were already using the approach.) Today, QFD is used successfully by manufacturers of automobiles, electronics, appliances, clothing, and construction equipment, by firms such as Mazda, Motorola, Xerox, IBM, Procter & Gamble, Hewlett-Packard, and AT&T. Two organizations, the American Supplier Institute, Inc., a nonprofit organization, and GOAL/QPC, a Massachusetts consulting firm, have publicized and developed the concept in the United States.

Under QFD, all operations of a company are driven by the voice of the customer, rather than by edicts of top management or the opinions or desires of design engineers. QFD departs from the traditional product planning process in which product concepts are originated by design teams or research and development groups, tested and refined, produced, and marketed. Often, a considerable amount of wasted effort and time is spent redesigning products and production systems until customer needs are met. If customer needs can be identified properly in the first place, then such wasteful effort is eliminated, which is the principal focus of QFD.

Product objectives are better understood and interpreted during the production process because all key design information is captured and synthesized. This approach helps to understand trade-offs in design, and promote consensus among managers. Use of QFD focuses on the drivers of customer satisfaction and dissatisfaction, making it a useful tool for competitive analysis of product quality by top management. Productivity as well as quality improvements generally result. Perhaps most significant, though, QFD reduces the time for new product development. QFD allows companies to simulate the effects of new design ideas and concepts. Through this benefit, companies can reduce product development time and bring new products into the market sooner, thus gaining competitive advantage. Details of the QFD process and its use are presented next.

QFD benefits companies through improved communication and teamwork between all constituencies in the value chain, such as between marketing and design, between design and manufacturing, and between purchasing and suppliers.

The House of Quality A set of matrixes is used to relate the voice of the customer to a product's technical requirements, component requirements, process control plans, and manufacturing operations. The first matrix, the customer requirement planning matrix shown in Figure 12.2, provides the basis for the QFD concept. The figure demonstrates why this matrix is often called the **House of Quality**.

Figure 12.2 The House of Quality

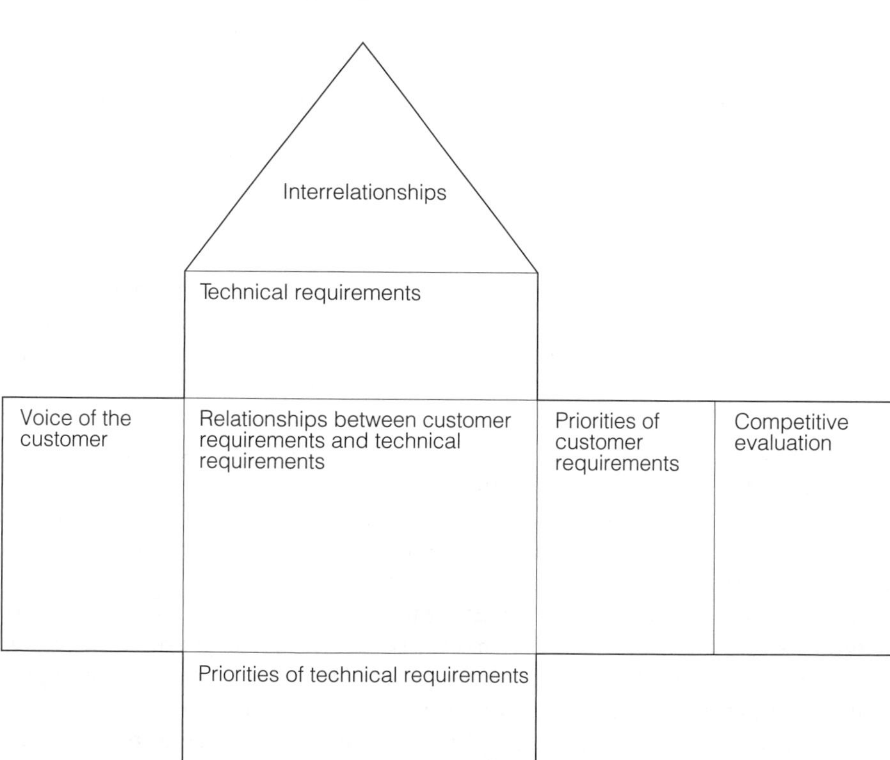

Building the House of Quality consists of six basic steps:

1. Identify customer requirements.
2. Identify technical requirements.
3. Relate the customer requirements to the technical requirements.
4. Conduct an evaluation of competing products or services.
5. Evaluate technical requirements and develop targets.
6. Determine which technical requirements to deploy in the remainder of the production/delivery process.

To illustrate the development of the House of Quality and the QFD process, the task of designing a new fitness center in a community with two other competing organizations is presented.

Step 1: Identify customer requirements. The voice of the customer is the primary input to the QFD process. As discussed in Chapter 5, many methods can be used to gather valid customer information. The most critical and most difficult step of the process is to capture the essence of the customer's needs and expectations. The customer's own words are vitally important in preventing misinterpretation by designers and engineers. Figure 12.3 shows the voice of the customer in the House of Quality for the fitness center, perhaps based on a telephone survey or focus groups. They are grouped into five categories: programs and activities, facilities, atmosphere, staff, and other. These groupings can easily be done using affinity diagrams, for example.

Step 2: List the technical requirements that provide the foundation for the product or service design. Technical requirements are design characteristics that describe the customer requirements as expressed in the language of the designer or engineer. Essentially, they are the "hows" by which the company will respond to the "whats"—customer requirements. They must be measurable, because the output is controlled and compared to objective targets. For the fitness center, these requirements include the number and type of program offerings and equipment, times, staffing requirements, facility characteristics and maintenance, fee structure, and so on. Figure 12.4 adds this information to the House of Quality.

The roof of the House of Quality shows the interrelationships between any pair of technical requirements. Various symbols denote these relationships. A typical scheme uses the symbol • to denote a very strong relationship, ○ for a strong relationship, and Δ to denote a weak relationship. These relationships indicate answers to questions such as, "How does a change in a technical characteristic affect others?" For example, increasing program offerings will probably require more staff, a larger facility, expanded hours, and higher costs; hiring more maintenance staff, building a larger facility, and buying more equipment will probably result in a higher membership fee. Thus, design decisions cannot be viewed in isolation. This relationship matrix helps to evaluate trade-offs.

Step 3: Develop a relationship matrix between the customer requirements and the technical requirements. Customer requirements are listed down the left column; technical requirements are written across the top. In the matrix itself, symbols indicate the degree of relationship in a manner similar to that used in the roof of the House of Quality. The purpose of the relationship matrix is to show whether the final technical requirements adequately address customer requirements. This assessment is usually based on expert experience, customer responses, or controlled experiments.

The lack of a strong relationship between a customer requirement and any technical requirement shows that the customer needs either are not addressed or

Figure 12.3 Voice of the Customer in the House of Quality

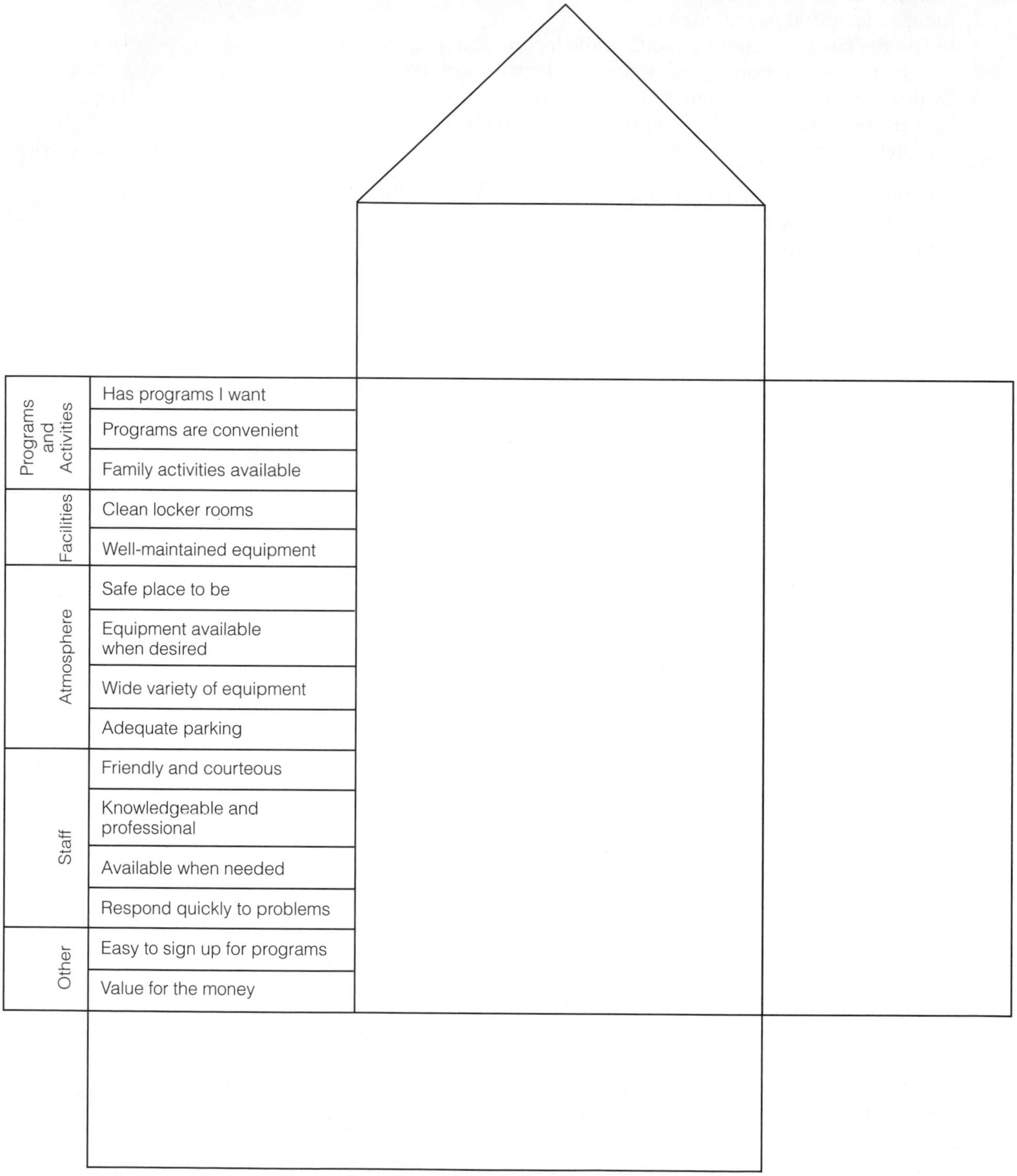

Programs and Activities	Has programs I want
	Programs are convenient
	Family activities available
Facilities	Clean locker rooms
	Well-maintained equipment
Atmosphere	Safe place to be
	Equipment available when desired
	Wide variety of equipment
	Adequate parking
Staff	Friendly and courteous
	Knowledgeable and professional
	Available when needed
	Respond quickly to problems
Other	Easy to sign up for programs
	Value for the money

Figure 12.4 Technical Requirements in the House of Quality

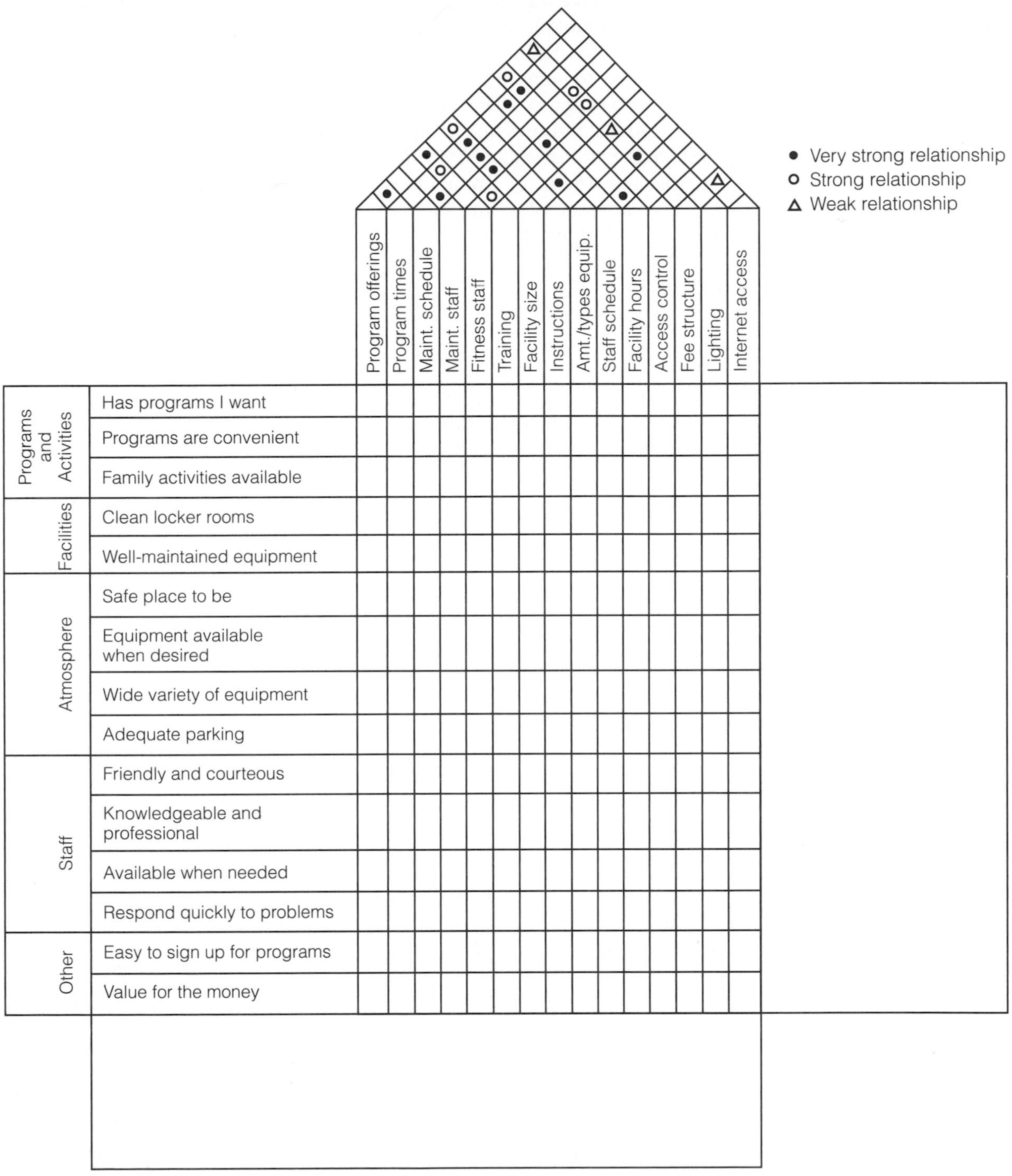

that the final design will have difficulty in meeting them. Similarly, if a technical requirement does not affect any customer requirement, it may be redundant or the designers may have missed some important customer need. For example, the customer requirement "clean locker rooms" bears a very strong relationship to the maintenance schedule and only a strong relationship to the number of maintenance staff. "Easy to sign up for programs" would probably bear a very strong relationship to Internet access and only a weak relationship to the hours the facility is open. Figure 12.5 shows an example of these relationships.

Step 4: Add competitor evaluation and key selling points. This step identifies importance ratings for each customer requirement and evaluates competitors' existing products or services for each of them (see Figure 12.6). Customer importance ratings represent the areas of greatest interest and highest expectations as expressed by the customer. Competitive evaluation highlights the absolute strengths and weaknesses in competing products. By using this step, designers can discover opportunities for improvement. It also links QFD to a company's strategic vision and indicates priorities for the design process. For example, if an important customer requirement receives a low evaluation on all competitors' products (for instance, "family activities available"), then by focusing on this need a company might gain a competitive advantage. Such requirements become key selling points and the basis for formulating marketing strategies.

Step 5: Evaluate technical requirements of competitive products and services and develop targets. This step is usually accomplished through intelligence gathering or product testing and then translated into measurable terms. These evaluations are compared with the competitive evaluation of customer requirements to determine inconsistencies between customer requirements and technical requirement but the evaluation of the related technical requirements indicates otherwise, then either the measures used are faulty or else the product has an image difference (either positive toward the competitor or negative toward the company's product), which affects customer perceptions. On the basis of customer importance ratings and existing product strengths and weaknesses, targets for each technical requirement are set, as shown in Figure 12.7. For example, customers rated programs and family activities of high importance while competitive evaluation shows them to be quite low. Setting a higher target for these requirements will help to meet this critical need and be a source of competitive advantage.

Step 6: Select technical requirements to be deployed in the remainder of the process. The technical requirements that have a strong relationship to customer needs, have poor competitive performance, or are strong selling points are identified during this step. These characteristics have the highest priority and need to be "deployed" throughout the remainder of the design and production process to maintain a responsiveness to the voice of the customer. Those characteristics not identified as critical do not need such rigorous attention. For example, program offerings, amount and types of equipment, facility hours, fee structure, and Internet access have been identified in Figure 12.7 as the key issues to address in designing the fitness center.

The QFD Process The House of Quality provides the marketing function with an important tool to understand customer needs and gives top management strategic direction. However, it is only the first step in the QFD process. The voice of the customer must be carried throughout the production/delivery process. Three other "houses of quality" are linked together to deploy the voice of the customer to (in a manufacturing setting) component parts characteristics, process plans, and

Figure 12.5 Relationship Matrix

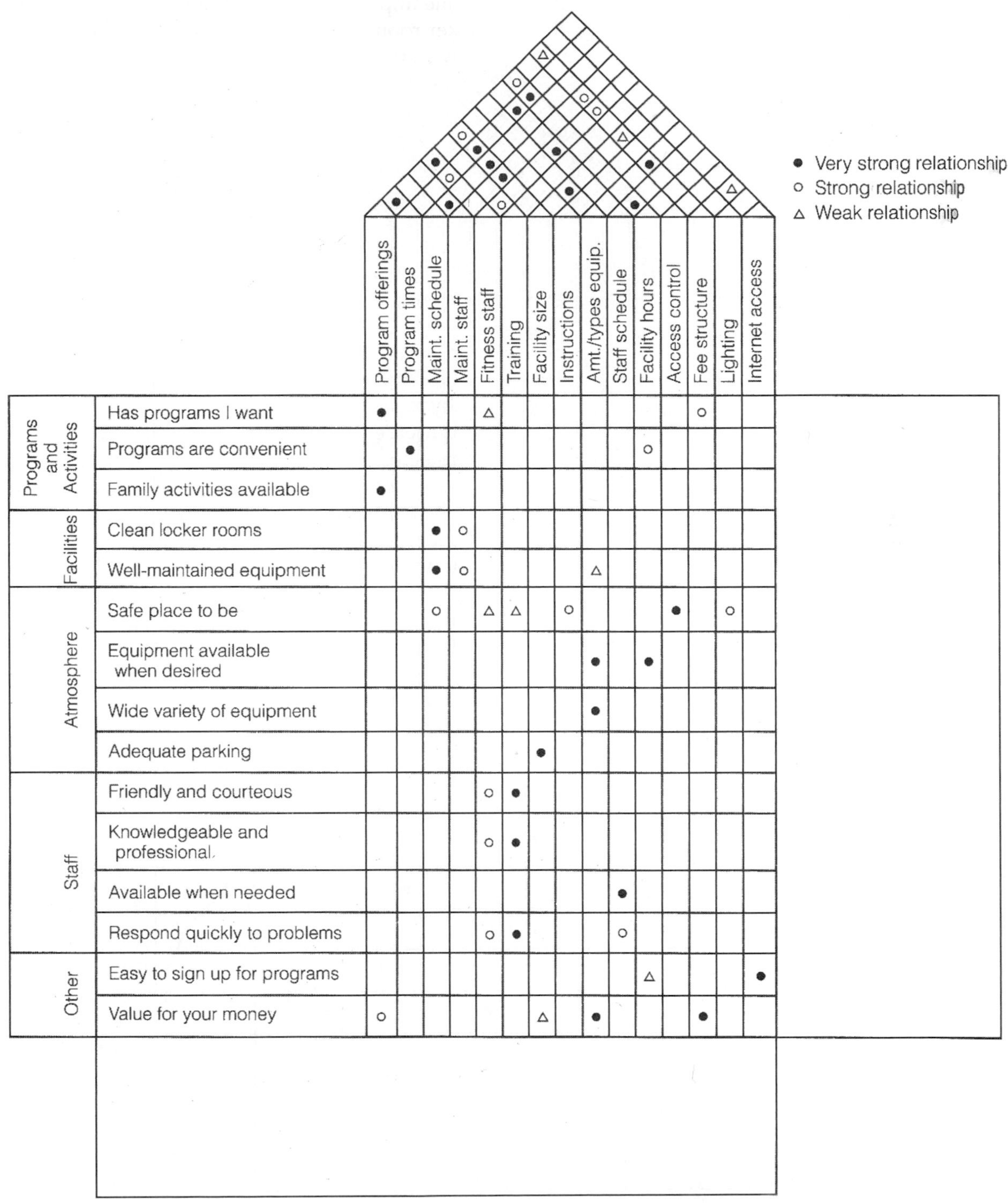

		Program offerings	Program times	Maint. schedule	Maint. staff	Fitness staff	Training	Facility size	Instructions	Amt./types equip.	Staff schedule	Facility hours	Access control	Fee structure	Lighting	Internet access
Programs and Activities	Has programs I want	●				△								○		
	Programs are convenient		●									○				
	Family activities available	●														
Facilities	Clean locker rooms			●	○											
	Well-maintained equipment			●	○					△						
Atmosphere	Safe place to be			○		△	△		○				●		○	
	Equipment available when desired									●		●				
	Wide variety of equipment									●						
	Adequate parking							●								
Staff	Friendly and courteous					○	●									
	Knowledgeable and professional					○	●									
	Available when needed										●					
	Respond quickly to problems					○	●				○					
Other	Easy to sign up for programs											△				●
	Value for your money	○						△		●				●		

Figure 12.6 Competitive Evaluation

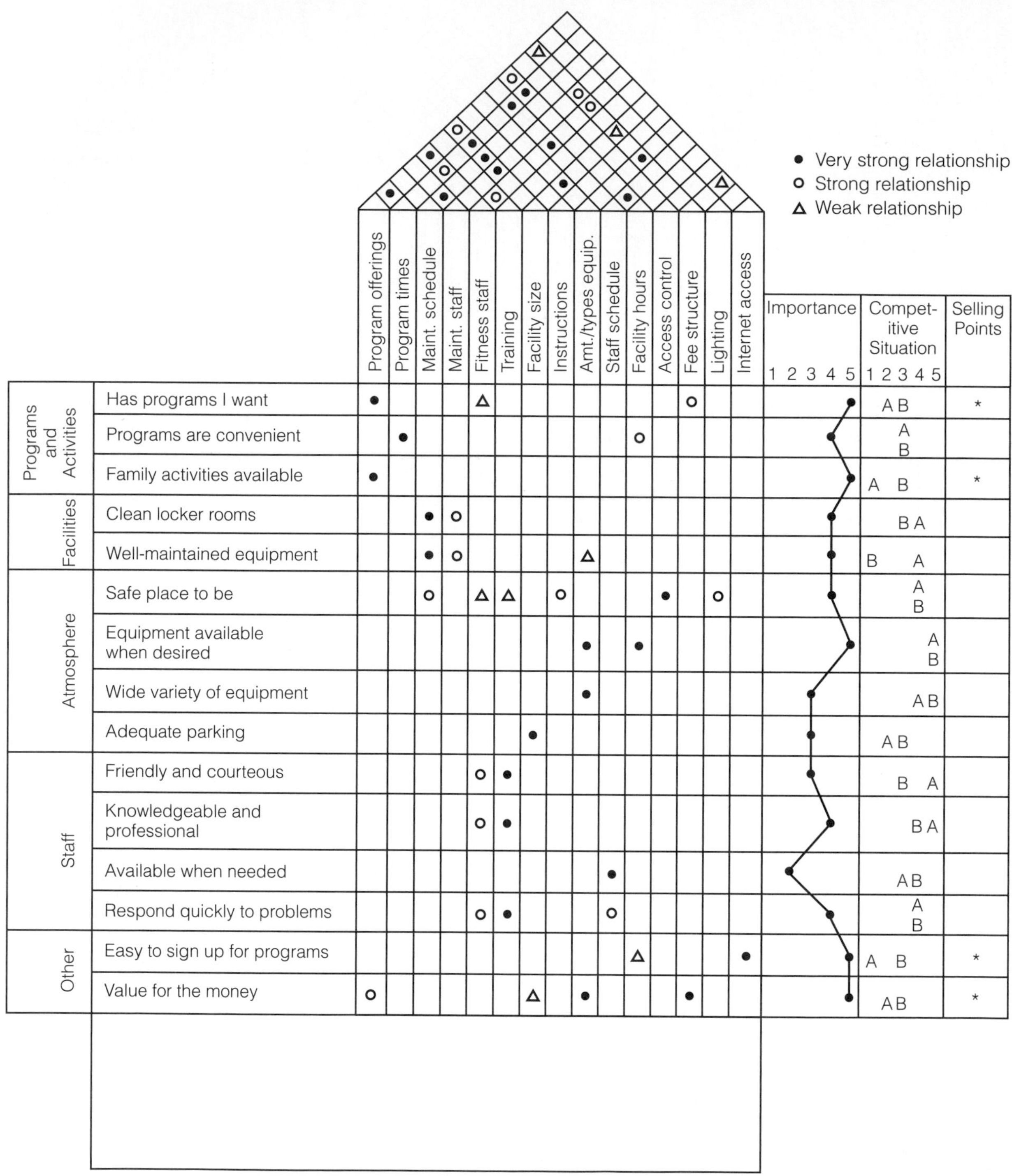

Category	Customer requirement	Program offerings	Program times	Maint. schedule	Maint. staff	Fitness staff	Training	Facility size	Instructions	Amt./types equip.	Staff schedule	Facility hours	Access control	Fee structure	Lighting	Internet access	Competitive Situation	Selling Points
Programs and Activities	Has programs I want	●				△								o			A B	*
	Programs are convenient		●									o					A B	
	Family activities available	●															A B	*
Facilities	Clean locker rooms			●	o												B A	
	Well-maintained equipment			●	o					△							B A	
Atmosphere	Safe place to be			o		△	△		o				●		o		A B	
	Equipment available when desired									●		●					A B	
	Wide variety of equipment									●							A B	
	Adequate parking							●									A B	
Staff	Friendly and courteous					o	●										B A	
	Knowledgeable and professional					o	●										B A	
	Available when needed										●						A B	
	Respond quickly to problems					o	●				o						A B	
Other	Easy to sign up for programs											△				●	A B	*
	Value for the money	o						△		●				●			A B	*

Figure 12.7 Completed House of Quality

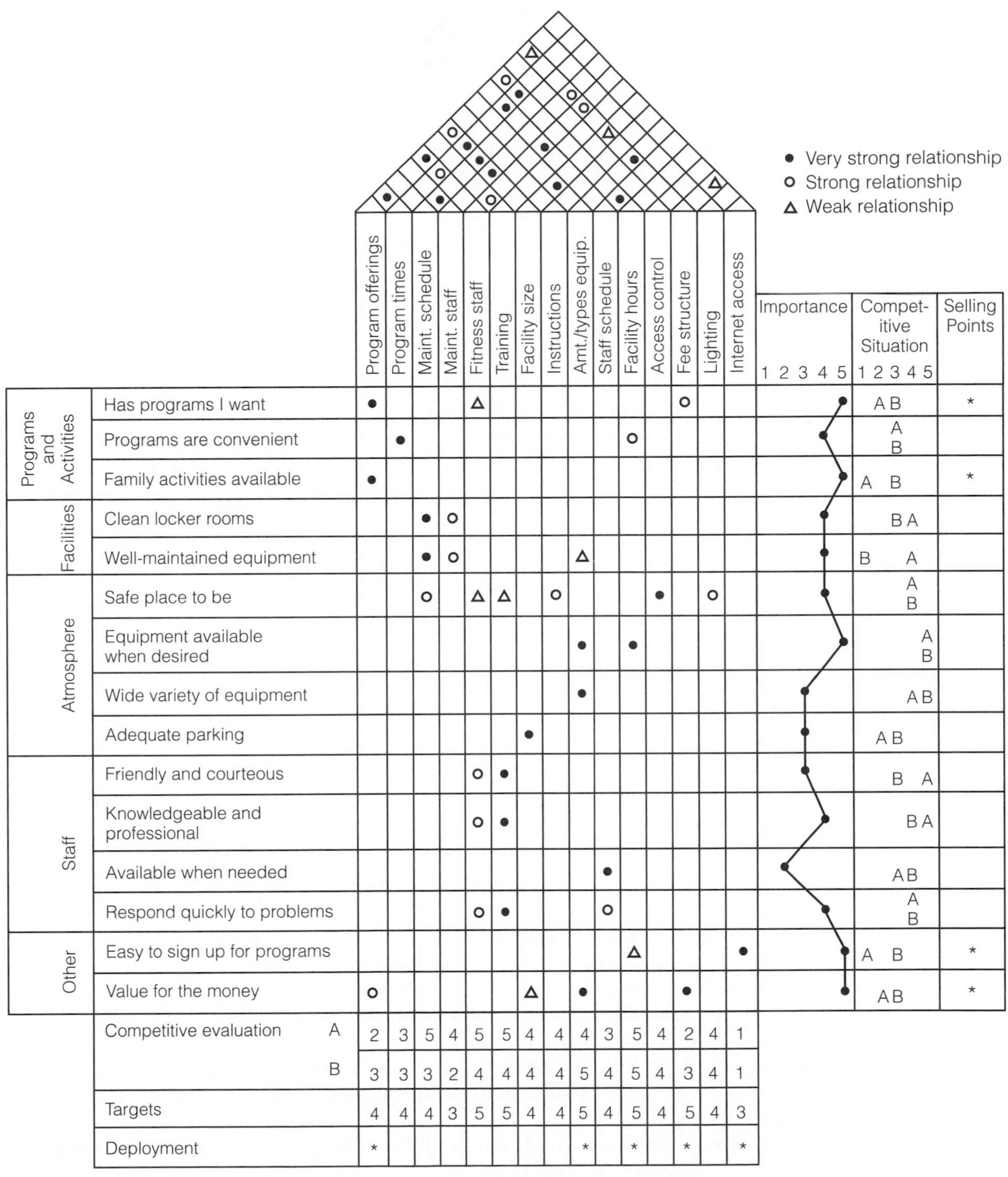

		Program offerings	Program times	Maint. schedule	Maint. staff	Fitness staff	Training	Facility size	Instructions	Amt./types equip.	Staff schedule	Facility hours	Access control	Fee structure	Lighting	Internet access	Competitive Situation	Selling Points
Programs and Activities	Has programs I want	●				△								○			A B	*
	Programs are convenient		●									○					A B	
	Family activities available	●															A B	*
Facilities	Clean locker rooms			●	○												B A	
	Well-maintained equipment			●	○					△							B A	
Atmosphere	Safe place to be			○		△	△		○				●		○		A B	
	Equipment available when desired									●		●					A B	
	Wide variety of equipment									●							A B	
	Adequate parking							●									A B	
Staff	Friendly and courteous					○	●										B A	
	Knowledgeable and professional					○	●										B A	
	Available when needed										●						A B	
	Respond quickly to problems					○	●				○						A B	
Other	Easy to sign up for programs											△				●	A B	*
	Value for the money	○						△		●				●			A B	*
	Competitive evaluation A	2	3	5	4	5	5	4	4	4	3	5	4	2	4	1		
	Competitive evaluation B	3	3	3	2	4	4	4	4	5	4	5	4	3	4	1		
	Targets	4	4	4	3	5	5	4	4	5	4	5	4	5	4	3		
	Deployment	*								*		*		*		*		

Figure 12.8 The Four Linked Houses of Quality

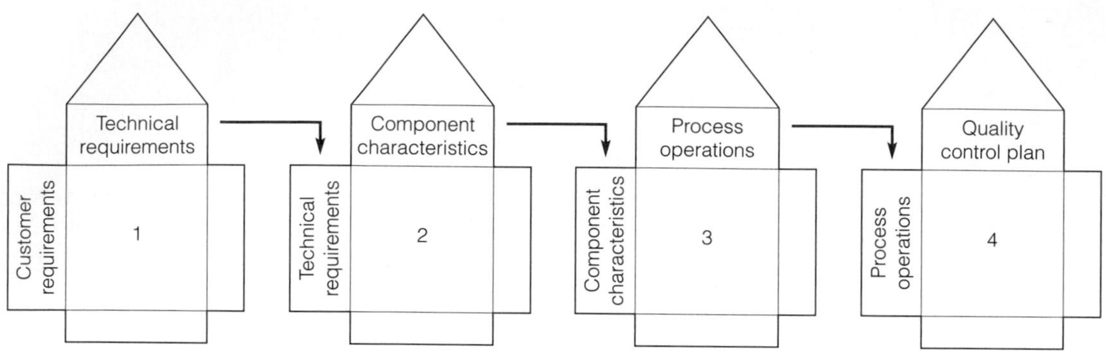

quality control. The second house is similar to the first house but applies to subsystems and components. The technical requirements from the first house are related to detailed requirements of subsystems and components (see Figure 12.8). At this stage, target values representing the best values for fit, function, and appearance are determined. For example, program offerings might be broken down into fitness programs, children's programs, family programs, and so on, each with its own unique set of design requirements, and hence, its own House of Quality.

In manufacturing, most of the QFD activities represented by the first two houses of quality are performed by product development and engineering functions. At the next stage, the planning activities involve supervisors and production line operators. In the third house, the process plan relates the component characteristics to key process operations, the transition from planning to execution. (For the fitness center, this step might involve creating a project plan for selecting, designing, and evaluating programs.) Key process operations are the basis for a *control point*. A control point forms the basis for a quality control plan delivering those critical characteristics that are crucial to achieving customer satisfaction, as specified in the last house of quality. At this point, for example, the fitness center might design membership surveys for evaluating programs, checklists for maintenance, performance appraisal approaches for the staff, and measures of equipment failures and problems. These activities are what must be measured and evaluated on a continuous basis to ensure that processes continue to meet the important customer requirements defined in the first House of Quality. Thus, the QFD process provides a thread from the voice of the customer, through design and production/delivery activities, to daily management and control. In that way, it provides the basis for more advanced methodologies such as design of experiments, and for effective implementation of statistical process control, which we discuss in Chapter 13.

The vast majority of applications of QFD in the United States concentrate on the first and, to a lesser extent, the second houses of quality.

Lawrence Sullivan, who brought QFD to the West, suggested that the third and fourth houses of quality offer far more significant benefits than the first two, especially in the United States.[13] In Japan, managers, engineers, and workers are more naturally cross-functional and tend to promote group effort and consensus thinking. In the United States, workers and managers are more vertically oriented and tend to suboptimize for individual and/or departmental achievements.

Companies in the United States tend to promote breakthrough achievements, which often inhibits cross-functional interaction. If a U.S. company can maintain the breakthrough culture with emphasis on continuous improvement through more effective cross-functional interactions as supported by QFD, it can establish a competitive advantage over competitors. The third and fourth houses of quality utilize the knowledge of about 80 percent of a company's employees—supervisors and operators. If their knowledge goes unused, this potential is wasted.

Design for Manufacturability

Designers must pay particular attention to cost, quality, and manufacturability in order to meet price targets that customers are willing to pay. A Samsung manager noted that 70 to 80 percent of quality, cost, and delivery time is determined in the initial design stages. This is one reason's for the company's obsession with reducing complexity early in the design cycle. As a result, Samsung has lower manufacturing costs, higher profit margins, quicker times to market, and more often than not, more innovative products than its competition.[14]

Simplifying designs can often improve both cost and quality. Mercedes-Benz, for example, saw its global leadership decline behind BMW and Lexus because of high costs and degrading quality. Although a technology leader, Mercedes' vehicles were packed with numerous electronic systems that need to be integrated and function seamlessly together, a very difficult task. Engineers typically designed new electronics for each model, adding to complexity and cost. One of the initiatives the company has undertaken to improve is to design less complex cars similar to what BMW did, for instance, using electronics architectures with common components that can be shared across many models.[15] By cutting the number of parts, material costs generally go down, inventory levels fall, the number of suppliers shrinks, and production time can be shortened.

Product design can significantly affect the cost of manufacturing (direct and indirect labor, materials, and overhead), redesign, warranty, and field repair; the efficiency by which the product can be manufactured, and the quality of the output.

Many aspects of product design can adversely affect manufacturability and, hence, quality.[16] Some parts may be designed with features difficult to fabricate repeatedly or with unnecessarily tight tolerances. Some parts may lack details for self-alignment or features for correct insertion. In other cases, parts so fragile or so susceptible to corrosion or contamination may be damaged in shipping or by internal handling. Sometimes a design simply has more parts than are needed to perform the desired functions, which increases the chance of assembly error. Thus, problems of poor design may show up as errors, poor yield, damage, or functional failure in fabrication, assembly, test, transport, and end use.

Designs with numerous parts increase the incidence of part mix-ups, missing parts, and test failures. Parts that are similar but not identical create the possibility that an assembler will use the wrong part. Parts without details to prevent insertion in the wrong orientation lead to more frequent improper assembly. Complicated assembly steps or tricky joining processes can cause incorrect, incomplete, unreliable, or otherwise faulty assemblies. Finally, the designer's failure to consider conditions to which parts will be exposed during assembly such as temperature, humidity, vibration, static electricity, and dust, may result in failures during testing or use.

Design for manufacturability (DFM) is the process of designing a product for efficient production at the highest level of quality. DFM is typically integrated into standard design processes, but because of the need for highly-creative solutions, it might be addressed in specialized "think-tank" departments in a company. Samsung, for example, supports a Value Innovation Program (VIP) Center, which has been described as "an invitation-only, round-the-clock, assembly line for ideas and profits where Samsung's top researchers, engineers, and designers come to solve their grittiest problems."[17] Typical projects might involve reducing material costs on a new printer by 30 percent, or reducing the number of steps needed to manufacture a new camcorder by 25 percent. Texas Instruments locates its design centers strategically throughout its facilities. These centers offer expertise and systems with extensive capability for electrical and mechanical computer-aided design, system engineering, and manufacturing, and allow the evaluation of parts that have the best quality history, producibility, reliability, and other special engineering requirements.

DFM is intended to prevent product designs that simplify assembly operations but require more complex and expensive components, designs that simplify component manufacture while complicating the assembly process, and designs that are simple and inexpensive to produce but difficult or expensive to service or support.

Table 12.1 summarizes important design guidelines for improving manufacturability and thus improving quality and reducing costs. Many industries have developed more specific guidelines. For example, guidelines for designing printed circuit boards include:

- Placing all components on the topside of the board
- Grouping similar components whenever possible
- Maintaining a 0.60-inch clearance for insertable components

Design and Environmental Responsibility

Environmental concerns have an unprecedented impact on product and process designs. Hundreds of millions of home and office appliances are disposed of each year. The problem of what to do with obsolete computers is a growing design and technological waste problem today.[18] Pressures from environmental groups clamoring for "socially responsive" designs, states and municipalities that are running out of space for landfills, and consumers who want the most for their money all cause designers and managers to look carefully at the concept of **design-for-environment**, or **DFE**.[19]

DFE is the explicit consideration of environmental concerns during the design of products and processes, and includes such practices as designing for recyclability and disassembly.

DFE offers the potential to create more desirable products at lower costs by reducing disposal and regulatory costs, increasing the end-of-life value of products, reducing material use, and minimizing liabilities. Recyclable products are designed to be taken apart and their components repaired, refurbished, melted down, or otherwise salvaged for reuse. For example, General Electric's plastics division, which serves the durable goods market, uses only thermoplastics in its products.[20] Unlike many other varieties of plastics, thermoplastics can be melted down and recast into other shapes and products, thus making them recyclable.

Many products are discarded simply because the cost of maintenance or repair is too high when compared with the cost of a new item. Now **design for disassembly** promises to bring back easy, affordable product repair. For example, Whirlpool Corporation is developing a new appliance designed for repairability, with its parts sorted for easy coding. Thus, repairability has the potential of pleasing customers, who would prefer to repair a product rather than discard it. At the same time,

Table 12.1 Design Guidelines for Quality Assurance

Guideline		Result
Minimize Number of Parts		
• Fewer parts and assembly drawings	→	Lower volume of drawings and instructions to control
• Less complicated assemblies	→	Lower assembly error rate
• Fewer parts to hold to required quality characteristics	→	Higher consistency of part quality
• Fewer parts to fail	→	Higher reliability
Minimize Number of Part Numbers		
• Fewer variations of like parts	→	Lower assembly error rate
Design for Robustness (Taguchi method)		
• Low sensitivity to component variability	→	Higher first-pass yield; less degradation of performance with time
Eliminate Adjustments		
• No assembly adjustment errors	→	Higher first-pass yield
• Eliminates adjustable components with high failure rates	→	Lower failure rate
Make Assembly Easy and Foolproof		
• Parts cannot be assembled wrong	→	Lower assembly error rate
• Obvious when parts are missing	→	Lower assembly error rate
• Assembly tooling designed into part	→	Lower assembly error rate
• Parts are self-securing	→	Lower assembly error rate
• No "force fitting" of parts	→	Less damage to parts; better serviceability
Use Repeatable, Well-Understood Processes		
• Part quality easy to control	→	Higher part yield
• Assembly quality easy to control	→	Higher assembly yield
Choose Parts That Can Survive Process Operations		
• Less damage to parts	→	Higher yield
• Less degradation of parts	→	Higher reliability
Design for Efficient and Adequate Testing		
• Less mistaking "good" for "bad" product and vice versa	→	Truer assessment of quality; less unnecessary rework
Lay Out Parts for Reliable Process Completion		
• Less damage to parts during handling and assembly	→	Higher yield; higher reliability
Eliminate Engineering Changes on Released Products		
• Fewer errors due to changeovers and multiple revisions/versions	→	Lower assembly error rate

Source: Reprinted with permission from D. Daetz, "The Effect of Product Design on Product Quality and Product Cost," *Quality Progress* vol. 20, no. 6, pp. 63–67, June 1987.

companies are challenged to consider fresh approaches to design that build both cost-effectiveness and quality into the product. For instance, even though it is more efficient to assemble an item using rivets instead of screws, this approach is contrary to a design-for-disassembly philosophy. An alternative might be an entirely new design that eliminates the need for fasteners in the first place.

Design for Excellence

Design for Excellence (DFX) is an emerging concept that includes many design-related initiatives such as concurrent engineering, design for manufacturability, design for assembly, design for environment, and other "design for" approaches.[21]

DFX objectives include higher functional performance, physical performance, user friendliness, reliability and durability, maintainability and serviceability, safety, compatibility and upgradeability, environmental friendliness, and psychological characteristics. DFX represents a total approach to product development and design involves the following activities:

- Constantly thinking in terms of how one can design or manufacture products better, not just solving or preventing problems
- Focusing on "things done right" rather than "things gone wrong"
- Defining customer expectations and going beyond them, not just barely meeting them or just matching the competition
- Optimizing desirable features or results, not just incorporating them
- Minimizing the overall cost without compromising quality of function

Target and Tolerance Design

After basic technical requirements have been established, designers must set specific dimensional or operational targets and tolerances for critical manufacturing or service characteristics. Although we will focus our attention on manufactured goods, similar considerations apply to services. Consider a typical microprocessor. The drawing in Figure 12.9 shows some of the critical dimensions and tolerances for the microprocessor. The "ratio" notation (0.514/0.588) denotes the permissible range of the dimension. Unless otherwise stated, the nominal dimension is the midpoint. Thus, the specification of 0.514/0.588 may be interpreted as a nominal dimension of 0.551 with a tolerance of plus or minus 0.037. Usually, this is written as 0.551 ± 0.037. The manufacturing-based definition of quality conformance to specifications is based on such tolerances.

Specifications apply to services as well. At Starbucks, the national chain of coffeehouses, milk must be steamed to at least 150 degrees Fahrenheit but never more than 170 degrees, and every espresso shot must be pulled within 23 seconds of service or tossed.[22] Government regulations often determine specifications for food and pharmaceutical products. For example, the U.S. Food and Drug

*Manufacturing specifications consist of nominal dimensions and tolerances. **Nominal** refers to the ideal dimension or the target value that manufacturing seeks to meet; **tolerance** is the permissible variation, recognizing the difficulty of meeting a target consistently.*

Figure 12.9 Microprocessor Specifications

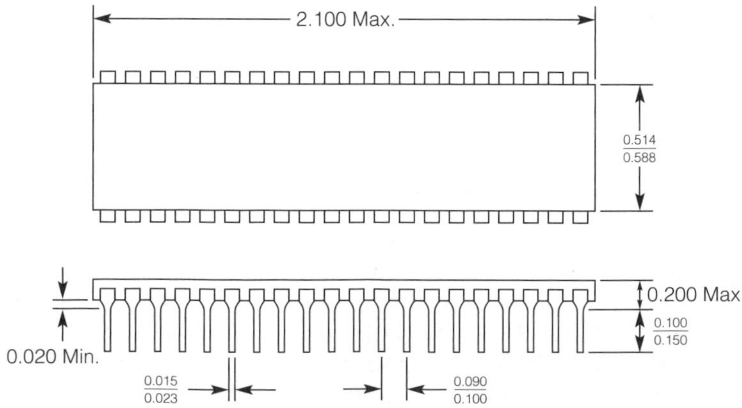

Administration (FDA) sets quality standards regarding the number of unsavory items that find their way into food products.[23] Packaged mushrooms are allowed to contain up to 20 maggots of any size per 100 grams of drained mushrooms or 15 grams of dried mushrooms, while 100 grams of peanut butter may have an average of 30 insect fragments and one rodent hair. (Need we say more?)

Tolerances are necessary because not all parts can be produced exactly to nominal specifications because of natural variations (common causes) in production processes due to the "5 Ms": men and women, materials, machines, methods, and measurement.

Tolerance design involves determining the permissible variation in a dimension. To design tolerances effectively, engineers must understand the necessary trade-offs. Narrow tolerances tend to raise manufacturing costs but they also increase the interchangeability of parts within the plant and in the field, product performance, durability, and appearance. Also, a tolerance reserve or factor of safety is needed to account for engineering uncertainty regarding the maximum variation allowable and compatibility with satisfactory product performance. Wide tolerances, on the other hand, increase material utilization, machine throughput, and labor productivity, but have a negative impact on product characteristics, as previously mentioned. Thus, factors operating to enlarge tolerances include production planning requirements; tool design, fabrication, and setup; tool adjustment and replacement; process yield; inspection and gauge control and maintenance; and labor and supervision requirements.

Traditionally, tolerances are set by convention rather than scientifically. A designer might use the tolerances specified on previous designs or base a design decision on judgment from past experience. Setting inappropriate tolerances can be costly. For instance, in one company, a bearing seat had to be machined on a large part, costing more than $1,000. Because of the precision tolerance specified by design engineers, one or two parts per month had to be scrapped when the tolerance was exceeded. A study revealed that the bearings being used did not require such precise tolerances. When the tolerance was relaxed, the problem disappeared. This one design change resulted in approximately $20,000 in savings per year.

All too often, tolerance settings fail to account for the impact of variation on product functionality, manufacturability, or economic consequences. In a review of Audi's TT Coupe when it was first introduced, automobile columnist Alan Vonderhaar noted, "There was apparently some problem with the second-gear synchronizer, a device that is supposed to ease shifts. As a result, on full-power upshifts from first to second, I frequently got gear clashes." He observed others with the same problem, from reading Internet newsgroups and concluded, "It appears to be an issue that surfaces just now and again, here and there throughout the production mix, suggesting it may be a tolerance issue—sometimes the associated parts are close enough to specifications to get along well, other times they're at the outer ranges of manufacturing tolerance and cause problems."[24]

DESIGN OPTIMIZATION

Designers of products and processes should make every effort to *optimize* their designs. A good analogy for understanding this concept is to consider the task of a major league baseball manager who must design the best player lineup. Although variation will be a factor among individuals as well as with the opposing team's defense, the manager would like to set the lineup that best plays to their strengths and overcomes their weaknesses.

Robust design refers to designing goods and services that are insensitive to variation in manufacturing processes and when consumers use them. Robust design is facilitated by design of experiments (see Chapter 10) to identify optimal levels for nominal dimensions and the use of the Taguchi loss function for optimizing tolerances.

Design optimization includes setting proper tolerances to ensure maximum product performance and making designs ***robust****, that is, insensitive to variations in manufacturing or the use environment.*

The Taguchi Loss Function

A scientific approach to tolerance design uses the **Taguchi loss function**, a concept introduced in Chapter 3. Recall that, as opposed to "goalpost" specifications, Taguchi suggests that no strict cut-off point divides good quality from poor quality. The following example supports this notion. The Japanese newspaper *Asahi Shimbum* (see http://www.asahi.com/english/english.html for current business and other news in Japan) published an example comparing the cost and quality of Sony televisions at two plants in Japan and San Diego.[25] The color density of all the units produced at the San Diego plant were within specifications, whereas some of those shipped from the Japanese plant were not (see Figure 12.10). However, the average loss per unit of the San Diego plant was \$0.89 greater than that of the Japanese plant. This increased cost occurred because workers adjusted units that were out of specification at the San Diego plant, adding cost to the process. Furthermore, a unit adjusted to minimally meet specifications was more likely to generate customer complaints than a unit close to the original target value, therefore incurring higher field service costs. Figure 12.10 shows that fewer U.S.-produced sets met the target value for color density. The distribution of quality in the Japanese plant was more uniform around the target value, and though some units were out of specification, the total cost was less. Taguchi measured quality as the variation from the target value of a design specification, and then translated that variation into an economic "loss function" that expresses the cost of variation in monetary terms.

In mathematical terms, Taguchi assumes that losses can be approximated by a quadratic function so that larger deviations from target correspond to increasingly larger losses. For the case in which a specific target value, T, is determined to produce the optimum performance, and in which quality deteriorates as the actual value moves away from the target on either side (called "nominal is best"), the loss function is represented by

$$L(x) = k(x - T)^2$$

where x is any actual value of the quality characteristic and k is some constant. Thus, $(x - T)$ represents the deviation from the target, and the loss increases by the square of the deviation. Figure 12.11 illustrates this function.

Figure 12.10 Variation in U.S.-Made Versus Japanese-Made Television Components

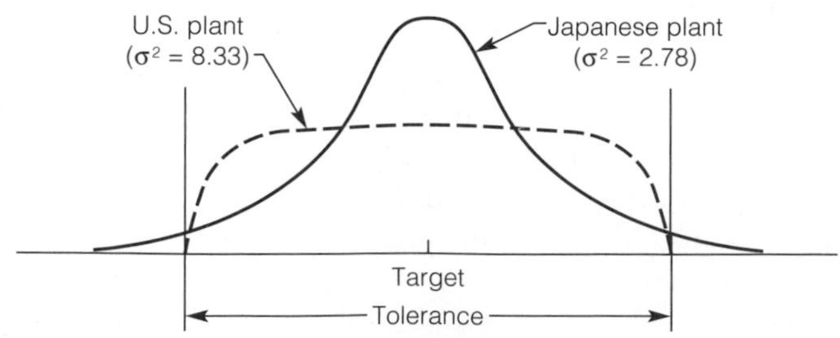

Figure 12.11 Nominal-Is-Best Loss Function

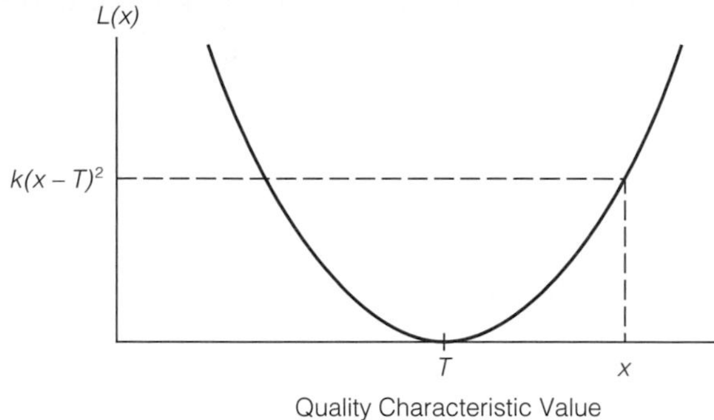

The constant, k, is estimated by determining the cost associated with a certain deviation from the target, as the following example illustrates. Assume that a certain quality characteristic has a specification of 0.500 ± 0.020. An analysis of company records reveals that if the value of the quality characteristic exceeds the target of 0.500 by the tolerance of 0.020 on either side, the product is likely to require an adjustment during the warranty period and cost $50 for repair. Then,

$$50 = k(0.020)^2$$
$$k = 50/0.0004 = 125{,}000$$

Therefore, the loss function is

$$L(x) = 125{,}000(x - T)^2$$

Thus, if the deviation is only 0.010, the estimated loss is

$$L(0.010) = 125{,}000(0.010)^2 = \$12.50$$

If the distribution of the variation about the target value is known, the average loss per unit can be computed by statistically averaging the loss associated with possible values of the quality characteristic. In statistical terminology, this average loss per unit is simply the expected value of the loss. To keep the mathematics simple, consider the following example.

Suppose that two processes, A and B, have the following distributions of a quality characteristic with specification 0.50 ± 0.02. In process A, the output of the process has values ranging from 0.48 to 0.52, all of which are equally likely. For process B, 60 percent of the output is expected to have a value of 0.50, 15 percent has a value of 0.49, and so on, as shown in the table below:

Value	Process A Probability	Process B Probability
0.47	0	0.02
0.48	0.20	0.03
0.49	0.20	0.15
0.50	0.20	0.60
0.51	0.20	0.15
0.52	0.20	0.03
0.53	0	0.02

Notice that the output from process A is spread equally over the range from 0.48 to 0.52 and lies entirely within specifications. In process B, output is concentrated near the target value, but does not entirely lie within specifications. Using the loss function

$$L(x) = 125{,}000(x - 0.50)^2,$$

the expected loss for each process can be computed as follows:

Value, x	Loss	Process A Probability	Weighted Loss	Process B Probability	Weighted Loss
0.47	112.5	0.00	0	0.02	2.25
0.48	50.0	0.20	10	0.03	1.50
0.49	12.5	0.20	2.5	0.15	1.875
0.50	0.0	0.20	0	0.60	0
0.51	12.5	0.20	2.5	0.15	1.875
0.52	50.0	0.20	10	0.03	1.50
0.53	112.5	0.00	0	0.02	2.25
		Expected loss	25.0		11.25

Clearly, process B incurs a smaller total expected loss even though some output falls outside specifications.

The expected loss is computed using a simple formula that involves the variance of the quality characteristic, σ^2, and the square of the deviation of the mean value from the target $D^2 = (\bar{x} - T)^2$. The expected loss is

$$EL(x) = k(\sigma^2 + D^2)$$

For instance, in process A, the variance of the quality characteristic is 0.0002 and $D^2 = 0$ because the mean value is equal to the target. Thus,

$$EL(x) = 125{,}000(0.0002 + 0) = 25$$

A similar computation can be used to determine the expected loss for process B.

To relate this calculation to the Sony television example cited above, k was determined to be 0.16. Because the mean of both distributions of color density fell on the target value, $D^2 = 0$ for both the U.S. and the Japanese plants. However, the variance of the distributions differed. For the San Diego plant, $\sigma^2 = 8.33$ and for the Japanese plant, $\sigma^2 = 2.78$. Thus, the average loss per unit was computed to be

$$\text{San Diego plant: } 0.16(8.33) = \$1.33$$

$$\text{Japanese plant: } 0.16(2.78) = \$0.44$$

or a difference of $0.89 per unit.

The expected loss provides a measure of variation that is independent of specification limits. Such a measure stresses continuous improvement rather than acceptance of the status quo simply because a product "conforms to specifications."

Not all quality characteristics have nominal targets with tolerances on either side. In some cases, such as impurities in a chemical process or fuel consumption, "smaller is better." In other cases, "larger is better" as with breaking strength or product life. The loss function for the smaller-is-better case is

$$L(x) = kx^2$$

and for the larger-is-better case is

$$L(x) = k(1/x^2)$$

These formulas can be applied in a manner similar to the previous examples. The following example shows how the Taguchi loss function may be used to set tolerances. Cassette tapes are still used in some handheld recording devices and in less expensive portable musical instrument recording devices. The desired speed of a cassette tape is 1.875 inches per second. Any deviation from this value causes a change in pitch and tempo and thus poor sound quality. Suppose that adjusting the tape speed under warranty when a customer complains and returns a device costs a manufacturer \$20. (This repair expense does not include other costs due to customer dissatisfaction and therefore is at best a lower bound on the actual loss.) Based on past information, the company knows the average customer will return a player if the tape speed is off the target by at least 0.15 inch per second. The loss function constant is computed as

$$20 = k(0.15)^2$$
$$k = 888.9$$

and thus the loss function is

$$L(x) = 888.9(x - 1.875)^2$$

At the factory, the adjustment can be made at a much lower cost of \$3, which consists of the labor to make the adjustment and additional testing. What should the tolerance be before an adjustment is made at the factory?

To use the loss function, set $L(x)$ = \$3 and solve for the tolerance:

$$3 = 888.9\,(\text{one-half tolerance})^2$$
$$\text{Tolerance} = \pm\sqrt{3/888.9} = \pm 0.058$$

Therefore, if the tape speed is off by more than 0.058 inches per second, adjusting it at the factory is more economical. Thus, the specifications should be 1.875 ± 0.058 or 1.817 to 1.933.

Design Failure Mode and Effects Analysis

Safety in consumer products represents a major issue in design, and certainly an important part of a company's public responsibilities. In a survey of more than 500 chief executives, more than one-third worked for firms that canceled the introduction of products because of liability concerns.

All parties responsible for design, manufacture, sales, and service of a defective product are now liable for damages.

According to the theory of strict liability, anyone who sells a product that is defective or unreasonably dangerous is subject to liability for any physical harm caused to the user, the consumer, or the property of either.[26] This law applies when the seller is in the business of selling the product, and the product reaches the consumer without a substantial change in condition even if the seller exercised all possible care in the preparation and sale of the product. The principal issue is whether a defect, direct or indirect, exists. If the existence of a defect can be established, the manufacturer usually will be held liable. A plaintiff need prove only that (1) the product was defective, (2) the defect was present when the product changed ownership, and (3) the defect resulted in injury. In 1997, Chrysler was ordered to pay \$262.5 million in a case involving defective latches on minivans; thus, the economic consequences can be significant.

Attention to design quality can greatly reduce the possibility of product liability claims as well as provide supporting evidence in defense arguments. Liability makes documentation of quality assurance procedures a necessity. A firm should record all evidence that shows the designer established test and monitoring procedures of critical product characteristics. Feedback on test and inspection results along with corrective actions taken must also be documented. Even adequate packaging and handling procedures are not immune to examination in liability suits, because packaging is still within the manufacturer's span of control. Managers should address the following questions:[27]

- Is the product reasonably safe for the end user?
- What could possibly go wrong with it?
- Are any needed safety devices absent?
- What kind of warning labels or instructions should be included?
- What would attorneys call "reasonable foreseeable use"?
- What are some extreme climatic or environmental conditions for which the product should be tested?
- What similarities does the product have with others that may have encountered previous problems?

One tool for proactively addressing such risks is **design failure mode and effects analysis (DFMEA)**, often simply called FMEA.[28] DFMEA was used by NASA in the 1960s and became popular in the automotive industry in the 1980s. Recently, it has found increasing application in health care. A Joint Commission for Accreditation of Healthcare Organizations standard lists DFMEA as a risk assessment tool, referring to it as "fault mode and effect analysis." The Institute for Healthcare Improvement defines FMEA as "a systematic, proactive method for evaluating a process to identify where and how it may fail and to assess the relative impact of different failures, in order to identify the parts of the process that are most in need of change."[29]

A DFMEA usually consists of specifying the following information for each design element or function:

- *Failure modes:* Ways in which each element or function can fail. This information generally takes some research and imagination. One way to start is with known failures that have occurred in the past. Documents such as quality and reliability reports, test results, and warranty reports provide useful information.
- *Effect of the failure on the customer:* Such as dissatisfaction, potential injury or other safety issue, downtime, repair requirements, and so on. Maintenance records, customer complaints, and warranty reports provide good sources of information. Consideration should be given to failures on the function of the end product, manufacturability in the next process, what the customer sees or experiences, and product safety.
- *Severity, likelihood of occurrence, and detection rating:* These are subjective ratings best done by a cross-functional team of experts. The severity rating is based on how serious the impact would be if the potential failure were to occur. Severity might be measured on a scale of 1 to 10, where a "1" indicates that the failure is so minor that the customer probably would not notice it, and a "10" might mean that the customer might be endangered. The occurrence rating is based on the probability of the potential failure occurring. This might be based on service history or field performance and provides an indication of the significance of the failure. The detection rating is based on how easily the potential failure could be detected prior to occurrence. Based on the severity of these assessments, a risk priority number (RPN) can be derived to identify critical failure modes that must be addressed.

- *Potential causes of failure:* Often failure is the result of poor design. Design deficiencies can cause errors either in the field or in manufacturing and assembly. Identification of causes might require experimentation and rigorous analysis.
- *Corrective actions or controls:* These controls might include design changes, mistake proofing, better user instructions, management responsibilities, and target completion dates.

After a DFMEA is completed, the organization should take corrective and preventive action to avoid the potential failures in the design or process. Figure 12.12 shows an example in health care. The risk priority number is the product of the severity, likelihood of occurrence, and detection ratings, whose scales are shown in Figure 12.13.

Using DFMEA will not only improve product functionality and safety, but also reduce external failure costs—particularly warranty costs, as well as decrease manufacturing and service delivery problems. It can also provide a defense against frivolous lawsuits. DFMEA should be conducted early in the design process to save costs and reduce cycle times, and provide a knowledge base to improve subsequent design efforts. This approach can also be used for processes to identify hazardous conditions that may endanger a worker or operational problems that can disrupt a production process and result in scrap, downtime, or other non-value-added costs.

Reliability Prediction and Optimization

Reliability—the ability of a product to perform as expected over time—is one of the principal dimensions of quality. Reliability is an essential aspect of both product and process design. Sophisticated equipment used today in such areas as transportation (airplanes), communications (satellites), and medicine (pacemakers) requires high reliability. High reliability can also provide a competitive advantage for many consumer goods. Japanese automobiles gained large market shares in the 1970s primarily because of their high reliability, and 2009 model Japanese brands still dominate the *Consumer Reports* annual ranking for predicted reliability in every vehicle category, although Ford has made significant improvements among domestic automakers.[30]

As the overall quality of products continues to improve, consumers expect higher reliability with each purchase; they simply are not satisfied with products that fail unexpectedly. However, the increased complexity of modern products makes high reliability more difficult to achieve. Likewise in manufacturing, the increased use of automation, complexity of machines, low profit margins, and time-based competitiveness make reliability in production processes a critical issue for survival of the business.

Basic Concepts and Definitions Like quality, reliability is often defined in a similar "transcendent" manner as a sense of trust in a product's ability to perform satisfactorily or resist failure. However, reliability is an issue that requires a more objective, quantitative treatment. Formally, reliability is defined as *the probability that a product, piece of equipment, or system performs its intended function for a stated period of time under specified operating conditions*. This definition has four important elements: probability, time, performance, and operating conditions.

First, reliability is defined as a *probability*, that is, a value between 0 and 1. Thus, it is a numerical measure with a precise meaning. Expressing reliability in this way provides a valid basis for comparison of different designs for products and systems. For example, a reliability of 0.97 indicates that, on average, 97 of 100 items will

Figure 12.12 Example of a DFMEA in Health Care

Description: Specimen collection/procession
Year(s): 2004
Location: Detroit

Process responsibility: Jane S.
Key date:

FMEA number: 2004-1
Prepared by: RDR Team
Revision date: 2/7/2005

Line No.	Process function/ requirements	Potential failure mode	Potential effect(s) of failure	Severity	Class	Potential cause(s)/ mechanism of failure	Occurrence	Current process controls	Detection	Risk priority number	Recommended action(s)	Responsibility and target completion date		Action result				
														Actions taken	New severity	New occurrence	New detection	New risk priority number
1.	1.0 Take specimen	1.1 Put in wrong tub	1.1.1 Run wrong task	8		Inadvertent error	3		9	192	Organics tubes by color, implement "pull" system of inventory mgmt.	Betty L	12/2/2004	Recommended actions done	9	1	1	9
		1.2 Not refrigerated on time	1.2.1 Ruin specimen	8		Inadvertent error	6		9	288	Implement tracking log & use of alarms, audit chart daily for completion	Betty L	11/25/2004	Recommended actions done	9	2	2	36
		1.3 Not centrifuged on time	1.3.1 Ruin specimen	8		Inadvertent error	6		9	288	Implement tracking log & use of alarms, audit chart daily for completion	Betty L	11/15/2004	Recommended actions done	9	1	8	72
		1.4 Shortage of tubes	1.4.1 Rework another	4		Work load	7		7	196	Pull system of inventory management	Betty L	12/02/2004		4	3	7	94
2	2.0 Centrifuge it	2.1 Equipment failure	2.1.1 can't run test	4		Aged equipment	2		10	80	Add to PM log	Kaye P	12/01/2004		4	2	6	48
		2.2 Insufficient run time	2.2.1 specimen	6		Inadvertent error	4		9	216	Set alarm to warn, provide process definition on RASIC chart, implement verification and audit daily	Kaye P	10/30/2004	Recommended actions done	9	1	2	18
3	3.0 Store/ refrigerate it	3.1 No Temperature log	3.1.1 Uncertainty of specimen	8		No the moniater	3	Acquire thermometer	10	190	Audit temperature log each shift	Kaye P	11/07/2004		6	3	6	106
		3.2 Temperature wrong	3.2.1 specimen tainted	8		Equipment failure	2		7	94	Add to PM log	Kaye P	10/30/2004		6	2	6	72
		3.3 Drop it	3.3.1 Ruin specimen	8		Inadvertent error	1		3	18	Work instruction	Kaye P	10/30/2004					

Source: Reprinted with permission from Dan Reid, "FMEA—Something Old, Something New," *Quality Progress*, May 2005, pp. 90–93.

Figure 12.13 Severity, Likelihood, and Detection Rating Scales

Severity Rating		Likelihood Detection of Rating				Occurrence Rating	
Rating	**Criteria**	**Rating**	**Failure probability**	**IPTO***	**IPMO****	**Rating**	**Detection**
10	Failure may seriously endanger patient.	10	Very high	>500	>500,000	10	Almost impossible
9	Failure involves regulatory noncompliance	9	Very high	333	333,333	9	Very remote
8	Failure causes patient high dissatisfaction.	8	High	125	125,000	8	Remote
7	Failure causes patient dissatisfaction	7	High	50	50,000	7	Very low
6	Failure causes disruption of patient ADL	6	Moderate	12.5	12,500	6	Low
5	Inconvenience for patient and multiple providers	5	Moderate	2.5	2,500	5	Moderate
4	Inconvenience at subsequent function; minor rework	4	Moderate	0.5	500	4	Moderately high
3	Slight inconvenience at next function; minor rework	3	Low	0.067	67	3	High
2	Slight inconvenience at delivery; minor rework	2	Very low	0.0067	7	2	Very high
1	Patient will probably not notice	1	Remote	0.00067	1	1	Almost certain

*Activities of daily living.

*Incident per thousand opportunities.
**Incident per million opportunities.

Source: Reprinted with permission form FMEA—"Something Old, Something New," *Quality Progress*, May 2005, pp. 90–93.

perform their function for a given period of time and under certain operating conditions. Often reliability is expressed as a percentage simply for descriptive purposes. The second element of the definition is *time*. Clearly a device having a reliability of 0.97 for 1,000 hours of operation is inferior to one having the same reliability for 5,000 hours of operation, assuming that the mission of the device is long life.

Performance is the third element and refers to the objective for which the product or system was made. The term *failure* is used when expectations of performance of the intended function are not met. Two types of failures can occur: ***functional failure*** *at the start of product life due to manufacturing or material defects such as a missing connection or a faulty component,* and ***reliability failure*** *after some period of use.* Examples of reliability failures include the following: a device does not work at all (car will not start); the operation of a device is unstable (car idles rough); or the performance of a device deteriorates (shifting becomes difficult). Because the nature of failure in each of these cases is different, the failure must be clearly defined.

The final component of the reliability definition is *operating conditions*, which involves the type and amount of usage and the environment in which the product is used. For example, typical operating conditions and environments for a wristwatch are summarized in Table 12.2. Notice that reliability must include extreme environments and conditions as well as the typical on-the-arm use.

By defining a product's intended environment, performance characteristics, and lifetime, a manufacturer can design and conduct tests to measure the probability of product survival (or failure). The analysis of such tests enable better prediction of reliability and improved product and process designs. Reliability engineers distinguish between inherent reliability, which is the predicted reliability determined by the design of the product or process, and the achieved reliability, which is the actual reliability observed during use. Actual reliability can be less than the inherent reliability due to the effects of the manufacturing process and the conditions of use.

Reliability Measurement In practice, reliability is determined by the number of failures per unit time during the duration under consideration (called the **failure rate**).

Table 12.2 Some Typical Watch Environments

Environment	Condition	Quantifiable Characteristics	Exposure Time
Typical use	On-the-arm	31°C (88°F)	16 hours/day
Transportation	In packing box	Vibration and shock (−20°C to +80°C)	Specifications for truck/rail/air shipping
Handling accident	Drop to hard floor	1,200 g, 2 milliseconds	1 drop/year
Extreme temperature	Hot, closed automobile	85°C (185°F)	4–6 hours, 5 times/year
Humidity and chemicals	Perspiration, salt, soaps	35°C (95°F) with 90% pH, rain	500 hours/year
Altitude	Pike's Peak	15,000 feet, −40°C	1 time

Source: Adapted from William R. Taylor, "Quality Assessed in New Products Via Comprehensive Systems Approach," *Industrial Engineering* 13, no. 3 (March 1981), 28–32.

The reciprocal of the failure rate is used as an alternative measure. Some products must be scrapped and replaced upon failure; others can be repaired. For items that must be replaced when a failure occurs, the reciprocal of the failure rate (having dimensions of time units per failure) is called the mean time to failure (MTTF). For repairable items, the mean time between failures (MTBF) is used.

In considering the failure rate of a product, suppose that a large group of items is tested or used until all fail, and that the time of failure is recorded for each item. Plotting the cumulative percentage of failures against time results in a curve such as the one shown in Figure 12.14. The slope of the curve at any point (that is, the slope of the straight line tangent to the curve) gives the instantaneous failure rate (failures per unit time) at any point in time. Figure 12.15 shows the failure rate curve, generally called a product life characteristics curve, corresponding to the cumulative failure curve in Figure 12.14. This curve was obtained by plotting the slope of the curve at every point. Notice that the slope of the curve, and thus the failure rate, may change over time. Thus, in Figure 12.15, the failure rate at 500 hours is 0.02 failures per hour, whereas the failure rate at 4,500 hours is 0.04 failures per hour. The average failure rate over any interval of time is the slope of the line between the two endpoints of the interval on the curve. As shown in Figure 12.16, the average failure rate over the entire 5,000-hour time period is 0.02 failures per hour. Many research institutes and large manufacturers conduct extensive statistical studies to identify distinct patterns of failure over time.

Gathering enough data about failures to generate as smooth a curve as is shown in Figure 12.16 is not always possible. If limited data are available, the failure rate is computed using the following formula:

$$\text{Failure rate} = \lambda = \frac{\text{Number of failures}}{\text{Total unit operating hours}}$$

or alternatively,

$$\lambda = \frac{\text{Number of failures}}{(\text{Units tested}) \times (\text{Number of hours tested})}$$

Figure 12.14 Cumulative Failure Curve Over Time

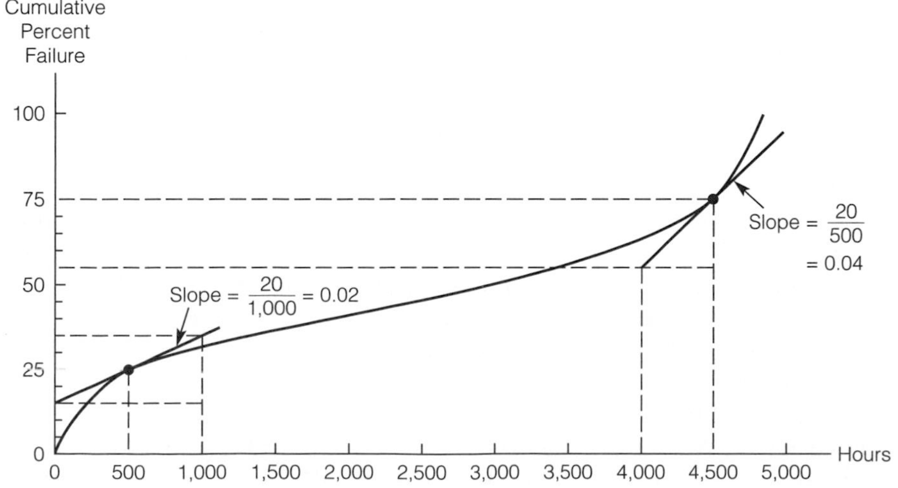

Figure 12.15 Failure Rate Curve

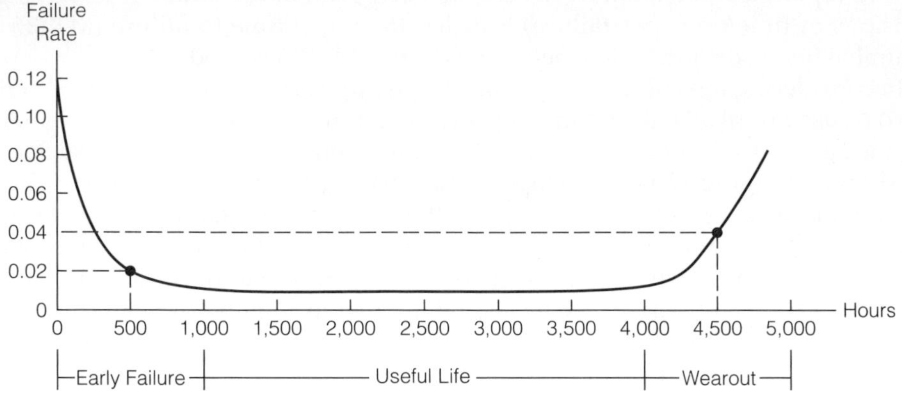

Figure 12.16 Average Failure Rate over a Time Interval

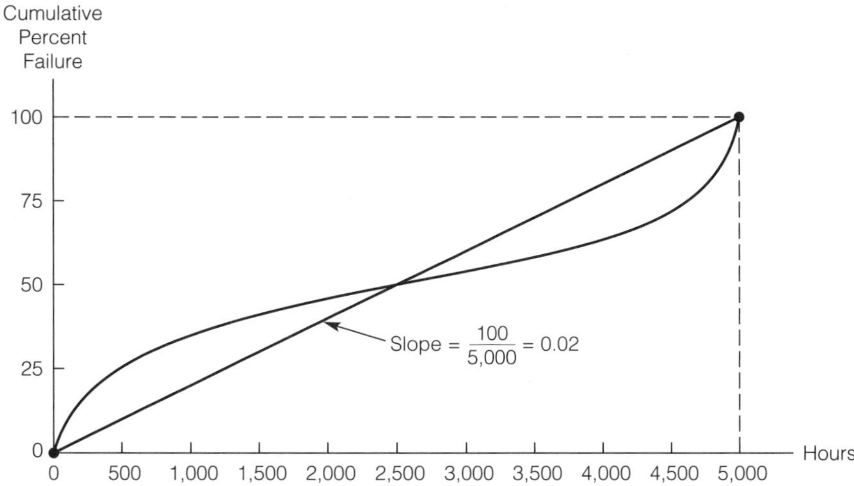

A fundamental assumption in this definition allows for different interpretations. Because the total unit operating hours equal the number of units tested times the number of hours tested, no difference occurs in total unit operating hours between testing 10 units for 100 hours or one unit for 1,000 hours. However, the difference in Figure 12.15 is clear because the failure rate varies over time. For example, if useful life began at 10 hours and the wearout period began at 200 hours, a failure would almost certainly occur before 1,000 hours, whereas a failure would not be likely to occur in 100-hour tests. During a product's useful life, however, the failure rate is assumed to be constant, and different test lengths during this period of time should show little difference. This assumption is the reason that time is an important element of the definition of reliability.

To illustrate the computation of λ, suppose that 10 units are tested over a 100-hour period. Four units failed with one unit each failing after 6, 35, 65, and 70 hours; the remaining six units performed satisfactorily until the end of the test. The total unit operating hours are

$$\begin{aligned} 1 \times 6 &= 6 \\ 1 \times 35 &= 35 \\ 1 \times 65 &= 65 \\ 1 \times 70 &= 70 \\ 6 \times 100 &= \underline{600} \\ & \quad 776 \end{aligned}$$

Therefore, λ = (4 failures)/(776 unit operating hours) = 0.00515 failures per hour. In other words, in a one-hour period, about 0.5 percent of the units would be expected to fail. On the other hand, over a 100-hour period, about (0.00515)(100) = 0.515 or 51.5 percent of the units would be expected to fail. In the actual test, only 40 percent failed. The failure rate curve in Figure 12.15 is an example of a typical product life characteristics curve for such components, for example, as semiconductors.

Many electronic components commonly exhibit a high, but decreasing, failure rate early in their lives (as evidenced by the steep slope of the curve), followed by a period of a relatively constant failure rate, and ending with an increasing failure rate.

In Figure 12.15, three distinct time periods are evident: early failure (from 0 to about 1,000 hours), useful life (from 1,000 to 4,000 hours), and wearout period (after 4,000 hours). The first is the early failure period, sometimes called the **infant mortality period**. Weak components resulting from poor manufacturing or quality control procedures will often lead to a high rate of failure early in a product's life. This high rate usually cannot be detected through normal test procedures, particularly in electronic semiconductors. Such components or products should not be permitted to enter the marketplace. The second phase of the life characteristics curve describes the normal pattern of random failures during a product's useful life. This period usually has a low, relatively constant failure rate caused by uncontrollable factors, such as sudden and unexpected stresses due to complex interactions in materials or the environment. These factors are usually impossible to predict on an individual basis. However, the collective behavior of such failures can be modeled statistically. Finally, as age takes over, the wearout period begins, and the failure rate increases.

New car owners generally experience this phenomenon. During the first few months of ownership, owners may have to return their car to the dealer to remove the initial bugs caused by poor workmanship or manufacturing processes, such as wheel alignment or rattles. Such defects are monitored by J. D. Power's Initial Quality metrics of which you are probably aware. During its prime lifetime, the car may have few failures; however, as parts begin to wear out, the number and rate of failures begin to increase until replacement becomes desirable.

Knowing the product life characteristics curve for a particular product helps engineers predict behavior and make decisions accordingly. For instance, if a manufacturer knows that the early failure period for a microprocessor is 600 hours, it can test the chip for 600 hours (or more) under actual or simulated operating conditions before releasing the chip to the market.

Knowledge of a product's reliability is also useful in developing warranties. As an illustration, consider a tire manufacturer who must determine a mileage warranty policy for a new line of tires. From engineering test data, the reliability curve shown in Figure 12.17 was constructed. This graph shows the probability of tread separation within a certain number of miles. Half the tires will fail by 36,500 miles,

Figure 12.17 Cumulative Probability for Tire Mileage

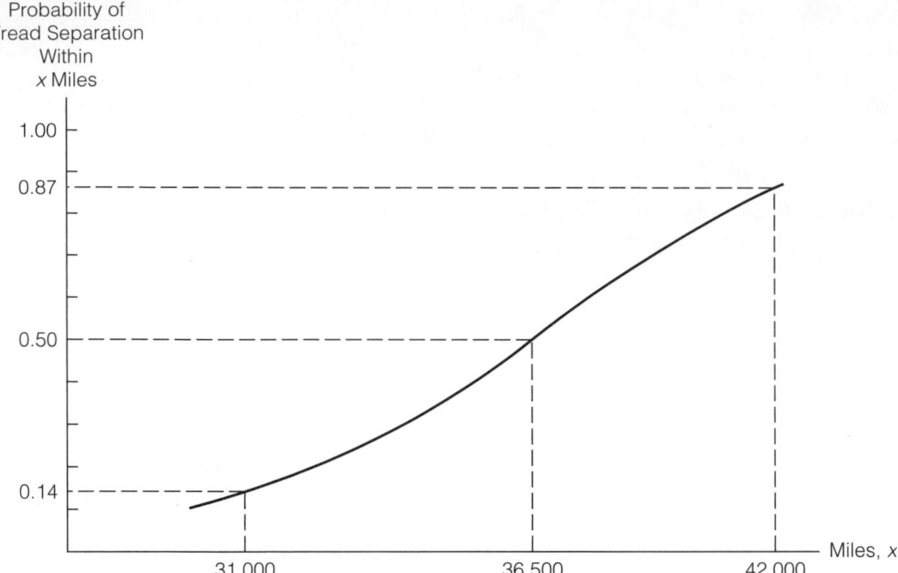

87 percent will wear out by 42,000 miles, and only 14 percent will wear out by 31,000 miles. Thus, if a 31,000-mile warranty is established, management can compute the expected cost of replacing 14 percent of the tires. On the other hand, these data may indicate a poor design in relation to similar products of competitors. Design changes might be necessary to improve reliability. Note that in this example time is not measured chronologically, but in terms of product usage.

Mathematics of Reliability Reliability was defined earlier as the probability that an item will *not* fail over a given period of time. However, the probability distribution of failures is usually a more convenient figure to use in reliability computations. Recall that during the useful life of a product the failure rate is assumed to be constant. Thus, the fraction of good items that fail during any time period is constant. One can assume then that the probability of failure over time can be modeled mathematically by an exponential probability distribution. Not only is this model mathematically justified, but it has been empirically validated for many observable phenomena, such as failures of lightbulbs, electronic components, and repairable systems such as automobiles, computers, and industrial machinery.

If λ is the failure rate, the probability density function representing failures is given by the exponential density

$$f(t) = \lambda e^{-\lambda t} \quad t \geq 0$$

The probability of failing during a time interval (t_1, t_2) can be shown to be

$$e^{-\lambda(t_2 - t_1)}$$

Specifically, the probability of failure in the interval $(0, T)$ is given by the cumulative distribution function

$$F(T) = 1 - e^{-\lambda T}$$

Because reliability is the probability of *survival*, the **reliability function** is calculated as

$$R(T) = 1 - F(T) = e^{-\lambda T}$$

This function represents the probability that the item will not fail within T units of time.

Consider, for example, an item having a reliability of 0.97 for 100 hours of normal use. Determine the failure rate λ by solving the equation $R = e^{-\lambda T}$ for λ. Substituting $R = 0.97$ and $T = 100$ into this equation yields

$$\begin{aligned} 0.97 &= e^{-\lambda(100)} \\ \ln 0.97 &= -100\lambda \\ \lambda &= -(\ln 0.97)/100 \\ &= 0.0304/100 \\ &\approx 0.0003 \text{ failure per hour} \end{aligned}$$

Thus, the reliability function is $R(T) = e^{-.0003T}$. The cumulative fraction of items that are expected to fail and survive after each 10-hour period may then be tabulated as given in Table 12.3. Note that the fraction failing in any 10-hour period is constant.

Reliability engineers characterize the instantaneous failure rate over time by what is called the **hazard function**, which is computed as follows:

$$h(t) = f(t)/[1 - F(t)] = f(t)/R(t)$$

The hazard function may be interpreted as the probability that an item that has not failed up to time t will fail immediately after time t. The failure rate curve shown in Figure 12.15 is an example of a hazard function. If the probability distribution of failures is known, it is easier to develop the failure rate curve using the hazard function formula instead of empirical data.

For the exponential distribution, the hazard function is as follows:

$$h(t) = \lambda e^{-\lambda t}/e^{-\lambda t} = \lambda$$

This simply states that the instantaneous failure rate is constant (as assumed during the useful life period in Figure 12.15). Note that the exponential distribution is not appropriate for characterizing the entire lifetime in Figure 12.15 because the hazard function is not constant over the entire range. The hazard function is useful when the distribution of failures is characterized by other probability distributions (a more advanced topic beyond the scope of this book).

Table 12.3 Cumulative Fraction Failing and Surviving

Time, T	Failures, $F(T)$	Survivors, $R(T)$
10	0.003	0.997
20	0.006	0.994
30	0.009	0.991
40	0.012	0.988
50	0.015	0.985
60	0.018	0.982
70	0.021	0.979
80	0.024	0.976
90	0.027	0.973
100	0.030	0.970

The reciprocal of the failure rate is often used in reliability computations. For nonrepairable items, $\theta = 1/\lambda$ is defined as the *mean time to failure* (MTTF). Thus, in the preceding example for $\lambda = 0.0003$ failure per hour, $\theta = 1/.0003 = 3{,}333$ hours. That is, one failure can be expected every 3,333 hours on the average. The probability distribution function of failures and the reliability function can be equivalently expressed using the MTTF as

$$F(T) = 1 - e^{-T/\theta}$$

and

$$R(T) = e^{-T/\theta}$$

Suppose, for example, that an electronic component has a failure rate of $\lambda = 0.0001$ failure per hour. The MTTF is $\theta = 1/0.0001 = 10{,}000$ hours. The probability that the component will not fail in 15,000 hours is

$$\begin{aligned} R(15{,}000) &= e^{-15{,}000/10{,}000} \\ &= e^{-1.5} \\ &= 0.223 \end{aligned}$$

For repairable items, θ is usually called the *mean time between failures* (MTBF). For example, suppose that a machine is operated for 10,000 hours and experiences four failures that are immediately repaired. The mean time between failures is

$$\text{MTBF} = 10{,}000/4 = 2{,}500 \text{ hours}$$

and the failure rate is

$$\lambda = 1/2{,}500 = 0.0004 \text{ failures per hour}$$

Computing System Reliability Many systems are composed of individual components with known reliabilities. The reliability data of individual components can be used to predict the reliability of the system at the design stage. Systems of components may be configured in *series*, in *parallel*, or in some mixed combination. Block diagrams are useful ways to represent system configurations where blocks represent functional components or subsystems. Engineers can use reliability calculations to predict performance and evaluate alternative designs to optimize performance within cost, size, or other constraints.

We first consider a **series system**, illustrated in Figure 12.18. In such a system, all components must function or the system will fail. If the reliability of component i is R_i, the reliability of the system is the product of the individual reliabilities, that is

$$R_S = R_1 R_2 \ldots R_n$$

This equation is based on the multiplicative law of probability. For example, suppose that a personal computer system is composed of the processing unit, graphics board,

Figure 12.18 Series System

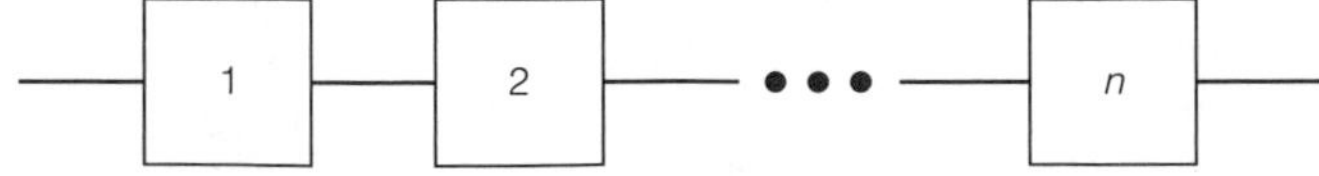

and DVD-ROM with reliabilities of 0.997, 0.980, and 0.975, respectively. The reliability of the system is therefore given by

$$R_S = (0.997)(0.980)(0.975) = 0.953$$

Note that when reliabilities are less than one, system reliability decreases as additional components are added in series. Thus, the more complex a series system is, the greater the chance of failure.

If the reliability function is exponential, for example, $R_i = e^{-\lambda_i T}$, then

$$\begin{aligned} R_S &= e^{-\lambda_1 T} e^{-\lambda_2 T} \cdots e^{-\lambda_n T} \\ &= e^{-\lambda_1 T - \lambda_2 T \cdots - \lambda_n T} \\ &= e^{-\left(\sum_{i=1}^{n} \lambda_i\right) T} \end{aligned}$$

Suppose that a two-component series system has failure rates of 0.004 and 0.001 per hour. Then

$$\begin{aligned} R_S(T) &= e^{-(0.004+0.001)T} \\ &= e^{-0.005T} \end{aligned}$$

The probability of survival for 100 hours would be

$$\begin{aligned} R_S(100) &= e^{-0.005(100)} \\ &= e^{-0.5} \\ &= 0.6065 \end{aligned}$$

Redundancy provides backup components that can be used when the failure of any one component in a system can cause a failure of the entire system. Redundant components can increase reliability dramatically. Redundancy is crucial to systems in which failures can be extremely costly, such as aircraft or satellite communications systems. Redundancy, however, increases the cost, size, and weight of the system.

Redundant components are designed in parallel system as illustrated in Figure 12.20. In such a system, failure of an individual component is less critical than in series systems; the system will successfully operate as long as one component functions. The reliability of the parallel system in Figure 12.19 is derived as follows. If $R_1, R_2, \ldots, R_n$ are the reliabilities of the individual components, the probabilities of failure are $1 - R_1, 1 - R_2, \ldots, 1 - R_n$, respectively. Because the system fails only if each component fails, the probability of system failure is

$$(1 - R_1)(1 - R_2) \ldots (1 - R_n)$$

Hence, the system reliability is computed as

$$R_S = 1 - (1 - R_1)(1 - R_2) \ldots (1 - R_n)$$

If all components have identical reliabilities R, then

$$R_S = 1 - (1 - R)^n$$

The computers on the space shuttle were designed with built-in redundancy in case of failure. Five computers were designed in parallel. Thus, for example, if the reliability of each is 0.99, the system reliability is

$$R_S = 1 - (1 - 0.99)^5 = 0.9999999999$$

Figure 12.19 Parallel System

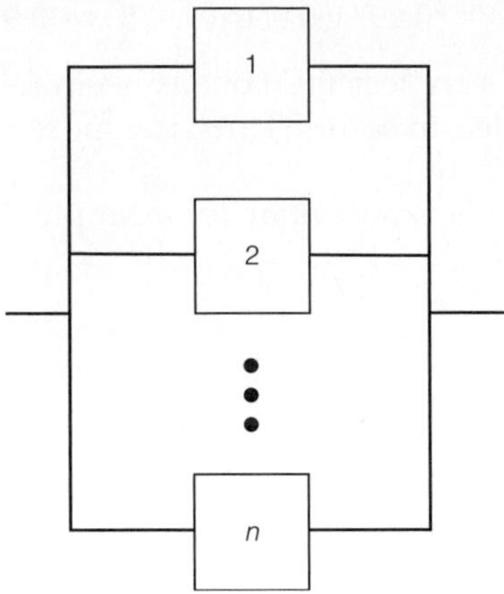

Most systems are composed of combinations of series and parallel systems. Consider the system shown in Figure 12.20(a). To determine the reliability of such a system, first compute the reliability of the parallel subsystem B:

$$R_B = 1 - (1 - 0.9)^3 = 0.999$$

This level of reliability is equivalent to replacing the three parallel components B with a single component B having a reliability of 0.999 in series with A, C, and D,

Figure 12.20 Series-Parallel System and Equivalent Parallel System Example 1

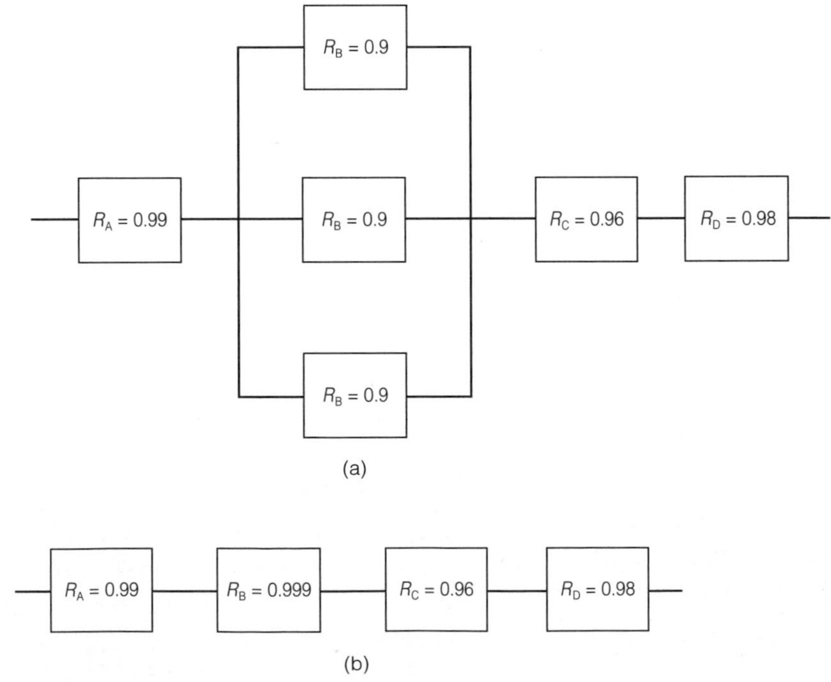

Figure 12.21 Series-Parallel System and Equivalent Parallel System Example 2

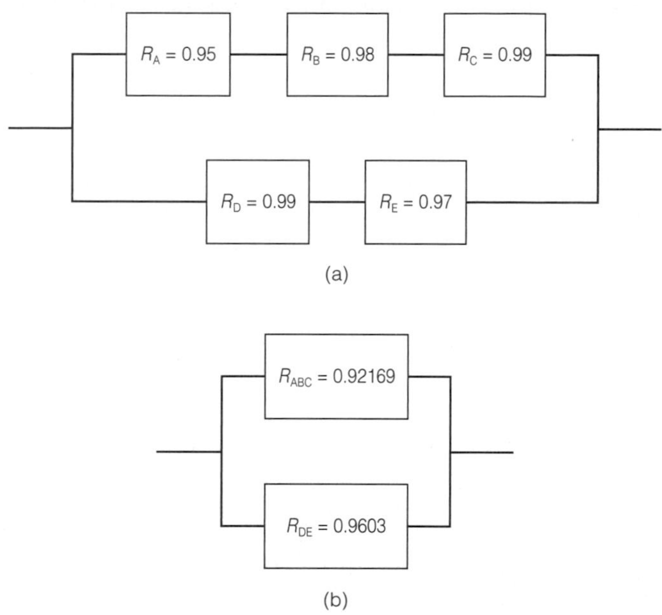

as shown in Figure 12.20(b). Next, compute the reliability of the equivalent series system:

$$R_S = (0.99)(0.999)(0.96)(0.98) = 0.93$$

A second type of series-parallel arrangement is shown in Figure 12.21(a). System reliability is determined by first computing the reliability of the series systems ABC and DE:

$$R_{ABC} = (0.95)(0.98)(0.99) = 0.92169$$

$$R_{DE} = (0.99)(0.97) = 0.9603$$

The result is an equivalent parallel system shown in Figure 12.21(b). The system reliability is then computed as

$$R_S = 1 - (1 - 0.92169)(1 - 0.9603) = 0.9969$$

By appropriately decomposing complex systems into series and/or parallel components as shown in these examples, the system reliability can be easily computed. Reliability requirements are determined during the product design phase. The designer may use these techniques to determine the effects of adding redundancy, substituting different components, or reconfiguring the design.

DESIGN VERIFICATION

Design verification is necessary to ensure that designs will meet customer requirements and can be produced to specifications.

The final phase of DFSS is verification of product and process designs. Sometimes verification is required by government regulation or for legal concerns. For products, reliability evaluation provides a means for obtaining data about product performance as both a verification approach and a means for design improvement. Verifying measurement systems and the capability of processes to meet specifications are also important in achieving Six Sigma performance. We introduce these approaches in this section.

Design Reviews

One approach often used to facilitate product development is the **design review**. The purpose of a design review is to stimulate discussion, raise questions, and generate new ideas and solutions to help designers anticipate problems before they occur. Generally, a design review is conducted in three major stages: preliminary, intermediate, and final. The preliminary design review establishes early communication between marketing, engineering, manufacturing, and purchasing personnel and provides better coordination of their activities. It usually involves higher levels of management and concentrates on strategic issues in design that relate to customer requirements and thus the ultimate quality of the product. A preliminary design review evaluates such issues as the function of the product, conformance to customer's needs, completeness of specifications, manufacturing costs, and liability issues. Eastman Chemical reviews designs for safety, reliability, waste minimization, patent position, toxicity information, environmental risks, product disposal, and other customer needs. It also conducts a market analysis of key suppliers' abilities to manage costs, obtain materials, maintain production, and ship reliably. AT&T Transmission Systems has a new product introduction center that evaluates designs based on manufacturing capabilities, recognizing that good designs both reduce the risk of manufacturing defects and improve productivity.

After the design is well established, an intermediate review takes place to study the design in greater detail to identify potential problems and suggest corrective action. Personnel at lower levels of the organization are more heavily involved at this stage. Finally, just before release to production, a final review is held. Materials lists, drawings, and other detailed design information are studied with the purpose of preventing costly changes after production setup.

Reliability Testing

The reliability of a product is determined principally by the design and the reliability of the components of the product. However, reliability is such a complex issue that it cannot always be determined from theoretical analysis of the design alone. Hence, formal testing is necessary, which involves simulating environmental conditions to determine a product's performance, operating time, and mode of failure. Testing is useful for a variety of other reasons. Test data are often necessary for liability protection, as means for evaluating designs or vendor reliability, and in process planning and selection. Often, reliability test data are required in military contracts. Testing is necessary to evaluate warranties and to avoid high costs related to early field failure. Good testing leads to good reliability and hence good quality.

Product testing is performed by various methods. The purpose of *life testing*, that is, running devices until they fail, is to measure the distribution of failures to better understand and eliminate their causes. However, such testing can be expensive and time-consuming. For devices that have long natural lives, life testing is not practical. **Accelerated life testing** involves overstressing components to reduce the time to failure and find weaknesses. This form of testing might involve running a motor faster than typically found in normal operating conditions. However, failure rates must correlate well to actual operating conditions if accelerated life testing is to be useful.

Other testing studies the robustness of products. Hewlett-Packard's popular HP-12c financial calculator, which is essentially unchanged since 1981 and still is a popular seller, undergoes a drop test in which engineers repeatedly drop it from desk height onto a hard floor. They also subject the keyboard to mechanical button-pushers to simulate the effects of 5 to 10 years of use.[31]

Semiconductors are the basic building blocks of numerous modern products such as MP3 players, automotive ignition systems, computers, and military weapons systems. Semiconductors have a small proportion of defects, called *latent defects*, which can cause them to fail during the first 1,000 hours of normal operation. After that, the failure rate stabilizes, perhaps for as long as 25 years, before beginning to rise again as components wear out. These infant mortalities can be as high as 10 percent in a new technology or as low as 0.01 percent in proven technologies. The sooner a faulty component is detected, the cheaper is its replacement or repair. A correction on an integrated circuit fabrication line costs about 50 cents; at the board level it might cost $5; at the system level about $50; and in the field, $500. If a printed circuit board contains 100 semiconductors, a failure rate of 0.01 percent would cause a board failure rate of 1 percent.

Burn-in, or *component stress testing,* involves exposing integrated circuits to elevated temperatures in order to force latent defects to occur. For example, a device that might normally fail after 300 hours at 25°C might fail in less than 20 hours at 150°C. Survivors are likely to have long, trouble-free operating lives. Studies and experience have demonstrated the economic advantages of burn-in. For example, a large-scale study of the effect of burn-in on enhancing reliability of dynamic MOS memories was conducted in Europe. The failure rate without burn-in conditioning and testing to eliminate infant mortality was 0.24 percent per thousand hours, whereas burn-in and testing reduced the rate to 0.02 percent per thousand hours. When considering the cost of field service and warranty work, for instance, reduction of semiconductor failure rates in a large system by an order of magnitude translates roughly into an average of one repair call per year versus one repair call per month. Because burn-in requires considerable time—48 to 96 hours is common—designers attempt to produce equipment that can perform some functional tests during the burn-in cycle rather than after. Modern systems exist to test and burn-in integrated circuits. One system has the capacity of 18,000 DRAMs (dynamic random access memory) per load and is flexible of the hardware. The system can accumulate and display information on the devices under test, both for real-time evaluation and for lot documentation.

Measurement System Evaluation

Accurately assessing performance depends on reliable measurement systems. Measuring quality characteristics generally requires the use of the human senses—seeing, hearing, feeling, tasting, and smelling—and the use of some type of instrument or gauge to measure the magnitude of the characteristic. Common types of measuring instruments used in manufacturing today fall into two categories: low-technology and high-technology. Low-technology instruments are primarily manual devices that have been available for many years; high-technology instruments describe those that depend on modern electronics, microprocessors, lasers, or advanced optics. The Bonus Materials folder for this chapter on the Premium website contains a discussion and some pictures of various types of measuring instruments.

BONUS MATERIALS

Metrology Gauges and instruments used to measure quality characteristics must provide correct information, which is assured through **metrology**—the science of measurement. Metrology is vital in our daily lives. Some examples include wondering whether you are getting a true gallon of gasoline at a gas station, whether the scanners at grocery stores are correctly reading the bar codes or if a box of cereal contains the amount stated on the package, or if the timers at a swim meet provide correct times.

Originally, metrology only measured the physical attributes of an object. Today, metrology is defined broadly as the collection of people, equipment, facilities, methods, and procedures used to assure the correctness or adequacy of measurements, and is a vital part of global competitiveness. In testifying before the U.S. Congress, the director of the Office of Standards Services at the National Institute of Standards and Technology noted that efficient national and international trade requires weights and measures organizations that assure uniform and accurate measures used in trade, national or regional measurement standards laboratories, standards development organizations, and accredited and internationally recognized calibration and testing laboratories.[32]

The need for metrology stems from the fact that every measurement is subject to error. The evaluation of data obtained from inspection and measurement is not meaningful unless the measurement instruments are accurate, precise, and reproducible.

Accuracy is defined as the difference between the true value and the observed average of a measurement. The lack of accuracy reflects a systematic bias in the measurement such as a gauge out of calibration, worn, or used improperly by the operator. Accuracy is measured as the amount of error in a measurement in proportion to the total size of the measurement. One measurement is more accurate than another if it has a smaller relative error.

Whenever variation is observed in measurements, some portion is due to measurement system error. Some errors are systematic (called bias); others are random. The size of the errors relative to the measurement value can significantly affect the quality of the data and resulting decisions.

Precision is defined as the closeness of repeated measurements to each other. Precision, therefore, relates to the variance of repeated measurements. A measuring instrument with a low variance is more precise than another having a higher variance. Low precision is the result of random variation that is built into the instrument, such as friction among its parts. This random variation may be the result of a poor design or lack of maintenance.

For example, suppose that two instruments measure a dimension whose true value is 0.250 inch. Instrument A may read 0.248 inch, whereas instrument B may read 0.259 inch. The relative error of instrument A is $(0.250 - 0.248)/0.250 = 0.8\%$; the relative error of instrument B is $(0.259 - 0.250)/0.250 = 3.6\%$. Thus, instrument A is said to be more accurate than instrument B. Now suppose that each instrument measures the dimension three times. Instrument A records values of 0.248, 0.246, and 0.251; instrument B records values of 0.259, 0.258, and 0.259. Instrument B is more precise than instrument A because its values are clustered closer together.

A measurement system may be precise but not necessarily accurate at the same time. The relationships between accuracy and precision are summarized in Figure 12.22. The figure illustrates four possible frequency distributions of 10 repeated measurements of some quality characteristic. In Figure 12.22 (a), the average measurement is not close to the true value. Moreover, a wide range of values fall around the average. In this case, the measurement is neither accurate nor precise. In Figure 12.22(b), even though the average measurement is not close to the true value, the range of variation is small. Thus, the measurement is precise but not accurate. In Figures 12.22(c) and (d), the average value is close to the true value—that is, the measurement

Figure 12.22 Accuracy Versus Precision

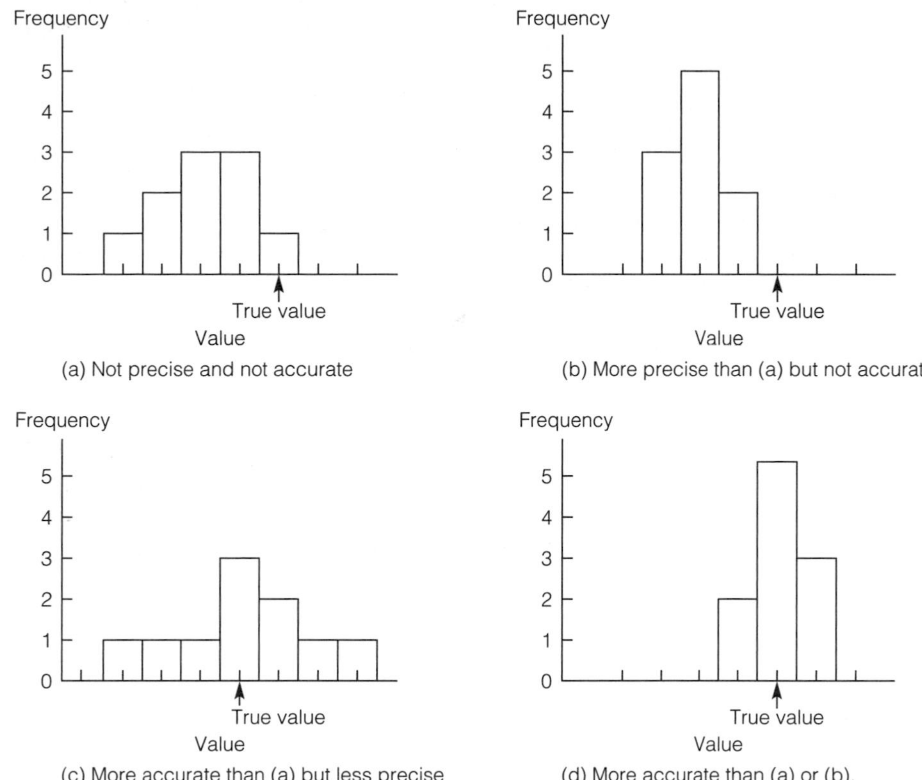

is accurate—but in 12.22(c) the distribution is widely dispersed and therefore not precise, whereas the measurement in 12.22(d) is both accurate and precise. Thus, Figure 12.22 demonstrates the vital nature of properly calibrating and maintaining all instruments used for quality measurements.

When a technician measures the same unit multiple times, the results will usually show some variability. **Repeatability**, or **equipment variation**, is the variation in multiple measurements by an individual using the same instrument. This measure indicates how precise and accurate the equipment is. Repeatability is influenced by the condition of the measurement instrument, its level of calibration (to be discussed shortly), environmental conditions such as noise or lighting, the worker's health and eyesight, and the process used to take the measurement. **Reproducibility**, or **operator variation**, is the variation in the same measuring instrument when it is used by different individuals to measure the same parts and indicates how robust the measuring process is to the operator and environmental conditions. Reproducibility is influenced by the training of the operators in the use of the instrument, clarity of the directions or procedures of the measurement process, calibration of gauges between workers, gauge maintenance, and worker health. Statistical approaches can be used to quantify and evaluate equipment and operator variation.

The importance of measurement analysis is summed up by the following equation:

$$\sigma^2_{\text{total}} = \sigma^2_{\text{process}} + \sigma^2_{\text{measurement}}$$

which states that the total observed variation in production output is the sum of the true process variation (which is what we actually want to measure) plus variation due to measurement. If the measurement variation is high, the observed results will be biased, and process capability measurements, for example, may look worse than they actually are. Thus, an objective of quality control is to reduce measurement error as much as possible.

Measurement System Evaluation and Verification The accuracy, repeatability, and reproducibility of any measurement system must be quantified and evaluated. Accuracy can be measured by comparing the observed average of a set of measurements to the true value of a reference standard. Repeatability and reproducibility require a study of variation and can be addressed through statistical analysis. A repeatability and reproducibility study is conducted in the following manner.[33]

1. Select m operators and n parts. Typically at least 2 operators and 10 parts are chosen. Number the parts so that the numbers are not visible to the operators.
2. Calibrate the measuring instrument.
3. Let each operator measure each part in a random order and record the results. Repeat this procedure for a total of r trials. At least two trials must be used. Let M_{ijk} represent the kth measurement of operator i on part j.
4. Compute the average measurement for each operator:

   $$\overline{x}_i = \left(\sum_j \sum_k M_{ijk}\right) / nr$$

   The difference between the largest and smallest average is

   $$\overline{x}_D = \max_i\{\overline{x}_i\} - \min_i\{\overline{x}_i\}$$

5. Compute the range for each part and each operator:

   $$R_{ij} = \max_k\{M_{ijk}\} - \min_k\{M_{ijk}\}$$

   These values show the variability of repeated measurements of the same part by the same operator. Next, compute the average range for each operator:

   $$\overline{R}_i = \left(\sum_j R_{ij}\right) / n$$

   The overall average range is then computed as

   $$\overline{\overline{R}} = \left(\sum_i \overline{R}_i\right) / m$$

6. Calculate a "control limit" on the individual ranges R_{ij}:

   $$\text{control limit} = D_4\overline{\overline{R}}$$

   where D_4 is a constant that depends on the sample size (number of trials, r) and can be found in Appendix B at the end of this book. Any range value beyond this limit might result from some assignable cause, not random error. Possible causes should be investigated and, if found, corrected. The operator should repeat these measurements using the same part. If no assignable cause is found, these values should be discarded and all statistics in step 5 as well as the control limit should be recalculated.

Once these basic calculations are made, an analysis of repeatability and reproducibility can be performed. The repeatability, or equipment variation (EV) is computed as

$$\text{EV} = K_1\overline{\overline{R}}$$

Reproducibility, or operator (sometimes called appraisal) variation (AV) is computed as

$$\text{AV} = \sqrt{(K_2\overline{x}_D)^2 - (\text{EV}^2/nr)}$$

(If the value under the radical is negative, then AV defaults to zero.) The constants K_1 and K_2 depend on the number of trials and number of operators, respectively. Some values of these constants are given in Table 12.4. These constants provide a 99 percent confidence interval on these statistics.

An overall measure of repeatability and reproducibility (R&R) is given by

$$\text{R\&R} = \sqrt{(\text{EV})^2 + (\text{AV})^2}$$

Repeatability and reproducibility are often expressed as a percentage of the tolerance of the quality characteristic being measured. The American Society for Quality suggests the following guidelines for evaluating these measures of repeatability and reproducibility:

- *Under 10 percent error:* This rate is acceptable.
- *10 to 30 percent error:* This rate may be acceptable based on the importance of the application, cost of the instrument, cost of repair, and so on.
- *Over 30 percent error:* Generally, this rate is not acceptable. Every effort should be made to identify the problem and correct it.

To illustrate a gauge repeatability and reproducibility study, suppose that a gauge used to measure the thickness of a gasket having a specification of 0.50 to 1.0 mm is to be evaluated. Ten parts have been selected for measurement by three operators. Each part is measured twice with the results as shown in the spreadsheet in Figure 12.23. (Slight rounding differences from manual calculations may be evident.)

The average measurement for each operator, $\overline{x}_i$, is

$$\overline{x}_1 = 0.830 \qquad \overline{x}_2 = 0.774 \qquad \overline{x}_3 = 0.829$$

Thus, $\overline{x}_D = 0.830 - 0.774 = 0.056$. The average range for each operator is

$$\overline{R}_1 = 0.037 \qquad \overline{R}_2 = 0.034 \qquad \overline{R}_3 = 0.017$$

The overall average range is $\overline{\overline{R}} = (0.037 + 0.034 + 0.017)/3 = 0.0293$. From Appendix B at the end of the book, $D_4 = 3.267$ because the two trials were conducted. Hence the control limit is $(3.267)\ (0.0293) = 0.096$. Because all range values fall below this

Table 12.4 Values of K_1 and K_2

Number of Trials	**2**	**3**	**4**	**5**
K_1	4.56	3.05	2.50	2.21
Number of Operators	**2**	**3**	**4**	**5**
K_2	3.65	2.70	2.30	2.08

Figure 12.23 Spreadsheet for Repeatability and Reproducibility Analysis (R&R.XLS)

	A	B	C	D	E	F	G	H	I	J	K	L	M	N
1	**Gauge Repeatability and Reproducibility**													
2	This spreadsheet is designed for up to three operators, three trials, and ten samples. Enter data ONLY in yellow shaded cells.													
3														
4	Number of operators			3		Upper specification limit				1				
5	Number of trials			2		Lower specification limit				0.5				
6	Number of samples			10										
7														
8	Data	Operator 1				Operator 2				Operator 3				
9		Trial				Trial				Trial				
10	Sample #	1	2	3	Range	1	2	3	Range	1	2	3	Range	
11	1	0.630	0.590		0.040	0.560	0.560		0.000	0.510	0.540		0.030	
12	2	1.000	1.000		0.000	1.040	0.960		0.080	1.050	1.010		0.040	
13	3	0.830	0.770		0.060	0.800	0.760		0.040	0.810	0.810		0.000	
14	4	0.860	0.940		0.080	0.820	0.780		0.040	0.810	0.810		0.000	
15	5	0.590	0.510		0.080	0.430	0.430		0.000	0.460	0.490		0.030	
16	6	0.980	0.980		0.000	1.000	1.040		0.040	1.040	1.000		0.040	
17	7	0.960	0.960		0.000	0.940	0.900		0.040	0.950	0.950		0.000	
18	8	0.860	0.830		0.030	0.720	0.740		0.020	0.810	0.810		0.000	
19	9	0.970	0.970		0.000	0.980	0.940		0.040	1.030	1.030		0.000	
20	10	0.640	0.720		0.080	0.560	0.520		0.040	0.840	0.810		0.030	
21	Range average				0.037				0.034				0.017	
22	Sample average				0.830				0.774				0.829	
23														
24												Tolerance analysis		
25	Average range	0.029		Repeatability (EV)						0.134		26.75%		
26	X-bar range	0.056		Reproducibility (AV)						0.147		29.37%		
27				Repeatability and Reproducibility (R&R)						0.199		39.73%		
28				Control limit for individual ranges						0.096				
29				Note: any ranges beyond this limit may be the result										
30				of assignable causes. Identify and correct. Discard										
31				values and recompute statistics.										

limit, no assignable causes of variation are suspected. Compute the repeatability and reproducibility measures:

$$EV = (4.56)(0.0293) = 0.134$$

$$AV = \sqrt{[(0.056)(2.70)]^2 - (0.134)^2/(10)(2)} = 0.147$$

$$R\&R = \sqrt{(0.134)^2 + (0.147)^2} = 0.199$$

If the tolerance of the gasket is 1.00 – 0.50 = 0.50, these measures expressed as a percent of tolerance are:

$$\text{Equipment variation} = 100(0.134)/0.50 = 26.8\%$$

$$\text{Operator variation} = 100(0.147)/0.50 = 29.4\%$$

$$\text{Total } R\&R \text{ variation} = 100(0.199)/0.50 = 39.8\%$$

Even though individually the equipment and operator variation may be acceptable, their combined effect is not. Efforts should be made to reduce the variation to an acceptable level.

Calibration

When we take any measurement, we need to ensure that the instrument used is capable of making the correct measurement; for instance, that a scale accurately measures weight. According to *The Quality Calibration Handbook*, **calibration** is the process of verifying the capability and performance of an item of measuring and test equipment compared to traceable measurement standards.[34] Measurements made using uncalibrated or inadequately calibrated equipment can lead to erroneous and costly decisions. For example, suppose that an inspector has a micrometer that is reading 0.002 inch too low. When measurements are made close to the upper limit, parts that are as much as 0.002 inch over the maximum tolerance limit will be accepted as good, whereas those at the lower tolerance limit or that are as much as 0.002 inch above the limit will be rejected as nonconforming. This can lead to failure or unsatisfactory performance of the end product and unnecessary costs associated with scrapping good parts.

One of the most important functions of metrology is ***calibration****—the comparison of a measurement device or system having a known relationship to national standards against another device or system whose relationship to national standards is unknown.*

The federal government has many calibration requirements that cover such areas as the accuracy for radio transmitter frequencies, aircraft altimeters, and automobile speedometers. Measures taken to assess compliance with a regulatory requirement must be made with a calibrated instrument.[35] The National Institute of Standards and Technology (NIST) maintains national measurement standards and provides technical advice on making measurements consistent with national standards. NIST works with various metrology laboratories in industry and government to assure that measurements made by different people in different places yield the same results. Thus, the measurement of "voltage" or "resistance" in an electrical component has a precise and universal meaning. This process is accomplished in a hierarchical fashion. NIST calibrates the reference-level standards of those organizations requiring the highest level of accuracy. These organizations calibrate their own working-level standards and those of other metrology laboratories. These working-level standards are used to calibrate the measuring instruments used in the field. The usual recommendation is that equipment be calibrated against working-level standards that are 10 times as accurate as the equipment. When possible, at least a four-to-one accuracy ratio between the reference and working-level standards is desired—that is, the reference standards should be at least four times as accurate as the working-level standards.

Many government regulations and commercial contracts require regulated organizations or contractors to verify that the measurements they make are *traceable* to a reference standard. For example, world standards exist for length, mass, and time. For other types of measurement, such as chemical measurements, industry standards exist. Organizations must be able to support the claim of traceability by keeping records that their own measuring equipment has been calibrated by laboratories or testing facilities whose measurements can be related to appropriate standards, generally national or international standards, through an unbroken chain of comparison.[36] The purpose of requiring traceability is to ensure that measurements are accurate representations of the specific quantity subject to measurement, within the uncertainty of the measurement. Not only should there be an unbroken chain of comparisons, each measurement should be accompanied by a statement of uncertainty associated with the farthest link in the chain from NIST—that is, the last facility providing the measurement value. This accountability can be assured by purchasing an instrument that is certified against a higher level (traceable) standard or by contracting with a calibration agency that has such standards to certify the instrument.

A typical calibration system involves the following activities:

- Evaluation of equipment to determine its capability
- Identification of calibration requirements
- Selection of standards to perform the calibration
- Selection of methods and procedures to perform the calibration
- Establishment of calibration frequency and rules for adjusting this frequency
- Establishment of a system to ensure that instruments are calibrated according to schedule
- Implementation of a documentation and reporting system
- Evaluation of the calibration system through an established auditing process

Smaller precision-manufactured parts, tighter tolerances, and the need to measure and verify parts faster, more accurately, and with greater repeatability are driving developments in metrology systems and equipment. How to manufacture and measure these cost-effectively is a challenge for both machine tool and metrology equipment manufacturers. To meet the anticipated industry needs, equipment manufacturers are looking for ways to optimize the functionality of measurement and inspection equipment using a wide range of sensor and mechanical technologies to reduce inspection time and costs. Multisensor data-gathering systems are being developed that incorporate tactile, vision, and laser-scanner systems. As production technology evolves, so too will the capabilities of metrology equipment to provide manufacturers with not only a means of inspection, but also valuable insights into the production process that will lead to higher quality at lower cost.[37]

Process Capability Evaluation

Process capability is important to both product designers and manufacturing engineers, and is critical to achieving Six Sigma performance. Knowing process capability allows one to predict, quantitatively, how well a process will meet specifications and to specify equipment requirements and the level of control necessary. For example, suppose that the inside diameter of a bushing that supports a steel shaft must be between 1.498 and 1.510 inches for an acceptable fit. If the diameter is too small, it can be enlarged through a rework process. However if it is too large, the part must be scrapped. If the variation in the machining process results in diameters that typically range from 1.495 to 1.515 inches, we would say that the process is not capable of meeting the specifications. Management then faces three possible decisions: (1) measure each piece and either rework or scrap nonconforming parts, (2) develop a better process by investing in new technology, or (3) change the design specifications.

***Process capability** is the range over which the natural variation of a process occurs as determined by the system of common causes, that is, what the process can achieve under stable conditions.*

Unfortunately, product design often takes place in isolation, with inexperienced designers applying tolerances to parts or products while having little awareness of the capabilities of the production process to meet these design requirements. Even experienced designers may be hard-pressed to remain up-to-date on the capabilities of processes that involve constant equipment changes, shifting technology, and difficult-to-measure variations in methods at scores of plants located hundreds or thousands of miles away from a centralized product design department. Process capability should be carefully considered in determining design specifications in a DFSS environment.

Process Capability Studies A **process capability study** is a carefully planned study designed to yield specific information about the performance of a process under specified operating conditions. Typical questions that are asked in a process capability study include the following:

- Where is the process centered?
- How much variability exists in the process?
- Is the performance relative to specifications acceptable?
- What proportion of output will be expected to meet specifications?
- What factors contribute to variability?

Many reasons exist for conducting a capability study. Manufacturing may wish to determine a performance baseline for a process, to prioritize projects for quality improvement, or to provide statistical evidence of quality for customers. Purchasing might conduct a study at a supplier plant to evaluate a new piece of equipment or to compare different suppliers. Engineering might conduct a study to determine the adequacy of R&D pilot facilities or to evaluate new processes.

Three types of studies are often conducted.

1. A *peak performance study* determines how a process performs under ideal conditions.
2. A *process characterization study* is designed to determine how a process performs under actual operating conditions.
3. A *component variability study* assesses the relative contribution of different sources of total variation.

The methods by which each study is conducted vary. A peak performance study is conducted under carefully controlled conditions over a short time interval to ensure that no special causes can affect variation. A process characterization study is performed over a longer time interval under actual operating conditions to capture the variations in materials and operators. A component variability study uses a designed experiment to control the sources of variability. Although this section considers a process characterization study, the general approach applies to a peak performance study with appropriate modifications.

The six steps in a process capability study are similar to those of any systematic investigation and include the following:

1. Choose a representative machine or segment of the process.
2. Define the process conditions.
3. Select a representative operator.
4. Provide materials that are of standard grade, with sufficient materials for uninterrupted study.
5. Specify the gauging or measurement method to be used.
6. Provide for a method of recording measurements and conditions, in order, on the units produced.

To obtain useful information, the sample size should be fairly large, generally at least 100. Process capability only makes sense if all special causes of variation have been eliminated and the process is in a state of statistical control (we will discuss this further in Chapter 13). For this discussion, we assume that the process is in control.

Two statistical techniques are commonly used to evaluate process capability. One is the frequency distribution and histogram, the other is the control chart. The use of frequency distributions and histograms is covered in this section, but the discussion of control charts is deferred to Chapter 13.

To illustrate the evaluation of process capability, let us consider the U-bolt data we used in Chapter 10 (Table 10.1). Using Microsoft Excel tools, we calculated the basic descriptive statistics for these data, and constructed a frequency distribution and histogram. These were shown in Figures 10.13. To recap, we saw that the mean dimension is $\overline{x} = 10.7171$, and the sample standard deviation $s = 0.0868$. The histogram suggests that the data are approximately normally distributed. Using this information, we can estimate the yield of conforming product for various manufacturing specifications analytically.

One of the properties of a normal distribution is that 99.73 percent of the observations will fall within three standard deviations from the mean. Thus, a process that is in control can be expected to produce a large percentage of output between $\mu - 3\sigma$ and $\mu + 3\sigma$, where μ is the process average. Therefore, the *natural tolerance limits* of the process are $\mu \pm 3\sigma$. A six standard deviation spread is commonly used as a measure of process capability. Thus, for the example, nearly all U-bolt dimensions are expected to fall between $10.7171 - 3(0.868) = 10.4566$ and $10.7171 + 3(0.0868) = 10.9766$. These calculations tell the production manager that if the design specifications are between 10.45 and 11.00, for instance, the process will be capable of producing nearly 100 percent conforming product.

Suppose, however, that design specifications are such that the dimension must lie between 10.55 and 10.90. Calculate the expected percentage of nonconforming U-bolts by computing the area under a normal distribution having a mean of 10.7171 and standard deviation 0.0868 to the left and right of these specifications, as illustrated in Figure 12.24. Converting 10.55 to a standard normal value yields $z = (10.55 - 10.7171)/0.0868 = -1.93$. Appendix A at the end of the book gives a value for the area to the *left* of $z = -1.93$ as $0.5000 - 0.4732 = 0.0268$. Similarly, the z value corresponding to 10.90 is $z = (10.90 - 10.7171)/0.0868 = 2.11$. The area to the *right* of $z = 2.11$ is $0.5000 - 0.4826 = 0.0174$. Therefore, the probability that a part will not meet specifications is $0.0268 + 0.0174 = 0.0442$ or, expressed as a percentage, is 4.42 percent, which is only slightly better than a 2-sigma level. Similar computations can be used to estimate the percentage of nonconforming parts for other tolerances.

Figure 12.24 Probability of Nonconforming Product with Specifications of 10.55 to 10.90

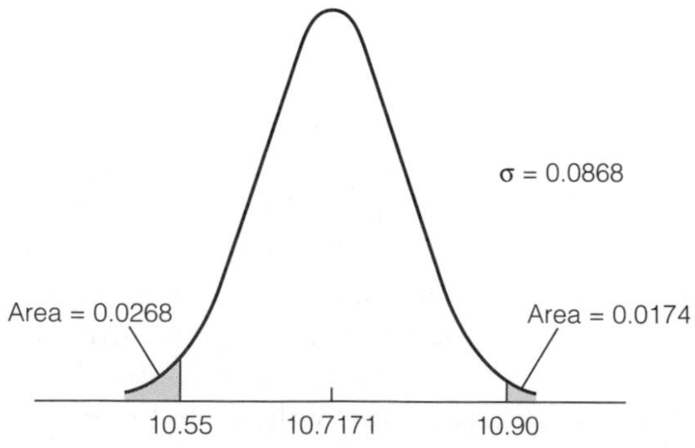

Figure 12.25 Examples of Process Variation Histograms and Specifications

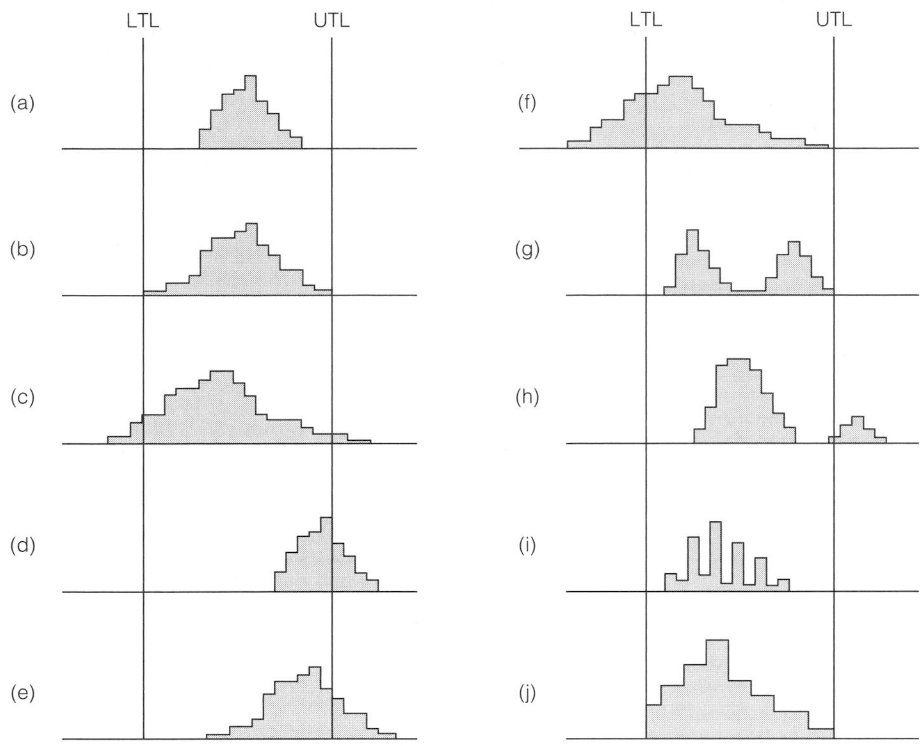

Not all process output will fit neatly into a normal curve; one can usually obtain important capability information directly from the histogram. Figure 12.25 shows some typical examples of process variation histograms that might result from a capability study. Figure 12.25(a) shows an ideal situation in which the natural variation is well within the specified tolerance limits. In Figure 12.25(b), the variation and tolerance limits are about equal; any shift of the distribution will result in nonconformances. The histogram in 12.25(c) shows a distribution with a natural variation greater than the specification limits; in this case, the process is not capable of meeting specifications. The histograms in Figures 12.25(d), (e), and (f) correspond to those in Figures 12.25(a), (b), and (c), except that the process is off-center from the specified tolerance limits. The capability of each is the same as in Figures 12.25(a), (b), and (c), but the shift in the mean of the distribution results in a higher level of nonconformance. Thus, in Figure 12.25(d), the process is capable; it is simply not adjusted correctly to the center of the specifications. In Figure 12.25(g), the bimodal shape suggests that perhaps the data were drawn from two different machines or that two different materials or products were involved. The small distribution to the right in Figure 12.25(h) may be the result of including pieces from a trial setup run while the machine was being adjusted. The strange distribution in Figure 12.25(i) might be the result of the measurement process, such as inadequate gauging or rounding of data, and not inherent in the process itself. Finally, the truncated distribution in Figure 12.25(j) is generally the result of sorting nonconforming parts; one would expect a smoother tail of the distribution on the left. Therefore, one must be careful to ensure that observed variation comes from the process itself, not from external influences. Thus, a good control system is a necessity, because a histogram alone will not provide complete information.

An important issue that is often ignored in process capability studies is the error resulting from using the sample standard deviation, s, rather than the true standard deviation, σ. A simple table can be constructed to find confidence intervals on the true value for σ for a given sample size. Such a table is shown in Table 12.5 and is easily explained by an example. For a given sample size, σ will be less than or equal to s times the factor in that row with probability p, where p is the column heading. Thus, for a sample size of 30, $\sigma \leq 0.744s$ with probability 0.005; $\sigma \leq 1.280s$ occurs 95 percent of the time; and so on. A 90 percent confidence interval for σ can be found by using the factors in the columns corresponding to $p = 0.050$ and $p = 0.950$. Thus, for a sample size of 30, a 95 percent confidence interval would be (0.825s, 1.280s). The interpretation of process capability information should be tempered by such an analysis.

The process capability index, C_p (sometimes called the process potential index), is defined as the ratio of the specification width to the natural tolerance of the process. C_p relates the natural variation of the process with the design specifications in a single, quantitative measure.

Process Capability Indexes In Figure 12.25 we saw that the distribution of process output can differ in both location and spread relative to the specifications. The relationship between the natural variation and specifications is often quantified by a measure known as the **process capability index**. In numerical terms, the formula is

$$C_p = \frac{\text{UTL} - \text{LTL}}{6\sigma}$$

where

UTL = upper tolerance limit
LTL = lower tolerance limit
σ = standard deviation of the process

The process capability index can be used for setting objectives and improving processes. Suppose that a quality manager in a firm has a process with a standard deviation of 1 and a tolerance spread of 8. The value of C_p for this situation is 1.33. The manager realizes that the natural spread is within specifications at this time, but new contracts call for increasing the value of the capability index. Targets are set for increasing the index to 1.66 within three months, to 2.00 within six months, and to 2.33 within a year. Given that the tolerance spread (UTL– LTL) is held at the previous level of 8, the following table shows the required process standard deviation for each phase of the project.

C_p	UTL – LTL	6σ	σ
1.33	8	6	1
1.66	8	4.8	0.8
2.00	8	4	0.67
2.33	8	3.43	0.57

Operationally, this task involves reducing the variability in the process from a standard deviation of 1.000 to 0.444, which results in the desired increase of C_p from the

Table 12.5 Ratio of Population to Sample Standard Deviation

Number of Samples	Fraction of Population Less Than or Equal to Value in Table 0.005	0.010	0.025	0.050	0.100	0.950	0.975	0.995
2	0.356	0.388	0.446	0.510	0.608	15.952	31.911	159.516
3	0.434	0.466	0.521	0.578	0.659	4.407	6.287	14.142
4	0.483	0.514	0.567	0.620	0.693	2.919	3.727	6.468
5	0.519	0.549	0.599	0.649	0.717	2.372	2.875	4.396
6	0.546	0.576	0.624	0.672	0.736	2.090	2.453	3.484
7	0.569	0.597	0.644	0.690	0.751	1.918	2.202	2.979
8	0.588	0.616	0.661	0.705	0.763	1.797	2.035	2.660
9	0.604	0.631	0.675	0.718	0.774	1.711	1.916	2.440
10	0.618	0.645	0.688	0.729	0.783	1.645	1.826	2.278
11	0.630	0.656	0.699	0.739	0.791	1.593	1.755	2.154
12	0.641	0.667	0.708	0.748	0.798	1.551	1.698	2.056
13	0.651	0.677	0.717	0.755	0.804	1.515	1.651	1.976
14	0.660	0.685	0.725	0.762	0.810	1.485	1.611	1.910
15	0.669	0.693	0.732	0.769	0.815	1.460	1.577	1.854
16	0.676	0.700	0.739	0.775	0.820	1.437	1.548	1.806
17	0.683	0.707	0.745	0.780	0.824	1.418	1.522	1.764
18	0.690	0.713	0.750	0.785	0.828	1.400	1.499	1.727
19	0.696	0.719	0.756	0.790	0.832	1.385	1.479	1.695
20	0.702	0.725	0.760	0.794	0.836	1.370	1.461	1.666
21	0.707	0.730	0.765	0.798	0.839	1.358	1.444	1.640
22	0.712	0.734	0.769	0.802	0.842	1.346	1.429	1.617
23	0.717	0.739	0.773	0.805	0.845	1.335	1.415	1.595
24	0.722	0.743	0.777	0.809	0.848	1.325	1.403	1.576
25	0.726	0.747	0.781	0.812	0.850	1.316	1.391	1.558
26	0.730	0.751	0.784	0.815	0.853	1.308	1.380	1.542
27	0.734	0.755	0.788	0.818	0.855	1.300	1.370	1.526
28	0.737	0.758	0.791	0.820	0.857	1.293	1.361	1.512
29	0.741	0.762	0.794	0.823	0.859	1.286	1.352	1.499
30	0.744	0.765	0.796	0.825	0.861	1.280	1.344	1.487
31	0.748	0.768	0.799	0.828	0.863	1.274	1.337	1.475
36	0.762	0.781	0.811	0.838	0.872	1.248	1.304	1.427
41	0.774	0.792	0.821	0.847	0.879	1.228	1.280	1.390
46	0.784	0.802	0.829	0.854	0.885	1.212	1.260	1.361
51	0.793	0.810	0.837	0.861	0.890	1.199	1.243	1.337
61	0.808	0.824	0.849	0.871	0.898	1.179	1.217	1.299
71	0.820	0.835	0.858	0.879	0.905	1.163	1.198	1.272
81	0.829	0.844	0.866	0.886	0.910	1.151	1.183	1.250
91	0.838	0.852	0.873	0.892	0.915	1.141	1.171	1.233
101	0.845	0.858	0.879	0.897	0.919	1.133	1.161	1.219

Source: Thomas D. Hall, "How Close Is s to σ?" Quality, no. 45, December 1991. Copyright © 1991 Quality. Reprinted with permission.

current level of 1.33 to the final level of 2.33, which might be accomplished using process improvement and technology upgrades.

Two important facts about the C_p index should be pointed out. One relates to process conditions and the other relates to interpretation of the values that have been calculated. First, the calculation of the C_p has no meaning if the process is not under statistical control. The natural spread (6σ) should be calculated using a sufficiently large sample to get a meaningful estimate of the population standard deviation (σ). Second, a C_p of 1.00 would require that the process be perfectly centered on the mean of the tolerance spread to prevent some units from being produced outside the limits. The goal of all units being produced within specifications with a C_p of 1.33 is much easier to achieve, and still easier with a C_p of 2.00. Many firms require C_p values of 1.66 or greater from their suppliers.

Many practitioners suggest a "safe" lower limit Cp of 1.5. A value above this level will practically guarantee that all units produced by a controlled process will be within specifications.

The previous discussion assumed that the process was centered; clearly the value of C_p does not depend on the mean of the process. To include information on process centering, one-sided indexes are often used. One-sided process capability indexes are as follows:

$$C_{pu} = \frac{\text{UTL} - \mu}{3\sigma} \text{ (upper one-sided index)}$$

$$C_{pu} = \frac{\mu - \text{LTL}}{3\sigma} \text{ (lower one-sided index)}$$

$$C_{pk} = \min(C_{pi}, C_{pu})$$

To illustrate these computations for the U-bolt example, we found a mean of 10.7171. Thus,

$$C_{pl} = \frac{10.717 - 10.50}{3(.0868)} = .83$$

$$C_{pu} = \frac{11.0 - 10.7171}{3(.0868)} = 1.086$$

$$C_{pk} = \min\{.83, 1.086\} = .83$$

We see that the process is more capable of satisfying the upper specification limit than the lower specification limit. The low value of C_{pk} indicates that the worst case is unacceptable. This index is often used in specifying quality requirements in purchasing contracts. Figure 12.26 shows a spreadsheet, available on the Premium website in the Excel templates folder, designed to compute these indexes.

We note that Six Sigma performance corresponds to process variation equal to half the design tolerance, or a C_p value of 2.0 (refer back to Figure 11.1). However, because Six Sigma allows a mean shift of up to 1.5 standard deviations from the target, C_{pk} must be held to 1.5.

Some controversy exists over C_p and C_{pk} as measures of process capability, particularly with respect to the economic loss function philosophy of Taguchi.[38] For example, a process may have a high C_{pk} even when its mean is off target and close to the specification limits, as long as the process spread is small.[39] Several alternative measures have been proposed and are discussed in one of the Bonus Materials documents for this chapter on the Premium website.

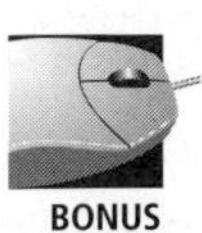
BONUS MATERIALS

Figure 12.26 Spreadsheet for Process Capability Calculations (PROCESS CAPABILITY.XLS)

	A	B	C	D	E	F	G	H	I	J	K	L	M	N	O	P
1	**Process Capability Analysis**															
2																
3	This spreadsheet is designed to handle up to 150 observations. Enter data ONLY in yellow-shaded cells.															
4																
5	**Nominal specification**				10.75		**Average**			10.7171			**Cp**	0.96		
6	**Upper tolerance limit**				11		**Standard deviation**			0.0868			**Cpl**	0.833		
7	**Lower tolerance limit**				10.5								**Cpu**	1.086		
8													**Cpk**	0.833		
9																
10	**DATA**	**1**	**2**	**3**	**4**	**5**	**6**	**7**	**8**	**9**	**10**	**11**	**12**	**13**	**14**	**15**
11	**1**	10.65	10.80	10.50	10.80	10.70	10.80	10.75	10.65	10.85	10.65	10.80	10.65			
12	**2**	10.75	10.85	10.80	10.80	10.70	10.70	10.85	10.70	10.80	10.55	10.70	10.85			
13	**3**	10.75	10.70	10.65	10.80	10.65	10.65	10.75	10.65	10.50	10.80	10.75	10.80			
14	**4**	10.60	10.65	10.65	10.70	10.60	10.75	10.80	10.85	10.65	10.65	10.70	10.60			
15	**5**	10.70	10.75	10.70	10.75	10.55	10.70	10.85	10.70	10.75	10.60	10.75	10.70			
16	**6**	10.60	10.90	10.85	10.75	10.65	10.65	10.60	10.75	10.75	10.60	10.65	10.65			
17	**7**	10.60	10.75	10.80	10.70	10.60	10.85	10.85	10.85	10.80	10.85	10.85	10.80			
18	**8**	10.75	10.75	10.70	10.70	10.70	10.60	10.65	10.85	10.75	10.65	10.70	10.65			
19	**9**	10.65	10.65	10.75	10.80	10.65	10.90	10.65	10.75	10.70	10.75	10.70	10.70			
20	**10**	10.60	10.60	10.75	10.80	10.75	10.85	10.75	10.75	10.70	10.65	10.60	10.65			

It is important to remember that C_p and C_{pk} are simply point estimates from some unknown distribution because they are based on samples. A confidence interval for C_{pk} can be expressed as:[40]

$$C_{pk} \pm z_{\alpha/2}\sqrt{\frac{1}{9n} + \frac{C_{pk}^2}{2n-2}}$$

For example, suppose the point estimate is 1.15 and the sample size $n = 45$. Using this formula, a 95 percent confidence interval is (0.89, 1.41). Although 1.15 may seem good, it is quite possible that the true population parameter is less than one because of sampling error. If a sample size of 400 were used instead to obtain the same point estimate, the confidence interval would be (1.06, 1.24), providing a better indication that the capability is indeed good.

Process capability indexes depend on the assumption that the distribution of output is normal. When a normal distribution does not apply, such as in the chemical industry, when suppliers often pick and choose material that will meet the specifications of customers (which often results in a uniform distribution), or when output is affected by tool wear and exhibits a highly skewed distribution, process capability indexes can be below 1 even though all measurements are within specification limits. Finally, process capability may be affected by measurement error. If the measurement error is large, then process capability indexes must be viewed with caution.

SUMMARY OF KEY POINTS AND TERMINOLOGY

BONUS MATERIALS

The Bonus Materials folder on the Premium website, provides a summary of key concepts and terminology introduced in this chapter.

Quality in Practice

Testing Audio Components at Shure, Inc.[41]

Shure Incorporated is a global, privately held company headquartered in Evanston, Illinois, with manufacturing facilities in Illinois, Texas, and Mexico, and sales offices in Germany and Hong Kong. Shure's mission is to deliver high-performing, quality, rugged and reliable audio products, and to provide superior customer service and support. Shure's philosophy is to be market-driven and customer-focused in their chosen markets. Each market segment has its own quality and reliability needs:

- *Performance Audio:* Musical performers and those who record and monitor their work on stage or in the studio. Anyone who has attended a rock concert can attest to the rough treatment microphones receive from the entertainers, some actually throwing them across the stage.
- *Presentation and Installation Audio:* Anywhere a sound system is installed, such as houses of worship, hotels, conference rooms, clubs, theaters, and auditoriums. Many users are unfamiliar with the acoustical characteristics of the equipment they are using and sound technicians are often not on site, so the equipment really needs to run by itself.
- *Radio and TV:* Broadcast industry both in studio and on location in the field. Technicians need to have total confidence in the equipment they are using on a live, remote broadcast, because they cannot go back and redo that on-the-spot interview.
- *Consumer Market:* Phonograph cartridges and low-cost microphones, including audiophiles, hip-hop DJs, and home recording. Scratch DJs literally take a record and pull it back and forth to the beat of a song, causing tremendous pressure on the phonograph stylus.
- *Mobile Communications:* Audio subsystems, such as hands-free cellular, within the automotive environment. Microphones need to perform in a variety of temperatures.

S.N. Shure began the company by launching a one-man operation in 1925 that sold radio parts kits. It was the microphone that marked the company's entry into manufacturing in 1932, and the microphone remains Shure's flagship product to this day. Because of its emphasis on engineering research, Shure products became known early on for their outstanding quality and durability. During World War II, Shure was awarded a U.S. government contract to provide microphones to the military, and needed to meet strict specifications for performance and ruggedness. Shure took the extra step to develop a rigorous in-house testing program that remains in place today.

In addition to microphones (both wired and wireless) and phonograph cartridges, Shure manufactures a number of other audio electronics products, including mixers, digital signal processors, personal monitoring systems, and digital feedback reducers. Shure's quality philosophy is reliability oriented. Products are tested for reliability well beyond the warranty period, with the goal of providing the customer long-term service and satisfaction. Testing is designed to simulate actual operating conditions. Shure has more than 80 test procedures in place. The following are a few examples:

- *Microphone Drop Test:* To determine whether a microphone is capable of dynamic shock stress. Initial performance data are taken on the mic. Then the mic is dropped numerous times onto a hardwood floor from a height of 6 feet at random angles. The mic is "talked out" after every two drops. After the drop tests, level and response are tested and compared to the initial data. Any unit not meeting original print specifications is considered a failure.
- *Perspiration Test:* To evaluate the corrosion resistance of painted/plated parts exposed to an acid solution simulating sweat. Parts are placed in a perspiration chamber that consists of a stand supporting the parts over a large glass jar containing acid solution. Parts are inspected daily for amounts of corrosion for a period of seven days. Parts are then compared to good control parts to determine amount of corrosion present.

- *Cable and Cable Assembly Flex:* To ensure that any cable that would normally be subjected to random twisting motion under tension will meet field requirements. Cable flex test equipment provides for two independent motions: rocking motion and rotation, and twisting motion and rotation. Cables not meeting flex life specification are considered a failure.
- *Sequential Shipping:* To evaluate the packaging effectiveness and mechanical integrity of the product under simulated shipping conditions. This test is used for all Shure products. Products packaged for shipping are given the following tests, in order: drop test, vibration test, and rough handling test. When the product is removed from its packaging, it must appear and operate as new. If appropriate, an electrical test is performed and compared to initial electrical test data.
- *Cartridge Drop and Scrape Test:* To determine ability of stylus to withstand accidental drops and side impacts. A cartridge mounted in a tone arm is dropped onto a moving record at least 100 times. The cartridge is scraped across a moving record 100 times. This test simulates and exceeds any abuse given to the cartridge and stylus in normal use.
- *Temperature Storage:* To determine ability to withstand extreme temperatures for extended periods of time. Initial performance data are taken. For high temperature, the product is placed in a preheated high temperature chamber for seven days. The product is allowed to stabilize at room temperature for 24 hours and then the same performance data are taken. For low temperature, the product is placed in a low temperature chamber for seven days, allowed to stabilize to room temperature for 24 hours, and tested.

By performing these and other rigorous tests, Shure consistently meets its goal of exceeding customers' product performance and reliability expectations.

Key Issues for Discussion

1. Describe how the definition of reliability presented in this chapter applies to the performance tests described here. Do these tests measure inherent reliability or achieved reliability?
2. For the examples of product testing provided in this case, discuss what quality/reliability measurements might be taken and how the data might be analyzed. For example, are the measurements attributes or variables? Would they be analyzed using descriptive statistics, Pareto charts, and so on?

Quality in Practice

Applying QFD in a Managed Care Organization[42]

Managed care was introduced in the United States nearly two decades ago as a means to maintain quality while managing costs. A managed care organization (MCO) contracts with physicians, hospitals, medical equipment companies, and home health agencies to provide services to its members (patients). The MCO markets its services and actively enrolls people. Once enrolled, members receive a handbook that explains how they can access the services offered by the MCO and its affiliated providers. The member handbook has become a main source of information regarding an increasingly complex array of benefits offered by the thousands of MCOs. Designing the handbook and creating its content are, therefore, important components of any MCO's business strategy. Unfortunately, a member satisfaction survey indicated that members have a poor understanding of their benefits. When members are unable to understand their benefits, the MCOs' member services switchboards are inundated with calls, resulting in frustration and anger and further delaying patient access to the MCOs' services. The MCO receives an average of 3,000 calls per day, with each call lasting an average of 3.2 minutes. Approximately 50 percent of these calls involve issues discussed in the member handbook. The MCO also spends more than $250,000 per year in providing supplemental materials to its members as a result of inadequacies in the member handbook.

To improve the handbook and member satisfaction, QFD was used to redesign it. The input for the QFD process was obtained through a series of focus groups. A total of 131 MCO customers participated in six focus group sessions. Participants were selected based on two criteria:

1. They had to have been members of a competing MCO—whose member handbook was used for comparison—for at least two years prior to joining the MCO being studied.
2. They had to have been members of the MCO being studied for at least two consecutive years.

The focus group process was then administered in two stages:

Stage 1. Participants were provided with a copy of the company's member handbook and the competitor's member handbook. Even though the participants had all used the competitor's member handbook, it was necessary to provide them with copies to ensure a fair comparison. They were allowed to take both handbooks home for one week to look them over.

Stage 2. The groups were brought together for a follow-up session that focused on data collection. Each session was facilitated by an independent researcher unaffiliated with the MCO, and each participant was provided lunch as a reward for participating in the study.

The six focus groups all followed these steps:

1. Determine customer requirements.
2. Measure the importance of the customer requirements.
3. Rate customer satisfaction with the company's current member handbook.
4. Rate satisfaction with the competitor's member handbook.
5. Develop a list of characteristics that are within the control of the company and could potentially improve the handbook. These characteristics are referred to as substitute quality characteristics.

The QFD process begins by capturing the voice of the customer or the customer requirements. The key customer requirements identified were ease of use, accuracy, timeliness, clarity, and consciousness. The technical requirements that describe how the organization will respond to each of the customer requirements were identified as follows:

- Font size
- Up-to-date information
- Use of pictures or illustrations
- Use of colors
- Glossary of terms
- Answers to frequently asked questions
- Expanded table of contents
- Offering the handbook in more than one language

After gathering the customer and technical requirements, the MCO determined there was a strong correlation between the substitute quality characteristic (technical requirement) of ease of use and the customer requirements of expanding the glossary of terms and the table of contents. Similarly, the following substitute quality characteristics had a moderate correlation with ease of use:

- Font size
- Use of pictures or illustrations
- Use of colors
- A question and answer section
- More language friendly

Providing updates had a weak correlation with ease of use.

The results of the MCO's QFD study resulted in the House of Quality shown in Figure 12.27. The numbers in the *Rate of Importance* column indicate the relative importance customers assigned to each requirement. The importance rating uses a numerical scale from 1 to 5, with 1 being low and 5 being high. Members were asked to use such a rating scale during the focus group sessions. Two customer requirements—ease of use and accuracy—were assigned high importance ratings of 4.5 and 5, respectively. The other three customer requirements—clarity, timeliness, and conciseness—received importance ratings of 3.8, 3.2, and 2.5, respectively.

The entries in the *Company Now* column indicate how customers rate the organization's performance with respect to their stated requirements. This rating is based on a numerical scale from 1 to 5, with 1 being poor and 5 being excellent. The entries in *Competitor X* column represent how the customers rate the chief competitor X with respect to their stated requirements. As is the case in the

Figure 12.27 House of Quality for the MCO Membership Handbook

Direction of improvement		
Maximize	↑	1
Target	×	0
Minimize	↓	–1

		Rate of importance	Font size	Updates	Photos or illustrations	Use of colors	Glossary of terms	Question and answer section	Table of contents	Laguage friendly	Competitive analysis	• Company now	• Competitor X	• Plan	• Rate of improvement	Absolute weight	Percentage of importance	Maximum = 29.5 Percentage of importance Minimum = 9.9	
		1	1	2	3	4	5	6	7	8	1	2	3	4	5	6	7		
Direction of improvement	1		↑	↑	↑	↑	↑	↑	↑	↑									
Ease of use	1	4.5	○	▽	○	○	●	○	●	○		3.2	4.3	4.5	1.4	6.3	25.2		1
Accuracy	2	5.0		●			▽	○		▽		3.1	4.1	4.6	1.5	7.4	29.5		2
Timeliness	3	3.2		●				▽				3.8	3.4	3.8	1.0	3.2	12.7		3
Clarity	4	3.8	▽	▽	○	▽	●	○	▽	○		2.6	3.7	3.9	1.5	5.7	22.7		4
Conciseness	5	2.5	▽		▽							4.1	3.3	4.1	1.0	2.5	9.9		5
Importance of the hows	1		108.1	427.9	153.4	98.2	460.0	244.7	249.1	173.0									
Percentage of importance of the hows	2		5.6	22.4	8.0	5.1	24.0	12.8	13.0	9.0									
Maximum = 24 Percentage of importance of the hows Minimum = 5.1	3																		
Competitive benchmarking results	4																		
• Company now	5		10	1	1	2	5	5	10	2									
• Competitor X	6		12	3	4	5	15	10	6	1									
• Plan	7		12	4	4	5	20	15	10	2									
			1	2	3	4	5	6	7	8									

Standard 9-3-1		
Strong	●	9
Moderate	○	3
Weak	▽	1

Source: Reprinted with permission from Vincent Omachonu & Paul Barach, "QFD in a Managed Care Organization," *Quality Progress*, November 2005, pp. 36–41.

Company Now column, these ratings are based on a numerical scale from 1 to 5, with 1 being poor and 5 being excellent. According to this study, the chief competitor's handbook is outperforming the MCO's handbook in ease of use, accuracy, and clarity, as perceived by its customers. The *Plan* column indicates where the company wishes to be with respect to each of the quality requirements stated by its customers. The plan for each requirement is determined by examining the MCO's position in relation to its competitor(s) and its customers' rate of importance. It is also based on the organization's strategic plan.

After taking all things into account, the MCO's QFD team set a goal of achieving a performance rating of 4.5 for ease of use, 4.6 for accuracy, 3.8 for timeliness, 3.9 for clarity, and 4.1 for conciseness. The MCO expects to achieve these levels of performance the next time its customers are surveyed. The *Rate of Improvement* column contains the ratio of the company's goal compared to where the company is today. It is determined by dividing the value in the *Plan* column by the value in the *Company Now* column for each requirement. The *Absolute Quality Weight* is determined by multiplying the rate of importance by the rate of improvement. It is an attempt to assign a weighted rate to what the customer considers to be important and the goal (value established in the *Plan* column).
The *Percentage of Importance* was determined by

transforming each absolute weight value into a percentage of the total absolute weight value (25.1).

After thoroughly looking at what is important to the MCO's customers, the company's current performance, its chief competitor's current position, and the goal, the MCO determined that accuracy is the most important requirement driving customer satisfaction, with nearly 30 percent of the demanded weight.

The figures in the *Importance of the Hows* row represent the sum of the products of each column symbol value and the corresponding demanded weight. The two most important technical requirements were glossary of terms and updates, with totals of 460 and 427.9, respectively. Each entry in the *Percentage of Importance of the Hows* row is divided by the sum of all the entries in that row and multiplied by 100 to convert it into a percentage.

The *Company Now* row gives the values of the measurable technical requirements. The QFD team examined and analyzed the chief competitor's member handbook and interviewed the sales and marketing representatives of both companies to determine the values of the technical requirements for the chief competitors marketing representatives participated in this study. They were selected based on their knowledge of and experience working with the two companies. The competitor outperformed the MCO under study in all aspects of the technical requirements, except language friendliness and table of contents. The most aggressive plans were targeted at the two technical requirements with the highest totals: glossary of terms and updates. The plan values represent the design targets for the team's effort for the redesign of the MCO's member handbook.

Following the redesign of the member handbook, the volume of calls associated with the issues addressed in the handbook decreased from 3,000 calls per day to 1,900 (about a 35 percent reduction). Member services telephone operators were able to attend to other important issues facing the members of the health plan. Besides increasing operational efficiency, this improvement enhanced member satisfaction and reduced employee frustration in having to repeatedly deal with these issues.

Key Issues for Discussion

1. Although this example of QFD involved the design of tangible items, why is it more difficult to implement in a service context as opposed to a pure manufacturing context?
2. Verify the calculations in the *Importance of the Hows* row and *Percentage of Importance of the Hows* row by showing the detailed calculations used to arrive at these figures.
3. What lessons can be learned and applied to other service organizations that seek to design or redesign their products and services?

Additional Quality in Practice features can be found in the Bonus Materials folder on the Premium website.

BONUS MATERIALS

Review Questions

1. Describe the product design and development process.
2. Discuss the importance of and impediments to reducing the time for product development.
3. What is Design for Six Sigma? Explain the four basic elements of DFSS and the various tools and methodologies that comprise this body of knowledge.
4. Explain concept engineering. Why is it an important tool for assuring quality in product and process design activities?
5. What are the principal benefits of QFD?
6. Outline the process of building the House of Quality. What departments and functions within the company should be involved in each step of the process?
7. How can product design affect manufacturability? Explain the concept and importance of design for manufacturability.

8. Summarize the key design practices for high quality in manufacturing and assembly.
9. Discuss environmental responsibility issues relating to product design facing businesses today.
10. Describe the basic approach to design for excellence.
11. Explain the difference between nominal dimensions and tolerances. How should tolerances be realistically set?
12. Explain the role of the Taguchi loss function in process and tolerance design.
13. What is design failure mode and effects analysis (DFMEA)? Provide a simple example illustrating the concept.
14. What is the importance of reliability and why has it become such a prominent area within the quality disciplines?
15. Define reliability. Explain the definition thoroughly.
16. What is the difference between a functional failure and a reliability failure?
17. What is the definition of failure rate? How is it measured?
18. Explain the differences and relationships between the cumulative failure rate curve and the failure rate curve.
19. How is the average failure rate over a time interval computed?
20. Explain the product life characteristics curve and how it can be used.
21. What is a reliability function? Discuss different ways of expressing this function.
22. Explain how to compute the reliability of series, parallel, and series-parallel systems.
23. Explain the purpose of design reviews and how they facilitate product development.
24. Describe different forms of product testing.
25. What does the term *latent defect* mean?
26. What is a "robust" design?
27. Provide some examples of low-tech and high-tech measuring instruments (see Bonus Materials).
28. Describe the science of metrology.
29. What is the difference between accuracy, precision, and reproducibility?
30. What is calibration and why is it important to a good quality assurance system?
31. How is an R&R study performed? What is its purpose?
32. Explain the term *process capability.* How can process capability generally be improved?
33. What are the three major types of process capability studies? Describe the methodology of conducting a process capability study.
34. Define the process capability indexes, C_p, C_{pl}, and C_{pu}, and explain how they may be used to establish or improve quality policies in operating areas or with suppliers.

PROBLEMS

Note: Data sets for several problems are available in the Excel workbook *C12Data* on the Premium website for this chapter. Click on the appropriate worksheet tab as noted in the problem (e.g., Prob. 12-5, etc.) to access the data.

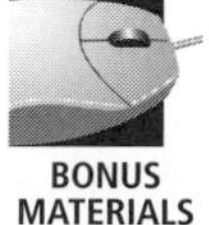

1. Tonia's Tasty Tacos conducted consumer surveys and focus groups and identified the most important customer expectations as
   - Tasty, moderately healthy food
   - Speedy service
   - An easy-to-read menu board
   - Accurate order filling
   - Perceived value

   Develop a set of technical requirements to incorporate into the design of a new facility and a House of Quality relationship matrix to assess how well your requirements address these expectations. Refine your design as necessary, based upon the initial assessment.
2. Newfonia, Inc., is working on a design for a new smart phone. Marketing staff conducted extensive surveys and focus groups with potential customers to determine the characteristics that the customers want and expect in a smart phone. Newfonia's studies have identified the most important customer expectations as
   - Initial cost
   - Reliability
   - Ease of use
   - Features
   - Operating cost
   - Compactness

   Develop a set of technical requirements to incorporate into the design of a House of Quality relationship matrix to assess how well your requirements address these expectations. Refine your design as necessary, based upon the initial assessment.
3. Tonia's Tasty Tacos (Problem 1) acquired some additional information. It found that consumers placed the highest importance on healthy food, followed by value, followed by order accuracy and service. The menu board was only casually noted as an important attribute in the surveys. Tonia faces three major competitors in this market: Grabby's, Tacoking, and Sandy's. Studies of their products yielded the information shown in the worksheet tab *Prob.12-3* in the Excel file *C12Data* on the Premium website for this chapter. Results of the consumer panel ratings for each of these competitors can also be found there (a 1–5 scale, with 5 being the best). Using this information, modify and extend your House of Quality from Problem 1 and develop a deployment plan for a new burger. On what attributes should the company focus its marketing efforts?

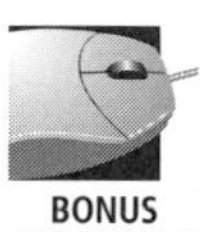

4. Newfonia, Inc. (Problem 2), faces three major competitors in this market: Oldphonia, Simphonia, and Colliefonia. It found that potential consumers placed the highest importance on reliability (measured by such things as freedom from operating system crashes and battery life), followed by compactness (weight/bulkiness), followed by flexibility (features, ease of use, and types of program modules available). The operating cost was only occasionally noted as an important attribute in the surveys. Studies of their products yielded the information shown in the table in the worksheet tab *Prob.12-4* in the Excel file *C12Data* on the Premium website for this chapter. Results of the consumer panel ratings for these competitors are also shown in that spreadsheet. Using this information, modify and extend your House of Quality from Problem 2 and develop a deployment plan for the new smartphone. On what attributes should the company focus its marketing efforts?

5. A genetic researcher at GenLab, Ltd. is trying to test two laboratory thermometers (that can be read to 1/100,000th of a degree Celsius) for accuracy and precision. She measured 25 samples with each and obtained the results found in the worksheet tab *Prob.12-5* in the Excel file *C12Data* on the Premium website for this chapter. The true temperature being measured is 0°C. Which instrument is more accurate? Which is more precise? Which is the better instrument?
6. Two scales were at Aussieburgers, Ltd. used to weigh the same 25 samples of hamburger patties for a fast-food restaurant in Australia. Results are shown in the workshet tab *Prob.12-6* in the Excel file *C12Data* on the Premium website for this chapter. The samples were weighed in grams, and the supplier has ensured that each patty weighs 114 grams. Which scale is more accurate? Which is more precise? Which is the better scale?
7. A blueprint specification for the thickness of a dishwasher part at PlataLimpia, Inc. is 0.325 ± 0.025 centimeters (cm). It costs $15 to scrap a part that is outside the specifications. Determine the Taguchi loss function for this situation.
8. A team was formed to study the dishwasher part at PlataLimpia, Inc. described in Problem 7. While continuing to work to find the root cause of scrap, they found a way to reduce the scrap cost to $10 per part.
   a. Determine the Taguchi loss function for this situation.
   b. If the process deviation from target can be held at 0.015 cm, what is the Taguchi loss?
9. A specification for the length of an auto part at PartsDimensions, Inc. is 5.0 ± 0.10 centimeters (cm). It costs $50 to scrap a part that is outside the specifications. Determine the Taguchi loss function for this situation.
10. A team was formed to study the auto part at PartsDimensions described in Problem 9. While continuing to work to find the root cause of scrap, the team found a way to reduce the scrap cost to $30 per part.
    a. Determine the Taguchi loss function for this situation.
    b. If the process deviation from target can be held at 0.020 cm, what is the Taguchi loss?
11. Ruido, Unlimited makes electronic soundboards for car stereos. Output voltage to a certain component on the board must be 12 ± 0.2 volts. Exceeding the limits results in an estimated loss of $50. Determine the Taguchi loss function.
12. An electronic component has a specification of 100 ± 3 ohms. Scrapping the component results in a $81 loss.
    a. What is the value of k in the Taguchi loss function?
    b. If the process is centered on the target specification with a standard deviation of 1 ohm, what is the expected loss per unit?
13. An automatic cookie machine must deposit a specified amount of 25 ± 0.2 grams (g) of dough for each cookie on a conveyor belt. If the machine either over- or underdeposits the mixture, it costs $0.02 to scrap the defective cookie.
    a. What is the value of k in the Taguchi loss function?
    b. If the process is centered on the target specification with a standard deviation of 0.06 g, what is the expected loss per unit?
14. A computer chip is designed so that the distance between two adjacent pins has a specification of 2.000 ± 0.002 millimeters (mm). The loss due to a defective chip is $2. A sample of 25 chips was drawn from the production process and the results, in mm, can be found in the worksheet tab *Prob.12-14* in the Excel file *C12Data* file on the Premium website for this chapter.
    a. Compute the value of k in the Taguchi loss function.
    b. What is the expected loss from this process based on the sample data?

15. In the production of transformers, any output voltage that exceeds 120 ± 15 volts is unacceptable to the customer. Exceeding these limits results in an estimated loss of $450. However, the manufacturer can adjust the voltage in the plant by changing a resistor that costs $2.25.
    a. Determine the Taguchi loss function.
    b. Suppose the nominal specification is 120 volts. At what tolerance should the transformer be manufactured, assuming that the amount of loss is represented by the cost of the resistor?
16. At Elektroparts Manufacturers' integrated circuit business, managers gathered data from a customer focus group and found that any output voltage that exceeds 120 ± 5 volts was unacceptable to the customer. Exceeding these limits results in an estimated loss of $200. However, the manufacturer can still adjust the voltage in the plant by changing a resistor that costs $2.00.
    a. Determine the Taguchi loss function.
    b. Suppose the nominal specification remains at 120 volts. At what tolerance should the integrated circuit be manufactured, assuming that the amount of loss is represented by the cost of the resistor?
17. Two processes, P and Q, are used by a supplier to produce the same component, Z, which is a critical part in the engine of the Air2Port 778 airplane. The specification for Z calls for a dimension of 0.24 mm ± 0.03. The probabilities of achieving the dimensions for each process based on their inherent variability are shown in the table found in the worksheet tab *Prob.12-17* in the Excel file *C12Data* for on the Premium website for this chapter. If $k = 60{,}000$, what is the expected loss for each process? Which would be the best process to use, based on minimizing the expected loss?
18. The average time to handle a call in a the Call-Nowait call processing center has a specification of 6 ± 1.25 minutes. The loss due to a mishandled call is $16. A sample of 25 calls was drawn from the process and the results, in minutes, can be found in the worksheet tab *Prob. 12-18* in the Excel file *C12Data* on the Premium website for this chapter.
    a. Compute the value of k in the Taguchi loss function.
    b. What is the expected loss from this process based on the sample data?
19. Compute the average failure rate during the intervals 0 to 40, 40 to 70, and 70 to 100, and 0 to 100, based on the information in Figure 12.28 and sketch the failure rate curve.

Figure 12.28 Cumulative Failure Curve

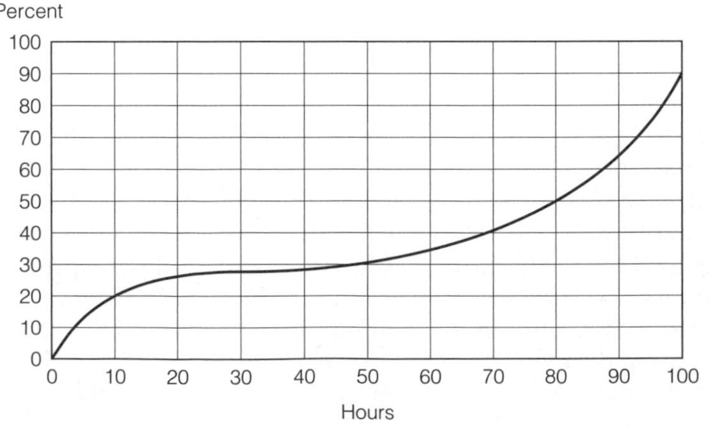

20. The life of a cell phone battery is normally distributed with a mean of 900 days and standard deviation of 50 days.
    a. What fraction of batteries is expected to survive beyond 975 days?
    b. What fraction will survive fewer than 800 days?
    c. Sketch the reliability function.
    d. What length of warranty is needed so that no more than 10 percent of the batteries will be expected to fail during the warranty period?
21. Lifetred, Inc., makes automobile tires that have a mean life of 75,000 miles with a standard deviation of 2,500 miles.
    a. What fraction of tires is expected to survive beyond 77,250 miles?
    b. What fraction will survive fewer than 68,750 miles?
    c. Sketch the reliability function.
    d. What length of warranty is needed so that no more than 10 percent of the tires will be expected to fail during the warranty period?
22. Massive Corporation's tested five motors in an 800-hour test. Compute the failure rate if, three failed after 200, 375, and 450 hours and the other two ran for the full 800 hours each.
23. Livelong, Inc.'s computer monitors have a failure rate of 0.00005 units per hour. Assuming an exponential distribution, what is the probability of failure within 10,000 hours? What is the reliability function?
24. An electronic component in a satellite radio has failure rate of $\lambda = 0.000015$. Find the mean time to failure (MTTF). What is the probability that the component will not have failed after 12,000 hours of operation?
25. The MTBF of an integrated circuit made by IceeU, Inc. is 18,000 hours. Calculate the failure rate.
26. A manufacturer of MP3 players purchases major electronic components as modules. The reliabilities of components differ by supplier (see diagram, below). Suppose that the configuration of the major components is given by:

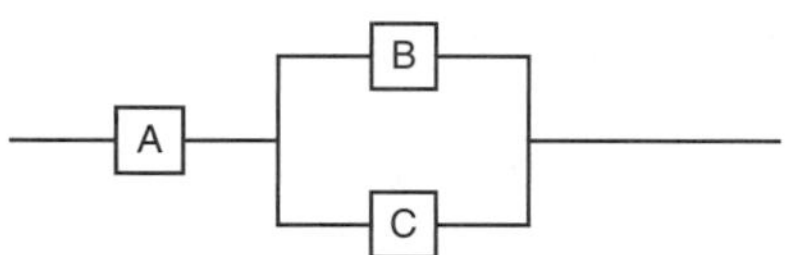

The components can be purchased from three different suppliers. The reliabilities of the components are as follows:

Component	Supplier 1	Supplier 2	Supplier 3
A	0.97	0.92	0.95
B	0.85	0.90	0.90
C	0.95	0.93	0.88

Transportation and purchasing considerations require that only one supplier be chosen. Which one should be selected if the radio is to have the highest possible reliability?

27. An electronic missile guidance system consists of the following components: Components A, B, C, and D have reliabilities of 0.98, 0.95, 0.85, and 0.99, respectively (see the following diagram). What is the reliability of the entire system?

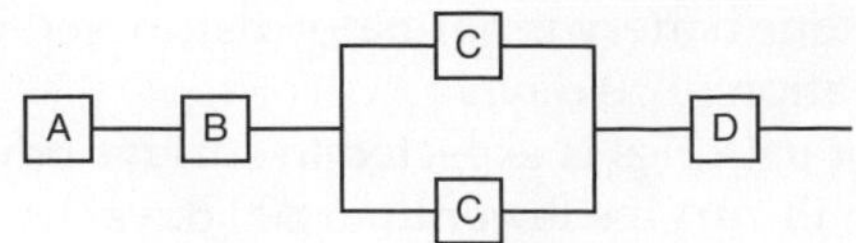

28. A Bestronics store processes customers through three work stations when they wish to buy a certain popular product. Modular components for the product must be checked electronically at two work stations before final checkout, where the cashier collects cash or credit cards for the sale.
    a. If workstation 1 has reliability of testing equipment of 0.98, workstation 2 has reliability of testing equipment of 0.92 and the final checkout register has a reliability of 0.90, what is the overall checkout system reliability?
    b. If the store manager wants to ensure at least a 90 percent system reliability, can she do so by dedicating two final checkout registers to the process, in parallel, each having a 0.90 reliability, with the same reliability at workstations 1 and 2?
29. Manuplex, Inc. has a complex manufacturing process, with three operations that are performed in series. Because of the nature of the process, machines frequently fall out of adjustment and must be repaired. To keep the system going, two identical machines are used at each stage; thus, if one fails, the other can be used while the first is repaired (see accompanying figure).

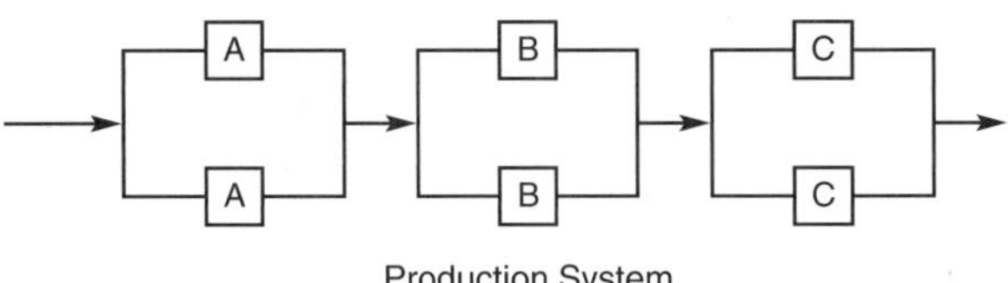

Production System

The reliabilities of the machines are as follows:

Machine	Reliability
A	0.70
B	0.80
C	0.95

    a. Analyze the system reliability, assuming only one machine at each stage (all the backup machines are out of operation).
    b. How much is the reliability improved by having two machines at each stage?
30. An automated production system at Autoprod, Inc. consists of three operations: turning, milling, and grinding. Individual parts are transferred from one operation to the next by a robot. Hence, if one machine or the robot fails, the process stops.
    a. If the reliabilities of the robot, turning center, milling machine, and grinder are 0.98, 0.90, 0.93, and 0.85, respectively, what is the reliability of the system?
    b. Suppose that two grinders are available and the system does not stop if one fails. What is the reliability of the system?

31. A gauge repeatability and reproducibility study at Frankford Brake Systems collected the data found in the worksheet *Prob.12-31* in the Excel file *C12Data* for on the Premium website for this chapter. Analyze these data. The part specification is 1.0 ± 0.06 mm.
32. A gauge repeatability and reproducibility study was made at Precision Parts, Inc., using three operators, taking three trials each on identical parts. The data that can be found in the worksheet tab *Prob.12-32* in the Excel file *C12Data* on the Premium website for this chapter were collected. Do you see any problems after analyzing these data? What should be done? The part specification for the collar that was measured was 1.6 ± 0.2 inches.
33. A machining process at the Mach3 Tool Co. has a required dimension on a part of 0.575 ± 0.007 inch. Twenty-five parts each were measured as found in the worksheet tab *Prob.12-33* in the Excel file *C12Data* on the Premium website for this chapter. What is its capability for producing within acceptable limits?
34. Adjustments were made in the process at the Mach3 Tool Co. discussed in Problem 33 and 25 more samples were taken. The results are given in the worksheet tab *Prob.12-34* in the Excel file *C12Data* on the Premium website for this chapter. What can you observe about the process? Is it now capable of producing within acceptable limits?
35. From the data for Kermit Theatrical Products, construct a histogram and estimate the process capability. If the specifications are 24 ± 0.03, estimate the percentage of parts that will be nonconforming. Finally, compute C_p, C_{pu}, and C_{pl}. Samples for three parts were taken as shown in the worksheet tab *Prob.12-35* in the Excel file *C12Data* on the Premium website for this chapter.
36. Samples for three parts made at River City Parts Co. were taken as shown in the worksheet tab *Prob.12-36* in the Excel file *C12Data* on the Premium website for this chapter. Data set 1 is for part 1, data set 2 is for part 2, and data set 3 is for part 3.
    a. Calculate the mean and standard deviations for each part and compare them to the following specification limits:

Part	Nominal	Tolerance
1	1.750	± 0.045
2	2.000	± 0.060
3	1.250	± 0.030

    b. Will the production process permit an acceptable fit of all parts into a slot with a specification of 5 ± 0.081 at least 99.73 percent of the time?
37. Omega Tecnology Ltd. (OTL) is a small manufacturing company that produces various parts for tool manufacturers. One of OTL's production processes involves producing a Teflon® spacer plate that has a tolerance of 0.05 to 0.100 cm in thickness. On the recommendation of the quality assurance (QA) department and over objections of the plant manager, OTL just purchased some new equipment to make these parts. Recently, the production manager was receiving complaints from customers about high levels of nonconforming parts. He suspected the new equipment, but neither QA nor plant management would listen. The manager discussed the issue with one of his production supervisors who mentioned that she had just collected some process data for a study that the quality assurance department was undertaking. The manager

decided that he would prove his point by showing that the new equipment was not capable of meeting the specifications. The data provided by the supervisor are shown in the worksheet tab *Prob.12-37* in the Excel file *C12Data* on the Premium website for this chapter. Perform a process capability study on these data and interpret your results.

38. Suppose that a refrigeration process at Coolfoods, Ltd. Has a normally distributed output with a mean of 25.0 and a variance of 1.44.
    a. If the specifications are 25.0 ± 3.25, compute C_p, C_{pk}, and C_{pm}. Is the process capable and centered?
    b. Suppose the mean shifts to 23.0 but the variance remains unchanged. Recompute and interpret these process capability indexes.
    c. If the variance can be reduced to 40 percent of its original value, how do the process capability indices change (using the original mean of 25.0)?
39. A process has upper and lower tolerance limits of 5.80 and 5.00, respectively. If the customer requires a demonstrated C_p of 2.0, what must the process standard deviation be? If both C_{pu} and C_{pl} must also be 2.0, determine the process mean using that calculated standard deviation assuming a normal distribution of output.
40. Clearly demonstrate that Six Sigma requires $C_p = 2.0$ and $C_{pk} = 1.5$.

PROJECTS, ETC.

1. Using whatever "market research" techniques are appropriate, define a set of customer attributes for
    a. Purchasing books at your college bookstore
    b. A college registration process
    c. A hotel room used for business
    d. A hotel room used for family leisure vacations

    For each case, determine a set of technical requirements and construct the relationship matrix for the House of Quality.
2. (This exercise would best be performed in a group.) Suppose that you were developing a small pizza restaurant with a dining area and local delivery. Develop a list of customer requirements and technical requirements and try to complete a House of Quality. What service standards might such an operation have?
3. Most children (and many adults) like to assemble and fly balsa-wood gliders. From your own experiences or from interviews with other students, define a set of customer requirements for a good glider. (Even better, buy one and test it to determine these requirements yourself.) If you were to design and manufacture such a product, how would you define a set of technical requirements for the design? Using your results, construct a relationship matrix for a House of Quality.
4. Fill in the following relationship matrix of a House of Quality for a screwdriver. By sampling your classmates, develop priorities for the customer attributes and use these and the relationships to identify key technical requirements to deploy.

	Price	Interchangeable bits	Steel shaft	Rubber grip	Ratchet capability	Plastic handle
Easy to use						
Does not rust						
Durable						
Comfortable						
Versatile						
Inexpensive						
Priority						

5. Discuss and prepare a report with examples on how DFMEA might be used in a service application rather than in a pure product design application.
6. Conduct an R&R study with a team of your fellow students to measure a set of sharpened pencils of various sizes. Use both an ordinary ruler and a metric ruler? What conclusions do you reach?
7. Visit several of the following metrology Web sites or find some new ones and summarize new ideas, concepts, or findings that are not discussed in this chapter.
   http://www.kinematics.com
   http://www.sandia.gov/psl
   http://www.metrology.org
   http://www.boulder.nist.gov
   http://www.nist.gov
   http://www.gecals.com
8. Visit a local machine shop, bakery, or similar factory to determine what type of measurements they perform, what instruments they use, how they use the data, and how they ensure the precision and accuracy of their instruments and gauges. Write a report of your findings.

CASES

Additional cases are available in the Bonus Materials folder on the Premium website.

BONUS MATERIALS

APPLYING QUALITY FUNCTION DEPLOYMENT TO A UNIVERSITY SUPPORT SERVICE[43]

This case is based on an application of QFD at Tennessee Technological University to their Research Resources Center (RRC), an internal service system. Originally created as a support facility for faculty and student research, the RRC has grown to offer many more services, including test preparation, manuscript preparation, resumes, flyers, brochures, faxing, copying, typing, and computer applications. The RRC is staffed weekdays from 7:30 A.M. to 4:30 P.M. with highly experienced support personnel. Jody, the head coordinator of the RRC, is proficient in specialty computer applications. She has a workstation at her disposal loaded with word-processing, graphics, and desktop publishing software. Peripherals such as a laser printer, color printer, and a full-page scanner allow her to generate high-quality output. Candy specializes in word processing, and Marie specializes in copying, collating, and stapling or binding. All three are proficient in most of the RRC functions.

Jobs can be classified as student, teacher, or rush. Most jobs are single-task oriented and can be completed by one RRC professional. The professional may be dependent on student workers to process job orders accurately and place them in the appropriate incoming jobs bin. Some jobs, however, are dependent on the other employees' functions. For instance, Candy types the tests, and Marie makes the copies and packages the final product. In these instances, Marie functions as an internal customer. She becomes dependent on another professional employee to accomplish her job.

Students involved in scholarship and work study programs are also employed part time to support RRC personnel. The RRC, functioning as a unit of the College of Business, is bound by the same regulations as other university offices: It has little control over the student employment selection process.

The responsibilities of the students include taking work orders and assisting customers in low-tech functions, such as making copies and finding research materials. No formal training is provided. The student workers are briefly informed of the RRC's functions and told to be courteous to customers. When student workers have questions, they ask one of the professionals. The student workers are primarily used as an interface between RRC professionals and customers.

A security issue is associated with some of the documents that the RRC processes. Some faculty members choose to have the RRC type and print their tests. In these instances, student workers cannot be involved in any process related to the test. The order is taken by one of the professionals, the job is executed, and the final product is locked in a file cabinet in a room where student workers are not allowed. Additionally, some student documents may not be handled by student workers. Project papers submitted for typing should not be viewed by a student worker who, by chance, may be in the same class and have the same assignment.

Because of limited space in the RRC, little distinction can be made between back office and front office. A counter is set up to the right of the door as customers walk in. All workers are stationed behind this counter. As customers need assistance, they are met at the counter by student workers who assist them. If a customer requires a job, then the appropriate work-order forms are filled out. During this time, the customer is in full view of the operations. Some frequent customers prefer to relay their job orders directly to the professionals. As a result of the customized nature of many of the jobs, this direct contact is sometimes appropriate. Some customers, however, prefer to do business with certain RRC representatives, which means that RRC professionals occasionally have to leave the work they are doing to serve the customer.

The area to the left of the counter is available for customer use (see Figure 12.29). Four large tables are centrally located for faculty members and students to use for study purposes. The waiting area is merely the area between the counter and these tables. Service lines are not structured, and service personnel attempt to serve customers on a first-come, first-served basis. When customers have work orders that can be completed quickly, they may choose to wait at the counter. Occasionally, a queue develops in front of the service counter.

QFD was used to analyze where a concerted effort might increase the RRC's quality level as perceived by the customer. Customer requirements were grouped along the five dimensions of service quality (in rank order of importance): reliability, responsiveness, assurance, empathy, and tangibles. These categories were further broken down into secondary requirements as shown in the House of Quality (Figure 12.30).

Figure 12.29 RRC Old Layout

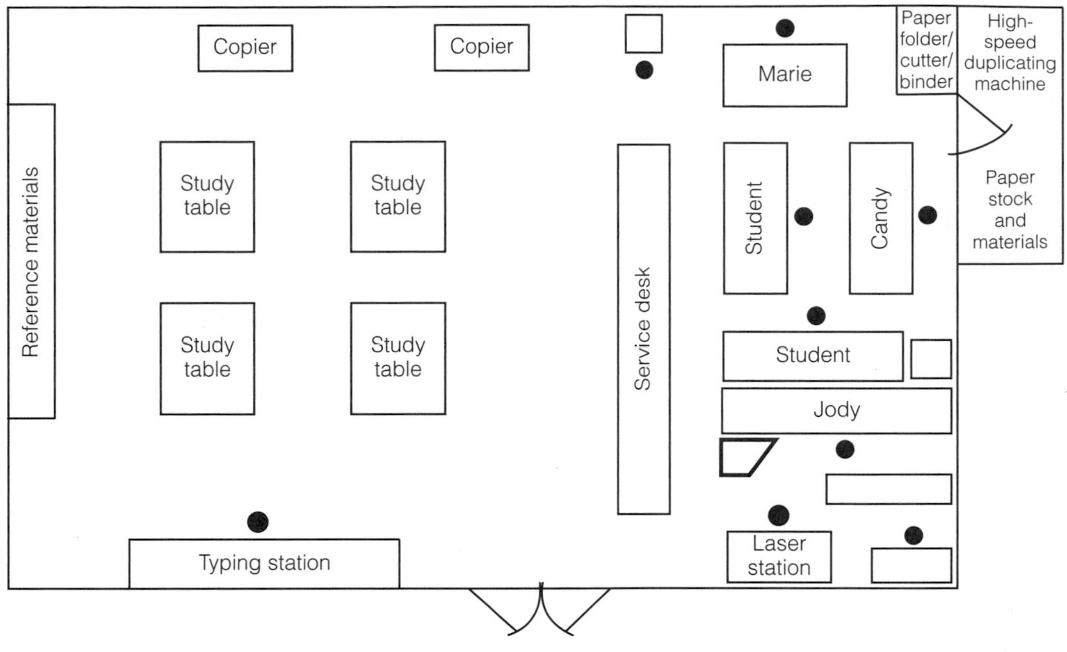

Source: Reprinted with permission from R. Nat Natarajan, Ralph E. Martz, and Kyouske Kurosaka, "Applying QFD to Internal Service System Design," *Quality Progress,* February 1999, 65–70. © 1999, American Society for Quality. No further distribution allowed without permission.

Key Issues for Discussion

1. Do you agree with the relative importance of measures of the voice of the customer in Figure 12.30? Explain why these rankings are reasonable, or provide counterarguments for a different ranking.
2. Using the relative importance ratings of the customer attributes and setting a scale of 1 = weak, 3 = medium, and 5 = strong for the relationship matrix, compute a weighted score for each of the technical requirements in Figure 12.30. Do your scores support the conclusions of the study in terms of the key service components to deploy in the QFD process?
3. What conclusions can you reach in terms of the key service components to deploy in the QFD process? What other recommendations might you suggest based on the information provided in this case? Propose an improved layout of the RRC and justify your proposal.

Black Elk Medical Center

Black Elk Medical Center (BEMC) is a quality-driven acute care hospital organization that includes three medical facilities that treat both inpatients and outpatients. BEMC has won numerous national and local quality awards. These included the J.D. Power awards in 2003 and 2004, First in Kentucky and Ohio in Hospital Quality Award by Anthem Insurance Co., and a listing as one of the Top Ten Hospitals. Black Elk's mission statement says: "We will strive for excellence in all services we provide compared to national standards."

In 2005, the Board of Trustees for Black Elk Medical Center set a goal to reduce the fall rate within the hospital nursing units below the national norm, defined by one national benchmark as 3.4 falls/1000 patient days. The current organizational fall rate for 2004 averaged 4.8 falls/1000

Figure 12.30 RRC House of Quality

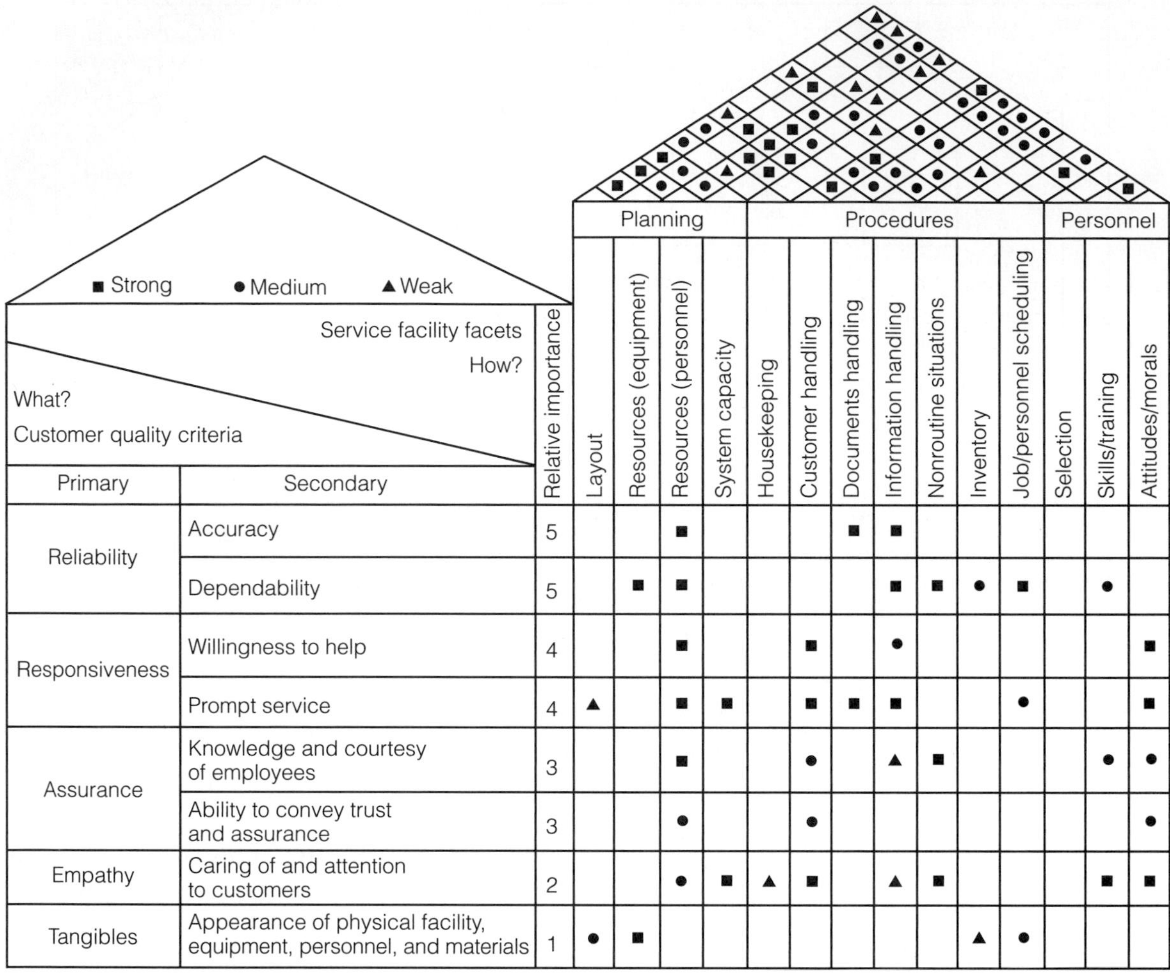

Primary	Secondary	Relative importance	Planning				Procedures							Personnel		
			Layout	Resources (equipment)	Resources (personnel)	System capacity	Housekeeping	Customer handling	Documents handling	Information handling	Nonroutine situations	Inventory	Job/personnel scheduling	Selection	Skills/training	Attitudes/morals
Reliability	Accuracy	5			■				■	■						
	Dependability	5		■	■					■	■	●	■		●	
Responsiveness	Willingness to help	4			■			■		●						■
	Prompt service	4	▲		■	■		■	■	■			●			■
Assurance	Knowledge and courtesy of employees	3			■			●		▲	■				●	●
	Ability to convey trust and assurance	3			●			●								●
Empathy	Caring of and attention to customers	2			●	■	▲	■		▲	■				■	■
Tangibles	Appearance of physical facility, equipment, personnel, and materials	1	●	■								▲	●			

Source: Reprinted with permission from R. Nat Natarajan, Ralph E. Martz, and Kyouske Kurosaka "Applying QFD to Internal Service System Design," *Quality Progress*, Vol. 31, No. 2, February 1999, pp. 65–70.

patient days and through first six months of 2005 average fall rate averaged 4.75 falls/1000 patient days. The fall rate at any health care institution is significant to elderly patients, and especially so to those that are 65 years of age and older. Many elderly patients fall, break a hip, or even die within one year of the fall. The Board set the fall reduction goal in conjunction with a new regulation, National Patient Safety Goal 9B, that stated that health care organizations must implement a fall reduction program and evaluate the effectiveness of the program no later than January 1, 2006.

Each health care organization was required to create or adopt a fall risk assessment process specific to the population served. The Joint Commission on Accreditation of Healthcare Organizations (JACHO) does not define a fall. Each health care organization must operationally define what they consider to be a fall, while meeting individual states' rules and regulations. The level of injury or type of injury must be tracked and documented to avoid counting near misses as falls. All age groups must be assessed for the risk of falling, not just the geriatric population. The health care organization also had to determine when the initial fall risk assessment was performed and the time frame for reassessments. Reassessments should be performed when a patient's condition changes, the patient is moved to another level of care, or when medications are ordered for the patient that would increase the risk of falling.

An 11-member interdisciplinary Fall Prevention Task Force was formed with representatives from Nursing, Facilities, Safety, Quality Management, Housekeeping, Plant Engineering, and Accreditation Services. The scope of the project was to assess the operations and environment at BEMC for actual or potential change to protect patients from accidental falls. The committee chair, Maureen Hebert, is the Long Term Care Administrator and has worked at Black Elk for over 18 years. Her responsibility includes providing patient care from acute care through a continuum of programs that include hospice, and long term care.

One of the first tasks was to perform an environmental assessment of all three acute care hospitals owned by Black Elk. The environment for each of the different nursing units is unique, which makes it more difficult to standardize and create hazard free environments. Task Force members visited each nursing unit and a patient room, which was invaluable for assessing risk factors and recommending or making appropriate changes. A standard checklist-style form was developed and helped to ensure a more thorough evaluation (see Figure 12.31).

Figure 12.31 Fall Checklist

FALL CHECKLIST (To be done on all falls)

1. Patient diagnosis: ________________________________
2. Number of days patient in hospital: ____ Today's date: _____
3. Patients fall risk level on day of admission: ____ Fall risk level day of fall ____
4. Was there a STAR up if patient was a high fall risk: YES ____ NO ____ N/A ____
5. Was fall risk level on patients caremap: YES ____ NO ____
6. If patient was a high fall risk, was "safety" on caremap as a problem?
   YES ____ NO ____ N/A ____
7. Was there documentation on the PFER that the fall letter was given and reviewed with the patient and/or family? YES ____ NO ____
8. If patient was high fall risk, was Q2hr toileting documented YES____ NO ____ N/A ____
9. Did patient have on "safety socks" YES ____ NO____
10. If necessary; was a walker/cane at bedside YES ____ NO ____ N/A____
11. Number of siderails up: ____ Was patient injured? ____
12. Was patient in restraints? YES ____ NO ____ Was Bed Alarm in use? YES ____ NO ____
13. Was any family at bedside: YES ____ NO ____
14. What was patient's mental status? _______ Number of nurse assistants on _____
15. What was the patient to nurse ratio? _______ What shift did the fall occur on?_______
16. Brief description of what happened, and was it witnessed?

Suppose that you were consulting for this organization. What would your next steps be? How would you use data gathered from the checklist? How would you design improved processes and systems to improve and control the incidence of falls, and to effectively and rapidly reduce the fall rate to be below 3.4 falls/1000 patient days?

NOTES

1. Peter Svensson, "It's not just computers: Gadgets crash," *The Cincinnati Enquirer*, April 3, 2003, A3.
2. H. James Harrington "Basic Block and Tackle" *Quality Digest*, March 2008.
3. Steven H. Wildstrom, "Price Wars Power Up Quality," *BusinessWeek*, September 18, 1995, 26.
4. Philip A. Himmelfarb, "Fast New-Product Development at Service Sector Companies," *Quality Digest*, April 1996, 41–44.
5. Justin Martin, "Ignore Your Customer," *Fortune*, May 1, 1995, 121–126.
6. Ames Rubber Corporation, Application Summary for the 1993 Malcolm Baldrige National Quality Award.
7. Don Clausing and Bruce H. Simpson, "Quality by Design," *Quality Progress*, January 1990, 41–44.
8. For the fascinating story of how Chrysler redesigned itself, along with their design process, see Brock Yates, *The Critical Path* (Boston: Little, Brown and Co., 1996).
9. C. M. Creveling, J. L. Slutsky, and D. Antis, Jr., *Design for Six Sigma in Technology and Product Development* (Upper Saddle River, NJ, Prentice Hall, 2003).
10. Charles Humber and Robert Launsby, "Straight Talk on DFSS," *Six Sigma Forum Magazine* 1, no. 4 (August 2002).
11. Christina Hepner Brodie, "A Polaroid Notebook: Concept Engineering," *Center for Quality of Management Journal* 3, no. 2 (1994), 7–14.
12. Laura Horton and David Boger, "How Bose Corporation Applied Concept Engineering to a Service," *Center for Quality of Management Journal* 3, no. 2 (1994), 52–59.
13. L. P. Sullivan, "Quality Function Deployment: The Latent Potential of Phases III and IV," in A. Richard Shores (ed.), *A TQM Approach to Achieving Manufacturing Excellence* (Milwaukee, WI: ASQC Quality Press, 1990), 265–279.
14. Peter Lewis, "A Perpetual Crisis Machine," *Fortune*, September 19, 2005, 58–76.
15. Gail Edmondson, "Mercedes' New Boss Rolls Up His Sleeves," *BusinessWeek*, October 17, 2005, 56.
16. Adapted from Douglas Daetz, "The Effect of Product Design on Product Quality and Product Cost," *Quality Progress*, June 1987, 63–67. © 1987, Hewlett-Packard Co. All rights reserved. Reprinted with permission.
17. Lewis (see note 14).
18. David Pescovitz, "Dumping Old Computers—Please Dispose of Properly," *Scientific American* 282, no. 2 (February 2000), 29; http://www.sciam.com/2000/0200issue/0200techbus2.html.
19. Early discussions of this topic can be found in Bruce Nussbaum and John Templeton, "Built to Last—Until It's Time to Take It Apart," *BusinessWeek*, September 17, 1990, 102–106. A more recent reference is Michael Lenox, Andrew King, and John Ehrenfeld, "An Assessment of Design-for-Environment Practices in Leading U.S. Electronics Firms," *Interfaces* 30, no. 3 (May/June 2000), 83–94.
20. Nussbaum and Templeton (see note 19).
21. DFX and DFSS: How QFD Integrates Them, Jui-Chin Jiang, Ming-Li Shiu and Mao-Hsiung Tu "A Smarter Way to Manufacture," *BusinessWeek*, April 30, 1990.
22. Jennifer Reese, "Starbucks: Inside the Coffee Cult," *Fortune*, December 9, 1996, 190–200.
23. Susan Dillingham, "A Little Gross Stuff in Food Is OK by FDA," *Insight*, May 22, 1989, 25.
24. Alan Vonderhaar, "Audi's TT Coupe's Ever So Close," *Cincinnati Enquirer*, November 27, 1999, F1, F2.
25. April 17, 1979; cited in L. P. Sullivan, "Reducing Variability: A New Approach to Quality," *Quality Progress* 17, no. 7 (July 1984), 15–21.
26. John H. Farrow, "Product Liability Requirements," *Quality Progress*, May 1980, 34–36; Mick Birmingham, "Product Liability: An Issue for Quality," *Quality*, February 1983, 41–42.
27. Randall Goodden, "Quality and Product Liability," *Quality Digest*, October 1995, 35–41.
28. R. Dan Reid, "FMEA—Something Old, Something New" *Quality Progress*, May 2005, 90–93.
29. "Failure Mode and Effects Analysis," Institute for Healthcare Improvement, 2004, p. 1.
30. Chris Woodyard, "Japanese makers maintain reign on reliability," *USA Today*, October 24, 2008, 4B.
31. Peter Svensson, "It's not just computers: Gadgets crash," *The Cincinnati Enquirer*, April 3, 2003, A3.
32. Statement made by Belinda Collins before the House Subcommittee on Technology, Committee on Science, June 29, 1995.
33. *ASQC Automotive Division Statistical Process Control Manual* (Milwaukee, WI: American Society for Quality Control, 1986).

34. Jay Bucher, *The Quality Calibration Handbook,* ASQ Quality Press, 2007.

35. Jennifer Pollock, "Built to Last, and Last . . ." *Fast Company,* May 2006, 83–84.

36. This section is adopted from NIST Calibration Services, available at http://www.nist.gov.

37. Jack Anderson, "The Future of Metrology," *Quality Digest*, January 31, 2008.

38. Paul F. McCoy, "Using Performance Indexes to Monitor Production Processes," *Quality Progress* 24, no. 2 (February 1991), 49–55; see also Fred A. Spring, "The Cpm Index," *Quality Progress* 24, no. 2 (February 1991), 57–61.

39. Helmut Schneider, James Pruett, and Cliff Lagrange, "Uses of Process Capability Indices in the Supplier Certification Process," *Quality Engineering* 8, no. 2 (1995–1996), 225–235.

40. Mark L. Crossley, "Size Matters. How Good Is your C_{pk}, Really?" *Quality Digest*, May 2000, 71–72.

41. Appreciation is expressed to Christine Schyvinck, VP Operations, Shure, Inc., for providing this case (October 2000).

42. Adapted from Vincent Omachonu and Paul Barach, "QFD in a Managed Care Organization," *Quality Progress*, November 2005, 36–41. © 2005, American Society for Quality. Reprinted with permission.

43. Adapted from R. Nat Natarajan, Ralph E. Martz, and Kyosuke Kurosaka, "Applying QFD to Internal Service System Design," *Quality Progress*, February 1999, 65–70. © 1999, American Society for Quality. Reprinted with permission.

CHAPTER 13

Statistical Process Control

Outline

QUALITY PROFILES: MESA Products, Inc., and Operations Management International, Inc.
IMPLEMENTING STATISTICAL PROCESS CONTROL
The Difference between Control and Capability
SPC METHODOLOGY
SPC Metrics
CONTROL CHARTS FOR VARIABLES DATA
Constructing $\bar{x}$- and R-Charts and Establishing Statistical Control
Estimating Process Capability
Process Monitoring and Control
Case Study: La Ventana Window Company
Interpreting Patterns in Control Charts
SPECIAL CONTROL CHARTS FOR VARIABLE DATA
$\bar{x}$- and s-Charts
Charts for Individuals
CONTROL CHARTS FOR ATTRIBUTES
Fraction Nonconforming (p) Chart
Variable Sample Size
np-Charts for Number Nonconforming
Charts for Nonconformances
Choosing between c- and u-Charts
SUMMARY OF CONTROL CHART CONSTRUCTION
DESIGNING CONTROL CHARTS
Basis for Sampling
Sample Size
Sampling Frequency
Location of Control Limits
SPC, ISO 9000:2000, AND SIX SIGMA
Controlling Six Sigma Processes
PRE-CONTROL
SUMMARY OF KEY POINTS AND TERMINOLOGY
QUALITY IN PRACTICE: Applying SPC to Pharmaceutical Product Manufacturing
QUALITY IN PRACTICE: Using a U-Chart in a Receiving Process
REVIEW QUESTIONS
PROBLEMS
Cases Morelia Mortgage Company
Murphy Trucking, Inc.
Day Industries

Deming's funnel experiment, described in Chapter 10, demonstrates that failure to distinguish between common causes and special causes of variation can actually increase the variation in a process. This problem often results from the mistaken belief that whenever process output is off target, some adjustment must be made. Knowing when to leave a process alone is an important step in maintaining control over a process. Equally important is knowing when to take action to prevent the production of nonconforming product.

Statistical process control (SPC) is a methodology for monitoring a process to identify special causes of variation and signaling the need to take corrective action when it is appropriate. When special causes are present, the process is deemed to be *out of control*. If the variation in the process is due to common causes alone, the process is said to be *in statistical control*. A practical definition of statistical control is that *both* the process averages and variances are constant over time.[1] SPC relies on *control charts*, one of the basic quality improvement tools that we briefly introduced in Chapter 13. SPC is a proven technique for improving quality and productivity. Many customers require their suppliers to provide evidence of statistical process control. Thus, SPC provides a means by which a firm may demonstrate its quality capability, an activity necessary for survival in today's highly competitive markets. SPC is quite effective for companies in the early stages of quality efforts; however, because it requires processes to show measurable variation, it is ineffective for quality levels approaching six sigma, and we will discuss this later in this chapter.

SPC has been an important tool in manufacturing, particularly in the automotive industry. The Automotive Industry Action Group's supplier requirements task force publishes an SPC manual that advocates that it be integrated into an organization's continual improvement activities and provides detailed guidance for applying SPC. However, SPC is not just for manufacturers, it is easily applied to service organizations. Table 13.1 lists just a few of the many potential applications of control charts for services. The key is in defining the appropriate quality measures to monitor. Most service processes can be improved through the appropriate application of control charts.

BONUS MATERIALS

In this chapter, we describe how to develop and use statistical process control to monitor manufacturing and service processes. A document in the Bonus Materials folder for this chapter on the Premium website provides an explanation of the statistical details for understanding the theory underlying control charts.

Table 13.1 Control Chart Applications in Service Organizations

Organization	Quality Measure
Hospital	Lab test accuracy Insurance claim accuracy On-time delivery of meals and medication
Bank	Check-processing accuracy
Insurance company	Claims-processing response time Billing accuracy
Post office	Sorting accuracy Time of delivery Percentage of express mail delivered on time
Ambulance	Response time
Police department	Incidence of crime in a precinct Number of traffic citations
Hotel	Proportion of rooms satisfactorily cleaned Checkout time Number of complaints received
Transportation	Proportion of freight cars correctly routed Dollar amount of damage per claim
Auto service	Percentage of time work completed as promised Number of parts out of stock

Quality Profiles

MESA Products, Inc., and Operations Management International, Inc.

MESA Products, Inc. is a small, privately held business that designs, manufactures and installs cathodic protection systems that control the corrosion of metal surfaces in underground and submerged structures, such as pipelines and tanks. MESA assembles more than 75,000 magnesium anodes each year, a product line that accounts for 30 percent of the company's material revenues. Beginning in 2002, MESA was instrumental in identifying and addressing an industry-wide issue of poor-quality magnesium anodes. Working with its key suppliers, the company implemented a comprehensive quality assurance specification for product acceptance, resulting in a significant improvement in the quality of the company's anodes. MESA then mounted an industry-wide awareness campaign to alert manufacturers and end users about the issue. As a result, the quality of anodes throughout the industry has improved.

Since its inception from a one-man service company in 1979 to a workforce of 75, MESA's philosophy has been to provide its customers with a quality product and outstanding service at a fair price. To achieve this goal, MESA focuses on teamwork and shared goals that include continuous improvement, continued growth and long-term success. A variety of tools help to improve performance, including "lean" manufacturing to reduce waste, certification for international quality standards by the International Organization for Standardization (ISO), and the Baldrige principles of performance excellence. A monthly balanced report card helps the company to review its performance and find ways to improve. For example, the report card process showed that MESA was routinely missing a target of shipping products within three days due to a lack of available inventory. MESA constructed a 5,000-square foot covered storage area, improving inventory availability and greatly facilitating timely shipments. From 2000 until MESA received a Baldrige Award in 2007, the company's on-time shipping performance improved from 93 percent to 97 percent, error rates went down 50 percent, throughput time in the magnesium assembly area improved by 82 percent, and assembly time of instrumentation equipment improved by 60 percent.

Headquartered in Greenwood Village, Colorado, Operations Management International, Inc. (OMI), operates and maintains more than 160 public and private sector wastewater and water treatment facilities in 29 states and facilities in Brazil, Canada, Egypt, Israel, Malaysia, New Zealand, Philippines, and Thailand. OMI's primary services are processing raw wastewater to produce clean, environmentally safe effluent and processing raw groundwater and surface water to produce clean, safe drinking water. OMI's "E3" motto, "Exceed our customers' expectations, empower our employees, enhance the environment," is the foundation for its Quality as a Business Strategy leadership system. Key enablers are the company's Linkage of Process Model, which defines relationships among processes, and its Family of Measures, a balanced scorecard of 20 integrated metrics. These measures of operational performance correspond to OMI's four strategic objectives—customer focus, business growth, innovation, and market leadership.

Improvement initiatives in the company's strategic plan are selected and crafted so that each initiative contributes significantly to achieving one or more strategic objectives and key customer requirements. In 2000, OMI had 26 improvement initiatives under way, each one assigned to a team led by a high-level executive. All teams write charters that state their purpose, objectives, and timeline for completion. A team charter also specifies which of OMI's more than 150 critical processes are involved, the metrics that will be used for evaluation, costs, required resources, and other information vital to the success of the initiative. Charters provide team members and company executives with the means for a quick and thorough analysis of progress toward planned goals. OMI received a 2000 Baldrige Award.

Source: Adapted from Malcolm Baldrige National Quality Award, Profiles of Winners, National Institute of Standards and Technology, Department of Commerce.

IMPLEMENTING STATISTICAL PROCESS CONTROL

In this section we provide some basic concept to understand SPC and how to implement it effectively.

The Difference between Control and Capability

Consider the data in Figure 13.1 (available in the Excel file *Quality Measurements* on the Premium website), which shows measurements of a quality characteristic for 30 samples from a manufacturing process with specifications 0.75 ± 0.25. Each row corresponds to a sample size of 5 taken every 15 minutes. The mean of each sample is also given in the last column. A frequency distribution and histogram of these data is

Figure 13.1 Thirty Samples of Quality Measurements

	A	B	C	D	E	F	G
1	**Quality Measurements**						
2				Observation			
3	Sample	1	2	3	4	5	Mean
4	1	0.682	0.689	0.776	0.798	0.714	0.732
5	2	0.787	0.860	0.601	0.746	0.779	0.755
6	3	0.780	0.667	0.838	0.785	0.723	0.759
7	4	0.591	0.727	0.812	0.775	0.730	0.727
8	5	0.693	0.708	0.790	0.758	0.671	0.724
9	6	0.749	0.714	0.738	0.719	0.606	0.705
10	7	0.791	0.713	0.689	0.877	0.603	0.735
11	8	0.744	0.779	0.660	0.737	0.822	0.748
12	9	0.769	0.773	0.641	0.644	0.725	0.710
13	10	0.718	0.671	0.708	0.850	0.712	0.732
14	11	0.787	0.821	0.764	0.658	0.708	0.748
15	12	0.622	0.802	0.818	0.872	0.727	0.768
16	13	0.657	0.822	0.893	0.544	0.750	0.733
17	14	0.806	0.749	0.859	0.801	0.701	0.783
18	15	0.660	0.681	0.644	0.747	0.728	0.692
19	16	0.816	0.817	0.768	0.716	0.649	0.753
20	17	0.826	0.777	0.721	0.770	0.809	0.781
21	18	0.828	0.829	0.865	0.778	0.872	0.834
22	19	0.805	0.719	0.612	0.938	0.807	0.776
23	20	0.802	0.756	0.786	0.815	0.801	0.792
24	21	0.876	0.803	0.701	0.789	0.672	0.768
25	22	0.855	0.783	0.722	0.856	0.751	0.793
26	23	0.762	0.705	0.804	0.805	0.809	0.777
27	24	0.703	0.837	0.759	0.975	0.732	0.801
28	25	0.737	0.723	0.776	0.748	0.732	0.743
29	26	0.748	0.686	0.856	0.811	0.838	0.788
30	27	0.826	0.803	0.764	0.823	0.886	0.820
31	28	0.728	0.721	0.820	0.772	0.639	0.736
32	29	0.803	0.892	0.740	0.816	0.770	0.804
33	30	0.774	0.837	0.872	0.849	0.818	0.830

Figure 13.2 Frequency Distribution and Histogram of Quality Measurements

Bin	Frequency
0.55	1
0.60	1
0.65	10
0.70	14
0.75	40
0.80	31
0.85	37
0.90	14
0.95	1
1.00	1
More	0

shown in Figure 13.2. The data form a relatively symmetric distribution with a mean of 0.762 and standard deviation 0.0738. Using these values, we find that $C_{pk} = 1.075$, indicating that the process capability is at least marginally acceptable.

Because the data were taken over an extended period of time, we cannot determine whether the process remained stable because the dimension of time is not considered in a histogram. Thus, histograms do not allow you to distinguish between common and special causes of variation. It is unclear whether any special causes of variation are influencing the capability index.

If we plot the mean of each sample against the time at which the sample was taken (because the time increments between samples are equal, the sample number is an appropriate surrogate for time), we obtain the run chart shown in Figure 13.3. The run chart suggests that the mean has shifted up around the time that sample 17 was taken. In fact, the process average for the first 16 samples is only 0.738, whereas the average for the remaining samples is 0.789. Therefore, although the overall average is close to the target specification, at no time was the actual process average centered near the target. We should conclude that this process is not in statistical control, and we should not pay much attention to the process capability calculations.

Process capability calculations make little sense if the process is not in statistical control because the data are confounded by special causes that do not represent the inherent capability of the process.

Control and capability are two different concepts. As shown in Figure 13.4, a process may be capable or not capable, or in control or out of control, independently of each other. Clearly, we would like every process to be both capable and in control. If a process is neither capable nor in control, we must first get it in a state of control by removing special causes of variation, and then attack the common causes to improve its capability. If a process is capable but not in control (as the previous example illustrated), we should work to get it back in control.

Figure 13.3 Run Chart of Sample Means

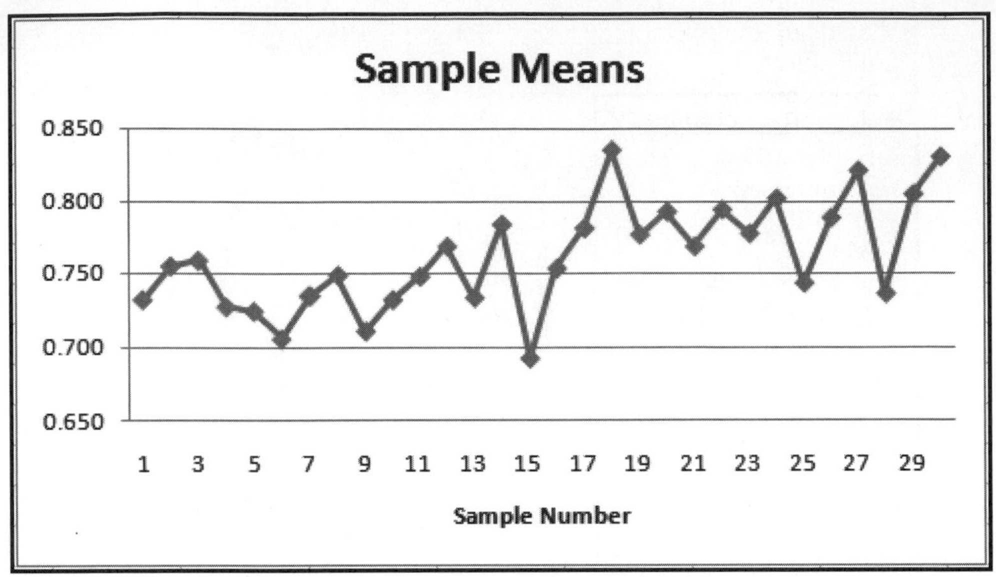

Figure 13.4 Capability versus Control (Arrows indicate the direction of appropriate management action)

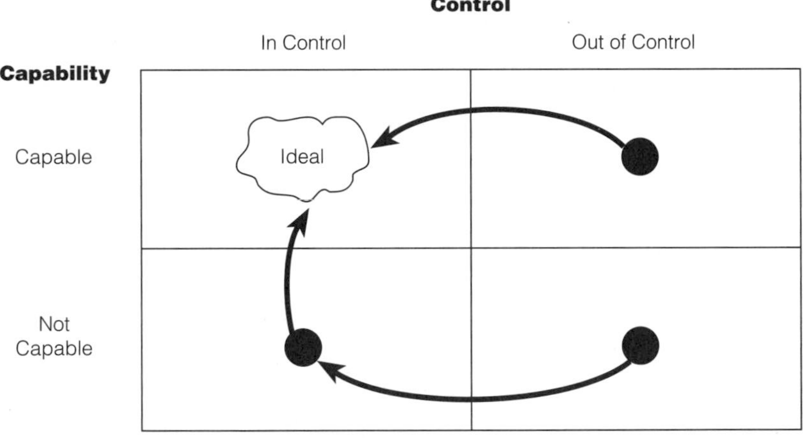

SPC METHODOLOGY

Control charts, like the other basic tools for quality improvement, are relatively simple to use. Control charts have three basic applications: (1) to establish a state of statistical control, (2) to monitor a process and signal when the process goes out of control, and (3) to determine process capability. The following is a summary of the steps required to develop and use control charts. Steps 1 through 4 focus on establishing a state of statistical control; in step 5, the charts are used for ongoing monitoring; and finally, in step 6, the data are used for process capability analysis.

1. Preparation
    a. Choose the variable or attribute to be measured.
    b. Determine the basis, size, and frequency of sampling.
    c. Set up the control chart.
2. Data collection
    a. Record the data.
    b. Calculate relevant statistics: averages, ranges, proportions, and so on.
    c. Plot the statistics on the chart.
3. Determination of trial control limits
    a. Draw the center line (process average) on the chart.
    b. Compute the upper and lower control limits.
4. Analysis and interpretation
    a. Investigate the chart for lack of control.
    b. Eliminate out-of-control points.
    c. Recompute control limits if necessary.
5. Estimation of process capability using the control chart data
6. Use as a problem-solving tool
    a. Continue data collection and plotting.
    b. Identify out-of-control situations and take corrective action.

SPC Metrics

Metrics used in SPC fall into one of two categories. An **attribute** is a performance characteristic that is either present or absent in the product or service under consideration. For example, a dimension is either within tolerance or out of tolerance, an order is complete or incomplete, or an invoice can have one, two, three, or any number of errors. Thus, attribute data are discrete and tell whether or not the characteristic conforms to specifications. Attributes often can be assessed by visual inspection, such as checking whether an order is filled properly prior to shipping; by comparing a measured dimension to specifications, such as determining whether the diameter of a shaft falls within specification limits of 1.60 ± 0.01 inch; or by counting, such as the number of incomplete solder joints on a circuit board. Attribute measurements are typically expressed as proportions or rates, for example, the fraction of orders that were not properly filled, number of shafts that do not meet specifications, or number of incomplete solder joints per circuit board.

The second type of performance characteristic is called a **variable**. Variable data are continuous (e.g., length, weight, and time). Variable measurements are concerned with the *degree* of conformance to specifications. Thus, rather than determining whether the diameter of a shaft simply meets a specification of 1.60 ± 0.01 inch, a measure of the actual value of the diameter is recorded. Variable measurements are generally expressed with such statistics as averages and standard deviations. Table 13.1 provides additional examples of both attributes and variables measurements.

Collecting attribute data is usually easier than collecting variable data because the assessment can usually be done more quickly by a simple inspection or count, whereas variable data require the use of some type of measuring instrument.

In a statistical sense, attributes inspection is less efficient than variables inspection; that is, it does not provide as much information. This means that attributes inspection requires a larger sample than variables inspection to obtain the same amount of statistical information about the quality of the product. This difference can become significant when inspection of each item is time-consuming or expensive. Most quality characteristics in services are attributes, which is perhaps one reason why service organizations have been slow to adopt measurement-based quality management approaches.

In the remainder of this chapter we discuss the construction, interpretation, and use of control charts following this methodology. Although many different charts are described, they differ only in the type of metric for which the chart is used; the basic approach described above applies to each of them.

CONTROL CHARTS FOR VARIABLES DATA

The charts most commonly used for variables data are the $\bar{x}$ chart ("x-bar" chart) and the *R*-chart (range chart). The $\bar{x}$-chart is used to monitor the centering of the process, and the *R*-chart is used to monitor the variation in the process. The range is used as a measure of variation simply for convenience, particularly when workers on the factory floor perform control chart calculations by hand. For large samples and when data are analyzed by computer programs, the standard deviation is a better measure of variability (discussed later).

Constructing $\bar{x}$- and *R*-Charts and Establishing Statistical Control

The first step in developing $\bar{x}$- and *R*-charts is to gather data. Usually, about 25 to 30 samples are collected. Samples between size 3 and 10 are generally used, with 5 being the most common. The number of samples is indicated by k, and n denotes the sample size. For each sample i, the mean (denoted $\bar{x}_i$) and the range (R_i) are computed. These values are then plotted on their respective control charts. Next, the *overall mean* and *average range* calculations are made. These values specify the center lines for the $\bar{x}$- and *R*-charts, respectively. The overall mean (denoted $\bar{\bar{x}}$ and often called the *grand average*) is the average of the sample means $\bar{x}_i$:

$$\bar{\bar{x}} = \frac{\sum_{i=1}^{k} \bar{x}_i}{k} \tag{13.1}$$

The average range ($\bar{R}$) is similarly computed, using the formula:

$$\bar{R} = \frac{\sum_{i=1}^{k} R_i}{k} \tag{13.2}$$

The average range and average mean are used to compute upper and lower control limits (UCL and LCL) for the *R*- and $\bar{x}$-charts. Control limits are easily calculated using the following formulas.

Control Limits for *R*-Chart:

$$\begin{aligned} UCL_R &= D_4\bar{R} \\ LCL_R &= D_3\bar{R} \end{aligned} \tag{13.3}$$

Control Limits for $\bar{x}$-Chart

$$\begin{aligned} UCL_{\bar{x}} &= \bar{\bar{x}} + A_2\bar{R} \\ LCL_{\bar{x}} &= \bar{\bar{x}} - A_2\bar{R} \end{aligned} \tag{13.4}$$

where the constants D_3, D_4, and A_2 depend on the sample size and can be found in Appendix B.

The control limits represent the range between which all points are expected to fall if the process is in statistical control. If any points fall outside the control limits or if any unusual patterns are observed, then some special cause has probably affected the process. The process should be studied to determine the cause. If special causes are present, then they are *not* representative of the true state of statistical control and the calculations of the center line and control limits will be biased. The corresponding data points should be eliminated, and new values for $\overline{\overline{x}}$, $\overline{R}$, and the control limits should be computed.

In determining whether a process is in statistical control, the R-chart is generally analyzed first. Because the control limits in the $\overline{x}$-chart depend on the average range, special causes in the R-chart may produce unusual patterns in the $\overline{x}$-chart, even when the centering of the process is in control. After statistical control is established for the R-chart, attention may turn to the $\overline{x}$-chart.

Estimating Process Capability

After a process has been brought to a state of statistical control by eliminating special causes of variation, the control chart statistics may be used to estimate process capability. This approach is not as accurate as that described in Chapter 12, because it uses an estimate of the standard deviation based on the average range rather than the true standard deviation of the original data. Nevertheless, it is a quick and useful method, provided that the distribution of the original data is reasonably normal.

Under the normality assumption, the standard deviation of the original data can be estimated as:

$$\hat{\sigma} = \overline{R}/d_2 \tag{13.5}$$

where d_2 is a constant that depends on the sample size and is also given in Appendix B. The natural variation of individual measurements is therefore given by $6\hat{\sigma}$. Using this along with the specifications, process capability indexes can easily be computed.

A word of caution deserves emphasis here. Control limits are often confused with specification limits. Specification dimensions are usually stated in relation to individual parts for "hard" goods, such as automotive hardware. However, in other applications, such as in chemical processes, specifications are stated in terms of average characteristics. Thus, control charts might mislead one into thinking that if all sample averages fall within the control limits, all output will be conforming.

Control limits relate to averages of samples, whereas specification limits relate to individual measurements.

This assumption is not true. A sample average may fall within the upper and lower control limits even though some of the individual observations are out of specification.

Because control limits are based on the sampling distribution of the mean, the standard error $(\sigma/\sqrt{n})$ becomes smaller with increasing sample sizes and therefore, the larger the sample size, the narrower the control limits.

Process Monitoring and Control

After a process is determined to be in control, the charts should be used on a daily basis to monitor performance, identify any special causes that might arise, and make corrections only as necessary. Unnecessary adjustments to a process result in nonproductive labor, reduced production, and increased variability of output as Deming taught.

It is more productive if the employees who run a process take the samples and chart the data. In this way, they can react quickly to changes in the process and make adjustments immediately. For greatest effectiveness, training of employees is essential. Many companies conduct in-house training programs to teach operators and supervisors the elementary methods of statistical quality control. Not only does this training provide the mathematical and technical skills that are required, but it also gives them increased quality consciousness.

Control charts indicate when to take action, and more importantly, when to leave a process alone.

Improvements in conformance typically follow the introduction of control charts in any process, particularly when the process is labor intensive. Apparently, management involvement in employees' work often produces positive behavioral modifications (as first demonstrated in the famous Hawthorne studies at the Western Electric Company). Under such circumstances, and as good practice, management and employees should revise the control limits periodically and determine a new process capability as improvements take place.

Control charts are designed to be used by employees in their work areas rather than by inspectors or quality control personnel. Under the philosophy of statistical process control, the burden of quality rests with the employees themselves. The use of control charts allows them to react quickly to special causes of variation. The range is used in place of the standard deviation for the very reason that it allows users to easily make the necessary computations to plot points on a control chart. Only simple calculations are required.

Case Study: La Ventana Window Company

The La Ventana Window Company (LVWC) manufactures original equipment and replacement windows for residential building and remodeling applications. LVWC landed a major contract as a supplier to Southwestern Vista Homes (SVH), a builder of residential communities in several major cities throughout the southwestern United States. Because of the large volume of demand, LVWC expanded its manufacturing operations to two shifts. Soon, they were working six days per week and hired additional workers and added on to their facility. The company based its manufacturing capability on its well-trained and dedicated employees, so it never felt the need to consider formal process control approaches. However, not long after La Ventana began shipping windows to Southwestern, it received some complaints about narrow, misfitting gaps between the upper and lower window sashes.

The plant manager suspected that the rapid expansion to a full two-shift operation, the pressures to produce higher volumes, and the push to meet just-in-time delivery requests were causing a breakdown in quality. He hired a quality consultant to train the shift supervisors and selected line workers in statistical process control methods.

As a trial project, the plant manager wants to evaluate the capability of a critical cutting operation that he suspects might be the source of the gap problem. The nominal specification for this cutting operation is 25.500 inches with a tolerance of 0.030 inch. Thus, the upper and lower specifications are LSL = 25.470 inch and USL = 25.530 inch. The consultant suggested inspecting five consecutive window panels in the middle of each shift over a 15-day period and recording the dimension of the cut. The worksheet *Case Data*, shown in Figure 13.5, in the Excel workbook *La Ventana Example* (available on the Premium website) shows the results of the data collection, along with the sample averages and ranges.

BONUS MATERIALS

The next step is to calculate the key statistics and trial control limits for the control charts. The overall mean is the sum of the sample averages divided by the number of samples (30), or equivalently, the average of the sample averages. The average range

Figure 13.5 La Ventana Case Data

	A	B	C	D	E	F	G	H	I	J	K	L
1	**La Ventana Window Company**											
2							**Observations**					
3	**Day-Shift**	**Operator**	**Sample**		**1**	**2**	**3**	**4**	**5**		**Average**	**Range**
4	1-1	Juanita	1		25.505	25.498	25.493	25.501	25.500		25.499	0.012
5	1-2	Tex	2		25.498	25.506	25.495	25.509	25.500		25.502	0.014
6	2-1	Juanita	3		25.493	25.500	25.503	25.511	25.493		25.500	0.018
7	2-2	Tex	4		25.496	25.496	25.496	25.505	25.500		25.499	0.009
8	3-1	Juanita	5		25.499	25.498	25.506	25.501	25.495		25.500	0.011
9	3-2	Tex	6		25.497	25.500	25.500	25.489	25.511		25.499	0.022
10	4-1	Juanita	7		25.502	25.500	25.508	25.500	25.500		25.502	0.008
11	4-2	Tex	8		25.498	25.497	25.503	25.502	25.498		25.500	0.006
12	5-1	Shane	9		25.482	25.485	25.484	25.466	25.491		25.482	0.025
13	5-2	Tex	10		25.492	25.504	25.510	25.500	25.509		25.503	0.018
14	6-1	Juanita	11		25.499	25.495	25.500	25.499	25.505		25.500	0.010
15	6-2	Tex	12		25.500	25.495	25.509	25.502	25.503		25.502	0.014
16	7-1	Juanita	13		25.504	25.500	25.495	25.497	25.489		25.497	0.015
17	7-2	Tex	14		25.503	25.501	25.500	25.500	25.513		25.503	0.013
18	8-1	Juanita	15		25.499	25.503	25.502	25.504	25.503		25.502	0.005
19	8-2	Tex	16		25.499	25.495	25.507	25.499	25.502		25.500	0.012
20	9-1	Juanita	17		25.492	25.498	25.506	25.507	25.502		25.501	0.015
21	9-2	Tex	18		25.498	25.500	25.500	25.495	25.493		25.497	0.007
22	10-1	Juanita	19		25.499	25.501	25.502	25.501	25.505		25.502	0.006
23	10-2	Tex	20		25.505	25.500	25.503	25.499	25.503		25.502	0.006
24	11-1	Shane	21		25.481	25.498	25.482	25.484	25.485		25.486	0.017
25	11-2	Tex	22		25.497	25.499	25.501	25.497	25.488		25.496	0.013
26	12-1	Juanita	23		25.514	25.505	25.512	25.494	25.495		25.504	0.020
27	2-2	Shane	24		25.474	25.481	25.505	25.499	25.492		25.490	0.031
28	13-1	Juanita	25		25.502	25.496	25.507	25.491	25.504		25.500	0.016
29	13-2	Tex	26		25.504	25.498	25.506	25.503	25.503		25.503	0.008
30	14-1	Juanita	27		25.498	25.497	25.511	25.494	25.487		25.497	0.024
31	14-2	Tex	28		25.500	25.506	25.494	25.497	25.506		25.501	0.012
32	15-1	Juanita	29		25.504	25.510	25.498	25.504	25.498		25.503	0.012
33	15-2	Tex	30		25.506	25.504	25.508	25.499	25.504		25.504	0.009

is the sum of the sample ranges divided by the number of samples, or, the average of the sample ranges. These can easily be found using the Excel AVERAGE function. The overall mean is $\bar{\bar{x}} = 25.499$, and the average range is $\bar{R} = 0.14$. You should verify these values using the spreadsheet data.

Because the sample size is 5, the factors used in computing the control limits found in Appendix B are $A_2 = 0.577$ and $D_4 = 2.114$. (For sample sizes of 6 or less, factor $D_3 = 0$; therefore, the lower control limit on the range chart is zero.) Using the formulas for the control limits (13.3 and 14.4), we have

$$\begin{aligned}
\text{LCR}_R &= D_3\bar{R} &&= 0 \\
\text{UCL}_R &= D_4\bar{R} = 2.114(0.0136) &&= 0.0288 \\
\text{LCL}_{\bar{x}} &= \bar{\bar{x}} - A_2\bar{R} = 25.499 - 0.577(0.014) &&= 25.491 \\
\text{UCL}_{\bar{x}} &= \bar{\bar{x}} + A_2\bar{R} = 25.499 - 0.577(0.014) &&= 25.507
\end{aligned}$$

To facilitate these calculations and to avoid the tedious task of either drawing control charts manually or constructing an Excel chart, we have created Excel templates for the control charts discussed in this book, all of which may be found in the *Excel Templates* folder on the Premium website. These templates include automatic calculation of statistics and control limits and the charts themselves (on separate tabs in the workbook). Some scaling of the chart display ranges may be necessary for certain data sets. Please note the following:

BONUS MATERIALS

- The templates are saved in Excel 97-2003 format to maintain compatibility with previous versions of Excel.
- You may need to rescale the vertical axis of the charts to make them more visually appealing. See the appropriate Excel help files for the version you are using.
- When a sample is deleted from a data set in the templates, do not enter zero for the data; instead, leave the cells blank. The charts are set up to interpolate between non-missing data points.
- When deleting special cause data, be sure to update the number of samples used in the calculations to compute the statistics or the control charts will not display correctly.

When a process is in statistical control, the points on a control chart fluctuate randomly between the control limits with no recognizable pattern.

The spreadsheet for $\bar{x}$- and R-charts is the Excel template *Xbar&R*. A portion of it for the La Ventana case data is shown in Figure 13.6. Figures 13.7 and 13.8 show the control charts.

Examining the range chart first, we see that sample 24 is clearly out of control. In the $\bar{x}$-chart, sample 24 is also outside the control limits, as are samples 9 and 21. If you look closely at the data, these samples have one characteristic in common: Shane was the operator during the time these samples were taken. In fact, these were the only times that Shane was running the process. On investigation, it was found that the regular operators, Juanita and Tex, were called away to troubleshoot a problem on another production line and replaced by Shane who usually works on the packaging line. Thus, we may attribute these anomalies to special causes of variation and should eliminate these from the control chart calculations.

After deleting the special cause samples from the data, the new charts appear to be in control as shown in Figures 13.9 and 13.10. Note that the control limits have changed somewhat; the new limits are:

$$\text{LCL}_R = 0$$
$$\text{UCL}_R = 0.0262$$
$$\text{LCL}_{\bar{x}} = 25.494$$
$$\text{UCL}_{\bar{x}} = 25.508$$

Now that statistical control has been established, process capability may be evaluated. Figure 13.11 shows the portion of the Excel template that calculates the process capability indexes. The Excel template uses equation (13.5) to calculate the natural variation in cell R6. The process capability indexes suggest that as long as the process remains in control, process capability is quite good; $C_p = 1.875$, $C_{pk} = 1.833$, and the process average is close to the nominal specification, as suggested by C_{pu} and C_{pl}.

The revised control limits, after removing special causes, should be used for continuing monitoring of the process. For example, suppose that the company collected new production data over the next 10 shifts. These are shown in Figure 13.12 (and are labeled "Additional Data" on the worksheet in the *La Ventana* workbook).

Figure 13.6 Portion of the Excel template Xbar&R for La Ventana Case Data

	A	B	C	D	E	F	G	H	I	J	K	L	M	N	O	P	Q	R
1	**X-bar and R-Chart**																	
2	This spreadsheet is designed for up to 50 samples, each of a constant sample size from 2 to 10. Enter data ONLY in yellow-shaded cells.																	
3	Enter the number of samples in cell E6 and the sample size in cell E7. Then enter your data in the grid below.																	
4	Click on sheet tabs for a display of the control charts. Specification limits may be entered in cells N7 and N8 for process capability.																	
5																		
6	Number of samples (<= 50)				30					Process Capability Calculations						Six sigma		0.035
7	Sample size (2 - 10)				5					Upper specification				25.53		Cp		1.71
8										Lower specification				25.47		Cpu		1.757
9	Grand Average		25.49918667		A2	D3	D4	d2								Cpl		1.664
10	Average Range		0.0136		0.577	0	2.114	2.326								Cpk		1.664
11																		
12	DATA	1	2	3	4	5	6	7	8	9	10	11	12	13	14	15	16	17
13	1	25.505	25.498	25.493	25.496	25.499	25.497	25.502	25.498	25.482	25.492	25.499	25.500	25.504	25.503	25.499	25.499	25.492
14	2	25.498	25.506	25.500	25.496	25.498	25.500	25.500	25.497	25.485	25.504	25.495	25.495	25.500	25.501	25.503	25.495	25.498
15	3	25.493	25.495	25.503	25.496	25.506	25.500	25.508	25.503	25.484	25.510	25.500	25.509	25.495	25.500	25.502	25.507	25.506
16	4	25.501	25.509	25.511	25.505	25.501	25.489	25.500	25.502	25.466	25.500	25.499	25.502	25.497	25.500	25.504	25.499	25.507
17	5	25.500	25.500	25.493	25.500	25.495	25.511	25.500	25.498	25.491	25.509	25.505	25.503	25.489	25.513	25.503	25.502	25.502
18	6																	
19	7																	
20	8																	
21	9																	
22	10																	
23	Average	25.4994	25.5016	25.5	25.4986	25.4998	25.4994	25.502	25.4996	25.4816	25.503	25.4996	25.5018	25.497	25.5034	25.5022	25.5004	25.501
24	LCLx-bar	25.4913	25.4913	25.491	25.4913	25.4913	25.4913	25.491	25.4913	25.4913	25.491	25.4913	25.4913	25.491	25.4913	25.4913	25.4913	25.491
25	Center	25.4992	25.4992	25.499	25.4992	25.4992	25.4992	25.499	25.4992	25.4992	25.499	25.4992	25.4992	25.499	25.4992	25.4992	25.4992	25.499
26	UCLx-bar	25.507	25.507	25.507	25.507	25.507	25.507	25.507	25.507	25.507	25.507	25.507	25.507	25.507	25.507	25.507	25.507	25.507
27																		
28	Range	0.012	0.014	0.018	0.009	0.011	0.022	0.008	0.006	0.025	0.018	0.01	0.014	0.015	0.013	0.005	0.012	0.015
29	LCLrange	0	0	0	0	0	0	0	0	0	0	0	0	0	0	0	0	0
30	Center	0.0136	0.0136	0.0136	0.0136	0.0136	0.0136	0.0136	0.0136	0.0136	0.0136	0.0136	0.0136	0.0136	0.0136	0.0136	0.0136	0.0136
31	UCLrange	0.02875	0.02875	0.0288	0.02875	0.02875	0.02875	0.0288	0.02875	0.02875	0.0288	0.02875	0.02875	0.0288	0.02875	0.02875	0.02875	0.0288

Figure 13.7 *R*-Chart for La Ventana Case

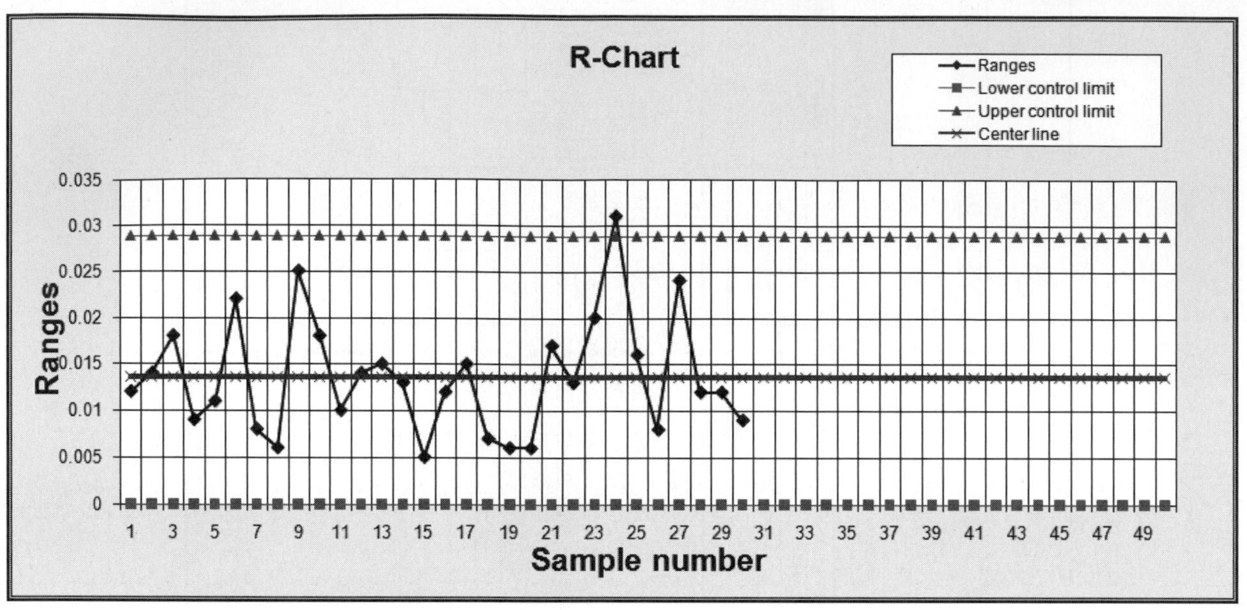

Figure 13.8 $\overline{x}$-Chart for La Ventana Case

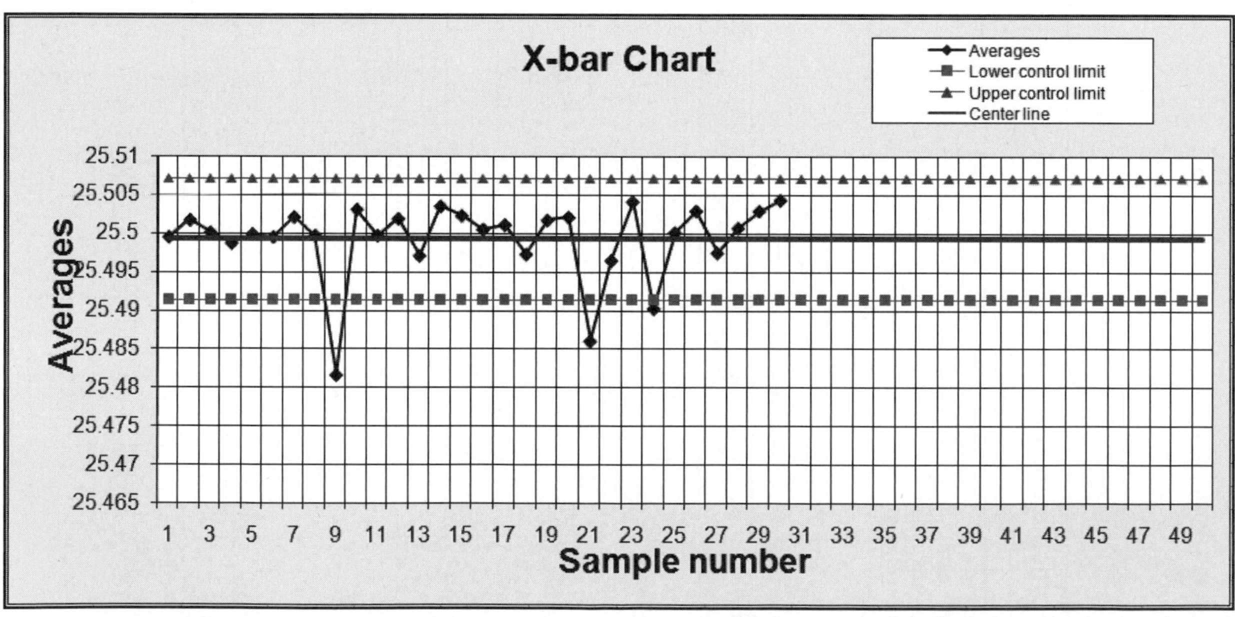

Figure 13.9 *R*-Chart for Revised Data

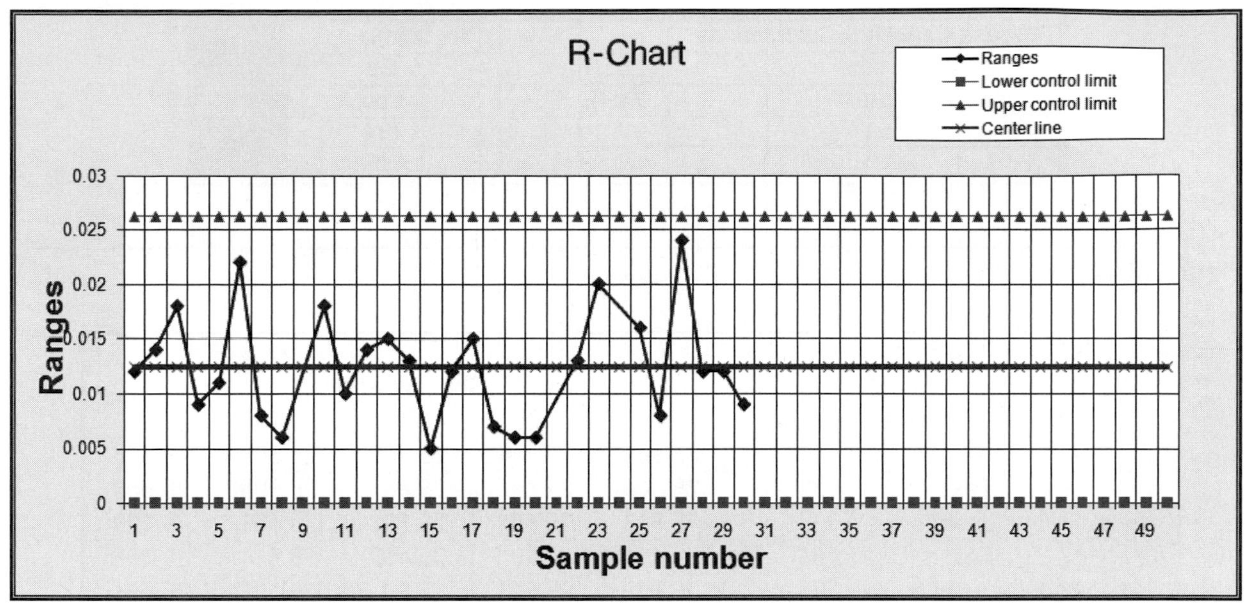

Figure 13.10 $\overline{x}$-Chart for Revised Data

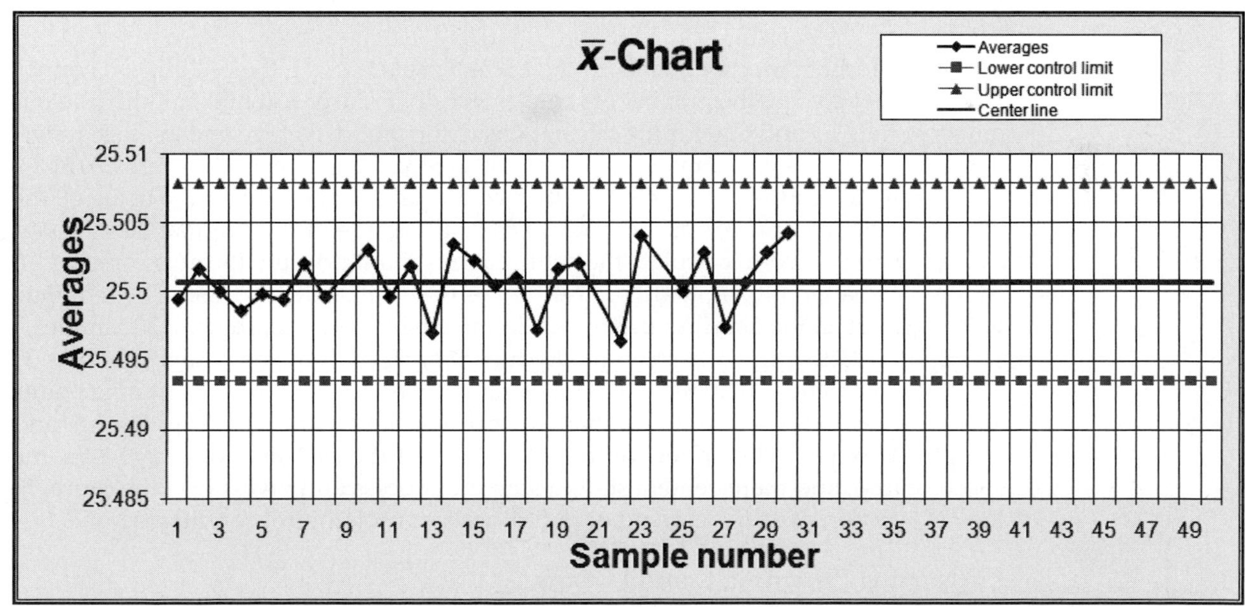

Figure 13.11 La Ventana Process Capability Calculations

Process Capability Calculations						Six sigma	0.032
Upper specification				25.53		Cp	1.875
Lower specification				25.47		Cpu	1.833
						Cpl	1.916
						Cpk	1.833

Figure 13.12 New Production Data for La Ventana

	A	B	C	D	E	F	G	H	I
1							Observations		
2	Day-Shift	Operator	Sample		1	2	3	4	5
3	16-1	Juanita	31		25.509	25.504	25.499	25.505	25.503
4	16-2	Tex	32		25.500	25.495	25.487	25.505	25.500
5	17-1	Juanita	33		25.513	25.504	25.506	25.498	25.489
6	17-2	Tex	34		25.494	25.503	25.492	25.514	25.495
7	18-1	Juanita	35		25.509	25.514	25.502	25.498	25.504
8	18-2	Tex	36		25.504	25.499	25.500	25.492	25.509
9	19-1	Juanita	37		25.499	25.507	25.513	25.497	25.511
10	19-2	Tex	38		25.501	25.509	25.510	25.507	25.495
11	20-1	Juanita	39		25.506	25.508	25.518	25.505	25.505
12	20-2	Tex	40		25.519	25.498	25.499	25.504	25.518

When adding additional data to the Excel template using the established control limits, do not change the number of samples in cell E6. Also, you must modify the formulas in cells C9 and C10 for the calculations of the grand average and average range. In cell C9, change the formula to read: =SUMIF(B13:*AE13*,">-99999",B23:*AE23*)/$E$6. We have italicized the changes; rather than computing the grand average using all the data, we only compute it using the data from the range of the original 30 samples, as this value is used to calculate the control limits. Similarly, the formula for cell C10 should be changed to: =SUMIF(B13:*AE13*,">-99999",B28:*AE28*)/$E$6. The template will still chart all the data, but use control limits established from the first 30 samples.

Figures 13.13 and 13.14 show the *R*- and $\bar{x}$-charts with the new data (samples 31 to 40). In the *R*-chart, it appears that the variation has increased as the last nine points all fall above the mean. In the $\bar{x}$-chart, it appears that the average is going up, and sample 39 exceeds the upper control limit. Both of these indications suggest some special cause, and management should stop the process and investigate the cause. In the next section, we will learn other indicators of out-of-control conditions.

Interpreting Patterns in Control Charts

The following list provides a set of general rules for examining a process to determine whether it is in control:

1. No points are outside control limits.
2. The number of points above and below the center line is about the same.

Figure 13.13 *R*-Chart with Additional Data

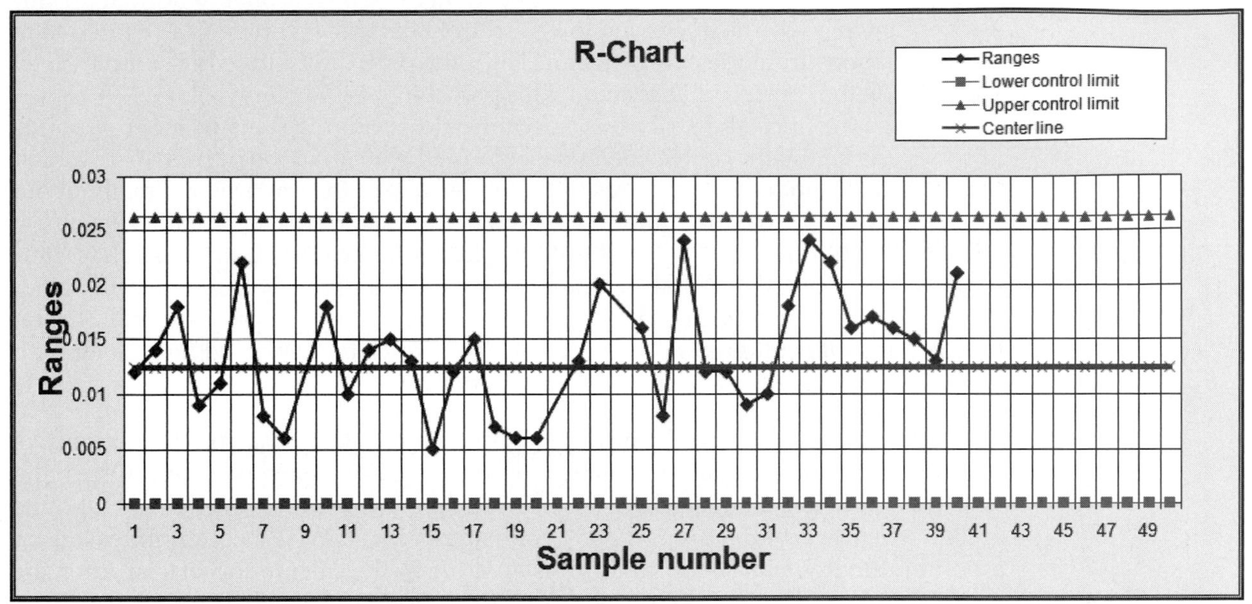

Figure 13.14 $\overline{x}$-Chart with Additional Data

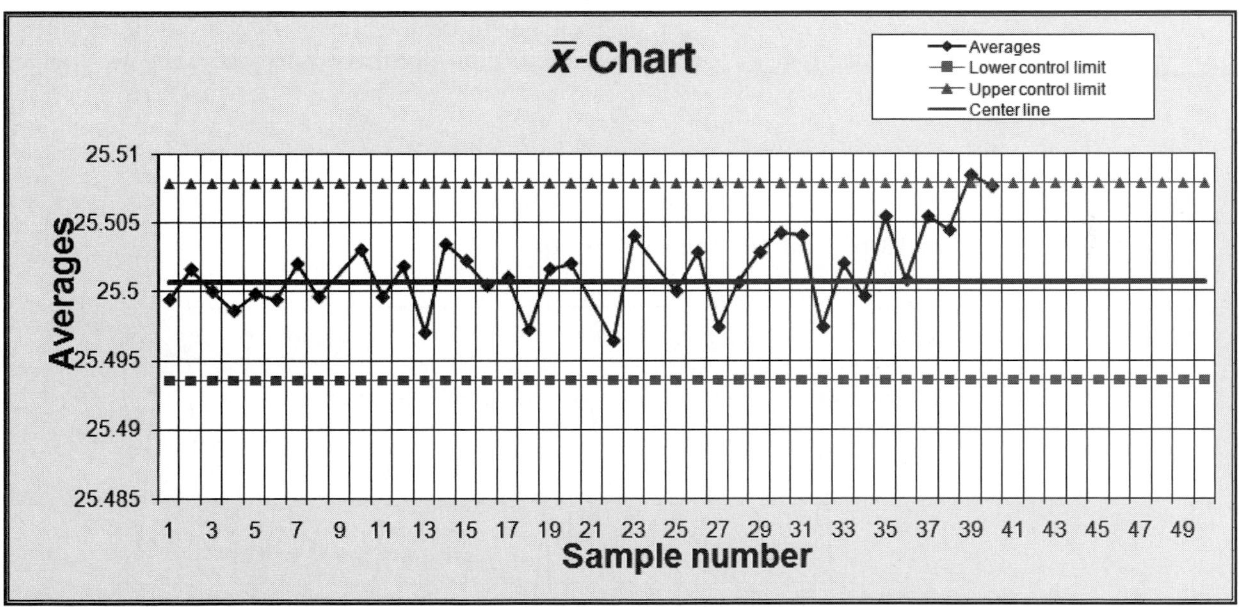

3. The points seem to fall randomly above and below the center line.
4. Most points, but not all, are near the center line, and only a few are close to the control limits.

The underlying assumption behind these rules is that the distribution of sample means is normal. This assumption follows from the central limit theorem of statistics, which states that the distribution of sample means approaches a normal distribution as the sample size increases regardless of the original distribution. Of course, for small sample sizes, the distribution of the original data must be reasonably normal for this assumption to hold. The upper and lower control limits are computed to be three standard deviations from the overall mean. Thus, the probability that any sample mean falls outside the control limits is small. This probability is the origin of rule 1.

Because the normal distribution is symmetric, about the same number of points fall above as below the center line. Also, because the mean of the normal distribution is the median, about half the points fall on either side of the center line. Finally, about 68 percent of a normal distribution falls within one standard deviation of the mean; thus, most—but not all—points should be close to the center line. These characteristics will hold provided that the mean and variance of the original data have not changed during the time the data were collected; that is, the process is stable. Several types of unusual patterns arise in control charts, which are reviewed here along with an indication of the typical causes of such patterns.[2]

One Point Outside Control Limits A single point outside the control limits (like we saw in the La Ventana case) is usually produced by a special cause. Often, the *R*-chart provides a similar indication. Once in a great while, however, such points are a normal part of the process and occur simply by chance. A common reason for a point falling outside a control limit is an error in the calculation of $\bar{x}$ or R for the sample. You should always check your calculations whenever this occurs. Other possible causes are a sudden power surge, a broken tool, measurement error, or an incomplete or omitted operation in the process.

Sudden Shift in the Process Average An unusual number of consecutive points falling on one side of the center line (see Figure 13.15) is usually an indication that the process average has suddenly shifted. Typically, this occurrence is the result of an external influence that has affected the process, which would be considered a special cause. In both the $\bar{x}$- and *R*-charts, possible causes might be a new operator, a new inspector, a new machine setting, or a change in the setup or method.

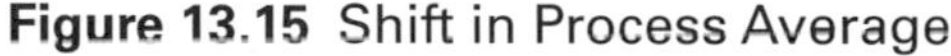

Figure 13.15 Shift in Process Average

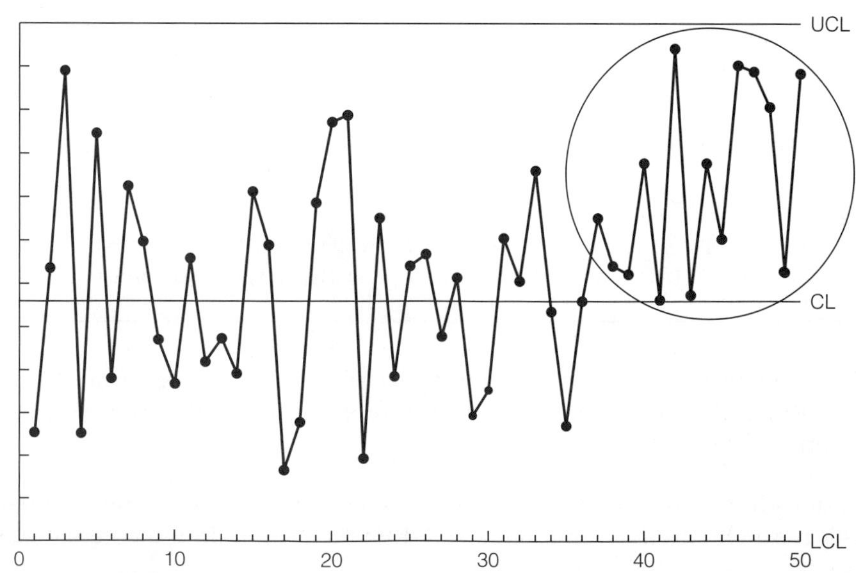

Figure 13.16 Examples of Rules for Detecting Shifts

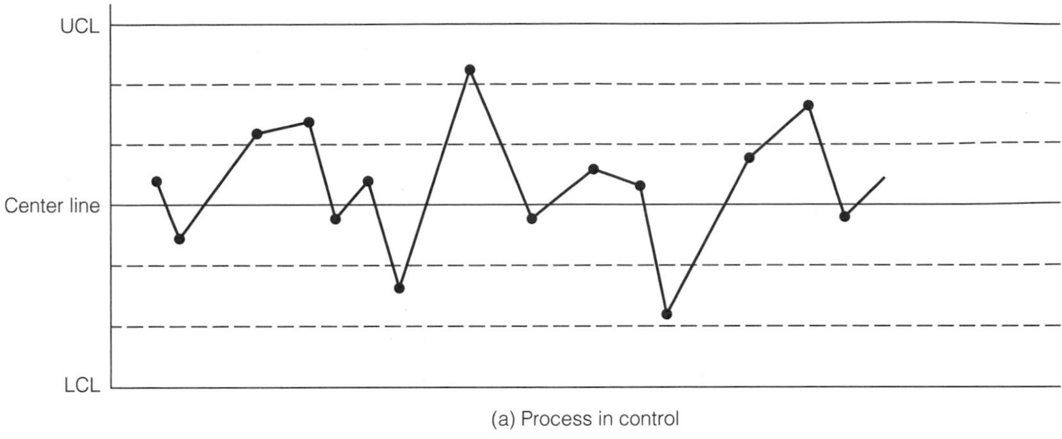

(a) Process in control

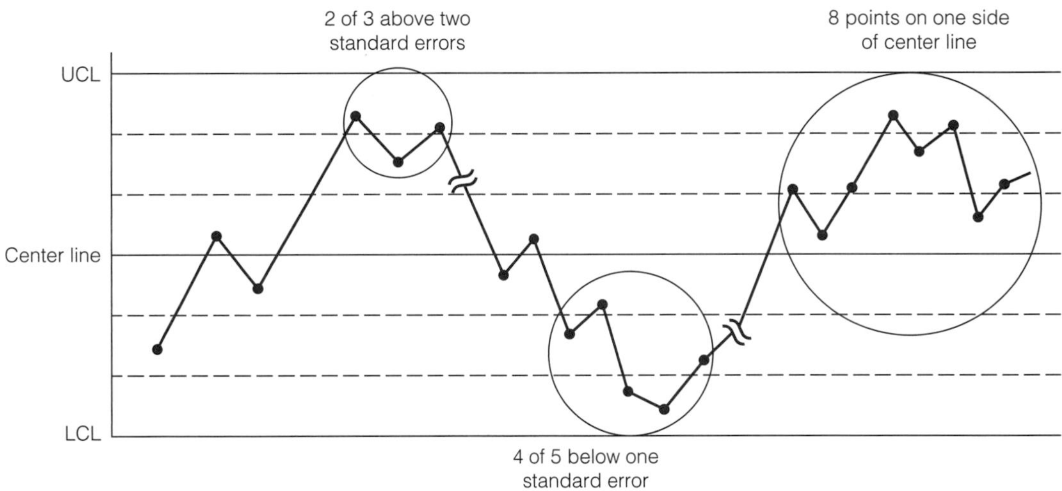

(b) Examples of out-of-control indicators

If the shift is up in the *R*-chart, as we observed with the additional data in the La Ventana Case, the process has become less uniform. Typical causes are carelessness of operators, poor or inadequate maintenance, or possibly a fixture in need of repair. If the shift is down in the *R*-chart, the uniformity of the process has improved. This shift might be the result of improved workmanship or better machines or materials. As mentioned, every effort should be made to determine the reason for the improvement and to maintain it.

Three rules of thumb are used for early detection of process shifts. A simple rule is that if eight consecutive points fall on one side of the center line, one could conclude that the mean has shifted. Second, divide the region between the center line and each control limit into three equal parts. Then if (1) two of three consecutive points fall in the outer one-third region between the center line and one of the control limits or (2) four out of five consecutive points fall within the outer two-thirds region, one would also conclude that the process has gone out of control. Examples are illustrated in Figure 13.16.

Figure 13.17 Cycles

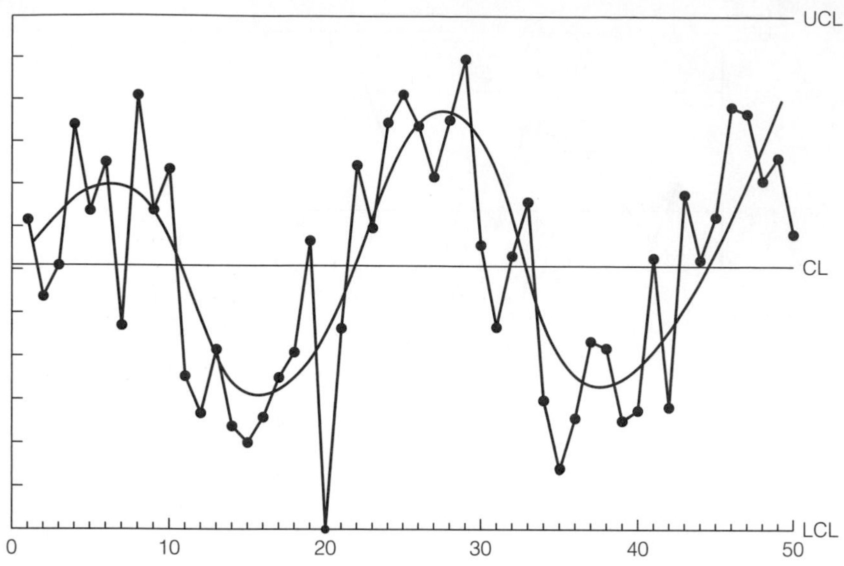

Cycles Cycles are short, repeated patterns in the chart, alternating high peaks and low valleys (see Figure 13.17). These patterns are the result of causes that come and go on a regular basis. In the $\bar{x}$-chart, cycles may be the result of operator rotation or fatigue at the end of a shift, different gauges used by different inspectors, seasonal effects such as temperature or humidity, or differences between day and night shifts. In the R-chart, cycles can occur from maintenance schedules, rotation of fixtures or gauges, differences between shifts, or operator fatigue.

Trends A trend is the result of some cause that gradually affects the quality characteristics of the product and causes the points on a control chart to gradually move up or down from the center line (see Figure 13.18), as we saw with the additional data in the La Ventana example. As a new group of operators gains experience on the job, for example, or as maintenance of equipment improves over time, a trend may occur. In the $\bar{x}$-chart, trends may be the result of improving operator skills, dirt or chip buildup in fixtures, tool wear, changes in temperature or humidity, or aging of equipment. In the R-chart, an increasing trend may be due to a gradual decline in material quality, operator fatigue, gradual loosening of a fixture or a tool, or dulling of a tool. A decreasing trend often is the result of improved operator skill or work methods, better materials, or improved or more frequent maintenance.

Hugging the Center Line Hugging the center line occurs when nearly all the points fall close to the center line (see Figure 13.19). In the control chart, it appears that the control limits are too wide. A common cause of hugging the center line is that the sample includes one item systematically taken from each of several machines, spindles, operators, and so on. A simple example will serve to illustrate this pattern. Suppose that one machine produces parts whose diameters average 7.508 with variation of only a few thousandths; a second machine produces parts whose diameters average 7.502, again with only a small variation. Taken together, parts from both machines

Figure 13.18 Trend

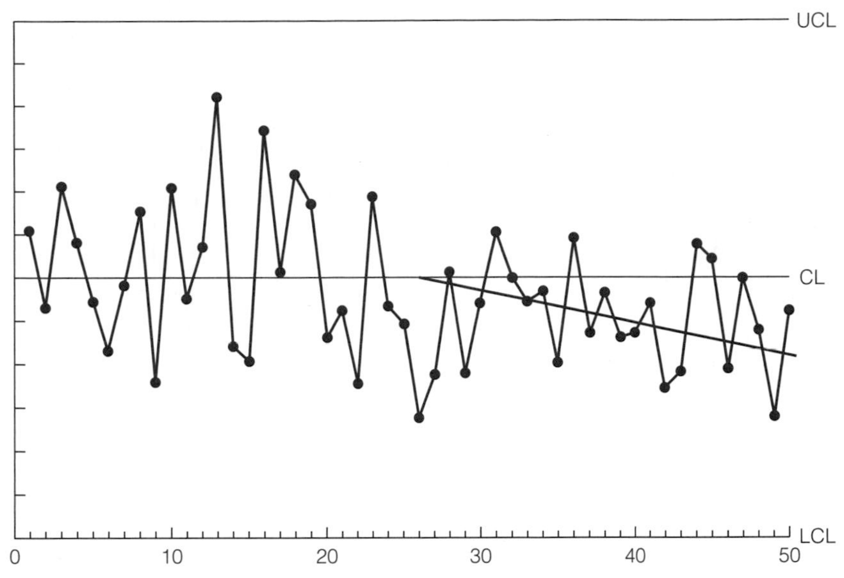

Figure 13.19 Hugging the Center Line

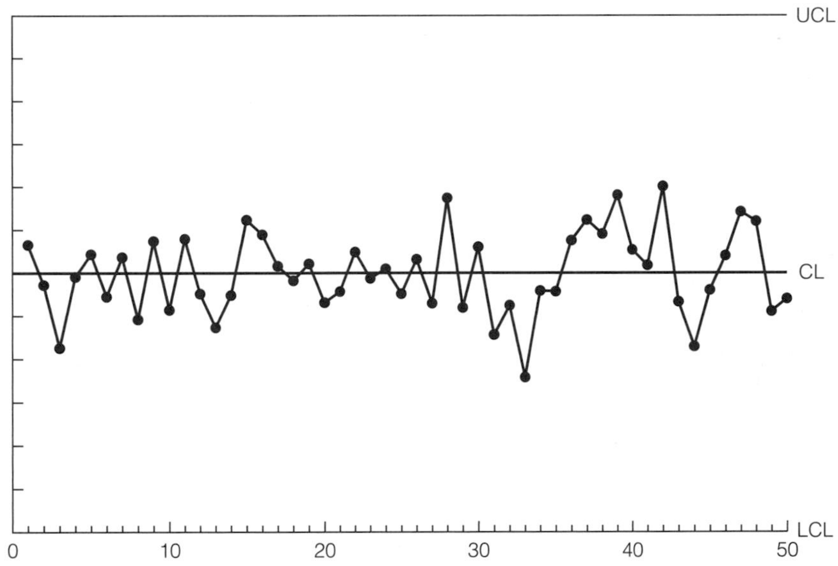

would yield a range of variation that would probably be between 7.500 and 7.510, and average about 7.505. Now suppose that one part from *each* machine is sampled, and a sample average computed to plot on an $\bar{x}$-chart. The sample averages will consistently be around 7.505, because one will always be high and the second will always be low. Even though a large variation will occur in the parts taken as a whole, should be constructed for *each* machine, spindle, operator, and so on. An often overlooked cause for

Figure 13.20 Hugging the Control Limits

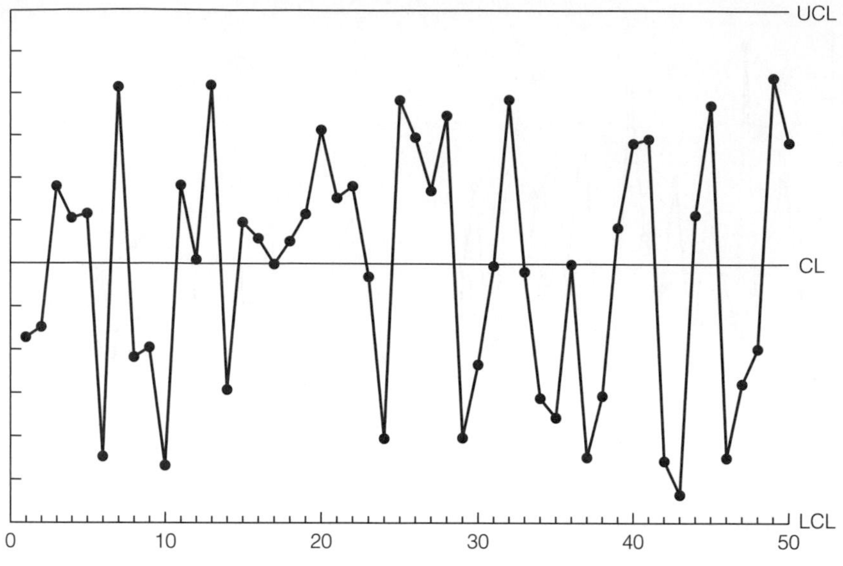

Figure 13.21 Illustration of Mixture

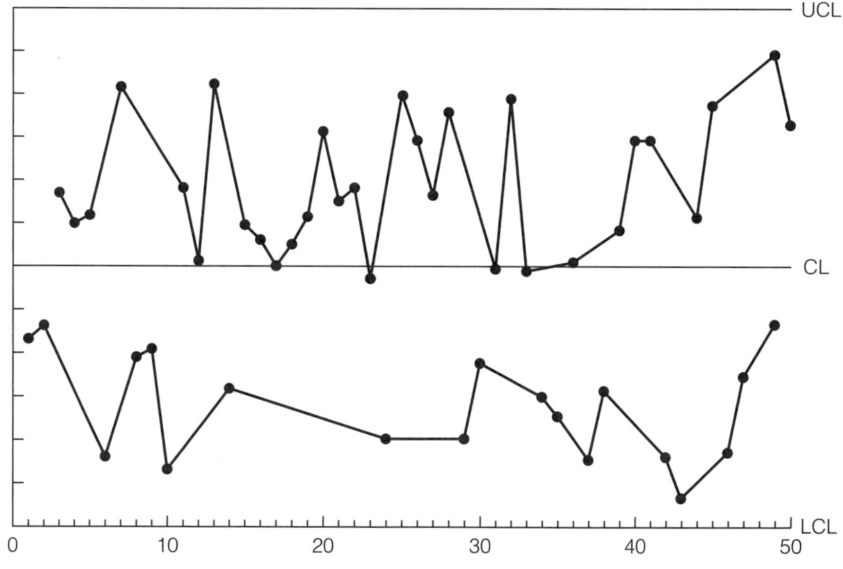

this pattern is miscalculation of the control limits, perhaps by using the wrong factor from the table, or misplacing the decimal point in the computations.

Hugging the Control Limits This pattern shows up when many points are near the control limits with few in between (see Figure 13.20). It is often called a mixture and is actually a combination of two different patterns on the same chart. A mixture can be split into two separate patterns, as Figure 13.21 illustrates. A mixture pattern can

Figure 13.22 Instability

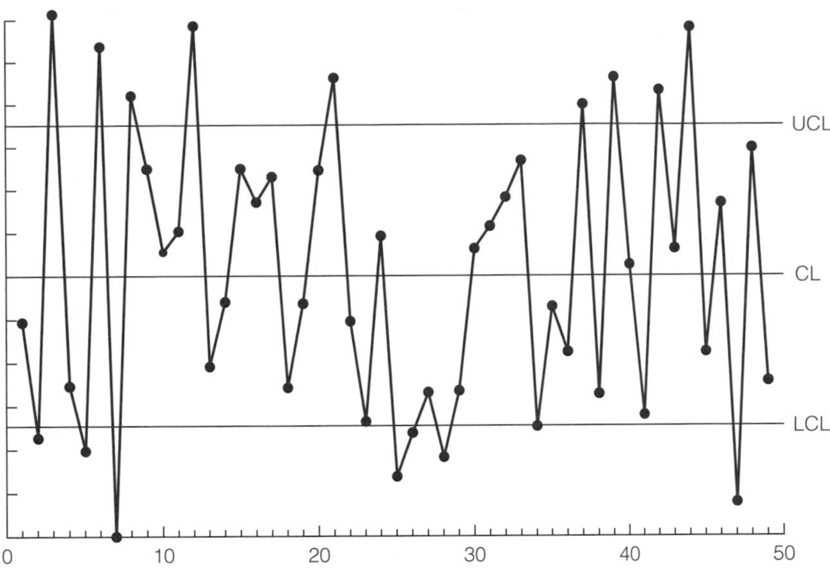

result when different lots of material are used in one process, or when parts are produced by different machines but fed into a common inspection group.

Instability Instability is characterized by unnatural and erratic fluctuations on both sides of the chart over a period of time (see Figure 13.22). Points will often lie outside both the upper and lower control limits without a consistent pattern. Assignable causes may be more difficult to identify in this case than with specific patterns. A frequent cause of instability is overadjustment of a machine, or the same reasons that cause hugging the control limits.

As suggested earlier, the *R*-chart should be analyzed before the $\bar{x}$-chart, because some out-of-control conditions in the *R*-chart may *cause* out-of-control conditions in the $\bar{x}$-chart. Figure 13.23 gives an example of this situation. The range in figure (a) shows a drastic trend downward. If you examine the $\bar{x}$-chart in figure (b), you will notice that the last several points seem to be hugging the center line. As the variability in the process decreases, all the sample observations will be closer to the true population mean, and therefore their average, $\bar{x}$, will not vary much from sample to sample. If this reduction in the variation can be identified and controlled, then new control limits should be computed for both charts as it indicates a process improvement.

The sample standard deviation is a more sensitive and better indicator of process variability than the range, especially for larger sample sizes. Thus, when tight control of variability is required, s should be used.

SPECIAL CONTROL CHARTS FOR VARIABLE DATA

Several alternatives to the popular $\bar{x}$- and *R*-charts for process control of variable measurements are available. This section discusses some of these alternatives.

Figure 13.23 Example of How Out-of-Control in an *R*-Chart May Affect the $\overline{x}$-Chart (a) Trend Down in Range. . .

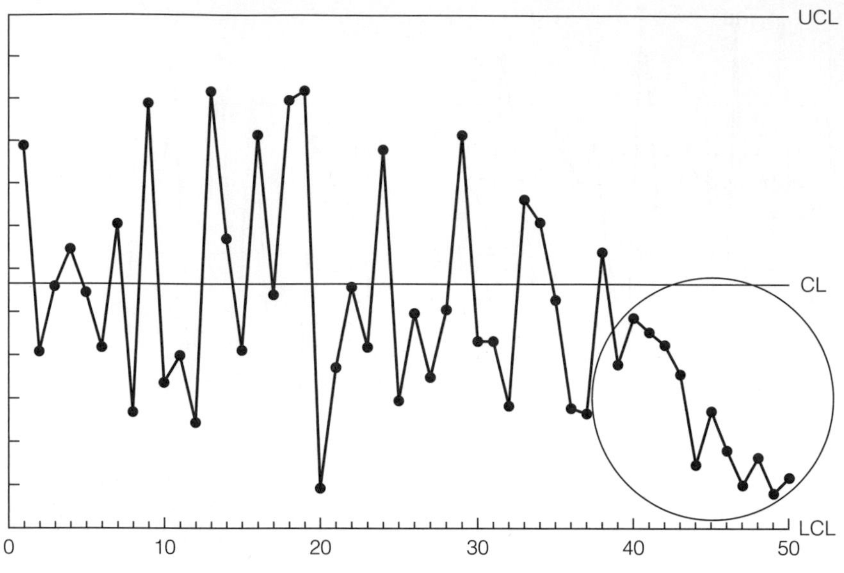

Figure 13.23 . . . (b) Causes Smaller Variation in $\overline{x}$-Chart

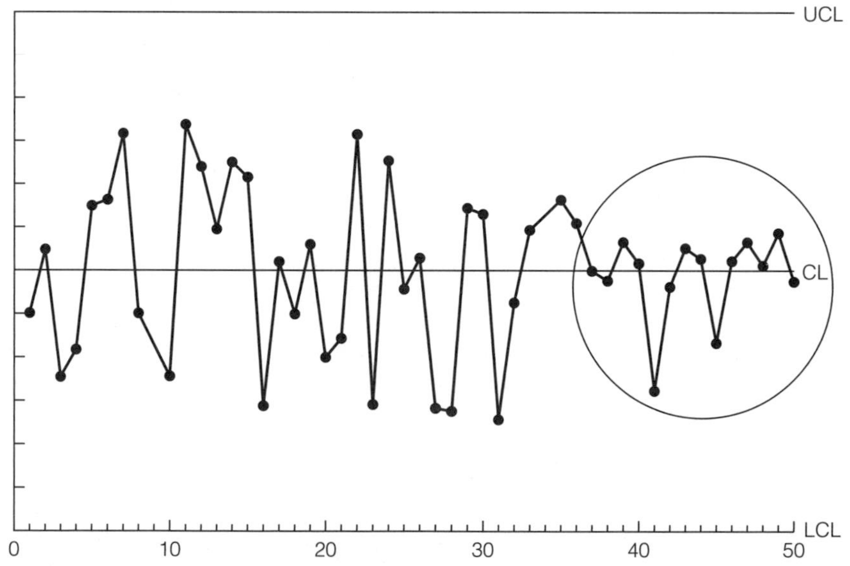

$\overline{x}$- and *s*-Charts

A better alternative to the *R*-chart to monitor variation is to compute and plot the standard deviation *s* of each sample. The sample standard deviation is computed as

$$s = \sqrt{\frac{\sum_{i=1}^{n}(x_i - \overline{x})^2}{n - 1}} \tag{13.6}$$

To construct an s-chart, compute the standard deviation for each sample. Next, compute the average standard deviation $\bar{s}$- by averaging the sample standard deviations over all samples. (Notice that this computation is analogous to computing $\bar{R}$.) Control limits for the s-chart are given by

$$\begin{aligned} UCL_s &= B_4\bar{s} \\ LCL_s &= B_3\bar{s} \end{aligned} \tag{13.7}$$

where B_3 and B_4 are constants found in Appendix B.

For the associated $\bar{x}$-chart, the control limits derived from the overall standard deviation are

$$\begin{aligned} UCL_{\bar{x}} &= \bar{\bar{x}} + A_3\bar{s} \\ LCL_{\bar{x}} &= \bar{\bar{x}} - A_3\bar{s} \end{aligned}$$

where A_3 is a constant found in Appendix B. Observe that the formulas for the control limits are equivalent to those for $\bar{x}$- and R-charts except that the constants differ.

Constructing $\bar{x}$- and s-Charts To illustrate the use of the $\bar{x}$- and s-charts, consider the data given in the Excel template *Xbar&S* in Figure 13.24. These data represent measurements of deviations in millimeters from a nominal specification for some machined part; thus, a value of 1 indicates 1 millimeter above the nominal, and so on. Samples of size 10 are used; for each sample, the mean and standard deviation have been computed.

The average (overall) mean is computed to be $\bar{\bar{x}} = -0.164$, and the average standard deviation is $\bar{s} = 1.467$. For samples of size 10, $B_3 = 0.284$, $B_4 = 1.716$, and $A_3 = 0.975$. Control limits for the s-chart are

$$\begin{aligned} LCL_s &= 0.284(1.467) = 0.417 \\ UCL_s &= 1.716(1.467) = 2.518 \end{aligned}$$

For the $\bar{x}$ -chart, the control limits are

$$\begin{aligned} LCL_{\bar{x}} &= -0.164 - 0.975(1.467) = -1.59 \\ UCL_{\bar{x}} &= -0.164 + 0.975(1.467) = 1.267 \end{aligned}$$

The $\bar{x}$- and s-charts are shown in Figures 13.25 and 13.26. This evidence indicates the process is not in control, and an investigation as to the reasons for the variation in the $\bar{x}$-chart, is warranted.

Charts for Individuals

In some situations, it may be inappropriate or undesirable to collect samples of multiple observations. For instance, in a chemical production process, sampling from a homogeneous mixture will result in little variation, except possibly from measurement error. In very low-volume production situations, a reasonable sample might cover a long period of time during which the process might have changed, thus not providing good information for control. In other situations, we might simply want to chart every observation, such as the waiting time of patients in an emergency room. With automated inspection for many manufacturing processes, the technology can easily collect quality data on every item produced. In all of these situations, the sample size for process control is $n = 1$, and a control chart for *individual measurements*—also called an *x-chart*—can be used.

Figure 13.24 Data and Calculations for $\overline{x}$- and *s*-Charts Example

	A	B	C	D	E	F	G	H	I	J	K	L	M	N	O	P	Q	R	S	T	U	V	W	X	Y	Z
1	**X-bar and s-Chart**																									
2	This spreadsheet is designed for up to 50 samples, each of a constant sample size from 2 to 10. Enter data ONLY in yellow-shaded cells.																									
3	Enter the number of samples in cell E6 and the sample size in cell E7. Then enter your data in the grid below.																									
4	Click on sheet tabs for a display of the control charts (some rescaling may be needed). Specification limits may be entered in cells N7 and N8 for process capability.																									
5																										
6	**Number of samples (<= 50)**				25					Process Capability Calculations							**Six sigma**	10.2								
7	**Sample size (2 - 10)**				10					**Upper specification**							**Cp**									
8										**Lower specification**							**Cpu**									
9	**Grand Average**		-0.164		A3	B3	B4	d2									**Cpl**									
10	**Avg. std. dev.**		1.4674343		0.975	0.284	1.716	3.078									**Cpk**									
11																										
12	**DATA**	**1**	**2**	**3**	**4**	**5**	**6**	**7**	**8**	**9**	**10**	**11**	**12**	**13**	**14**	**15**	**16**	**17**	**18**	**19**	**20**	**21**	**22**	**23**	**24**	**25**
13	**1**	1	-2	0	1	-3	-6	-3	0	2	0	-3	-1	-1	-3	-1	-1	-2	0	0	1	1	-1	0	1	2
14	**2**	-3	-1	-1	1	-1	2	-1	-2	0	0	-2	2	-3	-2	-1	-2	2	4	-3	2	0	0	0	0	-2
15	**3**	4	0	0	0	0	0	0	-3	-1	-2	2	0	0	2	-1	-2	-1	0	3	1	2	2	-1	0	1
16	**4**	2	3	0	2	-4	0	-2	-1	-1	-1	-1	-2	0	0	-2	0	0	0	3	1	1	-1	0	1	2
17	**5**	0	0	3	1	0	2	-1	-2	-3	-1	1	-1	1	-5	-1	1	-1	0	3	-3	2	2	1	1	-1
18	**6**	1	0	1	1	1	-1	-1	1	0	0	-2	2	-4	1	0	0	-1	3	1	2	0	2	0	2	2
19	**7**	-2	3	-2	2	0	2	-3	-3	1	-1	-2	2	1	1	-2	-2	2	0	0	1	1	-1	0	0	0
20	**8**	3	-2	0	0	-2	0	0	0	-2	-2	-1	-3	-1	-4	-1	0	-1	0	1	-2	1	0	0	0	1
21	**9**	0	-1	2	0	0	-3	-2	-3	-1	-2	1	-2	-1	-1	0	-1	1	1	2	3	1	0	-1	-1	-1
22	**10**	3	3	3	1	-2	0	-2	-2	0	0	1	0	-2	-3	-1	0	-2	0	-2	0	2	-1	0	0	2
23	**Average**	0.9	0.3	0.6	0.9	-1.1	-0.4	-1.5	-1.5	-0.5	-0.9	-0.6	-0.3	-1	-1.4	-1	-0.7	-0.3	0.8	0.8	0.6	1.1	0.2	-0.1	0.4	0.6
24	**LCLx-bar**	-1.59	-1.59	-1.59	-1.59	-1.59	-1.59	-1.59	-1.59	-1.59	-1.59	-1.59	-1.59	-1.59	-1.59	-1.59	-1.59	-1.59	-1.59	-1.59	-1.59	-1.59	-1.59	-1.59	-1.59	-1.59
25	**Center**	-0.16	-0.16	-0.16	-0.16	-0.16	-0.16	-0.16	-0.16	-0.16	-0.16	-0.16	-0.16	-0.16	-0.16	-0.16	-0.16	-0.16	-0.16	-0.16	-0.16	-0.16	-0.16	-0.16	-0.16	-0.16
26	**UCLx-bar**	1.267	1.267	1.267	1.267	1.267	1.267	1.267	1.267	1.267	1.267	1.267	1.267	1.267	1.267	1.267	1.267	1.267	1.267	1.267	1.267	1.267	1.267	1.267	1.267	1.267
27																										
28	**Std. Dev.**	2.234	2.003	1.647	0.738	1.595	2.503	1.08	1.434	1.434	0.876	1.713	1.829	1.633	2.366	0.667	1.059	1.494	1.476	2.098	1.838	0.738	1.317	0.568	0.843	1.506
29	**LCLs**	0.417	0.417	0.417	0.417	0.417	0.417	0.417	0.417	0.417	0.417	0.417	0.417	0.417	0.417	0.417	0.417	0.417	0.417	0.417	0.417	0.417	0.417	0.417	0.417	0.417
30	**Center**	1.467	1.467	1.467	1.467	1.467	1.467	1.467	1.467	1.467	1.467	1.467	1.467	1.467	1.467	1.467	1.467	1.467	1.467	1.467	1.467	1.467	1.467	1.467	1.467	1.467
31	**UCLs**	2.518	2.518	2.518	2.518	2.518	2.518	2.518	2.518	2.518	2.518	2.518	2.518	2.518	2.518	2.518	2.518	2.518	2.518	2.518	2.518	2.518	2.518	2.518	2.518	2.518

Figure 13.25 *s*-Chart

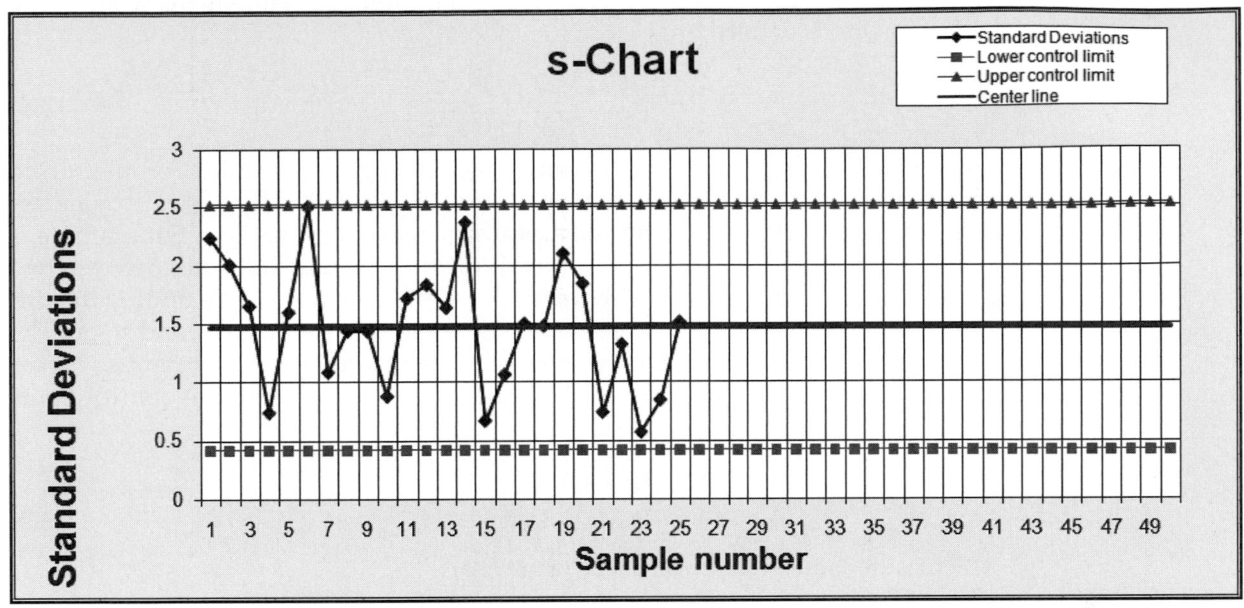

Figure 13.26 $\bar{x}$-Chart

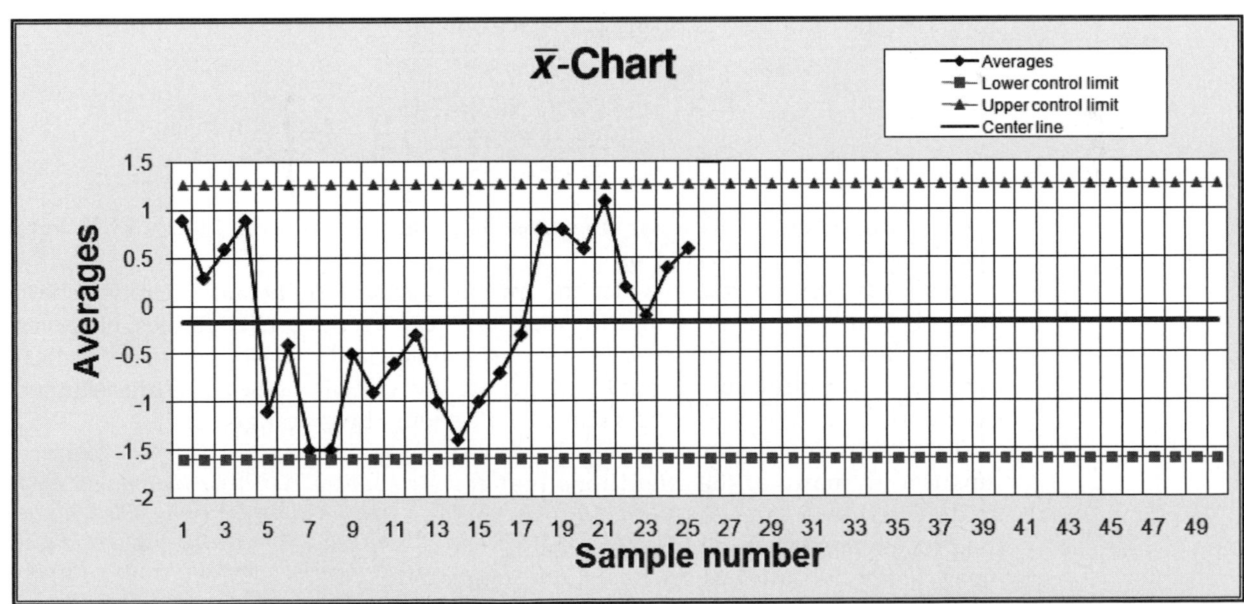

With individual measurements, the process standard deviation can be estimated and 3σ control limits used. As shown earlier, $\overline{R}/d_2$ provides an estimate of the process standard deviation. Thus, an x-chart for individual measurements would have 3σ control limits defined by

$$\begin{aligned} UCL_x &= \overline{x} + 3\overline{R}/d_2 \\ LCL_x &= \overline{x} - 3\overline{R}/d_2 \end{aligned} \tag{13.8}$$

Samples of size 1, however, do not furnish enough information for measuring process variability. One way of getting around this limitation is to use a moving average of the ranges, or a *moving range*, of n successive observations. For example, a moving range for $n = 2$ is computed by finding the absolute difference between two successive observations, a moving range for $n = 3$ is computed by finding the difference between the largest and smallest observations in groups of 3, and so on. The number of observations used in the moving range determines the constant d_2; hence, for $n = 2$, from Appendix B, $d_2 = 1.128$. The moving range chart has control limits defined by

$$\begin{aligned} UCL_R &= D_4\overline{R} \\ LCL_R &= D_3\overline{R} \end{aligned} \tag{13.9}$$

which is the same as in the ordinary range chart.

Constructing an x-Chart with Moving Ranges. Consider a set of observations measuring the percentage of cobalt in a chemical process as given in Figure 13.27 (Excel template *X&MR*). The moving range with $n = 2$ is computed as shown by taking absolute values of successive ranges and using the constants in Appendix B. For example, the first moving range is the difference between the first two observations, or $|3.75 - 3.80| = 0.05$. The second moving range is computed as $|3.80 - 3.70| = 0.10$, and so on.

Using the formulas (13.8) and (13.9), we obtain

$$\begin{aligned} LCL_R &= 0 \\ UCL_R &= (3.267)(0.352) = 1.15 \\ LCL_x &= 3.498 - 3(0.352)/1.128 = 2.56 \\ UCL_x &= 3.498 + 3(0.352)/1.128 = 4.43 \end{aligned}$$

The moving range chart shown in Figure 13.28 and the x-chart in Figure 13.29 indicate that the process is in control.

Some caution is necessary when interpreting patterns on the moving range chart. Points beyond control limits indicate assignable causes. Successive ranges, however, are correlated, and they may cause patterns or trends in the chart that are not indicative of out-of-control situations. On the x-chart, individual observations are assumed to be uncorrelated; hence, patterns and trends should be investigated.

Control charts for individuals offer the advantage of being able to draw specifications on the chart for direct comparison with the control limits.

In addition, charts for individuals are less sensitive to many of the conditions that can be detected by $\overline{x}$- and R-charts; for example, the process must vary a lot before a shift in the mean is detected. Also, short cycles and trends may appear on these charts and not on an $\overline{x}$- or R-chart. Finally, the assumption of normality of observations is more critical than for $\overline{x}$- and R-charts; when the normality assumption does not hold, greater chance for error is present.

Figure 13.27 Data and Calculations for *x*- and MR Chart

	A	B	C	D	E	F	G	H	I	J	K	L
1	**X and Moving Range Chart**											
2	This spreadsheet is designed for up to 75 observations and a moving range from 2 to 5. Enter data ONLY in yellow-shaded cells.											
3	Enter the number of samples in cell E6 and the sample size in cell E7. Then enter your data in the grid below.											
4	Click on sheet tabs to display the control charts (some rescaling may be needed).											
5												
6	**Number of samples (<= 75)**				25							
7	**Sample size for moving range(2 - 5)**				2							
8												
9	**Grand Average**		3.498		D3	D4	d2					
10	**Average Range**		0.352083333		0	3.267	1.13					
11												
12						**Moving**						
13	**Observation**	**Value**	**LCLx**	**CLx**	**UCLx**	**Range**	**LCLr**	**CLr**	**UCLr**			
14	1	3.75	2.5616	3.498	4.43439							
15	2	3.8	2.5616	3.498	4.43439	0.05	0	0.352	1.1503			
16	3	3.7	2.5616	3.498	4.43439	0.1	0	0.352	1.1503			
17	4	3.2	2.5616	3.498	4.43439	0.5	0	0.352	1.1503			
18	5	3.5	2.5616	3.498	4.43439	0.3	0	0.352	1.1503			
19	6	3.05	2.5616	3.498	4.43439	0.45	0	0.352	1.1503			
20	7	3.5	2.5616	3.498	4.43439	0.45	0	0.352	1.1503			
21	8	3.25	2.5616	3.498	4.43439	0.25	0	0.352	1.1503			
22	9	3.6	2.5616	3.498	4.43439	0.35	0	0.352	1.1503			
23	10	3.1	2.5616	3.498	4.43439	0.5	0	0.352	1.1503			
24	11	4	2.5616	3.498	4.43439	0.9	0	0.352	1.1503			
25	12	4	2.5616	3.498	4.43439	0	0	0.352	1.1503			
26	13	3.5	2.5616	3.498	4.43439	0.5	0	0.352	1.1503			
27	14	3	2.5616	3.498	4.43439	0.5	0	0.352	1.1503			
28	15	3.8	2.5616	3.498	4.43439	0.8	0	0.352	1.1503			
29	16	3.4	2.5616	3.498	4.43439	0.4	0	0.352	1.1503			
30	17	3.6	2.5616	3.498	4.43439	0.2	0	0.352	1.1503			
31	18	3.1	2.5616	3.498	4.43439	0.5	0	0.352	1.1503			
32	19	3.55	2.5616	3.498	4.43439	0.45	0	0.352	1.1503			
33	20	3.65	2.5616	3.498	4.43439	0.1	0	0.352	1.1503			
34	21	3.45	2.5616	3.498	4.43439	0.2	0	0.352	1.1503			
35	22	3.3	2.5616	3.498	4.43439	0.15	0	0.352	1.1503			
36	23	3.75	2.5616	3.498	4.43439	0.45	0	0.352	1.1503			
37	24	3.5	2.5616	3.498	4.43439	0.25	0	0.352	1.1503			
38	25	3.4	2.5616	3.498	4.43439	0.1	0	0.352	1.1503			

CONTROL CHARTS FOR ATTRIBUTES

Attribute data that can be observed and counted are useful in many practical situations. For instance, in printing packages for consumer products, color quality can be rated as acceptable or not acceptable. We may count the number of items with coloration problems. A hotel room's cleanliness is often assessed using a checklist. We may count the number of nonconforming quality characteristics per room.

One distinction that we must make is between an individual nonconformance and a nonconforming item. A **nonconformance** is a single nonconforming quality characteristic of a unit of work. In manufacturing we often use the term **defect**, and in service applications, we generally use the term **error** to describe a nonconformance. A unit of work may have several nonconformances. Thus, if a unit of work has one or more nonconformances, we term the entire unit **nonconforming**. Because certain attribute charts are used for nonconformances, whereas others are used for the number nonconforming, we must understand the difference.

Figure 13.28 Moving Range Chart

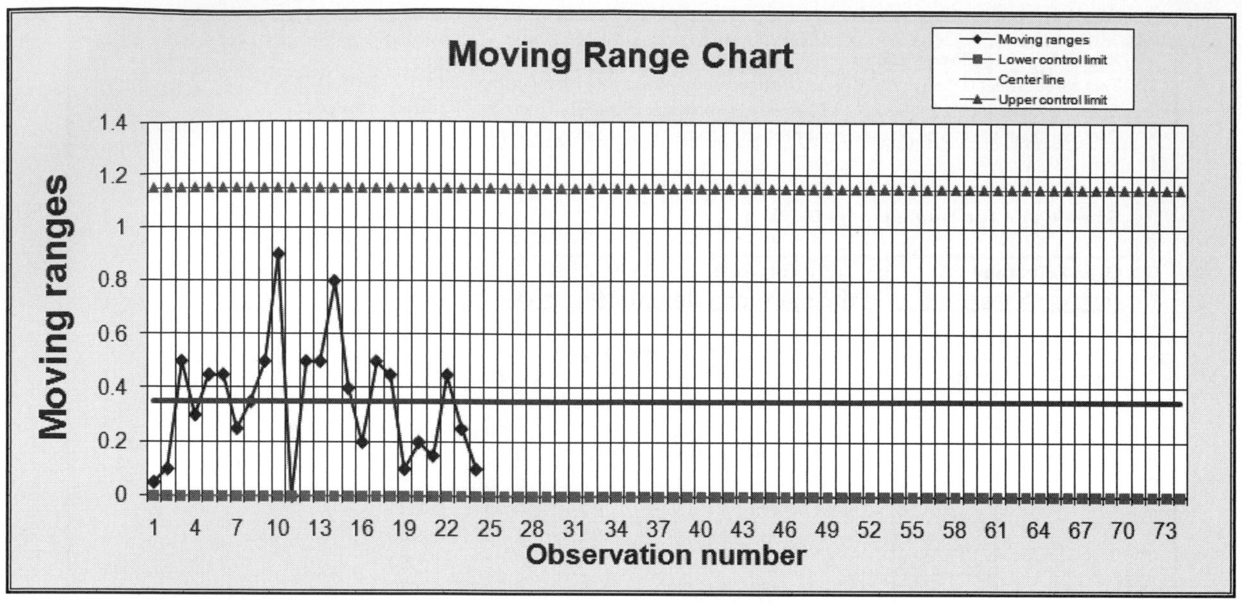

Figure 13.29 Individuals *x*-Chart

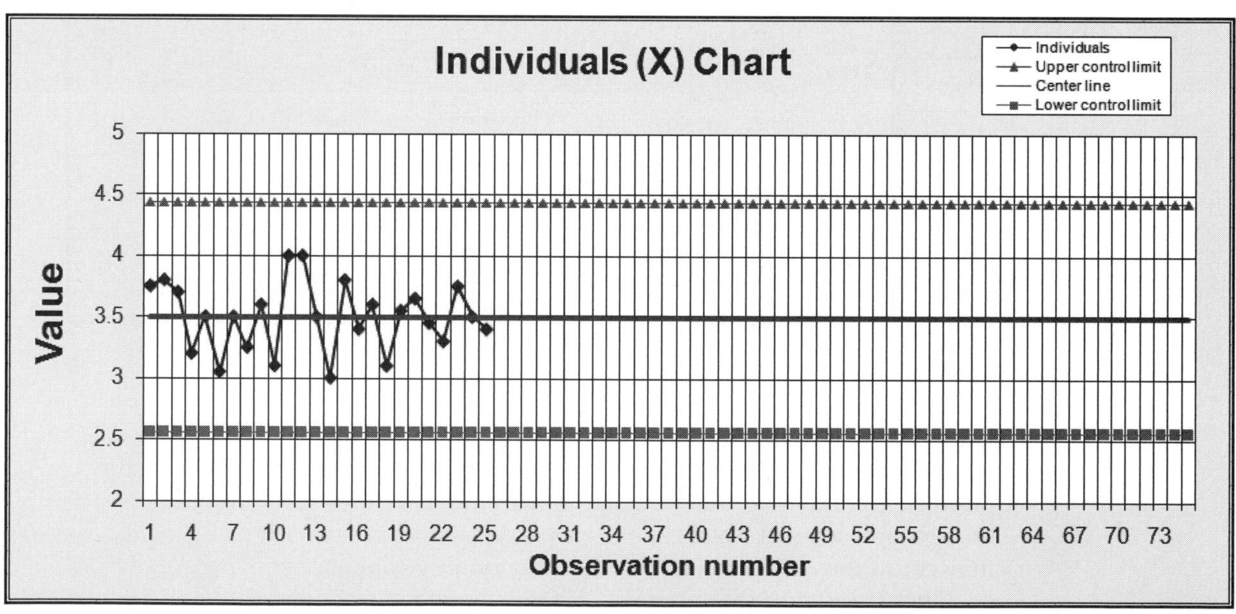

Fraction Nonconforming (*p*) Chart

A ***p*-chart** monitors the fraction of nonconforming items. As with variables data, a *p*-chart is constructed by first gathering 25 to 30 samples of the attribute being measured. The size of each sample should be large enough to have several nonconforming items. If the probability of finding a nonconforming item is small, a sample size of 100 or more items is usually necessary. Samples are chosen over time periods so that any special causes that are identified can be investigated.

Let us suppose that k samples, each of size n, are selected. If y represents the number nonconforming in a particular sample, the proportion nonconforming is y/n. Let p_i be the fraction nonconforming in the ith sample; the average fraction nonconforming for the group of k samples then is

$$\overline{p} = \frac{p_1 + p_2 + \cdots + p_k}{k} \tag{13.10}$$

This statistic reflects the average performance of the process. One would expect a high percentage of samples to have a fraction nonconforming within three standard deviations of $\overline{p}$. An estimate of the standard deviation is given by

$$s_{\overline{p}} = \sqrt{\frac{\overline{p}(1 - \overline{p})}{n}} \tag{13.11}$$

Therefore, upper and lower control limits are given by

$$\begin{aligned} \text{UCL}_p &= \overline{p} + 3s_{\overline{p}} \\ \text{LCL}_p &= \overline{p} - 3s_{\overline{p}} \end{aligned} \tag{13.12}$$

If LCL_p is less than zero, a value of zero is used.

Analysis of a p-chart is similar to that of an $\overline{x}$- or R-chart. Points outside the control limits signify an out-of-control situation. Patterns and trends should also be sought to identify special causes. However, a point on a p-chart below the lower control limit or the development of a trend below the center line indicates that the process might have improved, based on an ideal of zero defectives. Caution is advised before such conclusions are drawn, because errors may have been made in computation.

Constructing a *p*-Chart The operators of automated sorting machines in a post office must read the ZIP code on a letter and divert the letter to the proper carrier route. Over one month's time, 25 samples of 100 letters were chosen, and the number of errors was recorded. This information is summarized in Figure 13.30 (Excel template *p-chart*). The fraction nonconforming is found by dividing the number of errors by 100. The average fraction nonconforming, $\overline{p}$ is determined to be

$$\overline{p} = \frac{0.03 + 0.01 + \cdots + 0.01}{25} = 0.022$$

The standard deviation is computed as

$$s_{\overline{p}} = \sqrt{\frac{0.022(1 - 0.022)}{100}} = 0.01467$$

Thus, the upper control limit, UCL_p, is $0.022 + 3(0.01467) = 0.066$, and the lower control limit, LCL_p, is $0.022 - 3(0.01467) = -0.022$. Because this latter figure is negative, zero is used. The control chart for this example is shown in Figure 13.31. The sorting process appears to be in control. Any values found above the upper control limit or evidence of an upward trend might indicate the need for more experience or training of the operators.

Figure 13.30 Data and Calculations for *p*-Chart Example

	A	B	C	D	E	F	G	H	I	J	K	L	M
1	**Fraction Nonconforming (p) Chart**												
2	This spreadsheet is designed for up to 50 samples. Enter data ONLY in yellow-shaded cells.												
3	Click on the sheet tab to display the control chart (some rescaling may be needed).												
4													
5	**Average (p-bar)**		0.022										
6	**Avg. sample size**		100										
7										**Approximate Control Limits Using**			
8			**Sample**	**Fraction**	**Standard**					**Average Sample Size Calculations**			
9	**Sample**	**Value**	**Size**	**Nonconforming**	**Deviation**	**LCLp**	**CL**	**UCLp**		**LCLp**	**CL**	**UCLp**	
10	1	3	100	0.0300	0.014668	0	0.022	0.066		0	0.022	0.066005	
11	2	1	100	0.0100	0.014668	0	0.022	0.066		0	0.022	0.066005	
12	3	0	100	0.0000	0.014668	0	0.022	0.066		0	0.022	0.066005	
13	4	0	100	0.0000	0.014668	0	0.022	0.066		0	0.022	0.066005	
14	5	2	100	0.0200	0.014668	0	0.022	0.066		0	0.022	0.066005	
15	6	5	100	0.0500	0.014668	0	0.022	0.066		0	0.022	0.066005	
16	7	3	100	0.0300	0.014668	0	0.022	0.066		0	0.022	0.066005	
17	8	6	100	0.0600	0.014668	0	0.022	0.066		0	0.022	0.066005	
18	9	1	100	0.0100	0.014668	0	0.022	0.066		0	0.022	0.066005	
19	10	4	100	0.0400	0.014668	0	0.022	0.066		0	0.022	0.066005	
20	11	0	100	0.0000	0.014668	0	0.022	0.066		0	0.022	0.066005	
21	12	2	100	0.0200	0.014668	0	0.022	0.066		0	0.022	0.066005	
22	13	1	100	0.0100	0.014668	0	0.022	0.066		0	0.022	0.066005	
23	14	3	100	0.0300	0.014668	0	0.022	0.066		0	0.022	0.066005	
24	15	4	100	0.0400	0.014668	0	0.022	0.066		0	0.022	0.066005	
25	16	1	100	0.0100	0.014668	0	0.022	0.066		0	0.022	0.066005	
26	17	1	100	0.0100	0.014668	0	0.022	0.066		0	0.022	0.066005	
27	18	2	100	0.0200	0.014668	0	0.022	0.066		0	0.022	0.066005	
28	19	5	100	0.0500	0.014668	0	0.022	0.066		0	0.022	0.066005	
29	20	2	100	0.0200	0.014668	0	0.022	0.066		0	0.022	0.066005	
30	21	3	100	0.0300	0.014668	0	0.022	0.066		0	0.022	0.066005	
31	22	4	100	0.0400	0.014668	0	0.022	0.066		0	0.022	0.066005	
32	23	1	100	0.0100	0.014668	0	0.022	0.066		0	0.022	0.066005	
33	24	0	100	0.0000	0.014668	0	0.022	0.066		0	0.022	0.066005	
34	25	1	100	0.0100	0.014668	0	0.022	0.066		0	0.022	0.066005	

Figure 13.31 *p*-Chart

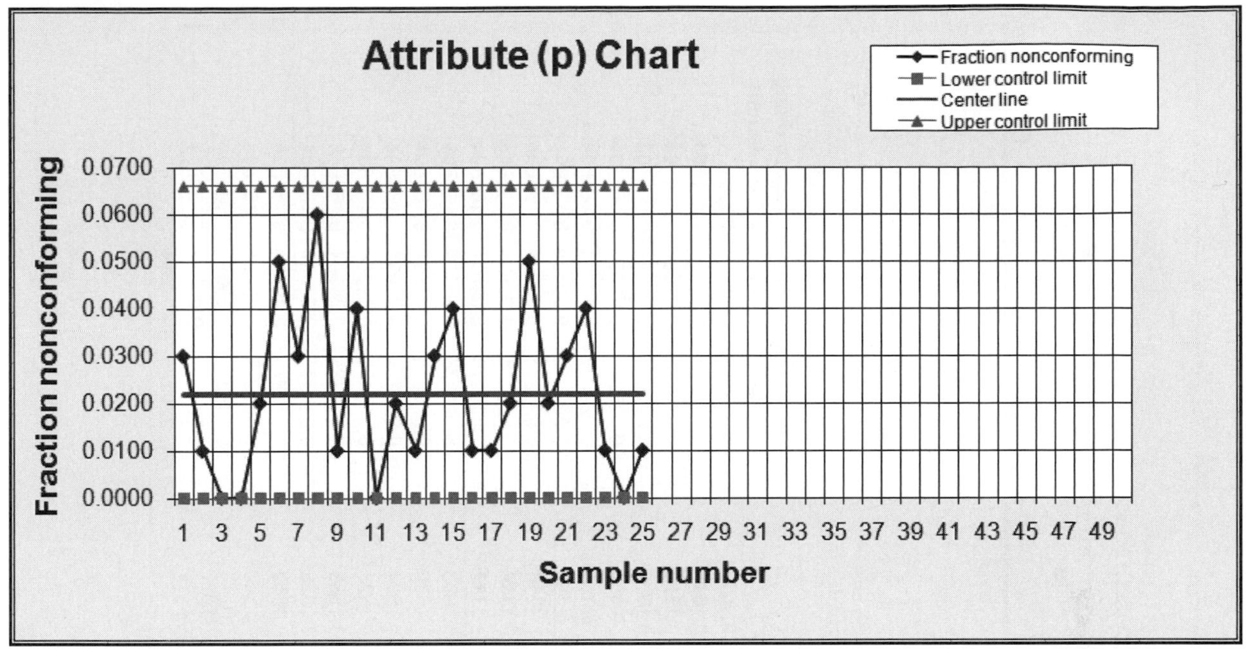

Variable Sample Size

Often 100 percent inspection is performed on process output during fixed sampling periods; however, the number of units produced in each sampling period may vary. In this case, the *p*-chart would have a variable sample size. One way of handling this variation is to compute a standard deviation for each individual sample. Thus, if the number of observations in the *i*th sample is n_i, control limits are given by

$$\bar{p} \pm 3\sqrt{\frac{\bar{p}(1-\bar{p})}{n_i}}$$

$$\text{where } \bar{p} = \frac{\Sigma \text{ number nonconforming}}{\Sigma n_i} \tag{13.13}$$

The data given in Figure 13.32 represent 20 samples with varying sample sizes. The value of $\bar{p}$ is computed as

$$\bar{p} = \frac{18 + 20 + 14 + \cdots + 18}{137 + 158 + 92 + \cdots + 160} = \frac{271}{2{,}980} = 0.0909$$

The control limits for sample 1 are

$$\text{LCL}_p = .0909 - 3\sqrt{\frac{.0909(1 - .0909)}{137}} = 0.017$$

$$\text{UCL}_p = .0909 + 3\sqrt{\frac{.0909(1 - .0909)}{137}} = 0.165$$

Because the sample sizes vary, the control limits are different for each sample. The *p* chart is shown in Figure 13.33. Note that points 13 and 15 are outside the control limits.

Figure 13.32 Data and Calculations for Variable Sample Size *p*-Chart Example

	A	B	C	D	E	F	G	H	I	J	K	L	M
1	**Fraction Nonconforming (p) Chart**												
2	This spreadsheet is designed for up to 50 samples. Enter data ONLY in yellow-shaded cells.												
3	Click on the sheet tab to display the control chart (some rescaling may be needed).												
4													
5	**Average (p-bar)**		0.090939597										
6	**Avg. sample size**		149										
7										**Approximate Control Limits Using**			
8			**Sample**	**Fraction**	**Standard**					**Average Sample Size Calculations**			
9	**Sample**	**Value**	**Size**	**Nonconforming**	**Deviation**	**LCLp**	**CL**	**UCLp**		**LCLp**	**CL**	**UCLp**	
10	1	18	137	0.1314	0.024565	0.017	0.091	0.1646		0.020275	0.09094	0.161604	
11	2	20	158	0.1266	0.022874	0.022	0.091	0.1596		0.020275	0.09094	0.161604	
12	3	14	92	0.1522	0.029976	0.001	0.091	0.1809		0.020275	0.09094	0.161604	
13	4	6	122	0.0492	0.026031	0.013	0.091	0.169		0.020275	0.09094	0.161604	
14	5	11	86	0.1279	0.031004	0	0.091	0.184		0.020275	0.09094	0.161604	
15	6	22	187	0.1176	0.021026	0.028	0.091	0.154		0.020275	0.09094	0.161604	
16	7	6	156	0.0385	0.02302	0.022	0.091	0.16		0.020275	0.09094	0.161604	
17	8	9	117	0.0769	0.026582	0.011	0.091	0.1707		0.020275	0.09094	0.161604	
18	9	14	110	0.1273	0.027414	0.009	0.091	0.1732		0.020275	0.09094	0.161604	
19	10	12	142	0.0845	0.024128	0.019	0.091	0.1633		0.020275	0.09094	0.161604	
20	11	8	140	0.0571	0.0243	0.018	0.091	0.1638		0.020275	0.09094	0.161604	
21	12	13	179	0.0726	0.02149	0.026	0.091	0.1554		0.020275	0.09094	0.161604	
22	13	5	196	0.0255	0.020537	0.029	0.091	0.1526		0.020275	0.09094	0.161604	
23	14	15	163	0.0920	0.022521	0.023	0.091	0.1585		0.020275	0.09094	0.161604	
24	15	25	140	0.1786	0.0243	0.018	0.091	0.1638		0.020275	0.09094	0.161604	
25	16	12	135	0.0889	0.024746	0.017	0.091	0.1652		0.020275	0.09094	0.161604	
26	17	16	186	0.0860	0.021082	0.028	0.091	0.1542		0.020275	0.09094	0.161604	
27	18	12	193	0.0622	0.020696	0.029	0.091	0.153		0.020275	0.09094	0.161604	
28	19	15	181	0.0829	0.021371	0.027	0.091	0.1551		0.020275	0.09094	0.161604	
29	20	18	160	0.1125	0.022731	0.023	0.091	0.1591		0.020275	0.09094	0.161604	

Figure 13.33 *p*-Chart for Variable Sample Size Example (Actual Sample Sizes Used)

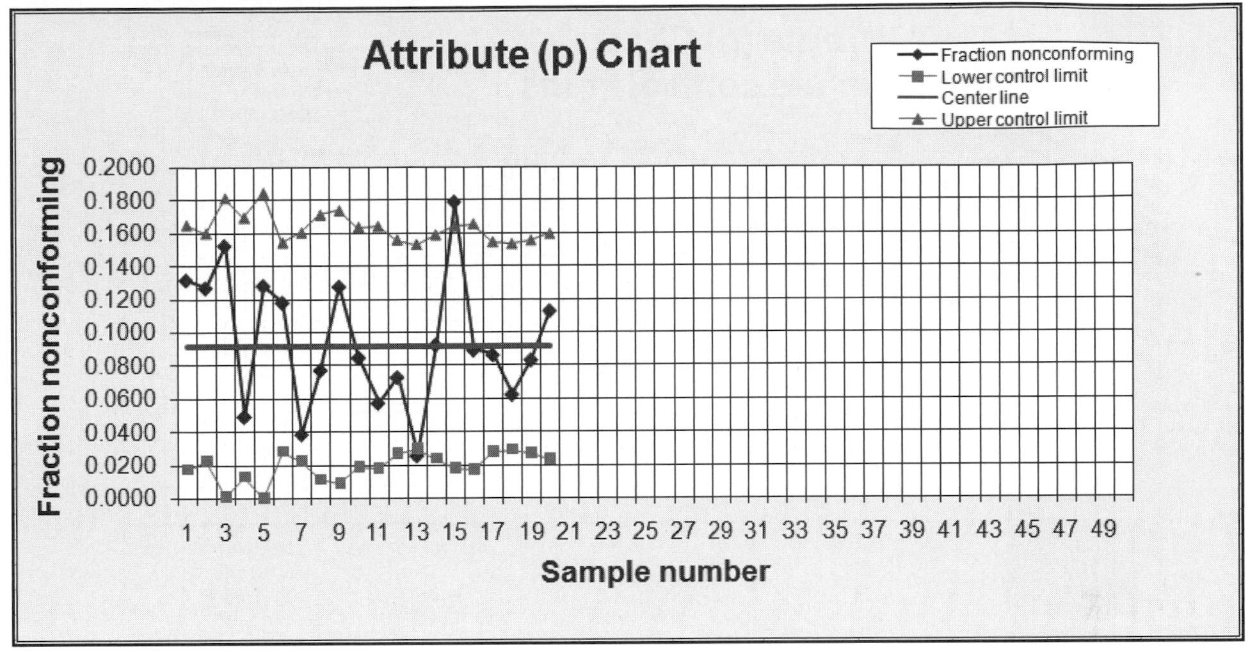

An alternative approach is to use the average sample size, $\overline{n}$, to compute approximate control limits. Using the average sample size, the control limits are computed as

$$UCL_p = \overline{p} + 3\sqrt{\frac{\overline{p}(1-\overline{p})}{\overline{n}}}$$

and

$$LCL_p = \overline{p} - 3\sqrt{\frac{\overline{p}(1-\overline{p})}{\overline{n}}} \quad (13.14)$$

These result in an approximation to the true control limits. For the data in Figure 13.32, the average sample size is $\overline{n} = 2{,}980/20 = 149$. Using this value, the upper control limit is calculated to be 0.1616, and the lower control limit is 0.0202. However, this approach has several disadvantages. Because the control limits are only approximate, points that are actually out of control may not appear to be so on this chart. Second, runs or nonrandom patterns are difficult to interpret because the standard deviation differs between samples as a result of the variable sample sizes. Hence, this approach should be used with caution. Figure 13.34 shows the control chart for this example with approximate control limits using the average sample size. Note the difference in sample 13; this chart shows that it is in control, whereas the true control limits show that this point is out of control.

As a general guideline, use the average sample size method when the sample sizes fall within 25 percent of the average. For this example, 25 percent of 149 is 37.25. Thus, the average could be used for sample sizes between 112 and 186. This guideline would exclude samples 3, 6, 9, 11, 13, and 18, whose control limits should be computed exactly. If the calculations are performed on a computer, sample size is not an issue.

Figure 13.34 *p*-Chart for Variable Sample Size Example (Average Sample Size Used)

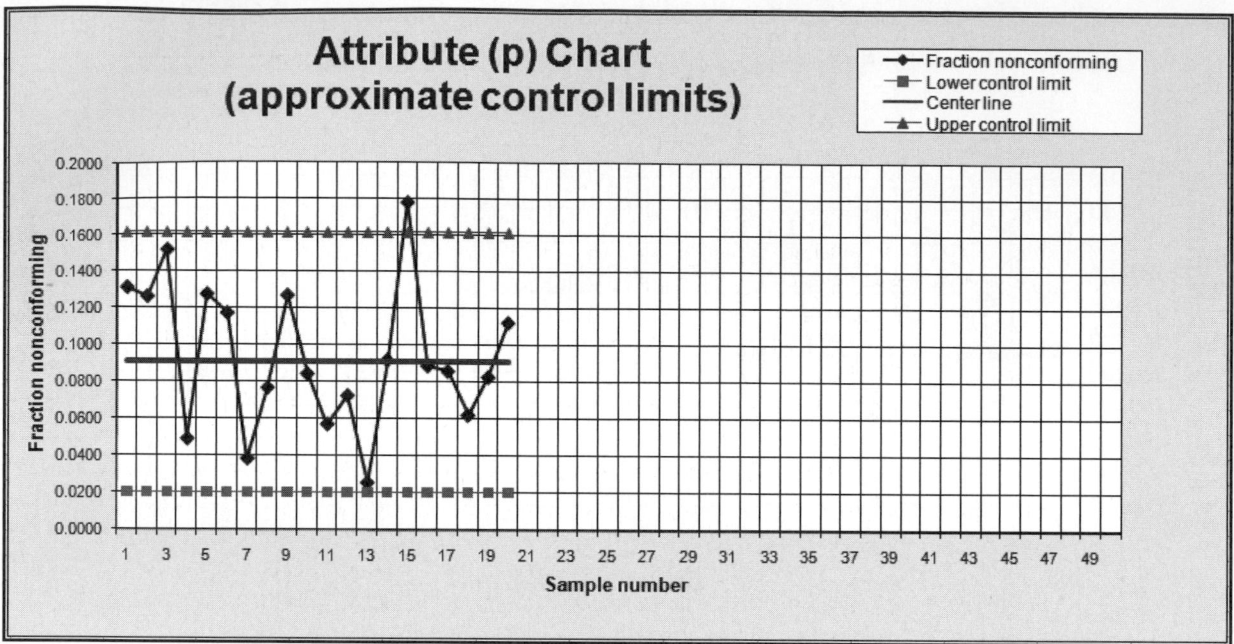

np-Charts for Number Nonconforming

In the *p*-chart, the fraction nonconforming of the *i*th sample is given by

$$p_i = y_i/n \tag{13.15}$$

where y_i is the number found nonconforming and n is the sample size. Multiplying both sides of the equation $p_i = y_i/n_i$ yields $y_i = np_i$. That is, the number nonconforming is equal to the sample size times the proportion nonconforming. Instead of using a chart for the fraction nonconforming, an equivalent alternative—a chart for the *number* of nonconforming items—is useful. Such a control chart is called an ***np*-chart**.

The *np*-chart is a control chart for the number of nonconforming items in a sample. To use the *np*-chart, the size of each sample *must be constant*. Suppose that two samples of sizes 10 and 15 each have four nonconforming items. Clearly, the fraction nonconforming in each sample is different, which would be reflected in a *p*-chart. An *np*-chart, however, would indicate no difference between samples. Thus, equal sample sizes are necessary to have a common base for measurement. Equal sample sizes are not required for *p*-charts, because the fraction nonconforming is invariant to the sample size.

The *np*-chart is a useful alternative to the *p*-chart because it is often easier to understand for production personnel—the *number* of nonconforming items is more meaningful than a fraction. Also, it requires only a count, making the computations simpler.

The control limits for the *np*-chart, like those for the *p*-chart, are based on the binomial probability distribution. The center line is the average number of nonconforming items per sample as denoted by $n\overline{p}$, which is calculated by taking k samples of size n, summing the number of nonconforming items y_i in each sample, and dividing by k. That is,

$$n\overline{p} = \frac{y_1 + y_2 + \cdots + y_k}{k} \tag{13.16}$$

Figure 13.35 Data and Calculations for *np*-Chart

	A	B	C	D	E	F	G	H
1	**Number Nonconforming (np) Chart**							
2	This spreadsheet is designed for up to 50 samples. Enter data ONLY in yellow-shaded cells.							
3	Each sample must have a constant sample size; enter this in cell C6.							
4	Click on the sheet tab to display the control chart (some rescaling may be needed).							
5								
6	**Sample size**		100					
7								
8	**Average (np-bar)**		2.2					
9	**Standard deviation**		1.466833324					
10								
11		**Number**						
12	**Sample**	**Nonconformin**	**LCLnp**	**CL**	**UCLnp**			
13	1	3	0	2.2	6.6005			
14	2	1	0	2.2	6.6005			
15	3	0	0	2.2	6.6005			
16	4	0	0	2.2	6.6005			
17	5	2	0	2.2	6.6005			
18	6	5	0	2.2	6.6005			
19	7	3	0	2.2	6.6005			
20	8	6	0	2.2	6.6005			
21	9	1	0	2.2	6.6005			
22	10	4	0	2.2	6.6005			
23	11	0	0	2.2	6.6005			
24	12	2	0	2.2	6.6005			
25	13	1	0	2.2	6.6005			
26	14	3	0	2.2	6.6005			
27	15	4	0	2.2	6.6005			
28	16	1	0	2.2	6.6005			
29	17	1	0	2.2	6.6005			
30	18	2	0	2.2	6.6005			
31	19	5	0	2.2	6.6005			
32	20	2	0	2.2	6.6005			
33	21	3	0	2.2	6.6005			
34	22	4	0	2.2	6.6005			
35	23	1	0	2.2	6.6005			
36	24	0	0	2.2	6.6005			
37	25	1	0	2.2	6.6005			

An estimate of the standard deviation is

$$s_{n\bar{p}} = \sqrt{n\bar{p}(1-\bar{p})} \tag{13.17}$$

where $\bar{p} = (n\bar{p})/n$. Using 3σ limits as before, the control limits are specified by

$$\begin{aligned} UCL_{n\bar{p}} &= n\bar{p} + 3\sqrt{n\bar{p}(1-\bar{p})} \\ LCL_{n\bar{p}} &= n\bar{p} - 3\sqrt{n\bar{p}(1-\bar{p})} \end{aligned} \tag{13.18}$$

The data for the post office example discussed earlier is given in Figure 13.35 (Excel template *np-chart*). The average number of errors found is:

$$n\bar{p} = \frac{3 + 1 + \cdots + 0 + 1}{25} = 2.2$$

Figure 13.36 *np*-Chart

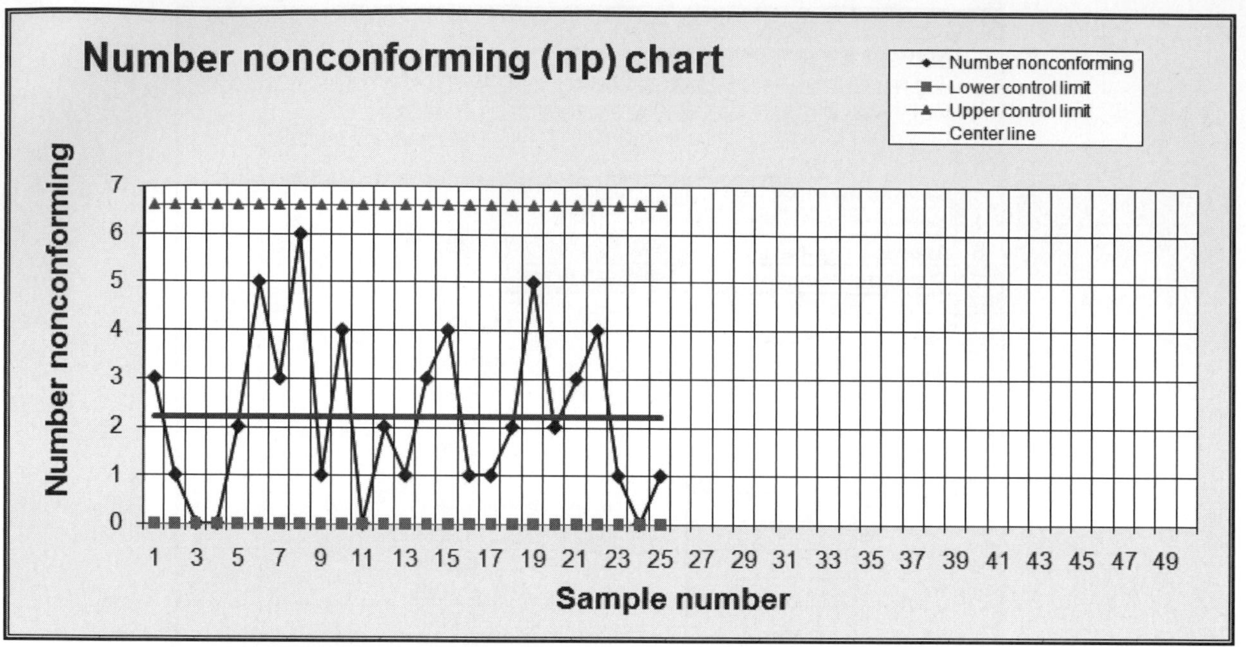

To find the standard deviation, we first compute

$$\bar{p} = \frac{2.2}{100} = 0.022$$

Then,

$$\begin{aligned} s_{n\bar{p}} &= \sqrt{2.2(1 - 0.022)} \\ &= \sqrt{2.2(0.978)} \\ &= \sqrt{2.1516} = 1.4668 \end{aligned}$$

The control limits are then computed as

$$\begin{aligned} \text{UCL}_{n\bar{p}} &= 2.2 + 3(1.4668) = 6.6 \\ \text{LCL}_{n\bar{p}} &= 2.2 - 3(1.4668) = -2.20 \end{aligned}$$

Because the lower control limit is less than zero, a value of 0 is used. The control chart for this example is given in Figure 13.36.

Charts for Nonconformances

In many situations, we may be interested not only in whether a unit of work is nonconforming, but also in how many nonconformances it has. For example, a hotel might be interested in measuring the number of nonconformances per room associated with housekeeping, or an electronics manufacturer might wish to measure the number of defects per circuit board during the manufacturing process. Two charts can be applied in such situations. The ***c*-chart** is used to control the total number of nonconformances per unit when subgroup size is constant. If subgroup sizes are variable, a ***u*-chart** is used to control the average number of nonconformances per unit.

Figure 13.37 Data and Calculations for *c*-Chart Example

	A	B	C	D	E	F	G
1	**Average Number of Nonconformances (c) Chart**						
2	This spreadsheet is designed for up to 50 samples. Enter data ONLY in yellow-shaded cells.						
3	Click on the sheet tab to display the control chart (some rescaling may be needed).						
4							
5	**Average (c-bar)**		1.8				
6	**Standard deviation**		1.341640786				
7							
8		**Number of**					
9	**Sample**	**Nonconformances**	**LCLc**	**CL**	**UCLc**		
10	1	2	0	1.8	5.824922		
11	2	3	0	1.8	5.824922		
12	3	0	0	1.8	5.824922		
13	4	1	0	1.8	5.824922		
14	5	3	0	1.8	5.824922		
15	6	5	0	1.8	5.824922		
16	7	3	0	1.8	5.824922		
17	8	1	0	1.8	5.824922		
18	9	2	0	1.8	5.824922		
19	10	2	0	1.8	5.824922		
20	11	0	0	1.8	5.824922		
21	12	1	0	1.8	5.824922		
22	13	0	0	1.8	5.824922		
23	14	2	0	1.8	5.824922		
24	15	4	0	1.8	5.824922		
25	16	1	0	1.8	5.824922		
26	17	2	0	1.8	5.824922		
27	18	0	0	1.8	5.824922		
28	19	3	0	1.8	5.824922		
29	20	2	0	1.8	5.824922		
30	21	1	0	1.8	5.824922		
31	22	4	0	1.8	5.824922		
32	23	0	0	1.8	5.824922		
33	24	0	0	1.8	5.824922		
34	25	3	0	1.8	5.824922		

The *c*-chart is based on the Poisson probability distribution. To construct a *c*-chart, first estimate the average number of defects per unit, $\bar{c}$, by taking at least 25 samples of equal size, counting the number of defects per sample, and finding the average. The standard deviation of the Poisson distribution is the square root of the mean and yields

$$s_c = \sqrt{\bar{c}} \tag{13.19}$$

Thus, 3σ control limits are given by

$$\begin{aligned} \text{UCL}_c &= \bar{c} + 3\sqrt{\bar{c}} \\ \text{LCL}_c &= \bar{c} - 3\sqrt{\bar{c}} \end{aligned} \tag{13.20}$$

Figure 13.37 shows the number of machine failures over a 25-day period (Excel template *c-chart*). The total number of failures is 45; therefore, the average number of failures per day is

$$\bar{c} = 45/25 = 1.8$$

Figure 13.38 *c*-Chart

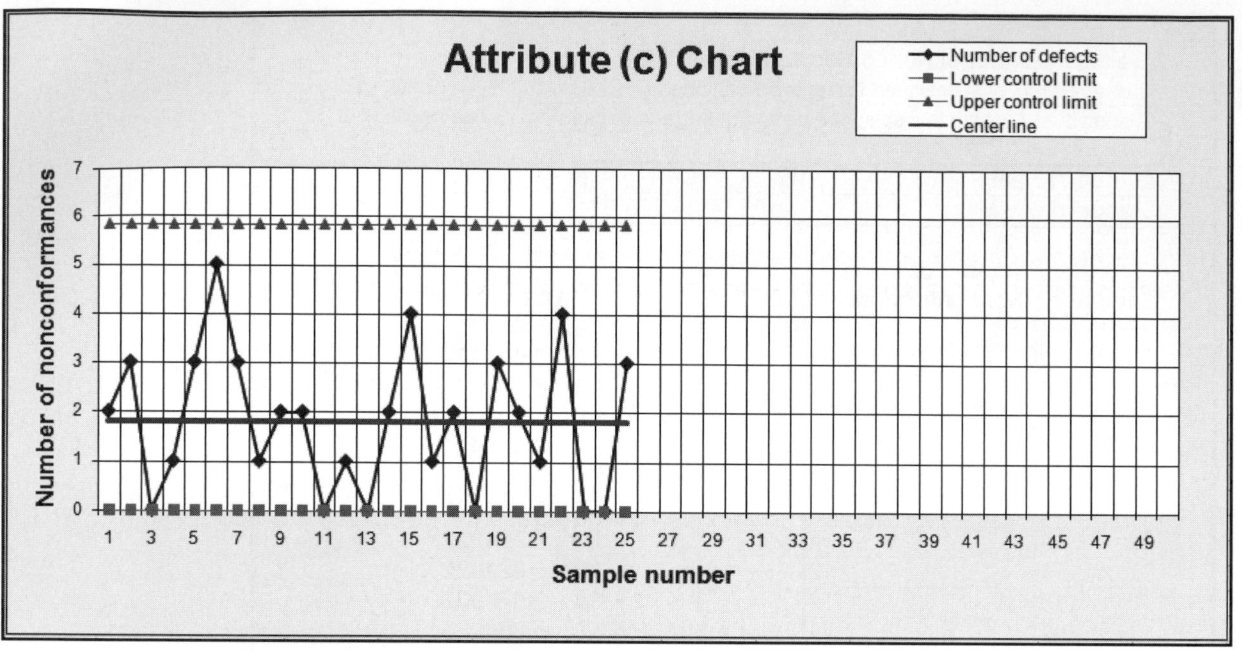

Control limits for a *c*-chart are therefore given by

$$UCL_c = 1.8 + 3\sqrt{1.8} = 5.82$$
$$LCL_c = 1.8 - 3\sqrt{1.8} = -2.22, \text{ or zero}$$

The chart is shown in Figure 13.38 and appears to be in control. Such a chart can be used for continued control or for monitoring the effectiveness of a quality improvement program.

As long as the subgroup size is constant, a *c*-chart is appropriate. In many cases, however, the subgroup size is not constant or the nature of the production process does not yield discrete, measurable units. For example, in administering daily drugs to patients, the opportunity for errors would vary by patient because the number of medications prescribed is often different. Simply counting the number of errors per day would not then be a valid comparison as the patient mix changes. Other applications, such as the production of textiles, photographic film, or paper, have no convenient set of items to measure. In such cases, a standard unit of measurement is used, such as defects per square meter or per square inch. The control chart for these situations is the *u*-chart.

The variable u represents the average number of defects per unit of measurement, that is $u = c/n$, where n is the size of the subgroup (such as square feet). The center line $\overline{u}$ for k samples each of size n_i is computed as follows:

$$\overline{u} = \frac{c_1 + c_2 + \cdots + c_k}{n_1 + n_2 + \cdots + n_k} \tag{13.21}$$

The standard deviation of the *i*th sample is estimated by

$$s_u = \sqrt{\overline{u}/n_i} \tag{13.22}$$

The control limits, based on three standard deviations for the ith sample, are then

$$\begin{aligned} \text{UCL}_u &= \bar{u} + 3\sqrt{\bar{u}/n_i} \\ \text{LCL}_u &= \bar{u} - 3\sqrt{\bar{u}/n_i} \end{aligned} \qquad (13.23)$$

similar to the p-chart with variable sample sizes. Note that if the size of the subgroups varies, so will the control limits. This is similar to the p-chart with variable sample size.

Suppose that a catalog distributor ships a variety of orders each day. The packing slips often contain errors such as wrong purchase order numbers, wrong quantities, or incorrect sizes. Because the sample size varies each day in the following example, a u-chart is appropriate. Figure 13.39 shows the error data collected during August (Excel template *u-chart*).

To construct the u-chart, first compute the number of errors per slip as shown in column 3. The average number of errors per slip, $\bar{u}$, is found by dividing the total number of errors (209) by the total number of packing slips (2,765):

$$\bar{u} = 209/2765 = 0.0756$$

The standard deviation for a particular sample size n_i is therefore

$$s_u = \sqrt{0.0756/n_i}$$

The control limits are shown in the spreadsheet. As with a p-chart, individual control limits will vary with the sample size. The control chart is shown in Figure 13.40. One point (#2) appears to be out of control.

One application of c-charts and u-charts is in a quality rating system. When some defects are considered to be more serious than others, they can be rated, or categorized, into different classes. For instance,

A – very serious
B – serious
C – moderately serious
D – not serious

Each category can be weighted using a point scale, such as 100 for A, 50 for B, 10 for C, and 1 for D.[3] These points, or demerits, can be used as the basis for a c- or u-chart that would measure total demerits or demerits per unit, respectively. Such charts are often used for internal quality control and as a means of rating suppliers.

Choosing between c- and u-Charts

The key issue in selecting between c- and u-charts to consider is *whether the sampling unit is constant*. For example, suppose that an electronics manufacturer produces circuit boards. The boards may contain various defects, such as faulty components and missing connections. Because the sampling unit—the circuit board—is constant (assuming that all boards are the same), a c-chart is appropriate to monitor the number of defects per unit. If the process produces boards of varying sizes with different numbers of components and connections, then a u-chart would apply.

Confusion often exists over which chart is appropriate for a specific application, because the c- and u-charts apply to situations in which the quality characteristics inspected do not necessarily come from discrete units.

Figure 13.39 Data and Calculations for *u*-Chart Example

	A	B	C	D	E	F	G	H
1	**Average Number of Nonconformances Per Unit (u) Chart**							
2	This spreadsheet is designed for up to 75 samples. Enter data ONLY in yellow-shaded cells.							
3	Click on the sheet tab to display the control chart (some rescaling may be needed).							
4								
5	**Average (u-bar)**		**0.075587703**					
6								
7			**Sample**					
8		**Number of**	**Unit**	**Defects**	**Standard**			
9	**Sample**	**Nonconformance**	**Size**	**per unit**	**Deviatior**	**LCLu**	**CL**	**UCLu**
10	1	8	92	0.0870	0.0286637	0	0.0756	0.1616
11	2	15	69	0.2174	0.0330979	0	0.0756	0.1749
12	3	6	86	0.0698	0.0296467	0	0.0756	0.1645
13	4	13	85	0.1529	0.0298206	0	0.0756	0.165
14	5	5	123	0.0407	0.0247898	0.0012	0.0756	0.15
15	6	5	87	0.0575	0.0294758	0	0.0756	0.164
16	7	3	74	0.0405	0.0319602	0	0.0756	0.1715
17	8	8	83	0.0964	0.0301777	0	0.0756	0.1661
18	9	4	103	0.0388	0.0270899	0	0.0756	0.1569
19	10	6	60	0.1000	0.0354936	0	0.0756	0.1821
20	11	7	136	0.0515	0.0235752	0.0049	0.0756	0.1463
21	12	4	80	0.0500	0.0307384	0	0.0756	0.1678
22	13	2	70	0.0286	0.0328607	0	0.0756	0.1742
23	14	11	73	0.1507	0.0321784	0	0.0756	0.1721
24	15	13	89	0.1461	0.0291428	0	0.0756	0.163
25	16	6	129	0.0465	0.0242064	0.003	0.0756	0.1482
26	17	6	78	0.0769	0.0311299	0	0.0756	0.169
27	18	3	88	0.0341	0.0293079	0	0.0756	0.1635
28	19	8	76	0.1053	0.0315369	0	0.0756	0.1702
29	20	9	101	0.0891	0.0273568	0	0.0756	0.1577
30	21	8	92	0.0870	0.0286637	0	0.0756	0.1616
31	22	2	70	0.0286	0.0328607	0	0.0756	0.1742
32	23	9	54	0.1667	0.0374135	0	0.0756	0.1878
33	24	5	83	0.0602	0.0301777	0	0.0756	0.1661
34	25	13	165	0.0788	0.0214034	0.0114	0.0756	0.1398
35	26	5	137	0.0365	0.023489	0.0051	0.0756	0.1461
36	27	8	79	0.1013	0.0309323	0	0.0756	0.1684
37	28	6	76	0.0789	0.0315369	0	0.0756	0.1702
38	29	7	147	0.0476	0.022676	0.0076	0.0756	0.1436
39	30	4	80	0.0500	0.0307384	0	0.0756	0.1678

Figure 13.40 *u*-Chart

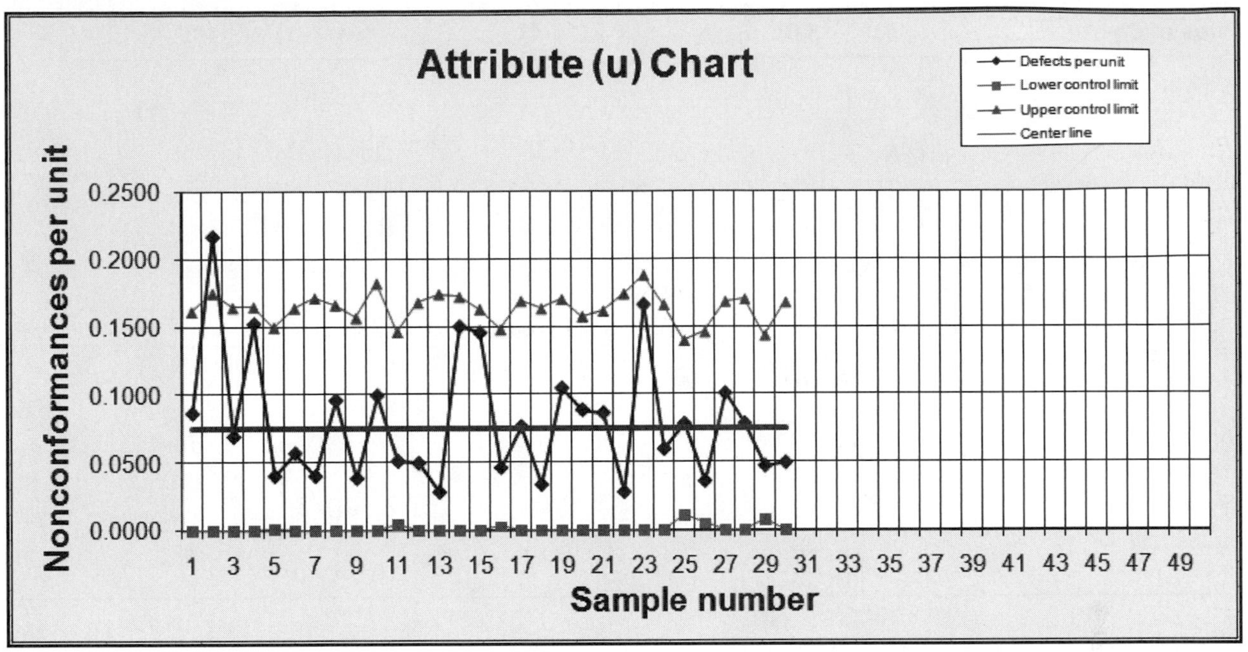

As another example, consider a telemarketing firm that wants to track the number of calls needed to make one sale. In this case, the firm has no physical sampling unit. However, an analogy can be made with the circuit boards. The sale corresponds to the circuit board, and the number of calls to the number of defects. In both examples, the number of occurrences in relationship to a constant entity is being measured. Thus, a *c*-chart is appropriate.

SUMMARY OF CONTROL CHART CONSTRUCTION

Table 13.2 summarizes the formulas used for constructing the different types of control charts discussed thus far. The Bonus Materials folder on the Premier website contains a discussion of some advanced types of control charts used in special situations. Figure 13.41 provides a summary of guidelines for chart selection.

A wide variety of commercial software is available to implement SPC. For example, one of the more recent packages is *CHARTrunner 2000*, product of PQ Systems (http://www.pqsystems.com). *CHARTrunner* generates SPC charts and performs statistical analyses using data that are collected, stored, and managed by other applications such as Microsoft Access or Excel, SQL Server, Oracle, text files, and many others. It generates control charts, as well as histograms, process capability results, Pareto charts, scatter diagrams, and others; performs curve fitting and linear regression; and allows users to customize out-of-control tests, select colors for sigma zones, display multiple sets of control limits, and save charts as image files. Software surveys can often be found in such professional publications as *Quality Progress* (http://www.asq.org) and *Quality Digest* (http://www.qualitydigest.com).

Table 13.2 Summary of Control Chart Formulas

Type of Chart	LCL	CL	UCL
$\bar{x}$ (with R)	$\bar{\bar{x}} - A_2\bar{R}$	$\bar{\bar{x}}$	$\bar{\bar{x}} + A_2\bar{R}$
R	$D_3\bar{R}$	$\bar{R}$	$D_4\bar{R}$
p	$\bar{p} - 3\sqrt{\bar{p}(1-\bar{p})/n}$	$\bar{p}$	$\bar{p} + 3\sqrt{\bar{p}(1-\bar{p})/n}$
$\bar{x}$ (with s)	$\bar{\bar{x}} - A_3\bar{s}$	$\bar{\bar{x}}$	$\bar{\bar{x}} + A_2\bar{s}$
s	$B_3\bar{s}$	$\bar{s}$	$B_4\bar{s}$
x	$\bar{x} - 3\bar{R}/d_2$	$\bar{x}$	$\bar{x} + 3\bar{R}/d_2$
np	$n\bar{p} - 3\sqrt{n\bar{p}(1-\bar{p})}$	$n\bar{p}$	$n\bar{p} + 3\sqrt{n\bar{p}(1-\bar{p})}$
c	$\bar{c} - 3\sqrt{\bar{c}}$	$\bar{c}$	$\bar{c} + 3\sqrt{\bar{c}}$
u	$\bar{u} - 3\sqrt{\bar{u}/n}$	$\bar{u}$	$\bar{u} + 3\sqrt{\bar{u}/n}$

Figure 13.41 Control Chart Selection

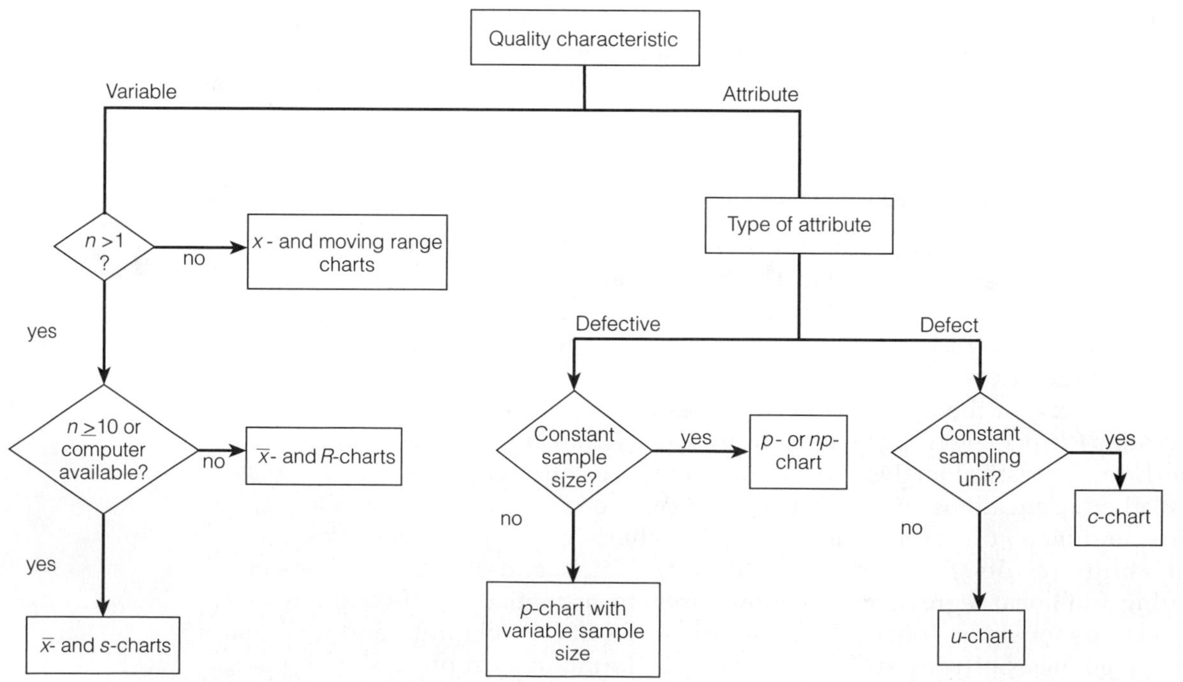

DESIGNING CONTROL CHARTS

Designers of control charts must consider four issues: (1) the basis for sampling, (2) the sample size, (3) the frequency of sampling, and (4) the location of the control limits.

Basis for Sampling

The purpose of a control chart is to identify the variation in a system that may change over time. In one case, a hospital was monitoring the waiting time in its emergency room. In constructing a control chart, five patients were chosen randomly over the course of each shift. In this example, it is unlikely that process conditions would remain stable over an entire working shift. Thus, little useful information was provided in the chart. First, any change in the process average during a shift would not be reflected in the data, and second, a change in the process level would cause points on the R-chart to be out of control, even if no change in the variability of the process actually occurred. A good sampling method should have the property that, if assignable causes are present, the chance of observing differences between samples is high, whereas the chance of observing differences within a sample is low. Samples that satisfy these criteria are called **rational subgroups**.

One approach to constructing rational subgroups is to use consecutive measurements over a short period of time. Consecutive measurements minimize the chance of variability within the sample while allowing variation between samples to be detected. This approach is useful when control charts are used to detect shifts in process level. One must also be careful not to overlap production shifts, different batches of material, and so on, when selecting the basis for sampling. Thus, the method of selecting samples should be chosen carefully so as not to bias the results.

In determining the method of sampling, samples should be chosen to be as homogeneous as possible so that each sample reflects the system of common causes or assignable causes that may be present at that point in time.

Sample Size

Sample size is a second critical design issue. A small sample size is desirable to minimize the opportunity for within-sample variation due to special causes. This issue is important because each sample should be representative of the state of control at one point in time. In addition, the cost of sampling should be kept low. The time an employee spends taking the sample measurements and plotting a control chart represents nonproductive time (in a strict accounting sense only!). On the other hand, control limits are based on the assumption of a normal distribution of the sample means. If the process is not normal, this assumption is valid only for large samples. Large samples also allow smaller changes in process characteristics to be detected with higher probability.

In practice, samples of about five have been found to work well in detecting process shifts of two standard deviations or larger. To detect smaller shifts in the process mean, larger sample sizes of 15 to 25 must be used.

Figure 13.42 shows the probability of detecting a shift in the mean in the next sample (that is, the probability of seeing the next point outside the 3σ control limit when the process has shifted some number of standard deviations) as a function of the sample size for an $\bar{x}$-chart. Thus, if a process has shifted 1.5 standard deviations,

Figure 13.42 Probability of Detecting a Shift in Mean

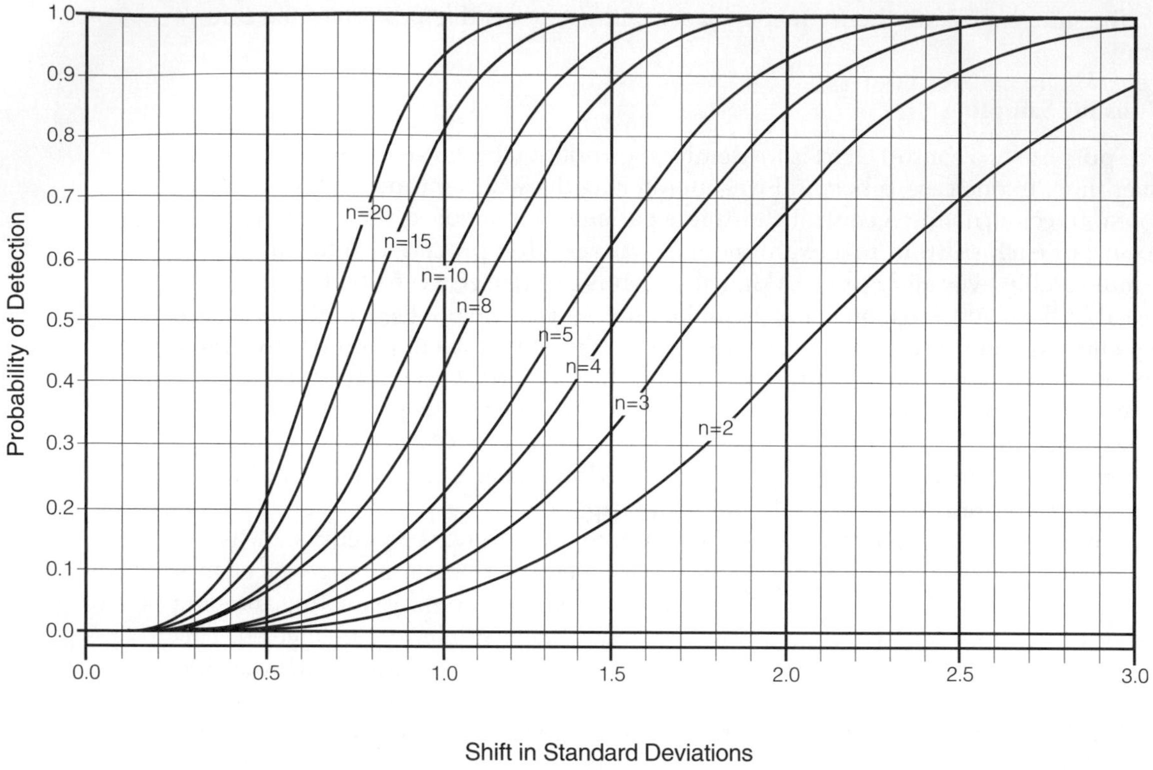

Source: Reprinted with permission from Lyle Dockendorf, "Choosing Appropriate Sample Subgroup Sizes for Control Charts," *Quality Progress* Vol. 25, no. 10, p. 160, October 1992. Copyright © 1992 American Society for Quality. No further distribution allowed without permission.

a sample size of 5 provides only a 64 percent chance of detection. For a 90 percent chance of detecting this particular process shift, a sample of at least 8 is needed.

For attributes data, too small a sample size can make a *p*-chart meaningless. Even though many guidelines such as "use at least 100 observations" have been suggested, the proper sample size should be determined statistically, particularly when the true portion of nonconformances is small. If p is small, n should be large enough to have a high probability of detecting at least one nonconformance. For example, if $p = 0.01$, then to have at least a 95 percent chance of finding at least one nonconformance, the sample size must be at least 300. Other approaches for determining attribute data sample sizes include choosing n large enough to provide a 50 percent chance of detecting a process shift of some specified amount, or choosing n so that the control chart will have a positive lower control limit. The reader is referred to the book by Montgomery in the bibliography for details on these calculations.

Sampling Frequency

The third design issue is the sampling frequency. Taking large samples on a frequent basis is desirable but clearly not economical. No hard-and-fast rules exist for the frequency of sampling. Samples should be close enough to provide an opportunity to detect changes in process characteristics as soon as possible and reduce the chances of producing a large amount of nonconforming output. However, they should not be so close that the cost of sampling outweighs the benefits that can be realized. This decision depends on the individual application and production volume.

Location of Control Limits

Using the analogy with errors in statistical hypothesis testing, a Type I error occurs when an incorrect conclusion is reached that a *special cause is present when in fact one does not exist* and results in the cost of trying to find a nonexistent problem. A Type II error occurs when *special causes are present but are not signaled in the control chart* because points fall within the control limits by chance. Because nonconforming products have a greater chance to be produced, a cost will eventually be incurred as a result. The size of a Type I error depends only on the control limits that are used; the wider the limits, the less chance of a point falling outside the limits, and consequently the smaller is the chance of making a Type I error. A Type II error, however, depends on the width of the control limits, the degree to which the process is out of control, and the sample size. For a fixed sample size, wider control limits increase the risk of making a Type II error. The traditional approach of using 3σ limits implicitly assumes that the cost of a Type I error is large relative to that of a Type II error; that is, a Type I error is essentially minimized. This situation will not always be the case, however.

Much research has been performed on economic design of control charts.[4] Cost models attempt to find the best combination of design parameters (center line, control limits, sample size, and sampling interval) that minimize expected cost or maximize expected profit. Certain costs are associated with making both Type I and Type II errors. A Type I error results in unnecessary investigation for an assignable cause, including costs of lost production time and special testing. A Type II error can be more significant. If an out-of-control process is not recognized, defectives that are produced may result in higher costs of scrap and rework in later stages of production or after the finished good reaches the customer. Unfortunately, the cost of a Type II error is nearly impossible to estimate because it depends on the number of nonconforming items—a quantity that is unknown.

The location of control limits is closely related to the risk involved in making an incorrect assessment about the state of control.

The costs associated with Type I and Type II errors conflict as control limits change. The tighter the control limits, the greater is the probability that a sample will indicate that the process is out of control. Hence, the cost of a Type I error increases as control limits are reduced. On the other hand, tighter control limits will reduce the cost of a Type II error, because out-of-control states will be more easily identified and the amount of defective output will be reduced. The costs associated with sampling and testing may include lost productive time when the process owner takes sample measurements, performs calculations, and plots the points on the control chart. If the testing is destructive, the value of lost units would also be included. Thus, larger sample sizes and more frequent sampling result in higher costs.

The sample size and frequency also affect the costs of Type I and Type II errors. As the sample size or frequency is increased, both Type I and Type II errors are reduced, because better information is provided for decision making. Table 13.3 summarizes this discussion of the three-way interaction of costs. In the economic design of control charts we must consider these simultaneously. Most models for such decisions can become quite complex and are beyond the scope of this text.

Table 13.3 Economic Decisions for Control Chart Construction

Source of Cost	Sample Size	Sampling Frequency	Control Limits
Type I error	Large	High	Wide
Type II error	Large	High	Narrow
Sampling and testing	Small	Low	—

As a practical matter, one often uses judgment about the nature of operations and the costs involved in making these decisions. Raymond Mayer suggests the following guidelines:

1. If the cost of investigating an operation to identify the cause of an apparent out-of-control condition is high, a Type I error becomes important, and wider control limits should be adopted. Conversely, if that cost is low, narrower limits should be selected.
2. If the cost of the defective output generated by an operation is substantial, a Type II error is serious, and narrower control limits should be used. Otherwise, wider limits should be selected.
3. If the cost of a Type I error and the cost of a Type II error for a given activity are both significant, wide control limits should be chosen, and consideration should be given to reducing the risk of a Type II error by increasing the sample size. Also, more frequent samples should be taken to reduce the duration of any out-of-control condition that might occur.
4. If past experience with an operation indicates that an out-of-control condition arises quite frequently, narrower control limits should be favored because of the large number of opportunities for making a Type II error. In the event that the probability of an out-of-control condition is small, wider limits are preferred.[5]

SPC, ISO 9000:2000, AND SIX SIGMA

ISO 9000:2000 places increased emphasis on the use of statistical methods compared with the previous version.[6] For example, the standards require "applicable methods, including statistical techniques" be identified and used for monitoring and measuring products and processes, and that through monitoring and measurement, the organization can demonstrate the ability of processes to meet requirements and that product requirements have been met. A new ISO standard, 11462-1, provides guidance for organizations wishing to use SPC to meet these requirements. The standard addresses the following elements:

- *Definition of SPC goals.* Such goals might include reducing variation around target values and compensating for process variation to ensure product conformity, reducing costs, indicating how the process is likely to behave in the future, and quantifying process capability.
- *Conditions for a successful SPC system.* These conditions include integration with a formal quality management system, management support, use of information for data-driven decisions and management reviews, and ensuring the competence of those who will be using the tools.
- *Elements of the SPC system.* These address the processes an organization should implement and actions it should take to ensure that a successful SPC system includes both operational and support activities. These elements can be

organized into a Plan-Do-Study-Act framework, and include a process documentation and control plan, definition of process targets and limits, data collection, measuring equipment, data recording and analysis, process control, short- and long-term process capability assessment, communication of results, and process improvement implementation and project management activities. This standard can provide useful assistance for organizations that are beginning to develop a formal SPC approach.

Controlling Six Sigma Processes[7]

SPC is a useful methodology for processes that operate at a low sigma level, for example 3-sigma or less. However, when the rate of defects is extremely low, standard control charts are not effective. For example, in using a *p*-chart for a process with a high sigma level, few defectives will be discovered even with large sample sizes. For instance, if $p = 0.001$, a sample size of 500 will only have an expected number of $500(0.001) = 0.5$ defects. Hence, most samples will have only zero or one defect, and the chart will provide little useful information for control. Using much larger sample sizes would only delay the timeliness of information and increase the chances that the process may have changed during the sampling interval. Small sample sizes will typically result in a conclusion that any observed defect indicates an out-of-control condition, thus, implying that a controlled process will have zero defects, which may be impractical. In addition, conventional SPC charts will have higher frequencies of false alarms and make it difficult to evaluate process improvements. These issues are important for Six Sigma Green Belts and Black Belts to understand.

One way of handling this situation is to use variable data rather than attribute data; however, this approach may be prohibitive from a cost or physical standpoint. An alternative for attribute data is to construct a **cumulative count of conforming (CCC) chart** to monitor the total number of conforming items until a defective item is found. The control limits for this type of chart are

$$\begin{aligned} LCL &= \ln(1-\alpha/2)/\ln(1-p) \\ CL &= \ln(0.5)/\ln(1-p) \\ UCL &= \ln(\alpha/2)/\ln(1-p) \end{aligned}$$

where α is the risk of a false alarm, for example, 0.0027, the value traditionally used for standard control charts. This level can be adjusted for different processes, depending on their criticality and costs of adjustments. A value that exceeds UCL indicates the process has likely improved; a value lower than LCL indicates deterioration of the process. Other advanced techniques are also available.

PRE-CONTROL[8]

Pre-control is a technique useful in operations such as machining, where quality characteristics are easily monitored and can be adjusted. It is valuable for monitoring process capability over time. A major advantage of pre-control is its direct relationship to specifications, which requires no recording, calculating, or plotting of data. The idea behind pre-control is to divide the tolerance range into zones by setting two *pre-control lines* halfway between the center of the specification and the tolerance limits (see Figure 13.43). The center zone, called the *green zone*, comprises one-half of the total tolerance. Between the pre-control lines and the tolerance limits are the *yellow zones*. Outside the tolerance limits are the *red zones*.

Figure 13.43 Pre-Control Ranges

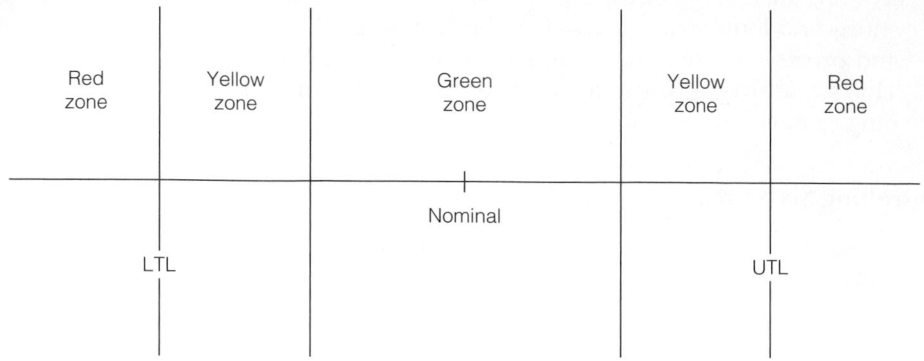

Pre-control is applied as follows. As a manufacturing run is initiated, five consecutive parts must fall within the green zone. If not, the production setup must be reevaluated before the full production run can be started. Once regular operations commence, two parts are sampled; if the first falls within the green zone, production continues, which eliminates the need to measure the second part. If the first part falls in a yellow zone, the second part is inspected. If the second part falls in the green zone, production can continue; if not, production should stop and a special cause should be investigated. If any part falls in a red zone, then action should be taken.

The rationale behind pre-control can be explained using basic statistical arguments. Suppose that the process capability is equal to the tolerance spread (see Figure 13.44). The area of each yellow zone is approximately 0.07, whereas that of the red zone is less than 0.01. The probability of two consecutive parts falling in a yellow zone is (0.07)(0.07) = 0.0049 if the process mean has not shifted. If $C_p > 1$, this probability is even less. Such an outcome would more than likely indicate a special cause. If both parts fall in the same yellow zone, you would conclude that the mean has shifted; if in different yellow zones, you would conclude that the variation has increased.

The frequency of sampling is often determined by dividing the time period between two successive out-of-control signals by six. Thus, if the process deteriorates, sampling frequency is increased; if it improves, the frequency is decreased. For example, the force necessary to break a wire used in electrical circuitry has a specification of 3 gm–7 gm. Thus, the pre-control zones are

Figure 13.44 Basis for Pre-Control Rules

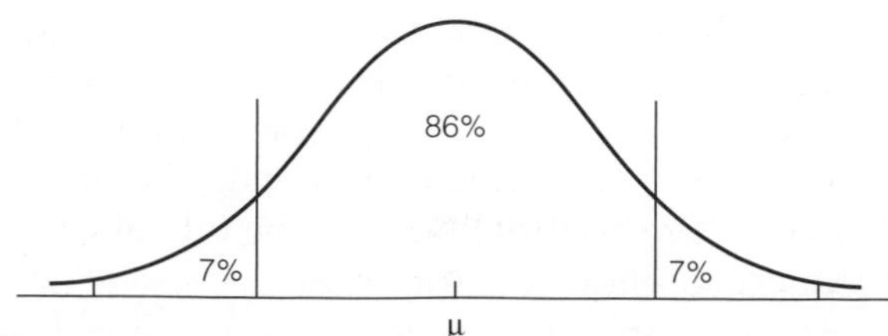

Range	Zone
<3	Red
3–4	Yellow
4–6	Green
6–7	Yellow
>7	Red

The following samples were collected:

Sample	First Measurement Value	Second Measurement Value
1	4.7	
2	4.5	
3	4.4	
4	4.2	
5	4.2	
6	4.0	
7	4.0	
8	3.7	3.6
9	6.5	3.5

For samples 1 through 7, the first measurement falls in the green zone; thus no further action need be taken. For sample 8, however, the first measurement falls in a yellow zone. The second measurement also falls in a yellow zone. The process should be stopped for investigation of a shift in the mean. At the next time of inspection, both pieces also fall in a yellow zone. In this case, the probable cause is a shift in variation. Again, the process should be stopped for investigation.

Pre-control is not an adequate substitute for control charts and should only be used when process capability is no greater than 88 percent of the tolerance, or equivalently, when C_p is at least 1.14. If the process mean tends to drift, then C_p should be higher.

If managers or operators are interested in detecting process shifts even though the product output falls within specifications, pre-control should not be used because it will not detect such shifts.

SUMMARY OF KEY POINTS AND TERMINOLOGY

BONUS MATERIALS

The Bonus Materials folder on the Premium website, provides a summary of key concepts and terminology introduced in this chapter.

QUALITY IN PRACTICE

APPLYING SPC TO PHARMACEUTICAL PRODUCT MANUFACTURING[9]

A Midwest pharmaceutical company manufactures (in two stages) individual syringes with a self-contained, single dose of an injectable drug. In the first stage, sterile liquid drug is filled into glass syringes and sealed with a rubber stopper. The remaining stage involves insertion of the cartridge into plastic syringes and the electrical "tacking" of the containment cap at a precisely determined length of the syringe. A cap that is "tacked" at a shorter than desired length (less than 4.920 inches) leads to pressure on the cartridge stopper and, hence, partial or complete activation of the syringe. Such syringes must then be scrapped. If the cap is "tacked" at a longer than desired length

(4.980 inches or longer), the tacking is incomplete or inadequate, which can lead to cap loss and potentially a cartridge loss in shipment and handling. Such syringes can be reworked manually to attach the cap at a lower position. However, this process requires a 100 percent inspection of the tacked syringes and results in increased cost for the items. This final production step seemed to be producing more and more scrap and reworked syringes over successive weeks.

At this point, statistical consultants became involved in an attempt to solve this problem and recommended SPC for the purpose of improving the tacking operation. The length was targeted as a critical variable to be monitored by $\bar{x}$- and R-charts, which eventually led to identifying the root cause of the problem. The actual case history contains instances in which desired procedures were not always followed. As such, this case illustrates well the properties, problems, pitfalls, and peculiarities in applying such charts, as well as the necessity of having well-trained quality specialists involved.

Operators of the final stage of this syringe assembly process were trained in the basics of process capability studies and control charting techniques. In an attempt to judge the capability of the process, the responsible technician was called in to adjust the tacking machine and to position and secure it at what seemed to be its best possible position. Then, 35 consecutive observations were taken (see Table 13.4), and a capability study was undertaken. The process had a sample mean of $\bar{\bar{x}} = 4.954$ inches, which was close to the nominal aim (or target) of 4.950 inches with a sample standard deviation of $s = 0.0083$ inches. Upper and lower specifications of 4.980 and 4.920 inches, respectively, gave an estimated $C_{pk} = 1.03$. Thus, it was determined that the process was minimally capable and could indeed produce the length desired.

To establish the control charts, the operators then collected 15 samples each of size 5 taken every 15 minutes. The $\bar{x}$- and R-charts are shown in Figure 13.45. These charts show that the process

Table 13.4 Initial 35 Consecutive Observations Taken for the Capability Study

4.95888	4.95533	4.94294	4.95422	4.96679	4.94487	4.95775	4.95710
4.96543	4.95603	4.95210	4.95311	4.95385	4.96014	4.95252	4.96633
4.96255	4.95287	4.93541	4.94840	4.96114	4.93901	4.95966	4.93667
4.95941	4.94539	4.96238	4.94337	4.95550	4.95482	4.96230	4.96175
4.96016	4.94626	4.95904					

Source: Adapted from LeRoy A. Franklin and Samar N. Mukherjee, "An SPC Case Study on Stabilizing Syringe Lengths," *Quality Engineering* 12, no. 1 (1999–2000), 65–71. Reprinted from Quality Engineering, courtesy of Marcel Dekker, Inc.

Figure 13.45 Initial $\bar{x}$ and R-Charts for the First 15 Samples

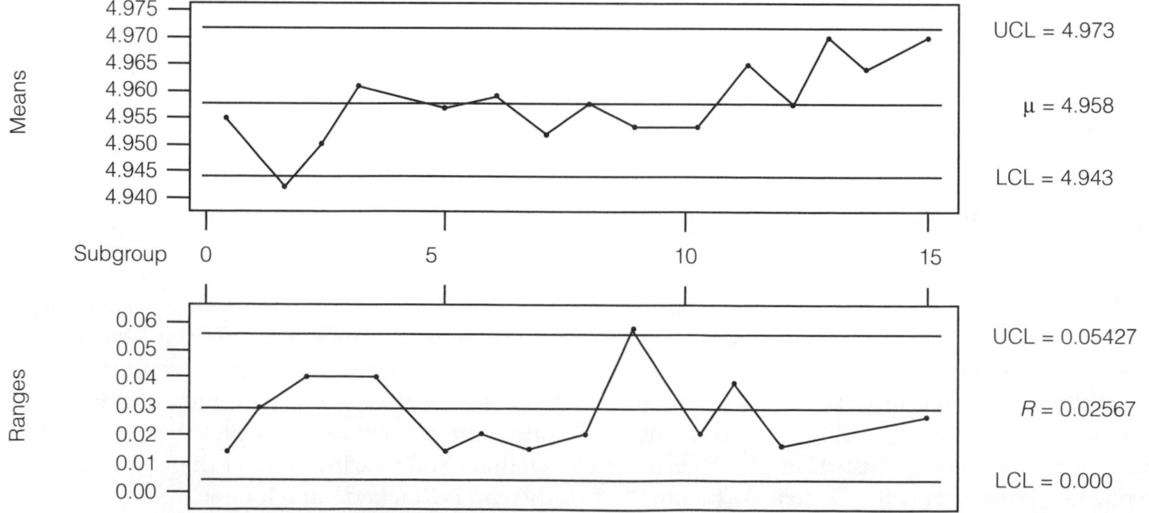

is already out of statistical control in both charts. Proper application of SPC procedures would have indicated that special causes should be identified and new control limits constructed. Unfortunately, the operators from this shift did not plot these points but only used the control limits they obtained to evaluate future measurements. The operators from this first shift continued to collect samples of size 5 every 15 minutes, but due to their unfamiliarity with charting, they never plotted these 15 new points either. At 4:00 P.M. of the same day, a new shift arrived and operators did plot this second set of 15 points using the control limits obtained from the first set of 15 points as shown in Figure 13.46. These charts show clearly that the centering was out of statistical control, with the average length far greater than desired. This conclusion was substantiated by operators noticing that the caps were not being tacked properly. The maintenance technician was immediately called in to adjust the machine properly.

After the first adjustment by the technician, the plot of the next sample taken 15 minutes later was already beyond the upper control limit for the $\bar{x}$-chart. Thus, the syringes were still too long, although the technician affirmed that he had set the height lower just 15 minutes earlier. The technician was recalled to readjust the machine. The second try was no better, and so the technician was called a third time to adjust the machine. This third try was successful in the sense that the length seemed to be reduced enough to have both the $\bar{x}$- and R-values inside their control limits.

This second shift operators continued sampling and collected 15 additional samples of size 5, at 15-minute intervals. They plotted these results (see Figure 13.47), but because no values were beyond the control limits, they took no action. It was at this point that the statistical consultants reviewed what had transpired. They not only determined that the original 15 points used to define the $\bar{x}$- and R-charts were themselves showing a process not under statistical control, but that the last 15 points also showed a process not under statistical control. The second shift workers had failed to notice the string of 15 points of the $\bar{x}$-chart all above the center line and failed to conclude that the center was "not where you wanted it." If they had, they would have once again called the technician to adjust the machine to lower the length of the syringes.

Fortunately, however, the consultants examined the R-chart as well as the $\bar{x}$-chart. Again, the last 14 points of R were all on one side of the center line, indicating a lack of statistical control. Careful examination of both charts revealed that the points of R were below the center and were indicating that the overall variation had been reduced by what the maintenance technician had done. Yet, in reading the $\bar{x}$-chart (after examining the R-chart), the length of the syringes seemed to have increased. The consultants contacted both the

Figure 13.46 $\bar{x}$ and R-Charts, Next 17 Samples

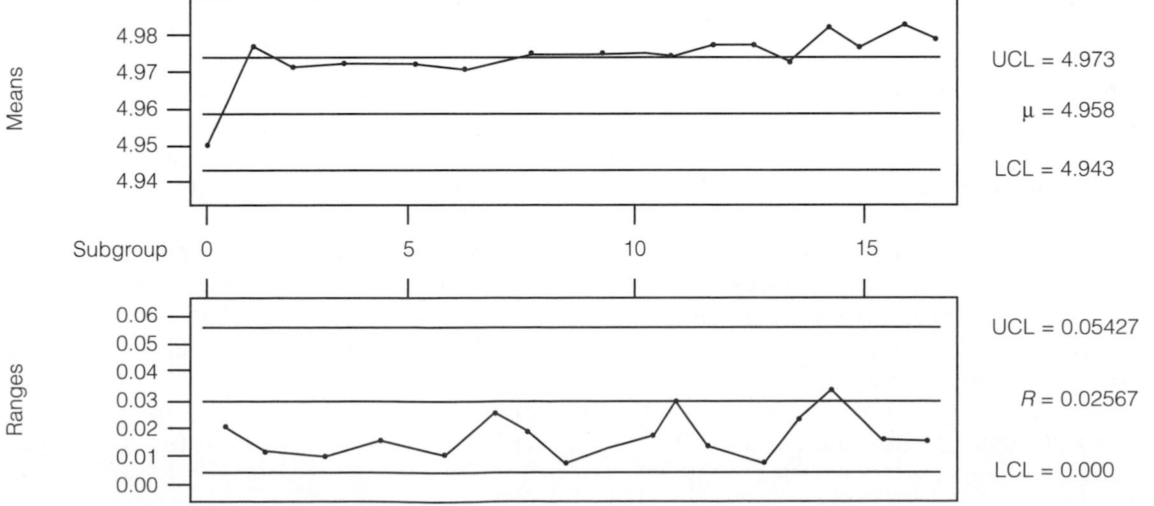

Figure 13.47 $\bar{x}$ and *R*-Charts for the Last 15 Samples

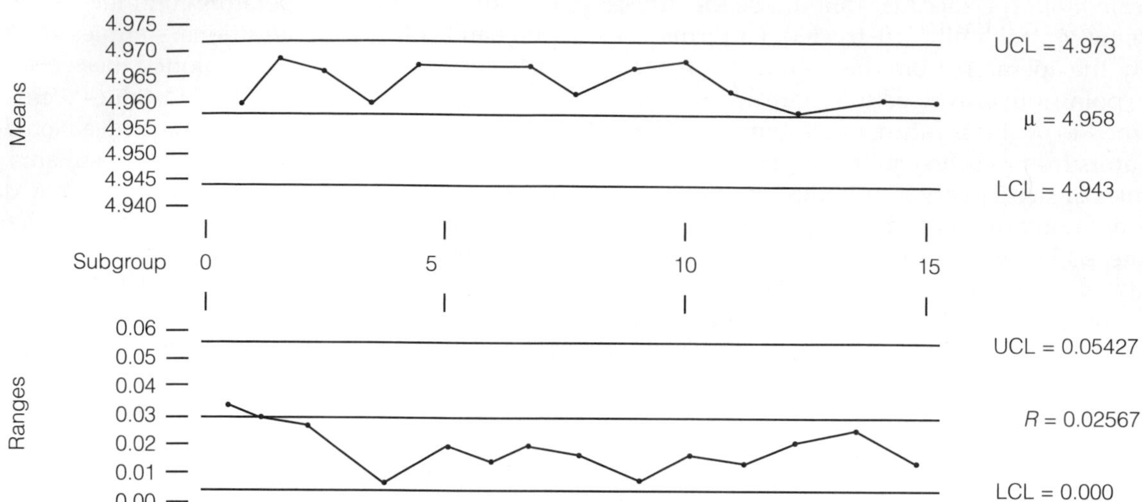

operators and the technician in order to try to find out what had happened to cause this confusing "good and bad" thing to occur. The maintenance technician's story was most revealing.

The maintenance technician said that for his first two (unsuccessful) attempts when he was told to adjust the process center (length of syringe) down, he moved the height adjustment stop down on its threaded shaft. However, he found it was difficult to tighten the locknut for this adjustment stop. The third time (the successful one), being frustrated that the thread of the shaft was too battered at the lower end of the stud, he actually moved the adjustment stop up even though he was asked to make the syringe lengths shorter. He thought this would result in still longer syringes being produced, but at least the locknut would hold. When he was told by the shift that the process was now producing the proper length syringes and that the operators were satisfied, he was mystified. He left wondering how a machine adjusted upward (toward longer lengths) could wind up producing shorter-length syringes!

The consultants realized the dramatic improvement (shortening) of the process variation told the important story. When the maintenance technician set the length of the adjustment cap where he was supposed to (lower), the threads were so worn as to make it impossible to hold the locknut in place. Thus, the vibration from the running machine (within about 15 minutes) loosened the locknut and adjustment cap quickly, resulting in drifts off center, producing syringes of erratic lengths. However, when the maintenance technician set the adjustment cap higher (which would make syringes longer), the threads there were good enough for the locknut to hold the cap in place. The lengths, indeed, were a little longer than what was targeted, but the variation had been so dramatically reduced that the overall effect was one of making acceptable syringes; that is, the syringes were a tiny bit longer than desired but very consistent in their length so no plotted points were beyond the upper control limit for the $\bar{x}$-chart.

The operators were satisfied with this situation because now the plotted points of the syringe lengths came under the upper control limit of the $\bar{x}$-chart, which convinced them that they were making syringes to the proper length. The consultants recommended to the managers that the threaded stud on which the adjustment stop moved be replaced. The repair work needed a special part that was fairly expensive and necessitated some downtime for the manufacturing process; nevertheless, on the strength of the control chart data and the explanation of the maintenance technician's and consultant's stories, the recommendation was implemented. Upon replacement of the threaded stud, waste and rework from the final step dropped to virtually zero over the period of many weeks.

Key Issues for Discussion

1. Using the data for the initial process capability study sample given in Table 13.4, compute the process capability indexes and construct a histogram for these data.
2. Explain why it was incorrect that the operators did not plot the initial data, find special causes, and compute new control limits. What might have happened had they done it correctly?
3. What lessons can be learned from this case?

Quality in Practice

Using a u-Chart in a Receiving Process[10]

CBT, Co. is a distributor of electrical automation and power transmission products. When the company began to implement a total quality management process, one manager was eager to collect data about the organization's receiving process because of a decrease in the organization's on-time deliveries. The manager suspected that the data entry person in the purchasing department was not entering data in the computer in a timely fashion; consequently, packages could not be properly processed for subsequent shipping to the customer.

A preliminary analysis indicated that the manager's notion was inaccurate. In fact, the manager was able to see that the data entry person was doing an excellent job. The analysis showed that handling packages that were destined for a branch operation in the same fashion as other packages created significant delays. A simple process change of placing a branch designation letter in front of the purchase order number told the receiving clerk to place those packages on a separate skid for delivery to the branch.

However, this analysis revealed a variety of other problems. Generally, anywhere from 65 to 110 packing slips were processed each day. These were found to contain many errors in addition to the wrong destination designation that contributed to the delays. Errors included

- Wrong purchase order
- Wrong quantity
- Purchase order not on the system
- Original order not on the system
- Parts do not match
- Purchase order was entered incorrectly
- Double shipment
- Wrong parts
- No purchase order

Many packing slips contained multiple errors. Table 13.5 shows the number of packing slips and total errors identified. A *u*-chart was constructed for each day to track the number of packing slip errors—defects—found. A *u*-chart was used because the sample size varied each day. Thus, the statistic monitored was the number of errors per packing slip. Figure 13.48 shows the *u*-chart that was constructed for this period. (This change in the branch designation took place on January 24, resulting in significant improvement, as shown on the chart.)

Although the chart shows that the process is in control (since the branch designation change), the average error rate of more than 9 percent still was not considered acceptable. After consolidating the types of errors into five categories, a Pareto analysis was performed. This analysis showed the following:

Category	Percentage
Purchase order error	35
Quantity error	22
No purchase order on system	17
Original order not on system	16
Parts error	10

The analysis is illustrated in Figure 13.49.

The first two categories accounted for more than half of the errors. The remedy for these problems was to develop a training module on

Table 13.5 CBT Company Packing Slip Error Counts

Date	Packing Slips	Errors	Date	Packing Slips	Errors
21 Jan	87	15	4 Mar	92	8
22 Jan	79	13	5 Mar	69	13
23 Jan	92	23	6 Mar	86	6
24 Jan	84	3	9 Mar	85	13
27 Jan	73	7	10 Mar	101	5
28 Jan	67	11	11 Mar	87	5
29 Jan	73	8	12 Mar	71	3
30 Jan	91	8	13 Mar	83	8
31 Jan	94	11	16 Mar	103	4
3 Feb	83	12	17 Mar	82	6
4 Feb	89	12	18 Mar	90	7
5 Feb	88	6	19 Mar	80	4
6 Feb	69	11	20 Mar	70	4
7 Feb	74	8	23 Mar	73	11
10 Feb	67	4	24 Mar	89	13
11 Feb	83	10	25 Mar	91	6
12 Feb	79	8	26 Mar	78	6
13 Feb	75	8	27 Mar	88	6
14 Feb	69	3	30 Mar	76	8
17 Feb	87	8	31 Mar	101	9
18 Feb	99	13	1 Apr	92	8
19 Feb	101	13	2 Apr	70	2
20 Feb	76	7	3 Apr	72	11
21 Feb	90	4	6 Apr	83	5
24 Feb	92	7	7 Apr	69	6
25 Feb	80	4	8 Apr	79	3
26 Feb	81	5	9 Apr	79	8
27 Feb	105	8	10 Apr	76	6
28 Feb	80	8	13 Apr	92	7
2 Mar	82	5	14 Apr	80	4
3 Mar	75	3	15 Apr	78	8

proper purchasing methods to ensure that vendors knew the correct information needed on the purchase orders. The third category—no purchase order on the computer system—caused receiving personnel to stage the orders until an investigation could find the necessary information. Because of this problem, the company realized it needed to revamp the original order-writing process. Specifically, both the order-writing and purchase order activities needed to be improved.

An analysis of the control chart in Figure 13.46 shows that the average error rate has gradually improved. To a large extent, this improvement was due to the recognition of the problems and enhanced communication among the constituents. While the full training program had not been implemented at the time this case was written, the company believed that a significant reduction in the error rate would result once the training was completed.

Key Issues for Discussion

1. Verify the computation of the center line and control limits in Figure 13.48.
2. What information might a separate chart for each error category provide? Would you recommend spending the time and effort to make these additional computations?

Figure 13.48 *u*-Chart for CBT Company Packing Slip Errors

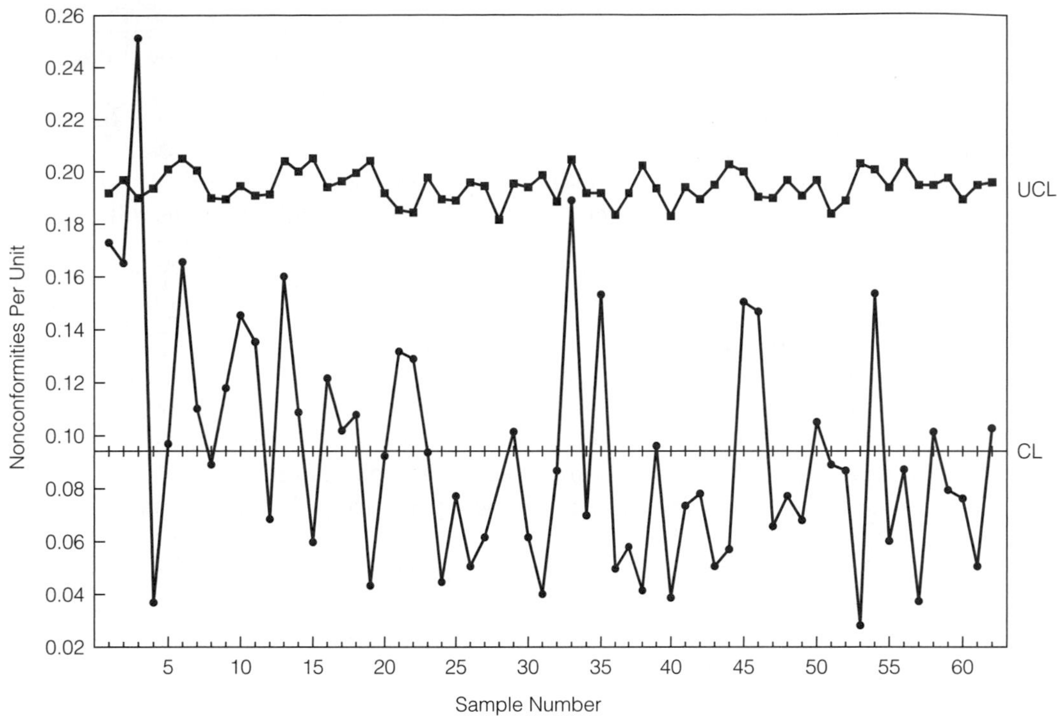

Figure 13.49 Pareto Analysis of Packing Slip Errors

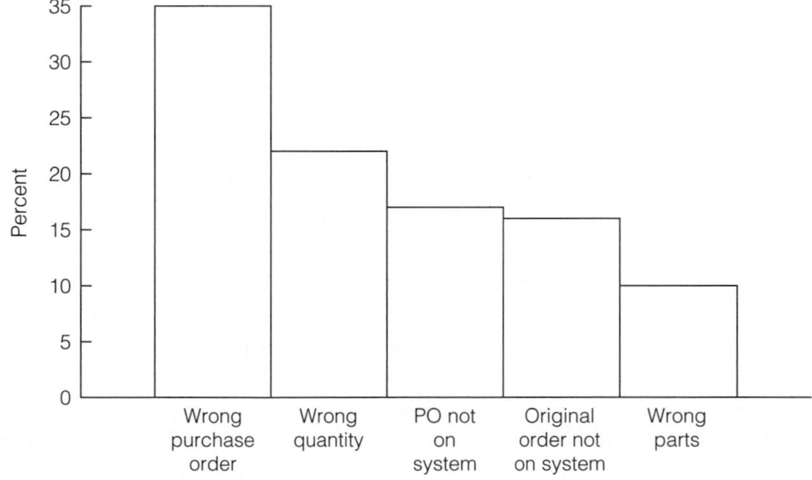

Review Questions

1. Define *statistical process control* and discuss its advantages.
2. What does the term *in statistical control* mean? Explain the difference between capability and control.
3. What are the disadvantages of simply using histograms to study process capability?
4. Discuss the three primary applications of control charts.
5. Describe the difference between variables and attributes data. What types of control charts are used for each?
6. Briefly describe the methodology of constructing and using control charts.
7. What does one look for in interpreting control charts? Explain the possible causes of different out-of-control indicators.
8. How should control charts be used by shop-floor personnel?
9. How are variables control charts used to determine process capability?
10. Describe the difference between *control limits* and *specification limits*.
11. Why is the s-chart sometimes used in place of the R-chart?
12. Describe some situations in which a chart for individual measurements would be used.
13. Explain the concept of a moving range. Why is a moving range chart difficult to interpret?
14. Explain the difference between *defects* and *defectives*.
15. Briefly describe the process of constructing a p-chart. What are the key differences compared with an $\bar{x}$-chart?
16. Does an np-chart provide any different information than a p-chart? Why would an np-chart be used?
17. Explain the difference between a c-chart and a u-chart.
18. Discuss how to use charts for defects in a quality rating system.
19. Describe the rules for determining the appropriate control chart to use in any given situation.
20. Suggest the appropriate control chart to use for the follow health-care measures:
    a. Falls per 1000 patients
    b. Rejected insurance claims per month
    c. Medication errors per patient
    d. Monthly dollar amount of insurance claim denials
    e. Admission time to emergency room
21. Explain the concept of rational subgroups.
22. What trade-offs are involved in selecting the sample size for a control chart?
23. Explain the economic trade-offs to consider when determining the sampling frequency to use in a control chart.
24. Discuss the implications of control limit location in terms of Type I and Type II errors.
25. Explain how SPC is reflected in the ISO 9000 standards.
26. How can SPC be used effectively in Six Sigma environments?
27. Describe approaches for applying PRE-Control.

PROBLEMS

Note: Data sets for many problems in this chapter are available in the Excel workbook *C13Data* in the Bonus Materials folder for this chapter on the Premium website. Click on the appropriate worksheet tab as noted in the problem (e.g., *Prob. 13-1*) to access the data. The Excel templates for control charts used in this chapter are also available in the Excel Templates folder on the website.

1. Tri-State Bank is investigating the processing time for loan applications. Samples were taken for 25 random days from 4 branches. These data can be found in the worksheet *Prob. 13-1.*
   a. Using Microsoft Excel® or similar software with statistical capability, construct a histogram for these 100 individual readings.
   b. Construct a run chart for the sample means.
   c. Interpret what the data show. Does the process appear to be in control?
2. Magnum Magnetics makes induction meters used in vending machines to test the validity of coins. Their specifications require the induction reading capability of the meters to fall between 0.25 and 0.50 Tesla (T) units. Quality analysts took 3 random test readings of 30 meters, as found in the worksheet *Prob. 13-2.*
   a. Using Microsoft Excel® or similar software with statistical capability, construct a histogram for these 90 individual readings.
   b. Construct a run chart for the sample means.
   c. Interpret what the data show. Does the process appear to be in control?
3. J. Phelps Swim Club is trying to calibrate their chlorine pump to ensure that the right amount of chlorine (1.0–1.5 ppm of free chlorine) is mixed into the water. Thirty samples of 3 readings at random times during the week were taken. These data can be found in the worksheet *Prob. 13-3.*
   a. Compute the mean and range of each sample, calculate control limits, and plot them on $\bar{x}$ and R control charts.
   b. Does the process appear to be in statistical control? Calculate descriptive statistics that may help you to determine the answer to this question. What evidence is there for your conclusion?
4. Mount Blanc Hospital is working on reducing waiting time in order to give customers better service in their waiting rooms. Fifty samples of size 5 were taken at random times from their main waiting room. These data can be found in the worksheet *Prob. 13-4.*
   a. Compute the mean and range of each sample, and control limits, and plot them on $\bar{x}$ and R control charts.
   b. Does the process appear to be in statistical control? Why or why not?
5. Twenty-five samples of size 4 resulted in statistics of $\bar{\bar{x}} = 30.0$ minutes and $\bar{R} = 2.5$ minutes for the Excellante Cleaning Company's average time to completely clean a rug. Compute control limits for $\bar{x}$- and R-charts and estimate the standard deviation of the process.
6. Twenty-five samples of size 6 resulted in statistics of $\bar{\bar{x}} = 8.0$ and $\bar{R} = 2.0$ for the Quality Service Company's average time to complete an order. Compute control limits for $\bar{x}$- and R-charts and estimate the standard deviation of the process.
7. In testing the temperature in an analysis process in Heritage DNA Labs, LLC, containing both positive and negative values, the data listed in the worksheet *Prob. 13-7* were obtained.
   a. Compute the mean, standard deviation and other descriptive statistics for the data.

b. Construct $\overline{x}$- and R-charts for these data. Determine whether the process is in control. If not, eliminate any assignable causes and compute revised limits.

8. While testing the voltage of a component used in a microcomputer for the Hertz Company, the data listed in the worksheet *Prob. 13-08* were obtained. Construct $\overline{x}$- and R-charts for these data. Determine whether the process is in control. If not, eliminate any assignable causes and compute revised limits.
9. The data for 25 samples of 4 items each, from the study at Tri-State Bank (*Prob. 13-01*, above) was further analyzed in an effort to use it for process control.
   a. Compute the mean and range of each sample, and control limits, and plot them on $\overline{x}$- and R-control charts.
   b. Does the process appear to be in statistical control? Why or why not?
10. The data for 30 samples of 3 items each, from the study at Magnum Magnetics (from *Prob. 13-02*, above) was further analyzed in an effort to use it for process control.
    a. Compute the mean and range of each sample, calculate the control limits, and plot them on $\overline{x}$- and R-control charts.
    b. Does the process appear to be in statistical control? Why or why not?
11. The data in worksheet *Prob. 13-11* represent processing time values for 40 samples of size 4 that were taken from Rapid Check Kiters, Inc.'s check processing firm over a 20-hour period.
    a. Compute the mean and standard deviation of all 40 samples for the sample data.
    b. Calculate the control limits and construct the $\overline{x}$- and R-charts, using the first 20 samples. Is the process under control at that point?
    c. Specifications for the process are 1.065 ± 0.14. If the process is under control, calculate the capability indexes, C_{pu}, C_{pl}, C_p, and C_{pk} using the part of the $\overline{x}$- and R-charts Excel template that calculates the process capability. What do the indexes indicate?
    d. After calculating the control limits, the last 20 samples were collected. When plotted using the control limits calculated earlier, does the process appear to be in statistical control? Why or why not? What should be done if it is not under control?
12. The data in worksheet *Prob. 13-12* list electrical resistance values (ohms) for 50 samples of size 5 that were taken from Babbage Chips, Inc.'s computer chip-making process over a 25-hour period.
    a. Compute the mean, standard deviation and other descriptive statistics for the data.
    b. Calculate the control limits and construct the $\overline{x}$- and R-charts, using the first 30 samples. Is the process under control at that point?
    c. Specifications for the process are 9.2 ± 3.2 ohms. If the process is under control, calculate the capability indexes, C_{pu}, C_{pl}, C_p, and C_{pk} using the part of the $\overline{x}$- and R-charts Excel template that calculates the process capability. What do the indexes indicate?
    d. After calculating the control limits, the last 20 samples were collected. When plotted using the control limits calculated earlier, does the process appear to be in statistical control? Why or why not? What should be done if it is not under control?
13. For each of the following control charts, assume that the process has been operating in statistical control for some time. What conclusions should the operators reach at this point?

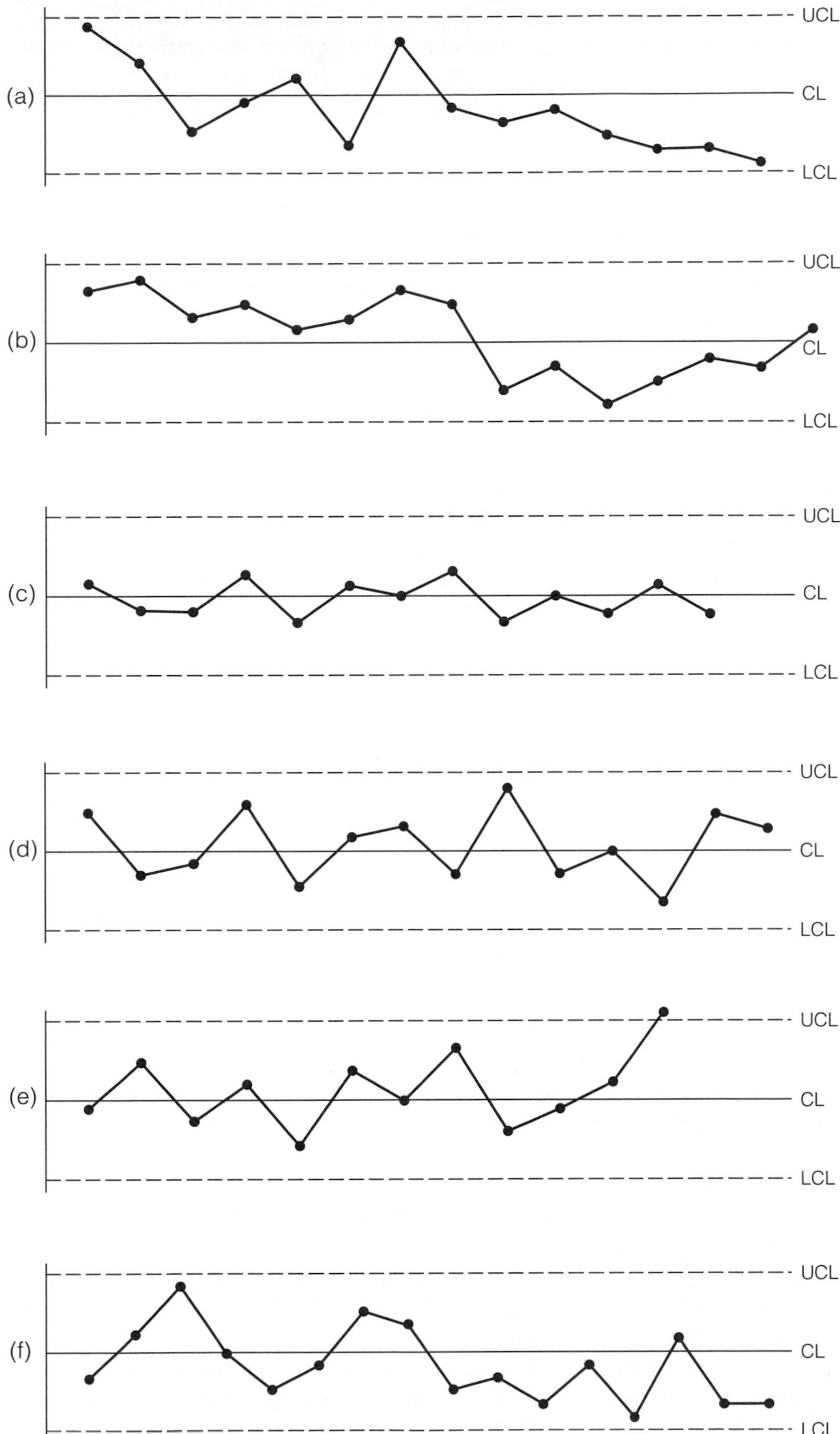
(a)
UCL
CL
LCL
(b)
UCL
CL
LCL
(c)
UCL
CL
LCL
(d)
UCL
CL
LCL
(e)
UCL
CL
LCL
(f)
UCL
CL
LCL

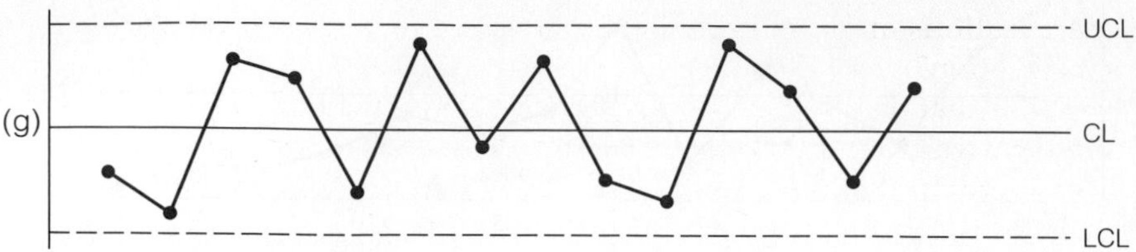

14. Discuss the interpretation of each of the following control charts:

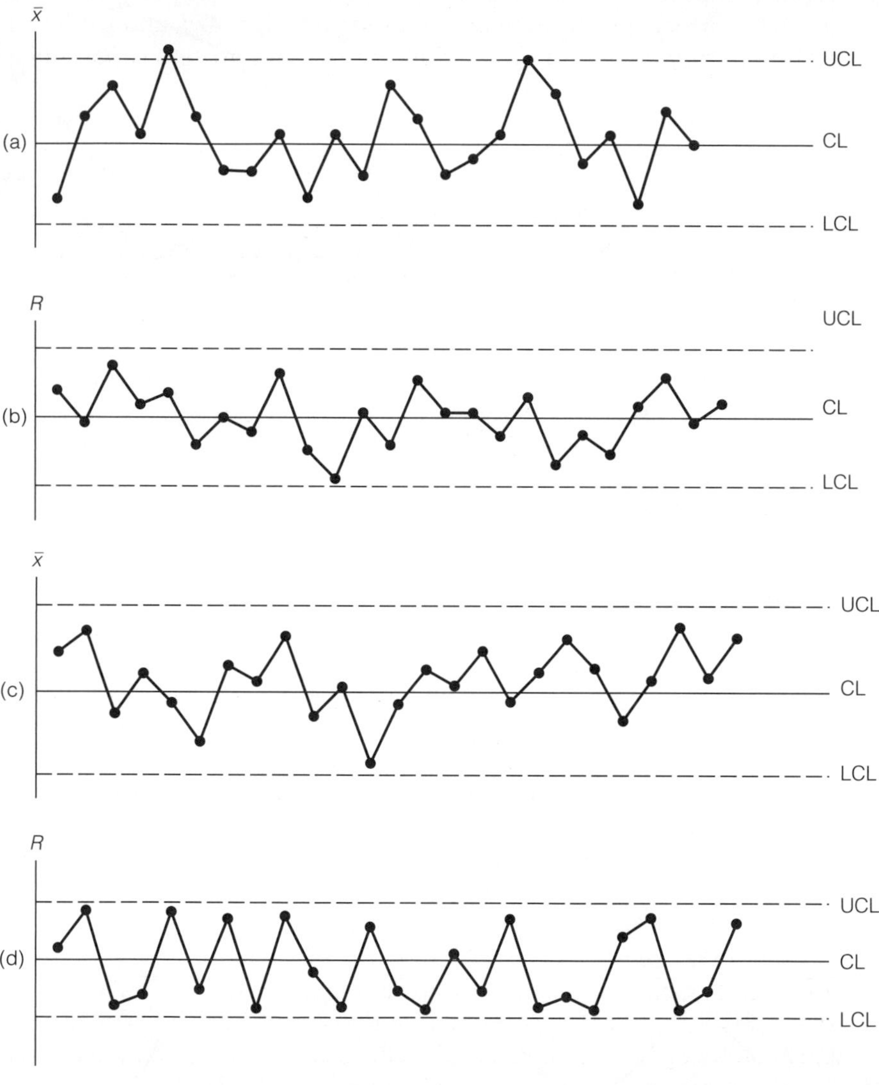

15. PCDrives has a manufacturing process that is normally distributed and has the sample means and ranges for 15 samples of size 5, found in the worksheet *Prob. 13-15*. Note that only sample statistics have been given, instead

of the raw data from the samples. Determine process capability limits. If specifications are determined to be 70 ± 25, what percentage will be out of specification?

16. Suppose that, in a review of the J. Phelps Swim Club data (*Prob. 13-03* worksheet), it was found that the values for the second sample had been recorded incorrectly and should have been 1.26, 1.22, and 1.21. In addition, the last value of the last sample was also recorded incorrectly. It should have been 1.25. After the two samples were revised, the process was considered under control, with an upper specification limit of USL = 1.5, and the lower specification limit at LSL = 1.0. Compute the process capability and the percent outside of specifications.
17. Suppose that in *Prob. 13-08* (part B) for the Hertz Company, after it was revised, the upper specification limit was set at USL = 475, and the lower specification limit was set at LSL = 325. Compute the process capability and the percent outside specifications that may be expected.
18. Fujiyama Electronics needs to construct $\bar{x}$- and s-charts for circuit boards that are purchased from an outside supplier. A critical dimension is the distance between two holes on the board that are supposed to be 5 cm apart. Use the data, consisting of 30 samples of size 4 found in the worksheet *Prob. 13-18*. What conclusions do you reach concerning the state of the process? Is it under control? Why or why not?
19. El Toro Grande Restaurante advertises that customers will have their orders taken within 3 minutes after being seated. Management wants to monitor average times, as it is such an important guarantee for business. Construct $\bar{x}$- and s-charts for the data given in the worksheet *Prob. 13-19*.
    a. Compute the mean and average standard deviation of each sample, calculate control limits, and plot them on control charts.
    b. Does the process appear to be in statistical control? Why or why not?
    c. Calculate the process capability statistics, using 3 minutes as the upper tolerance limit and zero as the lower tolerance limit. What recommendation would you make to management concerning the process, based on these findings?
20. Construct $\bar{x}$- and s-charts for the data for the Hertz Company from *Prob. 13-08* (part B) after the data was revised. Is the process in control?
21. Construct $\bar{x}$- and s-charts for the data for Babbage Chips from *Prob. 13-12*. Is the process in control? What recommendation would you make to management concerning the process, based on your analysis?
22. An injection molding machine at the Moby Molding Co. used to make plastic bottles has four molding heads. The outside diameter of the bottle is an important measure of process performance. The table in the worksheet *Prob.13-22* shows the results of 30 samples in which the data are coded by subtracting the actual value from the nominal dimension. Construct $\bar{x}$- and s-charts and discuss the results.
23. The sample means and standard deviations gathered in a calibration project by the Weighrite Corporation were observed for sample sizes of 10, as show in worksheet *Prob. 13-23*. Construct $\bar{x}$- and s-charts and discuss the results.
24. The temperature in a computer lab at Coyote University is very important for proper functioning of the computer equipment. The data in the worksheet *Prob. 13-24* shows the results of 30 samples of 5 each, taken at random at different times of day over a three month time period. Construct $\bar{x}$- and s-charts and discuss the results.

25. Calculate the process capability statistics for the outside diameters of the bottles made on the injection molding machine at the Moby Molding Co. (from *Prob.* 13-22). Use 0.12 as the upper tolerance limit and −0.10 as the lower tolerance limit for this important measure of process performance. What recommendation would you make to management concerning the process, based on these findings?
26. Calculate the process capability statistics for the temperature in the computer lab at Coyote University (from *Prob.* 13-24). Use 76 as the upper tolerance limit and 68 as the lower tolerance limit for this important measure. What recommendation would you make to management concerning the process, based on these findings?
27. Chief Henry Batter of the Gotham City Police Department is trying to reduce the time required to answer the phone at police headquarters (in fractions of a minute). The data in the worksheet for *Prob. 13-27* represent time in fractions of minutes for three individual readings taken at random for 25 days.
    a. Compute control limits for an x-chart (chart for individuals) using the statistic $\overline{R}/d_2$, with a 3-period moving range, as an estimate of the standard deviation.
    b. Construct an x-chart for individuals, using the data. Interpret the results.
28. Charlie Plato owns Charlie's China Emporium, which sells inexpensive cups, dishes, and bric-a-brack in a seaside resort. She has three checkout stations, which she would like to test to see if they are under control and capable. She considers sales of $36.50 per hour, per station, to be a representative average. Consider the data for 75 individual results of sales dollars per hour, per unit, shown in the worksheet *Prob. 13-28*.
    a. Compute control limits for an x-chart (chart for individuals) using the statistic $\overline{R}/d_2$ as an estimate of the standard deviation with a 3-period moving range.
    b. Construct an x-chart for individuals, using the data. Interpret the results.
29. Ricardo's Widgets makes a critical part for a popular brand of cell phones. Consider the data for 60 observations of a key dimension for the part, shown in the worksheet *Prob. 13-29*.
    a. Compute control limits for an x-chart using the statistic $\overline{R}/d_2$ as an estimate of the standard deviation, with a 4-period moving average for the range calculation.
    b. Construct an x-chart for "individuals" using the data. Interpret the results.
30. Thirty samples of 75 items each were inspected at the Yummy Candy Company and 75 **items** were found to be defective. Compute control limits for a p-chart for this process.
31. Thirty-five samples of 25 orders each at the Bakery Bread, Inc. were inspected, and 25 items were found to be defective. Compute control limits for a p-chart.
32. Samples of packages orders were taken at the R.A. Treinta Package Co. to determine if the orders were prepared correctly. The percent defectives for each sample are given in the worksheet *Prob. 13-33* for 25 samples. Five hundred orders are inspected each day for each sample. Construct a p-chart and interpret the results.
33. The fraction defective for a folding process in an Out-of-the-Box Co. plant is given in the worksheet *Prob. 13-33* for 25 samples. One hundred units are inspected each shift.
    a. Construct a p-chart and interpret the results.
    b. After the process was determined to be under control, process monitoring began, using the established control limits. The results of 25 more samples

are shown in the second part of the worksheet. Is there a problem with the process? If so, when should the process have been stopped, and steps taken to correct it?

34. The fraction defective of automotive pistons made by the Precision Piston Co. is given in the worksheet *Prob. 13-34* for 20 samples. Two hundred units are inspected each day. Construct a *p*-chart and interpret the results.
35. One hundred insurance claim forms are inspected daily at Full Life Insurance Co. over 25 working days, and the number of forms with errors have been recorded in the worksheet *Prob. 13-35*. Construct a *p*-chart. If any points occur outside the control limits, assume that assignable causes have been determined. Then construct a revised chart.
36. Samples of size 50 have been randomly selected during each of 30 shifts in a production process at Delgado Manufacturing, Inc. The data are given in the worksheet *Prob. 13-36*. Construct a *p*-chart and determine whether the process is in control. If not, eliminate any data points that appear to be due to assignable causes and construct a new chart.
37. SpeedyNetService.com, an Internet service provider (ISP), is concerned that the level of access of customers is decreasing, due to heavier use. The proportion of peak period time when a customer is likely to receive busy signals is considered a good measure of service level. The percentage of times a customer receives a busy signal during peak periods varies. Using a sampling process, the ISP set up control charts to monitor the service level, based on proportion of busy signals received. Construct the *p*-chart using on the sample data in the table in the worksheet *Prob.13-37*. What does the chart show? Is the service level good or bad, in your opinion?
38. Ellswater Hospital surveys all outgoing patients by means of a patient satisfaction questionnaire. The number of patients surveyed each month varies. Control charts that monitor the proportion of unsatisfied patients for key questions are constructed and studied. Construct a *p*-chart for the data in the worksheet *Prob. 13-38*, which represent responses to a question on satisfaction with hospital housekeeping services.
39. Construct an *np*-chart using the data in *Prob.13-35*, the Full Life Insurance Co. What does the chart show?
40. Construct an *np*-chart using the data in *Prob. 13-36* from Delgado Manufacturing Co. What does the chart show?
41. Calculate the centerline and control limits for a *c*-chart involving 40 samples and having a total of 1,000 defects and interpret their meaning.
42. Find 3σ control limits for a *c*-chart with an average number of defects equal to 18.
43. Calculate the centerline and control limits for a *c*-chart involving 35 samples and having a total of 350 defects and interpret the results.
44. Consider the sample data for defects per pizza in a new store being opened by Rob's Pizza Palaces in the worksheet *Prob. 13-44*. Construct a *c*-chart for these data. What does the chart show?
45. FarmaSuitica, Inc., a mail-order prescription drug vendor, measured the number of defects per standard 200 line order being picked in their distribution center. Construct a *c*-chart for data in the table in the worksheet *Prob. 13-43* and interpret the results.
46. A quality consultant was asked to analyze the data from order errors at the Audubon Books, Inc., distribution center as shown in the table in the worksheet *Prob. 13-46*. The data show the number of orders processed per month and the error found in those orders. Develop a run chart, a frequency

histogram, and a u-chart for these data. What insights do you get from each chart? What would you advise the distribution center manager to do about the errors?

47. Find 3σ control limits for a small u-chart with the following errors per sample unit. What do the limits show?

Errors	Sample Unit
5	92
3	136
4	70
8	78
7	165

48. Determine, using Figure 13.42, the appropriate sample size for detecting:
    a. A 1-sigma shift in the mean with a 0.80 probability.
    b. A 2-sigma shift with 0.95 probability
    c. A 2.5-sigma shift with 0.90 probability

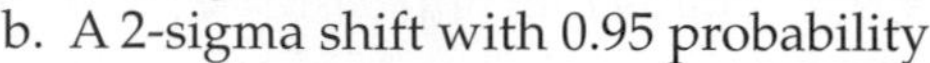

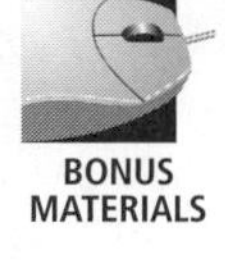

BONUS MATERIALS

For problems 49 through 51, see the Statistical Foundations of Control Charts Section in the Bonus Materials folder for this chapter on the Premium website.

49. What are the probability limits corresponding to a Type I error of $\alpha = 0.10$?
50 If control limits for a project are based on 2.75 standard deviations, what percentage of observations will be expected to fall beyond the limits?
51. What is the probability of observing 11 consecutive points on one side of the center line if the process is in control? 10 of 11 points? 9 of 11 points? How many points out of 11 on one side of the center would indicate lack of control?

CASES

I. MORELIA MORTGAGE COMPANY

The Morelia Mortgage Company (MMC) is a medium-sized mortgage lender that has continued to do well, despite the "meltdown" in the mortgage lending industry. Prior to the economic downturn, MMC was a principle supplier of lending services to Southwestern Desert Homes, a builder of residential communities in several major cities throughout the southwestern United States. Because it carefully selected clients who were able to make substantial downpayments for homes, and it avoided sub-prime or variable-rate mortgage lending, MMC has been shielded from the effects of "toxic mortgages" on its balance sheet. In fact, MMC expanded its mortgage refinancing and home remodeling credit operations to two shifts, as other lending company's ability to take on new clients contracted. Soon, they were working six days per week and hiring additional workers.

Not long after MMC began its second shift operations, it received some complaints about long mortgage processing times. This information alarmed Pete Purnell, CEO of Morelia Mortgage. He had retired early from a bank in a cold Midwestern city and decided that he wanted to relocate to the desert Southwest. He had hiked in the mountains and played golf during the first six months, but then realized that he needed more of a challenge than the recreational activities could provide. That was when he started Morelia Mortgage, using his experience in the mortgage and home loan business. MMC, under Pete's leadership, soon built a reputation as a high-quality, if somewhat conservative, lender. Among other things, the company was known for the capability of its well-trained and dedicated employees, who could generally complete the loan process in around 2–3 work days. Thus, Pete never felt the need to consider formal process control approaches. Now many customers were complaining that it took a week or two to close on a loan, even with an excellent credit score. In view of the recent complaints, Pete suspected that the rapid expansion to a full two-shift operation, the pressures to produce higher volumes, and the push to meet requests from high-profit customers was causing a breakdown in their quality.

On the recommendation of the V.P. for loan processing, Pete hired a quality consultant to train the process managers and certain loan workers in statistical process control methods. As a trial project, one process manager wanted to evaluate the capability of a critical operation that she suspects might be a major source of the delays. The nominal specification for this processing operation is 15.5 hours with a tolerance of 5 hours. Thus, the upper and lower specifications are LSL = 10.5 hours and USL = 20.5 hours. The consultant suggested inspecting five consecutive processing times, per loan worker, in the middle of each shift over a 15-day period and recording the completion times for loans that they had finished processing. The table in the worksheet *Morella Mortgage Case* in the workbook *C13CaseData* (available on the Premium website), shows 15 days' data collected for each shift, by loan worker.

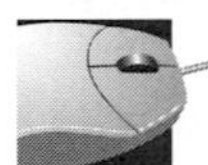

Assignment

1. Interpret the data in the *MMC Case* worksheet in the Excel workbook *C13CaseData* (available on the Premium website), establish a state of statistical control, and evaluate the capability of the process to meet specifications. Consider the following questions: What do the initial control charts tell you? Do any out-of-control conditions exist? If the process is not in control, what might be the likely causes, based on the information that is available? What is the process capability? What do the process capability indexes tell the company? Is MMC facing a serious problem that it needs to address? How might the company eliminate the problems of slow loan processing?
2. The process manager who initiated the trial project implemented the recommendations that resulted from the initial study. Because of her success in using control charts, MMC made a decision to continue using them on that process. After establishing control, one additional sample was taken over the next 20 shifts, shown in second part of the table in the *MMC Case* worksheet. Evaluate whether the process remains in control, and suggest any actions that should be taken. Consider the following issues: Does any evidence suggest that the process has changed relative to the established control limits? If any out-of-control patterns are suspected, what might be the cause? What should the company investigate?

II. Murphy Trucking, Inc.

Murphy Trucking, Inc. (MTI), supplies contract transportation services to many different manufacturing firms. One of its principal customers, Crawford Consumer Products (CCP), is actively improving quality by using the Malcolm Baldrige National Quality Award criteria. In an effort to improve supplier quality, Crawford Consumer Products mandated, last year, that all suppliers provide factual evidence of quality improvement efforts that lead to highly capable processes.

As part of its supplier development program, CCP held a seminar for all its suppliers to outline this initiative and provide initial assistance. The executive officers of MTI participated in this seminar and recognized that MTI was seriously lacking in its quality improvement efforts. More importantly, Jeff Blaine, who was the purchasing manager at CCP, told them privately that many errors had been found in MTI's shipping documents. CCP would not continue to tolerate this high number of errors; and if no improvements were made, it would seek transportation services elsewhere.

Rick Murphy, president and CEO of MTI, was concerned. During an off-site meeting, Murphy and other MTI executives developed a comprehensive blueprint to help MTI develop a total quality focus. One of the key objectives was to establish an SPC effort to gain control of key customer-focused processes and establish priorities for improvement.

The Billing Study after Process Improvement

In a good-faith attempt to respond to CCP's feedback, MTI turned its attention to its billing input errors and worked on them over the following six months. To gain some understanding of the situation, MTI conducted an initial (base case) study by sampling 20 bills of lading, each day, over a 20-day period. Initial results were dismal, with defective bills averaging a horrible 60 percent!

After process improvement and an intensive effort to train shipping clerks not to make errors, the company was ready to make another study to determine what progress had been made. The first set of tables in the *Murphy Case-Initial* worksheet in the Excel workbook *C13CaseData* on the Premium website shows the results of the initial study. The worksheet *Murphy Case-Revised* shows the results of the second study, after improvements were made. Both studies revealed that field employees were correcting the errors as they found them. In both cases, rework was costing the company almost $2 per error, but the number of errors had been substantially reduced between the two studies. However, field employees still were not always catching the errors, which led to field service and other problems.

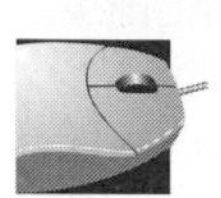
BONUS MATERIALS

Discussion Questions

1. At this point, MTI is unsure of how to interpret these results. You have been hired as a consultant by the executive committee to analyze these data and provide additional recommendations for integrating SPC concepts into MTI's quality system. Using the results from the base case data, determine the performance, that is, the process capability, in a qualitative and quantitative sense, of the billing input. What is the average rate of defective bills? Is the process in control? What error rates might the company expect in the future? What general conclusions do you reach?
2. Perform the same statistical analysis with the second set of data. How do the results differ? What is the average rate of defective bills? Is the process in control? What error rates might the company expect in the future? What general conclusions do you reach?

The Billing Study, Part II

The revelations from the initial study had been startling. The results from the second study were encouraging, but not yet where the company wanted to be. Rick Murphy personally led a group problem-solving session to address the root causes of the current error rate. During this session, the group members constructed a cause-and-effect diagram to help determine the causes of incorrect bills of lading.

Eight categories of causes were identified:

1. Incomplete shipper name or address
2. Incomplete consignee name or address
3. Missing container type
4. Incomplete description of freight
5. Weight not shown on bill of lading
6. Improper destination code
7. Incomplete driver's signature information
8. Inaccurate piece count

Using Deming's plan-do-study-act process, the group at Murphy designed a plan to examine all bills of lading over a 25-day period and count the number of errors in each of these categories. They repeated the study six months later to determine what progress, if any, had been made in error reduction. The second table in the *Murphy Case-Initial* worksheet and the second table in the worksheet *Murphy Case-Revised* show the data for the distribution of billing errors for these studies. Rick Murphy thought that the *p*-chart developed in the first study and reapplied to the second study provided significant information about the process; however, he was curious to find out whether another method could tell them more about the nature of the defects they were encountering.

Discussion Questions (cont.)

3. After developing *p*-charts for the first and second studies, you decide to analyze the data to determine whether the system is in control by constructing another appropriate control chart (other than a *p*-chart) that could better tell you about the nature of the defects. You also decide that it would be wise to construct a Pareto diagram to gain additional insight into the problem, and suggest recommendations to reduce billing errors.
4. Complete your analysis by using the three charts from each of the two studies to advise Rick and his managers at Murphy on

the next steps. How do the results differ from the first to the second study? Is the process in control? What error categories have improved? Which ones might the company need to work on immediately in order to bring about further improvements? What general conclusions do you reach?

III. Day Industries[11]

Day Industries is a medium-sized paint manufacturer. The process of making paint consists of four major steps: weigh-up, premix, milling, and letdown. In the weigh-up stage, the ingredients are added to a tank one at a time according to the formula. Next, the batch is mixed on a dispersion mixer; this premix stage takes about 30–60 minutes. Then the batch is pumped into an agitated vessel that contains a milling medium (small steel or titanium dioxide balls of consistent size), which reduces it to a specified particle size. Finally, the paint is removed from the mill and allowed to cool, then tested. Solvent is lost during the milling stage because of elevated temperatures; in the letdown stage, solvent is added to lower the viscosity to proper levels.

Viscosity, percent weight solids, and weight per gallon are all important quality characteristics because they determine the dry thickness, how well it applies to a surface, and corrosion properties. For a particular type of paint used by automotive companies to prevent corrosion, specifications are

Viscosity: 60–80
Weight solids: 60–65 percent
Weight per gallon: 12.6–13.5

The worksheet *Day Industries* in the Excel workbook *C13CaseData* (available on the Premium website) contains data for a series of batches that were produced. Using appropriate SPC charts or other statistical tools, evaluate how well the process is in control and its capability to meet requirements. Express your results in a report to the plant manager.

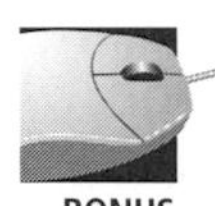
BONUS MATERIALS

NOTES

1. Robert W. Hoyer and Wayne C. Ellis, "A Graphical Exploration of SPC, Part 1," *Quality Progress* 29, no. 5 (May 1996), 65–73.

2. This discussion is adapted from James R. Evans, *Statistical Process Control for Quality Improvement: A Training Guide to Learning SPC* (Englewood Cliffs, NJ: Prentice Hall, 1991). Reprinted with permission of Prentice Hall, Upper Saddle River, NJ.

3. H. F. Dodge and M. N. Torrey, "A Check Inspection and Demerit Weighting Plan," *Industrial Quality Control* 13, no. 1 (July 1956), 5–12.

4. D. C. Montgomery, "The Economic Design of Control Charts: A Review and Literature Survey," *Journal of Quality Technology* 12, no. 2 (1980), 75–87.

5. Raymond R. Mayer, "Selecting Control Limits," *Quality Progress* 16, no 9 (1983), 24–26.

6. John E. West, "Do You Know Your SPC?" *Quality Digest*, July 2001, 51–56.

7. T.N. Goh and M. Xie, "Statistical Control of a Six Sigma Process," *Quality Engineering* 15, no. 4 (2003), 587–592.

8. Robert W. Traver, "Pre-Control: A Good Alternative to x-R-Charts," *Quality Progress* 18, no. 9 (September 1985).

9. Adapted from LeRoy A. Franklin and Samar N. Mukherjee, "An SPC Case Study on Stabilizing Syringe Lengths," *Quality Engineering* 12, no. 1 (1999–2000), 65–71. Reprinted from *Quality Engineering*, courtesy of Marcel Dekker, Inc.

10. We are grateful to Rick Casey for supplying this application.

11. Our thanks go to a former student, Jeffrey Day, for providing this case application.

Appendixes

A Areas for the Standard Normal Distribution
B Factors for Control Charts
C Random Digits

APPENDIX A

AREAS FOR THE STANDARD NORMAL DISTRIBUTION

Entries in the table give the area under the curve between the mean and z standard deviations above the mean. For example, for $z = 1.25$ the area under the curve between the mean and z is 0.3944.

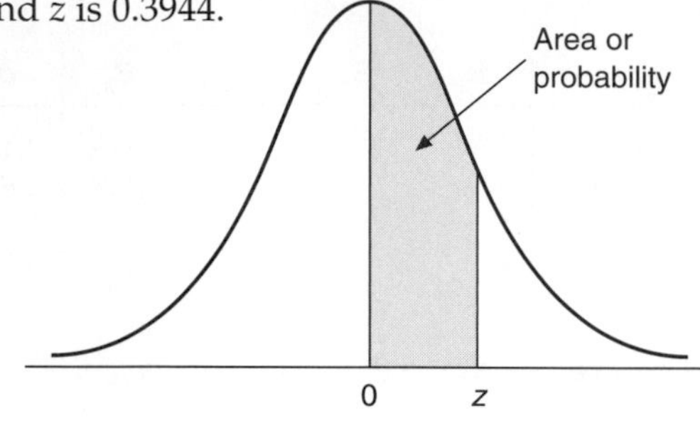

z	0.00	0.01	0.02	0.03	0.04	0.05	0.06	0.07	0.08	0.09
0.0	0.0000	0.0040	0.0080	0.0120	0.0160	0.0199	0.0239	0.0279	0.0319	0.0359
0.1	0.0398	0.0438	0.0478	0.0517	0.0557	0.0596	0.0636	0.0675	0.0714	0.0753
0.2	0.0793	0.0832	0.0871	0.0910	0.0948	0.0987	0.1026	0.1064	0.1103	0.1141
0.3	0.1179	0.1217	0.1255	0.1293	0.1331	0.1368	0.1406	0.1443	0.1480	0.1517
0.4	0.1554	0.1591	0.1628	0.1664	0.1700	0.1736	0.1772	0.1808	0.1844	0.1879
0.5	0.1915	0.1950	0.1985	0.2019	0.2054	0.2088	0.2123	0.2157	0.2190	0.2224
0.6	0.2257	0.2291	0.2324	0.2357	0.2389	0.2422	0.2454	0.2486	0.2518	0.2549
0.7	0.2580	0.2612	0.2642	0.2673	0.2704	0.2734	0.2764	0.2794	0.2823	0.2852
0.8	0.2881	0.2910	0.2939	0.2967	0.2995	0.3023	0.3051	0.3078	0.3106	0.3133
0.9	0.3159	0.3186	0.3212	0.3238	0.3264	0.3289	0.3315	0.3340	0.3365	0.3389
1.0	0.3413	0.3438	0.3461	0.3485	0.3508	0.3531	0.3554	0.3577	0.3599	0.3621
1.1	0.3643	0.3665	0.3686	0.3708	0.3729	0.3749	0.3770	0.3790	0.3810	0.3830
1.2	0.3849	0.3869	0.3888	0.3907	0.3925	0.3944	0.3962	0.3980	0.3997	0.4015
1.3	0.4032	0.4049	0.4066	0.4082	0.4099	0.4115	0.4131	0.4147	0.4162	0.4177
1.4	0.4192	0.4207	0.4222	0.4236	0.4251	0.4265	0.4279	0.4292	0.4306	0.4319
1.5	0.4332	0.4345	0.4357	0.4370	0.4382	0.4394	0.4406	0.4418	0.4429	0.4441
1.6	0.4452	0.4463	0.4474	0.4484	0.4495	0.4505	0.4515	0.4525	0.4535	0.4545
1.7	0.4554	0.4564	0.4573	0.4582	0.4591	0.4599	0.4608	0.4616	0.4625	0.4633
1.8	0.4641	0.4649	0.4656	0.4664	0.4671	0.4678	0.4686	0.4693	0.4699	0.4706
1.9	0.4713	0.4719	0.4726	0.4732	0.4738	0.4744	0.4750	0.4756	0.4761	0.4767
2.0	0.4772	0.4778	0.4783	0.4788	0.4793	0.4798	0.4803	0.4808	0.4812	0.4817
2.1	0.4821	0.4826	0.4830	0.4834	0.4838	0.4842	0.4846	0.4850	0.4854	0.4857
2.2	0.4861	0.4864	0.4868	0.4871	0.4875	0.4878	0.4881	0.4884	0.4887	0.4890
2.3	0.4893	0.4896	0.4898	0.4901	0.4904	0.4906	0.4909	0.4911	0.4913	0.4916
2.4	0.4918	0.4920	0.4922	0.4925	0.4927	0.4929	0.4931	0.4932	0.4934	0.4936
2.5	0.4938	0.4940	0.4941	0.4943	0.4945	0.4946	0.4948	0.4949	0.4951	0.4952
2.6	0.4953	0.4955	0.4956	0.4957	0.4959	0.4960	0.4961	0.4962	0.4963	0.4964
2.7	0.4965	0.4966	0.4967	0.4968	0.4969	0.4970	0.4971	0.4972	0.4973	0.4974
2.8	0.4974	0.4975	0.4976	0.4977	0.4977	0.4978	0.4979	0.4979	0.4980	0.4981
2.9	0.4981	0.4982	0.4982	0.4983	0.4984	0.4984	0.4985	0.4985	0.4986	0.4986
3.0	0.4986	0.4987	0.4987	0.4988	0.4988	0.4989	0.4989	0.4989	0.4990	0.4990

APPENDIX B

FACTORS FOR CONTROL CHARTS

	x-charts				*s*-Charts				*R*-charts					
n	A	A_2	A_3	c_4	B_3	B_4	B_5	B_6	d_2	d_3	D_1	D_2	D_3	D_4
2	2.121	1.880	2.659	0.7979	0	3.267	0	2.606	1.128	0.853	0	3.686	0	3.267
3	1.732	1.023	1.954	0.8862	0	2.568	0	2.276	1.693	0.888	0	4.358	0	2.574
4	1.500	0.729	1.628	0.9213	0	2.266	0	2.088	2.059	0.880	0	4.698	0	2.282
5	1.342	0.577	1.427	0.9400	0	2.089	0	1.964	2.326	0.864	0	4.918	0	2.114
6	1.225	0.483	1.287	0.9515	0.030	1.970	0.029	1.874	2.534	0.848	0	5.078	0	2.004
7	1.134	0.419	1.182	0.9594	0.118	1.882	0.113	1.806	2.704	0.833	0.204	5.204	0.076	1.924
8	1.061	0.373	1.099	0.9650	0.185	1.815	0.179	1.751	2.847	0.820	0.388	5.306	0.136	1.864
9	1.000	0.337	1.032	0.969	0.239	1.761	0.232	1.707	2.970	0.808	0.547	5.393	0.184	1.816
10	0.949	0.308	0.975	0.9727	0.284	1.716	0.276	1.669	3.078	0.797	0.687	5.469	0.223	1.777
11	0.905	0.285	0.927	0.9754	0.321	1.679	0.313	1.637	3.173	0.787	0.811	5.535	0.256	1.744
12	0.866	0.266	0.886	0.9776	0.354	1.646	0.346	1.610	3.258	0.778	0.922	5.594	0.283	1.717
13	0.832	0.249	0.850	0.9794	0.382	1.618	0.374	1.585	3.336	0.770	1.025	5.647	0.307	1.693
14	0.802	0.235	0.817	0.9810	0.406	1.594	0.399	1.563	3.407	0.763	1.118	5.696	0.328	1.672
15	0.775	0.223	0.789	0.9823	0.428	1.572	0.421	1.544	3.472	0.756	1.203	5.741	0.347	1.653
16	0.750	0.212	0.763	0.9835	0.448	1.552	0.440	1.526	3.532	0.750	1.282	5.782	0.363	1.637
17	0.728	0.203	0.739	0.9845	0.466	1.534	0.458	1.511	3.588	0.744	1.356	5.820	0.378	1.622
18	0.707	0.194	0.718	0.9854	0.482	1.518	0.475	1.496	3.640	0.739	1.424	5.856	0.391	1.608
19	0.688	0.187	0.698	0.9862	0.497	1.503	0.490	1.483	3.689	0.734	1.487	5.891	0.403	1.597
20	0.671	0.180	0.680	0.9869	0.510	1.490	0.504	1.470	3.735	0.729	1.549	5.921	0.415	1.585
21	0.655	0.173	0.663	0.9876	0.523	1.477	0.516	1.459	3.778	0.724	1.605	5.951	0.425	1.575
22	0.640	0.167	0.647	0.9882	0.534	1.466	0.528	1.448	3.819	0.720	1.659	5.979	0.434	1.566
23	0.626	0.162	0.633	0.9887	0.545	1.455	0.539	1.438	3.858	0.716	1.710	6.006	0.443	1.557
24	0.612	0.157	0.619	0.9892	0.555	1.445	0.549	1.429	3.895	0.712	1.759	6.031	0.451	1.548
25	0.600	0.153	0.606	0.9896	0.565	1.435	0.559	1.420	3.931	0.708	1.806	6.056	0.459	1.541

Source: Adapted from Table 27 of ASTM STP 15D ASTM *Manual on Presentation of Data and Control Chart Analysis.* © 1976 American Society for Testing and Materials, Philadelphia, PA.

Appendix C

Random Digits

63271	59986	71744	51102	15141	80714	58683	93108	13554	79945
88547	09896	95436	79115	08303	01041	20030	63754	08459	28364
55957	57243	83865	09911	19761	66535	40102	26646	60147	15702
46276	87453	44790	67122	45573	84358	21625	16999	13385	22782
55363	07449	34835	15290	76616	67191	12777	21861	68689	03263
69393	92785	49902	58447	42048	30378	87618	26933	40640	16281
13186	29431	88190	04588	38733	81290	89541	70290	40113	08243
17726	28652	56836	78351	47327	18518	92222	55201	27340	10493
36520	64465	05550	30157	82242	29520	69753	72602	23756	54935
81628	36100	39254	56835	37636	02421	98063	89641	64953	99337
84649	48968	75215	75498	49539	74240	03466	49292	36401	45525
63291	11618	12613	75055	43915	26488	41116	64531	56827	30825
70502	53225	03655	05915	37140	57051	48393	91322	25653	06543
06426	24771	59935	49801	11082	66762	94477	02494	88215	27191
20711	55609	29430	70165	45406	78484	31639	52009	18873	96927
41990	70538	77191	25860	55204	73417	83920	69468	74972	38712
72452	36618	76298	26678	89334	33938	95567	29380	75906	91807
37042	40318	57099	10528	09925	89773	41335	96244	29002	46453
53766	52875	15987	46962	67342	77592	57651	95508	80033	69828
90585	58955	53122	16025	84299	53310	67380	84249	25348	04332
32001	96293	37203	64516	51530	37069	40261	61374	05815	06714
62606	64324	46354	72157	67248	20135	49804	09226	64419	29457
10078	28073	85389	50324	14500	15562	64165	06125	71353	77669
91561	46145	24177	15294	10061	98124	75732	00815	83452	97355
13091	98112	53959	79607	52244	63303	10413	63839	74762	50289
73864	83014	72457	22682	03033	61714	88173	90835	00634	85169
66668	25467	48894	51043	02365	91726	09365	63167	95264	45643
84745	41042	29493	01836	09044	51926	43630	63470	76508	14194
48068	26805	94595	47907	13357	38412	33318	26098	82782	42851
54310	96175	97594	88616	42035	38093	36745	56702	40644	83514
14877	33095	10924	58013	61439	21882	42059	24177	58739	60170
78295	23179	02771	43464	59061	71411	05697	67194	30495	21157
67524	02865	39593	54278	04237	92441	26602	63835	38032	94770
58268	57219	68124	73455	83236	08710	04284	55005	84171	42596
97158	28672	50685	01181	24262	19427	52106	34308	73685	74246
04230	16831	69085	30802	65559	09205	71829	06489	85650	38707
94879	56606	30401	02602	57658	70091	54986	41394	60437	03195
71446	15232	66715	26385	91518	70566	02888	79941	39684	54315
32886	05644	79316	09819	00813	88407	17461	73925	53037	91904
62048	33711	25290	21526	02223	75947	66466	06232	10913	75336

Source: Reprinted from page 44 of *A Million Digits With 100,000 Normal Deviates,* by the Rand Corporation. New York: The Free Press, 1955. © 1955 by The Rand Corporation. Used by permission.

BIBLIOGRAPHY

Ahmed, Pervaiz K. and Mohammed Rafiq. "Integrated Benchmarking: A Holistic Examination of Select Techniques for Benchmarking Analysis." *Benchmarking for Quality Management & Technology* 5, 3 (1998): 225–242.

Allen, Derek R. and Morris Wolburn. *Linking Customer and Employee Satisfaction to the Bottom Line.* Milwaukee, WI: ASQ Quality Press, 2002.

Alukal, George, and Anthony Manos. "Lean Manufacturing." *The Quality Management Forum* 28, 3 (Summer 2002): 4–7.

American National Standard, Definitions, Symbols, Formulas, and Tables for Control Charts. ANSI/ASQC A1-1987. American Society for Quality Control, 310 W. Wisconsin Ave., Milwaukee, WI 53203.

American National Standard: Guide to Inspection Planning, ANSI/ASQC E-2-1984. Milwaukee, WI: American Society for Quality Control, 1984.

Andersen, Bjorn, and Tom Fagerhaug. *Performance Management Explained: Designing and Implementing Your State-of-the-Art System.* Milwuakee, WI: American Society for Quality, 2002.

Andersen, Bjorn. *Business Process Improvement Toolbox.* Milwaukee, WI: ASQ Quality Press, 1999.

AT&T Quality Steering Committee. *Achieving Customer Satisfaction.* Quality Technology Center, AT&T Bell Laboratories, 1990.

AT&T Quality Steering Committee. *Batting 1000: Using Baldrige Feedback to Improve Your Business.* AT&T Bell Laboratories, 1992.

AT&T Quality Steering Committee. *Policy Deployment.* AT&T Bell Laboratories, 1992.

AT&T Quality Steering Committee. *Process Quality Management & Improvement Guidelines.* AT&T Bell Laboratories, 1987.

AT&T Quality Steering Committee. *Process Quality Management & Improvement.* Quality Technology Center, AT&T Bell Laboratories, 1987.

Badracco, Joseph L. *Leading Quietly.* Boston: Harvard Business School Press, 2002.

Bauer, John E., Grace L. Duffy, and Russell T. Wescott (eds.). *The Quality Improvement Handbook.* Milwaukee, WI: ASQ Quality Press, 2002.

Bennis, Warren G., and Robert J. Thomas. *Geeks and Geezers.* Boston: Harvard Business School Press, 2002.

Bennis, Warren, Grechen M. Spreitzer, and Thomas G. Cummings (eds.). *The Future of Leadership: Today's Top Leadership Thinkers Speak to Tomorrow's Leaders.* San Francisco: Jossey-Bass, 2001.

Bens, Ingrid. *Facilitation at a Glance!* Cincinnati: AQP, 1999.

Berry, Leonard L., Valarie A. Zeithaml, and A. Parasuraman. "Five Imperatives for Improving Service Quality." *Sloan Management Review* (Summer 1990): 29–38.

Blackburn, Richard, and Benjamin Rosen. "Total Quality and Human Resources Management: Lessons Learned from Baldrige Award-Winning Companies." *Academy of Management Executive* 7, 3 (1993): 49–66.

Blanchard, Ken. *The Heart of a Leader: Insights on the Art of Influence.* Tulsa, OK: Honor Books, 1999.

Boser, Robert B., and Cheryl L. Christ. "Whys, Whens, and Hows of Conducting a Process Capability Study." Presentation at the ASQC/ASA 35th Annual Fall Technical Conference, Lexington, Kentucky, 1991.

Bossidy, Larry, Ram Charan, and Charles Burch. *Execution: The Discipline of Getting Things Done.* New York: Crown Books—Random House, 2002.

Box, G. E. P., and S. Bisgaard. "The Scientific Context of Quality Improvement." *Quality Progress* 20, 6, June 1987: 54–61.

Brager, Joan. "The Customer-Focused Quality Leader." *Quality Progress* 25, 5, May 1992, 51–53.

Brassard, Michael, and Diane Ritter. *The Memory Jogger II*. Methuen, MA: GOAL/QPC, 1994.

Brassard, Michael. *The Memory Jogger Plus+*. Methuen, MA: GOAL/QPC, 1989.

Breyfogle, Forrest W. III. *Implementing Six Sigma*, 2nd ed. New York: John Wiley & Sons, 2003.

Breyfogle, Forrest W. *Integrated Enterprise Excellence*—Vol. 3. Austin, TX: Citius Publishing, 2008.

Breyfogle, Forrest W., III, James M. Cupello, and Becki Meadows. *Managing Six Sigma*. New York: Wiley-Interscience, 2001.

Brocka, Bruce, and M. Suzanne Brocka. *Quality Management: Implementing the Best Ideas of the Masters*. Homewood, IL: Business One Irwin, 1992.

Brown, Bradford S. "Control Charts: The Promise and the Performance." Presentation at the ASQC/ASA 35th Annual Fall Technical Conference, Lexington, Kentucky, 1991.

Brown, Mark Graham. *Baldrige Award-Winning Quality: How to Interpret the Baldrige Criteria for Performance Excellence*, 17th ed. Milwaukee: ASQ Quality Press, 2008.

Brown, Mark Graham. *Winning Score : How to Design and Implement Organizational Scorecards*. New York: Productivity Press, 2007.

Brown, Mark Graham. *Keeping Score: Using the Right Metrics to Drive World-Class Performance*. New York: Quality Resources, 2006.

Brue, Greg. *Six Sigma for Managers*. New York, McGraw-Hill, 2002.

Buckingham, Marcus, and Curt Coffman. *First, Break All the Rules: What the World's Greatest Managers Do Differently*. New York: Simon and Schuster, 1999.

Burke, Charles J. "10 Steps to Best-Practices Benchmarking." *Quality Digest*, February 1996, 23–28.

Burns, T., and G. M. Stalker. *The Management of Innovation*. London: Tavistock, 1961.

Bush, David, and Kevin Dooley." The Deming Prize and the Baldrige Award: How They Compare." *Quality Progress* 22, 1, January 1989, 28–30.

Byrne, John. *Chainsaw: The Notorious Career of Al Dunlop in the Age of Profit-at-Any-Price*. New York: HarperBusiness, 2002.

Camison, Cesar. "Total Quality Management and Cultural Change: A Model of Organizational Development." *International Journal of Technology Management* 16, 4–6 (1998): 479.

Camp, Robert C. *Business Process Benchmarking: Finding and Implementing Best Practices*. Milwaukee, WI: ASQC Quality Press, 1995.

Carr, Maureen P., Francis W. Jackson, and Diane Cesarone. *The Crosswalk: Joint Commission Standards and Baldrige Criteria*. Oakbrook Terrace, IL : Joint Commission on Accreditation of Healthcare Organizations, 1997.

Case, Kenneth E., and Lynn L. Jones. *Profit Through Quality: Quality Assurance Programs for Manufacturers*. Norcross, GA: American Institute of Industrial Engineers, 1978.

Chatfield, Christopher. *Statistics for Technology: A Course in Applied Statistics*, 3rd ed. (Revised) New York: CRC Press, 1983.

Christison, William L. "Financial Information Is Key to Empowerment." *Quality Progress* 27, 7, July 1994, 47–48.

Cole, Robert E. "Corporate Strategy—Learning from the Quality Movement: What Did and Didn't Happen, and Why?" *California Management Review* 41, 1 (1998): 43.

Collins, James. *Good to Great: Why Some Companies Make the Leap . . . And Others Don't*. New York: HarperCollins, 2001.

Conger, J., and R. Kanugo. "Toward a Behavioral Theory of Charismatic Leadership in Organizational Settings." *Academy of Management Review*, October 1987: 637–647.

Conti, Tito. "Stakeholder-Based Strategies to Enhance Corporate Performance." *Denver, CO: Proceedings: Annual Quality Congress*, May 2002, 373–381.

Cooper, Robin, and Robert S. Kaplan. *The Design of Cost Management Systems: Text, Cases, and Readings*. New York: Prentice Hall, 1991.

Cullen, Thomas Patrick. *Managing Service Quality in the Hospitality Industry*. Ithaca, NY: Hotel School, Cornell University, 2000.

Cupello, James M. "A New Paradigm for Measuring TQM Progress." *Quality Progress* 27, 5, May 1994, 79–82.

DeCarly, Neil J., and W. Kent Sterett. "History of the Malcolm Baldrige Award." *Quality Progress* 23, 3, March 1990, 21–27.

Deming, W. Edwards. *Out of the Crisis*. Cambridge, MA: MIT Press, 2000.

Deming, W. Edwards. *The New Economics for Industry, Government, Education*, 2nd ed. Cambridge, MA: MIT Press, 2000.

DeToro, Irving, and Thomas McCabe. "How to Stay Flexible and Elude Fads." *Quality Progress*, March 1997, 55–60.

Donnell, Augustus, and Margaret Dellinger. *Analyzing Business Process Data: The Looking Glass*. AT&T Bell Laboratories, 1990.

Duncan, Acheson J. *Quality Control and Industrial Statistics*, 5th ed. Homewood, IL: Richard D. Irwin, 1986.

Duncan, W. Jack, and Joseph G. Van Matre. "The Gospel According to Deming: Is It Really New?" *Business Horizons*, July–August 1990, 3–9.

Dychtwald, Ken, Tamara J. Erickson, Robert Morison. *Workforce Crisis: How to Beat the Coming Shortage of Skills and Talent*. Cambridge, MA: Harvard Business School Press, 2006.

Easton, George S., and Sherry L. Jarrell. "The Effects of Total Quality Management on Organizational Performance: An Empirical Investigation." *The Journal of Business* 71, 2 (1998): 253.

Eckes, George. *The Six Sigma Revolution*. New York: John Wiley & Sons, 2001.

Emery, F. E., E. L. Trist, and J. Woodward. *Management and Technology.* London: Her Majesty's Stationery Office, 1958.

Eure, Rob. "E-Commerce (A Special Report): The Classroom—On the Job; Corporate E-Learning Makes Training Available Anytime, Anywhere." *The Wall Street Journal,* March 12, 2001, R33.

Evans, James R. *Quality and Performance Excellence: Management, Organization, and Strategy*, 5th ed. Cincinnati: Cengage Learning, 2008.

Evans, James R., and David L. Olson. *Introduction to Simulation and Risk Analysis*. Upper Saddle River, NJ: Prentice Hall, 2002.

Fitzsimmons, James A., and Mona J. Fitzsimmons. *New Service Development: Creating Memorable Experiences*. Thousand Oaks, CA: Sage Publications, 2000.

Ford, Matthew W. and James R. Evans. "Baldrige Assessment and Organizational Learning: The Need for Change Management." *Quality Management Journal* 8, 3, July 2001, 9–25.

Franz, Douglas. "To Put G. E. Online Meant Putting a Dozen Industries Online." *New York Times*, March 29, 2000.

Freund, Richard A. "Definitions and Basic Quality Concepts." *Journal of Quality Technology,* January 1985: 50–56.

Galford, Robert, Laurie Broedling, Edward G. Lawler, III, Tim Riley, et al. "Why Doesn't This HR Department Get Any Respect?" *Harvard Business Review* 76, 2, March/April 1998: 24–40.

Gantenbein, Douglas, and Marcia Stepanek. "Kaiser Takes the Cybercure." *Business Week*, February 7, 2000.

Garvin, David A. *Managing Quality*. New York: The Free Press, 1988.

George, Michael L. *Lean Six Sigma: Combining Six Sigma Quality with Lean Speed*. New York: McGraw-Hill, 2002.

Gitlow, H., S. Gitlow, A. Oppenheim, and R. Oppenheim. *Tools and Methods for the Improvement of Quality.* Homewood, IL: Irwin, 1989.

Godfrey, Blan. "Future Trends: Expansion of Quality Management Concepts, Methods and Tools to All Industries." *Quality Observer* 6, 9, September 1997, 40–43, 46.

Goetsch, David L., and Stanley B. Davis. *Understanding and Implementing ISO 9000:2000.* Upper Saddle River, NJ: Prentice Hall, 2002.

Goonan, Kathleen J., Joseph A. Muzikowski, and Particia K. Stoltz, *Journey to Excellence: How Baldrige Health Care Leaders Succeed*, Milwaukee, WI: ASQ Quality Press, 2009.

Grant, Eugene, L., and Richard S. Leavenworth. *Statistical Quality Control*, 7th ed. New York: McGraw-Hill, 1996.

Great Performances! AT&T Bell Laboratories, 1991.

Griffin, Ricky W., and Gregory Moorhead. *Organizational Behavior: Managing People and Organizations,* 9th ed. Mason, OH: Cengage Learning, 2010.

Griffith, Gary. *Quality Technician's Handbook,* 5th ed. New York: Prentice Hall, 2002.

Gryna, Frank M. *Work Overload: Redesigning Jobs to Minimize Stress and Burnout*. Milwaukee: ASQ Quality Press, 2004.

Gunter, Bert. "Process Capability Studies Part I: What Is a Process Capability Study?" *Quality Progress* 24, 2, February 1991, 97–99.

Haavind, Robert. *The Road to the Baldrige Award*. Boston: Butterworth-Heinemann, 1992.

Hackman, J. Richard. *Leading Teams: Setting the Stage for Great Performance.* Boston: Harvard Business School Press, 2002.

Hallowell, Roger. *Virtuous Cycles: Improving Service and Lowering Costs in E-Commerce*. Boston: Division of Research, Harvard Business School, 2001.

Harrington, H. James, and Kerim Tumay. *Simulation Modeling Methods.* New York: McGraw-Hill, 2000.

Harry, Mikel J. "Framework for Business Leadership." *Quality Progress*, April 2000.

Harry, Mikel J. *The Vision of Six Sigma: A Roadmap for Breakthrough*. Phoenix, AZ: Tri Star Publishing, 1997.

Hart, Christopher W. L., and Christopher E. Bogan. *The Baldrige*. New York: McGraw-Hill, 1992.

Hayes, Bob E. *Measuring Customer Satisfaction: Development and Use of Questionnaires*, 2nd ed. Milwaukee, WI: ASQC Quality Press, 1997.

Hayes, Glenn E. "Quality: Quandary and Quest." *Quality* 22, 7, July 1983, 18.

Henriques, Diana B., and Jacques Steinberg. "Right Answer, Wrong Score: Test Flaws Take Toll." *New York Times,* May 20, 2001; and Diana B. Henriques and Jacques Steinberg. "When a Test Fails the Schools, Careers and Reputations Suffer." *New York Times,* May 21, 2001. Source: http://deming.eng.clemson.edu/pub/psci/psn/inthenewsarchive.htm#2 (accessed June 24, 2009).

Herzberg, Frederick. "One More Time: How Do You Motivate Employees?" *Harvard Business Review* 46, (January/February 1968: 53–62.

Herzberg, Frederick. *Work and the Nature of Man*. Cleveland, OH: World, 1966.

Hesselbein, Frances, Marshall Goldsmith, and Richard Beckhard (eds.). *The Leader of the Future: New Visions, Strategies, and Practices for the next Era.* San Francisco: Jossey-Bass, Publishers, 1996.

Hiam, Alexander. *Closing the Quality Gap: Lessons from America's Leading Companies*. Englewood Cliffs, NJ: Prentice-Hall, 1992.

Hoerl, Roger W. "Six Sigma and the Future of the Quality Profession." *Quality Progress*, June 1998.

Hoffman, K. Douglas, and John E. G. Bateson. *Essentials of Services Marketing*. Fort Worth: Harcourt College Publishers, 2002.

Hradesky, John L. *Productivity and Quality Improvement*. New York: McGraw-Hill, 1988.

Hunt, V. Daniel. *Managing for Quality: Integrating Quality and Business Strategy*. Homewood, IL: Business One Irwin, 1993.

Hurley, Heather. "Cycle-Time Reduction: Your Key to a Better Bottom Line." *Quality Digest*, April 1996, 28–32.

Hutton, David W. *From Baldrige to the Bottom Line: A Road Map for Organizational Change and Improvement*. Milwaukee: ASQ Quality Press, 2000.

Janda, Swinder, Phillip J. Trocchia, and Kevin P. Gwinner. "Consumer Perceptions of Internet Retail Service Quality." *International Journal of Service Industry Management* 13, 5 (2002): 412–431.

Johnston, Robert. "The Determinants of Service Quality: Satisfiers and Dissatisfiers." *International Journal of Service Industry Management* 6, 5 (1995): 53.

Jugulum, Rajesh, and Philip Samuel. *Design for Lean Six Sigma* Hoboken, NJ: John Wiley & Sons, 2008.

Juran, J. M. *Juran on Quality by Design*. New York: The Free Press, 1992.

Juran, J. M. "Product Quality—A Prescription for the West." *Management Review*, June–July 1981.

Juran, J. M. "The Quality Trilogy." *Quality Progress* 19, August 1986, 19–24.

Juran, J. M., Editor, *A Historyof Managing for Quality*. Milwaukee, WI: ASQ Quality Press, 1995.

Kanfer, Ruth. "Motivation Theory in Industrial and Organizational Psychology." In Marvin D. Dunnette and Leaeta M. Hough (eds.). *Handbook of Industrial and Organizational Psychology*, 2nd ed., vol. 1. Palo Alto, CA: Consulting Psychologists Press, Inc., 1990, 75–170.

Kaplan, Robert S., and David P. Norton. *The Balanced Scorecard*. Boston: Harvard Business School Press, 1996.

Kaplan, Robert S., and David P. Norton. *The Strategy-Focused Organization: How Balanced Scorecard Companies Thrive in the New Business Environment*. Boston: Harvard Business School Press, 2000.

Katzenbach, Jon R. *Teams at the Top*. Boston: Harvard Business School Press, 1998.

Katzenbach, Jon R. and Douglas K. Smith. *The Wisdom of Teams*. New York: HarperBusiness, 2003.

Kenyon, David A. "Strategic Planning with the Hoshin Process." *Quality Digest*, May 1997, 55–63.

Kern, Jill P., John J. Riley, and Louis N. Jones (eds.). *Human Resources Management*. Quality and Reliability Series, sponsored by the ASQC Human Resources Division. New York: Marcel Dekker, Inc., and Milwaukee: ASQC Quality Press, 1987.

Kets de Vries, Manfred F.R. and Elizabeth Florent-Treacy, The New Global Leaders: Richard Branson, Percy Barnevik, and David Simon, pp. xiii–xiv, 40, 56–57. Copyright © 1999 Josey Bass, an Imprint of John Wiley & Sons, Inc. Reprinted by permission.

King, Carol A. "Service Quality Assurance Is Different." *Quality Progress* 18, 6, June 1985, 14–18.

Kivenko, Ken. "Improve Performance by Driving Out Fear." *Quality Progress* 27, 10, October 1994, 77–79.

Kloppenborg, Timpthy J. and Joseph A. Petrick, *Managing Project Quality.*Vienna, VA: Management Concepts, 2003.

Kouzes, James M., and Barry Z. Posner. *The Leadership Challenge*, 3rd ed. San Francisco: Jossey-Bass, 2002.

Kyrillidou, Martha, and Fred M. Heath. *Measuring Service Quality*. Champaign, IL: University of Illinois Graduate School of Library and Information Science, 2001.

Lapin, Lawrence L. *Statistics for Modern Business Decisions*, 4th ed. San Diego: Harcourt Brace Jovanovich, Inc., 1987.

Lawrence, P. R., and J. W. Lorsch. *Organization and Environment*. Boston: Harvard University, Division of Research, Graduate School of Business Administration, 1967.

Ledolter, J., and A. Swersey. "An Evaluation of Pre-Control." *Journal of Quality Technology* 29, 2, April 1997, 163–171.

Levy, Steven. *Insanely Great: The Life and Times of Macintosh: the Computer That Changed Everything*. New York: Viking, 1994.

Lewin, Kurt. *A Dynamic Theory of Personality*. New York: McGraw-Hill, 1935.

Lindsay, William M., and Joseph A. Petrick. *Total Quality and Organization Development*. Boca Raton, FL: CRC/St. Lucie Press, 1997.

Lloyd's Register Quality Assurance, Ltd. *Getting the Most from ISO 9000*. 1999.

Locke, E. A., and G. P. Latham. *Goal Setting: A Motivational Technique that Works!* Englewood Cliffs, NJ: Prentice Hall, 1984.

Lowe, J. *Jack Welch Speaks*. New York: John Wiley & Sons, 1998.

Lowenthal, Jeffrey N. *Six Sigma Project Management: A Pocket Guide*. Milwaukee, WI: ASQ Quality Press, 2001.

Malcolm Baldrige National Quality Award. *2009–10 Criteria for Performance Excellence*. National Institute of Standards and Technology, U.S. Department of Commerce.

Mayo, Elton. *The Human Problems of Industrial Civilization*. Cambridge, MA: Harvard Graduate School of Business, 1946.

Medina-Borja, Alexandra, and Konstantinos Triantis. "A Methodology to Evaluate Outcome Performance in Social Services and Government

Agencies." *Proceedings* 55th Annual Quality Congress, May 2001, 707–719.

Melan, Eugene H. *Process Management: A Systems Approach to Total Quality.* Portland, OR: Productivity Press, 1995.

Messmer, Max. "Rightsizing, Not Downsizing: How to Maintain Quality Through Strategic Staffing." *Industry Week*, August 3, 1993, 23–26.

Michelli, Joseph A. *The New Gold Standard*, New York: McGraw-Hill, 2008.

Miller, Ken. *The Change Agent's Guide to Radical Improvement*. Milwaukee: ASQ Quality Press, 2002.

Miner, John B. *Theories of Organizational Behavior.* Hinsdale, IL: Dryden Press, 1980.

Mittal, Banwari, and Jagdish N. Sheth. *Value Space: Winning the Battle for Market Leadership: Lessons from the World's Most Admired Companies*. New York: McGraw-Hill, 2001.

Mohrman, Susan Albers, Ramkrishnan V. Tenkasi, Edward E. Lawler, III, and Gerald E. Ledford, Jr. "Total Quality Management: Practice and Outcomes in the Largest U.S. Firms." *Employee Relations* 17, 3 (1995): 26–41.

Montgomery, D. C. *Introduction to Statistical Quality Control,* 4th ed. New York: John Wiley & Sons, 2000.

Morgan, Ronald B., and Jacke E. Smith. *Staffing the New Workplace: Selecting and Promoting for Quality Improvement*. Milwaukee, WI: ASQ Press, 1996.

Neely, Andrew, Chris Adams, and Mike Kennerley. *The Performance Prism: The Scorecard for Measuring and Managing Business Success.* New York: Financial Times-Prentice Hall, 2002. Performance Measurement Association. http://www.performanceportal.org.

Nelson, Lloyd S. "Control Charts for Individual Measurements." *Journal of Quality Technology* 14, 3, July 1982, 172–173.

Nemiro, Jill, Michael M. Beyerlein, Lori Bradley, Susan Beyerlein (eds.) *The Handbook of High Performance Virtual Teams: A Toolkit for Collaborating Across Boundaries*. San Francisco: Jossey-Bass John Wiley & Sons, 2008

Nogami, Glenda Y. "Eight Points for More Useful Surveys." *Quality Progress* 29, 10, October 1996, 93–96.

O'Dell, Karla, and C. Jackson Grayson, Jr. *If Only We Knew What We Know.* New York: Free Press, 1999.

Ohio Quality and Productivity Forum Roundtable. "Deming's Point Four: A Study." *Quality Progress* 21, 12, December 1988, 31–35.

Olian, Judy D., and Sara L. Rynes. "Making Total Quality Work: Aligning Organizational Processes, Performance Measures, and Stakeholders." *Human Resource Management* (Fall 1991) 303–333.

Ouelette, Steven M., and Michael V. Petrovich. "Daily Management and Six Sigma: Maximizing Your Returns." *Proceedings* ASQ 56th Annual Quality Congress, 2002.

Page, Harold S. "A Quality Strategy for the '80s." *Quality Progress* 16, 11, November 1983, 16–21.

Palmer, Brian, and Mike Ziemlanski. "Tapping Into People." *Quality Progress*, April 2000, 74–79.

Pande, Peter S., Robert P. Neuman, and Roland R. Cavanagh. *The Six Sigma Way Team Fieldbook: An Implementation Guide for Process Improvement Teams.* New York: McGraw-Hill Trade, 2001.

Parry, Pam. "Sears Delivers a Better QMS." *Quality Digest*, April 2006, 22–27.

Petrick, Joseph A., and Diana Furr. *Total Quality in Managing Human Resources*. Boca Raton, FL: CRC/St. Lucie Press, 1995.

Porter, Lyman W., Gregory A. Bigley, and Richard M. Steers. *Motivation and Work Behavior*, 7th ed. New York: McGraw-Hill, 2003.

Powell, Cash, Jr. "Empowerment, the Stake in the Ground for ABS." *Target,* January/February 1992.

Profiles of Malcolm Baldrige Award Winners. Boston: Allyn & Bacon, 1992.

Pyzdek, Thomas, *The Six Sigma Handbook.* New York: McGraw-Hill, 2003.

Pyzdek, Thomas. "Six Sigma Is Primarily a Management Program." *Quality Digest,* June 1999, 26.

Pyzdek, Thomas. *Pyzdek's Guide to SPC, Volume Two—Applications and Special Topics*. Milwaukee, WI: ASQ Quality Press, 1992.

Raju, P. S., and Subhash C. Lonial. "The Impact of Quality Context and Market Orientation on Organizational Performance in a Service Environment." *Journal of Service Research* 4, 2 (2001): 140–154.

Raturi, A., and D. McCutcheon. "An Epistemological Framework for Quality Management," working paper. Cincinnati, OH: University of Cincinnati, Department of Quantitative Analysis and Information Systems, March 1990.

Reilly, Norman B. *The Team Based Product Development Guidebook.* Milwaukee, WI: ASQ Quality Press, 1999.

Reimann, Curt W. "The Baldrige Award: Leading the Way in Quality Initiatives." *Quality Progress* 22, 7, July 1989, 35–39.

Reis, Dayr, Pahl, Joy, and Kuffel, Thomas. "Learning to Compete Through Quality." *The Quality Observer,* January 1997, 10–24.

Rice, George O. "Metrology." In Loren Walsh, Ralph Wurster, and Raymond J. Kimber (eds.). *Quality Management Handbook.* New York: Marcel Dekker, 1986, 517–530.

Robbins, C. L., and W. A. Robbins. "What Nurse Managers Should Know about Sampling Techniques." *Nursing Management* 20, 6, June 1989: 46–48.

Rosander, A. C. *Applications of Quality Control in the Service Industries.* New York: Marcel Dekker and ASQ Quality Press, 1985.

Rosander, A. C. *The Quest for Quality in Services.* Milwaukee, WI: ASQC Quality Press, 1989.

Rosenberg, Jarrett. "Five Myths about Customer Satisfaction." *Quality Progress* 29, 12, December 1996, 57–60.

Rosenfeld, Manny. "Only the Questions That Are Asked Can Be Answered." *Quality Progress,* April 1994, 71–73.

Rubinstein, Sidney P. "Quality and Democracy in the Workplace." Quality *Progress* 21, 4, April 1988, 25–28.

Rue, L. W., and L. Byars. *Management Skills and Applications,* 12th ed. New York: McGraw-Hill/Irwin, 2008.

Rust, Roland T., Christine Moorman, and Peter R. Dickson. *Getting Returns from Service Quality: Is the Conventional Wisdom Wrong?* Cambridge, MA: Marketing Science Institute, 2000.

Sample, Steven B. *The Contrarian's Guide to Leadership.* San Francisco: Jossey-Bass, 2001.

Sanes, Christina. "Customer Complaints = Golden Opportunities." *Transactions* 1993 ASQC Quality Congress, Boston, 45–51.

Scherkenbach, William W. *Deming's Road to Continual Improvement.* Knoxville, TN: SPC Press, 1991.

Schlesinger, Leonard A. "'Hardwiring' an Organization's Service Performance" Managing *Service Quality* 13, 1 (2003): 6–9.

Schmidt, Warren H., and Jerome P. Finnigan. *A Race Without a Finish Line.* San Francisco: Jossey-Bass Publishers, 1992.

Schneiderman, Arthur M. "Are There Limits to TQM?" *Strategy & Business* 11 (Second Quarter 1998): 35.

Schneiderman, Arthur M. "Why Balanced Scorecards Fail!" *Journal of Strategic Performance Measurement,* January 1999: 6.

Schneiderman, Arthur M. "Measurement, the Bridge between the Hard and Soft Sides." *Journal of Strategic Performance Measurement* 2, 2, April/May 1998: 14.

Scholtes, Peter R. "Communities as Systems." *Proceedings* ASQC 50th Annual Quality Congress (1996): 258–265.

Scholtes, P. R. *The Team Handbook,* 2nd ed. Madison, WI: Joiner Associates, 1996.

Semerad, James M. "Create a New Learning Environment." *APICS—The Performance Advantage,* April 1993, 34–37.

Sherman, Strat. "Stretch Goals: The Dark Side of Asking for Miracles." *Fortune,* November 13, 1995, 231–232.

Silverman, Lori with Annabeth L. Propst. *Critical SHIFT: The Future of Quality in Organizational Performance.* Milwaukee: ASQ Quality Press, 1999.

Simmons, David E., Mark A. Shadur, and Arthur P. Preston. "Integrating TQM and HRM." *Employee Relations* 17, 3 (1995): 75–86.

Smergut, Peter. "Total Quality Management and the Not-for-Profit." *Administration in Social Work,* 22, 3 (1998): 75.

Smith, Douglas K. and Robert C. Alexander. *Fumbling the Future: How Xerox Invented, Then Ignored the First Personal Computer.* New York: William Morrow and Co., 1988.

Snape, Ed, Adrian Wilkinson, Mick Marchington, and Ted Redman. "Managing Human Resources for TQM: Possibilites and Pitfalls." *Employee Relations* 17, 3 (1995), 42–51.

Snell, Scott A., and James W. Dean. "Integrated Manufacturing and Human Resource Management: A Human Capital Perspective." *Academy of Management Journal* 35, 3 (1992): 467–504.

Squires, Frank H. "What Do Quality Control Charts Control?" *Quality,* November 1982, 63.

St. Lawrence, Dennis, and Bob Stinnett. "Powerful Planning with Simple Techniques." *Quality Progress* 27, 7, July 1994, 57–64.

Stamatis, D. H. *Six Sigma and Beyond: Foundations of Excellent Performance.* Boca Raton, FL: St. Lucie/CRC Press, 2002.

Stewart, Thomas. *The Wealth of Knowledge.* New York: Currency, 2001.

Sutcliffe, Kathleen, Sim Sitkin, and Larry Browning. "Tailoring process management to situational requirements: Beyond the control and exploration dichotomy." from Robert E. Cole and W. Richard Scott [Eds.]. *The quality movement and organization theory.* Thousand Oaks, Calif.: Sage Publishing, 2000.

Taylor, Frederick W. *The Principles of Scientific Management.* New York: Harper & Row, 1911.

Taylor, Glenn L., and Martha N. Morgan. "The Reverse Appraisal: A Tool for Leadership Development" *Quality Progress* 28, 12, December 1995, 81–87.

Tedaldi, Michael, Fred Seaglione, and Vincent Russotti. *A Beginner's Guide to Quality in Manufacturing.* Milwaukee, WI: ASQC Quality Press, 1992.

Tedesco, Frank M. "Building Quality Goals into the Business Plan." *The Total Quality Review* 4, 1, March/April 1994: 31–34.

The Inc Team. *The Team Memory Jogger.* Madison, WI: Brian Joyner and Associates, Goal/QPC, 1995.

Tichy, Noel M., Andrew McGill, Andrew R. McGill (eds.). *The Ethical Challenge: How to Build Honest Business Leaders.* New York: John Wiley and Sons, 2003.

Tichy, Noel, and Eli Cohen. "The Teaching Organization." *Training and Development,* July 1998.

Tomas, Sam. "Six Sigma: Motorola's Quest for Zero Defects." *APICS, The Performance Advantage,* July 1991, 36–41.

Tomas, Sam. "What Is Motorola's Six Sigma Product Quality?" *American Production and Inventory Control Society 1990 Conference Proceedings.* Falls Church, VA: APICS, 27–31.

Tomas, Sam. "What Is Motorola's Six Sigma Product Quality?" *American Production and Inventory Control Society 1990 Conference Proceedings*. Falls Church, VA: APICS: 27–31.

U.S. Department of Commerce and Booz-Allen & Hamilton, Inc. "Total Quality Management (TQM): Implementer's Workshop." May 1990.

Van der Wiele, Ton, Alan Brown, Robert Millen, and Daniel Whelan. "Improvement in Organizational Performance and Self-Assessment Practices by Selected American Firms." *Quality Management Journal* 7, 4, October 2000, 8–22.

Van Gigch, John P. "Quality—Producer and Consumer Views." *Quality Progress* 10, 4, April 1977, 30–33.

Vance, Lonnie C. "A Bibliography of Statistical Quality Control Chart Techniques, 1970–1980." *Journal of Quality Technology* 15, 12, April 1983.

Wachniak, Ray. "World-Class Quality: An American Response to the Challenge." In M. Sepehri (ed.), *Quest for Quality: Managing the Total System*. Norcross, GA: Institute of Industrial Engineers, 1987.

Wadsworth, Harrison M., Kenneth S. Stephens, and A. Blanton Godfrey. *Modern Methods for Quality Control and Improvement*, 2nd ed. New York: John Wiley & Sons, 2002.

Waldman, David A. "A Theoretical Consideration of Leadership and Total Quality Management." *Leadership Quarterly* 4 (1993): 65–79.

Walton, Richard E. "From Control to Commitment in the Workplace." *Harvard Business Review* 63, 2, March/April 1985, 77–85.

Watson, Gregory H. Design for Six Sigma, Salem, NH: GOAL/QPC, 2005.

Watson, Gregory H. "Peter F. Drucker: Delivering Value to Customers." *Quality Progress* 35, 5, May 2002.

Welch, Jack, and John Byrne. *Jack: Straight from the Gut*. New York: Warner Books, 2001.

Welch, Jack, Rik Kirkland, and Geoffrey Colvin. "Jack: The Exit Interview." *Fortune*, September 17, 2001.

Whiteley, Richard C. *The Customer-Driven Company.* Reading, MA: Addison-Wesley, 1991.

Wilkerson, David, and Clifton Cooksey. *Customer Service Measurement.* Arlington, VA: Coopers & Lybrand, 1994.

Wong, Amy, and Amrik Sohal. "Customers' Perspectives on Service Quality and Relationship Quality in Retail Encounters." *Managing Service Quality* 12, 6, 2002: 424–433.

Yakhou, Mehenna, and Boubekeur Rahali. "Integration of Business Functions: Roles of Cross-Functional Information Systems." *APICS—The Performance Advantage* 2, 12, December 1992: 35–37.

Yee, William, and Ed Musselwhite. "Living TQM With Workforce 2000." *Transactions* 1993 ASQC Quality Congress. Boston, 141–146.

Zeithaml, A. Parasuraman, and Leonard L. Berry. *Delivering Quality Service*. New York: The Free Press, 1990.

Zemke, Ron. "The Emerging Art of Service Management." *Training* 29, January 1992: 36–42.

Zimmerman, Richard E., Linda Steinmann, and Vince Schueler. "Designing Customer Surveys That Work." *Quality Digest*,October 1996, 22–28.

Zubairi, Mazhar M. "Statistical Process Control Management Issues." 1985 IIE Fall Conference Proceedings. Reprinted in Mehran Sepehri (ed.), *Quest for Quality: Managing the Total System.* Norcross, GA: Industrial Engineering & Management Press, 1987.

INDEX

A

AACSB. *See* Association to Advance Collegiate Schools of Business
ABM. *See* activity-based management
ABM expert, 465
ABM master, 465
"Absolutes of Quality Management," 107
Academic Quality Improvement Project (AQIP), 71
accelerated life testing, 622–623
Accenture, 216
accessibility, 75, 180, 410, 416. *See also* data accessibility
accountability, 91, 424
accreditation agency, 132, 324
accuracy, 561, 624–*625*
Ackoff, Russell, 50
ACS. *See* American College of Surgeons (ACS)
ACSI. *See* American Customer Satisfaction Index
ACSI model, *195*
action
  in Deming's points, 93, 107
  in Juran's breakthrough sequence, 106
  plans, 157, 163–166
actionable
  defined, 376
  feedback, 226
  information, 191, 219, 224
  measures, 376
  results, 219, 375
activity-based costing, 390
activity-based management (ABM), 464
actual quality, 206–207
ADA. *See* Americans with Disabilities Act
ADAC Laboratories, *113*, 395
Adams, J. Stacy, 255
adjourning phase of teams, 269
adoption stage of life cycle, 450
Advanced Circuits, 206
AEP. *See* American Electric Power
aesthetics, as dimension of quality, 199
affinity diagrams, 204–205
after-action review, 322
Agency for Healthcare Research and Quality (AHRQ), 63
agendas, for meetings, 273
agility, 118, 312, 313
aging population, 14
Airbus, 364
airlines industry
  customer requirements for, 236
  quality in, 48, 58
Alcoa, 461–463
  leadership changes at, 461–463
  vision of, 462
alignment
  action plans and goals, 164
  brand, 293
  defined, 447
  employees and, 262
  of human resource plans, 170
  measures/strategies/processes and, 346, 366, 381–382
  organizational components and, 115, 166, 256
  of projects, 451
Alliance for Performance Excellence, 121
Alliance for Work-Life Progress, 246
Allied Signal, 133, 463
Amalgamated Clothing and Textile Workers, 33
Amazon.com, 228–230, 216
American business culture, 103
American College of Surgeons (ACS), 61
American Customer Satisfaction Index (ACSI), 194–*195*
  indexes produced by, 194
  model, *195*
  release of, 194
  results reported by, 194
  updating of, 194
American Electric Power (AEP), 423
American Express
  billing process at, 33
  change management at, 444
  DMAIC at, 536
  "label and link" at, 256
  organizational effectiveness measures at, 536
  quality at, 373
American Honda Motor Co., 289–291

American Management Association, 57
American Medical Colleges (AAMC), 63
American National Standards Institute (ANSI), 19, 128
American Productivity and Quality Center (APQC), 49, 112, 397–398
American Quality Foundation, 438
American Red Cross, 73, 448
American Society for Quality (ASQ), 8, 13–14, 19, 66. *See also* American Customer Satisfaction Index; Koalaty Kid
  Customer Satisfaction Index (ASCI), 194
  Honorary Members of, 109
  Human Development and Leadership Division, 424
  leadership competencies, 424
  quality principles, 13–14, 460
  school survey, 66
  in Six Sigma, 563
  standard terminology of, 19, 128
Americans with Disabilities Act (ADA), 416
Ames Rubber Corporation
  customer satisfaction, 52
  interlinking model for, 54, 205, 385
  performance measurements, 385
  product development at, 52, 54, 205, 585
  tool engineering, 54
  training at, 385
  work environment at, 270
AMR Research, Inc., 308
Analog Devices, 278, 368
analysis, 115–116, 130. *See also* Customer Value Analysis; design failure mode and effects analysis; failure mode and effects analysis; Measurement, Analysis and Improvement; Pareto analysis; statistical analysis
  at Branch-Smith, 181
  capability, 385
  cluster, 386
  at Corning, Incorporated, 67
  correlation, 164, 385, 512–513
  customer relationship management (CRM) and, 216
  cycle-time, 448, 561
  defined, 383
  in DMAIC, 534
  fishbone, 353
  "hard", 437
  at IBM, 384
  information, 123, 131
  for improvement, 132, 191, 201, 395
  for management, 139, 387–388
  matrix data, 171
  at Novel Connect, 417–418
  performance data, 225, 383–388
  predictive, 292
  process, 287
  process value, 448
  products, 200, 313
  progressive, *553*
  quality cost accounting and, 105
  regression, 293
  relationships in, 385
  repeatability spreadsheet, *628*
  reproducibility analysis, *628*
  results of, 223, 293
  segmentation, 385
  in Six Sigma, 265, 533–534
  spreadsheets, 385, 517, 530, *628*
  "soft", 437
  software for, 385
  staffing, 284
  statistical correlation, 135, 179, 220, 512–513
  strengths, weaknesses, opportunities, threats (SWOT), 164–165, 181–182, 429
  work method, 313
analysis of variance (ANOVA), 385, 510–512
analytic study, 505
ANOVA. *See* analysis of variance
ANSI. *See* American National Standards Institute
appraisal
  costs, 389
  performance, 278–279, 281
Appraisal Review Process, 49
APQC. *See* American Productivity and Quality Center
AQC. *See* Australian Quality Council (AQC)
AQIP. *See* Academic Quality Improvement Project (AQIP)
Arbol, Marvin, 238
Armstrong Building Products Operations (BPO), *113*, 367
arrow diagrams, 171
Artesyn Technologies, 103, *113*, 122
Arthur Andersen, 119
ASQ. *See* American Society for Quality
Assembly, 54
  at Boeing, 362–364
  charts, 313
  at DaimlerChrysler, 320
  in Deming's production system, 24
  at GM, 263
  in Japanese quality, 346–346
  in manufacturing, 51, 54, 313
assignable causes, 483
Association to Advance Collegiate Schools of Business (AACSB), 79, 80
assurance, 199, 504, 652, *654*. *See also* project quality assurance; quality assurance
AT&T
  benchmarking at, 339–340
  customer-supplier model, 195–196
  data management at, 393
  design engineers at, 260
  design review at, 622
  empowerment at, 260
  job enrichment at, 259
  methodology of, 311
  policy deployment at, 167

process focus, 22, 311
process management, 311
quality award, 10
steering team of, 428
training at, 259
team development, 269
workforce-focused outcomes, 373
attributes
charts for, 665, 687–701, *691*, *694*, *698*
customer, 223, 225, *235*
data, 665
at GE Fanuc, *517*
manufacturer, 17
and metrics, 665
product/service, 15, 17, 21, 27, 217, 225, 234, 266
raw, 90
role performance, *266*
Australian Business Excellence Award, 125–127
assessment criteria for, 126
framework, 125–126
Australian Business Review Weekly, 130
Australian Quality Council (AQC), 125
Automotive Industry Action Group, 660
autonomy, 258
availability, 172, 220
average characteristics, 667
average failure rate over a time interval, 614
average range, 666
Avis, 192
avoidable errors, 62
Avolio, B. J., 436
award programs. *See also* Baldrige Award; European Quality Award; Malcolm Baldrige National Quality Award; President's Quality Award
Australian Business Excellence Award, 137
Canadian Awards for Business Excellence, 125
categories, 74
Chinese National Quality Award, 127, 128
Deming Application Prize, 122–123
European Quality Award, 123–125
Excellence Award for Quality and Productivity, 10
Federal Quality Prototype Award, 10
"The Golden Hammer" Awards, 74
international, 122–133
J. D. Power Gold Plant Quality Award, 245
Lincoln Award for Excellence, 120
Mayor's Cup Quality Award, 127
Missouri Quality Award, 452
National Housing Quality Award (NHQA), 139
at Premier, 278
President's Quality Award (PQA), 74
Quality Improvement Prototype Award, 74
quality management, 111
Six Sigma Excellent Organization Award, 127–128
state, 75, 121
Team Excellence Award, 277
Xerox President's Award, 277

B

backward chaining, 542
balanced scorecard, 368–370
at IBM, 370
at Pearl River School District, 369
perspectives of, 368–369
at United States Postal Service, 402–404
Baldrige Award, 6, 10. *See also* Malcolm Baldrige National Quality Award
comparisons, 135–138
criteria for, 74
in education, 69
operational and financial results, 28
in performance excellence, 424
strategic planning cycle, 140
quality awareness, 10, 111
Baldrige Criteria for Performance Excellence, 111–122
analysis, 115, 116
areas to address in, 119–121
assessment findings, 457
business results as, 115
categories, 116
comparisons, 135–138
core values and concepts, 118–119, 447
customer focus and, 115
evolution of, 119
false starts stage, 451
framework, 74, 116
governance, 116
human resource focus in, 125
impacts of, 121
implementation of, 118–119
integration stage, 451–452
ISO and, 177
ISO compared to, 135–138
knowledge management, 115, 116
leadership and, 115, 116, 118, 424, 459
learning organization in, 456–457
measurement and, 115, 116
mission in, 117
as model in business, 120
national culture and, 128
process management in, 341–342
profile questions, 159
progress tools, 456
roadmap to, 451
at Saint Luke's Hospital, 440, 452–453
as self-assessment, 120–121, 456–459
Six Sigma and, 177–178
social responsibilities, 116
stages in, 451
status quo stage, 451
strategic planning and, 115, 177
sustaining stage, 451, 451

traction stage, 451
updates to, 115
values in, 117–118
visions in, 117–118
workforce focus, 115, 116
Baldrige, Malcolm, 6, 112
Baldrige organizational profile questions, 159
Bama Companies, *113*
Bandura, A., 255
Bank of Montreal, 208
Baptist Hospital Inc. (BHI), 366–367
BAR (Budget Accountability Report), 366
CARE, (Clinical Accountability Report of), 366
culture of, 169, 425
FOCUS-PDCA, 366
Hospital Information System (HIS) at, 394–395
human resource plans, 169
information management practices at, 366
leadership competencies at, 425
teams at, 263
training at, 286
Basecamp, 259
"Basic Elements of Improvement," 107, 108
Bass, B. M., 435
battery
discharge time data by brand, 511
testing experimental design, 509–510
Baxter Healthcare International
Baldrige and Six Sigma in, 137–138
responsibility in, 137
Baxter Quality Institute, 137
A Beautiful Mind, 336
behavioral frequency scale, 381
behavioral skills, 271
BellSouth, 27
Bell System, 7
Bell Telephone Laboratories, 7
BEMC. *See* Black Elk Medical Center
benchmarking, 338–340
at AT&T, 339–340
best practices and, 338, 339
breakthrough improvement and, 338–340
competitive, 339
customer satisfaction, 194
educational, 79–80
at General Mills, 339
at Graniterock Company, 339
internal, 397–398
International Benchmarking Clearinghouse, 386
measurement system, 37
at Mercy Hospital, 192
process, 339
reengineering and, 340
strategic, 339
at Xerox, 33, 35, 287, 339
Berkshire Hathaway, 228
best practices, 406–407, 448–449
Best Practices Knowledgebase, 406
Bezos, Jeff, 228–229
BHI. *See* Baptist Hospital Inc.
BI
customer feedback at, 217
Relationship Customer Satisfaction Index at, 217
Service Recovery Process at, 214
Transactional Customer Satisfaction Index at, 217
bias, 203, 219, 220, 224, 300, 492
Big Bear Stores, 229
Big Q, 11
black belt. *See* Six Sigma black belt
Black Elk Medical Center (BEMC), 653–656
Blaine, Jeff, 725
Blanchard, K. H., *433*–434
blogs, 203, 259
Blum, Jonathan, 277
BMW, 124, 199
Boeing
assembly lines at, 363
cultural changes and, 444
digital prototypes used at, 584
IPTs at, 262
information management systems at, 363–364
leadership system at, 51
measurements, 363–364
PBM developed by, 307, 311–312
product design at, 51, 311
stretch goals at, 338
Supplier On-Time Delivery Rate, 307
Boeing Aerospace Support (AS), *114*, 306–307, 311
Boeing Airlift and Tanker (A&T)
comparative data at, 386
financial measures at, 372
Human Resource Management at, 373
selecting measures and indicators at, 375
team development process, 262, 268–269
workforce-focused outcomes, 373
Boise, 543
"boomerang principle," 189
Bonsignore, Michael R., 464
Borders Books, 230
Bose Corporation, 587–588
Bostwick Viscosity Meter, 344
bottle plants, strategic planning case, 185
bottom-up planning, 164
bottom-up projects, 110, 537
Bowditch, James L., 255
Bowen, David E., 20
BPO. *See* Armstrong Building Products Operations; BPO (business process outsourcing)
BPO (business process outsourcing), 405
brainstorm, 262, 332, 353, 395, 566
brainwriting, 587
Branch-Smith Printing Division (BSPD), 180–182
complaint management, 213

data sharing at, 180–181, 213
employee selection of, 284
mission of, 180
Print Leadership Team (PLT), 181–182
QIP at, 332
SPP at, 180
statistical thinking, 481
strategic planning at, 180–182

breakthrough improvement, 338–340
benchmarking and, 338–340
defined, 339
objectives, 338
process, 339
reengineering and, 340
strategic, 339–340
stretch goals and, 338

breakthrough objectives, 338
Bronson Methodist Hospital, *114*
Brooks, Gayle, 416
Brown, Mark Graham, 375
BSPD. *See* Branch-Smith Printing Division
B2B (business-to-business), 396
BT Group, 215
Buffet, Warren, 228
builder, 424
Builder MT, 141
Buono, Anthony F., 255
burn-in, 55, 623
Burns, James M., *433*, 435
Bush, George W., 66
Business Excellence Model, 127, 399
Business Excellence organization, 137
business performance measures/indicators, 365
business practices, 20–25, 119, 459. *See also* specific types
business processes, 307–311. *See also* process management
business results, 116, *126*, 197, 292–*293*, 385
Business Roundtable, 431
business support activities, 55–56
business-to-business (B2B), 396
business-to-consumer (B2C), 396
Business Week, 8, 27
Byrne, John, 59

C

CAD (computer-aided design), 85, 415
Cadillac Motor Car Company
loyal customers, 193
mission of, 16
quality in, 16
simultaneous engineering at, 585

calibration, 138, 340, 389, 390, 629–630
call centers, 99, 176, 210, 320
CAM (computer-aided manufacturing), 415
Canadian Awards for Business Excellence, 125
capability. *See also* process capability
control and, 503, *517*, *662–664*
process, *540–541*
study, *710*
workforce, 282, 282–285

CARE, (Clinical Accountability Report of), 366
career development, 119, 270, 288, 294
Carlzon, Jan, 208
Case, Kenneth, 66
catchball process, 169
Caterpillar Financial Services Corporation (CSFC). *See also* Solar Turbines
data protection at, 431
DMEDI process at, 528
financial control mechanisms in, 431
information management at, 396
quality at, 57
Six Sigma within, 163, 528–529
strategic planning at, 162–163

causal relationships, *370*
causation, 492
cause-and-effect diagrams, 516, 518, 554–555
for billing errors, *576*
for causes of multiple trips, 566
facilitating understanding of, 374
general structure of, *554*
for hospital emergency admission, 554–555
indicators for, 369
Ishikawa, Kaoru, 554
in Japan, 554
key factors in, 384
measures for, 369
in multiple trips, *567*
in performance improvement, 385
prediction, 97
rational management decisions, 97

cause-and-effect modeling. *See* interlinking model
causes
assignable, 483
common, 482–483
DMAIC and, 179
failure, 514, 518
root, 270, 311, 337, 350, 353
special, 483
of variation, 62, 92, 94–96, 102, 482–483

CBS, 9
CCC chart. *See* cumulative count of conforming chart (CCC)
c-charts
applications of, 696, 697–701
u-charts versus, 696

CCL. *See* Center for Creative Leadership
CCP (Crawford Consumer Products), 725
CCR (Client Concern Resolution), 191
CE. *See* concept engineering Center for Creative Leadership (CCL), 437
Cedar Foundation. *See also* Texas Nameplate Company, Inc. (TNC)
commitment, 91
enthusiasm, 91
equality of opportunity, 91
leadership, 91
mission, 91

openness and accountability, 91
pursuit of excellence, 91
teamwork and partnership, 91
values of respect for the individual, 91
vision, 91
Center for Quality of Management (CQM), 227, 587
centering of process, 666–667, 711
center line, hugging, 678–680
Centers for Medicare and Medicaid Services (CMS), 63
Central Limit Theorem (CLT), 502–503
CGISS (Commercial, Government, and Industrial Solutions Sector), 6
"chain of customers," 56
Challenger space shuttle disaster, 9
change, 461–463. *See also* cultural change; strategic change
barriers to, 447–448
at Boeing AT&T, 375
in leadership, 68, 461–463
at Medrad, 284
organizational culture, 443–447
at PRO-Tec, 388
necessity for, 443
resistance to, 77, 422
strategic versus process, *444*
change management, *179*, 443–444, 463
changing nature of leadership (CNL), 437
Charismatic theory, 433
CHARTrunner, 701
charts. *See* specific charts
Chase Manhattan Bank, 392
Chase, Richard B., 318
checklists, 30, 318, 535, *655*
check sheets, 548
cautions, 549–550
for data collection, 549–550
for defect locations, 548, *551*
for defective items, 548
defined, 548
of dissatisfied responses, *577*
for recording times, 550, 566
Cherry Point Naval Air Station, 73
Chick-fil-A, 204
China
birth of quality assurance, 5
quality awards in, 127–128
Chinese Association for Quality (CAQ), 127
Chinese National Quality Award, 127
Christiansen, Delores, 64
Chrysler Corporation
design failure mode and effects analysis (DFMEA), 607
exciters/delighters at, 200
quality improvement, 4
simultaneous engineering at, 586
teams at, 264
Chugach School District (Alaska), 65
Chung Mong Koo, 421
CI. *See* confidence intervals; continuous improvement
Cigna, 178–179
Cincinnati Fiberglass, 323
Cincinnati Milacron, 264
Cincinnati Water Works (CWW), 350
CIP. *See* continuous improvement process (CIP)
circular organizational chart, 172
Citibank, 246
Clarke American Checks, Inc., 6
data accessibility at, 6
information management at, 375
operational and financial results, 28
performance indicators at, 375
quality engines at, 439
service quality, 6
S.T.A.R., 6
strategic planning, 439
termination Identification Process System (TIPS), 395
Client Concern Resolution (CCR), 191
Client Satisfaction Index (CSI), 192
Clifton Metal Works (CMW), 185–186
Clinton administration, 10, 74
CLT. *See* Central Limit Theorem
cluster analysis, 386
cluster sampling, 220, 491, 494–495
CMW (Clifton Metal Works), 185–186
CNH Capital, 561
CNL. *See* changing nature of leadership (CNL)
coaching, 434
Coca-Cola Company, 17
Codman, Ernest, 61
Cole, Robert, 455
Collins, Jim, 121
"command-and-control" attitude, 71
comment cards, 201
Commercial, Government, and Industrial Solutions Sector (CGISS), 6
commitment, 99, 109, 209–210
Cedar Foundation, 91
Customer support and, 209–210
in Deming's points, 106
to Excellence initiative, 452
in management, 108, 136, 252
organizational, 1, 79, 99, 109, 425
committee structure, 106
common causes of variation, 102, 482–483
Common Market, 128
communication, 272
communicator, 424
companywide quality 11
companywide quality control (CWQC),
beginnings of, 110
in Japan, 11
Compaq, 137
comparative data, 386–387
compensation, 274–276. *See also* rewards
competitive advantage
characteristics of, 25–26

customers want and needs and, 193
quality and, 25–29
competitive benchmarking, 339
competitive evaluation, 594, *596*
competitive success, 27, 306
competitors, 9, 14, 25, 26, 161
compliance, policies and procedures, 15
complaint management, 202
component stress testing. *See* burn-in
component variability study, 631
Comprehensive Local Education Plan (CLEP), 49
computer-aided design (CAD), 85, 342, 415
computer-aided manufacturing (CAM), 415
Computer Associates, 130
computer numerical controlled (CNC) equipment, 145–146
computing system reliability, 618–621
concept development, 587–588
at Bose Corporation, 587–588
concept engineering (CE) as, 587–588
customer environment and, 587
generation, 588
House of Quality as, 581–594
operationalizing, 588
overview of, 587
at Polaroid, 587–588
preliminary, 583–584
QFD as, *517*
requirements, 587
selection, 588
concept engineering (CE), 587–588
concurrent engineering, 585–586
confidence intervals (CI), 503–504
conflict management, 272
conformance
as dimension of quality, 17, 107, 198
problems, 537
conformance to requirements, 107
conformance to specifications, 10, 17, 105
degree of, 665
as flawed, 110
traditional view of, 10, 17, 111
consistency, 15
Consolidated School District (D15), 311
community support at, 432
process management for, 311
social responsibility at, 432
consultants, 15, 97, 137, 288
Consumer Product Safety Commission, 9
Consumer Reports, 9, 27, 609
consumers, 9, 13, 24, 193
Consumer's Checkbook, 423
consumer surveys, 392
content theories, 255
Continental Airlines, 215
continuous improvement (CI)
at Convergys, 404–408
defined, 558
Deming and, 23–24
forms of, 23
in Koalaty Kid program, 66–67
in knowledge management, 404–408
as lean production tool, 557, 558
learning cycle and, 24
at NYSE: CVG, 404–408
process focus and, 22–24
in statistical thinking, 480, 524
continuous improvement process (CIP), 65
continuous innovation, 455
continuous quality improvement (CQI), 33, 42, 62, 69, 121
continuous random variable, 490
control. *See also* companywide quality control; process control; quality control; statistical process control; statistical quality control; total quality control; Zero Quality Control
application of, 105
capability and, 503, *517*, 662–*664*
checkpoints, 168
defined, 319
improvement versus, *320*
Juran and, 106
visual, 557
control charts, 664–665, 666–727
applications of, 546–*548*
for attributes, 665, 687–701
calculation worksheets, *669*, *674*, 725, 726, 727
central limit theorem (CLT) and, 503
control, 667–668
control limits calculations, 666, 667, 669, 670, 676, 682–683, 686, 689, 691, 693–696, 697–699
cycles, 678
at Day Industries, 727
described, 546
designing, 703–706
development, 7, 482
economic decisions for constructing, *706*
at GE Fanuc, *517*
formulas, *702*
for hospitals, 546–547
hugging the center line, 678–680
hugging the control limit, *680*–681
indications on, 546
for individual measurement, 667, 683, 686
at La Ventana Window Company, 668–674
limits of, 546, 676
monitoring, 667–668
at Morelia Mortgage Company, 724–725
at Murphy Trucking, Inc. 725–727
one point outside limits, 676
or organizational effectiveness, 283
for output consistency, 7

pattern interpretation in, 546, 674–676
in pharmaceutical product manufacturing, 709–713
pre-control and, 707–709
process average shift, 676–678
process capability, 667
as process improvement tools, 481
purpose of, 703
quality problem identification, 7, 546
in receiving processes, 713–*715*
selection, 699, *702*–703
for service organizations, *660*
in Six Sigma, 542, 706–707
speical causes in, 705
special charts, 681–687
statistical control on, 666–667
structure of, *546*
summary of, 701–702
for surgery infections, *547*, *548*
for thickness data, 727
trends, 678
unusual patterns in, 667, 676–681
for variables data, 666–687
control limits. *See also* lower control limit; modified control limits; upper control limit
hugging, 678–681
location of, 705–706
for np-charts, 694–696
one point outside, 676
Convergys Corporation (NYSE: CVG), 404–408
best practices at, 406–407
continuous improvement (CI) for, 404–408
continuous improvement (CI) Pipeline Workflow, 406
continuous improvement (CI) Portal at, 405
continuous improvement (CI) Tools for, 407–408
TIP at, 407–408
Cooper, William, 3
Coors Brewing Company, 286–287
empowerment at, 251, 260, 264
training at, 286
Coors, Pete, 251
Copeland Companies, 543
COQ. *See* cost of qualify
Coral Springs, Florida, 28, 49, 209, 315
Core competencies, 175–177
at Apple, 176
conditions for, 175
in Coral Springs, Florida, 176–177
defined, 175
at Dell, 176
at Mercy Health System, 176
at Nordstrom, 175
at Novel Connect, 186
outsourcing, 176
overview, 175–176
at Premier, 280
at Procter & Gamble, 176
strategic work system design, 175–177
at Toyota, 175
vertical integration, 176
core processes. *See* Value-creation processes
Corning, Incorporated
empowerment at, 260
learning systems and, 67
Telecommunications Products Division (TPD), 314
Corporate Automation Plan, 402
corporate culture, 108, 251, 275, 279, 442. *See also* culture
corporate ladder, 171
corporate performance, 26, 43
Corporate Quality Manual, 137
corporate responsibility, 124
Corporate Responsibility Process (CPR), 430
Corporate social responsibility (CSR), 430–432
corrective action, 107, 311, 318, 352–353
correlation, 512–513
analysis, 385
statistical analysis, 27–28, 220, 512–513
statistical methodology, 96, 555–556
cost(s), 3. *See also* quality costs
activity-based, 390
appraisal, 389
external failure, 390
internal failure, 389
prevention, 389
of quality, 388–392
sampling, 491–492, 491–492
in Six Sigma, 561
cost of quality (COQ), 388–392
capturing and using, 390–391
classification, 389
matrix, 391
objectives of, 388–389
implementation of, 389
performance measures, 107, 372, 376
in service organizations, 391–392
in Six Sigma, 538
courage, 424
Covey, Stephen, 428
Coyote Community College, 414–417
Board of Governors (BOG), 415
LEARN at, 417
mission of, 415, 416
programs of, 414–415
stakeholders/requirements of, 416
students at, 415
CPR. *See* Corporate Responsibility Process (CPR)
CPS. *See* creative problem solving
CPV. *See* customer perceived value
CQI. *See* continuous quality improvement
CQM. *See* Center for Quality of Management
craftsmanship, age of, 5
Crawford Consumer Products (CCP), 725–726

"*Creating a Government That Works Better and Costs Less: Report of National Performance Review*," 74
creative problem solving (CPS), 336–337
creativity, 425
CRI. *See* Custom Research Inc.
critical defects, 378
critical-to-quality performance features (CTQs), 136, 226–227, 516–517, 532, *539*, 586
CRM. *See* customer relationship management (CRM)
Crosby, Patricia, 461–463
Crosby, Philip, 26, 461–463
Crosby philosophy, 106–108
Crosby's Absolutes of Quality Management, 107
Crosby's Basic Elements of Improvement, 107, 108
cross-functional teams, 22, 175, 264
 at Chrysler, 264
 developing and empowering, 268
 employees and, *252*
 key processes, 196
 at Medrad, 274, *284*
 at Ritz-Carlton Hotel Company, L.L.C., 165, 585
 at Solar Turbines, Inc,. 164
 in small businesses, 426
 in Six Sigma, 536
 at St. Luke's Hospital, 452
 Texas Nameplate Company, Inc. (TNC), 72
 at Veridian Homes, 140
Crownover, Dale, 72, 445
Crowther, Samuel, 7
CSFC. *See* Caterpillar Financial Services Corporation
CSI. *See* Client Satisfaction Index (CSI)
CSRs. *See* customer service representatives (CSR)
CTQs. *See* critical-to-quality performance features
cultural change, 103, 105, 328
 employee role in, 423
 managers and, 103, 253
 at Wainwright Industries, 446
cultural values, 443
culture
 American business, 103
 of Baptist Hospital, Inc., (BHI), 286, 366, 425
 change in, 443–447
 at Clarke American Checks, Inc., 6
 compliance, 75
 in Coral Springs, Florida, 49
 corporate, 442
 customer-focused, 208–217
 defined, 442
 dysfunctional corporate, 442
 of General Electric (GE), 251–252
 at Hillerich & Bradsby Co. (H&B), 103
 leadership in, 442
 at Motorola, Inc, 6
 national, 128
 organizational, 442–443
 of performance excellence, 75, 442, 445
 quality, 445
Cummins Engine Company, 33
cumulative count of conforming chart (CCC chart), 707
cumulative failure curve over time, *613*, *646*
Custom Research Inc. (CRI), 309
 benchmarking at, 309
customer(s)
 chains of, 56
 as consumers, 19
 contact, 210–211
 dissatisfaction, 131
 errors, 319
 expectations, 20–21, 198–199
 external, 19
 identifying, 195–198
 interaction, 59–60, 313, 561
 internal, 19–20, 196
 loyalty, 193, 213
 segmentation, 196–198
 in Six Sigma, 49, 135
 as total quality (TQ) practice, 25
 types, 196
 virtual, 216
customer benefit package, 193–194
customer contact
 employees, 208, 210–211
 requirements, 196–198, 211–212
customer culture, 208–217
 at BI, 214–215
 at TARP, 212
 at Tsutaya, 215–216
 commitments and support, 209–210
 complaint management/service recovery, 212–215
 contact requirements, 211–212
 creation, 208–217
 developing contact employees, 210–211
 management practices, 209
 moments of truth, 208–209
 partnerships and alliances, 215
 perspectives, 368
 technology, 215–217
customer-driven quality, 19–20, 118, 207
customer-driven quality cycle, 207
customer feedback, 258
 analyzing and using, 222–224
 at BI, 217
 At Graniterock, 220, 221, 223
 failed efforts, 224–225
 Hilton Hotel guest survey, 221
 importance rating of product/services, 234
 Likert scales, 219
 measuring engagement, 217–226
 perceived value, 225–226
 performance-importance comparison, 223
 performance ratings, 235
 satisfaction surveys, 218–222
 at Skilled Care Pharmacy, 224

customer focus, 20–21
  at Amazon.com, 228–230
  Baldrige Criteria for Performance Excellence and, 226–227
  Canadian National Quality Institute, 125
  as core value, 49
  European Excellence Award Framework, 124
  at Gold Star Chili, Inc., 241
  in ISO , 131
  measures, 20–21
  at Mercy Health System, 192
  outcomes, 372
  at Park Place Lexus, 191–192
  or performance excellence, 191
  in Six Sigma, 49, 135
  at Southwest Airlines, 208–209
  at 3M, 372, 582–583
customer importance survey, *222*
customer information, 205–208
  at Advanced Circuits, 206
  affinity diagram, 204–205
  comment cards, 201–202
  design production/service delivery and, 205–208
  direct contact, 202
  exploiting, 207
  focus groups, 202, 640
  formal surveys, 201–202
  field intelligence, 202
  gathering/analyzing, 201–205
  linking to design, production, and service delivery, 205–208
  listening and learning approach, 203–204
  monitoring by Internet, 202–203
  perceived quality, 207
  quality cycle, 207
  satisfaction surveys, 218–222
  study complaints, 202
customer needs, 198–205
  expectations, 196, 198–199
  at Frank Perdue, 198
  at Ideo, 198
  external customers, 200–201
  Ford Motor Company and, understanding, 198
  identification of, 198
  Kano classification system, 200
  quality dimensions, 198–199
  satisfaction/dissatisfaction of, 200
  service quality issues, 199–200
customer perceived value (CPV), 207, 225–226
CustomerPerfect!, 402
customer relationship management (CRM)
  aspects of, 216–217
  technology and, 216
customer requirements
  described, 196–198
  for airlines industry, 236
  classes of, 228
  in House of Quality, 591
customer satisfaction, 192–195
  benchmarking, 194
  boomerang principle, 189
  creating, 190
  delivery stage of, 227
  failure of, 224–224
  at FedEx, 57
  importance of, 192–*195*
  indicators of, 194, 372
  Likert scales for, 139
  measuring, 33, 218, 227
  at Ritz-Carlton Hotel Company, L.L.C., 193
  satisfaction index, 194–195
  in Six Sigma, 561
  surveys, 218–222
customer service, 292–294
customer service representatives (CSRs), 21, 239, 286, 350, 367
"Customer Site Visit" program, 90
customer-supplier partnerships, 22, 196, 215
Customer Value Analysis, 366
customization, 58, 313, 315–316
CWQC. *See* companywide quality control
cycles, 454, 457, 678
cycle time
  analysis, 448
  defined, 312, 330
  flexibility and, 371
  in Six Sigma, 561
Cycle Time Task Force, 309

D

D. *See* Consolidated School District (D15)
DADS (Digitally Assisted Dispatch System), 211
Daimler-Chrysler, 320
Dana Corporation-Spicer Driveshaft Division, *113*, 582–583
"dance cards," 558
"dangerous opportunity," 336
dashboards, 380–381
data. *See also* comparative data; performance data; raw data
  billing process, *576*, 726
  collection, 393–394, 532–533
  comparative, 386–387
  defined, 364
  at Juran Institute, 532–533
  management, 395
  at Pearl River School District (PRSD, 65
  protection, 395
  at Prudential Insurance Company, 394
  selecting measures and indicators, 374–375
  timely, 180, 196, 198, 204–205, 211, 258
  at Texas Nameplate Company, Inc. (TNC), 72, 90
  transforming, 22
  validity, 203, 309, 393, 429
data accessibility
  at Baptist Hospital (BI), 394
  at Clarke American Checks, Inc., 395

importance of, 394, 401
at Pearl River School District (PRSD), 65, 394
at Prudential Insurance Company, 394
at Wainwright Industries, 394
data mining, 385–386
data sharing
at Branch-Smith Printing Division (BSPD), 180–181, 213
at Clarke American's S.T.A.R., 6
in City of Coral springs and, 176
at Coors, Brewing, 251
at Commercial, Government, and Industrial Solutions Sector (CGISS), 6
at General Electric, 170, 251–252
at DuPont, 261
at EPA, 75
at Mercy Health System, 176
at Milliken, 393
at Ritz-Carlton Hotel Company, L.L.C., 61
at Solar Turbines Inc., 164
at STMicroelectronics, 322
data sheets, 548
Datsun, 16
David, Colin, 147
Day Industries, 727
Dean, James W. Jr., 20
debriefs, 322
decision making, 131, 272–273
decline stage of life cycle, 450
Deere & Company, 43–45
defectives, 18, 54–55, 100, 283, *530*
defect prevention, 322
defect rate, 322, 529
defects, 6–7, 20, 23, 27. *See also* Zero Defects
categories of, 31, 378
charts for, 7
checklist for, 30–31
check sheets for, 548, *551*
critical, 378
connotation, 30
defined, 30, 377–378
after experimental design optimization, 25, 52, 111, 455
latent, 623
major, 378
minor, 378
per million opportunities, 529
reducing, 23, 27
tracking, 317–318
defects per million opportunities (dpmo), 378, 529
defects per unit (DPU), 378
define, measure, analyze, design, and verify (DMADV), 586
define, measure, analyze, improve, control (DMAIC), 35–36, 135, 464, 586
define, measure, explore, design, implement (DMAIC) process, 531–536
at American Express, 536
analyze phase of, 517, 533–534
at Caterpillar Financial Services Corporation (CFSC), 528
control phase of, 517, 535
define phase of, 358–359, 517, 531–532
at GE Fanuc, 516–517
at Honeywell, 464
improve phase of, 517, 534–535
measure phase of, 517, 532–533
methodology for, 36, 135, 137, 336
at Midwest Bank, 358–359
in Six Sigma, 35, 135, 358, 531–536
techniques, 534
tools, 517
visual mapping of $Y = f(X)$, 533
at Xerox, 35–36
Delcor Homes, 133
delegating, 434
Dell Inc., process improvement at, 329–330
Dell, Michael, 329
Deming Application Prize, 122
criteria for, 92, 122, 123
introduced in Japan, 8, 92
Prize Committee, 122
winners of, 122
Deming chain reaction, 92–93
Deming cycle, 333–336
do stage, 335–336
focus of, 333
fundamentals of, 334–335
kaizen philosophy, 327–329
at Mercy Health System, 335
plan stage of, 333, 335
as process improvement methodology, 333–336
PSDA, 333
steps of, 333–334
study stage of, 333
Deming philosophy, 91–104
14 points of, 92–93, 99–104
chain reaction in, 92–93
comparisons of, 108
empowerment in, 260
foundations of, 92
funnel experiment, 484–490
motivation, 253
pay in, 97
people in, 245
Profound Knowledge system of, 96–97, 98–99
psychology and, 97–98
Red Bead experiment in, 484–489
seminars in, 103–104
statistical thinking and, 8, 94, 97
systems in, 93–95
theory of knowledge in, 96–97, 98
variation and, 95–96, 98
Deming, W. Edwards
Application prize, 92
education of, 91
in Japan, 8, 91–92
as "management guru," 92
MBNQA and, 112
production system viewed by, 23–24
quality assurance, 7, 9, 449
statistics and, 484
Deming's 14 points, 99
action in, 103–104
commitment in, 99

decision making in, 100–101
driving out fear and, 101–102
education in, 103
exhortations in, 102
improvement in, 101
inspection in, 100
leadership in, 423–424
Management by Objective (MBO), 102
original version of, 93, 143
philosophy in, 99–100
pride in workmanship and, 103
quotas in, 102
self-improvement in, 103
statistical thinking and, 484–490
teamwork in, 102
training in, 101
vision in, 99
de Pacotilla, Juan, 524–525
Department of Defense, 73
Deployment Grids, 280
Department of Labor (DOL), 74–75
Derr, Kenneth, 395
descriptive statistics, 495–497
design development, 43, 52–55, 589–603. *See also* House of quality; quality function deployment (QFD)
design failure mode and effects analysis (DFMEA), 607–609
design for environment (DFE), 600–601
Design for Excellence (DFX), 601–602
design for manufacturability (DFM), 599–600
design of experiments (DOE), 506–507
for disassembly, 600
of goods, 602–603
overview, 589
processes, 594–599
production, 599–600
quality guidelines, *601*
review, 584, 586, 603, 622
target and tolerance, 602–603
tools, 589–594
verification, 621–622
design development tools, 589–603
DFMEA, 607–609
reliability prediction, 609
design failure mode and effects analysis (DFMEA), 607–609
at Chrysler, 607
as design tool, 607–609
at NASA, 608
Institute for Healthcare Improvement, 608
safety and, 607–608
design for disassembly, 600
design for environment (DFE), 600–601
Design for Excellence (DFX), 601–602
design for manufacturability (DFM), 599–600
Design for Six Sigma (DFSS), 586–587
activities of, 586
applications of, 586–587
define, measure, analyze, design, and verify (DMADV) and, 586
at General Electric (GE), 586–587
tools for, 586
verification and, 621–622
design of experiments (DOE), 506–507
approach to, 506–507
wave soldering process and, 514–516
design of goods, 604
design optimization, 603–621
nominal-is-best loss function, 604–*605*
design failure mode and effects analysis (DFMEA), 607–609
overview, 603
reliability prediction and, 609
robust design, 604
Taguchi Loss Function, 604–607
U.S.-made versus Japanese-made TVs, *604*
design optimization tools
physics of failure, 607–609
redundancy, 619
Taguchi loss of function, 604–607
design processes, 583–585
design production, 205–208
design quality guidelines, *601*
design review, 622
design verification, 621–622
design verification tools, 621–637
burn-in, 623
calibration, 629–630
measurement system evaluations, 623–628
process capability evaluation, 630–631
process capability indexes, 634–637
process capability studies, 631–634
reliability testing, 609, 622–623
reviews, 622
detection rating scale, *611*
determination, 108
DFE. *See* design for environment (DFE)
DFM. *See* design for manufacturability (DFM)
DFMEA. *See* design failure mode and effects analysis
diagnostic journey, 106
diagrams. *See also* affinity diagrams; cause-and-effect diagrams; Pareto diagrams
affinity, 204–205
arrow, 171
interrelationship diagraph, 171
matrix, 171
scatter, 513, 555–556
tree, 171
Digitally Assisted Dispatch System (DADS), 211
direct customer contact, 202
directing, 434
discrete random variable, 490

Disney, 201, 442
dissatisfiers, 200
Distinguished Ad Agency (DAA), 469–470
distribution, *18*, *24*, *343*, *394*
DM. *See* DynMcDermott Petroleum Operations Company
DMADV. *See* define, measure, analyze, design, verify (DMAIC)
DMAIC. *See* define, measure, analyze, improve, control
DMEI. *See* Define, Measure, Explore, Design, Implement (DMEI)
Dodge, Harold, 7
DOE. *See* design of experiments
DOL (Department of Labor), 74
Domino's Pizza, 278
Douglas Aircraft, 11
Dover Corporation, 2 64
Dover, John, 524–425
Dow Chemical Company, 545
Dow Jones index, 545
Doyleston Hospital, Philadelphia, 200
dpmo. *See* defects per million opportunities
DPU. *See* defects per unit
drafts, for meetings, 273
drawdown systems, 307
Dresdner Kleinwort Wasserstein, 259
DRIVE process, 337
driving out fear, in Deming's 14 points, 101–102
drop test, 623, 638, 639
Drucker, Peter, 295
DuPont, 261
durability, as dimension of quality, 198
dynamic process, 505
DynMcDermott Petroleum Operations Company (DM), 57, 306–307
dysfunctional corporate culture, 442

E

Eastman Chemical Company
  complaints investigated at, 214–215
  design review, 622
  empowerment at, 261
  leadership system at, 51
  no-fault return policy of,
  quality assurance at, 51
  strategic planning at, 163
Eckes, George, 268
e-commerce, 42, 61, 256, 460
Economic Club of Chicago, 30
economics of quality, 107
education, 64–71. *See also* training
  Baldrige Award in, 65, 114
  benchmarking, 79, 80
  continuous improvement and, 49
  at Coyote Community College, 414–417
  delivery of, 287
  in Deming's 14 points, 103
  employee, 427, 456
  higher, 69–71
  needs, 287, 414
  programs, 414–415
  quality in, 64–71
  special opportunities in, 369
  steering committee, 427
  Testing Service, 79, 80
Educational Benchmarking Inc. (EBI), 79, 80
Educational Testing Service (ETS), 79
Edwards, George, 7
efficiency problems, 7
EFQM. *See* European Foundation for Quality Management (EFQM)
EI. *See* employee involvement
electronic medical record (EMR), 64
emerging leadership theories, 433
emotional intelligence theory, *433*, 436–437
empathy, as of quality, 199
employee(s), 21–22, 262, 292–294, 210–211. *See also* human resource management; workforce
  customer contact, 210–211
  empowered, 21–22, 49, 72, 208
  front-line, 13, 59, 100, 110, 170, 210–211, 277
  involvement of, 251–252, 277
  languages of, 105, 389
  morale of, 58, 66, 101, 251, 317, 330, 338, 384, 461
  motivating, 250, 253–256
  performance of, 446
  promotions, 301
  redundancy policy, 301–301
  retention of, 292–295, 300–301
  role of, 299
  role of in cultural 19–20
  selection of, 300–301
  in Six Sigma, 292–294
  statistical process control (SPC) and, 186
  systems thinking and, 94–95
  as team players, 20, 21–22, 299
  "voice of", 282, 402–403
  at Xerox, 33
employee involvement (EI), 251–252
employee satisfaction (ES)
  at AT&T, 256
  at FedEx, 59
  in Human Resource Plans, 170
  measuring, 281–282, 371, 403
  productivity, costs and, 384
  quality and, 59–60
  at Ritz-Carlton, 78
employee surveys
  at AT&T, 256
  in human resources, 181
  at Kenneth W. Monfort college of Business, 79, 80
  market, 92, 101
  at Marlow Industries, 283
  for satisfaction, 281
  self-determination versus, *262*
  at St. Luke's Hospital, Kansas City, 281

at Sunny fresh foods (SFF), 247
of workers, 90, 118
at Xerox, 33
empowerment, 259–261
EMR. *See* electronic medical record (EMR)
"enablers", 123, 124
ENBI Corporation, 328
energizing stage of life cycle, 450
engineering, 52–55. *See also* concept engineering; overengineering; reengineering; simultaneous engineering
cost of quality matrix in, 391
industrial, 54–55, 295
in manufacturing systems, 51
product design and, 52–53
tool, 54
total, 54
Enron, 119, 431
enterprise process model, 309
Enterprise Resource Planning (ERP), 382
enumerative studies, 505
environment, 14, 147–148, 157–162. *See also* design for environment; organizational environment; workforce environment
competitive, 159
concerns, 14
of Koalaty Kid program, 66–67
operating, 158, 307, 424
organizational, 116, 147–148
in strategic planning cycle, 140
in total quality (TQ), 453
leadership theories, 21–22, 121, 434, 436
environmental assessment, 164
environmental concerns, 14
Environmental Protection Agency (EPA), 75, 416
environmentally based theories, 255
EOQ. *See* European Organization for Quality Control
EPA. *See* Environmental Protection Agency (EPA)
EQA. *See* European Quality Award
equipment variation, 625
equivalent parallel system, *620*, 622
ergonomics, 196, 249, 289
Ernst, A. C., 448
ERP. *See* Enterprise Resource Planning
error rates, 322, 627
errors per million opportunities, (EPMO), 378
ethics, 13, 21, 115, 160, *267*
ETS. *See* Educational Testing Service
European Commission, 123
European Foundation for Quality Management (EFQM), 91, 123–125
European Organization for Quality Control (EOQ), 123
European Quality Award (EQA), 123
award process, 123
award winners, 125
framework, 123–125
Excel. *See* Microsoft Excel
excellence. *See* Australian Business Excellence Award; Baldrige Criteria for Performance Excellence; Business Excellence
Excellence21, 69–70. *See also* Canadian wards for Business Excellence; Lincoln Award for Excellence; Ohio Partnership for Excellence; performance excellence
at Motorola, 6, 69
at Xerox, 69
exciters/delighters, 200
executive leadership, 104, 436
exhortations, *93*, 102, *143*, 260
expected loss, 606
expected quality, 206–207
experienced meaningfulness, 258
experienced responsibility, 258
experimental design, 25, 111, 455
explicit knowledge, 396
external customers, 19
external failure costs, 390

F

facilitator, 266–267, 273
factorial experiments, 507–510
FADE. *See* focus, analyze, develop, execute
failure
causes of, 224–225
cumulative curve, *646*
effects of, *355*, *541*, 607–607
functional, 612
at GE Fanuc, 518
machine, 697–698
modes, 355
physics of, 613–618
reliability, 612
in Six Sigma, *540–541*
failure curve over time, 8, *646*
failure curve rate, *614*
failure mode and effects analysis (FMEA), 564, 608
failure rate, 613–*614*
causes of, 133, 329–330
curve, *614*
defined, 612–613
of electronic components, 329–330, 339, *612*, 615
mathematics of, 616
over time interval, 8, *613–614*
Family and Medical Leave Act, 299
family-owned enterprises, 71, 241, 286, 366
Fast Company magazine, 59, 276
FDA (U.S. Food and Drug Administration), 602–603
features, as dimension of quality, 198
Federal Aviation Agency (FAA), 413
federal government, quality in, 73–75
Federal Quality Institute (FQI), 74

Federal Quality Prototype Award, 10
Federal Trade Commission, 31
FedEx
credo of, 59
customer satisfaction at, 57
DADS at, 211
delivery services of, 211
employee satisfaction at, 59
guarantees of, 59
human resource management at, 59
motto of, 59
"no layoff" philosophy, 59
performance data at, 378–379
quality at, 57, 262
service quality indicator (SQI) at, 379
"SuperTracker" of, 61
training at, 287–288
feedback, 258. *See also* customer feedback
Feigenbaum, A. V., 11, 109–110, 459
Feigenbaum, Donald S., 459
Fidelity Investments, 61, 197–198
field intelligence, 202
final report
"is"/"should" process map, 331
finance/accounting, 55–56
financial accountability, 135, 459
financial measures, 372
financial outcomes, 372
financial perspectives, 368
finished goods inspection/testing, 55
finite population, 502
Finley, Michael, 268
FIR. *See* First Internet Reliable Bank
First in Service (FIS)®, 6
First Internet Reliable Bank (FIR), 238–240
First National Bank of Chicago, 376
FIS. *See* First in Service (FIS)
Fisher, R. A., 506
"fitness for use," 438
5S's (seiri, seiton, seiso, seiketsu, shitsuke), 557
5 Why technique, 534
Fleet Financial Group, 197
flexibility, 312
cycle time and, 371, 373
defined, 312
Florida Power and Light (FPL)
interlinking model at, 205
leadership at, 364
policy deployment at, 167
quality award, 10
flowcharts. *See also* process map
analysis process questions, 543
for answering phone *577*
AT&T and, 542–543
automobile service, 354
for auto service, 565–566
for Boise marketing/sales, 544–545
calls, 543, *577*
described, 542
development, 542
DMAIC and, 517
employees and, 542
for fast-food window, *571*
job descriptions, 314
LT billing process, *575*
for medical administration process, *577*
Microsoft Excel and, 542
for order fulfillment, 517, *565*
for patient registration process, *577*, *578*
as process improvement tools, 314
purpose of, 541–542
in Six Sigma, 541–545
at Timber and Wood Products Division of Boise Cascade, 543–545
time reduction and, 543
FMEA. *See* failure mode and effects analysis
focus, analyze, develop, execute (FADE), 337
focus groups, 202, 640
follower maturity, 434
Forbes, 404
Ford, Henry, Sr., 7, 175, 339
Ford Motor Company
2002 Revitalization Plan, 4
customer needs and, 4
"going back to basics," 7
Japanese management practices and, 7
lean production, 556
Quality Award of, 9
work system design, 175, 264
Ford, William, 4
formal supplier certification programs, 448
formal surveys, 201–202
forming phase of teams, 269
Fortune magazine, 212
Fort Wayne, Indiana, 562
FPL. *See* Florida Power and Light (FPL)
FQI (Federal Quality Institute), 74
fraction defective chart, *617*
fraction noncomforming p-charts, 688–693. *See also* control charts
Frederick C. Carder Elementary School, 66–67
Feigenbaum, A. V., 11, 109–110, 459–460
Feigenbaum, Donald S., 459–460
frequency distributions, 96, 495, 501, *624–625*, 632, *663*
Froedtert Memorial Lutheran Hospital, Milwaukee, 563
Frohman, Alan, 30
front-line personnel, 13, 59, 107, 110, 210–211
FSR. *See* Franchise Service Representatives
Full Range of Leadership, 436
full-scale production, 205
functional failure, 612
funnel, 489
funnel experiment, 484–490
results of, 490
rules for adjusting 489

future challenges, 12–14
fuzzy logic, 386

G

Gaebler, T., 364
gainsharing, 72, 274, 376
Galvin, Robert, 30, 133
Gantt, Henry, 249
Gap, 201
"garbage in, garbage out," 393
Gardner, Latoya, 276–277
Garvin, David A., 198, 259
Gates, Bill, 238
GE. *See* General Electric (GE)
GE Fanuc, 516–518
  ANOVA output for vendor/finish analysis, *519*
  Ball Grid Array (BGA), 516
  DMAIC at, 517
  Printed Wire Board (PWB) Fabricated Board Finishes, 516
  Six Sigma at, 516–518
  statistical analysis applied at, 516–518
  surface-mounted devices (SMDs), 516
Geisler, David, 261
Gellerman, Saul W., 254
Genecor, 271
Genentech, 271
General Electric (GE)
  business goals at, 538
  company culture of, 251–253
  design for environment (DFE) at, 600
  DFSS at, 586–587
  human resource plans at, 170
  as learning organization, 453–454
  management technique training offers, 201
  process control at, 319
  quality management, 10, 109
  reengineering at, 340
  Six Sigma at, 133, 134–134, 170
  Six Sigma black belt (SSBB) at, 441
  task force studies at, 10
  "Work-Out" program of, 251–252, 454
General Foods, 259
General Mills, 339
General Motors, 279
General Systems Company, 109–110
general systems theory, 94–95
Generally Accepted Auditing Standards, 431
Gilbreth, Frank, 249
Gilbreth, Lillian, 249
global markets, 13
Global Positioning System (GPS) techniques, 85
globalization, 13
GOAL/QPC, 171
"goalpost" specifications, 604
goals
  of AQIP, 71
  at Boeing, 338
  business, 33, 179, 287
  at Cigna, 179
  classification theories for, 255
  at General Electric (GE), 538
  at Medrad, 271
  at Motorola, 6, 52–53
  at Premier, 156, 158, 278, 280
  of process design, 312
  quality, 104, 105, 428
  for statistical process control (SPC), 529
  stretch, 338
  at Xerox, 33
Godfrey, A. Blanton, 224
"The Golden Hammer" Awards, 74
Golden Plaza Hotel, San Francisco, 298–299
Gold Star Chili, Inc. 241, 342–345
  background of, 241
  customer service representatives (CSRs) at, 343
  customer comment card, 345
  customer focus at, 241
  franchising process of, 342–*344*
  franchising steps, 344
  process management at, 342–345
  value-creation processes at, 342–343
Goleman, Daniel, *433*, 436
Good to Great: Why Some Companies Make the Leap . . . and Others Don't), 121
Goodnight, James, 271
Google, 246
Gore, Al, 74
governance, 430–431
  defined, 430
  principles, 431
  social responsibilities/leadership and, 116, 429–432
government safety regulations and recalls, 9
Graham, Julia, 445
grand average, 666
Graniterock Company, *222*, *223*, 481
  benchmarking at, 339
  company picnics at, 271
  customer importance survey, 222
  customer report card, 222–223
  statistical thinking at, 481
  workforce improvement, 281
Great man model, *433*
green belt. *See* Six Sigma green belt
GreenBook, 77
Green Built Homes, 140
green lawn parable, 470–471
GTE Directories, *114*
GTE Supply, 201
guarantees, 48, 209
guiding principles. *See* values

H

Hackman, J. R., 257–258
Hackman/Oldham Work Design Model, 257–258
Hagler, Ron, 524
Hamel, Gary, 175
Hammond, Joshua, 438
H&B. *See* Hillerich617 & Bradsby Co.
H&M. *See* Hennes & Mauritz
"hands-on"
  learning, 79
  project work, 117
Harrington, H. James, 1, 83, 581–582
Harvard Business Review, 368
hazard function, 617
health
  employee well-being and, 410
  screenings, 310

in workplace, 125, 196, 270, 410
health care industry, 61–64, 147. *See also* hospitals; Institute for Healthcare Improvement; Joint Commission on Accreditation of Healthcare Organizations; SSM Health Care
avoidable errors in, 62
design failure mode and effects analysis (DFMEA) in, *610*
overuse of services in, 62
quality in, 14, 325
quality problems in, 61–64
Six Sigma in, 147, 562
underutilization of services in, 62
variation of services in, 62
health maintenance organization (HMO), 63, 524–525
Hendricks, Kevin, 27
Hennes & Mauritz (H&M), 312
Hersey, P., *433*–434
Hershey Foods Corporation, 51
Hershey, Milton, 51
Herzberg, Frederick, 255
Herzberg's Two-Factor theory, 254–255
Hewitt Associates, 282–294
Hewlett-Packard, 8, 167, 514
hidden factory, 109, 561
higher education, 69–71
Higher Learning Commission, 71
high-performance management practices, 151, 227
high-performance work
defined, 256
designing systems, 256–273
managing, 273–283
organizations, 397
sustaining, 282–287
high-touch delivery framework, 79
Hillerich & Bradsby Co. (H&B), 103–104
Hillerich, Jack, 103
Hilton Hotels Corp., 20, 221
HIS (Hospital Information System), 394–395
Histograms, 548–550
cautions, 549–550
check sheets and, 549
defective item, *550*
described, 548–549
frequency distributions and, 499, 501, 548–549, *663*
Pareto, 501, *567*
of picking times, *566*, *567*
process variation, *633*
tool, 499
HMO. *See* health maintenance organization
HMO pharmacy crisis, 524–525
holding gains, 106
Home Depot, 135
Honda, 289–291
Honeywell, Inc., 120, 463–466
Hoover, Al, (PTA Health fund), 432
horizontal coordination, 11, 22, 288
Hoshin Kanri. *See* hoshin planning
hoshin planning, 167–168
Hospital Information System (HIS), 394
hospitals. *See also* specific hospitals
cause-and-effect, 554–555
control charts for, 324, 546–*548*
diagrams for, *555*
errors at, 62, 318
FADE at, 337
measurement in, 63, 324
patient services at, 19, 200
patient surveys, 325–326
staff behavior questions, 326
standards for, 61
House of Quality, 590–599
basis of, *590*
competitive evaluation, 594, *596*
completed, *597*
linking houses, *598*
for managed care organizations (MCOs), 63, 640–*641*
QFD and, 591–599
relationship matrix, *595*, *651*
steps for building, 591, 594
technical requirements in, 591, 594, *593*
Technological University RRC, 651–653
Voice of the Customer (VOC) in, *592*
House, Robert J., 255
HRM. *See* Human Resource Management (HRM)
Huawei Technologies, 37
Hubbard, James, 186
hugging center line, 678–680
hugging control limits, *680*–681
Hughes, T. D., 227
human resource focus
Baldrige Criteria for Performance Excellence and, 125, 177
in ERP, 382
in ISO , 181
at Nordam Europe, Ltd, 301
people focus in, 125
in QID, 182
in Six Sigma, 292–294
Human Resource Management (HRM). *See also* workforce
at Ames Rubber Corporation, 270
at AT&T, 232
at Convergys, 404
in Deming, 123, 245
described, 249
at FedEx, 59
at General Electric, 134
at Hewitt Associates, 292–294
information systems, 314
legalities, 279
School District #15 (D#15), 284
staff handbooks, 300
linking to business strategy, 169–170
at Medrad, 284
at Nordam Europe, Ltd., 300
objectives of, 249
planning, 155, 159, 428

practices of, 282
at Ritz-Carlton Hotel company, LLC, 60, 249, 314
scope of, 249–250
at Solar Turbines, 427
at St. Luke's Hospital, Kansas City, 423
at Xerox, 282
of workforce, 249–250
human resource plans, 169–170
humility, 424
Hurricane Katrina, 307
hypothesis testing, 504–505
Hyundai Motor Company, 323, 421–422

I

IBM. *See* International Business Machines
IBM Credit Corporation, 340
idea generation, *429*, 583
Ideo, 198
IHI. *See* Institute for Healthcare Improvement (IHI)
Imai, M., 167
Immelt, Jeffrey R., 429
implementation
of Baldrige Criteria for Performance Excellence, 118–119
of Crosby's Basic Elements of Improvement, 108
of ISO 9000, 132
of kaizen, 327
mistakes in performance excellence, 18, 62, 92–93, 317
of quality, 140
of Six Sigma, 265, 440
of total quality (TQ), 71
improper sampling, 492
improvement, 125. *See also* breakthrough improvement; continuous improvement; continuous improvement process; continuous quality improvement; process improvement methodologies; process improvement tools; quality improvement; quality improvement process; The Improvement Process
Ina Title Company, Japan, 506
indexes
American Customer Satisfaction, 194–195, 404
Client Satisfaction, 192
customer satisfaction, 194
Dow Jones, 545
employee satisfaction, 403
process capability, 634–637
quality cost, 390
Relationship Customer Satisfaction, 217
Transactional Customer Satisfaction, 217
indicators. *See also* Key Performance Indicator; service quality indicators
defined, 325, 365
lag, 369
lead, 369
measures and, 374–375
performance, 365
service quality, 379
individual measurement, 683–686
industrial engineering, 54–55
Industrial Quality Control, 8
Industrial Revolution, 5
infant mortality period, 615
infinite population, 503
information. *See also* data comparative
defined, 364–365
leading practices with, 365
technology, 60–61
information management
at Baptist Hospital, Inc. 366
at Caterpillar Financial Services Corporation (CSFC), 396
at Clarke American Checks, Inc., 375
costs, 389
indicators, 364
of resources, 393–395
in Six Sigma, 401–402
as total quality (TQ practice, 25
at Wainwright Industries, Inc. 366
infrastructure, 84, 448
Initial Quality Survey, 27
innovation, 118, 455
innovation perspectives, 368
inspection
in Deming's 14 points, 100
finished goods, 55
mass, 7, 8, 100
rate, 322
source, 558
instability, 453, 681
installation/service, 55
Institute for Healthcare Improvement (IHI), 63, 608
Institute of Medicine (IOM), 62
integrated product teams (IPTs), 262
integration, 447
integrity, 425
Intel Corporation, 340
interaction effect, 508–509
interconnected processes, 309
interlinking model, 383–386
for Ames Rubber Corporation, 54, 205, 385
defined, 383
at Florida Power and Light (FPL), 205
in House of Quality, *598*
at IBM, 384
for Johnson controls Inc. (JCI), 383–384
NMMC process, 385–386
relationships in, 384
at Seven-Eleven Japan, 205
internal audits, 439
internal benchmarking, 397–398
internal customers, 19–20, 196
internal failure costs, 389
internal perspectives, 368
International Business Machines (IBM)
balanced scorecard at, 370
cause-and-effect model for, 384
culture in, 442
interlinking model at, 383
job enrichment at, 259

modeling cause-and-effect relationships at, 370
process management at, 340
reengineering at, 341
selecting measures and indicators at, 375
training at, 259
International Consortium for Executive Development Research, 157
International Convention on Students' Circles, 265
International Organization for Standardization (IOS), 128, 661
International Quality Study (IQS), 448, 449
International Telephone and Telegraph (ITT), 106
Internet
banking over, 216, 238–240
customer service on, 202–203
reviews for consumers, 9
interrelationship diagraph, 171
interviews, employee satisfaction, 281
intraorganizational cooperation, 264
In2:InThinking Network, 99
involvement, 251–252, 277
IOS. *See* International Organization for Standardization
iPods, 287
IPTs. *See* integrated product teams
IQS. *See* International Quality Study
Ishikawa, Kaoru, 110, 264, 548
ISO 9000
Baldrige Criteria for Performance Excellence, compared to, 135–138
benefits of, 132–133
compared to Six Sigma, 135–138
and control charts, 542, 706–707
customer focus in, 129
human resource focus in, 181
implementation of, 132
leadership in, 438–440
process management in, 129, 341
quality management, 111, 138–139
quality policy, 438–440
registration, 132
resource management, 130
Six Sigma compared to, 135–138
standards, 128
strategic planning in, 177
ISO 9000-Fundamentals and Vocabulary, 129
ISO 9000:2000
comparison to Baldrige, 132
factors leading to, 130–131
improvements in, 130
Management Responsibility, 129
Measurement, Analysis, and Improvement, 130, 400
QS-9000, 131
quality management principles, 131–132
as response to dissatisfaction, 131
Resource Management, 130
standards, 128–129
structure of, 129–130
ISO audit, 181
ISO-Guidelines for Performance Improvements, 129
ISO-Requirements, 129
ITT (International Telephone and Telegraph), 106–107
ITT Avionics Division, 506–507

J

Janson Medical Clinic, *577–578*
Japan. *See also* Union of Japanese Scientists and Engineers
cause-and-effect diagram, 554
Deming in, 8, 91–92
job training in, 259
Juran in, 8
quality in, 7–8, 345–347
quality function deployment (QFD), 589
Seven-Eleven Stores in, 205
Japan Quality Medal, 123
JCAHO. *See* Joint Commission on Accreditation of Healthcare Organizations
JCI. *See* Johnson Controls, Inc.
J. D. Power associates, 27
Gold Plant Quality Award, 4
initial quality metrics, 615
Initial Quality Survey, 27
Jefferson, Thomas, 5
Jenks Public Schools (JPS), 48–49
drop out rates, 29
four "pillars" at, 48
learning approach at, 48–49
total quality (TQ) in, 48–49
Jiro, Kawakita, 204
JIT. *See* just-in-time scheduling
jobs
autonomy in, 259
core characteristics, 257–258
design of, 257–259
enlargement, 257
enrichment of, 259
rotation of, 259
satisfaction, 59–60, 257
training in Japan, 327–328
Johnson & Johnson, 270
Johnson Controls, Inc. (JCI), 193
Johnson, Samuel, 9
Joiner, Brian, 479–480
Joint Commission on Accreditation of Healthcare Organizations (JCAHO), 61–62
at Black elk Medical Center (BEMC), 654
creation of, 61
design failure mode and effects analysis (DFMEA), 608
standards set by, 324

Jostens, 215
JPS. *See* Jenks Public Schools
judgmental perspective, 15
judgment sampling, 491, 495
Juneman, Lou, 289, 292
Juran Center for Leadership in Quality, 424
Juran Institute, 106, 532–533
Juran, Joseph, 106
  background of, 104
  breakthrough sequence, 106
  in Japan, 21, 104
  as "management guru," 90
  Pareto principle and, 550
  quality assurance term, 7, 105
  statistical quality control techniques, 8, 105
Juran philosophy, 104–106
  breakthrough sequence, 106
  comparisons of, 108
  customer classifications, 197
  fear and, 102, 106
  quality culture, 445
  quality defined in, 105
  Quality Trilogy in, 105
Juran's breakthrough sequence, 106
JUSE. *See* Union of Japanese Scientists and Engineers
just-in-time scheduling (JIT), 53, 327

K

Kaiser Aluminum, 274
kaizen, 327–328
  at ENBI Corporation, 328
  focus of, 327
  implementation, 327
  philosophy, 328–329
  at Ritz-Carlton Hotel Company, 328–329
  success of, 328
kaizen blitz, 329
Kaizen Institute, 327
Kano classification system, 200
Kano, Noriaki, 200, 364
Kaplan, Robert, 368
KARLEE Company, 51, 528–529
Katayama, Mr., 16
Kearns, David, 9, 13, 287
Kelleher, Herb, 250
Kenneth W. Monfort College of Business (MCB), 69, 78–80, *114*
  "high-touch" at, 79
  mission of, 78
  quality within, 78–80
  value-based approach, 79–80
  vision, 78
  "wide-tech" at, 79
Kepner, Charles H., 537
key business drivers, 375, 376, 395
Key measurement and information management practices, 365
Key Performance Indicator (KPI), 79
key success factors, 147
KFC, 276–277
Kingsley Elementary school (Sullivan County, Tennessee), 68–69
  Koalaty Kid Express, 69
  steering team, 68
KJ method, 204
knowledge. *See also* information management; Profound Knowledge system; theory of knowledge
  assets, 396
  in Baldrige Criteria, 400–401
  explicit, 396
  in ISO 9000, 401
  management, 25, 395–400
  rapid knowledge transfer (RKT), 399–400
  of results, 258
  at Royal Mail, 398–399
  in Six Sigma, 401–402
  tacit, 396
  transfer, 396, 397–400
Koalaty Kid program, 66–67
  active involvement in, 67–68
  continuous improvement (CI) in, 66–67, 6869
  committed leadership in, 68
  environment of, 68
  Koalaty Kid Express, 69
Kodak, 31
Korea, 1. 13, 421
KPI. *See* Key Performance Indicator (KPI)

L

L. L. Bean, 209
La Ventana Window Company (LVWC), 668–674
labor intensity, 61, 315–316
labor unions, 22, 33, 92, 103–104
lagging measures, 369
Lands' End, 230, 313
Langford, David, 64–65
language, 18, 73, 76, 96, 105
LaRosa's Inc., 227–228
latent defects, 623
Laurent, Carly, 47–48
Lauzon, Armand, 252
Lawler, 255
Layoffs. *See* redundancy policy
layout, 215, 309, 557–558
LCL. *See* lower control limit (LCL)
Leader-Member Exchange, *433*
leadership, 31–35, 156–157, 423–438, 459. *See also* executive leadership; performance excellence
  at Alcoa, 461–463
  Baldrige Criteria for Performance Excellence and, 459
  at Baptist Hospital, Inc., (BHI), 425
  Categories of, 116
  at Caterpillar Financial Services Corporation (CFSC), 431
  at Cedar Foundation, 91
  change in, 443–448
  characteristics of, 424–425
  competencies for, 424
  at Consolidates School District 15, 432
  as core value, 49
  criteria for performance excellence, 115
  defined, 101

in Deming's 14 points, 101
effectiveness, 118
Florida Power and Light (FPL), 364
formal organized, 436, 437
governance and, 429–432
institute, 101
in ISO , 131
at Juran Center, 424
lack of, 101
leading practices for, 432–438
organizational structure and, 161, 398, 426
outcomes, 373–374
practice of, 425, 437–438
Quality Leadership Process, 32–33, 137
for quality, 32–34
at Ritz-Carlton Hotel Company, L.L.C., 117
at Saint Luke's Hospital (SLH), 422–423
in Six Sigma, 459
social responsibilities and, 13, 430–432
at Solar Turbines, Inc., 426–427, 431–432
at SSM Health Care, 430
stakeholders, 428
steering teams and, 428
strategy and, 156–157, 425
success and, 156
systems, 426–429
as total quality (TQ) practice, 25
leadership effectiveness model, *433*
leadership skills, 272
changing, 438
"hard," 437
"soft," 271
team, 272
leadership theories, 432–438
applied in Ritz-Carlton Hotel Company, L.L.C., 117, 436–437
applying in total quality (TQ) environment, 71
classification of, 433
emerging, 433
emotional intelligence, 433, 436–437
great group concept, 157
great leader concept, 157
perspectives on, 437–438
purpose of, 432
situational, 433–435
styles, 434
substitutes for, 433, 436
systems, 426–429
transactional, 433, 435
transformational, 433, 435–436
Leadership Through Quality, 9, 32–33
leading measures, 369
lean enterprise, 162, 464, 558
Lean Manufacturing Initiative, 137
lean production, 556–560
benefits of, 557
continuous improvement (CI) as tool of, 558
defined, 556
in financial institutions, 558
focus of, 557
enterprise, 558
manufacturing approach, 559
at Metro Health Hospital, 559–560
"phantom" capacity, 559
redesign and, 559–560
Six Sigma and, 31–36
at Sunset Manufacturing, Inc., 558
tools of, 557–558
of Toyota Motor Corporation, Ltd., 556–557
Lean Six Sigma, 31–36, 560
expert, 465
lean production versus, 560
master, 465
in manufacturing, 454
within Xerox, 31–36, 538
learner, 424
LEARN philosophy, 417
learning cycle of formal planning process, 180
performance and, 23–24
learning management system (LMS), 290
learning organizations
activities in, 455
at American Honda, 290
in Baldrige Criteria for Performance Excellence, 456–457
control in, 322
defined, 453
described, 455
developing, 454–455
General Electric (GE) as, 453–454
movement, 454
total quality (TQ) in, 453
learning perspectives, 368
Le Blanc, Honoré, 5
legal services, 56
Lemmie, Valerie, 527
Leonard, Denis, 450
Levi Strauss, 204
Levitt, Paul, 185
Lewis, Clarence Irving, 96
Lewis, James, 272
Lexus automobiles, 272
building quality in North America, 345–347
customer service linking at, 205
image of, 15
owners of, 208
liability, 9, 56, 197, 378, 390
life characteristics curve, 615
life cycle, 450–453
life testing, 622
Lightspeed Computed Tomography (CT) System, 587
likelihood, *611*
Likert scales, for customer satisfaction, 139
limitation stage of life cycle, 450
Lincoln Award for Excellence, 120
Lincoln Electric, 327
line organization, 173
line and staff organization, 173
Lipson, Charles, 512
Listening and learning approach, 203–205
Little q, 11
Livingstone, Mimi, 238
Locke, Edward, 255
Lockheed Missiles and Space Division, 264

"loss function," 604–607
Louisville Slugger, 103
Lowell, Francis, 338
lower control limit (LCL)), 666–667, 669, 676, 689
lower tolerance limit, 634, 636
loyalty, 193, 213
LT, Inc, 574–576
Luthans, Fred, 432
LVWC. *See* La Ventana Window Company (LVWC)
Lynch, Donald P., 537

M

Macy's Department Store, 196
Magnivision, 329
Maguire Miles, 460–461
main effect, 507–508
major defects, 378
Malcolm Baldrige National Quality Award (MBNQA), 6, 9, 10, 111. *See also* Baldrige Award
  application, 119–121
  Criteria for Performance Excellence, 111, 114–119, 288, 370
  Deming, W. Edwards and, 121–122
  evolution, 119
  examiners, 456
  history/purpose of, 112
  process management and, 341
  quality teams, 174
  recipients of, 113–114
  small businesses and, 120
  on state level, 120
Malcolm Baldrige National Quality Improvement Act (1987), 112
managed care organizations (MCOs), 639–642
  accreditation, 63
  applying QDF in, 639–642
  House of Quality for, 640–*641*
  quality assurance in, 63
management. *See also* activity-based management; change management; complaint management; customer relationship management; middle management; policy deployment; process management; quality management; senior management
  by facts, 118, 124
  language of, 388
  at Mazda, 374
  at Nucor Corporation, 275
  by planning, 167
  by processes, 124
  quality, environmental, health, and safety (QEHS) system, 140
  role in process improvement, 483–484
  skills, 272
  successful, 50
  systems approach, 131
  systems thinking and, 94–95
  teams, 174
  total quality management commitment of, 37, 76, 104, 186, 450
  title of, 172
  tools, 171
  traditional practices v. workforce engagement, 251
  workforce, 248–250
Management of Information, Knowledge, and Information Technology, 400–401
management by objective (MBO), 102
Managerial Grid model, *433*
managers, 56, 446, 449
manufacturers, 5
  costs, 9, 34, 94
  manufacturing assembly and, 54
  operations, 54, 94, 176
  quality in, 54, 322–333
  services versus, 313
manufacturing-based perspective, 17
manufacturing systems, 51
  assembly in, 54, 94
  design, 599–600
  finance/accounting, 55–56
  finished goods inspection/testing in, 55
  industrial engineering/process design in, 54–55
  installation/service in, 55
  key relationships in, 51
  Lean Manufacturing Initiative, 137
  marketing/sales in, 51–52
  packaging/shipping/warehousing in, 55
  product design/engineering in, 52–53
  production planning/scheduling, 54
  purchasing/receiving in, 53
  tool engineering in, 54
market evaluation, 584–585
marketing/sales, 51–52
market introduction, 584–585
marketplace measures, 372
market research, 10, 52, 105, 162, 200
market share, 26, 27, 57, *371*, *382–384*
market superiority, 25
Marlow Industries, 426
Marlow, Raymond, 426
Marriott, 21
Mary Kay Cosmetics, 339
Maslow, Abraham, 255
mass customization, 313
mass inspection, 8, 100
mastery descriptions, 280–281
MasteryWorks Inc., 246
mathematics of reliability, 616–618
matrices
  cost of quality, 391
  data analysis, 171
  diagrams, 171
  fixed pricing, 206
  House of Quality relationship, 591, 594, 651
  Imagimatrix, 411
  organizational structure, 173–174
  "prioritization," 137–138
  project life cycle accountability, 451

project selection, 539
relationship, *595*
scoring, 224
matrix-type organization, 173
maturation stage of life cycle, 450
Mayer, Raymond, 706
Mazda, 374
MBNA, 376
MBNQA. *See* Malcolm Baldrige National Quality Award
MBNQA teams, 174
MBO. *See* management by objective (MBO)
McAdam, Rodney, 450,
MCB. *See* Kenneth W. Monfort College of Business
McClelland, David, 255
McCombs, Tom, 461–463
McDonald's restaurant, 50, 350
McDonnel-Douglas Corporation, 11
McDonnell-Douglas Helicopter Company, 64
McGregor, Douglas, 255
MCI, 386
mean search
average, 666
and median, 676
overall, 666, 668–669
sample, *662*, *664*, 666
shift in, 663, 676–677, 703–704
mean square" (MS), 511
mean time between failures (MTBF), 613
mean time to failure (MTTF), 1, 613
measurements, 367–374. *See also* performance measurement systems
antiquated, 395
as Baldrige Criteria for Performance Excellence, 400–402
in customer engagement, 217–226
defined, 364, 367
in hospitals, 377
individual, 667, 683, 686
identification and selection of, 379–381
information management practices, 365
in insurance companies, 324
in performance, 277, 367–374
of process management, 312, 315, 376–379
quality control, 107
reliability, 612–616
sensory, 323
summits, 395
system error, 321
system evaluations, 155, 400, 623–628
U-bolts, 498, 632, 636
work, 99, 392
Measurement, Analysis and Improvement of Organizational Performance, 400
Measurement, Analysis, and Knowledge Management, 400
measurement-managed companies, 155, 400
measurement system evaluations, 626–628
measures. *See also* process measures
of Airbus, 364
business performance, 365, 366, 370–371, 383–384
customer-focused, 372
of dispersion, 495
of employee engagement, 281
financial, 372
"hard", 281
human resource, 281
indicators and, 364
lagging, 369
leadership, 373–374
leading, 369
linking to strategy, 375–376
marketplace, 372
organizational, 367
outcomes, 281, 370–374
process, 281, 373, 376–379
product/service, 370–371
selecting, 374–375, 379–381
"soft", 281
traceable, 629
workforce-focused, 372–373
Medical College of Wisconsin, 563
Medical error reduction, 563–564
Medical Information Data Access System, 395
Medrad
code of conduct at, 430
competencies at, 284
compensation at, 274
ethics within, 430
leadership system at, 51, 426, 430
learning/development process of, 287
process management at, 287
role profiles used at, 284
strategic planning at, 426
meetings, rules for effective, 272–273
Mehne, Patrick, 193
mentor, 424
Mercedes-Benz, 328, 599
Mercy Health System (MHS), 192
Best practice (BP) at, 386
Culture of Excellence Four Pillars, 192
comparative data at, 387
Dashboard Alert System, 383
performance measurement system at, 376
performance reviews at, 387
"Take the L.E.A.D" program, 19
MESA Products, Inc., 28, 336, *439*, *442*, 661
metrics, 665–666
Metro Health Hospital, 559–560
metrology, 393, 623–624
Michigan Studies, *433*
microprocessor specifications, *602*
Microsoft, 238, 448
Microsoft Excel
Analysis of variance (ANOVA) and, 510–512
best practices in, 448
cross-cutting themes, 137
data analysis tools, 497–501
descriptive statistics dialog box, 498–499
descriptive statistics results, 500
histogram dialog box, 499, 500

regression results, 513
spreadsheets and, 517, 530
statistical analysis with, 97, 385, 497–501
templates, 670–*671*
Middle East Quality Association, 13
Midwest Bank, PIVOT initiative, 358–359
Milliken, 393
Mind and the World (Lewis), 96
Minimum Standards for Hospitals, 61
minor defects, 378
Mintzberg, Henry, 162
mission
of Black Elk Medical Center (BEMC), 653
of Branch-Smith Printing Division, 180
of Cadillac Motor Car Company, 16
of Cedar Foundation, 91
of Clifton Metal Works, 185
of Coyote Community College, 415, 416
of Gold Star Chili, 241
of individual employees, 262
of Jenks Public Schools, 48, 49
of Joint Commission on Accreditation of Healthcare Organizations, 61–62
of MCB, 78, 79
of Mercy Hospital, 192
of National Committee for Quality Assurance (NCQA), 62
in organizational environment, 155, 158
of Pearl River School District (PRSD), 65
of Procter & Gamble, 210
of The Ritz-Carlton, 77
of University of Wisconsin-Stout, 70
U.S. Water Resource Agency, 84
Missouri Quality Award, 452
Mitsubishi, 589
mixture, 680–681
modern quality technology, 109
modified control limits, 674
moments of truth, 208–209
Monsanto, 277
Montgomery, Douglas C., 512
Morelia Mortgage Company, 724–725
motivation, 250, 253–256, 444
motivation theories, 250–256
categories of, 254
classification of, 255
systems and, 102
motivator, 424
Motorola, Inc.
Commercial/Government/Industrial Solutions Sector, 169, 197
end users and, 395
empowerment at, 260
excellence at, 6, 69–70
financial personnel at, 56
goals of, 6, 52, 133–134
human resource plans, 169
improvement process at, 6
kaizen in, 328
leadership system at, 51
Malcolm Baldrige Award, 113
organizational effectiveness measures at, 6
problem solving at, 338
process design at, 314–315
product design at, 52
quality influences on, 27, 30
Six Sigma within, 52–53, 133, 137, 338, 531
strategic planning at, 215
supplier training in, 22, 53, 215
Total Customer Satisfaction (TCS) at, 278
technical advisory boards at, 395
training at, 287, 288, 314
moving ranges, *682*, 686–687, *688*
Mt. Edgecumbe High School (Sitka, Alaska), 64
MTBF. *See* mean time between failures
MTI. *See* Murphy Trucking, Inc.
MTTF. *See* mean time to failure
Mulcahy, Anne, 260
multiple regression, 513
multiplicative law of probability, 618–619
Murphy, Rick, 727–726
Murphy Trucking, Inc. (MTI), 725–727
My Life and Work (Ford, Crowther), 7

N

NAICS. *See* North American Industry Classification System (NAICS)
NASA, 10, 73, 608
Nash General Hospital (Rocky Mount, North Carolina), 63
Nashua Corporation, 92
National Academy of Sciences, Institute of Medicine, 563
National Cash Register Company (NCR)
process improvement at, 326–327
root causes and, 327, 534
National Committee for Quality Assurance (NCQA), 62–63
National Healthcare Quality Report, 63
National Institute of Standards and Technology (NIST), 112, 115, 629
National Performance Assessment (NPA), 403
National Quality Institute (NQI), 125
National Quality Month, 10
National Quality Program, 112
Nationwide Insurance, 120
natural tolerance limits, 632, 634
Naval Air Systems Command, 11
navigator, 424
NCACS. *See* North Central Association of Colleges and Schools

NCQA. *See* National Committee for Quality Assurance (NCQA)
NCR. *See* National Cash Register Company
negotiation, 272
Net present value of the customer (NPVC), 197
Netflix, 216, 305–306
neural networks, 386
New England Deaconess Hospital, 63
Newsweek, 11
New York Times, 11
NGT. *See* nominal group technique (NGT)
Nissan Motor Car Company Limited, 6, 54
NIST. *See* National Institute of Standards and Technology
No Child Left Behind Act, 66
nominal, 602
nominal group technique (NGT), 273
nominal-is-best loss function, 604–*605*
noncomformance, *632*, 687. *See also* specific terms
noncomformities per unit, *632*
noncomparable data, 492
nonmanufacturing organizations, 56
nonsampling error, 492
Nordam Europe, Ltd., 300–302
Nordstrom, 22, 175
Norfolk Naval Shipyard, 73
normal distribution, 95, 490–491, 502–503, 632
norming phase of teams, 269
North American Industry Classification System (NAICS), 56
North Central Association of Colleges and Schools (NCACS), 416
North Mississippi Medical Center (NMMC), 28, 64, 162, 385–386, *439*
Norton, David, 368
not-for-profits, 71–73
Novak, David, 277
Novel Connect, 417
  core compentencies, 186–187
  customer focus, 242
  leadership, 470
  measurement, analysis, and knowledge management, 417–418
  organizational environment, 147–148
  performance measures, 417
  process improvements, 359
  workforce focus, 302
np-charts, 694–696
NPVC. *See* net present value of the customer
NQI. *See* (National Quality Institute)
NRS Corp, surveys, 141
Nucor Corporation, 274–276
  compensation at, 274–276
  management philosophy of, 274–274
  quality at, 274–275
  recruitment at, 275
NYS: CVG. *See* Convergys Corporation

O

Occupational Safety and Health Administration (OSHA), 403, 416
Office of Personnel Management, 74
Ohio State Studies, *433*
okyakusama, 190
Oldham, G. R., 257–258
OMI (Operations Management International, Inc.), *114*
"one-entry system," 309
"100-mile" rule, 272, 273
online learning, 291
operating conditions, 612
operating environments, *155*, 158, 307, 375, 424
operating practices, 328
operational definitions, 324, 370, 380, 532
operational variations, 483
Operations Management International, Inc. (OMI), *114*, 661
operator variation, 482, 625
optimize, 603
Oracle
  and control chart construction, 701
  information systems and, 382
Oregon State University (OSU), 69
organization. *See also* learning organization
  for breakthrough, 106
  as dynamic entity, 453
  matrix-type, 173
  reporting, 75
  third-party, 19, 218
organizational behavior, 433
organizational charts
  apparent structure, 172
  circular, 172
  team-based, 175
  traditional, 22
organizational culture, 442–447
organizational effectiveness measures, 12, 73, 261, *283*
organizational environment, 147–148, 157–162
  Baldrige profile questions, 159
  characteristics of, 158
  code of ethics, 160
  competitive, 159
  customer groups, 161
  description, 159
  indicators, 371
  market segments, 161
  mission statement, 158
  performance improvement system, 159, 277
  performance measures, 371
  profile, 158
  relationships, 159
  strategic challenges, 161–162
  strategic context, 159
  suppliers, 161
  values, 160, 277
  vision of, 158, 160
  workforce, 160–161 246–247
organizational performance, 171–175
organizational profile, 158
organizational structure
  apparent, 172
  context and, 159, 171–172
  defined, 171
  design, 159

factors in, 172
leadership and, 172, 424–432
performance excellence, 171–175
types of, 173–175
Organization for Standardization (IOS), 128, 430
Osborn, A. F., 336
Osborne, D., 364
OSHA. *See* Occupational Safety and Health Administration
OSU. *See* Oregon State University
OTC (over-the-counter), 330
out-of-control processes, 660, 677, 681–*682*
"out of specification," 667
outputs, 3, 22, 29, 128, 133, 333
"outside of the box," 338
outsourcing, 176
overall mean, 666
overengineering, 52
over-the-counter (OTC), 330
overuse of services, 62
ownership, 8, 10, 206, 248, 446

P

packaging/shipping/warehousing, 55
packing slip errors, *714–715*
Pal's Sudden Service, 155–156
benchmarking at, 383
business excellence process, 155–156
code of ethics, 160
core values, 160
process focus, 439
quality engines at, 439
SysDine at, 383
value creation processes for, 310
parallel system, *620*
parameters, 496
Pareto analysis, 390, 550–551, *715*
Pareto diagrams, 550
for activity time, *566*
analysis, 550–551, *715*
of customer calls, *552*
defect location, *551*
described, 550
histograms, 501
for progressive analysis, 551–*553*
at Rotor Clip Company, 551
Pareto distribution, 550
Pareto principle, 550
Pareto, Vilfredo, 550
Park Place Lexus (PPL), 191–192
Client Satisfaction Index (CSI) at, 192
DRIVE process at, 337
performance excellence at, 426
quality at, 57
strategic planning at, 163–164
Parnes, S. J., 336
participation, 27, 33, 397, 405
partnership development, 124
Patterson, John, 327
Pauli's Restaurant and Microbrewery, 237–238
PBM. *See* process based management
p-charts constructing, *688–694*
fraction nonconforming, 688–*694*
in funnel experiments, *485–487*
with variable sample size, 691–*694*
for zip code reader, 689
PDSA. *See* plan, do, study, act (PDSA)
peak performance study, 631
Pearl River School District (PRSD), 65–66, 369
balanced scorecard at, 369
continuous improvement (CI) at, 66
data accessibility at, 65, 394
learning system at, 65
Penemarl, James, 65
people
development and involvement, 124, 131
focus, 125
skills, 271, 272, 369
Peppers, Don, 190
PepsiCo, 352
perceived quality, 194–*195*, 207, 216
Perdue, Frank, 198
perfection, 15
performance
appraisal, 278–279
customer ratings of, 235, 371
defined, 256
as dimension of quality, 13–14, 198–199
improving, 159
indicators, 365
learning and, 247, 286–288
phase of teams, 269
reliability and, 612
performance data, 383–388
analyzing/using, 383–388
comparative data, 386–387
at FedEx, 59, 61, 211
at IBM, 384
interlinking, 383–384
at Mercy-Hospital, 387
at NMMC, 385–386
at PRO-TECH, 387–388
in reviews, 387–388, 440
at Trident Precision Manufacturing, Inc., *113*
performance excellence, 423–432
at American Electric Power (AEP), 423
in Baldrige Criteria, 459
in Baldrige framework, 424
barriers to, 447–448
best practices in, 448–449
building in organizations, 438–442
committing to, 99, 109, 209–210, 452
culture of, 246–247, 445
defined, 423
in Deming's 14 Points, 423–424
engagement principles, 250–253, 293
future trends, 459–461
key practices for, 155, 425
mistakes made in implementation, 18, 62, 92–93, 317
motivation principles, 253–256
organizational culture and, 442–447
at Park Place Lexus, 426

process, 35, 271–272
at Saint Luke's Hospital (SLH), 422–423, 440, 452–453
Stoner Excellence System, 428–429
success factors, 254
sustaining, 422, 449–459
theories, 255
workforce-focused practices, 247
performance-importance comparison, 223
performance management process (PMP), 280, 422–423
performance measurement systems, 367–382
alignment of, 381
continuous improvement and, 49
cost of quality and, 107, 388–392
designing effective, 374–382
Enterprise Resource Planning (ERP), 382
guidelines for, 375
linking to strategy, 375–376
mistakes made in, 18, 62, 92–93, 317
purposes of, 374
process-level, 376–379
selecting and identifying measures/indicators, 374–375, 379–381
scope of, 367–374
performance planning and development (PPD) process, 140
performing phase of teams, 269
perseverance, 425
personal learning, 118
personal quality checklist, 30–31
personal values, 30–31
personnel administration. *See* Human Resource Management (HRM)
personnel management. *See* Human Resource Management (HRM)
Peterson, Donald, 374
Peters, Tom, 251
"phantom" capacity, 559
pharmaceutical product manufacturing, 41–42, 524–525, 559
Philip Crosby Associates, 106–107
philosophy of quality management. *See also* Deming philosophy; Juran philosophy; kaizen philosophy; TQ philosophy
comparisons of, 108
Crosby philosophy, 106–108
for production, 173
various types, 109–111
PIMS Associates, Inc., 26,
plan-do-check-act (PDCA) cycle, 441
plan, do, study, act (PDSA), 49, 333, 707
planning. *See also* strategic planning; strategic planning process
bottom-up, 110, 164, 537
hoshin, 167–169
management by, 171
personnel, 169–170, 284
production, 54
project quality, 309
quality, 54
resource, 382, 427
top-down, 537
plan stage of Deming cycle, 333, 335
platform-team approach, 264, 582–583
PMA. *See* President's Management Agenda
PMP. *See* performance management process
PMTs. *See* process management team (PMTs)
Pompeo, Jack, 36
point estimates, 497
Poisson probability, 697
poka-yoke (mistakeproofing), 317–319
aspects of, 317
errors and, 318–319
levels of, 318
policy deployment, 167–169
at AT&T, 167
catchball process, 169
at Florida Power and Light, 167
grids, 280
at Hewlett-Packard, 167
management, 168–169
process of, 168–169
population, 496
finite, 502
mean, 496, 681
proportion, 496
ratio of, to sample standard deviation, 496, *635*
static, 505
Portland, Oregon, 218
PPL. *See* Park Place Lexus
PQA. *See* President's Quality Award
practices, 20–25. *See also* best practices
best-in-class selection, 339
in China, 36–37
high-performance management, 227, 277, 282
of Human Resource Management (HRM), 292–294, 285
implementing incorrect, 448
leadership, 31–36
leading to recognition, 276–278
leading to rewards, 276–278
operating, 328, 432
for strategic planning, 180–182
total quality, 20–25
universal, 448
Prahalad, C.K., 175
precision, 27, 40, 301, 624–*625*
pre-control, 707–709
basis for, 708
control charts and, 546, 709
green zone, 707
lines, 707
ranges, 708
red zone, 707
yellow zone, 707
predictive statistics, 496
preliminary concept development, 163, 583–584
Premier, Inc., 28, 156, 277–278
President's Advisory Commission on Consumer Protection and Quality, 62

President's Management Agenda (PMA), 74
President's Quality Award (PQA)
  aims of, 74
  compared to PMA, 74
  Federal Quality Institute (FQI), 74
  Quality Improvement Prototype Award, 74
  winners of, 74–75
Press Ganey Associates, 28
Press Ganey survey, 366
Pressler, Paul, 201
prevention costs, 389
"pride and joy" in work, 60, 76, 90, 250, 277
pride in workmanship, in Deming's 14 points, 90, 250, 277
Principles of Corporate Governance, 431
Printed Circuit Assembly–Encoder (PCA-Encoder), 514
Printed circuit board design, 600
Printed Wire (PWB) Fabricated Board Finishes, 516
"prioritization matrix," 137
probability, 490–491
  defined, 610
  of detecting shift in mean, 503
  distributions, 490–491
  of nonconforming product, 546, *632*
  of survival, 617
  for tire mileage, *616*
probe-and-learn, 455
problem(s)
  aging population and, 14
  benchmarks for, 37
  causes of, 98, 102, 106–107, 173, 179, 208
  conformance, 107, 252, 537
  created by variation, 102
  defined, 537
  diagnosis, 169, 354
  efficiency, 537
  financial, 12, 71, 167
  health care, 62
  implementation, 55, 169
  manufacturing, 37, 100, 107, 134
  process, 23, 25
  product design, 54–55, 69, 171, 537
  redefining/analyzing, 332
  service, 199–200, 246
  systemic, 22, 97
  technical, 53
  unstructured performance, 71, 537
  at Xerox, 33, 35
problem solving. *See also* creative problem solving
  categories of, 252
  defined, 336
  leadership and, 248
  process for, 336, 135–136, 251–252, 330, 332, 336–338
  at Ritz-Carlton Hotel Company, L.L.C., 60
  Six Sigma project teams, 265
  at SSM Health Care, 63
  systemic, 22, 97, 128, 455
  teams, 22, 49, 75, 143, 264, 270
  tools, 96, 106, 110, 171
process
  benchmarking, 35, 339
  change, 444
  defined, 22
  development, 584
  effectiveness outcomes, 373
  focus, 22–24
  function versus, 23
  implementation, 584–585
  mean, 529–530
  "mega-processes", 309
  monitoring, 325
  optimization, 125, 609
  owners, 307, 311, 342, 430
  problems, 336, 135–136, 251–252, 330, 332, 336–338
  simulation, 95
  variability, 73, 92, 95, 110, 199, 306, 312
process average, shift in, 530, 676–677
process based management (PBM), 307, 311–312
process capability, 630–637
  calculations, 632
  calculations spreadsheet, 530, 637
  defined, 630
  estimating, 632, 626–637
  evaluation of, 325
  indexes, 634–637
  management decisions in, 630
  probability computations, 490–491
  spreadsheet for, *637*
  statistical control and, 631, 636
  studies, 631–634
process capability index, 634–637
process characterization study, 631
process control, 319–326
  automobile service flowchart, 354
  at Cincinnati Fiberglass, 323
  components of, 319–320
  corrective actions, 322
  costs, 389
  at DaimlerChrysler, 320
  defined, 319
  error rates in, 322
  evaluations, 325
  medical administration process, 355
  monitoring, 325
  plan, 323
  and process management, 311
  in-process measures, 321–323
  in quality control, 320, 322–326
  at Ritz-Carlton, 323–324
  in services, 323–326
  at SSM Health Care, 321
  staff behavior questions, 326
  versus improvement, 320
process decision program chart, 171
process design, 312–319
  agility, 312, 313
  approaches, 313
  in the City of Coral Springs, 315
  flexibility, 312
  goal of, 312
  at Hennes & Mauritz, 312
  implementation, 584–585

industrial engineering and, 54–55
mistake-proofing, 317–319
at Motorola, Inc., 314
and process management, 311
at Ritz-Carlton, 314
standards for, 316–317
steps of, 314–315
process improvement, 326–330
akaizen blitz, 329
applying to order fulfillment, 565–568
automobile service flowchart, 354
continuous, 23, 326
at Dell Inc., 329–330
engaging workforce in, 246–247, 271–272
importance of, 326
Kaizen, 327–329
managers and, 483–484
medical administration process, 355
at Microsoft, 448
and process management, 311
at NCR, 326–327
opportunities, 329–330
at Procter & Gamble, 330, 327
at Ritz-Carlton, 328–329
in Six Sigma, 531–532
at Toyota, 327
process improvement methodologies, 330–338
automobile service flowchart, 354
benchmarking types, 338–340
at Branch-Smith Printing, 332
breakthrough improvement, 338–340
common themes of, 332
creative problem solving, 330–331, 336
custom, 336–338
Deming cycle, 23–24, 333–337
DMAIC stage, 358–359
"is" and "should" process map, 331
Juran's breakthrough cycle, 106
kaizen, 327–329
medical administration process, 355
At Mercy Health, 335
for PepsiCo, 352
PIVOT initiative, 358
quality improvement process (QIP), 332
reengineering, 340
at Siemens Energy and Automation, 352–353
theories, 255
Theory of Inventive Problem Solving (TRIZ), 338
process improvement tools
cause-and-effect diagrams, 516, 518, 554–555
check sheets, 548, 566
control charts as, 7, 546, 681, 707, 726
flowcharts, 314, 517, *565*, *571*, *575*
histograms, *633*
kaizen blitz, 329
Pareto diagrams, 550–551
poka-yoke (mistakeproofing), 317–319
run charts, 545–546, 663–*664*
scatter diagrams, 555–556
process-level measurements, 376–379
actionable, 376
alignment with strategic measurements, 381–382
defects in, 377–378
at Mercy Health System, 377
SMART (simple, measurable, actionable, related), 376
timely, 376
process management,
activities of, 311, 341, 342, 367
Baldrige Criteria for Performance Excellence and, 341–342
at Boeing Airlift and Tanker, 309
for Consolidated School District (D#15), 311
control and, 311
at Corning TPD, 314
defined, 309, 311
design and, 311
at Eastman Chemical Company, 214
enterprise process model, 309
frameworks, 311–312
at Gold Star Chili, Inc., 342–345
at IBM, 340
improvement and, 311
in ISO, 373, 401
measurements in, 312
at Medrad, 287
at Pal's Sudden Service, 310
practices for, 306,
requirements, 310
scope of, 532
in Six Sigma, 440–441
support, 308–309
at Texas Instruments (TI), 306
as total quality (TQ) practice, 25
value-creation, 308, 311, 342–343
process management teams (PMTs), 174
process map, *331*, 379
process measures
alignment with strategy, 381–382
generating, 376–379
identifying, 379–381
selecting, 374–375
types of, 380–381
Process Model, 661
process simplification, 448
Process Task Force, 309
process theories, 255
process value analysis, 448
process variation histograms, *633*
Procter & Gamble, 3
culture in, 442
customer support at, 209
cycle time reduction at, 330
OTC division of, 330
process improvement at, 327
recruitment at, 210
total quality (TQ) philosophy at, 3, 330
"voice of the company" department in, 402
Procter, William Cooper, 3
producers, 206
product(s)
liability, 9
measures of, 370–371

pharmaceutical manufacturing, 709–713
providing good, 15
quality, 10–11, 26, 372
quality dimensions of, 13–14, 198–199
teams, 262
testing, 55
product-based perspective, 15
product design, 52–53, 583–587
at Ames Rubber Company, 585
at Boeing, 363–364
control, 456
development process, 583–585
problems, 55
redesign, 559–560, 583
overview, 583
product designers, 18, 52
product design processes, 52–53, 583–587
at Caterpillar, 584
cost/manufacturability/quality and, 50
engineering and, 52–53
at IBM, 589
DMADV and, 586
engineering and, 52–53, 585–586
phases, 583–584
quality/social responsibility in, 13
self-assessement in, 456
in Six Sigma, 586–587
value-creation processes, 308
at Xerox, 33
product development
at Ames Rubber Corporation, 585
performance management and, 278
phases of, 583–584
process management and, 312
speed in, 518, 533, 585
streamlining, 34
at Xerox, 9
product-distribution cycle, 18
production 205–208. *See also* lean production
customer information and, 206–208
delivery processes and, 205–208, 591, 585–586, 594
Deming and, 23–24
design, 206–207
full-scale, 205
manufacturing systems and, 5, 207
non-, 276
philosophy of, 50, 205
planning, 54
pre-, 585
pull, 558
system, 23–24, 50, 317
tools, 585, 560
at Toyota Motor Corporation, Ltd., 12, 245, 327, 336, 449
variation and, 5, 18, 96, 323, 482
productivity, 3
"Productivity Improvement for the Federal Government" (Executive Order 12637), 73
product-liability judgments, 9
Product Realization, 129–130, 136, 226
product/service attributes, 21, 217
product/service measures, *234*, 385
professional depth, 79
profitability, 26
Profound Knowledge system, 93–94
components of, 93–94, 95–98
impacts of, 98–99
progressive analysis, *553*
project(s)
bottom-up, 164, 537
conception, 339
identification, 106
organizational structure, 309
pitfalls in, 538
quality control, 309
quality initiation, 12
quality planning, 54
ranking metric, 539–540
scheduling, 54
scoping, 536–537
selection matrix, 401, 539
success of, 538
teams, 263, 265–268
top-down in, 167, 169, 537
tracking, 342
as value-creation process, 308, 342–343
project management, 309
Project Management Body of Knowledge (PMBOK), 536
Project Management Institute, 536
project managers, 97, 272
project quality assurance. *See also* customer relationship management
Project Quality Recap, 309
project scoping, 532
promotion, of employees, 301
proof of need, 106
PRSD. *See* Pearl River School District psychology (PRSD)
PRO-TEC Coating Company, 28, 51, 248, *439*
PTA Health fund (Al Hoover/), 432
Public Company Accounting Reform and Investor Protection Act (2002), 431
public sector, 73–76
Publicizing extensively, as recognition program, 278
pull production, 558
purchasing/receiving, 53
Purdue University, 69
Purnell, Pete, 724
purpose, constancy of, 124
Pyzdek, Thomas, 540

Q

QBR. *See* Quarterly Business Reviews
QFD. *See* quality function deployment
QI. *See* quality improvement
QIP. *See* quality improvement process
QMI. *See* Quarterly Management Interaction
QMS. *See* quality management system
Qualcomm, Inc., 27
quality
accounting, 55–56
age of craftsmanship and, 5
assembly, 54
at American Express, 373
building, 4
business results and, 27–29

characteristics, 59, 96, 220
in China, 36–37
competitive advantage and, 25–29
conformance to specifications, 17, 107
cost of, 107, 388–392
culture, 75
current and future challenges, 12–14
customer-driven, 19–21, 15
defined, 3–4, 14–20
dimensions of, 13–14, 198–199
"doing it right the first time", 15, 107
early twentieth century, 7–8
in education, 64–71
employee engagement, 21–22, 250–253, 293
engineering, 52–53, 54–55
engines, 439
in federal government, 73–75
finance, 55–56
forces that influence, 174
future of, 13–14
goals, 104–105
"good news, bad news" about, 193
goods, inspection and testing, 55
at Honeywell, 463–466
in health care industry, 14, 61–64
history of, 4–14
implementation, 140, 448
importance of, 4–14
information technology, 60–61
installation and service, 55
integrating perspectives on, 17–19
initiatives, 12
in Japan, 110–112, 259, 264
Japanese, in North America, 345–347
as journey, 72, 450–453, 457
judgmental perspective for, 15
Kenneth W. Montort College of Business, 78–80
legal services, 56
levels of, 29
as management framework, 12–14, 139–141
maintaining, 4
manual, 104, 137, 439
in manufacturing, 50–51, 54, 322–323
manufacturing-based perspective, 17, 57–58
in marketing and sales, 51–52
in not-for-profits, 71–73
packaging, 55
performance measurements, 107, *662*
personal values and, 30–31
planning and scheduling, 54
policy, 438
post–World War II, 8
in practice, 31–38
problems, 55, 107
process design, 54–55
product-based perspective for, 15
product design, 52–53
profiles, 6
profitability and, 26
in public sector, 73–76
purchasing, 53
receiving parts and services, 53
revolution, 8–9
in services, 56–61, 58–59
shipping, 55
in Six Sigma, 12, 31–36
in small businesses, 71–73
stakeholder focus, 20–21
standards, 5, 16, 37, 91, 127–128, 316
in state/local government, 75–76
statistical methodology for, 495
surveys, 282
sustaining principles of, 176, 290, 452, 460
system, 50
systems thinking and, 50
teamwork, 21–22
three steps to, 109
transcendent value, 15
types of, 14–20
user-based perspective for, 16
value-based perspective for, 16–17
value chain in, 18
warehousing, 55
workforce, 59–60, 246–247
Xerox, 31–36
quality assurance, 56
defined, 4, 56
design guidelines for, 62, 112, 128, 129, *601*
history of, 5
in manufacturing, 51, 322–323
pioneers of, 7
total quality management (TQM) and, 4–5, 71
quality-based strategy, 43, 167
Quality Calibration Handbook, 629
quality circles, 264–265
development of, 264
functions of, 264–265
at Lockheed Missiles and Space Division, 264
quality control, 322–326
and control charts, *660*
at Daimler-Chrysler, 320
data collection for, 324, 532–533
effective systems, 323
in manufacturing, 322–323
measurement, 324
at Ritz-Carlton Hotel Company, L.L.C., 15, 323–324
in services, 323–326
Quality Control Award for Operations Business Units, 122
"quality-control czar," 422
Quality Control for Foremen, 110
Quality Control Handbook (Juran), 104
Quality Control: Principles, Practice, and Administration (Feigenbaum), 109
quality costs, 388–393
through activity based costing, 390–391
analyzing, 390–391
classification, 389–390
distribution of, 388–389
performance measurements and, 107, 392–393

planning, 389
in service organizations, 391–392
Quality Digest, 1, 12, 83
quality, environmental, health, and safety (QEHS) system, 140
"Quality First: Better Health Care for All Americans," 62
Quality Forum, 69
quality function deployment (QFD), 589–599
applications, 598, 651–653
benefits of, 590
as concept development, 587–588
House of Quality and, 590–594
in managed care organizations (MCOs), 63, 639–642
at Mitsubishi, 589
process, 594–99
Technological University RRC, 651–653
quality improvement (QI), 182, 332
Quality Improvement Council, 75
quality improvement process (QIP), 332
Quality Improvement Prototype Award, 10
Quality is Free (Crosby), 26
quality management, 10–15
quality management system (QMS), 441
quality organization, 5, 151, 173, 174, 445
Quality Progress, 460
Quality Trilogy, 105
Quarterly Business Reviews (QBR), 426
Quarterly Management Interaction (QMI), 426
"Quarterly Performance Audit," 368
QuEST Forum, 37
quincunx
in action, 95
experiment result, 96
Quinn, Feargal, 189–190
quotas, 93, 94, 99, 102, 104

R

radical redesign, 340
random variables, 490
rapid knowledge transfer (RKT), 399–*400*
Rath & Strong, 30
rational subgroups, 703
ratio of population to sample standard deviation, 496, *635*
raw data, 480
Raytheon, 119, 370
RBC. *See* Royal Bank of Canada
R-charts, 666–667
analysis, 681
constructing, 666–667
and cycles, 678, 686
at La Ventana, *672*
our-of-control in, *682*, 703
or revised data, *673*
in pharmaceutical product manufacturing, 710–*712*
shifts in, 676–677
spreadsheet for, 670
and trends, 678, 686
and variations, 674–*675*
Read, Carole, 578–578
Readilunch Restaurant, 578–579
Reagan, Ronald, 10, 73
recalls, of products, 9
receiving, 53, 713–*715*
recertification, 132
recognition, 274–278
defined, 274
practices leading to, 276–278
at Premier, Inc, 278
at Yum Brands, 277
recruitment, 300
at Baptist Hospital (BI), 169
at Kenneth W. Monfort College of Business, 78
at Nordam Europe, Ltd. 300
at Nucor Corporation, 300
at Oregon State University (OSU), 69
at Solar Turbines, 426
recycleability, 600
Red Bead experiment, 484–489
description, 484–485
first day's production, 485
fourth day's cumulative results, 487
fourth day's production, 486
lessons from, 486–489
run chart of fraction, 488
second day's cumulative results, 486
second day's production, 486
third day's cumulative results, 487
third day's production, 486
REDRESS (Resolve Employment Disputes Reach Equitable Solutions Swiftly), 403
redundancy, 301–302, 619
redundancy policy, 301–301
regeneration stage of life cycle, 450
registrar, 132
reengineering, 340
at American Red Cross, 73
at IBM Credit Corporation, 340
at Intel Corporation, 340
benchmarking and, 340
breakthrough improvement and, 340
at Caterpillar Financial Services Corporation (CSFC),
at GTE, 340
at Taco Bell, 340
regression, 513
Microsoft Excel results, 512–513
multiple, 513
simple, 513
reliability, 393, 609, 616–618, 622–623
basic concepts, 27, 609–612
computing system, 618–621
defined, 198, 199, 609, 612
DFMEA and, *610*
as dimension of quality, 199
failure, 198–199, 612
failure rate and, 618
function, 323, 395
of machines, *648*
mathematics of, 616–618
measurement, 219, 376–377, 393, 612–616
optimization and, 609
prediction, 135, 317, 609

severity, likelihood, and detection rating scales, *611*
testing, 55, 315, 323, 622–623
TMP Expert and, 465
reliability failure, 612
reliability function, 617
remedial action, 106, 322
remedial journey, 106
repeatability, 312, 625, 626–627
repeatability analysis spreadsheet, *628*
reproducibility, 625, 627
reproducibility analysis spreadsheet, *628*
Research Resources Center (RRC), 651–653
resistance measurements, 629
Resource Management, 393–395
resource planning, 382, *427*
response center, 210, 214
response changes, 508
responsiveness, 200
return on assets (ROA), 28, 31, 34, 281, 586
return on investment (ROI), 292, 293
return on quality (ROQ), 392–393
at Chase Manhattan Bank, 382–393
measuring, 382–393
practices leading to, 392
principles, 392
risk priority number (RPN), 563–564
risk taking, 21, 103, *266*, 279, 424, 426
Ritz, Caesar, 89
Ritz-Carlton Hotel Company, L.L.C., 60, 76–78, 323–324
Baldrige Award, 77
comparative data at, 386
Credo cards of, 117
credo of, 77
cross-functional teams at, 585
cultural resistance to change, 77, 447–448
customer satisfaction at, 60, 193
customers ranked by, 197
employees of, 60, 90, 117, 260
financial measures at, 372
Gold Standards of, 117
Guest Incident Action forms of, 213
guest-profiling system of, 61
human resource measures at, 60, 288
human resources at, 249
improvement process at, 77
information technology, 61
leadership at, 117–118
leadership theories applied in, 436–437
motto of, 77
organizational effectiveness measures at, 118
philosophy of, 117–118
project teams at, 165, 270
quality control at, 57, 90, 288
rewards at, 277
service process at, 77, 314
service quality in, 15, 76–78
service quality indicators (SQI) for, 77
steps of service of, 76–77, 118, 314
strategic planning at, 165
training at, 60, 117, 288
values, 118
vision, 76, 118
workforce-focused outcomes, 373
ROA. *See* return on assets (ROA)
Robbins, Harvey, 268
Roberts, Harry V., 30
Robert Wood Johnson University Hospital Hamilton (RWJ), *114*
robust design, 604
Rogers, Martha, 190
ROI. *See* return on investment (ROI)
rolled throughput yield (RTY), 378–379
Romanoff, Edward M., 464
root causes
audits and, 350
in China, 5
described, 1, 534
DMAIC and, 179, 534
list of, 337
in management frameworks, 311
at National Cash Register (NCR), 326–327
scientific approach to, 270
at UW-Stout, 70
versus symptoms, 110
ROQ. *See* return on quality (ROQ)
Rotor Clip Company, Inc., 551, 556
Royal Bank of Canada (RBC), 197
Royal Mail, 398–399
Royal Order of the Sacred Treasure, 92
RPN. *See* risk priority number
RRC. *See* Research Resources Center (RRC)
Rubbermaid, 200, 328
run charts, 31, 545–546, *663–664*
run chart of red beads produced, 488
Runyon, Marvin, 402
RWJ Hamilton. *See* Robert Wood Johnson University Hospital Hamilton

S

"safe" lower limits, 636
safety, 9
SAI. *See* Standards Australia International (SAI)
Saint Luke's Hospital (SLH), 422–423, 440, 452–453
salespersons, 85
sample, 496
mean, 497, *664*
proportion, 497
standard deviation, 497, 696
sample size, 703–704
and control charts, 703–704
and costs, 705
design issues, 703–704
frequency, 704–*706*
requirements, 319, 320
standard deviation, 5, 681–683
variable, 691–*694*
sample space, 490

sampling, 491–495. *See also* control charts; sample size
basis for, 491, 703
cluster, 491, 494–495
and constant unit, 699
and control limits, 667
cost of, 491–492
distributions, 501–503, 667
error, 492
factors in, 491
frequency, 490, 495, 704–*706*
improper,492, 493
judgment, 491, 495
methods of, 491
MIL-STD, for military standard, 8
plan for, 492
purpose of, 491–492
simple random, 491, 493–494
stratified random, 491, 494
systematic, 491, 492, 494
tables, 8
types of, 494
units, 699, *702*
Samsung Electronics Co. (SEC)
manufacturing costs at, 599
Six Sigma integration within, 338, 600
TRIZ at, 338
Value Innovation Program (VIP) center at, 600
Santa Cruz Guitar Company, 145–147
Santayana review, 455
Sarbanes-Oxley Act, 431
SAS Institute, Inc., 271
satisfiers, 200
SBQP. *See* Strategic Business and Quality Plan (SBQP)
Scandinavian Airlines System, 208
scatter chart, *513*
scatter diagrams, 555–556
s-charts, 682–*685*, *702*
Schneiderman, Art, 368
Scholtes, Peter, 98, 269, 272–273
Schulze, Horst, 117, 437
SCM. *See* supply chain management (SCM)
"scope creep," 536
scoring matrix, 224
scribes, 273
Scribner, Cynthia, 137
Sears, Roebuck and Co., 138–139
SEC. *See* Samsung Electronics Co.
SecurTrac, 563
segmentations, of markets, 196–198
seiri, seiton, seiso, seiketsu, shitsuke (5S's), 557, 558
self-assessment conduct, 456–459
defined, 456
elements of, 121, 458
findings, 457, 458
follow-up and, 458, 459
leveraging, 458–459
managers and, 458
opportunities for improvement (OFIs) and, 139
processes, 120–121
role of, 456
self-determination, 261
self-managed teams (SMTs), 268
Selit Corporation, 524
SELs. *See* senior executive leaders
Semco S/A, 172
Semler, Ricardo, 172
Senge, Peter, 453
senior executive leaders (SELs),
senior management, 459
responsibilities of, 157–158, 538
roles of, 60
Sensenbrenner, Joseph, 75
Sergesketter, Bernard F., 30–31
series-parallel system, 620, 622
series system, 618
service(s), 56–61, 76–78, 155–156, 162, 205–208, 289–292, 560–563
characteristics, 220
customers in, 15, 199–200, 292–294
defined, 56
delivery, 205–208, 211
in health care industry, 61–64
at Honda Motor Co., 289–292
indicators, 77, 379
information technology, 60–61
as labor intensive, 58, 61
manufacturing versus, 57–58, 313
organizations, 391–392, *660*
overuse of, 62
process control in, 212–215, 323–326
quality dimensions of, 13–14, 199
quality in, 6, 56–61, 199–200
Six Sigma in, 560–563
underutilization of, 62
variation in, 62
workforce, 59–60, 246–247
serviceability, dimension of quality, 13–14, 199
service process
components of, 315
data collection for, 324, 532–533
design considerations, 313–316
designers, 18, 52
at Motorola, 314–315
quality standards, 316
questions for, 316–317
at Ritz-Carlton Hotel Company, L.L.C., 314
service quality indicators (SQI), 77, *379*
Service Recovery Process, 213–215
service sector
changing personnel in, 57
growth of, 57
service system quality, 58–59
costs, 391–392
employees in, 315, 316
information technology in, 14, 60–61
key components of, 58, 316
Seven-Eleven Stores, 205
Seven Habits of Highly Effective People (Covey), 428
Seven QC Tools, 13, 115–117, 307, 541
severity, *611*
severity, likelihood, and detection rating scales, *611*
Sewell Cadillac, 193
Sewell, Carl, 193
SFF. *See* Sunny Fresh Foods
Shanghai Academy of Quality Management, 127
shared vision, 271
Share Food, 148
Sharp Healthcare, 28, *439*

Shenzhen Bureau of Quality and Technical Supervision, 127
Sheth, Narendra J., 512
Shewhart cycle, 333
Shewhart, Walter, 7
shift in process average, 676–677
Shingo, Shigeo, 317, 399
short-term thinking, 72, 169, 322, 328
Shure, Inc., 638
Shure, S. N., 638–639
Siemens Energy and Automation, 352
"silo" thinking, 398
"silver-bullet" solution, 328, 449
Simonic, Don, 461–463
simple, measurable, actionable, related, timely (SMART), 376
simple random sampling, 491, 493–494
simple regression, 513
simultaneous engineering, 585–586
Singhal, Vinrod, 27
single minute exchange of dies (SMED), 462, 558
Sistemas, Nick, 238
situational leadership theory, 433–435
Six Sigma, 147, 177–179, 226–227, 289, 292–294, 341–342, 401–402, 459
  in Allied Signal, 133
  application of, 177–179, 226–227, 289, 292–294, 341–342, 401–402, 459, 561, 563–564, 565–567
  Baldrige Criteria for Performance Excellence and, 136
  basics of, 178
  at Caterpillar Financial Services Corporation (CSFC), 528–529
  champions, 136, 265
  change, impetus for, 137
  characteristics of, 560
  in China, 5, 36–37, 127–128
  at Cigna, 178–179
  at CNH Capital, 561
  as collection of methods, 136–137, 401–402, 532–533
  competitive strategy, 178
  control charts in, 542, 706–707
  controlling processes of, 330–331, 707
  core values in, 49, 134
  critical to quality (CTQ), 136, 226–227, 516–517, 532, *539*
  customer focus in, 49, 135
  DMAIC methodology and, 531–536
  at DuPont, 561
  employee language, 531
  evolution of, 12, 133–135
  failures, 268
  financial applications of, 537, 562
  in Fort Wayne, Indiana, 562
  at General Electric (GE), 134, 135, 440–441
  at GE Fanuc, 516–518
  government and public agencies, 562
  in health care industry, 147, 562
  at Honeywell, 463–466
  human resource focus in, 134–135
  implementation of, 440–442
  information management in, 401–402
  integration, 441
  intelligence gathering, 441
  ISO compared to, 135–138
  kaizen, 558
  key concepts of, 531, 559, 560
  leadership in, 136, 435, 441, 459
  lean production and, 556–560
  managers and, 134–135, 440
  measures, 561
  medical error reduction with, 563–564
  at Motorola, Inc., 52–53
  order fulfillment process with, 565–567, 565–568
  organizational vision and, 538
  orientation, bottom-line, 441
  performance improvement, 177
  philosophy, 134
  pitfalls in, 538
  plan-do-check-act (PDCA) cycle, 441
  problem solving, 441
  process improvement tools in, 540–560, 534–535
  process management in, 136, 312, 341–342, 441
  project management for, 536–540
  project selection for, 341, 392, 401, 537–540
  projects, 396, 401–402, 441
  project types, 537–538
  quality in, 463–466
  as quality framework, 135
  quality level in, 529–531
  scoring models, 539
  Samsung Electronics Co. (SEC), 338, 600
  in services/small organizations, 560–563
  small organizations, 562–563
  statistical basis of, 529–531
  statistical bias of, 133
  strategic planning in, 136, 177–178
  success stories, 134
  teams, 265–268
  quality in, 463–466
  theoretical basis for, 529
  total quality management (TQM) comparisons, 135
  tools, 540
  training, 441, 540–541
  transactional, 560
Six Sigma black belt (SSBB), 265, 465
  at General Electric (GE), 134
  described, 465
  process management, 342, 707
  training, 265, 441, *541*
  at Xerox, 34
Six Sigma Excellent Organization Award, 127
Six Sigma green belt (SSGB), 265, 268, 465, 707
Six Sigma master black belt, 265, 465
Skandia, 395
Skilled Care Pharmacy, 41–42

customer grade card, 224
quality policy within, 42
scoring system, 224
skill variety, 258
Skinner, B. F., 255
Skyhigh Airlines, 413–414
SLRMC (Southwest Louisiana Regional Medical Center), 147
small businesses, 71–73
characteristics of, 71–72
"command-and-control" attitude in, 71
MBNQA and, 120
quality in, 71–73
Six Sigma in, 560–563
SMART. *See* simple, measureable, actionable, related, time (SMART)
SMED. *See* single minute exchange of dies
Smith, Aaron, 180
Smith, Bill, 133
Smith, Jennifer, 299
SMTs. *See* self-managed teams
"socially responsive" designs, 600
social responsibilities, 429–432
leadership/governance and, 429–432
scope of, 13
Social Responsibility Core Business Principle and Environmental, Health, and Safety Policy guide, 413
"soft skills," 271
software. *See also* Microsoft Excel
Access, 385, 701
CHARTrunner, 701
for ERP, 382
Excel, 385, 497–501, 669–*671*, 674, *684*, *687*, *690*, *695*, *697*, *700*
Oracle, 382, 701
Process Model, 661
Quality Gamebox, 502
SQL Server, 701
soikufu, 336
Solar Stoner Incorporated, 428
Solar Turbines Inc., 164, 431–432
committee structure, 427
leadership system at, 51, 426–427
organizational effectiveness measures at, 165
social responsibility at, 431–432
strategic planning at, 164
Solectron
change at, 444
Malcolm Baldrige Award, 113, 137
programs at, 271
rewards at, 277
in Six Sigma, 137
Solucient, 28
Sony, 134
Southwest Airlines, 201, 208–209, 250
Southwest Louisiana Regional Medical Center (SLRMC), 147
Southwestern Desert Homes, 724
Southwestern Vista Homes (SVH), 668
Spanyi, Andrew, 562
SPC. *See* statistical process control (SPC)
special causes, 98, 309, 483, 705
specification limits, 548, 636
specifications, 17, 531, *633*
speed of delivery, 15
Splaum, Don, 516
SPP. *See* strategic planning process
SPR (Strategic Petroleum Reserve), 306
spreadsheets, 30–31, 137, 171, *637*. *See also* specific types
SQC. *See* statistical quality control (SQC)
SQI. *See* service quality indicators
SQL Server, 701
Squires, Frank H., 484
SSBB. *See* Six Sigma black belt
SSGB. *See* Six Sigma green belt
SSM Health Care (SSMHC), 63–64, 166–167
Baldrige Award, 63, *114*
continuous quality improvement (CQI) at, 63
Corporate Responsibility Process (CRP) at, 430
customer satisfaction survey, 217
Nursing Shared Accountability, 166
patient satisfaction surveys at, 217
process management at, 310, 321
strategic planning at, 166–167
total quality (TQ) within, 217
SSMHC. *See* SSM Health Care
stable system, 483
stakeholders, 20–21, 270, *416*, 428–*429*
stakeholder value, 428–*429*
St. Luke's Hospital, Kansas City,
customer contact, 211–212
employee surveys at, 281
Human Resource Management (HRM) at, 423
"Leadership for Performance Excellence + Model" of, 422
quality journey of, 440, 452–453
standard error of mean, 502
standardization, 128, 430
standardized work, 557–558
Standards Australia International (SAI), 125
S.T.A.R. (suggestions, teams, actions, results), 6
Starbucks, 602
Stark, Ray, 464–465
State Farm Insurance, 431
state/local government, quality in, 75–76
state university case study, 357–358
static population, 505
statistical analysis
applied at GE Fanuc, 516–518
with Microsoft Excel, 497–501
statistical control, 660, 664, 666–667
statistical correlation analysis, 512–513, 555–556
statistical foundations, 490–495
probability distributions, 490–491

random variables, 490–491
sampling, 491–494
statistical inference, 496
statistical methodology, 495–513, 664–666
analytic study, 505
analysis of variance (ANOVA), 510–512
in application, 523–525
basics of, 495
confidence intervals, 503–504
"cookbook" approach, 97
correlation, 512–513, 555–556
descriptive statistics, 495–497
design of experiments (DOE), 506–507
enumerative study, 505
factorial experiments, 507–510
at General Electric, 516–519
hypothesis testing, 504–505
metrics, 665–666
Microsoft Excel, 497–501
predictive, 496
for quality, 514–516
regression analysis, 512–513
sampling distributions, 501–502
statistical analysis with Microsoft Excel, 497–501, 669–*671*, 674, *684*, *687*, *690*, *695*, *697*, *700*
statistical inference, 50, 496
tools, 540–541
statistical process control (SPC), 659–664. *See also* control charts
elements of, 660, 706–707
employees and, 661, 668, 724, 726
goals for, 529, 706
implementation, 662–664
at Mesa Products, Inc. 661
in pharmaceutical product manufacturing, 525–524
in service organizations, *660*
successful, 706
statistical quality control (SQC), 7
statistical sampling, 8, 482
statistical thinking, 480–490
applying, 482–484
at Branch-Smith Printing Division, 481
defined, 480
Deming philosophy and, 8, 484–490
at Graniterock Company, 481
principles of, 482–484
statistics, defined, 480
Steers, Richard M., 255
Steward, Douglas M., 318
STMicroelectronics
data sharing at, 322
marketplace measures at, 371
organizational effectiveness measures at, 371
quality control at, 113, 322
suppliers at, 322
validity checks at, 373
stockholders, 94, 154
Stoner, Inc.
business excellence system, 51, 428–429
leadership system at, 51, 428
workers at, 286
storming phase of teams, 269
strategic benchmarking, 339–340
Strategic Business and Quality Plan (SBQP), 167
strategic change, 443–445
strategic challenges, 161–162
strategic context, 159
strategic leadership, 157
strategic objectives, 165, 169, *170*, *369*, *377*, *429*
Strategic Petroleum Reserve (SPR), 306
strategic planning. *See also* performance excellence
at AT&T, 339–340
Baldrige Criteria for Performance Excellence and, 115–116, 140
cycle, 140
described, 115, 119, 154, 177
at Eastman Chemical Company, 163
Hoshin Kanri, 167–168
human resource plans, 169–170
implementation, 448
in ISO , 177
leading practices for, 156–157
linking measures to, 375–376
at Medrad, 426
at Motorola, Inc., 215
at Novel Connect, 187
at Park Place Lexus, 164
at Ritz-Carlton Hotel Company, L.L.C., 165
in Six Sigma, 136, 177–178
at Solar Turbines Inc., 164
at SSMHC, 166–167
tools, 171
as total quality (TQ) practice, 25
Strategic Planning Institute, 26
strategic planning process (SPP), 139
Strategic Vision, 4
Strategic work system design, 175–177, 186
strategy
defined, 153–154, 165
deployment, 162–165, 177
development, 162–165, 177
factors for, 170
leadership, 157
organizational structure and, 157–162
management tools, 171
measures and, 375–376
overview, 153–154
stratified random sampling, 491, 494
strengths, weaknesses, opportunities, threats (SWOT), 164–165
stretch goals, 338
Strong, Sarah, 299–300
study stage of Deming cycle, 333
suboptimization, 94, 398
substitutes for leadership theory, *433*, 436
success, 11–12, 21, 25, 110

suggestions, teams, actions, results (S.T.A.R.), 6
suggestion system, 252–253, 254
Sullivan, Lawrence, 598
sum of squared (SS) deviations, 511
Sun Microsystems, 27, 133, 282
Sunny Fresh Foods (SFF), 247–248
  employee surveys at, 247
  I-to-I (Initiate and Implement) process, 248
  leadership system at, 51
  "ramp in" schedule at, 256
  workers at, 247
Sunset Manufacturing, Inc., 558
superiority, 15, 25, 339
Superquinn, 189–190
"SuperTracker," 61
Supervisory contingency decision model, *433*
supplier(s)
  beneficial relationships, 131
  certification programs, 448
  customer bond, 100
  focus, 125
  identification of customer relationships, 196
  requirements for, 22, *195*
  at STMicroelectronics, 322
supply chain management (SCM), 101, 308, *310*, 373
supply chains, 394
supporting, 434
support processes, 308–309
surveys, 218–222. *See also* employee surveys
  barriers to change, 442
  companies, midsized to large, 557
  consumer, 392
  customer importance, 222
  customer satisfaction, 59, 141, 218–222
  employee, 282–283
  formal, 282
  at Graniterock, 222
  guest, 221
  Initial Quality Survey, 27
  by MasteryWorks, Inc., 246–247
  NRS Corp, surveys, 141
  patient satisfaction, 217
  at pearl River School District, *369*
  Press Ganey, 366
  satisfaction, 15
  at St. Luke's Hospital, 281
  Wall Street Journal, 59
  Workforce, 281
  Wyatt Company, 442
sustainability, 119, 422
sustainable growth, 154
Swaim, Jack, 137
Swissair, 316
SWOT. *See* strengths, weaknesses, opportunities, threats (SWOT)
SWOT analysis, system(s)
  defined, 164
  dynamics, 164–165
  organization's success and, 164–165
  planning, 164, 181–182, *429*
  Synder, 255
systematic error, 492
systematic sampling, 491, 492, 494
system, defined, 50

T

tacit knowledge, 396
Taguchi, Genichi, 110–111
Taguchi loss of function, 111, 604–607
  applications, 607
  expected loss, 606
  known distribution variation formula, 605–606
  larger-is-better formula, 607
  nominal-is-best, 604–*605*
  overview, 111, 604
  smaller-is-better formula, 606
  in U.S.-made versus Japanese-made TVs, 604
tangible errors, 318–319
tangibles, 199
Target, 230, 602–603
TARP. *See* Technical Assistance Research Programs, Inc. (TARP)
"Take the L.E.A.D" program, 192
task
  errors, 318
  identity, 258
  significance, 258
Taylor, Frederick W., 7, 248, 445
Taylor system, 7, 248–249
TCS (Total Customer Satisfaction), 133, 278
team(s)102. *See also* teamwork
  adjourning of, 269
  at AT&T, 268–269, 428
  at Baptist Hospital, Inc, 263
  at Boeing, 268–269
  building, 450
  at Chrysler Corporation, 264
  as cross-functional, 175, 264
  customer-focused, 174
  defined, 261
  development, 269
  facilitator, 266–267, 273
  failures, 267–268
  forming of, 269
  at GE Plastics, 134
  as intraorganizational, 264
  leaders, 266, 272
  life cycle of, 258
  management, 263
  members, 264–267, 272–273
  natural work, 263–264
  norming of, 269
  in organizational design/quality improvement, 172–175
  performance of, 269
  platform-team approach, 264, 582–583
  problem-solving, 262–263
  product, 326
  project, 263
  quality circles, 263–265
  roles/responsibilities, 266–267
  scribe, 267, 273
  self-directed work, 263
  self-managed, 263–264
  Six Sigma project, 265, 268
  skills, 272–273
  success factors, 269–270

sponsor, 266
steering, 428
storming of, 269
tasks of, 269
timekeeper, 267
training, 272
types of, 263–264
virtual, 263, 264
team-based organizational chart, 266–267
teamwork, 21–22, 261–268
Technical Assistance Research Programs, Inc. (TARP)
Technology, 214
complaint management and service recovery, 212
customer relationship management (CRM) and, 212–215
exploiting, 212
for training, 213
Technological University RRC, 651–643
applying QFD at, 652–653
House of Quality for, 652, 654
old layout for, *653*
telecommuting, 299–300
Tele-engineering, 85
telephone interviews, 203, 218–219
10-step monitoring/evaluation process for health care organizations, 325
Termination Identification Process System (TIPS), 395
testing, 55
Texas Instruments (TI)
Baldrige criteria in, 119–120, 457
benchmarking at, 339
best practices at, 398
job enrichment at, 259, 271
process management at, 306
quality control at, 135, 322
rapid knowledge transfer (RKT) at, 339
simulated classroom within, 203–204
teams at, 426
"texins", 271
training at, 270
workforce-focused outcomes, 373
Texas Nameplate Company, Inc. (TNC), 90–91
Baldrige Award, 72, 113
cross-functional team in, 72
"Customer Site Visit" program of, 90
data at, 90, 120
employees, 72, 90, 260
fear approach, 90
human resource measures at, 72
organizational effectiveness measures at, 173
leadership system at, 51
learning environment at, 90
performance results at, 90, 373
philosophy of, 72, 90
profit-sharing in, 72
quality, role of change in,173, 445
suppliers at, 322
training at, 72, 173
vision of, 445
TFEs. *See* thresholds for evaluation (TFEs)
The Improvement Process (TIP), 407
theory of inventive problem solving (TRIZ), 338
theory of knowledge, 94, 96–97
Theory X-theory Y model, *433*
"think-tank" departments, 600
third-party organizations, 19, 218
360-degree feedback, 279
3M, *113*, 135, 338, 372, 582–583
thresholds for evaluation (TFEs), *325*, 546–547
TI. *See* Texas Instruments
TI Defense Systems and Electronics Group, 119
Tichy, Noel, *433*
time, 612
closing, 204
failure rates, *614*
intervals, 613
TIP. *See* The Improvement Process
TIPS. *See* Termination Identification Process System (TIPS)
tire mileage probability, *616*
TNC. *See* Texas Nameplate Company, Inc.
tolerance design, 53, 602–603
tolerances
defined, 602
measurements, 320, 323, 628
necessity for, 10, 55, 603
in services, 316
settings for, 17, 111
based-specifications, 531
tool engineering, 54
tools, 171. *See also* specific types
top-down process, 167, 169, 287, 423, 455, 537
Toronto Plastics, Ltd., 133
Torque Traction Technologies, Inc., 582
Total Customer Satisfaction (TCS), 133, 278, 366
total productive maintenance (TPM), 558
total quality (TQ), 20–25
adoption of, 73
continuous improvement, 23–25
customers in, 20–21
defined, 11
Deming in, 24
employee engagement, 21–22
evolution of, 7, 11
implementation of, 71
introduced in Hungary,
key elements of, 110
in Korea, 1, 13, 421
leadership and, 434
measuring, 392–393
organizational charts, 173
practices, 25
principles of, 20
process focus, 22
at Procter & Gamble, 11
scope of, 10–11
stakeholder focus, 20–21
teamwork in, 22
techniques, 25
Total Quality Control (Feigenbaum), 11, 109, 459–460
total quality control (TQC)
aspects of, 109

coining of, 11, 109
linking to TQM, 11
total quality learning (TQL),
total quality management (TQM)
in China, 36
criticism of, 11–12
in Deming, 122
development of, 10–11
disappointments in, 11–12
role of in finances, 27
linking TQC/TQL to, 47, 70
performance excellence, 12
in Six Sigma, 135
at Xerox, 32
total quality management (TQM) toolbox, 540
total quality (TQ) philosophy, 453
Toyoda, Eiji,
Toyota Motor Corporation, Ltd.
core competencies, 175
guiding principles of, 557
lean production of, 556–557
Lexus division, 15
production system of, 175
quality culture, 449
suggestions system at, 251
workforce management, 245
TPD. *See* Corning Telecommunications Products Division
TPM. *See* total productive maintenance
TPM expert, 465
TPM master, 465
TQ. *See* total quality
TQC. *See* total quality control
TQL. *See* total quality learning
TQM. *See* Total Quality Management
traceable measurements, 629
Trader Joe's, 208
training, 289–292
at American Honda Motor Co., 289–292
at Ames Rubber Corporation, 385
at AT&T, 259
at Baptist Hospital, Inc. (BHI), 286
at Boeing Aerospace Support (AS), 307
at Chase Bank, 392–393
at Chuck E. Cheese, 287
components of, 287
at Coors Brewing Company, 286
costs of, 389
at Coyote Community College, 415
in Deming's 14 points, 143
at FedEx, 286, 287
at Gold Star Chili, Inc, 342–344
at Hewitt Associates, 292–293
at Honda Motor Company, 289–292
at Honeywell International, 463–464
at IBM, 259
in ISO 9000:2000, 288–289
in Japan, 259
at Marlow Industries, 282, 283
at Medrad, 287
at Midwest Bank, 358
at Motorola, Inc., 287
at Nordam Europe, 301
at Pal's Sudden Service, 287
at Park Place Lexus, 426
at Procter & Gamble, 461
at Ritz-Carlton Hotel Company, L.L.C., 270, 288, 323, 437
in Six Sigma,341, 440–441
at Solar Turbines, Inc, 427
at SSM Health care, 430
technology for, 408
at Texas Instruments, (TI), 270
total quality management (TQM), 135
Umslag, 286
At Wainwright Industries, Inc., 366
at Xerox, 287, 297
Transactional Customer Satisfaction Index, 217
transactional leadership theory, 435
transactional Six Sigma, 455, 560
transfer cycle time, 562
transformational leadership theory, *433*, 435–436
treatment errors, 318
treatments, in factors, 507
Treaty on European Union, 128
tree diagrams, 171
Tregoe, Benjamin B., 537
trends, 13, 678–*679*
Trident Precision Manufacturing, Inc., *113*
TRIZ. *See* theory of inventive problem solving
true standard deviation, 634, 667
"true value," 393
Tsutaya, 215
12 Customer-Contact Requirements, 211
Type I error, 705–706
Type II error, 705–706

U

UAW. *See* United Auto Workers (UAW)
u-charts, 699–701
applications of, 696, 698–699
c-charts versus, 699–701
constructing, 699
in receiving process, 713–*715*
UCL. *See* upper control limit (UCL)
Ulrich, Dave, *433*
Umslag, ehf, 286
uncritical projection of trends, 492
underutilization of services, 62
Union of Japanese Scientists and Engineers (JUSE), 8, 109, 110, 264
unions, 22
unit of work, 378
United Auto Workers (UAW), 4
United States, quality revolution in, 8–9
United Way of America, 73
universal theory of management, 99
University of Michigan Business School, 194
University of Northern Colorado, 69
University of Wisconsin-Stout
Baldrige Award, 69, 70
as "hidden treasure", 70
"Mission Driven-Market Smart" at, 70
student satisfaction at, 70

unstructured performance problems, 71, 537
upper control limit (UCL), 666–668, 674, 676, 689, 693
upper tolerance limit, 634, 636
U.S. Department of Commerce, 121
user-based perspective, 16
U.S. Postal Service, 120, 402–404
U.S. Water Resource Agency, 84–85

V

value(s),
  chain of, 14, 17–18
  creation, 158
  defined, 160
  organizational, 176, 196
  at Pal's Sudden Service, 160
  at Premier, 160
  suppliers and, 85
  at Walker Auto Sales and Service, 85
value-based perspective, 16–17
value-creation process, 342–343
Value Innovation Program (VIP), 600
values of K_1 and K_2, 627
variables, 490–491, 665, *692*. *See also* control charts
variation, 62, 95–96, *482*–483, 487
  "bullwhip" effect, 483
  in capacity utilization, 483
  in cash flows, 562
  in cause-and-effect diagrams, 554
  causes of, 102, 482–483
  Deming philosophy and, 92, 94, 99, 100, 336
  equipment, 625
  excessive, 96, 334
  measures, 511
  of organizations, 173
  operator, 625
  at Pal's Sudden Service, 383
  problems created by, 107, 483
  in process, 100, *633*
  in profound knowledge, 98–99
  production and, 5, 17–18, 96, 323
  quincunx and, 95–96
  reducing sources of, 105, 110
  reduction of, 100, 131, 311
  root causes and, 483
  of services, 62
  sources of in production process, 100, 482
  statistical method and, 95–96
  in systems, 487
  unpredictability and, 483
  unwanted, 323
  in U.S./Japanese TV components, *604*
  in yields, 507–508
Veridian Homes, quality frameworks, 139–141
"vertical job loading," 176
Vibration and Rotor Dynamics Laboratory, 432
VIP. *See* Value Innovation Program
virtual customers, 216
virtual teams, 263, 264
virtuous teaching style (VTC), 455–456
vision, 99
  ABM Master and, 465
  of Alcoa, 463
  balanced scorecard and, 368
  in Baldrige Criteria, 459
  at Baptist Hospital, Inc. (BHI), 425
  at Branch-Smith Printing, 180
  at Cedar Foundation, 91
  at Convergys, 405
  in Coral Springs, Florida, 49
  cultural values and, 443
  creation of, 99
  in Deming's 14 points, 99
  described, 158, 160
  at Eastman Chemical Company, 163
  employee role in, 140, 262
  at Jenks Public Schools, 48
  at J. S. Power, 4
  as key competencies, 284
  in leadership, 157, 425–426, 446, 451
  at Medrad, 284
  measurement systems and, 374, 375
  navigator in, 424
  in organizational environment, 25, 48, 158, 166, 425, 436
  policy deployment and, 167–168
  at Pal's Sudden Service, 160
  at Park Place Lexus, 164
  at Premier, 158–160
  at Saint Luke's Hospital, 422–423
  in senior leadership, 116
  shared, 271, 425, 435, 437, 448, 449
  stakeholders and, 174
  at Stoner, 429
  strategy and, 154, 165
  tangible, 157
  teamwork and, 443
  of Texas Nameplate Company, Inc. (TNC), 90
visual controls, 557
visual mapping of $Y = f(X)$, *533*
"vital few," 4, 118, 197, 375, 390
VOC. *See* Voice of the Customer
Voice of the Customer (VOC)
  in House of Quality, *592*
  at LaRosa's Inc., 227–228
  at U.S. Postal Service, 402
voltage measurements, 629
Vroom, Victor H., 255
VTC. *See* virtuous teaching style

W

Wainwright Industries, 366
  cultural change at, 446–447
  data accessibility at, 394
  empowerment in, 260
  information practices at, 366
  quality improvement at, 366
  suggestion system at, 252–253
  teams at, 446
  workforce of, 252–253
Waldenbooks, 230
Walker Auto Sales and Service (WASS), 85
Walker, Darren, 85
Wall Street Journal, 11, 59
Wal-Mart, 212–213
War Production Board, 8
WASS. *See* Walker Auto Sales and Service

waste elimination, 15
watch environments, *612*
Water Resource Agency, 84–85
Waterstone, 230
wave soldering process, 514–516
  data corresponding to first experiment, 515
  defects after experimental design optimization, 515
  DOE and,506, 514–516
  factors/levels of experimentation, 514
  at Hewlett-Packard India, Ltd., 514
Welch, Jack, 134, 454
well-being, 97, 178, 248, 425
Western Electric Company, 7
Westinghouse, 9, 264
Weston, Tex, 413
Wheelwright, S. C., 25
Whirlpool, 201
Whitney, Eli, 5
Wide Area Network (WAN), 85
wide-tech framework, 79
wikis, 259
Wilford, Sandra, 298–299
Willard, Daniel, 264
Williams, 255
Wilson Sporting goods, 483
The Wizard of Oz, 471–472
work design, 257–259
workers. *See* employee(s); workforce
workforce, 59–60
  appraisal, 278
  in Baldrige Criteria, 288
  capability, 282–284
  capacity, 284–285
  defined, 247–248
  development, 286–288, 415
  engaging in process improvement, 281–282
  in ISO 9000:2000, 288–289
  job satisfaction, 59–60
  learning, 286–288
  management of, 247–250, 273–282
  outcomes, 372–373
  retention of, 292–294, 300–301
  selection of, 300–301
  in Six Sigma, 289, 292–294
  360-degree feedback, 279
  as total quality (TQ) practice, 25
  of Wainwright Industries, 252–253, 260
work measurement, 99, 392
Work-Out program, 251–252, 454
work systems, 175–177, 186, 273–282. *See also* teamwork
  at Baptist Hospital, 263
  compensation, 274–276
  designing, 256–268
  empowerment and, 259–262
  job design, 257–259
  quality circles, 264–265
  recognition, 274–278
  rewards, 276–278
  self-determination versus empowerment, 262
  Six Sigma project teams, 265–268
  at Sunny Fresh Farms, 256
  sustaining, 282–288
  work design, 257–259
  at Xerox, 260
WorldCom, 119
World War II, 8
"wow factor," 27
Wright, Ann, 403
Wriston, Walter, 246
Wurtzel, Marvin, 562
Wyatt Company, 442

X

x-charts, 686–*687*
  applications, 666, 674–*675*
  for chemical process, 667, 683, 686
  constructing, 683
  constructing for statistical control, 666–667
  control limits for, 666–667, 683
  and cycles, 678
  for data/calculations, 668–674, *687*
  for individual measurements, 683, 686
  at La Ventana, *672*
  for machined part, 679
  with moving ranges, *682*, 686–687, *688*
  for revised data, *673*
  spreadsheet for, 670
  and trends, 678
  and variations, *684*
Xerox, 31–36, 260–261
  benchmarking at, 282, 339
  core values, 34–35
  customer satisfaction, 33, 34
  employees at, 33, 260
  empowerment at, 260
  evolution of quality at, 32
  Fuji-, 385
  Human Resource Management (HRM) at, 282
  interlinking model, 383
  Leadership Through Quality, 33–34
  Lean Six Sigma within, 31–36
  market share of, 32, 34
  market trends, 35
  Malcolm Baldrige National Quality Award, 33
  performance excellence process within, 34
  President's Award, 277
  Quality Forum hosted by, 69
  Quality Policy, 32, 34
  quality imperative within, 32
  restrengthening quality within, 34
  reward and recognition systems, 33
  suppliers and, 33
  training at, 33
Xerox Quality Policy, 32, 34

Y

yellow brick road to quality, 471–472
Yum Brands Inc., 277

Z

ZD. *See* Zero Defects
Zero Defects (ZD), 107–108
Zero Quality Control (ZQC), 317
ZQC. *See* Zero Quality Control (ZQC)
Zytec Corporation, 122

Businesses and Organizations Cited in this Book (continued)

FedEx
Fidelity Investments
First National Bank of Chicago
Florida Power and Light
Ford Motor Company
Frederick C. Carder Elementary School
Froedtert Memorial Lutheran Hospital, Milwaukee

Gap
GE Fanuc
Genecor
General Electric
General Foods
General Mills
General Motors
General Systems Company
Gilbert High School (Arizona)
Gold Star Chili, Inc.
Golden Plaza Hotel, San Francisco
Graniterock Company

Hennes & Mauritz
Herend Procelain Manufacturing
Hershey Foods Corporation
Hewlett-Packard
Hillerich & Bradsby Co.
Hilton Hotels Corp.
Hogan Center for Performance Excellence
Home Depot
Honda
Honeywell, Inc.
Hungarian Olympic committee
Hyundai Motor Company

IBM Credit Corporation, 370
Ina Title Company, Japan
International Organization for Standardization
International Telephone and Telegraph

Japan Quality Medal
Jenks Public Schools
John F. Welch Leadership Center (Crotonville)
Johnson & Johnson
Johnson Controls, Inc.
Joint Commission on Accreditation of Healthcare Organizations
Jostens
Juran Institute

Kaiser Aluminum
Kaizen Institute
KARLEE Company
Kenneth W. Monfort College of Business
KFC
Kingsley Elementary School (Sullivan County, Tennessee)
Kodak

L. L. Bean
Lands' End
LaRosa's Inc.
Levi Strauss
Lexus automobiles
Lockheed Missiles and Space Division
Lucas Sumitomo Brakes, Inc.

Macy's Department Store
Magnivision
Maguire Miles
Mariott
Marlow Industries
Mary Kay Cosmetics
MasteryWorks Inc.
Mazda
MCI
Medical College of Wisconsin
Medrad
Mercedes-Benz
Merrill Lynch Credit Corporation
Microsoft
Middletown Regional Hospital
Midwest Express Airlines
Milliken
Mitsubishi
Monsanto
Motorola, Inc.
Mt. Edgecumbe High School (Sitka, Alaska)

Nashua Corporation
National Academy of Sciences/Institute of Medicine
National Cash Register Company
National Committee for Quality Assurance
National Institute of Standards and Technology
National Quality Institute
National Semiconductor
Nationwide Insurance
Naval Air Systems Command
Netflix
New England Deaconess Hospital
Nissan Motor Car Company Limited,
Nordam Europe, Ltd.
North Central Association of Colleges and Schools
Nucor Corporation

Occupational Safety and Health Administration
Ohio Department of Transportation
Ohio Partnership for Excellence

continued on next page